CANADA

MAINE

ESOTA

Lake Superior

MICHIGAN

Lake Huron

WISCONSIN

Burlington
Montpelier
Augusta
VT. N.H.
Portland
Concord
Manchester

NEW
YORK

*Lake
Ontario*

Albany
Boston
MASS
Worcester
Springfield
Providence
R.I.

Rochester
Syracuse
Buffalo

polis
St. Paul

Grand
Rapids
Flint
Milwaukee
Lansing
Sterling Heights
Warren
Madison
Ann
Arbor
Detroit
Livonia
Lake Erie
Erie
PENN.
Bridgeport
New Haven
CT. Hartford
Stamford
Newark
Jersey City
New York

OWA

Cedar
Rapids
Davenport
Rockford
South
Bend
Toledo
Akron
Allentown
Harrisburg
Trenton
Philadelphia

na
oines

Chicago
Gary
Fort
Wayne
Cleveland
Youngstown
Pittsburgh
N.J.

ILLINOIS
Peoria
Urbana
Indianapolis
OHIO
Columbus
Dayton
Baltimore
Annapolis
Dover
DE.

Independence
Kansas City
Jefferson
City
Springfield
INDIANA
Cincinnati
WASHINGTON MD.
D.C.

St. Louis
Louisville
Frankfort
Lexington
W.VA.
Charleston
Richmond
Roanoke
Hampton
Norfolk
Newport News
Virginia Beach
Portsmouth
Chesapeake
VA.

Springfield
MISSOURI
Evansville
KENTUCKY
Nashville
Knoxville
Greensboro
Durham
Raleigh

ARKANSAS

Winston-
Salem
N.C.
Asheville
Charlotte
Chattanooga
TENNESSEE
Greenville
Columbia
S.C.

Little
Rock
Memphis

Huntsville
Atlanta
Augusta
Charleston

Shreveport
LOUISIANA
Jackson
Birmingham
Macon
Columbus
Savannah

ont
Baton Rouge
New Orleans
MISSISSIPPI
Biloxi
Montgomery
ALABAMA
GEORGIA
Pensacola
Tallahassee
Jacksonville
Mobile
FLORIDA

Gulf of Mexico

Orlando
St. Petersburg
Tampa

Hialeah
Fort Lauderdale
Hollywood
Miami

*ATLANTIC
OCEAN*

0	250	500 Miles
0	250	500 Kilometers

POPULOUS METROPOLITAN AREAS

■ Cities over 5 million

■ Cities over 1 million

○ Cities under 1 million

☆ State Capitals

IMPORTANT:

HERE IS YOUR REGISTRATION CODE TO ACCESS
YOUR PREMIUM McGRAW-HILL ONLINE RESOURCES.

For key premium online resources you need THIS CODE to gain access. Once the code is entered, you will be able to use the Web resources for the length of your course.

If your course is using **WebCT** or **Blackboard**, you'll be able to use this code to access the McGraw-Hill content within your instructor's online course.

Access is provided if you have purchased a new book. If the registration code is missing from this book, the registration screen on our Website, and within your WebCT or Blackboard course, will tell you how to obtain your new code.

Registering for McGraw-Hill Online Resources

MCGRAW-HILL

ONLINE RESOURCES

REGISTRATION CODE

2PD4-PNTO-KRE6-2G87-JE3R

To gain access to your McGraw-Hill web resources simply follow the steps below:

1. USE YOUR WEB BROWSER TO GO TO: **http://www.mhhe.com/brinkley11**
2. CLICK ON **FIRST TIME USER**.
3. ENTER THE REGISTRATION CODE* PRINTED ON THE TEAR-OFF BOOKMARK ON THE RIGHT.
4. AFTER YOU HAVE ENTERED YOUR REGISTRATION CODE, CLICK **REGISTER**.
5. FOLLOW THE INSTRUCTIONS TO SET-UP YOUR PERSONAL UserID AND PASSWORD.
6. WRITE YOUR UserID AND PASSWORD DOWN FOR FUTURE REFERENCE. KEEP IT IN A SAFE PLACE.

TO GAIN ACCESS to the McGraw-Hill content in your instructor's **WebCT** or **Blackboard** course simply log in to the course with the UserID and Password provided by your instructor. Enter the registration code exactly as it appears in the box to the right when prompted by the system. You will only need to use the code the first time you click on McGraw-Hill content.

Thank you, and welcome to your McGraw-Hill online resources!

Higher Education

Mc Graw Hill Higher Education

* YOUR REGISTRATION CODE CAN BE USED ONLY ONCE TO ESTABLISH ACCESS. IT IS NOT TRANSFERABLE.
0-07-293571-5 BRINKLEY: AMERICAN HISTORY: A SURVEY, 11E

AMERICAN HISTORY

A SURVEY

AMERICAN HISTORY

A SURVEY

Eleventh Edition

Alan Brinkley
Columbia University

Boston   Burr Ridge, IL   Dubuque, IA   Madison, WI   New York   San Francisco   St. Louis
Bangkok   Bogotá   Caracas   Kuala Lumpur   Lisbon   London   Madrid   Mexico City
Milan   Montreal   New Delhi   Santiago   Seoul   Singapore   Sydney   Taipei   Toronto

McGraw-Hill Higher Education ⚛
*A Division of The **McGraw-Hill** Companies*

AMERICAN HISTORY: A SURVEY

Published by McGraw-Hill, a business unit of The McGraw-Hill Companies, Inc. 1221 Avenue of the Americas, New York, NY, 10020. Copyright ©2003, 1999 by The McGraw-Hill Companies, Inc. All rights reserved. Previous editions ©1995, 1991 by McGraw-Hill, Inc. All rights reserved. ©1987, 1983 by Richard N. Current, T. H. W., Inc., Frank Freidel, and Alan Brinkley. All rights reserved. ©1979, 1971, 1966, 1964, 1961, 1959 by Richard N. Current, T. Harry Williams, and Frank Freidel. All rights reserved. No part of this publication may be reproduced or distributed in any form or by any means, or stored in a database or retrieval system, without the prior written consent of The McGraw-Hill Companies, Inc., including, but not limited to, in any network or other electronic storage or transmission, or broadcast for distance learning. Some ancillaries, including electronic and print components, may not be available to customers outside the United States.

This book is printed on acid-free paper.

5 6 7 8 9 0 QWD 0 9 8 7 6 5 4

ISBN 0-07-242436-2 (combined edition)
ISBN 0-07-249051-9 (volume I)
ISBN 0-07-249053-5 (volume II)

Publisher: *Lyn Uhl*
Senior sponsoring editor: *Steve Drummond*
Developmental editor: *Kristen Mellitt*
Lead project manager: *Susan Trentacosti*
Production supervisor: *Carol A. Bielski*
Freelance design coordinator: *Gino Cieslik*
Senior media producer: *Sean Crowley*
Supplement producer: *Nate Perry*
Supplement developmental editor: *Kate Scheinman*
Photo research coordinator: *Jeremy Cheshareck*
Photo researcher: *PhotoSearch, Inc.*
Cover design: *Gino Cieslik*
Interior design: *Maureen McCutcheon*
Typeface: *10/12 Garamond Book*
Compositor: *GTS Graphics, Inc.*
Printer: *Quebecor World Dubuque*

Cover photos: (Background image) © North Carolina Museum of Art/CORBIS; (Inset) Albert Bierstadt, "Bridal Veil Falls, Yosemite", 1871–1873. North Carolina Museum of Art. Photo: © North Carolina Museum of Art/CORBIS

Library of Congress Control Number: 2002106646

www.mhhe.com

*A*lan Brinkley is the Allan Nevins Professor of History at Columbia University. He is the author of *Voices of Protest: Huey Long, Father Coughlin, and the Great Depression*, which won the 1983 National Book award; *The Unfinished Nation: A Concise History of the American People*; *The End of Reform: New Deal Liberalism in Recession and War*; and *Liberalism and Its Discontents*. He was educated at Princeton and Harvard, and he has taught at Harvard (where he was awarded the Joseph R. Levenson Memorial Teaching Award), Princeton, the City University of New York Graduate School, and Oxford University, where he was the Harmsworth Professor of American History. He is a member of the American Academy of Arts and Sciences, a member of the board of the New York Council for the Humanities, and chairman of the board of the Century Foundation.

Brief Contents

Contents

Chapter One

THE MEETING OF CULTURES   2

Chapter Two

TRANSPLANTATIONS AND BORDERLANDS   32

Chapter Five

THE AMERICAN REVOLUTION 124

Chapter Six

THE CONSTITUTION AND THE NEW REPUBLIC 158

Chapter Nine

JACKSONIAN AMERICA   234

Chapter Ten

AMERICA'S ECONOMIC REVOLUTION   260

Chapter Eleven

COTTON, SLAVERY, AND THE OLD SOUTH   296

Chapter Twelve

ANTEBELLUM CULTURE AND REFORM   318

Chapter Thirteen

THE IMPENDING CRISIS   342

Chapter Fourteen

THE CIVIL WAR   370

Chapter Fifteen

RECONSTRUCTION AND THE NEW SOUTH 406

Chapter Sixteen

THE CONQUEST OF THE FAR WEST   440

Chapter Seventeen

INDUSTRIAL SUPREMACY   472

Chapter Eighteen

THE AGE OF THE CITY 498

Chapter Nineteen

FROM STALEMATE TO CRISIS 530

Chapter Twenty

THE IMPERIAL REPUBLIC   552

Chapter Twenty-One

THE RISE OF PROGRESSIVISM   574

Chapter Thirty-Two

THE CRISIS OF AUTHORITY   858

Preface

The past, of course, can never change. But our understanding of the past changes constantly; and as a result, so does the writing of history. Shifts in historical understanding occur for many reasons. They can be the results of discoveries of new evidence or new methods of interpreting familiar evidence. They can be products of new theories of history, or of human behavior. Most of all, they can be reflections of new questions, preoccupations, and concerns that emerge out of the events of the historian's own time.

Two such questions have led to significant changes in this new edition. Even before the terrible events of September 11, 2001, it was clear to most Americans that the recent history of the United States had become more embedded than ever before in the larger history of the world. The phenomenon of globalization—a central topic of modern public conversation—has become an invitation to historians to reconsider aspects of America's more distant past, where international forces also played an important role in the nation's history. The internationalization of the writing of American history is still in its infancy, and there are many areas of our past that have not yet been reconsidered in light of world events. Still, it is not too early to consider some of the ways we might draw new perspectives on our own past by looking at the histories of other societies. And so one of the goals of this new edition is to introduce some aspects of world history into the history of the United States.

Another aspect of our own time that has affected our understanding of the American past is the explosion of modern science and technology, and the tremendous impact of that explosion on many aspects of our society and culture. But while the specific advances in science and technology of our time may be new, the tremendous impact of science and technology on the development of the United States is not. Another goal of this new edition, therefore, is to incorporate a great deal more history of science and technology into the story of the American past.

Despite these and other changes, which are described in detail in the section immediately following this preface, I have tried to retain in this edition what I believe has long been the principal strength of this book: a balanced picture of the American past that connects the newer histories of society and culture that have emerged in the last several decades with the more traditional stories of politics, diplomacy, and great public events. The United States is a nation of extraordinary diversity, and we cannot hope to understand its history without understanding the experiences of the many different groups and cultures that have shaped it. But America is also a nation, whose people share a common political system, a connection to a national economy, and a familiarity with a shared and, in modern times, enormously powerful popular culture. To understand the American past, therefore, it is necessary to examine both the nation's considerable diversity and the powerful forces that have drawn it together and allowed it to survive and flourish.

As always, I am grateful to many people for their help in producing this new edition. I was particularly blessed to have the help of several gifted research assistants—James Delbourgo, Robert Lifset, Moshik Temkin, and Adrienne Sockwell—who contributed enormously to the new material in this edition as well as to the revision of existing sections. I appreciate the very helpful reviews of this book submitted by a group of talented scholars and teachers:

Joyce Appleby, *University of California at Los Angeles*

Kathren Brown, *Bowling Green State University*

Edward Carroll, *Heartland Community College*

Vincent Clark, *Johnson County Community College*

Charles L. Cohen, *University of Wisconsin, Madison*

Becky K. da Cruz, *Ozarks Technical Community College*

Gregory E. Dowd, *University of Notre Dame*

Nancy Gabin, *Purdue University*

Mark Goldman, *Tallahassee Community College*

Eliga Gould, *University of New Hampshire*

Marilyn Howard, *Columbus State Community College*

Richard R. Johnson, *University of Washington*

Juli Jones, *St. Charles Community College*

Michael Kassel, *University of Michigan, Flint*

Greg Kiser, *Northwest Arkansas Community College*

David Thomas Konig, *Washington University*

Michael Namorato, *University of Mississippi*

Melanie Perreault, *University of Central Arkansas*

Christiane Diehl Taylor, *Eastern Kentucky University*

Stephen Webre, *Louisiana Tech University*

Peter H. Wood, *Duke University*

I am grateful as well to the many people at McGraw-Hill who worked so hard on this new edition: Lyn Uhl and Kristen Mellitt, who patiently supervised the project from Boston; Susan Trentacosti, who skillfully managed the production of the book; Maria Victoria Paras, the careful and talented copy editor; Jeremy Cheshareck, who adeptly managed the illustrations; and Gino Cieslik, who is responsible for the attractive new design of the book. I was fortunate, as well, to have the assistance of the gifted photo researcher Debra Bull. My wife, Evangeline Morphos, as always, helped me to consider new approaches to the presentation of the past.

Finally, I am grateful to the students, teachers, and other readers of this book who have sent me unsolicited, but always welcome, comments, criticisms, and correc-tions. I hope they will continue to offer their reactions by sending them to me in care of the Department of History, Columbia University, New York, NY 10027; or by e-mail to ab65@columbia.edu.

Alan Brinkley
Columbia University
New York, NY

Although this book tells the large and complex story of the history of the United States, it has a very simple purpose. It aspires to be a thorough, balanced, and versatile account of America's past that instructors and students will find accessible and appropriate no matter what approach to the past a course chooses. It includes, as it has from its first edition, a careful, scrupulous examination of American political and diplomatic history. But it is, today, at least as committed to exploring the many other areas of the American past that are of interest to scholars and students alike.

Many of today's American history textbooks emerged out of the particular interests of their authors and their commitment to bringing new kinds of history to the attention of students—social history, regional histories, cultural history, women's history. This book, by contrast, exists to provide students and instructors with a broad account of a diverse American past, one in which no single approach or theme predominates. The eleventh edition is committed to representing the many newer forms of history that have emerged over a generation and more of scholarly innovation.

ORGANIZATION AND COVERAGE

American History: A Survey is organized in a way that reflects the typical United States history course. The thirty-four chapters follow the history of the United States chronologically, and the subheadings allow instructors to select portions of chapters to suit their syllabi. The text is divided into two volumes with an overlapping Chapter Fifteen that covers the "Reconstruction and the New South," providing flexibility for two-semester courses. While this organization makes it easy for instructors to use the text, it also allows for coverage of traditional topics in fresh ways.

NARRATIVE

The book is most notable for the balance among the many elements of the past it attempts to present and for its efforts to draw connections among them—to weave them together into a coherent narrative. In each new edition it has expanded its scope while maintaining the clear prose and the straightforward structure that have always made it so accessible and versatile for students and instructors. Today, the traditional political narrative is woven together with newer, equally important narratives: the history of women and gender, of race and ethnicity, of

economic growth and the changing character of labor of region and religion, of popular culture and intellectual life, and of the environment and the economy. *American History: A Survey* is at the cutting edge of the effort to put politics into social history and to put society and culture into political history.

ONE VOICE

One very distinctive feature of this book is that it represents the work of one author. Multiauthored books, of course, tend to bring together many scholars with different forms of expertise in different areas of the past. But a single author has the advantage of bringing a single, organizing conception to the book, of writing in a consistent style, and of providing greater unity and coherence to the narrative.

GLOBALIZATION

Recently, a great deal of attention has been given to the subject of thinking about and teaching the American experience in a way that places it in a larger international and global context. To study the history of our country in isolation from the many varied international influences and other national histories is to neglect an important part of the story. This edition attempts to present American history in a more international context, while preserving the distinctiveness of the nation's past. This coverage can be found within both the narrative of the text and in a new set of ten essays under the rubric "America and the World," placing events in American history in a global context.

CULTURAL HISTORY

The eleventh edition includes as well an expanded treatment of American culture, both through the integration of new cultural history into the text and through a well-received series of essays from the last edition titled "Patterns of Popular Culture." These essays examine ways in which popular culture has affected the lives of Americans at different times in the past and places that culture in a larger historical context. This edition includes one new "Patterns of Popular Culture" essay titled "The Golden Age of Comic Books" in Chapter 26.

THE NATURE OF HISTORICAL SCHOLARSHIP

The book is written in clear and accessible prose, but it does not condescend to students and does not shy away from complex issues and complicated debates. The "Where Historians Disagree" essays, which have always been a popular feature of this book, suggest its commitment to helping students understand the contested quality of much of the American past. This feature encourages them to think for themselves about what different aspects of our history actually mean.

CONTENT

American History: A Survey continues to win praise from both instructors and students for its balanced presentation of political, cultural, and social history, its clear and accessible prose, its reliable scholarship, its versatility of use, and its excellent map and illustration program. The "Patterns of Popular Culture," "The American Environment," and "Where Historians Disagree" features continue to provide exciting and informative presentations of cutting-edge scholarship. All of these strengths have been preserved and enhanced in the new eleventh edition.

This revision is in part a response to careful consideration of the comments and recommendations from instructors and scholars throughout the country. For example, in response to expert reviewer comments, the first four chapters have been thoroughly revised, drawing clearer connections between the history of the British colonies in North America and the larger, global context of migration and settlement, also known as the emergence of the "Atlantic world." In addition, extensive new material on environmental history has been added, in particular in Chapters 12, 18, 21, 22, 29, 30, 32, and 34. To meet the growing interest among today's students and scholars in science and technology, an expanded treatment of these topics is emphasized throughout the narrative. As always, the book gives particular attention to the very recent past, the history since the publication of the last edition, including the tumultuous events of September 11, 2001, and its aftermath.

PEDAGOGICAL FEATURES

The telling of a good story is only part of the task facing those who teach American history. Instructors also have to engage students in the enterprise of learning and the more actively engaged they are, the more they learn. Pedagogical tools within a textbook have become an important complement to the narrative, aiding students in participating actively in the learning process.

American History: A Survey has always provided students with clear, accessible, and useful pedagogical support. The eleventh edition continues this tradition by retaining the strong features of past editions, refining and updating these features, and adding several new ones.

Chapter Introductions and Conclusions

Each chapter opens with a short introduction that sets the stage for understanding the materials. Chapters then end with conclusions that highlight key themes. These features preserve the engaging narrative style while satisfying the pedagogical dictum: "tell them what they'll learn, teach them, then tell them what they have learned." The introductions and conclusions aid students in focusing on the main themes in the narrative.

Timelines

One of the most commonly voiced frustrations for instructors is that students lack a sense of chronology. Each chapter of this book contains a timeline focusing on significant events covered within the chapter narrative. These timelines have been placed at the beginning of each chapter and include events that correspond to many of the chapter subtitles, as well as other events sprinkled throughout the narrative.

Clear Headings and New Marginal Notes

Each chapter features clear thematic titles and precise headings that guide students through the narrative. An important and useful new pedagogical tool is the addition of marginal notes that highlight key terms and concepts contained within the narrative.

For Further Reference Sections

The bibliographies that conclude each chapter have been updated to provide students and instructors with assistance in accessing additional resources including books, films, and extensive website backup. At the end of each chapter, at the conclusion of the bibliographies, students will find our Online Learning Center logo and a line of text referring them to the website.

Expanded Integration of the Map Program with Both Text and Website

Because a sense of geography is essential to the study of history, the text includes a wealth of full-color maps. As instructors know very well, too often students just glance at maps without understanding them or engaging them critically. To address this, the author has created new captions for every map. These captions make specific reference to map content with questions. They are embedded with content cues for students. In addition, numerous maps in the book have a Web icon that links them to interactive versions on the Online Learning Center.

SUPPLEMENTS

 For the Instructor

Instructor's Manual
Prepared by Harvey H. Jackson, Jacksonville State University, and Bradley R. Rice, Clayton State College, this comprehensive Instructor's Manual is coordinated with both the text and Study Guide. The Instructor's Manual provides chapter summaries, themes and objectives for the instructor's use, suggestions for classroom discussion, map exercises, and interpretations to engage students.

Instructor's Manual for Advanced Placement Teachers
Prepared by Cheryl Lockhart, Amphitheater High School; William C. Bendt, Amphitheater High School; and Samuel Caruso, Catalina Foothills High School, this specially focused manual for AP teachers includes guiding questions; key terms, concepts, and names; controversy and debate material; and creative extensions such as group exercises and film recommendations.

Test Bank
Prepared by Tom DiPalma, William Rainey Harper College, this printed Test Bank provides multiple levels and types of questions for each chapter of the text. The 11th edition Test Bank gives five answer options for the multiple-choice questions to be compatible with the five-answer AP exam format.

Computerized Test Bank
Available in both Brownstone Diploma for Windows and Exam IV for Macintosh, this version of the test bank on CD-ROM allows instructors to customize each test to suit any course syllabus.

Overhead Transparency Acetates
This comprehensive package of 150 transparencies, most of them full-color, is designed to support the text's unique integrated art program.

U.S. History Video and CD-ROM Library
Contact your local sales representative for a complete listing of the many videos and CD-ROMs available from the Films for the Humanities American History catalog. Adoption requirements apply.

Instructor's Resource CD-ROM
This presentation manager organizes a diverse range of instructor's tools on one CD-ROM. Instructors can illustrate classroom lectures and discussions with text-specific PowerPoint presentations, or integrate images from a gallery of more than 800 maps and photographs into their own presentations. The Instructor's Manual and Test Bank are also included on this CD.

Instructor's Online Learning Center to Accompany
American History: A Survey
www.mhhe.com/brinkley11

At the homepage to the text-specific website, instructors will find a series of online tools to meet a wide range of classroom needs. The Instructor's Manual and most Power-Point presentations can be downloaded by instructors, but are password-protected to prevent tampering. Instructors can also create Web-based homework assignments or classroom activities by linking to the Student Online Learning Center, and can create an interactive course syllabus using McGraw-Hill's PageOut. *(www.mhhe. com/pageout).*

PageOut
www.mhhe.com/pageout

On the PageOut website, instructors can create their own course websites. PageOut requires no prior knowledge of HTML, no long hours of coding, and no design skills on the instructor's part. Simply plug the course information into a template and click on one of sixteen designs. The process takes no time at all and leaves instructors with a professionally designed website. Powerful features include an interactive course syllabus that lets instructors post content and links, an online gradebook, lecture notes, bookmarks, and even a discussion board where instructors and students can discuss course-related topics.

For the Student

Student Study Guide with Map Exercises
Prepared by Harvey H. Jackson and Bradley R. Rice, this Study Guide (available in two volumes) helps students to process and master important concepts covered in the text. For each chapter of the text, the Study Guide offers valuable pedagogical tools such as chapter summaries and reviews, chapter outlines that include the main theme of each chapter, objective questions, short answer and essay questions, and mapping exercises.

U.S. History Map Atlas
This is a valuable collection of more than fifty clear and colorful historical maps covering all major periods in American history. It is available for packaging with the textbook. Please contact your local sales representative for more information.

Web of Connections
This brief guide explores the many ways that the World Wide Web facilitates the study of history. It also includes a history of the Internet, instructions for navigating and searching the Web, a glossary of Web jargon, and lists of significant websites in history.

After the Fact Interactive CD-ROM—*The Visible and Invisible Worlds of Salem*
After the Fact Interactive CD-ROM—*Who Freed the Slaves?*
After the Fact Interactive CD-ROM—*USDA Government Inspected*
After the Fact Interactive CD-ROM—*From Rosie to Lucy*

After the Fact Interactive helps students practice the art of historical detection on real historical controversies. Rich, visually appealing modules on the Salem witch trials, the freeing of the slaves, the passage of the Meat Inspection Act of 1906, and the changing roles of women after World War II introduce them to the three basic steps taken by practicing historians: Ask, Research, and Argue; provide them with numerous rich original sources to examine, including video, audio, and images; and guide them in constructing an argument based on their research.

Student Online Learning Center to Accompany
American History: A Survey
www.mhhe.com/brinkley11

At the homepage to the text-specific website, students can link to an interactive study guide, including online essay questions, timelines, mapping exercises, and a variety of objective questions to guide students through the text material. Links to related websites make the student Online Learning Center a great place to begin Web-based research.

PowerWeb: American History
This online supplement is a collection of readings delivered electronically, along with other tools for conducting research in history. In addition, student study tools, Web research tips and exercises, and free access to the Northern Lights search engine are included. A card with a password for accessing PowerWeb has been packaged free with the textbook.

Qualifications
As a full-service publisher of quality education products, McGraw-Hill does much more than just sell textbooks to your students. We create and publish an extensive array of print, video, and digital supplements to support instruction on your campus. Orders of new (versus used) textbooks help us to defray the cost of developing such supplements, which is substantial. Please consult your McGraw-Hill sales representative to learn more about the availability of the supplements that accompany *American History: A Survey,* eleventh edition.

A Student's Guided Tour of
American History: A Survey

The author of *American History: A Survey* has made every effort to provide you with the most accurate, complete, and accessible textbook possible. With this goal in mind, he has included a number of helpful study aids within the text that augment the narrative and serve to heighten the drama and excitement of America's past. The following "Guided Tour" gives examples of many of these special features and suggests how to make the best use of them.

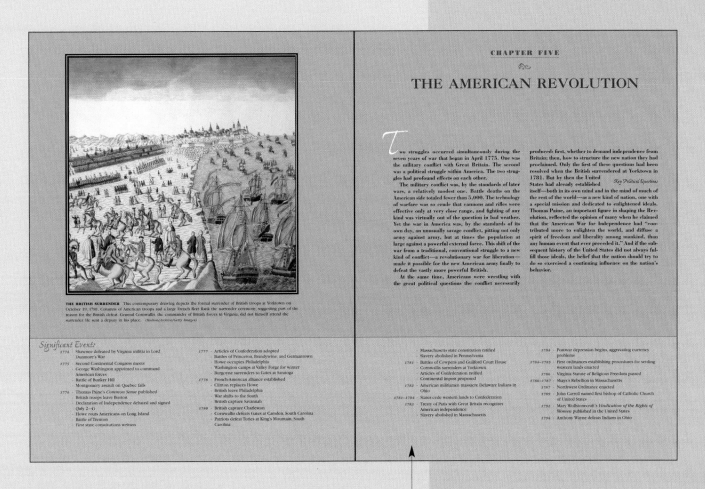

Chapter Introduction

Chapters open with a new introduction that focuses you on the main themes of the chapter and helps you see where the chapter is leading. In addition, new timelines that correspond to many of the chapter heads, as well as other events contained throughout the narrative, have been placed at the beginning of the chapters. These introductions, in addition to serving as a guide to the chapter, also are valuable for review in preparation for tests.

Maps

Maps are important tools that your instructors use to help tell the American story. This textbook includes a wealth of full-color maps that will enhance your study of our history. Captions that make specific reference to map content and include thought questions have been written for every map. In addition, many maps in the book feature a Web icon that links them to an interactive version on the text's Online Learning Center.

IMMIGRANT GROUPS IN COLONIAL AMERICA, 1760 Even though the entire Atlantic seaboard of what is now the United States had become a series of British colonies by 1760, the population consisted of people from many nations. As this map reveals, English settlers dominated most of the regions of North America. But note the large areas of German settlement in the western Chesapeake and Pennsylvania, the swath of Dutch settlement in New York and New Jersey; the Scotch-Irish regions in the western regions of the South; and the large areas in which Africans were becoming the majority of the population, even if subjugated by the white minority. • *What aspects of the history of these colonies help explain their ethnic composition?*

For an interactive version of this map go to www.mhhe.com/brinkley11ch3maps

English settlers as the "Pennsylvania Dutch," a corruption of their own word for "German": "Deutsch"). The Quaker colony became the most common destination for Germans, who came to America in growing numbers. (Among them were Moravians and Mennonites, with religious views similar in many ways to those of the Quakers.) Many German Protestants went to North Carolina as well, especially after the founding of New Bern in 1710 by a company of 600 German-speaking Swiss.

The most numerous of the newcomers were the Scotch-Irish—Scottish Presbyterians who had settled in northern Ireland (in the province of Ulster) in the early seventeenth century. The Ulster colonists had prospered for a time despite the barren soil and the constant, never wholly successful, struggle to suppress the Catholic natives. But in the first years of the eighteenth century, Parliament prohibited Ulster from exporting to England the woolens and other products that had become the basis of the northern Irish economy; at the same time, the English government virtually outlawed the practice of the Presbyterian religion in Ulster and insisted on conformity with the Anglican church. After 1710, moreover, the long-term

Interactive Maps

Interactive maps, related to those maps within the text distinguished by a Web icon, offer a variety of learning functions. On one level you can use the interactive maps to view topography, territories, borders, urban development, developing trends, and other such topics. On a second level, the interactive maps provide you with a multiple-choice quiz that tests your understanding of the information provided on the map, questions for deeper analysis, suggestions for projects, and an audio component that provides an overview of the map. Visit the site at www.mhhe.com/brinkley11.

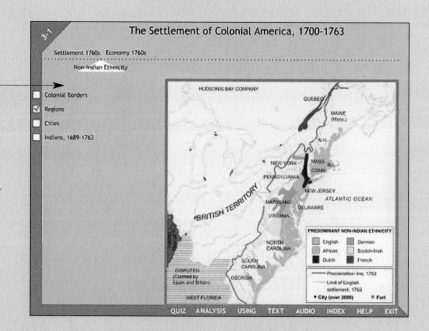

Where Historians Disagree

This well-received feature clearly demonstrates that history is not simply a collection of facts; rather, it consists of many stories that are often complex and open to interpretation. The "Where Historians Disagree" essays will help you to understand the contested quality of much of the American past. This feature will encourage you to think about what different aspects of our history actually mean and provide you with a taste of the thrill of historical investigation.

Where Historians Disagree
THE CHARACTER OF SLAVERY

No issue in American history has produced a richer literature or a more spirited debate than the nature of American slavery. The debate began even before the Civil War, when abolitionists strove to expose slavery to the world as a brutal, dehumanizing institution, while southern defenders of slavery tried to depict it as a benevolent, paternalistic system. That same debate continued for a time after the Civil War, but by the late nineteenth century, with white Americans eager for sectional conciliation, both northern and southern chroniclers of slavery began to accept a romanticized and unthreatening picture of the Old South and its "peculiar institution."

The first major scholarly examination of slavery was fully within this romantic tradition. Ulrich B. Phillips's *American Negro Slavery* (1918) portrayed slavery as an essentially benign institution in which kindly masters looked after submissive, childlike, and generally contented African Americans. Phillips's apologia for slavery remained the authoritative work on the subject for nearly thirty years.

In the 1940s, as concern about racial injustice increasingly engaged the attention of white Americans, challenges to Phillips began to emerge. In 1941, Melville J. Herskovits challenged Phillips's contention that black Americans retained little of their African cultural inheritance. In 1943, Herbert Aptheker published a chronicle of

(Historic New Orleans Collection)

(General Research Division, New York Public Library, Astor, Lenox and Tilden Foundations)

slave revolts as a way of challenging Phillips's claim that blacks were submissive and content.

A somewhat different challenge to Phillips emerged in the 1950s from historians who emphasized the brutality of the institution. Kenneth Stampp's *The Peculiar Institution* (1956) and, even more damningly, Stanley Elkins's *Slavery* (1959) described a labor system that did serious physical and psychological damage to its victims. Stampp and Elkins portrayed slavery as something like a prison, in which men and women had virtually no space in which to develop their own social and cultural lives. Elkins compared the system to Nazi concentration camps during World War II and likened the childlike "Sambo" personality of slavery to the distortions of character that many scholars believed the Holocaust had produced.

In the early 1970s, an explosion of new scholarship on slavery shifted the emphasis away from the damage the system inflicted on African Americans and toward the striking success of the slaves in building a culture of their own despite their enslavement. John Blassingame in 1973, echoing Herskovits's claims of thirty years earlier, argued that "the most remarkable aspect of the whole process of enslavement is the extent to which the American-born slaves were able to retain their ancestors' culture." Herbert Gutman, in *The Black Family in Slavery and Freedom* (1976) challenged the prevailing belief that slavery had weakened and even destroyed the African-American family. On the contrary, he argued, the black family survived slavery with impressive strength, although

with some significant differences from the prevailing form of the white family. Eugene Genovese's *Roll, Jordan, Roll* (1974) and other works revealed how African Americans manipulated the paternalist assumptions at the heart of slavery to build a large cultural space of their own within the system where they could develop their own family life, social traditions, and religious patterns. That same year, Robert Fogel and Stanley Engerman published their controversial *Time on the Cross*, a highly quantitative study that supported some of the claims of Gutman and Genovese about black achievement, but that went much further in portraying slavery as a successful and reasonably humane (if ultimately immoral) system. Slave workers, they argued, were better treated and lived in greater comfort than most northern industrial workers of the same era. Their conclusions produced a storm of criticism.

Some of the most important recent scholarship on slavery has focused on the role of women within it. Elizabeth Fox-Genovese's *Within the Plantation Household* (1988) examined the lives of both white and black women on the plantation. Rejecting the claims of some feminist historians that black and white women shared a common female identity born of their shared subordination to men, she portrayed slave women as defined by their dual roles as members of the plantation work force and anchors of the black family. Slave women, she argued, professed loyalty to their mistresses when forced to serve them as domestics; but their real loyalty remained to their own communities and families.

509

America in the World
THE ATLANTIC CONTEXT OF EARLY AMERICAN HISTORY

Most Americans understand that our nation has become intimately bound up with the rest of the world—that we live in a time that is sometimes called the "age of globalization." Most students of American history, however, have traditionally examined the nation's past in relative isolation. In recent years, scholars have begun to re-examine the way we explain the American past. They have revealed a host of new connections between what happened in the Americas and what was happening in the rest of the world. They have, in short, taken our modern notion of globalization and used it to explain some aspects of our more distant past. This re-examination has included the earliest period of European settlement of the Americas. Many scholars of early American history now examine what happened in the context of what has become known as the "Atlantic World."

The idea of an "Atlantic World" rests in part on the obvious connections between western Europe and the Spanish, British, French, and Dutch colonies in North and South America. All the early European civilizations of the Americas were part of a great imperial project launched by the major powers of Europe. The massive European immigration to the Americas beginning in the sixteenth century, the defeat and devastation of native populations, the creation of European agricultural and urban settlements, and the imposition of imperial regulations on trade, commerce, landowning, and political life—all of these forces reveal the influence of Old World imperialism on the history of the New World.

But the creation of empires is only one part of the creation of the Atlantic World. At least equally important—and closely related—is the expansion of commerce from Europe to the Americas. Although some Europeans traveled to the New World in search of religious freedom, or to escape oppression, or to search for adventure, the great majority of European immigrants were in search of economic opportunity. Not surprisingly, therefore, the European settlements in the Americas were almost from the start intimately connected to

Europe through the growth of commerce between them—commerce that grew more extensive and more complex with every passing year. The commercial relationship between America and Europe was responsible not just for the growth of trade, but also for the increases in migration over time—as the demand for labor in the New World drew more and more settlers from the Old World. Commerce was also the principal reason for the rise of slavery in the Americas, and for the growth of the slave trade between European America and Africa. The Atlantic World, in other words, included not just Europe and the Americas, but Africa as well.

Religion was another force binding together the Atlantic World. The vast majority of people of European descent were Christians and most of them maintained important religious ties to Europe. Catholics, of course, were part of a hierarchical church based in Rome and maintained close ties with the Vatican. But the Protestant faiths that predominated in North America were intimately linked to their European counterparts as well. New religious ideas and movements spread back and forth across the Atlantic with astonishing speed. Great revivals that began in Europe moved quickly to America. The "Great Awakening" of the mid-eighteenth century, for example, began in Britain and traveled to America in large part through the efforts of the English evangelist George Whitefield. American evangelists later carried religious ideas from the New World back to the Old.

The early history of European America was also closely bound up with the intellectual life of Europe. The Enlightenment—the cluster of ideas that emerged in Europe in the seventeenth and eighteenth centuries emphasizing the power of human reason—moved quickly to the Americas, producing considerable intellectual ferment throughout the New World, but particularly in the British colonies in North America and the Caribbean. The ideas of the British philosopher John Locke, for example, helped shape

the founding of Georgia. The English Constitution, and the idea of the "rights of Englishmen," shaped the way North Americans shaped their own concepts of politics. Many of the ideas that lay behind the American Revolution were products of British and continental philosophy that had traveled across the Atlantic. The reinterpretation of those idea by Americans to help justify their drive to independence—by, among others, Thomas Paine—moved back across the Atlantic to Europe and helped, among other things, to inspire the French Revolution. Scientific and technological knowledge—another product of the Enlightenment—moved rapidly back and forth across the Atlantic. Americans borrowed industrial technology from Britain. Europe acquired much of its early knowledge of electricity from experiments done in America. But the Enlightenment was only one part of the continuing intellectual connections within the Atlantic World, connections that spread artistic, scholarly, and political ideas widely through the lands bordering the ocean.

Instead of thinking of the early history of what became the United States simply as the story of the growth of thirteen small colonies along the Atlantic seaboard of North America, the idea of the "Atlantic World" encourages us to think of early American history as a vast pattern of exchanges and interactions—trade, migration, religious and intellectual exchange, and many other relationships—among all the societies bordering the Atlantic: western Europe, western Africa, the Caribbean, and North and South America.

(The I.N. Phelps Stokes Collection of American Historical Prints, Prints Division, The New York Public Library, Astor, Lenox and Tilden Foundations.)

22

America in the World

New "America in the World" features place America in a more global context. America has never existed in isolation from the rest of the world, and these essays demonstrate the importance of the many international influences and other national histories in the American story.

Patterns of Popular Culture

"Patterns of Popular Culture" essays spotlight ways in which popular culture has affected the lives of Americans at different times in the past and places that culture in a larger historical context. The author has selected a wide variety of high-interest topics ranging from *Horse Racing, Baseball and the Civil War, The Penny Press, The Slaves' Music, Rock Music in the Sixties, Lucy and Desi, The Age of Swing, Coney Island, The Wild West Show, Yellow Journalism*, and *The Golden Age of Comic Books*. (See the Contents for a complete listing.)

Patterns of Popular Culture
HORSE RACING

There were few respites from the daily struggle for survival for the first European settlers in North America. Men and women attended church and celebrated major religious holidays, but there was little in most of their lives that twentieth-century Americans would recognize as leisure or popular culture. For relatively affluent colonists, however, one sport emerged very early as an enduringly popular form of entertainment: horse racing.

It was natural, perhaps, that horse racing would become so appealing in the seventeenth and eighteenth centuries, when horses were, for most people, the only source of transportation over land other than walking. Those who could afford to own horses considered them part of the essential equipment of life. But people also formed attachments to their horses and prided themselves on their beauty and speed. Eventually, such attachments led to the creation of a spectator sport in which that beauty and speed were the central attractions.

Informal horse racing began almost as soon as Europeans settled the English colonies. Formal racing followed quickly. The first race track in North America—New Market (named for a popular race course in England)—was established in 1665 near the site of present-day Garden City, on Long Island in New York. It was, from the beginning, a showcase for horses bred in America by Americans, and in 1751 the track's authorities decreed that no imported horses could race there. For a time, New Market (and other horse racing sites) were

dominated by English military officers stationed in the colonies. But tracks quickly developed a much wider appeal, and soon horse racing had spread up and down the Atlantic coast. By the time of the American Revolution, it was popular in almost every colony. It had a particularly avid following in Maryland, Virginia, and South Carolina; and it was moving as well into the newly settled areas of the Southwest. Andrew Jackson was a founder of the first racing track in Nashville, Tennessee, in the early nineteenth century. Kentucky—whose native bluegrass was early recognized as ideal for grazing horses—had eight tracks by 1800.

Like almost everything else in the life of early America, the world of

OAKLAND HOUSE AND RACE COURSE This 1840 painting by Robert Brammer and August A. Von Smith portrays an early race course in Louisville, Kentucky, which provided entertainment to affluent white southerners. *(Oakland House and Race Course, Louisville, 1840. By Robert Brammer and August A. Von Smith. Collection of The Speed Art Museum, Louisville, Kentucky. Purchase, Museum Art fund, 56.19)*

horse racing was bounded by lines of class and race. For many years, it was considered the exclusive preserve of "gentlemen," so much so that in 1674 a court in Virginia fined James Bullocke, a tailor, for proposing a race, "it being contrary to Law for a Labourer to make a race, being a sport only for Gentlemen." But while white aristocrats retained control of racing, they were not the only people who participated in it. Southern aristocrats often trained young male slaves as jockeys for their horses, just as northern horse owners employed the services of free blacks as riders. In the North and the South, African Americans eventually emerged as some of the most talented and experienced trainers of racing horses. And despite social and legal

THE ECLIPSE-HENRY MATCH RACE "Match races" between famous horses were a popular feature of early nineteenth-century horse racing. This famous 1823 race on Long Island, New York, pitted prize-winning horses from the North and the South against one another. American Eclipse, the northern entry, won. *(Private collection)*

pressures, free blacks and poor whites often staged their own, informal races, which proved highly popular among lower-class men and women and which helped give racing a slightly disreputable image among more conservative white aristocrats.

Racing also began early to reflect the growing sectional rivalry between the North and the South. In 1824, the Union Race Course on Long Island established an astounding $24,000 purse for a race between two famous thoroughbreds: American Eclipse (from the North) and Sir Henry (from the South). American Eclipse won two of the three heats, but a southern racehorse prevailed in another such celebrated contest in 1836. These inter-sectional races, which drew enormous crowds and created tremendous publicity, continued into the 1850s, until the North-South rivalry began to take a more deadly form.

Horse racing remained popular after the Civil War, but two developments changed its character considerably. One was the successful effort to drive African Americans out of the sport. At least until the 1890s, black jockeys and trainers remained central to racing. At the first Kentucky Derby in 1875, fourteen of the fifteen horses had African-American riders. One black man, Isaac Murphy, became one of the greatest jockeys of all time, the winner of three Kentucky Derbys and a remarkable 44 percent of all races in which he rode. Gradually, however, the same social dynamics that enforced racial segregation on so many other areas of American life in this era penetrated racing as well. By the beginning of the twentieth century, through a combination of harassment, intimidation, and formal discrimination, white jockeys and the organized jockey clubs had driven almost all

black riders, and many black trainers, out of the sport.

The second change was the introduction of formalized betting to the sport. Informal wages had been part of racing almost from the beginning, but in the late nineteenth century race tracks themselves began creating betting systems as a way to lure customers to the races. At the same time that the breeding of racehorses was moving into the hands of enormously wealthy families (many of them the beneficiaries of new industrial fortunes), the audience for racing was becoming increasingly working class and lower middle class. The people who now came to tracks were mostly white men, and some white women, lured to the races not by a love of horses—which were coming now to play a less central role in their everyday lives—but by the usually futile hope of quick and easy riches through gambling.

---

his commitment to the agrarian ideal, found himself obliged as president to confront and accommodate them.

JEFFERSON THE PRESIDENT

Privately, Thomas Jefferson may well have considered his victory over John Adams in 1800 to be what he later termed it: a revolution "as real . . . as that of 1776." Publicly, however, he was restrained and conciliatory as he assumed office, attempting to minimize the differences between the two parties and to calm the passions that the bitter campaign had aroused. "We are all republicans, we are all federalists," he said in his inaugural address. And during his eight years in office, he did much to prove those words correct. There was no complete repudiation of Federalist policies, no true "revolution." Indeed, at times Jefferson seemed to outdo the Federalists at their own work—most notably in overseeing a remarkable expansion of the territory of the United States.

The Federal City and the "People's President"

Symbolic of the relative unimportance of the federal government during the Jeffersonian era was the character *The District of Columbia* of the newly founded national capital, the city of Washington. John Adams had moved to the new seat of government during the last year of his administration. There were many at that time who expected the raw, uncompleted town to emerge soon as a great and majestic city, a focus for the growing nationalism that the Federalists were pro-

moting. The French architect Pierre L'Enfant had designed the capital on a grand scale, with broad avenues radiating out from the uncompleted Capitol building, set on one of the area's highest hills. Washington was, many Americans believed, to become the Paris of the United States.

In reality, however, throughout Jefferson's presidency—and indeed through most of the nineteenth century—Washington remained little more than a straggling, provincial village. Although the population increased steadily from the 3,200 counted in the 1800 census, it

SAVING THE FORESTS

From the earliest days of European settlement in North America, people depended for their very survival on forests—for building homes, barns, fences, and wagons; for heating buildings; for powering locomotives, forging iron, tanning leather, making soap. Next to food, wood was the most basic resource in the American economy.

It was also the most wasted. Trees were essential to new settlements, but they were also the chief obstacle to those settlements. East of the Mississippi River, creating new farming communities usually meant cutting down forests. Although trees were cut for lumber and fuel, the main reason for their removal was simply clearing. Within a decade or two, few signs would remain that the

new cornfield or pasture had ever been a forest at all.

The American forest seemed so endless that few worried about conserving it. As a result, the nineteenth-century inhabitants of the United States destroyed trees at an astonishing rate. By 1850, over 100 million acres of land—an area roughly the size of modern California—had been cleared since the time of the first colonists. Moreover, the rate of forest destruction was increasing, so that over the next ten years another 40 million acres were cleared—as if the entire state of Georgia had been deforested in a single decade.

Although most Americans still regarded their forests as limitless, a few began to voice concern about what

might happen if deforestation continued at this rapid pace. The most influential of these was a remarkable Vermonter named George Perkins Marsh. A scholar who read a dozen or more European languages, Marsh served as the U.S. ambassador to Turkey from 1849 to 1854, and to Italy from 1860 until his death in 1882. During his many years living on the shores of the Mediterranean, Marsh became interested in the environmental effects of classical civilizations. He gathered evidence from his travels and readings to demonstrate that deforestation had wreaked havoc with the earth.

The result was one of the most important books in the history of American conservation. Published in 1864, Marsh's *Man and Nature* warned of the dangerous consequences that might result if the United States did not stop destroying its forests. Losing access to lumber and fuel was the least of the problems he named. Much more important, he said, was the forest's role in stabilizing the natural environment. According to Marsh's theories, trees slowed the rate at which water drained from the soil. They prevented erosion, maintained soil fertility, and stabilized the flow of natural springs and streams. Removing them laid the groundwork for environmental disaster. In the end, it would turn the landscape into a desert.

For proof of his claims, Marsh offered evidence from around the world. He described springs he had known as a child in Vermont that had since dried up as the trees around them were cleared. As evidence that cutting down forests could lead to desertification, he pointed to North Africa and the Middle East, holding them up as examples of

A NEWLY CLEARED FARM, 1790s Clearing forests was the essential first step toward establishing a new farm and thereby "improving" land. Farmers killed trees by stripping their bark and then planted crops amid the remaining stumps. Settlers used lumber to build houses and barns, erect fences, and supply fireplaces with fuel. *(Bettmann/Corbis)*

EARLY LUMBERING IN MICHIGAN As pioneer farmers moved west, a parallel migration of woodcutters took place. By the second half of the nineteenth century, pine lumber was being shipped by rail out of the north woods of Maine, New York, Michigan, and Minnesota to supply farmers on the treeless prairies with the construction materials and fuel that were essential to an agricultural economy. *(Bettmann/Corbis)*

GEORGE PERKINS MARSH For most of his career, Marsh was an attorney, diplomat, and politician. (He served three times in the U.S. House of Representatives.) But his most enduring legacy was his impact, through his writings, on the early years of the movement in America to protect nature from human exploitation and destruction. *(Culver Pictures, Inc.)*

what America might become if its citizens refused to heed his warnings. Only a strong commitment to conserving the forest and other natural resources could save the nation from its folly. "Man has too long forgotten," he wrote, "that the earth was given to him for usufruct [use without damage] alone, not for consumption, still less for profligate waste."

Marsh's book drew wide attention from scientists and politicians all over the United States. From the 1870s forward, increasing numbers of Americans began to express concern about the future of the nation's forests, and laws started to be passed for their protection and restoration. Although many of Marsh's theories about the climatic influence of forests would eventually prove to be overstated or wrong, they became the basis for several influential policies. Laws in the 1870s offered free

land on the Great Plains to settlers who planted trees there (although such stands of trees did not increase rainfall as Marsh and the authors of the laws had hoped). More important was Marsh's influence on the conservation of existing forests.

His most important success occurred in the state of New York. Many people were worried that falling water levels in the Erie Canal might threaten the lifeblood of the state's economy and foreshadow problems for New York City's water supply. Following Marsh's theories, they attributed the problem to deforestation in the state's heavily lumbered Adirondack Mountains. As a result of their efforts, the state legislature passed a law in 1885 creating a huge "forest reserve" there. To guarantee that the Adirondacks would remain "forever wild," defenders saw that a clause to this effect was

inserted into the new state constitution in 1894. The Adirondack Forest Reserve was a model for the nation as a whole. In 1891, seeking specifically to protect watersheds, Congress passed the Forest Reserve Act, empowering the president to set aside any "public lands wholly or in part covered with timber or under growth." The act became the basis for the National Forest system of the United States. Conservation of the forest reserves soon emerged as a chief political objective of Theodore Roosevelt's presidency. Saving the forests had become national policy, in no small measure because of the book Marsh had published four decades earlier.

Roosevelt added land to several existing parks and also created new ones: Crater Lake in Oregon, Mesa Verde in Utah, Platt in Oklahoma, and Wind Cave in South Dakota.

The Hetch Hetchy Controversy

The contending views of the early conservation movement came to a head beginning in 1906 in a sensational controversy over the Hetch Hetchy Valley in Yosemite

National Park. Hetch Hetchy (a name derived from a local Indian term meaning "grassy meadows") was a spectacular, high-walled valley highly popular with naturalists such as Muir and his fellow Sierra Club members. But many residents of San Francisco, worried about finding enough water to serve their growing population, saw Hetch Hetchy as an ideal place for a dam, which would create a large reservoir for the city—a plan that Muir and others furiously opposed.

In 1906, San Francisco suffered a devastating earthquake and fire. Widespread sympathy for the city strengthened their case for the dam; and Theodore Roosevelt—who had initially expressed some sympathy for Muir's position—turned the decision over to his chief forester, Gifford Pinchot. As the principal exponent of the rational use of nature, Pinchot had no interest in Muir's aesthetic and spiritual arguments. He approved construction of the dam.

For over a decade, a battle raged between naturalists and the advocates of the dam, a battle that consumed the energies of John Muir for the rest of his life and that eventually, many believed, helped *Competing Conservationist* kill him. "Dam Hetch Hetchy!" *Visions* Muir once said. "As well dam for water-tanks the people's cathedrals and churches, for no holier temple has ever been consecrated by the heart of man." To Pinchot, the issue was the practical one of

The American Environment

This feature provides exciting and informative essays of cutting-edge scholarship that highlight environmental history, as well as the history of science and technology. Topics include the biological invasion of colonial times, altering the flow of water in the early 1800s, and pesticide spraying in more recent times. These essays will deepen your understanding of and interest in a very important field of history. (See the Contents for a complete listing.)

THE ARRIVAL OF THE ENGLISH

England's first documented contact with the New World came only five years after Spain's. In 1497, John Cabot (like Columbus a native of Genoa) sailed to the northeastern coast of North America on an expedition sponsored by King Henry VII. Other English navigators

John Cabot continued Cabot's unsuccessful search for a northwest passage through the New World to the Orient. They explored other areas of North America during the sixteenth century. But even though England claimed dominion over the lands its explorers surveyed, nearly a century passed before the English made any serious efforts to establish colonies there. Like other European nations, England had to experience an internal transformation before it could begin settling new lands. That transformation occurred in the sixteenth century.

The Commercial Incentive

Part of the attraction of the New World to the English was its newness, its contrast to their own troubled land. America seemed a place where human settlement could start anew, where a perfect society could be created without the flaws and inequities of the Old World. Such dreams began to emerge in England only a few years after Columbus's voyages. They found classic expression in Sir Thomas More's *Utopia* (published in Latin in 1516, translated into English thirty-five years later), which described a mythical and nearly perfect society on an imaginary island supposedly discovered by a companion of Amerigo Vespucci in the waters of the New World.

More's picture of an ideal community was, among other things, a comment on the social and economic ills of the England of his own time. The people of Tudor England suffered from frequent and costly European wars, from almost constant religious strife, and above all from a harsh economic transformation of the countryside. Because the

The Enclosure Movement worldwide demand for wool was growing rapidly, many landowners were finding it profitable to convert their land from fields for crops to pastures for sheep. The result was a significant growth in the wool trade. But that meant land worked at one time by serfs and later by rent-paying tenants was steadily enclosed for sheep runs and taken away from the farmers. Thousands of evicted tenants roamed the countryside in gangs, begging from (and at times robbing) the more fortunate householders through whose communities they passed.

The government passed various laws designed to halt enclosures, relieve the worthy poor, and compel the ablebodied or "sturdy beggars" to work. Such laws had little effect. The enclosure movement continued unabated, and relatively few of the dislocated farmers could find reemployment in raising sheep or manufacturing wool. By removing land from cultivation, the enclosure movement

also limited England's ability to feed its population, which grew from 3 million in 1485 to 4 million in 1603. Both because of the dislocation of farmers and the restriction of the food supply, therefore, the nation had a serious problem of surplus population.

Amid this growing distress, a rising class of merchant capitalists was prospering from the expansion of foreign trade. At first, England had exported little except raw wool; but new merchant capitalists helped create a domestic cloth industry that allowed them to begin marketing finished goods at home and abroad. At first, most exporters did business almost entirely as individuals. In time, however, some merchants joined forces and formed chartered companies. Each such

Chartered Companies enterprise operated on the basis of a charter acquired from the monarch, which gave the company a monopoly for trading in a particular region. Among the first of these were the Muscovy Company (1555), the Levant Company (1581), the Barbary Company (1585), the Guinea Company (1588), and the East India Company (1600). Investors in these companies often made fantastic profits from the exchange of English manufactures, especially woolens, for exotic goods; and they felt a powerful urge to continue the expansion of their profitable trade.

Central to this drive was the emergence of a new concept of economic life known as mercantilism, which was gaining favor throughout Europe. Mercantilism rested on the assumption that the nation as a whole was the principal actor in the economy, not the individuals within it. The goal of economic activity should be to increase the nation's total wealth. Mercantilists believed that the world's wealth was finite. One person or nation could grow rich only at the expense of another. A nation's economic health depended, therefore, on extracting as much wealth as possible from foreign lands and exporting as little wealth as possible from home.

The principles of mercantilism guided the economic policies of virtually all the European nation-states in the sixteenth and seventeenth cen-

Mercantilism turies. Mercantilism greatly enhanced the position of the new merchant capitalists, whose overseas ventures were thought to benefit the entire nation and to be worthy of government assistance. It also increased competition among nations. Every European state was trying to find markets for its exports while trying to limit its imports. One result was the increased attractiveness of acquiring colonies, which could become the source of goods that a country might otherwise have to buy from other nations.

In England, the mercantilistic program thrived at first on the basis of the flourishing wool trade with the European continent, and particularly with the great cloth market in Antwerp. Beginning in the 1550s, however, that glutted market collapsed, and English merchants found themselves obliged to look elsewhere for

---

Marginal Notes

The text provides you with an important and new study tool with the addition of marginal notes that complement the narrative. These highlight key terms, events, and concepts as they appear within the narrative. Not only are these useful to you as you read through the text, they also serve as a valuable review tool for test preparation.

---

taking steps to make the party's hold on the courts secure. By the Judiciary Act of 1801, passed by the lame duck Congress, the Federalists reduced the number of

The Judiciary Act of 1801 Supreme Court justiceships by one but greatly increased the number of federal judgeships as a whole. Adams quickly appointed Federalists to the newly created positions. Indeed, there were charges that he stayed up until midnight on his last day in office to finish signing the new judges' commissions. These officeholders became known as the "midnight appointments."

Even so, the Republicans viewed their victory as almost complete. The nation, they believed, had been saved from tyranny. A new era could now begin, one in which the true principles on which America had been founded would once again govern the land. The exuberance with which the victors viewed the future—and the importance they attributed to the Federalists' defeat—was evident in the phrase Jefferson himself later used to describe his election. He called it the "Revolution of 1800." It remained to be seen how revolutionary it would really be.

CONCLUSION

The writing of the Constitution of 1787 was the single most important political event in the history of the United States, and a notable event in the political history of the modern world. In creating a "federal" system of dispersed and divided authority—authority divided among national and state governments, authority divided among an executive, a legislature, and a judiciary—the young nation sought to balance its need for an effective central government against its fear of concentrated and despotic power. The ability of the delegates to the Constitutional Convention to compromise again and again to produce the ultimate structure gave evidence of the deep yearning among them for a stable political system. The same willingness to compromise allowed the greatest challenge to the ideals of the new democracy—slavery—to survive intact.

The writing and ratifying of the Constitution settled some questions about the shape of the new nation. The first twelve years under the government created by the Constitution solved others. And yet by the year 1800, a basic disagreement about the future of the nation—a disagreement personified by the differences between committed nationalist Alexander Hamilton and the self-proclaimed champion of democracy Thomas Jefferson—remained unresolved and was creating bitter divisions and conflicts within the political world. The election of Thomas Jefferson to the presidency that year opened a new chapter in the nation's public history. It also brought to a close, at least temporarily, savage political conflicts that had seemed to threaten the nation's future.

FOR FURTHER REFERENCE

Charles Beard, *An Economic Interpretation of the Constitution of the United States* (1913) is one of the seminal works of modern American historical inquiry, although its interpretation is no longer widely accepted. Gordon Wood, *The Creation of the American Republic* (1969) is the leading analysis of the intellectual path from the Declaration of Independence to the American Constitution. Jack Rakove, *Original Meanings: Politics and Ideas in the Making of the Constitution* (1996) connects the politics of the 1780s with the political ideas embedded in the Constitution. Stanley Elkins and Eric McKitrick, *The Age of Federalism* (1993) provides a detailed overview of political and economic development in the 1790s. Joyce Appleby, *Capitalism and a New Social Order: The Republican Vision of the 1790s* (1984) highlights liberal and capitalist impulses unleashed after the ratification of the Constitution. Joseph Ellis is the author of several highly regarded books on the founders: *After the Revolution: Profiles of Early American Culture* (1979), which examines some of the framers of the new nation; *American Sphinx: The Character of Thomas Jefferson* (1997); *Founding Brothers: The Revolutionary Generation* (2000); and *Passionate Sage: The Character and Legacy of John Adams* (1993). David McCullough, *John Adams* (2001) is a vivid, sympathetic, and outstandingly popular biography.

For quizzes, Internet resources, references to additional books and films, and more, consult this book's Online Learning Center at www.mhhe.com/brinkley11.

For Further Reference

For Further Reference lists at the end of every chapter highlight the most significant books available about topics covered in the chapter and can help you do further research or follow up on a topic of particular interest to you.

ILLUSTRATIONS

MAPS

CHARTS

AMERICAN HISTORY

A SURVEY

FROBISHER AND THE ESKIMOS In 1577, the English explorer Martin Frobisher embarked on an elusive search that enchanted a generation of Europeans—the search for the "Northwest Passage," a waterway through North America to the Pacific. He sailed into the Arctic regions of eastern Canada, deep into Baffin Bay, before finding his route blocked by impassable ice. Along the way, he encountered groups of Baffinland Eskimos, who—as this John White drawing (repainted by his contemporary Hans Sloan) shows—attacked his party. Even outnumbered, the Frobisher party had the advantage of firearms and escaped serious harm. *(British Museum, London/The Bridgeman Art Library)*

Significant Events

14,000–12,000 B.C.	Asians begin migrating to North America across the Bering Strait
1347	Black Death begins in Europe
1480s	Portuguese explorers travel down west coast of Africa in search of sea route to Asia
1492	Columbus sails west from Spain in search of Asia, reaches Bahama Islands in the Caribbean
1494	Papal decree divides New World between Spain and Portugal
1497	John Cabot establishes first English claim in North America
1502	First African slaves arrive in Spanish America

CHAPTER ONE

THE MEETING OF CULTURES

The discovery of America did not begin with Christopher Columbus. It began many thousands of years earlier when human beings first crossed an ancient land bridge over the Bering Strait into what is now Alaska and—almost certainly without realizing it—began to people a new continent. No one is certain when these migrations began; recent estimates suggest between 12,000 and 14,000 years ago, but some scholars believe the first crossings were much earlier. They were probably a result of the development of new stone tools—spears and other hunting implements—with which it became possible to pursue the large animals that regularly crossed between Asia and North America. Year after year, a few at a time, these nomadic peoples—all of them apparently from a Mongolian stock similar to that of modern-day eastern Siberia—entered the new continent and moved ever deeper into its heart. Ultimately, perhaps as early as 9,000 B.C., the migrations reached the southern tip of South America. By the end of the fifteenth century A.D., when the first important contact with Europeans occurred, America was the home of many millions of men and women. Scholars estimate that more than 50 million people—and perhaps as many as 75 million, more than lived in Europe—lived in the Americas by 1500 and that as many as 10 million lived in the territory that now constitutes the United States.

AMERICA BEFORE COLUMBUS

As settlement spread, the peoples of the different regions of America began to adapt themselves to their surroundings. For many centuries, they lived primarily in small nomadic bands, subsisting through hunting, fishing, and occasionally primitive agriculture, depending on the resources of the lands in which they lived. Gradually, however, they developed substantial civilizations—some of them of vast size and power. There was as much variety among the civilizations of the Americas as among the civilizations of Europe, Asia, and Africa.

The Civilizations of the South

The most elaborate of these societies emerged in South and Central America and in Mexico. In Peru, the Incas created a powerful empire of perhaps 6 million people. They developed a complex political system and a large network of paved roads that welded together the populations of many tribes under a single rule. In Central America and on the Yucatán peninsula of Mexico, the Mayas built a sophis-

ticated culture with a written language, a numerical system similar to the Arabic (and superior to the Roman), an accurate calendar, and an advanced agricultural system. They were succeeded by the Aztecs, a once-nomadic warrior tribe from the north. In the late thirteenth century, the *Incas, Mayans, and Aztecs* Aztecs established a precarious rule over much of central and southern Mexico and built elaborate administrative, educational, and medical systems comparable to the most advanced in Europe at the time. The Aztecs also developed a harsh religion that required human sacrifice. Their Spanish conquerors discovered the skulls of 100,000 victims in one location when they arrived in 1519. That was one reason why many Europeans came to consider the Aztecs "savages" despite their impressive accomplishments (and despite the holy wars and witch burnings in the Christian world, which show that the Aztecs were not alone in finding religious justification for killing).

The economies of these societies were based primarily on agriculture, but there were also substantial cities. In them lived, among others, many of the warriors and priests

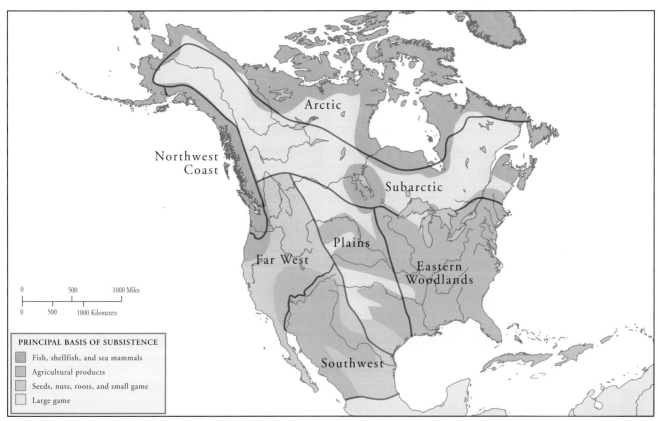

HOW THE EARLY NORTH AMERICANS LIVED This map shows the various ways in which the native tribes of North America supported themselves before the arrival of European civilization. Like most precommercial peoples, the native Americans survived largely on the resources available in their immediate surroundings. Note, for example, the reliance on the products of the sea of the tribes along the northern coastlines of the continent, and the way in which tribes in relatively inhospitable climates in the North—where agriculture was difficult—relied on hunting large game. Most native Americans were farmers. ◆ *What different kinds of farming would have emerged in the very different climates of the agricultural regions shown on this map?*

 For an interactive version of this map go to www.mhhe.com/brinkley11ch1maps

who ruled the empires and formed their hereditary elites. Some of these cities were as large as the greatest capitals of Europe. Tenochtitlán, the Aztec capital built on the site of present-day Mexico City, had a population of over 100,000 in 1500 and an impressive complex of majestic public buildings—including temples equal in size to the great pyramids of Egypt. The Mayas (at Mayapán and elsewhere) and the Incas (in such cities as Cuzco and Machu Picchu) produced similarly elaborate settlements with striking religious and ceremonial structures of their own. These achievements are all the more remarkable for their having been attained without some of the important technologies that Asian and European civilizations possessed. The Incas, for example, never had any system of writing or any equivalent for paper. And as late as the sixteenth century, no American society had yet developed wheeled vehicles.

The Civilizations of the North

The peoples north of Mexico—in the lands that became the United States and Canada—did not develop empires as large or political systems as elaborate as those of the Incas, Mayas, and Aztecs. They did, however, build complex civilizations of great variety. Societies that subsisted on hunting, gathering, fishing, or some combination of the three emerged in the northern regions of the continent.

Complex and Varied Civilizations The Eskimos of the Arctic Circle fished and hunted seals; their civilization spanned thousands of miles of largely frozen land, which they traversed by dogsled. The big-game hunters of the northern forests led nomadic lives based on pursuit of moose and caribou. The tribes of the Pacific Northwest, whose principal occupation was salmon fishing, created substantial permanent settlements along the coast and engaged in constant and often violent competition with one another for access to natural resources.

Another group of tribes spread through relatively arid regions of the Far West and developed successful communities—many of them quite wealthy and densely populated—based on fishing, hunting small game, and gathering. Other societies in North America were primarily agricultural. Among the most elaborate were those in the Southwest. The people of that region built large irrigation systems to allow farming on their relatively dry land, and they constructed substantial towns that became centers of trade, crafts, and religious and civic ritual. Their densely populated settlements at Chaco Canyon and elsewhere consisted of stone and adobe terraced structures, known today as pueblos, many of which resembled the large apartment buildings of later eras in size and design. In the Great Plains region, too, most tribes were engaged in sedentary farming (corn and other grains) and lived in substantial permanent settlements, although there were some small nomadic tribes that subsisted by hunting buffalo. (Only in the eighteenth century, after Europeans had introduced the horse to North America, did buffalo hunting begin to support a large population in the region; at that point, many once-sedentary farmers left the land to pursue the great migratory buffalo herds.)

The eastern third of what is now the United States—much of it covered with forests and inhabited by people who have thus become known as the Woodland Indians—had the greatest food resources of any region of the continent. Many tribes lived there, and most of them engaged simultaneously in farming, hunting, gathering, and fishing. In the South there were for a time substantial permanent settlements and large trading networks based on the corn and other grains grown in the rich lands of the Mississippi River valley. As in the Southwest, cities emerged as trading and political centers. Among them was Cahokia (near present-day St. Louis), which at its peak in 1200 A.D. had a population of 40,000 and contained a great complex of large earthen mounds.

INDIANS OF NEW FRANCE The drawing is by the cartographer Charles Bécard de Granville, who was employed by the French government to make maps of its territories in North America. Granville also produced drawings of the flora and fauna of the region and of the natives he encountered. This depiction of Indian hunters traveling by river dates from approximately 1701. *(Gilcrease Institute)*

WHY DO HISTORIANS SO OFTEN DIFFER?

There was a time, early in the twentieth century, while the professional study of history was still relatively new, when many historians believed that questions about the past could be answered with the same certainty and precision that questions in other, more scientific fields could be answered. By using precise methods of research and analysis, and by deploying armies of scholars to sift through available records and produce careful, closely argued accounts of the past, it would be possible to create something close to definitive histories that would survive without controversy for many generations. Scholars who believed this were known as "positivists," and they shared the views of such European thinkers as Auguste Comte and Thomas Henry Huxley that real knowledge can only be derived from direct, scientific observation of clear "facts." Historians, therefore, set out to answer questions for which extensive archival or statistical evidence was available.

Although a vigorous debate continues to this day over whether historical research can or should be truly objective, almost no historian any longer accepts the "positivist" claim that history could ever be anything like an exact science. Disagreement about the past is, in fact, at the very heart of the

effort to understand history—just as disagreement about the present is at the heart of efforts to understand our own time. Critics of contemporary historical scholarship often denounce the way historians are constantly revising earlier interpretations; some denounce the act of interpretation itself. History, they claim, is "what happened." Historians should "stick to the facts." That scholars almost always find it impossible to do so helps account for the many controversies surrounding the historical profession today.

Historians differ with one another both because the "facts" are seldom as straightforward as their critics claim, and because facts by themselves mean almost nothing without an effort to assign meaning to them. There are, of course, some historical "facts" that are not in dispute. Everyone agrees, for example, that the Japanese bombed Pearl Harbor on December 7, 1941, or that Abraham Lincoln was elected president in 1860. But many other "facts" are much harder to determine—among them, for example, the question of how large the American population was before the arrival of Columbus, which is discussed later in this chapter. How many slaves resisted slavery? This sounds like a reasonably straightforward question, but it is

(Library of Congress)

almost impossible to answer with any certainty—in part because the records of slave resistance are spotty, and in part because the definition of "resistance" is a matter of considerable dispute.

Even when a set of facts is reasonably clear and straightforward, historians disagree—sometimes quite radically—over what they mean. Those disagreements can be the result of

CAHOKIA INDIAN MOUNDS The great earthen mounds constructed by the Cahokia Indians near present-day St. Louis have endured into modern times as part of the Missouri landscape. One of them is pictured here, rising above a farm field. *(Missouri Historical Society)*

political and ideological disagreements. Some of the most vigorous debates in recent decades have been between scholars who believe that economic interests and class divisions are the key to understanding the past, and those committed to other assumptions who believe that ideas and culture are at least as important as material interests. The disagreements can be a result of the particular perspectives that people of different backgrounds bring to the study of the past. Whites and people of color, men and women, people from the American South and people from the North, young people and older people: these and many other points of difference find their way into scholarly disagreements. And debates can be a result as well of differences over methodology—differences, for example, between those who believe that quantitative studies can answer important historical questions and those who believe that other, less precise methods come closer to the truth.

Most of all, perhaps, historical interpretation changes in response to the time in which it is written. Historians may strive to be "objective" in their work, but no one can be entirely free from the assumptions and concerns of the present. In the 1950s, the omnipresent shadow of the Cold War had a profound effect on the way most historians viewed the past and produced much work that seemed to validate the American democratic experience in contrast to the new and dangerous alternatives that seemed to be challenging it at the time. In the 1960s, concerns about racial justice and disillusionment with the Vietnam War altered the way many historians thought. Those events introduced a much more critical tone to scholarship and turned the attention of scholars away from politics and government and toward the study of society and culture.

Many areas of scholarship in the late twentieth century are embroiled in a profound debate over whether there is such a thing as "truth." The world, some scholars argue, is simply a series of "narratives" constructed by people who view life in very different and often highly personal ways. "Truth" does not really exist. Everything is a product of interpretation. Not many historians embrace such radical ideas; most would agree that interpretations, to be of any value, must rest on a solid foundation of observable facts. But historians do recognize that even the most compelling

(Jim Pickerell/Black Star)

facts are subject to many different interpretations and that the process of understanding the past is a forever continuing—and forever contested—process.

The agricultural societies of the Northeast were more mobile than those in other regions. Farming techniques there were designed to exploit the land quickly rather than to develop permanent settlements. Natives often cleared the land by setting forest fires or cutting into trees to kill them. They then planted crops—corn, beans, squash, pumpkins, and others—among the dead or blackened trunks. After a few years, when the land became exhausted or the filth from a settlement began to accumulate, they moved on and established themselves elsewhere. In some parts of eastern North America, villages dispersed every winter and families foraged for themselves in the wilderness until warm weather returned; those who survived then reassembled to begin farming again.

Many of the tribes living east of the Mississippi River were linked together loosely by common linguistic roots. The largest of the language groups was the Algonquin tribes, which lived along the Atlantic seaboard from Canada to Virginia. More elaborately organized was the Iroquois Confederation, which emerged in the mid-fifteenth century, centered in what is now upstate New York. The Iroquois included at least five distinct northern "nations"—the Seneca, Cayuga, Onondaga, Oneida, and Mohawk—and had links as well with the Cherokees and the Tuscaroras farther south, in the Carolinas and Georgia. The third largest language group—the Muskogean—included the tribes in the southernmost region of the eastern seaboard: the Chickasaws, Choctaws, Creeks, and Seminoles. Alliances among the various Indian societies (even among those with common languages) were fragile, since the peoples of the Americas did not think of themselves as members of a single civilization. When Europeans arrived and began to threaten their way of life, Indians generally

Mobile Societies

THE AMERICAN POPULATION BEFORE COLUMBUS

No one knows how many people lived in the Americas in the centuries before Columbus. But scholars and others have spent more than a century and have written many thousands of pages debating the question nevertheless. Interest in this question survives, despite the near impossibility of answering it, because the debate over the pre-Columbian population is closely connected to the much larger debate over the consequences of European settlement of the Western Hemisphere.

Throughout the nineteenth century, Native Americans—in the midst of their many losing battles against the spread of white civilization—spoke often of the great days before Columbus when there were many more people in their tribes. They drew from their own rich tradition of oral history handed down through storytelling from one generation to another. The painter and ethnographer George Catlin, who spent much time among the tribes in the 1830s painting portraits of a race that he feared was "fast passing to extinction," listened to these oral legends and estimated that there had been 16 million Indians in North America before the Europeans came.

Most other white Americans who thought about this issue dismissed such claims as preposterous and insisted that the native population could not have been even as large as a million. Indian civilization was far too primitive, they claimed, to have been able to sustain so large a population.

In the early twentieth century, an ethnologist at the Smithsonian Institution, James Mooney, set out to find a method of estimating the early North American population that would be more scientific than the methods of the previous century, which were essentially guesses. He drew from early accounts of soldiers and missionaries in the sixteenth century and in 1928 came up with the implausibly precise figure of 1.15 million natives who lived north of Mexico in the early sixteenth century. That was a larger figure than nineteenth-century writers had suggested, but still much smaller than the Indians themselves claimed. A few years later, the anthropologist Alfred Kroeber used many of Mooney's methods to come up with an estimate of the population of the entire Western Hemisphere—considerably larger than Mooney's, but much lower than Catlin's.

(Biblioteca Mediceo Laurenxiana, Firenze/IKONA, Rome)

He concluded in 1934 that there were 8.4 million people in the Americas in 1492, half in North America and half in the Caribbean and South America. His conclusions remained largely uncontested until the 1960s.

These low early estimates reflected, more than anything else, an assumption that the arrival of the Europeans did not much reduce the native population. Given that assumption, it seemed reasonable to assume that the

viewed the threat in terms of how it affected their own community and tribe, not in terms of how it affected any larger "Indian nation." Only rarely did tribes unite in opposition to challenges from whites.

Tribal Cultures

The enormous diversity of economic, social, and political structures among the North American Indians makes large generalizations about their cultures difficult. In the last centuries before the arrival of Europeans, however, Native Amer- *Agricultural Revolution* icans—like peoples in other areas of the world—were experiencing an agricultural revolution. In all regions of the United States (if in varying degrees from place to place), tribes were becoming more sedentary and were developing new sources of food, clothing, and shelter. Most regions were experiencing significant population growth. Virtually all were developing the sorts of elaborate social customs and rituals that only relatively stationary societies can produce. Religion was as important to Indian

society as it was to most other cultures and was usually closely bound up with the natural world on which the tribes depended. Native Americans worshipped many gods, whom they associated variously with crops, game, forests, rivers, and other elements of nature. Some tribes created elaborate, brightly colored totems as part of their religious ritual; most staged large festivals on such important occasions as harvests or major hunts.

As in other parts of the world, the societies of North America tended to divide tasks according to gender. All tribes assigned women the jobs of caring for children, preparing meals, and gathering certain foods. But the allocation of other tasks varied from one society to another. Some tribal groups (notably the Pueblos of the Southwest) reserved farming tasks almost entirely for men. Among others (including the Algonquins, the Iroquois, and the Muskogees), women tended the fields, while men engaged in hunting, warfare, or clearing land. Iroquois women and children were often left alone for extended periods while men were away hunting or fighting battles. As a result, women tended to control the social and economic

relatively low numbers of Indians that Europeans encountered in the late sixteenth and seventeenth centuries reflected the numbers of natives living in the Americas in earlier centuries as well. A dramatic change in the scholarly approach to the early population came as a result of the discovery by a number of scholars in the 1960s and 1970s that the early tribes had been catastrophically decimated by European plagues not long after the arrival of Columbus—meaning that the numbers Europeans observed even in the late 1500s were already dramatically smaller than the numbers in 1492. Drawing on early work by anthropologists and others who discovered evidence of widespread deaths by disease, historians such as William McNeill in 1976 and Alfred Crosby a decade later produced powerful accounts of the near extinction of some tribes and the dramatic depopulation of others in a pestilential holocaust with few parallels in history. Almost all scholars now accept that much, perhaps most, of the native population was wiped out by disease—smallpox, measles, tuberculosis, and other plagues imported from Europe—

before white settlers began serious efforts to count.

The belief that the native population was much bigger in 1492 than it would be a few decades later has helped spur much larger estimates of how many people were in America before Columbus. Henry Dobyns, an anthropologist who was one of the earliest scholars to challenge the early, low estimates, claimed in 1966 that there were between 10 and 12 million people north of Mexico in 1492, and between 90 and 112 million in all of the Americas. He reached those figures by concluding that epidemics had destroyed 95 percent of the pre-Columbian population. He then took the best information on the population after Columbus and multiplied it by 20. No subsequent scholar has made so high a claim, and most historians have concluded that the 95 percent figure of deaths by disease is too high except for a few, relatively isolated areas such as Hispaniola. But most subsequent estimates have been much closer to Dobyns's than to Kroeber's. The geographer William M. Denevan, for example, argued in 1976 that the American population in 1492 was around 55 mil-

lion and that the population north of Mexico was under 4 million. Those are among the lowest of modern estimates, but still dramatically higher than the nineteenth-century numbers.

The vehemence with which scholars, and at times the larger public, have debated these figures is not just because it is very difficult to determine population size. It is also because the debate over the population is part of the debate over whether the arrival of Columbus—and the millions of Europeans who followed him—was a great advance in the history of civilization (as most Americans believed in 1892 when they joyously celebrated the 400th anniversary of Columbus's voyage) or an unparalleled catastrophe that virtually exterminated a large and flourishing native population (as some Americans and Europeans argued during the far more somber commemoration of the 500th anniversary in 1992). How to balance the many achievements of European civilization in the New World after 1492 against the terrible destruction of native peoples that accompanied it is, in the end, less a historical question, perhaps, than a moral one.

organization of the settlements and played powerful roles within families (which in many tribes were traced back "matrilineally," or through the mother's line).

EUROPE LOOKS WESTWARD

Europeans were almost entirely unaware of the existence of the Americas before the fifteenth century. A few early wanderers—Leif Eriksson, an eleventh-century Norse seaman, and perhaps others—had glimpsed parts of the New World and had demonstrated that Europeans were capable of crossing the ocean to reach it. But even if their discoveries had become common knowledge (and they did not), there would have been little incentive for others to follow. Europe in the Middle Ages (roughly 500–1500 A.D.) was not an adventurous civilization. Divided into innumerable small duchies and kingdoms, its outlook was overwhelmingly provincial. Subsistence agriculture predominated, and commerce was limited; few merchants looked beyond the bound-

aries of their own regions. The Roman Catholic Church exercised a measure of spiritual authority over most of the continent, and the Holy Roman Empire provided at least a nominal political center. Even so, real power was for the most part widely dispersed; only rarely could a single leader launch a great venture. Gradually, however, conditions in Europe changed so that by the late fifteenth century interest in overseas exploration had grown.

Commerce and Nationalism

Two important and related changes provided the first incentive for Europeans to look toward new lands. One was a result of the significant growth in Europe's population in the fifteenth century. The Black Death, a catastrophic epidemic of the bubonic plague that began in Constantinople in 1347, had decimated Europe, killing (according to some estimates) more than a third of the people of the continent and debilitating its already limited economy. But a century and a half later, the population had

IROQUOIS WOMEN This 1734 French engraving shows Iroquois women at work in a settlement somewhere in what is now upstate New York. In the foreground, women are cooking. Others are working in the fields. Men spent much of their time hunting and soldiering, leaving the women to govern and dominate the internal lives of the villages. Property in Iroquois society was inherited through the mother, and women occupied positions of great honor and authority within the tribes. *(Library of Congress)*

THE INDIAN VILLAGE OF SECOTON (C. 1585), BY JOHN WHITE John White created this illustration of life among the Eastern Woodland Indians in coastal North Carolina. It shows the diversified agriculture practiced by the natives: squash, tobacco, and three varieties of corn. The hunters shown in nearby woods suggest another element of the native economy. At bottom right, Indians perform a religious ritual, which White described as "strange gestures and songs." *(British Museum)*

rebounded. With that growth came a rise in land values, a reawakening of commerce, and a general increase in prosperity. Affluent landlords were

A Reawakening of Commerce

becoming eager to purchase goods from distant regions, and a new merchant class was emerging to meet their demand. As trade increased, and as advances in navigation and shipbuilding made long-distance sea travel more feasible, interest in developing new markets, finding new products, and opening new trade routes rapidly increased.

Paralleling the rise of commerce in Europe, and in part responsible for it, was the rise of new governments that were more united and powerful than the feeble political entities of the feudal past. In the western areas of Europe, the authority of the distant pope and the even more distant Holy Roman Emperor was necessarily weak. As a result, strong new monarchs were emerging there and cre-

Centralized Nation-States

ating centralized nation-states, with national courts, national armies, and—perhaps most important—national tax systems. As these ambitious kings and queens consolidated their power and increased their wealth, they became eager to enhance the commercial growth of their nations.

Ever since the early fourteenth century, when Marco Polo and other adventurers had returned from Asia bearing exotic goods (spices, fabrics, dyes) and even more exotic tales, Europeans who hoped for commercial glory had dreamed above all of trade with the East. For two centuries, that trade had been limited by the difficulties of the long, arduous overland journey to the Asian courts. But in the fourteenth century, as the maritime capabilities of several western European societies increased, there began to be serious talk of finding a faster, safer sea route to Asia. Such dreams gradually found a receptive audience in the courts of the new monarchs. By the late fifteenth century, some of them were ready to finance daring voyages of exploration.

The first to do so were the Portuguese. They were the preeminent maritime power in the fifteenth century, in large part because of the work of one man, Prince Henry the Navigator. Henry's own principal interest was not in

Prince Henry the Navigator

finding a sea route to Asia, but in exploring the western coast of Africa. He dreamed of establishing a Christian empire there to aid in his country's wars against the Moors of northern Africa; and he hoped to find new stores of gold. The explorations he began did not fulfill his own hopes, but they ultimately led farther than he had dreamed. Some of Henry's mariners went as far south as Cape Verde, on Africa's west coast. In 1486 (six years after Henry's death), Bartholomeu Dias rounded the southern tip of Africa (the Cape of Good Hope); and in 1497–1498 Vasco da Gama proceeded all the way around the cape to India. In 1500, the next fleet bound for India, under the command of Pedro Cabral, was blown westward off its southerly course and happened upon the coast of Brazil. But by then another man, in the service of another country, had already encountered the New World.

Christopher Columbus

Christopher Columbus, who was born and reared in Genoa, Italy, obtained most of his early seafaring experience in the service of the Portuguese. As a young man, he became intrigued with the possibility, already under discussion in many seafaring circles, of reaching Asia by going not east but west. Columbus's hopes rested on several basic misconceptions. He believed that the world was far smaller than it actually is. He also believed that the Asian continent extended farther eastward than it actually does. He assumed, therefore, that the Atlantic was narrow enough to be crossed on a relatively brief voyage. It did not occur to him that anything lay to the west between Europe and Asia.

Columbus failed to win support for his plan in Portugal, so he turned to Spain. The Spaniards were not yet as advanced a maritime people as the Portuguese, but they were at least as energetic and ambitious. And in the fifteenth century, the marriage of Spain's two most powerful regional rulers, Ferdinand of Aragon and Isabella of Castile, had produced the strongest monarchy in Europe. Like other young monarchies, it soon grew eager to demonstrate its strength by sponsoring new commercial ventures.

Columbus appealed to Queen Isabella for support for his proposed westward voyage. In 1492, having consolidated the monarchy's position within Spain itself, Isabella agreed to Columbus's request. Commanding ninety men

Columbus's First Voyage

and three ships—the *Niña,* the *Pinta,* and the *Santa María*— Columbus left Spain in August 1492 and sailed west into the Atlantic on what he thought was a straight course for Japan. Ten weeks later, he sighted land and assumed he

CHRISTOPHER COLUMBUS In this somewhat idealized drawing, created several years after Christopher Columbus's historic voyage to the New World, Columbus stands in the bow of his ship, a suit of armor ready at his feet, approaching a shore in the New World that he believed was in fact part of Asia. *(Library of Congress)*

had reached his target. In fact, he had landed on an island in the Bahamas. When he pushed on and encountered Cuba, he assumed he had reached China. He returned to Spain in triumph, bringing with him several captured natives as evidence of his achievement. (He called the natives "Indians" because he believed they were from the East Indies in the Pacific.)

But Columbus had not, of course, encountered the court of the great khan in China or the fabled wealth of the Indies. A year later, therefore, he tried again, this time with a much larger expedition. As before, he headed into the Caribbean, discovering several other islands and leaving a small and short-lived colony on Hispaniola. On a third voyage, in 1498, he finally reached the mainland and cruised along the northern coast of South America. When he passed the mouth of the Orinoco River (in present-day Venezuela), he concluded for the first time that what he had discovered was not in fact an island off the coast of China, as he had assumed, but a separate continent; such a large freshwater stream, he realized, could emerge only from a large body of land. Still, he remained convinced that Asia was only a short distance away. And although he failed in his efforts to sail around the northeastern coast of South America to the Indies (he was blocked by the Isthmus of Panama), he returned to Spain believing that he had explored at least the fringes of the Far East. He continued to believe that until he died.

Columbus's celebrated accomplishments made him a popular hero for a time, but he ended his life in obscurity. When Europeans at last gave a name to the New World, they ignored him. The distinction went instead to a Florentine merchant, Amerigo Vespucci, a member of a later Portuguese expedition to the New World who wrote a series of vivid descriptions of the lands he visited and who recognized the Americas as new continents.

Columbus has been celebrated for centuries as the "Admiral of the Ocean Sea" (a title he struggled to have officially bestowed on him during his lifetime) and as a representative of the new, secular, scientific impulses of Renaissance Europe. But Columbus was also a deeply religious man, even something of a mystic. His voyages

Religious Motives for Exploration

were inspired as much by his conviction that he was fulfilling a divine mission as by his interest in geography and trade. A strong believer in biblical prophecies, he came to see himself as a man destined to advance the coming of the millennium. "God made me the messenger of the new heaven and the new earth," he wrote near the end of his life, "and he showed me the spot where to find it." A similar combination of worldly and religious passions lay behind many subsequent efforts at exploration and settlement of the New World.

Partly as a result of Columbus's initiative, Spain began to devote greater resources and energy to maritime exploration and gradually replaced Portugal as the leading seafaring nation. The Spaniard Vasco de Balboa fought his way across the Isthmus of Panama in 1513 and became the first known European to gaze westward upon the great ocean that separated America from China and the Indies. Seeking access to that ocean, Ferdinand

Ferdinand Magellan

Magellan, a Portuguese in the employ of the Spanish, found the strait that now bears his name at the southern end of South America, struggled through the stormy narrows and into the ocean (so calm by contrast that he christened it the "Pacific"), then proceeded to the Philippines. There Magellan died in a conflict with the natives, but his expedition went on to complete the first known circumnavigation of the globe (1519–1522). By 1550, Spaniards had explored the coasts of North America as far north as Oregon in the west and Labrador in the east, as well as some of the interior regions of the continent.

BALBOA DISCOVERING THE PACIFIC The Spanish historian Herrera created this engraving to commemorate Vasco de Balboa's discovery of the Pacific Ocean, which he encountered after fighting his way across the Isthmus of Panama. Balboa's contemporaries called the Pacific *"El Mar del Sur,"* the "South Sea." *(Bettmann/Corbis)*

The Conquistadores

In time, Spanish explorers in the New World stopped thinking of America simply as an obstacle to their search for a route to the East. They began instead to consider it a possible source of wealth rivaling and even surpassing the original Indies. On the basis of Columbus's discoveries, the Spanish claimed for themselves the whole of the New World, except for a piece of it (today's Brazil) that was reserved by a papal decree for the Portuguese. By the mid-sixteenth century, the Spanish were well on their way to establishing a substantial American empire.

The early Spanish colonists, beginning with those Columbus brought on his second voyage, settled on the islands of the Caribbean, where they tried to enslave the Indians and find gold. They had little luck in either effort. But then, in 1518, Hernando Cortés led a small military expedition of about 600 men into Mexico. Cortés had been a Spanish government official in Cuba for fourteen years and to that point had achieved little success. But when he heard stories of great treasures in Mexico, he decided to go in search of them. He met strong and resourceful resistance from the Aztecs and their powerful emperor, Montezuma. The first Spanish assault on Tenochtitlán, the Aztec capital, failed. But Cortés and his army had, unknowingly, unleashed an assault on the Aztecs far more devastating than military attack: they had exposed the natives to smallpox. A smallpox epidemic decimated the population and made it possible for the Spanish

Cortés Conquers the Aztecs

to triumph in their second attempt at conquest. The Spanish saw the epidemic as vindication of their efforts. When the Christians were exhausted from war, one follower of Cortés said at the time, "God saw fit to send the Indians smallpox." Through his ruthless suppression of

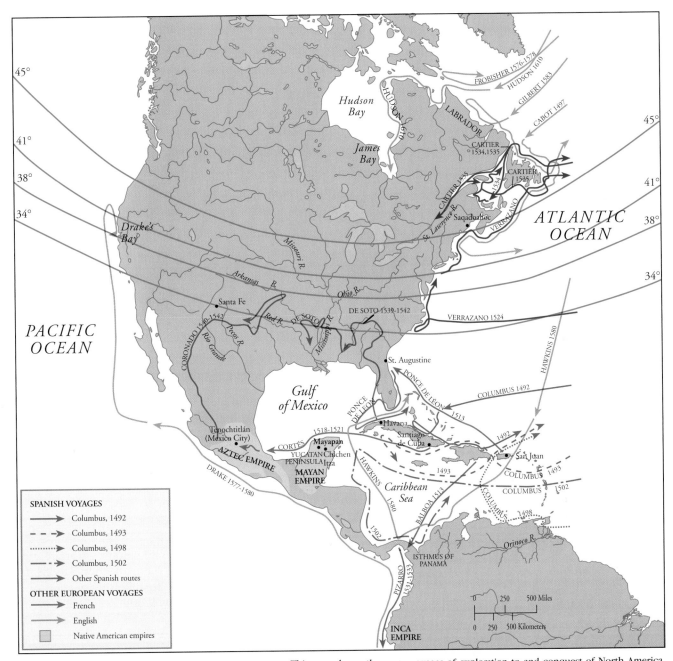

EUROPEAN EXPLORATION AND CONQUEST, 1492–1583 This map shows the many voyages of exploration to and conquest of North America launched by Europeans in the late fifteenth and sixteenth centuries. Note how Columbus and the Spanish explorers who followed him tended to move quickly into the lands of Mexico, the Caribbean, and Central and South America, while the English and French explored the northern territories of North America. ◆ *What factors might have led these various nations to explore and colonize these different areas of the New World?*

 For an interactive version of this map go to www.mhhe.com/brinkley11ch1maps

the surviving natives, Cortés established a lasting reputation as the most brutal of the Spanish *conquistadores* (conquerors).

The news that silver was to be found in Mexico attracted the attention of other Spaniards. From the island colonies and from Spain itself, a wave of conquistadores descended on the mainland in search of fortune—a movement comparable in some ways to the nineteenth-

century gold rushes elsewhere in the world, but far more vicious. Francisco Pizarro, who conquered Peru (1532–1538) and revealed to Europeans the wealth of the Incas, opened the way for other advances into South America. His one-time deputy Hernando de Soto, in a futile search for gold, silver, and jewels, led several expeditions (1539–1541) through Florida west into the continent and became the first white man known to have

THE MEXICANS STRIKE BACK In this vivid scene from the Duran Codex, Mexican artists illustrate a rare moment in which Mexican warriors gained the upper hand over the Spanish invaders. Driven back by native fighters, the Spanish have taken refuge in a room in the royal palace in Tenochtitlán while brightly attired Mexican warriors besiege them. Although the Mexicans gained a temporary advantage in this battle, the drawing illustrates one of the reasons for their inability to withstand the Spanish in the longer term. The Spanish soldiers are armed with rifles and crossbows, while the Indians carry only spears and shields. *(Oronoz Archivo)*

crossed the Mississippi River. Francisco Coronado traveled north from Mexico (1540–1542) into what is now New Mexico in a similarly fruitless search for gold and jewels; in the process, he helped open the Southwest of what is now the United States to Spanish settlement.

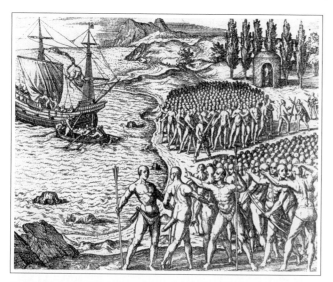

PIZARRO IN PERU A European artist depicted Pizarro's arrival on the coast of Peru in the early 1530s, where he was greeted by crowds of hostile Indians. By 1538, Pizarro had conquered the empire of the Incas. *(British Museum)*

The story of the Spanish warriors is one of great military daring and achievement. It is also a story of remarkable brutality and greed. The conquistadores subjugated and, *Brutality and Greed* in some areas (through a combination of warfare and disease), almost exterminated the native populations. In this horrible way, they made possible the creation of a vast Spanish empire in the New World.

The Spanish Empire

Spanish exploration, conquest, and colonization in America was primarily a work of private enterprise, carried on by individual leaders, with little direct support from the government at home. Those who wished to launch expeditions to the New World had first to get licenses from the crown. Those who obtained licenses *(encomiendas)* were permitted to exact labor and tribute from the natives in specific areas, a system the Spanish had first used in dealing with the Moors in Spain itself. Settlers did not receive actual land grants, but the control of the labor in a territory in effect gave them control of the land.

A license did no more than confer rights; colonizers had to equip and finance their expeditions on their own and assume the full risk of loss or ruin. They might succeed and make a fortune; they might fail—through

DE SOTO IN NORTH AMERICA This gruesome drawing portrays Spanish troops under Hernando de Soto massacring a group of Mobile Indians in what is now Alabama, in the winter of 1540–1541. De Soto had been governor of Cuba, but in 1539 he sailed to Florida with 600 troops and for the next several years traveled through large areas of what would later become the southern United States until dying of fever in 1542. Here, as elsewhere, his troops dealt with the Indian tribes they encountered along the way with unrestrained brutality. *(Rare Books and Special Collections/Library of Congress)*

shipwreck, natural disaster, incompetence, or bad luck—and lose everything, including their lives, as many adventurers did. The New World did not always attract good or intelligent immigrants, but in the beginning it seldom attracted the fainthearted.

Spanish America

Lured by dreams of treasure, Spanish explorers, conquistadores, and colonists established a vast empire for Spain in the New World. New European diseases and Spanish military power forced the previously powerful Aztec and Incan empires into submission. The history of the Spanish empire spanned three distinct periods. The first was the age of discovery and exploration—beginning with Columbus and continuing through the first two decades of the sixteenth century. The second was the age of the conquistadores, in which Spanish military forces (aided by the diseases they unleashed) established their dominion over the lands once ruled by natives. The third phase began in the 1570s, when new Spanish laws—the Ordinances of Discovery—banned the most brutal military

Ordinances of Discovery

conquests. From that point on, the Spanish expanded their presence in America through colonization.

The first Spaniards to arrive in the New World, the conquistadores, had been interested in only one thing: getting rich. And in that they were fabulously successful. For 300 years, beginning in the sixteenth century, the mines in Spanish America yielded more than ten times as much gold and silver as the rest of the world's mines put together. These riches made Spain for a time the wealthiest and most powerful nation on earth.

After the first wave of conquest, however, most Spanish settlers in America traveled to the New World for other reasons. Many went in hopes of creating a profitable agricultural economy. Unlike the conquistadores, who left little but destruction behind them, these settlers helped establish elements of European civilization in America that permanently altered both the landscape and the social structure.

At least as important as a force for colonization was the Catholic Church. When Pope Innocent VIII signed a treaty with Ferdinand and Isabella of Spain in 1486, acknowledging Spain's claim to most of the Americas from Mexico south, he established one binding condition: that

OUTPOSTS ON THE NORTHERN FRONTIER OF NEW SPAIN
(Not simultaneous; through the 18th century)

- Missions
- Forts (Sometimes with missions)
- Settlements

World divided into Spanish and Portuguese hemispheres: Treaty of Tordesillas (1494)

Aztec Empire at the time of Spanish Conquest

Inca Empire at the time of Spanish Conquest

Colonial boundaries and provincial names are for the late 18th century

SPANISH AMERICA From the time of Columbus's initial voyage in 1492 until the mid-nineteenth century, Spain was the dominant colonial power in the New World. From the southern regions of South America to the northern regions of the Pacific northwest, Spain controlled one of the world's vastest empires. Note how much of the Spanish empire was simply grafted upon the earlier empires of native peoples—the Incas in what is today Chile and Peru, and the Aztecs across much of the rest of South America, Mexico, and the Southwest of what is now the United States. ◆ *What characteristics of Spanish colonization would account for their preference for already settled regions?*

For an interactive version of this map go to www.mhhe.com/brinkley11ch1maps

Catholicism would be the only religion of the new terri-

Catholic Missions

tories. Spain abided by that condition. As a result, the character-istic Spanish settlements in the new world were highly religious in character. Although the Spanish founded sev-eral commercial and military centers in the sixteenth cen-tury, the most common settlement by the early seven-teenth century was the mission. Missions had commercial

lives, to be sure. But their primary purpose, at least at first, was converting natives to Catholicism. There were usually military garrisons connected to the missions, to protect them from hostile natives. *Presidios* (military bases) often grew up nearby to provide additional protection. Other Spaniards went to America to spread the Christian reli-gion. Indeed, after the era of the conquistadores came to a close in the 1540s, the missionary impulse became one of the principal motives for European emigration to America. Priests or friars accompanied all colonizing ventures. Through the work of zealous missionaries, the gospel of the Catholic Church ultimately extended throughout South and Central America, Mexico, and into the South and Southwest of the present United States.

Northern Outposts

The Spanish fort established in 1565 at St. Augustine, Florida, became the first permanent European settlement in the present-day United States. It served as a military outpost, an administrative center for Franciscan mission-

St. Augustine

aries, and a headquarters for unsuccessful campaigns among North American natives that were ultimately abandoned. It did not mark the beginning of a substantial effort at colonization in the region.

A more substantial colonizing venture began thirty years later in the Southwest. In 1598, Don Juan de Oñate traveled north from Mexico with a party of 500 men and claimed for Spain some of the lands of the Pueblo Indians that Coronado had passed through over fifty years before. The Spanish migrants began to establish a colony, modeled roughly on those the Spanish had created farther south, in what is now New Mexico. Oñate distributed *encomiendas,* and the Spanish began demanding tribute from the local Indians (and at times commandeering them as laborers). Spanish colonists founded Santa Fe in 1609.

Oñate's harsh treatment of the natives (who greatly outnumbered the small Spanish population) threatened the stability of the new colony and led to his removal as governor in 1606. Over time, relations between the Spanish and the Pueblos improved. Substantial numbers of Pueblos converted to Christianity under the influence of Spanish missionaries. Others entered into important trading relationships with the Spanish. The colony remained precarious nevertheless because of the danger from Apache and Navajo raiders, who threatened the Spanish and Pueblos alike. Even so, the New Mexico settlement continued to grow. By 1680, there were over 2,000 Spanish colonists living among about 30,000 Pueblos. The economic heart of the colony was not the gold and precious metals the early Spanish explorers had tried in vain to find. It was cattle and sheep, raised on the *ranchos* that stretched out around the small towns Spanish settlers established.

In 1680, the colony was nearly destroyed when the Pueblos rose in revolt. Despite the widespread conversions to Catholicism, most natives (including the converts) continued to practice their own religious rituals—

Pueblo Revolt of 1680

rituals that sustained their sense of tribal identity. In 1680, Spanish priests and the colonial government, which was closely tied to the missionaries, launched one of their periodic efforts to suppress these rituals. In response, an Indian religious leader named Pope led an uprising that killed hundreds of European settlers (including twenty-one priests), captured Santa Fe, and drove the Spanish temporarily from the region. But twelve years later the Spanish returned, resumed seizing Pueblo lands, and crushed a last revolt in 1696.

Spanish exploitation of the Pueblos did not end. But after the revolts, many Spanish colonists realized that they could not prosper in New Mexico if they remained constantly in conflict with a native population that greatly outnumbered them. They tried to solve the problem in two ways. On the one hand, the Spanish intensified their efforts to assimilate the Indians—baptizing Indian children at birth and enforcing observance of Catholic rituals. On the other hand, they now permitted the Pueblos to own land; they stopped commandeering Indian labor; they replaced the encomienda system with a less demanding and oppressive one; and they tacitly tolerated the practice of tribal religious rituals.

These efforts were at least partially successful. After a while, there was significant intermarriage between Europeans and Indians. Increasingly, the Pueblos came to consider the Spanish their allies in the continuing battles with the Apaches and Navajos. By 1750, the Spanish population had grown modestly to about 4,000. The Pueblo population had declined (through disease, war, and migration) to about 13,000, less than half what it had been in 1680. New Mexico had by then become a reasonably stable but still weak and isolated outpost of the Spanish empire.

The Empire at High Tide

By the end of the sixteenth century, the Spanish empire had become one of the largest in the history of the world. It included the islands of the Caribbean and the coastal areas of South America that had been the first targets of the Spanish expeditions. It extended to Mexico and southern North America, where a second wave of colonizers had established outposts.

Spain's Vast Empire

Most of all, the empire spread southward and westward into the vast landmass of South America—the areas that are now Chile, Argentina, and Peru. In 1580, when the Spanish and Portuguese monarchies temporarily united, Brazil came under Spanish jurisdiction as well.

It was, however, a colonial empire very different from the one the English would establish in North America beginning in the early seventeenth century. Although the earliest Spanish ventures in the New World had been largely independent of the throne, by the end of the sixteenth century the monarchy had extended its authority directly into the governance of local communities. Colonists had few opportunities to establish political institutions independent of the crown. There was also a significant economic difference between the Spanish empire and the later British one. The Spanish were far more successful than the British would be in extracting great surface wealth—gold and silver—from their American colonies. But for the same reason, they concentrated relatively less energy on making agriculture and commerce profitable in their colonies. The strict and inflexible commercial policies of the Spanish government made things worse. *Rigid Royal Control* To enforce the collection of duties and to provide protection against pirates, the government established rigid and restrictive regulations. They required all trade with the colonies to go through a single Spanish port and only a few colonial ports, in fleets making but two voyages a year. The system stifled the economic development of the Spanish areas of the New World.

There was also an important difference between the character of the population in the Spanish empire and that of the colonies to the north. Almost from the beginning, the English, Dutch, and French colonies in North America concentrated on establishing permanent settlement and family life in the New World. The Europeans in North America reproduced rapidly after their first difficult years and in time came to outnumber the natives. The Spanish, by contrast, ruled their empire but did not people it. In the first century of settlement, fewer than 250,000 settlers in the Spanish colonies were from Spain itself or from any other European country. Only about 200,000 more arrived in the first half of the seventeenth century. Some additional settlers came from various outposts of Spanish civilization in the Atlantic—the Azores, the Cape Verde Islands, and elsewhere; but even with these other sources, the number of European settlers in Spanish America remained very small relative to the native population. Despite the ravages of disease and war, the vast majority of the population of the Spanish Empire continued to consist of natives. The Spanish, in other words, imposed a small ruling class upon a much larger existing population; they did not create a self-contained European society in the New World as the English would attempt to do in the north. The story of the *A Collision of Cultures* Spanish Empire, therefore, is the story of a collision between two cultures that had been developing for centuries along completely different lines followed by a partial fusion of those cultures.

Biological and Cultural Exchanges

The lines separating the races in the Spanish Empire gradually grew less distinct than they would be in the English colonies to the north, but European and native cultures never entirely merged. Indeed, significant differences remain today between European and Indian cultures throughout South and Central America. Nevertheless, the arrival of whites launched a process of interaction between different peoples that left no one unchanged.

Europeans would not have been exploring the Americas at all without their early contacts with the natives. From them, they first learned of the *Increasing Levels of Exchange* rich deposits of gold and silver. After that, the history of the Americas became one of increasing levels of exchanges—some beneficial, some catastrophic—among different peoples and cultures.

The first and most profound result of this exchange was the importation of European diseases to the New World. It would be difficult to exaggerate the consequences of the exposure of Native Americans to such illnesses as influenza, measles, chicken pox, mumps, typhus, and above all smallpox—diseases to which Europeans had over time developed at least a partial immunity but to which Native Americans were tragically vulnerable. Millions died.

Native groups inhabiting some of the large Caribbean islands and some areas of Mexico were virtually extinct within fifty years of their first contact with whites. On Hispaniola—where the Dominican Republic and Haiti are today and where Columbus landed and established a small, short-lived colony in the 1490s—the native population quickly declined from approximately 1 million to about 500. In the Mayan areas *Demographic Catastrophe* of Mexico, as much as 95 percent of the population perished within a few years of their first contact with the Spanish. Some groups fared better than others; some (although far from all) of the tribes north of Mexico, whose contact with European settlers came later and was often less intimate, were spared the worst of the epidemics. But most areas of the New World experienced a demographic catastrophe at least as grave as, and in many places far worse than, the Black Death that had killed at least a third of the population of Europe two centuries before.

The decimation of native populations in the southern regions of the Americas was not, however, purely a result of this inadvertent exposure to infection. It was also a result of the conquistadores' quite deliberate policy of subjugation and extermination. Their brutality was in part a reflection of the ruthlessness with which Europeans waged war in all parts of the world. It was also a result of *Deliberate Subjugation and Extermination* their conviction that the natives were "savages"—uncivilized peoples whom they considered somehow not fully human. Paradoxically, the brutality was also a consequence of the high level of development of some native societies. Had the natives truly been as primitive as Europeans wanted to believe, there would have been little need to destroy them. But organized into substantial empires, they posed a threat to the conquistadores' ambitions.

That, more than anything else, accounts for the thoroughness with which the Spanish set about obliterating native cultures. They razed cities and dismantled temples

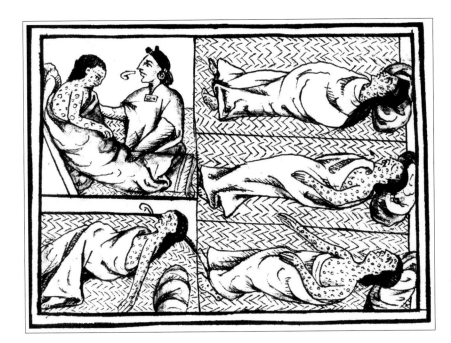

SMALLPOX AMONG THE INDIANS Far more devastating to the Indians of America than the military ventures of Europeans were deadly diseases carried to the New World by invaders from the old. Natives had developed no immunity to the infectious diseases of Europe, and they died by the hundreds of thousands from such epidemics as measles, influenza, and (as depicted here by a European artist) smallpox. *(Biblioteca Mediceo Laurenxiana, Firenze/IKONA, Rome)*

and monuments. They destroyed records and documents (one reason why modern scholars have been able to learn so little about the histories of these native societies). They systematically killed Indian warriors, leaders, and priests. They tried, in short, to eliminate the underpinnings of existing native civilizations so as to bring the Indian population fully under Spanish control and to remove all obstacles to the spread of Christianity. By the 1540s, the combined effects of European diseases and European military brutality had all but destroyed the empires of Mexico and South America and had largely eliminated native resistance to the Spanish.

Not all aspects of the exchange were so disastrous to the natives. The Europeans introduced important new crops to America (among them sugar and bananas), domestic livestock (cattle, pigs, and sheep), and perhaps most significantly the horse, which had disappeared from the Western Hemisphere in the Ice Age and now returned aboard Spanish ships in the sixteenth century. The Europeans imported these things for their own use. But Indian tribes soon learned to cultivate the new crops, and European livestock proliferated rapidly and spread widely among natives. In the past, most tribes had possessed no domesticated animals at all other than dogs. The horse, in particular, became central to the lives of many natives and transformed their societies.

New Crops and Agricultural Techniques

The exchange was at least as important (and more beneficial) to the Europeans. In both North and South America, the arriving white peoples learned new agricultural techniques from the natives, techniques often better adapted to the character of the new land than those they had brought with them from Europe. They discovered new crops, above all maize (corn), which became an important staple among the settlers. Columbus

took it back to Europe from his first trip to America, and it soon spread through much of Europe as well. Such American foods as squash, pumpkins, beans, sweet potatoes, tomatoes, peppers, and potatoes also found their way back to Europe and in the process revolutionized European agriculture. Agricultural discoveries ultimately proved more important to the future of Europe than the gold and silver the conquistadores valued so highly.

In South America, Central America, and Mexico, a society emerged in which Europeans and natives lived in intimate, if unequal, contact with one another. As a result, Indians adopted many features of European civilization, although those features seldom survived the transfer to America unchanged. Many natives gradually came to learn Spanish or Portuguese, but in the process they created a range of dialects, combining the European languages with their own. European missionaries—through both persuasion and coercion—spread Catholicism through most areas of the Spanish Empire. But native Christians tended to connect the new creed with features of their old religions, creating a hybrid of faiths that were, while essentially Christian, nevertheless distinctively American.

Colonial officials were expected to take their wives with them to America, but among the ordinary settlers—the majority—European men outnumbered European women by at least ten to one. Not surprisingly, therefore, the Spanish immigrants had substantial sexual contact with native women. Intermarriage became frequent, and before long the population of the colonies came to be dominated (numerically, at least) by

A Complex Racial Hierarchy

people of mixed race, or *mestizos*. Through much of the Spanish Empire, as a result, an elaborate racial hierarchy developed, with Spanish at the top, natives at the bottom, and people of mixed races distributed in between. Racial categories, however, were much more fluid than the Spanish wanted to believe and could not long remain fixed. Over time, the wealth and influence of a family often came to define its place in the "racial" hierarchy more decisively than race itself. A successful or powerful person could become "Spanish" regardless of his or her actual racial ancestry.

The frequency of intermarriage suggests a great deal about how the society of the Spanish Empire was taking shape. It reveals, of course, that men living alone in a strange land craved female companionship and the satisfactions of family life and that they sought those things in the only places they could—among the native population. It shows the desperate need for labor among the white settlers, including the domestic labor that native wives could provide; in some cases, intermarriage was a form of labor recruitment. Finally, it suggests why the lines separating the races in the areas of Spanish settlement did not remain as distinct as they did in the later English colonies, which were peopled largely by families and in which intermarriage with natives was consequently rare.

Intermarriage was not, however, just a result of the needs and desires of white men. Some Indian women *Reasons for Intermarriage* entered marriages to white men only under coercion, but the extent of intermarriage suggests that not all women resisted. Native women might have seen some advantage in marrying Spanish men because the male populations of their tribes were so depleted by warfare or enslavement by the Spaniards. There were also long-established customs of intermarriage among some Indian tribes as a way of forming or cementing alliances. Since many Indians considered the white settlers little more foreign than some rival native groups, that custom probably contributed to the frequency of intermarriage as well.

Natives were the principal labor source for the Europeans. Virtually all the commercial, agricultural, and mining enterprises of the Spanish and Portuguese colonists depended on an Indian work force. Different labor systems emerged in different areas of the empire. In some places, Indians were sold into slavery. More often, colonists used a wage system closely related, but not identical, to slavery, by which Indians were forced to work in *Varied Labor Systems* the mines and on the plantations for fixed periods, unable to leave without the consent of their employers. Such work forces survived in some areas of the South American mainland for many centuries. So great was the need for native labor that European settlers were less interested in acquiring land than they were in gaining control over Indian villages, which could become a source of labor and tribute to landlords.

Even so, the native population could not meet all the labor needs of the colonists—particularly since the native population had declined (and in some places virtually vanished) because of disease and war. As early as 1502, therefore, European settlers began importing slaves from Africa.

Africa and America

Most of the black men and women who were forcibly taken to America came from a large region in west Africa below the Sahara Desert, known as Guinea. It was the home of a wide variety of peoples and cultures. Since over half of all the new arrivals in the New World between 1500 and 1800 were Africans, those cultures, too, greatly affected the character of American civilization. Europeans and white Americans came to portray African society as primitive and uncivilized (in part to justify the enslavement of Africa's people). But most Africans were, in fact, civilized peoples with well-developed economies and political systems.

Humans began settling in west Africa at least 10,000 years ago. By the fifteenth century A.D., they had developed extensive civilizations and complex political systems. The residents of upper Guinea had substantial commercial contact with the Mediterranean world—trading ivory, gold, and slaves for finished goods. Largely as a result, they became *Ghana and Mali* early converts to Islam. After the collapse of the ancient kingdom of Ghana around 1100 A.D., the even larger empire of Mali emerged and survived well into the fifteenth century. Its great city, Timbuktu, became fabled as a trading center and a seat of education.

Africans further south were more isolated from Europe and the Mediterranean. They were also more politically fragmented. The central social unit in much of the south was the village, which usually consisted of members of an extended family group. Some groups of villages united in small kingdoms—among *Benin, Congo, and Songhay* them Benin, Congo, and Songhay. But no large empires emerged in the south comparable to the Ghana and Mali kingdoms farther north. Nevertheless, these southern societies developed extensive trade—in woven fabrics, ceramics, and wooden and iron goods, as well as crops and livestock—both among themselves and, to a lesser degree, with the outside world.

The African civilizations naturally developed economies that reflected the climates and resources of their lands. In upper Guinea, fishing and rice cultivation, supplemented by the extensive trade with Mediterranean lands, were the foundation of the economy. Farther south, Africans grew wheat and other food crops, raised livestock, and fished. There were some more nomadic tribes in the interior, which subsisted largely on hunting and gathering and developed less elaborate social systems. But most Africans were sedentary people,

SCULPTURE OF DJENNE Many of the Africans forcibly exported from their homes to America in the seventeenth and eighteenth centuries were natives of Mali, the seat of an ancient east African civilization. This terra cotta sculpture, discovered in the 1940s, dates from between 600 and 900 years ago. It may be an image of an ancestor created for use in a family shrine. *("Seated Prisoner", 11th/ 16th Century, Djenne, Founders Society Purchase, Robert H. Tannahill Foundation Fund. Photograph ©1995 The Detroit Institute of the Arts)*

linked together by elaborate political, economic, and familial relationships.

Like many Native American societies, but unlike those in Europe, African societies tended to be matrilineal—which means that people traced their heredity through, and inherited property from, their mothers rather than their fathers. When a couple married, the husband left his own family to join the family of his wife. Like most other peoples, Africans divided work by gender, but the nature of that division varied greatly from place to place. Women

Matrilineal Societies

played a major role, often the dominant role, in trade; in many areas they were the principal farmers (while the men hunted, fished, and raised livestock); everywhere, they managed child care and food preparation. Most tribes also divided political power by gender, with men choosing leaders and systems for managing what they defined as male affairs and women choosing parallel leaders to handle female matters. Tribal chiefs generally were men (although in some places there was a female counterpart), but the position customarily passed down not to the chief's son but to the son of the chief's eldest sister. African societies, in short, were characterized by a greater degree of sexual equality than those of most other parts of the world.

In those areas of west Africa where indigenous religions had survived the spread of Islam (which included most of the lands south of the empire of Mali), people worshipped many gods, whom they associated with various aspects of the natural world and whose spirits they believed lived in trees, rocks, forests, and streams. Most Africans also developed forms of ancestor worship and took great care in tracing family lineage; the most revered priests (who were often also important social and political leaders as well) were generally the oldest people.

African societies had elaborate systems of social ranks (or hierarchies). Small elites of priests and nobles stood at the top. Most people belonged to a large middle group of farmers, traders, crafts workers, and others. At the bottom of society were slaves—men and women who were put into bondage after being captured in wars or because of criminal behavior or unpaid debts. Slavery was not usually permanent; people were generally placed in bondage for a fixed period and in the meantime retained certain legal protections (including the right to marry). Their children, moreover, did not inherit their parents' condition of bondage. The slavery that Africans would experience at the hands of the Europeans was to be very different; but the existence of slavery among Africans themselves helped make their enslavement by Europeans easier.

The African slave trade began long before the European migration to the New World. As early as the eighth century A.D., west Africans began selling slaves to traders from the Mediterranean. They were responding to a demand from affluent families who wanted black men and women as domestic servants. They were also responding to more general labor shortages in some areas of Europe and North Africa. When Portuguese sailors began exploring the coast of Africa in the fifteenth century, they too bought slaves—usually criminals and people captured in war—and took them back to Portugal, where there was a small but steady demand.

In the sixteenth century, however, the market for slaves grew dramatically as a result of the rising European demand for sugar cane. The small areas of sugar cultivation in the Mediterranean were proving inadequate, and production soon moved to the island of Madeira off the African coast, which became a Portuguese colony. Not long after that, it moved to the Caribbean islands and Brazil. Sugar was a labor-intensive crop, and the demand

Growth of the African Slave Trade

for workers in these new areas increased rapidly. European slave traders responded to that demand by increasing the recruitment of workers from along the coast of west Africa (and from some areas of east Africa as well). As the demand increased, African kingdoms warred with one another in an effort to capture potential slaves to exchange for European goods. At first the slave traders were overwhelmingly Portuguese and, to a lesser extent, Spanish. By the seventeenth century, the Dutch had won control of most of the slave market. In the eighteenth century, the English dominated it. (Despite some recent claims, Jews were never significantly involved in the slave trade.) By 1700 slavery had begun to spread well beyond its original locations in the Caribbean and South America and into the English colonies to the north.

Most Americans understand that our nation has become intimately bound up with the rest of the world—that we live in a time that is sometimes called the "age of globalization." Most students of American history, however, have traditionally examined the nation's past in relative isolation. In recent years, scholars have begun to re-examine the way we explain the American past. They have revealed a host of new connections between what happened in the Americas and what was happening in the rest of the world. They have, in short, taken our modern notion of globalization and used it to explain some aspects of our more distant past. This re-examination has included the earliest period of European settlement of the Americas. Many scholars of early American history now examine what happened in the "New World" in the context of what has become known as the "Atlantic World."

The idea of an "Atlantic World" rests in part on the obvious connections between western Europe and the Spanish, British, French, and Dutch colonies in North and South America. All the early European civilizations of the Americas were part of a great imperial project launched by the major powers of Europe. The massive European immigration to the Americas beginning in the sixteenth century, the defeat and devastation of native populations, the creation of European agricultural and urban settlements, and the imposition of imperial regulations on trade, commerce, landowning, and political life—all of these forces reveal the influence of Old World imperialism on the history of the New World.

But the creation of empires is only one part of the creation of the Atlantic World. At least equally important—and closely related—is the expansion of commerce from Europe to the Americas. Although some Europeans traveled to the New World in search of religious freedom, or to escape oppression, or to search for adventure, the great majority of European immigrants were in search of economic opportunity. Not surprisingly, therefore, the European settlements in the Americas were almost from the start intimately connected to

Europe through the growth of commerce between them—commerce that grew more extensive and more complex with every passing year. The commercial relationship between America and Europe was responsible not just for the growth of trade, but also for the increases in migration over time—as the demand for labor in the New World drew more and more settlers from the Old World. Commerce was also the principal reason for the rise of slavery in the Americas, and for the growth of the slave trade between European America and Africa. The Atlantic World, in other words, included not just Europe and the Americas, but Africa as well.

Religion was another force binding together the Atlantic World. The vast majority of people of European descent were Christians and most of them maintained important religious ties to Europe. Catholics, of course, were part of a hierarchical church based in Rome and maintained close ties with the Vatican. But the Protestant faiths that predominated in North America were intimately linked to their European counterparts as well. New religious ideas and movements spread back and forth across the Atlantic with astonishing speed. Great revivals that began in Europe moved quickly to America. The "Great Awakening" of the mid-eighteenth century, for example, began in Britain and traveled to America in large part through the efforts of the English evangelist George Whitefield. American evangelists later carried religious ideas from the New World back to the Old.

The early history of European America was also closely bound up with the intellectual life of Europe. The Enlightenment—the cluster of ideas that emerged in Europe in the seventeenth and eighteenth centuries emphasizing the power of human reason—moved quickly to the Americas, producing considerable intellectual ferment throughout the New World, but particularly in the British colonies in North America and the Caribbean. The ideas of the British philosopher John Locke, for example, helped shape

the founding of Georgia. The English Constitution, and the idea of the "rights of Englishmen," shaped the way North Americans shaped their own concepts of politics. Many of the ideas that lay behind the American Revolution were products of British and continental philosophy that had traveled across the Atlantic. The reinterpretation of those ideas by Americans to help justify their drive to independence—by, among others, Thomas Paine—moved back across the Atlantic to Europe and helped, among other things, to inspire the French Revolution. Scientific and technological knowledge—another product of the Enlightenment—moved rapidly back and forth across the Atlantic. Americans borrowed industrial technology from Britain. Europe acquired much of its early knowledge of electricity from experiments done in America. But the Enlightenment was only one part of the continuing intellectual connections within the Atlantic World, connections that spread artistic, scholarly, and political ideas widely through the lands bordering the ocean.

Instead of thinking of the early history of what became the United States simply as the story of the growth of thirteen small colonies along the Atlantic seaboard of North America, the idea of the "Atlantic World" encourages us to think of early American history as a vast pattern of exchanges and interactions—trade, migration, religious and intellectual exchange, and many other relationships—among all the societies bordering the Atlantic: western Europe, western Africa, the Caribbean, and North and South America.

(The I.N. Phelps Stokes Collection of American Historical Prints, Prints Division, The New York Public Library, Astor, Lenox and Tilden Foundations.)

THE ARRIVAL OF THE ENGLISH

England's first documented contact with the New World came only five years after Spain's. In 1497, John Cabot (like Columbus a native of Genoa) sailed to the northeastern coast of North America on an expedition sponsored by King Henry VII. Other English navigators

John Cabot | continued Cabot's unsuccessful search for a northwest passage

through the New World to the Orient. They explored other areas of North America during the sixteenth century. But even though England claimed dominion over the lands its explorers surveyed, nearly a century passed before the English made any serious efforts to establish colonies there. Like other European nations, England had to experience an internal transformation before it could begin settling new lands. That transformation occurred in the sixteenth century.

The Commercial Incentive

Part of the attraction of the New World to the English was its newness, its contrast to their own troubled land. America seemed a place where human settlement could start anew, where a perfect society could be created without the flaws and inequities of the Old World. Such dreams began to emerge in England only a few years after Columbus's voyages. They found classic expression in Sir Thomas More's *Utopia* (published in Latin in 1516, translated into English thirty-five years later), which described a mythical and nearly perfect society on an imaginary island supposedly discovered by a companion of Amerigo Vespucci in the waters of the New World.

More's picture of an ideal community was, among other things, a comment on the social and economic ills of the England of his own time. The people of Tudor England suffered from frequent and costly European wars, from almost constant religious strife, and above all from a harsh economic transformation of the countryside. Because the

The Enclosure Movement | worldwide demand for wool was growing rapidly, many land-

owners were finding it profitable to convert their land from fields for crops to pastures for sheep. The result was a significant growth in the wool trade. But that meant land worked at one time by serfs and later by rent-paying tenants was steadily enclosed for sheep runs and taken away from the farmers. Thousands of evicted tenants roamed the countryside in gangs, begging from (and at times robbing) the more fortunate householders through whose communities they passed.

The government passed various laws designed to halt enclosures, relieve the worthy poor, and compel the able-bodied or "sturdy beggars" to work. Such laws had little effect. The enclosure movement continued unabated, and relatively few of the dislocated farmers could find reemployment in raising sheep or manufacturing wool. By removing land from cultivation, the enclosure movement

also limited England's ability to feed its population, which grew from 3 million in 1485 to 4 million in 1603. Both because of the dislocation of farmers and the restriction of the food supply, therefore, the nation had a serious problem of surplus population.

Amid this growing distress, a rising class of merchant capitalists was prospering from the expansion of foreign trade. At first, England had exported little except raw wool; but new merchant capitalists helped create a domestic cloth industry that allowed them to begin marketing finished goods at home and abroad. At first, most exporters did business almost entirely as individuals. In time, however, some merchants joined forces and formed chartered companies. Each such

enterprise operated on the ba- | *Chartered Companies*

sis of a charter acquired from the monarch, which gave the company a monopoly for trading in a particular region. Among the first of these were the Muscovy Company (1555), the Levant Company (1581), the Barbary Company (1585), the Guinea Company (1588), and the East India Company (1600). Investors in these companies often made fantastic profits from the exchange of English manufactures, especially woolens, for exotic goods; and they felt a powerful urge to continue the expansion of their profitable trade.

Central to this drive was the emergence of a new concept of economic life known as mercantilism, which was gaining favor throughout Europe. Mercantilism rested on the assumption that the nation as a whole was the principal actor in the economy, not the individuals within it. The goal of economic activity should be to increase the nation's total wealth. Mercantilists believed that the world's wealth was finite. One person or nation could grow rich only at the expense of another. A nation's economic health depended, therefore, on extracting as much wealth as possible from foreign lands and exporting as little wealth as possible from home.

The principles of mercantilism guided the economic policies of virtually all the European nation-states in the sixteenth and seventeenth cen- |

turies. Mercantilism greatly en- | *Mercantilism*

hanced the position of the new merchant capitalists, whose overseas ventures were thought to benefit the entire nation and to be worthy of government assistance. It also increased competition among nations. Every European state was trying to find markets for its exports while trying to limit its imports. One result was the increased attractiveness of acquiring colonies, which could become the source of goods that a country might otherwise have to buy from other nations.

In England, the mercantilistic program thrived at first on the basis of the flourishing wool trade with the European continent, and particularly with the great cloth market in Antwerp. Beginning in the 1550s, however, that glutted market collapsed, and English merchants found themselves obliged to look elsewhere for

THE DOCKS OF BRISTOL, ENGLAND By the eighteenth century, when this scene was painted, Bristol had become one of the principal English ports serving the so-called triangular trade among the American colonies, the West Indies, and Africa. The lucrativeness of that trade is evident in the bustle and obvious prosperity of the town. Even earlier, however, Bristol was an important port of embarkation for the thousands of English settlers migrating to the New World. *(Docks and Quay. English School (18th Century). City of Bristol Museum and Art Gallery/ The Bridgeman Art Library, London)*

overseas trade. The establishment of colonies seemed to

Richard Hakluyt's Argument for Colonies

be a ready answer to that and other problems. Richard Hakluyt, an Oxford clergyman and the outstanding English propagandist for colonization, argued that colonies would not only create new markets for English goods, they would also help alleviate poverty and unemployment by siphoning off the surplus population. For the poor who remained in England "idly to the annoy of the whole state," there would be new work as a result of the prosperity the colonies would create. Perhaps most important, colonial commerce would allow England to acquire products from its own new territories for which the nation had previously been dependent on foreign rivals—products such as lumber, naval stores, and, above all, silver and gold.

The Religious Incentive

In addition to these economic motives for colonization, there were also religious ones, rooted in the events of the European and English Reformations. The Protestant Reformation began in Germany in 1517, when Martin Luther openly challenged some of the basic practices and beliefs of the Roman Catholic Church—until then, the supreme religious authority and also one of the strongest political authorities throughout western Europe. Luther, an Augustinian monk and ordained priest, challenged the Catholic belief that salvation could be achieved through good works or through loyalty (or payments) to the church itself. He denied the church's claim that God communicated to the world through the pope and the clergy. The Bible, not the church, was the authentic voice of God, Luther claimed, and salvation was to be found not through "works" or through the formal practice of religion, but through faith alone. Luther's challenge quickly won him a wide following among ordinary men and women in northern Europe. He himself insisted that he was not revolting against the church, that his purpose was to reform it from within. But when the pope excommunicated him in 1520, Luther defied him and began to lead his followers out of the Catholic Church entirely. A schism within European Christianity had begun that was never to be healed.

As the spirit of the Reformation spread rapidly throughout Europe, creating intellectual ferment and (in some places) war, other dissidents began offering alternatives

Doctrine of Predestination | to orthodox Catholicism. The Swiss theologian John Calvin was, after Luther, the most influential reformer and went even further than Luther had in rejecting the Catholic belief that human institutions could affect an individual's prospects for salvation. Calvin introduced the doctrine of predestination. God "elected" some people to be saved and condemned others to damnation; each person's destiny was determined before birth, and no one could change that predetermined fate. But while individuals could not alter their destinies, they could strive to know them. Calvinists believed that the way people led their lives might reveal to them their chances of salvation. A wicked or useless existence would be a sign of damnation; saintliness, diligence, and success could be signs of grace. Calvinism created anxieties among its followers, to be sure; but it also produced a strong incentive to lead virtuous, productive lives. The new creed spread rapidly throughout northern Europe and produced (among other groups) the Huguenots in France and the Puritans in England.

The English Reformation began, however, more because of a political dispute between the king and the pope than as a result of these doctrinal revolts. In 1529 King Henry VIII became angered by the pope's refusal to

The English Reformation | grant him a divorce from his Spanish wife (who had failed to bear him the son he desperately wanted). In response, he broke England's ties with the Catholic Church and established himself as the head of the Christian faith in his country. He made relatively few other changes in English Christianity, however, and after his death the survival of Protestantism remained in doubt for a time. When Henry's Catholic daughter Mary ascended the throne, she quickly restored England's allegiance to Rome and harshly persecuted those who refused to return to the Catholic fold. Many Protestants were executed (the origin of the queen's enduring nickname, "Bloody Mary"); others fled to the European continent, where they came into contact with the most radical ideas of the Reformation. Mary died in 1558, and her half-sister, Elizabeth, became England's sovereign. Elizabeth once again severed the nation's connection with the Catholic Church (and, along with it, an alliance with Spain that Mary had forged).

JOHN CALVIN Next to Martin Luther, John Calvin was the most important figure of the European Reformation. His belief in predestination was central to the Puritan faith of early New England. *(Bettman/Corbis)*

The Church of England, as the official religion was now known, satisfied the political objectives of the queen, but it failed to satisfy the religious desires of many English Christians. Large groups of Catholics continued to claim allegiance to the pope. Others, affected by the teachings of the European Reformation, believed the new Church of England had abandoned Rome without abandoning Rome's offensive beliefs and practices. Under Elizabeth, the church began to incorporate some of the tenets of Calvinism, but never enough to satisfy its critics—particularly the many exiles who had fled the country under Mary and who now returned, bringing their new, more radical religious ideas with them. They continued to clamor for reforms that would "purify" the church; as a result, they became known as "Puritans."

A few Puritans took what were, by the standards of the time, genuinely radical positions. They were known as Separatists, and they were deter- | *Puritan Separatists* mined to worship as they pleased | in their own independent congregations. That determination flew in the face of English law—which outlawed unauthorized religious meetings, required all subjects to attend regular Anglican services, and levied taxes to support the established church. The radicalism of the Separatists was

ELIZABETH I The flemish artist Marcus Gheeraerts the younger moved to England in 1568 (along with his father, also a painter) as a Protestant refugee from his homeland. In approximately 1593 he painted this portrait of the English queen, portraying her as she was seen by many of her contemporaries: a strong, confident ruler presiding over an ambitious, expansionist nation. She stands here on a map of England. *(National Portrait Gallery, London)*

visible in other ways as well, including their rejection of prevailing assumptions about the proper religious roles of women. Many Separatist sects, perhaps most prominently the Quakers, permitted women to serve as preachers and to assume a prominence in other religious matters that would have been impossible in the established church.

Most Puritans resisted separatism. Still, their demands were by no means modest. They wanted to simplify Anglican forms of worship. They wanted to reduce the power of the bishops, who were appointed by the crown and who were, in many cases, openly corrupt and highly extravagant. Perhaps above all they wanted to reform the local clergy, a group composed in large part of greedy, uneducated men with little interest in (or knowledge of) theology. The more moderate Puritans wished, in short, to see the church give more attention to its spiritual role and less to its worldly ambitions. No less than the Separatists, they grew increasingly frustrated by the refusal of either

the political or ecclesiastical leaders of the nation to respond to their demands.

Puritan discontent, already festering, grew rapidly after the death of Elizabeth, the last of the Tudors, and the accession to the throne of James I, a Scotsman and the first of the *Puritan Discontent* Stuarts, in 1603. James believed kings ruled by divine right, and he felt no obligation to compromise with his opponents. He quickly antagonized the Puritans, a group that included most of the rising businessmen, by resorting to arbitrary taxation, by favoring English Catholics in the granting of charters and other favors, and by supporting "high church" forms of ceremony. By the early seventeenth century, some religious nonconformists were beginning to look for places of refuge outside the kingdom. Along with the other economic and social incentives for colonization, such religious discontent helped turn England's gaze to distant lands.

The English in Ireland

England's first experience with colonization came not in the New World, but in a land separated from Britain only by a narrow stretch of sea: Ireland. The English had long laid claim to the island and had for many years maintained small settlements in the area around Dublin. Only in the second half of the sixteenth century, however, did serious efforts at large-scale colonization begin. Through the 1560s and 1570s, would-be colonists moved through Ireland, capturing territory and attempting to subdue the native population. In the process they developed many of the assumptions that would guide later English colonists in America.

The most important of these assumptions was that the native population of Ireland—approximately 1 million people, loyal to the Catholic Church, with their own language (Gaelic) and their own culture—was a collection of wild, vicious, and ignorant "savages." The Irish lived in ways the English considered crude and wasteful ("like beasts"), and they fought back against the intruders with a ferocity that the English considered barbaric. Such people could not be tamed, the English concluded. They certainly could not be assimilated into English society. They must, therefore, be suppressed, isolated, and if necessary destroyed. Eventually, they might be "civilized," but only after they were thoroughly subordinated.

Whatever barbarities the Irish may have inflicted on the colonizers, the English more than matched in return. Sir Humphrey Gilbert, who was later to establish the first British colony in the New World (an unsuccessful venture in Newfoundland), served for a time as governor of one Irish district and suppressed native rebellions with extraordinary viciousness. Gilbert was an educated and supposedly civilized man. But he considered the natives somehow less than human, and therefore not entitled to whatever decencies civilized people reserved for their treatment of one another. As a result, he managed to justify, both to himself and to others, such atrocities as beheading Irish soldiers after they were killed in battle. Gilbert himself, Sir Walter Raleigh, Sir Richard Grenville, and others active in Ireland in the mid-sixteenth century derived from their experiences there an outlook they would take to America, where they made similarly vicious efforts to subdue and subjugate the natives.

The Irish experience led the English to another important (and related) assumption about colonization: that English settlements in distant lands must retain a rigid separation from the native populations. In Ireland, English *The Plantation Model* colonizers established what they called "plantations," transplantations of English society in a foreign land. Unlike the Spanish in America, the English in Ireland did not try simply to rule a subdued native population; they tried to build a complete society of their own, peopled with emigrants from England itself. The new society would exist within a "pale of settlement," an area physically separated from the natives. That concept, too, they would take with them to the New World, even though in Ireland, as later in America, the separation of peoples and the preservation of "pure" English culture proved impossible.

The French and the Dutch in America

English settlers in North America, unlike those in Ireland, were to encounter not only natives but also other Europeans who were, like them, driven by mercantilist ideas to establish economic outposts abroad. To the south and southwest was the Spanish Empire. Spanish ships continued to threaten English settlements along the coast for years. But except for Mexico and scattered outposts such as those in Florida and New Mexico, the Spanish made little serious effort to colonize North America.

England's more formidable North American rivals in the early sixteenth century were the French. France founded its first permanent settlement in America at Quebec in 1608, less than a year after the English started their first colony at Jamestown. The French colony's population grew very slowly. Few French Catholics felt any inclination to leave their homeland, and French Protestants who might have wished to emigrate were excluded from the colony. The French, however, exercised an influence in the New World disproportionate to their numbers, largely because of their relationships with Native Americans. Unlike the English, who for many years hugged the coastline and traded with the Indians of the interior through intermediaries, the French forged close, direct ties with natives deep inside the continent. French Jesuit missionaries were among the first to penetrate Indian societies, and they established some of the first contacts between the two peoples. More important still were the *coureurs de bois*—adventurous fur traders and trappers—who also penetrated far into the wilderness and developed an extensive trade that became one of the underpinnings of the French colonial economy.

Coureurs de Bois

The fur trade was, in fact, more an Indian than a French enterprise. The *coureurs de bois* were, in many ways, little more than agents for the Algonquins and the Hurons, who were the principal fur traders among the Indians of the region and from whom the French purchased their pelts. The French traders were able to function only to the degree that they could form partnerships with the Indians. Successful partnerships often resulted from their ability to become virtually a part of native society, living among the Indians and at times marrying Indian women. The fur trade helped open the way for the other elements of the French presence in North America—the agricultural estates (or *seignuries*) along the St. Lawrence River, the development of trade and military centers at Quebec and Montreal, and the creation of an alliance with the Algonquins and others—that enabled the French to compete with the more numerous British in the contest for control of North America. That alliance also brought the French into conflict with the Iroquois, the Algonquins' ancient enemies, who assumed the central role in the English fur trade. An early result of these tensions was a 1609 attack led by Samuel de Champlain, the founder of Quebec, on a band of Mohawks, apparently at the instigation of his Algonquin trading partners.

The Dutch, too, were establishing a presence in North America. Holland had won its independence from Spain in the early seventeenth century and was one of the leading trading nations of the world. Its merchant fleet was larger than England's, and its traders were active not only in Europe but also in Africa, Asia, and—increasingly—America. In 1609 an English explorer in the employ of the Dutch, Henry Hudson, sailed up the river that was to be named for him in what is now New York State. Because the river was so wide, he believed for a time that he had found the long-sought water route through the continent to the Pacific. He was wrong, of course, but his explorations led to a Dutch claim on territory in America and to the establishment of a permanent Dutch presence in the New World.

Henry Hudson

For more than a decade after Hudson's voyage, the Dutch maintained an active trade in furs in and around New York. In 1624, the Dutch West India Company established a series of permanent trading posts on the Hudson, Delaware, and Connecticut Rivers. The company actively encouraged settlement of the region—not just from Holland itself, but from such other parts of northern Europe as Germany, Sweden, and Finland. It transported

New Amsterdam

THE "RESTITUTION" OF NEW AMSTERDAM This is a detail from an elaborate engraving created to celebrate the "Restitutio" (or return) of New Amsterdam to the Dutch in 1673. England had captured New Amsterdam in 1664 and made claim to the entire province of New Netherland. But in 1672, war broke out between England and the Netherlands, and the Dutch recaptured their lost province. In celebration of that event, this heroic picture of the Dutch fleet in New York was created for sale in the Netherlands. Early in 1674, at the conclusion of the war, the Dutch returned the colony to England. *(Museum of the City of New York)*

whole families to the New World and granted vast feudal estates to landlords (known as "patroons") on condition that they bring still more immigrants to America. The result was the colony of New Netherland and its principal town, New Amsterdam, on Manhattan Island. Its population, diverse as it was, remained relatively small; the colony was only loosely united, with chronically weak leadership.

The First English Settlements

The first enduring English settlement in the New World was established at Jamestown, in Virginia, in 1607. But for nearly thirty years before that, English merchants and adventurers had been engaged in a series of failed efforts to create colonies in America. Through much of the sixteenth century, the English had mixed feelings about the New World. They knew of its existence and were intrigued by its possibilities. Under the strong leadership of Elizabeth I, they were developing a powerful sense of nationalism that encouraged dreams of expansion. At the same time, however, England was leery of Spain, which remained the dominant force in America and, it seemed, the dominant naval power in Europe.

But much changed in the 1570s and 1580s. English "sea dogs" such as Sir Francis Drake staged successful raids on

The Spanish Armada Spanish merchant ships and built confidence in England's ability to challenge Spanish sea power. More important was the attempted invasion of England by the Spanish Armada in 1588. Philip II, the powerful Spanish king, had recently united his nation with Portugal. He was now determined to end England's challenges to Spanish commercial supremacy and to bring the English back into the Catholic Church. He assembled one of the largest military fleets in

the history of warfare—known to history as the "Spanish Armada"—to carry his troops across the English Channel and into England itself. Philip's bold venture turned into a fiasco when the smaller English fleet dispersed the Armada and, in a single stroke, ended Spain's domination of the Atlantic. The English now felt much freer to establish themselves in the New World.

The pioneers of English colonization were Sir Humphrey Gilbert and his half-brother Sir Walter Raleigh—both friends of Queen Elizabeth, and both veterans of the earlier colonial efforts in Ireland. In 1578 Gilbert obtained from Elizabeth a patent granting him the exclusive right for six years "to inhabit and possess at his choice all remote and heathen lands not in the actual possession of any Christian prince."

After numerous setbacks, Gilbert led an expedition to Newfoundland in 1583 and took possession of it in the queen's name. He proceeded southward along the coast, looking for a good place to *Gilbert's Expedition to Newfoundland* build a military outpost that might eventually grow into a profitable colony. But a storm sank his ship, and he was lost at sea.

Roanoke

Raleigh was undeterred by Gilbert's misfortune. The next year, he secured from Elizabeth a six-year grant similar to Gilbert's and sent a small group of men on an expedition to explore the North American coast. They returned with two captive Indians and glowing reports of what they had seen. They were particularly enthusiastic about an island the natives called Roanoke and about the area of the mainland just beyond it (in what is now North Carolina).

ROANOKE A drawing by one of the English colonists in the ill-fated Roanoke expedition of 1585 became the basis for this engraving by Theodore DeBry, published in England in 1590. A small European ship carrying settlers approaches the island of Roanoke, at left. The wreckage of several larger vessels farther out to sea and the presence of Indian settlements on the mainland and on Roanoke itself suggest some of the perils the settlers encountered. *(New York Public Library)*

Raleigh asked the queen for permission to name the entire region "Virginia" in honor of Elizabeth, "the Virgin Queen." But while Elizabeth granted the permission, she did not offer the financial assistance Raleigh had hoped his flattery would produce. So he turned to private investors to finance another expedition.

In 1585 Raleigh recruited his cousin, Sir Richard Grenville, to lead a group of men (most of them from the *The First Roanoke Colony* English plantations in Ireland) to Roanoke to establish a colony. Grenville deposited the settlers on the island, remained long enough to antagonize the natives by razing an Indian village as retaliation for a minor theft, and returned to England. The following spring, Sir Francis Drake unexpectedly arrived in Roanoke. With supplies and reinforcements from England long overdue, the beleaguered colonists boarded Drake's ships and left.

Raleigh tried again in 1587, sending an expedition carrying ninety-one men, seventeen women (two of them pregnant), and nine children—the nucleus, he hoped, of

a viable "plantation." The settlers landed on Roanoke and attempted to take up where the first group of colonists had left off. (Shortly after arriving, one of the women— the daughter of the commander of the expedition, John White—gave birth to a daughter, Virginia Dare, the first American-born child of English parents.) White returned to England after several weeks (leaving his daughter and granddaughter behind) in search of supplies and additional settlers; he hoped to return in a few months. But the hostilities with Spain intervened, and White did not return to the island for three years. When he did, in 1590, he found the island utterly deserted, with no clue to the settlers' fate other than the cryptic inscription "Croatoan" carved on a post. Some have argued that the colonists were slaughtered by the Indians in retaliation for Grenville's (and perhaps their own) hostilities. Others have contended that they left their settlement and joined native society, ultimately becoming entirely assimilated. But no conclusive solution to the mystery of the "Lost Colony" has ever been found.

The Roanoke disaster marked the end of Sir Walter Raleigh's involvement in English colonization of the New World. In 1603, when James I succeeded Elizabeth to the throne, Raleigh was accused of plotting against the king, stripped of his monopoly, and imprisoned for more than a decade. Finally (after being released for one last ill-fated maritime expedition), he was executed by the king in 1618. No later colonizer would receive grants of land in the New World as vast or undefined as those Raleigh and Gilbert had acquired. But despite the discouraging example of these early experiences, the colonizing impulse remained alive.

In the first years of the seventeenth century, a group of London merchants to whom Raleigh had assigned his charter rights decided to renew the attempt at colonization in Virginia. A rival group of merchants, from Plymouth and other West Country towns, were also interested in American ventures and were sponsoring voyages of exploration farther north, up to Newfoundland, where West Country fishermen had been going for many years. In 1606 James I issued a new charter, which divided America

New Colonial Charters

between the two groups. The London group got the exclusive right to colonize in the south, and the Plymouth merchants received the same right in the north. Through their efforts, the first enduring English colonies were planted in America.

CONCLUSION

The lands that Europeans eventually named the Americas were the home of many millions of people before the arrival of Columbus. Having migrated from Asia thousands of years earlier, the pre-Columbian Americans spread throughout the Western Hemisphere and eventually created great civilizations. Among the most notable of them were the Incas in Peru, and the Mayas and Aztecs in Mexico. In the regions north of what was later named the Rio Grande, the human population was smaller and the civilizations less advanced than they were further south. Even so, North American natives created a cluster of civilizations that thrived and expanded. There were probably 10 million people living north of Mexico by the time Columbus arrived.

In the century after European contact, these native populations suffered a series of catastrophes that all but destroyed the civilizations they had built: brutal invasions by Spanish and Portuguese conquistadores and, even more devastating, a series of plagues inadvertently imported by Europeans that decimated native populations. By the middle of the sixteenth century, the Spanish and Portuguese—no longer faced with effective resistance from the native populations—had established colonial control over all of South America and much of North America, creating one of the largest empires in the world.

In the parts of North America that would eventually become the United States, the European presence was for a time much less powerful. The Spanish established an important northern outpost in what is now New Mexico, a society in which Europeans and Indians lived together intimately, if unequally. They created a fort at St. Augustine, Florida. On the whole, however, the North American Indians remained largely undisturbed by Europeans until the English, French, and Dutch migrations began in the early seventeenth century.

FOR FURTHER REFERENCE

Alvin M. Josephy, ed., *America in 1492: The World of the Indian Peoples Before the Arrival of Columbus* (1993) and Brian M. Fagan, *The Great Journey: The Peopling of Ancient America* (1987) provide introductions to pre-Columbian history. William M. Denevan, ed., *The Native Population of the Americas in 1492* (1976) and Russell Thornton, *American Indian Holocaust and Survival: A Population History since 1492* (1987) are important contributions to the debate over the size and character of the American population before Columbus. Alfred Crosby, *The Columbian Exchange: Biological and Cultural Consequences of 1492* (1972) explores the results of European-Indian contact in both the Americas and Europe.

D. W. Meinig, *The Shaping of America, Vol. I: Atlantic America, 1492–1800* (1986) is an account of the early contacts between Europeans and the New World. Gary Nash, *Red, White and Black: The Peoples of Early America* (1982) provides a brief, multiracial survey of colonial America. Philip Curtin, *The Atlantic Slave Trade: A Census* (1969) has become the indispensable starting point for understanding African forced migration to the Americas. One outstanding collection of essays that summarizes modern scholarship on colonial America is Jack P. Greene and J.R.Pole, eds., *Colonial British America: Essays in the New History of the Early Modern Era* (1984). *Columbus and the Age of Discovery* (1991) is a seven-part documentary film series on Christopher Columbus, his era, and his legacy.

For quizzes, Internet resources, references to additional books and films, and more, consult this book's Online Learning Center at www.mhhe.com/brinkleyll.

THE INCONVENIENCIES
THAT HAVE HAPPENED TO SOME PER-
SONS WHICH HAVE TRANSPORTED THEMSELVES
from *England* to *Virginia*, without prouisions necessary to sustaine themselues, hath
greatly hindred the Progresse of that noble Plantation: For preuention of the like disorders
heereafter, that no man suffer, either through ignorance or misinformation; it is thought requisite to publish this short declaration: wherein is contained a particular of such neces-
saries, as either priuate families or single persons shall haue cause to furnish themselues with, for their better
support at their first landing in Virginia; whereby also greater numbers may receiue in part,
directions how to prouide themselues.

Apparrell.	li.	s.	d.
One Monmouth Cap	00	01	10
Three falling bands		01	03
Three shirts		07	06
One waste-coate		02	02
One suite of Canuase		07	06
One suite of Frize		10	00
One suite of Cloth		15	00
Three paire of Irish stockins		04	00
Foure paire of shooes		08	08
One paire of garters		00	10
One doozen of points		00	03
One paire of Canuase sheets		08	00
Seuen ells of Canuase, to make a bed and boulster, to be filled in *Virginia* 8.s. One Rug for a bed 8. s. which with the bed seruing for two men, halfe is	08	00	
Fiue ells coorse Canuase, to make a bed at Sea for two men, to be filled with straw, iiij.s.		05	00
One coorse Rug at Sea for two men, will cost vj.s. is for one		04	00

Victuall.			
Eight bushels of Meale	02	00	00
Two bushels of pease at 3.s.		06	00
Two bushels of Oatemeale 4.s. 6.d.		09	00
One gallon of *Aquauitæ*		02	06
One gallon of Oyle		03	06
Two gallons of Vineger 1.s.		02	00
	03	03	00

Armes.			
One Armour compleat, light		17	00
One long Peece, fiue foot or fiue and a halfe, neere Musket bore	01	02	00
One sword		05	00
One belt		01	00
One bandaleere		01	06
Twenty pound of powder		18	00
Sixty pound of shot or lead, Pistoll and Goose shot		05	00
	03	09	06

Tooles.	li.	s.	d.
Fiue broad howes at 2.s. a piece		10	00
Fiue narrow howes at 16.d. a piece		06	08
Two broad Axes at 3.s. 8.d. a piece		07	04
Fiue felling Axes at 18.d. a piece		07	06
Two steele hand sawes at 16.d. a piece		02	08
Two two-hand sawes at 5. s. a piece		10	00
One whip-saw, set and filed with box, file, and wrest		10	00
Two hammers 12.d. a piece		02	00
Three shouels 18.d. a piece		04	06
Two spades at 18.d. a piece		03	00
Two augers 6.d. a piece		01	00
Sixe chissels 6.d. a piece		03	00
Two percers stocked 4.d. a piece		00	08
Three gimlets 2.d. a piece		00	06
Two hatchets 21.d. a piece		03	06
Two frowes to cleaue pale 18.d.		03	00
Two hand bills 20. a piece		03	04
One grindlestone 4.s.		04	00
Nailes of all sorts to the value of	02	00	00
Two Pickaxes		03	00
	06	02	08

Houshold Implements.			
One Iron Pot		07	00
One kettle		06	00
One large frying pan		02	06
One gridiron		01	06
Two skillets		05	00
One spit		02	00
Platters, dishes, spoones of wood		04	00
	01	08	00

For Sugar, Spice, and fruit, and at Sea for 6. men. | 00 | 12 | 06 |

So the full charge of Apparrell, Victuall, Armes, Tooles,
and houshold stuffe, and after this rate for each person,
will amount vnto about the summe of | 12 | 10 | 00 |
The passage of each man is | 06 | 00 | 00 |
The fraight of these prouisions for a man, will be about
halfe a Tun, which is | 01 | 10 | 00 |
So the whole charge will amount to about | 20 | 00 | 00 |

Nets, hookes, lines, and a tent must be added, if the number of people be greater, as also some kine.
And this is the vsuall proportion that the Virginia Company doe
bestow vpon their Tenants which they send.

Whosoeuer transports himselfe or any other at his owne charge vnto *Virginia*, shall for each person so transported before Midsummer 1625.
haue to him and his heires for euer fifty Acres of Land vpon a first, and fifty Acres vpon a second diuision.

Imprinted at London by FELIX KYNGSTON. 1622.

ADVICE TO MIGRANTS This 1622 handbill by the Virginia Company of London provides a detailed list of items that people contemplating a voyage to America should plan to take with them. The list reflects the company's awareness of how few finished goods were yet available in America (and also their realization that they themselves could profit from selling such goods to their passengers). *(Rare Books Division, New York Public Library, Astor, Lenox and Tilden Foundations)*

Significant Events

CHAPTER TWO

TRANSPLANTATIONS AND BORDERLANDS

The Roanoke fiasco dampened the colonizing enthusiasm in England—for a time. But the lures of the New World—the presumably vast riches, the abundant land, *Lure of the New World* the opportunities for religious freedom, the chance to begin anew—were too strong to be suppressed for very long. Propagandizers such as Richard Hakluyt kept the image of America alive in English society. By the early seventeenth century, the effort to establish permanent colonies in the New World resumed.

The first of these new efforts were much like the earlier, failed ones. They were largely private ventures, with little planning or direction from the English government. They were small, fragile settlements, and generally unprepared for the hardships they were to face. They met with terrible disasters.

Several things characterized these first permanent English settlements. First, the colonies were business enterprises. They were financed by private companies, and, in most cases, they were expected to produce a profit. Second, as in Ireland, there were few efforts to blend English society with the society of the natives. The Europeans attempted, as best they could, to isolate themselves from the Indians and create enclosed societies *Characteristics of English* that would be entirely their *Settlements* own—"transplantations" of the English world they had left behind. Third, almost nothing worked out as they had planned—largely because the English could not effectively isolate themselves from the world around them, a world populated by Native American tribes, but also by colonists, explorers, and traders from Spain, France, and the Netherlands, and immigrants from other parts of Europe. The English colonies were, in short, part of a complex and rapidly changing society. However much the settlers tried to re-create English society in the New World, American society very quickly began to develop its own habits and institutions.

THE EARLY CHESAPEAKE

After James I issued his 1606 charters to the London and Plymouth Companies, the principal obstacle to founding new American colonies was, as usual, money. The Plymouth group made an early, unsuccessful attempt to establish a colony at Sagadoahoc, on the coast of Maine; but in the aftermath of that failure, it largely abandoned its colonizing efforts. The London Company, by contrast, moved quickly and decisively. Only a few months after receiving its charter, it launched a colonizing expedition headed for Virginia—a party of 144 men aboard three ships: the *Godspeed,* the *Discovery,* and the *Susan Constant.*

The Founding of Jamestown

Only 104 men survived the journey. They reached the American coast in the spring of 1607, sailed into the Chesapeake Bay and up a river they named the James, and established their colony on a peninsula extending from the river's northern bank. They called it Jamestown. The colonists had chosen their site poorly. In an effort to avoid the mistakes of Roanoke (whose residents were assumed to have been killed by Indians), they selected what they believed to be an easily defended location—an inland setting that they believed would offer them security. But the site was low and swampy, hot and humid in the summer, and prey to outbreaks of malaria. It was surrounded by thick woods, which were difficult to clear for cultivation. And it lay within the territories of powerful local Indians, a confederation led by the imperial chief Powhatan.

The result could hardly have been more disastrous. For seventeen years, one wave of English settlers after another attempted to make Jamestown a habitable and profitable colony. Every effort failed. The town became instead a place of misery and death; and the London Company, which had sponsored it in the hope of vast profits, saw itself drained of funds and saddled with seemingly endless losses. All that could be said of Jamestown at the end of this first period of its existence was that it had survived.

The initial colonists, too many of whom were adventurous gentlemen and too few of whom were willing laborers, ran into serious difficulties from the moment they landed. Much like the Indians to the south who had succumbed quickly to European diseases when first exposed to them, these English settlers had had no prior exposure, and thus no immunity, to the infections of the new land. Malaria, in particular, debilitated the colony, killing some and weakening others so they could do virtually no work. Because the promoters in London demanded a quick return on their investment, the colonists spent much of their limited and dwindling energy on futile searches for gold. They made only slightly more successful efforts to

Early Problems

pile up lumber, tar, pitch, and iron for export. Growing food was a low priority.

The London Company promoters had little interest in creating a family-centered community, and at first they sent no women to Jamestown. The absence of English women made it difficult for the settlers to establish any semblance of a "society." The colonists were seldom able (and also seldom willing) to intermarry with native women, and hence Jamestown was at first an entirely male settlement. Without women, settlers could not establish real households, could not order their domestic lives, and had difficulty feeling any sense of a permanent stake in the community.

Greed and rootlessness contributed to the failure to grow sufficient food; inadequate diets contributed to the colonists' vulnerability to disease; the ravages of disease made it difficult for the settlers to recover from their early mistakes. The result was a community without the means to sustain itself. By January 1608, when ships appeared with additional men and supplies, all but 38 of the first 104 colonists were dead. Jamestown, now facing extinction, survived the crisis largely because of the efforts of twenty-seven-year-old Captain John Smith. He was already a famous world traveler, the hero of implausible travel narratives he had written and published. But he was also a capable organizer. Leadership in the colony had been divided among the several members of a council who quarreled continually. In the fall of 1608, however, Smith became council president and asserted his will. He imposed work and order on the community. He also organized raids on neighboring Indian villages to steal food and kidnap natives. During the colony's second winter, fewer than a dozen (in a population of about 200) died. By the summer of 1609, when Smith was deposed from the council and returned to England to receive treatment for a serious powder burn, the colony was showing promise of survival.

John Smith

Reorganization

The London Company (now calling itself the Virginia Company) was, in the meantime, dreaming of bigger things. In 1609 it obtained a new charter from the king, which increased its power over the colony and enlarged the area of land to which it had title. The company raised additional capital by selling stock to "adventurers" who would remain in England but share in future profits. It attracted new settlers by offering additional stock to "planters" who were willing to migrate at their own expense. And it provided free passage to Virginia for poorer people who would agree to serve the company for seven years. In the spring of 1609, confident that it was now poised to transform Jamestown into a vibrant, successful venture, the company launched a "great fleet" of nine vessels with about 600 people (including some women and children) aboard—headed for Virginia.

More disaster followed. One of the Virginia-bound ships was lost at sea in a hurricane. Another ran aground on one of the Bermuda islands and was unable to free itself for months. Many of those who reached Jamestown, still weak from their long and stormy voyage, succumbed to fevers before the cold weather came. The winter of 1609–1610 became known as the "starving time," a period worse than anything before. The local Indians, antagonized by John Smith's raids and other hostile actions by the early English settlers, killed off the livestock in the woods and kept the colonists barricaded within their palisade. The Europeans lived on what they could find: "dogs, cats, rats, snakes, toadstools, horsehides," and even the "corpses of dead men," as one survivor recalled. The following May, the migrants who had run aground and been stranded on Bermuda finally arrived in Jamestown. They found only about 60 people (out of 500 residents the previous summer) still alive—and those so weakened by the ordeal that they seemed scarcely human. There seemed no point in staying on. The new arrivals took the survivors onto their ship, abandoned the settlement, and sailed downriver for home.

The Starving Time

That might have been the end of Jamestown had it not been for an extraordinary twist of fate. As the refugees proceeded down the James toward the Chesapeake Bay, they met an English ship coming up the river—part of a fleet bringing supplies and the colony's first governor, Lord De La Warr. The departing settlers agreed to turn around and return to Jamestown. New relief expeditions with hundreds of colonists soon began to arrive, and the effort to turn a profit in Jamestown resumed.

De La Warr and his successors (Sir Thomas Dale and Sir Thomas Gates) imposed a harsh and rigid discipline on the colony. They organized settlers into work gangs. They sentenced offenders to be flogged, hanged, or broken on the wheel. But this communal system of labor did not function effectively for long. Settlers often evaded work, "presuming that howsoever the harvest prospered, the general store must maintain them." Governor Dale soon concluded that the colony would fare better if the colonists had personal incentives to work. He began to permit the private ownership and cultivation of land. Landowners would repay the company with part-time work and contributions of grain to its storehouses.

De La Warr's Harsh Discipline

Under the leadership of these first, harsh governors, Virginia was not always a happy place. But it survived and even expanded. New settlements began lining the river above and below Jamestown. The expansion was partly a result of the order and discipline the governors at times managed to impose. It was partly a product of increased military assaults on the local Indian tribes, which provided protection for the new settlements. But it also occurred because the colonists had at last discovered a marketable crop: tobacco.

Tobacco

Europeans had become aware of tobacco soon after Columbus's first return from the West Indies, where he had seen the Cuban natives smoking small cigars *(tabacos)*, which they inserted in the nostril. By the early seventeenth century, tobacco from the Spanish colonies was already in wide use in Europe. Some critics denounced it as a poisonous weed, the cause of many diseases. King James I himself led the attack with

THE GROWTH OF THE CHESAPEAKE, 1607–1750 This map shows the political forms of European settlement in the region of the Chesapeake Bay in the seventeenth and early eighteenth centuries. Note the several different kinds of colonial enterprises: the royal colony of Virginia, controlled directly by the English crown after the failure of the early commercial enterprises there; and the proprietary regions of Maryland, northern Virginia, and North Carolina, which were under the control of powerful English aristocrats. ◆ *Did these political differences have any significant effect on the economic activities of the various Chesapeake colonies?*

TOBACCO PLANT This 1622 woodcut, later hand-colored, represents the tobacco plant cultivated by English settlers in Virginia in the early seventeenth century after John Rolfe introduced it to the colonists. On the right is an image of a man smoking the plant through a very large pipe. *(Hulton/Archive/Getty Images)*

Expansion

Even the discovery of tobacco cultivation was not enough to help the Virginia Company. By 1616, there were still no profits, only land and debts. Nevertheless, the promoters continued to hope that the tobacco trade would allow them finally to turn the corner. In 1618, they launched a last great campaign to attract settlers and make the colony profitable.

Part of that campaign was an effort to recruit new settlers and workers to the colony. The company established what they called the "headright" system. Headrights were fifty-acre grants of land, which new settlers could acquire in a variety of ways. Those who already lived in the colony received 100 acres apiece. Each new settler received a single headright for himself or herself. This system encouraged family groups to migrate together, since the more family members traveled to America, the larger the land-holding the family would receive. In addition, anyone (new settler or old) who paid for the passage of other immigrants to Virginia would receive an additional headright for each new arrival—thus, it was hoped, inducing the prosperous to import new laborers to America. Some colonists were able to assemble sizable plantations with the combined headrights they received for their families and their servants. In return, they contributed a small quitrent (one shilling a year for each headright) to the company.

The Headright System

The company added other incentives as well. To diversify the colonial economy, it transported ironworkers and other skilled craftsmen to Virginia. In 1619, it sent 100 Englishwomen to the colony (which was still overwhelmingly male) to become the wives of male colonists. (The women could be purchased for 120 pounds of tobacco and enjoyed a status somewhere between indentured servants and free people, depending on the good will—or lack of it—of their husbands.) It promised the colonists the full rights of Englishmen (as provided in the original charter of 1606), an end to the strict and arbitrary rule of the communal years, and even a share in self-government. On July 30, 1619, in the Jamestown church, delegates from the various communities met as the House of Burgesses. It was the first meeting of an elected legislature, a representative assembly, within what was to become the United States.

A month later, another event in Virginia established a very different but no less momentous precedent. As John Rolfe recorded, "about the latter end of August" a Dutch ship brought in "20 and odd Negroes." The status and fate of these first Africans in the English colonies remains obscure. There is some reason to believe that the colonists did not consider them slaves, that they thought of them as servants to be held for a term of years and then freed, like the white servants with whom the planters were already familiar. For a time, moreover, the use of black labor remained limited.

A Counterblaste to Tobacco (1604), in which he urged his people not to imitate "the barbarous and beastly manners of the wild, godless, and slavish Indians, especially in so vile and stinking a custom." Other critics were concerned because England's tobacco purchases from the Spanish colonies meant a drain of English gold to the Spanish importers. Still, the demand for tobacco soared.

Then in 1612, the Jamestown planter John Rolfe began to experiment in Virginia with a harsh strain of tobacco that local Indians had been growing for years. He produced crops of high quality, and he found ready buyers in England. Tobacco cultivation quickly spread up and down the James. The character of this tobacco economy—its profitability, its uncertainty, its land and labor demands—transformed Chesapeake society in fundamental ways.

Emergece of the Tobacco Economy

Of most immediate importance, perhaps, was the pressure tobacco cultivation created for territorial expansion. Tobacco growers needed large areas of farmland to grow their crops; and because tobacco exhausted the soil after only a few years, the demand for land increased even more. English farmers began establishing plantations deeper and deeper in the interior, isolating themselves from the center of European settlement at Jamestown and encroaching on territory the natives considered their own.

Although Africans continued to trickle steadily into the colony, planters continued to prefer European indentured servants until at least the 1670s, when such servants began to become scarce and expensive. But whether or not anyone realized it at the time, the small group of black people who arrived in 1619 marked a first step toward the enslavement of Africans within what was to be the American republic.

The expansion of the colony was able to proceed only because of effective suppression of the local

Suppression of the Powhatan Indians

Indians, who resisted the expanding English presence. For two years, Sir Thomas Dale led unrelenting assaults against the Powhatan Indians and in the process kidnapped the great chief Powhatan's daughter Pocahontas. When Powhatan refused to ransom her, she converted to Christianity and in 1614 married John Rolfe. (Pocahontas accompanied her husband back to England, where, as a Christian convert and a gracious woman, she stirred interest in projects to "civilize" the Indians. She died while abroad.) At that point, Powhatan ceased his attacks on the English in the face of overwhelming odds. But after his death several years later, his brother, Opechancanough, became head of the native confederacy and resumed the effort to defend tribal lands from European encroachments. On a March morning in 1622, tribesmen called on the white settlements as if to offer goods for sale, then suddenly attacked. Not until 347 whites of both sexes and all ages (including John Rolfe) lay dead or dying were the Indian warriors finally forced to retreat. The surviving English struck back mercilessly at the Indians and turned back the threat for a time. Only after Opechancanough led another unsuccessful uprising in 1644 did the Powhatans finally cease to challenge the eastern regions of the colony.

By then the Virginia Company in London was defunct.

Demise of the Virginia Company

The company had poured virtually all its funds into its profitless Jamestown venture and in the aftermath of the 1622 Indian uprising faced imminent bankruptcy. In 1624, James I revoked the company's charter, and the colony came under the control of the crown. It would remain so until 1776.

Exchanges of Agricultural Technology

The hostility the early English settlers expressed toward their Indian neighbors was in part a result of their conviction that their own civilization was greatly superior to that of the natives—and perhaps above all that they were more technologically advanced. The English, after all, had great ocean-going vessels, muskets and other advanced implements of weaponry, and many other tools that the Indians had not developed. Indeed, when John Smith and other early Jamestown residents grew frustrated at their

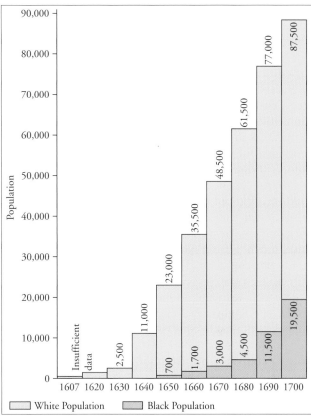

THE NON-INDIAN POPULATION OF THE CHESAPEAKE, 1607–1700 This graph shows the very rapid growth of the population of the Chesapeake during its first century of European settlement. Note the very dramatic increases in the first half of the century, and the somewhat slower increase in the later decades. If the forcibly imported slave population were not counted in the last two decades of the century, the non-Indian population would have grown virtually not at all. ◆ *What impact would the growth of African slavery have had on the rate of immigration by Europeans?*

inability to find gold and other precious commodities, they often blamed the backwardness of the natives. The Spanish in South America, Smith once wrote, had grown rich because the natives there had built advanced civilizations and mined much gold and silver. If Mexico and Peru had been as "ill peopled, as little planted, laboured and manured as Virginia," he added, the Spanish would have found no more wealth than the English did.

Yet the survival of Jamestown was, in the end, largely a result of agricultural technologies developed by Indians and borrowed by the English. Native agriculture was far better adapted to the soil and climate of Virginia than the agricultural traditions the English settlers brought with them. The Indians of Virginia were not nomadic hunters, but settled farmers whose villages were surrounded by neatly ordered fields in which grew a variety of crops—beans, pumpkins, vegetables, and above all maize (known to us as corn),

Indian Agricultural Techniques

which had been previously unknown to the English. Some of the Indian farmlands stretched over hundreds of acres and supported substantial populations.

The English settlers did not adopt all the Indian agricultural techniques. Natives cleared fields not, as the English did, by cutting down and uprooting all the trees. Instead they killed trees in place by "girdling" them (that is, making deep incisions around the base) in the areas in which they planted or setting fire to their roots; and they planted crops not in long, straight rows, but in curving patterns around the dead tree trunks. But in other respects, the English learned a great deal from the Indians about how to grow food in the New World. In particular, they quickly recognized the great value of corn, which proved to be easier to cultivate and to produce much greater yields than any of the European grains the English had known at home. Corn was also attractive to the settlers because its stalks could be a source of sugar and it spoiled less easily than other grains. The English also learned the advantages of growing beans alongside corn to enrich the soil. An early settler in New England (where the English also learned how to cultivate corn from the natives) wrote that the Indians had taught the settlers "to cull out the finest seede, to observe the fittest season, to keepe distance for holes, and fit measure for hills, to worme it, and weede it; to prune it, and dresse it as occasion shall require."

Maryland and the Calverts

Maryland was founded under circumstances very different from those of Virginia, but it nonetheless developed in ways markedly similar to its neighbor to the south. The new colony was the dream of George Calvert, the first Lord Baltimore, a recent convert to Catholicism and a shrewd businessman. Calvert envisioned establishing a colony both as a great speculative venture in real estate and as a retreat for English Catholics, many of whom felt oppressed by the Anglican establishment at home. He died before he could receive a charter from the king. But in 1632, his son Cecilius, the second Lord Baltimore, received a charter remarkable not only for the extent of the territory it granted him—an area that encompassed parts of what are now Pennsylvania, Delaware, and Virginia, in addition to present-day Mary-land—but also for the powers it bestowed on him. He and his heirs were to hold their province as "true and absolute lords and proprietaries," and were to acknowledge the ultimate sovereignty of the king only by paying an annual fee to the crown.

Proprietary Rule

Lord Baltimore named his brother, Leonard Calvert, governor and sent him with another brother to oversee the settlement of the province. In March 1634, two ships—the *Ark* and the *Dove*—bearing 200 to 300 passengers entered the Potomac River and turned into one of its eastern

THE MARYLAND PROPRIETOR, C. 1670 In a detail of a portrait by the court painter to King Charles II, the young Cecilius Calvert reaches for a map of Maryland. His grandfather and namesake, the second Lord Baltimore (1606–1675), holds it out to him. George Calvert, the father of the elder Cecilius, began negotiations to win a royal charter for Maryland; his son completed them in 1632 and became the first proprietor of the colony. He published the map shown here in 1635 as part of an effort to attract settlers to the colony. By the time this portrait was painted, Lord Baltimore's son, Charles, was governor of Maryland. The boy Cecilius, the heir apparent, died in 1681 before he could assume his title. *(Enoch Pratt Free Library)*

tributaries. On a high and dry bluff, these first arrivals laid out the village of St. Mary's (named, diplomatically, for the queen). The neighboring Indians, who were more worried about rival tribes in the region than they were about the new arrivals, befriended the settlers, provided them with temporary shelter, sold them land, and supplied them with corn. Unlike the Virginians, the early Marylanders experienced no Indian assaults, no plagues, no starving time.

The Calverts had invested heavily in their American possessions, and they needed to attract many settlers to make the effort profitable. As a result, they had to encourage the immigration of Protestants as well as their fellow English Catholics, who were both relatively few in number (about 2 percent of the population of England) and generally reluctant to emigrate. The Protestant settlers (mostly Anglicans) outnumbered the Catholics from the start, and the Calverts quickly realized that Catholics would always be a minority in the colony. They prudently adopted a pol-

Religious Toleration

icy of religious toleration. To appease the non-Catholic majority, Calvert appointed a Protestant as governor in 1648. A year later, he sent from England the draft of an "Act Concerning Religion," which assured freedom of worship to all Christians.

Nevertheless, politics in Maryland remained plagued for years by tensions between the Catholic minority (which included the proprietor) and the Protestant majority. Zealous Jesuits and crusading Puritans frightened and antagonized their opponents with their efforts to establish the dominance of their own religion. At one point, the Protestant majority barred Catholics from voting and repealed the Toleration Act. There was frequent violence, and in 1655 a civil war temporarily unseated the proprietary government and replaced it with one dominated by Protestants. The English in Maryland were spared serious conflict with Indians, but they made up for that by inflicting decades of conflict and instability on themselves.

Although Maryland's government ultimately came to resemble those of other American colonies, with a two-house assembly and a governor appointed from abroad, the distribution of real power in the colony differed sharply from that in other parts of English America. The proprietor retained absolute authority to distribute land as he wished. Lord Baltimore initially granted large estates to his relatives and to other English aristocrats, so that a landed aristocracy quickly established itself in Maryland. By 1640, a severe labor shortage in the colony had forced a change in the land grant procedure; and Maryland, like Virginia, adopted a "headright" system—a grant of 100 acres to each male settler, another 100 for his wife and each servant, and 50 for each of his children. But the great landlords of the colony's earliest years remained powerful even as the population grew larger and more diverse. Like Virginia, Maryland became a center of tobacco cultivation; and like Virginia, planters worked their land with the aid, first, of indentured servants imported from England and then, beginning late in the seventeenth century, with slaves imported from Africa. Settlement and trade remained dispersed, centered on scattered large plantations, and few towns of any significance emerged.

Turbulent Virginia

By the mid-seventeenth century, the Virginia colony had survived its early disasters, and both its population and the complexity and profitability of its economy were increasing. It was also growing more politically contentious, as emerging factions within the province began

Virginia's Westward Expansion

to compete for the favor of the government. Perhaps the most important dispute involved policy toward the natives. As settlement moved west, further into Indian lands, border conflicts grew increasingly frequent. Much of the tension within English Virginia in the late seventeenth century revolved around how to respond to those conflicts.

Sir William Berkeley arrived in Virginia in 1642 at the age of thirty-six, appointed governor by King Charles I. With but one interruption he remained in control of the government until the 1670s. Berkeley was popular at first as he sent explorers across the Blue Ridge Mountains to open up the western interior of Virginia. He organized the force that put down the 1644 Indian uprising, captured Opechancanough, and (against Berkeley's orders) shot and killed him. The defeated Indians ceded a large area of land to the English, but Berkeley agreed to prohibit white settlement west of a line he negotiated with the tribes.

This attempt to protect Indian territory—like many such attempts later in American history—was a failure from the start, largely because of the rapid growth of the Virginia population. Oliver Cromwell's victory in 1649 in the English Civil War (see pp. 49–50) and the flight of many of his defeated opponents to the colony contributed to what was already a substantial population increase. Between 1640 and 1650, Virginia's population doubled from 8,000 to 16,000. By 1660, it had more than doubled again, to 40,000. As the choice lands along the tidewater became scarce, new arrivals and indentured servants completing their terms or escaping from their masters pressed westward into the piedmont. By 1652, English settlers had established three counties in the territory promised to the Indians. Unsurprisingly, there were frequent clashes between natives and whites.

By the 1660s, Berkeley had become a virtual autocrat in the colony. When the first burgesses were elected in 1619,

Berkeley's Autocratic Rule

all men aged seventeen or older were entitled to vote. By 1670, the vote was restricted to landowners, and elections were rare. The same burgesses, loyal and subservient to the governor, remained in office year after year. Each county continued to have only two representatives, even though some of the new counties of the interior contained many more people than the older ones of the tidewater area. Thus the more recent settlers in the "backcountry" were underrepresented or (if living in areas not yet formally organized as counties) not represented at all.

Bacon's Rebellion

In 1676, backcountry unrest and political rivalries combined to create a major conflict. Nathaniel Bacon, a wealthy young graduate of Cambridge University, arrived in Virginia in 1673. He purchased a substantial farm in the west and won a seat on the governor's council. He established himself, in other words, as a member of the backcountry gentry—one of the influential, propertied landowners who were emerging in the western region of the state and becoming leaders in their areas.

But the new backcountry gentry was squabbling with the leaders of the tidewater region in the east. They dis-

Backcountry Grievances

agreed on many issues, but above all on policies toward the natives. The backcountry settlements were in constant danger of attack from Indians, because many of these settlements were being established on lands reserved for the tribes by treaty. White settlers in western Virginia had long resented the governor's attempts to hold the line of settlement steady so as to avoid antagonizing the natives. That policy was, they believed, an effort by the eastern aristocracy to protect its dominance by holding down the white population in the west. (In reality, the policy was at least as much an effort by Berkeley to protect his own lucrative fur trade with the Indians.)

Bacon, an aristocratic man with great political ambitions, had additional reasons for unhappiness with Berkeley. He resented his exclusion from the inner circle of the governor's council (the so-called Green Spring group, whose members enjoyed special access to patronage). Bacon also fumed about Berkeley's refusal to allow him a piece of the Indian fur trade. He was developing grievances that made him a natural leader of an opposing faction.

Bloody events thrust him into that role. In 1675, some Doeg Indians—angry about the European intrusions into their lands—raided a western plantation and killed a white servant. Bands of local whites struck back angrily and haphazardly, attacking not only the small Doeg tribe but the powerful Susquehannock as well. The Indians responded with more raids on plantations and killed many more white settlers. As the fighting escalated, Bacon and other concerned landholders—unhappy with the governor's cautious response to their demand for help—defied Berkeley and struck out on their own against the Indians. Berkeley dismissed Bacon from the governor's council and proclaimed him and his men rebels. At that point what had started as an unauthorized assault on the Indians became a military challenge to the colonial government, a conflict known as Bacon's Rebellion. It was the largest and most powerful insurrection against established authority in the history of the colonies, one that would not be surpassed until the Revolution.

Twice, Bacon led his army east to Jamestown. The first time he won a temporary pardon from the governor; the second time, after the governor reneged on the agreement, he burned the city and drove the governor into exile. In the midst of widespread social turmoil throughout the colony, Bacon stood on the verge of taking command of Virginia. Instead, he died suddenly of dysentery; and Berkeley, his position bolstered by the arrival of British troops, soon managed to regain control. In 1677, the Indians (aware of their inability to defeat the white forces militarily) reluctantly signed a new treaty that opened additional lands to white settlement.

Bacon's Rebellion was significant for several reasons. It was part of the continuing struggle to define the boundary between Indian and white lands in Virginia; it showed how unwilling the English settlers were to abide by earlier agreements with the natives, and

Significance of Bacon's Rebellion

how unwilling the Indians were to tolerate further white movement into their territory. It revealed the bitterness of the competition between eastern and western landowners. But it also revealed something that Bacon himself had never intended to unleash: the potential for instability in the colony's large population of free, landless men. These men—most of them former indentured servants, propertyless, unemployed, with no real prospects—had formed the bulk of Bacon's constituency during the rebellion. They had become a large, unstable, floating population eager above all for access to land. Bacon had for a time maintained his popularity among them by exploiting their hatred of Indians. Gradually, however, he found himself unintentionally leading a movement that reflected the animosity of these landless men toward the landed gentry of which Bacon himself was a part.

One result was that landed people in both eastern and western Virginia began to recognize a common interest in preventing social unrest from below. That was one of several reasons that they turned increasingly to the African slave trade to fulfill their need for labor. Enslaved blacks might pose dangers too, but the events of 1676 suggested that the perils of importing a large white subordinate class were even greater.

THE GROWTH OF NEW ENGLAND

The first enduring settlement in New England—the second in English America—resulted from the discontent of a congregation of Puritan Separatists in England.

Religious Repression

For years, Separatists had been periodically imprisoned and even executed for defying the government and the Church of England; some of them, as a result, began to contemplate leaving England altogether in search of freedom to worship as they wished.

Plymouth Plantation

It was illegal to leave England without the consent of the king. In 1608, however, a congregation of Separatists from the hamlet of Scrooby began emigrating quietly, a few at a time, to Leyden, Holland, where they could worship without interference. Holland, however, was unsatisfying to them in other ways. As foreigners, they were barred from the Dutch craft guilds and had to work at unskilled and poorly paid jobs. They were also troubled by the effects of the tolerant atmosphere of Dutch society, which seemed to pose as much of a threat to their dream of a close-knit Christian community as had the repression in England. They watched with alarm as their children began to drift away from their families and their church and into Dutch society. As a result, some of the Separatists decided to move again, this time across the Atlantic, where they hoped to create the kind of community they wanted and where they could spread "the gospel of the Kingdom of Christ in those remote parts of the world."

Leaders of the Scrooby group obtained permission from the Virginia Company to settle in Virginia. From the king, they received informal assurances that he would "not molest them, provided they carried themselves peaceably." (This was a historic concession by the crown, for it opened English America to settlement not only by the Scrooby group but by other dissenting Protestants.) Several English merchants agreed to advance the necessary funds in exchange for a share in the profits of the settlement at the end of seven years.

The migrating Puritans "knew they were pilgrims" even before they left Holland, their leader and historian, William Bradford, later wrote. In September 1620 they left the port of Plymouth, on the English coast, in the *Mayflower* with thirty-five "saints" (Puritan Separatists) and sixty-seven "strangers" (people who were not full members of the leaders' church) aboard. By the time they sighted land in November, it was too late in the year to go on. Their original destination was probably the mouth of the Hudson River, in what is now New York. But they found themselves instead on Cape Cod. After exploring the region for a while, they chose a site for their settlement in the area just north of the cape, an area Captain John Smith had named "Plymouth" (after the English port from which the Puritans had sailed) during an exploratory journey some years before. Plymouth lay outside the London Company's territory, and the settlers realized they had no legal basis for settling there. As a result, *The Mayflower Compact* forty-one of the "saints" signed a document, the Mayflower Compact, which established a civil government and proclaimed their allegiance to the king. Then, on December 21, 1620, the Pilgrims stepped ashore at Plymouth Rock.

They settled on cleared land that had once been an Indian village until, three years earlier, a mysterious epidemic—known as "the plague" and probably brought to the region by earlier European explorers—had swept through the region and substantially depopulated it. The Pilgrims' first winter was a difficult one; half the colonists perished from malnutrition, disease, and exposure. But the colony survived.

The Pilgrims' experience with the Indians was, for a time at least, very different from the experiences of the early English settlers farther south. That was in part because the remaining natives in the region—their numbers thinned by disease—were significantly weaker than their southern neighbors and realized they had to get along with the Europeans. It was also probably because the Pilgrims were less actively hostile to the natives than the colonists in Virginia were. In the end, the survival and growth of the colony depended crucially on the assistance they received from natives. Important *Relations with the Indians* Indian friends—Squanto and Samoset, among others—showed them how to gather seafood, cultivate corn, and hunt local animals. Squanto, a Pawtuxet who had earlier been captured by an English explorer and taken to Europe, spoke English and was of particular help to the settlers in forming an alliance with the local Wampanoags, under Chief Massasoit. After the first harvest, in 1621, the settlers marked the alliance by inviting the Indians to join them in an October festival, the first Thanksgiving.

The relationship between settlers and natives was never an equal one. The Pilgrims were few and weak, but the epidemic-ravaged Wampanoags were even weaker, particularly in the face of the firearms the English had brought with them. (They became weaker still sixteen years after the *Mayflower* arrived when a smallpox epidemic—a result of contact with English settlers—swept through the region with devastating consequences.)

The Pilgrims could not hope to create rich farms on the sandy, marshy soil, and their early fishing efforts produced no profits. In 1622, the military officer Miles Standish, one of the leaders of the colony, established a semimilitary regime to impose discipline on the settlers. Eventually the Pilgrims began to grow enough corn and other crops to provide them with a modest trading surplus. They also developed a small fur trade with the Abenaki Indians of Maine. From time to time new colonists arrived from England, and in a decade the population reached 300.

The people of "Plymouth Plantation," as they called their settlement, chose William Bradford again and again to be *William Bradford* their governor. As early as 1621, he persuaded the Council for New England (the successor to the old Plymouth Company, which had charter rights to the territory) to give them legal permission to live there. He ended the communal labor plan Standish had helped create, distributed land among the families, and thus, as he explained it, made "all hands very industrious." He and a group of fellow "undertakers" took over the colony's debt to its original financiers in England and, with earnings from the fur trade, finally paid it off—even though the financiers had repeatedly cheated them and had failed to send them promised supplies.

The Pilgrims were always a poor community. As late as the 1640s, they had only one plow among them. But they clung to the belief that God had put them in the New World to live as a truly Christian community; and they were, on the whole, content to live their lives in what they considered godly ways.

At times, they spoke of serving as a model for other Christians. Governor Bradford wrote in retrospect: "As

The story of the Pilgrims and the first Thanksgiving remains one of the oldest and best known in American history. But there is another pilgrim story that is much less familiar. The colonists at Plymouth, like those up and down the Atlantic seaboard (and like the Spanish and Portugese settlers who preceded them to their south), did not travel alone. They brought with them to America a host of other organisms, plants, and animals that were familiar to Europeans but completely unknown to the Indians. The colonization of America was as much a biological invasion as a cultural one. It helped transform the American landscape.

In some respects, the invasion was devastating. The English, like the Spanish, brought with them deadly epidemics such as smallpox and debilitating illnesses such as tuberculosis, previously unknown in North America. Indian immune systems were not equipped with antibodies that could defend against those diseases. Thirteen years after the Pilgrims arrived, a devastating smallpox epidemic wiped out much of the Indian population around Plymouth. The native communities there, as elsewhere in America, experienced population declines of 50 to 90 percent as a result of these epidemics, which would continue for centuries.

The disappearance of so many Indians was itself a profound change in the American landscape. But Indians who survived the epidemics often formed relationships with the colonists in ways that made other profound changes in the environment. The fur trade caused some of the most important of those changes. Indians were eager for goods they could trade with the colonists; and the colonists' demand for furs encouraged some tribes (and some colonists as well) to hunt native animals much more intensively than ever before. Animal populations declined as hunting pressure increased, so much so that areas like New England had lost most of their large mammals—as well as smaller ones such as deer, moose, wild turkeys, and wolves—within two centuries of the first settlements. Their departure made room for the domesticated grazing animals that colonists brought with them: cattle, sheep, hogs, and horses. Most of these animals had been entirely absent from Indian America.

Increasing their livestock became one of the colonists' overriding goals. As the herds expanded, so did the colonists' need for new land. They cut down forests to create new pastures. Cattle and horses enabled the colonists to cultivate much more land than had the tribes, because the animals made it possible to plant crops using plows. Indians had depended on hoes for their farming, which required much more human labor and thus limited the amount of land that one person or family could tend.

Although some of the crops the colonists planted were in fact Indian—corn being the most important—many were brought across the Atlantic as seeds. Wheat, rye, barley, and oats soon appeared in colonists' fields and quickly spread wherever the colonists went. In their gardens, colonial women tended vegetables and herbs that were a mixture of Indian and European crops. Cabbages, peas, and potatoes lent variety to the colonial diet. Herbs added flavorings to otherwise bland meals, furnished medicines for healing, and supplied the color in homespun fabrics. In the

one small candle may light a thousand, so the light here kindled hath shone to many, yea in some sort to our whole nation." But the Pilgrims were less committed to grand designs, less concerned about how they were viewed by others, than the Puritans who settled the larger and more ambitious English colonies to their north.

The Massachusetts Bay Experiment

Turbulent events in England in the 1620s (combined with the example of the Plymouth colony) created strong interest in colonization among other groups of Puritans. James I had been creating serious tensions for years between himself and Parliament through his effort to claim the divine right of kings and by his harsh, repressive policies toward the Puritans. The situation worsened after his death in 1625, when he was succeeded by his son, Charles I. By trying to restore Roman Catholicism to England and destroy religious nonconformity, he started the nation down the road that in the 1640s would lead to civil war. The Puritans were particular targets of Charles's policies. Some were imprisoned for their beliefs, and

many began to consider the climate of England intolerable. The king's disbanding of Parliament in 1629 (it was not to be recalled until 1640) ensured that there would be no political solution to the Puritans' problems.

In the midst of this political and social turmoil, a group of Puritan merchants began organizing a new enterprise designed to take advantage of opportunities in America. At first their interest was largely an *Massachusetts Bay Company* economic one. They obtained a grant of land in New England for most of the area now comprising Massachusetts and New Hampshire; they acquired a charter from the king (who was evidently unaware that they were Puritans) allowing them to create the Massachusetts Bay Company and to establish a colony in the New World; and they bought equipment and supplies from a defunct fishing and trading company that had attempted (and failed) to establish a profitable enterprise in North America. In 1629, they were ready to dispatch a substantial group of settlers to New England.

Among the members of the Massachusetts Bay Company, however, were a number of Puritans who saw the enter-

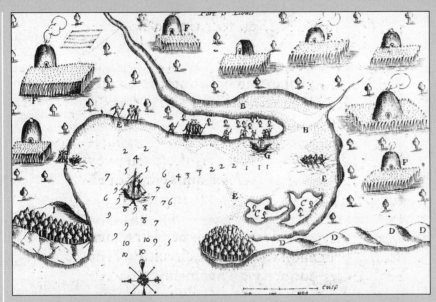

CHAMPLAIN'S MAP OF PLYMOUTH PLANTATION, 1605 When Samuel de Champlain visited Plymouth, Massachusetts, in 1605, he drew this map of the bay showing numerous Indian settlements in the vicinity. The many cornfields suggest what a prosperous community this was. Fifteen years later, when the Pilgrims arrived, most of these Indians would be dead from European diseases. *(Houghton Library, Harvard University)*

To enable their imported animals and plants to thrive, colonists sought to re-create the ecological conditions under which they had lived on the other side of the Atlantic. They divided their lands into the familiar functional units of a peasant agricultural system: grain fields, pastures, hay meadows, woodlots, orchards, gardens, barnyards. They built fences to separate the places reserved for animals from the places where crops grew. And so the fence—a construction almost entirely absent from Indian America—became for the colonists a symbol of "improvement," a sign that the landscapes of the New World were becoming more like those of the Old.

When the Pilgrims celebrated their first November harvest, they were partly thanking their Indian neighbors for the corn and wild meat they had shared. But they were also giving thanks for their own crops and animals, on which not just their survival but their sense of safety and familiarity depended. Those other, nonhuman, pilgrims were in fact one of the foundations on which the whole of colonial society would be built.

orchards around their homesteads, colonists planted apples, pears, plums, cherries, and other fruit trees. From apples came one of the colonists' favorite beverages, cider, and from orchards generally came fresh fruit, preserves, and other sweeteners that found their way to colonial tables.

prise as something more than a business venture. They began to consider emigrating themselves and creating a haven for Puritans in New England. Members of this faction met secretly in Cambridge in the summer of 1629 and agreed to buy out the other investors and move en masse to America.

As governor, the new owners of the company chose *John Winthrop* John Winthrop, an affluent, university-educated gentleman with a deep piety and a forceful character. Winthrop had been instrumental in organizing the migration, and he commanded the expedition that sailed for New England in 1630: seventeen ships and 1,000 people (who were, unlike the earlier migrants to Virginia, mostly family groups). It was the largest single migration of its kind in the seventeenth century. Winthrop carried with him the charter of the Massachusetts Bay Company, which meant that the colonists would be responsible to no company officials in England, only to themselves.

Unlike the two previous English settlements in America—Jamestown and Plymouth—the Massachusetts migration quickly produced several different new settle-ments. The port of Boston, at the mouth of the Charles River, became the company's headquarters and the colony's capital. But in the course of the next decade colonists moved into a number of other new towns in eastern Massachusetts: Charlestown, Newtown (later renamed Cambridge), Roxbury, Dorchester, Watertown, Ipswich, Concord, Sudbury, and others.

The Massachusetts Bay Company soon transformed itself into a colonial government. According to the original company charter, the eight stockholders (or "freemen") were to meet as a general court to choose officers and adopt rules for the corporation. But this commercial definition of government, which concentrated authority in what was in effect a corporate board of directors, quickly gave way to a more genuinely political system. The definition of "freemen" changed to include all male citizens, not just the stockholders. John Winthrop dominated colonial politics just as he had dominated the original corporation, but after 1634 he and most other officers of the colony had to face election each year.

Unlike the Separatist founders of Plymouth, the founders of Massachusetts had no intention of breaking

PORTRAIT OF A BOSTON WOMAN Anne Pollard, a member of the original Winthrop expedition to Boston, was 100 years old when this portrait was painted in 1721. In 1643, thirteen years after her arrival in Massachusetts, she married a Boston innkeeper with whom she had 13 children. After her husband's death in 1679, she continued to manage the tavern on her own. When she died in 1725, at the age of 104, she left 130 direct descendants. The artist who painted this early portrait is unknown, but is assumed to be an American working in the relatively primitive style common in New England before the arrival in 1729 of the first academically trained portraitists from England. *(Courtesy of the Massachusetts Historical Society)*

COLONIAL CURRENCY This seal was created in 1690 by the Massachusetts Bay Company to validate the paper "bills of credit" with which colonists conducted many financial transactions. Paper money met considerable resistance at first. Many people doubted its value and would not accept it, preferring instead the Spanish silver coins that were in wide circulation at the time. Gradually, however, a shortage of silver required increasing reliance on this and other paper devices. *(Courtesy of the Massachusetts Historical Society)*

away from the Church of England. Yet if they continued to feel any real attachment to the Anglican establishment, they gave little sign of it in their behavior. In every town, *The Congregational Church* | the community church had (in the words of the prominent minister John Cotton) "complete liberty to stand alone," unlike churches in the highly centralized Anglican structure in England. Each congregation chose its own minister and regulated its own affairs. In both Plymouth and Massachusetts, this form of parish organization eventually became known as the Congregational Church.

The Massachusetts Puritans were not grim or joyless, as many observers would later portray them. They were, however, serious and pious people. They strove to lead useful, conscientious lives of thrift and hard work, and they honored material success as evidence of God's favor.

"We here enjoy God and Jesus Christ," Winthrop wrote to his wife soon after his arrival; "is this not enough?" He and the other Massachusetts founders believed they were founding a holy commonwealth—a "city upon a hill"—that could serve as a model for the rest of the world.

If Massachusetts was to become a beacon to others, it had first to maintain its own "holiness." The clergy and the | *A Theocratic Society* government worked closely together to ensure that it did. Ministers had no formal political power, but they exerted great influence on church members, who were the only people who could vote or hold office. The government in turn protected the ministers, taxed the people (members and nonmembers alike) to support the church, and enforced the law requiring attendance at services. Dissidents had no more freedom of worship in America than the Puritans themselves had had in England. Colonial Massachusetts was, in effect, a "theocracy," a society in which the line between the church and the state was hard to see.

Like other new settlements, the Massachusetts Bay colony had early difficulties. During their first winter, an unusually severe one, nearly a third of the colonists died;

others left in the spring. But more rapidly than Jamestown or Plymouth, the colony grew and prospered. The Pilgrims and neighboring Indians helped with food and advice. Incoming settlers, many of them affluent, brought needed tools and other goods, which they exchanged for the cattle, corn, and other produce of the established colonists and the natives. The large number of family groups in the colony (a sharp contrast to the early years at Jamestown) helped ensure a feeling of commitment to the community and a sense of order among the settlers. It also allowed the population to reproduce itself more rapidly. The strong religious and political hierarchy ensured a measure of social stability.

The Expansion of New England

As the population grew, more and more people arrived in Massachusetts who did not accept all the religious tenets

Growing Religious Dissent | of the colony's leaders or who were not Puritan "saints" and hence could not vote. The Massachusetts government considered religious dissent as much a threat to the community as heresy or treason. Newcomers had a choice of conforming to the religious practices of the colony or leaving. Many left, helping to begin a process that would spread settlement throughout present-day New England and beyond.

The Connecticut Valley, about 100 miles west of the edge of European settlement around Boston, began attracting English families as early as the 1630s, despite claims to those lands by the Dutch. The Connecticut settlers were attracted by the valley's fertile lands (a contrast to the stony, unproductive soil around Boston) and by its isolation from the intensely religious character of Massachusetts Bay. The valley appealed in particular to Thomas Hooker, a minister of Newtown (Cambridge), who defied the Massachusetts government in 1635 and led his congregation through the wilds to establish the town of Hartford. Four years later, the people of Hartford and of two other newly founded upriver towns, Windsor and Wethersfield, established a colonial government of their own and adopted a constitution known as the Fundamental Orders of Connecticut. This created a government similar to that of Massachusetts Bay but gave a larger proportion of the men the right to vote and hold office. (Women were barred from voting virtually everywhere.)

Another Connecticut colony, the project of a Puritan minister and a wealthy merchant from England, grew up around New Haven on the Connecticut coast. It reflected impatience not with the orthodoxy of Massachusetts Bay, but with what its founders considered the increasing religious laxity in Boston. The Fundamental Articles of New Haven (1639) established a religious government even stricter than that in Boston. New Haven remained independent until 1662, when a royal

THE GROWTH OF NEW ENGLAND, 1620–1750 The European settlement of New England, as this map reveals, traces its origins primarily to two small settlements on the Atlantic coast. The first was the Pilgrim settlement at Plymouth, which began in 1620 and spread out through Cape Cod, southern Massachusetts, and the islands of Martha's Vineyard and Nantucket. The second, much larger settlement began in Boston in 1630 and spread rapidly through western Massachusetts, north into New Hampshire and Maine, and south into Connecticut. ◆ *Why would the settlers of Massachusetts Bay have expanded so much more rapidly and expansively than those of Plymouth?*

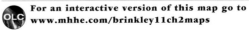

For an interactive version of this map go to
www.mhhe.com/brinkley11ch2maps

charter combined it with Hartford to create the colony of Connecticut.

Rhode Island had its origins in the religious and political dissent of Roger Williams, an engaging but controversial young minister who lived for a time in Salem, Massachusetts. Even John Winthrop, who considered

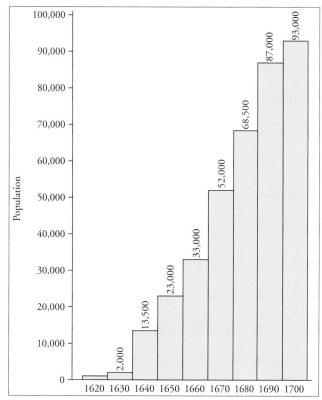

THE NON-INDIAN POPULATION OF NEW ENGLAND, 1620–1700
As in the Chesapeake colonies, the European population of New England grew very rapidly after settlement began in 1620. The most rapid rate of growth, unsurprisingly, came in the first thirty years, when even a modest wave of immigraton could double or triple the small existing population. But the largest numbers of new immigrants arrived between 1650 and 1680. ◆ *What events in England in those years might have led to increased emigration to America in that period?*

Williams a heretic, called him a "sweet and amiable" man, and William Bradford described him as "a man godly and zealous, having many precious parts." But he was, Bradford added, "very unsettled in judgment." Williams, a confirmed Separatist, argued that the Massachusetts church should abandon all allegiance to the Church of England. More disturbing to the clergy, he called for a complete separation of church and state—to protect the church from the corruption of the secular world. The colonial government, alarmed at this challenge to its spiritual authority, banished him. During the bitter winter of 1635–1636, he took refuge with Narragansett tribesmen; the following spring he bought a tract of land from them and, with a few followers, created the town of Providence on it. Other communities of dissidents followed him to what became Rhode Island, and in 1644 Williams obtained a charter from Parliament permitting him to establish a government. Rhode Island's government gave no support to the church and allowed "liberty in religious concernments." For a time, it was the only colony in which members of all faiths (including Jews) could worship without interference.

Roger Williams

An even greater challenge to the established order in Massachusetts Bay emerged in the person of Anne Hutchinson, an intelligent and charismatic woman from a substantial Boston family. Hutchinson had come to Massachusetts with her husband in 1634 as part of a community led by the minister John Cotton. She shared Cotton's belief that only the "elect" were entitled to any religious or political authority. Living a righteous life was not enough to earn a place among the elect; to be a saint, it was necessary to have undergone a conversion experience—something relatively few residents of Massachusetts had done.

Hutchinson antagonized the leaders of the colony by arguing much more vehemently than Cotton that the members of the Massachusetts clergy who were not among the elect had no right to spiritual office. She claimed that her own uninspiring minister was among the nonelect and that he had no right to exercise any authority over his congregation. Over time she made the same claim about many other clergy as well and eventually charged that all the ministers in Massachusetts—with the exception of John Cotton and her own brother-in-law—were not among the elect. Such teachings (which her critics called "Antinomianism," from the Greek meaning "hostile to the law") were a serious threat to the spiritual authority of the established clergy. Hutchinson also created alarm by affronting prevailing assumptions about the proper role of women in Puritan society. She was not a retiring, deferential wife and mother, but a powerful religious figure in her own right.

Anne Hutchinson

Hutchinson developed a large following among women, to whom she offered an active role in religious affairs. She also attracted support from others (merchants, young men, and dissidents of many sorts) who resented the oppressive character of the colonial government. As her influence grew, and as she began to deliver open attacks on some members of the clergy, the Massachusetts leadership mobilized to stop her. Hutchinson's followers were numerous and influential enough to prevent Winthrop's reelection as governor in 1636, but the next year he returned to office and put her on trial for heresy. Hutchinson embarrassed her accusers by displaying a remarkable knowledge of theology; but because she continued to defy clerical authority (and because she claimed she had herself communicated directly with the Holy Spirit—a violation of the Puritan belief that the age of such revelations had passed), she was convicted of sedition and banished as "a woman not fit for our society." Her unorthodox views had challenged both religious belief and social order in Puritan Massachusetts. With her family and some of her followers, she moved to Rhode Island. Later still, she moved south into New Netherland (later New York), where in 1643 she died during an Indian uprising.

Alarmed by Hutchinson's heresy, male clergy began to restrict further the already limited public activities of women within congregations and to control other activi-

ANNE HUTCHINSON PREACHING IN HER HOUSE IN BOSTON
Anne Hutchinson was alarming to many of Boston's religious leaders not only because she openly challenged the authority of the clergy, but also because she implicitly challenged norms of female behavior in Puritan society. *(Bettmann/Corbis)*

ties she had inspired. As a result, many of Hutchinson's followers began to migrate out of Massachusetts Bay, especially to New Hampshire and Maine.

Colonies had been established there in 1629 when two English proprietors, Captain John Mason and Sir Ferdinando Gorges, had received a grant from the Council *New Hampshire and Maine* for New England and divided it along the Piscataqua River to create two separate provinces. But despite their lavish promotional efforts, few settlers had moved into these northern regions until the religious disruptions in Massachusetts Bay. In 1639, John Wheelwright, a disciple of Anne Hutchinson, led some of his fellow dissenters to Exeter, New Hampshire. Other groups—of both dissenting and orthodox Puritans—soon followed. New Hampshire became a separate colony in 1679. Maine remained a part of Massachusetts until 1820.

Settlers and Natives

Indians were less powerful rivals to the early New England immigrants than natives were to the English settlers further south. By the mid-1630s, the native population, small to begin with, had been almost extinguished by the epidemics. The surviving Indians sold much of their land to the English (a great boost to settlement, since much of it had already been cleared). Some natives—known as "praying Indians"—even converted to Christianity and joined Puritan communities.

Indians provided crucial assistance to the early settlers as they tried to adapt to the new land. Whites learned from the natives about vital local food crops: corn, beans, pumpkins, and potatoes. They *Importance of Indian Assistance* also learned such crucial agricultural techniques as annual burning for fertilization and planting beans to replenish exhausted soil. Natives also served as important trading partners to European immigrants, particularly in the creation of the thriving North American fur trade. They were an important market for such manufactured goods as iron pots, blankets, metal-tipped arrows, eventually guns and rifles, and (often tragically) alcohol. Indeed, commerce with the Indians was responsible for the creation of some of the first great fortunes in British North America and for the emergence of wealthy families who would exercise influence in the colonies (and later the nation) for many generations. The relationship between whites and Indians, in New England as throughout the areas of European settlement in the Americas, was one of constant interaction, in which each group influenced the other in crucial ways.

But as in other areas of white settlement, there were also conflicts; and the early peaceful relations between whites and Indians did not last. Tensions soon developed as a result of the white colonists' enormous appetite for land, an appetite that grew as the white population of the colonies increased. The expanding white demand for land was also a result of a change in the colonists' agrarian economy. As the wild animals of the region began to disappear from overhunting, colonists began to concentrate more and more on raising domesticated animals: cattle, sheep, hogs, horses, and others. Increasing their livestock became one of the colonists' overriding goals. As the herds expanded, so did the colonists' need for new land. As a result, they moved steadily into territories such as the Connecticut Valley, where the natives were more numerous and more powerful than they had been along the Massachusetts coast. White settlers in those areas came into conflict with the local tribes.

The character of those conflicts—and the brutality with which whites assaulted their Indian foes—emerged in part out of changing Puritan attitudes toward the natives. At *Shifting Attitudes* first, many white New Englanders had looked at the Indians with a slightly condescending admiration. Before long, however, they came to view them primarily as "heathens" and "savages," and hence as a constant threat to the existence of a godly community in the New World. Some Puritans believed the solution to the Indian "problem"

A PEQUOT VILLAGE DESTROYED An English artist drew this view of a fortified Pequot village in Connecticut surrounded by English soldiers and their allies from other tribes during the Pequot War in 1637. The invaders massacred more than 600 residents of the settlement. *(Rare Book Division, New York Public Library)*

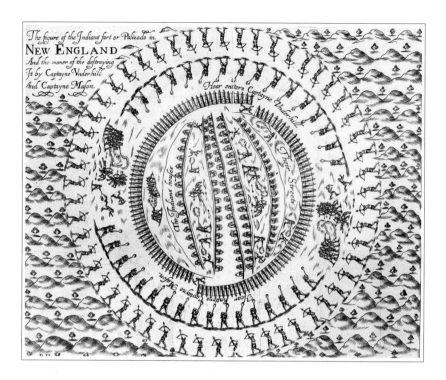

was to "civilize" the natives by converting them to Christianity and European ways, and some English missionaries had modest success in producing converts. One such missionary, John Eliot, even translated the Bible into an Algonquian language. Other Puritans, however, envisioned a harsher "solution": displacing or, if that failed, exterminating the natives.

To the natives, the threat from the English was very direct. European settlers were penetrating deeper and deeper into the interior, seizing land, clearing forests, driving away much of the wild game on which the tribes depended for food. English farmers often let their livestock run wild, and the animals often destroyed natives' crops. The Indian population in the region had been declining for years as a result of epidemic diseases. Now land and food shortages worsened their plight. There had been more than 100,000 Indians in New England at the beginning of the seventeenth century; by 1675, only 10,000 remained. This decline created despair among New England natives. It drove some Indians to alcoholism and others to conversion to Christianity. But it also produced conflict.

The Pequot War, King Philip's War, and the Technology of Battle

The first major conflict came in 1637, when hostilities broke out between English settlers in the Connecticut Valley

The Pequot War

and the Pequot Indians of the region. It was a result of competition between the white settlers and the Pequots over trade with the Dutch in New Netherland and friction over land. In what became known as the Pequot War, En-

glish settlers allied with the Mohegan and Narragansett Indians (who were also rivals of the Pequots). The greatest savagery in the conflict was the work of the English. In the bloodiest act of the war, white raiders under Captain John Mason marched against a palisaded Pequot stronghold and set it afire. Hundreds of Indians died, burned to death in the flaming stockade or killed as they attempted to escape. Those who survived were hunted down, captured, and sold as slaves. The Pequot tribe was almost wiped out.

The most prolonged and deadly encounter between whites and Indians in the seventeenth century began in 1675, a conflict that the English would remember for generations as King Philip's War. As in the earlier Pequot War in Connecticut, an Indian tribe—in this case the Wampanoags, under the leadership of a chieftain known to the white settlers as King Philip and among his own people as Metacomet—rose up to resist English incursions into their lands. The Wampanoags had not always been hostile to the settlers; indeed, Metacomet's grandfather had once forged an alliance with the English. But by the 1670s, they had become convinced that only armed resistance could protect them from the movement of the English into their lands and, more immediately, from the efforts by the colonial governments to impose English law on the natives. (A court in Plymouth had recently tried and hanged several Wampanoags for murdering a member of their own tribe.)

For three years, the natives—well organized and armed with guns—terrorized a string of Massachusetts towns, destroy-

King Philip's War

ing twenty of them and causing the deaths of as many as a thousand people (including at least one-sixteenth of the white males in the colony). The war greatly weakened both the society and economy of Massachusetts. But the white settlers fought back and gradually prevailed, beginning in 1676 when Massachusetts leaders joined forces with the Mohawks, long-time rivals of the Wampanoags, and recruited guides, spies, and soldiers from among the so-called praying Indians of the region. While white militiamen attacked Indian villages and destroyed native food supplies, a group of Mohawks ambushed Metacomet and shot and killed him, then bore his severed head to Boston to present to the colonial leaders. After that the fragile alliance that Metacomet had managed to forge among local tribes collapsed. Europeans were soon able to crush the uprising. Some Wampanoag leaders were executed; others were sold into slavery in the West Indies. The Wampanoags and their allies, their populations depleted and their natural resources reduced, were now powerless to resist the English.

Yet these victories by the white colonists did not end the danger to their settlements. This was in part because other Indians in other tribes survived, and were still capable of attacking English settlements. It was also because the New England settlers faced competition not only from the natives but also from the Dutch and the French, who claimed the territory on which some of the outlying settlements were established. The French, in particular, would pose a constant threat to the English through their alliance with the Algonquins. In later years, they would join forces with Indians in their attacks on the New England frontier.

The character of the Pequot War, King Philip's War, and many other conflicts between natives and settlers in the years that followed was crucially affected by earlier exchanges of technology between the English and the

Flintlock Musket

tribes. In particular, the Indians made effective use of a relatively new weapon introduced to New England by Myles Standish and others: the flintlock rifle. It replaced the earlier staple of colonial musketry, the matchlock rifle, which proved too heavy, cumbersome, and inaccurate to be useful in the kind of combat characteristic of Anglo-Indian struggles. The matchlock had to be steadied on a fixed object and ignited with a match before firing; the flintlock could be held up without support and fired without a match. (Indians using bows and arrows often outmatched settlers using the clumsy matchlocks.)

Many English settlers were slow to give up their cumbersome matchlocks for the lighter flintlocks. But the Indians recognized the advantages of the newer rifles right away and began purchasing them in large quantities as part of their regular trade with the colonists. Despite rules forbidding colonists to instruct natives on how to use and repair the weapons, the natives learned to handle the rifles, and even to repair them, very effectively on their own. They even built a substantial forge for shaping and repairing rifle parts. In King Philip's War, the very high casualties on both

sides were a result of the use of these more advanced rifles.

Indians also used more traditional military technologies in their conflicts with the English—especially the construction of forts. The Narragansetts, allies of the Wampanoags in King Philip's War, built an enormous fort in the Great Swamp of Rhode Island in 1675, which became the site of one of the bloodiest battles of the war before English attackers burned it down. After that, a band of Narragansetts set out to build a large stone fort, with the help of a member of the tribe who had learned masonry while working with the English. When English soldiers discovered the stone fort in 1676, after the end of King Philip's War, they killed most of its occupants and destroyed it. In the end, the technological skills of the Indians (both those they borrowed from the English and those they drew from their own traditions) were no match for the overwhelming advantages of the English settlers in both numbers and firepower.

THE RESTORATION COLONIES

By the end of the 1630s, English settlers had established six significant colonies in the New World: Virginia, Massachusetts, Maryland, Connecticut, Rhode Island, and New Hampshire. (Maine remained officially part of Massachusetts until after the American Revolution.) But for nearly thirty years after Lord Baltimore received the charter for Maryland in 1632, the English government launched no additional colonial ventures. It was preoccupied with troubles of its own at home.

The English Civil War

England's problems had begun during the rule of James I, who attracted widespread opposition before he died in 1625 *Origins* but never openly challenged Parliament. His son, Charles I, was not so prudent. After he dissolved Parliament in 1629 and began ruling as an absolute monarch, he steadily alienated a growing number of his subjects—and the members of the powerful Puritan community above all. Finally, desperately in need of money, Charles called Parliament back into session and asked it to levy new taxes. But he antagonized the members by dismissing them twice in two years. In 1642, some of them organized a military challenge to the king, thus launching the English Civil War.

The conflict between the Cavaliers (the supporters of the king) and the Roundheads (the forces of Parliament, who were mostly Puritans) lasted seven years. Finally, in 1649, the Roundheads defeated the king's forces, captured Charles himself, and—in an action that horrified not only much of continental Europe at the time but also future generations of English men and women—beheaded the monarch. To replace him, they elevated the stern Roundhead leader Oliver Cromwell to the position of "protector," from which he ruled for the next nine years. When Cromwell died in 1658, his son and heir proved unable to maintain his authority. Two years later, King Charles II, son of the beheaded monarch, returned from exile and claimed the throne.

Among the many results of the Stuart Restoration was

New Proprietary Colonies

the resumption of colonization in America. Charles II quickly began to reward faithful courtiers with grants of land in the New World; and in the twenty-five years of his reign, he issued charters for four additional colonies: Carolina, New York, New Jersey, and Pennsylvania. The new colonies were all proprietary ventures (modeled on Maryland rather than on Virginia and Massachusetts), thus exposing an important change in the nature of American settlement. No longer were private companies interested in launching colonies, realizing at last that there were no quick profits to be had in the New World. The goal of the founders of the new colonies was not so much quick commercial success as permanent settlements that would provide proprietors with land and power.

The Carolinas

Carolina (a name derived from the Latinate form of "Charles") was, like Maryland, carved in part from the original Virginia grant. Charles II awarded the territory to a group of eight court favorites, all prominent politicians already active in colonial affairs. In successive charters issued in 1663 and 1665, the eight proprietors received joint title to a vast territory stretching south to the Florida peninsula and west to the Pacific Ocean. Like Lord Baltimore, they received almost kingly powers over their grant.

Also like Lord Baltimore, they expected to profit as landlords and land speculators. They reserved large estates for themselves, and they proposed to sell or give away the rest in smaller tracts (using a headright system similar to those in Virginia and Maryland) and to collect

Incentives for Settlement

annual payments ("quitrents") from the settlers. Although committed Anglicans themselves, they welcomed any settlers they could get. The charter of the colony guaranteed religious freedom to everyone who would worship as a Christian. The proprietors also promised a measure of political freedom; laws were to be made by a representative assembly. With these incentives, they hoped to attract settlers from the existing American colonies and thus to avoid the expense of financing expeditions from England.

Their initial efforts failed dismally, and some of the original proprietors gave up. But one man—Anthony Ashley Cooper, soon to become the earl of Shaftesbury—persisted. Cooper convinced his partners to finance migrations to Carolina from England. In the spring of 1670, the first of these expeditions—a party of 300—set out from England. Only 100 people survived the difficult voyage; those who did established a settlement in the Port Royal area of the Carolina coast. Ten years later they founded a city at the junction of the Ashley and Cooper Rivers, which in 1690 became the colonial capital. They called it Charles Town. (It was later renamed Charleston.)

The earl of Shaftesbury, troubled by the instability in England, wanted a planned and well-ordered community. With the aid of the English philosopher John

Fundamental Constitution for Carolina

Locke, he drew up the Fundamental Constitution for Carolina in 1669, which created an elaborate system of land distribution and an elaborately designed social order. In fact, however, Carolina developed along lines quite different from the almost utopian vision of Shaftesbury and Locke. For one thing, the colony was never really united in anything more than name. The northern and southern regions remained widely separated and were socially and economically distinct from one another. The northern settlers were mainly backwoods farmers, largely isolated from the outside world, scratching out a meager existence through subsistence agriculture. They developed no important aristocracy and for many years imported virtually no African slaves. In the south, fertile lands and the good harbor at Charles Town promoted a more prosperous economy and a more aristocratic society. Settlements grew up rapidly along the Ashley and Cooper Rivers, and colonists established a flourishing trade in corn, lumber, cattle, pork, and (beginning in the 1690s) rice—which was to become the colony's principal commercial crop. Traders from the interior used Charles Town to market furs and hides they had acquired from Indian trading partners; some also marketed Indian slaves, generally natives captured by rival tribes and sold to the white traders.

Southern Carolina very early developed close ties to the large (and now overpopulated) English colony on the island of Barbados. For many years, Barbados was Carolina's most important trading partner. During the first ten years of settlement, most of the new settlers in Carolina were Barbadians, some of whom arrived with large groups of African workers and established themselves quickly as substantial landlords. African slavery had taken root on Barbados earlier than in any of the mainland colonies (see pp. 54–57); and the white Caribbean migrants—tough, uncompromising profit seekers—established a similar slave-based plantation society in Carolina. (The proprietors, four of whom had a financial interest in the African slave trade, encouraged the importation of Africans.)

For several decades, Carolina remained one of the most unsta-

North and South Carolina

ble of all the English colonies in America. There were tensions between the small farmers of the Albemarle region in the north and the wealthy planters in the south. There were conflicts between the rich Barbadians in southern Carolina and the smaller landowners around them. After Lord Shaftesbury's death, the proprietors proved unable to establish order, and in 1719 the colonists seized control

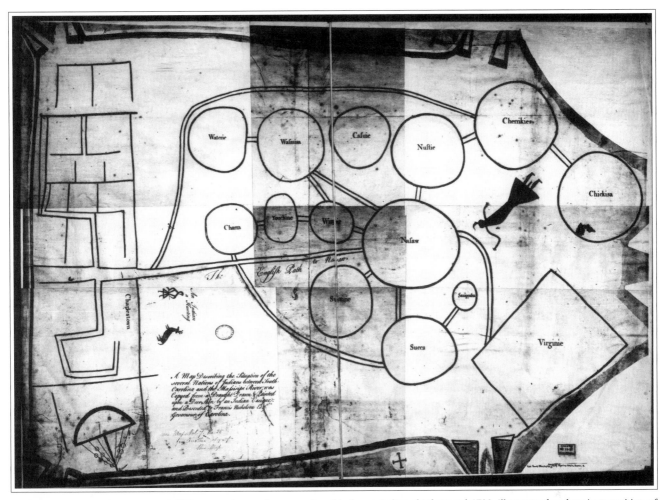

CHARLESTON, SOUTH CAROLINA This unusual map, drawn on deerskin by an Indian chief around 1730, illustrates the close juxtaposition of the ordered English settlement in Charleston, South Carolina, seen on the left, and the more fluid Indian settlements near the town, on the right. *(Hulton/Archive/Getty Images)*

of the colony from them. Ten years later, the king divided the region into two royal colonies, North and South Carolina.

New Netherland, New York, and New Jersey

In 1664, one year after he issued the Carolina charter, Charles II granted to his brother James, the duke of York, all the territory lying between the Connecticut and Delaware Rivers. But much of the territory included in the grant was already claimed by the Dutch, who had established substantial settlements at New Amsterdam and other strategic points beginning in 1624.

The emerging conflict between the English and the Dutch in America was part of a larger commercial rivalry between the two nations in the seventeenth century throughout the world. But the English particularly resented the Dutch presence in America, because it served as a wedge between the northern and southern English colonies and because it provided bases for Dutch smugglers

evading English customs laws. And so in 1664, an English fleet under the command of Richard Nicolls sailed into the *Capture of New Amsterdam* lightly defended port of New Amsterdam and extracted a surrender from the arbitrary and unpopular Dutch governor, Peter Stuyvesant, who had failed to mobilize resistance to the invasion. Under the Articles of Capitulation, the Dutch colony surrendered to the British and received in return assurances that the Dutch settlers would not be displaced. Several years later, in 1673, the Dutch briefly reconquered New Amsterdam. But they lost it for good in 1674.

James, the duke of York, his title to New Netherland now clear, renamed the colony New York and prepared to govern a colony of extraordinary diversity. New York contained not only Dutch and English, but Scandinavians, Germans, French, Africans (imported as slaves by the Dutch West India Company), and members of several different Indian tribes. There were, of course, many different religious faiths among these groups. James made no effort to impose his own Roman Catholicism on the colony. Like

NEW AMSTERDAM The small Dutch settlement on Manhattan Island, known before 1664 as New Amsterdam, fell to the English in 1664. This painting shows buildings clustered at the southern tip of the island, which remained the center of what became New York City until the nineteenth century. *(Bettmann/Corbis)*

other proprietors before him, he remained in England and delegated powers to a governor and a council. But he provided for no representative assembly, perhaps because a parliament had executed his own father, Charles I. The laws did, however, establish local governments and guarantee religious toleration. Despite these concessions, there were immediate tensions over the distribution of power in the colony. The great Dutch "patroons" (large landowners) survived with their economic and political power largely intact. James granted large estates as well to some of his own political supporters in an effort to create a class of influential landowners loyal to him. Power in the colony thus remained widely and unequally dispersed—among wealthy English landlords, Dutch patroons, fur traders (who forged important alliances with the Iroquois), and the duke's political appointees. Like Carolina, New York would for many years be a highly factious society.

It was also a growing and generally prosperous colony. By 1685, when the duke of York ascended the English throne as James II, New York contained approximately 30,000 people, about four times as many as when James had received his grant twenty years before. Most of them still lived within the Hudson Valley, close to the river itself, with the largest settlement at its mouth, in the town of New York (formerly New Amsterdam).

Originally, James's claims in America extended south of the Hudson to the Delaware Valley and beyond. But shortly after receiving his charter, he gave a large portion of that land to a pair of political allies, Sir John Berkeley and Sir George Carteret, both of whom were also Carolina proprietors. Carteret named the territory New Jersey, after the island in the English channel on which he had been born. In 1702, after nearly a decade of political squabbling and economic profitlessness, the proprietors ceded control of the territory back to the crown and New Jersey became a royal colony.

Establishment of New Jersey

Like New York (from which much of the population had come), New Jersey was a place of enormous ethnic and religious diversity. But unlike New York, New Jersey developed no important class of large landowners; most of its residents remained small farmers. Nor did New Jersey (which, unlike New York, had no natural harbor) produce any single important city.

The Quaker Colonies

Pennsylvania, like Massachusetts, was born out of the efforts of dissenting English Protestants to find a home for their own religion and their own distinctive social order. The

The Society of Friends

Society of Friends originated in mid-seventeenth-century England and grew into an important force as a result of the preachings of George Fox, a Nottingham shoemaker, and Margaret Fell. Their followers came to be known as Quakers because Fox urged them to "tremble at the name of the Lord." Unlike the Puritans, Quakers rejected the concepts of predestination and original sin. All people had divinity within themselves (an "Inner Light," which could guide them along the path of righteousness), and all who cultivated that divinity could attain salvation. Also unlike the Puritans, Quakers granted women a position within the church generally equal to that of men. Women and men alike could become preachers and define church doctrine. A symbol of that sexual equality was the longtime partnership between Fox and Fell.

Of all the Protestant sectarians of the time, the Quakers were the most anarchistic and the most democratic. They had no church government, only periodic meetings of representatives from congregations. They had no paid clergy, and in their worship they spoke up one by one as the spirit moved them. Disregarding distinctions of gender and class, they addressed one another with the terms "thee" and "thou," words then commonly used in other parts of English society only in speaking to servants and social inferiors. And as confirmed pacifists, they refused to fight in wars. The Quakers were unpopular enough in England as a result of these beliefs and practices. They increased their unpopularity by occasionally breaking up other religious groups at worship. Many were jailed.

As a result, like the Puritans before them, the Quakers looked to America for asylum. A few went to New England. But except in Rhode Island, they were greeted there with fines, whippings, and banishment; three men and a woman who refused to leave were actually put to death. Others migrated to northern Carolina, and there became the fastest-growing religious community in the region. They were soon influential in colonial politics. But many Quakers wanted a colony of their own. As a despised sect, they had little chance of getting the necessary royal grant without the aid of someone influential at court. But fortunately for Fox and his followers, a number of wealthy and prominent men had become attracted to the faith.

William Penn

One of them was William Penn—the son of an admiral in the Royal Navy who was a landlord of valuable Irish estates. He had received the gentleman's education expected of a person of his standing, but he resisted his father in being attracted to untraditional religions. Converted to the doctrine of the Inner Light, the younger Penn became an evangelist for Quakerism. With George Fox, he visited the European continent and found Quakers there who, like Quakers in England, longed to emigrate to the New World. He set out to find a place for them to go.

Penn turned his attention first to New Jersey, half of which belonged to two fellow Quakers after 1764. Penn himself became an owner and proprietor of part of the colony. But in 1681, after the death of his father, he received from the king an even more valuable grant of lands. Penn had inherited his father's Irish lands and also his father's claim to a large debt from the king. Charles II, short of cash, paid the debt with a grant of territory between New York and Maryland—an area larger than England and Wales combined and which (unknown to him) contained more valuable soil and minerals than any

A QUAKER MEETING An anonymous artist painted this view of a Quaker meeting in approximately 1790. Because the Society of Friends (or Quakers) believed that all people were equal in the eyes of God, they appointed no ministers and imposed no formal structure on their religious services. Members of the congregation stood up to speak at will. *(Museum of Fine Arts, Boston, Bequest of Maxim Karolik)*

other province of English America. Penn would have

Pennsylvania Founded

virtually total authority within the province. At the king's insistence, the territory was named Pennsylvania, after Penn's late father.

Like most proprietors, Penn wanted Pennsylvania to be profitable for him and his family. And so he set out to attract settlers from throughout Europe through informative and honest advertising in several languages. Pennsylvania soon became the best known of all the colonies among ordinary people in England and on the continent. It also became the most cosmopolitan. Settlers flocked to the province from throughout Europe, joining several hundred Swedes and Finns who had been living in a small trading colony—New Sweden—established in 1638 at the mouth of the Delaware River. But the colony was never profitable for Penn and his descendants. Indeed, Penn himself, near the end of his life, was imprisoned in England for debt and died in poverty in 1718.

Penn was more than a mere real estate promoter, however, and he sought to create in Pennsylvania what he called a holy experiment. He helped create a liberal Frame of Government with a representative assembly. In 1682, he sailed to America and personally supervised the laying out of a city between the Delaware and the Schuylkill Rivers, which he named Philadelphia ("Brotherly Love"). With its rectangular streets, like those of Charles Town, Philadelphia helped set the pattern for most later cities in America. Penn believed, as had Roger Williams, that the land belonged to the Indians, and he was careful to see that they were reimbursed for it, as well as to see that they were not debauched by the fur traders' alcohol. Indians respected Penn as an honest white man, and during his lifetime the colony had no major conflicts with the natives. More than any other English colony, Pennsylvania prospered from the outset (even if its proprietor did not), because of Penn's successful recruitment of emigrants, his thoughtful planning, and the region's mild climate and fertile soil.

But the colony was not without conflict. By the late 1690s, some residents of Pennsylvania were beginning to resist the nearly absolute power of the proprietor. Residents of the southern areas of the colony, in particular, complained that the government in Philadelphia was unresponsive to their needs. As a result, a substantial

Charter of Liberties

opposition emerged to challenge Penn. Pressure from these groups grew to the point that in 1701, shortly before he departed for England for the last time, Penn agreed to a Charter of Liberties for the colony. The charter established a representative assembly (consisting, alone among the English colonies, of only one house), which greatly limited the authority of the proprietor. The charter also permitted "the lower counties" of the colony to establish their own representative assembly. The three counties did so in 1703 and as a result became, in effect, a separate colony: Delaware—although until the American Revolution, it had the same governor as Pennsylvania.

BORDERLANDS AND MIDDLE GROUNDS

The English colonies clustered along the Atlantic seaboard of North America eventually united, expanded, and became a great nation. But in the seventeenth and early eighteenth centuries, their future was not all clear. In those years, they were small, frail settlements surrounded by other, competing societies and settlements. The British Empire in North America was, in fact, a much smaller and weaker one than the great Spanish Empire to the South, and not, on the surface at least, clearly stronger than the enormous French empire to the North.

The continuing contest for control of North America, and the complex interactions among the diverse peoples populating the continent, were most clearly visible in areas around the borders of English settlement—the Caribbean and along the northern, southern, and western borders of the coastal colonies.

The Caribbean Islands

The Chesapeake was the site of the first permanent English settlements in the New World. Throughout the first half of the seventeenth century, however, the most important destinations for English immigrants were the islands of the Caribbean and the northern way station of Bermuda. More than half the

The English Caribbean

English migrants to the New World in the early seventeenth century settled on these islands. The island societies had close ties to English North America from the beginning and influenced the development of the mainland colonies in several ways. But they were also surrounded by, and sometimes imperiled by, outposts of the Spanish Empire.

Before the arrival of Europeans, most of the Caribbean islands had substantial native populations—the Arawaks, the Caribs, and the Ciboney. But

Imperial Conflict

beginning with Christopher Columbus's first visit in 1492, and accelerating after the Spanish established their first colony on Hispaniola in 1496, the native population was all but wiped out by European epidemics. Indians were never a significant factor in European settlement of the Caribbean. Indeed, by the time significant European settlement of the islands began, many were almost entirely deserted.

The Spanish Empire claimed title to all the islands in the Caribbean, but there was substantial Spanish settlement only on the largest of them: Cuba, Hispaniola, and Puerto Rico. English, French, and Dutch traders began settling on some of the smaller islands early in the sixteenth century, although these weak colonies were always vulnerable to Spanish attack. After Spain and the Netherlands went to war in 1621 (distracting the Spanish navy and leaving the English in the Caribbean relatively unmolested), the pace of English colonization increased. By mid-century, there were several substantial English settlements on the islands, the most important of them on

MAKING MOLASSES IN BARBADOS African slaves, who constituted the vast majority of the population of the flourishing sugar-producing island of Barbados, work here in a sugar mill grinding sugar cane and then boiling it to produce refined sugar, molasses, and—after a later distillation process not pictured here—rum. *(Arents Collections, Rare Books Division, New York Public Library. Astor, Lenox and Tilden Foundations)*

Antigua, St. Kitts, Jamaica, and Barbados. Even so, through the seventeenth century, the English settlements in the Caribbean were the targets of almost constant attacks and invasions by the Spanish, the Portuguese, the French, the Dutch, and the remaining Indians of the region. The world of the Caribbean was a violent and turbulent place.

The Caribbean colonies built their economies on raising crops for export. In the first years of the seventeenth century, English settlers experimented unsuccessfully with tobacco and cotton. But they soon discovered that the most lucrative crop was sugar, for which there was a substantial and growing market in Europe. Sugar cane could also be distilled into rum, for which there was also a booming market abroad. Within a decade of the introduction of sugar cultivation to the West Indies, planters were devoting almost all of their land to sugar cane. In their appetite for more land for sugar cane, they cut down forests and destroyed the natural habitats of many animals, and greatly reduced the amount of land available for growing food.

Because sugar was a labor-intensive crop, and because the remnant of the native population was too small to provide a work force, English planters quickly found it necessary to import laborers. As in the Chesapeake, they began by bringing indentured servants from England. But the arduous work discouraged white laborers; many found it impossible to adapt to the harsh tropical climate so different from that of England. By mid-century, therefore, the *Sugar and Slavery* English planters in the Caribbean (like the Spanish colonists who preceded them) were relying more and more heavily on an enslaved African work force, which soon substantially outnumbered them.

On Barbados and other islands where a flourishing sugar economy developed, the English planters were a tough, aggressive, and ambitious breed. Some of them grew enormously wealthy; and since their livelihoods depended on their work forces, they expanded and solidified the system of African slavery there remarkably quickly. By the late seventeenth century, there were four times as many African slaves as there were white settlers. By then the West Indies had ceased to be an attractive destination for ordinary English immigrants; most now went to the colonies on the North American mainland instead.

Masters and Slaves in the Caribbean

A small white population, much of it enjoying great economic success, and a large African population, all of it in bondage, was a potentially explosive combination. As in other English colonies in the New World in which Africans

SUGAR PLANTATION IN THE ANTILLES This nineteenth-century engraving shows a sugar plantation in one of the Caribbean islands of the Antilles. Although the picture gives the sense of an idyllic landscape, sugar plantations were notoriously rugged places for the African slaves who worked there (and whose quarters can be seen on the left). *(Explorer/Mary Evans Picture Library)*

came to outnumber Europeans, whites in the Caribbean *Slave Revolts* grew fearful of slave revolts. They had good reason, for there were at least seven major slave revolts in the islands, more than the English colonies of North America experienced in their entire history as slave societies. As a result, white planters monitored their labor forces closely and often harshly. Beginning in the 1660s, all the islands enacted legal codes to regulate relations between masters and slaves and to give white people virtually absolute authority over Africans. A master could even murder a slave with virtual impunity.

There was little in either the law or in the character of the economy to compel planters to pay much attention to the welfare of their workers. Many white slaveowners concluded that it was cheaper to buy new slaves periodically than to protect the well-being of those they already owned, and it was not uncommon for masters literally to work their slaves to death. Few African workers survived more than a decade in the brutal Caribbean working environment—they were either sold to planters in North America or died. Even whites,

who worked far less hard than did the slaves, often succumbed to the harsh climate; most died before the age of forty—often from tropical diseases to which they had no immunity.

Establishing a stable society and culture was extremely difficult for people living in such harsh and even deadly conditions. Many of the whites were principally interested in getting rich and had no long-term commitment to the *Unstable Societies* islands. Those who could returned to England with their fortunes and left their estates in the hands of overseers. A large proportion of the European settlers were single men, and many of them either died or left at a young age. Those who remained, many of them common white farmers and laborers living in desperate poverty, were too poor to contribute much to the development of the society. Europeans in the Caribbean lacked many of the institutions that gave stability to the North American settlements: church, family, community. That was one reason that the white population remained such a small minority on the islands. Like much of the Spanish Empire, the Caribbean colonies of England were governed by a small white ruling class governing a much larger population of Africans and (in some places) natives. But as in the English colonies on the mainland, there was little intermarriage between whites and blacks.

Africans in the Caribbean faced even greater difficulties, of course, but they managed to create a world of their own despite the hardships. They started families (although many of them were broken up by death or the slave trade); they sustained African religious and social traditions (and resisted Christianity); and within the rigidly controlled world of the sugar plantations, they established patterns of resistance.

The Caribbean settlements were connected to the North American colonies in many ways. They were an *Connection to British North America* | important part of the Atlantic trading world in which many Americans became involved—a source of sugar and rum and a market for goods made in the mainland colonies and in England. They were the principal source of African slaves for the mainland colonies; well over half the slaves in North America came from the islands, not directly from Africa. And because Caribbean planters established an elaborate plantation system earlier than planters in North America, they provided models that many mainland people consciously or unconsciously copied. In the American South, too, planters grew wealthy at the expense of poor whites and, above all, of African slaves.

The Southwestern Borderlands

By the end of the seventeenth century, the Spanish empire had established only a small presence in the regions that became the United States. In Mexico and regions further south, the Spanish had established a sophisticated and impressive empire. Their capital, Mexico City, was the most dazzling metropolis in the Americas. The Spanish residents, well over a million of them, enjoyed much greater prosperity than all but a few English settlers in North America.

But the principal Spanish colonies north of Mexico— *Spain's Northern Colonies* | Florida, Texas, New Mexico, Arizona, and California—were relatively unimportant economically to the empire. They attracted religious minorities, Catholic missionaries, independent ranchers fleeing the heavy hand of imperial authority, and Spanish troops defending the northern flank of the empire. But they remained weak and peripheral parts of the great empire to their south.

New Mexico was the most prosperous and populous of these Spanish outposts. Once the Spanish quelled the Pueblo revolt there in 1680 (see p. 17), they worked effectively with the natives of the region to develop a flourishing agriculture, profiting from the knowledge the Pueblos had developed over the years of how to grow grain in these arid lands. By the early nineteenth century, New Mexico had a non-Indian population of over 10,000—the largest European settlement west of the Mississippi and north of Mexico—and it was steadily expanding through the region. But New Mexico was prosperous only when compared to other borderlands. Its residents were far less successful than the Spanish in Mexico and other more densely settled regions.

The Spanish began to colonize California once they realized that other Europeans—among them English merchants and French and Russian trappers—were beginning to establish a presence in the region. Formal Spanish | *California* | settlement of California began in the 1760s, when the governor of Baja California was ordered to create outposts of the empire further north. Soon a string of missions, forts (or *presidios*), and trading communities were springing up along the Pacific coast, beginning with San Diego and Monterey in 1769 and eventually San Francisco (1776), Los Angeles (1781), and Santa Barbara (1786). As in other areas of European settlement, the arrival of the Spanish in California had a devastating effect on the native population, which died in great numbers from the diseases the colonists imported. The best estimates suggest that the native population of the region (approximately 65,000 at the time of the first Spanish settlements) had declined by two-thirds by 1820. As the new settlements spread, however, the Spanish insisted that the remaining natives convert to Catholicism. That explains the centrality of missions in almost all the major Spanish outposts in California. But the Spanish colonists were also intent on creating a prosperous agricultural economy, and they enlisted Indian laborers to help them do so. California's Indians had no choice but to accede to the demands of the Spanish, although there were frequent revolts by natives against the harsh conditions imposed upon them. Already decimated by European diseases generations earlier, the tribes now declined further as a result of malnutrition and overwork at the hands of the Spanish missions.

In the late seventeenth and early eighteenth centuries, the Spanish considered the greatest threat to the northern borders of their empire to be the growing ambitions of the French. In the 1680s, French explorers traveled down the Mississippi Valley to the mouth of the river and claimed the lands they had traversed for their king, Louis XIV, in 1682. They called the territory Louisiana. Fearful of French incursions further west, and unsettled by the nomadic Indians driven into the territory by the French, the Spanish began to fortify their claim to Texas by establishing new forts, missions, and settlements there, including San Fernando (later San Antonio) in 1731. The region that is now Arizona was also becoming increasingly tied to the Spanish empire. Northern Arizona was a part of the New Mexico colony and was governed from Santa Fe. The rest of Arizona (from Phoenix south) was controlled by the Mexican region of Sonora. As in California, much of the impetus for these settlements came from Catholic missionaries (in this case Jesuits), eager to convert the natives. But the missionary project met with little success. Unlike the sedentary Pueblos around Santa Fe, the Arizona natives were nomadic peoples, unlikely to settle down or to Christianize, frequently at war with rival tribes, and—like natives elsewhere—tragically vulnerable to smallpox, measles, and other diseases carried into the region by the Spanish. As had happened earlier in California, epidemics reduced the native population of Arizona by two-thirds in the early eighteenth century.

The Spanish colonies in the Southwest were not the nucleus of a large and expanding society. They were, rather, the sparsely populated edges of the great Spanish empire to the South—created less to increase the wealth of the empire than to defend it from threats by other European powers in the North. Nevertheless, these Spanish outposts helped create enduring societies very *Importance of the Spanish Borderlands* unlike those being established by the English along the Atlantic seaboard. The Spanish colonies were not committed to displacing the native populations, but rather to enlisting them. They sought to convert them to Catholicism, to recruit them (sometimes forcibly) as agricultural workers, and to cultivate them as trading partners. The Spanish did not generally consider the natives to be their equals, certainly, and they did not often treat them very well. But neither did they consider them merely as obstacles to their own designs, as many English settlers in the East did.

The Southeast Borderlands

A more direct challenge to English ambitions in North America was the Spanish presence in the southeastern areas of what is now the United States. After the establishment of the Spanish claim to Florida in the 1560s (see p. 17), missionaries and traders began moving northward into Georgia and westward into what is now known as the panhandle, and some ambitious Spaniards began to dream of expanding their empire still further north, into what became the Carolinas, and perhaps beyond. The founding of Jamestown in 1607 dampened those hopes and replaced them with fears. The English colonies, they believed, could threaten their existing settlements in Florida and Georgia. As a result, the Spanish built forts in both regions to defend themselves against the slowly increasing English presence there. Throughout the eighteenth century, the area between the Carolinas and Florida was the site of continuing tension, and frequent conflict, between the Spanish and the English—and, to a lesser degree, between the Spanish and the French, who were threatening their northwestern borders with settlements in Louisiana and in what is now Alabama.

There was no formal war between England and Spain *Hostilities in the Southeast* in these years, but that did not dampen the hostilities in the Southeast. English pirates continually harassed the Span-

ish settlements and, in 1668, actually sacked St. Augustine. Both sides in this conflict sought to make use of the native tribes. The English encouraged Indians in Florida to rise up against the Spanish missions. The Spanish, for their part, offered freedom to African slaves owned by English settlers in the Carolinas if they agreed to convert to Catholicism. About 100 Africans accepted the offer, and the Spanish later organized some of them into a military regiment to defend the northern border of New Spain. The English correctly viewed the Spanish recruitment of their slaves as an effort to undermine their economy. By the early eighteenth century, the constant fighting in the region had driven almost all the Spanish settlers out of Florida. The Spanish presence was almost entirely confined to St. Augustine on the Atlantic coast and Pensacola on the Gulf Coast, and to the modest colonies that surrounded the forts there. Because they were so few and so weak, they came to rely—far more than most British did—on natives and Africans and intermarried frequently with them.

Eventually, after more than a century of conflict in the southeastern borderlands, the English prevailed—acquiring Florida in the aftermath of the Seven Years' War (known in America as the French and Indian war; see pp. 101–105) and rapidly populating it with settlers from their colonies to the North. Before that point, however, protecting the southern boundary of the British empire in North America was a continual concern to the English and contributed in crucial ways to the founding of the colony of Georgia.

The Founding of Georgia

Georgia was unique in its origins. Its founders were a group of unpaid trustees led by General James Oglethorpe, a member of Parliament and military hero. They were interested in economic success, but they were driven primarily by military and philanthropic motives. They *James Oglethorpe's Vision* wanted to erect a military barrier against the Spanish lands on the southern border of English America, and they wanted to provide a refuge for the impoverished, a place where English men and women without prospects at home could begin anew.

The need for a military buffer between South Carolina and the Spanish settlements in Florida was particularly urgent in the first years of the eighteenth century. In a 1676 treaty, Spain had recognized England's title to lands already occupied by English settlers. But conflict between the two colonizing powers had continued. In 1686, a force of Indians and Creoles from Florida, directed by Spanish agents, attacked and destroyed an outlying South Carolina settlement south of the treaty line. And when hostilities broke out again between Spain and England in 1701 (known in England as Queen Anne's War and on the continent as the War of the Spanish Succession), the fighting renewed in America as well. That war ended in 1713, but another European conflict with similar repercussions for the New World was continually expected.

Oglethorpe, himself a veteran of the most recent Spanish war, was keenly aware of the military advantages of an English colony south of the Carolinas. Yet his interest in settlement rested even more on his philanthropic commitments. As head of a parliamentary committee investigating English prisons, he had grown appalled by the plight of honest debtors rotting in confinement. Such prisoners, and other poor people in danger of succumbing to a similar fate, could, he believed, become the farmer-soldiers of the new colony in America.

In 1732, King George II granted Oglethorpe and his fellow trustees control of the land between the Savannah and Altamaha Rivers. Their colonization policies reflected the vital military purposes of the colony. They limited the size of landholdings to make the settlement compact and easier to defend against Spanish and Indian attacks. They excluded Africans, free or slave; Oglethorpe *Georgia's Military Rationale* feared slave labor would produce internal revolts, and that disaffected slaves might turn to the Spanish as allies. The trustees prohibited rum (both because Oglethorpe disapproved of it on moral grounds and because the trustees feared its effects on the natives). They strictly regulated trade with the Indians, again to limit the possibility of wartime insurrection. They also excluded Catholics for fear they might collude with their coreligionists in the Spanish colonies to the south.

Oglethorpe himself led the first colonial expedition to Georgia, which built a fortified town at the mouth of the Savannah River in 1733 and later constructed additional forts south of the Altamaha. In the end, only a few debtors were released from jail and sent to Georgia. Instead, the trustees brought hundreds of impoverished tradesmen and artisans from England and Scotland and many religious refugees from Switzerland and Germany. Among the immigrants was a small group of Jews. English settlers made up a lower proportion of the European population of Georgia than of any other English colony.

The strict rules governing life in the new colony stifled its early development and ensured the failure of Oglethorpe's vision. Settlers in Georgia—many of whom were engaged in labor-intensive agriculture—needed a work force as much as those in other southern colonies. Almost from the start they began demanding the right to buy slaves. Some opposed the restrictions on the size of individual property holdings. Many resented the nearly absolute political power of Oglethorpe and the trustees. As a result, newcomers to the region generally preferred to settle in South Carolina, where there were fewer restrictive laws.

Oglethorpe (whom some residents of Georgia began calling "our perpetual dictator") at first bitterly resisted the demands of the settlers for social and political reform. Over time, however, he wearied of the conflict in the colony and grew frustrated at its failure to grow. He also suffered military disappointments, such as a 1740 assault on the Spanish outpost at St. Augustine, Florida, which ended in failure. Oglethorpe, now disillusioned with his American venture, began to loosen his grip. Even before the 1740 defeat, the trustees had removed the limitation on individual landholdings. In 1750, they removed the ban on slavery. A year later they ended the prohibition of rum and returned control of the colony to the king, who immediately permitted the summoning of a representative assembly. Georgia continued to grow more slowly than the other southern colonies, but in other ways it now developed along lines roughly similar to those of South Carolina. By 1770, there were over 20,000 non-Indian residents of the colony, nearly half of them African slaves.

Middle Grounds

The struggle for the North American continent was not just one among competing European empires. It was also a contest between the new immigrants and the native populations—between Spanish, English, French, Dutch, and other colonists, on the one hand, and the many Indian tribes with whom they shared the continent, on the other.

In some parts of the British empire—Virginia and New England, for example—English settlers fairly quickly established their dominance, subjugating and displacing most natives until they had established societies that were dominated almost entirely by Europeans. But in other regions, the balance of power was for many years far more precarious. Along the western borders of English settlement, in particular, Europeans and Indians lived together *Conflict and Accommodation* in regions in which neither side was able to establish clear dominance. In these "middle grounds," as they have been called, the two populations—despite frequent conflicts—carved out ways of living together, with each side making concessions to the other.

These were the peripheries of empires, in which the influence of formal colonial governments was virtually invisible. European settlers, and the soldiers scattered in forts throughout these regions to protect them, were unable to displace the Indians. So they had to carve out on their own a relationship with the tribes. In that relationship, the Europeans found themselves obliged to adapt to tribal expectations at least as much as the Indians had to adapt to European ones. Both French and British settlers gradually learned to do so.

To the Indians, the European migrants were both menacing and appealing. They feared the power of these strange people: their guns, their rifles, their forts. But they also wanted the French and British settlers to behave like "fathers"—to help them mediate their own internal disputes, to offer them gifts, to help them moderate their

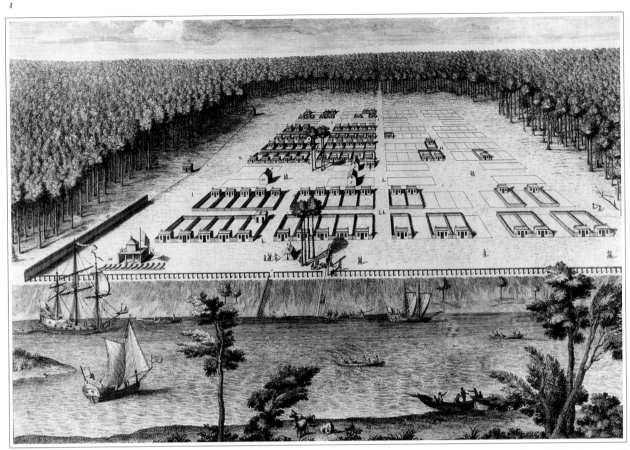

SAVANNAH IN 1734 This early view of the English settlement at Savannah by an English artist shows the intensely orderly character of Georgia in the early moments of European settlement there. As the colony grew, its residents gradually abandoned the rigid plan created by Georgia's founders. *(I.N. Phelps Stokes Collection of American Historical Prints, New York Public Library)*

conflicts. Europeans came from a world in which the formal institutional and military power of a nation or empire governed relationships between societies. But the natives had no understanding of the modern notion of a "nation" and thought much more in terms of ceremony and kinship. Gradually, Europeans learned to fulfill at least some of their expectations—to settle disputes among tribes, to moderate conflicts within tribes, to participate solemnly in Indian ceremonies, and to offer gifts as signs of respect.

In the seventeenth century, before many English settlers had entered the interior, the French were particularly adept *Mutually Beneficial Relations* at creating mutually beneficial relationships with the tribes. French migrants in the interior regions of the continent were often solitary fur traders, and some of them welcomed the chance to form close relationships with—even to marry within—the tribes. They also recognized the importance of treating tribal chiefs with respect and channeling gifts and tributes through them. By the mid-eighteenth century, French influence in the interior was in decline, and British settlers gradually became the dominant European group in the "middle grounds." It took the British a considerable time to learn the lessons that the French had long ago absorbed—that simple commands and raw force were

ineffective in creating a workable relationship with the tribes; that they too had to learn to deal with Indian leaders through gifts and ceremonies and mediation. Eventually they did so, and in large western regions—especially those around the Great Lakes—they established a precarious peace with the tribes that lasted for several decades.

But as the British (and after 1776) American presence in the region grew, the balance of power between Europeans and *The Shifting Balance* natives shifted. Newer settlers had difficulty adapting to the complex rituals of gift-giving and mediation that the earlier migrants had developed. The stability of the relationship between the Indians and whites deteriorated. By the early nineteenth century, the "middle ground" had collapsed, replaced by a European world in which Indians were ruthlessly subjugated and eventually removed. Nevertheless, it is important to recognize that for a considerable period of early American history, the story of the relationship between whites and Indians was not simply a story of conquest and subjugation, but also—in some regions—a story of a difficult but stable accommodation and mutual adaptation. The Indians were not simply victims in the story of the growth of European settlement in North America. They were also important actors, sometimes obstructing and sometimes facilitating the development of the new societies.

THE EVOLUTION OF THE BRITISH EMPIRE

The English colonies in America had originated as quite separate projects, and for the most part they grew up independent of one another. But by the mid-seventeenth century, the growing commercial success of the colonial ventures was producing pressure in England for a more rational, uniform structure to the empire.

The Drive for Reorganization

Imperial reorganization, many people in England claimed, would increase the profitability of the colonies and the power of the English government to supervise them. Above all, it would contribute to the success of the mercantile system, the foundation of the English economy. Colonies would provide a market for England's manufactured goods and a source of supply for raw materials it could not produce at home, thus promoting the principal goal of the mercantile system—increasing the to-

Mercantilism

tal wealth of the nation. But for the new possessions truly to promote mercantilist goals, England would have to exclude foreigners (as Spain had done) from its colonial trade. According to mercantilist theory, any wealth flowing to another nation could come only at the expense of England itself. Hence the British government sought to monopolize trade relations with its colonies.

In theory, the mercantile system offered benefits to the colonies as well by providing them with a ready market for the raw materials they produced and a source for the manufactured goods they did not. But some colonial goods were not suitable for export to England, which itself produced wheat, flour, and fish and had no interest in obtaining them from America. Colonists also found it more profitable at times to trade with the Spanish, French, or Dutch even in goods that England did import. Thus, a considerable trade soon developed between the English colonies and non-English markets.

For a time, the English government made no serious efforts to restrict this challenge to the principles of mercantilism, but gradually it began passing laws to regulate colonial trade. During Oliver Cromwell's "Protectorate," in 1650 and 1651, Parliament passed laws to keep Dutch ships out of

The Navigation Acts

the English colonies. After the Restoration, the government of Charles II adopted three Navigation Acts designed to regulate colonial commerce even more strictly. The first of them, in 1660, closed the colonies to all trade except that carried in English ships. This law also required the colonists to export certain items, among them tobacco, only to England or English possessions. The second act, in 1663, provided that all goods being shipped from Europe to the colonies had to pass through England on the way; that would make it possible for England to tax them. The third act, in 1673, was a response to the widespread evasion of the first two

laws by the colonial shippers, who frequently left port claiming to be heading for another English colony but then sailed to a foreign port. It imposed duties on the coastal trade among the English colonies, and it provided for the appointment of customs officials to enforce the Navigation Acts. These acts formed the legal basis of England's mercantile system in America for a century.

The system created by the Navigation Acts had obvious advantages for England. But it had some advantages for the colonists as well. By restricting all trade to British ships, the laws encouraged the colonists (who were themselves legally British subjects) to create an important shipbuilding industry of their own. And because the English wanted to import as many goods as possible from their own colonies (as opposed to importing them from other, rival nations), they encouraged—and at times subsidized—the development of American production of goods they needed, among them iron, silk, and lumber. Despite the bitter complaints the laws provoked in America in the late seventeenth century, and the even more bitter conflicts they would help to provoke decades later, the system of the Navigation Acts served the interests of the British and the Americans alike reasonably well through most of the eighteenth century.

The Dominion of New England

Enforcement of the Navigation Acts required not only the stationing of customs officials in America, but the establishment of an agency in England to oversee colonial affairs. In 1679, Charles II attempted to increase his control over Massachusetts (which behaved at times as if its leaders considered it an independent nation) by stripping the colony of its authority over New Hampshire and chartering a separate, royal colony there whose governor he would himself appoint. Five years later, after the Massachusetts General Court defied instructions from Parliament to enforce the Navigation Acts, Charles revoked the Massachusetts corporate charter and made it a royal colony.

Charles II's brother and successor, James II, who came to the throne in 1685, went much further. In 1686, he created a single Dominion of New England, which combined the government of Massachusetts with the governments of the rest of the New England colonies and, in

Sir Edmund Andros

1688, with those of New York and New Jersey as well. He eliminated the existing assemblies within the new Dominion and appointed a single governor, Sir Edmund Andros, to supervise the entire region from Boston. Andros was an able administrator but a stern and tactless man; his rigid enforcement of the Navigation Acts, his brusque dismissal of the colonists' claims to the "rights of Englishmen," and his crude and arbitrary tactics made him quickly and thoroughly unpopular. He was particularly despised in Massachusetts, where he tried to strengthen the Anglican Church.

The "Glorious Revolution"

James II was not only losing friends in America; he was making powerful enemies in England by attempting to exercise autocratic control over Parliament and the courts. He was also appointing his fellow Catholics to high office, inspiring fears that he would try to reestablish Catholicism as England's official religion. By 1688, his popular support had all but vanished.

Until 1688, James's heirs were two daughters—Mary and Anne—both of whom were Protestant. But in that year the king had a son and made clear that the boy would be raised a Catholic. Some members of Parliament were so alarmed that they invited the king's daughter Mary and her husband, William of Orange, ruler of the Netherlands and Protestant champion of Europe, to assume the throne together. When William and Mary arrived in England with a small army, James II (perhaps remembering what had happened to his father, Charles I) offered no resistance and fled to France. As a result of this bloodless coup, which the English called "the Glorious Revolution," William and Mary became joint sovereigns.

When Bostonians heard of the overthrow of James II, they moved quickly to unseat his unpopular viceroy in New England. Andros managed to escape an angry mob, but he was arrested and imprisoned as he sought to flee the city dressed as a woman. The new *End of the Dominion* sovereigns in England chose not to contest the toppling of Andros and quickly acquiesced in what the colonists had, in effect, already done: abolishing the Dominion of New England and restoring separate colonial governments. They did not, however, accede to all the colonists' desires. In 1691, they combined Massachusetts with Plymouth and made it a royal colony. The new charter restored the General Court, but it gave the crown the right to appoint the governor. It also replaced church membership with property ownership as the basis for voting and office-holding and required the Puritan leaders of the colony to tolerate Anglican worship.

Andros had been governing New York through a lieutenant governor, Captain Francis Nicholson, who enjoyed the support of the wealthy merchants and fur traders of the province—the same groups who had dominated the colony for years. Other, less favored colonists—farmers, mechanics, small traders, and shopkeepers—had a long accumulation of grievances against both Nicholson and his allies. The leader of the New York dissidents was Jacob Leisler, a German immigrant and a prosperous merchant who had married into a prominent Dutch family but had never won acceptance as one of the colony's ruling class. Much like Nathaniel Bacon in Virginia, the ambitious Leisler resented his exclusion and eagerly grasped the opportunity to challenge the colonial elite. In May 1689, when news of the Glorious Revolution in England and the fall of Andros in Boston reached New York, Leisler raised a militia, captured the city fort, drove Nicholson into exile, and proclaimed himself the new head of government in New York. For two years, he tried in vain to stabilize his power in the colony amid fierce factional rivalry. In 1691, when William and Mary appointed a new governor, Leisler briefly resisted this challenge to his authority. Although he soon yielded, his hesitation allowed his many political enemies to charge him with treason. He and one of his sons-in-law were hanged, drawn, and quartered. Fierce rivalry between what became known as the "Leislerians" and the "anti-Leislerians" dominated the politics of New York for many years thereafter.

In Maryland, many people erroneously assumed when they heard news of the Glorious Revolution that their proprietor, the Catholic Lord Baltimore, who was living in England, had sided with the Catholic James II and opposed *John Coode's Rebellion* William and Mary. So in 1689, an old opponent of the proprietor's government, John Coode, started a new revolt as head of an organization calling itself "An Association in Arms for the Defense of the Protestant Religion, and for Asserting the Right of King William and Queen Mary to the Province of Maryland and All the English Dominions." The insurgents drove out Lord Baltimore's officials. Through an elected convention, they chose a committee to run the government and petitioned the crown for a charter as a royal colony. In 1691, William and Mary complied, stripping the proprietor of his authority. The colonial assembly established the Church of England as the colony's official religion and forbade Catholics to hold public office, to vote, or even to practice their religion in public. Maryland became a proprietary colony again in 1715, but only after the fifth Lord Baltimore joined the Anglican Church.

As a result of the Glorious Revolution, the colonies revived their representative assemblies and successfully thwarted the plan for colonial unification. In the process, they legitimized the idea that the colonists had some rights within the empire, that the English government needed to consider their views in making policies that affected them. But the Glorious Revolution in America was not, as many Americans later came to believe, a clear demonstration of American resolve to govern itself or a clear victory for colonial self-rule. In New York and Maryland, in particular, the uprisings had more to do with local factional and religious divisions than with any larger vision of the nature of the empire. And while the insurgencies did succeed in eliminating the short-lived Dominion of New England, their ultimate results were governments that increased the crown's potential authority in many ways. As the first century of English settlement in America came to its end and as colonists celebrated their victories over arbitrary British rule, they were in fact becoming more a part of the imperial system than ever before.

CONCLUSION

The English colonization of North America was part of a larger effort by several European nations to expand the reach of their increasingly commercial societies. Indeed, for many years, the British empire in America was among the smallest and weakest of the imperial ventures there, overshadowed by the French to the North and the Spanish to the South.

In the British colonies along the Atlantic seaboard, new agricultural and commercial societies gradually emerged—in the South centered on the cultivation of tobacco and cotton, and reliant on slave labor; and in the northern colonies centered on more traditional food crops and based mostly on free labor. Substantial trading centers emerged in such cities as Boston, New York, Philadelphia, and Charleston, and a growing proportion of the population became prosperous and settled in these increasingly complex communities. By the early eighteenth century, English settlement had spread from northern New England (in what is now Maine) south into Georgia.

But this growing British empire coexisted with, and often found itself in conflict with, the presence of other Europeans—most notably the Spanish and the French—in other areas of North America. In these borderlands, societies did not assume the settled, prosperous form they were taking in the Tidewater and New England. They were raw, sparsely populated settlements in which Europeans, including over time increasing numbers of English, had to learn to accomodate not only one another but also the still-substantial Indian tribes with whom they shared these interior lands. By the middle of the eighteenth century, there was a significant European presence across a broad swath of North America—from Florida to Maine, and from Texas to Mexico to California—only a relatively small part of it controlled by the British. But changes were underway within the British empire that would soon lead to its dominance through a much larger area of North America.

FOR FURTHER REFERENCE

William Cronon, *Changes in the Land: Indians, Colonists, and the Ecology of New England* (1983) examines the social and environmental effects of English settlement in colonial America. Richard White, *The Middle Ground: Indians, Empires, and Republics in the Great Lakes Region, 1650–1815* (1991) is an important study of the accommodations that Indians and early European settlers made in the continental interior. James H. Merrell, *The Indians' New World* (1991), and *Into the American Woods: Negotiators on the Pennsylvania Frontier* (1999) are among the best examinations of the impact of European settlement on eastern tribes. Perry Miller, *The New England Mind: From Colony to Province* (1953) is a classic exposition of the Puritan intellectual milieu. Michael Kammen, *Colonial New York* (1975) illuminates the diversity and pluralism of New York under the Dutch and the English. Edmund Morgan, *American Slavery, American Freedom* (1975) is a compelling narrative of political and social development in early Virginia. Peter Wood, *Black Majority* (1974) describes the early importance of slavery in the founding of South Carolina. Richard S. Dunn, *Sugar and Slaves: The Rise of the Planter Class in the English West Indies, 1624–1713* (1972) is important for understanding the origins of British colonial slavery. David J. Weber, *The Spanish Frontier in North America* (1992) examines the northern peripheries of the Spanish empire.

For quizzes, Internet resources, references to additional books and films, and more, consult this book's Online Learning Center at www.mhhe.com/brinkley11.

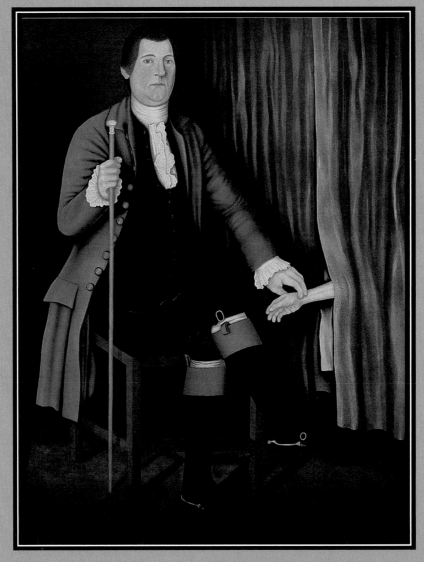

DR. WILLIAM GLEASON The American artist Winthrop Chandler painted this image of a doctor examining a female patient in 1780. The doctor obviously considers it inappropriate to view a woman lying in bed, so he takes her pulse as she slips her hand through the curtain obscuring her. *(Ohio State Historical Society)*

Significant Events

1636	Harvard College founded in Massachusetts
1640	Instability in tobacco markets begins
1647	Massachusetts law requires a public school in every town
1650	Population of New England begins to grow by natural increase
1662	Halfway Covenant established in New England
1670s	Flow of indentured servants declines
	Slave traders begin importing slaves directly from Africa to North America
1685	Edict of Nantes revoked in France; Huguenots begin migrating to North America
1690s	Rice production becomes central to South Carolina economy
	Slave trade expands as prices decline

CHAPTER THREE

SOCIETY AND CULTURE IN PROVINCIAL AMERICA

*T*he British colonies were, most people in both England and America believed, outposts of the British world. And it is true that as the colonies grew and became more prosperous, they also became more English. The colonists adopted the tastes, styles, and customs of England, bought goods made in England, read books and pamphlets published in England, and modeled most of their political, cultural, and educational institutions on their English equivalents. Some of the early settlers had come to America to escape what they considered English tyranny. But by the early eighteenth century, many, perhaps most, colonists considered themselves Englishmen just as much as the men and women in England itself did.

At the same time, however, life in the colonies was diverging in many ways from that in England simply by the nature of the New World. The physical environment was very different—vaster and less tamed. The

Diverging Societies

population was more diverse as well. Beginning with the Dutch settlements in New York, the area that would become the United States was a magnet for immigrants from many lands other than England: Scotland, Ireland, the European continent, as well as migrants from the Spanish and French empires already established in America. And beginning with the first importation of slaves into Virginia, English North America became the destination for thousands of forcibly transplanted Africans. At least equally important, Europeans and Africans were interacting constantly with a native population that for many years outnumbered them. Despite the efforts of the colonists to isolate themselves from Indian society and create a culture all their own, the European and Native American worlds could not remain entirely separate.

To the degree that the colonists emulated English society, they were becoming more and more like one another. To the degree that they were shaped by the character of their own regions, they were becoming more and more diverse. Indeed, the pattern of society in some areas of North America resembled that of other areas scarcely at all. Although Americans would ultimately discover that they had enough in common to join together to form a single nation, these regional differences continued to affect their society well beyond the colonial period.

1691 · Official toleration of Catholics ends in Maryland
1692 · Witchcraft trials begin in Salem
1693 · College of William and Mary founded in Virginia
1697 · Royal African Company monopoly of slave trade broken; slave importations begin to increase
1701 · Yale College founded in Connecticut
1708–1709 · First major migration of Palatinate Germans to North America begins
1710 · Major Scotch-Irish migrations to North America begin
· German Swiss establish settlements in North Carolina
1720 · Cotton Mather initiates smallpox inoculations in Massachusetts

1734 · Great Awakening begins in Massachusetts
· Peter Zenger tried in New York
1739 · George Whitefield arrives in North America
· Great Awakening intensifies
· Stono slave rebellion in South Carolina
1740s · Indigo production begins in South Carolina
1746 · College of New Jersey founded at Princeton
1754 · King's College (later Columbia University) founded in New York
1755 · Academy and College of Philadelphia (later University of Pennsylvania) founded
1764 · Major ironworks established in New Jersey

THE COLONIAL POPULATION

Not until long after the beginning of European colonization did Europeans and Africans in North America outnumber the native population. But after uncertain

Immigration and Natural Increase

beginnings at Jamestown and Plymouth, the nonnative population grew rapidly and substantially, through continued immigration and through natural increase, until by the late seventeenth century Europeans and Africans became the dominant population groups along the Atlantic coast.

A few of the early English settlers were members of the upper classes—usually the younger sons of the lesser gentry, men who stood to inherit no land at home and aspired to establish estates for themselves in America. For the most part, however, the early English population was very unaristocratic. It included some members of the emerging middle class, businessmen who migrated to America for religious or commercial reasons, or (like John Winthrop) both. But the dominant element was English laborers. Some came to the New World independently. The religious dissenters who formed the bulk of the population of early New England, for example, were men and women of modest means who arranged their own passage, brought their families with them, and established themselves immediately on their own land. But in the Chesapeake, at least three-fourths of the immigrants in the seventeenth century arrived as indentured servants.

Indentured Servitude

The system of temporary servitude in the New World developed out of existing practices in England. Young men and women bound themselves to masters for a fixed term of servitude (usually four to five years). In return they received passage to America, food, and shelter. Upon comple-

Origins

tion of their terms of service, male indentures were supposed to receive such benefits as clothing, tools, and

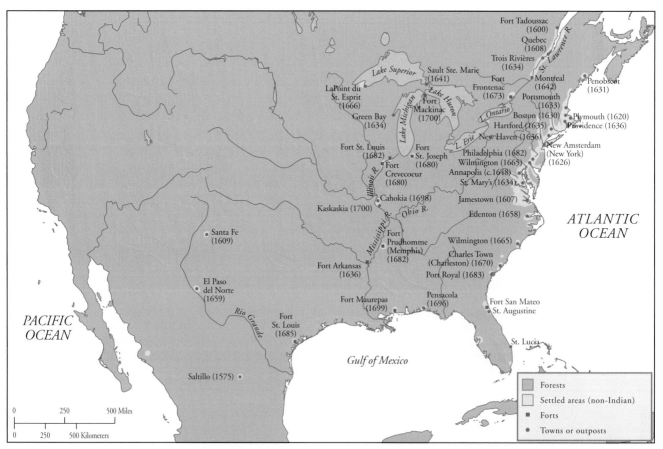

AMERICA IN 1700 This map reveals how tiny a proportion of North America was settled by Europeans in 1700, nearly a century after the first English settlements there. The largest area of settlement was the thin fringe of colonies along the northern Atlantic seaboard. There were additional scattered settlements, almost all of them tiny, in eastern Canada, along the southern Atlantic coast, in the Mississippi valley, and in the Southwest. ◆ *What would account for the isolated colonies in noncoastal areas of North America?*

 For an interactive version of this map go to www.mhhe.com/brinkley11ch3maps

occasionally land; in reality, however, many left service without anything at all, unprepared and unequipped to begin earning livings on their own. Roughly one-fourth of the indentures in the Chesapeake were women, most of whom worked as domestic servants. Because men greatly outnumbered women in the region in the seventeenth century, they could reasonably expect to marry when their terms of servitude expired. Male domestic servants, however, usually had no such options.

Most indentured servants came to the colonies voluntarily, but not all. Beginning as early as 1617, the English government occasionally dumped shiploads of convicts in America to be sold into servitude, although some criminals, according to Captain John Smith, "did chuse to be hanged ere they would go thither, and were." The government also sent prisoners taken in battles with the Scots and the Irish in the 1650s, as well as other groups deemed undesirable: orphans, vagrants, paupers, and those who were "lewd and dangerous." Other involuntary immigrants were neither dangerous nor indigent but simply victims of kidnapping, or "impressment," by aggressive and unscrupulous investors and promoters.

It was not difficult to understand why the system of indentured servitude proved so appealing to those in a position to employ workers and servants in colonial America—particularly once it became clear, as it quickly did, that the Indian population could not easily be transformed into a servile work force. The indenture system provided a means of coping with the severe labor shortage in the New World. In the Chesapeake, the headright system (by which masters received additional land grants for every servant they imported) offered another incentive. For the servants themselves, the attractions were not always so clear. Those who came voluntarily often did so to escape troubles in England; others came in the hope of establishing themselves on land or in trades of their own when their terms of service expired. Yet the reality often differed sharply from the hope.

By the late seventeenth century, indentured servants and people who had begun as indentures had become one of the largest elements of the population. Some former indentures managed to establish themselves successfully as farmers, tradespeople, or artisans. Others (mostly

Realities of Indentured Servitude

males) found themselves without land, without employment, without families, and without prospects. A large floating population of young single men—such as those who supported Bacon's Rebellion—emerged in some areas. They traveled restlessly from place to place in search of work or land and were a potential (and at times actual) source of social unrest, particularly in the Chesapeake. Even free laborers who did find employment or land and settled down with families often did not stay put for very long. The phenomenon of families simply pulling up stakes and moving to another, more promising location every several years was

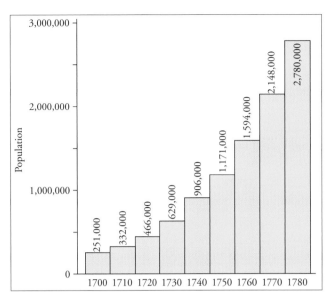

THE NON-INDIAN POPULATION OF NORTH AMERICA, 1700–1780 The European population of North America grew much more dramatically in the eighteenth century than it had in the seventeenth, exceeding 2 million by 1770. But unlike the seventeenth century, the most important reason for this expansion was natural increase (children born in America), replacing immigration from Europe. ◆ *Why would the natural increase have been so much larger than in the past?*

one of the most prominent characteristics of the colonial population.

Indentured servitude remained an important source of population growth well into the eighteenth century, but beginning in the 1670s the flow began to decline substantially. A decrease in the English birth rate and an increase in English prosperity reduced the pressures on many men and women who might otherwise have considered emigrating. After 1700, those who did travel to America as indentured servants generally avoided the southern colonies, where working conditions were arduous and prospects for advancement were slim, and settled in the mid-Atlantic colonies, especially Pennsylvania and New York, where they could anticipate better opportunities. In the Chesapeake, landowners themselves began to find the indenture system less attractive, in part because they were troubled by the instability that former servants created or threatened to create. That was one reason for the increasing centrality of African slavery in the southern agricultural economy.

Birth and Death

At first, new arrivals in most colonies, whatever their background or status, could anticipate great hardship: inadequate food, frequent epidemics, and in an appalling number of cases, early death. Gradually, however, conditions of settlement improved enough to allow the non-Indian population to begin to expand. By the end of the seventeenth

SERVANTS FOR SALE The *South Carolina Gazette* of Charles Town ran this advertisement in November 1749 to announce the arrival of a group of English "indentures"—men and women who had accepted passage to America in exchange for their agreement to sell themselves as servants for a fixed period of years once they arrived. Indentures were the most common form of labor in most of the colonies during much of the seventeenth century, but by 1749 the system was already beginning to die out—replaced in the South by the enslavement of Africans. The appeal at the end of this advertisement for help in capturing two German indentures who had run away was similar to many such advertisements in many southern papers over the next century appealing for help in finding runaway slaves. *(Charleston Library Society)*

century, the non-Indian population in the English colonies of North America had grown to over a quarter of a million, of whom about 25 percent were Africans.

Although immigration remained for a time the greatest source of population increase, the most important long-range factor in the growth of the non-Indian colonial population was its ability to reproduce itself. Marked improvement in the reproduction rate began in New England and the mid-Atlantic colonies in the second half of the seventeenth century, and after the 1650s natural

Exceptional Longevity in New England

increase became the most important source of population growth there. The New England population more than quadrupled through reproduction alone in the second half of the seventeenth century. This was less a result of unusual fertility (families in England and in other colonies were probably equally fertile) than of exceptional longevity. Indeed, the life spans of residents of some areas of New England were nearly equal to those of people in the twentieth century. In the first generation of American-born colonists, according to one study, men who survived infancy lived to an average age of seventy-one, women to seventy. The next generation's life expectancy declined somewhat—to sixty-five for men who survived infancy—but remained at least ten years higher than the English equivalent and approximately twenty years higher than life expectancy in the South. Scholars disagree on the reasons for these remarkable life spans, but contributing factors probably include the cool climate and the relatively disease-free environment it produced, clean water (a stark contrast to England in these years), and the absence of large population centers that might breed epidemics.

Conditions improved much more slowly in the South. The mortality rates for whites in the Chesapeake region remained markedly higher than those elsewhere until the mid-eighteenth century (and the mortality rates for Africans higher still). Throughout the seventeenth century, the average life expectancy for white men in the region was just over forty years, and for white women slightly less. One in four children died in infancy, and fully half died before the age of twenty. The high death rate among adults meant that only about a third of all marriages lasted more than ten years; thus those children who survived infancy often lost one or both of their parents before reaching maturity. Widows, widowers, and orphans formed a substantial proportion of the white population of the Chesapeake. The continuing ravages of disease (particularly malaria) and the prevalence of salt-contaminated water kept the death rate high in the South; only after the settlers developed immunity to the local diseases (a slow process known as "seasoning") did life expectancy increase significantly. Population growth was substantial in the region, but largely as a result of immigration.

Natural increases in the population, wherever they occurred, were in large part a result of a steady improvement in the sex ratio through the seventeenth century. In the early years of settlement, more than three-quarters of the white population of the Chesapeake consisted of men. And even in New England, which from the beginning had attracted more families (and thus more women) than the southern colonies, 60 percent of the white inhabitants in 1650 were male. Gradually, however, more women began to arrive in the colonies; and increasing birth rates, which of course produced roughly equal numbers of males and females, contributed to shifting the sex ratio as well. Not until well into the eighteenth century did the ratio begin to match that in England (where women were a slight majority), but by the late seventeenth century, the proportion of males to females in all the colonies was becoming more balanced.

More Balanced Sex Ratio

Medicine in the Colonies

The very high death rates of women who bore children illustrate the primitive nature of medical knowledge and practice in the colonies. Seventeenth- and eighteenth-century physicians had little or no understanding of infection and sterilization. As a result, many people died from infections contracted during childbirth or surgery from dirty instruments or dirty hands. Because communities were unaware of bacteria, many were plagued with infectious diseases transmitted by garbage or unclean water.

One result of the limited extent of medical knowledge was that it was relatively easy for people to enter the field, even without any professional training. The biggest beneficiaries of this ease of access were women, who established themselves in considerable numbers as midwives. Midwives assisted women in childbirth, but they also dis-

Midwives

pensed other medical advice— usually urging their patients to use herbs or other natural remedies. Midwives were popular because they were usually friends and neighbors of the people they treated, unlike physicians, who were few and therefore not often well known to their patients. Male doctors felt threatened by the midwives and struggled continually to drive them from the field, although they did not make substantial progress in doing so until the nineteenth century.

Midwives and doctors alike practiced medicine on the basis of the prevailing assumptions of their time, most of them derived from the theory of "humoralism" popularized by the great second-century Roman physican Galen. Galen argued that the human body was governed by four "humors" that were lodged in four bodily fluids: yellow bile (or "choler"), black bile ("melancholy"), blood, and phlegm. In a healthy body, the four humors existed in balance. Illness represented an imbalance and suggested the need for removing from the body the excesses of whatever fluid was causing the imbalance. That was the rationale that lay behind the principal medical techniques of the seventeenth century: purging, expulsion, and bleeding. Bleeding was the most extreme of the treatments (and the most destructive), and it was practiced mostly by male physicians. Midwives preferred more homeopathic treatments and favored "pukes" and laxatives. The great majority of early Americans, however, had little contact with physicians, or even midwives, and sought instead to deal with illness on their own, confident that their own abilities were equal to those of educated physicians— which, given the state of medical knowledge, was often true. The assumption that treating illness was the exclusive province of trained professionals, so much a part of the twentieth century, lay far in the distance in the colonial era.

That seventeenth-century medicine rested so much on ideas produced 1,400 years before is evidence of how little support there was for the scientific method—which rests on experimentation and observation rather than on inherited faiths—in England and America at the time. Bleeding, for example, had been in use for hundreds of years, during which time there had been no evidence at all that it helped people recover from illness; indeed, if anyone had chosen to look for it, there was considerable evidence that bleeding could do great harm. But what would seem in later eras to be the simple process of testing scientific assumptions was not yet a common part of Western thought. That was one reason that the birth of the Enlightenment in the late seventeenth century—with its faith in human reason and its belief in the capacity of individuals and societies to create better lives—was important not just to politics but to science.

Women and Families in the Chesapeake

The importance of reproduction in the labor-scarce society of seventeenth-century America had particularly significant effects on women. The high sex ratio meant that few women remained unmarried for long. The average European woman in America married for the first time at twenty or twenty-one years of age, considerably earlier than in England; in some areas of the Chesapeake, the average bride was three to four years younger. In the Chesapeake, the most important factor affecting women and families remained, until at least the mid-eighteenth century, the extraordinarily high mortality

Male Authority Undermined

rate. Under those circumstances, the traditional male-centered family structure of England—by which husbands and fathers exercised firm, even dictatorial control over the lives of their wives and children—was difficult to maintain. Because so few families remained intact for long, rigid patterns of male authority were constantly undermined. Standards of sexual behavior were also more flexible in the South than they were in England or other parts of America. Because of the large numbers of indentured servants who were forbidden to marry until their terms of service expired, premarital sexual relationships were frequent. Female servants who became pregnant before the expiration of their terms could expect harsh treatment: heavy fines, whippings if no one could pay the fines, an extra year or two of service added to their contract, and the loss of their children after weaning. Bastard children were themselves bound out as indentures at a very early age. On the other hand, a pregnant woman whose term of service expired before the birth of her child or whose partner was able to buy her remaining time from her master might expect to marry quickly. Over a third of Chesapeake marriages occurred with the bride already pregnant.

Women in the Chesapeake could anticipate a life consumed with childbearing. The average wife became pregnant every two years. Those who lived long enough bore an average of eight children apiece (up to five of whom typically died in infancy or early childhood). Since childbirth was one of the most frequent causes of female death, relatively few women survived to see all their children grow to maturity.

For all the hardships women encountered in the seventeenth-century South, they also enjoyed more power and a greater level of freedom than women in other areas (or than southern women in later years). Because men were plentiful and women scarce, females had consider-

Greater Independence in the South

able latitude in choosing husbands. (They also often had no fathers or other male relatives nearby trying to control their choices.) Because women generally married at a much younger age than men, they also tended to outlive their husbands (even though female life expectancy was somewhat shorter than male). Widows were often left with several children and with responsibility for managing a farm or plantation, a circumstance of enormous hardship but one that also gave them significant economic power.

Widows seldom remained unmarried for long, however. Those who had no grown sons to work the tobacco farms and plantations had particular need for male assistance, and marriage was the surest way to secure it. Since many widows married men who were themselves widowers, complex combinations of households were frequent. With numerous stepchildren, half brothers, and half sisters living together in a single household, women often had to play the role of peacemaker—a role that may have further enhanced their authority within the family.

The high mortality rate in the seventeenth-century Chesapeake also created large numbers of orphans, many with no property and no extended family on which to rely. Much earlier than in England or in the northern American colonies, therefore, Maryland and Virginia created special courts and other institutions to protect and control orphaned children.

By the early eighteenth century, the character of the Chesapeake population was beginning to change, and with it the nature of the typical family. Life expectancy was increasing; indentured servitude was in decline; and natural reproduction was becoming the principal source of white population increase. The sex ratio was becoming more equal. One result of these changes was that life for white

Revival of Patriarchy

people in the region became less perilous and less arduous. Another result was that women lost some of the power that their small numbers had once given them. As families grew more stable, traditional patterns of male authority revived. By the mid-eighteenth century, southern families were becoming highly "patriarchal," that is, dominated by the male head of the family.

Women and Families in New England

In New England, where many more immigrants arrived with family members and where death rates declined quickly, family structure was much more stable than it was in the Chesapeake and hence much more traditional. Because the sex ratio was reasonably balanced, most men could expect to marry.

Women, however, remained in the minority; and as in the Chesapeake, they married young, began producing children early, and continued to do so well into their

THE GRAVE OF MARY MOORE Female mortality was very high in early eighteenth-century New England, because so many women died in childbirth—which was very likely the cause of death of the young woman whose grave this headstone marks and who died at age 19. The grim carving of a winged skull at the top of the stone was a common symbol at the time of the victory of the soul over death. *(Kevin Fleming/Corbis)*

thirties. In contrast to the South, however, northern children were more likely to survive (the average family raised six to eight children to maturity), and families were

Male-Dominated New England

more likely to remain intact. Fewer New England women became widows, and those who did generally lost their husbands later in life. Hence women were less often cast in roles independent of their husbands. Young women, moreover, had less control over the conditions of marriage, both because there were fewer unmarried men vying for them and because their fathers were more often alive and able to exercise control over their choice of husbands.

Among other things, increased longevity meant that, unlike in the Chesapeake (where three-fourths of all children lost at least one parent before the age of twenty-one), white parents in New England usually lived to see their children and even their grandchildren grow to maturity. Still, the lives of most New England women were nearly as consumed by childbearing and child rearing as those of women in the Chesapeake. Even women who lived into their sixties spent the vast majority of their mature years with young children in the home. The longer lives in New England also meant that parents continued to control their children far longer than did parents in the South. Although they were less likely than parents in England actually to "arrange" marriages for their children, few sons and daughters could choose spouses entirely independent of their parents' wishes. Men usually depended on their fathers for land—generally a prerequisite for beginning families of their own. Women needed dowries from their parents if they were to attract desirable husbands. Stricter parental supervision of children meant, too, that fewer women became pregnant before marriage than in the South (although even in Puritan New England the premarital pregnancy rate was not insubstantial—as high as 20 percent in some communities).

For New Englanders more than for residents of the Chesapeake, family relationships and the status of women were defined in part by religious belief. In the South, established churches were relatively weak. But in New England the Puritan church was a powerful institutional and social presence. In theory, the Puritan belief that men and women were equal before God and hence equally capable of interpreting the Bible created possibilities for women to emerge as spiritual leaders. But in reality, religious authority remained securely in the hands of men, who used it in part to reinforce a highly patriarchal view of society. The case of Anne Hutchinson—a woman who became an important religious figure only to be disciplined and expelled by the male church hierarchy—is an example of both the possibilities and the limits of female spiritual power.

Puritanism placed a high value on the family, which was not only the principal economic unit but also the principal religious unit within every community. In one sense, then, Puritan women played important roles within their families because their culture valued the position of wife and mother. At the same time, however, Puritanism reinforced the idea of nearly absolute male authority and the assumption of female weakness

The Patriarchal Puritan Family

and inferiority. Women were expected to be modest and submissive. (Such popular girls' names as Prudence, Patience, Chastity, and Comfort suggest something about Puritan expectations of female behavior.) A wife was expected to devote herself almost entirely to serving the needs of her husband and household.

Women were of crucial importance to the New England agricultural economy. Not only did they bear and raise children who at relatively young ages became part of the work force, but they themselves were continuously engaged in tasks vital to the functioning of the farm—gardening, raising poultry, tending cattle, spinning, and weaving, as well as cooking, cleaning, and washing.

The Beginnings of Slavery in British America

Almost from the beginning of European settlement in America, there was a demand for black servants to supplement the always scarce southern labor supply. The demand grew rapidly once tobacco cultivation became a staple of the Chesapeake economy. But the supply of African laborers was limited during much of the seventeenth century, because the Atlantic slave trade did not at first serve the English colonies in America. Portuguese slavers, who had dominated the trade since the sixteenth century, shipped captive men and women from the west coast of Africa to the new European colonies in South America and the Caribbean. Gradually, however, Dutch and French navigators joined the slave trade. A substantial commerce in slaves grew up within the Americas, particularly between the Caribbean islands and the southern colonies of English America. By the late seventeenth century, the supply of black workers in North America was becoming plentiful.

As the commerce in slaves grew more extensive and more sophisticated, it also grew more horrible. Before it ended in the nineteenth century, it was responsible for the forced immigration of as many as 11 million Africans to North and South America and the Caribbean. (Until the late eighteenth century, the number of African immigrants to

The Middle Passage

the Americas was higher than that of Europeans.) Native African chieftains captured members of enemy tribes in battle, tied them together in long lines, or "coffles," and sold them in the flourishing slave marts on the African coast. Then, after some haggling on the docks between the European traders and the African suppliers, the terrified victims were packed into the dark, filthy holds of ships for the horrors of the "middle passage"—the journey to America. For weeks, sometimes even months, the black

The debate among historians over how and why white Americans created a system of slave labor in the seventeenth century—and how and why they determined that people of African descent and no others should populate that system—has been a long and unusually heated one. At its center is the question of whether slavery was a result of white racism or helped to create it.

In 1950, Oscar and Mary Handlin published an influential article, "Origins of the Southern Labor System," which noted that many residents of the American colonies (and of England) lived in varying degrees of "unfreedom" in the seventeenth century, although none resembling slavery as it came to be known in America. The first Africans who came to America lived for a time in conditions not very different from those of white indentured servants. But slavery came ultimately to differ substantially from other conditions of servitude. It was permanent bondage, and it passed from one generation to the next. That it emerged in America, the Handlins argued, resulted from efforts by colonial legislatures to increase the available labor force. That it included African Americans and no others was because black people had few defenses and few defenders. Racism emerged to justify slavery; it did not cause slavery.

In 1959, Carl Degler became the first of a number of important histori-

ans to challenge the Handlins. In his essay "Slavery and the Genesis of American Race Prejudice," he argued that Africans had never been like other servants in the Chesapeake; that "the Negro was actually never treated as an equal of the white man, servant or free." Racism was strong "long before slavery had come upon the scene." It did not result from slavery, but helped cause it. Nine years later, Winthrop D. Jordan argued similarly that white racism, not economic or legal conditions, produced slavery. In *White Over Black* (1968) and other, earlier writings, Jordan argued that Europeans had long viewed people of color—and black Africans in particular—as inferior beings appropriate for serving whites. Those attitudes migrated with

white Europeans to the New World, and white racism shaped the treatment of Africans in America—and the nature of the slave labor system—from the beginning.

George Fredrickson has echoed Jordan's emphasis on the importance of racism as an independent factor reinforcing slavery; but unlike Jordan, he has argued that racism did not precede slavery. "The treatment of blacks," he wrote, "engendered a cultural and psycho-social racism that after a certain point took on a life of its own. . . . Racism, although the child of slavery, not only outlived its parent but grew stronger and more independent after slavery's demise."

Peter Wood's *Black Majority* (1974), a study of seventeenth-century

(*View of Mulberry (House and Street) by Thomas Coram. Gibbes Museum of Art/Carolina Art Association*)

prisoners remained chained in the bowels of the slave ships. Conditions varied from one ship to another. Some captains took care to see that their potentially valuable cargo remained reasonably healthy. Others accepted the deaths of numerous Africans as inevitable and tried to cram as many as possible into their ships to ensure that enough would survive to yield a profit at journey's end. On such ships, the African prisoners were sometimes packed together in such close quarters that they were unable to stand, hardly able to breathe. Some ships supplied them with only minimal food and water. Women were often victims of rape and other sexual abuse. Those who died en route were simply thrown overboard. Upon ar-

rival in the New World, slaves were auctioned off to white landowners and transported, frightened and bewildered, to their new homes.

The first black laborers arrived in English North America before 1620, and as English seamen began to establish themselves in the slave trade, the flow of Africans to the colonies gradually increased. But North America was always a much less important market for Africans than were other parts of the New World, especially the Caribbean islands and Brazil, whose labor-intensive sugar economies created an especially large demand for slaves. Fewer than 5 percent of the Africans imported to the Americas went directly to the English colonies on

South Carolina, moved the debate back away from racism and toward social and economic conditions. Wood demonstrated that blacks and whites often worked together on relatively equal terms in the early years of settlement. But as rice cultivation expanded, finding white laborers willing to do the arduous work became more difficult. The forcible importation of African workers, and the creation of a system of permanent bondage, was a response to a growing demand for labor and to fears among whites that without slavery a black labor force would be difficult to control. Similarly, Edmund Morgan's *American Slavery, American Freedom* (1975) argued that the southern labor system was at first relatively flexible and later grew more rigid. In colonial Virginia, he claimed, white settlers did not at first intend to create a system of permanent bondage. But as the tobacco economy grew and created a high demand for cheap labor, white landowners began to feel uneasy about their dependence on a large group of dependent white workers, since such workers were difficult to recruit and control. Thus slavery was less a result of racism than of the desire for white landowners to find a reliable and stable labor force. Racism, Morgan contended, was a result of slavery, an ideology created to justify a system that had been developed to serve other needs. And David Brion Davis, in *The Problem of Slavery in the Age of Revolution* (1975), argued that while prejudice against blacks had a long history, racism as a systematic ideology was crystallized during the American Revolution—as Americans such as Thomas Jefferson struggled to explain the paradox of slavery existing in a republic committed to individual freedom.

Robin Blackburn's *The Making of New World Slavery* (1996) is perhaps the most emphatic statement of the economic underpinnings of slavery. Why, he asks, did the American colonies create a thriving slave labor system at a time when slavery had almost entirely died out in Europe? He concedes that race was a factor; Africans were "different" in appearance, culture, and religion from European colonists, and it was easier to justify enslaving them than it was to justify enslaving English, French, or Spanish workers. But the real reasons for slavery were hardheaded economic decisions by ambitious entrepreneurs, who realized very early that a slave-labor system in the labor-intensive agricultural world of the American South and the Caribbean was more profitable than a free-labor system. Slaveowning planters, he argues, not only enriched themselves; they created wealth that benefited all of colonial society and provided significant capital for the rapidly developing economy of England.

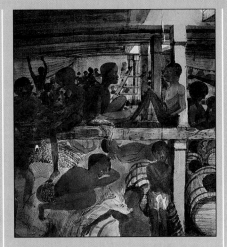

(National Maritime Museum, London)

Thus, slavery served the interests of a powerful combination of groups: planters, merchants, governments, industrialists, and consumers. Race may have been a rationale for slavery, allowing planters and traders to justify to themselves the terrible human costs of the system. But the most important reason for the system was not racism, but the pursuit of profit—and the success of the system in producing it. Slavery was not, according to Blackburn, an antiquated remnant of an older world. It was, he uncomfortably concludes, a recognizably modern labor system that, however horrible, served the needs of an emerging market economy.

the mainland. Most blacks who ended up in what became the United States spent time first in the West Indies. Not until the 1670s did traders start importing blacks directly from Africa to North America. Even then, however, the flow remained small for a time, mainly because a single group, the Royal African Company of England, maintained a monopoly on trade in the mainland colonies and managed as a result to keep prices high and supplies low.

A turning point in the history of the African population in North America came in the mid-1690s, when the Royal African Company's monopoly was finally broken. With the trade now opened to English and colonial merchants on a competitive basis, prices fell and the number of Africans arriving in North America rapidly increased. By the end of the century, only about one in ten of the residents of the colonies was African (about 25,000 in all). But because Africans were so heavily concentrated in a few southern colonies, they were already beginning to outnumber Europeans in some areas. The high ratio of men to women among African immigrants (there were perhaps two males to one female in most areas) retarded the natural increase of the black population. But in the Chesapeake at least, more new slaves were being born by 1700 than were being imported from Africa. In South Carolina, by contrast, the difficult conditions of rice cultivation—and the high death rates of those who worked in the rice

Growing Slave Population

AFRICANS BOUND FOR AMERICA Shown here are the below-deck slave quarters of a Spanish vessel en route to the West Indies. A British warship captured the slaver, and a young English naval officer (Lt. Francis Meynell) made this watercolor sketch on the spot. The Africans seen in this picture appear somewhat more comfortable than prisoners on some other slave ships, who were often chained and packed together so tightly that they had no room to stand or even sit. *(National Maritime Museum, London)*

fields—ensured that the black population would barely be able to sustain itself through natural increase until much later.

Between 1700 and 1760, the number of Africans in the colonies increased tenfold to about a quarter of a million. A relatively small number (16,000 in 1763) lived in New England; there were slightly more (29,000) in the middle colonies. The vast majority, however, continued to live in the South. By then the flow of free white laborers to that region had all but stopped, and Africans had become securely established as the basis of the southern work force.

It was not entirely clear at first that the status of black laborers in America would be fundamentally different from that of white indentured servants. In the rugged conditions of the seventeenth-century South, it was often *Uncertain Status* difficult for Europeans and Africans to maintain strictly separate roles. In some areas—South Carolina, for example, where the number of African arrivals swelled more quickly than anywhere else—whites and blacks lived and worked together for a time on terms of relative equality. Some blacks were treated much like white hired servants, and some were freed after a fixed term of servitude. A few Africans themselves became landowners, and some apparently owned slaves of their own.

By the early eighteenth century, however, a rigid distinction had become established between black and white. (See "Where Historians Disagree," pp. 72–73.) Masters were contractually obliged to free white servants after a fixed term of servitude. There was no such necessity to free black workers, and the assumption slowly spread that blacks would remain in service permanently. Another incentive for making the status of Africans rigid was that the children of slaves provided white landowners with a self-perpetuating labor force.

White assumptions about the inferiority of people of color contributed to the growing rigidity of the system. Such assumptions came naturally to the English settlers. They had already defined themselves as a superior race in their relations with the native Indian population (and earlier in their relations with the Irish). The idea of subordinating a supposedly inferior race was, therefore, already established in the English imagination by the time substantial numbers of Africans appeared in America.

In the early eighteenth century, colonial assemblies began to pass "slave codes," limiting the rights of blacks in law and ensuring almost absolute authority to white masters. One factor, and one factor only, determined whether a person *Slave Codes* was subject to the slave codes: color. In contrast to the colo-

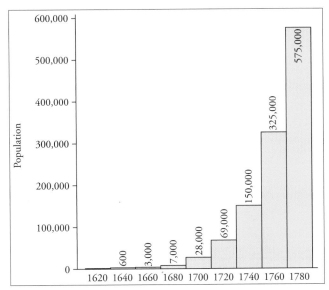

THE AFRICAN POPULATION OF THE BRITISH COLONIES, 1620–1780 From tiny beginnings in the seventeenth century, the African population of the British colonies grew rapidly in the eighteenth century. The growth of slavery was a result of both supply (a readily available population of African workers in the Caribbean islands) and demand (the growth of tobacco, rice, and cotton cultivation in larger areas of the South). The slave population in the colonies also increased naturally in this period at a far greater rate than in the past, largely because living conditions for African workers improved. ◆ *Why would slaveowners have invested in better conditions for their slaves?*

THE PENNSYLVANIA DUTCH This painting of a gentleman in traditional dress was a familiar subject of Pennsylvania Dutch folk art in the eighteenth century. The Pennsylvania Dutch were, in fact, German immigrants. They were known to their neighbors in Pennsylvania as "Dutch" because that was how their native word for their nationality ("Deutsch") sounded to most English-speakers. *(Free Library of Philadelphia)*

nial societies of Spanish America, where people of mixed race had a different (and higher) status than pure Africans, English America recognized no such distinctions. Any African ancestry was enough to classify a person as black.

Changing Sources of European Immigration

The diverse character of the early colonial population was a result of the mingling of the English with Indians and Africans. But it was also a result of substantial immigration from other parts of Europe. By the early eighteenth century, the flow of immigrants from England itself began to decline substantially—a result of better economic conditions there and of new government restrictions on emigration in the face of massive depopulation in some regions of the country. But as English immigration declined, French, German, Swiss, Irish, Welsh, Scottish, and Scandinavian immigration continued and increased.

The earliest, although not the most numerous, of these non-English European immigrants were the French Calvinists, or Huguenots. A royal proclamation, the Edict of Nantes of 1598, had allowed them to become practically a state within the state in Roman Catholic France. In 1685, however, the French government revoked the edict.

Huguenots and Pennsylvania Dutch

Soon after that, Huguenots began leaving the country. A total of about 300,000 left France in the following decades, and a small proportion of them

traveled to the English colonies in North America. Many German Protestants suffered similarly from the arbitrary religious policies of their rulers; and all Germans, Catholics as well as Protestants, suffered from the devastating wars with King Louis XIV of France (the "Sun King"). The Rhineland of southwestern Germany, the area known as the Palatinate, experienced particular hardships. Because it was close to France, its people were particularly exposed to slaughter and their farms to ruin at the hands of invaders. The unusually cold winter of 1708–1709 dealt a final blow to the precarious economy of the region. More than 12,000 Palatinate Germans sought refuge in England, and approximately 3,000 of them soon found their way to America. They arrived in New York and tried at first to make homes in the Mohawk Valley, only to be ousted by the powerful landlords of the region. Some of the Palatines moved farther up the Mohawk, out of reach of the patroons; but most made their way to Pennsylvania, where they received a warm welcome (and where they ultimately became known to

IMMIGRANT GROUPS IN COLONIAL AMERICA, 1760 Even though the entire Atlantic seaboard of what is now the United States had become a series of British colonies by 1760, the population consisted of people from many nations. As this map reveals, English settlers dominated most of the regions of North America. But note the large areas of German settlement in the western Chesapeake and Pennsylvania; the swath of Dutch settlement in New York and New Jersey; the Scotch-Irish regions in the western regions of the South; and the large areas in which Africans were becoming the majority of the population, even if subjugated by the white minority. ◆ *What aspects of the history of these colonies help explain their ethnic composition?*

 For an interactive version of this map go to www.mhhe.com/brinkley11ch3maps

English settlers as the "Pennsylvania Dutch," a corruption of their own word for "German": "Deutsch"). The Quaker colony became the most common destination for Germans, who came to America in growing numbers. (Among them were Moravians and Mennonites, with religious views similar in many ways to those of the Quakers.) Many German Protestants went to North Carolina as well, especially after the founding of New Bern in 1710 by a company of 600 German-speaking Swiss.

The most numerous of the newcomers were the Scotch-Irish—Scottish Presbyterians who had settled in

northern Ireland (in the province of Ulster) in the early seventeenth century. The Ulster colonists had prospered for a time despite the barren soil and the constant, never wholly successful, struggle to suppress the Catholic natives. But in the first years of the eighteenth century, Parliament prohibited Ulster from exporting to England the woolens and other products that had become the basis of the northern Irish economy; at the same time, the English government virtually outlawed the practice of the Presbyterian religion in Ulster and insisted on conformity with the Anglican church. After 1710, moreover, the long-term leases of many Scotch-Irish expired; English landlords doubled and even tripled the rents. Thousands of tenants embarked for America.

Often coldly received at the colonial ports, many of the Scotch-Irish pushed out to the edges of European settlement. There they occupied land without much regard for who actually claimed to own it, whether absentee whites, Indians, or the colonial governments. They believed that, as one colonist said "it was against the laws of God and nature that so much land should

Scotch-Irish | be idle while so many Christians wanted it to labor on and to raise bread." They were as ruthless in their displacement and suppression of the Indians as they had been with the native Irish Catholics.

Immigrants from Scotland itself and from southern Ireland added other elements to the colonial population in the eighteenth century. Scottish Highlanders, some of them Roman Catholics who had been defeated in rebellions in 1715 and 1745, immigrated into several colonies, North Carolina above all. Presbyterian Lowlanders, faced in Scotland with high rents in the country and unemployment in the towns, left for America in large numbers shortly before the American Revolution, joining earlier groups of Scots, who had arrived in the late seventeenth century. They became a significant influence in New Jersey and Pennsylvania and helped established Presbyterianism as an important religion in those colonies. The Catholic Irish migrated steadily over a long period, and by the time of the Revolution they were almost as numerous as the Scots, although less conspicuous. Many of them had by then abandoned their Roman Catholic religion and with it much of their ethnic identity.

Continuing immigration and natural increase contributed to a rapid population growth in the colonies in the eighteenth century. In 1700, the non-Indian population of the colonies totaled less than 250,000; by 1775, it was over 2 million—a nearly tenfold increase. Throughout the colonial period, the non-Indian population nearly doubled every twenty-five years.

THE COLONIAL ECONOMIES

To those who remained in Europe, and even to some who settled in North America, the English colonies often appeared so small and isolated as to seem virtually at the end of the world. But from the beginning, almost all the English colonies were commercial ventures and were

Rapid Population Growth | tied in crucial ways to other economies. They developed substantial trade with the native population of North America, with the French settlers to the north, and, to a lesser extent, with Spanish colonists to the south and west. And over time they developed an even more substantial trade within the growing Atlantic economy of the sixteenth and seventeenth centuries, of which they became a critical part.

American colonists engaged in a wide range of economic pursuits. But except for a few areas in the West where the small white populations subsisted largely on the fur and skin trade with the Indians, farming dominated all areas of European and African settlement throughout the seventeenth and eighteenth centuries. Some farmers engaged in simple subsistence agriculture; but whenever possible American farmers attempted to grow crops for the local, intercolonial, and export markets.

The Southern Economy

In the Chesapeake region, tobacco early established itself as the basis of the economy. A strong European demand for the crop enabled some planters to grow enormously wealthy and at times allowed the region as a whole to pros-

Tobacco

per. But production frequently exceeded demand, and as a result the price of tobacco periodically suffered severe declines. The first major bust in the tobacco economy occurred in 1640, and the boom-and-bust pattern continued throughout the colonial period and beyond. Growing more tobacco only made the problem of overproduction worse, but Chesapeake farmers never understood that. Those planters who could afford to do so expanded their landholdings, enlarged their fields, and acquired additional laborers. After 1700, tobacco plantations employing several dozen slaves or more were common.

The staple of the economies of South Carolina and Georgia was rice production. By building dams and dikes along the low-lying coastline with its many tidal rivers, farmers managed to create rice paddies that could be flooded and then drained. Rice cultivation was arduous work, performed standing knee-deep in the mud of malarial swamps under a blazing sun, surrounded by insects. It was a task so difficult and unhealthful that white laborers generally refused to perform it. As a result, planters in South Carolina and Georgia were even more dependent than those elsewhere on African slaves. It was not only because Africans could be compelled to perform these difficult tasks that whites found them so valuable. It was also because they were much better at the work than whites. They showed from the beginning a greater resistance than whites to malaria and other local diseases (although the impact of disease on African workers was by no means inconsiderable). And they proved more adept at performing the basic agricultural tasks required, in part because some of them had come from rice-producing regions of west Africa (a fact that has led some historians to argue that Africans were responsible for introducing rice cultivation to America in the early seventeenth century). It was also because most Africans were more accustomed to hot and humid climates such as those of the rice-growing regions than were the Europeans.

In the early 1740s, another staple crop contributed to the South Carolina economy: indigo. Eliza Lucas, a young

SELLING TOBACCO This late-seventeenth-century label was used in the sale of American tobacco in England. The drawing depicts Virginia as a land of bright sunshine, energetic slaves, and prosperous, pipe-smoking planters. *(American Heritage)*

Antiguan woman who managed her family's North American plantations, experimented with cultivating the West

Indigo

Indian plant (which was the source of a blue dye in great demand in Europe) on the mainland. She discovered that it could grow on the high ground of South Carolina, which was unsuitable for rice planting, and that its harvest came while the rice was still growing. Indigo became an important complement to rice and a popular import in England.

Because of the South's early dependence on large-scale cash crops, the southern colonies developed less of a commercial or industrial economy than the colonies of the North. The trading in tobacco and rice was handled largely by merchants based in London and, later, in the northern colonies. Few cities of more than modest size developed in the South. No substantial local merchant communities emerged. A pattern was established that would characterize the southern economy, and differentiate it from that of other regions, for more than two centuries.

Northern Economic and Technological Life

In the North, as in the South, agriculture continued to dominate, but it was agriculture of a more diverse kind. Agriculture, however, did not remain the only major economic activity in the North because conditions for farming were less favorable there than in the South. In northern New England, in particular,

More Diverse Agriculture in the North

colder weather and hard, rocky soil made it difficult for colonists to develop the kind of large-scale commercial farming system that southerners were creating. Conditions for agriculture were better in southern New England and the middle colonies, where the soil was fertile and the weather more temperate. New York, Pennsylvania, and the Connecticut River valley were the chief suppliers of wheat to much of New England and to parts of the South. Even there, however, a substantial commercial economy emerged alongside the agricultural one.

Almost every colonist engaged in a certain amount of industry at home. Occasionally these home industries provided families with surplus goods they could trade or sell. Beyond these domestic efforts, craftsmen and artisans established themselves in colonial towns as cobblers, blacksmiths, riflemakers, cabinetmakers, silversmiths, and printers. In some areas, entrepreneurs harnessed water power to run small mills for grinding grain, processing cloth, or milling lumber. And in several places, large-scale shipbuilding operations began to flourish.

The first effort to establish a significant metals industry in the colonies was an ironworks established in Saugus, Massachusetts, in the 1640s after iron ore deposits had been discovered in the region. Iron technology was already advancing rapidly in England, and the colonists attempted to transfer those skills to America. The Saugus works used water power to drive a bellows, which controlled the heat in a charcoal furnace. The carbon from the burning charcoal helped remove the oxygen from the ore and thus reduced its melting temperature. As the ore melted, it trickled down into molds or was taken in the form of simple "sow bars" to a nearby forge to be shaped into iron objects such as pots and anvils. There was also a mill suitable for turning the "sow bars" into narrow rods that blacksmiths could cut into nails. The Saugus works was a technological success; indeed, it could boast technological capabilities equal to any ironworks in Europe at the time. But it was a financial failure.

Saugus Ironworks

It began operations in 1646; in 1668, its financial problems forced it to close its doors.

Metal works, however, gradually became an important part of the colonial economy. The largest industrial enterprise anywhere in English North America was the ironworks of the German ironmaster Peter Hasenclever in northern New Jersey. Founded in 1764 with British capital, it employed several hundred laborers, many of them imported from ironworks in Germany. There were other, smaller ironmaking enterprises in every northern colony (with particular concentrations in Massachusetts, New Jersey, and Pennsylvania), and there were ironworks as well in several of the southern colonies. Even so, these and other growing industries did not become the basis for the kind of explosive industrial growth that Great Britain experienced in the late eighteenth century—in part because English parliamentary regulations such as the Iron Act of 1750 restricted metal processing in the colonies. Similar prohibitions limited the manufacture of

COMMERCE IN NEW ENGLAND This late-eighteenth-century painting of the home, wharves, countinghouse, and fleet of a prosperous New England fisherman gives some indication of how commerce was expanding even in such relatively small places as Duxbury, Massachusetts. The owner, Joshua Winsor, was active in the mackerel and cod fishing industry. The painting—evidently an effort to celebrate Winsor's great material success and record it for posterity—was by his son-in-law, Dr. Rufus Hathaway. *(A View of Mr. Joshua Winsor's House, 1793–95. By Rufus Hathaway. Museum of American Folk Art, New York. Promised anonymous gift.)*

woolens, hats, and other goods. But the biggest obstacles to industrialization in America were an inadequate labor supply, a small domestic market, and inadequate transportation facilities and energy supplies.

More important than manufacturing were industries that exploited the natural resources of the continent. By the mid-seventeenth century, the flourishing fur trade of earlier years was in decline. Taking its place were lumbering, mining, and fishing, particularly in the waters off the New England coast. These industries provided commodities that could be exported to England in exchange for manufactured goods. And they helped produce the most distinctive feature of the northern economy: a thriving commercial class.

Extractive Industries

The Extent and Limits of Technology

Despite the technological progress that was occurring in some parts of America in the seventeenth and eighteenth centuries, much of colonial society was conspicuously lacking in even very basic technological capacities. Up to half the farmers in the colonies were so primitively equipped that they did not even own a plow. Substantial numbers of households owned no pots or kettles for cooking. And only about half the households in the colonies owned guns or rifles—with rural people almost as unlikely to have firearms as urban people. The relatively low levels of ownership of these and other elementary tools was not because such things were difficult to make, but because most Americans remained too poor or too isolated to be able to afford them. Many households had few if any candles, because they were unable to afford candle molds or tallow (wax), or because they had no access to commercially produced candles. In the early eighteenth century, very few farmers owned wagons. Most made do with two-wheeled carts, which could be hauled by hand (or by horse) around the farm but which were not very efficient for transporting crops to market. The most commonly owned tool on American farms was the axe, which suggests how much time most farmers had to spend clearing land.

Even so, few colonists were self-sufficient in the late seventeenth and early eighteenth centuries. The popular image of early American households is of people who had little connection to the market, who grew their own food, made their own clothes, and bought little from anyone else. In fact, relatively few colonial families owned spinning wheels or looms, which suggests that most people purchased whatever yarn and cloth they needed, or could afford, from merchants. Most farmers who grew grain took it to centralized facilities for processing.

Myth of Self-Sufficiency

In general, unsurprisingly, people who lived in isolated or poor areas owned fewer tools and had less access to advanced technologies than did those in more populous or affluent areas. But throughout the colonies, the ability of people to acquire manufactured implements lagged far behind the economy's capacity to produce them.

The Rise of Colonial Commerce

Perhaps the most remarkable feature of colonial commerce in the seventeenth century was that it was able to survive at all. American merchants faced such bewildering and intimidating obstacles, and lacked so many of the basic institutions of trade, that they managed to stay afloat only with great difficulty. There was, first, no commonly accepted medium of exchange. The colonies had almost no specie (gold or silver coins). They experimented at times with different forms of paper currency—tobacco certificates, for example, which were secured by tobacco stored in warehouses; or land certificates, secured by property. Such paper was not, however, acceptable as payment for any goods from abroad and it was in any case ultimately outlawed by Parliament. For many years, colonial merchants had to rely on a haphazard barter system or on crude money substitutes such as beaver skins.

Shortage of Currency

A second obstacle was the near impossibility of imposing order on their trade. In the fragmented, jerry-built commercial world of colonial America, no merchants could be certain that the goods on which their commerce relied would be produced in sufficient quantity; nor could they be certain of finding adequate markets for them. Few channels of information existed to inform traders of what they could expect in foreign ports; vessels sometimes stayed at sea for several years, journeying from one market to another, trading one commodity for another, attempting to find some way to turn a profit. Engaged in this chaotic commerce, moreover, were an enormous number of small, fiercely competitive companies, which made the problem of stabilizing the system even more acute.

Despite these and other problems, commerce in the colonies not only survived but grew. There was an elaborate coastal trade, through which the colonies did business with one another and with the West Indies, largely in such goods as rum, agricultural products, meat, and fish. The mainland colonies received sugar, molasses, and slaves from the Caribbean markets in return. There was as well an expanding transatlantic trade, which linked the North American colonies in an intricate network of commerce with England, continental Europe, and the west coast of Africa. This commerce has often been described, somewhat inaccurately, as the "triangular trade," suggesting a neat process: merchants carried rum and other goods from New England to Africa; exchanged their merchandise for slaves, whom they then transported to the West Indies (hence the term "middle passage" for the dreaded journey—it was the second of the three legs of the voyage); and then exchanged the slaves for sugar and molasses,

Triangular Trade

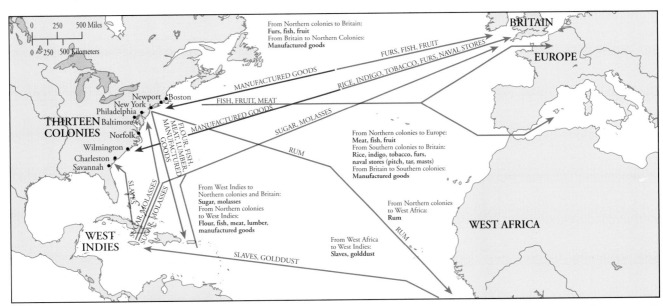

From Northern colonies to Britain:
Furs, fish, fruit
From Britain to Northern Colonies:
Manufactured goods

FURS, FISH, FRUIT

MANUFACTURED GOODS

RICE, INDIGO, TOBACCO, FURS, NAVAL STORES

BRITAIN

EUROPE

THIRTEEN COLONIES

Newport · Boston
New York
Philadelphia ·
Baltimore ·
Norfolk ·
Wilmington ·
Charleston ·
Savannah ·

FISH, FRUIT, MEAT

MANUFACTURED GOODS

SUGAR, MOLASSES

FLOUR, FISH, MEAT, LUMBER, MANUFACTURED GOODS

RUM

From Northern colonies to Europe:
Meat, fish, fruit
From Southern colonies to Britain:
**Rice, indigo, tobacco, furs,
naval stores (pitch, tar, masts)**
From Britain to Southern colonies:
Manufactured goods

From West Indies to
Northern colonies and Britain:
Sugar, molasses
From Northern colonies
to West Indies:
**Flour, fish, meat, lumber,
manufactured goods**

From Northern colonies
to West Africa:
Rum

WEST AFRICA

SLAVES
SUGAR, MOLASSES
SUGAR, MOLASSES

RUM

WEST INDIES

From West Africa
to West Indies:
Slaves, golddust

SLAVES, GOLDDUST

0   250   500 Miles
0   250   500 Kilometers

THE "TRIANGULAR TRADE" This map illustrates the complex pattern of trade that fueled the colonial American economy in the seventeenth and eighteenth centuries. A simple explanation of this trade is that the American colonies exported raw materials (agricultural products, furs, and others) to Britain and Europe and imported manufactured goods in return. But while that explanation is accurate, it is not complete, largely because the Atlantic trade was not a simple exchange between America and Europe, but a complex network of exchanges involving the Caribbean, Africa, and the Mediterranean. Note the important exchanges between the North American mainland and the Caribbean islands; the important trade between the American colonies and Africa; and the wide range of European and Mediterranean markets in which Americans were active. Not shown on this map, but also very important to colonial commerce, was a large coastal trade among the various regions of British North America. ◆ *Why did the major ports of trade emerge almost entirely in the northern colonies?*

 For an interactive version of this map go to www.mhhe.com/brinkley11ch3maps

which they shipped back to New England to be distilled into rum. In fact, the system was almost never so simple. The "triangular" trade in rum, slaves, and sugar was in fact part of a maze of highly diverse trade routes: between the northern and southern colonies, America and England, America and Africa, the West Indies and Europe, and other combinations.

Out of this complex and highly risky trade emerged a group of adventurous entrepreneurs who by the mid-eighteenth century were beginning to constitute a distinct merchant class. Concentrated in the port cities of the North (above all, Boston, New York, and Philadelphia), they enjoyed protection from foreign competition within the English colonies—the British Navigation Acts had excluded all non-British ships from the colonial carrying trade. They

Emerging Merchant Class

had access to a market in England for such American products as furs, timber, and ships. That did not, however, satisfy all their commercial needs. Many colonial products—fish, flour, wheat, and meat, all of which England could produce for itself—required markets altogether outside the British empire. Ignoring laws restricting colonial trade to England and its possessions, many merchants developed markets in the French, Spanish, and Dutch West Indies, where prices were often higher than in the British colonies. The profits from this commerce enabled the colonies to import the manufactured goods they needed from Europe.

In the course of the eighteenth century, the colonial commercial system began to stabilize. In some cities, the more successful merchants expanded their operations so greatly that they were able to dominate some sectors of trade and curb some of the destabilizing effects of competition. Merchants managed, as well, to make extensive contacts in the English commercial world, securing their positions in certain areas of transatlantic trade. But the commercial sector of the American economy remained open to newcomers, largely because it—and the society on which it was based—was expanding so rapidly.

The Rise of Consumerism

Among relatively affluent residents of the colonies, the growing prosperity and commercialism of British America created both new appetites and new opportunities to satisfy them. The result was a growing preoccupation with the consumption of material goods—and of the association of possessions with social status.

One thing that spurred the growth of eighteenth-century consumerism was the increasing division of American societies by class. As the difference between the upper and lower classes became more glaring, people of means became more intent on demonstrating their own membership in the upper ranks of society. The ability to purchase and display consumer goods was an important way of doing so, particularly for affluent people in cities and towns, who did not have large estates with which they could demonstrate their success. But the growth of

Growing Consumerism

consumerism was also a product of the early stages of the industrial revolution. Although there was relatively little industry in America in the eighteenth century, England and Europe were making rapid advances and producing more and more affordable goods for affluent Americans to buy. The new manufacturing was dependent, of course, on customers for its products. In an increasingly commericial society, therefore, there were many people committed to creating a social climate in which purchasing consumer goods could be considered a positive social good.

To facilitate the new consumer appetites, merchants and traders began advertising their goods in journals and newspapers. Agents of urban merchants—the ancestors of the traveling salesman—fanned out through the countryside, attempting to interest wealthy landowners and planters in the luxury goods now available to them. George and Martha Washington, for example, spent considerable time and money ordering elegant furnishings for their home at Mount Vernon, goods that were shipped to them mostly from England and Europe.

One feature of a consumer society is that things that once were considered luxuries quickly come to be seen as necessities once they are readily available. In the colonies, items that became commonplace after having once been expensive luxuries included tea, household linens, glassware, manufactured cutlery, crockery, and furniture,

Social Consequences

and many other things. Another result of consumerism is the association of material goods—of the quality of a person's home and possessions and clothing, for example—with virtue and "refinement." The ideal of the cultivated "gentleman" and the gracious "lady" became increasingly powerful throughout the colonies in the eighteenth century, and many colonists strove to emulate that ideal. In part that meant striving to become educated and "refined"—"gentlemanly" or "ladylike" in speech and behavior. Americans read books on manners and fashion. They bought magazines about London society. And they strove to develop themselves as witty and educated conversationalists. They also commissioned portraits of themselves and their families, devoted large portions of their homes to entertainment, built shelves and cases in which they could display

TEA PARTY IN THE TIME OF GEORGE I This painting by an unknown artist dates from the 1720s and shows a prosperous Virginian posing with a fashionable and expensive tea service, some of it from China. His eagerness to display his possessions in this way is a sign of the growing interest in the badges of refinement among colonial Americans of means in the eighteenth century. *(Colonial Williamsburg Foundation)*

fashionable possessions, constructed formal gardens, and lavished attention on their wardrobes and hairstyles.

The growing importance of consumption and refinement was visible in the public spaces as well. Eighteenth-century cities—in America as in England and Europe—began to plan their growth to ensure that there would be elegant and gracious public squares, parks, and boulevards. In the past, social interaction in American communities had largely been between neighbors and relatives, or at most among members of church congregations. Now that a wider "society" was emerging within cities, it became important to create not just private but also public stages for social display.

PATTERNS OF SOCIETY

Although there were sharp social distinctions in the colonies, the well-defined and deeply entrenched class system of England failed to reproduce itself in America. In England, where land was scarce and the population large, the relatively small number of people who owned property had enormous power over the great majority who did not; the imbalance between land and population became a foundation of the English economy and the *Social Mobility* cornerstone of its class system. In America, the opposite was true. Land was abundant, and people were scarce. Aristocracies emerged in America, to be sure. But they tended to rely less on landownership than on control of a substantial work force, and they were generally less secure and less powerful than their English counterparts. Far more than in England, there were opportunities in America for social mobility—both up and down.

There emerged, too, new forms of community whose structure reflected less the British model than the realities of the American environment. These forms varied greatly from one region to another, but several basic—and distinctly American—types emerged.

The Plantation

The plantation defined a distinctive way of life for many white and black southerners that would survive, in varying forms, until the Civil War. The first plantations emerged in the early settlements of Virginia and Maryland, once tobacco became the economic basis of the Chesapeake.

In a few cases, plantations were of enormous size—much like some of the great estates of England. The Maryland plantation of Charles Carroll of Carrollton, reputedly the wealthiest man in the colonies, covered 40,000 acres and contained 285 slaves. On the whole, however, seventeenth-century colonial plantations were rough and relatively small estates. In the early days in Virginia, they were little more than crude clearings where landowners and indentured servants worked side by side in conditions so horrible that death was an everyday occurrence. Even in

later years, when the death rate declined and the landholdings became more established, plantation work forces seldom exceeded thirty people.

The economy of the plantation, like all agricultural economies, was a precarious one. In good years, successful growers could earn great profits and expand their operations. But since they could not *Vagaries of the Plantation Economy*

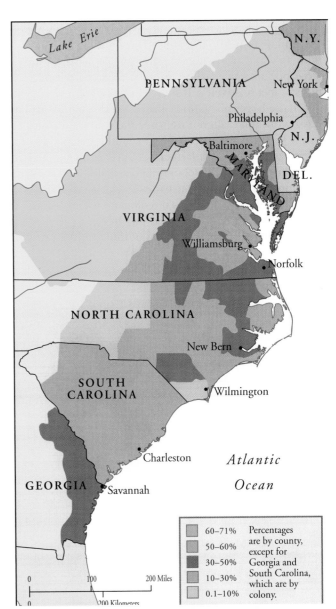

AFRICAN POPULATION AS A PROPORTION OF TOTAL POPULATION, c. 1775 This map illustrates the parts of the colonies in which the slave population was a large proportion of the whole—in some areas actually a majority. The densest African population was in Tidewater Virginia, but there were black majorities as well in South Carolina and parts of North Carolina. The slave population was smallest in the western regions of the southern colonies and in the area north of the Chesapeake, although there remained a significant African population in parts of New Jersey and New York (some slave, some free). ◆ *What explains the dense concentrations of slaves in these areas of the South?*

control their markets, even the largest planters were constantly at risk. When prices for their crops fell—as tobacco prices did, for example, in the 1660s—they faced ruin.

Because plantations were often far from cities and towns—which were, in any case, relatively few in the South—they tended to become self-contained communities. Residents lived in close proximity to one another in a cluster of buildings that included the "great house" of the planter himself (a house that was usually, although not always, far from great), the service buildings, the barns, and the cabins of the slaves. Wealthier planters often created something approaching a full town on their plantations, with a school (for white children only), a chapel, and a large population. Smaller planters lived more modestly, but still in a relatively self-sufficient world.

On the larger plantations, the presence of a substantial slave work force altered not only the economic, but the family lives of the planter class. Plantation mistresses, unlike the wives of small farmers, could rely on servants to perform ordinary household chores and could thus devote more time to their husbands and children than their counterparts in other parts of colonial society. But there were also frequent sexual liaisons between their husbands or sons and black women of the slave community. Southern women generally learned to pretend not to no-

tice these relationships, but they were almost certainly a source of anxiety and resentment. Black women, naturally, had even greater cause to resent such liaisons.

Southern society was highly stratified. Even though the fortunes of planters could rise and fall quickly, at any given time there were always wealthy landowners who exer- *Stratified Southern Society* cised much greater social and economic influence than their less prosperous neighbors. Within given areas, great landowners controlled not only the lives of those who worked on their own plantations but also the livelihoods of small farmers who could not effectively compete with the wealthy planters and thus depended on them to market crops and receive credit. Small farmers, working modest plots of land with few or no slaves to help them, formed the majority of the southern agrarian population, but it was the planters who dominated the southern agrarian economy. Most landowners lived in rough cabins or houses, with their servants or slaves nearby. Relatively few lived in anything resembling aristocratic splendor.

Plantation Slavery

African slaves, of course, lived very differently. On the smaller farms with only a handful of slaves, there was not always a rigid social separation between whites and

MULBERRY PLANTATION, 1770 This painting of a rice plantation in South Carolina is unusual in placing the slave quarters in the forefront of the picture. The steep roofs of the slave cabins, which were built by the slaves themselves, reflected African architectural styles. The high roofs helped keep the cabins cool by allowing the heat to rise into the rafters. The master's house and adjacent chapel, built in more conventionally European style, is in the background. *(*View of Mulberry (House and Street) *by Thomas Coram, Gibbes Museum of Art/Carolina Art Association)*

blacks. But by the mid-eighteenth century, over three-fourths of all blacks lived on plantations of at least ten slaves; nearly half lived in communities of fifty slaves or more. In these larger establishments, Africans developed a society and culture of their own—influenced by their white masters, to be sure, but also partly independent of them.

Although whites seldom encouraged formal marriages among slaves, Africans themselves developed a strong and elaborate family structure. Slaves attempted to construct nuclear families, and they managed at times to build stable households, even to work together growing their own food in gardens provided by their masters. But such efforts were in constant jeopardy. Any family member could be sold at any time to another planter, even to one in another colony. As a result, the black family evolved along lines in many ways different from its white counterpart. Africans placed special emphasis on extended kinship networks. They even created surrogate "relatives" for those who were separated entirely from their own families. They adapted themselves, in short, to difficult conditions over which they had limited control.

African workers also developed languages of their own. In South Carolina, for example, the early slaves communicated with one another in Gullah, a hybrid of English and African tongues, that not only reinforced a sense of

Slave Culture

connection with their African ancestry but enabled them to engage in conversations their white masters could not understand. There emerged, too, a distinctive slave religion, which blended Christianity with African folklore and which became a central element in the emergence of an independent black culture.

Nevertheless, slave society was subject to constant intrusions from and interaction with white society. African house servants, for example, at times lived in what was, by the standards of slavery, great luxury; but they were also isolated from their own community and under constant surveillance from whites. Black women were subject to usually unwanted sexual advances from owners and overseers and hence to bearing mulatto children, who were rarely recognized by their white fathers but who were generally accepted as members of the slave community. On some plantations, African workers received kindness and even affection from their masters and mistresses and at times displayed genuine devotion in return. On others, they encountered physical brutality and occasionally even sadism, against which they were virtually powerless.

There were occasional acts of individual resistance by slaves against masters, and at least twice during the colonial period there were actual slave rebellions. In the most

Stono Rebellion

important such revolt, the so-called Stono Rebellion in South Carolina in 1739, about 100 Africans rose up, seized weapons, killed several whites, and attempted to escape south to Florida. Whites quickly crushed the uprising and

executed most participants. The most frequent form of resistance was simply running away, but for most slaves that provided no real solution either. There was nowhere to go.

Most slaves, male and female, worked as field hands (with women shouldering the additional burdens of cooking and child rearing). But on the larger plantations that aspired to genuine self-sufficiency, some slaves learned trades and crafts: blacksmithing, carpentry, shoemaking, spinning, weaving, sewing, midwifery, and others. These skilled craftsmen and craftswomen were at times hired out to other planters. Some set up their own establishments in towns or cities and shared their profits with their owners. On occasion, they were able to buy their freedom. There was a small free black population living in southern cities by the time of the Revolution.

The Puritan Community

A very different form of community emerged in Puritan New England, but one that was also distinctively American. The characteristic social unit in New England was not the isolated farm, but the town. Each new settlement drew up a "covenant" among its members, binding all residents

Patterns of Settlement

together in a religious and social commitment to unity and harmony. Some such settlements consisted of people who had immigrated to America together (occasionally, entire Puritan congregations who had traveled to the New World as a group). More often, they consisted of people who had met during their voyage or after their arrival in America.

The structure of the towns reflected the spirit of the covenant. Colonists laid out a village, with houses and a meetinghouse arranged around a central pasture, or "common." They also divided up the outlying fields and woodlands of the town among the residents; the size and location of a family's field depended on the family's numbers, wealth, and social station. But wherever their lands might lie, families generally lived in the village with their neighbors close by, reinforcing the strong sense of community.

Once established, a town was generally able to run its own affairs, with little interference from the colonial government. Residents held a yearly "town meeting" to decide important questions and to choose a group of "selectmen," who governed until the next meeting. Only adult males were permitted to participate in the meeting. But

Puritan Democracy

even among them, important social distinctions remained, the most crucial of which was membership in the church. Only those residents who could give evidence of grace, of being among the elect (the "visible saints") confident of salvation as a result of a conversion experience, were admitted to full membership, although other residents of the town were still required to attend church services.

The English system of primogeniture—the passing of all inherited property to the firstborn son—did not take root in New England. Instead, a father divided up his lands among all his sons. His control of this inheritance was one of the most effective means of exercising power over the male members of his family. Often a son would reach his late twenties before his father would allow him to move into his own household and work his own land. Even then, sons would usually continue to live in close proximity to their fathers. Young women were generally more mobile than their brothers, since they did not stand to inherit land; their dowries and their inheritances consisted instead of movable objects (furniture, household goods, occasionally money or precious objects) and thus did not tie them to a particular place.

The early Puritan community, in short, was a tightly knit society. The town as a whole was bound together by its initial covenant, by the centralized layout of the village, by the power of the church, and by the town meeting. The family was held together by the rigid patriarchal structure that limited opportunities for younger members (males in particular) to strike out on their own. Yet as the years passed and the communities grew, this communal structure experienced strains. This was partly because of the increasing commercialization of New England society. But it was also a result of other pressures that developed even within purely agricultural communities, pressures that were a result primarily of population growth.

As towns grew larger, residents tended to cultivate lands farther and farther from the community center. Some moved out of the town center to be nearer their lands and thus began to find themselves far away from the church. Some groups of outlying residents would eventually *Population Pressure* apply for permission to build a church of their own, which was usually the first step toward creation of a wholly new town. Such applications were frequently the occasion for bitter quarrels between the original townspeople and those who proposed to break away.

The practice of distributing land through the patriarchal family structure also helped create tensions in the Puritan community. In the first generations, fathers generally

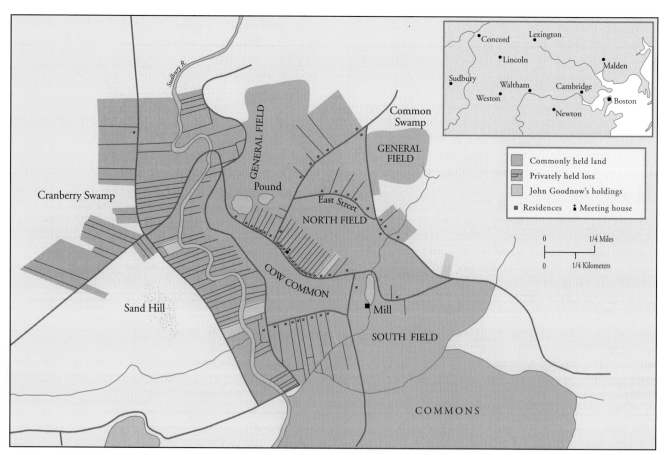

THE NEW ENGLAND TOWN: SUDBURY, MASSACHUSETTS, 17TH CENTURY Just as the plantation was a characteristic social form in the southern colonies, the town was the most common social unit in New England. This map shows the organization of Sudbury, Massachusetts, a town just west of Boston, in its early years in the seventeenth century. Note the location of the houses, which are grouped mostly together around a shared pasture (or "commons") and near the church. Note, too, the outlying fields, which were divided up among residents of the town, even though they were often not connected to the land on which they lived. The map illustrates the holdings of a single resident of Sudbury, John Goodnow, whose house was on the Common, but whose lands were scattered over a number of areas of Sudbury. ◆ *What aspects of New England life might help explain the clustering of residences at the center of the town? (From Sumner Chilton Powell,* Puritan Village: The Formation of a New England Town. *Copyright © 1963 by Wesleyan University. Reprinted by permission from Wesleyan University Press)*

controlled enough land to satisfy the needs of all their sons. After several generations, however, when such lands were being subdivided for the third or fourth time, there was often too little to go around, particularly in communities surrounded by other towns, with no room to expand outward. The result was that in many communities, groups of younger residents began breaking off and moving elsewhere—at times far away—to form towns of their own where land was more plentiful.

Even within the family, economic necessity often undermined the patriarchal model to which most Puritans, in theory at least, subscribed. It was not only the sons

Generational Conflict

who needed their fathers (as a source of land and wealth); fathers needed their sons, as well as their wives and daughters, as a source of labor to keep the farm and the household functioning. Thus, while in theory men had nearly dictatorial control over their wives and children, in reality relationships were more contractual, with the authority of husbands and fathers limited by economic necessity (and, of course, bonds of affection).

The Witchcraft Phenomenon

The gap between the expectation of a cohesive, united community and the reality of an increasingly diverse and fluid one was difficult for early New Englanders to accept. At times, such tensions could produce bizarre and disastrous events. One example was the widespread hysteria in the 1680s and 1690s over supposed witchcraft—the human exercise of Satanic powers—in New England.

The most famous outbreak (although by no means the only one) was in Salem, Massachusetts, where adolescent girls began to exhibit strange behavior and leveled accusations of witchcraft against several West Indian servants steeped in voodoo lore. The hysteria they produced

Salem Witch Trials

spread throughout the town, and before it was over, hundreds of people (most of them women) were accused of witchcraft. As the crisis in Salem grew, accusations shifted from marginal women like the West Indians to more prominent and substantial people. Nineteen residents of Salem were put to death before the trials finally ended in 1692; the girls who had been the original accusers later recanted and admitted that they had made up the story.

But the Salem experience was only one of many. Accusations of witchcraft spread through many New England towns in the early 1690s (and indeed had emerged regularly in Puritan society for many years before). Research into the background of accused witches reveals that most were middle-aged women, often widowed, with few or no children. Many accused witches were of low social position, were often involved in domestic conflicts, had frequently been accused of other crimes, and were considered abrasive by their neighbors. Others were women

A STUDY OF WITCHCRAFT This pamphlet, originally published in 1697 near the height of the witchcraft phenomenon in New England, was one of many contemporary studies to take the idea of witchcraft seriously. Belief in witches as agents of Satan was widespread in early New England society (and in many other parts of the Christian world as well), and many of the charges that seem preposterous in our time appeared entirely plausible, even among educated people, in theirs. *(Courtesy Peabody Essex Museum, Salem, MA)*

who, through inheritance or enterprise, had come into possession of substantial land and property on their own and hence also challenged the gender norms of the community. Puritan society had little tolerance for "independent" women. That so many "witches" were women who were not securely lodged within a male-dominated family structure (and that many seemed openly to defy the passive, submissive norms society had created for them) suggests that tensions over gender roles played a substantial role in generating the crisis.

Above all, however, the witchcraft controversies were a reflection of the highly religious character of these societies. New Englanders believed in the power of Satan and his ability to assert his power in the world. Belief in witchcraft was not a marginal superstition, rejected by the mainstream. It was a common feature of Puritan religious conviction.

Cities

To call the commercial centers that emerged along the Atlantic

Growth of Colonial Cities

coast in the eighteenth century "cities" would be to strain the modern definition of that word. Even the

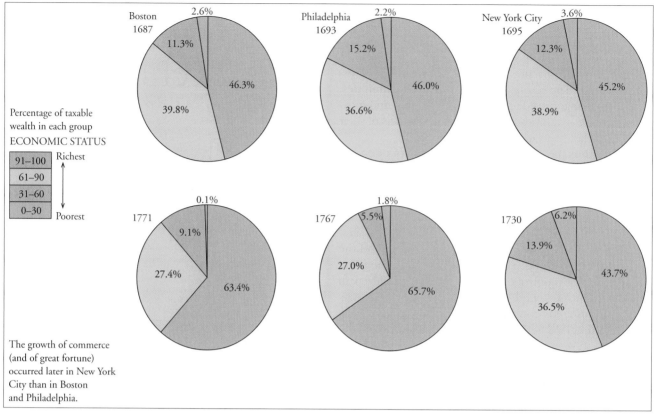

WEALTH DISTRIBUTION IN COLONIAL CITIES, 1687–1771 Although the gap between rich and poor in colonial America was not as large as it would become in the nineteenth and twentieth centuries, the rise of commerce in the early eighteenth century did produce increasing inequality. This chart shows the distribution of wealth in three important commercial cities—Boston, Philadelphia, and New York. The upper pie charts show the distribution of wealth in the late seventeenth century, and the lower charts show how that distribution had changed by the mid or late eighteenth centuries. Note the heavy concentration of wealth in the top ten percent of the population in the seventeenth century, and the even heavier concentration of wealth in Boston and Philadelphia in the eighteenth century. In New York, by contrast, wealth distribution became slightly more equal between 1695 and 1730, because of the breaking up of the great Dutch estates once the colony came under the control of the British. In later years, New York would show the same pattern of growing inequality that Boston and Philadelphia experienced. ◆ *What aspects of colonial commerce helped concentrate so much wealth in the hands of a relatively small group?*

largest colonial community was scarcely bigger than a modern small town. Yet by the standards of the eighteenth century, cities did indeed exist in America. In the 1770s the two largest ports—Philadelphia and New York—had populations of 28,000 and 25,000, respectively, which made them larger than most English urban centers. Boston (16,000), Charles Town (later Charleston), South Carolina (12,000), and Newport, Rhode Island (11,000), were also substantial communities by the standards of the day.

Colonial cities served as trading centers for the farmers of their regions and as marts for international trade. Their leaders were generally merchants who had acquired substantial estates. Disparities of wealth were features of almost all communities in America, but in cities they seemed particularly glaring. Moving beside them were the numerous minor tradesmen, workers, and indigents, dressed simply and living in crowded and often filthy conditions. More than in any other area of colonial

life (except, of course, in the relationship between masters and slaves), social distinctions were real and visible in urban areas.

There were other distinctive features of urban life as well. Cities were the centers of much of what industry there was in the colonies, such as ironworks and distilleries for turning imported molasses into exportable rum. They were the locations of the most advanced schools and the most sophisticated cultural activities, and of shops where imported goods could be bought. In addition, they were communities with peculiarly urban social problems: crime, vice, pollution, epidemics, traffic. Unlike smaller towns, cities were required to establish elaborate governments. They set up constables' offices and fire departments. They developed systems for supporting the urban poor, whose numbers grew steadily and became especially large in times of economic crisis.

Commercial and Cultural Importance

METHODISM IN AMERICA Methodism is the branch of Protestantism derived from the teachings of John Wesley and others, who argued that Christians should live by "rule and method." Methodists were among the first traveling evangelists. One of the most prominent of them in America was George Whitfield, one of the leaders of the Great Awakening. Eventually, Methodism itself split into a number of denominations. This church, the first Episcopal Methodist Church in America, established in New York in 1784, was an example of the splintering of Methodism. *(Museum of the City of New York)*

Cities were also particularly vulnerable to fluctuations in trade. When a market for a particular product became glutted and prices fell, the effects on residents of a town—merchants and those whose livelihoods derived from commerce—could be severe. In the countryside, the impact was generally more muted. Finally, and of particular importance for the political future of the colonies, cities became places where new ideas could circulate and be discussed. Because there were printers, it was possible to have regular newspapers. Books and other publications from abroad introduced new intellectual influences. And the taverns and coffeehouses of cities provided forums in which people could gather and debate the issues of the day. It was not surprising that when the revolutionary crisis began to build in the 1760s and 1770s, it was first visible in the cities.

AWAKENINGS AND ENLIGHTENMENTS

Two powerful forces were competing in American intellectual life in the eighteenth century. One was the traditional outlook of the sixteenth and seventeenth centuries, with its emphasis on a personal God, intimately involved with the world, keeping watch over individual lives. The other was the new spirit of the Enlightenment, a movement that was sweeping both Europe and America, which stressed the importance of science and human reason. The old views supported such phenomena as the belief in witchcraft, and they placed great value on a stern moral code in which intellect was less important than faith. The Enlightenment, by contrast, suggested that people had substantial control over their own lives and the course of their societies, that the world could be explained and therefore could be structured along rational scientific lines. Much of the intellectual climate of colonial America was shaped by the tension between these two impulses.

The Pattern of Religions

Religious toleration flourished in America to a degree unmatched in any European nation, not because Americans deliberately sought to produce it but because conditions virtually required it. Settlers in America brought with them so many different religious practices that it proved impossible to impose a single religious code on any large area.

Roots of Religious Toleration

The Church of England was established as the official faith in Virginia, Maryland, New York, the Carolinas, and Georgia. Except in Virginia and Maryland, however, the laws establishing the Church of England as the official colonial religion were largely ignored. Even in New England, where the Puritans had originally believed that they were all part of a single faith, there was a growing tendency in the eighteenth century for different congregations to affiliate with different denominations, especially Congregationalism and Presbyterianism. In parts of New York and New Jersey, Dutch settlers had established their own Calvinist denomination, Dutch Reformed, which survived after the colonies became part of the British Empire. American Baptists (of whom Roger Williams is considered the first) developed a great variety of sects. All Baptists shared the belief that rebaptism, usually by total immersion, was necessary when believers reached maturity. But while some Baptists remained Calvinists (believers in predestination) others came to believe in salvation by free will.

Protestants extended toleration to one another more readily than they did to Roman Catholics. Many Protestants in America, like many in England, feared and hated the pope. New Englanders, in particular, viewed their Catholic neighbors in New France (Canada) not only as *Anti-Catholicism* commercial and military rivals but also as dangerous agents of Rome. In most of the English colonies, however, Roman Catholics were too few to cause serious conflict. They were most numerous in Maryland, and even there they numbered no more than 3,000. Perhaps for that reason they suffered their worst persecution in that colony. After the overthrow of the original proprietors in 1691, Catholics in Maryland not only lost their political rights but also were forbidden to hold religious services except in private houses.

Jews in provincial America totaled no more than about 2,000 at any time. The largest community lived in New York City. Smaller groups settled in Newport and Charleston, and there were scattered Jewish families in all the colonies. Nowhere could they vote or hold office. Only in Rhode Island could they practice their religion openly.

By the beginning of the eighteenth century, some Americans were growing troubled by the apparent decline in religious piety in their society. The movement of the population westward and the wide scattering of settlements had caused many communities to lose touch with organized religion. The rise of commercial prosperity created a more secular outlook in urban areas. The progress of science and free thought in Europe—and the importation of Enlightenment ideas to America—caused at least some colonists to doubt traditional religious beliefs.

Concerns about weakening piety surfaced as early as the 1660s in New England, where the Puritan oligarchy warned of a decline in the power of the church. Sabbath after Sabbath, ministers preached sermons of despair (known as "jeremiads"), deploring the signs of waning piety. By the standards of other societies or other eras, the Puritan faith remained remarkably strong. But New Englanders measured their faith by their own standards, and to them the "declension" of religious piety seemed a serious problem.

Jeremiads

The Great Awakening

By the early eighteenth century, similar concerns were emerging in other regions and among members of other faiths. Everywhere, colonists were coming to believe, religious piety was in decline and opportunities for spiritual regeneration were dwindling. The result was the first great American revival: the Great Awakening.

The Great Awakening began in earnest in the 1730s, reached its climax in the 1740s, and brought a new spirit of religious fervor that many Americans believed was reversing the trend away from piety. The revival had particular appeal to women (who constituted the majority of converts) and to younger sons of the third or fourth generation of settlers—those who stood to inherit the least land and who faced the most uncertain futures. The rhetoric of the revival emphasized the potential for every person to break away from the constraints of the past and start anew in his or her relationship with God. Such beliefs may have reflected the desires of many people to break away from their families or communities and start a new life.

Powerful evangelists from England helped spread the revival. John and Charles Wesley, the founders of Methodism, visited Georgia and other colonies in the 1730s. George Whitefield, a powerful open-air preacher and for a time an associate of the Wesleys, made several evangelizing tours through the colonies and drew tremendous crowds. But the outstanding preacher of the Great Awakening was the New England Congregationalist Jonathan Edwards, a deeply orthodox Puritan but a highly original theologian. From his pulpit in Northampton, Massachusetts, Edwards attacked the new doctrines of easy salvation for all. He preached anew the traditional Puritan ideas of the absolute sovereignty of God, predestination, and salvation by God's grace alone. His vivid descriptions of hell could terrify his listeners.

The Great Awakening led to the division of existing congregations (between "New Light" revivalists and "Old Light" traditionalists) and to the founding of new ones. It also affected areas of society outside the churches. Some of the revivalists denounced book learning as a hindrance to salvation, and some communities repudiated secular education altogether. But other evangelists saw education as a means of furthering religion, and they founded or led schools for the training of New Light ministers.

Old Lights and New Lights

GEORGE WHITEFIELD Whitefield succeeded John Wesley as leader of the Calvinistic Methodists in Oxford, England. Like Wesley, he was a major force in promoting religious revivalism in both England and America. He made his first missionary journey to the New World in 1738 and returned in the mid-1740s for a celebrated journey through the colonies that helped spark the Great Awakening. *(National Portrait Gallery, London)*

The Enlightenment

The Great Awakening caused one great upheaval in the culture of the colonies. The Enlightenment, a very different—and in many ways competing—phenomenon, caused another. It began in Europe, but it came to America in force in the early eighteenth century.

The Enlightenment was to a large degree the product of some of the great scientific and intellectual discoveries in Europe in the seventeenth century. As scientists and other thinkers discovered natural laws that they believed regulated the workings of nature, they came to celebrate the power of human reason and scientific inquiry. Enlightenment thinkers argued that reason, not just faith, could create progress and advance knowledge. They argued that humans had a moral sense on which they could rely to tell the difference between right and wrong; that they did not need always to turn to God for guidance in

making decisions. They insisted that men and women could, through the power of their own reason, move civilization to ever greater heights.

In celebrating reason, the Enlightenment slowly helped undermine the power of traditional authority—something the Great Awakening did as well. But unlike the Great Awakening, the Enlightenment encouraged men and women to look to themselves—not to God—for guidance as to how to live their lives and to shape society. Enlightenment thought, with its *Traditional Authority Challenged* emphasis on human rationality, encouraged a new emphasis on education. It helped create a heightened interest in politics and government (for through governments, the believers in reason argued, society had its best chance of bettering itself). Most Enlightenment figures did not challenge religion and insisted that rational inquiry would support, not undermine Christianity. But they challenged the notion of some religious groups that the answer to all questions about human society should, or could, come directly from God.

In the early seventeenth century, Enlightenment ideas in America were largely borrowed from abroad—from such earlier giants as Francis Bacon and John Locke, and from contemporary Enlightenment thinkers in England and Scotland. Few Americans had yet made important contributions of their own to the new age of science and reason. Later, however, such Americans as Benjamin Franklin, Thomas Jefferson, Thomas Paine, and James Madison made their own vital contributions to the Enlightenment tradition.

Education

Even before Enlightenment ideas became common in America, colonists had placed a high value on education, despite the difficulties they confronted in gaining access to it. Some families tried to teach their children to read and write at home, although the heavy burden of work in most agricultural households limited the time available for schooling. In Massachusetts, a 1647 law required every town to support a public school, and while many communities failed to comply, a modest network of educational establishments emerged as a result. Elsewhere, the Quakers and other sects operated church schools. And in some communities, widows or unmarried women conducted "dame schools" by holding private classes in their homes. In cities, master craftsmen set up evening schools for their apprentices; at least a hundred such schools appeared between 1723 and 1770.

Only a relatively small number of children received education beyond the primary level; but white male Americans, at least, achieved a high degree of literacy. By the time of *High White Literacy Rates* the Revolution, well over half of all white men could read and write, a rate substantially

Books were scarce and expensive in colonial America, and many families owned only one: the Bible. But starting very early in the life of the English colonies, men and women had another important source of information: almanacs, the most popular nonreligious literature in early America.

Almanacs had been popular in Europe since at least the mid-sixteenth century. They first appeared in America in 1638 or 1639 when printers in Cambridge, Massachusetts began publishing the *Philomath Almanac,* which combined an elaborate calendar of religious holidays with information about astronomy, astrology, and, as time went on, other popular interests. By the 1680s, the *Farmer's Almanac* began to rival the *Philomath.* It was a heavily illustrated publication that set a pattern for the future by adding medical advice, practical wisdom, navigational information, and humor. It also indulged in the European custom of prognostication; through a combination of superstition, popular folklore, and astronomical (and astrological) devices, it predicted weather patterns throughout the year, crop yields, and many other things. Almanac predictions were notoriously unreliable; but in the absence of any better alternatives, many people relied on them nevertheless.

By 1700, there were dozens, perhaps hundreds, of almanacs circulating

POOR RICHARD'S ALMANACK This page from a 1757 edition of *Poor Richard's Almanack* illustrates the wide range of material that almanacs presented to their readers—an uplifting poem, a calendar of holidays and weather predictions, and such scattered pieces of advice and wisdom as "A rich rogue is like a fat hog, who never does good till as dead as a log." *(New York Public Library)*

throughout the colonies and even in the sparsely settled lands to the west and north. The most popular almanacs sold tens of thousands of copies every year. Most families had at least one, and many had several. "It is easy to prove," one almanac writer claimed in the mid-eighteenth century, "that no book we read (except the Bible) is so much valued and so serviceable to the community." America was a multilingual society, and although most almanacs were in English, some appeared in French, Dutch, Hebrew, Norwegian, Spanish, German, and various Indian languages. For five years just after the Revolution, Benjamin Banneker of Maryland was the only African-American almanac writer, publishing a book that occasionally included harsh commentary on slavery and the slave trade.

The best-known almanac in the colonies in the years before the American Revolution was published by Benjamin Franklin, a printer's son who ran away from an apprenticeship in his older brother's print shop in Rhode Island and eventually settled in Philadelphia. There, from 1732 to 1758, he published *Poor Richard's Almanack* under the pseudonym Richard Saunders. "I endeavor'd to make it both entertaining and useful," Franklin later wrote in his autobiography. "And observing that it was generally read, . . . I consider'd it as a proper vehicle for conveying instruction among the com-

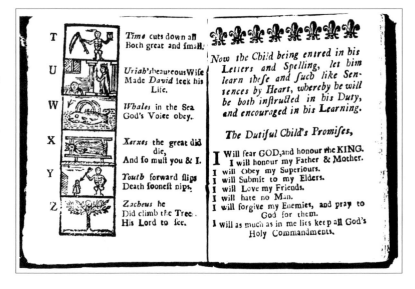

A "DAME SCHOOL" PRIMER More than the residents of any other region of North America (and far more than those of most of Europe), the New England colonists strove to educate their children and achieved perhaps the highest level of literacy in the world. Throughout the region, young children attended institutions known as "dame schools" (because the teachers were almost always women) and learned from primers like this one. Puritan education emphasized both basic skills (the alphabet and reading) and moral and religious precepts, as this sample page suggests. *(American Antiquarian Society)*

mon people, who bought scarcely any other books." In issue after issue, Franklin accompanied his calendars, astronomical information, and other standard almanac fare with "proverbial sentences, chiefly such as inculcated industry and frugality." One of his favorite proverbs, which he said illustrated how difficult it was for a poor man always to act honestly, was "It is hard for an empty sack to stand upright." Poor Richard's many sayings became among the most familiar passages in America. Franklin was among many writers who used the almanac to promote the new scientific discoveries of his time and to try to discredit what he considered the backward superstitions that stood in the way of knowledge. He was particularly contemptuous of astrology.

Almanacs were virtually the only widely read publications in America that contained popular humor, and they are one of the best sources today for understanding what early Americans considered funny. Not unlike later generations, they delighted in humor that ridiculed the high and mighty (aristocrats, lawyers, clergymen, politicians), that made fun of relationships between men and women, and that expressed stereotypes about racial and ethnic groups. In the 1760s and 1770s, almanac humor was often used to disguise political ideas, in the way it

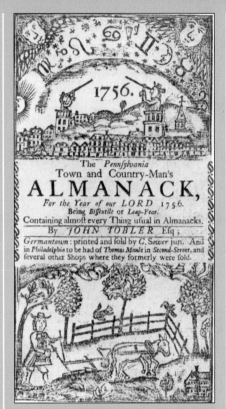

TOWN AND COUNTRY-MAN'S ALMANACK
As the population of colonial cities and towns grew, almanacs—originally targeted mainly at farmers—began to make explicit appeal to townspeople as well. *(Sinclair Hamilton Collection, Princeton, New Jersey)*

ridiculed British officials and American Tories. During the war itself, humorous

anecdotes about military officers and political leaders reflected the uneasy views of Americans about the long and difficult struggle.

During and after the Revolution, much almanac humor consisted of admiring anecdotes about the man who was by then perhaps the most famous and beloved man in America—Poor Richard himself, Benjamin Franklin. Much less reverential, and probably funnier to readers, was the often ribald ethnic and racial humor in many almanacs. In *Beer's Almanac* of 1801, an Irishman boasted that he had owned a large estate in Ireland before leaving for America. Why, he was asked, had he left it to come to the United States? "Ah," he replied, "It was indeed under a small encumbrance; for another man's land lay right a top of it."

Almanacs remained enormously popular throughout the nineteenth century, and some are still published today. But they had their greatest influence in the early years of European settlement when, for thousands of Americans, they were virtually the only source of printed information people had. "A good Almanac," the printer Isaac Briggs wrote in 1798, in a preface to one of his own, "is, like iron, far more valuable (although much less valued) than gold, if we estimate its value by its absolute usefulness to the common purposes of life."

---

higher than in most European countries. The large number of colonists who could read helped create a market for the first widely circulated publications in America other than the Bible: almanacs. (See pp. 92–93.) The literacy rate for women lagged behind that of men until the nineteenth century; and while opportunities for further education were scarce for males, they were almost nonexistent for females. Nevertheless, in their early years colonial girls often received the same home-based education as boys, and their literacy rate too was substantially higher than that of their European counterparts. African slaves had virtually no access to education. Occasionally a master or mistress would teach slave children to read and write, but they had few real incentives to do so. Indeed, as the slave system became more firmly entrenched, strong

social (and ultimately legal) sanctions developed to discourage any efforts to promote black literacy, lest it encourage slaves to question their station. Indians, too, remained largely outside the white educational system—to a large degree by choice; most tribes preferred to educate their children in their own way. But some white missionaries and philanthropists established schools for Native Americans and helped create a small but significant population of Indians literate in spoken and written English.

Nowhere was the intermingling of the influences of traditional religiosity and the new spirit of the Enlightenment clearer than in the colleges and universities that grew up in colonial America. Of the six colleges in operation by 1763, all but two were founded by religious groups primarily for the training of preachers. Yet in almost all, the influences of the new scientific, rational approach to knowledge could be felt. Harvard, the first American college, was established in 1636 by the General Court of Massachusetts at the behest of Puritan theologians, who wanted to create a training center for ministers. Two years later, in 1638, instruction began in Cambridge. The college was named for a Charlestown minister, John Harvard, who had died and left his library and half his estate to the college. Decades later, in 1693, William and Mary College (named for the English king and queen) was established in Williamsburg, Virginia, by Anglicans; like Harvard, it was conceived as an academy to train clergymen. In 1701, conservative Congregationalists, dissatisfied with what they considered the growing religious liberalism of Harvard, founded Yale (named for one of its first benefactors, Elihu Yale) in New Haven, Connecticut. Out of the Great Awakening emerged the College of New Jersey, founded in 1746 and known later as Princeton (after the town in which it is located). One of its first presidents was Jonathan Edwards.

Despite the religious basis of these colleges, students at most of them could derive something of a liberal education from the curricula, which included not only theology, but logic, ethics, physics, geometry, astronomy, rhetoric, Latin, Hebrew, and Greek. From the beginning, Harvard attempted not only to provide an educated ministry but also to "advance learning and perpetuate it to

Liberal Curricula

posterity." Members of the Harvard faculty made strenuous efforts to desseminate new scientific ideas—particularly the ideas of Copernican astronomy—to a larger public, often publishing their ideas in popular almanacs. By doing so, they hoped to stamp out popular belief in astrology, which they considered pagan superstition.

King's College, founded in New York in 1754 and later renamed Columbia, was even more devoted to the spread of secular knowledge. It had no theological faculty and was interdenominational from the start. The Academy and College of Philadelphia, which became the University of Pennsylvania, was a completely secular institution, founded in 1755 by a group of laymen under the inspiration of Benjamin Franklin. It offered courses in utilitarian subjects—mechanics, chemistry, agriculture, government, commerce, and modern languages—as well as in the liberal arts. It also became the site of the first medical school in British America, founded in 1765.

The Spread of Science

The clearest indication of the spreading influence of the Enlightenment in America was an increasing interest in scientific knowledge. Most of the early colleges established chairs in the natural sciences and introduced some of the advanced scientific theories of Europe, including Copernican astronomy and Newtonian physics, to their students. But the most vigorous promotion of science in these years occurred outside the colleges, through the private efforts of amateurs and the activities of scientific societies. Leading merchants, planters, and even theologians became corresponding members of the Royal Society of London, the leading English scientific organization. Benjamin Franklin, the most celebrated amateur scientist in America, won international fame through his experiments with electricity and most notably through his experimental proof of the nature of lightning and electricity and his invention of the lightning rod. His 1752 demonstration, using a kite, of his theory that lightning and electricity were the same was widely celebrated in the colonies.

The high value that influential Americans were beginning to place on scientific knowledge was clearly demonstrated by the most daring and controversial scientific experiment of the eighteenth century: inoculation against

Smallpox Inoculation

smallpox. The Puritan theologian Cotton Mather heard, reportedly from his own slave, of the practice of deliberately infecting people with mild cases of smallpox in order to immunize them against the deadly disease. He learned, too, that experiments in inoculation were being conducted, with some success, in England. Mather was not, certainly, a wholly committed scientist. He continued to believe that disease was a punishment for sin. Yet despite strong opposition from many of his neighbors, he urged inoculation on his fellow Bostonians during an epidemic in the 1720s. The results confirmed the effectiveness of the technique. Other theologians (including Jonathan Edwards) took up the cause, along with many physicians. By the mid-eighteenth century, inoculation had become a common medical procedure in America.

Concepts of Law and Politics

In seventeenth- and eighteenth-century law and politics, as in other parts of their lives, Americans of European descent believed that they were re-creating in the New World the practices and institutions of the Old. But as in other areas, they managed, without meaning to or even realizing it, to create something very different.

Changes in the law in America resulted in part from the scarcity of English-trained lawyers, who were almost unknown in the colonies until after 1700. Not until well into the eighteenth century did authorities in England try to impose the common law and the statutes of the realm upon the provinces. By then, it was already too late. Although the American legal system adopted most of the essential elements of the English system, including such ancient rights as trial by jury, significant differences had already become well established. Pleading and court procedures were simpler in America than in England, and punishments were different. Instead of the gallows or

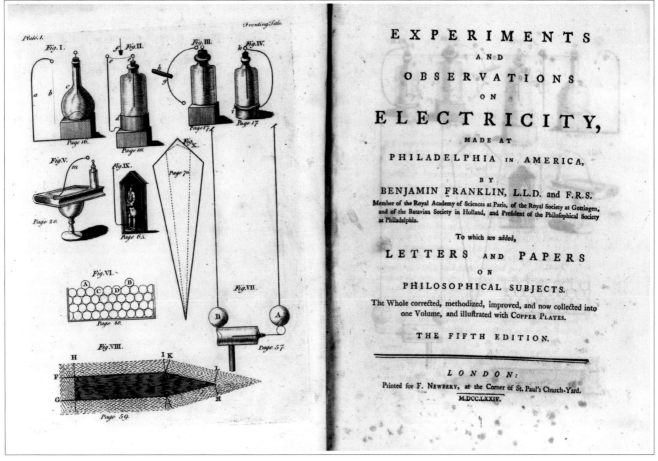

BENJAMIN FRANKLIN ON ELECTRICITY The discovery of electricity was one of the great scientific events of the eighteenth century, even though large-scale practical use of electrical energy emerged much later. Benjamin Franklin was one of the first Americans, and certainly the most famous American, to experiment with electricity. This is the frontispiece for a book, originally published in 1750 in Philadelphia, that describes his "experiments and observations." The pages shown here are from the London edition, which appeared in 1774. (*© Hulton Getty/Getty Images*)

prison, colonists more commonly resorted to the whipping post, the branding iron, the stocks, and (for "gossipy" women) the ducking stool. In a labor-scarce society, it was not in the interests of communities to execute or incarcerate potential workers. Crimes were redefined. In England, a printed attack on a public official, whether true or false, was considered libelous. In the 1734–1735 trial of the New York publisher John Peter Zenger, who was powerfully defended by the Philadelphia lawyer Andrew Hamilton, the courts ruled that criticisms of the government were not libelous if factually true—a verdict that removed some restrictions on the freedom of the press. There was a subtle but decisive transformation in legal philosophy. Some colonists came to think of law as a reflection of the divine will; others saw it as a result of the natural order. In neither case did they consider it an expression of the power of an earthly sovereign.

Even more significant for the future of the relationship between the colonies and England were important emerging differences between the American and British political systems. Because the royal government was so far away, Americans created a group of institutions of their *Colonial Governments* own that gave them—in reality, if not in theory—a large measure of self-government. In most colonies, local communities grew accustomed to running their own affairs with minimal interference from higher authorities. Communities also expected to maintain strict control over their delegates to the colonial assemblies, and those assemblies came to exercise many of the powers that Parliament exercised in England (even though in theory Parliament remained the ultimate authority in America). Provincial governors appointed by the crown had broad powers on paper, but in fact their influence was sharply limited. They lacked control over appointments and

PUNISHMENT IN NEW ENGLAND New England communities prescribed a wide range of punishments for misconduct and crime in the seventeenth and eighteenth centuries. Among the more common punishments were public humiliations—placing offenders in stocks, forcing them to wear badges of shame, or, as in this woodcut, publicly ducking them in a stream or pond to create both discomfort and embarrassment. *(The British Museum)*

contracts; such influence resided largely in England or with local colonial leaders. They could never be certain of their tenure in office; because governorships were patronage appointments, a governor could be removed any time his patron in England lost favor. And in many cases, governors were not even familiar with the colonies they were meant to govern. Some governors were native-born Americans, but most were Englishmen who came to the colonies for the first time to assume their offices. The result of all this was that the focus of politics in the colonies became a local one. The provincial governments became accustomed to acting more or less independently of Parliament, and a set of assumptions and expectations about the rights of the colonists began to take hold in America that policymakers in England did not share. These differences caused few problems before the 1760s, because the British did little to exert the authority they believed they possessed. But when, beginning in 1763, the English government began attempting to tighten its control over the American colonies, a great imperial crisis developed.

CONCLUSION

What began as a few small, isolated, precarious settlements in the wilderness had evolved by the mid-eighteenth century into a large and complex society. The English colonies in America grew steadily between the 1650s and the 1750s: in population, in the size of their economies, and in the sophistication—and diversity—of their cultures. In many ways the colonies had become more like England by the mid-eighteenth century than they had been during their frail early years. In other ways, life in America and life in Britain had begun to diverge.

Many distinct societies developed in the colonies, but the greatest distinction was between the colonies of the North and those of the South. In the North, society was dominated by relatively small family farms and by towns *Regional Differences* and cities of growing size. A thriving commercial class was developing, and with it an increasingly elaborate urban culture. In the South, there were many family farms as well. But there were also large plantations cultivating tobacco, rice, indigo, and cotton for export. By the late sev-

enteenth century, these plantations were relying heavily on African workers who had been brought to the colonies forcibly as slaves. There were few significant towns and cities in the South, and little commerce other than the marketing of crops.

The colonies did, however, also have much in common. Most white Americans accepted common assumptions about racial inequality. That enabled them to tolerate (and at times celebrate) the enslavement of African men and women and to justify a campaign of displacement and often violence against Native Americans that would continue for two centuries. Most white Americans (and, in different ways, most nonwhite Americans as well) were deeply religious. The Great Awakening, therefore, had a powerful impact throughout the colonies, North and South. And most white colonists shared a belief in certain basic principles of law and politics, which they considered embedded in the English constitution, and which in the years after the 1750s would lead to a great imperial crisis.

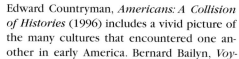

FOR FURTHER REFERENCE

Edward Countryman, *Americans: A Collision of Histories* (1996) includes a vivid picture of the many cultures that encountered one another in early America. Bernard Bailyn, *Voyagers to the West: A Passage in the Peopling of America on the Eve of the Revolution* (1986) reveals the complexity and scope of European emigration to North America. Bailyn's *The Origin of American Politics* (1968) remains an excellent introduction to colonial politics. David Hackett Fischer, *Albion's Seed* (1989) suggests four major folkways for English migrants to America. Jack P. Greene, *Pursuits of Happiness: The Social Development of Early Modern British Colonies and the Formation of American Culture* (1986) is a broad portrait of life in early American communities. Laurel Thatcher Ulrich, *Good Wives: Image and Reality in the Lives of Women in Northern New England,* *1650–1750* (1982) examines women's roles in colonial New England. John Demos, *The Unredeemed Captive: A Family Story of Early America* (1994) is a vivid, unconventional account of the experiences of a New England girl captured by Indians. Robin Blackburn, *The Making of New World Slavery: From the Baroque to the Modern, 1492–1800* (1997) includes an important examination of the character of the institution in colonial America. Kathleen M. Brown, *Good Wives, Nasty Wenches, and Anxious Patriarchs: Gender, Race and Power in Colonial Virginia* (1996) places gender at the center of the development of slavery in the Chesapeake. Rhys Isaac, *The Transformation of Virginia, 1740–1790* (1982) uses the methods of cultural anthropology in an influential study of the world of the colonial Virginia gentry.

OLC

For quizzes, Internet resources, references to additional books and films, and more, consult this book's Online Learning Center at www.mhhe.com/brinkley11.

THE BOSTON MASSACRE (1770), BY PAUL REVERE This is one of many sensationalized engravings, by Revere and others, of the conflict between British troops and Boston laborers that became important propaganda documents for the Patriot cause in the 1770s. Among the victims of the massacre listed by Revere was Crispus Attucks, probably the first black man to die in the struggle for American independence. *(Burstein Collection/Corbis)*

Significant Events

1713 ·	Treaty of Utrecht concludes Queen Anne's War
1718 ·	New Orleans founded to serve French plantation economy in Louisiana
1744–1748 ·	King George's War
1749 ·	French construct fortresses in Ohio Valley
1754 ·	Albany Plan for intercolonial cooperation rejected
·	Battle of Fort Duquesne begins French and Indian War
1756 ·	Seven Years' War begins in Europe
1757 ·	British policies provoke riots in New York
1758 ·	Pitt returns authority to colonial assemblies
·	British capture Louisbourg fortress and Fort Duquesne
1759 ·	British forces under Wolfe capture Quebec
1760 ·	George III becomes king

CHAPTER FOUR

THE EMPIRE IN TRANSITION

s late as the 1750s, few Americans saw any reason to object to their membership in the British Empire. The imperial system provided them with many benefits: opportunities for trade and commerce, military protection, political stability. And those benefits were accompanied by few costs; for the most part, the English government left the colonies alone. While Britain did attempt to regulate the colonists' external trade, those regulations were usually so laxly administered that they could be easily circumvented. Some Americans predicted that the colonies would ultimately develop to a point where greater autonomy would become inevitable. But few expected such a change to occur soon.

By the mid-1770s, however, the relationship between the American colonies and their British rulers had become so strained, so poisoned, so characterized by suspicion and resentment that the once seemingly unbreakable bonds of empire were ready to snap. And in the spring of 1775, the first shots were fired in a war that would ultimately win America its independence.

The revolutionary crisis emerged as a result of both longstanding differences between the colonies and England and particular events in the 1760s and 1770s. Ever since the first days of settlement in North America, the ideas and institutions of the colonies had been *Sources of Crisis* diverging from those in England in countless ways. Only because the relationship between America and Britain had been so casual had those differences failed to create serious tensions in the past. Beginning in 1763, however, the British government embarked on a series of new policies toward its colonies—policies dictated by changing international realities and new political circumstances within England itself—that brought the differences between the two societies into sharp focus. In the beginning, most Americans reacted to the changes with relative restraint. Gradually, however, as crisis followed crisis, a large group of Americans found themselves fundamentally disillusioned with the imperial relationship. By 1775, that relationship was, for all practical purposes, damaged beyond repair.

LOOSENING TIES

After the Glorious Revolution of 1688 in England and the collapse of the Dominion of New England in America, the English government (which became the British government after 1707, when a union of England and Scotland created Great Britain) made no serious or sustained effort to tighten its control over the colonies for over seventy years. During those years, it is true, an increasing number of colonies were brought under the direct control of the king. New Jersey in 1702, North and South Carolina in 1729, Georgia in 1754—all became royal colonies, bringing the total to eight; in all of them, the king had the power to appoint the governors and other colonial officials. During those years, Parliament also passed new laws supplementing the original Navigation Acts and strengthening the mercantilist program— laws restricting colonial manufactures, prohibiting paper currency, and regulating trade. On the whole, however, the British government remained uncertain and divided about the extent to which it ought to interfere in colonial affairs. The colonies were left, within broad limits, to go their separate ways.

A Tradition of Neglect

In the fifty years after the Glorious Revolution, the British Parliament established a growing supremacy over the *Growing Power of Parliament* king. During the reigns of George I (1714–1727) and George II (1727–1760), both of whom were German born and unaccustomed to English ways, the prime minister and his fellow cabinet ministers began to become the nation's real executives. They held their positions not by the king's favor but by their ability to control a majority in Parliament.

These parliamentary leaders were less inclined than the seventeenth-century monarchs had been to try to tighten imperial organization. They depended heavily on the support of the great merchants and landholders, most of whom feared that any such experiments would require large expenditures, would increase taxes, and would diminish the profits they were earning from the colonial trade. The first of the modern prime ministers, Robert Walpole, deliberately refrained from strict enforcement of the Navigation Acts, believing that relaxed trading restrictions would stimulate commerce.

Meanwhile, the day-to-day administration of colonial affairs remained decentralized and inefficient. There was no colonial office in London. The nearest equivalent was the *Decentralized Colonial Administration* Board of Trade and Plantations, established in 1696—a mere advisory body that had little role in any actual decisions. Real authority rested in the Privy Council (the central administrative agency for the government as a whole), the admiralty, and the treasury. But those agencies were responsible for administering laws at home as well as overseas; none could concentrate on colonial affairs alone. To complicate matters further, there was considerable overlapping and confusion of authority among the departments.

Few of the London officials, moreover, had ever visited America; few knew very much about conditions there. What information they did gather came in large part from agents sent to England by the colonial assemblies to lobby for American interests, and these agents, naturally, did nothing to encourage interference with colonial affairs. (The best known of them, Benjamin Franklin, represented not only his own colony, Pennsylvania, but also Georgia, New Jersey, and Massachusetts.)

It was not only the weakness of administrative authority in London and the policy of neglect that weakened England's hold on the colonies. It was also the character of the royal officials in America—among them the governors, the collectors of customs, and naval officers. Some of these officeholders were able and intelligent men; most were not. Appointments generally came as the result of bribery or favoritism, not as a reward for merit. Many appointees remained in England and, with part of their salaries, hired substitutes to take their places in America. Such deputies received paltry wages and thus faced great temptations to augment their incomes with bribes. Few resisted the temptation. Customs collectors, for example, routinely waived duties on goods when merchants paid them to do so. Even honest and well-paid officials usually found it expedient, if they wanted to get along with their neighbors, to yield to the colonists' resistance to trade restrictions.

Resistance to imperial authority centered in the colonial legislatures. By the 1750s the American assemblies had claimed the right to levy taxes, make appropriations, approve appointments, and pass laws for their respective colonies. Their legislation was subject to veto by the governor or the Privy Council. But the assemblies had leverage over the governor through their control of the colonial budget, and they could circum- *Powerful Colonial Legislatures* vent the Privy Council by repassing disallowed laws in slightly altered form. The assemblies came to look upon themselves as little parliaments, each practically as sovereign within its colony as Parliament itself was in England. In 1754, the Board of Trade reported to the king, regarding the members of the New York assembly, that they "have wrested from Your Majesty's governor the nomination of all offices of government, the custody and direction of the public military stores, the mustering and direction of troops raised for Your Majesty's service, and in short almost every other part of executive government."

The Colonies Divided

Despite their frequent resistance to the authority of London, the colonists continued to think of themselves as loyal English subjects. In many respects, in fact, they felt

AN APPEAL FOR COLONIAL UNITY This sketch, one of the first American editorial cartoons, appeared in Benjamin Franklin's Philadelphia newspaper, the *Pennsylvania Gazette*, on May 9, 1754. It was meant to illustrate the need for intercolonial unity and, in particular, for the adoption of Franklin's Albany Plan. *(Library Company of Philadelphia)*

stronger ties to England than they did to one another. "Fire and water," an English traveler wrote, "are not more heterogeneous than the different colonies in North America." New Englanders and Virginians viewed each other as something close to foreigners. A Connecticut man denounced the merchants of New York for their "frauds and unfair practices," while a New Yorker condemned Connecticut because of the "low craft and cunning so incident to the people of that country." Only an accident of geography, it seemed, connected these disparate societies to each other.

Yet for all their differences, the colonies could scarcely avoid forging connections with one another. The growth of the colonial population produced an almost continuous line of settlement along the seacoast and led to the gradual construction of roads and the rise of intercolonial trade. The colonial postal service helped increase communication. In 1691, it had operated only from Massachusetts to New York and Pennsylvania. In 1711, it extended to New Hampshire in the North; in 1732, to Virginia in the South; and ultimately, all the way to Georgia.

Still, the colonists were loath to cooperate even when, in 1754, they faced a common threat from their old rivals, the French, and *Albany Plan* France's Indian allies. A conference of colonial leaders—with delegates from Pennsylvania, Maryland, New York, and New England—was meeting in Albany in that year to negotiate a treaty with the Iroquois, as the British government had advised the colonists to do. The delegates stayed on to talk about forming a colonial federation for defense against the Indians. Benjamin Franklin proposed, and the delegates tentatively approved, a plan by which Parliament would set up in America "one general government" for all the colonies (except Georgia and Nova Scotia). Each colony would "retain its present constitution," but would grant to the new general government such powers as the authority to govern all relations with the Indians. The central government would have a "president general" appointed and paid by the king (just as colonial governors were) and a legislature (a "grand council") elected by the colonial assemblies.

War with the French and Indians was already beginning when this Albany Plan was presented to the colonial assemblies. None approved it. "Everyone cries, a union is necessary," Franklin wrote to the Massachusetts governor, "but when they come to the manner and form of the union, their weak noodles are perfectly distracted."

THE STRUGGLE FOR THE CONTINENT

In the late 1750s and early 1760s, a great war raged through North America, changing forever the balance of power both within the continent and between it and the rest of the world. The war in America was part of a titanic struggle between England and France for dominance in world trade and naval power. The British victory in that struggle, known in Europe as the Seven Years' War, rearranged global power and cemented England's role as the world's great commercial and imperial nation. It also cemented its control of most of the settled regions of North America.

In America, however, the conflict was the final stage in a long battle among the three principal powers in northeastern North America: the English, the French, and the Iroquois. For more than a century prior to the conflict—which was known in America as the French and Indian War—these three groups had maintained an uneasy balance of power. The events of the 1750s upset that balance, produced a prolonged and open conflict, and established a precarious dominance for the English societies throughout the region.

The French and Indian War was important to the English colonists in America for another reason as well. By bringing the Americans into closer contact with British authority than ever before, it raised to the surface some of the underlying tensions in the colonial relationship.

New France and the Iroquois Nation

The French and the English had coexisted relatively peacefully in North America for nearly a century. But by the 1750s, as both English and French settlements expanded, religious and commercial tensions began to produce new frictions and new conflicts. The crisis began in part because of the expansion of the French presence in America in the late seventeenth century—a result of

New Sources of Conflict | Louis XIV's search for national unity and increased world power. France began to devote new attention to the development of its North American territories, and French settlement rapidly expanded. The lucrative fur trade drew immigrant French peasants deeper into the wilderness. Missionary zeal drew large numbers of French Jesuits into the interior in search of potential converts. The bottomlands of the Mississippi River valley attracted French farmers discouraged by the short growing season in Canada.

By the mid-seventeenth century, the French Empire in America comprised a vast territory. Louis Joliet and Father Jacques Marquette, French explorers of the 1670s, journeyed together by canoe from Green Bay on Lake Michigan as far south as the junction of the Arkansas and Mississippi Rivers. A year later, René Robert Cavelier, Sieur de La Salle, began the explorations that in 1682 took him to the delta of the Mississippi, where he claimed the surrounding country for France and named it Louisiana in the king's honor. Subsequent traders and missionaries wandered to the southwest as far as the Rio Grande; and the explorer Pierre Gaultier de Varennes, Sieur de La Verendrye, pushed westward in 1743 from Lake Superior to a point within sight of the Rocky Mountains. The French had by then revealed the outlines of, and laid claim to, the whole continental interior.

To secure their hold on these enormous claims, they founded a string of widely separated communities, *France's North American Empire* | fortresses, missions, and trading posts. Fort Louisbourg, on Cape Breton Island, guarded the approach to the Gulf of St. Lawrence. Would-be feudal lords established large estates (*seigneuries*) along the banks of the St. Lawrence River; and on a high bluff above the river stood the fortified city of Quebec, the center of the French Empire in America. To the south was Montreal, and to the west Sault Sainte Marie and Detroit. On the lower Mississippi emerged plantations much like those in the southern colonies of English America, worked by black slaves and owned by "Creoles" (white immigrants of French descent). New Orleans, founded in 1718 to service the French plantation economy, soon was as big as some of the larger cities of the Atlantic seaboard; Biloxi and Mobile to the east completed the string of French settlement.

But the French were not, of course, alone in the continental interior. They shared their territories with a large and powerful Indian population—in regions now often labeled the "middle ground" (see pp. 59–60)—and their relations with the natives were crucial to the shaping of their empire. They also shared the interior with a growing number of English traders and settlers, who had been moving beyond the confines of the colonial boundaries in the East. Both the French and the English were aware that the battle for control of North America would be determined in part by which group could best win the allegiance of native tribes—as trading partners and, at times, as military allies. The Indians, for their part, were principally concerned with protecting their independence. Whatever alignments they formed with the European societies growing up around them were generally marriages of convenience, determined by which group offered the most attractive terms.

The English—with their more advanced commercial economy—could usually offer the Indians better and more plentiful goods. But the French offered something that was often more important: tolerance. Unlike the English settlers, most of whom tried to impose their own social norms on the Native Americans they encountered, the French settlers in the interior generally adjusted their own behavior to Indian patterns. French fur traders frequently married Indian women and adopted tribal ways. Jesuit missionaries interacted comfortably with the natives and converted them to Catholicism by the thousands without challenging most of their social customs. By the mid-eighteenth century, therefore, the French had better and closer relations with most of the tribes of the interior than did the English.

The most powerful native group, however, had a rather different relationship with the French. The Iroquois Confederacy—the five Indian nations (Mohawk, Seneca, Cayuga, Onondaga, and Oneida) that had formed a defensive al- | *The Iroquois Confederacy* | liance in the fifteenth century—had been the most powerful tribal presence in the Northeast since the 1640s, when they had fought—and won—a bitter war against the Hurons. Once their major competitors were largely gone from the region, the Iroquois forged an important commercial relationship with the English and Dutch along the eastern seaboard—although they continued to trade with the French as well. Indeed, the key to the success of the Iroquois in maintaining their independence was that they avoided too close a relationship with either group and astutely played the French and the English off against each other. As a result, they managed to maintain an uneasy balance of power in the Great Lakes region.

The principal area of conflict among these many groups was the Ohio Valley. The French claimed it. Several competing Indian tribes (many of them refugees from lands farther east, driven into the valley by the English expansion) lived there. English settlement was expanding into it. And the Iroquois were trying to establish a presence there as traders. With so many competing groups jostling for influence, the Ohio Valley quickly became a potential battleground.

Anglo-French Conflicts

As long as England and France remained at peace in Europe, and as long as the precarious balance in the North American interior survived, the tensions among the English, French, and Iroquois remained relatively mild. But after the Glorious Revolution in England, the English throne

European Seeds of Conflict passed to one of Louis XIV's principal enemies, William III, who was also the stadholder (chief magistrate) of the Netherlands and who had long opposed French expansionism. William's successor, Queen Anne (the daughter of James II), ascended the throne in 1702 and carried on the struggle against France and its new ally, Spain. The result was a series of Anglo-French wars that continued intermittently in Europe for nearly eighty years.

The wars had important repercussions in America. King William's War (1689–1697) produced a few, indecisive clashes between the English and French in northern New England. Queen Anne's War, which began in 1701 and continued for nearly twelve years, generated more substantial conflicts: border fighting with the Spaniards in the South as well as with the French and their Indian allies in the North. The Treaty of Utrecht, which brought the conflict to a close in 1713, transferred substantial areas of French territory in North America to the English, including Acadia (Nova Scotia) and Newfoundland. Two decades later, European rivalries led to still more conflicts in America. Disputes over British trading rights in the Spanish colonies produced a war between England and Spain and led to clashes between the British in Georgia and the Spaniards in Florida. (It was in the context of this conflict that the last English colony in America, Georgia, was founded in 1733; see pp. 58–59.) The Anglo-Spanish conflict soon merged with a much larger European war, in which England and France lined up on opposite sides of a territorial dispute between Frederick the Great of Prussia and Maria Theresa of Austria. (France supported Prussia, in the hope of seizing the Austrian Netherlands; England supported Austria, to keep Holland from the French.) The English colonists in America were soon drawn into the struggle, which they called King George's War; and between 1744 and 1748 they engaged in a series of conflicts with the French. New Englanders captured the French bastion at Louisbourg on Cape Breton Island; but the peace treaty that finally ended the conflict forced them (in bitter disappointment) to abandon it.

In the aftermath of King George's War, relations among the English, French, and Iroquois in North America quickly deteriorated. The Iroquois (in what in retrospect appears a major blunder) began for the first time to grant trading concessions in the interior to English merchants. In the context of the already tense Anglo-French relationship in America, that decision set in motion a chain of events disastrous for the Iroquois Confederacy. The French feared that the English were using the concessions as a first step toward expansion into French lands (which to some extent they were). They began in 1749 to construct new fortresses in the Ohio Valley. The English interpreted the French activity as a threat to their western settlements. They protested and began making military preparations and building fortresses of their own. The balance of power that the Iroquois had strove to maintain for

so long rapidly disintegrated, and the five Indian nations allied themselves with the British and assumed an essentially passive role in the conflict that followed.

Fort Necessity For the next five years, tensions between the English and the French increased. In the summer of 1754 the governor of Virginia sent a militia force (under the command of an inexperienced young colonel, George Washington) into the Ohio Valley to challenge French expansion. Washington built a crude stockade (Fort Necessity) not far from the larger French outpost, Fort Duquesne, on the site of what is now Pittsburgh. After the Virginians staged an unsuccessful attack on a French detachment, the French countered with an assault on Fort Necessity, trapping Washington and his soldiers inside. After a third of them died in the fighting, Washington surrendered.

That clash marked the beginning of the French and Indian War, the American part of the much larger Seven Years' War that spread through Europe at the same time. It was the climactic event in the long Anglo-French struggle for empire.

The Great War for the Empire

The French and Indian War lasted nearly nine years, and it proceeded in three distinct phases. The first of these phases lasted from the Fort Necessity debacle in 1754 until the expansion of the war to Europe in 1756. It was primarily a local, North American conflict, which the English colonists managed largely on their own.

Braddock Defeated The British provided modest assistance during this period, but they provided it so ineptly that it had little impact on the struggle. The British fleet failed to prevent the landing of large French reinforcements in Canada; and the newly appointed commander in chief of the British army in America, General Edward Braddock, failed miserably in a major effort in the summer of 1755 to retake the crucial site at the forks of the Ohio River where Washington had lost the battle at Fort Necessity. A French and Indian ambush a few miles from the fort left Braddock dead and what remained of his forces in disarray.

The local colonial forces, meanwhile, were preoccupied with defending themselves against raids on their western settlements by the Indians of the Ohio Valley. Virtually all of them (except the Iroquois) were now allied with the French, having interpreted the defeat of the Virginians at Fort Duquesne as evidence of British weakness. Even the Iroquois, who were nominally allied with the British, remained fearful of antagonizing the French. They engaged in few hostilities and launched no offensive into Canada, even though they had, under heavy English pressure, declared war on the French. By late 1755, many English settlers along the frontier had withdrawn to the east of the Allegheny Mountains to escape the hostilities.

THE SIEGE OF LOUISBOURG, 1758 The fortress of Louisbourg, on Cape Breton Island in Nova Scotia, was one of the principal French outposts in eastern Canada during the French and Indian War. It took a British fleet of 157 ships nearly two months to force the French garrison to surrender. "We had not had our Batteries against the Town above a Week," wrote a British soldier after the victory, "tho we were ashore Seven Weeks; the Badness of the Country prevented our Approaches. It was necessary to make Roads for the Cannon, which was a great Labour, and some Loss of Men; but the spirits the Army was in is capable of doing any Thing." *(New Brunswick Museum)*

The second phase of the struggle began in 1756, when the governments of France and England formally opened hostilities and a truly international conflict (the Seven Years' War) began. In Europe, the war was marked by a realignment within the complex system of alliances. France allied itself with its former enemy, Austria; England joined France's former ally, Prussia. The fighting now spread to the West Indies, India, and Europe itself. But the principal struggle remained the one in North America, where so far England had suffered nothing but frustration and defeat.

Beginning in 1757, William Pitt, the English secretary of state (and future prime minister), began to transform the *William Pitt Takes Charge* war effort in America by bringing it for the first time fully under British control. Pitt himself began planning military strategy for the North American conflict, appointing military commanders, and issuing orders to the colonists. Military recruitment had slowed dramatically in America after the defeat of Braddock. To replenish the army, British commanders began forcibly enlisting colonists (a practice known as "impressment"). Officers also began to seize supplies and equipment from local farmers and tradesmen and compelled colonists to offer shelter to British troops—all

generally without compensation. The Americans had long ago become accustomed to running their own affairs and had been fighting for over two years without much assistance or direction from the British. They resented these new impositions and firmly resisted them—at times, as in a 1757 riot in New York City, violently. By early 1758, the friction between the British authorities and the colonists was threatening to bring the war effort to a halt.

Beginning in 1758, therefore, Pitt initiated the third and final phase of the war by relaxing many of the policies that Americans found obnoxious. He agreed to reimburse the colonists for all supplies requisitioned by the army. He returned control over military recruitment to the colonial assemblies (which resulted in an immediate and dramatic increase in enlistments). And he dispatched large numbers of additional troops to America.

Finally, the tide of battle began to turn in England's favor. The French had always been outnumbered by the British colonists; after 1756, they suffered as well from a series of poor harvests. As a result, they were unable to sustain their early military successes. By mid-1758, the British regulars in America (who did the bulk of the actual fighting) and the colonial militias were seizing one French stronghold after another. Two brilliant English generals, Jeffrey Amherst and James Wolfe, captured the fortress at Louisbourg in July 1758; a few months later Fort Duquesne fell without a fight.

Siege of Quebec

The next year, at the end of a siege of Quebec, supposedly impregnable atop its towering cliff, the army of General James Wolfe struggled up a hidden ravine under cover of darkness, surprised the larger forces of the Marquis de Montcalm, and defeated them in a battle in which both commanders died. The dramatic fall of Quebec on September 13, 1759, marked the beginning of the end of the American phase of the war. A year later, in September 1760, the French army formally surrendered to Amherst in Montreal.

Not all aspects of the struggle were as romantic as Wolfe's dramatic assault on Quebec. The British resorted at times to such brutal military expedients as population dispersal. In Nova Scotia, for example, they uprooted several thousand French inhabitants, whom they suspected of disloyalty, and scattered them throughout the English colonies. (Some of these Acadians eventually made their way to Louisiana, where they became the ancestors of the present-day Cajuns.) Elsewhere, English and colonial troops inflicted even worse atrocities on the Indian allies of the French—for example, offering "scalp bounties" to those who could bring back evidence of having killed a native. The French and their Indian allies retaliated, and hundreds of families along the English frontier perished in brutal raids on their settlements.

Peace finally came after the accession of George III to the British throne and the resignation of Pitt, who, unlike the new king, wanted to continue hostilities. The British achieved most of Pitt's

Peace of Paris

aims nevertheless in the Peace of Paris, signed in 1763. Under its terms, the French ceded to Great Britain some of their West Indian islands and most of their colonies in India. They also transferred Canada and all other French territory east of the Mississippi, except New Orleans, to Great Britain. They ceded New Orleans and their claims west of the Mississippi to Spain, thus surrendering all title to the mainland of North America.

The French and Indian War had profound effects on the British Empire and the American colonies. It greatly expanded England's territorial claims in the New World. At the same time, it greatly enlarged Britain's debt; financing the vast war had been a major drain on the treasury. It also generated substantial resentment toward the Americans among British leaders. Officials in England were contemptuous of the colonists for what they considered American military ineptitude during the war; they were angry that the colonists had made so few financial contributions to a struggle waged largely for American benefit; they were particularly bitter that some colonial merchants had been selling food and other goods to the French in the West Indies throughout the conflict. All

these factors combined to persuade many English leaders that a major reorganization of the empire, giving London increased authority over the colonies, would be necessary in the aftermath of the war.

The war had an equally profound but very different effect on the American colonists. It forced them, for the first time, to act in concert against a common foe. The friction of 1756–1757 over British requisition and impressment policies, and the 1758 return of au-

Consequences of the Seven Years' War

thority to the colonial assemblies, established an important precedent in the minds of the colonists: it seemed to confirm the illegitimacy of English interference in local affairs. For thousands of Americans—the men who served in the colonial armed forces—the war was an important socializing experience. The colonial troops, unlike the British regiments, generally viewed themselves as part of a "people's army." The relationship of soldiers to their units was, the soldiers believed, in some measure voluntary; their army was a communal, not a coercive or hierarchical, organization. The contrast with the British regulars, whom the colonists widely resented for their arrogance and arbitrary use of power, was striking; and in later years, the memory of that contrast helped to shape the American response to British imperial policies.

For the Indians of the Ohio Valley, the third major party in the French and Indian War, the British victory was disastrous. Those tribes that had allied themselves with the French had earned the enmity of the victorious English. The Iroquois Confederacy, which had allied itself with Britain, fared only slightly better. English officials saw the passivity of the Iroquois during the war (a result of their effort to hedge their bets and avoid antagonizing the French) as evidence of duplicity. In the aftermath of the peace settlement, the Iroquois alliance with the British quickly unraveled, and the Iroquois Confederacy itself began to crumble from within. The Iroquois nations would continue to contest the English for control of the Ohio Valley for another fifty years; but increasingly divided and increasingly outnumbered, they would seldom again be in a position to deal with their white rivals on terms of military or political equality.

THE NEW IMPERIALISM

With the treaty of 1763, England found itself truly at peace for the first time in more than fifty years. But the difficult experiences of the previous decade had convinced many English leaders that they could no longer govern their empire as casually as they had in the past. Saddled with enormous debts from the many years of fighting, England was desperately in need of new revenues from its empire. Responsible for vast new lands in the New World, the imperial government could not long avoid expanding its involvement in its colonies.

THE THIRTEEN COLONIES IN 1763 This map is a close-up of the thirteen colonies at the end of the Seven Years' War. Like the previous map, it shows the line of settlement established by the Proclamation of 1763 (the red line), as well as the extent of actual settlement in that year (the green line). Note that in the middle colonies (North Carolina, Virginia, Maryland, and southern Pennsylvania), settlement had already reached the red line—and in one small area of western Pennsylvania moved beyond it—by the time of the Proclamation of 1763. Note also the string of forts established beyond the Proclamation line. ◆ *How do the forts help to explain the efforts of the British to restrict settlement? And how does the extent of actual settlement help explain why it was so difficult for the British to enforce their restrictions?*

 For an interactive version of this map go to www.mhhe.com/brinkley11ch4maps

Burdens of Empire

The experience of the French and Indian War, however, suggested that such increased involvement would not be easy to achieve. Not only had the colonists proved so resistant to British control that Pitt had been forced to relax his policies in 1758, but the colonial assemblies had continued after that to respond to British needs slowly and grudgingly. Unwilling to be taxed by Parliament to support the war effort, the colonists were generally reluctant to tax themselves as well. Defiance of imperial trade regulations and other British demands continued, and even increased, through the last years of the war.

The problems of managing the empire became more difficult after 1763 because of a basic shift in Britain's imperial design. In the past, the English had viewed their colonial empire primarily in terms of trade; they had opposed acquisition of territory for its own sake. But by the

Commercial versus Territorial Imperialists

mid-eighteenth century, a growing number of English and American leaders (including both William Pitt and Benjamin Franklin) were beginning to argue that land itself was of value to the empire—because of the population it could support, the taxes it could produce, and the imperial splendor it would confer. The debate between the old commercial imperialists and the new territorial ones came to a head at the conclusion of the French and Indian War. The mercantilists wanted England to return Canada to France in exchange for Guadeloupe, the most commercially valuable of the French "sugar islands" in the West Indies. The territorialists, however, prevailed. The acquisition of the French territories in North America was a victory for, among others, Benjamin Franklin, who had long argued that the American people would need these vast spaces to accommodate their rapid and, he believed, limitless growth. Franklin and his supporters in the colonies were soon to discover, however, that the new acquisitions brought with them unexpected problems.

With the territorial annexations of 1763, the area of the British Empire was suddenly twice as great as it had been, and the problems of governing it were thus considerably more complex. Some argued that the empire should restrain rapid settlement in the western territories. To allow Europeans to move into the new lands too quickly, they warned, would run the risk of stirring up costly conflicts with the Indians. Restricting settlement would also keep the land available for hunting and trapping.

Other colonists wanted to see the new territories opened for immediate development, but they disagreed among themselves about who should control the western lands. Colonial governments made fervent, and often conflicting, claims of jurisdiction. Others argued that control should remain in England, and that the territories should be considered entirely new colonies, unlinked to the existing settlements. There were, in short, a host of problems and pressures that the British could not ignore.

At the same time, the government in London was running out of options in its effort to find a way to deal with

Britain's Staggering War Debt

its staggering war debt. Landlords and merchants in England itself were objecting strenuously to increases in what they already considered excessively high taxes. The necessity of stationing significant numbers of British troops on the Indian border after 1763 was adding even more to the cost of defending the American settlements. And the halfhearted response of the colonial assemblies to the war effort had suggested that in its search for revenue, England could not rely on any co-

operation from the colonial governments. Only a system of taxation administered by London, the leaders of the empire believed, could effectively meet England's needs.

At this crucial moment in Anglo-American relations, with the imperial system in desperate need of redefinition, the English government experienced a series of changes as a result of the accession to the throne of a new king. George III assumed power in 1760 on the death of his grandfather. And he brought two particularly unfortunate qualities to the office. First, he was determined, unlike his two predecessors, to be an active and responsible monarch. In part because of pressure from his ambitious mother, he removed from power the longstanding and relatively stable coalition of Whigs, who had (under Pitt and others) governed the empire for much of the century and whom the new king mistrusted. In their place, he created a new coalition of his own through patronage and bribes and gained an uneasy control of Parliament. The new ministries that emerged as a result of these changes were inherently unstable, each lasting in office an average of only about two years.

The king had serious intellectual and psychological limitations that compounded his political difficulties. He suffered, apparently, from a rare disease that produced intermittent bouts of insanity. (Indeed, in the last years of his long reign he was, according to most accounts, a virtual lunatic, confined to the palace and unable to perform

George III's Shortcomings

any official functions.) Yet even when George III was lucid and rational, which in the 1760s and 1770s was most of the time, he was painfully immature (he was only twenty-two when he ascended the throne) and insecure—striving constantly to prove his fitness for his position but time and again finding himself ill equipped to handle the challenges he seized for himself. The king's personality, therefore, contributed to both the instability and the intransigence of the British government during these critical years.

More immediately responsible for the problems that soon emerged with the colonies, however, was George Grenville, whom the king made prime minister in 1763. Grenville, a brother-in-law of William Pitt, did not share Pitt's sympathy with the American point of view. He agreed instead with the prevailing opinion within Britain that the colonists had been too long indulged and that they should be compelled to obey the laws and to pay a part of the cost of defending and administering the empire. He promptly began trying to impose a new system of control upon what had been a loose collection of colonial possessions in America.

The British and the Tribes

The western problem was the most urgent. With the departure of the French, settlers and traders from the English colonies had begun immediately to move over the

GEORGE III George III was 22 years old when he ascended the throne in 1760, and for many years almost all portraits of him were highly formal, with the king dressed in elaborate ceremonial robes. This more informal painting dates from much later in his reign, after he had begun to suffer from the mental disorders that eventually consumed him. After 1810, he was blind and permanently deranged, barred from all official business by the Regency Act of 1811. His son (later King George IV) served as regent in those years. *(The Granger Collection)*

mountains and into the upper Ohio Valley. The Indians of the region objected to this intrusion into their land and commerce; and an alliance of tribes, under the Ottawa chieftain Pontiac, struck back. To prevent an escalation of the fighting that might threaten western trade, the British government issued a ruling—the Proclamation of 1763—forbidding settlers to advance beyond a line drawn along the Appalachian Mountains.

The Proclamation of 1763 was appealing to the British for several reasons. It would allow London, rather than the provincial governments and their land-hungry con-

Proclamation of 1763 | stituents, to control the west-
ward movement of the white population. Hence, westward expansion would proceed in an orderly manner, and conflicts with the tribes, which were both militarily costly and dangerous to trade, might be limited. Slower western settlement would also slow the

population exodus from the coastal colonies, where England's most important markets and investments were. And it would reserve opportunities for land speculation and fur trading for English rather than colonial entrepreneurs.

Although the tribes were not enthusiastic about the Proclamation, which required them to cede still more land to the white settlers, many tribal groups supported the agreement as the best bargain available to them. The Cherokee, in particular, worked actively to hasten the drawing of the boundary, hoping to put an end to white encroachments for good. Relations between the western tribes and the British improved in at least some areas after the Proclamation, partly as a result of the work of the Indian superintendents the British appointed. John Stuart was in charge of Indian affairs in the southern colonies and Sir William Johnson in the northern ones. Both were sympathetic to Native American needs and lived among the tribes; Johnson married a Mohawk woman, Mary Brant, who was later to play an important role in the American Revolution.

In the end, however, the Proclamation of 1763 failed to meet even the modest expectations of the Native Americans. It had some effect in limit-
ing colonial land speculation in | *White Encroachment*
the West and in controlling the fur trade, but on the crucial point of the line of settlement it was almost completely ineffective. White settlers continued to swarm across the boundary and to claim lands farther and farther into the Ohio Valley. The British authorities tried repeatedly to establish limits to the expansion. In 1768, Stuart and Johnson negotiated new agreements with the western tribes creating a supposedly permanent boundary (which, as always, increased the area of white settlement at the expense of Native Americans). But these treaties (signed respectively at Hard Labor Creek, South Carolina, and Fort Stanwix, New York) also failed to stop the white advance. Within a few years, the 1768 agreements were replaced with new ones, which pushed the line of settlement still farther west.

The Colonial Response

The Grenville ministry soon moved to increase its authority in the colonies in more direct ways. Regular British troops, London announced, would now be stationed permanently in America; and under the Mutiny Act of 1765 the colonists were required to assist in provisioning and maintaining the army. Ships of the British navy were assigned to patrol American waters and search for smugglers. The customs service was reorganized and enlarged. Royal officials were ordered to take up their colonial posts in person instead of sending substitutes. Colonial manufacturing was to be restricted, so that it would not compete with the rapidly expanding industry of Great Britain.

The Sugar Act of 1764, designed in part to eliminate the illegal sugar trade between the continental colonies and the

NORTH AMERICA IN 1763 The victory of the English over the French in the Seven Years' War (or, as it was known in America, the French and Indian War) reshaped the map of colonial North America. Britain gained a vast new territory, formerly controlled by France—Canada, and a large area west of the Mississippi River, thus more than doubling the size of the British Empire in America. French possessions in the New World dwindled to a few islands in the Caribbean. Spain continued to control a substantial empire in the North American interior. The red line along the western borders of the English colonies represents the line of settlement established by Britain in 1763. White settlers were not permitted to move beyond that line. ◆ *Why did the British wish to restrict settlement of the western lands?*

 For an interactive version of this map go to www.mhhe.com/brinkley11ch4maps

French and Spanish West Indies, raised the duty on sugar (while lowering the duty on molasses, further damaging the market for sugar grown in the colonies). It also estab-

Sugar, Currency, and Stamp Acts

lished new vice-admiralty courts in America to try accused smugglers—thus depriving them of the benefit of sympathetic local juries. The Currency Act of 1764 required the colonial assemblies to stop issuing paper money (a widespread practice during the war) and to retire on schedule all the paper money already in circulation. Most momentous of all, the Stamp Act of 1765 imposed a

tax on most printed documents in the colonies: newspapers, almanacs, pamphlets, deeds, wills, licenses.

The new imperial program was an effort to reapply to the colonies the old principles of mercantilism. And in some ways, it proved highly effective. British officials were soon collecting more than ten times as much annual revenue from America as before 1763. But the new policies created many more problems than they solved.

The colonists may have resented the new imperial regulations, but at first they found it difficult to resist them effectively. For one thing, Americans continued to

PREPARING TO MEET THE PAXTON BOYS The "Paxton Boys" were residents of western Pennsylvania who were declared outlaws by the assembly in Philadelphia after they launched an unauthorized attack on neighboring Conestoga Indians. Instead of surrendering, they armed themselves and marched on Philadelphia. This engraving satirizes the haphazard military preparations in the city for the expected invasion. An accompanying poem, expressing the contempt some colonists felt toward the urbanized, pacifist Quakers of Philadelphia, commented: "To kill the Paxtonians, they then did Advance, With Guns on their Shoulders, but how did they Prance." Benjamin Franklin finally persuaded the Paxton rebels not to attack in return for greater representation in the legislature. *(Library Company of Philadelphia)*

harbor as many grievances against one another as against the authorities in London. Often, the conflicts centered around tensions between the established societies of the Atlantic coast and the newer, more precarious areas of white settlement further west—areas often known as the "backcountry." Residents of the backcountry often

Paxton Boys

felt isolated from, and underrepresented in, the colonial governments. They sometimes felt beleaguered because they lived closer to the worlds of the Indian tribes than the societies of the East. In 1763, for example, a band of people from western Pennsylvania known as the Paxton Boys descended on Philadelphia with demands for relief from colonial (not British) taxes and for money to help them defend themselves against Indians; the colonial government averted bloodshed only by making concessions to them.

In 1771, a small-scale civil war broke out as a result of the so-called Regulator movement in North Carolina. The

Regulator Movement

Regulators were farmers of the Carolina upcountry who organized in opposition to the high taxes that local sheriffs (appointed by the colonial governor) collected. The western counties were badly underrepresented in the colonial assembly, and the Regulators failed to win redress of their

grievances there. Finally they armed themselves and began resisting tax collections by force. To suppress the revolt, Governor William Tryon raised an army of militiamen, mostly from the eastern counties, who defeated a band of 2,000 Regulators in the Battle of Alamance. Nine on each side were killed, and many others were wounded. Afterward, six Regulators were hanged for treason.

The bloodshed was exceptional, but bitter conflicts within the colonies were not. After 1763, however, the new policies of the British government began to create common grievances among virtually all colonists that to some degree counterbalanced these internal divisions. For under the Grenville program, as the Americans saw it, all people—in all classes, in all colonies—would suffer.

Indeed, there was something in the Grenville program to antagonize virtually everyone. Northern merchants believed they would suffer from restraints on their commerce, from the closing of opportunities for manufacturing, and from the increased burden of taxation. Settlers in the northern backcountry resented the closing of the West to land speculation and fur trading. Southern planters, in debt to English merchants, feared having to pay additional taxes and losing their ability to ease their debts by speculating in western land. Professionals—ministers, lawyers, professors, and others—depended on merchants and planters for their livelihood and thus shared their concerns about the effects of English law. Small farmers, the largest group in the colonies, believed they would suffer from increased taxes and from the abolition of paper money, which had enabled them to pay their loans. Workers in towns opposed the restraints on manufacturing.

The new restrictions came, moreover, at the beginning of an economic depression. The British government, by pouring money into the colonies to finance the fighting, had stimulated a wartime boom; that flow of funds stopped after the peace in 1763, precipitating an economic bust. Now the authori-

Postwar Depression

ties in London proposed to aggravate the problem by taking money out of the colonies. The imperial policies would, many colonists feared, doom them to permanent economic stagnation and a declining standard of living.

In reality, most Americans soon found ways to live with (or circumvent) the new British policies. The American economy was not, in fact, being destroyed. But economic anxieties were rising in the colonies nevertheless, and they created a growing sense of unease, particularly in the cities—the places most directly affected by British policies and the places where resistance first arose. Urban Americans were worried about the periodic economic slumps that were occurring with greater and greater frequency. They had been shocked by the frightening depression of the early 1760s. They were alarmed by the growth of a large group within the population who were unemployed or semi-employed, and who were in either case a destabilizing element in the community. The result of all these anxieties was a feeling in some colonial cities—and particularly in Boston, the city suffering the worst economic problems—that something was deeply amiss.

Whatever the economic consequences of the British government's programs, the political consequences were—in the eyes of the colonists, at least—far worse. Perhaps nowhere else in the late-eighteenth-century world did so large a proportion of the people take an ac-

Political Consequences of the Grenville Program

tive interest in public affairs. That was partly because Anglo-Americans were accustomed (and deeply attached) to very broad powers of self-government; and the colonists were determined to protect those powers. The keys to self-government, they believed, were the provincial assemblies; and the key to the power of the provincial assemblies was their long-established right to give or withhold appropriations for the colonial governments. By attempting to circumvent the colonial assemblies, raise extensive revenues directly from the public, and provide salaries directly and unconditionally to royal officials in America, the British government was challenging the basis of colonial political power: control over public finance. Home rule, therefore, was not something new and different that the colonists were striving to

attain. It was something old and familiar that they desired to keep. The movement to resist the new imperial policies, a movement for which many would ultimately fight and die, was thus at the same time democratic and conservative. It was a movement to conserve liberties Americans believed they already possessed.

STIRRINGS OF REVOLT

By the mid-1760s, therefore, a hardening of positions had begun in both England and America that would bring the colonies into increasing conflict with the mother country. The victorious war for empire had given the colonists a heightened sense of their own importance and a renewed commitment to protecting their political autonomy. It had given the British a strengthened belief in the need to tighten administration of the empire and a strong desire to use the colonies as a source of revenue. The result was a series of events that, more rapidly than anyone could imagine, shattered the English Empire in America.

The Stamp Act Crisis

Even if he had tried, Prime Minister Grenville could not have devised a better method for antagonizing and unifying the colonies than the Stamp Act of 1765. The Sugar Act of a

Effects of the Stamp Act

year earlier had affected few people other than the New England merchants whose trade it hampered. But the new tax fell on all Americans, of whatever section, colony, or class. And it evoked particular opposition from some of the most powerful members of the population. Merchants and lawyers were obliged to buy stamps for ships' papers and legal documents. Tavern owners, often the political leaders of their neighborhoods, were required to buy stamps for their licenses. Printers—the most influential group in distributing information and ideas in colonial society—had to buy stamps for their newspapers and other publications.

The actual economic burdens of the Stamp Act were, in the end, relatively light; the stamps were not very expensive. What made the law obnoxious to the colonists was not so much its immediate cost as the precedent it seemed to set. In the past, Americans had rationalized the taxes and duties on colonial trade as measures to regulate commerce, not raise money. Some Americans had even managed to persuade themselves that the Sugar Act, which was in fact designed primarily to raise money, was not fundamentally different from the traditional imperial duties. The Stamp Act, however, they could interpret in only one way. It was a direct attempt by England to raise revenue in the colonies without the consent of the colonial assemblies. If this new tax passed without resistance, the door would be open for more burdensome taxation in the future.

THE ALTERNATIVES OF WILLIAM BURG In the aftermath of the Boston Tea Party, and in response to the Coercive Acts Great Britain enacted to punish the colonists, the First Continental Congress called on Americans to boycott British goods until the Acts were repealed. In this drawing, a prosperous Virginia merchant is seen signing a pledge to honor the nonimportation agreement— unsurprisingly given the alternative, visible in the background of the picture: tar and feathers hanging from a post labeled "A Cure for the Refractory." *(Colonial Williamsburg Foundation)*

Few colonists believed that they could do anything more than grumble and buy the stamps—until the Virginia House of Burgesses sounded what one colonist called a "trumpet of sedition" that aroused Americans to action almost everywhere. The "trumpet" was the collective voice of a group of young Virginia aristocrats. They hoped, among other things, to challenge the power of tidewater planters who (in alliance with the royal governor) dominated Virginia politics. Foremost among the malcontents was Patrick Henry, who had already achieved fame for his fiery oratory and his occasional defiance of British authority. Henry made a dramatic speech to the House of Burgesses in May 1765, concluding with a vague prediction that if present policies were not revised, George III, like earlier tyrants, might lose his head. There were shocked cries of "Treason!" and, according to one witness, an immediate apology from Henry (although many years later he was quoted as having made the defiant reply: "If this be treason, make the most of it").

Henry introduced a set of resolutions declaring that Americans possessed the same rights as the English, especially the right to be taxed only by their own representatives; *Virginia Resolves* that Virginians should pay no taxes except those voted by the Virginia assembly; and that anyone advocating the right of Parliament to tax Virginians should be deemed an enemy of the colony. The House of Burgesses defeated the most extreme of Henry's resolutions, but all of them were printed and circulated as the "Virginia Resolves" (creating an impression in other colonies that the people of Virginia were more militant than they actually were).

In Massachusetts at about the same time, James Otis persuaded his fellow members of the colonial assembly to call an intercolonial congress for action against the new tax. In October 1765, the Stamp Act Congress met in New York with delegates from nine colonies and decided to petition the king and the two houses of Parliament. Their petition conceded that Americans owed to Parliament "all due subordination," but it denied that the colonies could rightfully be taxed except through their own provincial assemblies.

Meanwhile, in several colonial cities crowds began taking the law into their own hands. During the summer of 1765 serious riots broke out up and down the coast, the *Sons of Liberty* largest of them in Boston. Men belonging to the newly organized Sons of Liberty terrorized stamp agents and burned the stamps. The agents, themselves Americans, hastily resigned; and the sale of stamps in the continental colonies virtually ceased. In Boston, a crowd also attacked such pro-British "aristocrats" as the lieutenant governor, Thomas Hutchinson (who had privately opposed passage of the Stamp Act but who, as an officer of the crown, felt obliged to support it once it became law). The protestors pillaged Hutchinson's elegant house and virtually destroyed it.

The Stamp Act crowd actions raise the question of whether the protests in the colonies represented more than opposition to British policy. That the protesters seemed often to target symbols of affluence (such as Hutchinson's lavish home) as well as symbols of authority suggests that resentment of disparities of wealth (which had grown increasingly visible in colonial cities) played at least some role in fueling the anger among ordinary citizens. But opposition to British policy and protests against it were widespread, embracing rich and poor alike. Whatever basis in class resentments there may have been to the protests was almost certainly less important in the end than the larger political and ideological foundation.

The Stamp Act crisis was a dangerous moment in the relationship between the colonies and the British government. But the crisis subsided, largely because England backed down. The authorities in London did not relent because of the resolutions by the colonial assemblies, the petitions from the Stamp Act Congress, or the riots in

were strong and vociferous, and they insisted that unless England compelled the colonists to obey the Stamp Act, they would soon cease to obey any laws of Parliament. So on the same day, to satisfy such critics, Parliament passed the Declaratory Act, asserting Parliament's authority over the colonies "in all cases whatsoever." In their rejoicing over the repeal of the Stamp Act, most Americans paid little attention to this sweeping declaration of power.

The Townshend Program

The reaction in England to the Rockingham government's policy of appeasement was less enthusiastic than it was in America. English landlords, a powerful political force, angrily protested that the government had "sacrificed the landed gentlemen to the interests of traders and colonists." They feared that backing down from taxing the colonies would lead the government to increase taxes on them. The king finally bowed to their pressure and dismissed the Rockingham ministry. To replace it, he called upon the aging but still powerful William Pitt to form a government. Pitt had been a strong critic of the Stamp Act and had a reputation in America as a friend of the colonists (even though his acceptance of a peerage in 1766 had disillusioned some of his American admirers). Once in office, however, Pitt (now Lord Chatham) was so hobbled by gout and at times so incapacitated by mental illness that the actual leadership of his administration fell to the chancellor of the exchequer, Charles Townshend—a brilliant, flamboyant, and at times reckless politician known to his contemporaries variously as "the Weathercock" and "Champagne Charlie."

Among Townshend's first challenges was dealing with the continuing American grievances against Parliament. The greatest of them, now that the Stamp Act had failed, involved the Mutiny (or Quartering) Act of 1765, which required the colonists to provide quarters and supplies for *Mutiny Act* the British troops in America. The British considered this a reasonable requirement. The troops were stationed in North America to protect the colonists from Indian or French attack and to defend the frontiers; lodging the troops in coastal cities was simply a way to reduce the costs to England of supplying them. To the colonists, however, the law was another assault on their liberties.

They did not so much object to quartering the troops or providing them with supplies; they had been doing that voluntarily ever since the last years of the French and Indian War. They resented that these contributions were now mandatory, and they considered it another form of taxation without consent. They responded with defiance. The Massachusetts Assembly refused to vote the mandated supplies to the troops. The New York Assembly soon did likewise, posing an even greater challenge to imperial authority, since the army headquarters were in New York City.

"THE TORY'S DAY OF JUDGMENT" A mob of American Patriots hoists a Loyalist neighbor up a flagpole in this woodcut, which is obviously sympathetic to the victim. The crowd is shown as fat, rowdy, and drunken. Public humiliations of Tories were not infrequent during the war. More common, however, was seizure of their property. *(Library of Congress)*

American cities. They changed their attitude because of economic pressure. Even before the Stamp Act, many New Englanders had stopped buying English goods to protest the Sugar Act of 1764. Now the colonial boycott spread, and the Sons of Liberty intimidated those colonists who were reluctant to participate in it. The merchants of England, feeling the loss of much of their colonial market, begged Parliament to repeal the Stamp Act; and stories of unemployment, poverty, and discontent arose from English seaports and manufacturing towns.

The Marquis of Rockingham, who succeeded Grenville as prime minister in July 1765, tried to appease both the *Parliament Retreats* English merchants and the American colonists, and he finally convinced the king to kill the Stamp Act. On March 18, 1766, Parliament repealed it. Rockingham's opponents

To enforce the law and to try again to raise revenues in the colonies, Townshend steered two measures through Parliament in 1767. The first disbanded the New York Assembly until the colonists agreed to obey the Mutiny Act.

Internal and External Taxes (By singling out New York, Townshend thought he would avoid Grenville's mistake of arousing all the colonies at once.) The second levied new taxes (known as the Townshend Duties) on various goods imported to the colonies from England—lead, paint, paper, and tea. The colonists could not logically object to taxation of this kind, Townshend reasoned, because it met standards they themselves had accepted. Benjamin Franklin, as a colonial agent in London trying to prevent the passage of the Stamp Act, had long ago argued for the distinction between "internal" and "external" taxes and had denounced the stamp duties as internal taxation. Townshend himself had considered the distinction laughable; but he was nevertheless imposing duties on what he believed were clearly external transactions.

Townshend's efforts to satisfy colonial grievances were to no avail. The new duties were no more acceptable to Americans than the stamp tax. Townshend might call them external taxes, but colonial merchants and, indirectly, colonial consumers would have to pay them. Their purpose, Americans believed, was the same as that of the Stamp Act: to raise revenue from the colonists without their consent. And the suspension of the New York Assembly, far from isolating New York, aroused the resentment of all the colonies. They considered this assault on the rights of one provincial government a precedent for the annihilation of the rights of all of them.

The Massachusetts Assembly took the lead in opposing the new measures by circulating a letter to all the colonial governments urging them to stand up against every tax, external or internal, imposed by Parliament. At first, the circular evoked little response in some of the legislatures (and ran into strong opposition in Pennsylvania's). Then Lord Hillsborough, secretary of state for the colonies, issued a circular letter of his own from London in which he warned that assemblies endorsing the Massachusetts letter would be dissolved. Massachusetts defiantly reaffirmed its support for the circular. (The vote in the Assembly was 92 to 17, and for a time "ninety-two" became a patriotic rallying cry throughout British America.) The other colonies, including Pennsylvania, promptly rallied to the support of Massachusetts.

In addition to his other unpopular measures, Townshend tried to strengthen enforcement of commercial regulations in the colonies by, among other things, establishing a new board of customs commissioners in America. Townshend hoped the new board would stop the rampant corruption in the colonial customs houses, and to some extent his hopes were fulfilled. The new commissioners virtually ended smuggling in Boston, their headquarters, although smugglers continued to carry on a busy trade in other colonial seaports.

The Boston merchants—accustomed, like all colonial merchants, to loose enforcement of the Navigation Acts and doubly aggrieved now that the new commission was diverting the lucrative smuggling trade elsewhere—were *Colonial Boycotts* indignant, and they took the lead in organizing another boycott. In 1768, the merchants of Philadelphia and New York joined them in a nonimportation agreement, and later some southern merchants and planters also agreed to cooperate. Colonists boycotted British goods subject to the Townshend Duties; and throughout the colonies, American homespun and other domestic products became suddenly fashionable, while English luxuries fell from favor.

Late in 1767, Charles Townshend suddenly died—before the consequences of his ill-conceived program had become fully apparent. The question of dealing with colonial resistance to the Townshend Duties fell, therefore, to the new prime minister, Lord North. Hoping to break the nonimportation agreement and divide the colonists, Lord North secured the repeal of all the Townshend Duties except the tax on tea in March 1770.

The Boston Massacre

The withdrawal of the Townshend Duties never had a chance to pacify colonial opinion. Before news of the repeal reached America, an event in Massachusetts raised colonial resentment to a new level of intensity. The colonists' harassment of the new customs commissioners in Boston had grown so intense *Competition for Scarce Employment* that the British government had placed four regiments of regular troops inside the city. The presence of the "redcoats" was a constant affront to the colonists' sense of independence and a constant reminder of what they considered British oppression. Everywhere they went, Bostonians encountered British soldiers—often arrogant and intrusive, sometimes coarse and provocative. There was particular tension between the redcoats and Boston laborers. Many British soldiers, poorly paid and poorly treated by the army, wanted jobs in their off-duty hours; and they competed with local workers in an already tight market. Clashes between them were frequent.

On the night of March 5, 1770, a few days after a particularly intense skirmish between workers at a ship-rigging factory and British soldiers who were trying to find work there, a crowd of dockworkers, "liberty boys," and others began pelting the sentries at the customs house with rocks and snowballs. Hastily, Captain Thomas Preston of the British regiment lined up several of his men in front of the building to protect it. There was some scuffling; one of the soldiers was knocked down; and in the midst of it all, apparently, several British soldiers fired into the crowd, killing five people (among them a mulatto sailor, Crispus Attucks).

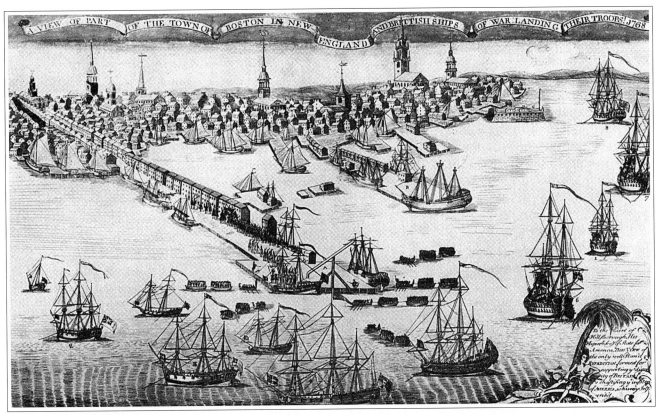

THE BRITISH IN BOSTON, 1768 British troops arrived in Boston on September 30, 1768, marched into the city, and pitched tents on the Boston common. The soldiers were charged with ensuring the safety of British customs officers, who three months earlier had been driven from the city by local residents and had appealed to England for protection. The presence of the troops became a continuing irritant in relations between the colonists and the British government. This 1770 engraving by Paul Revere shows troops embarking from British naval vessels at Long Wharf and marching "with insolent Parade" up King Street into the city. *(Henry Francis du Point Winterthur Museum)*

This murky incident, almost certainly the result of panic and confusion, was quickly transformed by local resistance leaders into the "Boston Massacre"—a graphic symbol of British oppression and brutality. The victims became popular martyrs; the event became the subject of such lurid (and inaccurate) accounts as the widely circulated pamphlet Innocent Blood Crying to God from the Streets of Boston. A famous engraving by Paul Revere, widely reproduced and circulated, portrayed the massacre as a carefully organized, calculated assault on a peaceful crowd. A jury of Massachusetts colonists found the British soldiers guilty of manslaughter and sentenced them to a token punishment. Colonial pamphlets and newspapers, however, convinced many Americans that the soldiers were guilty of official murder. Year after year, resistance leaders marked the anniversary of the massacre with demonstrations and speeches. The leading figure in fomenting public outrage over the Boston Massacre was Samuel Adams, the most effective radical in the colonies. Adams (a distant cousin of John Adams, second president of the United States) was born in 1722 and was thus somewhat older than other leaders of colonial protest. As a member of an earlier generation with strong ties to New England's Puritan past, he was particularly inclined to

Samuel Adams

view public events in stern moral terms. A failure in business, he had occupied several political and governmental positions. His real importance, however, was as an unflagging voice expressing outrage at British oppression. England, he argued, had become a morass of sin and corruption; only in America did public virtue survive. He spoke frequently at Boston town meetings; and as one unpopular English policy followed another—the Townshend Duties, the placement of customs commissioners in Boston, the stationing of British troops in the city (with its violent results)—his message attracted increasing support. In 1772, he proposed the creation of a "committee of correspondence" in Boston to publicize the grievances against England throughout the colony. He became its first head. Other colonies followed Massachusetts's lead, and there grew up a loose network of political organizations that kept the spirit of dissent alive through the 1770s.

The Philosophy of Revolt

Although a superficial calm settled on the colonies for approximately three years after the Boston Massacre, the crises of the 1760s had helped arouse enduring ideological challenges to England and had produced powerful instruments for publicizing colonial grievances. Gradually a political outlook gained a following in America that would ultimately serve to justify revolt.

The ideas that would support the Revolution emerged from many sources. Some were drawn from religious (particularly Puritan) sources or from the political experiences of the colonies. Others came from abroad. Most important, perhaps, were the "radical" ideas of those in Great Britain who stood in opposition to their government. Some were Scots, who considered the English state tyrannical. Others were embittered "country Whigs," who felt excluded from power and considered the existing system corrupt and oppressive. Drawing from some of the great philosophical minds of earlier generations—most notably John Locke—these English dissidents framed a powerful argument against their government.

Central to this emerging ideology was a new concept of what government should be. Because humans were inherently corrupt and selfish, government was necessary

England's Balanced Constitution to protect individuals from the evil in one another. But because any government was run by corruptible people, the people needed safeguards against its possible abuses of power. Most people in both England and America considered the English constitution the best system ever devised to meet these necessities. By distributing power among the three elements of society—the monarchy, the aristocracy, and the common people—the English political system ensured that no individual or group could exercise authority unchecked by another. Yet by the mid-seventeenth century, dissidents in both England and America had become convinced that the constitution was in danger. A single center of power—the king and his ministers—was becoming so powerful that it could not be effectively checked, and the system was becoming a corrupt and dangerous tyranny.

Such arguments found little sympathy in most of England. The English constitution was not a written document or a fixed set of unchangeable rules. It was a general sense of the "way things are done," and most people in England were willing to accept changes in it. Americans, by contrast, drew from their experience with colonial charters, in which the shape and powers of government were permanently inscribed on paper. They resisted the idea of a flexible, changing set of basic principles.

One basic principle, Americans believed, was the right of people to be taxed only with their own consent—a belief that gradually took shape in the widely repeated slogan, "No taxation without representation." Whatever the nature of a tax—whether internal or external, whether designed to raise revenue or to control trade—it could not be levied without the consent of the colonists themselves.

This clamor about "representation" made little sense to the English. According to English constitutional theory, members of Parliament did not represent individuals or particular geographical areas. Instead, each member represented the interests of the whole nation and indeed the whole empire, no matter where the member happened to come from. The many boroughs of England that had no representative in Parliament, the whole of Ireland, and the colonies thousands of miles away—all were thus represented in the Parliament at London, even though they elected no representatives of their own. This was the theory of "virtual" representation. But Americans, drawing from their experiences with their town meetings and their colonial assemblies, believed in "actual" representation. Every community was entitled to its own representative, elected by the people of that community and directly responsible to them. Since the colonists had none of their own representatives in Parliament, it followed that they were not represented there. Americans believed that the colonial assemblies played the same role within the colonies that Parliament did within England. The empire, the Americans argued, was a sort of federation of commonwealths, each with its own legislative body, all tied together by common loyalty to the king.

Such ideas illustrated a fundamental difference of opinion between England and America over the nature of sovereignty—over the question of where ultimate power lay. By arguing that Parliament had the *Virtual versus Actual Representation* right to legislate for England and for the empire as a whole, but that only the provincial assemblies could legislate for the individual colonies, Americans were in effect arguing for a division of sovereignty. Parliament would be sovereign in some matters; the assemblies would be sovereign in others. To the British, such an argument was absurd. In any system of government there must be a single, ultimate authority. And since the empire was, in their view, a single, undivided unit, there could be only one authority within it: the English government of king and Parliament.

The Tea Excitement

An apparent calm in America in the first years of the 1770s disguised a growing sense of resentment at the increasingly heavy-handed British enforcement of the Navigation Acts. The customs commissioners, who remained in the colonies despite the repeal of the Townshend Acts, were mostly clumsy, intrusive, and arrogant officials. They harassed colonial merchants and seamen constantly with petty restrictions, and they also enriched themselves through graft and through illegal seizures of merchandise.

Colonists also kept revolutionary sentiment alive through writing and talking. Dissenting leaflets, pamphlets, and books circulated widely through the colonies. In towns and *Revolutionary Discourse* cities, men gathered in churches, schools, town squares, and above all in taverns to discuss politics and express their growing disenchantment with English policy. The rise of revolutionary ideology was not simply a result of the ideas of intellectuals. It was also a product of a social process by which ordinary people heard, discussed, and absorbed new ideas.

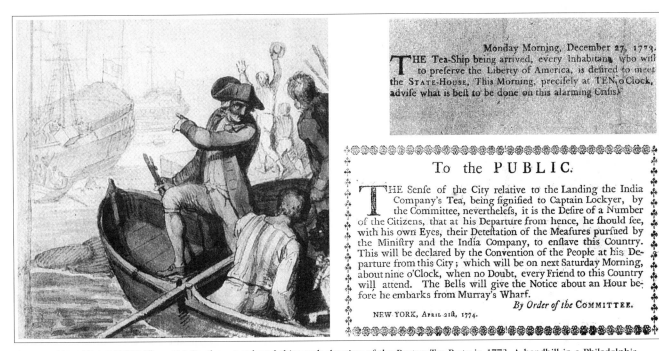

THE BOSTON TEA PARTY The artist Ramberg produced this wash drawing of the Boston Tea Party in 1773. A handbill in a Philadelphia newspaper ten days later and another distributed in New York the following April illustrate how quickly the spirit of resistance spread to other colonies. *(Left, Metropolitan Museum of Art;* Upper Right, *Chicago Historical Society;* Bottom Right, *Bettmann/Corbis)*

The popular anger lying just beneath the surface was also visible in occasional acts of rebellion. At one point, colonists seized a British revenue ship on the lower Delaware River. And in 1772, angry residents of Rhode Island boarded the British schooner *Gaspée,* set it afire, and sank it in Narragansett Bay. The British response to the *Gaspée* affair further inflamed American opinion. Instead of putting the accused attackers on trial in colonial courts, the British sent a special commission to America with power to send the defendants back to England for trial.

What finally revived the revolutionary fervor of the 1760s, however, was a new act of Parliament—one that the English government had expected to be relatively uncontroversial. It involved the business of selling tea. In 1773, Britain's East India Company (which had an official monopoly on trade with the Far East) was sitting on large stocks of tea that it could not sell in England. It was on the verge of bankruptcy. In an effort to save the company, the government passed the Tea Act of 1773, which gave the company the right to export its merchandise directly to the colonies without paying any of the navigation taxes that were imposed on the colonial merchants, who had traditionally served as the middlemen in such transactions. With these privileges, the East India Company could undersell American merchants and monopolize the colonial tea trade.

The act angered many colonists for several reasons. First, it enraged influential colonial merchants, who feared being replaced and bankrupted by a powerful monopoly. The East India Company's decision to grant franchises to certain American merchants for the sale of their tea created further resentments among those excluded from this lucrative trade. More important, however, the Tea Act revived American passions about the issue of taxation without representation. The law provided no new tax *The Tea Act* on tea. But the original Townshend duty on the commodity—the only one of the original duties that had not been repealed—survived. It was the East India Company's exemption from that duty that put the colonial merchants at such a grave competitive disadvantage. Lord North assumed that most colonists would welcome the new law because it would reduce the price of tea to consumers by removing the middlemen. But resistance leaders in America argued that it was another insidious example of the results of an unconstitutional tax. Many colonists responded by boycotting tea.

The boycott was an important event in the history of colonial resistance. Unlike earlier protests, most of which had involved relatively small numbers of people, the boycott mobilized large segments of the population. It also helped link the colonies together in a common experience of mass popular protest. Particularly important to the movement were the activities of colonial women, who were among the principal consumers of tea and now became leaders of the effort to boycott it.

Women had played a significant role in resistance activities from the beginning. Several women (most prominently Mercy Otis Warren) had been important in writing the dissident literature—in Warren's case satirical plays—that did much to fan colonial resentments in the 1760s. Women had participated actively in anti-British riots and crowd activities in the 1760s; they had formed an

In colonial Massachusetts, as in many other American colonies in the 1760s and 1770s, taverns (or "public houses," as they were often known) were crucial to the development of popular resistance to British rule. The Puritan culture of New England created some resistance to taverns, and there were continuing efforts by reformers to regulate or close them to reduce the problems caused by "public drunkenness," "lewd behavior," and anarchy. But as the commercial life of the colonies expanded, and as increasing numbers of people began living in towns and cities, taverns became a central institution in American social life—and eventually in its political life as well.

Taverns were appealing, of course, because they provided alcoholic drinks in a culture where the craving for alcohol—and the extent of drunk-

enness—was very high. But taverns had other attractions as well. There were few other places where people could meet and talk openly in public, and to many colonists the life of the tavern came to seem the only vaguely democratic experience available to them. Gradually, many came to see the attacks on the public houses as efforts to increase the power of existing elites and suppress the freedoms of ordinary people. The tavern was a mostly male institution, just as politics was considered a mostly male concern. And so the fusion of male camaraderie and political discourse emerged naturally out of the tavern culture.

As the revolutionary crisis deepened, taverns and pubs became the central meeting places for discussions of the ideas that fueled resistance to British polices. Educated and uneducated men alike joined in animated discussions of events. Those who could not read—and there were many—could learn about the contents of revolutionary pamphlets from listening to tavern discussions. They could join in the discussion of the new republican ideas emerging in the Americas by participating in tavern celebrations of, for example, the anniversaries of resistance to the Stamp Act. Those anniversaries inspired elaborate toasts in public houses throughout the colonies. Such toasts were the equivalents of political speeches, and illiterate men could learn much from them about the political concepts that were circulating through the colonies.

Taverns were important sources of information in an age before any wide distribution of newspapers. Tavernkeepers were often trusted informants and confidants to the Sons of Liberty and other activists, and

TAVERN BILLIARDS Gentlemen in Hanover Town, Virginia gather for a game of billiards in a local tavern in this 1797 drawing by Benjamin Henry Latrobe. *(Maryland Historical Society, Baltimore)*

they were fountains of information about the political and social turmoil of the time. Taverns were also the settings for political events. In 1770, for example, a report circulated through the taverns of Danvers, Massachusetts about a local man who was continuing to sell tea despite the colonial boycott. The Sons of Liberty brought the seller to the Bell Tavern and persuaded him to sign a confession and apology before a crowd of defiant men in the public room.

Almost all politicians found it necessary to visit taverns in colonial Massachusetts if they wanted any real contact with the public. Samuel Adams spent considerable time in the public houses of Boston, where he sought to encourage resistance to British rule while taking care to drink moderately so as not to erode his stature as a leader. His cousin John Adams was somewhat more skeptical of taverns, more sensitive to the vices they encouraged. But he, too, recognized their political value. In taverns, he once said, "bastards, and legislatores are frequently begotten."

THE SCALES OF JUSTICE This sign for a Hartford tavern promises hospitality (from "the charming Patroness") and "entertainment" as well as food and drink. *(The Connecticut Historical Society, Hartford)*

informal organization—the Daughters of Liberty—that occasionally mocked their male counterparts as insufficiently militant. The Sons of Liberty, they wrote in a 1768 poem, were "Supinely asleep, and depriv'd of their Sight . . . strip'd of their Freedom, and rob'd of their Right." Now, as the sentiment for a boycott grew, some women

mobilized as never before, determined (as the Daughters of Liberty had written) "that rather than Freedom, we'll part with our Tea."

In the last weeks of 1773, with strong popular support, leaders in various colonies made plans to prevent the East India Company from landing its cargoes in colonial ports.

In Philadelphia and New York, determined colonists kept the tea from leaving the company's ships. In Charleston, they stored it away in a public warehouse. In Boston, after failing to turn back the three ships in the harbor, local

Boston Tea Party   patriots staged a spectacular drama. On the evening of December 16, 1773, three companies of fifty men each, masquerading as Mohawks, passed through a tremendous crowd of spectators (which served to protect them from official interference), went aboard the three ships, broke open the tea chests, and heaved them into the harbor. As the electrifying news of the Boston "tea party" spread, other seaports followed the example and staged similar acts of resistance of their own.

When the Bostonians refused to pay for the property they had destroyed, George III and Lord North decided on a policy of coercion, to be applied only against Massachusetts—the chief center of resistance. In four acts of 1774, Parliament closed the port of Boston, drastically reduced the powers of self-government in the colony, permitted royal officers to be tried in other colonies or in England when accused of crimes, and provided for the quartering of troops in the colonists' barns and empty houses.

Parliament followed these Coercive Acts—or, as they were more widely known in America, Intolerable Acts—

Coercive Acts   with the Quebec Act, which was separate from them in origin and quite different in purpose. Its object was to provide a civil government for the French-speaking Roman Catholic inhabitants of Canada and the Illinois country. The law extended the boundaries of Quebec to include the French communities between the Ohio and Mississippi Rivers. It also granted political rights to Roman Catholics and recognized the legality of the Roman Catholic Church within the enlarged province. In many ways it was a tolerant and long overdue piece of legislation. But in the inflamed atmosphere of the time, many people in the thirteen English-speaking colonies considered it a threat. They were already alarmed by rumors that the Church of England was scheming to appoint a bishop for America who would impose Anglican authority on all the various sects. Since the line between the Church of England and the Church of Rome had always seemed to many Americans dangerously thin, the passage of the Quebec Act convinced some of them that a plot was afoot in London to subject Americans to the tyranny of the pope. Those interested in western lands, moreover, believed that the act would hinder westward expansion.

The Coercive Acts, far from isolating Massachusetts, made it a martyr to residents of other colonies and sparked

Consequences   new resistance up and down the coast. Colonial legislatures passed a series of resolves supporting Massachusetts.

PAYING THE EXCISEMAN This eighteenth-century satirical drawing by a British artist depicts Bostonians forcing tea down the throat of a customs official, whom they have tarred and feathered. In the background, colonists are dumping tea into the harbor (presumably a representation of the 1773 Boston Tea Party); and on the tree at right is a symbol of the Stamp Act, which the colonists had defied eight years earlier. *(Metropolitan Museum of Art)*

Women's groups throughout the colonies mobilized to extend the boycotts of British goods and to create substitutes for the tea, textiles, and other commodities they were shunning. In Edenton, North Carolina, fifty-one women signed an agreement in October 1774 declaring their "sincere adherence" to the anti-British resolutions of their provincial assembly and proclaiming their duty to do "every thing as far as lies in our power" to support the "publick good."

COOPERATION AND WAR

Revolutions do not simply happen. They need organizers and leaders. Beginning in 1765, colonial leaders developed a variety of organizations for converting popular discontent into direct action—organizations that in time formed the basis for an independent government.

New Sources of Authority

The passage of authority from the royal government to the colonists themselves began on the local level, where the tradition of autonomy was already strong. In colony after colony, local institutions responded to the resistance movement by simply seizing authority on their own. At times, entirely new, extralegal bodies emerged semi-spontaneously and began to perform some of the functions of government. In Massachusetts in 1768, for example, Samuel Adams called a convention of delegates from the towns of the colony to sit in place of the General Court, which the governor had dissolved. The Sons of Liberty, which Adams had helped organize in Massachusetts and which sprang up elsewhere as well, became another source of power. Its members at times formed disciplined bands of vigilantes who made certain that all colonists respected the boycotts and other forms of popular resistance. And in most colonies, committees of prominent citizens began meeting to perform additional political functions.

The most effective of these new groups were the committees of correspondence, which Adams had inaugurated in Massachusetts in 1772. Virginia later established the first intercolonial committees of correspondence, which made possible continuous cooperation among the colonies. Virginia also took the greatest step of all toward united action in 1774 when, after the royal governor dissolved the assembly, a rump session met in the Raleigh Tavern at Williamsburg, declared that the Intolerable Acts menaced the liberties of every colony, and issued a call for a Continental Congress. Variously elected by the assemblies and by extralegal meetings, delegates from all the thirteen colonies except Georgia were present when, in September 1774, the First Continental Congress convened in Carpenter's Hall in Philadelphia. They made five major decisions. First,

First Continental Congress

in a very close vote, they rejected a plan (proposed by Joseph Galloway of Pennsylvania) for a colonial union under British authority (much like the earlier Albany Plan). Second, they endorsed a statement of grievances, whose tortured language reflected the conflicts among the delegates between moderates and extremists. The statement reflected the influence of the moderates by seeming to concede Parliament's right to regulate colonial trade and by addressing the king as "Most Gracious Sovereign"; but it also included a more extreme demand for the repeal of all the oppressive legislation passed since 1763. Third, they approved a series of resolutions that a Suffolk County, Massachusetts, convention had passed, recommending, among other things, that the colonists make military preparations for defense against possible attack by the British troops in Boston. Fourth, they agreed to nonimportation, nonexportation, and nonconsumption as means of stopping all trade with Great Britain, and they formed a "Continental Association" to enforce the agreements. And fifth, when the delegates adjourned, they agreed to meet again the next spring, thus indicating that they considered the Continental Congress a continuing organization.

Through their representatives in Philadelphia the colonies had, in effect, reaffirmed their autonomous status within the empire and declared something close to economic war to maintain that position. The more optimistic of the Americans hoped that this economic warfare alone would win a quick and bloodless victory, but the more pessimistic had their doubts. "I expect no redress, but, on the contrary, increased resentment and double vengeance," John Adams wrote to Patrick Henry; "we must fight." And Henry replied, "By God, I am of your opinion."

During the winter, the Parliament in London debated proposals for conciliating the colonists. Lord Chatham (William Pitt), the former prime minister, urged the

RECRUITING PATRIOTS This Revolutionary War recruiting poster tries to attract recruits by appealing to their patriotism (asking them to defend "the liberties and independence of the United States"), their vanity (by showing the "handsome clothing" and impressive bearing of soldiers), and their greed (by offering them "a bounty of twelve dollars" and "sixty dollars a year"). *(Library of Congress)*

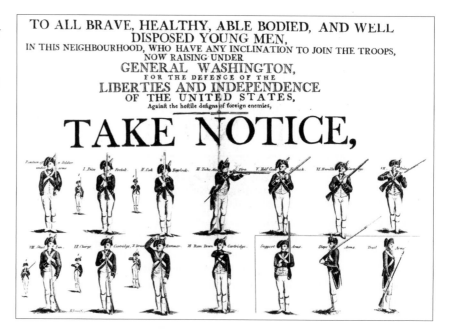

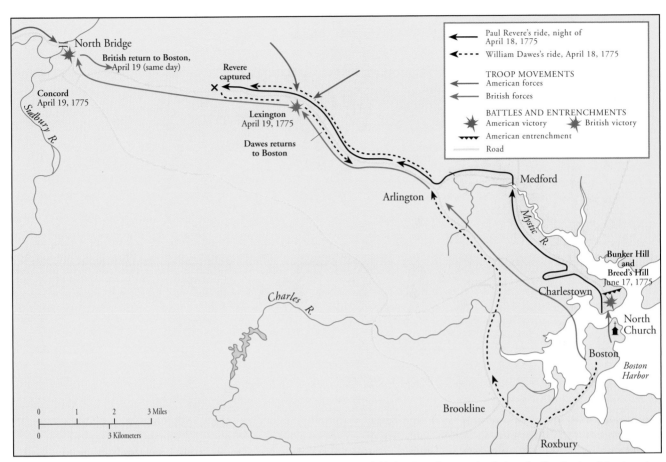

THE BATTLES OF LEXINGTON AND CONCORD, 1775 This map shows the fabled series of events that led to the first battle of the American Revolution. On the night of April 18, 1775, Paul Revere and William Dawes rode out from Boston to warn the outlying towns of the approach of British troops. Revere was captured just west of Lexington, but Dawes escaped and returned to Boston. The next morning, British forces moved out of Boston toward Lexington, where they met armed American minutemen on the Lexington common and exchanged fire. The British dispersed the Americans in Lexington. But they next moved on to Concord, where they encountered more armed minutemen, clashed again, and were driven back toward Boston. All along their line of march, they were harassed by riflemen. ◆ *What impact did the battles of Lexington and Concord (and the later battle of Bunker Hill, also shown on this map) have on colonial sentiment toward the British?*

withdrawal of troops from America. Edmund Burke called

The Conciliatory Propositions

for the repeal of the Coercive Acts. But their efforts were in vain. Lord North finally won approval early in 1775 for a series of measures known as the Conciliatory Propositions, but they were in fact far less conciliatory than the approaches Burke or Chatham had urged. Parliament now proposed that the colonies, instead of being taxed directly by Parliament, would tax themselves at Parliament's demand. With this offer, Lord North hoped to divide the American moderates, who he believed represented the views of the majority, from the extremist minority. But his offer was probably too little and, in any case, too late. It did not reach America until after the first shots of war had been fired.

Lexington and Concord

For months, the farmers and townspeople of Massachusetts had been gathering arms and ammunition and training as "minutemen," preparing to fight on a minute's notice. The Continental Congress had approved preparations for a defensive war, and the citizen-soldiers awaited an aggressive move by the British regulars in Boston.

In Boston, General Thomas Gage, commanding the British garrison, knew of the military preparations in the countryside but considered his army too small to do anything until reinforcements arrived. He resisted the advice of less cautious officers, who assured him that the Americans would never dare actually to fight, that they would back down quickly before any show of British force. Major John Pitcairn, for example, insisted that a single "small action," such as the burning of a few towns, would "set everything to rights."

When General Gage received orders from England to arrest the rebel leaders Sam Adams and John Hancock, known to be in the vicinity of Lexington, he still hesitated. But when he

General Thomas Gage

heard that the minutemen had stored a large supply of gunpowder in Concord (eighteen miles from Boston), he at last decided to act. On the night of April 18, 1775, he sent a

The Retreat

From Concord to Lexington of the Army of Wild Irish Asses Defeated by the Brave American Militia
Mr Deacon Mr Loeings Mr Mulikens Mr Bonds Houses and Barn all Plunderit and Burnt on April 19.th

THE BRITISH RETREAT FROM CONCORD, 1775 This American cartoon satirizes the retreat of British forces from Concord after the battle there on April 19, 1775. Patriot forces are lined up on the left, and the retreating British forces (portrayed with dog heads, perhaps because many of the soldiers were "wild" Irish) straggle off at right—some fleeing in panic, others gloating over the booty they have plundered from the burning homes above. In its crude and exaggerated way, the cartoon depicts the success of Patriot forces at the Old North Bridge in Concord in repulsing a British contingent under the command of Lord Percy. As the redcoats retreated to Lexington and then to Boston, they continued to encounter fire from colonial forces, not arrayed in battle lines as shown here, but hidden along the road. One British soldier described the nightmarish withdrawal: "We were fired on from Houses and behind Trees . . . the Country was . . . full of Hills, Woods, stone Walls . . . which the Rebels did not fail to take advantage of." *(Anne S.K. Brown Military Collection, Brown University Library)*

detachment of about 1,000 soldiers out from Boston on the road to Lexington and Concord. He intended to surprise the colonials and seize the illegal supplies without bloodshed.

But patriots in Boston were watching the British movements closely, and during the night two horsemen, William Dawes and Paul Revere, rode out to warn the villages and farms. When the British troops arrived in Lexington the next day, several dozen minutemen awaited them on the town common. Shots were fired and minutemen fell; eight of them were killed and ten more wounded. Advancing to Concord, the British discovered that the Americans had hastily removed most of the powder supply, but the British burned what was left of it. All along the road from Concord back to Boston, farmers hiding behind trees, rocks, and stone fences harassed the British with continual gunfire. By the end of the day, the British had lost almost three times as many men as the Americans.

The first shots—the "shots heard round the world," as Americans later called them—had been fired. But who had fired them? According to one of the minutemen at

Lexington, Major Pitcairn had shouted to the colonists on his arrival, "Disperse, ye rebels!" When the Americans ignored the command, he had given the order to fire. British officers and soldiers told a different story. They claimed that the minutemen had fired first, that only after seeing the flash of American guns had the British begun to shoot. Whatever the truth, the rebels succeeded in circulating their account well ahead of the British version, adorning it with lurid tales of British atrocities. The effect was to rally to the rebel cause thousands of colonists, north and south, who previously had had little enthusiasm for it.

It was not immediately clear to the British, and even to many Americans, that the skirmishes at Lexington and Concord were the first battles of a war. Many saw them as simply another example of the tensions that had been afflicting Anglo-American relations for years. But whether *The Revolution Begins* they recognized it at the time or not, the British and the Americans had taken a decisive step. The War for Independence had begun.

CONCLUSION

When the French and Indian War ended in 1763, it might have seemed reasonable to expect that relations between the English colonists in America and Great Britain itself would have been cemented more firmly than ever. America and Britain had fought together in a great war against the French and their Indian allies. They had won impressive victories. They had vastly expanded the size of the British Empire.

But in fact the end of the French and Indian War altered the imperial relationship forever, in ways that ultimately drove Americans to rebel against English rule and begin a war for independence. To the British, the lesson of the war was that the colonies in America needed firmer control from London. The empire was now much bigger, and it needed better administration. The war had produced great debts, and the Americans—among the principal beneficiaries of the war—should help pay them. And so for more than a decade after the end of the fighting, the British tried one strategy after another to tighten control over and extract money from the colonies, all of them in the end failures.

To the colonists, this effort to tighten imperial rule was both a betrayal of the sacrifices they had made in the war and a challenge to their long-developing assumptions about the rights of English people to rule themselves. Gradually, white Americans came to see in the British policies evidence of a conspiracy to establish tyranny in the New World. And so throughout the 1760s and 1770s, the colonists developed ever more overt and effective forms of resistance. By the time the first shots were fired in the American Revolution in 1775, Britain and America—not long before bonded so closely to one another that most white Americans considered themselves as English as any resident of London—had come to view each other as two very different societies. Their differences, which came to seem irreconcilable, propelled them into a war that would change the course of history.

FOR FURTHER REFERENCE

Fred Anderson, *The Crucible of War: The Seven Years' War and the Fate of Empire in British North America, 1754–1766* (2000) is an excellent account of the critical years in which the British Empire transformed itself through its colonial wars in America. David Armitage, *The Ideological Origins of the British Empire* (2000) examines the ideas of those who promoted and sought to justify Britain's imperial ambitions. Francis Jennings, *The Ambiguous Iroquois Empire* (1984) examines the critical role of the Iroquois in the conflicts over empire in North America. Richard Bushman, *King and People in Colonial Massachusetts* (1987) traces the fracture between Massachusetts colonists and the imperial government. Gary Nash, *The Urban Crucible: The Northern Seaports and the Origins of the American Revolution* (1979) argues that increasing class stratification in northern cities contributed to the coming of the American Revolution. Robert R. Palmer, *The Age of Democratic Revolution: Vol. 1, The Challenge* (1959) and J. G. A. Pocock, *The Machiavellian Moment* (1975) both place the American Revolution in the context of a transatlantic political culture. Bernard Bailyn, *The Ideological Origins of the American Revolution* (1967) was one of the first works by an American historian to emphasize the importance of English republican political thought for the revolutionary ideology of the American colonists.

For quizzes, Internet resources, references to additional books and films, and more, consult this book's Online Learning Center at www.mhhe.com/brinkley11.

THE BRITISH SURRENDER This contemporary drawing depicts the formal surrender of British troops at Yorktown on October 19, 1781. Columns of American troops and a large French fleet flank the surrender ceremony, suggesting part of the reason for the British defeat. General Cornwallis, the commander of British forces in Virginia, did not himself attend the surrender. He sent a deputy in his place. *(Hulton/Archive/Getty Images)*

Significant Events

1774 · Shawnee defeated by Virginia militia in Lord Dunmore's War

1775 · Second Continental Congress meets
· George Washington appointed to command American forces
· Battle of Bunker Hill
· Montgomery assault on Quebec fails

1776 · Thomas Paine's *Common Sense* published
· British troops leave Boston
· Declaration of Independence debated and signed (July 2–4)
· Howe routs Americans on Long Island
· Battle of Trenton
· First state constitutions written

1777 · Articles of Confederation adopted
· Battles of Princeton, Brandywine, and Germantown
· Howe occupies Philadelphia
· Washington camps at Valley Forge for winter
· Burgoyne surrenders to Gates at Saratoga

1778 · French-American alliance established
· Clinton replaces Howe
· British leave Philadelphia
· War shifts to the South
· British capture Savannah

1780 · British capture Charleston
· Cornwallis defeats Gates at Camden, South Carolina
· Patriots defeat Tories at King's Mountain, South Carolina

CHAPTER FIVE

THE AMERICAN REVOLUTION

Two struggles occurred simultaneously during the seven years of war that began in April 1775. One was the military conflict with Great Britain. The second was a political struggle within America. The two struggles had profound effects on each other.

The military conflict was, by the standards of later wars, a relatively modest one. Battle deaths on the American side totaled fewer than 5,000. The technology of warfare was so crude that cannons and rifles were effective only at very close range, and fighting of any kind was virtually out of the question in bad weather. Yet the war in America was, by the standards of its own day, an unusually savage conflict, pitting not only army against army, but at times the population at large against a powerful external force. This shift of the war from a traditional, conventional struggle to a new kind of conflict—a revolutionary war for liberation—made it possible for the new American army finally to defeat the vastly more powerful British.

At the same time, Americans were wrestling with the great political questions the conflict necessarily produced: first, whether to demand independence from Britain; then, how to structure the new nation they had proclaimed. Only the first of these questions had been resolved when the British surrendered at Yorktown in 1781. But by then the United States had already established *Key Political Questions* itself—both in its own mind and in the mind of much of the rest of the world—as a new kind of nation, one with a special mission and dedicated to enlightened ideals. Thomas Paine, an important figure in shaping the Revolution, reflected the opinion of many when he claimed that the American War for Independence had "contributed more to enlighten the world, and diffuse a spirit of freedom and liberality among mankind, than any human event that ever preceded it." And if the subsequent history of the United States did not always fulfill those ideals, the belief that the nation should try to do so exercised a continuing influence on the nation's behavior.

THE STATES UNITED

Although many Americans had been expecting a military conflict with Britain for months, even years, the actual beginning of hostilities in 1775 found the colonies generally unprepared for the enormous challenges awaiting them. America was an unformed nation, with a population less than a third as large as the 9 million of Great Britain, and with vastly inferior economic and military resources. It faced the task of mobilizing for war against the world's greatest armed power. Americans faced that task, moreover, deeply divided about what they were fighting for.

Defining American War Aims

Three weeks after the battles of Lexington and Concord, the Second Continental Congress met in the State House in Philadelphia, with delegates from every colony except Georgia, which sent no representative until the following autumn. The members agreed to support the war. But they disagreed, at times profoundly, about its purpose.

At one pole was a group led by the Adams cousins (John and Samuel), Richard Henry Lee of Virginia, and others, who favored complete independence from Great Britain. At the other pole was a group led by such moderates as John Dickinson of Pennsylvania, who hoped for modest reforms in the imperial relationship that would permit an early reconciliation with Great Britain. Most of the delegates tried to find some middle ground between these positions. They demonstrated their uncertainty in *Olive Branch Petition* two very different declarations, which they adopted in quick succession. They approved one last, conciliatory appeal to the king, the "Olive Branch Petition." Then, on July 6, 1775, they adopted a more antagonistic "Declaration of the Causes and Necessity of Taking Up Arms." It proclaimed that the British government had left the American people with only two alternatives, "unconditional submission to the tyranny of irritated ministers or resistance by force."

The attitude of much of the public mirrored that of the Congress. At first, most Americans believed they were fighting not for independence but for a redress of grievances within the British Empire. During the first year of fighting, however, many of them began to change their minds, for several reasons. First, the costs of the war—human and financial—were so high that the original war aims began to seem too modest to justify them. Second, what lingering affection American Patriots retained for England greatly diminished when the British began trying to recruit Indians, African slaves, and foreign mercenaries (the hated Hessians) against them. Third, and most important, colonists came to believe that the British government was forcing them toward independence by rejecting the Olive Branch Petition and instead enacting a

"Prohibitory Act," which closed the colonies to all overseas trade and made no concessions to American demands except an offer to pardon repentant rebels. The British enforced the Prohibitory Act with a naval blockade of colonial ports.

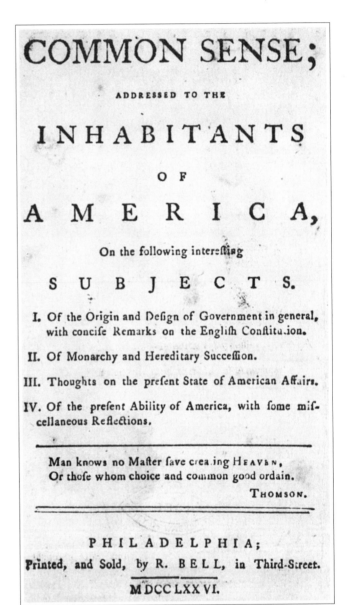

COMMON SENSE Shown here is the title page of the first edition of Thomas Paine's influential pamphlet, published anonymously in Philadelphia on January 10, 1776. Paine served in Washington's army during the campaigns in New Jersey and at the same time wrote a series of essays designed to arouse support for the Patriot cause. They were collectively titled *The Crisis* (the first of them contains the famous phrase "These are the times that try men's souls"). In later years Paine took an active part in the French Revolution, on behalf of which he published *The Rights of Man* (1791–1792). He also wrote *The Age of Reason* (1794–1796), which attacked conventional Christian beliefs and promoted his own "deist" philosophy. He returned to America in 1802 and spent the last years before his death in 1809 in poverty and obscurity. (*Library of Congress*)

But the growing support for independence remained to a large degree unspoken until January 1776, when an impassioned pamphlet appeared that galvanized many Americans. It was called, simply, *Common Sense*. Its author, unmentioned on the title page, was Thomas Paine, who had emigrated from England to America fifteen months before (with letters of introduction from Benjamin

Common Sense

Franklin, whom he had met in London). Long a failure in various trades, Paine now proved a brilliant success as a revolutionary propagandist. His pamphlet helped change the American outlook toward the war. Paine wished to expose the folly of continuing to believe reconciliation with Britain was possible. He wanted to turn the anger of Americans away from the specific parliamentary measures they were resisting and toward what he considered the root of the problem—the English constitution itself. It was not enough, he argued, for Americans to continue blaming their problems on particular ministers, or even on Parliament. It was the king, and the system that permitted him to rule, that was to blame. It was, he argued, simple common sense for Americans to break completely with a government that could produce so corrupt a monarch as George III, a government that could inflict such brutality on its own people, a government that could drag Americans into wars in which America had no interest. The island kingdom of England was no more fit to rule the American continent, he claimed, than a satellite was fit to rule the sun.

The Decision for Independence

Common Sense sold more than 100,000 copies in its first few months. (Given the size of the American population at the time, that would be the equivalent of selling 8 million copies today.) To many of its readers it was a revelation. Although sentiment for independence remained far from unanimous, support for the idea grew rapidly in the first months of 1776.

In the midst of all this, the Continental Congress (meeting again in Philadelphia) was moving slowly and tentatively toward a final break with England. It declared American ports open to the ships of all nations except Great Britain. It entered into communication with foreign powers. It recommended to the various

The Declaration of Independence

colonies that they establish new governments independent of the British Empire, as in fact most already were doing. Congress also appointed a committee to draft a formal declaration of independence. On July 2, 1776, it adopted a resolution: "That these United Colonies are, and, of right, ought to be, free and independent states; that they are absolved from all allegiance to the British crown, and that all political connexion between them and the state of Great Britain is, and ought to be, totally dissolved." Two days

later, on July 4, Congress approved the Declaration of Independence itself, which provided the formal justifications for the actions the delegates had in fact taken two days earlier.

Thomas Jefferson, a thirty-three-year-old delegate from Virginia, wrote most of the Declaration, with help from Benjamin Franklin and John Adams. As Adams later observed, Jefferson said little in the document that was new. Its virtue lay in the eloquence with which it expressed beliefs already widespread in America. In particular, it expressed ideas that had been voiced throughout the colonies in the preceding months in the form of at least ninety other, local "declarations of independence"—declarations drafted up and down the coast by town meetings, artisan and militia organizations, county officials, grand juries, Sons of Liberty, and colonial assemblies. Jefferson borrowed heavily from these texts, both for the ideas he expressed and, to some extent, for the precise language he used.

The document was in two parts. In the first, the Declaration restated the familiar contract theory of John Locke: that governments were formed to protect the rights of life, liberty, and property; Jefferson gave the theory a more idealistic tone by referring instead to the rights of "life, liberty and the pursuit of happiness." In the second part, the Declaration listed the alleged crimes of the king, who, with the backing of Parliament, had violated his "contract" with the colonists and thus had forfeited all claim to their loyalty.

The Declaration's ringing endorsement of the idea that "all men are created equal"—a phrase borrowed from an earlier document by Jefferson's fellow Virginian George Mason—later helped movements of liberation and reform of many kinds in the United States and abroad. It helped inspire, among other things, the French Revolution's own Declaration of the Rights of Man. More immediately, the Declaration—and its bold claim that the American colonies were now a sovereign nation, "The United States of America"—led to increased foreign aid for the struggling rebels and prepared the way for France's intervention on their side. The Declaration also encouraged American Patriots, as those opposing the British called themselves, to fight on and to reject the idea of a peace that stopped short of winning independence. At the same time it created deep divisions within American society.

Responses to Independence

At the news of the Declaration of Independence, crowds in Philadelphia, Boston, and other places gathered to cheer, fire guns and cannons, and ring church bells. But there were many in America who did not rejoice. Some had disapproved of the war from the beginning. Others had been willing to support it only so long as its aims did not conflict with their basic loyalty to the king. Such

Through most of its long life, the debate over the origins of the American Revolution has tended to reflect two broad schools of interpretation. One sees the Revolution largely as a political and intellectual event and argues that the revolt against Britain was part of a defense of ideals and principles. The other views the Revolution as a social and economic phenomenon and contends that material interests were at its heart.

The Revolutionary generation itself portrayed the conflict as a struggle over ideals, and their interpretation prevailed through most of the nineteenth century. For example, George Bancroft wrote in 1876 that the Revolution "was most radical in its character, yet achieved with such benign tranquillity that even conservatism hesitated to censure." Its aim, he argued, was to "preserve liberty" against British tyranny.

But in the early twentieth century, historians influenced by the reform currents of the progressive era began to identify social and economic forces that they believed had contributed to the rebellion. In a 1909 study of New York, Carl Becker wrote that two questions had shaped the Revolution: "The first was the question of home rule; the second was

(Anne S.K. Brown Military Collection, Brown University Library)

the question . . . of who should rule at home." The colonists were not only fighting the British; they were also engaged in a kind of civil war, a contest for power between radicals and conservatives that led to the "democratization of American politics and society."

Other "progressive" historians elaborated on Becker's thesis. In *The American Revolution Considered as a Social Movement* (1926), J. Franklin Jameson argued that "the stream of revolution, once started, could not be confined within narrow banks, but spread abroad upon the land. . . . Many economic desires, many social aspirations, were set free by the political struggle, many aspects of society profoundly altered by the forces thus let loose." In a 1917 book, Arthur M. Schlesinger maintained that colonial merchants, motivated by their own interest in escaping the restrictive policies of British mercantilism, aroused American resistance in the 1760s and 1770s.

Beginning in the 1950s, a new generation of scholars began to re-emphasize the role of ideology and to de-emphasize the role of economic interests. Robert E. Brown (in 1955) and Edmund S. Morgan (in 1956) both argued that most eighteenth-century white Americans, regardless of station, shared basic political principles and that the social and economic conflicts the progressives had identified were not severe. The rhetoric of the Revolution, they suggested, was not propaganda, but a real reflection of the colonists' ideas. Bernard Bailyn, in

---

people were a minority, but a substantial one. They called themselves Loyalists; supporters of independence called them Tories.

In the aftermath of the Declaration of Independence, the colonies began to call themselves states—a reflection of their belief that each province was now in some respects a separate and sovereign entity. And as states, they had to create new governments to replace the royal governments that independence had repudiated. By 1781, most states had produced written constitutions that established republican governments; some of these constitutions survived, with only minor changes, for decades to come.

Divided Americans

At the national level, however, the process of forming a government was more halting and less successful. For a time, Americans were uncertain whether they even wanted a real national government; the Continental Congress had not been much more than a coordinating

mechanism, and virtually everyone considered the individual colonies (now states) the real centers of authority. Yet fighting a war required a certain amount of central direction. Americans began almost immediately to do something they would continue to do for more than two centuries: balance the commitment to state and local autonomy against the need for some centralized authority.

In November 1777, Congress adopted the Articles of Confederation (which were not finally ratified until 1781). They did little more than confirm the weak, decentralized system already in operation. The Continental Congress would survive as the chief coordinating agency of the war effort. Its powers over the individual states would be very limited. Indeed, the Articles did not make it entirely clear that the Congress was to be a real government at all. As a result, the new nation had to fight a war for its own survival with a weak and

Articles of Confederation

The Ideological Origins of the American Revolution (1967), demonstrated the complex roots of the ideas behind the Revolution and argued that this carefully constructed political stance was not a disguise for economic interests but a genuine ideology that itself motivated the colonists to act. The Revolution, he claimed, "was above all else an ideological, constitutional, political struggle and not primarily a controversy between social groups undertaken to force changes in the organization of the society or the economy."

By the late 1960s, however, a group of younger historians—many of them influenced by the New Left—were challenging the ideological interpretation again by illuminating social and economic tensions within colonial society that they claimed helped shape the Revolutionary struggle. Jesse Lemisch and Dirk Hoerder pointed to the actions of mobs in colonial cities as evidence of popular resentment of both American and British elites. Joseph Ernst re-emphasized the significance of economic pressures on colonial merchants and tradesmen. Gary Nash, in *The Urban Crucible* (1979), emphasized the role of growing economic distress in colonial cities in creating a climate in which Revolutionary sentiment could flourish. Edward

(Gift of Edgar William and Bernice Chrysler Garbisch, © 1998 Board of Trustees, National Gallery of Art, Washington)

Countryman and Rhys Isaac both pointed to changes in the nature of colonial society and culture, and in the relationship between classes in eighteenth-century America, as a crucial prerequisite for the growth of the Revolutionary movement.

Some newer social interpretations of the Revolution attempt to break free of the old debate pitting ideas against interests. The two things are not in competition with, but rather reinforce

one another, more recent scholars argue. "Everyone has economic interests," Gary Nash has written, "and everyone . . . has an ideology." Only by exploring the relationships between the two can historians hope fully to understand either. Also, as Linda Kerber has written, newer interpretations have "reinvigorated the Progressive focus on social conflict between classes and extended it to include the experience not only of rich and poor but of a wide variety of interest groups, marginal communities, and social outsiders." That extension of focus to previously little-studied groups includes work by Mary Beth Norton on women, Silvia Frey on slaves, and Colin Calloway on Native Americans.

A decade ago, Gordon Wood, in *The Radicalism of the American Revolution* (1992), helped revive an interpretation of the Revolution that few historians have embraced in recent decades: that it was a genuinely radical event, which led to the breakdown of such longstanding patterns of society as deference, patriarchy, and traditional gender relations. Class conflict and radical goals may not have caused the Revolution; but the Revolution had a profound, even radical, ideological impact on society nevertheless.

uncertain central government, never sure of its own legitimacy.

Mobilizing for War

The new governments of the states and the nation faced a series of overwhelming challenges: raising and organizing armies, providing them with the supplies and equipment they needed, and finding a way to pay for it all. Without access to the British markets on which the colonies had come to depend, finding necessary supplies was exceptionally difficult. Shortages persisted to the end.

America had many gunsmiths, but they could not come close to meeting the wartime demand for guns and ammunition, let alone the demand for heavy arms. Although Congress created a government arsenal at Springfield, Massachusetts, in 1777, the Americans managed to manufacture only a small fraction of the equipment they used. They relied heavily on weapons and materiel they were able to

capture from the British. But they got most of their war supplies from European nations, mainly from France.

Financing the war proved in many ways the most nettlesome problem. Congress had no authority to levy taxes directly on the people; it had to requisition funds from the state governments. But hard money was scarce in America, and the states were little better equipped to raise it than Congress was. None of them contributed more than a small part of their expected share. Congress tried to raise money by selling long-term bonds, but few Americans could afford them and those who could generally preferred to invest in more profitable ventures, such as privateering. In the end, the government had no choice but to issue paper money. Continental currency came from the printing presses in large and repeated batches. The states printed sizable amounts of paper currency of their own.

The result, predictably, was inflation. Prices rose to fantastic heights, and the value of paper money plummeted.

VOTING FOR INDEPENDENCE The Continental Congress actually voted in favor of independence from Great Britain on July 2, 1776. July 4, the date Americans now celebrate as Independence Day, is when the Congress formally approved the Declaration of Independence. This painting by Edgar Pine-Savage re-creates the scene in Philadelphia as delegates from the various colonies made their momentous decision. *(Historical Society of Pennsylvania)*

Many American farmers and merchants began to prefer doing business with the British, who could pay for goods in gold or silver coin. (That was one reason why George

Financing the War

Washington's troops suffered from severe food shortages at Valley Forge in the winter of 1777–1778; many Philadelphia merchants would not sell to them.) Congress tried repeatedly to stem the inflationary spiral. All such efforts failed. In the end, the new American government was able to finance the war effort only by borrowing heavily from other nations.

After the first great surge of patriotism faded in 1775, few Americans volunteered for military service. As a result, the states had to resort to persuasion and force: to paying bounties to attract new recruits and to drafting them. Even when it was possible to recruit substantial numbers of militiamen, they remained under the control of their respective states. Congress quickly recognized the disadvantages of this decentralized system and tried, with some success, to correct it. In the spring of 1775, it created a Continental army with a single commander in chief. George Washington, the forty-three-year-old Virginia planter-aristocrat who had commanded colonial forces

during the French and Indian War, possessed more experience than any other American-born officer available. He had also been an early advocate of independence. Above all, he was admired, respected, and trusted by nearly all Patriots. He was the unanimous choice of the delegates, and he took command in June 1775.

Congress had chosen well. Throughout the war, Washington kept faithfully at his task, despite difficulties and discouragements that would have daunted a lesser man. He had to deal with serious problems of morale among soldiers who consistently received short rations and low pay; open mutinies

General George Washington

broke out in 1781 among the Pennsylvania and New Jersey troops. The Continental Congress, Washington's "employers," always seemed too little interested in supplying him with manpower and equipment and too much interested in interfering with his conduct of military operations. During the discouraging winter of Valley Forge, some congressmen and army officers apparently even conspired unsuccessfully (in the so-called Conway Cabal, named for Thomas Conway, one of its alleged leaders) to replace Washington as commander in chief.

REVOLUTIONARY SOLDIERS Jean Baptiste de Verger, a French officer serving in America during the Revolution, kept a journal of his experiences illustrated with watercolors. Here he portrays four American soldiers carrying different kinds of arms: a black infantryman with a light rifle, a musketman, a rifleman, and an artilleryman. *(Anne S.K. Brown Military Collection, Brown University Library)*

Washington was not without shortcomings as a military commander. But he was, in the end, a great war leader. With the aid of foreign military experts such as the Marquis de Lafayette from France and Baron von Steuben from Prussia, he succeeded in building and holding together an army of fewer than 10,000 men that, along with state militias, ultimately prevailed against the great-

Foreign Assistance

est military power in the world. Even more important, perhaps, in a new nation still unsure of either its purposes or its structure, with a central government both weak and divided, Washington provided the army—and the people—with a symbol of stability around which they could rally. He may not have been the most brilliant of the country's early leaders, but in the crucial years of the war, at least, he was the most successful in holding the new nation together.

THE WAR FOR INDEPENDENCE

On the surface, at least, all the advantages in the military struggle between America and Great Britain appeared to lie with the British. They possessed the greatest

navy and the best-equipped army in the world. They had access to the resources of an empire. They had a coherent structure of command. The Americans, by contrast, were struggling to create a new army and a new government at the same time that they were trying to fight a war.

Yet the United States had advantages that were not at first apparent. Americans were fighting on their own ground, while the English were far from their own land (and their own resources). The American Patriots were, on the whole, deeply committed to the conflict; the British people only halfheartedly supported the war. Beginning in 1777, more-

American Advantages

over, the Americans had the benefit of substantial aid from abroad, when the American war became part of a larger world contest in which Great Britain faced the strongest powers of Europe—most notably France—in a struggle for imperial supremacy.

The American victory was not, however, simply the result of these advantages. It was not simply a result, either, of the remarkable spirit and resourcefulness of the people and the army. It was a result, too, of a series of egregious blunders and miscalculations by the British in the early stages of the fighting, when England could (and probably should) have won. And it was, finally, a result of the transformation

BATTLE OF GERMANTOWN On October 4, 1777, Washington launched an attack on General Howe's camp at Germantown, near Philadelphia. Although the Patriots were successful in the first hours of the battle, a heavy fog confused them and allowed the British finally to force them to retreat. This 1782 painting re-creates a part of the battle: an attack by American forces led by "Mad Anthony" Wayne. *(Valley Forge Historical Society)*

of the war—which proceeded in three different phases—into a new kind of conflict that the British military, for all its strength, could not win.

The First Phase: New England

For the first year of the fighting—from the spring of 1775 to the spring of 1776—the British remained uncertain about whether or not they were actually engaged in a war. Many English authorities continued to believe that what was happening in America was a limited, local conflict and that British forces were simply attempting to quell pockets of rebellion in the contentious area around Boston. Gradually, however, colonial forces took the offensive and made almost the entire territory of the American colonies a battleground.

After the British withdrawal from Concord and Lexington in April 1775, American forces besieged the army of General Thomas Gage in Boston. The Patriots suffered severe casualties in the Battle of Bunker Hill (actually fought on Breed's Hill) on June 17, 1775, and were ultimately driven from their position there. But they inflicted much

Bunker Hill

greater losses on the enemy than the enemy inflicted on them. Indeed, the British suffered their heaviest casualties of the entire war at Bunker Hill. After the battle, the Patriots continued to tighten the siege.

By the first months of 1776, the British had concluded that Boston was not the best place from which to wage war. Not only was it in the center of the most fervently anti-British region of the colonies, it was also tactically indefensible—a narrow neck of land, easily isolated and besieged. By late winter, in fact, Patriot forces had surrounded the city and occupied strategic positions on the heights. On March 17, 1776 (a date still celebrated in Boston as Evacuation Day), the British departed Boston for Halifax in Nova Scotia with hundreds of Loyalist refugees. Less than a year after the firing of the first shots, the Massachusetts colonists had driven the British—temporarily—from American soil.

Elsewhere, the war proceeded fitfully and inconclusively. To the south, at Moore's Creek Bridge in North Carolina, a band of Patriots crushed an uprising of Loyalists on February 27, 1776, and in the process discouraged a British plan to invade the southern states. The British had expected substantial aid from local Tories in the

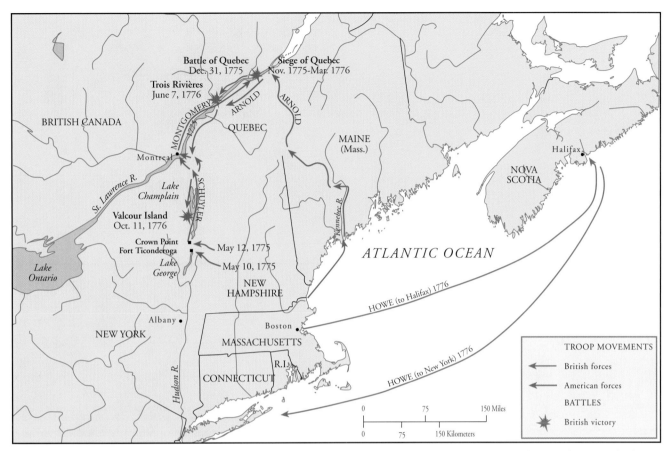

THE REVOLUTION IN THE NORTH, 1775–1776 After initial battles in and around Boston, the British forces left Massachusetts and (after a brief stay in Halifax, Canada) moved south to New York. ◆ *Why would the British have considered New York a better base than Boston?* In the meantime, American forces moved north in an effort to capture British strongholds in Montreal and Quebec, with little success.

 For an interactive version of this map go to www.mhhe.com/brinkley11ch5maps

South; they realized now that such aid might not be as effective as they had hoped. To the north, Americans launched an invasion of Canada—hoping to remove the

Invasion of Canada

British threat and win the Canadians to their cause. Benedict Arnold, the commander of a small American force, threatened Quebec in late 1775 and early 1776 after a winter march of incredible hardship. Richard Montgomery, coming to his assistance, combined his forces with Arnold's and took command of both. Montgomery died in the assault on the city; and although a wounded Arnold kept up the siege for a time, the Quebec campaign ended in frustration. Congress sent a civilian commission to Canada, headed by the seventy-year-old Benjamin Franklin. But Franklin also failed to win the allegiance of the northern colonists. Canada was not to become part of the new nation.

The British evacuation of Boston in 1776 was not, therefore, so much a victory for the Americans as a reflection of changing English assumptions about the war. By the spring of 1776, it had become clear to the British that

the conflict was not a local phenomenon in the area around Boston. The American campaigns in Canada, the agitation in the South, and the growing evidence of colonial unity all suggested that England must be prepared to fight a much larger conflict. The departure of the British, therefore, marked a shift in strategy more than an admission of defeat. It signaled the beginning of a new phase in the war.

The Second Phase: The Mid-Atlantic Region

The next phase of the war, which lasted from 1776 until early 1778, was when the British were in the best position to win. Indeed, had it not been for a series of blunders and misfortunes, they probably would have crushed the rebellion then. During this period the struggle became, for the most part, a traditional, conventional war. And in that, the Americans were woefully overmatched.

The British regrouped quickly after their retreat from Boston. During the summer of 1776, in the weeks immediately following the Declaration of Independence,

THE BATTLE OF BUNKER HILL, 1775 British troops face Patriot forces outside Boston on June 17, 1775, in the first great battle of the American Revolution. The British ultimately drove the Americans from their positions on Breed's Hill and Bunker Hill, but only after suffering enormous casualties. General Gage, the British commander, reported to his superiors in London after the battle: "These people show a spirit and conduct against us they never showed against the French." This anonymous painting reveals the array of British troops and naval support and also shows the bombardment and burning of Charlestown from artillery in Boston. *(Gift of Edgar William and Bernice Chrysler Garbisch,* © *1998 Board of Trustees, National Gallery of Art, Washington)*

the waters around New York City grew crowded with the most formidable military force Great Britain had ever sent abroad. Hundreds of men-of-war and troopships and 32,000 disciplined soldiers arrived, under the command of the affable William Howe. Howe felt no particular hostility toward the Americans. He hoped to awe them into submission rather than fight them, and he believed that most of them, if given a chance, would show their loyalty to the king. In a meeting with commissioners from Congress, he offered them a choice between submission with royal pardon and a battle against overwhelming odds.

To oppose Howe's impressive array, Washington could muster only about 19,000 poorly armed and trained sol-

British Take New York

diers, even after combining the Continental army with state militias; he had no navy at all. Even so, the Americans quickly rejected Howe's offer and chose to continue the war—a decision that led inevitably to a succession of rapid defeats. The British pushed the defenders off Long Island, compelled them to abandon Manhattan, and then drove them

in slow retreat over the plains of New Jersey, across the Delaware River, and into Pennsylvania.

For eighteenth-century Europeans, warfare was a seasonal activity. Fighting generally stopped in cold weather. The British settled down for the winter at various points in New Jersey, leaving an outpost of Hessians (German mercenaries) at Trenton on the Delaware River. But Washington did not sit still. On Christmas night 1776, he boldly recrossed the icy river, surprised and scattered the Hessians, and occupied the town. Then he advanced to Princeton and drove a British force from their base in the college there. But Washington was unable to hold either Princeton or Trenton, and he finally took refuge for the rest of the winter in the hills around Morristown, New Jersey.

For their campaigns of 1777 the British devised a strategy to cut the United States in two. Howe would move north from New York City up the Hudson to Albany, while an-

Britain's Strategy

other British force would come south from Canada to meet him. One of the younger British officers, the dashing

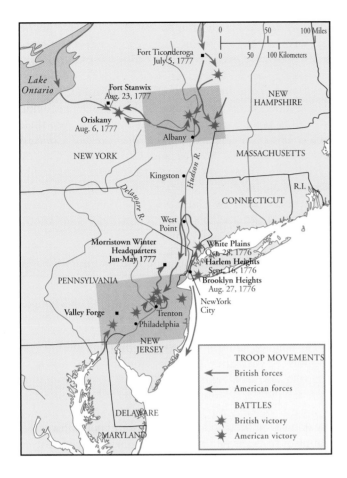

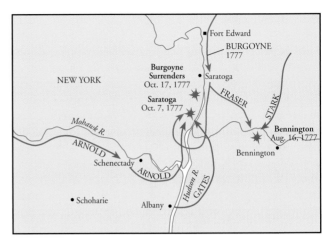

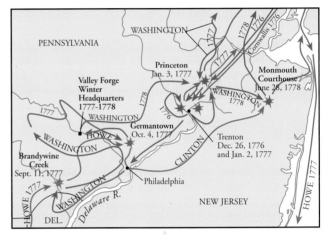

THE REVOLUTION IN THE MIDDLE COLONIES, 1776–1778 These maps illustrate the major campaigns of the Revolution in the middle colonies—New York, New Jersey, and Pennsylvania—between 1776 and 1778. The large map on the left shows the two prongs of the British strategy: first, a movement of British forces south from Canada into the Hudson Valley; and second, a movement of other British forces, under General William Howe, out from New York. The strategy was designed to trap the American army in between the two British movements. ◆ *What movements of Howe helped thwart that plan?* The two smaller maps on the right show a more detailed picture of some of the major battles. The upper ones reveal the surprising American victory at Saratoga. The lower ones show a series of inconclusive battles between New York and Philadelphia in 1777 and 1778.

 For an interactive version of this map go to www.mhhe.com/brinkley11ch5maps

John Burgoyne, secured command of this northern force and planned a two-pronged attack along both the Mohawk and the upper Hudson approaches to Albany.

But after setting this plan in motion, Howe himself abandoned it. He decided instead to launch an assault on the rebel capital Philadelphia—an assault that would, he hoped, discourage the Patriots, rally the Loyalists, and bring the war to a speedy conclusion. He removed the bulk of his forces from New York by sea, landed at the head of the Chesapeake Bay, brushed Washington aside at the Battle of Brandywine Creek on September 11, and proceeded north to Philadelphia, which he was able to occupy with little resistance. Meanwhile, Washington, after an unsuccessful October 4 attack at Germantown (just outside Philadelphia), went into winter quarters at Valley Forge. The Continental Congress, now dislodged from its capital, reassembled at York, Pennsylvania.

Howe's move to Philadelphia left Burgoyne to carry out the campaign in the north alone. Burgoyne sent Colonel Barry St. Leger up the St. Lawrence River toward Lake Ontario and the headwaters of the Mohawk, while Burgoyne himself advanced directly down the upper Hudson Valley. He got off to a flying start. He seized Fort Ticonderoga easily and with it an enormous store of powder and supplies; this caused such dismay in Congress that the delegates removed General Philip Schuyler from command of American forces in the north and replaced him with Horatio Gates.

By the time Gates took command, Burgoyne had already experienced two staggering defeats. In one of them—at Oriskany, New York, on August 6—a Patriot band of German farmers led by Nicholas Herkimer held off a force of Indians and Tories commanded by St. Leger. That gave Benedict Arnold time to go to the relief of Fort

Stanwix and close off the Mohawk Valley to St. Leger's advance.

In the other battle—at Bennington, Vermont, on August 16—New England militiamen under the Bunker Hill veteran John Stark severely mauled a British detachment that Burgoyne had sent out to seek supplies. Short of materials, with all help cut off, Burgoyne fought several costly engagements and then withdrew to Saratoga, where Gates surrounded him. On October 17, 1777, Burgoyne ordered what was left of his army, nearly 5,000 men, to surrender to the Americans.

To the Patriots, the New York campaign was a remarkable victory. News of it reverberated throughout the new *Patriot Victory at Saratoga* nation and through Europe as well. The British surrender at Saratoga became a major turning point in the war—above all, perhaps, because it led directly to an alliance between the United States and France.

The British failure to win the war during this period, a period in which they had overwhelming advantages, was *British Blunders* in large part a result of their own mistakes. And in assessing them, the role of William Howe looms large. He abandoned his own most important strategic initiative—the northern campaign—leaving Burgoyne to fight alone. And even in Pennsylvania, where he chose to engage the enemy, he refrained from moving in for a final attack on the weakened Continental army, even though he had several opportunities. Instead, he repeatedly allowed Washington to retreat and regroup; and he permitted the American army to spend a long winter unmolested in Valley Forge, where—weak and hungry—they might have been easy prey for British attack. Some believed that Howe did not want to win the war, that he was secretly in sympathy with the American cause. His family had close ties to the colonies, and he himself was linked politically to those forces within the British government that opposed the war. Others pointed to personal weaknesses: Howe's apparent alcoholism, his romantic attachment (he spent the winter of 1777–1778 in Philadelphia with his mistress when many were urging him to move elsewhere). But the most important problem, it seems clear, was his failure to understand the nature of the war that he was fighting—or even to understand that it was truly a war.

The Iroquois and the British

The campaign in upstate New York was not just a British defeat. It was a setback for the ambitious efforts of several Iroquois leaders, who hoped to involve Indian forces in the English military effort, believing that a British victory would help stem white movement onto tribal lands. The Iroquois Confederacy had declared itself a neutral in the war in 1776, but not all its members were content to remain passive in the northern campaign. Among those who worked to expand the Native American role in the war were a Mohawk brother and sister, Joseph and Mary Brant. Both were people of stature within the Mohawk nation: Joseph was a celebrated warrior; Mary was a magnetic woman and the widow of Sir William Johnson, the British superintendent of Indians, who had achieved wide popularity among the tribes. The Brants persuaded their own tribe to contribute to the British cause and attracted the support of the Seneca and Cayuga as well. They played an important role in Burgoyne's unsuccessful campaigns in the north.

But the alliance was also a sign of the growing divisions within the Iroquois Confederacy. Only three of the six nations of the Confederacy supported the British. The *Divisions in the Iroquois Confederacy* Oneida and the Tuscarora backed the Americans; the Onondaga split into several factions. The three-century-old Confederacy, weakened by the aftermath of the French and Indian War, continued to unravel.

The alliance had other unhappy consequences for the Iroquois. A year after Oriskany, Indians joined British troops in a series of raids on outlying white settlements in upstate New York. Months later, Patriot forces under the command of General John Sullivan harshly retaliated, wreaking such destruction on tribal settlements that large groups of Iroquois fled north into Canada to seek refuge. Many never returned.

Securing Aid from Abroad

The failure of the British to crush the Continental army in the mid-Atlantic states, combined with the stunning American victory at Saratoga, was a turning point in the war. It transformed the conflict and ushered it into a new and final phase.

Central to this transformation of the war was American success in winning support from abroad—indirect support from several European nations, and direct support from France. Even before the Declaration of Independence, Congress dispatched representatives to the capitals of Europe to negotiate commercial treaties with the governments there; if America was to leave the British Empire, it would need to cultivate new trading partners. Such treaties would, of course, require European governments to recognize the United States as an independent nation. John Adams called the early American representatives abroad *Militia Diplomats* "militia diplomats." Unlike the diplomatic regulars of Europe, they had little experience with the formal art and etiquette of Old World diplomacy. Since transatlantic communication was slow and uncertain (it took from one to three months for a message to cross the Atlantic), they had to interpret the instructions of Congress very freely and make crucial decisions entirely on their own.

The most promising potential ally for the United States was France. King Louis XVI, who had come to the throne in 1774, and his astute foreign minister, the Count de Vergennes, were eager to see Britain lose a crucial part of its empire. Through a series of covert bargains, facilitated by the creation of a fictional trading firm and the use of secret agents on both sides (among them the famed French dramatist Caron de Beaumarchais), France began supplying the Americans large quantities of much-needed supplies. But the French government remained reluctant to provide the United States with what it most wanted: diplomatic recognition.

Finally, Benjamin Franklin himself went to France to represent the United States. A natural diplomat, Franklin became a popular hero among the French—aristocrats and common people alike. His popularity there greatly helped the American cause. Of even greater help was the news of the American victory at Saratoga, which arrived in London on December 2, 1777, and in Paris two days later. On February 6, 1778—in part to forestall a British peace offensive that Vergennes feared might persuade the Americans to abandon the war—France formally recognized the United States as a sovereign nation and laid the groundwork for greatly expanded assistance to the American war effort.

France's intervention made the war an international conflict. In the course of the next two years, France, *Pivotal French Aid* | Spain, and the Netherlands all drifted into another general war with Great Britain in Europe, and all contributed both directly and indirectly to the ultimate American victory. But France was America's truly indispensable ally. Not only did it furnish the new nation with most of its money and munitions; it also provided a navy and an expeditionary force that proved invaluable in the decisive phase of the revolutionary conflict.

The Final Phase: The South

The last phase of the military struggle in America was very different from either of the first two. The British government had never been fully united behind the war in the first place; after the defeat at Saratoga and the intervention of the French, it imposed new limits on its commitment to the conflict. Instead of a full-scale military struggle against the American army, therefore, the British decided to try to enlist the support of those elements of the American population—a majority, they continued to believe—who were still loyal to the crown; in other words, they would work to undermine the Revolution from within. Since the British believed Loyalist sentiment was strongest in the southern colonies (despite their earlier failure to enlist Loyalist support in North Carolina), the main focus of their effort shifted there; and so it was in the South, for the most part, that the final stages of the war occurred.

The new strategy was a dismal failure. British forces spent three years (from 1778 to 1781) moving through the South, fighting small battles and large, and attempting to neutralize the territory through which they traveled. All such efforts ended in frustration. The British badly overestimated the extent of Loyalist sentiment. There were many Tories in Georgia and the Carolinas, some of them disgruntled members of the Regulator movement. But there were also many more Patriots than the British had believed. In Virginia, support for independence was as fervent as in Massachusetts. And even in the lower South, Loyalists often refused to aid the British because they feared reprisals from the Patriots around them. The British also harmed their own cause by encouraging southern slaves to desert their owners in return for promises of emancipation. Many slaves (perhaps five percent of the total) took advantage of this offer, despite the great difficulty of doing so. But white southerners were aghast; and even many who might otherwise have been inclined to support the crown now joined the Patriot side, which posed no such threat to slavery. The British also faced severe logistical problems in the South. Patriot forces could move at will throughout the region, living off the resources of the countryside, blending in with the civilian population and leaving the British unable to distinguish friend from foe. The British, by contrast, suffered all the disadvantages of an army in hostile territory.

It was this phase of the conflict that made the war truly "revolutionary"—not only because it introduced a new kind of combat, but also because it had the effect of mobilizing and politicizing large groups of the population who had previously remained aloof from the struggle. With the war expanding into previously isolated communities, with many civilians forced to involve themselves whether they liked it or not, the political climate of the United States grew more heated than ever. And support for independence, far from being crushed as the British had hoped, greatly increased.

That was the context in which the important military encounters of the last years of the war occurred. In the North, where significant num- *Revolutionary Consequences of the Southern Campaign* bers of British troops remained, the fighting settled into a relatively quiet stalemate. Sir Henry Clinton replaced the hapless William Howe in 1778 and moved what had been Howe's army from Philadelphia back to New York. There the British troops stayed for more than a year, with Washington using his army to keep watch around them. The American forces in New York did so little fighting in this period that Washington sent some troops west to fight hostile Indians who had been attacking white settlers. In that same winter, George Rogers Clark, under orders from the state of Virginia—not from either Washington or Congress—led a daring expedition over the mountains and captured settlements in the Illinois country from the British and their Indian allies.

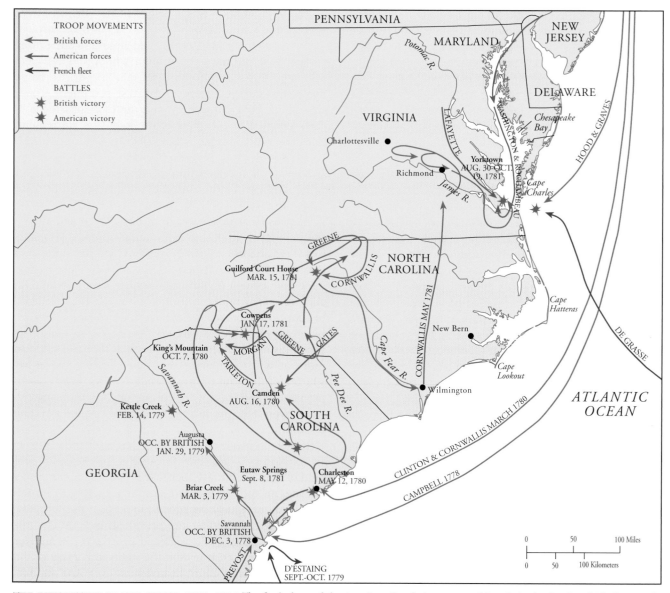

THE REVOLUTION IN THE SOUTH, 1778–1781 The final phase of the American Revolution occurred largely in the South, which the British thought would be a more receptive region for their troops. ◆ *Why did they believe that?* This map reveals the many, scattered military efforts of the British and the Americans in those years, none of them conclusive. It also shows the final chapter of the Revolution around the Chesapeake Bay and the James River. ◆ *What errors led the British to their surrender at Yorktown?*

 For an interactive version of this map go to www.mhhe.com/brinkley11ch5maps

During this period of relative calm, General Benedict Arnold shocked the American forces—and Washington in particular—by becoming a traitor. Arnold had been one of the early heroes of the war, but now, convinced that the American cause was hopeless, he conspired with British agents to betray the Patriot stronghold at West Point on the Hudson River. The scheme unraveled before Arnold could complete it, and he fled to the safety of the British camp, where he spent the rest of the war.

In the meantime, decisive fighting was in progress in the South. The British did have some significant military successes during this period. On December 29, 1778,

they captured Savannah, on the coast of Georgia; and on May 12, 1780, they took the port of Charleston, South Carolina. They also inspired some Loyalists to take up arms and advance with them into the interior. But although the British were able to win conventional battles, they were constantly harassed as they moved through the countryside by Patriot guerrillas led by such resourceful fighters as Thomas Sumter, Andrew Pickens, and Francis Marion, the "Swamp Fox."

Moving inland to Camden, South Carolina, Lord Cornwallis (Clinton's choice as British commander in the South) met and crushed a Patriot force under Horatio

THE BRITISH ON THE HUDSON, 1776 In one of the largest troop movements of the Revolution, English commanders sent 13,000 British and Hessian troops up the Hudson River to drive George Washington and his Patriot army from strongholds in the palisades above the river. The British took nearly 3,000 prisoners when the Patriots surrendered on November 16, 1776. Thomas Davies painted this watercolor of the British landing at the time. *(Emmet Collection. Miriam & Ira D. Wallach Division of Art, Prints & Photographs, The New York Public Library, Astor, Lenox and Tilden Foundations)*

Gates on August 16, 1780. Congress recalled Gates, and Washington gave the southern command to Nathanael *Nathanael Greene* Greene, a Quaker and a former blacksmith from Rhode Island and probably the ablest of all the American generals of the time next to Washington himself.

Even before Greene joined the southern army, the tide of battle began to turn against Cornwallis. At King's Mountain (near the North Carolina–South Carolina border) on October 7, 1780, a band of Patriot riflemen from the backwoods killed, wounded, or captured an entire force of 1,100 New York and South Carolina Tories that Cornwallis was using as auxiliaries. Once Greene arrived, he confused and exasperated Cornwallis further by dividing the American forces into small, fast-moving contingents and refraining from a showdown in open battle. One of the contingents inflicted what Cornwallis admitted was "a very unexpected and severe blow" at Cowpens on January 17, 1781. Finally, after receiving reinforcements, Greene combined all his forces and maneuvered to meet the British on ground of his own choosing, at Guilford Court House, North Carolina. After a hard-fought bat-

tle there on March 15, 1781, Greene withdrew from the field; but Cornwallis had lost so many men that he decided at last to abandon the Carolina campaign.

Cornwallis withdrew to the port town of Wilmington, North Carolina, to receive supplies being sent to him by sea; later he moved north to launch raids in the interior of Virginia. But Clinton, concerned for the army's safety, ordered him to take up a position on the peninsula between the York and James Rivers and wait for ships to carry his troops to New York or Charleston. So Cornwallis retreated to Yorktown and began to build fortifications there.

George Washington—along with the Count Jean Baptiste de Rochambeau, commander of the French expeditionary force in America, and Admiral François Joseph Paul de Grasse, commander of the French fleet in American waters—set out to trap *Yorktown* Cornwallis at Yorktown. Washington and Rochambeau marched a French-American army from New York to join other French forces under Lafayette in Virginia, while de Grasse sailed with additional troops for Chesapeake Bay and the York River.

The American Revolution was a result of specific tensions and conflicts between imperial Britain and its colonies along the Atlantic coast of North America. But it was also a part, and a cause, of what historians have come to call an "age of revolutions," which spread through much of the world in the last decades of the eighteenth century and the first decades of the nineteenth.

The modern idea of revolution—the overturning of old systems and regimes and the creation of new ones—was a product to a large degree of the ideas of the Enlightenment. Among those ideas was the notion of popular sovereignty, articulated by the English philosopher John Locke and others. It introduced the idea that political authority did not derive from the divine right of kings or the inherited authority of aristocracies but from the consent of the governed. A related Enlightenment idea was the concept of individual freedom, which challenged the traditional belief that governments had the right to prescribe the way people act, speak, and even think. Champions of individual freedom in the eighteenth century—among them the French philosopher Voltaire—advocated religious toleration (an end to discrimination against those who did not embrace a nation's dominant or official religion) and freedom of thought and expression. The Swiss-French Enlightenment theorist Jean Jacques Rousseau helped spread the idea of political and legal equality for all people—the end of special privileges for aristocrats and elites, the right of all citizens to participate in

STORMING THE BASTILLE This painting portrays the storming of the great Parisian fortress and prison, the Bastille, on July 14, 1789. The Bastille was a despised symbol of royal tyranny to many of the French, because of the arbitrarily arrested and imprisoned people who were sent there. The July assault was designed to release the prisoners, but in fact the revolutionaries found only seven people in the vast fortress. Even so, the capture of the Bastille—which marked one of the first moments in which ordinary Frenchmen joined the Revolution—became one of the great moments in modern French history. The anniversary of the event, "Bastille Day," remains the French national holiday. *(Photo Bulloz/Musee Carnavalet)*

These joint operations, perfectly timed and executed, caught Cornwallis between land and sea. After a few shows of resistance, he capitulated on October 17, 1781 (four years to the day after the surrender of Burgoyne at Saratoga). Two days later, as a military band played the old tune "The World Turn'd Upside Down," Cornwallis, claiming to be ill, sent a deputy who formally surrendered the British army of more than 7,000 men.

Except for a few skirmishes, the fighting was now over; but the United States had not yet won the war. British forces continued to hold the seaports of Savannah, Charleston, Wilmington, and New York. Before long, a British fleet met and defeated Admiral de Grasse's fleet in the West Indies, ending Washington's hopes for further French naval assistance. For more than a year, although there was no significant further combat between British and American forces, it remained possible that the war might resume and the struggle for independence might still be lost.

Winning the Peace

Cornwallis's defeat provoked outcries in England against continuing the war. Lord North resigned as prime minister; Lord Shelburne emerged from the political wreckage to succeed him; and British emissaries appeared in France to talk informally with the American diplomats there, of whom the three principals were Benjamin Franklin, John Adams, and John Jay.

The Americans were under instructions to cooperate fully with France in their negotiations with England. But Vergennes insisted that France could not agree to any settlement of the war with England until its ally Spain had achieved its principal war aim: winning back Gibraltar

the formation of policies and laws. Together, these Enlightenment ideas formed the basis for challenges to existing social orders in many parts of the western world, and eventually beyond it.

The American Revolution was the first and in many ways most influential of the Enlightenment-derived uprisings against established orders. It served as an inspiration to people in other lands who were trying to find a way to oppose unpopular regimes. In 1789, a little over a decade after the beginning of the American Revolution, revolution began in France—at first through a revolt by the national legislature against the king and then through a series of increasingly radical challenges to established authority. The monarchy was abolished (and the king and queen publicly executed in 1793), the authority of the Catholic church was challenged and greatly weakened, and at the peak of revolutionary chaos during the Jacobin period (1793–1794), over 40,000 suspected enemies of the revolution were executed and hundreds of thousands of others imprisoned. The radical phase of the revolution came to an end in 1799, when Napoleon Bonaparte, a young general, seized power and began to build a new French empire. But France's *ancien regime* of king and aristocracy never wholly revived.

Together, the French and American revolutions helped inspire uprisings in many other parts of the Atlantic world. In 1791, a major slave uprising began in Haiti and soon attracted over 100,000 rebels. The slave army defeated both the white settlers of the island and the French colonial armies sent to quell their rebellion. Under the leadership of Toussaint L'Ouverture, they began to agitate for independence; and on January 1, 1804, a few months after Toussaint's death, Haiti established its independence.

The ideas of these revolutions spread next into Spanish and Portuguese colonies in the Americas, particularly among the so-called *creoles,* people of European ancestry born in America. In the late eighteenth century, they began to resist the continuing authority of colonial officials sent from Spain and Portugal and to demand a greater say in governing their own lands. When Napoleon invaded Spain and Portugal in 1807, the French armies weakened the ability of the European regimes to sustain authority over their American colonies. In the years that followed, revolutions swept through much of Latin America and established independent nations throughout the New World. Mexico became an independent nation in 1821 and provinces of Central America that had once been part of Mexico (Guatemala,

El Salvador, Honduras, Nicaragua, and Costa Rica) established their independence three years later. Simon Bolivar, modeling his efforts on those of George Washington, led a great revolutionary movement that won independence for Brazil in 1822 and also helped lead revolutionary campaigns in Venezuela, Ecuador, and Peru—all of which won their independence in the 1820s. At about the same time, Greek patriots—drawing from the examples of other revolutionary nations—launched a movement to win their independence from the Ottoman empire, which finally succeeded in 1830.

The age of revolutions left many new, independent nations in its wake. It did not, however, succeed in establishing the ideals of popular sovereignty, individual freedom, and political equality in all the nations it affected. Slavery survived in the United States and in many areas of Latin America. New forms of aristocracy and even monarchy emerged in France, Mexico, Brazil, and elsewhere. Women—many of whom had hoped the revolutionary age would win new rights for them—made few legal or political gains in this era. But the ideals that the revolutionary era introduced to the Western world continued to shape the histories of nations throughout the nineteenth century and beyond.

---

from the British. There was no real prospect of that happening soon, and the Americans began to fear that the alliance with France might keep them at war indefinitely. As a result, Franklin, Jay, and Adams began proceeding on their own, without informing Vergennes, and signed a preliminary treaty with Great Britain on November 30, 1782. Franklin, in the meantime, skillfully pacified Vergennes and avoided an immediate rift in the French-American alliance.

The British and Americans reached a final settlement —the Treaty of Paris—on September 3, 1783, when both Spain and France agreed to end hostilities. It was, on the whole, remarkably favorable to *Treaty of Paris* the United States in granting a clear-cut recognition of its independence and a generous, though ambiguous cession of territory—from the southern boundary of Canada to the northern boundary of

Florida and from the Atlantic to the Mississippi. With good reason Americans celebrated in the fall of 1783 as the last of the British occupation forces embarked from New York and General Washington, at the head of his troops, rode triumphantly into the city.

WAR AND SOCIETY

Historians have long debated whether the American Revolution was a social as well as a political revolution. Some have argued that the colonists were struggling not only over the question of home rule, but over "who should rule at home." Others claim that domestic social and economic concerns had little to do with the conflict. (See "Where Historians Disagree," pp. 128–129.) Whatever the motivations of Americans, however, there can be little doubt that the War for Independence had important effects on the nature of American society.

Loyalists and Minorities

The losers in the American Revolution included not only the British but also American Loyalists. There is no way to be sure how many Americans remained loyal to England during the Revolution, but it is clear that there were many—at least a fifth (and some estimate as much as a third) of the white population. Their motivations were varied. Some were officeholders in the imperial government, who stood to lose their positions as a result of the Revolution. Others were merchants engaged in trade closely tied to the imperial system. (Most merchants, however, supported the Revolution.) Still others were people who lived in relative isolation and who thus had not been exposed to the wave of discontent that had turned so many Americans against Britain; they had simply retained their traditional loyalties. There were cultural and ethnic minorities who feared that an independent America would not offer them sufficient protection. There were settled, cautious people who feared social instability. And there were those who, expecting the British to win the war, were simply currying favor with the anticipated victors.

What happened to these men and women during the war is a turbulent and at times tragic story. Hounded by Patriots in their communities, harassed by legislative and judicial actions, the position of *The Loyalists' Plight* many Loyalists became intolerable. Up to 100,000 fled the country. Those who could afford to—for example, the hated Tory governor of Massachusetts, Thomas Hutchinson—moved to England, where many lived in difficult and lonely exile. Others of more modest means moved to Canada, establishing the first English-speaking community in the province of Quebec. Some returned to America after the war and, as the earlier passions and resentments faded, managed to reenter the life of the nation. Others remained abroad for the rest of their lives.

Most Loyalists were people of average means, but a substantial minority consisted of men and women of wealth. They left behind large estates and vacated important positions of social and economic leadership. Even some who remained in the country saw their property confiscated and their positions forfeited. The result was new opportunities for Patriots to acquire land and influence, a situation that produced significant social changes in many communities.

It would be an exaggeration, however, to claim that the departure of the Loyalists was responsible for anything approaching a social revolution or that the Revolution created a general assault on the wealthy and powerful in America. When the war ended, those who had been wealthy at its beginning were, for the most part, still wealthy. Most of those who had wielded social and political influence continued to wield it. Indeed, the distribution of wealth and power changed more rapidly after the war than it had changed during it.

The war had a significant effect on other minorities as well, and on certain religious groups in particular. No sect suffered more than the Anglicans, many of whose members were Loyalists. In Virginia and Maryland, where the colonial governments had recognized Anglicanism as the official religion and had imposed a tax for its maintenance, the new Revolutionary regimes disestablished the church and eliminated the subsidy. In other states, Anglicans had received aid from England, which also ceased with the outbreak of war. By the time the fighting ended, many Anglican parishes no longer even had clergymen, for there were few ministers to take the place of those who had died or who had left the country as Loyalist refugees. Anglicanism survived in America, but the losses during the Revolution permanently weakened it. The Revolution also weakened the Quakers in Pennsylvania and elsewhere. They incurred widespread unpopularity because of their pacifism. Their refusal to support the war destroyed much of the social and political prestige they had once enjoyed, and the church never fully recovered.

Disestablishment of the Anglican Church

While the war was weakening the Anglicans and the Quakers, it was improving the position of the Roman Catholic Church. On the advice of Charles Carroll of Carrollton, a Maryland statesman and Catholic lay leader, most American Catholics supported the Patriot cause during the war. The French alliance brought Catholic troops and chaplains to the country, and the gratitude with which most Americans greeted them did much to erode old hostilities toward Catholics, whom Americans had in the past often denounced as agents of the devil. The church did not greatly increase its numbers as a result of the Revolution, but it did gain considerable strength as an institution. Not long after the end of the war, the Vatican provided the United States with its own Catholic hierarchy. (Until then, Catholic bishops in Europe had controlled the American church.) Father John Carroll (also of Maryland) was named head of Catholic missions in America in 1784 and, in 1789, the first American bishop. In 1808 he became archbishop of Baltimore.

The War and Slavery

For the largest of America's minorities—the African-American population—the war had limited, but nevertheless profound, significance. For some, it meant freedom, because many slaves took advantage of the British presence in the South in the final years of the war to escape. The British enabled many of them to leave the country—

not out of any principled commitment to emancipation, but as a way of disrupting the American war effort. In South Carolina, for example, nearly a third of all slaves defected during the war. Africans had constituted over 60 percent of the population in 1770; by 1790, that figure had declined to about 44 percent.

For other African Americans, the Revolution meant an increased exposure to the concept, although seldom to the reality, of liberty. Most black Americans could not read, but few could avoid exposure to the new and exciting ideas circulating through the towns and cities, and even at times on the plantations, where they lived. At times, they attempted to apply those ideas to themselves. The results included incidents in several communities in which African Americans engaged in open resistance to white control. In Charleston, South Carolina, for example, Thomas Jeremiah, a free black, was executed in 1775 after Patriot leaders accused him of conspiring to smuggle British guns to South Carolina slaves. It also produced some eloquent efforts by black writers (mostly in the North) to articulate the lessons of the revolution for their people. "Liberty is a jewel which was handed Down to man from the cabinet of heaven," the black New Englander Lemuel Hayes wrote in 1776. "Even an African has Equally good a right to his Liberty in common with Englishmen. . . . Shall a man's Couler Be the Decisive Criterion wherby to Judg of his natural right?"

African American Desire for Freedom

That was one reason why in South Carolina and Georgia—where slaves constituted half or more of the population—there was great ambivalence about the revolution. Slaveowners opposed British efforts to emancipate their slaves, but they also feared that the revolution itself would foment slave rebellions. The same fears helped prevent English colonists in the Caribbean islands (who were far more greatly outnumbered by African slaves) from joining with the continental Americans in the revolt against Britain. In much of the North, the combination of revolutionary sentiment and evangelical Christian fervor helped spread antislavery sentiments widely through society. But in the South, white support for slavery survived. Southern churches rejected the antislavery ideas of the North and worked instead to develop a rationale for slavery—in part by reinforcing ideas about white superiority, in part by encouraging slaveowners to make slavery more humane.

As in so many other periods of American history, the Revolution exposed the continuing tension between the nation's commitment to liberty and its commitment to slavery. To people in our time, and even to some people in revolutionary times, it seems obvious that liberty and slavery are incompatible with one another. But to many white Americans in the eighteenth century, especially in the South, that did not seem obvious. Many white southerners believed, in fact, that enslaving Africans—whom they considered inferior and unfit for citizenship—was the best way to ensure liberty for white people. They feared the impact of free black people living alongside whites. They also feared that without slaves, it would be necessary to recruit a servile white workforce in the South, and that the resulting inequalities would jeopardize the survival of liberty. One of the ironies of the American Revolution, therefore, was that white Americans were fighting both to secure freedom for themselves and to preserve slavery for others.

Tension between Liberty and Slavery

Native Americans and the Revolution

Most Indians viewed the American Revolution with considerable uncertainty. The American Patriots tried to persuade them to remain neutral in the conflict, which they described as a "family quarrel" between the colonists and Britain that had nothing to do with the tribes. The British, too, generally sought to maintain Indian neutrality, fearing that native allies would prove unreliable and uncontrollable. Most tribes ultimately chose to stay out of the war.

To some Indians, however, the Revolution threatened to replace a ruling group in which they had developed at least some measure of trust (the British) with one they considered generally hostile to them (the Patriots). The British had consistently sought to limit the expansion of white settlement into Indian land (even if unsuccessfully); the Americans had spearheaded the encroachments. Thus some Native Americans, among them those Iroquois who participated in the Burgoyne campaign in upper New York, chose to join the English cause. Still others took advantage of the conflict to launch attacks of their own.

In the western Carolinas and Virginia, a Cherokee faction led by Dragging Canoe launched a series of attacks on outlying white settlements in the summer of 1776. Patriot militias responded with overwhelming force, ravaging Cherokee lands and forcing Dragging Canoe and many of his followers to flee west across the Tennessee River. Those Cherokee who remained behind agreed to a new treaty by which they gave up still more land. Not all Native American military efforts were so unsuccessful. Some Iroquois, despite the setbacks at Oriskany, continued to wage war against white Americans in the West and caused widespread destruction in large agricultural areas of New York and Pennsylvania—areas whose crops were of crucial importance to the Patriot cause. And although the retaliating United States armies inflicted heavy losses on the Indians, the attacks continued throughout the war.

In the end, however, the Revolution generally weakened the position of Native Americans in several ways. The Patriot victory increased the white demand for western lands; many American whites associated restrictions on settlement with British oppression and expected the new nation to remove the obstacles. At the same time, white attitudes toward the tribes, seldom friendly in the

Taking Sides

best of times, took a turn for the worse. Many whites deeply resented the assistance the Mohawk and other Indian nations had given the British and insisted on treating them as conquered people. Others adopted a paternalistic view of the tribes that was only slightly less dangerous to them. Thomas Jefferson, for example, came to view the Native Americans as "noble savages" uncivilized in their present state but redeemable if they were willing to adapt to the norms of white society.

Among the tribes themselves, the Revolution both revealed and increased the deep divisions that made it difficult for them to form a common front to resist the growing power of whites. In 1774, for example, the Shawnee Indians in western Virginia had attempted to

Growing Divisions among the Indians

lead an uprising against white settlers moving into the lands that would later become Kentucky. They attracted virtually no allies and (in a conflict known as Lord Dunmore's War) were defeated by the colonial militia and forced to cede more land to white settlers. The Cherokee generated little support from surrounding tribes in their 1776 battles. And the Iroquois, whose power had been eroding since the end of the French and Indian War, were unable to act in unison in the Revolution. The Iroquois nations that chose to support the British attracted little support from tribes outside the Confederacy (many of whom resented the long Iroquois domination of the interior) and even from other tribes within the Iroquois nation.

Nor did the conclusion of the Revolutionary War end the fighting between white Americans and Indians. Bands of Native Americans continued to launch raids against white settlers on the frontier. White militias, often using such raids as pretexts, continued to attack Indian tribes who stood in the way of expansion. Perhaps the most vicious massacre of the era occurred in 1782, after the British surrender, when white militias slaughtered a peaceful band of Delaware Indians at Gnadenhuetten in Ohio. They claimed to be retaliating for the killing of a white family several days before, but few believed this band of Delaware (who were both Christian converts and pacifists) had played any role in the earlier attack. The white soldiers killed ninety-six people, including many women and children. Such massacres did not become the norm of Indian-white relations. But they did reveal how little the Revolution had done to settle the basic conflict between the two peoples.

Women's Rights and Women's Roles

The long Revolutionary War, which touched the lives of almost every region, naturally had a significant effect on American women. The departure of so many men to fight in the Patriot armies left wives, mothers, sisters, and daughters in charge of farms and businesses. Some women handled these tasks with great success. In other cases, inexperience, inflation, the unavailability of male labor, or the threat of enemy troops led to failures and dislocations. Some women whose husbands or fathers went off to war did not have even a farm or shop to fall back on. Many cities and towns developed significant populations of impoverished women, who on occasion led popular protests against price increases. On a few occasions, hungry women rioted and looted for food. On several other occasions (in New Jersey and Staten Island), women launched attacks on occupying British troops, whom they were required to house and feed at considerable expense.

Not all women, however, stayed behind when the men went off to war. Sometimes by choice, but more often out of economic necessity or because they had been driven from their homes by the enemy (and by the smallpox and dysentery the British army carried with it), women flocked in increasing numbers to the camps of the Patriot

Women of the Army

armies to join their male relatives. George Washington looked askance at these female "camp followers," convinced that they were disruptive and distracting (even though his own wife, Martha, spent the winter of 1778–1779 with him at Valley Forge). Other officers were even more hostile, voicing complaints that reflected a high level of anxiety over this seeming violation of traditional gender roles (and also, perhaps, over the generally lower-class backgrounds of the camp women). One described them in decidedly hostile terms: "their hair falling, their brows beady with the heat, their belongings slung over one shoulder, chattering and yelling in sluttish shrills as they went and spitting in the gutters." In fact, however, the women were of significant value to the new army. It had not yet developed an adequate system of supply and auxiliary services, and it profited greatly from the presence of women. They increased army morale, and they performed such necessary tasks as cooking, laundry, and nursing.

But female activity did not always remain restricted to "women's" tasks. In the rough environment of the camps, traditional gender distinctions proved difficult to maintain. Considerable numbers of women became involved, at least intermittently, in combat—including the legendary Molly Pitcher (so named because she carried pitchers of water to soldiers on the battlefield). Molly Pitcher watched her husband fall during one encounter and immediately took his place at a field gun. A few women even disguised themselves as men so as to be able to fight.

After the war, of course, the soldiers and the female camp followers returned home. The experience of combat had little visible impact on how society (or on how women themselves) defined female roles in peacetime.

THE BRITISH INFANTRY The world's greatest military power raised its armies in almost haphazard fashion. Command of a British regiment was a favor to well-positioned gentlemen, who received a cash reward for every man they enlisted. With that incentive, they were hardly picky, and the foot soldiers of the British army were mostly men who could be persuaded (or tricked) into enlisting through a combination of liquor and cash. Even so, the rough-and-ready quality of the British infantry made them good soldiers on the whole. This drawing portrays a British encampment during the American Revolution. As with the colonial armies, the British troops attracted women, seen at left, some of whom served as "camp followers," doing chores to help the soldiers. The soldiers themselves wore highly ornamental uniforms that were in many ways very impractical. To keep himself properly groomed and attired could take a soldier up to three hours a day. *(Anne S.K. Brown Military Collection, Brown University Library)*

The Revolution did, however, call certain assumptions about women into question in other ways. The emphasis on liberty and the "rights of man" led some women to begin to question their position in society as well. "By the way," Abigail Adams wrote to her husband John Adams in 1776, "in the new code of laws which I suppose it will be necessary for you to make, I desire you would remember the ladies and be more generous and favorable to them than your ancestors. Do not put such unlimited power into the hands of the Husbands."

Adams was calling for a very modest expansion of women's rights. She wanted new protections against abusive and tyrannical men. A few women, however, went further. Judith Sargent Murray, one of the leading essayists of the late eighteenth century, wrote in 1779 that women's minds were as good as men's and that girls as well as boys therefore deserved access to education. Murray later became one of the leading defenders of the works of the English feminist Mary Wollstonecraft, whose *Vindication of the Rights of Women* was published in the United States in 1792. After reading it, Murray rejoiced that Americans were beginning to understand "the Rights of Women" and that future generations of women would inaugurate "a new era in female history."

In most respects, however, the new era did not arrive. Some political leaders—among them Benjamin Franklin and Benjamin Rush—voiced support for the education of *Calls for Women's Rights* women and for other feminist reforms. Yale students in the 1780s debated the question "Whether women ought to be admitted into the magistracy and government of empires and republics." And there was for a time wide discussion of the future role of women in a new republic that had broken with so many other traditions already. But few concrete reforms became either law or common social practice.

In colonial society, under the doctrines of English common law, an unmarried woman had some legal rights (to own property, to enter contracts, and others), but a married woman had virtually no rights at all. She could own no property and earn no independent wages; everything she owned and everything she earned belonged to her husband. She had no legal authority over her children; the father was, in the eyes of the law, the autocrat of the family. Because a married woman had no property rights, she could not engage in any legal transactions (buying or selling, suing or being sued, writing wills). She could not vote. Nor could she obtain a divorce; that, too, was a right reserved almost exclusively for men. That was what Abigail Adams (who herself enjoyed a very happy marriage) meant when she appealed to her husband not to put "such unlimited power into the hands of the Husbands."

The Revolution did little to change any of these legal customs. In some states, it did become easier for women to obtain divorces. And in New Jersey, women obtained the right to vote (although that right was repealed in 1807). Otherwise, there were few advances and some setbacks—including widows' loss of the right to regain their dowries from their husbands' estates. That change left many widows without any means of support and was one of the reasons for the increased agitation for female education: such women needed a way to support themselves.

The Revolution, in other words, far from challenging the patriarchal structure of American society, actually confirmed and strengthened it. Few American women challenged the belief that they occupied a special sphere distinct from men. Most accepted that their place remained in the family. Abigail Adams, in the same letter in which she asked her husband to "remember the ladies," urged him to "regard us then as Beings placed by providence under your protection and in imitation of the Supreme Being make use of that power only for our happiness." Nevertheless, the revolutionary experience did contribute to a subtle but important alteration of women's expectations of their status within the family. In the past, they had often been little better than servants in their husbands' homes; men and women both had generally viewed the wife as a clear subordinate, performing functions in the family of much less importance than those of the husband. But the Revolution encouraged people of both genders to reevaluate the contribution of women to the family and the society.

One reason for this was the participation of women in the revolutionary struggle itself. And part was a result of the reevaluation of American life during and after the revolutionary struggle. As the republic searched for a cultural identity for itself, it began to

A Strengthened Patriarchal Structure

place additional value on the role of women as mothers. The new nation was, many Americans liked to believe, producing a new kind of citizen, steeped in the principles of liberty. Mothers had a particularly important task, therefore, in instructing their children in the virtues the republican citizenry was expected now to possess. Wives were still far from equal partners in marriage, but their ideas, interests, and domestic roles received increased respect.

The War Economy

Inevitably, the Revolution produced important changes in the structure of the American economy. After more than a century of dependence on the British imperial system,

American trade suddenly found itself on its own. No longer did it have the protection of the great British navy; on the contrary, English ships now attempted to drive American vessels from the seas. No longer did American merchants have access to the markets of the empire; those markets were now hostile ports—including, of course, the most important source of American trade: England itself.

Yet while the Revolution disrupted traditional economic patterns, in the long run it strengthened the American economy. Well before the war was over, American ships had learned to evade the British navy with light, fast, easily maneuverable vessels. Indeed, the Yankees began to prey on British commerce with hundreds of privateers. For many shipowners, privateering proved to be more profitable than ordinary peacetime trade. More important in the long run, the end of imperial restrictions on American shipping opened up enormous new areas of trade to the nation. Colonial merchants had been violating British regulations for years, but the rules of empire had nevertheless inhibited American exploration of many markets. Now, enterprising merchants in New England and elsewhere began to develop new commerce in the Caribbean and in South America. By the mid-1780s, American merchants were developing an important new pattern of trade with Asia; and by the end of that decade, Yankee ships were regularly sailing from the eastern seaboard around Cape Horn to the Pacific coast of North America, there exchanging manufactured goods for hides and furs, and then proceeding across the Pacific to barter for goods in China. There was also a substantial increase in trade among the American states.

When English imports to America were cut off—first by the prewar boycott, then by the war itself—there were desperate efforts throughout the states to stimulate domestic manufacturing of certain necessities. No great industrial expansion resulted, but there were several signs of the economic growth that was to come in the next century. Americans began to make their own cloth—"homespun," which became both patriotic and fashionable—to replace the now unobtainable British fabrics. It would be some time before a large domestic textile industry would emerge, but the nation was never again to rely exclusively on foreign sources for its cloth. There was, of course, pressure to build factories for the manufacture of guns and ammunition. And there was a growing general awareness that America need not forever be dependent on other nations for manufactured goods.

New Patterns of Trade

The war stopped well short of revolutionizing the American economy; not until the nineteenth century would that begin to occur. But it did serve to release a wide range of entrepreneurial energies that, despite the temporary dislocations, encouraged growth and diversification.

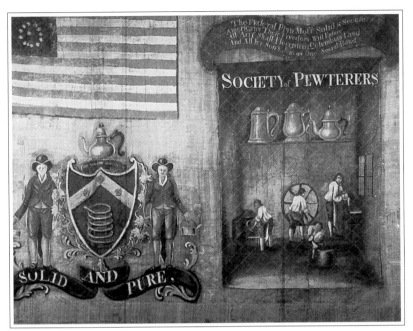

BANNER OF THE SOCIETY OF PEWTERERS Members of the American Society of Pewterers carried this patriotic banner when they marched in a New York City parade in July 1788. Its inscription celebrates the adoption of the new federal Constitution and predicts a future of prosperity and freedom in "Columbia's Land." The banner also suggests the growing importance of American manufacturing, which had received an important boost during the Revolution when British imports became unavailable. *(New-York Historical Society)*

THE CREATION OF STATE GOVERNMENTS

At the same time that Americans were struggling to win their independence on the battlefield, they were also struggling to create new institutions of government to replace the British system they had repudiated. That struggle continued for more than fifteen years, but its most important phase occurred during the war itself, at the state level.

The Assumptions of Republicanism

If Americans agreed on nothing else when they began to build new governments for themselves, they agreed that those governments would be republican. To them, that meant a political system in which all power came from the people, rather than from some supreme authority (such as a king). The success of such a government depended on the nature of its citizenry. If the population consisted of sturdy, independent property owners imbued with civic virtue, then the republic could survive. If it consisted of a few powerful aristocrats and a great mass of dependent workers, then it would be in danger. From the beginning, therefore, the ideal of the small freeholder (the independent landowner) was basic to American political ideology.

Importance of Civic Virtue

Another crucial part of that ideology was the concept of equality. The Declaration of Independence had given voice to that idea in its most ringing phrase: "All men are created equal." It was a belief that stood in direct contrast to the old European assumption of an inherited aristocracy. The innate talents and energies of individuals, not their positions at birth, would determine their roles in society. Some people would inevitably be wealthier and more powerful than others. But all people would have to earn their success. There would be no equality of condition, but there would be equality of opportunity.

In reality, of course, the United States was never a nation in which all citizens were independent property holders. From the beginning, there was a sizable dependent labor force—the white members of which were allowed many of the privileges of citizenship, the black members of which were allowed virtually none. American women remained both politically and economically subordinate. Native Americans were systematically exploited and displaced. Nor was there ever full equality of opportunity. American society was more open and more fluid than that of most European nations, but the condition of a person's birth was almost always a crucial determinant of success.

Persistent Inequality

Nevertheless, in embracing the assumptions of republicanism, Americans were adopting a powerful, even revolutionary, ideology, and their experiment in statecraft became a model for many other countries. It made the United States for a time the most admired and studied nation on earth.

The First State Constitutions

Two states—Connecticut and Rhode Island—already had governments that were republican in all but name even before the Revolution. They simply deleted references to

England and the king from their charters and adopted them as constitutions. The other eleven states, however, produced new documents.

The first and perhaps most basic decision was that the constitutions were to be written down, because Americans believed the vagueness of England's unwritten constitution had produced corruption. The second

Written Constitutions and Strong Legislatures

decision was that the power of the executive, which Americans believed had grown too great in England, must be limited. Pennsylvania eliminated the executive altogether. Most other states inserted provisions limiting the power of governors over appointments, reducing or eliminating their right to veto bills, and preventing them from dismissing the legislature. Most important, every state forbade the governor or any other executive officer from holding a seat in the legislature, thus ensuring that, unlike in England, the two branches of government would remain wholly separate.

But the new constitutions did not embrace direct popular rule. In Georgia and Pennsylvania, the legislature consisted of one popularly elected house. But in every other state, there was an upper and a lower chamber, and in most cases, the upper chamber was designed to represent the "higher orders" of society. There were property requirements for voters—some modest, some substantial— in all states.

Revising State Governments

By the late 1770s, Americans were growing concerned about the apparent divisiveness and instability of their new state governments, which were having trouble accomplishing anything at all. Many believed the problem was one of too much democracy. As a result, most of the states began to revise their constitutions to limit popular power. Massachusetts was the first to act on the new concerns. By waiting until 1780 to ratify its first constitution, Massachusetts allowed these changing ideas to shape its government, and the state produced a constitution that served as a model for others.

Two changes in particular differentiated the Massachusetts and later constitutions from the earlier ones. The first was a change in the process of constitution writing itself. Most of the first documents had been written by state legislatures and thus could easily be amended (or violated) by them. Massachusetts, and later other states, sought a way to protect the constitutions from ordinary politics and created the constitutional convention: a special assembly of the people that would meet only for the purpose of writing the constitution and that would never (except under extraordinary circumstances) meet again.

The second change was a significant strengthening of the executive, a reaction to what many believed was the instability of the original state governments that had weak governors. The 1780 Massachusetts constitution made the governor one of the strongest in any state. He was to be elected directly by the people;

Shift to Strong Executives

he was to have a fixed salary (in other words, he would not be dependent on the good will of the legislature each year for his wages); he would have significant appointment powers and a veto over legislation. Other states followed. Those with weak or nonexistent upper houses strengthened or created them. Most increased the powers of the governor. Pennsylvania, which had no executive at all at first, now produced a strong one. By the late 1780s, almost every state had either revised its constitution or drawn up an entirely new one in an effort to produce stability in government.

Toleration and Slavery

The new states moved far in the direction of complete religious freedom. Most Americans continued to believe that religion should play some role in government, but they did not wish to give special privileges to any particular denomination. The privileges that churches had once enjoyed were now largely stripped away. In 1786, Virginia enacted the Statute of Religious Liberty, written by Thomas Jefferson, which called for the complete separation of church and state.

Statute of Religious Liberty

More difficult to resolve was the question of slavery. In areas where slavery was already weak—in New England, where there had never been many slaves, and in Pennsylvania, where the Quakers opposed slavery— it was abolished. Even in the South, there were some pressures to amend or even eliminate the institution; every state but South Carolina and Georgia prohibited further importation of slaves from abroad, and South Carolina banned the slave trade during the war. Virginia passed a law encouraging manumission (the freeing of slaves).

Nevertheless, slavery survived in all the southern and border states. There were several reasons: racist assumptions among whites about the inferiority of blacks; the enormous economic investments many white southerners had in their slaves; and the inability of even such men as Washington and Jefferson, who had moral misgivings about slavery, to envision any alternative to it. If slavery were abolished, what would happen to the black people in America? Few whites believed blacks could be integrated into American society as equals. In maintaining slavery, Jefferson once remarked, Americans were holding a "wolf by the ears." However unappealing it was to hold on to it, letting go would be even worse.

A FREE BLACK MAN John Singleton Copley, the great American portraitist of the Revolutionary age, painted this picture of a young African American in 1777–78. He was probably a worker on New England fishing boats who appeared in another Copley painting ("Watson and the Shark"). It is one of a relatively small number of portrayals of the free blacks in the North in this era, and one of even a smaller number that portrays them realistically and seriously. *(Head of a Negro, 1777–1778. By John Singleton Copley. Oil on canvas, 53.3 × 41.3 cm. Founders Society Purchase, Gibbs-Williams Fund. Photograph © 1986 The Detroit Institute of Arts)*

THE SEARCH FOR A NATIONAL GOVERNMENT

Americans were much quicker to agree on state institutions than they were on the structure of their national government. At first, most believed that the central government should remain a relatively weak and unimportant force and that each state would be virtually a sovereign nation. It was in response to such ideas that the Articles of Confederation emerged.

The Confederation

The Articles of Confederation, which the Continental Congress had adopted in 1777, provided for a national government much like the one already in place. Congress remained the central—indeed the only—institution of national authority. Its powers expanded to give it author-

ity to conduct wars and foreign relations and to appropriate, borrow, and issue money. But it did not have power to regulate trade, draft troops, or levy taxes directly on the people. For troops and taxes it had to make formal requests to the state legislatures, which could—and often did—refuse them. There was no separate executive; the "president of the United States" was merely the presiding officer at the sessions of Congress. Each state had a single vote in Congress, and at least nine of the states had to approve any important measure. All thirteen state legislatures had to approve any amendment of the Articles.

Limited Power of the National Government

During the process of ratifying the Articles of Confederation (which required approval by all thirteen states), broad disagreements over the plan became evident. The small states had insisted on equal state representation, but the larger states wanted representation to be based on population. The smaller states prevailed on that issue. More important, the states claiming western lands wished to keep them, but the rest of the states demanded that all such territory be turned over to the national government. New York and Virginia had to give up their western claims before the Articles were finally approved. They went into effect in 1781.

The Confederation, which existed from 1781 until 1789, was not a complete failure, but it was far from a success. It lacked adequate powers to deal with interstate issues or to enforce its will on the states, and it had little stature in the eyes of the world.

Diplomatic Failures

Evidence of the low esteem in which the rest of the world held the Confederation was its difficulty in persuading Great Britain (and to a lesser extent Spain) to live up to the terms of the peace treaty of 1783.

Postwar Disputes with Britain and Spain

The British had promised to evacuate American territory, but British forces continued to occupy a string of frontier posts along the Great Lakes within the United States. Nor did the British honor their agreement to make restitution to slaveowners whose slaves the British army had confiscated. There were also disputes over the northeastern boundary of the new nation and over the border between the United States and Florida, which Britain had ceded back to Spain in the treaty. Most American trade remained within the British Empire, and Americans wanted full access to British markets; England, however, placed sharp restrictions on that access.

In 1784, Congress sent John Adams as minister to London to resolve these differences, but Adams made no headway with the English, who were never sure whether he represented a single nation or thirteen different ones. Throughout the 1780s, the British government refused

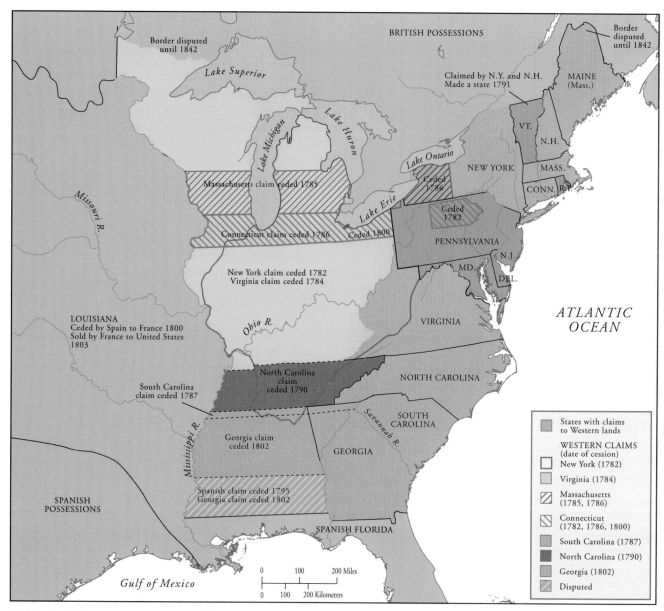

THE CONFLICT OVER WESTERN LANDS The American victory in the Revolution transformed the colonies into "states" within a new nation whose central government claimed at least some sovereignty over the individual units. An early conflict between national and state power took place over the state claims to western lands—claims established during the colonial period. This map shows the extensive western lands claimed by most of the original thirteen colonies to land in the West, and it illustrates the shifting nature of those claims over time—as colonies and then states transferred land to one another. The new national government gradually persuaded the states to give it control of the western lands, and in 1784 and 1785 it issued ordinances governing the process of settling those lands. ◆ *Why did the national government consider it important for the states to give up their claim to these territories?*

even to send a diplomatic minister to the American capital.

Confederation diplomats agreed to a treaty with Spain in 1786. The Spanish accepted the American interpreta-

Regional Differences over Diplomatic Policy

tion of the Florida boundary. In return the Americans recognized the Spanish possessions in North America and accepted limits on the right of United States vessels to navigate the Mississippi for twenty years.

Southern states, incensed at the idea of giving up their access to the Mississippi, blocked ratification, further weakening the government's standing in world diplomacy.

The Confederation and the Northwest

The Confederation's most important accomplishment was its resolution of some of the controversies involving the western lands. When the Revolution began, only a few

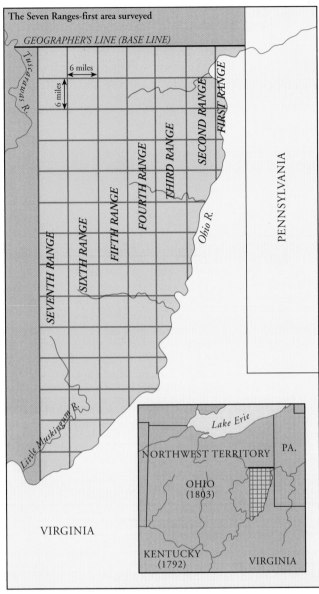

The Seven Ranges-first area surveyed

GEOGRAPHER'S LINE (BASE LINE)

6 miles

6 miles

Tuscarawas R.

FIRST RANGE

SECOND RANGE

THIRD RANGE

FOURTH RANGE

FIFTH RANGE

SIXTH RANGE

SEVENTH RANGE

PENNSYLVANIA

Ohio R.

Little Muskingum R.

VIRGINIA

Lake Erie

NORTHWEST TERRITORY

PA.

OHIO
(1803)

VIRGINIA

KENTUCKY
(1792)

VIRGINIA

* Four sections
reserved for
subsequent sales

Section 16
reserved for
school funds

36	30	24	18	12	6
35	29*	23	17	11*	5
34	28	22	16	10	4
33	27	21	15	9	3
32	26*	20	14	8*	2
31	25	19	13	7	1

6 miles

1 mile

A

B
C
D E

One Section = 640 acres (1 mile square)
A Half section = 320 acres
B Quarter section = 160 acres
C Half-quarter section = 80 acres
D & E Quarter-quarter section = 40 acres

One township (six miles square)

LAND SURVEY: ORDINANCE OF 1785 In the Ordinance of 1785, the Congress established a new system for surveying and selling western lands. These maps illustrate the way in which the lands were divided in an area of Ohio. Note the highly geometrical grid pattern that the Ordinance imposed on these lands. Each of the squares in the upper map was subdivided into 36 sections, as illustrated in the lower map. ◆ *Why was this grid pattern so appealing to the planners of the western lands?*

thousand whites lived west of the Appalachian divide; by 1790 their numbers had increased to 120,000. The Confederation had to find a way to include these new settlements in the political structure of the new nation. The landed states began to yield their claims to the national government in 1781, and by 1784 the Confederation controlled enough land to permit Congress to begin making policy for the national domain.

The Ordinance of 1784, based on a proposal by Thomas Jefferson, divided the western territory into ten self-governing districts, each of which could petition Congress for statehood when its population equaled the number of free inhabitants of the smallest existing state. Then, in the Ordinance of 1785, Congress created a system for surveying and selling the western lands. The territory north of the Ohio River was to be surveyed and marked off into neat rectangular townships, each divided into thirty-six identical sections. In every township four sections were to be set aside for the United States; the revenue from the sale of one of the other sections was to support creation of a public school. Sections were to be sold at auction for no less than one dollar an acre.

The Ordinances of 1784 and 1785

The organization of the western territories established a pattern that would dominate much of the landscape of the United States for centuries to come: the grid. (See "The American Environment," pp. 152–153.) The 1785 Ordinance, in short, made a dramatic and indelible mark on the American landscape.

The original ordinances proved highly favorable to land speculators and less so to ordinary settlers, many of whom could not afford the price of the land. Congress compounded the problem by selling much of the best land to the Ohio and Scioto Companies before making it available to anyone else. Criticism of these policies led to the passage in 1787 of another law governing western settlement—legislation that became known as the "Northwest Ordinance." The 1787 Ordinance abandoned the ten districts established in 1784 and created a single Northwest Territory out of the lands north of the Ohio; the territory could be divided subsequently into between three and five territories. It also specified a population of 60,000 as a minimum for statehood, guaranteed freedom of religion and the right to trial by jury to residents of the Northwest, and prohibited slavery throughout the territory.

Northwest Ordinance

Among the many environmental changes that people have wrought upon the American landscape is one so familiar that we seldom notice it—except, perhaps, when we look down upon the land from the air and see, in almost all regions of the nation, the unmistakable square and rectangular patterns that make up the most characteristic of American geographical forms: the grid. The grid did not come naturally to America. It was imposed upon the land—but not until after several centuries of European settlement in the New World and several experiments with other systems.

Methods of dividing up land into specific pieces of property that individuals can own or control are known as "cadastral" systems. Several different versions of them emerged in the Americas. The Spanish, for instance, had given a few of their most prominent colonists in New Mexico, Texas, and California vast estates *(encomiendas)*, which were defined less by the actual boundaries of the land—which remained somewhat informal and undefined—than by the right of the owners to claim payments in labor or crops from the people who lived there. The Dutch created a similar land system along the banks of the Hudson River in

New York, where most of the tenants were European immigrants rather than Indians. The cadastral systems of the Spanish and the Dutch encouraged and reinforced social hierarchy—giving great power to large landholders at the expense of those who worked the land—and discouraged social fluidity.

The English colonies had at least two major cadastral systems. One was the New England town system, in which a large tract of land was granted by charter to a small group of proprietors, who then divided it up for the benefit of individual settlers. All original colonists were given house lots near the church and meetinghouse in the center of town, but each also received tracts of land for traditional agricultural uses, often widely scattered in different parts of the town. In the South, land was surveyed according to a much more informal system called "metes and bounds"—which in practice amounted to virtually no system at all. People wanting to buy land went to the county courthouse and purchased a claim to a given number of acres. They then went more or less wherever they chose and marked out the allotted number of acres. The result was a crazy-quilt pattern of properties, many of them overlapping

because many owners did not know of a prior claim to the land they were surveying. The southern system was cheap and at first easy to administer, but it produced so many conflicts over who owned what land that claimants were often forced to battle one another in court for decades. Prior to the Revolution, in short, there were highly variable methods for dividing up land in America, most of them loose, informal, and unstable.

When the new government of the United States met in the wake of the Revolution to settle various problems of the new nation, one of their most important tasks was to decide which cadastral system was most appropriate for the republic—and particularly for the vast western territories ceded to the national government by the states in 1781 that became known as the "public domain." Clearly, a semi-feudal system of large land estates like that of the Spanish or Dutch was inappropriate for a republic like the United States. Members of Congress were also eager to avoid the random irregularities and legal conflicts associated with southern metes and bounds. They therefore turned to a modified version of the New England town system. Shortly after the end of

METES AND BOUNDS, NORTH CAROLINA The lack of a standardized survey system in the southern colonies produced crazy-quilt field patterns that persist to this day. The irregular fence lines and property boundaries one sees when flying over the southern landscape reflect the metes and bounds surveys that were made centuries ago. *(Comstock)*

the Revolution, they passed what would become one of the great founding laws in American history, the Land Ordinance of 1785. This act was as important to the future shape of the American landscape as the Constitution was to the future shape of American government.

The Ordinance originally applied only to what was then called the Northwest Territory—present-day Ohio, Indiana, Michigan, Illinois, and Wisconsin—but it became a model for all subsequent land systems administered by the federal government. One of its most important features was its requirement that lands be surveyed before they could be purchased, thus circumventing the problems of the southern system. To make sure that surveyed tracts did not overlap, the authors of the ordinance turned to a familiar Enlightenment symbol of rationality and order: the Cartesian coordinate plane that Renee Descartes had offered as a foundation for his new mathematics—in other words, a grid composed of square or rectangular areas.

Lands west of the Ohio River were divided into square townships six miles to a side, each containing thirty-six square miles, or "sections." Surveyors walked along each side of a section and located its four corners to eliminate confusion about where one section ended and another began. Townships were sold in two ways: either as thirty-six-square-mile units to large proprietors who broke them up and resold them as speculations, or as one-square-mile sections to smaller landowners.

The environmental effects of the 1785 Ordinance are almost impossible to exaggerate. The modern landscape of the West and Midwest would be unrecognizable without it. As one flies today from Pennsylvania to Ohio, one instantly recognizes the shift from random field shapes near the Atlantic coast to the rigid north-south, east-west rectilinear patterns of the grid further inland. Except for modern interstate highways, most roads still follow the edges of the original section lines. Farmers still plow their fields within the boundaries set by the original surveyors and still preserve many of the old gnarled "witness trees" the surveyors used to mark section corners. American cities and towns—from New York to Seattle—mimic the national grid in the rectangular layout of their streets and lots. We live in a rectilinear world.

The 1785 Ordinance accomplished its goals with great success. It surveyed the public domain according to a regular system, prevented unnecessary litigation over property rights, and speeded the development of western lands. But it was not without problems. It encouraged a dispersed form of settlement—farm families a fixed distance, often a half mile or more, from their neighbors—that undermined the community ideals that the Ordinance's model, the New England town system, had sought to promote. It led people to arrange their fields and roads according to a rigid north-south, east-west alignment, regardless of local topography. Finally, when the surveyors eventually reached the arid West, where a dry climate made traditional eastern farming impossible, the square mile units of the grid proved inappropriate both for livestock raising and for irrigation.

Despite these social and environmental problems, however, the grid is here to stay. Once drawn, property boundaries can survive for centuries and even millennia after the society that originally drew them has disappeared. In writing the 1785 Ordinance, members of Congress made an indelible mark on the American landscape.

THE GRID, ILLINOIS Starting at the point where the Ohio River crosses the Pennsylvania-Ohio border, government surveyors applied the Land Ordinance of 1785 to most parts of the United States. The uniform checkerboard pattern of the national grid is visible to any traveler who flies or drives across this terrain. *(Comstock)*

The western lands south of the Ohio River received less attention from Congress, and development was more chaotic there. The region that became Kentucky and Tennessee developed rapidly in the late 1770s, and in the 1780s speculators and settlers began setting up governments and asking for recognition as states. The Confederation Congress was never able to resolve the conflicting claims in that region successfully.

Indians and the Western Lands

On paper at least, the western land policies of the Confederation created a system that brought order and stability to the process of white settlement in the Northwest. But in reality, order and stability came slowly and at great cost, because much of the land the Confederation was neatly subdividing and offering for sale consisted of territory claimed by the Indians of the region. Congress tried to resolve that problem in 1784, 1785, and 1786 by persuading Iroquois, Choctaw, Chickasaw, and Cherokee leaders to sign treaties ceding substantial western lands in the North and South to the United States. But those agreements proved ineffective. In 1786, the leadership of the Iroquois Confederacy repudiated the treaty it had signed two years earlier and threatened to attack white settlements in the disputed lands. Other tribes had never really accepted the treaties affecting them and continued to resist white movement into their lands.

Violence between whites and Indians on the Northwest frontier reached a crescendo in the early 1790s. In 1790 and again in 1791, a group of tribes led by the famed Miami warrior Little Turtle, defeated United States forces in two major battles near what is now the

Battle of Fallen Timbers | western border of Ohio; in the second of those battles, on November 4, 1791, 630 white Americans died in fighting at the Wabash River (the greatest military victory Indians had ever or would ever achieve in their battles with whites). Efforts to negotiate a settlement failed because of the Miami's insistence that no treaty was possible unless it forbade white settlement west of the Ohio River. Negotiations did not resume until after General Anthony Wayne led 4,000 soldiers into the Ohio Valley in 1794 and defeated the Indians in the Battle of Fallen Timbers.

A year later, the Miami signed the Treaty of Greenville, ceding substantial new lands to the United States (which was now operating under the Constitution of 1789) in exchange for a formal acknowledgment of their claim to the territory they had managed to retain. In doing so, the United States was affirming that Indian lands could be ceded only by the tribes themselves. That hard-won assurance, however, proved a frail protection against the pressure of white expansion westward in later years.

LITTLE TURTLE Little Turtle led the Miami confederacy in its wars with the United States in what is now Ohio and Indiana in the early 1790s. For a time he seemed almost invincible, but in 1794 Little Turtle was defeated in the Battle of Fallen Timbers. In this sketch (a rough copy of a painting attributed to Gilbert Stuart), Little Turtle wears a medal bearing the likeness of George Washington, awarded him by the United States after the signing of the Treaty of Greenville. *(Bettmann/Corbis)*

Debts, Taxes, and Daniel Shays

The postwar depression, which lasted from 1784 to 1787, increased the perennial American problem of an inadequate money supply, a problem that weighed particu- | *Postwar Depression* larly heavily on debtors. In dealing with this problem, Congress most clearly demonstrated its weakness.

The Confederation itself had an enormous outstanding debt that it had accumulated during the Revolutionary War, and few means with which to pay it. It had sold war bonds that were now due to be repaid; it owed money to its soldiers; it had substantial debts abroad. But it had no power to tax. It could only make requisitions of the states, and it received only about one-sixth of the money it requisitioned. The fragile new nation was faced with the grim prospect of defaulting on its obligations.

This alarming possibility brought to the fore a group of leaders who would play a crucial role in the shaping of the republic for several decades. Committed nationalists, they sought ways to increase the powers of the central government and to meet its financial obligations. Robert Morris, the head of the Confederation's treasury; Alexander Hamilton, his young protégé; James Madison of Virginia; and others called for a "continental impost"—a 5 percent duty on imported goods to be levied by Congress and used to fund the debt. Many Americans, however, feared that the impost plan would concentrate too much financial power in the hands of Morris and his allies in Philadelphia. Congress failed to approve the impost in 1781 and again in 1783. Angry and discouraged, the nationalists largely withdrew from any active involvement in the Confederation.

Political Disputes over Economic Issues

The states had war debts, too, and they generally relied on increased taxation to pay them. But poor farmers, already burdened by debt and now burdened again by new taxes, considered such policies unfair, even tyrannical. They demanded that the state governments issue paper currency to increase the money supply and make it easier for them to meet their obligations. Resentment was especially high among farmers in New England, who felt that the states were squeezing them to enrich already wealthy bondholders in Boston and other towns.

Throughout the late 1780s, therefore, mobs of distressed farmers rioted periodically in various parts of New England. Dissidents in the Connecticut Valley and the Berkshire Hills of Massachusetts, many of them Revolutionary veterans, rallied behind Daniel Shays, a former captain in the Continental army. Shays issued a set of demands that included paper money, tax relief, a moratorium on debts, the relocation of the state capital from Boston to the interior, and the abolition of imprisonment for debt. During the summer of 1786, the Shaysites concentrated on preventing the collection of debts, private or public, and used force to keep courts from sitting and sheriffs from selling confiscated property. In Boston, members of

Shays's Rebellion

DANIEL SHAYS AND JOB SHATTUCK Shays and Shattuck were the principal leaders of the 1786 uprising by poor farmers in Massachusetts demanding relief from their indebtedness. Shattuck led an insurrection in the east, which collapsed when he was captured on November 30. Shays organized the rebellion in the west, which continued until finally dispersed by state militia in late February 1787. The following year, state authorities pardoned Shays; even before that, the legislature responded to the rebellion by providing some relief to the impoverished farmers. These drawings are part of a hostile account of the rebellion published in 1787 in a Boston almanac. *(National Portrait Gallery, Smithsonian Institution/Art Resource, NY)*

the legislature, including Samuel Adams, denounced Shays and his men as rebels and traitors. When winter came, the rebels advanced on Springfield, hoping to seize weapons from the arsenal there. An army of state militiamen, financed by a loan from wealthy merchants, set out from Boston to confront them. In January 1787, this army met Shays's band and dispersed his ragged troops.

As a military enterprise, Shays's Rebellion was a failure, although it produced some concessions to the aggrieved farmers. Shays and his lieutenants, at first sentenced to death, were later pardoned, and Massachusetts offered the protesters some tax relief and a postponement of debt payments. The rebellion had more important consequences for the future of the United States, for it added urgency to a movement already gathering support throughout the new nation—the movement to produce a new, national constitution.

CONCLUSION

Between a small, inconclusive battle on a village green in New England in 1775 and a momentous surrender at Yorktown in 1781, the American people fought a great and terrible war against the mightiest military nation in the world. No one outside America, and few within it, would have predicted in 1775 that the makeshift armies of the colonies could withstand the armies and navies of the British empire. But a combination of luck, brilliance, determination, and timely aid from abroad allowed the Patriots, as they began to call themselves, to make full use of the advantages of fighting on their home soil and to frustrate British designs time and again.

The war was not just a historic military event. It was also a great political one, for it propelled the colonies to unite, to organize, and—in July 1776—to declare their independence. Having done so, they fought with even greater determination, defending now not just a set of principles, but an actual, fledgling nation. By the end of the war, they had created new governments at both the state and national level and had begun experimenting with new political forms that would distinguish the United States from any previous nation in history.

The war was also important for its effects on American society—for the way it shook (although never overturned) the existing social order; for the way it caused women to question (although seldom openly to challenge) their place in society; and for the way it spread notions of liberty and freedom throughout a society that in the past had often been rigidly hierarchical and highly deferential. Even African-American slaves absorbed some of the ideas of the Revolution, although it would be many years before they would be in any position to make very much use of them.

Victory in the American Revolution solved many of the problems of the new nation, but it also produced others. What should the United States do about its relations with the Indians and with its neighbors to the north and south? What should it do about the distribution of western lands? What should it do about slavery? How should it balance its commitment to liberty with its need for order? These questions bedeviled the new national government in its first years of existence and ultimately led Americans to create a new political order.

FOR FURTHER REFERENCE

Robert Middlekauf, *The Glorious Cause: The American Revolution, 1763–1789* (1985), a volume in the Oxford History of the United States, is a thorough, general history of the Revolution. Edward Countryman, *The American Revolution* (1985) is a useful, briefer overview. Gordon Wood, *The Radicalism of the American Revolution* (1992) emphasizes the profound political change that the Revolution produced. Charles Royster, *A Revolutionary People at War: The Continental Army and American Character* (1979) suggests the importance of military service for American men. Mary Beth Norton, *Liberty's Daughters: The Revolutionary Experience of American Women, 1750–1800* (1980) demonstrates that the Revolution had a significant impact on the lives of American women as well. Eric Foner, *Tom Paine and Revolutionary America* (1976) connects the leading pamphleteer of the Revolution with urban radicalism in Philadelphia. Pauline Maier, *American Scripture* (1997) is a penetrating study of the making of the Declaration of Independence, and of its impact on subsequent generations of Americans. Colin Calloway, *The American Revolution in Indian Country* (1995) is a new and important study on an often neglected aspect of the war. Sylvia R. Frey, *Water from the Rock: Black Resistance in a Revolutionary Age* (1991), argues that the American Revolution was a major turning point in the history of slavery in the American South. *Liberty* (1997), is a compelling six-hour PBS documentary film history of the American Revolution, from its early origins in the 1760s.

For quizzes, Internet resources, references to additional books and films, and more, consult this book's Online Learning Center at www.mhhe.com/brinkley11.

THE AMERICAN STAR Frederick Kemmelmeyer painted this tribute to George Washington sometime in the 1790s. It was one of many efforts by artists and others to create an iconography for the new republic. *(Metropolitan Museum of Art)*

Significant Events

CHAPTER SIX

THE CONSTITUTION AND THE NEW REPUBLIC

*B*y the late 1780s, most Americans had grown deeply dissatisfied with the deficiencies of the Confederation: with the government's apparent inability to deal with factiousness and instability; with its failure to handle economic problems effectively; and perhaps most of all with the frightening powerlessness it had displayed in the face of Shays's Rebellion. A decade earlier, Americans had deliberately avoided creating a genuine national government, fearing that it would encroach on the sovereignty of the individual states. Now they reconsidered. In 1787, they created a new government defined by the Constitution of the United States.

Deficiencies of the Confederation Government

The American Constitution derived most of its principles from the state documents that had preceded it. But it was also a remarkable achievement in its own right. Out of the contentious atmosphere of a fragile new nation, Americans fashioned a system of government that has survived for more than two centuries as one of the stablest and most successful in the world.

William Gladstone, the great nineteenth-century British statesman, once called the Constitution the "most wonderful work ever struck off at a given time by the brain and purpose of man." The American people in the years to come generally agreed. Indeed, to them the Constitution took on some of the characteristics of a sacred document, a holy mystery. Later generations viewed its framers as men almost godlike in their wisdom. Many considered its provisions an unassailable "fundamental law," from which all public policies, all political principles, all solutions of controversies must spring.

The adoption of the Constitution did not complete the creation of the republic. It only defined the terms in which debate over the future of government would continue. Americans may have agreed that the Constitution was a nearly perfect document, but they disagreed—at times fundamentally—on what that document meant. They still do. Out of such disagreements emerged the first great political battles of the new nation.

- Judiciary Act of 1789 is passed
- French Revolution begins
- 1791 · Hamilton issues "Report on Manufactures"
- First Bank of the United States chartered
- Vermont becomes fourteenth state
- 1792 · Washington reelected without opposition
- Kentucky becomes fifteenth state
- 1793 · Citizen Genet affair challenges American neutrality
- 1794 · Whiskey Rebellion quelled in Pennsylvania
- Jay's Treaty signed

- 1795 · Pinckney's Treaty signed
- 1796 · John Adams elected president
- Tennessee becomes sixteenth state
- 1798 · XYZ Affair precipitates state of quasi war with France
- Alien and Sedition Acts passed
- Virginia and Kentucky Resolutions passed
- 1800 · Jefferson and Burr tie vote in electoral college
- 1801 · Jefferson becomes president after Congress confirms election
- Judiciary Act of 1801 passed

FRAMING A NEW GOVERNMENT

So unpopular and ineffectual had the Confederation Congress become by the mid-1780s that it began to lead an almost waiflike existence. In 1783, its members timidly withdrew from Philadelphia to escape from the clamor of army veterans demanding back pay. They took refuge for a while in Princeton, New Jersey, then moved

A Weak Central Government

to Annapolis, and in 1785 settled in New York. Through all of this, the delegates were often conspicuous largely by their absence. Only with great difficulty did Congress secure a quorum to ratify the treaty with Great Britain ending the Revolutionary War. Eighteen members, representing only eight states, voted on the Confederation's most important piece of legislation, the Northwest Ordinance. In the meantime, a major public debate was beginning over the future of the Confederation.

Advocates of Centralization

Weak and unpopular though the Confederation was, it had for a time satisfied a great many—probably a majority—of the people. They believed they had fought the Revolutionary War to avert the danger of what they considered remote and tyrannical authority; now they wanted to keep political power centered in the states, where they could carefully and closely control it.

But during the 1780s, some of the wealthiest and most powerful groups in the country began to clamor for a more genuinely national government capable of dealing with the nation's problems—

Supporters of a Strong National Government

particularly the economic problems that most directly afflicted them. Some military men, many of them members of the exclusive and hereditary Society of the Cincinnati (formed by Revolutionary army officers in 1783), were disgruntled at the refusal of Congress to fund their pensions. They began aspiring to influence and invigorate the national government; some even envisioned a form of military dictatorship and flirted briefly (in 1783, in the so-called Newburgh Conspiracy) with a direct challenge to Congress, until George Washington intervened and blocked the potential rebellion.

American manufacturers—the artisans and "mechanics" of the nation's cities and towns—wanted to replace the various state tariffs with a uniformly high national duty. Merchants and shippers wanted to replace the thir-

GEORGE WASHINGTON AT MOUNT VERNON Washington was in his first term as president in 1790 when an anonymous folk artist painted this view of his home at Mount Vernon, Virginia. Washington appears in uniform, along with members of his family, on the lawn. After he retired from office in 1797, Washington returned happily to his plantation and spent the two years before his death in 1799 "amusing myself in agricultural and rural pursuits." He also played host to an endless stream of visitors from throughout the country and Europe. *(Gift of Edgar William and Bernice Chrysler Garbisch, © 1998 Board of Trustees, National Gallery of Art, Washington)*

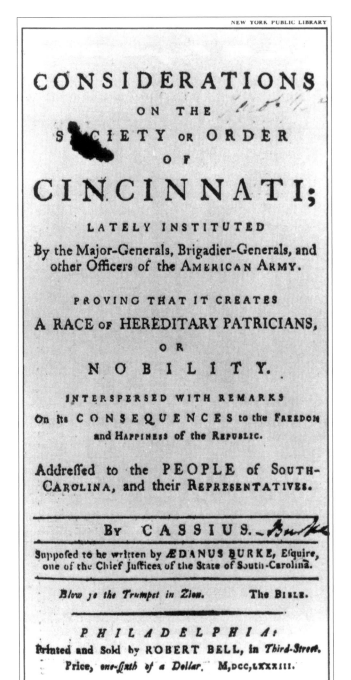

A BROADSIDE AGAINST "NOBILITY" This 1783 pamphlet was one of many expressions of the broad democratic sentiment that the Revolution unleashed in American society. The Society of the Cincinnati was an organization created shortly after the Revolution by men who had served as high-ranking officers in the Patriot Army. To many Americans, however, the Society—membership in which was to be hereditary—looked suspiciously like the inherited aristocracies of England. This pamphlet, printed in Philadelphia but intended for South Carolinians, warns of the dangers the Society supposedly posed to the "Freedom and Happiness of the Republic." *(New York Public Library)*

teen different (and largely ineffective) state commercial policies with a single, national one. Land speculators wanted the "Indian menace" finally removed from their western tracts. People who were owed money wanted to stop the states from issuing paper money, which would lower the value of what they received in payment. Investors in Confederation securities wanted the government to fund the debt and thus enhance the value of their securities. Large property owners looked for protection from the threat of mobs, a threat that seemed particularly menacing in light of such episodes as Shays's Rebellion. By 1786, these diverse demands had grown so powerful that the issue was no longer whether the Confederation should be changed but how drastic the changes should be. Even the defenders of the existing system reluctantly came to agree that the government needed strengthening at its weakest point—its lack of power to tax.

The most resourceful of the reformers was Alexander Hamilton, political genius, New York lawyer, one-time military aide to General Washington, and illegitimate son of a Scottish merchant in the West Indies. From the beginning, *Alexander Hamilton* Hamilton had been unhappy with the Articles of Confederation and the weak central government they had created. He now called for a national convention to overhaul the entire document. He found an important ally in James Madison of Virginia, who persuaded the Virginia legislature to convene an interstate conference on commercial questions. Only five states sent delegates to the meeting, held in Annapolis, Maryland, in 1786; but the delegates approved a proposal drafted by Hamilton (who was representing New York) recommending that Congress call a convention of special delegates from all the states to gather in Philadelphia the next year and consider ways to "render the constitution of the Federal government adequate to the exigencies of the union."

At that moment, in 1786, there seemed little possibility that the Philadelphia convention would attract any more interest than the meeting at Annapolis had attracted. Only by winning the support of George Washington, the centralizers believed, could they hope to prevail. But Washington at first showed little interest in joining the cause. Then, early in 1787, the news of Shays's Rebellion spread throughout the nation. Thomas Jefferson, then the American minister in Paris, was not alarmed. "I hold," he confided in a letter to James Madison, "that a little rebellion, now and then, is a good thing, and as necessary in the political world as storms in the physical." But Washington took the news less calmly. "There are combustibles in every State which a spark might set fire to," he exclaimed. "I feel infinitely more than I can express for the disorders which have arisen. Good God!" In May, he left his home at Mount Vernon in Virginia for the Constitutional Convention in Philadelphia. His support gave the meeting immediate credibility.

A Divided Convention

Fifty-five men, representing all the states except Rhode Island, attended one or more sessions of the convention that sat in the Philadelphia State House from May to September 1787. These "Founding Fathers," as they would

The Founding Fathers

later become known, were on the whole relatively young men; their average age was forty-four, and only one delegate (Benjamin Franklin, then eighty-one) was of advanced age. They were well educated by the standards of their time. Most represented the great propertied interests of the country, and many feared what one of them called the "turbulence and follies" of democracy. Yet all were also products of the American Revolution and retained the Revolutionary suspicion of concentrated power.

The convention unanimously chose Washington to preside over its sessions and then closed its business to the public and the press. The members then ruled that each state delegation would have a single vote. Major decisions would not require unanimity, as they did in Congress, but only a simple majority. Virginia, the most populous state, sent the best-prepared delegation to Philadelphia. James Madison (thirty-six years old) was its intellectual leader. He had devised a detailed plan for a new "national" government, and the Virginians used it to control the agenda from the moment the convention began.

Edmund Randolph of Virginia began the discussion by proposing that "a national government ought to be established, consisting of a supreme Legislative, Executive, and Judiciary." Despite its vagueness, it was a drastic proposal. It called for the creation of a government very different from the existing Confederation, which, among other things, had no executive branch. But so committed were the delegates to fundamental reform that they approved this resolution after only perfunctory debate. Then Randolph introduced the details of Madison's

The Virginia Plan

plan. The Virginia Plan (as it came to be known) called for a new national legislature consisting of two houses. In the lower house, the states would be represented in proportion to their population; thus the largest state (Virginia) would have about ten times as many representatives as the smallest (Delaware). Members of the upper house were to be elected by the lower house under no rigid system of representation; thus some of the smaller states might at times have no members at all in the upper house.

The proposal aroused immediate opposition among delegates from Delaware, New Jersey, and other small states. Some responded by arguing that Congress had called the convention "for the sole and express purpose of revising the Articles of Confederation" and had no authority to do more than that. Eventually, however, William Paterson of New Jersey submitted a substantive alternative to the Virginia Plan, a proposal for a "federal" as opposed to a "national" government. The New Jersey Plan preserved the existing one-house legislature, in which each state had equal representation, but it gave Congress expanded powers to tax and to regulate commerce. The delegates voted to table Paterson's proposal, but not without taking note of the substantial support for it among small-state representatives.

The Virginia Plan remained the basis for discussion. But its supporters realized they would have to make concessions to the small states if the convention was ever to reach a general agreement. They soon conceded an important point by agreeing to permit the members of the upper house to be elected by the state legislatures rather than by the lower house of the national legislature. Thus each state would be sure of always having at least one member in the upper house.

But many questions remained. Would the states be equally represented in the upper house, or would the large states have more members than the small ones? Would slaves (who could not vote) be counted as part of the population in determining the

Small States versus Large States

size of a state's representation in Congress, or were they to be considered simple property? Delegates from states with large and apparently permanent slave populations—especially those from South Carolina—wanted to have it both ways. They argued that slaves should be considered persons in determining representation. But they wanted slaves to be considered property if the new government were to levy taxes on each state on the basis of population. Representatives from states where slavery had disappeared or was expected soon to disappear argued that slaves should be included in calculating taxation but not representation. No one argued seriously for giving slaves citizenship or the right to vote.

Compromise

The delegates bickered for weeks. By the end of June, as both temperature and tempers rose to uncomfortable heights, the convention seemed in danger of collapsing. Benjamin Franklin, who remained a calm voice of conciliation through the summer, warned that if they failed, the delegates would "become a reproach and by-word down to future ages. And what is worse, mankind may hereafter, from this unfortunate instance, despair of establishing governments by human wisdom, and leave it to chance, war and conquest." Partly because of Franklin's soothing presence, the delegates refused to give up.

Finally, on July 2, the convention agreed to create a "grand committee," with a single delegate from each state (and with Franklin as chairman), to resolve the disagreements. The committee produced a proposal that became the basis of the "Great Compromise." Its most impor-

The Great Compromise

tant achievement was resolving the difficult problem of representation. The proposal called for a legislature in which the states would be represented in the lower house on the basis of population, with each slave counted as three-fifths of a free person in determining the basis for both representation and direct taxation. (The three-fifths formula was based on the false assumption that a slave was three-fifths as productive as a free worker and thus contributed only three-fifths as much wealth to the state.) The committee proposed that in the upper house, the states should be represented equally with two members apiece. The proposal broke the deadlock. On July 16, 1787, the convention voted to accept the compromise.

Over the next few weeks, while several committees worked on the details of various parts of the emerging constitution, the convention as a whole agreed to another important compromise on the explosive issue of slavery. The representatives of the southern states feared that the power to regulate trade might interfere with the cotton economy, which relied heavily on sales abroad, and with slavery. In response, the convention agreed that the new legislature would not be permitted to tax exports; Congress would also be forbidden to impose a duty of more than $10 a head on imported slaves, and it would have no authority to stop the slave trade for twenty years. To those delegates who viewed the continued existence of slavery as an affront to the principles of the new nation, this was a large and difficult concession. They agreed to it because they feared that without it the Constitution would fail.

The convention disposed of other differences of opinion it was unable to harmonize by evasion or omission—leaving important questions alive that would surface again in later years. The Constitution provided no definition of citizenship. Most important was the absence of a list of individual rights, which would restrain the powers of the national government in the way that bills of rights restrained the state governments. Madison opposed the idea, arguing that specifying rights that were reserved to the people would, in effect, limit those rights. Others, however, feared that without such protections the national government might abuse its new authority.

The Constitution of 1787

Many people contributed to the creation of the American Constitution, but the single most important of them was James Madison—the most creative political thinker of his

James Madison

generation. Madison created the Virginia Plan, from which the final document ultimately emerged, and he did most of the drafting of the Constitution itself. But Madison's most important achievement was in helping resolve two important philosophical questions that had served as obstacles to the creation of an effective national government: the question of sovereignty and the question of limiting power.

THE CONVENTION AT PHILADELPHIA This engraving of delegates at work, created in 1823, is one of countless efforts in the early nineteenth century to re-create imaginatively the great constitutional convention in Philadelphia in 1787. It appeared in an early *History of the United States of America* by Rev. Charles A. Goodrich. *(General Research Division, New York Public Library, Astor, Lenox and Tilden Foundations)*

The question of sovereignty had been one of the chief sources of friction between the colonies and Great Britain, and it continued to trouble Americans as they attempted to create their own government. How could both *The Question of Sovereignty* the national government and the state governments exercise sovereignty at the same time? Where did ultimate sovereignty lie? The answer, Madison and his contemporaries decided, was that all power, at all levels of government, flowed ultimately from the people. Thus neither the federal government nor the state governments were truly sovereign. All of them derived their authority from below. The opening phrase of the Constitution (devised by Robert Morris) was "We the people of the United States"—an expression of the belief that the new government derived its power not from the states but from its citizens.

Resolving the problem of sovereignty made possible one of the distinctive features of the Constitution—its distribution of powers between the national and state governments. It was, Madison wrote at the time, "in strictness, neither a national nor a federal Constitution, but a composition of both." The Constitution and the government it created were to be the "supreme law" of the land; no state would have the authority to defy it. The federal government was to have broad powers, including the power to tax, to regulate commerce, to control the currency, and to pass such laws as would be "necessary and proper" for carrying out its other responsibilities. Gone was the stipulation of the Articles that "each State shall retain

The Constitution—America's most powerful symbol of national identity and the nation's most important source of authority—has inspired debate from the moment it was drafted. Today, as throughout American national history, views of the Constitution reflect the political views of those who seek to interpret it. Some argue that the Constitution is a flexible document intended to evolve in response to society's evolution. Others argue that it has a fixed meaning, rooted in the "original intent" of the framers and that to move beyond that is to deny its value.

Historians, too, disagree about why the Constitution was written and what it meant; and their debate has also reflected contemporary beliefs about what the Constitution should mean. To some scholars, the creation of the federal system was an effort to preserve the ideals of the Revolution by eliminating the disorder and contention that threatened the new nation; it was an effort to create a strong national government capable of exercising real authority. To others, the Constitution was an effort to protect the economic interests of existing elites, even at the cost of betraying the principles of the Revolution. And to still others, the Constitution was designed to protect individual freedom and to limit the power of the federal government.

The first influential exponent of the heroic view of the Constitution as the culmination of the Revolution was John Fiske, whose book *The Critical Period of American History* (1888) painted a grim picture of political life

(General Research Division, New York Public Library, Astor, Lenox and Tilden Foundations)

under the Articles of Confederation. The nation, Fiske argued, was reeling under the impact of a business depression; the weakness and ineptitude of the national government; the threats to American territory from Great Britain and Spain; the inability of either the Congress or the state governments to make good their debts; the interstate jealousies and barriers to trade; the widespread use of inflation-producing paper money; and the lawlessness that culminated in Shays's Rebellion. Only the timely adoption of the Constitution, Fiske claimed, saved the young republic from disaster.

Fiske's view met with little dissent until 1913, when Charles A. Beard published a powerful challenge to it in *An Economic Interpretation of the Constitution of the United States*, which became one of the most influential works of American history in the twentieth century. According to Beard, the 1780s had been a "critical period" not for the nation as a whole but only for

certain conservative business interests who feared that the decentralized political structure of the republic imperiled their financial position. Such men, he claimed, wanted a government able to promote industry and trade, protect private property, and perhaps most of all, make good the public debt—much of which was owed to them. The Constitution was, Beard claimed, "an economic document drawn with superb skill by men whose property interests were immediately at stake" and who won its ratification over the opposition of a majority of the people. Were it not for their impatience and determination, he argued in a later book (1927), the Articles of Confederation might have formed a perfectly satisfactory, permanent form of government.

Beard's view of the Constitution influenced more than a generation of historians. As late as the 1950s, for example, Merrill Jensen argued in *The New Nation* (1950) that the 1780s were not years of chaos and despair, but a time of hopeful striving. He agreed with Beard that only the economic interests of a small group of wealthy men could account for the creation of the Constitution. To them, the Constitution was notable chiefly for the way it abridged the democratic possibilities of the new nation.

But in the 1950s—in the aftermath of a great world crisis that many scholars believed called into question the desirability of giving free reign to popular passions—a series of powerful challenges to the Beard thesis emerged. The Constitution, many

every power, jurisdiction, and right not expressly delegated to the United States in Congress assembled." On the other hand, the Constitution accepted the existence of separate states and left important powers in their hands.

In addition to solving the question of sovereignty, the Constitution produced a solution to a problem that was particularly troubling to Americans: the problem of concentrated authority. Nothing so frightened the leaders of the new nation as the prospect of creating a tyrannical government. Indeed, that fear had been one of the chief obstacles to the creation of a national government at all. Drawing from the ideas of the French philosopher Baron de Montesquieu, most Americans had long believed that the best

way, perhaps the only way, to avoid tyranny was to keep government close to the people. A republic, they thought, must remain confined to a relatively small area; a large nation would breed corruption and despotism because the rulers would be so distant from most of the people that there would be no way to control them. In the first years of the new American nation, these assumptions had led to the belief that the individual states must remain sovereign and that a strong national government would be dangerous.

Madison, however, helped break the grip of these assumptions by arguing that a large republic would be less, not more, likely to produce tyranny, because it would contain so many different factions that no single group would

scholars now began to argue, was not an effort to preserve property, but an enlightened effort to ensure stability and order. Robert E. Brown, for example, argued in 1956 that "absolutely no correlation" could be shown between the wealth of the delegates to the Constitutional Convention and their position on the Constitution. Forrest McDonald, in *We the People* (1958), looked beyond the convention itself to the debate between the Federalists and the Antifederalists and concluded similarly that there was no consistent relationship between wealth and property and support for the Constitution. Instead, opinion on the new system was far more likely to reflect local and regional interests. Areas suffering social and economic distress were likely to support the Constitution; states that were stable and prosperous were likely to oppose it. There was no intercolonial class of monied interests operating in concert to produce the Constitution. The cumulative effect of these attacks greatly weakened Beard's argument; few historians any longer accepted his thesis without reservation.

In the 1960s, a new group of scholars began to revive an economic interpretation of the Constitution—one that differed from Beard's in important ways but that nevertheless emphasized social and economic factors as motives for supporting the federal system. Jackson Turner Main argued, in *The Anti-federalists* (1961), that supporters of the Constitution, while not perhaps the united creditor class that Beard described, were nevertheless economi-

cally distinct from critics of the document. The Federalists, he argued, were "cosmopolitan commercialists," eager to advance the economic development of the nation; the Antifederalists, by contrast, were "agrarian localists," fearful of centralization. Gordon Wood's important study, *The Creation of the American Republic* (1969), de-emphasized economic grievances but nevertheless suggested that the debate over the state constitutions in the 1770s and 1780s reflected profound social divisions and that those same divisions helped shape the argument over the federal Constitution. The Federalists, he suggested, were largely traditional aristocrats. They had become deeply concerned by the instability of life under the Articles of Confederation and were particularly alarmed by the decline in popular deference toward social elites. The creation of the Constitution was part of a larger search to create a legitimate political leadership based on the existing social hierarchy; it reflected the efforts of elites to contain what they considered the excesses of democracy.

In more recent years, as contemporary debates over the Constitution have intensified, historians have continued to examine the question of "intent." Did the framers intend a strong, centralized political system; or did they intend to create a decentralized system with a heavy emphasis on individual rights? The answer, according to Jack Rakove's *Original Meanings* (1996), is both— and many other things as well. The Constitution, he argues, was not the

product of a single intelligence or of a broad consensus. It was the result of a long and vigorous debate through which the views of many different groups found their way into the document. James Madison, generally known as the father of the Constitution, was a strong nationalist, who believed that only a powerful central government could preserve stability in a large nation and keep narrow factionalism in check. Alexander Hamilton, Madison's ally in the battle, also saw the Constitution as a way to protect order and property, as a way to defend the nation against the dangers of too much liberty. But if Madison and Hamilton feared too much liberty, they also feared too little. And that made them receptive to the vigorous demands of the "anti-Federalists" for protections of individual rights, which culminated in the Bill of Rights. The framers differed as well in their views of the proper relationship between the federal government and the state governments. Madison favored unquestioned federal supremacy, and even tried to insert a clause in the Constitution giving Congress the right to invalidate state laws. Many others involved in the debate wanted to preserve the rights of the states and saw in the federal system—and in its unusual division of sovereignty among different levels and branches of government—a guarantee against too much national power. The Constitution is not, Rakove argues, "infinitely malleable." But neither does it have a fixed meaning that can be a reliable guide to how we interpret it today.

ever be able to dominate it. (In this, he drew from—among other sources—the Scottish philosopher David Hume.) This idea of many centers of power "checking each other"

Separation of Powers

and preventing any single, despotic authority from emerging not only made possible the idea of a large republic, but also helped shape the internal structure of the federal government. The Constitution's most distinctive feature was its "separation of powers" within the government, its creation of "checks and balances" among the legislative, executive, and judicial branches. The array of forces within the government would constantly compete with (and often frustrate) one another. Congress would have two

chambers, the Senate and the House of Representatives, each with members elected in a different way and for different terms, and each checking the other, since both would have to agree before any law could be passed. The president would have the power to veto acts of Congress. The federal courts would have protection from both the executive and the legislature because judges and justices, once appointed by the president and confirmed by the Senate, would serve for life.

The "federal" structure of the government, which divided power between the states and the nation, and the system of "checks and balances," which divided power among various elements within the national government itself, were designed to protect the United States from the kind of despotism Americans believed had emerged in England. But they were also designed to protect the nation from another kind of despotism, perhaps equally menacing: the tyranny of the people. Fear of the "mob," of an "excess of democracy," was at least as important to the framers as fear of a single tyrant. Shays's Rebellion had been only one example, they believed, of what could happen if a nation did not defend itself against the unchecked exercise of popular will. Thus in the new government, only the members of the House of Representatives would be elected directly by the people. Senators, the president, and federal judges would be insulated in varying degrees from the public.

On September 17, 1787, thirty-nine delegates signed the Constitution, doubtless sharing the feelings that Benjamin Franklin expressed at the end: "Thus I consent, Sir, to this Constitution, because I expect no better, and because I am not sure it is not the best."

Federalists and Antifederalists

The delegates at Philadelphia had greatly exceeded their instructions from Congress and the states. Instead of making simple revisions to the Articles of Confederation, they had produced a plan for a completely different form of government. They feared, therefore, that the Constitution might never be ratified under the rules of the Articles of Confederation, which required unanimous approval by the state legislatures. So the convention changed the rules. The Constitution specified that the new government would come into existence among the ratifying states when any nine of the thirteen had ratified

it. The delegates recommended to Congress that special state conventions, not state legislatures, consider the document.

The old Confederation Congress, now overshadowed by the events in Philadelphia, passively accepted the convention's work and submitted it to the states for approval. All the state legislatures except Rhode Island's elected delegates to ratifying conventions, most of which began meeting by early 1788. Even before the ratifying conventions convened, however, a great national debate on the new Constitution had begun—in the state legislatures, in mass meetings, in the columns of newspapers, and in ordinary conversations. Occasionally, passions rose to the point that opposing factions came to blows. In at least one place—Albany, New York—such clashes resulted in injuries and death.

Supporters of the Constitution had a number of advantages. They were better organized than their opponents, and they had the support of the two most eminent men in America, Franklin and Washington. (Washington, for example, had declared that the nation faced a choice between the Constitution and disunion.) And they seized an appealing label for themselves: "Federalists"—the term that opponents of centralization had once used to describe themselves—thus implying that they were less committed to a "nationalist" government than in fact they were. The Federalists also had the support of the ablest political philosophers of their time: Alexander Hamilton, James Madison, and John Jay. Those three men, under the joint pseudonym "Publius," wrote a series of essays—widely published in newspapers throughout the nation—explaining the meaning and virtues of the Constitution. The essays were

The Federalist Papers

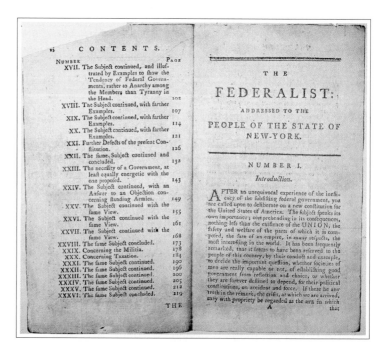

FEDERALIST #1 The Federalist Papers, gathered together here in a book distributed to the people of New York, began as essays, letters, and articles published in newspapers throughout America during the debate over the Constitution. Its authors—James Madison, Alexander Hamilton, and John Jay—were defenders of the new Constitution and wrote these essays to explain its value and importance. They remain today one of the most important American contributions to political theory. *(The Granger Collection)*

later issued as a book, and they are known today as The Federalist Papers. They are among the greatest American contributions to political theory.

The Federalists called their critics "Antifederalists," implying that their rivals had nothing to offer except opposition and chaos. But the Antifederalists had serious and

The Antifederalists

intelligent arguments of their own. They presented themselves as the defenders of the true principles of the Revolution. The Constitution, they believed, would betray those principles by establishing a strong, potentially tyrannical, center of power in the new national government. The new government, they claimed, would increase taxes, obliterate the states, wield dictatorial powers, favor the "well born" over the common people, and put an end to individual liberty. But their biggest complaint was that the Constitution lacked a bill of rights, a concern that revealed one of the most important sources of their opposition: a basic mistrust of human nature and of the capacity of human beings to wield power. (Some contemporaries, and some later scholars, described them as "men of little faith.") The Antifederalists argued that any government that centralized authority would inevitably produce despotism. Their demand for a bill of rights was a product of this belief: no government could be trusted to protect the liberties of its citizens; only by enumerating the natural rights of the people could there be any assurance that those rights would be preserved.

At its heart, then, the debate between the Federalists and the Antifederalists was a battle between two fears. The Federalists were afraid, above all, of disorder, anarchy, chaos; they feared the unchecked power of the masses, and they sought in the Constitution to create a govern-

Debating the Constitution

ment that would function at some distance from popular passions and that would be strong enough to act against threats to order and stability. The Antifederalists were not anarchists. They too recognized the need for an effective government. But they were much more afraid of the state than they were of the people, much more concerned about the dangers of concentrated power than about the dangers of popular will. They opposed the Constitution for some of the same reasons the Federalists supported it: because it placed obstacles between the people and the exercise of power.

Despite the Antifederalist efforts, ratification proceeded quickly (although not without occasional difficulty) during the winter of 1787–1788. The Delaware convention was the first to act, when it ratified the Constitution unanimously. The New Jersey and Georgia conventions did the same. In the larger states of Pennsylvania and Massachusetts, the Antifederalists put up a more determined struggle but lost in the final vote. New Hampshire ratified the document in June 1788—the ninth state to do so. It was now theoretically possible for the Constitution to go into effect.

A new government could not hope to flourish, however, without the participation of Virginia and New York, the two biggest states, whose conventions remained closely divided. By the end of June, first Virginia and then New York had consented to the Constitution by narrow margins. The New York convention yielded to expediency—even some of the most staunchly Antifederalist delegates feared that the state's commercial interests would suffer if, once the other states gathered under the "New Roof," New York were to remain outside. Massachusetts, Virginia, and New York all ratified, on the assumption that a bill of rights would be added to the Constitution. The North Carolina convention adjourned without taking action, waiting to see what happened to the amendments. Rhode Island, whose leaders had opposed the Constitution almost from the start, did not even call a convention to consider ratification.

Completing the Structure

The first elections under the Constitution took place in the early months of 1789. Almost all the newly elected congressmen and senators had favored ratification, and many had served as delegates to the Philadelphia convention. There was never any real doubt about who would be the first president. George Washington had presided at the Constitutional Convention, and many who had favored ratification did so only because they expected him to preside over the new government as well. Washington received the votes of all the presidential electors. John Adams, a leading Federalist, became vice president. After a journey from Mount Vernon marked by elaborate celebrations along the way, Washington was inaugurated in New York—the national capital for the time being—on April 30, 1789.

The first Congress served in many ways almost as a continuation of the Constitutional Convention, because its principal responsibility was filling in the various gaps in the Constitution. Its most important task was drafting a bill

The Bill of Rights

of rights. By early 1789, even Madison had come to agree that some sort of bill of rights was essential to legitimize the new government in the eyes of its opponents. Congress approved twelve amendments on September 25, 1789; ten of them were ratified by the states by the end of 1791. What we know as the Bill of Rights is these first ten amendments to the Constitution. Nine of them placed limitations on Congress by forbidding it to infringe on certain basic rights: freedom of religion, speech, and the press; immunity from arbitrary arrest; trial by jury; and others. The Tenth Amendment reserved to the states all powers except those specifically withheld from them or delegated to the federal government.

On the subject of the federal courts, the Constitution said only: "The judicial power of the United States shall be vested in one Supreme Court, and in such inferior courts as the Congress may from time to time ordain and establish." It was left to Congress to determine the number of Supreme Court judges to be appointed and the kinds of lower courts to be organized. In the Judiciary Act of 1789, Congress provided for a Supreme Court of six members, with a chief justice and five associate justices; thirteen district courts with one judge apiece; and three circuit courts of appeal, each to consist of one of the district judges sitting with two of the Supreme Court justices. In the same act, Congress gave the Supreme Court the power to make the final decision in cases involving the constitutionality of state laws.

The Constitution referred indirectly to executive departments but did not specify what or how many there should be. The first Congress created three such departments—state, treasury, and war—and also established the *The Cabinet* offices of the attorney general and postmaster general. To the office of secretary of the treasury, Washington appointed Alexander Hamilton of New York, who at age thirty-two was an acknowledged expert in public finance. For secretary of war he chose a Massachusetts Federalist, General Henry Knox. As attorney general he named Edmund Randolph of Virginia, sponsor of the plan on which the Constitution had been based. As secretary of state he chose another Virginian, Thomas Jefferson, who had recently served as minister to France.

FEDERALISTS AND REPUBLICANS

The resolution of these initial issues, however, did not resolve the deep disagreements about the nature of the new government. On the contrary, for the first twelve years under the Constitution, American politics was characterized by a level of acrimony seldom matched in any period since. The framers of the Constitution had dealt with many disagreements not by solving them but by papering them over with a series of vague compromises; as a result, the conflicts survived to plague the new government.

At the heart of the controversies of the 1790s was the same basic difference in philosophy that had been at the heart of the debate over the Constitution. On one side stood a powerful group that believed America required a strong, national government: that the country's mission was *Competing Visions* to become a genuine nation-state, with centralized authority, a complex commercial economy, and a proud standing in world affairs. On the other side stood another group—a minority at first, but one that gained strength during the decade—that envisioned a far more modest central government. American society should not, this group believed, aspire to be highly commercial or urban. It should remain predominantly rural and agrarian, and it should have a central government of modest size and powers that would leave most power in the hands of the states and the people. The centralizers became known as the Federalists and gravitated to the leadership of Alexander Hamilton. Their opponents took the name Republicans and gathered under the leadership of James Madison and Thomas Jefferson.

Hamilton and the Federalists

For twelve years, control of the new government remained firmly in the hands of the Federalists. That was in part because George Washington had always envisioned a strong national government and as president had quietly supported those who were attempting to create one. His enormous prestige throughout the nation was one of the Federalists' greatest assets. But Washington also believed that the presidency should remain above political controversies, and so he avoided any personal involvement in the deliberations of Congress. As a result, the dominant figure in his administration became his talented secretary of the treasury, Alexander Hamilton, who exerted more influence on domestic and foreign policy than anyone else both during his term of office and, to an almost equal extent, after his resignation in 1794.

Of all the national leaders of his time, Hamilton was one of the most aristocratic in personal tastes and politi-

BANK NOTE How to create a stable currency was one of the greatest challenges facing the new American nation. This fifty dollar bank note illustrates the principal form paper money assumed in the early republic. It was issued in 1797 by a bank in Philadelphia, and its value was directly tied to the stability of the bank itself. Only many years later did the national government assume control of printing and distributing currency. *(Eric P. Newman Numismatic Education Society)*

cal philosophy—ironically, perhaps, since his own origins as an illegitimate child in the Caribbean had been so humble. Far from embracing the republican ideals of the virtue of the people, he believed that a stable and effective government required an enlightened ruling class. Thus, the new government needed the support of the wealthy and

Assuming the Debt

powerful; and to get that support it needed to give those elites a stake in its success. Hamilton proposed, therefore, that the new government take responsibility for the existing public debt. Many of the miscellaneous, uncertain, depreciated certificates of indebtedness that the old Congress had issued during and after the Revolution were now in the hands of wealthy speculators; the government should call them in and exchange them for uniform, interest-bearing bonds, payable at definite dates. (This policy was known as "funding" the debt.) He also recommended that the federal government "assume" (or take over) the debts the states had accumulated during the Revolution; this assumption policy would encourage state as well as federal bondholders to look to the central government for eventual payment. Hamilton did not, in other words, envision paying off and thus eliminating the debt. He wanted instead to create a large and permanent national debt, with new bonds being issued as old ones were paid off. The result, he believed, would be that creditors—the wealthy classes most likely to lend money to the government—would have a permanent stake in seeing the government survive.

Hamilton also wanted to create a national bank. At the time, there were only a few banks in the country, located principally in Boston, Philadelphia, and New York. A new, national bank would help fill the void that the absence of a well-developed banking system had created. It would provide loans and currency to businesses. It would give the government a safe place to deposit federal funds. It would help collect taxes and disburse the government's expenditures. It would keep up the price of government bonds through judicious bond purchases. The bank would be chartered by the federal government, would have a monopoly of the government's own banking business, and would be controlled by directors, of whom one-fifth would be appointed by the government. It would provide a stable center to the nation's small and feeble banking system.

The funding and assumption of debts would require new sources of revenue, since the government would now have to pay interest on the loans it was accepting. Up to now, most government revenues had come from the

Hamilton's Report on Manufacturing

sale of public lands in the West. Hamilton proposed two new kinds of taxes. One was an excise to be paid by distillers of alcoholic liquors, a tax that would fall most heavily on the whiskey distillers of the backcountry, especially in Pennsylvania, Virginia, and North Carolina—small farmers who converted part of

their corn and rye crop into whiskey. The other was a tariff on imports, which not only would raise revenue but would also protect American manufacturing from foreign competition. In his famous "Report on Manufactures" of 1791, he laid out a grand scheme for stimulating the growth of industry in the United States and wrote glowingly of the advantages to the nation of a healthy manufacturing base.

The Federalists, in short, offered more than a vision of how to stabilize the new government. They offered a vision of the sort of nation America should become—a nation with a wealthy, enlightened ruling class, a vigorous, independent commercial economy, and a thriving industrial sector; a nation able to play a prominent role in world economic affairs.

Enacting the Federalist Program

Few members of Congress objected to Hamilton's plan for funding the national debt, but many did oppose his proposal to accept the debt "at par," that is at face value. The old certificates had been issued to merchants and farmers in payment for war supplies

Debating Hamilton's Program

during the Revolution, or to officers and soldiers of the Revolutionary army in payment for their services. But many of these original holders had sold their bonds during the hard times of the 1780s to speculators, who had bought them at a fraction of their face value. Many members of Congress believed if the federal government was to assume responsibility for these bonds, some of them should be returned to the original purchasers. James Madison, now a representative from Virginia, proposed dividing the federally funded bonds between the original purchasers and the speculators. But Hamilton's allies insisted that such a plan was impractical and that the honor of the government required that it pay the bondholders themselves, not the original lenders who had sold their bonds of their own accord. Congress finally passed the funding bill Hamilton wanted.

Hamilton's proposal that the federal government assume the state debts encountered greater difficulty. His opponents argued that if the federal government took over the state debts, the people of states with few debts would have to pay taxes to service the larger debts of other states. Massachusetts, for example, owed far more money than did Virginia. Hamilton and his supporters struck a bargain with the Virginians to win passage of the bill.

The deal involved the location of the national capital. The capital had moved from New York back to Philadelphia in 1790. But the Virginians wanted a new capital near them in the South. Hamilton met with Thomas Jefferson (after Jefferson's return from France) and agreed over dinner

Location of the Capital

to provide northern support for placing the capital in the South in exchange for Virginia's votes for the assumption bill. The bargain called for the construction of a new capital city on the banks of the Potomac River, which divided Virginia and Maryland, on land to be selected by Washington himself. The government would move there by the beginning of the new century.

Hamilton's bank bill sparked the most heated debate, the first of many on this controversial issue. Hamilton argued that creation of a national bank was compatible with

Bank of the United States the intent of the Constitution, even though the document did not explicitly authorize it. But Madison, Jefferson, Randolph, and others argued that Congress should exercise no powers that the Constitution had not clearly assigned it. Nevertheless, both the House and the Senate finally agreed to Hamilton's bill. Washington displayed some uncertainty about its legality at first, but he finally signed it. The Bank of the United States began operations in 1791, under a charter that granted it the right to continue for twenty years.

Hamilton also had his way with the excise tax, although protests from farmers later forced revisions to reduce the burden on the smaller distillers. He won passage, too, of a new tariff in 1792, although it raised rates less than he had wished.

Once enacted, Hamilton's program had many of the effects he had intended and won the support of influential segments of the population. It quickly restored public credit; the bonds of the United States were soon selling at home and abroad at prices even above their par value. Speculators (among them many members of Congress) reaped large profits as a result. Manufacturers profited from the tariffs, and merchants in the seaports benefited from the new banking system.

Others, however, found the Hamilton program less appealing. Small farmers, who formed the vast majority of the population, complained that they had to bear a disproportionate tax burden. Not only did they have to pay property taxes to their state governments, but they bore the brunt of the excise tax on distilleries and, indirectly, the tariff. A feeling grew among many Americans that the Federalist program served the interests not of the people but of small, wealthy elites. Out of this feeling an organized political opposition arose.

The Republican Opposition

The Constitution had made no reference to political parties, and the omission was not an oversight. Most of the framers—and George Washington in particular—believed that organized parties were dangerous and should be avoided. Disagreement on particular issues was inevitable, but most of the founders believed that such disagreements need not and should not lead to the formation of permanent factions. "The public good is disregarded in the conflicts of rival parties," Madison had written in The Federalist Papers (in Number 10, perhaps the most influential of all the essays), "and . . . measures are too often decided, not according to the rules of justice and the rights of the minor party, but by the superior force of an interested and overbearing majority."

Yet within just a few years after ratification of the Constitution, Madison and others became convinced that Hamilton and his followers had become just such an "interested and overbearing majority." Not *Establishment of the Federalist Party* only had the Federalists enacted a program that many of these leaders opposed. More ominously, Hamilton himself had, in their eyes, worked to establish a national network of influence that embodied all the worst features of a party. The Federalists had used their control over appointments and the awarding of government franchises, and all the other powers of their offices, to reward their supporters and win additional allies. They had encouraged the formation of local associations—largely aristocratic in nature—to strengthen their standing in local communities. They were doing many of the same things, their opponents believed, that the corrupt British governments of the early eighteenth century had done.

Because the Federalists appeared to be creating such a menacing and tyrannical structure of power, their critics felt, there was no alternative but to *Formation of the Republican Party* organize a vigorous opposition. The result was the emergence of an alternative political organization, which called itself the Republican Party. (This first "Republican" Party is not a direct ancestor of the modern Republican Party, which was born in the 1850s.) By the late 1790s, the Republicans were going to even greater lengths than the Federalists to create an apparatus of partisan influence. In every state they formed committees, societies, and caucuses. Republican groups were corresponding with one another across state lines. They were banding together to influence state and local elections. And they were justifying their actions by claiming that they and they alone represented the true interests of the nation—that they were fighting to defend the people against a corrupt conspiracy by the Federalists. Just as Hamilton believed that the network of supporters he was creating represented the only legitimate interest group in the nation, so the Republicans believed that their party organization represented the best interests of the people. Neither side was willing to admit that it was acting as a party; neither would concede the right of the other to exist. This institutionalized factionalism is known to scholars as the "first party system."

From the beginning, the preeminent figures among the Republicans were Thomas Jefferson and James Madison. Indeed, the two men were such intimate collaborators with such similar political philosophies that it is sometimes difficult to distinguish the contributions of one

THE JEFFERSONIAN IDYLL American artists in the early nineteenth century were drawn to tranquil rural scenes, symbolic of the Jeffersonian vision of a nation of small, independent farmers. By 1822, when Francis Alexander painted this pastoral landscape, the simple agrarian republic it depicts was already being transformed by rapid economic growth. *(Gift of Edgar William and Bernice Chrysler Garbisch, © 1998 Board of Trustees, National Gallery of Art, Washington)*

from those of the other. But Jefferson, the more magnetic personality of the two, gradually emerged as the most prominent spokesman for the Republicans. Jefferson considered himself a farmer. (He was, in fact, a substantial planter; but he had spent relatively little time in recent years at his estate in Virginia.) He believed in an agrarian republic, most of whose citizens would be sturdy, independent farmer-citizens tilling their own soil.

Jefferson did not scorn commercial activity; he assumed farmers would market their crops in the national and even international markets. Nor did he oppose industry; he believed the United States should develop some manufacturing capacity. But he was suspicious of large cities, feared urban mobs as "sores upon the body politic," and opposed the development of an advanced industrial economy because it would, he feared, increase the number of propertyless workers packed in cities. In short, Jefferson envisioned a decentralized society, dominated by small property owners engaged largely in agrarian activities.

The difference between the Federalist and Republican social philosophies was visible in, among other things, reactions to the French Revolution. As that revolution grew

Differences over the French Revolution

increasingly radical in the 1790s, with its attacks on organized religion, the overthrow of the monarchy, and eventually the execution of the king and queen, the Federalists expressed horror. But the Republicans generally applauded the democratic, anti-aristo-

cratic spirit they believed the French Revolution embodied. Some even imitated the French radicals (the Jacobins) by cutting their hair short, wearing pantaloons, and addressing one another as "Citizen" and "Citizeness."

Although both parties had supporters in all parts of the country and among all classes, there were regional and economic differences. The Federalists were most numerous in the commercial centers of the Northeast and in such southern seaports as Charleston; the Republicans were most numerous in the rural areas of the South and the West.

As the 1792 presidential election—the nation's second—approached, both Jefferson and Hamilton urged Washington to run for another term. The president reluctantly agreed. But while most Americans considered Washington above the partisan battle, he was actually much more in sympathy with the Federalists than with the Republicans. And during his presidency, Hamilton remained the dominant figure in government.

ESTABLISHING NATIONAL SOVEREIGNTY

The Federalists consolidated their position—and attracted wide public support for the new national government—by dealing effectively with two problems the old Confederation had been unable fully to resolve. They helped stabilize the nation's western lands, and they strengthened America's international position.

Securing the Frontier

Despite the Northwest Ordinance, the Confederation Congress had largely failed to tie the outlying western areas of the country firmly to the government. Farmers in western Massachusetts had risen in revolt; settlers in Vermont, Kentucky, and Tennessee had toyed with the idea of separating from the Union. At first, the new government under the Constitution faced similar problems.

In 1794, farmers in western Pennsylvania raised a major challenge to federal authority when they refused to pay a whiskey excise tax and began terrorizing the tax collectors (much as colonists had done at the time of the Stamp Act). But the federal government did not leave settlement of the so-called Whiskey Rebellion to Pennsyl-

Whiskey Rebellion

vania, as the Confederation Congress had left Shays's Rebellion to Massachusetts. At Hamilton's urging, Washington called out the militias of three states, raised an army of nearly 15,000 (a larger force than he had commanded against the British during most of the Revolution), and personally led the troops into Pennsylvania. As the militiamen approached Pittsburgh, the center of the resistance, the rebellion quickly collapsed.

The federal government won the allegiance of the whiskey rebels by intimidating them. It won the loyalties of other frontier people by accepting their territories as new states in the Union. The last of the original thirteen colonies joined the Union once the Bill of Rights had been appended to the Constitution—North Carolina in 1789 and Rhode Island in 1790. Then Vermont, which had had its own state government since the Revolution, became the fourteenth state in 1791 after New York and New Hampshire finally agreed to give up their claims to it. Next came Kentucky, in 1792, when Virginia gave up its claim to that region. After North Carolina finally ceded its western lands to the Union, Tennessee became first a territory and, in 1796, a state.

Native Americans and the New Nation

The new government faced a greater challenge, inherited from the Confederation, in the more distant areas of the Northwest and the Southwest, where Indians (occasionally in alliance with the British and Spanish) continued to challenge the republic's claim to tribal lands. The ordinances of 1784–1787, establishing the terms of white settlement in the West, had produced a series of border conflicts with Indian tribes resisting white settlement in their lands. The new government inherited these clashes, which continued with few interruptions for nearly a decade. Although the United States eventually defeated virtually every Indian challenge (if often at great cost), it was clear that the larger question of who was to control the lands of the West—the United States or the Indian nations—remained unanswered.

These clashes revealed another issue the Constitution had done little to resolve: the place of the Indian nations within the new federal structure. The Constitution barely mentioned Native Americans. Article I excluded "Indians not taxed" from being counted in the population totals that de-

Indians and the Constitution

termined the number of seats states would receive in the House of Representatives; and it gave Congress the power to "regulate Commerce with foreign Nations, and among the several States, and with the Indian tribes." Article VI bound the new government to respect treaties negotiated by the Confederation, most of which had been with the tribes. But none of this did very much to clarify the precise legal standing of Indians or Indian nations within the United States.

On the one hand, the Constitution seemed to recognize the existence of the tribes as legal entities. On the other hand, it made clear that they were not "foreign Nations" (in the same sense that European countries were); nor were their members citizens of the United States. The tribes received no direct representation in the new gov-

A COMMENT ON THE WHISKEY REBELLION
Although Thomas Jefferson and other Republicans claimed to welcome occasional popular uprisings, the Federalists were horrified by such insurgencies as Shays's Rebellion in Massachusetts and, later, the Whiskey Rebellion in Pennsylvania. This Federalist cartoon portrays the rebels as demons who pursue and eventually hang an unfortunate "exciseman" (tax collector), who has confiscated two kegs of rum. *(Atwater Kent Museum)*

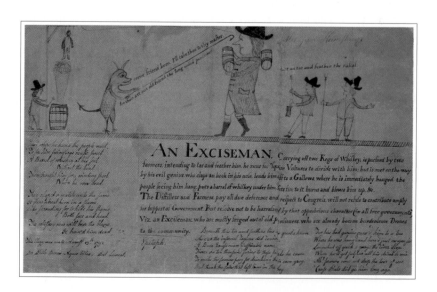

ernment. Above all, the Constitution did not address the major issue that would govern relations between whites and Indians: land. Indian nations lived within the boundaries of the United States, yet they claimed (and the white government at times agreed) that they had some measure of sovereignty within their own lands. But neither the Constitution nor common law offered any clear guide to the rights of a "nation within a nation" or to the precise nature of tribal sovereignty, which ultimately depended on control of land. Thus, the relationship between the tribes and the United States remained to be determined by a series of treaties, agreements, and judicial decisions in a process that has continued for two centuries.

Maintaining Neutrality

Not until 1791—eight years after the end of the Revolution—did Great Britain send a minister to the United States, and then only because Madison and the Republicans were threatening to place special trade restrictions on British ships. That was one of many symbols of the difficulty the new government had in establishing its legitimacy in the eyes of the British. Another crisis in Anglo-American relations emerged in 1793 when the new French government, created by the revolution of 1789, went to war with Great Britain and its allies. Both the president and Congress took steps to establish American neutrality in that conflict. But the neutrality quickly encountered severe tests.

The first challenge to American neutrality came from revolutionary France and its first diplomatic representative to America, the brash and youthful Edmond Genet. Instead of landing at Philadelphia and presenting himself immediately to the president, Genet disembarked at Charleston.

Citizen Genet

There he made plans to use American ports to outfit French warships, encouraged American shipowners to serve as French privateers, and commissioned the aging George Rogers Clark to lead a military expedition against Spanish lands to the south. (Spain was at the time an ally of Great Britain and an enemy of France.) In all of this, Genet was brazenly ignoring Washington's policies and flagrantly violating the Neutrality Act. His conduct infuriated Washington (who provided "Citizen Genet," as he was known, with an icy reception in Philadelphia) and the Federalists; it also embarrassed all but the most ardent admirers of the French Revolution among the Republicans. Washington eventually demanded that the French government recall him, but by then Genet's party was out of power in France. (The president granted him political asylum in the United States, and he settled with his American wife on a Long Island farm.) The neutrality policy had survived its first serious test.

A second and even greater challenge came from Great Britain. Early in 1794, the Royal Navy began seizing hundreds of American ships engaged in trade in the French West Indies, outraging public opinion in the United States. Anti-British feeling rose still higher at the report that the governor general of Canada had delivered a warlike speech to the Indians on the northwestern frontier. Hamilton was deeply concerned. War would mean an end to imports from England, and most of the revenue for maintaining his financial system came from duties on those imports.

Jay's Treaty and Pinckney's Treaty

This was, Hamilton believed, no time for ordinary diplomacy. He did not trust the State Department to reach a settlement with Britain. Jefferson had resigned as secretary of state in 1793 to devote more time to his political activities, but his successor, Edmund Randolph, was even more ardently pro-French than Jefferson had been. So Hamilton persuaded Washington to name a special commissioner to England: John Jay, chief justice of the United States Supreme Court and a staunch New York Federalist. Jay was instructed to secure compensation for the recent British assaults on American shipping, to demand withdrawal of British forces from the frontier posts, and to negotiate a new commercial treaty.

The long and complex treaty Jay negotiated in 1794 failed to achieve these goals. But it was not without merit. It settled the conflict with Britain and helped prevent what had seemed likely to become a war between the two nations. It established undisputed American sovereignty over the entire Northwest. And it produced a reasonably satisfactory commercial relationship with Britain, whose *Jay's Treaty* trade was important to the United States. Nevertheless, when the terms became public in America, there were bitter public denunciations of it for having failed to extract enough promises from the British. Jay himself was burned in effigy in various parts of the country. Opponents of the treaty—nearly all the Republicans and even some Federalists, encouraged by agents of France—went to extraordinary lengths to defeat it in the Senate. The American minister to France, James Monroe, and even the secretary of state, Edmund Randolph, joined the desperate attempt to prevent ratification. But in the end the Senate ratified what was by then known as Jay's Treaty.

Among other things, the treaty made possible a settlement of America's conflict with the Spanish, because it raised fears in Spain that the British and the Americans might now join together to challenge Spanish possessions in *Pinckney's Treaty* North America. When Thomas Pinckney arrived in Spain as a special negotiator, he had no difficulty in gaining nearly everything the United States had sought from the Spaniards for more than a decade. Under Pinckney's Treaty (signed in 1795), Spain recognized the right of Americans to navigate the Mississippi to its mouth and to deposit goods at New Orleans for reloading on oceangoing ships; agreed to fix the northern boundary of Florida where Americans always had insisted it should be, along the 31st parallel; and required Spanish authorities to prevent the Indians in Florida from launching raids across the border.

THE DOWNFALL OF THE FEDERALISTS

The Federalists' impressive triumphs did not ensure their continued dominance in the national government. On the contrary, success seemed to produce problems of its own—problems that eventually led to their downfall.

Since almost all Americans in the 1790s agreed that there was no place in a stable republic for an organized opposition, the emergence of the Republicans as powerful contenders for popular favor seemed to the Federal-

MOUNT VERNON George and Martha Washington lavished enormous attention to their home at Mount Vernon, importing materials and workmen from Europe to create a house that they hoped would rival some of the elegant country homes of England. This detail from a mantle suggests the degree to which they—like many wealthy planters and merchants of their time—strove to bring refinement and gentility to their lives. *(Paul Rocheleau/Rebus, Inc.)*

ists a grave threat to national stability. Beginning in the late 1790s, when major international perils confronted the government as well, the Federalists could not resist the temptation to move forcefully against the opposition. Facing what they believed was a stark choice between respecting individual liberties and preserving stability, the Federalists chose stability. The result was political disaster. After 1796, the Federalists never won another election. The popular respect for the institutions of the federal government, which they had worked so hard to produce among the people, survived. But the Federalists themselves gradually vanished as an effective political force.

The Election of 1796

Despite strong pressure from his many admirers to run for a third term as president, George Washington insisted on retiring from office in 1797. In a "Farewell Address" to the American people (actually a long letter, composed in part by Hamilton and published in a *Washington's Farewell Address* Philadelphia newsletter), he reacted sharply to the Republicans. His reference to the "insidious wiles of foreign influence" was not just an abstract warning against international entanglements; it was also a specific denunciation of those Republicans who had been conspiring with the French to frustrate the Federalist diplomatic program.

With Washington out of the running, no obstacle remained to an open expression of the partisan rivalries that had been building over the previous eight years. Jefferson was the uncontested candidate of the Republicans in 1796. The Federalists faced a more difficult choice. Hamilton, the personification of Federalism, had created too many enemies to be a credible candidate. So Vice President John Adams, who had been directly associated with none of the unpopular Federalist measures, became his party's nominee for president.

The Federalists were still clearly the dominant party, and there was little doubt of their ability to win a majority of the presidential electors. But without Washington to mediate, they fell victim to fierce factional rivalries that almost led to their undoing. Hamilton and many other Federalists (especially in the South) were not reconciled to Adams's candidacy and favored his running mate Thomas Pinckney instead. And when, as expected, the Federalists elected a majority of the presidential electors, some of these Pinckney supporters declined to vote for Adams; he managed to defeat Jefferson by only three electoral votes. Because a still larger number of Adams's supporters declined to vote for Pinckney, Jefferson finished second in the balloting and became vice president. (The Constitution provided for the candidate receiving the second highest number of electoral votes to become vice presi-

JOHN ADAMS Adams's illustrious career as Revolutionary leader, diplomat, and president marked the beginning of four generations of public distinction among members of his family. His son, John Quincy Adams, served as secretary of state and president. His grandson, Charles Francis Adams, was one of the great diplomats of the Civil War era. His great-grandson, Henry Adams, was one of America's most distinguished historians and writers. *(Adams National Historic Site, Quincy, Massachusetts)*

dent—hence the awkward result of men from different parties serving in the nation's two highest elected offices. The Twelfth Amendment, adopted in 1804, reformed the electoral system to prevent such situations.)

Adams thus assumed the presidency under inauspicious circumstances. He presided over a divided party, which faced a strong and resourceful Republican opposition committed to its extinction. Adams himself was not *Divided Federalists* even the dominant figure in his own party; Hamilton remained the most influential Federalist, and Adams was never able to challenge him effectively. The new president was one of the country's most accomplished and talented statesmen, but he had few skills as a politician. Austere, rigid, aloof, he had little talent at conciliating differences, soliciting support, or inspiring enthusiasm. He was a man of enormous, indeed intimidating rectitude, and he seemed to assume that his own virtue and the correctness of his positions would alone be enough to sustain him. He was usually wrong.

The Quasi War with France

American relations with Great Britain and Spain improved as a result of Jay's and Pinckney's Treaties. But the nation's relations with revolutionary France quickly deteriorated. French vessels captured American ships on the high seas and at times imprisoned the crews. When the South Carolina Federalist Charles Cotesworth Pinckney, brother of Thomas Pinckney, arrived in France, the government refused to receive him as the official representative of the United States.

Some of President Adams's advisers favored war, most notably Secretary of State Thomas Pickering, a stern New Englander who detested France. But Hamilton recommended conciliation, and Adams agreed. In an effort to stabilize relations, Adams appointed a bipartisan commission—consisting of Charles Cotesworth Pinckney, the recently rejected minister; John Marshall, a Virginia Federalist, later chief justice of the Supreme Court; and Elbridge Gerry, a Massachusetts Republican but a personal friend of the president—to negotiate with France. When the Americans arrived in Paris in 1797, three agents of the French foreign minister, Prince Talleyrand, demanded a loan for France and a bribe for French officials before any negotiations could begin. Pinckney responded succinctly and angrily: "No! No! Not a sixpence!"

When Adams heard of the incident, he sent a message to Congress denouncing the French insults and urging preparations for war. He then turned the report of the American commissioners over *The XYZ Affair* to Congress, after deleting the names of the three French agents and designating them only as "Messrs. X, Y, and Z." When the report was published, it created widespread popular outrage at France's actions and strong support for the Federalists' response. For nearly two years after the "XYZ Affair," as it became known, the United States found itself engaged in an undeclared war with France.

Adams persuaded Congress to cut off all trade with France, to repudiate the treaties of 1778, and to authorize American vessels to capture French armed ships on the high seas. In 1798, Congress *The Quasi War* created a Department of the Navy and appropriated money for the construction of new warships. The navy soon won a number of duels with French vessels and captured a total of eighty-five ships, including armed merchantmen. The United States also began cooperating closely with the British and became virtually an ally of Britain in the war with France.

In the end, France chose to conciliate the United States before the conflict grew. Adams sent another commission to Paris in 1800, and the new French government (headed now by "first consul" Napoleon Bonaparte) agreed to a treaty with the United States that canceled the old agreement of 1778 and established new commercial

THE XYZ AFFAIR The sensational "XYZ Affair" of 1798 is the subject of this American political cartoon. The five-headed figure in the center represents the Directory of the French government; he is demanding "money, money, money" from the three diplomats at left who were in Paris representing the United States. The monster at the top right is operating a guillotine—a symbol of the violence and terror of the later stages of the French Revolution. *(The Granger Collection)*

arrangements. As a result, the "quasi war" came to a reasonably peaceful end. In the process, the United States had at last freed itself from the entanglements and embarrassments of the "perpetual" alliance with France it had forged during the Revolution.

Repression and Protest

The conflict with France helped the Federalists increase their majorities in Congress in 1798. Armed with this new strength, they began to consider ways to silence the

Alien and Sedition Acts

Republican opposition. The result was some of the most controversial legislation in American history: the Alien and Sedition Acts.

The Alien Act placed new obstacles in the way of foreigners who wished to become American citizens, and it strengthened the president's hand in dealing with aliens. The Sedition Act allowed the government to prosecute those who engaged in "sedition" against the government. In theory only libelous or treasonous activities were subject to prosecution; but since such activities were subject to widely varying definitions, the law made it possible for the federal government to stifle virtually any opposition. The Republicans interpreted the new laws as part of a Federalist campaign to destroy them and fought back.

President Adams signed the new laws but was cautious in implementing them. He did not deport any aliens, and he prevented the government from launching a major crusade against the Republicans. But the legislation had a significant repressive effect nevertheless. The Alien Act helped discourage immigration and encouraged some foreigners already in the country to leave. And the administration made use of the Sedition Act to arrest and convict

ten men, most of them Republican newspaper editors whose only crime had been to criticize the Federalists in government.

Republican leaders pinned their hopes for a reversal of the Alien and Sedition Acts on the state legislatures. (The Supreme Court had not yet established its sole right to nullify congressional legislation, and

Virginia and Kentucky Resolutions

there were many who believed that the states had that power too.) The Republicans laid out a theory for state action in two sets of resolutions in 1798–1799, one written (anonymously) by Jefferson and adopted by the Kentucky legislature and the other drafted by Madison and approved by the Virginia legislature. The Virginia and Kentucky Resolutions, as they were known, used the ideas of John Locke to argue that the federal government had been formed by a "compact" or contract among the states and possessed only certain delegated powers. Whenever it exercised any undelegated powers, its acts were "unauthoritative, void, and of no force." If the parties to the contract, the states, decided that the central government had exceeded those powers, the Kentucky Resolution claimed, they had the right to "nullify" the appropriate laws.

The Republicans did not win wide support for nullification; only Virginia and Kentucky declared the congressional statutes void. The Republicans did, however, succeed in elevating their dispute with the Federalists to the level of a national crisis. By the late 1790s, the entire nation was as deeply and bitterly divided politically as it would ever be in its history. State legislatures at times resembled battlegrounds. Even the United States Congress was plagued with violent disagreements. In one celebrated incident in the chamber of the House of Representatives,

CONGRESSIONAL BRAWLERS This cartoon lampoons a celebrated fight on the floor of the House of Representatives in 1798 between Matthew Lyon, a Republican from Vermont, and Roger Griswold, a Federalist from Connecticut. The conflict began when Griswold insulted Lyon by attacking his military record in the Revolutionary War. Lyon replied by spitting in Griswold's face. Two weeks later, Griswold attacked Lyon with his cane, and Lyon seized a pair of fire tongs and fought back. That later scene is depicted (and ridiculed) here. Other members of Congress are portrayed as enjoying the spectacle. On the wall is a picture entitled "Royal Sport," showing animals fighting. *(New York Public Library)*

Matthew Lyon, a Republican from Vermont, responded to an insult from Roger Griswold, a Federalist from Connecticut, by spitting in Griswold's eye. Griswold attacked Lyon with his cane. Lyon fought back with a pair of fire tongs, and the two men ended up wrestling on the floor.

The "Revolution" of 1800

These bitter controversies shaped the 1800 presidential election. The presidential candidates were the same as four years earlier: Adams for the Federalists, Jefferson for the Republicans. But the campaign of 1800 was very different from the one preceding it. Indeed, it may have been the ugliest in American history. Adams and Jefferson themselves displayed reasonable dignity, but their supporters showed no such restraint. The Federalists accused Jefferson of being a dangerous radical and his followers of being wild men who, if they should come to power, would bring on a reign of terror comparable to that of the French Revolution. The Republicans portrayed Adams as a tyrant conspiring to become king, and they accused the Federalists of plotting to subvert human liberty and impose slavery on the people. There was considerable personal invective as well. For example, it was during this campaign that the story of Jefferson's alleged romantic involvement with a slave woman on his plantation was first widely aired.

The Election of 1800

The election was close, and the crucial contest was in New York. There, Aaron Burr had mobilized an organization of Revolutionary War veterans, the Tammany Society, to serve as a Republican political machine. And through Tammany's efforts, the Republicans carried the city by a large majority, and with it the state. Jefferson was, apparently, elected.

But an unexpected complication soon jeopardized the Republican victory. The Constitution called for each elector to "vote by ballot for two persons." The normal practice was for an elector to cast one vote for his party's presidential candidate and another for the vice presidential candidate. (The difficulties in sustaining this delicate practice in a highly partisan environment had led in 1796 to the election of Jefferson as vice president under his opponent, Adams.) To avoid a tie between Jefferson and Aaron Burr (the Republican vice presidential candidate in 1800), the Republicans had intended for one elector to refrain from voting for Burr. But the plan went awry. When the votes were counted, Jefferson and Burr each had 73. No candidate had a majority. According to the Constitution the House of Representatives had to choose between the two leading candidates when no one had a majority; in this case, that meant deciding between Jefferson and Burr. Each state delegation would cast a single vote.

The new Congress, elected in 1800 with a Republican majority, was not to convene until after the inauguration of the president, so it was the Federalist Congress that had to decide the question. Some Federalists hoped to use the situation to salvage the election for their party; others wanted to strike a bargain with Burr and elect him. But after a long deadlock, several leading Federalists, most prominent among them Alexander Hamilton, concluded that Burr (whom many suspected of having engineered the deadlock in the first place) was too unreliable to trust with the presidency. On the thirty-sixth ballot, Jefferson was elected.

After the election of 1800, the only branch of the federal government left in Federalist hands was the judiciary. The Adams administration spent its last months in office taking steps to make the party's hold on the courts secure. By the Judiciary Act of 1801, passed by the lame duck Congress, the Federalists reduced the number of

 The Judiciary Act of 1801

Supreme Court justiceships by one but greatly increased the number of federal judgeships as a whole. Adams quickly appointed Federalists to the newly created positions. Indeed, there were charges that he stayed up until midnight on his last day in office to finish signing the new judges' commissions. These officeholders became known as the "midnight appointments."

Even so, the Republicans viewed their victory as almost complete. The nation, they believed, had been saved from tyranny. A new era could now begin, one in which the true principles on which America had been founded would once again govern the land. The exuberance with which the victors viewed the future—and the importance they attributed to the Federalists' defeat—was evident in the phrase Jefferson himself later used to describe his election. He called it the "Revolution of 1800." It remained to be seen how revolutionary it would really be.

CONCLUSION

The writing of the Constitution of 1787 was the single most important political event in the history of the United States, and a notable event in the political history of the modern world. In creating a "federal" system of dispersed and divided authority—authority divided among national and state governments, authority divided among an executive, a legislature, and a judiciary—the young nation sought to balance its need for an effective central government against its fear of concentrated and despotic power. The ability of the delegates to the Constitutional Convention to compromise again and again to produce the ultimate structure gave evidence of the deep yearning among them for a stable political system. The same willingness to compromise allowed the greatest challenge to the ideals of the new democracy—slavery—to survive intact.

The writing and ratifying of the Constitution settled some questions about the shape of the new nation. The first twelve years under the government created by the Constitution solved others. And yet by the year 1800, a basic disagreement about the future of the nation—a disagreement personified by the differences between committed nationalist Alexander Hamilton and the self-proclaimed champion of democracy Thomas Jefferson—remained unresolved and was creating bitter divisions and conflicts within the political world. The election of Thomas Jefferson to the presidency that year opened a new chapter in the nation's public history. It also brought to a close, at least temporarily, savage political conflicts that had seemed to threaten the nation's future.

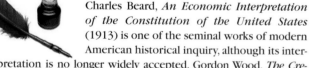

FOR FURTHER REFERENCE

Charles Beard, *An Economic Interpretation of the Constitution of the United States* (1913) is one of the seminal works of modern American historical inquiry, although its interpretation is no longer widely accepted. Gordon Wood, *The Creation of the American Republic* (1969) is the leading analysis of the intellectual path from the Declaration of Independence to the American Constitution. Jack Rakove, *Original Meanings: Politics and Ideas in the Making of the Constitution* (1996) connects the politics of the 1780s with the political ideas embedded in the Constitution. Stanley Elkins and Eric McKitrick, *The Age of Federalism* (1993) provides a detailed overview of political and economic development in the 1790s. Joyce Appleby, *Capitalism and a New Social Order: The Republican Vision of the 1790s* (1984) highlights liberal and capitalist impulses unleashed after the ratification of the Constitution. Joseph Ellis is the author of several highly regarded books on the founders: *After the Revolution: Profiles of Early American Culture* (1979), which examines some of the framers of the new nation; *American Sphinx: The Character of Thomas Jefferson* (1997); *Founding Brothers: The Revolutionary Generation* (2000); and *Passionate Sage: The Character and Legacy of John Adams* (1993). David McCullough, *John Adams* (2001) is a vivid, sympathetic, and outstandingly popular biography.

For quizzes, Internet resources, references to additional books and films, and more, consult this book's Online Learning Center at www.mhhe.com/brinkley11.

THE RISE OF CULTURAL NATIONALISM

In many respects, American cultural life in the early nineteenth century seemed to reflect the Republican vision of the nation's future. Opportunities for education increased; the nation's literary and artistic life began to free itself from European influences; and American religion began to confront and adjust to the spread of Enlightenment rationalism. In other respects, however, the new culture was posing a serious challenge to Republican ideals.

Patterns of Education

Central to the Republican vision of America was the concept of a virtuous and enlightened citizenry. Jefferson himself called emphatically for a national "crusade against ignorance." Republicans believed, therefore, in the creation of a nationwide system of public schools to create the educated electorate they believed a republic required. All male citizens (the nation's prospective voters) should, they argued, receive free education. They were unable to realize that dream, although their efforts to do so sustained a vision that in later years would produce much more substantial results.

Importance of a Virtuous Citizenry

Some states endorsed the principle of public education for all in the early years of the republic, but none actually created a working system of free schools. A Massachusetts law of 1789 reaffirmed the colonial laws by which each town was obligated to support a school, but there was little enforcement. In Virginia, the state legislature ignored Jefferson's call for universal elementary education and for advanced education for the gifted. As late as 1815, not a single state had a comprehensive public school system.

Instead, schooling became primarily the responsibility of private institutions, most of which were open only to those who could afford to pay for them. In the South and in the mid-Atlantic states, religious groups ran most of the schools. In New England and elsewhere, private academies were usually more secular, many of them modeled on schools founded by the Phillips family at Andover, Massachusetts, in 1778, and at Exeter, New Hampshire, three years later. By 1815, there were thirty such private secondary schools in Massachusetts, thirty-seven in New York, and several dozen more scattered throughout the country. Many were frankly aristocratic in outlook, training their students to become members of the nation's elite. There were a few schools open to the poor, but not nearly enough to accommodate everyone, and the education they offered was usually clearly inferior to that provided at more exclusive schools.

Private Schooling

Private secondary schools such as those in New England, and even many public schools, accepted only male students. The Republicans, like most of their contemporaries, clung to a paternal vision of society, in which virtuous white men presided benevolently over a world in which all other groups—including women—were dependents. Yet the early nineteenth century did see some important advances in female education.

In the eighteenth century, women had received very little education of any kind, and the female illiteracy rate at the time of the Revolution was very high—at least 50 percent. At the same time, however, Americans had begun to place a new value on the contribution of the "republican mother" to the training of the new generation. That raised an important question: If mothers remained ignorant, how could they raise their children to be enlightened? Beginning as early as the 1770s and accelerating thereafter, such concerns led to the creation of a network of female academies throughout the nation (usually for the daughters of affluent families). In 1789, Massachusetts required that its public schools serve females as well as males. Other states, although not all, soon followed.

New Educational Opportunities for Women

MORAVIAN BOYS' SCHOOL, C. 1800 This drawing illustrates the interior of a boys' school in North Carolina, run by Moravian Germans. The Moravians were a German Protestant sect many of whose members emigrated to America in the 1750s. One large group founded Bethlehem, Pennsylvania, and another established settlements in western North Carolina. Their belief in social improvement contributed to their interest in education and also to the creation of several short-lived Utopian communities. *(Courtesy of Moravian Archives, Winston-Salem, North Carolina)*

But there were strict limits to this new belief in education for women. Most men, at least, assumed that female education should serve only to make women better wives and mothers. Women therefore had no need for advanced or professional training; there was no reason for colleges and universities to make space for female students. Some women, however, aspired to more. In 1784, Judith Sargent Murray published an essay defending women's rights to education, a defense set in terms very different from those used by most men. Men and women were equal in intellect and potential, Murray argued. Women, therefore, should have precisely the same educational opportunities as men. What was more, they should have opportunities to earn their own living, to establish a role for themselves in society apart from their husbands and families. Murray's ideas became an inspiration to later generations of women, but during most of her own lifetime (1751–1820) they attracted relatively little support.

Reformers who believed in the power of education *Indian Education* to reform and redeem ignorant and "backward" people spurred a growing interest in Indian education. Because Jefferson and his followers liked to think of Native Americans as "noble savages" (uncivilized, but unlike their view of African Americans, not necessarily innately inferior), they hoped that schooling the Indians in white culture would tame and "uplift" the tribes. Although white governments did little to promote Indian education, missionaries and mission schools proliferated among the tribes.

Almost no white people in the early nineteenth century believed that there was a need to educate African Americans, almost all of whom were still slaves. In a few northern states, some free black children attended segregated schools. In the South, slaveowners generally tried to prevent their black workers from learning to read or write, fearful that knowledge would make them unhappy with their condition. Some African Americans managed to acquire some education despite these obstacles, by teaching themselves and their own children. But the numbers of literate slaves remained very small.

Higher education was even less widely available than education at lower levels, despite republican hopes for a *Higher Education* wide dispersion of advanced knowledge. (Jefferson himself founded the University of Virginia to promote that ideal.) The number of colleges and universities in America grew from nine at the start of the Revolution to twenty-two by 1800 and continued to increase thereafter. None of the new schools, however, was truly public. Even those established by state legislatures (in Georgia, North Carolina, Vermont, Ohio, and South Carolina, for example) relied on private contributions and on tuition fees. Scarcely more than one white man in a thousand (and no women, blacks, or Indians at all) had access to any college

education, and those few who did attend universities were almost without exception members of prosperous, propertied families.

The education that the colleges provided was, moreover, exceedingly limited—narrow training in the classics and a few other areas and intensive work in theology. Indeed, the clergy was the only profession for which college training was generally a prerequisite. A few institutions attempted to provide their students advanced training in other fields. The College of William and Mary in Virginia, the University of Pennsylvania, and Columbia College in New York all created law schools before 1800, but most lawyers continued to train for their profession simply by apprenticing themselves to practicing attorneys.

Medicine and Science

The University of Pennsylvania created the first American medical school in the eighteenth century. In the early nineteenth century, however, most doctors studied medicine by working with an established practitioner. Some American physicians believed in applying new scientific methods to medicine and struggled against age-old prejudices and superstitions. Efforts to teach anatomy, for example, encountered strong public hostility because of the dissection of cadavers that the study required. Municipal authorities had virtually no understanding of medical science and almost no idea of what to do in the face of the severe epidemics that so often swept their populations; only slowly did they respond to the warnings of Benjamin Rush, a pioneering Philadelphia physician, and others that lack of adequate sanitation programs was to blame for disease.

Individual patients often had more to fear from their doctors than from their illnesses. Even the leading advocates of scientific medicine often embraced useless and dangerous treatments. Benjamin Rush, for example, was an advocate of the new and supposedly scientific techniques of bleeding and purging, and many of his patients died. George Washington's death in 1799 was probably less a result of the minor throat infection that had afflicted him than of his physicians' efforts to cure him by bleeding and purging.

The medical profession also used its newfound commitment to the "scientific" method to justify expanding its *Decline of Midwifery* own control to kinds of care that had traditionally been outside its domain. Most childbirths, for example, had been attended by female midwives. In the early nineteenth century, physicians began to handle deliveries themselves and to demand restrictions on the role of midwives. Among the results of that change was a narrowing of opportunities for women (midwifery was an important female occupation) and a restriction of access

THE PENNSYLVANIA HOSPITAL As the ideas of the Enlightenment spread through American culture in the eighteenth and nineteenth centuries, encouraging the belief that every individual was a divine being and could be redeemed from even the most miserable condition, hospitals and asylums—such as this institution in Pennsylvania—began to emerge to provide settings for the redemption of the poor, the ill, and the deviant. *(Library Company of Philadelphia)*

to childbirth care for poor mothers (who could have afforded midwives, but who could not pay the higher physicians' fees).

Education and professional training in the early republic—in medicine and in many other fields—thus fell far short of the Jeffersonian vision. Indeed, efforts to promote education and increase professionalism often had the effect of strengthening existing elites rather than eroding them. Nevertheless, the ideal of equal educational opportunity survived, and in later decades it would become a vital force behind universal public education.

Cultural Aspirations in the New Nation

Many Americans in the Jeffersonian era may have repudi-

Establishment of a National Culture

ated the Federalist belief in political and economic centralization, but most embraced another form of nationalism with great fervor. Having won political independence from Europe, they aspired now to a form of cultural independence. In the process, they dreamed of an American literary and artistic life that would rival the greatest achievements of Europe. As a popular "Poem on the Rising Glory of America" had predicted as early as 1772, Americans believed that their "happy land" was destined to become the "seat of empire" and the "final stage" of civilization, with "glorious works of high invention and of wond'rous art." The United States, another eighteenth-century writer had proclaimed, would serve as "the last and greatest theatre for the improvement of mankind."

Such nationalism found expression, among other places, in early American schoolbooks. The Massachusetts geographer Jedidiah Morse, author of *Geography Made*

Easy (1784), said the country must have its own textbooks to prevent the aristocratic ideas of England from infecting the people. The Connecticut schoolmaster and lawyer Noah Webster argued similarly that the American students should be educated as patriots, their minds filled with nationalistic, American thoughts. "As soon as he opens his lips," Webster wrote, "he should rehearse the history of his own country; he should lisp the praise of liberty, and of those illustrious heroes and statesmen who have wrought a revolution in her favor."

Further to encourage a distinctive American culture and help unify the new nation, Webster insisted on a simpli-

Noah Webster

fied and Americanized system of spelling—"honor" instead of "honour," for example. His *American Spelling Book,* first published in 1783 and commonly known as the "blue-backed speller," eventually sold over 100 million copies, to become the best-selling book (except for the Bible) in the entire history of American publishing. Webster also wrote grammars and other schoolbooks. His school dictionary, issued in 1806, was republished in many editions and was eventually enlarged to become (in 1828) *An American Dictionary of the English Language.* His speller and his dictionary established a national standard of words and usages. Although Webster's Federalist political views fell into disfavor in the early nineteenth century, his cultural nationalism remained popular and influential.

Those Americans who aspired to create a more elevated national literary life faced a number of obstacles. There was, to be sure, a large potential audience for a national literature—a substantial reading public, created in part by the wide circulation of newspapers and political pamphlets during the Revolution. But there were few opportunities for would-be American authors to get their work before the public. Printers preferred to publish popular works by English writers (for which they had to pay no royalties); magazine publishers filled their pages largely with items clipped from British periodicals. Only those American writers willing to pay the cost and bear the risk of publishing their own works could compete for public attention.

Even so, a growing number of American authors struggled to create a strong native literature so that, as the poet Joel Barlow wrote, "true ideas of glory may be implanted in the minds of men here, to take the place of the false and destructive ones that have degraded the species in other countries." Barlow himself, one of a group of Connecticut writers known as the "Hartford Wits," published an epic poem, *The Columbiad,* in 1807, in an effort to convey the special character of American civilization. The acclaim it received helped to encourage other native writers.

Among the most ambitious was the Philadelphian Charles Brockden Brown. Like many Americans, he was attracted to the relatively new literary form of the novel, which had become popular in England in the late eighteenth century and had been successfully imported to America. But Brown sought to do more than simply imitate the English forms; he tried to use his novels to give voice to distinctively American themes, to convey the "soaring passions and intellectual energy" of the new nation. His obsession with originality led him to produce a body of work characterized by a fascination with horror and deviant behavior. Perhaps as a result, his novels failed to develop a large popular following.

Much more successful was Washington Irving, a

Washington Irving | resident of New York State who won wide acclaim for his satirical histories of early American life and his powerful fables of society in the New World. His popular folk tales, recounting the adventures of such American rustics as Ichabod Crane and Rip Van Winkle, made him the widely acknowledged leader of American literary life in the early nineteenth century and one of the few writers of that era whose works would continue to be read by later generations.

Perhaps the most influential works by American authors in the early republic were not poems, novels, or stories, but works of history that glorified the nation's past. Mercy Otis Warren, who had been an influential playwright and agitator during the 1770s, continued her literary efforts with a three-volume *History of the Revolution,* published in 1805 and emphasizing the heroism of the American struggle. Mason Weems, an Anglican clergyman, published a eulogistic *Life of Washington* in 1806, which became one of the best-selling books of the era. Weems had little interest in historical accuracy. He portrayed the aristocratic former president as a homespun man possessing simple republican virtues. (He also invented, among other things, the famous story of the young Washington

cutting down a cherry tree.) History, like literature, was serving as a vehicle for instilling a sense of nationalism in the American people.

Religious Skepticism

The American Revolution weakened traditional forms of religious practice by detaching churches from government and by elevating ideas of individual liberty and reason that challenged many ecclesiastical traditions. By the 1790s, only a small proportion of white Americans (perhaps as few as 10 percent) were members of formal churches, and ministers were complaining often about the "decay of vital piety." Religious traditionalists were particularly alarmed about the emergence of new, "rational" theologies that reflected modern, scientific attitudes and de-emphasized the role of God in the world.

Some Americans, including Jefferson and Franklin, embraced "deism," which had originated among Enlighten- | *Deism* ment philosophers in France. Deists accepted the existence of God, but considered Him a remote being who, after having created the universe, had withdrawn from direct involvement with the human race and its sins. Books and articles attacking religious "superstitions" attracted wide readerships and provoked much discussion, among them Thomas Paine's *The Age of Reason,* published in parts between 1794 and 1796. Paine once declared that Christianity was the "strangest religion ever set up," for "it committed a murder upon Jesus in order to redeem mankind from the sin of eating an apple."

Religious skepticism also produced the philosophies of "universalism" and "unitarianism," which emerged at first as dissenting views within the New England Congregational Church. Disciples of these new ideas rejected the Calvinist belief in predestination, arguing that salvation was available to all. They rejected, too, the idea of the Trinity. Jesus was only a great religious teacher, they claimed, not the Son of God. So wide was the gulf between these dissenters and the Congregationalist establishment that it finally became a permanent schism. James Murray (who later married Judith Sargent Murray) founded the Universalist Church as a separate denomination in Gloucester, Massachusetts, in 1779; the Unitarian Church was established in Boston three years later.

Some Americans believed that the spread of rationalism marked the end of traditional, evangelistic religion in the new nation. But quite the contrary was true. In fact, most Americans continued to hold strong religious beliefs (even if the widespread popular fervor of the Great Awakening of the 1730s had largely faded). What had declined was their commitment to organized churches and denominations, which many considered too formal and traditional for their own zealous religious faith. Deism, Universalism, Unitarianism, and other "rational" religions seemed more powerful than they actually were because for a time traditional evangelicals were confused and disorganized. But beginning in 1801, traditional religion staged a dramatic comeback in the form of a wave of revivalism known as the Second Great Awakening.

The Second Great Awakening

The origins of the Second Awakening lay in the efforts of conservative theologians of the 1790s to fight the spread of religious rationalism, and in the efforts of church establishments to revitalize their organizations.

Leaders of several different denominations participated in the evangelizing efforts that drove the revival. Presbyterians tried to arouse the faithful on the western fringe of white settlement, and conservatives in the church became increasingly militant in response to so-called New Light dissenters (people who had altered their religious views to make them more compatible with the world of scientific rationalism). Methodism, which John Wesley had founded in England, spread to America in the 1770s and became a formal denomination in 1784 under the leadership of Francis Asbury. Authoritarian and hierarchical in structure, the Methodist Church sent itinerant preachers throughout the nation to win recruits; it soon became the fastest-growing denomination in America. Almost as successful were the Baptists, who were themselves relatively new to America; they found an especially fervent following in the South.

By 1800, the revivalist energies of all these denominations were combining to create the greatest surge *Cane Ridge* of evangelical fervor since the first Great Awakening sixty years before. Beginning among Presbyterians in several eastern colleges (most notably at Yale, under the leadership of President Timothy Dwight), the new awakening soon spread rapidly throughout the country, reaching its greatest heights in the western regions. In only a few years, a large proportion of the American people were mobilized by the movement, and membership in those churches embracing the revival—most prominently the Methodists, the Baptists, and the Presbyterians—was mushrooming. At Cane Ridge, Kentucky, in the summer of 1801, a group of evangelical ministers presided over the nation's first "camp meeting"—an extraordinary revival that lasted several days and impressed all who saw it with its size (some estimated that 25,000 people attended) and its fervor. Such events became common in subsequent years, as the Methodists in particular came to rely on them as a way to "harvest" new members. The Methodist circuit-riding preacher Peter Cartwright won national fame as he traveled from region to region exhorting his listeners to embrace the church. Even Cartwright, however, was often unprepared for the results of his efforts—a religious frenzy that at times produced convulsions, fits, rolling in the dirt, and the twitching "holy jerks."

The message of the Second Great Awakening was not entirely consistent, but its basic thrust was clear. Individuals must readmit God and Christ into their daily lives, must embrace a fervent, active piety, and must reject the skeptical rationalism that threatened traditional beliefs. Even so, the wave of revivalism did not serve to restore the religious ideas of the past. Few of the revivalist denominations any longer accepted the idea of predestination; and the belief that a person could affect his or her own destiny, rather than encouraging irreligion as many had feared, added intensity to the individual's search for salvation. The Awakening, in short, combined a more active piety with a belief in God as an active force in the world whose grace could be attained through faith and good works.

The Second Awakening did not revive the strength of the old religious institutions any more than it revived old religious ideas. Instead, it accelerated the growth of different sects and denominations and helped create a broad popular acceptance of the idea that men and women could belong to different Protestant churches and still be committed to essentially the same Christian faith. Finally, the new evangelicalism—by spreading religious fervor into virtually every area of the nation, including remote regions where no formal church had ever existed—provided a vehicle for establishing a sense of order and social stability in communities still searching for an identity.

Message of the Great Awakening

One of the most striking features of the Second Great Awakening was the preponderance of women within it. Young women, in particular, were drawn to the revivalism, and female converts far outnumbered males. In some areas, church membership became overwhelmingly female as a result. One reason for this was that women were more numerous in certain regions than men. Adventurous young men often struck out on their own and moved west; women, for the most part, had no such options. Their marriage prospects thus diminished and their futures plagued with uncertainty, some women discovered in religion a foundation on which to build their lives. But even where there was no shortage of men, women flocked to the revivals in enormous numbers, which suggests that they were responding to their changing economic roles as well. The movement of industrial work out of the home (where women had often contributed to the family economy through spinning and weaving) and into the factory—a process making rapid strides in the early nineteenth century (see p. 277)—robbed older women, in particular, of one of their most important social roles. Younger, unmarried women with more mobility could follow the work out of the home and into the factory with less difficulty, but that

METHODIST CAMP MEETING, 1837 Camp (or revival) meetings were popular among some evangelical Christians in America as early as 1800. By the 1820s, there were approximately 1,000 meetings a year, most of them in the South and the West. After one such meeting in 1806, a participant wrote: "Will I ever see anything more like the day of Judgement on this side of eternity—to see the people running, yes, running from every direction to the stand, weeping, shouting, and shouting for joy. . . . O! Glorious day they went home singing shouting." This lithograph, dated 1837, suggests the degree to which women predominated at many revivals. *(The Granger Collection)*

movement, too, created personal and social strains. Religious enthusiasm helped compensate for the losses and adjustments these transitions produced; it also provided access to a new range of activities associated with the churches—charitable societies ministering to orphans and the poor, missionary organizations, and others—in which women came to play important roles.

Although revivalism was most widespread within white society, it penetrated other cultures as well. In some areas of the country, revivals were open to people of all races, and many blacks not only attended but eagerly embraced the new religious fervor. Out of these revivals, in fact, emerged a substantial group of black preachers, who became important figures within the slave community. Some of them translated the apparently egalitarian religious message of the Second Awakening—that salvation was available to all—into a similarly egalitarian message for blacks in the present world. For example, out of black revival meetings in Virginia arose an elaborate plan in 1800 (devised by Gabriel Prosser, the brother of a black preacher) for a slave rebellion and attack on Richmond. The plan was discovered and the rebellion forestalled by whites, but revivalism continued to stir racial unrest in the South.

African Americans and the Revivals

The spirit of revivalism was particularly strong in these years among Native Americans, although very different in its origins and expression from revivalism in white or black society. It drew heavily from earlier tribal experiences. In the 1760s, the Delaware prophet Neolin had sparked a widespread revival in the Old Northwest with a message combining Christian and Indian imagery and bringing to Native American religion a vision of a personal God, intimately involved in the affairs of man. Neolin had also called for Indians to rise up in defense of their lands and had denounced the growth of trade and other relationships with white civilization. His vehement statements had helped stimulate the Indian military efforts of 1763 and beyond.

The dislocations and military defeats Indians suffered in the aftermath of the American Revolution created a sense of crisis among many of the eastern tribes in particular; as a result, the 1790s and early 1800s became another era of Indian religious fervor and prophecy. Presbyterian and Baptist missionaries were active among the southern tribes and sparked a great wave of conversions. But the most important revivalism came from the efforts of another great prophet: Handsome Lake, a Seneca whose seemingly miraculous

Indians and the Second Great Awakening

"rebirth" after years of alcoholism helped give him a special stature within his tribe. Handsome Lake, like Neolin before him, called for a revival of traditional Indian ways. That meant repudiating the individualism of white society, which Handsome Lake argued had penetrated tribal life with alarming results, and restoring the communal quality of the Indian world. (He claimed to have met Jesus, who instructed him to "tell your people they will become lost when they follow the ways of the white man.") Handsome Lake's message spread through the scattered Iroquois communities that had survived the military and political setbacks of previous decades and inspired many Indians to give up whiskey, gambling, and other destructive customs derived from white society.

But the revival did not, in fact, lead to a true restoration of traditional Iroquois culture. Instead, Handsome Lake encouraged Christian missionaries to become active within the tribes, and he urged Iroquois men to abandon their roles as hunters (partly because so much of their hunting land had been seized by whites) and become sedentary farmers instead. Iroquois women, who had traditionally done the farming, were to move into more domestic roles. When some women resisted the change, Handsome Lake denounced them as witches.

The Second Great Awakening also had important ef-
Freethinkers fects on those Americans who did not accept its teachings. The rational "freethinkers," whose skeptical philosophies had done so much to produce the revivals, were in many ways victims of the new religious fervor. They did not disappear after 1800, but their influence rapidly declined, and for many years they remained a small and defensive minority within American Christianity. Instead, the dominant religious characteristic of the new nation became a fervent evangelicalism, which would survive into the mid-nineteenth century and beyond.

STIRRINGS OF INDUSTRIALISM

Despite the hopes of Jefferson and his followers that the United States would remain a simple agrarian republic, the nation took its first, tentative steps in these years toward its transformation into exactly the sort of urban, industrial society the early Republicans had warned against. Americans of the Jeffersonian era were welcoming a series of technological advances that would ultimately help ensure that the United States too would be transformed.

Technology in America

Americans imported some of these technological advances from England. (See "America in the World," pp. 190–191.) The British government attempted to protect the nation's manufacturing preeminence by preventing the export of textile machinery or the emigration of skilled mechanics. Despite such efforts, immigrants arrived in the United

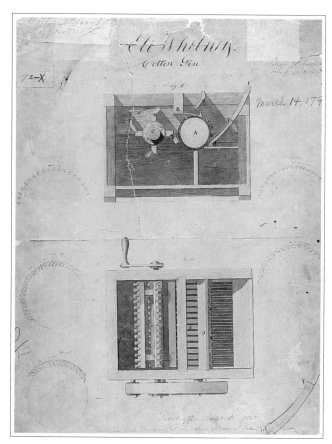

THE COTTON GIN Eli Whitney's cotton gin revolutionized the cotton economy of the South by making the processing of short-staple cotton simple and economical. These 1794 drawings are part of Whitney's application for a federal patent on his device. (*National Archives*)

States with advanced knowledge of English technology, eager to introduce the new machines to America. Samuel Slater, for example, used the knowledge he had acquired before leaving England to build a spinning mill for the Quaker merchant Moses Brown in Pawtucket, Rhode Island, in 1790. It was the first modern factory in America.

America in the early nineteenth century also produced several important inventors of its own. Among them was Oliver Evans, of Delaware, who devised a number of ingenious new machines: an automated flour mill, a card-making machine, and others. He made several important improvements in the steam engine, and in 1795 he published America's first textbook of mechanical engineering: *The Young Mill-Wright's and Miller's Guide.* His own flour mill, which began operations in 1787, required only two men to operate: one of them emptying a bag of wheat into the machinery, another putting the lid on the barrels of flour and rolling them away.

Even more influential for the future of the nation were the inventions of the Massachusetts-born, Yale-educated Eli Whitney, who revolutionized both cotton production and weapons manufacturing. The growth of the textile industry in England had created an enormous demand for cotton, a demand that planters in the American South were finding impossible to meet. Their greatest obstacle was separating the seeds from cotton fiber—a difficult and time-consuming process that was essential before cotton could be sold. Long-staple, or Sea Island, cotton, with its smooth black seeds and long fibers, was easy to clean, but it grew successfully only along the Atlantic coast or on the offshore islands of Georgia and South Carolina. There was not nearly enough of it to satisfy the demand. Short-staple cotton, by contrast, could grow inland through vast areas of the South. But its sticky green seeds were extremely difficult to remove. A skilled worker could clean no more than a few pounds a day by hand. Then, in 1793, Whitney, who was working at the time as a tutor on the Georgia plantation of General Nathanael Greene's widow, invented a machine

Eli Whitney's Cotton Gin that performed the arduous task quickly and efficiently. It was dubbed the cotton gin ("gin" was an abbreviation for "engine"), and it transformed the life of the South.

Mechanically, the gin was very simple. A toothed roller caught the fibers of the cotton boll and pulled them between the wires of a grating. The grating caught the seeds while a revolving brush removed the lint from the roller's teeth. With the device, a single operator could clean as much cotton in a few hours as a group of workers had once needed a whole day to do. The results were pro-

found. Soon cotton growing spread into the upland South, and within a decade the total crop increased eightfold. African-American slavery, which with the decline of tobacco production some had considered a dwindling institution, regained its importance, expanded, and became more firmly fixed upon the South.

The cotton gin not only changed the economy of the South, it also helped transform the North. The large supply of domestically produced fiber *The Cotton Gin's Impact on the North* was a strong incentive to entrepreneurs in New England and elsewhere to develop an American textile industry. Few northern states could hope to thrive on the basis of agriculture alone; by learning to turn cotton into yarn and thread, they could become industrially prosperous instead. The manufacturing preeminence of the North, which emerged with the development of the textile industry in the 1820s and 1830s, helped drive a wedge between the nation's two most populous regions—one becoming increasingly industrial, the other more firmly wedded to agriculture—and ultimately contributed to the coming of the Civil War. It also helped ensure the eventual Union victory.

Whitney also made a major contribution to the development of modern warfare and in the process made a

PAWTUCKET BRIDGE AND FALLS One reason for the growth of the textile industry in New England in the early nineteenth century was that there were many sources of water power in the region to run the machinery in the factories. That was certainly the case with Slater's Mill, one of the first American textile factories, which was located in Pawtucket, Rhode Island, alongside a powerful waterfall. This view was painted by an anonymous artist in the 1810s. *(Rhode Island Historical Society)*

While Americans were engaged in a revolution to win their independence, they were also taking the first steps toward an at least equally important revolution—one that was already in progress in England and Europe. It was the emergence of modern industrialism. Historians differ over precisely when the industrial revolution began, but it is clear that by the end of the eighteenth century it was well underway in many parts of the world. By the end of the nineteenth century, the global process of industrialization had transformed the societies of Britain, most of continental Europe, Japan, and the United States. Its social and economic consequences were complex and profound, and continue today to shape the nature of global society.

For Americans, the industrial revolution was largely a product of rapid changes in Great Britain, the nation with which they had the closest relations. Britain was the first nation to develop significant industrial capacity. The factory system took root in England in the late eighteenth century, revolutionizing the manufacture of cotton thread and cloth. One invention followed another in quick succession. Improvements in weaving drove improvements in spinning, and these changes created a demand for new devices for carding (combing and straightening the fibers for the spinner). Water, wind, and animal power continued to be important in the

textile industry; but more important was the emergence of steam power—which began to proliferate after the appearance of James Watt's advanced steam engine (patented in 1769). Cumbersome and inefficient by modern standards, Watt's engine was nevertheless a major improvement over the earlier "atmospheric" engine of Thomas Newcomen. England's textile industry quickly became the most profitable in the world and it helped encourage comparable advances in other fields of manufacturing as well. Despite the efforts of the British government to prevent the export of English industrial technology, knowledge of the new machines reached other nations quickly, usually through the emigration of people who had learned the technology in British factories.

America benefited the most from English technology, because it received more immigrants from Great Britain than from any other country. But English technology spread quickly to the nations of continental Europe as well. Belgium was the first, developing a significant coal, iron, and armaments industry in the early nineteenth century. France—profiting from the immigration of approximately fifteen thousand British workers with advanced technological skills—had created a substantial industrial capacity in textiles and metals by the end of the 1820s, which in turn contributed to a great boom in railroad construction

later in the century. German industrialization progressed rapidly after 1840, beginning with coal and iron production and then, in the 1850s, moving into large-scale railroad construction. By the late nineteenth century, Germany had created some of the world's largest industrial corporations. In Japan, the sudden intrusion of American and European traders helped cause the so-called Meiji reforms of the 1880s, and 1890s, which launched a period of rapid industrialization there as well.

Industrialization changed not just the world's economies, but also its societies. First in England, and then in Europe, America, and Japan, social systems underwent wrenching changes. Hundreds of thousands of men and women moved from rural areas into cities to work in factories, where they experienced both the benefits and the costs of industrialization. The standard of living of the new working class, when objectively quantified, was usually significantly higher than that of the rural poor. Many of those who moved from farm to factory experienced some improvement in nutrition and other material circumstances, and even in their health. But there were psychological costs to being suddenly uprooted from one way of life and thrust into another, fundamentally different. Those costs could outweigh the material gains. There was little in most workers' prior experience to prepare them for the nature of industrial labor.

contribution to other industrial techniques. During the two years of undeclared war with France (1798 and 1799), Americans were deeply troubled by their lack of sufficient armaments for the expected hostilities. Production of muskets—each carefully handcrafted by a skilled gunsmith—was discouragingly slow. Whitney devised a machine to make each part of a gun according to an exact pattern. Tasks could thus be divided among several workers, and one laborer could assemble a weapon out of parts made by several others. Before long, manufacturers of sewing machines, clocks, and many other complicated products were using the same system.

The new technological advances were relatively isolated phenomena during the early years of the nineteenth

century. Not until at least the 1840s did the nation begin to develop a true manufacturing economy. But the inventions of this period were crucial in making the eventual transformation possible.

Transportation Innovations

One of the prerequisites for industrialization is an efficient system for transporting raw materials to factories and finished goods to markets. The United States had no such system in the early years of the republic. Without such a system, there could be no domestic market extensive enough to justify large-scale production. But work was under way that would ultimately remove the transportation obstacle.

It was disciplined, routinized work with a fixed and rigid schedule, a sharp contrast to the varying, seasonal work pattern of the rural economy. Nor were many factory workers prepared for life in the new industrial towns and expanding cities. Industrial workers experienced, too, a fundamental change in their relationship with their employers. Unlike rural landlords and local aristocrats, factory owners and managers—the new class of industrial capitalists, many of them accumulating unprecedented wealth—were usually remote and inaccessible figures. They dealt with their workers impersonally and the result was a growing schism between the two classes—each lacking access to or understanding of the other. Working men and women throughout the globe began thinking of themselves as a distinct class, with common goals and interests. And their efforts simultaneously to adjust to their new way of life and to resist its most damaging aspects sometimes created great social turbulence. Battles between workers and employers became a characteristic feature of industrial life throughout the world.

Life in industrial nations changed at every level. Populations in industrial countries grew rapidly, and people began to live longer. At the same time, industrial cities began to produce great increases in pollution, crime, and—until modern sanitation systems emerged—infectious disease. Around

THE ENGLISH CANAL AGE Industrialization in England contributed, as it did in America, to the building of new transportation facilities to serve the growing commercial markets of the new economy. Among the most popular such facilities were canals, among them the Regent's Canal in London, pictured here in the 1820s. *(Guildhall Library, Corporation of London/The Bridgeman Art Library)*

the industrial world, middle classes expanded and came, in varying degrees, to dominate the economy (although not always the culture or the politics) of their nations.

Not since the agrarian revolution thousands of years earlier, when many humans had turned from hunting to farming for sustenance, had there been an economic change of a magnitude comparable to the industrial revolution. Centuries of traditions, of social patterns, and of cultural and religious assumptions were challenged and often shattered. The tentative stirrings of industrial activity in the United States in the early nineteenth century, therefore, were part of a vast movement that over the course of the next century was to transform much of the globe.

There were several ways to solve the problem of the small American market. One was to look for customers overseas, and American merchants continued their efforts to do that. Among the first acts of the new Congress when it met in 1789 were two tariff bills giving preference to American ships in American ports, helping to stimulate an expansion of domestic shipping. More important—indeed the principal reason for the growth of American trade in this period—was the outbreak of war in Europe in the 1790s, allowing Yankee merchant vessels to take over most of the carrying trade between Europe and the Western Hemisphere. As early as 1793, the young republic had a merchant marine and a foreign trade larger than those of any country except England. In proportion to its population, the United

States had more ships and international commerce than any country in the world. And the shipping business was growing fast. Between 1789 and *Rapid Growth of American Shipping* 1810, the total tonnage of American vessels engaged in overseas traffic rose from less than 125,000 to nearly 1 million. American ships had carried only 30 percent of the country's exports in 1789; they were carrying over 90 percent in 1810. The figures for imports increased even more dramatically, from 17.5 percent to 90 percent in the same period.

Another solution to the problem of limited markets was to develop new markets at home, by improving transportation between the states and into the interior of the continent. Progress was slower here than in international

A SCENE OF THE ROAD The watercolorist George Tattersall painted this image of a stagecoach negotiating the rough roads and bridges that were beginning to link together the disparate regions of early nineteenth-century America. *(Highways and Byeways of the Forest, A Scene of "The Road." Sketch by George Tattersall. Museum of Fine Arts, Boston)*

shipping, but some improvements were occurring nevertheless. In river transportation, a new era began with the development of the steamboat. A number of inventors began experimenting with steam-powered craft in the late eighteenth century; John Fitch exhibited a forty-five-foot vessel with paddles operated by steam to some of the delegates at the Constitutional Convention in 1787. But the real breakthrough was Oliver Evans's development of a high-pressure engine, lighter and more efficient than James Watt's, which made steam more feasible for powering boats (and, eventually, the locomotive) as well as mill machinery.

The inventor Robert Fulton and the promoter Robert
Robert Fulton's Steamboat | R. Livingston were principally responsible for perfecting the steamboat and bringing it to the attention of the nation. Their *Clermont,* equipped with paddle wheels and an English-built engine, sailed up the Hudson in the summer of 1807, demonstrating the practicability of steam navigation (even though it took the ship thirty hours to go 150 miles). In 1811, a partner of Livingston's, Nicholas J. Roosevelt (a remote ancestor of Theodore Roosevelt), intro-

duced the steamboat to the West by sending the *New Orleans* from Pittsburgh down the Ohio and Mississippi. The next year, this vessel began a profitable career of service between New Orleans and Natchez.

Meanwhile, what was to become known as the "turnpike era" had begun. In 1792, a
corporation constructed a toll | *The Turnpike Era*
road running the sixty miles from Philadelphia to Lancaster, with a hard-packed surface of crushed rock. This venture proved so successful that several other companies laid out similar turnpikes (so named from the kind of tollgate frequently used) from other cities to neighboring towns. Since the turnpikes had to produce profits for the companies that built them, construction costs had to be low enough and the prospective traffic heavy enough to ensure an early and ample return. As a result these roads, radiating from eastern cities, ran comparatively short distances and through thickly settled areas. No private operators were willing to build similar highways over the mountains and into the less populated interior. State governments and the federal government eventually had to finance them.

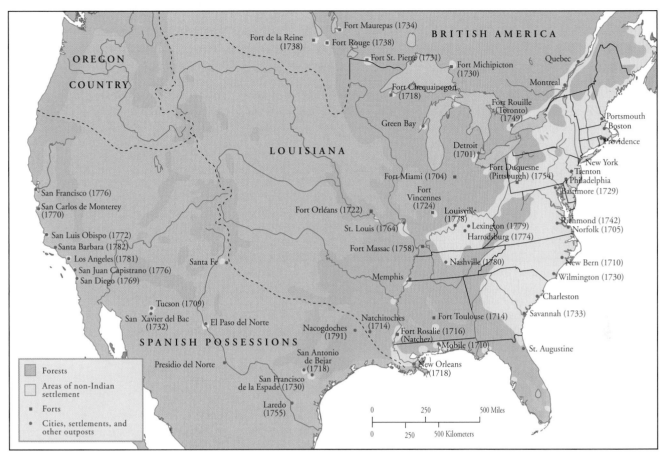

AMERICA IN 1800 This map illustrates how substantially the non-Indian settlement of British North America (much of it by 1800 the United States) had expanded since 1700. On p. 66, a similar map shows a tiny fringe of settlement along the Atlantic seaboard. Note the new areas of settlement here: west of the orginal thirteen colonies—including, in Kentucky, an area that reaches almost to the Mississippi River. Significant settlements are also now visible along the Gulf Coast, especially in the territory around New Orleans. Scattered non-Indian settlements are visible in the Southwest and along the coast of California, as well as in southern Canada (where the settlements were largely forts). ◆ *How does this map help explain the spread of settlement south from Pittsburgh into western Virginia and Kentucky?*

 For an interactive version of this map go to ww.mhhe.com/brinkley11ch7maps

The Rising Cities

Despite all the changes and all the advances, America in the early nineteenth century remained an overwhelmingly rural and agrarian nation. Only 3 percent of the non-Indian population lived in towns of more than 8,000 at the time of the second census in 1800. Ten percent lived west of the Appalachian Mountains, far from what urban centers there were. Much of the country remained a wilderness. Even the nation's largest cities could not begin to compare, either in size or in cultural sophistication, with such European capitals as London and Paris.

Yet here too there were signs of change. The leading American cities might not yet have become world capitals, but they were large and complex enough to rival the important secondary cities of Europe. Philadelphia, with 70,000 residents, and New York, with 60,000, were becoming major centers of commerce and learning. They were developing a distinctively urban culture. So too were the next largest cities of the new nation: Baltimore (26,000 in 1800), Boston (24,000), and Charleston (20,000).

People living in towns and cities lived differently from the vast majority of Americans who continued to work as farmers. Among other things, urban life produced affluence, and affluent people sought amenities that would not have entered the imaginings of all but the wealthiest farmers. They sought increasing elegance and refinement in their homes, their grounds, and their dress. They also looked for diversions—music, theater, dancing, and, for many people, one of the most popular entertainments of all, horse racing. (See "Patterns of Popular Culture," pp. 194–195.)

Urban Life

Much remained to be done before this small and still half-formed nation would become a complex modern society. It was still possible in the early nineteenth century to believe that those changes might not ever occur. But forces were already at work that, in time, would lastingly transform the United States. And Thomas Jefferson, for all

There were few respites from the daily struggle for survival for the first European settlers in North America. Men and women attended church and celebrated major religious holidays, but there was little in most of their lives that twentieth-century Americans would recognize as leisure or popular culture. For relatively affluent colonists, however, one sport emerged very early as an enduringly popular form of entertainment: horse racing.

It was natural, perhaps, that horse racing would become so appealing in the seventeenth and eighteenth centuries, when horses were, for most people, the only source of transportation over land other than walking. Those who could afford to own horses considered them part of the essential equipment of life. But people also formed attachments to their horses and prided themselves on their beauty and speed. Eventually, such attachments led to the creation of a spectator sport in which that beauty and speed were the central attractions.

Informal horse racing began almost as soon as Europeans settled the English colonies. Formal racing followed quickly. The first race track in North America—New Market (named for a popular race course in England)—was established in 1665 near the site of present-day Garden City, on Long Island in New York. It was, from the beginning, a showcase for horses bred in America by Americans, and in 1751 the track's authorities decreed that no imported horses could race there. For a time, New Market (and other horse racing sites) were

dominated by English military officers stationed in the colonies. But tracks quickly developed a much wider appeal, and soon horse racing had spread up and down the Atlantic coast. By the time of the American Revolution, it was popular in almost every colony. It had a particularly avid following in Maryland, Virginia, and South Carolina; and it was moving as well into the newly settled areas of the Southwest. Andrew Jackson was a founder of the first racing track in Nashville, Tennessee, in the early nineteenth century. Kentucky—whose native bluegrass was early recognized as ideal for grazing horses—had eight tracks by 1800.

Like almost everything else in the life of early America, the world of

horse racing was bounded by lines of class and race. For many years, it was considered the exclusive preserve of "gentlemen," so much so that in 1674 a court in Virginia fined James Bullocke, a tailor, for proposing a race, "it being contrary to Law for a Labourer to make a race, being a sport only for Gentlemen." But while white aristocrats retained control of racing, they were not the only people who participated in it. Southern aristocrats often trained young male slaves as jockeys for their horses, just as northern horse owners employed the services of free blacks as riders. In the North and the South, African Americans eventually emerged as some of the most talented and experienced trainers of racing horses. And despite social and legal

OAKLAND HOUSE AND RACE COURSE This 1840 painting by Robert Brammer and August. A. Von Smith portrays an early race course in Louisville, Kentucky, which provided entertainment to affluent white southerners. *(Oakland House and Race Course, Louisville, 1840. By Robert Brammer and August A. Von Smith. Collection of The Speed Art Museum, Louisville, Kentucky. Purchase, Museum Art fund, 56.19)*

his commitment to the agrarian ideal, found himself obliged as president to confront and accommodate them.

JEFFERSON THE PRESIDENT

Privately, Thomas Jefferson may well have considered his victory over John Adams in 1800 to be what he later termed it: a revolution "as real . . . as that of 1776." Publicly, however, he was restrained and conciliatory as

he assumed office, attempting to minimize the differences between the two parties and to calm the passions that the bitter campaign had aroused. "We are all republicans, we are all federalists," he said in his inaugural address. And during his eight years in office, he did much to prove those words correct. There was no complete repudiation of Federalist policies, no true "revolution." Indeed, at times Jefferson seemed to outdo the Federalists at their own work—most notably in overseeing a remarkable expansion of the territory of the United States.

THE ECLIPSE-HENRY MATCH RACE "Match races" between famous horses were a popular feature of early nineteenth-century horse racing. This famous 1823 race on Long Island, New York, pitted prize-winning horses from the North and the South against one another. American Eclipse, the northern entry, won. *(Private collection)*

pressures, free blacks and poor whites often staged their own, informal races, which proved highly popular among lower-class men and women and which helped give racing a slightly disreputable image among more conservative white aristocrats.

Racing also began early to reflect the growing sectional rivalry between the North and the South. In 1824, the Union Race Course on Long Island established an astounding $24,000 purse for a race between two famous thoroughbreds: American Eclipse (from the North) and Sir Henry (from the South). American Eclipse won two of the three heats, but a southern racehorse prevailed in another such celebrated contest in 1836. These inter-sectional races, which drew enormous crowds and created tremendous publicity, continued into the 1850s, until the North-South rivalry began to take a more deadly form.

Horse racing remained popular after the Civil War, but two developments changed its character considerably. One was the successful effort to drive African Americans out of the sport. At least until the 1890s, black jockeys and trainers remained central to racing. At the first Kentucky Derby in 1875, fourteen of the fifteen horses had African-American riders. One black man, Isaac Murphy, became one of the greatest jockeys of all time, the winner of three Kentucky Derbys and a remarkable 44 percent of all races in which he rode. Gradually, however, the same social dynamics that enforced racial segregation on so many other areas of American life in this era penetrated racing as well. By the beginning of the twentieth century, through a combination of harassment, intimidation, and formal discrimination, white jockeys and the organized jockey clubs had driven almost all

black riders, and many black trainers, out of the sport.

The second change was the introduction of formalized betting to the sport. Informal wages had been part of racing almost from the beginning, but in the late nineteenth century race tracks themselves began creating betting systems as a way to lure customers to the races. At the same time that the breeding of racehorses was moving into the hands of enormously wealthy families (many of them the beneficiaries of new industrial fortunes), the audience for racing was becoming increasingly working class and lower middle class. The people who now came to tracks were mostly white men, and some white women, lured to the races not by a love of horses—which were coming now to play a less central role in their everyday lives—but by the usually futile hope of quick and easy riches through gambling.

The Federal City and the "People's President"

Symbolic of the relative unimportance of the federal government during the Jeffersonian era was the character

The District of Columbia | of the newly founded national capital, the city of Washington. John Adams had moved to the new seat of government during the last year of his administration. There were many at that time who expected the raw, uncompleted town to emerge soon as a great and majestic city, a focus for the growing nationalism that the Federalists were pro-

moting. The French architect Pierre L'Enfant had designed the capital on a grand scale, with broad avenues radiating out from the uncompleted Capitol building, set on one of the area's highest hills. Washington was, many Americans believed, to become the Paris of the United States.

In reality, however, throughout Jefferson's presidency—and indeed through most of the nineteenth century—Washington remained little more than a straggling, provincial village. Although the population increased steadily from the 3,200 counted in the 1800 census, it

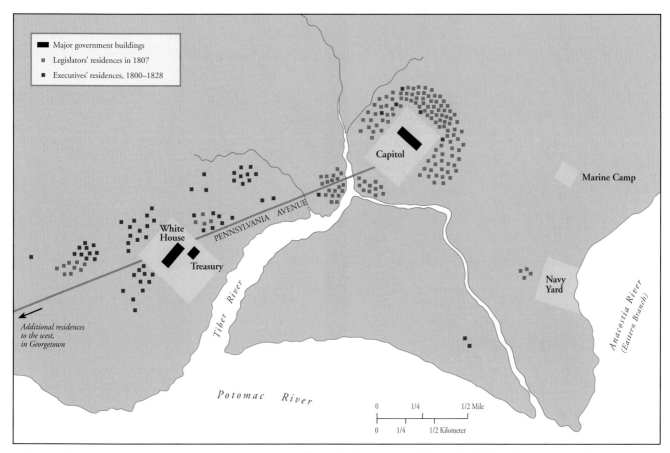

WASHINGTON, D.C. IN THE EARLY NINETEENTH CENTURY The nation's capital moved from New York to Washington in 1800, into a new city designed on a grand scale by the French planner Pierre L'Enfant. But in the early eighteenth century, it remained little more than a village in a marshy tract of land, which helped create hot, humid summers. This map shows the location of the principal government buildings in the early Republic, and also the sites of the homes of members of the executive and legislative branches. Note how the homes of executive officials clustered around the White House and the Treasury, while those of legislators clustered around the Capitol. ◆ *How did the geography of the city help shape the relationship between the executive and legislative branches?*

never rivaled that of New York, Philadelphia, or the other major cities of the nation. The city remained a raw, inhospitable community with few public buildings of any consequence. Members of Congress viewed Washington not as a home but as a place to visit briefly during sessions of the legislature and leave as quickly as possible. Most lived in a cluster of simple boardinghouses in the vicinity of the Capitol. It was not unusual for a member of Congress to resign his seat in the midst of a session to return home if he had an opportunity to accept the more prestigious post of member of his state legislature.

Jefferson set out as president to act in a spirit of democratic simplicity in keeping with the frontier-like character of the unfinished federal city. He was a wealthy and aristocratic planter by background, the owner of more than 100 slaves, and a man of rare cultivation and sophistication; but he conveyed to the public an image of plain, almost crude disdain for pretension. He walked like an ordinary citizen to and from his inauguration at the Capitol, instead of riding in a coach at the head of a procession. In the presidential mansion, which had not yet acquired the

name "White House," he disregarded the courtly etiquette of his predecessors (in part, no doubt, because as a widower he had no first lady to take charge of social affairs). At state dinners, he let his guests scramble pell-mell for places at the table. He did not always bother to dress up, once prompting the fastidious British ambassador to complain of being received by the president in coat and pantaloons that were "indicative of utter slovenliness and indifference to appearances."

Yet Jefferson managed nevertheless to impress most of those who knew him. He was a brilliant conversationalist, a gifted writer, and one of the nation's most intelligent and creative men, with perhaps a wider range of interests and accomplishments than any public figure in American history. In addition to politics and diplomacy, he was an active architect, educator, inventor, scientific farmer, and philosopher-scientist.

Jefferson was, above all, a shrewd and practical politician. On the one hand, he went to great lengths to eliminate the aura of majesty surrounding the presidency that he *Jefferson the Politician*

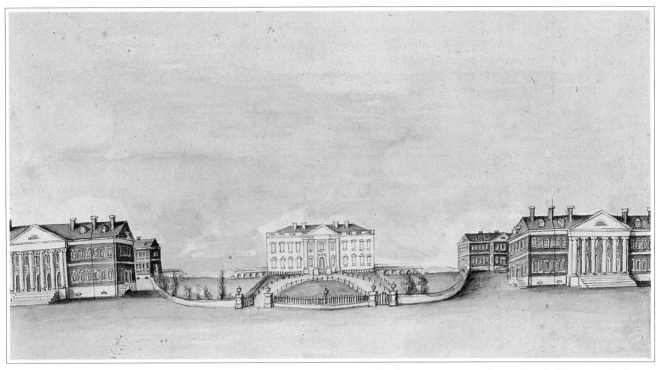

"WASHINGTON CITY, 1821" This 1821 painting by a French artist shows one of Washington's most significant vistas: looking across Lafayette Park at the North Facade of the White House. The painting suggests both the grandeur to which the new capital aspired and the relative crudeness and simplicity of the city as it then existed. *(I.N. Phelps Stokes Collection, Miriam and Ira D. Wallach Division of Art, Prints and Photographs, The New York Public Library, Astor, Lenox and Tilden Foundations)*

THOMAS JEFFERSON This 1805 portrait by the noted American painter Rembrandt Peale shows Jefferson at the beginning of his second term as president. It also conveys (through the simplicity of dress and the slightly unkempt hair) the image of democratic simplicity that Jefferson liked to project. *(New-York Historical Society)*

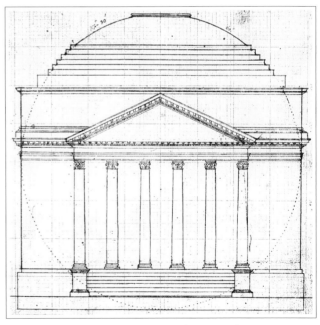

JEFFERSON THE ARCHITECT Among his many other accomplishments, Thomas Jefferson was one of the most gifted architects in early America. This rotunda is the centerpiece of the central campus of the University of Virginia, which Jefferson designed near the end of his life. Earlier, he designed his own home near Charlottesville, Monticello; and his proposal for a president's mansion in Washington placed second in a blind competition. *(University of Virginia Library)*

believed his predecessors had created. At the same time, however, Jefferson worked hard to exert influence as the leader of his party, giving direction to Republicans in Congress by quiet and sometimes even devious means. Although the Republicans had objected strenuously to the efforts of their Federalist predecessors to build a network of influence through patronage, Jefferson, too, used his powers of appointment as an effective political weapon. Like Washington before him, he believed that federal offices should be filled with men loyal to the principles and policies of the administration. By the end of his first term about half the government jobs, and by the end of his second term practically all of them, were in the hands of loyal Republicans.

When Jefferson ran for reelection in 1804, he won overwhelmingly. The Federalist presidential nominee, Charles C. Pinckney, could not even carry most of the party's New England strongholds. Jefferson won 162 electoral votes to Pinckney's 14, and the Republican majorities in both houses of Congress increased.

Dollars and Ships

Under Washington and Adams, the Republicans believed, the government had been needlessly extravagant. Yearly federal expenditures had nearly tripled between 1793 and 1800. Hamilton had, as he had intended, increased the public debt and created an extensive system of internal taxation, including the hated whiskey excise tax.

The Jefferson administration moved deliberately to re-*Limiting the Federal Government* verse the trend. In 1802, it persuaded Congress to abolish all internal taxes, leaving customs duties and the sale of western lands as the only sources of revenue for the government. Meanwhile, Secretary of the Treasury Gallatin drastically reduced government spending, cutting the already small staffs of the executive departments to minuscule levels. Although Jefferson was unable to retire the entire national debt as he had hoped, he did cut it almost in half (from $83 million to $45 million) during his presidency.

Jefferson also scaled down the armed forces. He reduced the tiny army of 4,000 men to 2,500. He cut the navy from twenty-five ships to seven and reduced the number of officers and sailors accordingly. Anything but the smallest of standing armies, he argued, might menace civil liberties and civilian control of government. And a large navy, he feared, might promote overseas commerce, which Jefferson believed should remain secondary to agriculture. Yet Jefferson was not a pacifist. At the same time that he was reducing the size of the army and navy, he was helping to establish the United States Military Academy at West Point, founded in 1802. And when trouble began brewing overseas, he began again to build up the fleet.

Such trouble appeared first in the Mediterranean, off the coast of northern Africa. For years the Barbary states of North Africa—Morocco, Algiers, Tunis, and Tripoli (now part of Libya)—had been demanding protection money from all nations whose ships sailed the Mediterranean. Even Great Britain gave regular contributions to the pirates. During the 1780s and *Challenging the Barbary Pirates* 1790s the United States agreed to treaties providing for annual tribute to the Barbary states, but Jefferson was reluctant to continue this policy of appeasement. "Tribute or war is the usual alternative of these Barbary pirates," he said. "Why not build a navy and decide on war?"

In 1801, the pasha of Tripoli forced Jefferson's hand. Unsatisfied by the American response to his extortionate demands, he ordered the flagpole of the American consulate chopped down—a symbolic declaration of war. Jefferson responded cautiously, building up the American fleet in the region over the next several years. Finally, in 1805, the United States reached an agreement with the pasha that ended American payments of tribute to Tripoli but required the United States to pay a substantial (and humiliating) ransom of $60,000 for the release of American prisoners seized by Barbary pirates.

Conflict with the Courts

Having won control of the executive and legislative branches of government, the Republicans looked with suspicion on the judiciary, which remained largely in the hands of Federalist judges. Soon after Jefferson's first inauguration, his followers in Congress launched an attack on this last preserve of the opposition. Their first step was the repeal of the Judiciary Act of 1801, thus eliminating the judgeships to which Adams had made his "midnight appointments."

The debate over the courts led to one of the most important judicial decisions in the history of the nation. Feder-*Judicial Review* alists had long maintained that the Supreme Court had the authority to nullify acts of Congress (although the Constitution said nothing specifically to support the claim), and the Court itself had actually exercised the power of judicial review in 1796 when it upheld the validity of a law passed by the legislature. But the Court's authority in this area would not be secure, it was clear, until it actually declared a congressional act unconstitutional.

In 1803, in the case of *Marbury* v. *Madison* it did so. William Marbury, one of *Marbury v. Madison* Adams's "midnight appointments," had been named a justice of the peace in the District of Columbia. But his commission, although signed and sealed, had not been delivered to him before Adams left office. Once Jefferson became president, the new secretary of state, James Madison, was responsible for transmitting appointments. He had refused to hand over the commission. Marbury applied to the Supreme Court for an order directing Madison to perform his official duty. In its historic ruling, the Court found that Marbury had a right to his commission but that the Court had no authority to order Madison to deliver it. On the surface,

WEST POINT Creating a professional military was an important task for the leaders of the early republic. Without an army, they realized, it would be difficult for the United States to win respect in the world. The establishment of the United States Military Academy at West Point (whose parade ground is pictured here) was, therefore, an important event in the early history of the republic. *(U.S. Military Academy, West Point)*

therefore, the decision was a victory for the administration. But of much greater importance than the relatively insignificant matter of Marbury's commission was the Court's reasoning in the decision.

The original Judiciary Act of 1789 had given the Court the power to compel executive officials to act in such matters as the delivery of commissions, and it was on that basis that Marbury had filed his suit. But the Court ruled that Congress had exceeded its authority in creating that statute: that the Constitution had defined the powers of the judiciary, and that the legislature had no right to expand them. The relevant section of the 1789 act was therefore void. In seeming to deny its own authority, the Court was in fact radically enlarging it. The justices had repudiated a relatively minor power (the power to force the delivery of a commission) by asserting a vastly greater one (the power to nullify an act of Congress).

The chief justice of the United States at the time of the *John Marshall* ruling (and until 1835) was John Marshall, one of the towering figures in the history of American law. A leading Federalist and prominent Virginia lawyer, he had served John Adams as secretary of state. (It had been Marshall, ironically, who had neglected to deliver Marbury's commission in the

closing hours of the administration.) In 1801, just before leaving office, Adams had appointed him chief justice, and almost immediately Marshall established himself as the dominant figure on the Court, shaping virtually all its most important rulings—including, of course, *Marbury* v. *Madison*. Through a succession of Republican administrations, he battled to give the federal government unity and strength. In so doing, he established the judiciary as a branch of government coequal with the executive and the legislature—a position that the founders of the republic had never clearly indicated it should occupy.

Jefferson recognized the threat that an assertive judiciary could pose to his policies. Even while the Marbury case was still pending, he was preparing for a renewed assault on this last Federalist stronghold. He urged Congress to impeach obstructive judges, and Congress attempted to oblige him. After successfully removing from office a district judge, John Pickering of New Hampshire (on the perhaps specious grounds that he was insane and thus unfit for office), the Republicans targeted a justice of the Supreme Court itself: Justice Samuel Chase, a highly partisan *Impeachment of Samuel Chase* Federalist. Chase had certainly been injudicious; he had, for example, delivered stridently partisan speeches from the bench. But he had committed no crime. Some Republicans argued, however, that impeachment was not merely a criminal proceeding. Congress could properly impeach a judge for political reasons—for obstructing the other branches of the government and disregarding the will of the people.

At Jefferson's urging, the House impeached Chase and sent him to trial before the Senate early in 1805. But Republican leaders were unable to get the necessary two-thirds' vote for conviction in the Senate. Chase's acquittal set an important precedent. It helped establish that impeachment would not become a purely political weapon, that something more than partisan disagreement would have to underlie the process. Marshall remained secure in his position as chief justice. And the judiciary survived as a powerful force within the government—more often than not ruling on behalf of the centralizing, expansionary policies that the Republicans had been trying to reverse.

DOUBLING THE NATIONAL DOMAIN

In the same year that Jefferson became president of the United States, Napoleon Bonaparte made himself ruler of France with the title of first consul. In the year that Jefferson was reelected, Napoleon named himself emperor. The two men had little in common. Yet for a time they were of great help to each other in international politics—until Napoleon's ambitions moved from Europe to America and created conflict and estrangement.

Jefferson and Napoleon

Having failed in a grandiose plan to seize India from the British Empire, Napoleon began turning his imperial ambitions in a new direction: he began to dream of restoring French power in the New World. The territory east of the Mississippi, which France had ceded to Great Britain in 1763, was now mostly part of the United States and lost to France forever. But Napoleon wanted to regain the lands west of the Mississippi, which now belonged to Spain, over which Napoleon now exercised heavy influence. Under the secret Treaty of San Ildefonso of 1800 between the French and the Spanish, France regained title to Louisiana, which included almost the whole of the Mississippi Valley to the west of the river, plus New Orleans near its mouth. The Louisiana Territory would, Napoleon hoped, become the heart of a great French empire in America.

Also part of Napoleon's empire in the New World were the sugar-rich and strategically valuable West Indian islands that still belonged to France—Guadeloupe, Martinique, and above all Santo Domingo. But unrest among the Caribbean slaves posed a threat to Napoleon's hopes for the islands. Africans in Santo Domingo (inspired by the French Revolution as some American slaves had been inspired by the American Revolution) revolted and created a republic of their own, under the remarkable black leader Toussaint L'Ouverture. Taking advantage of a truce in his war with England, Napoleon sent an army to the West Indies. It crushed the insurrection and restored French authority; but the incident was an early sign of the problems Napoleon would have in realizing his ambitions in America.

Jefferson was unaware at first of Napoleon's imperial ambitions in America, and for a time he pursued a foreign policy that reflected his well-known admiration for France. He appointed as American minister to Paris the ardently pro-French Robert R. Livingston. He worked to secure ratification of the Franco-American settlement of 1800 and began observing the terms of the treaty even before it was ratified. The Adams administration had joined with the British in recognizing and supporting the rebel regime of Toussaint L'Ouverture in Santo Domingo; Jefferson assured the French minister in Washington that the American people, especially those of the slaveholding states, did not approve of the black revolutionary, who was setting a bad example for their own slaves. He even implied that the United States might join with France in putting down the rebellion (although nothing ever came of the suggestion).

Toussaint L'Ouverture

Jefferson began to reconsider his position toward France when he heard rumors of the secret transfer of Louisiana. "It completely reverses all the political relations of the U.S.," he wrote to Livingston in April 1802. Always before, America had looked to France as its "natural friend." But there was on the earth "one single spot" whose possessor was "our natural and habitual enemy." That spot was New Orleans, the outlet through which the produce of the fast-growing western regions of the United States traveled to the markets of the world. If France should actually seize New Orleans, Jefferson said, then "we must marry ourselves to the British fleet and nation."

Importance of New Orleans

Jefferson was even more alarmed when, in the fall of 1802, he learned that the Spanish intendant at New Orleans (who still governed the city, since the French had not yet taken formal possession of the region) had announced a disturbing new regulation. American ships sailing the Mississippi River had for many years been accustomed to depositing their cargoes in New Orleans for transfer to oceangoing vessels. The intendant now forbade the practice—even though Spain had guaranteed Americans that right in the Pinckney Treaty of 1795—thus effectively closing the lower Mississippi to American shippers.

Westerners demanded that the federal government do something to reopen the river. The president faced a dilemma. If he yielded to the frontier clamor and tried to change the policy by force, he would run the risk of a major war with France. If he ignored the westerners' demands, he might lose political support. But Jefferson saw another solution. He instructed Robert Livingston, the American ambassador in Paris, to negotiate the purchase of New Orleans. Livingston on his own authority proposed that the French sell the United States the vast western part of Louisiana as well.

In the meantime, Jefferson persuaded Congress to appropriate funds for an expansion of the army and the construction of a river fleet, and he deliberately gave the impression that American forces might soon descend on New Orleans and that the United States might form an alliance with Great Britain if the problems with France were not resolved. Perhaps that was why Napoleon *Napoleon's Offer* suddenly decided to accept Livingston's proposal and offer the United States the entire Louisiana Territory.

Napoleon had good reasons for the decision. His plans for an American empire had already gone seriously awry, partly because a yellow fever epidemic had wiped out much of the French army in the New World and partly be-

cause the expeditionary force Napoleon wished to send to reinforce them and take possession of Louisiana had been frozen into a Dutch harbor through the winter of 1802–1803. By the time the harbor thawed in the spring of 1803, Napoleon was preparing for a renewed war in Europe. He would not, he realized, have the resources now to secure an American empire.

The Louisiana Purchase

Faced with Napoleon's startling proposal, Livingston and James Monroe, whom Jefferson had sent to Paris to assist in the negotiations, had to decide first whether they

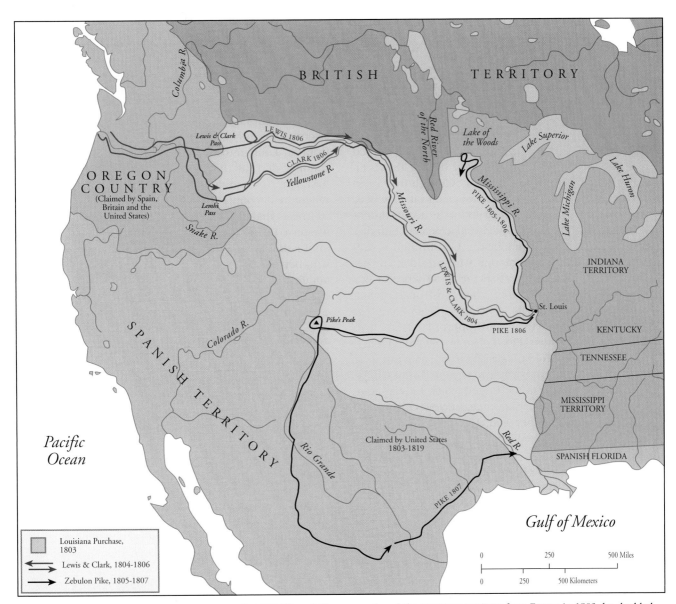

EXPLORING THE LOUISIANA PURCHASE, 1804–1807 When Jefferson purchased the Louisiana territory from France in 1803, he doubled the size of the nation. But few Americans knew what they had bought. The Lewis and Clark Expedition set out in 1804 to investigate the new territories, and this map shows their route, along with that of another inveterate explorer Zebulon Pike. Note the vast distances the two parties covered (including, in both cases, a great deal of land outside the Louisiana Purchase). Note, too, how much of this enormous territory lay outside the orbit of even these ambitious explorations. ◆ *How did the American public react to the addition of these new territories?*

 For an interactive version of this map go to ww.mhhe.com/brinkley11ch7maps

should even consider making a treaty for the purchase of the entire Louisiana Territory, since they had not been authorized by their government to do so. But fearful that Napoleon might withdraw the offer, they decided to proceed without further instructions from home. After some haggling over the price—Napoleon's negotiator Barbe-Marbois asked for and got somewhat more than the minimum amount Napoleon had set—Livingston and Monroe signed the agreement on April 30, 1803.

By the terms of the treaty, the United States was to pay a total of 80 million francs ($15 million) to the French government. The United States was also to grant certain exclusive commercial privileges to France in the port of New Orleans and was to incorporate the residents of Louisiana into the Union with the same rights and privileges as other citizens. The boundaries of the purchase were not clearly defined; the treaty simply specified that Louisiana would occupy the "same extent" as it had when France and Spain had owned it.

In Washington, the president was both pleased and embarrassed when he received the treaty. He was pleased with the terms of the bargain but uncertain whether the United States had authority to accept it, since he had always insisted that the federal government could rightfully exercise only those powers explicitly assigned to it. Nowhere did the Constitution say anything about the acquisition of new territory. But Jefferson's advisers persuaded him that his treaty-making power under the Constitution would justify the purchase of Louisiana. The president finally agreed, trusting, as he said, "that the good sense of our country will correct the evil of loose construction when it shall produce ill effects." The Republican Congress promptly approved the treaty and appropriated money to implement its provisions. Finally, late in 1803, the French assumed formal control of Louisiana from Spain just long enough to turn the territory over to General James Wilkinson, the commissioner of the United States and the commander of a small occupation force. In New Orleans, beneath a bright December sun, United States soldiers lowered the recently raised French tricolor and raised the American flag in its place.

Jefferson's Quandary

The government organized the Louisiana Territory much as it had organized the Northwest Territory, with the assumption that its various territories would eventually become states. The first of these was admitted to the Union as the state of Louisiana in 1812.

Lewis and Clark Explore the West

Meanwhile, several ambitious explorations were revealing the geography of the far-flung new territory to white Americans, few of whom had ever ventured much beyond the Mississippi River. In 1803, even before Napoleon's offer to sell Louisiana, Jefferson helped plan an expedition that was to cross the continent to the Pacific Ocean,

gather geographical facts, and investigate prospects for trade with the Indians. He named as its leader his private secretary and Virginia neighbor, the thirty-two-year-old Meriwether Lewis, a veteran of Indian wars skilled in the ways of the wilderness. Lewis chose as a colleague the twenty-eight-year-old William Clark, who—like George Rogers Clark, his older brother—was an experienced frontiersman and Indian fighter. In the spring of 1804, Lewis and Clark, with a company of four dozen men, started up the Missouri River from St. Louis. With the Shoshone woman Sacajawea as their guide, they eventually crossed the Rocky Mountains, descended the Snake and Columbia Rivers, and in the late autumn of 1805 camped on the Pacific coast. In September 1806, they were back in St. Louis with elaborate records of the geography and the Indian civilizations they had observed along the way, and a lengthy diary recounting their experiences.

While Lewis and Clark were still on their journey, Jefferson dispatched other explorers to other parts of the Louisiana Territory. Lieutenant Zebulon Montgomery Pike, twenty-six years old, led an expedition in the fall of 1805 from St. Louis into the upper Mississippi Valley. In the summer of 1806, he set out again up the valley of the Arkansas River and into what later became Colorado, where he encountered, but failed in his attempt to climb, the peak that now bears his name. His account of his western travels created an enduring (and inaccurate) impression among many Americans in the East that the land between the Missouri River and the Rockies was an uncultivable desert. Pike believed it ought to be left forever to the nomadic Indian tribes.

Zebulon Pike

The Burr Conspiracy

Jefferson's triumphant reelection in 1804 suggested that most of the nation approved the new territorial acquisition. But some New England Federalists raged against it. They realized that the more the West grew and the more new states joined the Union, the less power the Federalists and their region would retain. In Massachusetts, a group of the most extreme Federalists, known as the Essex Junto, concluded that the only recourse for New England was to secede from the Union and form a separate "Northern Confederacy." If a northern confederacy was to have any hope for lasting success as a separate nation, the Federalists believed, it would have to include New York and New Jersey as well as New England. But the leading Federalist in New York, Alexander Hamilton, refused to support the secessionist scheme. "Dismemberment of our empire," he wrote, "will be a clear sacrifice of great positive advantages without any counterbalancing good, administering no relief to our real disease, which is democracy."

Essex Junto

Federalists in New York then turned to Hamilton's greatest political rival: Vice President Aaron Burr, a politician

NEW ORLEANS IN 1803 Because of its location near the mouth of the Mississippi River, New Orleans was the principal port of western North America in the early nineteenth century. Through it, western farmers shipped their produce to markets in the east and Europe. This 1803 painting celebrates the American acquisition of the city from France as part of the Louisiana Purchase. *(Chicago Historical Society)*

without prospects in his own party, because Jefferson had never forgiven him for the 1800 election deadlock. Burr accepted a Federalist proposal that he become their candidate for governor of New York in 1804, and there were rumors (unsupported by any evidence) that he had also agreed to support the Federalist plans for secession. Hamilton accused Burr of plotting treason and made numerous private remarks, widely reported in the press, about Burr's

Hamilton and Burr

"despicable" character. When Burr lost the election, he blamed his defeat on Hamilton's malevolence. "These things must have an end," Burr wrote. He challenged Hamilton to a duel.

Dueling had by then already fallen into some disrepute in America, but many people still considered it a legitimate institution for settling matters of "honor." Hamilton feared that refusing Burr's challenge would brand him a coward. And so, on a July morning in 1804, the two men met at Weehawken, New Jersey. Hamilton was mortally wounded; he died the next day.

The resourceful and charismatic Burr was now a political outcast who had to flee New York to avoid an indict-

ment for murder. He found new outlets for his ambitions in the West. Even before the duel, he had begun corresponding with prominent white settlers in the Southwest, especially with General James Wilkinson, now governor of the Louisiana Territory. Burr and Wilkinson, it seems clear, hoped to lead an expedition that would capture Mexico from the Spanish. "Mexico glitters in all our eyes," Burr wrote; "the word is all we wait for." But there were also rumors that they wanted to separate the Southwest from the United States and create a western empire that Burr would rule. There is little evidence that these rumors were true.

Whether the rumors were true or not, many of Burr's opponents—including, ultimately, Jefferson himself—chose to believe them. When Burr led a group of armed followers down the Ohio River by boat in 1806, disturbing reports flowed into Washington (the most alarming from Wilkinson, who had suddenly turned against Burr and who now informed the president that treason was afoot) that an attack on New Orleans was imminent. Jefferson ordered Burr and his men arrested as traitors. Burr was brought to Richmond for trial. Determined to win a conviction, Jefferson carefully managed the government's case from Washington. But Chief Justice Marshall, presiding over the trial on circuit duty, limited the evidence the government could present and defined the charge in such a way that the jury had little choice but to acquit him.

The Burr "conspiracy" was in part the story of a single man's soaring ambitions and flamboyant personality. But it was also a symbol of the larger perils still facing the new nation. With a central government that remained deliberately weak, with vast tracts of land only nominally controlled by the United States, with ambitious political leaders willing, if necessary, to circumvent normal channels in their search for power, the legitimacy of the federal government, and indeed the existence of the United States as a stable and united nation, remained to be fully established.

EXPANSION AND WAR

The Napoleonic Wars   Two very different conflicts were taking shape in the later years of Thomas Jefferson's presidency that would, together, draw the United States into a difficult and frustrating war. One was the continuing tension in Europe, which in 1803 escalated once again into a full-scale conflict (the Napoleonic Wars). As the fighting escalated, both the British and the French took steps to prevent the United States from trading with (and thus assisting) the other.

The other conflict was in North America itself, a result of the ceaseless westward expansion of white settlement, which was now stretching to the Mississippi River and beyond, colliding again with Native American populations committed to protecting their lands and their trade from intruders. In both the North and the South, the threatened tribes mobilized to resist white encroachments. They began as well to forge connections with British forces in Canada and Spanish forces in Florida. The Indian conflict on land therefore became intertwined with the European conflict on the seas, and ultimately helped cause the War of 1812, an unpopular conflict with ambiguous results.

Conflict on the Seas

The early nineteenth century saw a dramatic expansion of American shipping in the Atlantic. Britain retained significant naval superiority, but the British merchant marine was preoccupied with commerce in Europe and Asia and devoted little energy to trade with America. Thus the United States stepped effectively into the void and developed one of the most important merchant marines in the world, which soon controlled a large proportion of the trade between Europe and the West Indies.

In 1805, at the Battle of Trafalgar, a British fleet virtually destroyed what was left of the French navy. Because France could no longer challenge the British at sea, Napoleon now chose to pressure England through economic rather than naval means. The result was what he called the Continental System, designed to close the European continent to British trade. Napoleon issued a series of decrees (one in Berlin in 1806 and another in Milan in 1807) barring British ships and neutral ships that had called at British ports from landing their cargoes at any European port controlled by France or its allies. The British government replied to Napoleon's decrees by establishing—through a series of "orders in council"—a blockade of the European coast. The blockade required that any goods being shipped to Napoleon's Europe be carried either in British vessels or in neutral vessels stopping at British ports—precisely what Napoleon's policies forbade.

American ships were caught between Napoleon's Berlin and Milan decrees and Britain's orders in council. If *America's Predicament* they sailed directly for the European continent, they risked being captured by the British navy; if they sailed by way of a British port, they risked seizure by the French. Both of the warring powers were violating America's rights as a neutral nation. But most Americans considered the British, with their greater sea power, the worse offender. British ships pounced on Yankee merchantmen all over the ocean; the French could do so only in European ports. Particularly infuriating to Americans, British vessels stopped United States ships on the high seas and seized sailors off the decks, making them victims of "impressment."

Impressment

The British navy—with its floggings, low pay, and terrible shipboard conditions—was known as a "floating hell" to its sailors. Few volunteered. Most had to be "impressed" (forced) into the service. At every opportunity they deserted. By 1807, many of these deserters had joined the American merchant marine or the American navy. To check this loss of vital manpower, the British claimed the right to stop and search American merchant ships (although at first not naval vessels) and reimpress deserters. They did not claim the right to take native-born Americans, but they did claim the right to seize naturalized Americans born on British soil. In practice, the British navy often made no such distinctions, impressing British deserters and native-born Americans alike into service.

In the summer of 1807, the British went to more provocative extremes in an incident involving a vessel of the American navy. Sailing from *Chesapeake-Leopard Incident* Norfolk, with several alleged deserters from the British navy among the crew, the American naval frigate *Chesapeake* encountered the British ship *Leopard*. When the

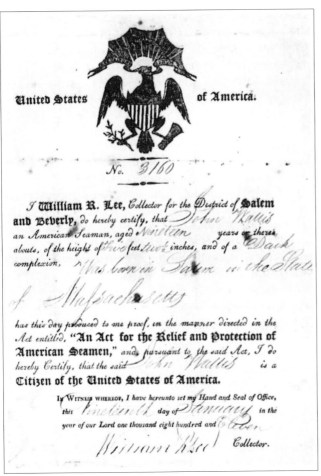

PROTECTION FROM IMPRESSMENT To protect American sailors from British impressment, the federal government issued official certificates of United States citizenship—known as "protection papers." But British naval officers, aware that such documents were often forged, frequently ignored them. *(Essex Institute, Salem, Massachusetts)*

American commander, James Barron, refused to allow the British to search the *Chesapeake,* the *Leopard* opened fire. Barron had no choice but to surrender, and a boarding party from the *Leopard* dragged four men off the American frigate.

When news of the *Chesapeake-Leopard* incident reached the United States, there was great popular clamor for revenge. If Congress had been in session, it might have declared war. But Jefferson and Madison tried to maintain the peace. Jefferson expelled all British warships from American waters, to lessen the likelihood of future incidents. Then he sent instructions to his minister in England, James Monroe, to demand that the British government renounce impressment. The British government disavowed the action of the officer responsible for the *Chesapeake-Leopard* affair and recalled him; it offered compensation for those killed and wounded in the incident; and it promised to return three of the captured sailors (one of the original four

had been hanged). But the British refused to renounce impressment.

"Peaceable Coercion"

In an effort to prevent future incidents that might bring the nation again to the brink of war, Jefferson presented a drastic measure to Congress when it reconvened late in 1807. The Republican legislators promptly enacted it into law. It was known as the Embargo, and it became one of the most controversial political issues of its time. The Embargo prohibited American ships from leaving the United States for any foreign port anywhere in the world. (If it had specified only British and French ports, Jefferson reasoned, it could have been evaded by means of false clearance papers.) Congress also passed a "force act" to give the government power to enforce the Embargo.

The Embargo

The law was widely evaded, but it was effective enough to create a serious depression through most of the nation. Hardest hit were the merchants and shipowners of the Northeast, most of them Federalists. Their once lucrative shipping business was at a virtual standstill, and they were losing money every day. They became convinced that Jefferson had acted unconstitutionally.

The election of 1808 came in the midst of the Embargo-induced depression. James Madison, Jefferson's secretary of state and political ally, won the presidency. But the Federalists ran much more strongly than they had in 1804. The Embargo was clearly a growing political liability, and Jefferson decided to back down. A few days before leaving office, he approved a bill ending his experiment with what he called "peaceable coercion."

To replace the Embargo, Congress passed the Non-Intercourse Act just before Madison took office. The new law reopened trade with all nations but Great Britain and France. A year later, in 1810, Congress allowed the Non-Intercourse Act to expire and replaced it with Macon's Bill No. 2, which reopened free commercial relations with Britain and France, but authorized the president to prohibit commerce with either belligerent if one should continue violating neutral shipping after the other had stopped. Napoleon, in an effort to induce the United States to reimpose the Embargo against Britain, announced that France would no longer interfere with American shipping. Madison announced that an embargo against Great Britain alone would automatically go into effect early in 1811 unless Britain renounced its restrictions on American shipping.

Non-Intercourse Act

In time, the new, limited embargo, although less well enforced than the earlier one had been, hurt the economy of England enough that the government repealed its blockade of Europe. But the repeal came too late to prevent war. In any case, naval policies were only part of the reason for tensions between Britain and the United States.

The "Indian Problem" and the British

Given the ruthlessness with which white settlers in North America had dislodged Indian tribes to make room for expanding settlement, it was hardly surprising that ever since the Revolution many Native Americans had continued to look to England—which had historically attempted to limit western expansion—for protection. The British in Canada, for their part, had relied on the tribes as partners in the lucrative fur trade and as potential military allies.

There had been relative peace in the Northwest for *William Henry Harrison* | over a decade after Jay's Treaty and Anthony Wayne's victory over the tribes at Fallen Timbers in 1794. But the 1807 war crisis following the *Chesapeake-Leopard* incident revived the conflict between Indians and white settlers. Two important (and very different) leaders emerged to oppose one another in the conflict: William Henry Harrison and Tecumseh.

The Virginia-born Harrison, already a veteran Indian fighter at age twenty-six, went to Washington as the congressional delegate from the Northwest Territory in 1799. He was a committed advocate of growth and development in the western lands, and he was largely responsible for the passage in 1800 of the so-called Harrison Land Law, which enabled white settlers to acquire farms from the public domain on much easier terms than before.

In 1801, Jefferson appointed Harrison governor of the Indiana Territory to administer the president's proposed solution to the "Indian problem." *Jefferson's Offer* Jefferson offered the Native Americans a choice: they could convert themselves into settled farmers and assimilate—become a part of white society; or they could migrate to the west of the Mississippi. In either case, they would have to give up their claims to their tribal lands in the Northwest.

Jefferson considered the assimilation policy a benign alternative to continuing conflict between Indians and white settlers, conflict he assumed the tribes were destined to lose. But to the tribes, the new policy seemed far from benign, especially given the bludgeonlike efficiency with which Harrison set out to implement it. He played off one tribe against another and used threats, bribes, trickery, and whatever other tactics he felt would help him conclude treaties. By 1807, the United States had extracted from reluctant tribal leaders treaty rights to eastern Michigan, southern Indiana, and most of Illinois. Meanwhile, in the Southwest, white Americans were taking millions of acres from other tribes in Georgia, Tennessee,

THE TREATY OF GREENVILLE An unknown member of General Anthony Wayne's staff painted this scene of Indians and U.S. officers signing a treaty in Greenville, Ohio, in 1795, by which twelve tribes agreed to surrender the southern half of the territory to the United States in exchange for payment of about 1/8 cent per acre. *(Chicago Historical Society)*

and Mississippi. The Indians wanted desperately to resist, but the separate tribes were helpless by themselves against the power of the United States. They might have accepted their fate passively but for the emergence of two new factors.

One factor was the policy of the British authorities in Canada. After the *Chesapeake* incident and the surge of anti-British feeling throughout the United States, the British colonial authorities began to expect an American invasion of Canada and took desperate measures for their own defense. Among those measures were efforts to renew friendship with the Indians—friendship badly frayed by the Battle of Fallen Timbers, in which the British had refused to provide assistance to the tribes—and efforts to provide them with increased supplies. "Are the Indians to be employed in case of a rupture with the United States?" the lieutenant governor of upper Canada asked Sir James Craig, governor general of the province, in 1807. The governor replied: "If we do not employ them, there cannot exist a moment's doubt that they will be employed against us."

Tecumseh and the Prophet

The second, and more important, factor intensifying the

The Prophet's Message

border conflict was the rise of two remarkable Native American leaders. One was Tenskwatawa, a charismatic religious leader and orator known as the Prophet. He had experienced a mystical awakening in the process of recovering from alcoholism. Having freed himself from what he considered the evil effects of white culture, he began to speak to his people of the superior virtues of Indian civilization and the sinfulness and corruption of the white world. In the process, he inspired a religious revival that spread through numerous tribes and helped unite them. Like Neolin before him, and like his contemporary to the east, Handsome Lake, Tenskwatawa demonstrated the power of religious leaders to mobilize Indians behind political and military objectives. The Prophet's headquarters at the confluence of Tippecanoe Creek and the Wabash River (known as Prophetstown) became a sacred place for people of many tribes and attracted thousands of Indians from throughout the Midwest. Out of their common religious experiences, they began to consider joint political and military efforts as well.

The Prophet's brother Tecumseh—"the Shooting Star," chief of the Shawnees—emerged as the leader of these more secular efforts. Tecumseh understood, as few

Tecumseh's Strategy

other Indian leaders had, that only through united action could the tribes hope to resist the advance of white civilization. Beginning in 1809, after tribes in Indiana had ceded vast lands to the United States, he set out to unite all the Indians of the Mississippi Valley, north and south. Together, he promised, they would halt white expansion, recover the whole Northwest, and make the Ohio River the boundary between the United States and the Indian country. He maintained that Harrison and others, by negotiating treaties with individual tribes, had obtained no real title to land. The land belonged to all the tribes; none of them could rightfully cede any of it without the consent of the others. "The Great Spirit gave this great island to his red children. He placed the whites on the other side of the big water," Tecumseh told Harrison. "They were not contented with their own, but came to take ours from us. They have driven us from the sea to the lakes—we can go no farther."

In 1811, Tecumseh left Prophetstown and traveled down the Mississippi to visit the tribes of the South and persuade

Battle of Tippecanoe

them to join the alliance. During his absence, Governor Harrison saw a chance to destroy the growing influence

TECUMSEH Tecumseh's efforts to unite the tribes of the Mississippi Valley against further white encroachments on their lands led him ultimately into an alliance with the British after the Battle of Tippecanoe in 1811. In the War of 1812, he was commissioned a brigadier general by the British and fought against the United States in the Battle of the Thames. He is shown in this painting (by the daughter of an English officer stationed near Detroit) wearing British military trousers. *(Fort Malden National Historical Park)*

JAMES AND DOLLEY MADISON James Madison may have been the most brilliant of the early leaders of the republic, but he was also one of the most serious and humorless, as this grim portrait suggests. His wife (born Dolley Payne in North Carolina and raised a Quaker in Virginia) was twenty-six when she married the forty-three-year-old Madison in 1794. Her charm and social grace made her one of her husband's greatest political assets. She acted as hostess for Thomas Jefferson, a widower, while her husband was secretary of state. And she presided over a lively social life during her eight years in the White House as first lady. *(New-York Historical Society)*

of the two Native American leaders. He camped near Prophetstown with 1,000 soldiers, and on November 7, 1811, he provoked a fight. Although the white forces suffered losses as heavy as those of the natives, Harrison drove off the Indians and burned the town. The Battle of Tippecanoe (named for the creek near the fighting) disillusioned many of the Prophet's followers, who had believed that his magic would protect them. Tecumseh returned to find the confederacy in disarray. But there were still many warriors eager for combat, and by the spring of 1812 they were active along the frontier, from Michigan to Mississippi, raiding white settlements and terrifying white settlers.

The bloodshed along the western borders was largely a result of the Indians' own initiative, but Britain's agents in Canada had encouraged and helped supply the uprising. To Harrison and most white residents of the regions, there seemed only one way to make the West safe for Americans. That was to drive the British out of Canada and annex that province to the United States—a goal that many westerners had long cherished for other reasons as well.

Florida and War Fever

While white "frontiersmen" in the North demanded the conquest of Canada, those in the South wanted the United States to acquire Spanish Florida, a territory that included the present state of Florida and the southern areas of what are now Alabama, Mississippi, and Louisiana. The territory was a continuing threat to whites in the southern United States. Slaves escaped across the Florida border; Indians in Florida launched frequent raids north into white settlements along the border. But white southerners also coveted Florida because through it ran rivers that could provide residents of the Southwest with access to valuable ports on the Gulf of Mexico.

In 1810, American settlers in West Florida (an area that is part of Mississippi and Louisiana today) seized the Spanish fort at Baton Rouge and asked the federal government to annex the territory to the United States. President Madison happily agreed and then began planning to get the rest of Florida, too. The desire for Florida became yet another motivation for war with Britain. Spain was Britain's ally, and a war with Britain might provide a pretext for taking Spanish territory.

By 1812, war fever was growing on both the northern

War Hawks

and southern borders of the United States. In the congressional elections of 1810, voters from these regions elected a large number of representatives of both parties eager for war with Britain. They became known as the "war hawks." Some of them were ardent nationalists fired by passion for territorial expansion—among them two men, both recently elected to the House of Representatives, who would play a great role in national politics for much of the next four decades: Henry Clay of Kentucky and John C. Calhoun of South Carolina. Others were men impassioned in their defense of Republican values. Together, they formed a powerful coalition in favor of war.

Clay became Speaker of the House in 1811, and he filled committees with those who shared his eagerness for war. He appointed Calhoun to the crucial Committee on Foreign Affairs, and both men began agitating for the conquest of Canada. Madison still hoped for peace. But he shared the concerns of other Republicans about the dangers to American trade, and he was losing control of Congress. On June 18, 1812, he gave in to the pressure and approved a declaration of war against Britain.

THE WAR OF 1812

Preoccupied with their struggle against Napoleon in Europe, the British were not eager for an open conflict with the United States. Even after the Americans declared war, Britain largely ignored them for a time. But in the fall of 1812, Napoleon launched a catastrophic campaign against Russia that left his army in disarray and his power in Europe diminished. By late 1813, with the French Empire on its way to final defeat, Britain was able to turn its military attention to America.

Battles with the Tribes

Americans entered the War of 1812 with great enthusiasm, but events on the battlefield soon cooled their ardor. In the summer of 1812, American forces invaded Canada through Detroit. They soon had to retreat back to Detroit and in August surrendered the fort there. Other invasion efforts also failed. In the meantime, Fort Dearborn (Chicago) fell before an Indian attack.

Things went only slightly better for the United States on the seas. At first, American frigates won some spectac-

Early Defeats

ular victories over British warships, and American privateers destroyed or captured many British merchant ships, occasionally braving the coastal waters of the British Isles themselves and burning vessels within sight of the shore. But by 1813, the British navy—now less preoccupied with Napoleon—was counterattacking effectively, driving the American frigates to cover and imposing a blockade on the United States.

The United States did, however, achieve significant early military successes on the Great Lakes. First, the Americans took command of Lake Ontario, which permitted them to raid and burn York (now Toronto), the capital of Canada. American forces then seized control of Lake Erie, mainly through the work of the youthful Oliver Hazard Perry, who en-

Put-In-Bay

gaged and dispersed a British fleet at Put-In-Bay on September 10, 1813. This made possible, at last, another invasion of Canada by way of Detroit, which Americans could now reach easily by water. William Henry Harrison, the American commander in the West, pushed up the river Thames into upper Canada and on October 5, 1813, won a victory notable for the death of Tecumseh, who was serving as a brigadier general in the British army. The Battle of the Thames weakened and disheartened the Native Americans of the Northwest and greatly diminished their ability to defend their claims to the region.

In the meantime, another white military leader was striking an even harder blow at the tribes of the Southwest. The Creeks, whom Tecumseh had aroused on a visit to the South and whom the Spanish had supplied with weapons, had been attacking white settlers near the Florida border. Andrew Jackson, a wealthy Tennessee planter and a general in the state militia, temporarily abandoned plans for an invasion of Florida and set off in pursuit of them. On March 27, 1814, in the Battle of Horseshoe Bend, Jackson's men took terrible revenge on the Indians—slaughtering women and children along with warriors—and broke the resistance of the Creeks. The tribe agreed to cede most of its lands to the United States and retreated westward, farther into the interior. The battle also won Jackson a commission as major general in the United States Army, and in that capacity he led his men farther south into Florida and, on November 7, 1814, seized the Spanish fort at Pensacola.

Battles with the British

The victories over the tribes were not enough to win the war. After the surrender of Napoleon in 1814, England prepared to invade the United States. A British armada sailed up the Patuxent River from Chesapeake Bay and landed an army that marched a short distance overland to Bladensburg, on the outskirts of Washington, where it dispersed a poorly trained force

The British Invasion

of American militiamen. On August 24, 1814, the British troops entered Washington and put the government to flight. Then they set fire to several public buildings, including the White House, in retaliation for the earlier American burning of the Canadian capital at York. This was the low point of American fortunes in the war.

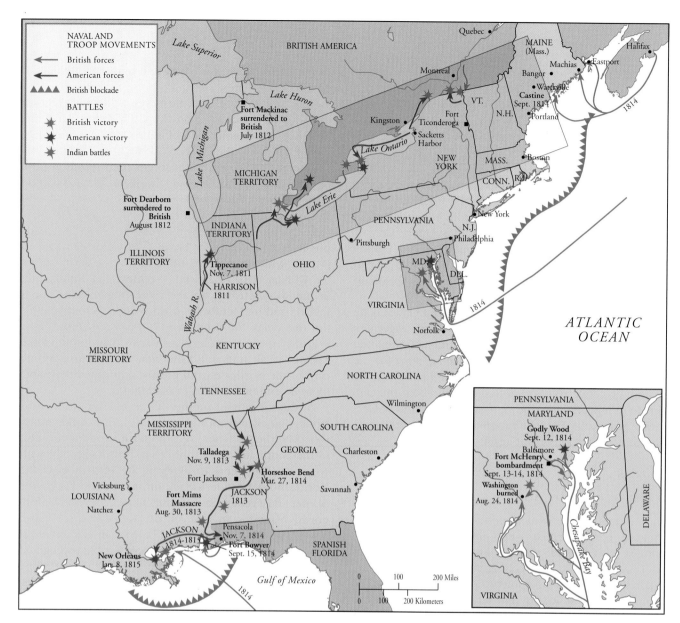

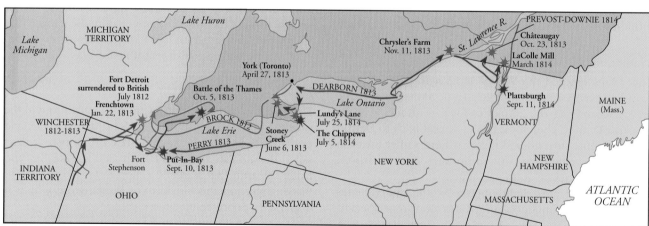

THE WAR OF 1812 These three maps illustrate the military maneuvers of the British and the Americans during the War of 1812. The large map at top shows all the theaters of the war, from New Orleans to southern Canada. The detail at bottom shows the extended land and water battle along the Canadian border and in the Great Lakes. The detail in the bottom right corner of the upper map shows the fighting around Washington and Baltimore. Note how in all these theaters, there are about the same number of British and American victories. ◆ *What brought this inconclusive war finally to an end?*

For an interactive version of this map go to ww.mhhe.com/brinkley11ch7maps

THE BURNING OF WASHINGTON This dramatic engraving somewhat exaggerates the extent of the blazes in Washington when the British occupied the city in August 1814. But the invaders did set fire to the Capitol, the White House, and other public buildings in retaliation for the American burning of the Canadian capital at York. *(Bettmann/Corbis)*

Leaving Washington in partial ruins, the invading army proceeded up the bay toward Baltimore. But Baltimore harbor, guarded by Fort McHenry, was prepared. To block the approaching fleet, the American garrison had sunk several ships to clog the entry to the harbor, thus forcing the British to bombard the fort from a distance. Through the night of September 13, Francis Scott Key, a Washington lawyer who was on board one of the British ships trying to secure the release of an American prisoner, watched the bombardment. The next morning, "by the dawn's early light," he could see the flag on the fort still flying; he recorded his pride in the moment by scribbling a poem— "The Star-Spangled Banner"—on the back of an envelope. The British withdrew from Baltimore, and Key's words were soon set to the tune of an old English drinking song. In 1931, "The Star-Spangled Banner" became the official national anthem.

Meanwhile, American forces repelled another British invasion in northern New York at the Battle of Platts-burgh, on September 11, 1814, which turned back a much larger British naval and land force and secured the northern border of the United States. In the South, a formidable array of battle-hardened British veterans, fresh from the campaign against the French in Spain, landed below New Orleans and prepared to advance north up the Mississippi. Awaiting the British was Andrew Jackson with a motley collection of Tennesseans, Kentuckians, Creoles, blacks, pirates, and regular army troops behind earthen fortifications. On January 8, 1815, the British advanced, but their exposed forces were no match for Jackson's well-protected men. After the Americans had repulsed several waves of attackers, the British finally retreated, leaving behind 700 dead (including their commander, Sir Edward

Battle of New Orleans

THE BOMBARDMENT OF FORT MCHENRY
The British bombardment of Fort McHenry in
Baltimore harbor in September 1814 was of
modest importance to the outcome of the War of
1812. It is remembered as the occasion for Francis
Scott Key to write his poem "The Star-Spangled
Banner," which recorded his sentiments at seeing
an American flag still flying over the fort "by the
dawn's early light." *(I.N. Phelps Stokes Collection of
American Historical Prints, The New York Public
Library)*

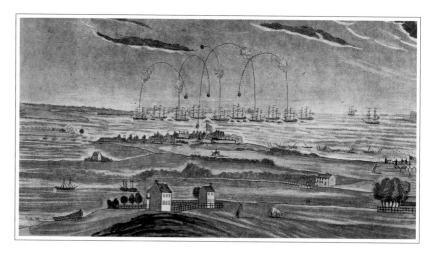

Pakenham), 1,400 wounded, and 500 prisoners. Jackson's
losses were eight killed and thirteen wounded. Only later
did news reach North America that the United States and
Britain had signed a peace treaty several weeks before the
Battle of New Orleans.

The Revolt of New England

With a few notable exceptions, such as the Battles of Put-In-
Bay and New Orleans, the military operations of the United
States between 1812 and 1815 consisted of a series of humiliating failures. As a result, the American government
faced increasing popular opposition as the contest dragged
on. In New England, opposition both to the war and to the
Republican government that was waging it was so extreme
that some Federalists celebrated British victories. In
Congress, in the meantime, the Republicans had continual
trouble with the Federalist opposition, led by a young
congressman from New Hampshire, Daniel Webster, who
missed no opportunity to embarrass the administration.

By now the Federalists were a minority in the country
as a whole, but they were still the majority party in New
England. Some of them began to dream again of creating
a separate nation in that region, which they could dominate and in which they could escape what they saw as the
tyranny of slaveholders and backwoodsmen. Talk of secession revived and reached a climax in the winter of
1814–1815.

On December 15, 1814, delegates from the New
England states met in Hartford,
Connecticut, to discuss their
grievances. Those who favored secession at the Hartford
Convention were outnumbered by a comparatively moderate majority. But while the convention's report only
hinted at secession, it reasserted the right of nullification
and proposed seven amendments to the Constitution
(presumably as the condition of New England's remaining
in the Union)—amendments designed to protect New
England from the growing influence of the South and the
West.

Hartford Convention

Because the war was going badly and the government
was becoming desperate, the New Englanders assumed
that the Republicans would have to agree to their demands. Soon after the convention adjourned, however,
the news of Jackson's smashing victory at New Orleans
reached the cities of the Northeast. A day or two later,
reports arrived from abroad of a negotiated peace. In the
euphoria of this apparent triumph, the Hartford Convention and the Federalist party came to seem futile, irrelevant, even treasonable. The failure of the secession effort
was a virtual death blow to the Federalist Party.

The Peace Settlement

Peace talks between the United States and Britain had begun even before fighting in the War of 1812 began. But serious negotiations did not begin until August 1814, when
American and British diplomats met in Ghent, Belgium.
John Quincy Adams, Henry Clay, and Albert Gallatin led
the American delegation.

Although both sides began with extravagant demands,
the final treaty did little except
end the fighting itself. The
Americans gave up their demand for a British renuncia-
tion of impressment and for the cession of Canada to the
United States. The British abandoned their call for the creation of an Indian buffer state in the Northwest and made
other, minor territorial concessions. The negotiators
referred other disputes to arbitration. Hastily drawn up,
the treaty was signed on Christmas Eve 1814.

Treaty of Ghent

Both sides had reason to accept this skimpy agreement. The British were exhausted and in debt from their
prolonged conflict with Napoleon and eager to settle the
lesser dispute in North America. The Americans realized
that with the defeat of Napoleon in Europe, the British
would no longer have much incentive to interfere with
American commerce. Indeed, by the end of 1815, impressment had all but ceased.

Other settlements followed the Treaty of Ghent and
contributed to a long-term improvement in Anglo-Ameri-

ATTACKING THE FEDERALISTS A Republican cartoonist derided the secession efforts of New England Federalists at the Hartford Convention in this cartoon. It portrays timid men representing Massachusetts, Connecticut, and Rhode Island preparing to leap into the arms of George III. *(Library of Congress)*

can relations. A commercial treaty in 1815 gave Americans the right to trade freely with England and much of the British Empire. The Rush-Bagot agreement of 1817 provided for mutual disarmament on the Great Lakes; eventually (although not until 1872) the Canadian-American boundary became the longest "unguarded frontier" in the world.

Rush-Bagot Agreement

For the other parties to the War of 1812, the Indian tribes east of the Mississippi, the Treaty of Ghent was of no lasting value. It required the United States to restore to the tribes lands seized by white Americans in the fighting, but those provisions were never enforced. Ultimately, the war was another disastrous blow to the capacity of Native Americans to resist white expansion. Tecumseh, their most important leader, was dead. The British, their most important allies, were gone from the Northwest. The alliance that Tecumseh and the Prophet had forged was in disarray. And the end of the war spurred a great new drive by white settlers deeper into the West, into land the Indians were less than ever able to defend.

CONCLUSION

Thomas Jefferson called his election to the presidency the "Revolution of 1800," and his supporters believed that his victory would bring a dramatic change in the character of the nation—a retreat from Hamilton's dreams of a powerful, developing nation with great stature in the world; a return to an ideal of a simple agrarian republic happily isolated from the corruption and intrigue of Europe.

But American society was changing rapidly in the early nineteenth century, making it virtually impossible for the

Jeffersonian dream to prevail. The nation's population was expanding and diversifying. Its cities were growing, and its commercial life was becoming ever more important. In 1803, Jefferson himself made one of the most important contributions to the growth of the United States: the Louisiana Purchase, which dramatically expanded the physical boundaries of the nation—and which began extending white settlement deeper into the continent. In the process, it greatly widened the battles between Europeans and Native Americans.

The growing national pride and commercial ambitions of the United States gradually created another serious conflict with Great Britain: the War of 1812, a war that went badly for the Americans on the whole, but that was settled finally in 1814 on terms at least mildly favorable to the United States. By then, the bitter party rivalries that had characterized the first years of the republic had to some degree subsided, and the nation was poised to enter what became known as the "Era of Good Feelings." It was to be an era in which good feelings did not last for very long.

FOR FURTHER REFERENCE

Joseph J.Ellis, *American Sphinx: The Character of Thomas Jefferson* (1997) is a perceptive study of the man. Henry Adams, *History of the United States During the Administration of Jefferson and Adams,* 9 vols. (1889–1891) is one of the great literary achievements of early American historiography. Frank Bergon, ed., *The Journals of Lewis and Clark* (1989) is a concise abridgment of these fascinating accounts of their explorations. James Ronda, *Lewis and Clark Among the Indians* (1984) examines the exploration from a Native American perspective. Thomas C.Cochran, *Frontiers of Change: Early Industrialization in America* (1981) summarizes economic development in the early republic. Jeanne Boydston, *Home and Work: Housework, Wages, and the Ideology of Labor in the Early Republic* (1990) argues that the cultural status of women declined as the market revolution began to transform the American economy. Drew McCoy, *The Elusive Republic: Political Economy in Jeffersonian America* (1980) traces the Jeffersonian struggle to keep the United States free from European-style corruption and decay. Paul Finkleman, *Slavery and the Founders: Race and Liberty in the Age of Jefferson* (1996) considers the problem of slavery in the early Republic. Donald Hickey, *The War of 1812:A Forgotten Conflict* (1989) is an account of the war. J.C.A. Stagg, *Mr. Madison's War: Politics, Diplomacy, and Warfare in the Early American Republic, 1783–1830* (1983) argues that James Madison led the United States to war against Great Britain in order to preserve vital American commercial interests, but that he underestimated New England opposition to the war.

For quizzes,Internet resources, references to additional books and films, and more, consult this book's Online Learning Center at www.mhhe.com/brinkley11.

FOURTH OF JULY PICNIC AT WEYMOUTH LANDING (C.1845), BY SUSAN MERRETT Celebrations of Independence Day, like this one in eastern Massachusetts, became major festive events throughout the United States in the early nineteenth century, a sign of rising American nationalism. *(Art Institute of Chicago)*

Significant Events

1813 · Francis Lowell establishes textile factories in Waltham, Massachusetts

1815 · U.S. signs treaties with tribes taking western lands from Indians

1816 · Second Bank of the United States chartered
· Monroe elected president
· Tariff protects textile industry from foreign competition
· Indiana enters Union

1817 · Madison vetoes internal improvements bill
· Mississippi enters Union

1818 · Jackson invades Florida, ends first Seminole War
· Illinois enters Union

CHAPTER EIGHT

VARIETIES OF AMERICAN NATIONALISM

*L*ike a "fire bell in the night," as Thomas Jefferson put it, the issue of slavery arose after the War of 1812 to threaten the unity of the nation. The debate began when the territory of Missouri applied for admission to the Union, raising the question of whether it would be a free or a slaveholding state. But the larger issue, one that would arise again and again to plague the republic, was whether the vast new western regions of the United States would ultimately move into the orbit of the North or the South.

The Growing Crisis over Slavery

The Missouri crisis, which Congress settled by compromise in 1820, was significant at the time not only because it was a sign of the sectional crises to come but because it stood in such sharp contrast to the rising American nationalism of the years following the war. Whatever forces might be working to pull the nation apart, stronger ones were acting for the moment to draw it together. The American economy was experiencing remarkable growth. The federal government was acting in both domestic and foreign policy to assert a vigorous nationalism. Above all, perhaps, a set of widely (although never universally) shared sentiments and ideals worked to bind the nation together: the memory of the Revolution, the veneration of the Constitution and its framers, the belief that America had a special destiny in the world. These beliefs combined to produce among many Americans a vibrant, even romantic, patriotism.

Every year, Fourth of July celebrations reminded Americans of their common struggle for independence, as fife-and-drum corps and flamboyant orators appealed to patriotism and nationalism. When the Marquis de Lafayette, the French general who had aided the United States during the Revolution, traveled through the country in 1824, crowds in every region and of every party cheered him in frenzied celebration.

And on July 4, 1826—the fiftieth anniversary of the adoption of the Declaration of Independence—an event occurred which to many seemed to confirm that the United States was a nation specially chosen by God. On that remarkable day, Americans were to learn, two of the greatest of the country's founders and former presidents—Thomas Jefferson, author of the Declaration, and John Adams, whom Jefferson had called "its ablest advocate and defender"—died within hours of each other. Jefferson's last words, those at his bedside reported, were "Is it the Fourth?" And Adams comforted those around him moments before his death by saying, "Thomas Jefferson still survives."

For a time, it was possible for many Americans to overlook the very different forms their nationalism took—and to ignore the large elements of their population who were excluded from the national self-definition altogether. But the vigorous economic and territorial expansion this exuberant nationalism produced ultimately brought those differences to the fore.

1819 · Commercial panic destabilizes economy	1822 · Rocky Mountain Fur Company established
· Spain cedes Florida to United States in Adams-Onís Treaty	1823 · Monroe Doctrine proclaimed
· Supreme Court hears *Dartmouth College* v. *Woodward* and *McCulloch* v. *Maryland*	1824 · John Quincy Adams wins disputed presidential election
· Alabama enters Union	· Supreme Court rules in *Gibbons* v. *Ogden*
1819–1820 · Stephen H. Long explores Kansas, Nebraska, and Colorado	1826 · Thomas Jefferson and John Adams die on July 4
1820 · Missouri Compromise enacted	1827 · Creek Indians cede lands to Georgia
· Monroe reelected president without opposition	1828 · "Tariff of abominations" passed
1821 · Mexico wins independence from Spain	· Andrew Jackson elected president
· William Becknell opens trade between U.S. territories and New Mexico	

A GROWING ECONOMY

The end of the War of 1812 allowed the United States to resume the economic growth and territorial expansion that, despite the Republicans' hopes for a simple agrarian society, had characterized the first decade of the nineteenth century. A vigorous postwar boom led to a disastrous bust in 1819. Brief though it was, the collapse was evidence that the United States continued to lack some of the basic institutions necessary to sustain long-term growth. In the years to follow, there were strenuous efforts to introduce stability to the expanding economy.

Banking, Currency, and Protection

The War of 1812 may have stimulated the growth of manufacturing, but it also produced chaos in shipping and banking, and it exposed dramatically the inadequacy of the existing transportation and financial systems. The aftermath of the war, therefore, saw the emergence of a series of political issues connected with national economic development: reestablishing the Bank of the United States (the first Bank's charter had expired in 1811, and Congress had declined to renew it), protecting the new industries, and providing a nationwide network of roads and waterways.

Postwar Issues

The wartime experience underlined the need for another national bank. After the expiration of the first Bank's charter, a large number of state banks had begun operations. They issued vast quantities of bank notes but did not always bother to retain a large enough reserve of gold or silver to redeem the notes on demand. The notes passed from hand to hand more or less as money, but their actual value depended on the reputation of the bank that issued them. Thus there was a wide variety of notes, of widely differing value, in circulation at the same time. The result was a confusion that made honest business difficult and counterfeiting easy.

Congress dealt with the currency problem by chartering a second Bank of the United States in 1816. It was essentially the same institution Hamilton had founded in 1791 except that it had more capital than its predecessor. The national bank could not forbid state banks from issuing currency, but its size and power enabled it to dominate the state banks. It could compel them to issue only sound notes or risk being forced out of business.

Second Bank of the United States

Congress also acted to promote the already burgeoning manufacturing sector of the nation's economy, which the war (by cutting off imports) had greatly stimulated. Manufactured goods had been so scarce during the conflict that, even with comparatively unskilled labor and inexperienced management, new factories could start operations virtually assured of quick profits.

The American textile industry had experienced a particularly dramatic growth. The first census of manufacturing, in 1810, listed 269 cotton and 24 woolen mills in the country. But the Embargo of 1807 and the War of 1812 had spurred a tremendous expansion. Between 1807 and 1815, the total number of cotton spindles increased more than fifteenfold, from 8,000 to 130,000. Until 1814, the textile factories—most of them in New England—produced only yarn and thread; families operating handlooms at home did the actual weaving of cloth. Then the Boston merchant Francis Cabot Lowell, after examining textile machinery in England, developed a power loom that was better than its English counterpart. In 1813, Lowell organized the Boston Manufacturing

Growth of the Textile Industry

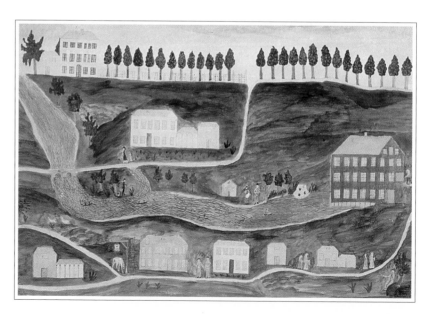

AN EARLY MILL IN NEW ENGLAND This early folk painting of about 1814 shows the small town of East Chelmsford, Massachusetts—still primarily agrarian, with its rural houses, open fields, and grazing livestock, but with a small textile mill already operating along the stream, at right. A little more than a decade later, the town had been transformed into a major manufacturing center and renamed for the family that owned the mills: Lowell. (Part of the Town of Chelmsford. *By Miss Warren. Abby Aldrich Rockefeller Folk Art Center, Williamsburg, Virginia*)

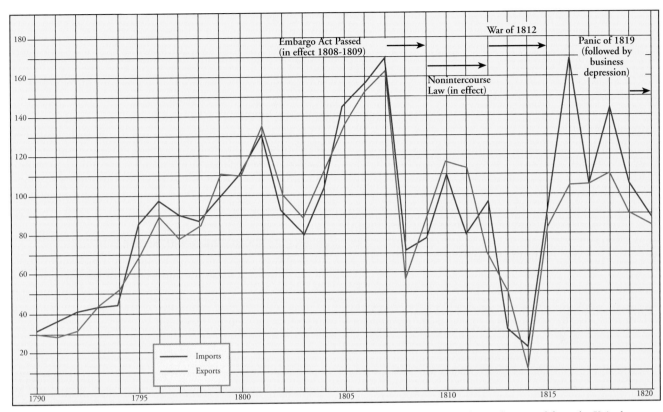

AMERICAN IMPORTS AND EXPORTS, 1790–1820 This chart shows the pattern of goods imported to and exported from the United States—the level of foreign trade, and the balance between goods bought and goods sold. Americans were heavily dependent on Britain and Europe for "finished" or "manufactured" goods in these years; and as you can see, imports grew as rapidly as, and often even more rapidly than, exports. Note how the nation's disputes with European powers depressed both exports and imports from about 1808 to 1814. ◆ *How does this chart help explain Congress's passage of a protective tariff law in 1816?*

Company and, at Waltham, Massachusetts, founded the first mill in America to carry on the processes of spinning and weaving under a single roof. Lowell's company was an important step in revolutionizing American manufacturing and in shaping the character of the early industrial work force. (See pp. 278–281.)

But the end of the war suddenly dimmed the prospects for American industry. British ships—determined to recapture their lost markets—swarmed into American ports and unloaded cargoes of manufactured goods, many priced below cost. As one English leader explained to Parliament, it was "well worth while to incur a loss upon the first exportation, in order, by the glut, to stifle in the cradle those rising manufactures in the United States, which war had forced into existence, contrary to the natural course of things." The "infant industries" cried out for protection against these tactics, arguing that they needed time to grow strong enough to withstand the foreign competition.

In 1816, protectionists in Congress won passage of a

A Protective Tariff

tariff law that effectively limited competition from abroad on a wide range of items, among the most important of which was cotton cloth. There were objections from agricultural interests, who would have to pay higher prices for manu-

factured goods as a result. But the nationalist dream of creating an important American industrial economy prevailed.

Transportation

The nation's most pressing economic need in the aftermath of the war, however, was for improvements in its transportation system. Without a better transportation network, manufacturers would not have access to the raw materials they needed and would not be able to send their finished goods to markets within the United States. So an old debate resumed: Should the federal government help to finance roads and other "internal improvements"?

The idea of using government funds to finance road building was not a new one.

Government-Funded Roads

When Ohio entered the Union in 1803, the federal government agreed that part of the proceeds from the government's sale of public lands there should finance road construction. In 1807, Jefferson's secretary of the treasury, Albert Gallatin, proposed that revenues from the Ohio land sales should help finance a National Road from the Potomac River to the Ohio River. Both Congress and the president approved.

After many delays, construction of the National Road finally began in 1811 at Cumberland, Maryland, on the Potomac; and by 1818, this highway—with a crushed stone surface and massive stone bridges—ran as far as Wheeling, Virginia, on the Ohio River. Meanwhile the state of Pennsylvania gave $100,000 to a private company to extend the Lancaster pike westward to Pittsburgh. Over both of these roads a heavy traffic soon moved: stagecoaches, Conestoga wagons, private carriages, and other vehicles, as well as droves of cattle. Despite high tolls, the roads made transportation costs across the mountains lower than ever before—still too high to permit the long-distance hauling of such bulky loads as wheat or flour, but low enough to justify transporting commodities with a high value in proportion to their weight, such as textiles. Manufactures moved from the Atlantic seaboard to the Ohio Valley in unprecedented quantities.

At the same time, on the rivers and the Great Lakes, steam-powered shipping was expanding rapidly. The development of steamboat lines was already well under-way before the War of 1812, thanks to the technological advances introduced by Robert Fulton and others. The war had retarded expansion of the system for a time, but by 1816, river steamers were beginning to journey up and down the Mississippi to the Ohio River, and up the Ohio as far as Pittsburgh.

Steamboats

Within a few years, steamboats were carrying far more cargo on the Mississippi than all the earlier forms of river transport—flatboats, barges, and others—combined. They stimulated the agricultural economy of the West and the South, by providing much readier access to markets at greatly reduced cost. They enabled eastern manufacturers to send their finished goods west much more readily.

Despite the progress with steamboats and turnpikes, there remained serious gaps in the nation's transportation network, as experience during the War of 1812 had shown. Once the British blockade cut off Atlantic shipping, the coastal roads became choked by the unaccustomed volume of north-south traffic. Long lines of wagons waited

DECK LIFE ON THE *PARAGON*, 1811–1812 The *North River Steamboat Clermont*, launched in 1806 by the inventor Robert Fulton and propelled by an engine he had developed, traveled from Manhattan to Albany (about 150 miles) in thirty-two hours. That was neither the longest nor the fastest steam voyage to date, but the *Clermont* proved to be the first steam-powered vessel large enough and reliable enough to be commercially valuable. Within a few years Fulton and his partner Robert R. Livingston had several steamboats operating profitably around New York. The third vessel in their fleet, the *Paragon*, shown here in a painting by the Russian diplomat and artist Pavel Petrovich Svinin, could carry 150 people and contained an elegant dining salon fitted with bronze, mahogany, and mirrors. Svinin called it "a whole floating town," and Fulton told a friend that the *Paragon* "beats everything on the globe, for made as you and I are we cannot tell what is in the moon." (*Metropolitan Museum of Art*)

for a chance to use the ferries that were still the only means of crossing most rivers. Oxcarts, pressed into emergency service, took six or seven weeks to go from Philadelphia to Charleston. In some areas there were serious shortages of goods that normally traveled by sea, and prices rose to new heights. Rice cost three times as much in New York as in Charleston, flour three times as much in Boston as in Richmond—all because of the difficulty of transportation. There were military consequences, too. On the northern and western frontiers, the absence of good roads had frustrated American campaigns.

In 1815, with this wartime experience in mind, President Madison called the attention of Congress to the "great importance of establishing throughout our country the roads and canals which can be best executed under the national authority," and suggested that a constitutional amendment would resolve any doubts about Congress's authority to provide for their construction. Representative John C. Calhoun promptly introduced a bill that would have used the funds owed the government by the Bank of the United States to finance internal improvements. "Let us, then, bind the republic together with a perfect system of roads and canals," Calhoun urged. "Let us conquer space."

Congress passed Calhoun's internal improvements bill, but President Madison, on his last day in office (March 3, 1817), vetoed it. He supported

Vetoing Internal Improvements

the purpose of the bill, he explained, but he still believed that Congress lacked authority to fund the improvements without a constitutional amendment. And so on the issue of internal improvements, at least, the nationalists fell short of their goals. It remained for state governments and private enterprise to undertake the tremendous task of building the transportation network necessary for the growing American economy.

EXPANDING WESTWARD

One reason for the growing interest in internal improvements was the sudden and dramatic surge in westward expansion in the years following the War of 1812. "Old America seems to be breaking up and moving westward," wrote an English observer at the time. By the time of the census of 1820, white settlers had pushed well beyond the Mississippi River, and the population of the western regions was increasing more rapidly than that of the nation as a whole. Almost one of every four white Americans lived west of the Appalachians in 1820; ten years before, only one in seven had resided there.

The Great Migrations

The westward movement of the white American population was one of the most important developments of the nineteenth century. It had a profound effect on the nation's economy, bringing vast new regions into the emerging capitalist system. It had great political ramifications, which ultimately became a major factor in the coming of the Civil War. And like earlier movements west, it thrust peoples of different cultures and traditions into intimate association with one another—with

Reasons for Westward Expansion

effects that were ultimately disastrous for some, but important on all sides. There were several important reasons for this expansion. Population pressures and economic pressures pushed many Americans from the East; the availability of new lands and the decline of Indian resistance drew them to the West.

The pressures driving white Americans out of the East came in part from the continued growth of the nation's population—both through natural increase and through immigration. Between 1800 and 1820, the population nearly doubled—from 5.3 million to 9.6 million. The growth of cities absorbed some of that increase, but most Americans were still farmers. The agricultural lands of the East were by now largely occupied, and some of them were exhausted. In the South, the spread of the plantation system, and of a slave labor force, limited opportunities for new settlers.

Meanwhile, the West itself was becoming increasingly attractive to white settlers. The War of 1812 had helped diminish (although it did not wholly eliminate) one of the traditional deterrents to western expansion: Native American opposition. And in the aftermath of the war, the federal government continued its policy of pushing the remaining tribes farther and farther west. A series of treaties in 1815 wrested more land from the Indians. In the meantime, the government was erecting a chain of stockaded forts along the Great Lakes and the upper Mississippi

The Factor System

to protect the frontier. It also created a "factor" system, by which government factors (or agents) supplied the tribes with goods at cost. This not only worked to drive Canadian traders out of the region, it also helped create a situation of dependency that made Native Americans themselves easier to control.

Now that fertile lands were secure for white settlement, migrants from throughout the East flocked to what was then known as the Old Northwest (now called part of the Midwest). The Ohio and Monongahela Rivers were the main routes westward, until the completion of the Erie Canal in 1825. The pioneers reached the river by traveling along the turnpike to Pittsburgh or along the National Road to Wheeling, or by sailing down one of its tributaries—such as the Kanawha, the Cumberland, or the Tennessee. Once on the Ohio, they floated downstream on flatboats bearing all their possessions, then left the river (often at Cincinnati, which was becoming one of the region's—and the nation's—principal cities) and pressed on overland with wagons, handcarts, packhorses, cattle, and hogs.

1838.
Mai.
18th

From St. Louis up on the Mississippi.

Start from St. Louis at Noon. Weather clear.

Alton, on the Western side of the Hill
N° 1 — 4.

Fort Snelling from the East

FORT SNELLING This is an 1838 sketch of Fort Snelling (at the juncture of the Minnesota and Mississippi Rivers), containing instructions for reaching it from St. Louis. It was one of a string of fortifications built along the western edge of European settlement along the Great Lakes and the upper Mississippi in the first three decades of the nineteenth century. The forts were designed to protect the new white communities from hostile Indians. Fort Snelling stands today in Minnesota as a "living history" site. *(Minnesota Historical Society)*

White Settlers in the Old Northwest

Having arrived at their destination, preferably in the spring or early summer, most settlers built lean-tos or cabins, then hewed clearings out of the forest and put in *Frontier Life* | crops of corn to supplement the wild game they caught and the domestic animals they had brought with them. It was a rough existence, plagued by loneliness, poverty, dirt, and disease. Men, women, and children worked side by side in the fields—and at times had virtually no contact for weeks or months at a time with anyone outside their own families.

Life in the western territories was not, however, as solitary and individualistic as later myth suggested. Migrants often journeyed westward in groups, and sometimes stayed together, formed new communities, and built schools, churches, stores, and other institutions. The labor shortage in the interior led neighbors to develop systems of mutual aid, gathering periodically to raise a barn, clear land, harvest crops, or make quilts. Gradually, the settlers built a thriving farm economy based largely on family units of modest size and committed to the cultivation of grain and the raising of livestock.

Another common feature of life in the Northwest (and indeed in much of early-nineteenth-century America) was mobility. Individuals and families were constantly on the *A Mobile Society* move, settling for a few years in one place, then selling their land (often at a significant profit, given the rapidly rising price of farm properties in the region) and settling again somewhere else. When new areas for settlement opened farther to the west, it was often the people already on the western edges of white settlement—rather than those who remained in the East—who flocked to them first.

The Plantation System in the Southwest

In the Southwest, the new agricultural economy emerged along different lines—just as the economy of the Old South had long been different from that of the Northeast. The principal attraction there was cotton. The cotton lands in the uplands of the Old South had lost much of their fertility through overplanting and erosion. But the market for cotton continued to grow, so there was no lack of ambitious farmers seeking fresh soil in a climate suitable for the crop. In the Southwest, around the end of the Appalachian range, stretched a broad zone within which cotton could thrive. That zone included what was to become known as the Black Belt of central Alabama and Mississippi, a vast prairie with a dark, productive soil of rotted limestone.

The advance of southern settlement meant the spread of cotton, plantations, and slavery. The first arrivals in an uncultivated region were usually ordinary people like the settlers farther north, small farmers | *Cotton and the Expansion of Slavery* who made rough clearings in the forest. But wealthier planters soon followed. They bought up the cleared or partially cleared land, while the original settlers moved farther west and started over again.

The large planters made the westward journey in a style quite different from that of the first pioneers. Over the alternately dusty and muddy roads came great caravans consisting of herds of livestock, wagonloads of household goods, long lines of slaves, and—bringing up the rear—the planter's family riding in carriages. Success in the wilderness was by no means assured, even for the wealthiest settlers. But many planters soon expanded small clearings into vast cotton fields. They replaced the cabins of the early pioneers with more sumptuous log dwellings and ultimately with imposing mansions that symbolized the emergence of a newly rich class. In later years, these western planters would assume the airs of a longstanding aristocracy. But by the time of the Civil War, few planter families in the Southwest had been there for more than one or two generations.

The rapid growth of the Northwest and Southwest resulted in the admission of four new states to the Union in the immediate aftermath of the War of 1812: Indiana in 1816, Mississippi in 1817, Illinois in 1818, and Alabama in 1819.

Trade and Trapping in the Far West

Not many Anglo-Americans yet knew much about or were much interested in the far western areas of the continent. But a significant trade nevertheless began to develop between these western regions and the United States early in the nineteenth century, and it grew steadily for decades.

Mexico, which continued to control Texas, California, and much of the rest of the Southwest, won its independence from Spain in 1821. Almost immediately, it opened its northern territories to trade with the United States, hoping to revive an economy that had grown stagnant during its war with Spain. American traders poured into the region—overland into Texas and New Mexico, by sea into California. Merchants from the United States quickly displaced Indian traders who had dominated trade with Mexico in some areas of the Southwest. They also displaced some of the same Mexicans who had hoped this new commerce would improve their fortunes. In New Mexico, for example, the Missouri trader William Becknell began in 1821 to offer American manufactured goods for sale, priced considerably below the inferior Mexican goods that had dominated the market in the past. Mexico effectively lost its markets in its own colony, and a steady traffic of commercial wagon trains was moving back and forth along the Santa Fe Trail between Missouri and New Mexico.

Becknell and those who followed him diverted an established trade from Mexico to the United States. Fur traders created a wholly new commerce with the West. Before the War of 1812, John Jacob Astor's American Fur Company had established Astoria as a trading post at the mouth of the Columbia River in Oregon. But when the war came, Astor sold his suddenly imperiled interests to the Northwestern Fur Company, a British concern operating out of Canada. After the war Astor centered his own operations in the Great Lakes area, from which he eventually extended them westward to the Rockies. Other companies carried on operations up the Missouri and its tributaries and into the Rocky Mountains.

Astor's American Fur Company

At first, fur traders did most of their business by purchasing pelts from the Indians. But increasingly, white trappers entered the region and began to hunt beaver on their own. Substantial numbers of Anglo-Americans and French Canadians moved deep into the Great Lakes region and beyond to join the Iroquois and other Indians in pursuit of furs.

THE RENDEZVOUS The annual rendezvous of fur trappers and traders was a major event in the lives of the lonely men who made their livelihoods gathering furs. It was also a gathering of representatives of the many cultures that mingled in the Far West, among them Anglo-Americans, French Canadians, Indians, and Hispanics. *(Denver Public Library)*

The trappers, or "mountain men," who began trading

Mountain Men

in and exploring the Far West were, without knowing it, the first wedge of a white movement into those lands that would ultimately dominate the region and transform it. Even in small numbers, they were developing important relationships with the existing residents of the West—Indian and Mexican—and altering the character of society there. White trappers were almost without exception relatively young single men. Not surprisingly, many of them entered into sexual relationships with Indian and Mexican women. They also recruited them as helpers in the difficult work of preparing furs and skins for trading. Perhaps two-thirds of the white trappers married Indian or Hispanic women while living in the West, and their marriages (according to one study) lasted an average of fifteen years and produced an average of three children.

As the trappers moved west from the Great Lakes region, they began to establish themselves in what is now Utah and in parts of New Mexico. In 1822, Andrew and William Ashley founded the Rocky Mountain Fur Company and recruited white trappers to move permanently into the Rockies in search of furs, which were becoming increasingly scarce farther east. The Ashleys dispatched supplies annually to their trappers in exchange for furs and skins. The arrival of the supply train became the occasion for a gathering of scores of mountain men, some of whom lived much of the year in considerable isolation.

But however isolated their daily lives, these mountain

The Fur Trade and the Market Economy

men were closely bound up with the expanding market economy of the United States. Some were employees of the Rocky Mountain Fur Company (or some other, similar enterprise), earning a salary in return for providing a steady supply of furs. Others were nominally independent but relied on the companies for credit; they were almost always in debt and hence economically bound to the companies. Some trapped entirely on their own and simply sold their furs for cash, but they too depended on merchants from the East for their livelihoods. And it was to those merchants that the bulk of the profits from the trade flowed.

Many trappers and mountain men lived peacefully and successfully with the Native Americans and Mexicans whose lands they came to share. But some did not. Jedediah S. Smith, a trapper who became an Ashley partner, founded his own fur company to profit from trade in the northern Rockies in 1826. He also led a series of forays deep into Mexican territory that ended in disastrous battles with the Mojaves and other tribes. When an 1827 expedition to Oregon he had organized was attacked by Indians he managed to escape. Sixteen other members of his party of twenty died. Four years later, he set out for

New Mexico and was killed by Comanches, who took the weapons he was carrying and sold them to Mexican settlers.

Eastern Images of the West

Americans in the East were only dimly aware of the world the trappers were entering and helping to reshape. Smith and others became the source of dramatic (and often exaggerated) popular stories. But the trappers themselves did not often write of their lives or draw maps of the lands they explored.

More important in increasing eastern awareness of the West were explorers, many

Stephen Long's Expedition

of them dispatched by the United States government with instructions to chart the territories they visited. In 1819 and 1820, with instructions from the War Department to find the sources of the Red River, Stephen H. Long led nineteen soldiers on a journey up the Platte and South Platte Rivers through what is now Nebraska and eastern Colorado (where he discovered a peak that would be named for him), and then returned eastward along the Arkansas River through what is now Kansas. He failed to find the headwaters of the Red River. But he wrote an influential report on his trip, including an assessment of the region's potential for future settlement and development that echoed the dismissive conclusions of Zebulon Pike fifteen years before. "In regard to this extensive section of

PLATTE RIVER CROSSING The trails to the West, along which hundreds of thousands of white, English-speaking people migrated in the antebellum period, were filled with hardships: steep hills, rugged mountains with narrow passes through them, broad deserts, and rivers—some broad, some rapid—that had to be crossed, in the absence of bridges, with makeshift rafts and barges. Joseph Goldsborough Bruff, who traveled to California along the Overland trail, sketched this crossing on the Platte River, which runs from Nebraska into the Missouri River. *(Reproduced by permission of The Huntington Library, San Marino, California)*

country between the Missouri River and the Rocky Mountains," Long wrote, "we do not hesitate in giving the opinion that it is almost wholly unfit for cultivation, and of course uninhabitable by a people depending upon agriculture for their subsistence." On the published map of his expedition, he labeled the Great Plains the "Great American Desert."

THE "ERA OF GOOD FEELINGS"

The expansion of the economy, the growth of white settlement and trade in the West, the creation of new states—all reflected the rising spirit of nationalism that was permeating the United States in the years following the War of 1812. That spirit found reflection for a time in the character of national politics.

The End of the First Party System

Ever since 1800, the presidency seemed to have been the special possession of Virginians. After two terms in office Jefferson chose his secretary of state, James Madison of

The Virginia Dynasty

Virginia, to succeed him, and after two more terms, Madison secured the presidential nomination for his secretary of state, James Monroe, also of Virginia. Many in the North were expressing impatience with the so-called Virginia Dynasty, but the Republicans had no difficulty electing their candidate in the listless campaign of 1816. Monroe

received 183 ballots in the electoral college; his Federalist opponent, Rufus King of New York, received only 34— from Massachusetts, Connecticut, and Delaware.

Monroe was sixty-one years old when he became president. In the course of his long career, he had served as a soldier in the Revolution, as a diplomat, and most recently as a cabinet officer. He entered office under what seemed to be remarkably favorable circumstances. With the decline of the Federalists, his party faced no serious opposition. With the conclusion of the War of 1812, the nation faced no important international threats. American politicians had dreamed since the first days of the republic of a time in which partisan divisions and factional disputes might come to an end. In the prosperous postwar years, Monroe attempted to use his office to realize that dream.

He made that clear, above all, in the selection of his cabinet. For secretary of state, he chose the New Englander and former Federalist John Quincy Adams. Jefferson, Madison, and Monroe had all served as secretary of state before becoming president; Adams, therefore, immediately became the heir apparent, suggesting that the "Virginia Dynasty" would soon come to an end. Speaker of the House Henry Clay declined an offer to be secretary of war, so Monroe named John C. Calhoun instead. In his other appointments, too, Monroe took pains to include both northerners and southerners, easterners and westerners, Federalists and Republicans.

Soon after his inauguration, Monroe did what no president since Washington had done: he made a goodwill

THE TRIUMPHANT TOUR OF JAMES MONROE After James Monroe's enormously successful tour of the northern and eastern states in 1818, midway through his first term as president, there was widespread self-congratulation through much of the United States for the apparent political unity that had gripped the nation. Only a few years earlier, the northeast had been the bastion of Federalist party opposition to the Republican governments of the early nineteenth century. At one point, some Federalist leaders had even proposed secession from the United States. But now a Virginia Republican president had been greeted as a hero in the former Federalist strongholds. This book, published in 1820 (when Monroe ran virtually unopposed for re-election), is an account of the president's triumphant tour and a short account of his life— an early version of the now familiar campaign biography. *(Collection of David J. and Janice L. Frent)*

tour through the country. In New England, so recently the

Monroe's Goodwill Tour | scene of rabid Federalist discontent, he was greeted everywhere with enthusiastic demonstrations. The *Columbian Centinel,* a Federalist newspaper in Boston, commenting on the "Presidential Jubilee" in that city, observed that an "era of good feelings" had arrived. And on the surface, at least, the years of Monroe's presidency did appear to be an "era of good feelings." In 1820, Monroe was reelected without opposition. For all practical purposes, the Federalist Party had now ceased to exist.

John Quincy Adams and Florida

Like his father, the second president of the United States, John Quincy Adams had spent much of his life in diplomatic service. And even before becoming secretary of state, he had become one of the great diplomats in American history. He was also a committed nationalist, and he considered his most important task to be the promotion of American expansion.

His first challenge was Florida. The United States had already annexed West Florida, but that claim was in dispute. Most Americans, moreover, still believed the nation should gain possession of the entire peninsula. In 1817, Adams began negotiations with the Spanish minister, Luis de Onís, in hopes of resolving the dispute and gaining the entire territory for the United States.

In the meantime, however, events were taking their own course in Florida itself. Andrew Jackson, now in command of American troops along the Florida frontier,

The Seminole War | had orders from Secretary of War Calhoun to "adopt the necessary measures" to stop continuing raids on American territory by Seminole Indians south of the border. Jackson used those orders as an excuse to invade Florida, seize the Spanish forts at St. Marks and Pensacola, and order the hanging of two British subjects on the charge of supplying and inciting the Indians. The operation became known as the Seminole War.

Instead of condemning Jackson's raid, Adams urged the government to assume responsibility for it. The United States, he told the Spanish, had the right under international law to defend itself against threats from across its borders. Since Spain was unwilling or unable to curb those threats, America had simply done what was necessary. Jackson's raid demonstrated to the Spanish that the United States could easily take Florida by force. Adams implied that the nation might consider doing so.

Onís realized, therefore, that he had little choice but to come to terms with the Americans. Under the provisions of the Adams-Onís Treaty of 1819, Spain ceded all of

Adams-Onís Treaty | Florida to the United States and gave up its claim to territory north of the 42nd parallel in the Pacific Northwest. In return, the American government gave up its claims to Texas.

SEMINOLE DANCE This 1838 drawing by a U.S. military officer portrays a dance by Seminole Indians near Fort Butler in Florida. It was made in the midst of the prolonged Second Seminole War, which ended in 1842 with the removal of most of the tribe from Florida to reservations west of the Mississippi. *(Reproduced by permission of The Huntington Library, San Marino, California)*

The Panic of 1819

But the Monroe administration had little time to revel in its diplomatic successes, for the nation was falling victim to a serious economic crisis: the Panic of 1819. It followed a period of high foreign demand for American farm goods and thus of exceptionally high prices for American farmers (all as a result of the disruption of European agriculture caused by the Napoleonic Wars). The rising prices for farm goods had stimulated a land boom in the western United States. Fueled by speculative investments, land prices soared.

The availability of easy credit to settlers and speculators—from the government (under the land acts of 1800 and 1804), from state banks and wildcat banks, even for a time from the rechartered Bank of the United States—fueled the land boom. Beginning in 1819, however, new management at the national bank began tightening credit, calling in loans, and foreclosing mortgages. This precipitated a series of failures by state banks, and the result was a financial panic, which many Americans, particularly those in the West, blamed on the national bank. Thus began a process that would eventually make the Bank's existence one of the nation's most burning political issues. Six years of depression followed.

Some Americans saw the Panic of 1819 and the wide-

Boom and Bust

spread distress that followed as a warning that rapid economic growth and territorial expansion would destabilize the nation and threaten its survival. But by 1820 most Americans were irrevocably committed to the idea of growth and expansion. Public debate in the future would revolve less around whether growth was good or bad than around how to encourage and control it.

SECTIONALISM AND NATIONALISM

For a brief but alarming moment in 1819–1820, the increasing differences between the North and the South threatened the unity of the United States—until the Missouri Compromise averted a sectional crisis for a time. The forces of nationalism continued to assert them-

selves, and the federal government began to assume the role of promoter of economic growth.

The Missouri Compromise

When Missouri applied for admission to the Union as a state in 1819, slavery was already well established there.

Tallmadge Amendment

Even so, Representative James Tallmadge, Jr. of New York proposed an amendment to the Missouri statehood bill that would prohibit the further introduction of slaves into Missouri and provide for the gradual emancipation of those already there. The Tallmadge Amendment provoked a controversy that was to rage for the next two years.

Since the beginning of the republic, partly by chance and partly by design, new states had come into the Union more or less in pairs, one from the North, another from the South. In 1819, there were eleven free states and eleven slave states; the admission of Missouri would upset

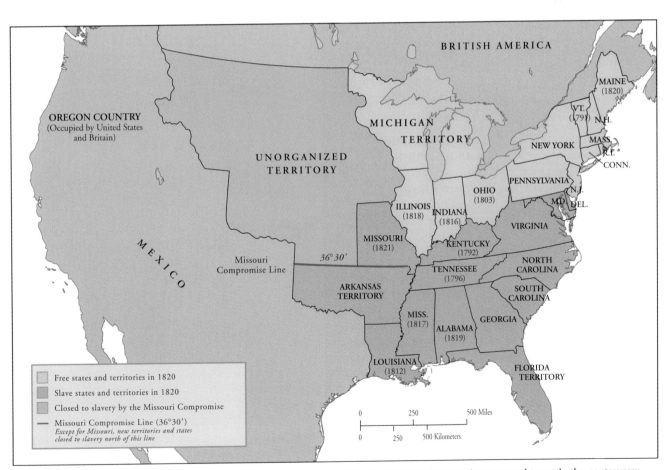

THE MISSOURI COMPROMISE, 1820 This map illustrates the way in which the Missouri Compromise proposed to settle the controversy over slavery in the new western territories of the United States. The compromise rested on the virtually simultaneous admission of Missouri and Maine to the Union, one a free state and the other a slave one. Note the red line extending beyond the southern border of Missouri, which in theory established a permanent boundary between areas in which slavery could be established and areas where it could not be. • *What precipitated the Missouri Compromise?*

 For an interactive version of this map go to ww.mhhe.com/brinkley11ch8maps

that balance and increase the political power of the North over the South. Hence the controversy over slavery and freedom in Missouri.

Complicating the Missouri question was the application of Maine (previously the northern part of Massachusetts)

Compromise

for admission as a new (and free) state. Speaker of the House Henry Clay informed northern members that if they blocked Missouri from entering the Union as a slave state, southerners would block the admission of Maine. But Maine ultimately offered a way out of the impasse, as the Senate agreed to combine the Maine and Missouri proposals into a single bill. Maine would be admitted as a free state, Missouri as a slave state. Then Senator Jesse B. Thomas of Illinois proposed an amendment prohibiting slavery in the rest of the Louisiana Purchase territory north of the southern boundary of Missouri (the 36° 30′ parallel). The Senate adopted the Thomas Amendment, and Speaker Clay, with great difficulty, guided the amended Maine-Missouri bill through the House.

Nationalists in both North and South hailed this settlement—which became known as the Missouri Compromise—as a happy resolution of a danger to the Union. But the debate over it had revealed a strong undercurrent of sectionalism that was competing with—although at the moment failing to derail—the powerful tides of nationalism.

Marshall and the Court

John Marshall served as chief justice of the United States for almost thirty-five years, from 1801 to 1835, and he dominated the Court more fully than anyone else before or since. More than anyone but the framers themselves, he molded the development of the Constitution: strengthening the judicial branch at the expense of the executive and legislative branches, increasing the power of the federal government at the expense of the states, and advancing the interests of the propertied and commercial classes.

Committed to promoting commerce, the Marshall Court staunchly defended the inviolability of contracts. In *Fletcher* v. *Peck* (1810), which arose out of a series of notorious land frauds in Georgia, the Court had to decide whether the Georgia legislature of 1796 could repeal the act of the previous legislature granting lands under shady circumstances to the Yazoo Land Companies. In a unanimous decision, Marshall held that a land grant was a valid contract and could not be repealed even if corruption was involved.

Dartmouth College v. *Woodward* (1819) further ex-

Dartmouth College v. Woodward

panded the meaning of the contract clause of the Constitution. Having gained control of the New Hampshire state government, Republicans tried to revise Dartmouth College's charter (granted by King George III in 1769) to convert the private college into a state university. Daniel Webster, a Dartmouth graduate and brilliant orator, argued the college's case. The Dartmouth charter, he insisted, was a contract, protected by the same doctrine that the Court had already upheld in *Fletcher* v. *Peck.* Then, according to legend, he brought some of the justices to tears with an irrelevant passage that concluded: "It is, sir, . . . a small college. And yet there are those who love it." The Court ruled for Dartmouth, proclaiming that corporation charters such as the one the colonial legislature had granted the college were contracts and thus inviolable. The decision placed important restrictions on the ability of state governments to control corporations.

In overturning the act of the legislature and the decisions of the New Hampshire courts, the justices also implicitly claimed for themselves the right to override the decisions of state courts. But advocates of states' rights, especially in the South, continued to challenge its right to do so. In *Cohens* v. *Virginia* (1821), Marshall explicitly

JOHN MARSHALL The imposing figure in this early photograph is John Marshall, the most important chief justice of the Supreme Court in American history. A former secretary of state, Marshall served as chief justice from 1801 until his death in 1835 at the age of 80. Such was the power of his intellect and personality that he dominated his fellow justices throughout that period, regardless of their previous party affiliations or legal ideologies. Marshall established the independence of the Court, gave it a reputation for nonpartisan integrity, and established its powers, which were only vaguely described by the Constitution. *(National Archives and Records Administration)*

affirmed the constitutionality of federal review of state court decisions. The states had given up part of their sovereignty in ratifying the Constitution, he explained, and their courts must submit to federal jurisdiction; otherwise, the federal government would be prostrated "at the feet of every state in the Union."

Meanwhile, in *McCulloch* v. *Maryland* (1819), Marshall confirmed the "implied powers" of Congress by upholding the constitutionality of the Bank of the United States. The

Confirming Implied Powers

Bank had become so unpopular in the South and the West that several of the states tried to drive branches out of business by outright prohibition or by confiscatory taxes. This case presented two constitutional questions to the Supreme Court: Could Congress charter a bank? And if so, could individual states ban it or tax it? Daniel Webster, one of the Bank's attorneys, argued that establishing such an institution came within the "necessary and proper" clause of the Constitution and that the power to tax involved a "power to destroy." If the states could tax the Bank at all, they could tax it to death. Marshall adopted Webster's words in deciding for the Bank.

In the case of *Gibbons* v. *Ogden* (1824), the Court strengthened Congress's power to regulate interstate commerce. The state of New York had granted the steamboat company of Robert Fulton and Robert Livingston the exclusive right to carry passengers on the Hudson River to New York City. Fulton and Livingston then gave Aaron Ogden the business of carrying passengers across the river between New York and New Jersey. But Thomas Gibbons, with a license granted under an act of Congress, began competing with Ogden for the ferry traffic. Ogden brought suit against him and won in the New York courts. Gibbons appealed to the Supreme Court. The most important question facing the justices was whether Congress's power to give Gibbons a license to operate his ferry superseded the state of New York's power to grant Ogden a monopoly. Marshall claimed that the power of Congress to regulate interstate commerce (which, he said, included navigation) was "complete in itself" and might be "exercised to its utmost extent." Ogden's state-granted monopoly, therefore, was void.

The decisions of the Marshall Court established the primacy of the federal government over the states in regulating the economy and opened the way

Establishing Federal Primacy

for an increased federal role in promoting economic growth. They protected corporations and other private economic institutions from local government interference. They were, in short, highly nationalistic decisions, designed to promote the growth of a strong, unified, and economically developed United States.

The Court and the Tribes

The nationalist inclinations of the Marshall Court were visible as well in a series of decisions concerning the legal status of Indian tribes within the United States. But these decisions did not simply affirm the supremacy of the United States; they also carved out a distinctive position for Native Americans within the constitutional structure.

The first of the crucial Indian decisions was in the case of *Johnson* v. *McIntosh* (1823). Leaders of the Illinois and Pinakeshaw tribes had sold parcels of their land to a group of white settlers (including Johnson) but had later signed a treaty with the federal government ceding territory that included those same parcels to the United States. The government proceeded to grant homestead rights to new white settlers (among them McIntosh) on the land claimed by Johnson. The Court was asked to decide which claim had precedence. Marshall's ruling, not surprisingly, favored the United States. But in explaining it, he offered a preliminary definition of the place of Indians within the nation. The tribes had a basic right to their tribal lands, he said, that preceded all other American law. Individual American citizens could not buy or take land from the tribes; only the federal government—the supreme authority—could do that.

Even more important was the Court's 1832 decision in *Worcester* v. *Georgia,* in which the Court invalidated a Georgia law that attempted to regulate access by U.S. citizens

Worcester v. Georgia

to Cherokee country. Only the federal government could do that, Marshall claimed, thus taking another important step in consolidating federal authority over the states (and over the tribes). In doing so, he further defined the nature of the Indian nations. The tribes, he explained, were sovereign entities in much the same way Georgia was a sovereign entity—"distinct political communities, having territorial boundaries within which their authority is exclusive." In defending the power of the federal government, he was also affirming, indeed expanding, the rights of the tribes to remain free from the authority of state governments.

The Marshall decisions, therefore, did what the Constitution itself had not done: they defined a place for Indian tribes within the American political system. The tribes had basic property rights. They were sovereign entities not subject to the authority of state governments. But the federal government, like a "guardian" governing its "ward," had ultimate authority over tribal affairs—even if that authority was, according to the Court, limited by the government's obligation to protect Indian welfare. These provisions were seldom enough to defend Indians from the steady westward march of white civilization, but they formed the basis of what legal protections they had.

The Latin American Revolution and the Monroe Doctrine

Just as the Supreme Court was asserting American nationalism in the shaping of the country's economic life, so the Monroe administration was asserting nationalism in foreign policy. As always, American diplomacy was

CHEROKEE LEADERS Sequoyah, left (who also used the name George Guess), was a mixed-blood Cherokee who translated his tribe's language into writing through an elaborate alphabet of his own invention, pictured here. He opposed Indian assimilation into white society and saw the preservation of the Cherokee language as a way to protect the culture of his tribe. He moved to Arkansas in the 1820s and became a chief of the western Cherokee tribes. Major George Lowery, shown on the right, was also a mixed-blood Cherokee and served as assistant principal chief of the Cherokee from 1828 to 1838. He supported acculturation but remained a Cherokee nationalist. He wears a U.S. presidential medal around his neck. *(Left, National Anthropological Archives, Smithsonian; Right, Gilcrease Institute)*

principally concerned with Europe. But in the 1820s, dealing with Europe forced the United States to develop a policy toward Latin America.

Americans looking southward in the years following *Revolution in Latin America* the War of 1812 beheld a gigantic spectacle: the Spanish Empire in its death throes, a whole continent in revolt, new nations in the making. Already the United States had developed a profitable trade with Latin America and was rivaling Great Britain as the principal trading nation there. Many believed the success of the anti-Spanish revolutions would further strengthen America's position in the region.

In 1815, the United States proclaimed neutrality in the wars between Spain and its rebellious colonies, implying a partial recognition of the rebels' status as nations. Moreover, the United States sold ships and supplies to the revolutionaries, a clear indication that it was not genuinely neutral but was trying to help the insurgents. Finally, in 1822, President Monroe established diplomatic relations with five new nations—La Plata (later Argentina), Chile, Peru, Colombia, and Mexico—making the United States the first country to recognize them.

In 1823, Monroe went further and announced a policy that would ultimately be known *The Monroe Doctrine* (beginning some thirty years later) as the "Monroe Doctrine," even though it was primarily the work of John Quincy Adams. "The American continents," Monroe declared, ". . . are henceforth not to be considered as subjects for future colonization by any European powers." The United States would consider any foreign challenge to the sovereignty of existing American nations an unfriendly act. At the same time, he proclaimed, "Our policy in regard to Europe . . . is not to interfere in the internal concerns of any of its powers."

The Monroe Doctrine emerged directly out of America's relations with Europe in the 1820s. Many Americans feared that Spain's European allies (notably France) would as- *American Fears* sist Spain in an effort to retake its lost empire. Even more troubling to Adams (and many other Americans) was the fear that Great Britain had designs on Cuba. Adams wanted to keep Cuba in Spanish hands until it fell (as he believed it ultimately would) to the Americans.

The Monroe Doctrine had few immediate effects, but it was important as an expression of the growing spirit of nationalism in the United States in the 1820s. And it established the idea of the United States as the dominant power in the Western Hemisphere.

THE REVIVAL OF OPPOSITION

After 1816, the Federalist Party offered no presidential candidate and soon ceased to exist as a national political force. The Republican Party (which considered itself not a party at all but an organization representing the whole of the population) was the only organized force in national politics.

By the late 1820s, however, partisan divisions were emerging once again. In some respects, the division mir-

New Political Divisions | rored the schism that had produced the first party system in the 1790s. The Republicans had in many ways come to resemble the early Federalist regimes in their promotion of economic growth and centralization. And the opposition, like the opposition in the 1790s, objected to the federal government's expanding role in the economy. There was, however, a crucial difference. At the beginning of the century, the opponents of centralization had also often been opponents of economic growth. Now, in the 1820s, the controversy involved not whether but how the nation should continue to expand.

The "Corrupt Bargain"

Until 1820, when the Federalist Party effectively ceased

End of the Caucus System | operations and James Monroe ran for reelection unopposed, presidential candidates were nominated by caucuses of the two parties in Congress. But in 1824, "King Caucus" was overthrown. The Republican caucus nominated William H. Crawford of Georgia, the secretary of the treasury and the favorite of the extreme states' rights faction of the party. But other candidates received nominations from state legislatures and won endorsements from irregular mass meetings throughout the country.

One of them was Secretary of State John Quincy Adams, who held the office that was the traditional stepping-stone to the presidency. But as he himself ruefully understood, he was a man of cold and forbidding manners, with little popular appeal. Another contender was Henry Clay, the Speaker of the House. He had a devoted personal following and a definite and coherent program: the "American System," which proposed creating a great home market for factory and farm producers by raising the protective tariff, strengthening the national bank, and financing internal improvements. Andrew Jackson, the fourth major candidate, had no significant political record—even though he had served briefly as a representative in Congress and was now a new member of the United States Senate. But he was a military hero and had the help of shrewd political allies from his home state of Tennessee.

Jackson received more popular and electoral votes than any other candidate, but not a majority. He had 99 electoral votes to Adams's 84, Crawford's 41, and Clay's 37. *Election of 1824*

The Twelfth Amendment to the Constitution (passed in the aftermath of the contested 1800 election) required the House of Representatives to choose among the three candidates with the largest numbers of electoral votes. Crawford was seriously ill and not a plausible candidate. Clay was out of the running, but he was in a strong position to influence the result. Jackson was Clay's most dangerous political rival in the West, so Clay supported Adams, in part because, alone among the candidates, he was an ardent nationalist and a likely supporter of the American System. With Clay's endorsement, Adams won election in the House.

The Jacksonians believed their large popular and electoral pluralities entitled their candidate to the presidency, and they were enraged when he lost. But they grew angrier still when Adams named Clay his secretary of state. The State Department was the well-established route to the presidency, and Adams thus appeared to be naming Clay as his own successor. The outrage the Jacksonians expressed at what they called a "corrupt bargain" haunted Adams throughout his presidency.

The Second President Adams

Throughout Adams's term in the White House, the political bitterness arising from the "corrupt bargain" charges thoroughly frustrated his policies. Adams proposed an ambitiously nationalist program reminiscent of Clay's American System. But Jacksonians in Congress blocked most of it.

Adams also experienced diplomatic frustrations. He appointed delegates to an international conference that the Venezuelan liberator, Simón Bolívar, had called in Panama in 1826. But Haiti was one of the participating nations, and southerners in Congress opposed the idea of white Americans mingling with the black delegates. Congress delayed approving the Panama mission so long that the American delegation did not arrive until after the conference was over.

Adams also lost a contest with the state of Georgia, which wished to remove the remaining Creek and Cherokee Indians from the state to gain additional soil for cotton planters. The United States government, in a 1791 treaty, had guaranteed that land to the Creeks; but in 1825, white Georgians had extracted a new treaty from William McIntosh, the leader of one faction in the tribe and a longtime advocate of Indian cooperation with the United States. Adams believed the new treaty had no legal force, since McIntosh clearly did not represent the wishes of the tribe; and he refused to enforce the treaty, setting up a direct conflict between the president and the state.

JOHN QUINCY ADAMS This photograph of the former president was taken shortly before his death in 1848—almost twenty years after he had left the White House—when he was serving as a congressman from Massachusetts. During his years as president, he was—as he had been throughout his life—an intensely disciplined and hard-working man. He rose at four in the morning and made a long entry in his diary for the previous day. He wrote so much that his right hand at times became paralyzed with writer's cramp, so he taught himself to write with his left hand as well. *(Brown Brothers)*

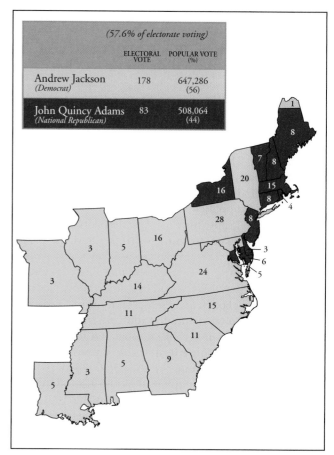

(57.6% of electorate voting)		
	ELECTORAL VOTE	POPULAR VOTE (%)
Andrew Jackson *(Democrat)*	178	647,286 (56)
John Quincy Adams *(National Republican)*	83	508,064 (44)

THE ELECTION OF 1828 As this map shows, Andrew Jackson's victory over John Quincy Adams was one of the most decisive in American history for a challenger facing an incumbent president. ◆ *What accounts for this decisive repudiation of President Adams?*

 For an interactive version of this map go to ww.mhhe.com/brinkley11ch8maps

The governor of Georgia defied the president and proceeded with plans for Indian removal. Adams found no way to stop him.

Even more damaging to the administration was its

Tariff of Abominations support for a new tariff on imported goods in 1828. This measure originated with the demands of Massachusetts and Rhode Island woolen manufacturers, who complained that the British were dumping textiles on the American market at artificially low prices. But to win support from middle and western states, the administration had to accept duties on other items. In the process, it antagonized the original New England supporters of the bill; the benefits of protecting their manufactured goods from foreign competition now had to be weighed against the prospects of having to pay more for raw materials. Adams signed the bill, earning the animosity of southerners, who cursed it as the "tariff of abominations."

Jackson Triumphant

By the time of the 1828 presidential election, a new two-party system had begun to emerge out of the divisions among the Republicans. On one side stood the supporters of John Quincy Adams, who called themselves the National Republicans and who supported the economic nationalism of the preceding years. Opposing them were the followers of Andrew Jackson, who took the name Democratic Republicans and who called for an assault on privilege and a widening of opportunity. Adams attracted the support of most of the remaining Federalists; Jackson appealed to a broad coalition that opposed the "economic aristocracy."

THE RISE OF MASS POLITICS

On March 4, 1829, an unprecedented throng—thousands of Americans from all regions of the country, in-

Jackson's Inauguration

cluding farmers, laborers, and others of modest social rank—crowded before the Capitol in Washington, D.C., to witness the inauguration of Andrew Jackson. After the ceremonies, the boisterous crowd poured down Pennsylvania Avenue, following their hero to the White House. There, at a public reception open to all, they filled the state rooms to overflowing, trampling one another, soiling the carpets, ruining elegantly upholstered sofas and chairs in their eagerness to shake the new president's hand. "It was a proud day for the people," wrote Amos Kendall, one of Jackson's closest political associates. "General Jackson is their own President." To other observers, however, the scene was less appealing. Justice of the Supreme Court Joseph Story, a friend and colleague of John Marshall, looked on the inaugural levee, as it was called, and remarked with disgust: "The reign of King 'Mob' seems triumphant."

The Expanding Electorate

What some have called the "age of Jackson" did not much advance the cause of economic equality. The distribution of wealth and property in America was little different at the end of the Jacksonian era than it was at the start. But it did mark a transformation of American politics that extended the right to vote widely to new groups.

ANDREW JACKSON This portrait suggests something of the fierce determination that characterized Andrew Jackson's military and political careers. Shattered by the death of his wife a few weeks after his election as president—a death he blamed (not entirely without reason) on the attacks his political opponents had leveled at her—he entered office with a steely determination to live by his own principles and give no quarter to his adversaries. *(New-York Historical Society)*

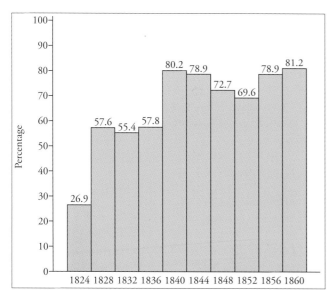

PARTICIPATION IN PRESIDENTIAL ELECTIONS, 1824–1860
This chart reveals the remarkable increase in popular participation in presidential elections in the years after 1824. Participation almost doubled between 1824 and 1828, and it increased substantially again beginning in 1840 and continuing through and beyond the Civil War. ◆ *What accounts for this dramatic expansion of the electorate? Who remained outside the voting population in these years?*

Until the 1820s, relatively few Americans had been permitted to vote. Most states restricted the franchise to white

Broadening the Franchise

males who were property owners or taxpayers or both, effectively barring an enormous number of the less affluent from the voting rolls. But beginning even before Jackson's election, the rules governing voting began to expand. Changes came first in Ohio and other new states of the West, which, on joining the Union, adopted constitutions that guaranteed all adult white males the right to vote and gave all voters the right to hold public office. Older states, concerned about the loss of their population to the West and thinking that extending the franchise might encourage some residents to stay, began to grant similar political rights to their citizens, dropping or reducing their property ownership or taxpaying requirements. Eventually, every state democratized its electorate to some degree, although some much later and less fully than others.

Change provoked resistance, and at times the democratic trend fell short of the aims of the more radical reformers, as when Massachusetts held its constitutional convention in 1820. Reform-minded delegates complained that in the Massachusetts government the rich were better represented than the poor, both because of restrictions on voting and officeholding and because of a peculiar system

JACKSONIAN AMERICA

When the French aristocrat Alexis de Tocqueville visited the United States in 1831, one feature of American society struck him as "fundamental": the "general equality of condition among the people." Unlike older societies, in which privilege and wealth passed from generation to generation within an entrenched upper class, America had no rigid distinctions of rank. "The government of democracy," he wrote in his classic study *Democracy in America* (1835–1840), "brings the notion of political rights to the level of the humblest citizens, just as the dissemination of wealth brings the notion of property within the reach of all the members of the community."

De Tocqueville

Yet Tocqueville also wondered how long the fluidity of American society could survive in the face of the growth of manufacturing and the rise of the factory system. Industrialism, he feared, would create a large class of dependent workers and a small group of new aristocrats. For, as he explained it, "at the very moment at which the science of manufactures lowers the class of workmen, it raises the class of masters."

Americans, too, pondered the future of their democracy in these years of economic and territorial expansion. Some feared that the nation's rapid growth would produce social chaos and insisted that the country's first priority must be to establish order and a clear system of authority. Others argued that the greatest danger facing the nation was privilege and that society's goal should be to eliminate the favored status of powerful elites and make opportunity more widely available. Advocates of this latter vision seized control of the federal government in 1829 with the inauguration of Andrew Jackson.

Jackson and his followers were not egalitarians. They did nothing to challenge the existence of slavery; they supervised one of the harshest assaults on American Indians in the nation's history; and they accepted the necessity of economic inequality and social gradation. Jackson himself was a frontier aristocrat, and most of those who served him were people of wealth and standing. They were not, however, usually aristocrats by birth. They had, they believed, risen to prominence on the basis of their own talents and energies, and their goal in public life was to ensure that others like themselves would have the opportunity to do the same.

The "democratization" of government over which Andrew Jackson presided was accompanied by a lofty rhetoric of equality and aroused the excitement of working people. To the national leaders who promoted that democratization, however, its purpose was not to aid farmers and laborers. Still less was it to assist the truly disenfranchised: African Americans (both slave and free), women, Native Americans. It was to challenge the power of eastern elites for the sake of the rising entrepreneurs of the South and the West.

Equality of Opportunity

1832 · Democrats hold first national party convention
· Jackson vetoes bill to recharter Bank of the United States
· Jackson reelected president
1832–1833 · Nullification crisis erupts
1833 · Jackson and Taney remove federal deposits from Bank of the United States
· Commercial panic disrupts economy
1834 · Indian Trade and Intercourse Act renewed
1835 · Roger Taney succeeds Marshall as chief justice of the Supreme Court
· Federal debt retired
1835–1840 · Tocqueville publishes *Democracy in America*
1835–1842 · Seminole War

1836 · Jackson issues "specie circular"
· Martin Van Buren elected president
1837 · Supreme Court rules in *Charles River Bridge* case
1837–1842 · Commercial panic and depression
1838 · "Aroostook War" fought in Maine and Canada
1839 · Whigs hold their first national convention
1840 · William Henry Harrison elected president
· Independent Treasury Act passed
1841 · Harrison dies
· John Tyler becomes president
1842 · Dorr Rebellion hastens reform in Rhode Island
· Webster-Ashburton Treaty signed

DETAIL FROM *THE VERDICT OF THE PEOPLE* (1855), BY GEORGE CALEB BINGHAM This scene of an election-day gathering is peopled almost entirely by white men. Women and blacks were barred from voting, but among white males political rights expanded substantially in the 1830s and 1840s. *(Bank of America)*

Significant Events

But issues seemed to count for little in the end, as the campaign degenerated into a war of personal invective. The Jacksonians charged that Adams as president had been guilty of gross waste and extravagance and had used public funds to buy gambling devices (a chess set and a billiard table) for the White House. Adams's supporters hurled even worse accusations at Jackson. They called him a murderer and distributed a "coffin handbill," which listed, within coffin-shaped outlines, the names of militiamen whom Jackson was said to have shot in cold blood during the War of 1812. (The men had been deserters who were legally executed after sentence by a court-martial.) And they called his wife a bigamist. Jackson had married his beloved Rachel at a time when the pair incorrectly believed her first husband had divorced her. (When Jackson's wife first read of the accusations against her shortly after the election, she collapsed, and a few weeks later, died; not without reason, Jackson blamed his opponents for her death.)

Jackson's victory was decisive, but sectional. He won 56 percent of the popular vote and an electoral majority of 178 votes to 83. Adams swept virtually all of New England and *Jackson Triumphant* showed significant strength in the mid-Atlantic region. Nevertheless, the Jacksonians considered their victory as complete and as important as Jefferson's in 1800. Once again, the forces of privilege had been driven from Washington. Once again, a champion of democracy would occupy the White House and restore liberty to the people and to the economy. America had entered, some Jacksonians claimed, a new era of democracy, the "era of the common man."

CONCLUSION

In the aftermath of the War of 1812, a vigorous nationalism came increasingly to characterize the political and popular culture of the United States. In all regions of the country, white men and women celebrated the achievements of the early leaders of the republic, the genius of the Constitution, and the success of the nation in withstanding serious challenges both from without and within. Party divisions faded to the point that James Monroe, the fifth president, won reelection in 1820 without opposition.

But the broad nationalism of the so-called era of good feelings disguised some deep divisions within the United States. Indeed, the character of American nationalism differed substantially from one region, and one group, to another. Battles continued between those who favored a strong central government committed to advancing the economic development of the nation and those who wanted a decentralization of power to open opportunity to more people. Battles continued as well over the role of slavery in American life—and in particular over the place of slavery in the new western territories that the United States was rapidly populating (and wresting from the tribes). The Missouri Compromise of 1820 postponed the day of reckoning on that issue—but only for a time, as Andrew Jackson would discover soon after becoming president in 1829.

FOR FURTHER REFERENCE

Frederick Jackson Turner, *The Frontier in American History* (1920), is the classic statement of American exceptionalism. Turner argued that the western frontier endowed the United States with a distinctive, individualist, and democratic national character. John Mack Faragher, *Women and Men on the Overland Trail* (1979) was an early and influential book in the "new western history" that challenged Turner; his *Sugar Creek* (1987) portrays the society of the Old Northwest in the early nineteenth century.

Robert V. Remini, *Andrew Jackson and the Course of American Empire: 1767–1821* (1977) emphasizes Andrew Jackson's importance in American territorial expansion in the South prior to 1821 and in the development of American nationalism. Morton J. Horwitz, *The Transformation of American Law, 1780–1865* (1977), an important work in American legal history, connects changes in the law to changes in the American economy. Ernest R. May, *The Making of the Monroe Doctrine* (1975) presents the history of a leading principle of American foreign policy.

For quizzes, Internet resources, references to additional books and films, and more, consult this book's Online Learning Center at www.mhhe.com/brinkley11.

by which members of the state senate represented property rather than simply people. But Daniel Webster, one of the conservative delegates, opposed democratic changes on the grounds that "power naturally and necessarily follows property" and that "property as such should have its weight and influence in political arrangement." Webster and the rest of the conservatives could not prevent the reform of the rules for representation in the state senate; nor could they prevent elimination of the property requirement for voting. But, to the dismay of the radicals, the new constitution required that every voter be a taxpayer and that the governor be the owner of considerable real estate.

More often, however, the forces of democratization prevailed in the states. In the New York convention of 1821, for example, conservatives led by James Kent insisted that a taxpaying requirement for suffrage was not enough and that, at least in the election of state senators, the property qualification should survive. Kent argued that society "is an association for the protection of property as well as of life" and that "the individual who contributes only one cent to the common stock ought not to have the same power and influence in directing the property concerns of the partnership as he who contributes his thousands." But reformers, citing the Declaration of Independence, maintained that life, liberty, and the pursuit of happiness, not property, were the main concerns of society and government. The property qualification was abolished.

The wave of state reforms was generally peaceful, but in Rhode Island democratization efforts created considerable instability. The Rhode Island constitution (which was still basically the old colonial charter) barred more than half the adult males of the state from voting. The conservative legislature, chosen by this restricted electorate, consistently blocked all efforts at reform. In 1840, the lawyer and activist Thomas L. Dorr and a group of his followers formed a "People's party," held a convention, drafted a new constitution, and submitted it to a popular vote. It was overwhelmingly approved. The existing legislature, however, refused to accept the Dorr document and submitted

The Dorr Rebellion

a new constitution of its own to the voters. It was narrowly defeated. The Dorrites, in the meantime, had begun to set up a new government, under their own constitution, with Dorr as governor; and so, in 1842, two governments were claiming legitimacy in Rhode Island. The old state government proclaimed that Dorr and his followers were rebels and began to imprison them. Meanwhile, the Dorrites made a brief and ineffectual effort to capture the state arsenal. The Dorr Rebellion, as it was known, quickly failed. Dorr himself surrendered and was briefly imprisoned. But the episode helped pressure the old guard to draft a new constitution, which greatly expanded the suffrage.

The democratization process was far from complete. In much of the South, election laws continued to favor the planters and politicians of the older counties and to limit the influence of more newly settled western areas. Slaves, of course, were disenfranchised by definition; they were

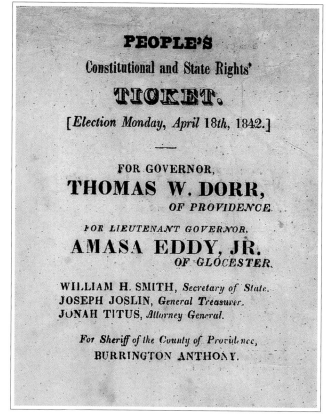

THE DORR REBELLION The democratic sentiments that swept much of the nation in the 1830s and 1840s produced, among many other things, the Dorr Rebellion (as its opponents termed it) in Rhode Island. Thomas Dorr was one of many Rhode Islanders who denounced the state's constitution, which limited voting rights to a small group of property owners known as "freeholders." The dissidents crafted a new constitution and submitted it to a vote; a majority of the state's citizens approved it. But the legislature refused to acknowledge its legitimacy, and the result was two separate elections in 1842 for the same state offices. Dorr ran for governor under the new constitution, and was elected by a majority of the people. This "ticket" was what his supporters placed in ballot boxes as they cast their votes. Another candidate, Samuel King, ran under the old constitution, and was elected by the freeholders. Both men were inaugurated, and not until President Tyler threatened federal intervention on behalf of King did the Dorr movement crumble. A year later, however, the state ratified a new constitution extending the franchise. *(Courtesy The Rhode Island Historical Society, RHi X5 304)*

not considered citizens and were believed to have no legal or political rights. Free blacks could not vote anywhere in the South and hardly anywhere in the North. Pennsylvania, in fact, amended its state constitution in 1838 to strip blacks of the right to vote they had previously enjoyed. In no state could women vote. Nowhere was the ballot secret, and often voters had to cast a spoken vote rather than a written one, which meant that political bosses could, and often did, bribe and intimidate them.

Despite the persisting limitations, however, the number of voters increased far more rapidly than did the population as a whole. Indeed, one of the most striking political   *Democratic Reforms* trends of the early nineteenth century was the change in

To many Americans in the 1820s and 1830s, Andrew Jackson was a champion of democracy, a symbol of a spirit of anti-elitism and egalitarianism that was sweeping American life. In the twentieth century, however, historians have disagreed sharply not only in their assessments of Jackson himself, but in their portrayal of American society in his era.

The "progressive" historians of the early twentieth century tended to see the politics of Jackson and his supporters as a forerunner of their own generation's battles against economic privilege and political corruption. Frederick Jackson Turner encouraged scholars to see Jacksonianism as the product of the democratic West: a protest by the people of the frontier against the conservative aristocracy of the East, which they believed restricted their own freedom and opportunity. Jackson represented those who wanted to make government responsive to the will of the people rather than to the power of special interests. The culmination of this progressive interpretation of Jacksonianism was the publication in 1945 of Arthur M. Schlesinger, Jr.'s *The Age of Jackson*. Schlesinger was less interested in the

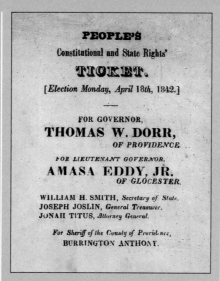

(Courtesy The Rhode Island Historical Society, RHi X5 304)

regional basis of Jacksonianism than Turner's disciples had been. He saw support for Jackson not just among western farmers, but also among urban laborers in the East. Jacksonian democracy, he argued, was the effort "to control the power of the capitalist groups, mainly Eastern, for the benefit of non-capitalist groups, farmers and laboring men, East, West, and South." He portrayed Jacksonianism as an early version of mod-

ern reform efforts (in the progressive era and the New Deal) to "restrain the power of the business community."

Richard Hofstadter, in an influential 1948 essay in *The American Political Tradition*, sharply disagreed. He argued that Jackson was the spokesman of rising entrepreneurs—aspiring businessmen who saw the road to opportunity blocked by the monopolistic power of eastern aristocrats. The Jacksonians opposed special privileges only to the extent those privileges blocked their own road to success. They were less sympathetic to the aspirations of those below them. Similarly, Bray Hammond, writing in 1957, argued that the Jacksonian cause was "one of enterpriser against capitalist," of rising elites against entrenched ones. Other historians, exploring the ideological origins of the movement saw Jacksonianism less as a democratic reform movement than as a nostalgic effort to restore a lost (and largely imagined) past. Marvin Meyer's *The Jacksonian Persuasion* (1957) argued that Jackson and his followers looked with misgivings on the new industrial society emerging around them and yearned instead for a restoration of the agrarian, republican virtues of an earlier time.

---

the method of choosing presidential electors and the dramatic increase in popular participation in the process. In 1800, the legislature had chosen the presidential electors in ten of the states, and the people in only six. By 1828, electors were chosen by popular vote in every state but South Carolina. In the presidential election of 1824, fewer than 27 percent of adult white males had voted. In the election of 1828, the figure rose to 58 percent and in 1840 to 80 percent.

The Legitimization of Party

The high level of voter participation was only partly the result of an expanded electorate. It was also the result of a growing interest in politics and a strengthening of party organization and, perhaps equally important, party loyalty. Although party competition was part of American politics almost from the beginning of the republic, acceptance of the idea of party was not. For more than thirty years, most Americans who had opinions about the

nature of government considered parties evils to be avoided and thought the nation should seek a broad consensus in which permanent factional lines would not exist. But in the 1820s and 1830s, those assumptions gave way to a new view: that permanent, institutionalized parties were a desirable part of the political process, that indeed they were essential to democracy.

The elevation of the idea of party occurred first at the state level, most prominently in New York. There Martin Van Buren led a dissident political faction (known as the "Bucktails" or the "Albany Regency"). In the years after the War of 1812, this group began to challenge the established political leadership—led by the aristocratic governor, De Witt Clinton—that had dominated the state for years. Factional rivalries were not new, of course. But the way Van Buren and his followers posed their challenge was new. Refuting the traditional view of a political party as undemocratic, they argued that only an institutionalized party, based in the populace at large, could ensure genuine democracy. The alternative was the sort of closed

Historians of the 1960s began examining Jacksonianism in entirely new ways: looking less at Jackson himself, less at the rhetoric and ideas of his supporters, and more at the nature of American society in the early nineteenth century. Lee Benson's *The Concept of Jacksonian Democracy* (1961)—a pathbreaking work of quantitative history—emphasized the role of religion and ethnicity in determining political divisions in the 1830s. If there was an egalitarian spirit alive in America in those years, it extended well beyond the Democratic Party and the followers of Jackson. Edward Pessen's *Jacksonian America* (1969) revealed that the democratic rhetoric of the age disguised the reality of an increasingly stratified society, in which inequality was growing more, not less, severe. Richard McCormick (1963) and Glyndon Van Deusen (1963) similarly emphasized the pragmatism of Jackson and the Democrats and deemphasized clear ideological and partisan divisions.

Scholars in more recent years have also paid relatively little attention to Jackson and the Democratic Party and instead have focused on a series of broad social changes occurring in the early and mid-nineteenth century which some have called a "market revolution." Those changes had profound effects on class relations, and the political battles of the era reflected only a part of their impact. Sean Wilentz, in *Chants Democratic* (1984), identified the rise in the 1820s of a powerful class identity among workers in New York, who were attracted less to Jackson himself than to the idea that power in a republic should be widely dispersed. John Ashworth, in *"Agrarians"* and *"Aristocrats"* (1983), and Harry Watson, in *Liberty and Power* (1990), have also seen party politics as a reflection of much larger social changes. The party system was an imperfect reflection of a struggle between people committed to unrestricted opportunities for all white men and those committed to advancing the goals of capitalists, in part through government action.

Recent scholarship may have turned the focus of discussion away from Jackson and the Democratic Party and toward the larger society. But its success in revealing inequality and oppression in antebellum America has produced some withering reassessments of Jackson himself. In *Fathers and Children: Andrew Jackson and the Subjugation of the American Indian* (1975), Michael Rogin portrays Jackson as a man obsessed with escaping from the imposing shadow of the revolutionary generation. He would lead a new American revolution, not against British tyranny but against those who challenged the ability of white men to control the continent. He displayed special savagery toward American Indians, whom he pursued, Rogin argued, with an almost pathological violence and intensity. Alexander Saxton, in *The Rise and Fall of the White Republic* (1990), likewise points to the contradiction between the image of the age of Jackson as a time of expanding democracy and the reality of constricted rights for women, blacks, and Indians. The Democratic Party, he argues, was committed above all to defending slavery and white supremacy.

But the portrayal of Jackson as a champion of the common man has not vanished from scholarly life. The leading Jackson biographer of the postwar era, Robert V. Remini, has noted the flaws in Jackson's concept of democracy; but within the context of his time, Remini claims, Jackson was a genuine "man of the people."

---

elite that Clinton had created. In the new kind of party the Bucktails proposed, ideological commitments would be less important than loyalty to the party itself. Preservation of the party as an institution—through the use of favors, rewards, and patronage—would be the principal goal of the leadership. Above all, for a party to survive, it must have a permanent opposition. Competing parties would give each political faction a sense of purpose; they would force politicians to remain continually attuned to the will of the people; and they would check and balance each other in much the same way that the different branches of government checked and balanced one another.

By the late 1820s, this new idea of party was spreading beyond New York. The election of Jackson in 1828, the result of a popular movement that seemed to stand apart from the usual political elites, seemed further to legitimize the idea of party as a popular, democratic institution. "Parties of some sort must exist," said a New York newspaper. "'Tis in *The Second Party System* | the nature and genius of our government." Finally, in the 1830s, a fully formed two-party system began to operate at the national level, with each party committed to its own existence as an institution and willing to accept the legitimacy of its opposition. The anti-Jackson forces began to call themselves Whigs. Jackson's followers called themselves Democrats (no longer Democratic Republicans), thus giving a permanent name to what is now the nation's oldest political party.

"President of the Common Man"

Unlike Thomas Jefferson, Jackson was no democratic philosopher. The Democratic Party, much less than Jefferson's Republicans, embraced no clear or uniform ideological position. But Jackson himself did embrace a distinct, if simple, theory of democracy. It should offer "equal protection and equal benefits" to all its white male citizens and favor no region or class over another. In practice, that meant an assault on what Jackson and his associates considered the citadels of the eastern aristocracy and an effort to extend opportunities to the rising classes of the West and the South. It also meant a firm commitment to the

ELECTION SCENE Frequent and often boisterous campaign rallies were characteristic of electoral politics in the 1840s, when party loyalties were high and political passions intense—as this 1845 drawing by Alfred Jacob Miller of a rally in Catonsville, Maryland, suggests. *(M. and M. Karolik Collection of American Watercolors and Drawings, 1800–1875. Museum of Fine Arts, Boston.)*

continuing subjugation of African Americans and Indians (and, although for different reasons, women), for the Jacksonians believed that only by keeping these "dangerous" elements from the body politic could the white-male democracy they valued be preserved.

Jackson's first targets were the entrenched officeholders in the federal government, many of whom had been in place for a generation or more. "Office is considered as a species of property," Jackson told Congress in a bitter denunciation of the "class" of permanent officeholders, "and government rather as a means of promoting individual interests than as an instrument created solely for the service of the people." Official duties, he believed, could be made "so plain and simple that men of intelligence may readily qualify themselves for their performance." Offices belonged to the people, he argued, not to the entrenched officeholders. Or, as one of his henchmen, William L. Marcy of New York, more cynically put it, "To the victors belong the spoils."

In the end, Jackson removed a total of no more than one-fifth of the federal officeholders

The Spoils System

during his eight years in office, many of them less for partisan reasons than because they had misused government funds or engaged in other corruption. Proportionally, Jackson dismissed no more than jobholders than Jefferson had dismissed during his presidency. But by embracing the philosophy of the "spoils system," a system already well entrenched in a number of state governments, the Jackson administration helped make the right of elected officials to appoint their own followers to public office an established feature of American politics.

Jackson's supporters also worked to transform the process by which presidential candidates won their party's nominations. They had long resented the congressional caucus, a process they believed worked to restrict access to the office to those favored by entrenched elites and a process Jackson himself had avoided in 1828. In 1832, the president's followers staged a national party convention to renominate him for the presidency—one year after the Anti-Masons (see p. 251) became the first party to hold such a meeting. In later generations, some would see the party convention as a source of corruption and political exclusivity. But those who created it in the 1830s considered it a great triumph for democracy. Through the convention, they believed, power would arise directly from the people, not from aristocratic political institutions such as the caucus.

The spoils system and the political convention did serve to limit the power of two entrenched elites—permanent officeholders and the exclusive party caucus. Yet neither really transferred power to the peo-

Limited Nature of Democratic Reform

ple. Appointments to office almost always went to prominent political allies of the president and his associates. Delegates to national conventions were less often common men than members of local party organizations. Political opportunity within the party was expanding, but much less so than Jacksonian rhetoric suggested.

"OUR FEDERAL UNION"

Jackson's commitment to extending power beyond entrenched elites led him to want to reduce the functions of the federal government. A concentration of power in Washington would, he believed, restrict opportunity to people with political connections. But Jackson also believed in forceful presidential leadership and was strongly committed to the preservation of the Union. Thus at the same time that Jackson was promoting an economic program to reduce the power of the national government, he was asserting the supremacy of the Union in the face of a potent challenge. For no sooner had he entered office than his own vice president—John C. Calhoun—began to champion a controversial (and, in Jackson's view, dangerous) constitutional theory: nullification.

Calhoun and Nullification

Calhoun was forty-six years old in 1828, with a distinguished past and an apparently promising future. But the smoldering issue of the tariff created a dilemma for him. Once he had been an outspoken protectionist and had strongly supported the tariff of 1816. But by the late 1820s, many South Carolinians had come to believe that the "tariff of abominations" was responsible for the stagnation of

their state's economy—even though the stagnation was largely a result of the exhaustion of South Carolina's farmland, which could no longer compete effectively with the newly opened and fertile lands of the Southwest. Some exasperated Carolinians were ready to consider a drastic remedy—secession.

Calhoun's future political hopes rested on how he met this challenge in his home state. He did so by developing a theory that he believed offered a *Calhoun's Theory of Nullification* more moderate alternative to secession: the theory of nullification. Drawing from the ideas of Madison and Jefferson and their Virginia and Kentucky Resolutions of 1798–1799 and citing the Tenth Amendment to the Constitution, Calhoun argued that since the federal government was a creation of the states, the states—not the courts or Congress—were the final arbiters of the constitutionality of federal laws. If a state concluded that Congress had passed an unconstitutional law, then it could hold a special convention and declare the federal law null and void within the state. The nullification doctrine—and the idea of using it to nullify the 1828 tariff—quickly attracted broad support in South Carolina. But it did nothing to help Calhoun's standing within the new administration, in part because he had a powerful rival in Martin Van Buren.

The Rise of Van Buren

Van Buren was about the same age as Calhoun and equally ambitious. He had won election to the governorship of *Martin Van Buren* New York in 1828 and then resigned in 1829 when Jackson appointed him secretary of state. Alone among the figures in the Jackson administration, Van Buren soon established himself as a member both of the official cabinet and of the president's unofficial circle of political allies, known as the "Kitchen Cabinet" (which included such Democratic newspaper editors as Isaac Hill of New Hampshire and Amos Kendall and Francis P. Blair of Kentucky). Van Buren's influence with the president was unmatched and grew stronger still as a result of a quarrel over etiquette that drove a wedge between the president and Calhoun.

Peggy O'Neale was the attractive daughter of a Washington tavern keeper with whom both Andrew Jackson and his friend John H. Eaton had taken lodgings while serving as senators from Tennessee. O'Neale was married, but rumors circulated in Washington in the mid-1820s that she and Senator Eaton were having an affair. O'Neale's husband died in 1828, and she and Eaton were soon married. A few weeks later, Jackson named Eaton secretary of war and thus made the new Mrs. Eaton a cabinet wife. The rest of the administration wives, led by Mrs. Calhoun, refused to receive her. Jackson (remembering the effects of public slander directed against his own

JOHN C. CALHOUN This photograph, by Matthew Brady, captured Calhoun toward the end of his life, when he was torn between his real commitment to the ideals of the Union and his equally fervent commitment to the interests of the South. The younger generation of southern leaders, who would dominate the politics of the region in the 1850s, were less idealistic and more purely sectional in their views. *(Library of Congress)*

MARTIN VAN BUREN As leader of the so-called Albany Regency in New York in the 1820s, Van Buren helped create one of the first modern party organizations in the United States. Later, as Andrew Jackson's secretary of state and (after 1832) vice president, he helped bring party politics to the national level. So it was ironic that in 1840, when he ran for reelection to the presidency, he lost to William Henry Harrison, whose Whig Party made effective use of many of the techniques of mass politics that Van Buren himself had pioneered. *(Library of Congress)*

THE WEBSTER-HAYNE DEBATE This painting by G. P. A. Healy portrays Daniel Webster's famous reply to Senator Robert Y. Hayne of South Carolina during their dramatic 1830 debate. Until 1860, it hung in the Senate chamber where the debate took place. Today it is in Faneuil Hall in Boston. Webster challenged Hayne's contention that the Union was simply a voluntary association of independent states. The people, not the states, had made the Constitution, he argued, and no state could reject the Union. Rejecting the South's position, which he described as "Liberty first and Union afterwards," Webster called dramatically for "Liberty and Union, now and forever, one and inseparable." Webster's speech was widely distributed throughout the North, and schoolchildren memorized its most famous passages for generations. *(Courtesy Boston Art Commission 1998)*

late wife) was furious and demanded that the members of the cabinet accept her into their social world. Calhoun, under pressure from his wife, refused. Van Buren, a widower, befriended the Eatons and thus ingratiated himself with Jackson. By 1831, partly as a result of the Peggy Eaton affair, Jackson had chosen Van Buren to succeed him in the White House, apparently ending Calhoun's dreams of the presidency.

The Webster-Hayne Debate

In January 1830, as the controversy over nullification grew more intense, a great debate occurred in the United States Senate over another sectional controversy. In the midst of a routine debate over federal policy toward western lands, a senator from Connecticut suggested that all land sales and surveys be temporarily discontinued. Robert Y. Hayne, a young senator from South Carolina, responded, charging that slowing down the growth of the West was a way for the East to retain its political and economic power. Although he had no real interest in western lands, he hoped his stance would attract support from westerners in Congress for South Carolina's drive to lower the tariff. Both the South and the West, he argued, were victims of the tyranny of the Northeast. He hinted that the two regions might combine to defend themselves against that tyranny.

Daniel Webster, now a senator from Massachusetts and a nationalistic Whig, answered Hayne the next day. He attacked Hayne, and through him Calhoun, for what he considered their challenge *States' Rights versus National Power* to the integrity of the Union—in effect, challenging Hayne to a debate not on public lands and the tariff but on the issue of states' rights versus national power. Hayne, coached by Calhoun, responded with a defense of the theory of nullification. Webster then spent two full afternoons delivering what became known as his "Second Reply to Hayne," a speech that northerners quoted and revered for years to come. He concluded with the ringing appeal: "Liberty and Union, now and forever, one and inseparable!"

CHARLESTON, 1831 The little-known South Carolina artist S. Bernard painted this view of Charleston's East Battery in 1831. Then, as now, residents and vistors liked to stroll along the battery and watch the activity in the city's busy harbor. But Charleston in the 1830s was a less important commercial center than it had been a few decades earlier. By then, overseas traders were increasingly avoiding southern ports and doing more and more business in New York. *(Yale University Art Gallery)*

Both sides now waited to hear what President Jackson thought of the argument. The answer became clear at the annual Democratic Party banquet in honor of Thomas Jefferson. After dinner, guests delivered a series of toasts. The president arrived with a written text in which he had underscored certain words: "Our Federal Union—It must be preserved." While he spoke, he looked directly at Calhoun. The diminutive Van Buren, who stood on his chair to see better, thought he saw Calhoun's hand shake and a trickle of wine run down his glass as he responded to the president's toast with his own: "The Union, next to our liberty most dear." The two most important figures in government had drawn sharp lines between themselves.

The Nullification Crisis

In 1832, finally, the controversy over nullification produced a crisis when South Carolinians responded angrily to a congressional tariff bill that offered them no relief from the 1828 "tariff of abominations." Almost immediately, the legislature summoned a state convention, which voted to nullify the tariffs of 1828 and 1832 and to forbid the collection of duties within the state. At the same time, South Carolina elected Hayne to serve as governor and Calhoun (who resigned as vice president) to replace Hayne as senator.

Jackson insisted that nullification was treason and that those implementing it were traitors. He strengthened the federal forts in South Carolina and ordered a warship and several revenue ships to Charleston. When Congress convened early in 1833, Jackson proposed a force bill authorizing the president to use the military to see that acts of Congress were obeyed. Violence seemed a real possibility.

Calhoun faced a predicament as he took his place in the Senate. Not a single state had come to South Carolina's support. Even South Carolina itself was divided and could not hope to prevail in a showdown with the federal government. But the timely intervention of Henry Clay, newly elected to the Senate, averted a crisis. Clay devised a compromise by which the tariff would be lowered gradually so that, by 1842, it would reach approximately the same level as in 1816. The compromise and the force bill were passed on the same day, March 1, 1833. Jackson signed them both. In South Carolina, the convention reassembled and repealed its nullification of the tariffs. But unwilling to allow Congress to have the last word, the convention nullified the force act—a purely symbolic act, since the tariff toward which the force act was directed had already been repealed. Calhoun and his followers claimed a victory for nullification, which had, they insisted, forced the revision of the

Compromise

tariff. But the episode taught Calhoun and his allies that no state could defy the federal government alone.

THE REMOVAL OF THE INDIANS

There had never been any doubt about Andrew Jackson's attitude toward the Indian tribes that continued to live in the eastern states and territories of the United States. He wanted them to move west, beyond the Mississippi, out of the way of expanding white settlement. Jackson's antipathy toward the Native Americans had a special intensity because of his own earlier experiences leading military campaigns against tribes along the Southern border. But in most respects, his views were little different from those of most other white Americans.

White Attitudes Toward the Tribes

In the eighteenth century, many white Americans had considered the Indians "noble savages," peoples without real civilization but with an inherent dignity that made civilization possible among them. By the first decades of the nineteenth century, this vaguely paternalistic attitude (the attitude of Thomas Jefferson, among others) was giving way to a new and more hostile one, particularly among the whites in the western states and territories whom Jackson came to represent. Such whites were coming to view Native Americans simply as "savages," not only uncivilized but uncivilizable. That was one reason for the commitment to Indian removal: the belief that whites should not be expected to live in close proximity to the "savage" Indians, that Indian cultures and societies were unworthy of respect.

Changing Attitudes Toward the Indians

White westerners favored removal as well because they feared that continued contact between the expanding white settlements and the Indians would produce endless conflict and violence. Most of all, however, they favored Indian removal because of their own insatiable desire for territory. The tribes possessed valuable land in the path of expanding white settlement. Whites wanted it.

Legally, only the federal government had authority to negotiate with the Indians over land, a result of Supreme Court decisions that established the tribes as, in effect, "nations within the nation." The tribal nations that the Court identified were not, however, securely rooted in Native American history. The large tribal aggregations with which white Americans dealt were, in fact, relatively new entities. Most Indians were accustomed to thinking in much more local terms. They created these larger tribes when they realized they would need some collective strength to deal with whites; but as new and untested political entities, the tribes were often weak and divided. The Marshall Court had seemed to acknowledge this in declaring the tribes not only sovereign nations, but also dependent ones, for whom the federal government must take considerable responsibility. Through most of the nineteenth century, the government interpreted that responsibility as finding ways to move the Native Americans out of the way of expanding white settlement.

The Black Hawk War

The federal government had already taken substantial strides toward removing Native Americans from the East by the time Jackson entered the White House. But substantial tribal enclaves remained. In the Old Northwest, the long process of expelling the woodland Indians culminated in a last battle in 1831–1832, between white settlers in Illinois and an alliance of Sauk (or Sac) and Fox Indians under the fabled and now aged warrior Black Hawk. An earlier treaty had ceded tribal lands in Illinois to the United States; but Black Hawk and his followers refused to recognize the legality of the agreement, which a rival tribal faction had signed. Hungry and resentful, a thousand of them crossed the river and reoccupied vacant lands in Illinois. White settlers in the region feared that the resettlement was the beginning of a substantial invasion, and they assembled the Illinois state militia and federal troops to repel the "invaders."

The Black Hawk War, as it became known, was notable chiefly for the viciousness of the white military efforts. White leaders in western Illinois vowed to exterminate the "bandit collection of Indians"

Sauk and Fox Indians Defeated

BLACK HAWK AND WHIRLING THUNDER After his defeat by white settlers in Illinois in 1832, the famed Sauk warrior Black Hawk and his son, Whirling Thunder, were captured and sent on a tour by Andrew Jackson, displayed to the public as trophies of war. They showed such dignity through the ordeal that much of the white public quickly began to sympathize with them. This portrait, by John Wesley Jarvis, was painted on the tour's final stop, in New York City. Black Hawk wears the European-style suit, while Whirling Thunder wears native costume to emphasize his commitment to his tribal roots. Soon thereafter, Black Hawk returned to his tribe, wrote a celebrated autobiography, and died in 1838. *(Bettman/Corbis)*

and attacked them even when Black Hawk attempted to surrender. The Sauks and Foxes, defeated and starving, retreated across the Mississippi into Iowa. White troops (and some bands of Sioux whom they encouraged to join the chase) pursued them as they fled and slaughtered most of them. United States troops captured Black Hawk himself and sent him on a tour of the East, where Andrew Jackson was one of many curious whites who arranged to meet him. (Abraham Lincoln served as a captain of the militia, but saw no action, in the Black Hawk War; Jefferson Davis was a lieutenant in the regular army.)

The "Five Civilized Tribes"

More troubling to the government in the 1830s were the

Agrarian Tribes of the South

tribes remaining in the South. In western Georgia, Alabama, Mississippi, and Florida lived what were known as the "Five Civilized Tribes"—the Cherokee, Creek, Seminole, Chickasaw, and Choctaw—most of whom had established settled agricultural societies with successful economies. The Cherokees in Georgia had formed a particularly stable and sophisticated culture, with their own written language and a formal constitution (adopted in 1827) that created an independent Cherokee Nation. They were more closely tied to their lands than many of the more nomadic tribes to the north.

Even some whites argued that the Cherokees, unlike other tribes, should be allowed to retain their eastern lands, since they had become such a "civilized" society and had, under pressure from missionaries and government agents, given up many of their traditional ways. Cherokee men had once been chiefly hunters and had left farming mainly to women. By now the men had given up most of their hunting and (like most white men) took over the farming themselves; Cherokee women, also like their white counterparts, restricted themselves largely to domestic tasks.

The federal government, to which the Constitution had

Removal Act

delegated the power to negotiate with the tribes, had worked steadily through the first decades of the nineteenth century to negotiate treaties with the southern Indians that would remove them to the West and open their lands for white settlement. But the negotiating process often did not proceed fast enough to satisfy the region's whites. The State of Georgia's independent effort to dislodge the Creeks, over the objection of President Adams, was one example of this impatience. That same impatience became evident early in Jackson's administration, when the legislatures in Georgia, Alabama, and Mississippi began passing laws to regulate the tribes remaining in their states. They received assistance in these efforts from Congress, which in 1830 passed the Removal Act (with Jackson's approval), which appropriated money to finance federal negotiations with

the southern tribes aimed at relocating them to the West. The president quickly dispatched federal officials to negotiate nearly a hundred new treaties with the remaining tribes. Thus, the southern tribes faced a combination of pressures from both the state and federal governments. Most tribes were too weak to resist, and they ceded their lands in return for only token payments. Some, however, balked.

In Georgia, the Cherokees tried to stop the white encroachments by appealing to the Supreme Court. The Court's decisions in *Cherokee Nation* v. *Georgia,* and *Worcester* v. *Georgia* in 1831 and 1832 (see p. 229) seemed at least partially to vindicate the tribe. But Jackson's longtime hostility toward Native Americans and his longtime commitment to their removal left him with little sympathy for the Cherokees and little patience with the Court. He was eager to retain the support of white southerners and westerners in the increasingly bitter partisan battles in which his administration was becoming engaged. That was one reason why the president had vigorously supported (and even actively encouraged) Georgia's efforts to remove the Cherokees before the Court decision. His reaction to Marshall's rulings reflected his belief that the justices were using the issue to express their hostility to the larger aims of his presidency. When the chief justice announced the decision in *Worcester* v. *Georgia,* Jackson reportedly responded with contempt. "John Marshall has made his decision," he was reported to have said. "Now let him enforce it." The decision was not enforced.

In 1835, the federal government extracted a treaty from a minority faction of the

Cherokee Resistance

Cherokees, none of them a chosen representative of the Cherokee Nation. The treaty ceded the tribe's land to Georgia in return for $5 million and a reservation west of the Mississippi. The great majority of the 17,000 Cherokees did not recognize the treaty as legitimate and refused to leave their homes. But Jackson would not be thwarted. He sent an army of 7,000 under General Winfield Scott to round them up and drive them westward at bayonet point.

Trails of Tears

About 1,000 Cherokee fled across the state line to North Carolina, where the federal government eventually provided a small reservation for them in the Smoky Mountains, which survives today. But most of the rest made the long, forced trek to "Indian Territory" (which later became Oklahoma) beginning in the winter of 1838. Along the way, a Kentuckian observed: "Even aged females, apparently nearly ready to drop in the grave, were travelling with heavy burdens attached to their backs, sometimes on frozen ground and sometimes on muddy streets, with no covering for their feet."

Indian Removal

Thousands, perhaps an eighth or more of the emigrés, perished before or soon after reaching their unwanted destination. In the harsh new reservations in which they were now forced to live, the survivors never forgot the hard journey. They called their route "The Trail Where They Cried," the Trail of Tears. Jackson claimed that the "remnant of that ill-fated race" was now "beyond the reach of injury or oppression," apparently trying to convince himself or others that he had supported removal as a way to protect the tribes.

The Cherokees were not alone in experiencing the hardships of the Trail of Tears. Between 1830 and 1838, virtually all the "Five Civilized Tribes" were expelled from the southern states and forced to relocate in the new Indian Territory, which Congress had officially created by the Indian Intercourse Act of 1834. The Choctaws of Mississippi and western Alabama were the first to make

the trek, beginning in 1830. The army moved out the Creeks of eastern Alabama and western Georgia in 1836. The Chickasaw in northern Mississippi began the long march westward a year later, and the Cherokees, finally, a year after that. The government thought the Indian Territory was safely distant from existing white settlements and consisted of land that most whites considered undesirable. It had the additional advantage, the government believed, of being on the eastern edge of what earlier white explorers had christened the "Great American Desert," land unfit for habitation. It seemed unlikely that whites would ever seek to settle along the western borders of the Indian Territory; and thus the prospect of whites surrounding the reservation and producing further conflict seemed remote.

Only the Seminoles in Florida managed to resist the pressures to relocate, and even their success was limited. Like other tribes, the Seminoles had agreed under pressure

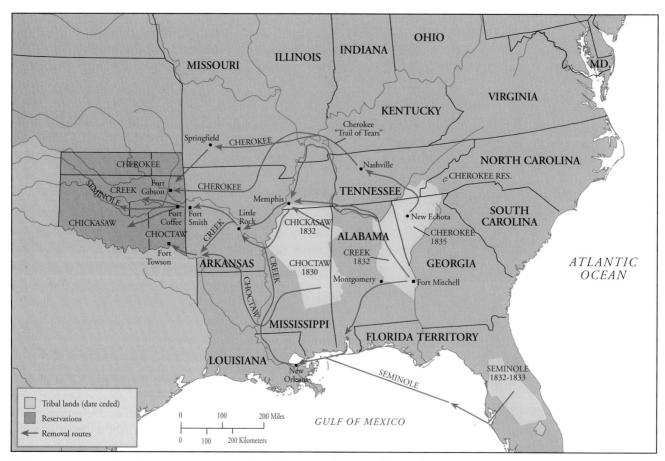

THE EXPULSION OF THE TRIBES, 1830–1835 Andrew Jackson was famous well before he became president for his military exploits against the tribes. Once in the White House, he ensured that few Indians would remain in the southern states of the nation, now that white settlement was increasing there. The result was a series of dramatic "removals" of Indian tribes out of their traditional lands and into new territories west of the Mississippi—mostly in Oklahoma. Note the very long distance many of these tribes had to travel. ◆ *Why was the route of the Cherokees, shown in the upper portion of the map, known as the "Trail of Tears"?*

 For an interactive version of this map go to ww.mhhe.com/brinkley11ch8maps

AN INTER-TRIBAL NEGOTIATION
The devastating policies of the Jackson administration—which forced thousands of Native Americans to relocate from their lands—produced a wide range of desperate responses among the Indians themselves. Some tried to ally themselves with the American government, among them a group of Iroquois shown in this painting in "white man's clothes," negotiating on Washington's behalf with Shawnee, Miami, and other western tribes. Red Jacket, the Iroquois leader shown in the center, made little progress. The western Indians jeered at him for the failure of the Iroquois to defend their lands, and Red Jacket left humiliated. *(Smithsonian American Art Museum, Washington, DC/Art Resource, NY)*

to a settlement (the 1832–1833 treaties of Payne's Landing), by which they ceded their lands to the government and agreed to move to Indian Territory within three years. Most did move west, but a substantial minority, under the leadership of the chieftain Osceola, refused to leave and staged an uprising beginning in 1835 to defend their lands. (Joining the Indians in their struggle was a group of runaway black slaves who had been living with *The Seminole War* the tribe.) The Seminole War dragged on for years. Jackson sent troops to Florida, but the Seminoles with their African-American associates were masters of guerrilla warfare in the jungly Everglades. Even after Osceola had been treacherously captured by white troops while under a flag of truce and had died in prison; even after white troops had engaged in a systematic campaign of extermination against the resisting Indians and their black allies; even after 1,500 white soldiers had died and the federal government had spent $20 million on the struggle—even then, followers of Osceola remained in Florida. Finally, in 1842, the government abandoned the war. By then, many of the Seminoles had been either killed or forced westward. But the relocation of the Seminoles, unlike the relocation of most of the other tribes, was never complete.

The Meaning of Removal

By the end of the 1830s, virtually all the important Indian societies east of the Mississippi (with such exceptions as the Seminoles and a few Cherokee in the South and some tribal enclaves in northern Michigan and Wisconsin) had been removed to the West. The tribes had ceded over 100 million acres of eastern land to the federal government; they had received in return about $68 million and 32 million acres in the far less hospitable lands west of the Mississippi between the Missouri and Red Rivers. There they lived, divided by tribe into a series of carefully defined reservations, in a territory surrounded by a string of United States forts to keep them in (and to keep most whites out), in a region whose climate and topography bore little relation to anything they had known before. Eventually, even this forlorn enclave would face incursions from white civilization.

What were the alternatives to the removal of the eastern Indians? There was probably never any realistic possibility that the government could stop white expansion westward. White people had already been penetrating the West for nearly two centuries, and such penetrations were certain to continue. But did that expansion really require removal?

There were, in theory at least, several alternatives to the brutal removal policy. There *Alternatives to Removal* were many examples in the West of white settlers and native tribes living side by side and creating a shared (if not necessarily equal) world. In the pueblos of New Mexico, in the fur trading posts of the Pacific Northwest, in parts of Texas and California, settlers from Mexico, Canada, and the United States had created societies in which Indians and whites were in intimate contact with each other. Even during the famous Lewis and Clark expedition, white explorers had lived with western Indians on terms of such intimacy that many of them contracted venereal disease from Indian sexual partners. Sometimes these close contacts between whites and Indians were beneficial to both sides, even reasonably equal. Sometimes they were cruel and exploitive. But the early multiracial societies of the West did not separate whites and Indians. They demonstrated ways in which the two cultures could interact, each shaping the other.

By the mid-nineteenth century, however, white Americans had adopted a different model as they contemplated westward expansion. Much as the early British settlers along the Atlantic coast had established "plantations," from which natives were, in theory, to be excluded, so the westward-moving whites of later years came to imagine the territories they were entering as virgin land, with no preexisting civilization. Native Americans, they believed, could not be partners—either equal or subordinate—in the creation of new societies in the West. They were obstacles, to be removed and, as far as possible, isolated. Indians, Andrew Jackson once said, had "neither the intelligence, the industry, the moral habits, nor the desire of improvement" to be fit partners in the project of extending white civilization westward. By dismissing Native American cultures in that way, white Americans justified to themselves a series of harsh policies that they believed (incorrectly) would make the West theirs alone.

JACKSON AND THE BANK WAR

Jackson was quite willing to use federal power against rebellious states and against the tribes. On economic issues, however, he was consistently opposed to concentrating power either in the federal government or in powerful and, in his view, aristocratic institutions associated with it. An early example of his skeptical view of federal power was his 1830 veto of a congressional measure providing a subsidy to the proposed Maysville Road in Kentucky. The bill was unconstitutional, Jackson argued, because the road in question lay entirely within Kentucky and was not, therefore, a part of "interstate commerce." But the bill was also unwise, he believed, because it committed the government to what Jackson considered extravagant expenditures.

Jackson's Opposition to Concentrated Power

Jackson's opposition to federal power and aristocratic privilege lay behind the most celebrated episode of Jackson's presidency: the war against the Bank of the United States.

Biddle's Institution

The Bank of the United States in the 1830s was a mighty institution indeed, and it is not surprising that it would attract Jackson's wrath. Its stately headquarters in Philadelphia seemed to symbolize its haughty image of itself. It had branches in twenty-nine other cities, making it the most powerful and far-flung financial institution in the nation. By law,

Nicholas Biddle

the Bank was the only place that the federal government could deposit its own funds; the government, in turn, owned one-fifth of the bank's stock. The Bank did a tremendous business in general banking. It provided credit to growing enterprises; it issued bank notes, which served as a dependable medium of exchange throughout the country; and it exercised a restraining effect on the less well-managed state banks. Nicholas Biddle, who served as president of the Bank from 1823 on, had done much to put the institution on a sound and prosperous basis. Nevertheless, Andrew Jackson was determined to destroy it.

Opposition to the Bank came from two very different groups: the "soft-money" faction and the "hard-money" faction. Advocates of soft money—people who wanted more currency in circulation and believed that issuing bank notes unsupported by gold and silver was the best way to circulate more currency—consisted largely of state bankers and their allies. They objected to the Bank of the United States because it restrained the state banks from issuing notes freely. The hard-money people believed that gold and silver were the only basis for money. They condemned all banks that issued bank notes, including the Bank of the United States. The soft-money advocates were believers in rapid economic growth and speculation; the hard-money forces embraced older ideas of "public virtue" and looked with suspicion on expansion and speculation.

Hard and Soft Money

Jackson himself supported the hard-money position. Many years before, he had been involved in some grandiose land and commercial speculations based on paper credit. His business had failed, and he had fallen deeply into debt as a result of the Panic of 1797. After that, he was suspicious of all banks and all paper currency. But as president he was also sensitive to the complaints of his many soft-money supporters in the West and the South. He made it clear that he would not favor renewing the charter of the Bank of the United States, which was due to expire in 1836.

Biddle was a Philadelphia aristocrat, unaccustomed to politics. But in his efforts to save the Bank, he began granting financial favors to influential men who he thought might help him preserve the bank. In particular, he turned to Daniel Webster and cultivated a close personal friendship with him. He named Webster the Bank's legal counsel and director of its Boston branch; Webster was also a frequent, heavy borrower from the Bank. Perhaps unsurprisingly, he helped Biddle win the support of other important figures, among them Henry Clay.

Clay, Webster, and other advisers persuaded Biddle to apply to Congress in 1832 for a bill to renew the Bank's charter. That was four years ahead of the date the original charter was scheduled to expire. But forcing a vote now would allow the Bank to become a major issue in the 1832

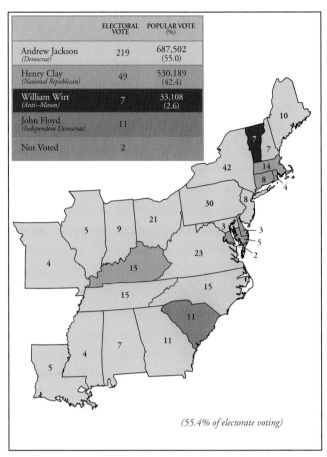

	ELECTORAL VOTE	POPULAR VOTE (%)
Andrew Jackson *(Democrat)*	219	687,502 (55.0)
Henry Clay *(National Republican)*	49	530,189 (42.4)
William Wirt *(Anti--Mason)*	7	33,108 (2.6)
John Floyd *(Independent Democrat)*	11	
Not Voted	2	

(55.4% of electorate voting)

THE ELECTION OF 1832 Jackson's re-election victory in 1832 was almost as decisive as his earlier victory in 1828. ◆ *What changes are visible in party loyalties since the previous election?*

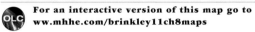

For an interactive version of this map go to ww.mhhe.com/brinkley11ch8maps

national elections. Congress passed the recharter bill; Jack-

Jackson's Veto

son, predictably, vetoed it; and the Bank's supporters in Congress failed to override the veto. Just as Clay had hoped, the 1832 campaign now centered on the future of the Bank.

Clay himself ran for president that year as the unanimous choice of the National Republicans, who held a nominating convention in Baltimore late in 1831. But the bank war failed to provide him with the winning issue for which he had hoped. Jackson, with Van Buren as his running mate, overwhelmingly defeated Clay (and several minor party candidates) with 55 percent of the popular vote and 219 electoral votes (more than four times as many as Clay received). These results were a defeat not only for Clay, but also for Biddle.

The "Monster" Destroyed

Jackson was now more determined than ever to destroy the "monster" Bank as quickly as possible. He could not legally abolish the institution before the expiration of its charter. Instead, he tried to weaken it. He decided to re-move the government's de-posits from the Bank. His secre-tary of the treasury believed

Removal of Government Deposits

that such an action would destabilize the financial system and refused to give the order. Jackson fired him and appointed a new one. When the new secretary similarly balked, Jackson fired him too and named a third, more compliant secretary: Attorney General Roger B. Taney, his close friend and loyal ally. Taney began placing the government's deposits not in the Bank of the United States, as it had in the past, but in a number of state banks (which Jackson's enemies called "pet banks").

The arrogant Nicholas Biddle, whom Jacksonians derisively called "Czar Nicholas," did not give in without a fight. "This worthy President," he wrote sarcastically, "thinks that because he has scalped Indians and imprisoned Judges, he is to have his way with the Bank. He is mistaken." When the administration began to transfer funds directly from the Bank of the United States to the pet banks (as opposed to the initial practice of simply depositing new funds in those banks), Biddle called in loans and raised interest rates, explaining that without the government deposits the Bank's resources were stretched too thin. He realized his actions were likely to cause financial distress. He hoped a short recession would persuade Congress to recharter the Bank. "Nothing but the evidence of suffering," he told a colleague, would "produce any effect in Congress." By now, the struggle had become not just a conflict over policy and principle, but a bitter and even petulant personal battle between two proud men—both of them acting recklessly in an effort to humiliate and defeat the other.

As financial conditions worsened in the winter of 1833–1834, supporters of the Bank blamed Jackson's policies for the recession. They organized meetings around the country and sent petitions to Washington urging a rechartering of the Bank. But the Jacksonians blamed the recession on Biddle and refused to budge. When distressed citizens appealed to the president for help, he dismissively answered, "Go to Biddle."

Finally, Biddle contracted credit too far even for his own allies in the business community, who began to fear that in his effort to save his own bank he was threatening their interests. Some of them did "go to Biddle." A group of New York and Boston merchants protested (as one of them reported) that the business community "ought not and would not sustain him in further pressure, which he very well knew was not necessary for the safety of the bank, and in which his whole object was to coerce a charter." To appease the business community, Biddle at last reversed himself and began to grant credit in abundance and on reasonable terms. His vacillating and unpopular tactics ended his chances of winning a recharter of the Bank.

Jackson had won a consider-able political victory. But when

Jackson Victorious

"THE DOWNFALL OF MOTHER BANK" This 1832 Democratic cartoon celebrates Andrew Jackson's destruction of the Bank of the United States. The president is shown here driving away the Bank's corrupt supporters by ordering the withdrawal of government deposits. *(New-York Historical Society)*

the Bank of the United States died in 1836, the country lost a valuable, albeit flawed, financial institution and was left with a fragmented and chronically unstable banking system that would plague the economy for more than a century.

The Taney Court

In the aftermath of the Bank War, Jackson moved against the most powerful institution of economic nationalism of all: the Supreme Court. In 1835, when John Marshall died, the president appointed as the new chief justice his trusted ally Roger B. Taney. Taney did not bring a sharp break in constitutional interpretation, but he gradually helped modify Marshall's vigorous nationalism.

Perhaps the clearest indication of the new judicial mood

Charles River Bridge v. Warren Bridge

was the celebrated case of *Charles River Bridge* v. *Warren Bridge* of 1837. The case involved a dispute between two Massachusetts companies over the right to build a bridge across the Charles River between Boston and Cambridge. One company had a

longstanding charter from the state to operate a toll bridge and claimed that this charter guaranteed it a monopoly of the bridge traffic. Another company had applied to the legislature for authorization to construct a second, competing bridge that would—since it would be toll free—greatly reduce the value of the first company's charter.

The first company contended that in granting the second charter the legislature was engaging in a breach of contract and noted that the Marshall Court, in the *Dartmouth College* case and other decisions, had ruled that states had no right to abrogate contracts. But now Taney, speaking for the Democratic majority on the Court, supported the right of Massachusetts to award the second charter. The object of government, Taney maintained, was to promote the general happiness, an object that took precedence over the rights of contract and property. A state, therefore, had the right to amend or abrogate a contract if such action was necessary to advance the well-being of the community. Such an abrogation was clearly necessary in the case of the Charles River Bridge, he argued, because the original bridge company, by exercising a monopoly, was benefiting from unjustifiable privilege. (It did not help the first company that its members were largely Boston aristocrats and that it was closely associated with elite Harvard College; the challenging company, by contrast, consisted largely of newer, aspiring entrepreneurs—the sort of people with whom Jackson and his allies instinctively identified.) The decision reflected one of the cornerstones of the Jacksonian ideal: that the key to democracy was an expansion of economic opportunity, which would not occur if older corporations could maintain monopolies and choke off competition from newer companies.

THE CHANGING FACE OF AMERICAN POLITICS

Jackson's forceful—some claimed tyrannical—tactics in crushing first the nullification movement and then the Bank of the United States helped galvanize a growing opposition coalition that by the mid-1830s was ready to assert itself in national politics. It began as a gathering of national political leaders opposed to Jackson's use of power. Denouncing the president as "King Andrew I," they began to refer to themselves as Whigs, after the party in England that had traditionally worked to limit the

Birth of the Whig Party | power of the king. With the emergence of the Whigs, the nation once again had two competing political parties. What scholars now call the "second party system" had begun what turned out to be its relatively brief life.

Democrats and Whigs

The two parties were different from one another in their philosophies, in their constituencies, and in the character of their leaders. But they became increasingly alike in the way they approached the process of electing their followers to office.

Democrats in the 1830s envisioned a future of steadily expanding economic and political opportunities for

Democrats' Emphasis on Opportunity | white males. The role of government should be limited, they believed, but it should include efforts to remove obstacles to opportunity and to avoid creating new ones. That meant defending the Union, which Jacksonians believed was essential to the dynamic economic growth they favored. It also meant attacking centers of corrupt privilege. As Jackson himself said in his farewell address, the society of America should be one in which "the planter, the farmer, the mechanic, and the laborer, all know that their success depends on their own industry and economy," in which artificial privilege would stifle no one's opportunity. Among the most radical members of the party—the so-called Locofocos, mainly workingmen and small businessmen and professionals in the

Northeast—sentiment was strong for a vigorous, perhaps even violent assault on monopoly and privilege far in advance of anything Jackson himself ever contemplated.

The political philosophy that became known as Whiggery was very different. It

Whigs' Call for Economic Union | favored expanding the power of the federal government, encouraging industrial and commercial development, and knitting the country together into a consolidated economic system. Whigs embraced material progress enthusiastically; but unlike the Democrats, they were cautious about westward expansion, fearful that rapid territorial growth would produce instability. Their vision of America was of a nation embracing the industrial future and rising to world greatness as a commercial and manufacturing power. Thus while Democrats were inclined to oppose legislation establishing banks, corporations, and other modernizing institutions, Whigs generally favored such measures.

To some extent, the constituencies of the two major parties reflected these diffuse philosophies. The Whigs were strongest among the more substantial merchants and manufacturers of the Northeast; the wealthier planters of the South (those who favored commercial development and the strengthening of ties with the North); and the ambitious farmers and rising commercial class of the West—usually migrants from the Northeast—who advocated internal improvements, expanding trade, and rapid economic progress. The Democrats drew more support from smaller merchants and the workingmen of the Northeast; from southern planters suspicious of industrial growth; and from westerners—usually with southern roots—who favored a predominantly agrarian economy and opposed the development of powerful economic institutions in their region. Whigs tended to be wealthier than Democrats, to have more aristocratic backgrounds, and to be more commercially ambitious.

But Whigs and Democrats alike were more interested in winning elections than in maintaining philosophical purity. And both parties made frequent adjustments in their public postures to attract the largest possible number of voters. In New York, for example, the Whigs worked to develop a popular

Anti-Masons | following by making a connection to a movement known as Anti-Masonry. The Anti-Mason movement had emerged in the 1820s in response to widespread resentment against the secret, exclusive, and hence supposedly undemocratic, Society of Freemasons. Such resentments greatly increased in 1826 when a former Mason, William Morgan, mysteriously disappeared (and was assumed to have been murdered) from his home in Batavia, New York, shortly before he was scheduled to publish a book purporting to expose the secrets of Freemasonry. Whigs seized on the Anti-Mason frenzy to launch harsh attacks on Jackson and Van Buren (both

Freemasons), implying that the Democrats were part of the antidemocratic conspiracy. In the process, the Whigs presented themselves as opponents of aristocracy and exclusivity. They were, in other words, attacking the Democrats with the Democrats' own issues.

Religious and ethnic divisions also played an important role in determining the constituencies of the two parties. Irish and German Catholics, among the largest of the recent immigrant groups, tended to support the Democrats, who appeared to share their own vague aver-*Cultural Issues* sion to commercial development and entrepreneurial progress and who seemed to respect their family- and community-centered values and habits. Evangelical Protestants gravitated toward the Whigs because they associated the party with constant development and improvement, goals their own faith embraced. These and other ethnic, religious, and cultural tensions were often more influential in determining party alignments than any concrete political or economic proposals.

The Whig Party was more successful at defining its positions and attracting a constituency than it was in uniting behind a national leader. No single person was ever able to command the loyalties of the party in the way Andrew Jackson commanded the loyalties of the Democrats. Instead, Whigs tended to divide their loyalties among three figures, each of whom was so substantial a figure that together they became known as the "Great Triumvirate": Henry Clay, Daniel Webster, and John Calhoun.

Clay won support from many of those who favored his *Clay's American System* program for internal improvements and economic development, what he called the American System; but his image as a devious operator and his identification with the West proved serious liabilities. He ran for president three times and never won. Daniel Webster, the greatest orator of his era, won broad support with his passionate speeches in defense of the Constitution and the Union; but his close connection with the Bank of the United States and the protective tariff, his reliance on rich men for financial support, and his excessive and often embarrassing fondness for brandy prevented him from developing enough of a national constituency to win him the office he so desperately wanted. John C. Calhoun, the third member of what became known as the Great Triumvirate, never considered himself a true Whig, and his identification with the nullification controversy in effect disqualified him from national leadership in any case. But he had tremendous strength in the South, supported a national bank, and shared with Clay and Webster a strong animosity toward Andrew Jackson.

The problems that emerged from this divided leadership became particularly clear *Election of 1836* in 1836. The Democrats were united behind Andrew Jackson's personal choice for president, Martin Van Buren. The Whigs could not even agree on a single candidate. Instead, they ran several candidates, hoping to profit from the regional strength of each. Webster represented the party in New England; Hugh Lawson White of Tennessee ran in the South; and the former Indian fighter and hero of the War of 1812 from Ohio, William Henry Harrison, was the candidate in the middle states and the West. Party leaders hoped the three candidates together might draw enough votes from Van Buren to prevent his getting a majority and throw the election to the House of Representatives, where the Whigs might be able to elect one of their own leaders. In the end, however, Van Buren won easily, with 170 electoral votes to 124 for all his opponents.

Van Buren and the Panic of 1837

Andrew Jackson retired from public life in 1837, the most beloved political figure of his age. Martin Van Buren was very different from his predecessor and far less fortunate. He was never able to match Jackson's personal popularity, and his administration encountered economic difficulties that devastated the Democrats and helped the Whigs.

Van Buren's success in the 1836 election was a result in part of a nationwide economic boom that was reaching its height in that year. Canal and railroad builders were at a peak of activity. Prices were rising, money was plentiful, and credit was easy as banks increased their loans and notes with little regard to their reserves of cash. The land business, in particular, was booming. Between 1835 and 1837, the government sold nearly 40 million acres of public land, nearly three-fourths of it to speculators, who purchased large tracts in hopes of reselling them at a profit. These land sales, along with revenues the government received from the tariff of 1833, created a series of substantial federal budget surpluses and made possible a steady reduction of the national debt (something Jackson had always advocated). From 1835 to 1837, the government for the first and only time in its history was out of debt, with a substantial surplus in the Treasury.

Congress and the administration now faced the question of what to do with the Treasury surplus. Reducing the tariff was *Distribution Act* not an option, since no one wanted to raise that thorny issue again. Instead, support grew for returning the federal surplus to the states. In 1836, Congress passed a "distribution" act requiring the federal government to pay its surplus funds to the states each year in four quarterly installments as interest-free, unsecured loans. No one expected the "loans" to be repaid. The states spent the money quickly, mainly to encourage construction of highways, railroads, and canals. The distribution of the surplus thus gave further stimulus to the economic boom. At the same time, the withdrawal of federal funds strained the state (or "pet") banks in which they had been deposited by the government; they had to call in their own loans to make the transfer of funds to the state governments.

"THE TIMES," 1837 This savage caricature of the economic troubles besetting the United States in 1837 illustrates, among other things, popular resentment of the hard-money orthodoxies of the time. A sign on the Custom House reads: "All bonds must be paid in Specie." Next door, the bank announces: "No specie payments made here." Women and children are shown begging in the street, while unemployed workers stand shoeless in front of signs advertising loans and "grand schemes." *(New-York Historical Society)*

Congress did nothing to check the speculative fever, with which many congressmen themselves were badly infected. Webster, for one, was buying up thousands of acres in the West. But Jackson, always suspicious of paper currency, was unhappy that the government was selling good land and receiving in return various state bank notes worth no more than the credit of the issuing bank.

In 1836, not long before leaving office, he issued a presidential order, the "specie circular." It provided that in payment for public lands the government would only accept gold or silver coins or currency securely backed by gold or silver. Jackson was right to fear the speculative fever but wrong in thinking the specie circular would cure it. On the contrary, it produced a financial panic that

Panic of 1837

began in the first months of Van Buren's presidency. Hundreds of banks and businesses failed. Unemployment grew. Bread riots broke out in some of the larger cities. Prices fell, especially the price of land. Many railroad and canal projects failed. Several of the debt-burdened state governments ceased to pay interest on their bonds, and a few

repudiated their debts, at least temporarily. It was the worst depression in American history to that point, and it lasted for five years. It was a political catastrophe for Van Buren and the Democrats.

Both parties bore some responsibility for the panic. The distribution of the Treasury surplus, which had weakened the state banks and helped cause the crash, had been a Whig measure. Jackson's specie circular, which had started a run on the banks as land buyers rushed to trade in their bank notes for specie, was also to blame. But the depression was only partly a result of federal policies. England and western Europe were facing panics of their own, which caused European (and especially English) investors to withdraw funds from America, putting an added strain on American banks. A succession of crop failures on American farms reduced the purchasing power of farmers and required increased imports of food, which sent more money out of the country. But whatever its actual causes, the Panic of 1837 occurred during a Democratic administration, and the Democrats paid the political price for it. The Van Buren administration, which strongly opposed government intervention in the economy, did little to fight the depression. Some of the steps it took—borrowing money to pay government debts and accepting only specie for payment of taxes—may have made things worse. Other efforts failed in Congress: a "preemption" bill that would have given settlers the right to buy government land near them before it was opened for public sale, and another bill lowering the price of land. Van Buren did succeed in establishing a ten-hour workday on all federal projects, by presidential order, but he had only a few legislative achievements.

The most important and controversial of them was the *Independent Treasury* creation of a new financial system to replace the Bank of the United States. Under Van Buren's plan, known as the "independent treasury" or "subtreasury" system, the government would place its funds in an independent treasury at Washington and in subtreasuries in other cities. No private banks would have the government's money or name to use as a basis for speculation; the government and the banks would be "divorced."

Van Buren called a special session of Congress in 1837 to consider the proposal, which failed in the House. In 1840, the last year of Van Buren's presidency, the administration finally succeeded in driving the measure through both houses of Congress.

The Log Cabin Campaign

As the campaign of 1840 approached, the Whigs realized that they would have to settle on one candidate for president this time if they were to have any hope of winning. As a result, they held their first national nominating convention in Harrisburg, Pennsylvania, in December 1839. Passing over the controversial Henry Clay, who had expected the nomination, the convention chose William Henry Harrison and, for vice president, John Tyler of Virginia. Harrison was a descendant of the Virginia aristocracy but had spent his adult life in the Northwest. He was a renowned soldier, a famous Indian fighter, and a popular national figure. The Democrats nominated Van Buren. But because they were not much more united than the Whigs, they failed to nominate a vice presidential candidate, leaving the choice of that office to the electors.

The 1840 campaign was the first in which the new popular "penny press" carried news of the candidates to a large audience of workers and tradespeople. It also illustrated how fully the concept of party competition, the subordination of ideology to immediate political needs, had established itself in America. The Whigs—who had emerged as a party largely because of their opposition to Andrew Jackson's common-man democracy, who in most regions represented the more affluent elements of the *New Techniques of Political Campaigning* population, and who favored government policies that would aid business—presented themselves in 1840 as the party of the common people. So, of

WHIG HEADQUARTERS, 1840 The Whig Party in 1840 managed to disguise its relatively elite character by portraying its presidential candidate, the patrician General William Henry Harrison, as a man of the people—a man born in a log cabin who enjoyed drinking hard cider from a jug. Pictures of log cabins abounded during the Whig campaign. One of them is visible in this drawing of a party rally in Philadelphia. *(Stock Montage, Inc.)*

course, did the Democrats. Both parties used the same techniques of mass voter appeal, the same evocation of simple, rustic values. What mattered now was not the philosophical purity of the party but its ability to win votes. The Whig campaign was particularly effective in portraying William Henry Harrison, a wealthy member of the frontier elite with a considerable estate, as a simple man of the people who loved log cabins and hard cider. They accused Van Buren of being an aloof aristocrat who used cologne, drank champagne, and ate from gold plates. The Democrats had no defense against the combination of these campaign techniques and the effects of the depression. Harrison won the election with 234 electoral votes to 60 for Van Buren and with a popular vote majority of 53 percent.

The Frustration of the Whigs

Despite their decisive victory, the Whigs found their four years in power frustrating and divisive ones. In large part, that was because their popular new president, "Old Tippecanoe," William Henry Harrison, died of

A BEAUTIFUL GOBLET OF
WHITE·HOUSE CHAMPAGNE

AN UGLY *MUG* OF
LOG·CABIN HARD CIDER

AN ATTACK ON VAN BUREN This "pull card," made during the 1840 presidential campaign, which Van Buren lost to William Henry Harrison, satirizes the president as an aristocratic dandy. The card displays Van Buren grinning while he drinks champagne in the White House. Pulling a tab on the card changes his champagne glass to a mug of hard cider (with Harrison's initials on it) and changes his expression from delight to revulsion. *(Division of Political History, American History Museum, Smithsonian Institution, Washington, D.C.)*

pneumonia one month after taking office. Vice President Tyler succeeded him. Control of the administration thus fell to a man with whom the Whig party leadership had relatively weak ties. Harrison had generally deferred to Henry Clay and Daniel Webster, whom he named secretary of state. Under Tyler, things soon changed.

Tyler was a former Democrat who had left the party in reaction to what he considered Jackson's excessively egalitarian program and imperious methods. But there were still signs of his Democratic past in his approach to public policy. The president did agree to bills abolishing Van Buren's independent treasury system and raising tariff rates. But he refused to support Clay's attempt to recharter a Bank of the United States. And he vetoed several internal improvement bills that Clay and other congressional *Whigs Break with Tyler* | Whigs sponsored. Finally, a conference of congressional Whigs read Tyler out of the party. Every cabinet member but Webster resigned; five former Democrats took their places. When Webster, too, left the cabinet, Tyler appointed Calhoun, who had rejoined the Democratic Party, to replace him.

A new political alignment was emerging. Tyler and a small band of conservative southern Whigs were preparing to rejoin the Democrats. Joining the "common man's party" of Jackson and Van Buren was a faction with decidedly aristocratic political ideas, who thought that government had an obligation to protect and even expand the institution of slavery, and who believed in states' rights with almost fanatical devotion.

Whig Diplomacy

In the midst of these domestic controversies, a series of incidents in the late 1830s brought Great Britain and the United States once again to the brink of war. Residents of the eastern provinces of Canada launched a rebellion against the British colonial government in 1837, and some of the rebels chartered an American steamship, the *Caroline,* to ship supplies across the Niagara River to them from New York. British authorities in Canada seized the *Caroline* and burned it, killing one American in the process. The British government refused either to disavow the attack or to provide compensation for it, and resentment in the

THE PENNY PRESS

On September 3, 1833, a small newspaper appeared in New York City for the first time: the *New York Sun*, published by a young former apprentice from Massachusetts named Benjamin Day. It was four pages long; it contained mostly trivial local news, with particular emphasis on sex, crime, and violence; and it sold for a penny. It launched a new age in the history of American journalism, the age of the "penny press."

Before the advent of the penny press, newspapers in America were produced almost entirely by and for

the upper classes. Some published mainly business news; others worked to advance the aims of a political party. All were far too expensive for most ordinary citizens to buy. But several important changes in the business of journalism and the character of American society paved the way for Benjamin Day and others to challenge the established press. New technologies—the steam-powered cylinder printing press, new machines for making paper, railroads and canals for distributing issues to a larger market—made it possible to publish newspapers inexpensively and to sell them widely. A rising popular literacy rate, a result in part of the spread of public education, created a bigger reading public.

The penny press was also a response to the changing culture of the 1820s and 1830s. The spread of an urban, market economy contributed to the growth of the penny press by drawing a large population of workers, artisans, and clerks—the genesis of an industrial working class and a modern middle class—into large cities, where they became an important market for the new papers. The spirit of democracy—symbolized by the popularity of Andrew Jackson and the rising numbers of white male voters across the country—helped create an appetite for journalism that spoke to and for "the people," rather than the parties or the upper classes. Hence Benjamin Day's slogan for his new paper: "It Shines for ALL." *The Sun*, and other

papers like it, were self-consciously egalitarian. They were eager to tweak and embarrass the rich and powerful (through their popular gossip columns). They were also committed to feeding the appetites of the people of modest means, who constituted most of their readership. "Human interest stories" helped solidify their hold on the working public. Condescending stories about poor black men and women—ridiculing their subjects' illiteracy and their accents—were also popular among their virtually all-white readership.

Within six months of its first issue, the *Sun* had the largest circulation in New York—8,000 readers, more than twice its nearest competitors. Its success encouraged others to begin publishing penny papers of their own. James Gordon Bennett's *New York Herald*, which began publication in 1835, soon surpassed the *Sun* in popularity with its lively combination of sensationalism and local gossip and with its aggressive pursuit of national and international stories. The *Herald* pioneered a "letters to the editor" column. It was the first paper to have regular reviews of books and the arts. It even launched the first daily sports section. By 1860, it had the largest circulation of any daily newspaper in the world: more than 77,000.

Not all the new penny papers were as sensationalist as the *Sun* and the *Herald*. Both the *Philadelphia Public Ledger* and the *Baltimore Sun*, founded in 1836 and 1837

THE NEW YORK SUN This 1834 front page of the *Sun*, which had begun publication a year earlier, contains advertisements, light stories, a description of a slave auction in Charleston, S.C., and homespun advice: "Life is short. The poor pittance of several years is not worth being a villain for." *(Collection of the New-York Historical Society)*

United States ran high. But the British soon had reasons for

The Caroline Affair

anger as well. Authorities in New York, attempting to exploit the *Caroline* affair, arrested a Canadian named Alexander McLeod and charged him with the murder of the American who had died in the incident. The British government, expressing majestic rage, insisted that McLeod could not be accused of murder because he had acted under official orders. The foreign secretary, the bellicose Lord Palmerston, demanded McLeod's release and threatened that his execution would bring "immediate and frightful" war.

Webster as secretary of state did not think McLeod was worth a war, but he was powerless to release him. The

prisoner was under New York jurisdiction and had to be tried in the state courts, a peculiarity of American jurisprudence that the British did not seem to understand. A New York jury did what Webster could not: it defused the crisis by acquitting McLeod.

At the same time, tensions flared over the boundary between Canada and Maine, which

Aroostook War

had been in dispute since the Treaty of 1783. In 1838, groups of Americans and Canadians, mostly lumberjacks, began moving into the Aroostook River region in the disputed area, precipitating a violent brawl between the two groups that became known as the "Aroostook War."

respectively, strove to provide more serious coverage of the news. The *Baltimore Sun* even developed a Washington bureau, the first of the penny papers to do so. The *New York Tribune,* founded in 1841 by Horace Greeley (later a major antislavery leader and a Republican presidential candidate), hired some of the most important writers of the day—among them Charles A. Dana, Margaret Fuller, Henry James, and William Dean Howells—and prided itself on serious reporting and commentary. All of it was tinged with a conspicuous sympathy for socialism (Greeley once hired Karl Marx as a London correspondent) and for the aspirations of working people. As serious as the *Tribune,* but more sober and self-consciously "objective" in its reportage, was the *New York Times,* which Henry Raymond founded in 1851. "We do not mean to write as if we were in a passion—unless that shall really be the case," the *Times* huffily proclaimed in its first issue, in an obvious reference to Greeley and his impassioned reportage; "and we shall make it a point to get into a passion as rarely as possible."

But the *Times*'s dutiful restraint and self-conscious respectability was rare in the penny press. More typical was the front page of the June 4, 1836 *Herald,* devoted in its entirety to the sensational murder of a prostitute by a frequent patron of brothels. "Why is not the militia called?" Bennett's paper asked breathlessly at the beginning of the main story. "We give . . . testimony up to the latest hour. . . . The mystery of the bloody drama increases—increases—increases."

No papers in the 1830s had yet begun to use the large banner headlines of modern tabloids. None had photographs, and only a few—Bennett's *Herald* notable among them—ran drawings to accompany their stories with any regularity. But within their columns of unbroken newsprint lay the origins of the press we know today. They were the first papers to pay their reporters and thus began the process of turning journalism into a profession. They were the first to rely heavily on advertisements and often devoted up to half their space to paid advertising. They reached beyond the business world and the political clubs and communicated with a genuinely mass market. They were often sensationalist and usually opinionated. But they were often also aggressive in uncovering serious and important news—in police stations, courts, jails, streets, and private homes as well as in city halls, state capitals, Washington, and the world.

THE FIRST "EXTRA" This 1840 "special edition" of the *New York Sun* was innovative in two ways. It was probably the first "extra" edition of any daily newspaper in America. It was also one of the first examples of large and (in this case at least) lurid illustration in the daily press. This dramatic picture accompanies a story about the explosion of the ship. *(Print Collection Miriam and Ira D. Wallach Division. New-York Public Library, Astor, Lenox and Tilden Foundation)*

Several years later, there were yet more Anglo-American problems. In 1841, an American ship, the *Creole,* sailed from Virginia for New Orleans with more than 100 slaves aboard. En route the slaves mutinied, took possession of the ship, and took it to the Bahamas. British officials there declared the slaves free, and the English government refused to overrule them. Many Americans, especially southerners, were furious.

At this critical juncture, a new government eager to reduce the tensions with the United States came to power in Great Britain. In the spring of 1842, it sent Lord Ashburton, an admirer of America, to negotiate an agreement on the Maine boundary and other matters. The result of his negotiations with Secretary of State Webster and representatives from Maine and Massachusetts was the Webster-Ashburton Treaty of 1842. Its terms established a firm northern boundary between the United States and Canada along the Maine-New Brunswick border that survives to this day; the new border gave the United States a bit more than half of the previously disputed territory. Other, smaller provisions placated Maine and Massachusetts and protected critical trade routes in both the northern United States and southern Canada. In a separate exchange of notes, Ashburton eased the memory of the *Caroline* and *Creole* affairs by expressing regret and promising no

Webster-Ashburton Treaty

future "officious interference" with American ships. The Webster-Ashburton treaty was generally popular in America, and in its aftermath Anglo-American relations substantially improved.

During the Tyler administration, the United States established its first diplomatic relations with China. In 1842, Britain forced China to open certain ports to foreign trade. Eager to share the new privileges, American mercantile interests persuaded Tyler and Congress to send a commissioner—Caleb Cushing—to China to negotiate a treaty giving the United States some part in the China trade. In the Treaty of Wang Hya, concluded in 1844,

Treaty of Wang Hya

Cushing secured most-favored-nation provisions giving Americans the same privileges as the English. He also won for Americans the right of "extraterritoriality"—the right of Americans accused of crimes in China to be tried by American, not Chinese, officials. In the next ten years, American trade with China steadily increased.

In their diplomatic efforts, at least, the Whigs were able to secure some important successes. But by the end of the Tyler administration, the party could look back on few other victories. In the election of 1844, the Whigs lost the White House. They were to win only one more national election in their history before a great sectional crisis arose that would shatter their party and, for a time, the Union.

CONCLUSION

The election of Andrew Jackson to the presidency in 1828 marked not only the triumph of a particular vision of government and democracy. It represented as well the emergence of a new political world. Throughout the American nation, the laws governing political participation were loosening and the number of people permitted to vote (which eventually included most white males, but almost no one else) was increasing. Along with this expansion of the electorate was emerging a new spirit of party politics. Parties had once been reviled by American leaders as contributing to the spirit of faction. Now a new set of ideas was emerging that saw in institutionalized parties not a challenge, but a contribution to democracy. Party competition would be a way of containing and muting disagreements that might otherwise run amok. It would be another of the healthy restraints—another part of the system of checks and balances—that made American government work.

Jackson's Legacy

Andrew Jackson was a party man, and he set out as president to entrench his party, the Democrats, in power. He was also a fierce defender of his region, the West, and

a sharp critic of what he considered the stranglehold of the aristocratic East on the nation's economic life. He sought to limit the role of the federal government in economic affairs, fearful that it would serve to entrench existing patterns of wealth and power. He worked to destroy the Bank of the United States, which he considered a corrupt vehicle of aristocratic influence. Jackson was, finally, a nationalist. And he confronted the greatest challenge to American unity yet to have emerged in the young nation—the nullification crisis of 1832–1833—with a strong assertion of the power and importance of the Union. These positions won him broad popularity and ensured his reelection in 1832 and the election of his designated successor, Martin Van Buren, in 1836.

But the Democrats were not the only ones to have learned the lessons of the age of parties. A new coalition of anti-Jacksonians, who called themselves the Whigs, launched a powerful new party that used much of the same anti-elitist rhetoric the Democrats had used to win support for their own much more nationalist program. Their emergence culminated in the campaign of 1840 with the election of the first Whig president.

FOR FURTHER REFERENCE

Arthur M. Schlesinger, Jr., *The Age of Jackson* (1945) represents Jacksonian politics as an eastern, urban democratic movement of working men and upper-class intellectuals. Bray Hammond, *Banks and Politics in America from the Revolution to the Civil War* (1957) challenges Schlesinger by arguing that the Bank War was essentially a struggle between different groups of capitalist elites. Harry L. Watson, *Liberty and Power: The Politics of Jacksonian America* (1990) provides an important

newer synthesis of Jacksonian politics. Donald B. Cole, *Martin Van Buren and the American Political System* (1984) examines the emergence of modern notions of party through the career of Van Buren. Richard Hofstadter, *The Idea of a Party System: The Rise of Legitimate Opposition in the United States, 1740–1840* (1969) traces the growing acceptance of the idea of partisan competition. Daniel Walker Howe, *The Political Culture of the American Whigs* (1979) analyzes the careers of several leading Whig politicians including the Whig triumvirate of Calhoun,

Clay, and Webster. William V. Freehling, *Prelude to Civil War: The Nullification Controversy in South Carolina* (1966) argues that South Carolina planters' anxiety over the fate of slavery was at the heart of the nullification crisis. Francis P. Prucha, *American Indian Policy in the Formative Years* (1962) is an overview of early Indian policy by the leading scholar of the subject. Michael Rogin, *Fathers and Children:Andrew Jackson and the Destruction of American Indians* (1975) offers a more radical and idiosyncratic perspective on Jackson's career as an Indian fighter using the methods of psychoanalysis. Sean Wilentz, *Chants Democratic:New York City and the Rise of the American Working Class, 1788–1850* (1984) is an important study of working-class ideology during the Jacksonian period.

For quizzes, Internet resources, references to additional books and films, and more, consult this book's Online Learning Center at www.mhhe.com/brinkley11.

THE LOWELL MILLS Fifteen years earlier, Lowell, Massachusetts, had been a small farming village known as East Chelmsford. By the 1840s, when Fitzhugh Lane painted *The Middlesex Company Woolen Mills,* the town had become one of the most famous manufacturing centers in America and a magnet for visitors from around the world. Lane's painting shows female workers, who dominated the labor force in Lowell, entering the factory. *(American Textile History Museum, Lowell, Massachusetts)*

Significant Events

1813	Lowell establishes textile mill at Waltham, Massachusetts
1817–1825	Erie Canal constructed
1830	Baltimore and Ohio becomes first American railroad to begin operations
1830s	Major immigration from southern (Catholic) Ireland begins
	Factory system spreads in textile and shoe industries
	First national craft unions founded
1832	Cholera plague
1834	Women workers at Lowell mills stage strike
	Cyrus McCormick patents mechanical reaper

CHAPTER TEN

AMERICA'S ECONOMIC REVOLUTION

When the United States entered the War of 1812, it was still an essentially agrarian nation. There were, to be sure, cities in America, several of substantial size. In some of them there was a flourishing mercantile economy, based largely on overseas trade. There was also modest but growing manufacturing activity, concentrated mainly in the Northeast. But the overwhelming majority of Americans were farmers and tradespeople, working within an economy that was still mainly local.

By the time the Civil War began in 1861, the United States had transformed itself. Most Americans were still *The Market Revolution* rural people, to be sure. But even most American farmers were now part of a national, and increasingly international, market economy. Above all, perhaps, the United States had developed a major manufacturing sector and was beginning to challenge the industrial nations of Europe for supremacy. The nation had experienced the first stage of its industrial revolution; and while the changes that revolution produced were far from complete, most Americans understood that their world had changed irrevocably.

These dramatic changes—changes that affected not just the economy, but society, culture, and politics—did not have the same impact everywhere. The Northeast, and its new economic ally the Northwest, were rapidly developing a complex, modern economy and society, increasingly dominated by large cities, important manufacturing, and profitable commercial farming. It was in many ways an unequal society, but it was also a fluid one, firmly committed to the ideal of free labor. Relatively few white Americans yet lived west of the Mississippi River, but parts of those western lands, too, were becoming part of large-scale commercial agriculture and other enterprises and were creating links to the capitalist economy of the Northeast.

In the South and Southwest, there were changes, too. Southern agriculture, particularly cotton farming, flour- *Regional Divergences* ished as never before in response to the growing demand from textile mills in New England and elsewhere. But while the southern states were becoming increasingly a part of the national and international capitalist world, they also remained much less economically developed than their northern counterparts. And as the North became ever more committed to the fluidity and mobility of its free-labor system, the South was becoming more and more resolute in its defense of slavery.

The industrial revolution, which was doing so much to draw the nation into a single, integrated economy, was also working to isolate—and, increasingly, to alarm—the residents of one of its regions. The economic revolution was transforming the nation. It was also dividing it.

1837 · Native American Association begins efforts to restrict immigration
· Oberlin becomes first American coeducational college
· Mt. Holyoke College for women opens

1842 · Massachusetts Supreme Court, in *Commonwealth* v. *Hunt*, declares unions and strikes legal
· P. T. Barnum opens American Museum in New York

1844 · Samuel F. B. Morse sends first telegraph message

1845 · Irish potato famine begins, spurring major emigration to America
· Native American Party formed to combat immigration

· Female Labor Reform Association established at Lowell

1846 · Rotary press invented, making possible rapid printing of newspapers
· Associated Press organized

1847 · John Deere begins manufacturing steel plows

1848 · Failed revolution in Germany spurs emigration to America
· Wisconsin enters Union

1850 · Nativists form Supreme Order of the Star-Spangled Banner to oppose immigration

1852 · American Party (Know-Nothings) formed

THE CHANGING AMERICAN POPULATION

The American industrial revolution was a result of many factors. Before it could occur, the United States needed a population large enough both to grow its own food and to provide a work force for the industrial economy. It needed a transportation and communications system capable of sustaining commerce over a large geographical area. It needed the technology to permit manufacturing on a large scale. And it needed systems of business organization capable of managing large industrial enterprises. By 1860, the northern regions of the nation had acquired at least the beginnings of all those things.

The American Population, 1820–1840

Between 1820 and 1840, not only did the population of the United States dramatically increase, but much of it became concentrated in the industrial centers of the Northeast and Northwest, where it provided a labor force for the growing factory system. Three trends characterized the American population in these years, all of them contributing in various ways to economic growth. The population was increasing rapidly. Much of it was migrating westward. And much of it was moving to towns and cities.

The American population had stood at only 4 million in 1790. By 1820, it had reached 10 million; by 1830, nearly 13 million; and by 1840, 17 million. The United States was growing much more rapidly in population than Britain or Europe. One reason for this substantial population growth was improvements in public health. *Reasons for Population Increase* The number and ferocity of epidemics (such as the great cholera plague of 1832)—which had periodically decimated urban and even rural populations in America—slowly declined, as did the nation's mortality rate as a whole. The population increase was also a result of a high birth rate. In 1840, white women bore an average of 6.14 children each, a decline from the very high rates of the eighteenth century but still substantial enough to produce rapid population increases, particularly since a larger proportion of children could expect to grow to adulthood than had been the case a generation or two earlier.

Immigration, choked off by wars in Europe and economic crises in America, contributed little to the American population in the first three decades of the nineteenth century but rapidly revived beginning in the 1830s. Of the total 1830 population of nearly 13 million, the foreign-born numbered fewer than 500,000. But the number of immigrants climbed to 60,000 in 1832 and nearly 80,000 in 1837. Reduced transportation costs and increasing economic opportunities in America helped stimulate the immigration boom, as did deteriorating economic conditions in some areas of Europe. The migrations introduced new groups to the United States. In particular, the number of immigrants arriving from the southern (Catholic) counties of Ireland began to grow, marking the beginning of a

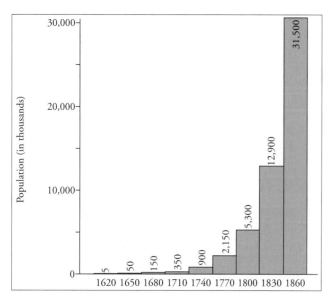

POPULATION GROWTH, 1620–1860 From its tiny beginnings in the seventeenth century, the American population grew rapidly and dramatically so that by 1860—with over 31 million people—the United States was one of the most populous countries in the world. ◆ *How did this growing population contribute to the nation's economic transformation?*

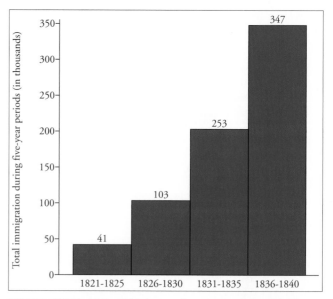

IMMIGRATION, 1820–1840 Among the sources of the nation's growing population in the nineteenth century was rapidly increasing immigration. This graph shows how rapidly immigration to the United States increased in the 1820s and 1830s. The 347,000 immigrants in the last half of the 1830s was almost nine times the number in the first half of the 1820s. ◆ *Where did most of these new immigrants settle?*

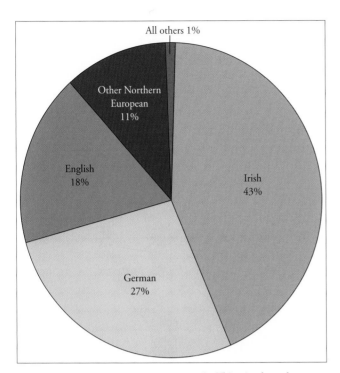

All others 1%

Other Northern European 11%

English 18%

German 27%

Irish 43%

SOURCES OF IMMIGRATION, 1820–1840 This pie chart shows where the large numbers of immigrants portrayed in the previous chart came from. Note the very large number of Irish immigrants. ◆ *Why were the Irish among the most likely immigrant groups to become part of the industrial work force?*

tremendous influx of Irish Catholics that was to continue through the three decades before the Civil War.

Much of this new European immigration flowed into the rapidly growing cities of the Northeast. But urban growth was a result of substantial internal migration as well. As the agricultural regions of New England and other areas grew less profitable, more and more people picked up stakes and moved—some to more promising agricultural regions in the West, but many to eastern cities. In 1790, one person in thirty had lived in a city (defined as a community of 8,000 or more); in 1820, one in twenty; and in 1840, one in twelve. The largest such cities were in the Northeast.

The rise of New York City was particularly dramatic. By 1810 it was the largest city in the United States. That was partly a result of its superior natural harbor. It was also a result of the Erie Canal (completed in 1825), which gave the city unrivaled access to the interior. New York's growth was a result, too, of liberal state laws that made the city attractive for both foreign and domestic commerce.

Immigration and Urban Growth, 1840–1860

The growth of cities accelerated dramatically between
Rapid Urbanization | 1840 and 1860. The population of New York, for example, rose

from 312,000 to 805,000. (New York's population would have numbered 1.2 million in 1860 if Brooklyn, which was then a separate municipality, had been included in the total.) Philadelphia's population grew over the same twenty-year period from 220,000 to 565,000; Boston's from 93,000 to 177,000. By 1860, 26 percent of the population of the free states was living in towns (places of 2,500 people or more) or cities (8,000 people or more), up from 14 percent in 1840. That percentage was even higher for the industrializing states of the Northeast. (In the South, by contrast, the increase of urban residents was only from 6 percent in 1840 to 10 percent in 1860.)

The booming agricultural economy of the western regions of the nation produced significant urban growth as well. Between 1820 and 1840, communities that had once been small western villages or trading posts became major cities: St. Louis, Pittsburgh, Cincinnati, Louisville. All of them benefited from strategic positions on the Mississippi River or one of its major tributaries. All of them became centers of the growing carrying trade that connected the farmers of the Midwest with New Orleans and, through it, the cities of the Northeast. After 1830, however, substantial shipping began from the Mississippi River to the Great Lakes, creating major new urban centers that gradually superseded the river ports. Among them were Buffalo, Detroit, Milwaukee, Cleveland, and—most important in the end—Chicago.

The enlarged urban population was in part simply a reflection of the growth of the national population as a whole, which rose by more than a third—from 23 million to over 31 million—in the decade of the 1850s alone. By 1860, the American population was larger than Britain's and quickly approaching that of France and Germany. Urban growth was also a result of the continuing, indeed increasing, flow of people into cities from the farms of the Northeast, which continued to decline because of competition from Europe and the American West (and because of the relative disadvantages of their own *Surging Immigration* soil). Immigration from abroad continued to increase as well. The number of foreigners arriving in the United States in 1840—84,000—was the highest for any one year to that point in the nineteenth century. But in later years, even that number would come to seem insignificant. Between 1840 and 1850, more than 1.5 million Europeans moved to America, three times the number of arrivals in the 1830s; in the last years of that decade, average annual immigration was almost 300,000. Of the 23 million people in the United States in 1850, 2.2 million (almost 10 percent) were foreign-born. Still greater numbers arrived in the 1850s—over 2.5 million. Almost half the residents of New York City in the 1850s were recent immigrants. In St. Louis, Chicago, and Milwaukee, the foreign-born outnumbered those of native birth. Few immigrants settled in the South. Only 500,000 lived in

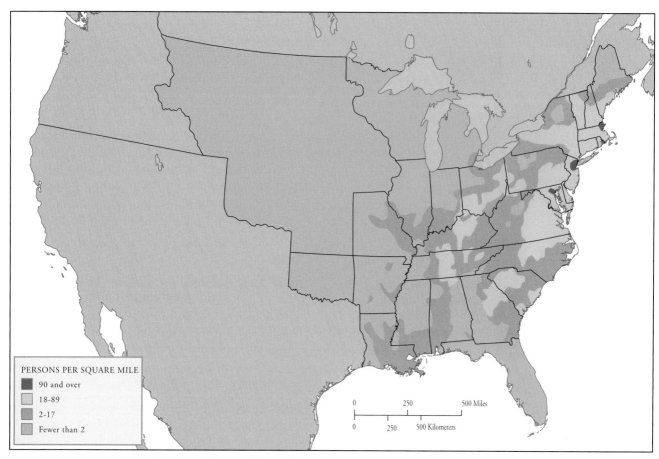

PERSONS PER SQUARE MILE

- 90 and over
- 18-89
- 2-17
- Fewer than 2

0   250   500 Miles

0   250   500 Kilometers

AMERICAN POPULATION DENSITY, 1820 The population of the United States in 1820 was still overwhelmingly rural and agrarian and was still concentrated largely in the original thirteen states, although settlement was growing in the Ohio River valley to the west. Note how few areas of the country were populated really densely: a small area in northeastern Massachusetts, the area around New York City, and the area in Maryland adjoining Baltimore. ◆ *What accounts for the density in these areas?*

BROADWAY, NEW YORK By the 1830s, New York had emerged as America's leading commercial city, and this picture of the bustling street life at Broadway and Canal Street suggests something of the growing energy of urban economies in the early years of industrialization. *(I.N. Phelps Stokes Collection, Miriam and Ira D. Wallach Division of Art, Prints and Photographs, The New York Public Library, Astor, Lenox and Tilden Foundations)*

BROADWAY, NEW-YORK.

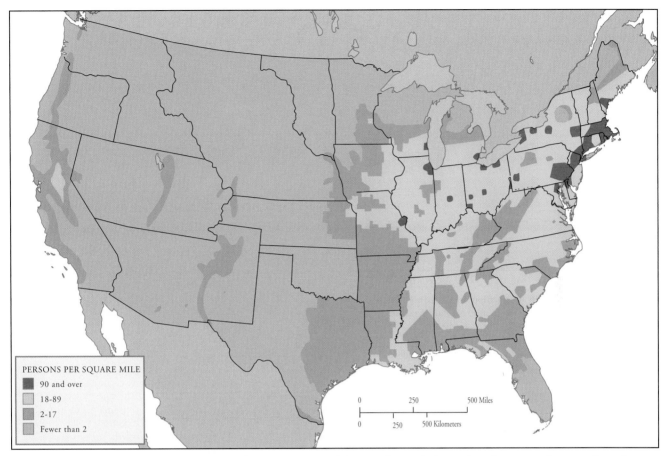

AMERICAN POPULATION DENSITY, 1860 By 1860, the population of the United States had spread much more evenly across the entire country. Communities that had once been small trading posts emerged as major cities. Among them were St. Louis, Pittsburgh, Cincinnati, and Louisville. In the meantime, the Erie Canal had opened up a large and prosperous market area for New York City. Note the larger and more numerous areas of dense population, including many in the Midwest. ◆ *What accounts for the growing population density in some areas of the deep South?*

PERSONS PER SQUARE MILE

- 90 and over
- 18-89
- 2-17
- Fewer than 2

the slave states in 1860, and a third of these were concentrated in Missouri, mostly in St. Louis.

The newcomers came from many different countries

German and Irish Immigrants

and regions: England, France, Italy, Scandinavia, Poland, and Holland. But the overwhelming majority came from Ireland and Germany. In 1850, the Irish constituted approximately 45 percent and the Germans over 20 percent of the foreign-born in America. By 1860, there were more than 1.5 million Irish-born and approximately 1 million German-born people in the United States. There were several reasons for this flood of immigration. In Germany, the economic dislocations of the industrial revolution had caused widespread poverty, and the collapse of the liberal revolution there in 1848 also persuaded many Germans to emigrate. In Ireland, the oppressiveness and unpopularity of English rule drove many people to emigrate. But these political factors were dwarfed in the mid-nineteenth century by the greatest disaster in Ireland's history: a catastrophic

failure of the potato crop (and other food crops) that caused the devastating "potato famine" of 1845–1849. Nearly a million people died of starvation and disease. Well over a million more emigrated to the United States.

The Irish and German patterns of settlement in America were very different. The great majority of the Irish settled in the eastern cities, where they swelled the ranks of unskilled labor. Most Germans moved on to the Northwest, where they became farmers or went into business in the western towns. One reason for the difference was wealth: German immigrants generally arrived with at least some money; the Irish had practically none. Another important reason was gender. Most German immigrants were members of family groups or were single men, for whom movement to the agricultural frontier was both possible and attractive. Many Irish immigrants were young, single women, for whom movement west was much less plausible. They were more likely to stay in the eastern cities, where factory and domestic work was available.

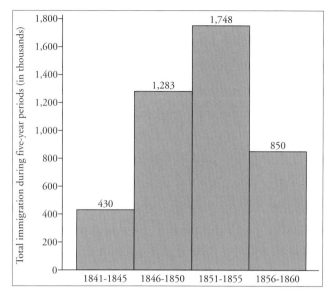

IMMIGRATION, 1840–1860 Immigration continued to increase in the forty years before the Civil War. This chart illustrates the much higher levels of growth than in the previous forty years. The low point in this era was the first half of the 1840s, in which 430,000 new immigrants entered the United States. That was significantly higher than the largest number of the previous twenty years. In the early 1850s, the number of immigrants grew to nearly two million. ◆ *What events in Europe contributed to this increase?*

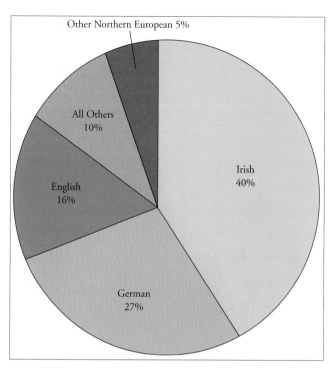

SOURCES OF IMMIGRATION, 1840–1860 Although the extent of immigration increased dramatically in the two decades after 1840, the sources of it remained remarkably stable. Note how closely the distribution of immigrant groups portrayed in this pie chart parallels that in the similar chart for the 1820–1840 period. ◆ *What were some of the differences between what German and Irish immigrants did once they arrived in America?*

The Rise of Nativism

Needless to say, the vast new foreign-born population had a profound effect on the character of American society. Some native-born Americans saw in the new immigration a source of great opportunity. Industrialists and other employers welcomed the arrival of a large supply of cheap labor, which they believed would help them keep wage rates low. Land speculators and others with investments in the sparsely populated West hoped that many of the immigrants would move into the region and help expand the population, and thus the market for land and goods, there. Political leaders in western states and territories hoped the immigrants would, by swelling their population, also increase the political influence of the region. Wisconsin, for example, permitted foreign-born residents to become voters as soon as they had declared their intention of seeking citizenship and had resided in the state for a year; other western states soon followed its lead. In eastern cities, too, urban political organizations eagerly courted immigrant voters, hoping to enhance their own political strength.

Other Americans, however, viewed the growing foreign-born population with alarm. Their fears led to the rise of what is known as "nativism," a defense of native-born people and a hostility to the foreign-born, usually combined with a desire to stop or slow immigration.

The emerging nativism took many forms. Some of it was a result of simple racism. Many nativists (conveniently overlooking their own immigrant heritage) argued that the new immigrants were inherently inferior to older-stock Americans. Some viewed them with the same contempt and prejudice—and the same low estimate of their potential abilities—with which they viewed African Americans. Many nativists avoided racist arguments but argued nevertheless that the newcomers were socially unfit to live alongside people of older stock, that they did not bring with them sufficient standards of civilization. Evidence for that, they claimed, was the wretched urban and sometimes rural slums in which they lived. (Many nativists seemed to assume that such wretchedness was something immigrants chose, rather than the result of their extreme poverty.) Others—especially workers—complained that because foreigners were willing to work for low wages, they were stealing jobs from the native labor force. Protestants, observing the success of Irish Catholics in establishing footholds in urban politics, warned that the church of Rome was gaining a foothold in American government. Whig politicians were outraged because so

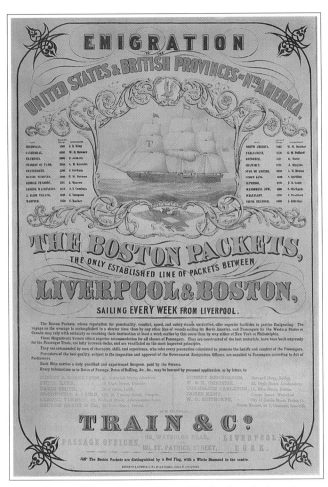

AN APPEAL TO EMIGRANTS This widely distributed advertising card was one of many appeals to potential English and Irish travelers to America in the 1830s and 1840s. Like many such companies, it tried to attract both affluent passengers (by boasting of "superior accommodations") and working-class people of modest means. *(Courtesy of The Bostonian Society/Old State House)*

A "KNOW NOTHING" FLAG The American Party, which began as a secret organization with the popular nickname "Know Nothings" (from their refusal to divulge any information about their activities), was in the forefront of antebellum campaigns against immigration— as this flag (which refers to the older-stock white members of the party as "Native Americans") suggests. The Know Nothings were particularly alarmed about the rising number of Catholic immigrants to the United States and warned that this "monster" (Catholicism) was "only waiting for the hour to approach to plant its flag of tyranny, persecution, and oppression among us." *(Photo Courtesy of Milwaukee County Historical Society)*

many of the newcomers voted Democratic. Others complained that the immigrants corrupted politics by selling their votes. Many older-stock Americans of both parties feared that immigrants would bring new, radical ideas into national life.

Out of these tensions and prejudices emerged a number of new secret societies created to combat what nativists had come to call the "alien menace." Most of them originated in the Northeast. Some later spread to

Native American Party

the West and even to the South. The first of these, the Native American Association, began agitating against immigration in 1837. In 1845, nativists held a convention in Philadelphia and formed the Native American Party (unaware that the term they used to describe themselves would one day become a common label for American Indians). Anti-immigrant sentiment crested in

the 1850s. Many of the nativist groups combined in 1850 to form the Supreme Order of the Star-Spangled Banner. It endorsed a list of demands that included banning Catholics or the foreign-born from holding public office, more restrictive naturalization laws, and literacy tests for voting. The order adopted a strict code of secrecy, which included the secret password, used in lodges across the country, "I know nothing." Ultimately, members of the movement became known as the "Know-Nothings."

Gradually, the Know-Nothings turned their attention to party politics, and after the election of 1852 they created a

The Know-Nothings

new political organization that they called the American Party. In the East, the new organization scored an immediate and astonishing success in the elections of 1854: the Know-Nothings cast a large vote in Pennsylvania and New York and won control of the state government in Massachusetts. Elsewhere, the progress of the Know-Nothings was more modest. Western members of the party, because of the presence of many German voters in the area, found it expedient not to oppose naturalized Protestants. After 1854, the strength of the Know-Nothings declined. The Know-Nothing Party's most lasting impact was its contribution to the collapse of the existing party system (organized around the Whig and Democratic parties) and the creation of new national political alignments.

"AMERICANS SHALL RULE AMERICA" Thomas Swann, a Maryland railroad magnate, was elected mayor of Baltimore in 1856 as the candidate of the American (or "Know-Nothing") Party after a campaign characterized by widespread violence and disorder and by a strident denunciation of immigrants. This cartoon lambasting the American Party's activities in Baltimore conveys the opponents' image of the Know-Nothings as a party of drunken hooligans. *(Maryland Historical Society)*

TRANSPORTATION, COMMUNICATIONS, AND TECHNOLOGY

Just as the industrial revolution required an expanding population, it also required an efficient and effective system of transportation and communications. Without such a system, merchants and manufacturers would be unable to ship their goods to distant markets or communicate effectively with trading partners in other regions. Without such a system, the industrial work force would not have access to the food supplies it needed to sustain itself. The first half of the nineteenth century saw dramatic changes in transportation and communications in the United States.

Both transportation and communications required, in turn, significant advances in technological knowledge—as did many other areas of the economy. The antebellum era was notable as well for remarkable technological advances.

The Canal Age

From 1790 until the 1820s, the so-called turnpike era, Americans had relied largely on roads for internal transportation. But in a country as large as the United States was becoming, roads alone (and the mostly horse-drawn vehicles that used them) were not adequate for the nation's expanding needs. And so, in the 1820s and 1830s, Americans began to turn to other means of transportation as well.

The larger rivers, especially the Mississippi and the Ohio, had been important transportation routes for years, but most of the traffic on them consisted of flat barges—little more than rafts—that floated downstream laden with cargo and were broken up at the end of their journeys because they could not navigate back upstream. To return north, shippers had to send goods by land or by agonizingly slow upstream vessels that sometimes took up to four months to travel the length of the Mississippi.

These rivers had become vastly more important by the 1820s, as steamboats grew in number and improved in design. *Steamboats* The new riverboats carried the corn and wheat of northwestern farmers and the cotton and tobacco of southwestern planters to New Orleans in a fraction of the time of the old barges. From New Orleans, oceangoing ships took the cargoes on to eastern ports. Steamboats also developed a significant passenger traffic, and companies built increasingly lavish vessels to compete for this lucrative trade (even though most passengers could not afford the luxurious amenities and slept in the hold or on the deck).

But neither the farmers of the West nor the merchants of the East were wholly satisfied with this pattern of trade. Farmers would pay less to transport their goods (and eastern consumers would pay less to consume them) if they could ship them directly eastward to market, rather than by the roundabout river-sea route; and northeastern merchants, too, could sell larger quantities of their manufactured goods if they could transport their

BUILDING THE ERIE CANAL This lithograph by Anthony Imbert suggests something of the enormous engineering challenges that the builders of the Erie Canal faced. This picture shows excavations at Lockport, New York, where a horse-powered crane and a large crew of Irish immigrant workers clear boulders from the channel. Imbert created these and other images to illustrate a book published in 1825 to celebrate the completion of the canal. *(Building the Erie Canal. Lithograph by Anthony Imbert. From Cadwallader Colden's* Memoir on the Celebration of the Completion of the New York Canals. *The Metropolitan Museum of Art, Harris Brisbane Dick Fund, 1941. (41.51))*

merchandise more directly and economically to the West. New highways across the mountains provided a partial solution to the problem. But the costs of hauling goods overland, although lower than before, were still too high for anything except the most compact and valuable merchandise. The thoughts of some merchants and entrepreneurs began, therefore, to turn to an alternative: canals.

A team of four horses could haul one and a half tons of goods eighteen miles a day on the turnpikes. But the same

Economic Advantages of Canals

four horses, walking along the "towpaths" next to canals while yoked to barges, could draw a boatload of a hundred tons twenty-four miles a day. By the 1820s, the economic advantages of canals had generated a booming interest in expanding the water routes to the West. Canal building was too expensive for private enterprise, and the job of digging canals fell largely to the states. The ambitious state governments of the Northeast took the lead in constructing them. New York was the first to act. It had the natural advantage of a good land route between the Hudson River and Lake Erie through

the only real break in the Appalachian chain. But the engineering tasks were still imposing. The distance was more than 350 miles, several times as long as any of the existing canals in America. The route was interrupted by high ridges and a wilderness of woods. After a long public debate over whether the scheme was practical, canal advocates prevailed when De Witt Clinton, a late but ardent convert to the cause, became governor in 1817. Digging began on July 4, 1817.

The building of the Erie Canal was the greatest construction project Americans had ever undertaken. The canal itself was simple: basically a ditch forty feet wide and four feet deep, with towpaths along the banks for the horses or mules that were to draw the canal boats. But hun-

The Erie Canal

dreds of difficult cuts and fills, some of them enormous, were required to enable the canal to pass through hills and over valleys; stone aqueducts were necessary to carry it across streams; and eighty-eight locks, of heavy masonry with great wooden gates, were needed to permit ascents and descents. The Erie Canal was not just an engineering triumph, but an immediate financial success. It opened in

THE FLOW OF WATER

No element of the North American landscape was more basic to the development of the young republic than water. The earliest settlements on the eastern seaboard were all at the ocean's edge, where they had ready access to transatlantic trade. Each major city in the new nation—Boston, New York, Philadelphia, Baltimore, Charleston, New Orleans—began life as a port. The interior trade of the continent was concentrated almost entirely along natural watercourses. Water was the catalyst that made trade and settlement possible.

Thus it is not surprising that some of the earliest large-scale manipulations of the American landscape had to do with redirecting the flow of water. Until the 1820s, most crops raised west of the Appalachians traveled to market by floating downstream toward New Orleans on the Ohio, the Mississippi, or the Missouri River. The great wave of canal building that swept the nation in the 1820s and 1830s was designed to divert that southward flow of commerce north toward the Great Lakes and east to the port towns on the Atlantic coast. The most dramatic success was, of course, the Erie Canal, which enabled New York City to capture the trade of the Great Lakes and the Ohio Valley. The emergence of New York as the greatest metropolis on the continent occurred at the same time that settlement exploded on the shores of the Great Lakes, and both

were encouraged by the canal. The canal also contributed to the decline of agriculture in New England, as farmers on marginal land found themselves unable to compete with abundant grain crops from the western prairies.

In addition to rearranging the American agricultural landscape, canals had unexpected ecological consequences. The Erie Canal introduced to Lake Ontario the sea lamprey, a parasitic fish that attaches itself to other fish and weakens or kills them by sucking their blood. It had never before inhabited the Great Lakes, but it began to put pressure on the lake's native whitefish, trout, and salmon. A complex redistribution of the lake's fish population was the long-term result, with many species declining and even disappearing.

If canals created an artificial system of waterways, dams created an equally artificial system of power that altered traditional ways of consuming energy in the American economy. The industrial revolution came to the United States not with the steam engine but with the waterwheel. Falling water had been used since the earliest colonial times to grind flour and saw lumber. But large-scale exploitation of water power did not occur until New England capitalists used British technology to mechanize the production of textiles. The best known of the New England textile towns is probably Lowell, Massachusetts, which is justly renowned in American history for the

new labor system it introduced in its factories. But Lowell's success would have been impossible had the city not harnessed the potential energy of the Merrimack River to drive its factories.

The implications of this new use of water were dramatic. Formerly, the energy that had driven the American economy had been biologically limited by the strength of horses and human workers. Now an even larger share of the energy came from rivers (until they were supplanted by coal-powered steam). The harnessing of water power had disastrous results for certain fish species, like the salmon, which formerly had swum upstream to spawn. As dams blocked major rivers of the east coast to create power sources, salmon disappeared from most of their former homes.

The typical industrial town of the water power era had certain features that are evident even today. It was always located beside a natural waterfall or rapids where a river dropped quickly from a higher to a lower elevation. A dam upstream from the town diverted water into a complicated network of canals and underground conduits. These diverted water to the factories, which straddled the natural drop in elevation. As the water flowed beneath the buildings, it turned large waterwheels and turbines. Long leather belts transmitted the resulting energy to driveshafts running the length of the factory.

WATER-POWERED FACTORY ON THE GREEN RIVER, MASSACHUSETTS American factories in the early nineteenth century depended much more on water than on steam. They were typically located near major falls or rapids on large rivers, so that canals could divert water through wheels and turbines beneath the factory, supplying power to the machinery within. (Bettmann/Corbis)

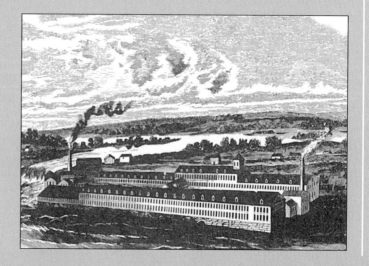

THE GREAT NEW YORK FIRE OF DECEMBER 16, 1835 One of the most devastating fires in New York City's history destroyed hundreds of buildings on December 16, 1835. Without an effective municipal water supply, firefighters had to bring water to the scene in tank carts and hand-pump it onto the flames. The fire encouraged New York citizens to support construction of the Croton Aqueduct. *(Bettmann/Corbis)*

that the workers lived nearest the factories, in flimsy structures erected on the floodplain, while managers and owners lived on the hillsides in more expensive houses that were less exposed to flooding.

The final elements of the new water landscape of nineteenth-century America were in the cities. To increase their supply of drinking water and to protect themselves from frequent fires, the great port cities of the east coast constructed great reservoir systems like New York's Croton Aqueduct, completed in 1842, which brought water from dozens of miles away. A little later, they introduced sewers to dispose of dangerous urban wastes downstream from drinking supplies. As a result, the water-borne epidemics of cholera that had devastated the United States in 1832, 1849, and 1866 had nearly vanished by the end of the century.

Ports, canals, dams, factories, reservoirs, sewers: today these are familiar features of the American landscape. At the time they were constructed, however, they constituted a revolution in the way Americans traveled, worked, drank, bathed, and protected themselves from disease. Controlling the flow of water was among the greatest environmental and technological changes of the nineteenth century.

Water power towns lived and died with water. In winter, when rivers froze with ice, factories sometimes had to shut down for lack of power. (The same was true of canals: the canal economy regularly went into hibernation during the winter months, with trade coming nearly to a standstill between December and April.) Worse, water power towns were regularly subject to flooding during storms and spring runoffs, and could suffer devastating destruction from the very source that ordinarily sustained them. This was one reason why the housing in such towns was often arranged so

THE CROTON AQUEDUCT BRINGS WATER TO NEW YORK CITY, 1842 When the Croton Aqueduct was completed, bringing water from the upper Hudson Valley to the southern tip of Manhattan, the residents of New York City staged an immense celebration. A new fountain was built in honor of the event. The aqueduct continues to supply the city with water today. *(The Research Library, The New York Public Library)*

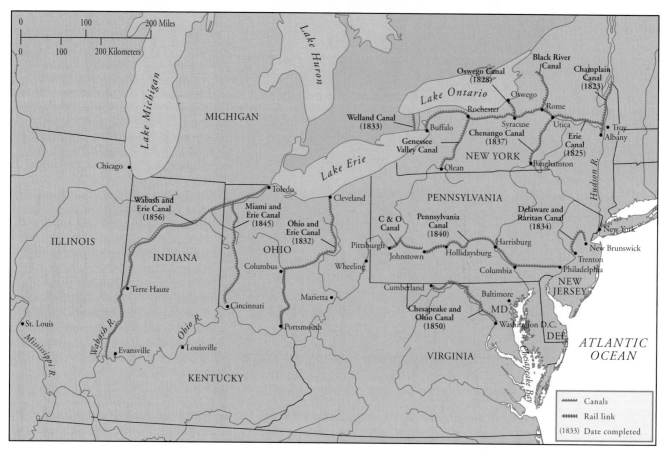

CANALS IN THE NORTHEAST, 1823–1860 The great success of the Erie Canal, which opened in 1825, inspired decades of energetic canal building in many areas of the United States, as this map illustrates. But none of the new canals had anything like the impact of the original Erie Canal, and thus none of New York's competitors—among them Baltimore, Philadelphia, and Boston—were able to displace it as the nation's leading commercial center. ◆ *What form of transportation ultimately displaced the canals?*

 For an interactive version of this map go to www.mhhe.com/brinkley11ch10maps

October 1825, amid elaborate ceremonies and celebrations, and traffic was soon so heavy that within about seven years tolls had repaid the entire cost of construction. By providing a route to the Great Lakes, the canal gave New York direct access to Chicago and the growing markets of the West. New York could now compete with (and increasingly replace) New Orleans as a destination for agricultural goods (particularly wheat) and other products of the West, and as a source for manufactured goods to be sold in the region.

The system of water transportation—and the primacy of New York—extended farther when the states of Ohio and Indiana, inspired by the success of the Erie Canal, provided water connections between Lake Erie and the Ohio River. These canals helped connect them by an inland water route all the way to New York, although it was still necessary to transfer cargoes several times between canal, lake, and river craft. One of the immediate results of these new transportation routes was increased white settlement in the Northwest, because canals made

it easier for migrants to make the westward journey and to ship their goods back to eastern markets.

Rival cities along the Atlantic seaboard took alarm at the prospect of New York's acquiring so vast a hinterland (the area supplying goods to and buying products from a port). These other cities believed that New York's phenomenal growth would come at their expense. But they had limited success in catching up. Boston, its way to the Hudson River blocked by the Berkshire Mountains, did not even try to connect itself to the West by canal; its hinterland would remain confined largely to New England. Philadelphia and Baltimore had the still more formidable Allegheny Mountains to contend with. They made a serious effort at canal building, nevertheless, but with discouraging results. Pennsylvania's effort ended in an expensive failure. Maryland constructed part of the Chesapeake and Ohio Canal beginning in 1828, but completed only the stretch between Washington, D.C., and Cumberland, Maryland, and thus never crossed the mountains. In the South, Richmond and

RACING ON THE RAILROAD Peter Cooper, who in later years was best known as a philanthropist and as the founder of the Cooper Union in New York City, was also a successful iron manufacturer. Cooper designed and built the first steam-powered locomotive in America in 1830 for the Baltimore and Ohio railroad. On August 28 of that year, he raced his locomotive (the "Tom Thumb") against a horse-drawn railroad car. This sketch depicts the moment when Cooper's engine overtook the horse-car. *(Museum of the City of New York)*

Charleston also aspired to build water routes to the Ohio Valley, but never completed them.

In the end, canals did not provide a satisfactory route to the West for any of New York's rivals. Some cities, however, saw their opportunity in a different and newer means of transportation. Even before the canal age had reached its height, the era of the railroad was already beginning.

The Early Railroads

Railroads played no more than a secondary role in the nation's transportation system in the 1820s and 1830s, but railroad pioneers laid the groundwork in those years for the great surge of railroad building in midcentury that would link the nation together as never before. Eventually, railroads became the primary transportation system for the United States, and they remained so until the construction of the interstate highway system in the mid-twentieth century.

Railroads emerged from a combination of technological and entrepreneurial innovations. The technological breakthroughs included the invention of tracks, the creation of steam-powered locomotives, and the development of railroad cars that could serve as public carriers of passengers and freight. By 1804, both English and American inventors had experimented with steam engines for propelling land vehicles. In 1820, John Stevens ran a locomotive and cars around a circular track on his New Jersey estate. And in 1825, the Stockton and Darlington Railroad in England opened a short length of track and became the first line to carry general traffic.

American entrepreneurs, especially in those northeastern cities that sought better communication with the West, quickly grew interested in the English experiment.

Technological Basis of the Railroad

The first company to begin actual operations was the Baltimore and Ohio, which opened a thirteen-mile stretch of track in 1830. In New York, the Mohawk and Hudson began running trains along the sixteen miles between Schenectady and Albany in 1831. By 1836, more than a thousand miles of track had been laid in eleven states.

But there was not yet a true railroad system. Even the longest of the lines was comparatively short in the 1830s, and most of them served simply to connect water routes, not to link one railroad to another. Even when two lines did connect, the tracks often differed in gauge (width), so that cars from one line often could not fit onto the tracks of another. Schedules were erratic, and wrecks were frequent. But railroads made some important advances in the 1830s and 1840s. The introduction of heavier iron rails improved the roadbeds. Steam locomotives became more flexible and powerful. Redesigned passenger cars became stabler, more comfortable, and larger.

Railroads and canals were soon competing bitterly. For a time, the Chesapeake and Ohio Canal Company blocked the advance of the Baltimore and Ohio Railroad through the narrow gorge of the upper Potomac, which it controlled; and the state of New York prohibited railroads from hauling freight in competition with the Erie Canal and its branches. But railroads had so many advantages that when they were able to compete freely with other forms of transportation they almost always prevailed.

Competition between Railroads and Canals

The Triumph of the Rails

After 1840, railroads gradually supplanted canals and all other modes of transport. In 1840, there were 2,818 miles of railroad tracks in the United States; by 1850, there were

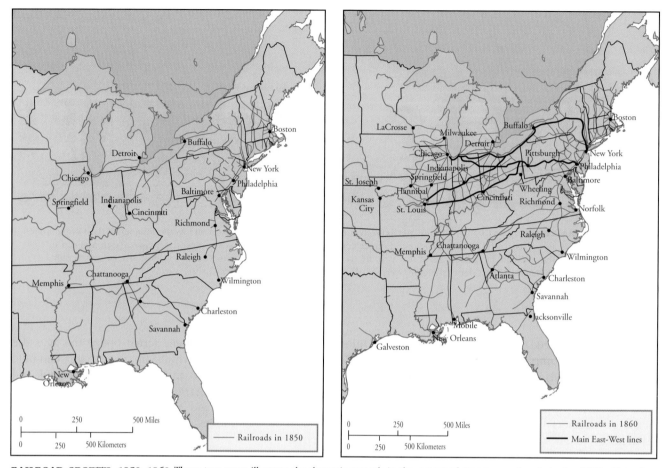

RAILROAD GROWTH, 1850–1860 These two maps illustrate the dramatic growth in the extent of American railroads in the 1850s. Note the particularly extensive increase in mileage in the upper Midwest (known at the time as the Northwest). Note too the relatively smaller increase in railroad mileage in the South. Railroads forged a close economic relationship between the upper Midwest and the Northeast, and weakened the Midwest's relationship to the South. ◆ *How did this contribute to the South's growing sense of insecurity within the Union?*

 For an interactive version of this map go to www.mhhe.com/brinkley11ch10maps

9,021. An unparalleled burst of railroad construction followed in the 1850s, tripling the amount of trackage in just ten years. The most comprehensive and efficient system was in the Northeast, which had twice as much trackage per square mile as the Northwest and four times as much as the South. But the expansion of the rails left no region untouched. Railroads were even reaching west of the Mississippi, which was spanned at several points by great iron bridges. One line ran from Hannibal to St. Joseph on the Missouri River, and another was under construction between St. Louis and Kansas City.

An important change in railroad development—one that would profoundly affect the nature of sectional align-

Consolidation

ments—was the trend toward the consolidation of short lines into longer lines (known as "trunk lines"). By 1853, four major railroad trunk lines had crossed the Appalachian barrier to connect the Northeast with the Northwest. Two, the New York Central and the New York and Erie,

gave New York City access to the Lake Erie ports. The Pennsylvania railroad linked Philadelphia and Pittsburgh, and the Baltimore and Ohio connected Baltimore with the Ohio River at Wheeling. From the terminals of these lines, other railroads into the interior touched the Mississippi River at eight points. Chicago became the rail center of the West, served by fifteen lines and more than a hundred daily trains. The appearance of the great trunk lines tended to divert traffic from the main water routes—the Erie Canal and the Mississippi River. By lessening the dependence of the West on the Mississippi, the railroads helped weaken further the connection between the Northwest and the South.

Capital to finance the railroad boom came from many sources. Private American investors provided part of the necessary funding, and railroad companies borrowed large sums from abroad. But local governments—states, counties, cities, towns—also often contributed capital, because they were eager to have railroads serve them. This support came in the form of loans, stock subscriptions, subsidies, and donations of land for rights-of-way. The railroads obtained substantial additional assistance from the federal government in the form of public land grants. In 1850, Senator Stephen A. Douglas of Illinois and other railroad-minded politicians persuaded Congress to grant federal lands to aid the Illinois Central, which was building from Chicago toward the Gulf of Mexico. Other states and their railroad promoters demanded the same privileges, and by 1860, Congress had allotted over 30 million acres to eleven states to assist railroad construction.

Innovations in Communications and Journalism

Facilitating the operation of the railroads was an important innovation in communications: the magnetic telegraph. Telegraph lines extended along the tracks, connecting one station with another and aiding the scheduling and routing of trains. But the telegraph had an importance to the nation's economic development beyond its contribution to the railroads. On the one hand, it permitted instant communication between distant cities, tying the nation together as never before. On the other hand, it helped reinforce the schism between the North and South. Like railroads, telegraph lines were far more extensive in the North than in the South, and they helped similarly to link the North to the Northwest (and thus to separate the Northwest further from the South).

The telegraph had burst into American life in 1844, *The Telegraph* | when Samuel F. B. Morse, after several years of experimentation, succeeded in transmitting from Baltimore to Washington the news of James K. Polk's nomination for the presidency. The relatively low cost of constructing wire systems made the Morse telegraph system seem the ideal answer to the problems of long-distance communication. By 1860, more than 50,000 miles of wire connected most parts of the country; and a year later, the Pacific telegraph, with 3,595 miles of wire, opened between New York and San Francisco. By then, nearly all the independent lines had joined in one organization, the Western Union Telegraph Company.

New forms of journalism also drew communities together into a common communications system. In 1846, Richard Hoe invented the steam cylinder rotary press, making it possible to print newspapers rapidly *The Associated Press* | and cheaply. The development of the telegraph, together with the introduction of the rotary press, made possible much speedier collection and distribution of news than ever before. In 1846, newspaper publishers from around the nation formed the Associated Press to promote cooperative news gathering by wire; no longer did they

THE CYLINDRICAL PRESS The revolving cylindrical press revolutionized newspaper (and other) publishing in the decades before the Civil War by making possible the printing of large numbers of papers relatively quickly. This ten-cylinder model dates from about 1850. *(Bettmann/Corbis)*

have to depend on the cumbersome exchange of newspapers for out-of-town reports.

Major metropolitan newspapers began to appear in the larger cities of the Northeast. In New York alone, there were Horace Greeley's *Tribune,* James Gordon Bennett's *Herald,* and Henry J. Raymond's *Times.* All gave serious attention to national and even international events and had substantial circulations beyond the city.

In the long run, journalism would become an important unifying factor in American life. In the 1840s and 1850s, *Fueling Sectional Discord* however, the rise of the new journalism helped to feed sectional discord. Most of the major magazines and newspapers were in the North, reinforcing the South's sense of subjugation. Southern newspapers tended to have smaller budgets and reported largely local news. Few had any impact outside their immediate communities. The combined circulation of the *Tribune* and the *Herald* exceeded that of all the daily newspapers published in the South put together. Above all, the news revolution—along with the revolutions in transportation and communications that accompanied it—contributed to a growing awareness within each section of how the other sections lived and of the deep differences that had grown up between the North and the South—differences that would ultimately seem irreconcilable.

COMMERCE AND INDUSTRY

By the middle years of the nineteenth century, the United States had developed the beginnings of a modern capitalist economy and an advanced industrial capacity. This emerging economy created *Impact of the Market Economy* enormous wealth and changed the face of all areas of the

CHICAGO, 1858 This photograph of the busy freight depot and grain elevators of the Illinois Central Railroad illustrates the rapid growth of Chicago in the 1850s as the great trading center of the central part of the United States. *(Chicago Historical Society)*

nation. But it did not, of course, affect everyone equally. Some classes and regions benefited from the economic development far more than others.

The Expansion of Business, 1820–1840

American business grew rapidly in the 1820s and 1830s, partly because of population growth and the transportation revolution, but also because of the daring, imagination, and ruthlessness of a new generation of entrepreneurs.

One important change came in the retail distribution of goods, which was becoming increasingly systematic and efficient. In the larger cities, stores specializing in groceries, dry goods, hardware, and other lines appeared, although residents of smaller towns and villages still depended on general stores (stores that did not specialize and carried small selections of a great many different kinds of merchandise). In these less populous areas, many people did much of their business by barter.

The organization of business was also changing. Individuals or limited partnerships continued to operate most businesses, and the dominating figures were still the great merchant capitalists, who generally had sole ownership of their enterprises. In some larger businesses, however, the individual merchant capitalist was giving way to the corporation. Corporations had the advantage of combin-

Advantages of the Corporation

ing the resources of a large number of shareholders, and they began to develop particularly rapidly in the 1830s, when some legal obstacles to

their formation were removed. Previously, a corporation could obtain a charter only by a special act of the state legislature—a cumbersome process that stifled corporate growth. By the 1830s, however, states were beginning to pass general incorporation laws, under which a group could secure a charter merely by paying a fee.

The new laws also permitted a system of limited liability, which meant that individual stockholders risked losing only the value of their own investment if a corporation should fail, and that they were not liable (as they had been in the past) for the corporation's larger losses. The rise of these new corporations made possible the accumulation of much greater amounts of capital and hence made possible much larger manufacturing and business enterprises.

Investment alone, however, still provided too little capital to meet the demands of the most ambitious businesses. Such businesses relied heavily on credit, and their bor-

Inadequate Credit

rowing often created dangerous instability. Credit mechanisms remained very crude in the early nineteenth century. The government alone could issue official currency, but the official currency consisted only of gold and silver (or paper certificates backed literally by gold and silver), and there was thus too little of it to support the growing demand for credit. Under pressure from corporate promoters, many banks issued large quantities of bank notes—unofficial currency that circulated in much the same way that government currency did but was of much less stable value. Banks issued these notes to meet the growing demand for capital for expanding business ventures. But the notes had value only to the degree that the bank could sustain public confidence in their value; and some banks issued so many notes that their own reserves could not cover them. As a result, bank failures were frequent, and bank deposits were often insecure. The difficulty of obtaining credit for business investment remained, therefore, an impediment to economic growth.

The Emergence of the Factory

The most profound economic development in mid-nineteenth-century America was the rise of the factory. Before the War of 1812, most of what manufacturing there was in the United States took place within private households or in small, individually operated workshops. Men and women built or made products by hand, or with simple machines such as hand-operated looms. Gradually, however, improved technology and increasing demand produced a fundamental change. It came first in the New England textile industry. There, beginning early in the nineteenth century, entrepreneurs were beginning to make use of new and larger machines driven by water power that allowed them to bring textile operations together under a single roof. This factory system, as it came to be known, spread rapidly in the 1820s and began to make serious inroads into the old home-based system of spinning thread and weaving cloth.

Factories also penetrated the shoe industry, concentrated in eastern Massachusetts. Shoes were still largely *Transformation of the Shoe Industry* | handmade, but manufacturers were beginning to employ workers who specialized in one or another of the various tasks involved in production. Some factories began producing large numbers of identical shoes in ungraded sizes and without distinction as to rights and lefts. By the 1830s, factory production was spreading from textiles and shoes into other industries and from New England to other areas of the Northeast.

Between 1840 and 1860, American industry experienced even more dramatic growth as the factory system spread rapidly. In 1840, the total value of manufactured goods produced in the United States stood at $483 million; ten years later the figure had climbed to over $1 billion; and in 1860 it reached close to $2 billion. For the first time, the value of manufactured goods was approximately equal to that of agricultural products.

Of the approximately 140,000 manufacturing establishments in the country in 1860, 74,000 were located in the Northeast. Moreover, they included most of the larger enterprises. The Northeast had only a little more than half *The Industrial Northeast* | the mills and factories in the United States; but the plants there were so large that the region produced more than two-thirds of the nation's manufactured goods. Of the

1,311,000 workers in manufacturing in the United States, about 938,000 were employed in the mills and factories of New England and the mid-Atlantic states.

Advances in Technology

Even the most highly developed industries were still relatively immature. American cotton manufacturers, for example, produced goods of coarse grade; fine items continued to come from England. But by the 1840s, significant advances were in progress. Machine technology advanced more rapidly in the United States in the mid-nineteenth century than in any other country in the world—partly because Americans were still catching up with the more advanced technologies of Europe and had to move quickly in order to compete; and partly because the American economy was growing so rapidly that the rewards of technological innovation were very great. Change was so rapid, in fact, that some manufacturers built their new machinery out of wood; by the time the wood wore out, they reasoned, improved technology would have made the machine obsolete. By the beginning of the 1830s, American technology had become so advanced—particularly in textile manufacturing—that industrialists in Britain and Europe were beginning to travel to the United States to learn new techniques, instead of the other way around.

Among the most important was in the manufacturing of machine tools—the tools used to make machinery parts. The government supported much of the research and development of machine tools, often in connection with supplying the military. For example, a government armory in Springfield, Massachusetts, developed two important tools—the turret lathe (used for cutting screws and other metal parts) and the universal milling machine (which replaced the hand chiseling of complicated parts and dies with a machine process that could ensure that all milling would be identical)—early in the nineteenth century. The precision grinding machine (which became critical to, among other things, the construction of sewing machines) was designed in the 1850s to help the United States Army produce standardized rifle parts. The federal armories such as those at Springfield and Harpers Ferry, Virginia, where these and other tools were developed, became the breeding ground for many technological discoveries, and a magnet for craftsmen and factory owners looking for ideas that could be of use to them. By the 1840s, the machine tools used in the factories of the Northeast were already better than those in most European factories.

One of the principal results of the creation of better machine tools was that the principle of interchangeable parts, | *Interchangeable Parts* which Eli Whitney and Simeon North had tried to introduce into gun factories they had designed decades earlier, now found its way into many industries. Eventually, interchangeability would revolutionize watch and clock making, the manufacturing of locomotives, the creation of steam engines, and the making of many farm tools. It would also help make possible such newer devices as bicycles, sewing machines, typewriters, cash registers, and eventually the automobile.

Industrialization was also profiting from the introduction of new sources of energy. Coal was replacing wood and water power as fuel for many factories. The production of coal, most of it mined around Pittsburgh in western Pennsylvania, leaped from 50,000 tons in 1820 to 14 million tons in 1860. The new power source made it possible to locate mills away from running streams and thus permitted industry to expand still more widely.

The great technological advances in American industry owed much to American inventors, as the patent *Technological Innovations* records of the time make clear. In 1830, the number of inventions patented was 544; by 1850, the figure had risen to 993; and in 1860, it stood at 4,778. Several industries provide particularly vivid examples of how a technological innovation could produce a major economic change. In 1839, Charles Goodyear, a New England hardware merchant, discovered a method of vulcanizing rubber (treating it to give it greater strength and elasticity); by 1860, his process had found over 500 uses and had helped create a major American rubber industry. In 1846, Elias Howe of Massachusetts constructed a sewing machine; Isaac Singer made improvements on it, and the Howe-Singer machine was soon being used in the manufacture of ready-to-wear clothing. A few years later, during the Civil War, it would supply the Northern troops with uniforms.

Innovations in Corporate Organization

The merchant capitalists—entrepreneurs who were engaged primarily in foreign and domestic trade and who at times invested some of their profits in small-scale manufacturing ventures—remained figures of importance in the 1840s. In such cities as New York, Philadelphia, and Boston, influential mercantile groups operated shipping lines to southern ports—carrying off cotton, rice, and sugar—or dispatched fleets of trading vessels to the ports of Europe and Asia. Among their vessels were the famous clippers, the fastest (and most beautiful) sailing ships afloat. In their heyday in the late 1840s and early 1850s, the clippers could average 300 miles a day, which compared favorably with the best time of contemporary steamships.

But merchant capitalism was declining by the middle of *Decline of Merchant Capitalism* the century. This was partly because British competitors were stealing much of America's export trade. But the more important reason for the decline was the discovery by the merchants themselves that there were greater opportunities for profit in manufacturing than in trade. That was one reason why industries developed first in the Northeast: an affluent merchant class already existed there and had the money and the will to finance them.

By the 1840s, the corporate form of organization was spreading rapidly, particularly in the textile industry. Ownership of American enterprise was gradually moving away from individuals and families and toward its highly dispersed modern form: many stockholders, each owning a relatively small proportion of the total. But whatever the form of business organization—and there continued to be many different forms—industrial capitalists soon became the new ruling class, the aristocrats of the Northeast, with far-reaching economic and political influence.

MEN AND WOMEN AT WORK

However sophisticated industrial firms became technologically and administratively, manufacturers still relied above all on a supply of labor. In the 1820s and 1830s, factory labor came primarily from the native-born population. After 1840, the growing immigrant population became the most important new source of workers.

Recruiting a Native Work Force

Recruiting a labor force was not an easy task in the early years of the factory system. Ninety percent of the American people in the 1820s still lived and worked on farms. City residents, although increasing in number, were still relatively few, and the potential workers among them even fewer. Many urban residents were skilled artisans—independent craft workers who owned and managed their own shops as small businessmen; they were not likely to flock to factory jobs. The available unskilled workers were not numerous enough to form a reservoir from which the new industries could draw.

The beginnings of an industrial labor supply came instead from the transformation of American agriculture in the nineteenth century. The *Transformation of American Agriculture* opening of vast, fertile new farmlands in the Midwest, the improvement of transportation systems, the development of new farm machinery—all combined to increase food production dramatically. New farming methods were also less labor intensive than the old ones; the number of workers required to produce large crops in the West was much smaller than the number required to produce smaller crops in the Northeast. No longer did each region have to feed itself entirely from its own farms; it could

WOMEN AT WORK This early photograph of female millworkers standing before their machines suggests something of the primitive quality of early factories—dimly lit, cramped, with conditions that offered little protection against accidents. All the women in this picture are wearing hair tightly pulled back, to prevent it from being caught in one of the machines. *(Courtesy George Eastman House)*

import food from other regions. As as result, farmers and their families began to abandon some of the relatively unprofitable farming areas of the East. In the Northeast, and especially in New England, where poor land had always placed harsh limits on farm productivity, rural people began leaving the land to work in the factories.

Two systems of recruitment emerged to bring this new labor supply to the expanding textile mills. One, common in the mid-Atlantic states (especially in such major manufacturing centers as New York and Philadelphia), brought whole families from the farm to the mill. Parents tended looms alongside their children, some of whom were no more than four or five years old. The second system, common in Massachusetts, enlisted young women, mostly farmers' daughters in their late teens and early twenties. It was known as the Lowell or Waltham system, after the factory towns in which it first emerged. Many of these women worked for several years in the factories, saved their wages, and returned home to marry and raise children. Others married men they met in the factories or in town and remained part of the industrial world. But they often stopped working in the mills and took up domestic roles instead.

Labor conditions in these early years of the factory system were significantly better than those in English industry, better too than they would ultimately become in much of the United States. The employment of young children created undeniable hardships. But the misery was not as great as in European factories, since working children in America usually remained under the supervision of their parents. In England, by contrast, asylum authorities often hired out orphans to factory owners who showed little concern for their welfare and kept them in something close to slavery.

Even more different from the European labor system was a second labor system, common in Lowell and factory *The Lowell System* towns like it. This was a system that relied heavily, indeed almost exclusively, on young unmarried women. In England and other areas of industrial Europe, the conditions of work for women were often horrifyingly bad. A British parliamentary investigation revealed, for example, that women workers in the coal mines endured unimaginably wretched conditions. Some had to crawl on their hands and knees, naked and filthy, through cramped, narrow tunnels, pulling heavy coal carts behind them. It was little wonder that English visitors to America considered the Lowell mills a female paradise by contrast. The Lowell workers lived in clean boardinghouses and dormitories, which the factory owners maintained for them. They were well fed and carefully supervised. Because many New Englanders considered the employment of women to be vaguely immoral, the factory owners placed great emphasis on maintaining a proper environment for their employees, enforcing strict curfews and requiring regular church attendance. Employers quickly dismissed women suspected of immoral conduct. Wages for the Lowell workers were low, but generous by the standards of the time. The women even found time to write and publish a monthly magazine, the *Lowell Offering*.

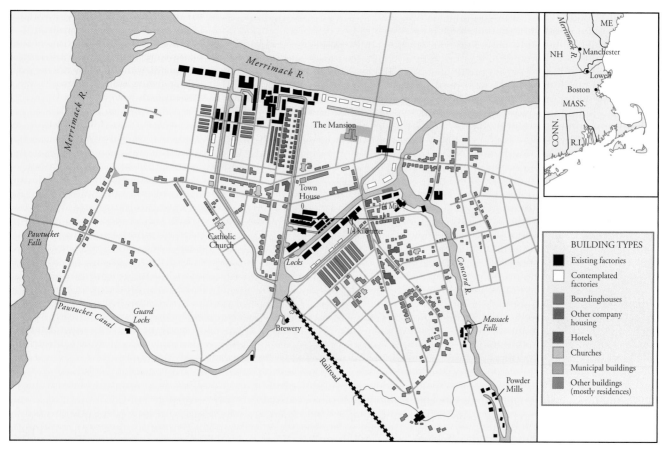

LOWELL, MASSACHUSETTS, 1832 Lowell was one of the leading manufacturing centers of New England in the 1830s, and one of the largest textile centers in America. Lowell relied heavily on women workers. Company owners—in deference to popular uneasiness about women working outside the home—created a paternalistic system of boarding houses for them, where they could be carefully supervised. This map shows the clusters of boarding houses adjacent to groups of factories. Note how concentrated the manufacturing center of the town was, and how the transportation system (rail and water) served the factories. Note also the many churches, which women workers were usually required to attend. ◆ *What happened to this labor system in the 1840s and 1850s?*

Yet even these relatively well-treated workers often *Women Workers* found the transition from farm life to factory work difficult, even traumatic. Uprooted from everything familiar, forced to live among strangers in a regimented environment, many women suffered from severe loneliness and disorientation. Still more had difficulty adjusting to the nature of factory work—the repetition of fixed tasks hour after hour, day after day. That the women had to labor from sunrise to sunset was not in itself a new experience; many of them had worked similarly long days on the farm. But that they now had to spend those days performing tedious, unvarying chores, and that their schedules did not change from week to week or season to season, made the adjustment to factory work especially painful. But however uncomfortable women may have found factory work, they had few other options. They were barred from such manual labor as construction or from work as sailors or on the docks. Most of society considered it unthinkable for women to travel the country alone, as many men did, in

search of opportunities. Work in the mills was in many cases virtually the only alternative to returning to farms that could no longer support them.

The paternalistic factory system of Lowell did not, in any case, survive for long. In the competitive textile market as it developed in the 1830s and 1840s—a market prey to the booms and busts that afflicted the American economy as a whole—manufacturers found it *Decline of the Lowell* difficult to maintain the high liv- *System* ing standards and reasonably attractive working conditions with which they had begun. Wages declined; the hours of work lengthened; the conditions of the boardinghouses deteriorated as the buildings decayed and overcrowding increased.

In 1834, mill workers in Lowell organized a union—the Factory Girls Association—which staged a strike to protest a 25 percent wage cut. Two years later, the association struck again—against a rent increase in the boardinghouses. Both strikes failed, and a recession in 1837 virtually destroyed the organization. Eight years

FOUR WOMEN WEAVERS This tintype shows four young women employed in the textile factories of Lowell, Massachusetts. Neatly dressed in matching uniforms, they conveyed the image the factory managers wanted the public to absorb: that women could work in the mills and still be protected from the rough and tumble world of industrialization. *(American Textile History Museum. Lowell, Massachusetts)*

later the Lowell women, led by the militant Sarah Bagley, created the Female Labor Reform Association and began agitating for a ten-hour day and for improvements in conditions in the mills. The new association not only made demands of management; it also turned to state government and asked for legislative investigation of conditions in the mills. By then, however, the character of the factory work force was changing again. The mill girls were gradually moving into other occupations: teaching, domestic service, or marriage. And textile manufacturers were turning to a less contentious labor supply: immigrants.

The Immigrant Work Force

The rapidly increasing supply of immigrant workers after 1840 was a boon to manufacturers and other entrepreneurs. At last they had access to a source of labor that was both large and inexpensive. These new workers, because of their vast numbers and their unfamiliarity with their new country, had even less leverage than the women they at times displaced. As a result, they often encountered far worse working conditions. Construction gangs, made up increasingly of Irish immigrants, performed the heavy, unskilled work on

Economic Advantages of Immigrant Labor

turnpikes, canals, and railroads under often intolerable conditions. Because most of these workers had no marketable skills and because of native prejudice against them, they received wages so low—and received them so intermittently, since the work was seasonal and uncertain—that they generally did not earn enough to support their families in even minimal comfort. Many of them lived in flimsy shanties, in grim conditions that endangered the health of their families (and reinforced native prejudices toward the "shanty Irish").

Irish workers began to predominate in the New England textile mills as well in the 1840s, and their arrival accelerated the deterioration of working conditions there. There was far less social pressure on owners to provide a decent environment for Irish workers than there had been to provide the same for native women. Employers began paying piece rates (wages tied to how much a worker produced) rather than a daily wage and employed other devices to speed up production and use the labor force more profitably and efficiently. By the mid-1840s, Lowell—once a model for foreign visitors of enlightened industrial development—had become a squalid slum. Similarly miserable working-class neighborhoods were emerging in other northeastern cities.

In almost all industrial areas, factories themselves were becoming large, noisy, unsanitary, and often dangerous places to work. The average workday was extending to *Harsh Work Conditions* twelve, often fourteen hours. Wages were declining, so that even skilled male workers could hope to earn only from $4 to $10 per week, while unskilled laborers were likely to earn only about $1 to $6 per week. Women and children, whatever their skills, also earned less than most men. Conditions were still not as bad as in most factory towns in England and Europe, but neither were American factories the models of cleanliness, efficiency, and human concern that many people had once believed them to be.

The Factory System and the Artisan Tradition

It was not only the mill workers who suffered from the transition to the modern factory system. It was also the skilled artisans whose trades the factories were displacing. The artisan tradition was as much a part of the older, republican vision of America as the tradition of sturdy, independent, yeoman farmers. Independent craftsmen considered themselves embodiments of the American ideal; they clung to a vision of economic life that was in some ways very different from that the new capitalist class was promoting. It was a vision based not just on the idea of individual, acquisitive success (although they were not, of course, averse to profits) but also on a sense of a "moral community." Skilled artisans valued their independence; they also valued the stability and relative equality within their economic world.

The factory system threatened that world with obsolescence. Some artisans made *Deskilling* successful transitions into small-scale industry. But others found themselves unable to compete with the new factory-made goods that sold for a fraction of the artisans' prices. In the face of this competition from industrial capitalists, craftsmen began early in the nineteenth century to form organizations—workingmen's political parties and the first American labor unions—to protect their endangered positions and to resist the new economic order in which they sensed they would have no role. As early as the 1790s, printers and cordwainers took the lead. The cordwainers—makers of high-quality boots and shoes—suffered from the competition of the new shoe factories capitalists were building in New England and elsewhere. The development of mass-production methods threatened their livelihoods; it also threatened their independence and their status in their communities. Members of other skilled trades—carpenters, joiners, masons, plasterers, hatters, and shipbuilders—felt similarly vulnerable.

In such cities as Philadelphia, Baltimore, Boston, and *National Trade Unions* New York, the skilled workers of each craft formed societies for mutual aid. During the 1820s and 1830s, the craft societies began to combine on a citywide basis and set up central organizations known as trade unions. With the widening of markets, the economies of cities were interconnected, so workers soon realized there were advantages in joining forces and established national unions or federations of local ones. In 1834, delegates from six cities founded the National Trades' Union; and in 1836, the printers and the cordwainers set up their own national craft unions.

This early craft union movement fared poorly. Labor leaders struggled against the handicap of hostile laws and hostile courts. The common law, as interpreted by the courts in the industrial states, viewed a combination among workers as, in itself, an illegal conspiracy. Adverse court decisions, however, were not the only things obstructing the rising unions. The Panic of 1837, a dramatic financial collaspe that produced a severe recession, weakened the movement further. Still, the failure of these first organizations did not end the efforts by workers—artisans and factory operatives alike—to gain some control over their productive lives.

Fighting for Control

Workers at all levels of the emerging industrial economy made continuous efforts to improve their lots. They tried, with little success, to persuade state legislatures to pass laws setting a maximum workday. Two states—New Hampshire in 1847 and Pennsylvania in 1848—actually passed ten-hour laws, limiting the workday unless the workers agreed to an "express contract" calling for more time on the job. Such measures were virtually without impact, however, because employers could simply require prospective employees to sign the "express contract" as a condition of hiring. Three states—Massachusetts, New Hampshire, and Pennsylvania—passed laws regulating child labor. But again, the results were minimal. The laws simply limited the workday to ten hours for children unless their parents agreed to something longer; employers had little difficulty persuading parents to consent to additional hours.

Perhaps the greatest legal victory of industrial workers came in Massachusetts in 1842, when the supreme court of the *Commonwealth v. Hunt* state, in *Commonwealth* v. *Hunt*, declared that unions were lawful organizations and that the strike was a lawful weapon. Other state courts gradually accepted the principles of the Massachusetts decision. On the whole, however, the union movement of the 1840s and 1850s remained generally ineffective. Some workers were reluctant to think of themselves as members of a permanent laboring force and resisted joining unions. But even those unions that did manage to recruit significant numbers of industrial workers were usually not large enough or strong enough to stage strikes, and even less frequently strong enough to win them.

Artisans and skilled workers, despite their setbacks in the 1830s, had somewhat greater success than did factory workers. But their unions often had more in common with preindustrial guilds than with modern labor organizations. In most cases, their primary purpose was to protect the favored position of their members in the labor force by restricting admission to the skilled trades. The organizing effort that had floundered in the 1830s revived impressively in the 1850s. Among the new organizations skilled workers created were the National Typographical Union, founded in 1852, the Stone Cutters in 1853, the Hat Finishers in 1854, and the Molders and the Machinists, both in 1859.

Virtually all the early craft unions excluded women, even though female workers were numerous in almost

Female Protective Unions every industry and craft. As a result, women began establishing their own protective unions by the 1850s, often with the support of middle-class female reformers. Like the male craft unions, the female protective unions had little power in dealing with employers. They did, however, serve an important role as mutual aid societies for women workers.

Despite these persistent efforts at organization and protest, the American working class in the 1840s and 1850s was notable for its relatively modest power. In England, workers were becoming a powerful, united, and often violent economic and political force. They were creating widespread social turmoil and helping to transform the nation's political structure. In America, nothing of the sort happened. Many factors combined to inhibit the growth of effective labor resistance. Among the most important was the flood of immigrant laborers into the country. The newcomers were usually willing to work for lower wages than native workers. Because they were so numerous, manufacturers had

America's Divided Working Class

little difficulty replacing disgruntled or striking workers with eager immigrants. Ethnic divisions and tensions—both between natives and immigrants and among the various immigrant groups themselves—often led workers to channel their resentments into internal bickering rather than into their shared grievances against employers. There was, too, the sheer strength of the industrial capitalists, who had not only economic but also political and social power and could usually triumph over even the most militant challenges.

PATTERNS OF INDUSTRIAL SOCIETY

The industrial revolution was making the United States—and particularly its more economically developed regions—dramatically wealthier by the year. It was also making society more unequal, and it was transforming social relationships and everyday life at almost every level—from the workplace to the family.

The Rich and the Poor

The commercial and industrial growth of the United States greatly elevated the average income of the American people. But what evidence there is—and it is admittedly

THE SHOP AND WAREHOUSE OF DUNCAN PHYFE Duncan Phyfe was a celebrated and (as this watercolor by John Rubens Smith suggests) prosperous furniture maker in New York for many decades, serving the growing population of affluent households in search of refinement and display. The elegant Georgian details on Phyfe's shop on Fulton Street suggest how even places of business were adapting to the new conception of opulence. *(The Metropolitan Museum of Art, Rogers Fund, 1922(22.28.1) Photograph © 1982 The Metropolitan Museum of Art)*

CENTRAL PARK To affluent New Yorkers, the construction of the city's great Central Park was important because it provided them with an elegant setting for their daily carriage rides—an activity ostensibly designed to expose the riders to fresh air but that was really an occasion for them to display their finery to their neighbors. *(Museum of the City of New York)*

sketchy—suggests that this increasing wealth was being distributed highly unequally.

Increasing Inequality in Wealth

Substantial groups of the population, of course, shared hardly at all in the economic growth: slaves, Indians, landless farmers, and many of the unskilled workers on the fringes of the manufacturing system. But even among the rest of the population, disparities of income were marked. Wealth had always been unequally distributed in the United States, to be sure. Even in the era of the Revolution, according to some estimates, 45 percent of the wealth was concentrated in the hands of about 10 percent of the population. But by the mid-nineteenth century, that concentration had become far more pronounced. In Boston in 1845, for example, 4 percent of the citizens are estimated to have owned more than 65 percent of the wealth; in Philadelphia in 1860, 1 percent of the population possessed more than half the wealth. Among the American people overall in 1860, according to scholarly estimates, 5 percent of the families possessed more than 50 percent of the wealth.

There had been wealthy classes in America almost from the beginning of European settlement. But the extent and character of wealth was changing in response to the commercial revolution of the mid-nineteenth century. Merchants and industrialists were accumulating enormous fortunes; and because there was now a significant number of rich people living in cities, a distinctive culture of wealth began to emerge. In large cities, people of great wealth gathered together in neighborhoods of astonishing opulence. They founded clubs and developed elaborate social rituals. They looked increasingly for ways to display their wealth—in the great mansions they built, the showy carriages in which they rode, the lavish household goods they accumulated, the clothes they wore, the elegant social establishments they patronized. New York, which had more wealthy families than anywhere else, developed a particularly elaborate high society. The construction of the city's great Central Park, which began in the 1850s, was in part a result of pressure from the members of high society, who wanted an elegant setting for their daily carriage rides.

There was also a significant population of genuinely destitute people emerging in the growing urban centers of the nation. These were people who were not merely poor,

The Urban Poor

AMERICA'S ECONOMIC REVOLUTION **285**

in the sense of having to struggle to sustain themselves— most Americans were poor in that sense. They were almost entirely without resources, often homeless, dependent on charity or crime or both for survival. Substantial numbers of people actually starved to death or died of exposure.

Some of these "paupers," as contemporaries called them, were recent immigrants who had failed to find work or to adjust to life in the New World. Some were widows and orphans, stripped of the family structures that allowed most working-class Americans to survive. Some were people suffering from alcoholism or mental illness, unable to work. Others were victims of native prejudice—barred from all but the most menial employment because of race or ethnicity. The Irish were particular victims of such prejudice.

Among the worst victims were free blacks. African-American communities in antebellum northern cities were small by later standards, but most major urban areas *African-American Poverty* had significant black populations. Some of these African Americans were descendants of families that had lived in the North for generations. Others were former slaves who had escaped from the South or been released by their masters or had bought their freedom; some former slaves, once free, then worked to buy the freedom of relatives left behind. In material terms, at least, life was not always much better for them in the North than it had been in slavery. Most had access only to very menial jobs, which usually paid too little to allow workers to support their families or educate their children; in bad times many had access to no jobs at all. In most parts of the North, blacks could not vote, could not attend public schools, indeed could not use any of the public services available to white residents. Most blacks preferred life in the North, however arduous, to life in the South because it permitted them at least some level of freedom. But that freedom did not bring anything approaching equality.

Social Mobility

One might expect the contrasts between conspicuous wealth and conspicuous poverty in antebellum America to have encouraged more class conflict than actually occurred. But a number of factors operated to quell resentments. For one thing, however much the relative economic position of American workers may have been declining, the absolute living standard of most laborers was improving. Life, in material terms at least, was usually better for factory workers than it had been on the farms or in the European societies from which they had migrated. They ate better, they were often better clothed and housed, and they had greater access to consumer goods.

There was also a significant amount of mobility within the working class, which helped to limit discontent.

Opportunities for social mobility, for working one's way up the economic ladder, were limited, but the opportunities *Social Mobility* did exist. A few workers did manage to move from poverty to riches by dint of work, ingenuity, and luck—a very small number, but enough to support the dreams of those who watched them. And a much larger number of workers managed to move at least one notch up the ladder—for example, becoming in the course of a lifetime a skilled, rather than an unskilled, laborer. Such people could envision their children and grandchildren moving up even further.

More common than social mobility was geographical mobility, which was even more extensive in the United States than in Europe, where it was considerable. America had a huge expanse of uncultivated land in the West, much of it open for settlement for the first time in the 1840s and 1850s. Some workers saved money, bought land, and moved west to farm it. The historian Frederick Jackson Turner later referred to the availability of western lands as a "safety valve" for discontent, a basic explanation for the relative lack of social conflict in the antebellum United States. But few urban workers, and even fewer poor ones, could afford to make such a move or had the expertise to know how to work land even if they could have bought it. Much more common was the movement of laborers from one industrial town to another. Restless, questing, sometimes hopeful, sometimes despairing, these frequently moving people were often the victims of layoffs, looking for better opportunities elsewhere. Their search may seldom have led to a marked improvement in their circumstances, but the rootlessness of this large segment of the work force—one of the most distressed segments—made effective organization and protest far more difficult.

There was, finally, another "safety valve" for working-class discontent: politics. Economic opportunity may not have greatly expanded in the nineteenth century, but opportunities to participate in politics did. And to many white, male working people, access to the ballot seemed to offer a way to help guide their society and to feel like a significant part of their communities.

Middle-Class Life

For all the visibility of the very rich and the very poor in antebellum society, the fastest-growing group in America was the middle class. The expansion of the middle class was in part a result of the growth of the industrial economy and the increasing commercial life that accompanied it. Economic development opened many more opportunities for people to own or work *Rapidly Expanding Middle* in businesses, to own shops, to *Class* engage in trade, to enter professions, and to administer organizations. In earlier times, when ownership of land had been the only real basis of wealth, society had been divided between people with little or no land (people Europeans generally called peasants) and a landed gentry (which in Europe usually became an inherited aristocracy). Once commerce and industry became a source of wealth, these rigid distinctions broke down; and many people could become prosperous without owning land, but by providing valuable services to the new economy or by owning capital other than land.

Middle-class life in the years before the Civil War rapidly established itself as the most influential cultural form of urban America. Middle-class families lived in solid and often substantial homes. Their rowhouses lined city streets, larger in size and more elaborate in design than the cramped, functional rowhouses in working-class neighborhoods—but also far less lavish than the great houses of the very rich. Like the wealthy, middle-class people tended to own their homes. Workers and artisans were increasingly becoming renters—a relatively new phenomenon in American cities that spread widely in the early nineteenth century.

Middle-class women tended to remain in the home and care for the children and the household, although increasingly they were also able to hire servants—usually young, unmarried immigrant women who put in long hours of arduous work for very little money. One of the aspirations of middle-class women in an age when doing the family's laundry could take an entire day was to escape from some of the drudgery of housework.

New household inventions altered, and greatly improved, the character of life in *New Household Inventions* middle-class homes. Perhaps the most important was the invention of the cast-iron stove, which began to replace fireplaces as the principal vehicle for cooking and also as an important source of heat. These wood- or coal-burning devices were hot, clumsy, and dirty by the standards of the twentieth century; but compared to the inconvenience and danger of cooking on an open hearth, they seemed a great luxury to nineteenth-century families. Stoves gave cooks more control over the preparation of food and allowed them to cook several things at once.

Middle-class diets were changing rapidly in the antebellum years, and not just because of the wider range of cooking the stove made possible. The expansion and diversification of American agriculture, and the ability of farmers to ship goods to urban markets by rail from distant regions greatly increased the variety of food available in cities. Fruits and vegetables were difficult to ship over long distances in an age with little refrigeration, but families had access to a greater variety of meats, grains, and dairy products than they had had in the past. A few households acquired iceboxes in the years before the Civil War, and the sight of wagons delivering large chunks of ice to wealthy and middle-class homes began to become a familiar part of urban life. Iceboxes allowed their owners to keep fresh meat and dairy products for as long as several days without

spoilage. Most families, however, did not yet have any kind of refrigeration. Preserving food for them meant curing meat with salt and preserving fruits in sugar. Diets were generally much heavier and starchier than they are today, and middle-class people tended to be considerably stouter than would be fashionable in the twentieth century.

Middle-class homes came to differentiate themselves from those of workers and artisans in other ways as well. They were more elaborately decorated and furnished, with *Growing Class Distinctions* goods made available for the first time through factory production of household goods. Houses that had once had bare walls and floors now had carpeting, wallpaper, and curtains. The spare, simple styles of eighteenth-century homes gave way to the much more elaborate, even baroque household styles of the early Victorian era—styles increasingly characterized by crowded, even cluttered rooms, dark colors, lush fabrics, and heavy furniture and draperies. Middle-class homes also became larger. It became less common for children to share beds and for all family members to sleep in the same room. Parlors and dining rooms separate from the kitchen—once a luxury reserved largely for the wealthy—became the norm for the middle class as well. Some urban middle-class homes had indoor plumbing and indoor toilets by the 1850s—a significant advance over the outdoor wells and privies that had been virtually universal only a few years earlier (and that remained common among working-class people).

The Changing Family

The new industrializing society of the northern regions of the United States produced profound changes in the nature and function of the family. At the heart of the transformation was the movement of families from farms to urban areas, where jobs, not land, were the most valued commodities. The patriarchal system of the countryside, where fathers controlled their children's futures by controlling the distribution of land to them, could not survive the move to a city or town. Sons and daughters were much more likely to leave the family in search of work than they had been in the rural world.

Another important change was the shift of income-earning work out of the home and into the shop, mill, or factory. In the early decades of the nineteenth century (and for many years before that), the family itself had been the principal unit of economic activity. Family farms, family shops, and family industries were the norm throughout most of the United States. Men, women, and children worked together, sharing tasks and jointly earning the income that sustained the family. But in the middle years of the nineteenth century, there were important changes.

Those changes occurred even among the farming population, which continued to constitute the majority of the American people. As farming spread to the fertile lands of

PASTORAL AMERICA, 1848 This painting by the American artist Edward Hicks suggests the degree to which Americans continued to admire the "Peaceable Kingdom" (the name of another, more famous Hicks work) of the agrarian world. Hicks entitled this work *An Indian Summer view of the Farm w. Stock of James C. Cornell of Northampton Bucks county Pennsylvania. That took the Premium in the Agricultural Society, October the 12, 1848.* It portrays the diversified farming of a prosperous Pennsylvania family, shown here in the foreground with their cattle, sheep, and workhorses. In the background stretches a field ready for plowing and another ready for harvesting. *(National Gallery of Art, Washington)*

the Northwest and as the size and profitability of farms

Declining Economic Role of the Family

expanded, agricultural work became more commercialized. Farm owners in need of labor began to rely less on their families (which often were not large enough to satisfy the demand) and more on hired male workers. These farmhands performed many of the tasks that on smaller farms had once been the jobs of the women and children of the family. As a result, farm women tended to work increasingly at domestic tasks—cooking, sewing, gardening, and dairying—a development that spared them from some heavy labor but that also removed them from the principal income-producing activities of the farm. Farm women in the new agricultural regions of the Northwest tended, therefore, to have a lower economic status within the family (and within the community) than their earlier counterparts in the East, who had been more crucial to the family economy. (See Chapter 11 for a discussion of family relations in the agrarian South.)

In the industrial economy of the rapidly growing cities, there was an even more significant decline in the traditional economic function of the family. The urban household itself became less important as a center of production. Instead, most income earners left home each day to work elsewhere. A sharp distinction began to emerge between the public world of the workplace—the world of commerce and industry—and the private world of the family. The world of the family was now dominated not by production, but by housekeeping, child rearing, and other primarily domestic concerns. It was also a world dominated by women.

Accompanying (and perhaps in part caused by) the changing economic function of the family was a decline in the

Falling Birth Rates

birth rate. In 1800, the average American woman could be expected to give birth to approximately seven children during her childbearing years. By 1860, the average woman bore five children. The birth rate fell most quickly in urban areas and among middle-class women. Mid-nineteenth-century Americans had access to some birth control devices, which undoubtedly contributed in part to the change. There was also a significant rise in abortions, which remained legal in some states until after the Civil War and which, according to some estimates, may have

NATHAN HAWLEY AND FAMILY Nathan Hawley, seated at center in this 1801 painting, was typical of many early-nineteenth-century fathers in having a very large family. Nine members are visible here. Hawley at the time was the warden of the Albany County jail in New York, and the painting was by William Wilkie, one of the inmates there. The painting suggests that Hawley was a man of modest but not great means. His family is fashionably dressed, and there are paintings on the walls—signs of style and affluence. But the house is very simply furnished, without drapes for the windows, with a simple painted floor cloth in the front room, and a bare floor in the back. *(Collection of the Albany Institute of History and Art)*

terminated as many as 20 percent of all pregnancies in the 1850s. But the most important cause of the declining birth rate was almost certainly changes in sexual behavior—including increased abstinence.

The deliberate effort among middle-class men and women, in particular, to limit family size was a reflection of a much larger shift in the nature of society in the mid-nineteenth-century North. In a world in which the economy was becoming increasingly organized, in which production was moving out of the home, in which individuals were coming to expect more from the world, in which people placed more emphasis on calculations about the future, making careful decisions about bearing children seemed important. It expressed the increasingly secular, rationalized, and progressive orientation of the rapidly developing American North.

Women and the "Cult of Domesticity"

The emerging distinction between the public and private worlds, between the workplace and the home, accompanied (and helped cause) increasingly sharp distinctions between the social roles of men and women. Those distinctions affected not only factory workers and farmers,

but members of the growing middle class as well. There had, of course, always been important differences between the male and female spheres in American society. Women had long been denied many legal and political rights enjoyed by men; within the family, the husband and father had traditionally ruled, and the wife and mother had generally bowed to his demands and desires. It had long been practically impossible for most women to obtain divorces, although divorces initiated by men were often easier to arrange. (Men were also far more likely than women to win custody of children in case of a divorce.) In most states, husbands retained almost absolute authority over both the property and persons of their wives. Wife beating was illegal in only a few areas, and the law did not acknowledge that rape could occur within marriage. Women traditionally had very little access to the worlds of business or politics. Indeed, custom in most communities dictated that women never speak in public before mixed audiences.

Most women also had much less access to education than men, a situation that survived into the mid-nineteenth *Female Education* century. Although they were encouraged to attend school at the elementary level, they were strongly discouraged—and in most cases effectively barred—from pursuing higher education. Oberlin in Ohio became the first col-lege in America to accept female students; it permitted four to enroll in 1837, despite criticism that coeducation was a rash experiment approximating free love. Oberlin authorities were confident that "the mutual influence of the sexes upon each other is decidedly happy in the cultivation of both mind & manners." But few other insti-tutions shared their views. Coeducation remained extraor-dinarily rare until long after the Civil War; and only a very few women's colleges—such as Mount Holyoke, founded in Massachusetts by Mary Lyon in 1837—emerged.

However unequal the positions of men and women were in the preindustrial era, those positions were gener-ally defined within the context of a household in which all members played crucial roles in generating family income. In the middle-class family of the new industrial society, however, the husband was assumed to be the principal, usually the only, income producer. The wife was now expected to remain in the home and to engage in largely domestic activities.

The result was an important shift in the middle-class concept of the woman's place within the family and of the family's place within the larger society. The proper role of women became a subject of broad discussion in

New Roles for Women | middle-class society in the mid-nineteenth century; and out of this discussion came a widespread view of women as guardians of the "domestic virtues." Their role as mothers, entrusted with the nurturing of the young, seemed more central to the family than it had in the past. And their role as wives—as companions and helpers to their husbands—grew more important as well. Middle-class women, no longer producers, now became more impor-tant as consumers. They learned to place a high value on keeping a clean, comfortable, and well-appointed home, on entertaining, and on dressing elegantly and stylishly.

Occupying their own "separate sphere," some women began to develop a distinctive female culture. Friendships

Women's Separate Sphere | among women became increas-ingly intense; women began to form their own social networks (and, ultimately, to form female clubs and associations that were of great impor-tance to the advancement of various reforms). A distinc-tive feminine literature began to emerge to meet the demands of middle-class women. There were romantic novels (many of them by female writers), which focused on the private sphere that women now inhabited. There were women's magazines, of which the most prominent was *Godey's Lady's Book,* edited after 1837 by Sarah Hale, who had earlier founded a women's magazine of her own. The magazine scrupulously avoided dealing with public controversies or political issues and focused instead on fashions, shopping and homemaking advice, and other purely domestic concerns. Politics and religion were inappropriate for the magazine, Hale explained in 1841, because "other subjects are more important for our sex and more proper for our sphere."

By the standards of a later era, the increasing isolation of women from the public world seems to be a form of op-pression and discrimination. And it is true that few men con-sidered women fit for business, politics, or the professions. On the other hand, most middle-class men—and many middle-class women as well—considered the new female sphere a vehicle for expressing special qualities that made women in some ways superior to men. Women were to be the custodians of morality and benevolence, just as the home— | *Benefits and Costs* shaped by the influence of women—was to be a refuge from the harsh, competitive world of the marketplace. It was women's responsibility to provide religious and moral instruction to their children and to counterbalance the ac-quisitive, secular impulses of their husbands. Thus the "cult of domesticity," as some scholars have called it, brought both benefits and costs to middle-class women. It allowed them to live lives of greater material comfort than in the past, and it placed a higher value on their "female virtues" and on their roles as wife and mother. At the same time, it left women increasingly detached from the public world, with fewer outlets for their interests and energies.

The costs of that detachment were particularly clear among unmarried women of the middle class. By the 1840s, the ideology of domesticity had grown so powerful that few genteel women would any longer consider working (as many had in the past) in shops or mills, and few employers would consider hiring them. But unmarried women never-theless required some income-producing activity. They had few choices. Some could become teachers or nurses, profes-sions that seemed to call for the same female qualities that made women important within the home; and both those professions began in the 1840s and 1850s to attract signifi-cant numbers of women, although not until the Civil War did females begin to dominate them. Otherwise, unmarried fe-males were largely dependent on the generosity of relatives.

Middle-class people gradually came to consider work by women outside the house-hold to be unseemly, something | *Working Class Women* characteristic of the lower classes—as indeed it was. Working-class women could not afford to stay home and cultivate the "domestic virtues." They had to produce in-come for their families. They continued to work in fac-tories and mills, but under conditions far worse than those that the original, more "respectable" women work-ers had enjoyed. They also frequently found employment in middle-class homes. Domestic service became one of the most frequent sources of female employment. In other words, now that production had moved outside the household, women who needed to earn money had to move outside their own households to do so.

Leisure Activities

Leisure time was scarce for all but the wealthiest Americans in the mid-nineteenth century. Most people worked long hours. Saturday was a normal working day.

One of the characters Huckleberry Finn encountered in his journey down the Mississippi in Mark Twain's famous novel was a roguish traveling actor who called himself "the Duke of Bridgewater." The Duke improvised performances almost anywhere there was anyone willing to pay. One of his favorite encores, he claimed, was "Hamlet's soliloquy . . . the most celebrated thing in Shakespeare." He recited it with bravado, and with very little fidelity to the original text:

> To be, or not to be; that is the bare bodkin
> That makes calamity of so long life.

The events of Twain's novel were set in the years before the Civil War,

THE PARK THEATER This 1821 watercolor by John Searle shows the interior of the Park Theater in New York, which had recently been rebuilt after a fire. The play is a farce by the English playwright William T. Moncrieffe. The faces in the audience are all portraits of real New Yorkers at the time. (© Collection of the New York Historical Society)

when Shakespeare's work was familiar to Americans of all ages, classes, and regions. From elegant theaters in the great eastern cities, to makeshift stages and rickety "opera houses" in farming villages and mining towns in the West, Americans gathered to watch productions of Shakespeare's plays just as they gathered to watch now-forgotten comedies and melodramas written in their own time. Whether performed by famous actors or by hand-to-mouth hustlers like Twain's "Duke," Shakespeare was entertainment for the masses.

Performances of Shakespeare had begun in America as early as 1750, but public interest in his plays reached its peak in the 1830s, 1840s, and 1850s, when theater was the single most popular performing art throughout the United States, and Shakespeare the single most popular playwright. Many, perhaps most, performances of Shakespearean plays were irreverent, inaccurate, and romanticized. Tragedies were rewritten with happy endings. Comedies were interlaced with contemporary, regional humor. Texts were reworked with American dialect, and plays were abbreviated and sandwiched into programs containing other popular work of the time. So familiar were many Shakespearean plots that audiences took delight in seeing them parodied in productions such as "Julius Sneezer," "Hamlet and Egglet," and "Much Ado About a Merchant of Venice."

People from all walks of life went regularly to the theater and mingled with one another in ways that would become unusual in later eras. Seating was often divided by class—a tier of boxes for the wealthiest patrons, orchestra seats for the middle class, and balconies for those too poor to sit anywhere else (and for virtually all non-white members of the audience). But despite these distinctions, going to the theater was a vibrantly democratic

experience of a kind seldom visible in twentieth-century America except occasionally at sports events.

One result was that American audiences were often noisy, rambunctious, and—at least in the eyes of many actors—obnoxious. Men and women did not sit quietly in theaters as most do today. They shouted out reactions to the plays, taunted actors, and occasionally—as in an 1832 performance of *Richard III* in New York—climbed onto the stage and joined the performance, mingling with the actors during a battle scene and charging across the stage as if they were soldiers.

The leading Shakespearean actors of the antebellum era became figures of enormous public interest, and at times could spur great popular passion. Evidence of that came from events in New York City in 1849. The celebrated American actor Edwin Forrest—beloved by working-class audiences as a great patriot and a common man who had risen to greatness—gave a performance of *Macbeth* on the same evening that a renowned English actor, William Macready, was performing the same play elsewhere in the city. Many New Yorkers believed that the aloof, aristocratic Macready, and through him the city's wealthy elites, were attempting to humiliate Forrest. Forrest supporters crowded into Macready's performance and hooted him off the stage. Three days later, Macready tried again at the Astor Place Opera House. Ten thousand people, most of them Forrest enthusiasts, gathered outside and tried to force their way into the theater. Militia, called out for the occasion, fired into the crowd killing at least 22 and wounding more than 150. It was one of the bloodiest civil conflicts of the first half of the nineteenth century.

Shakespeare remained popular throughout the Civil War. In 1864 enthusiastic crowds greeted a performance in New York of *Julius Caesar,*

THE ASTOR PLACE RIOT This later watercolor of the Astor Place riot in 1849 conveys something of the violence and bedlam that the great rivalry between Edwin Forrest and William Macready produced. Here, anti-English mobs demonstrate outside the theater in which the English actor Macready was performing. During the rioting, they set the theater on fire, and the turmoil only subsided when the Seventh Regiment guard was called out. *(The Great Riot at the Astor Place Opera House, New York, Thursday Evening, May 10, 1849. Published by N. Currier, 1849. Museum of the City of New York, The Harry T. Peters Collection)*

THE BOOTHS IN *JULIUS CAESAR* The Booths were America's leading acting family in the 1860s, and this photograph by Matthew Brady captures a rare event: the appearance together in a play of Edwin Booth, the most famous and talented member of the family, and two of his acting brothers, John Wilkes (left, remembered today as Lincoln's assassin but well known at the time as a popular actor) and Junius Brutus Booth, Jr. (right). They are performing Shakespeare's *Julius Caesar* in New York. *(Library of Congress)*

featuring three members of America's most celebrated theatrical family: William Junius Booth, an aging giant who had been the foremost tragic actor of his generation, and his two sons Edwin and John Wilkes. "No playgoer has seen Shakespere [sic] presented with attraction more likely to draw and charm the true lover of the drama since the days when Shakespere himself appeared in his own plays," the *New York Herald* editorialized in a fit of civic pride. "Only English cities could hope to rival us in this."

Edwin Booth went on to become America's most revered actor of the last half of the nineteenth century, renowned in particular for his performances of *Hamlet* and other great Shakespearean roles at the Booth Theater he founded in New York. His

brother, John Wilkes, is best remembered leaping to the stage of Ford's Theater in Washington on April 14, 1865 after having fatally shot Abraham Lincoln. His famous exclamation at the time, "Sic semper tyrannis," was the motto of the state of Virginia. But it was better known as the phrase Brutus supposedly uttered after killing Julius Caesar, an event most familiar to nineteenth-century audiences—and to Booth himself—from performances of Shakespeare's play.

Huckleberry Finn was published in 1884, when the broad popularity of Shakespeare that Twain described was already beginning to fade. By the end of the nineteenth century, Shakespeare's work was beginning to be treated with much more gravity and was starting to be associated with the educated upper classes. The great

Shakespearean actors of these later years had no large followings among workers and ordinary people. They were favorites of the aristocracy, who sought to protect them and the plays they performed from being debased by common audiences they considered incapable of understanding them. A clear distinction had grown up between "high culture," of which Shakespeare was now a part, and "lowbrow culture," from which Shakespeare was gradually excluded. That distinction has survived into our own time.

Vacations—paid or unpaid—were rare. For most people, Sunday was the only respite from work; and Sundays were generally reserved for religion and rest. Almost no commercial establishments did any business at all on Sunday, and even within the home most families frowned upon playing games or engaging in other kinds of entertainment on the Sabbath. For many working-class and middle-class people, therefore, holidays took on a special importance. That was one reason for the strikingly elaborate Fourth of July celebrations throughout the country in the nineteenth century. The celebrations were not just expressions of patriotism. They were a way of enjoying one of the few holidays from work available to most Americans.

In rural America, where most people still lived, the erratic pattern of farmwork gave many people some relief from the relentless working schedules of city residents. For urban people, however, leisure was something to be seized in what few free moments they had. Men gravitated to taverns for drinking, talking, and game-playing. Women gathered in one another's homes for conversation, card games, or to share work on such household tasks as sewing. For educated people, whose numbers were rapidly expanding, reading became one of the principal leisure activities. Newspapers and magazines proliferated rapidly, and books—novels, histories, autobiographies, biographies, travelogues, and others—became staples of affluent homes. Women were particularly avid readers, and women writers created a new genre of fiction specifically for females—the "sentimental novel," which often offered idealized visions of women's lives and romances (see pp. 338–339).

There was also a vigorous culture of public leisure, even if many families had to struggle to find time or means to participate in it. In larger cities, theaters were becoming increasingly popular; and while some of them catered to particular social groups, others attracted audiences that crossed class lines. Wealthy people, middle-class people, workers and their *Minstrel Shows* families: all could sometimes be found watching a performance of Shakespeare or a melodrama based on a popular novel or an American myth. Minstrel shows—in which white actors mimicked (and ridiculed) African-American culture—became increasingly popular (see pp. 428–429). Public sporting events—boxing, horse racing, cockfighting (already becoming controversial), and others—often attracted considerable crowds. Baseball—not yet organized into professional leagues—was beginning to attract large crowds when played in city parks or fields on the edges of towns (see pp. 388–389). A particularly exciting event in many communities was the arrival of the circus—a traveling entertainment with roots in the middle ages that continued to entertain, delight, and bamboozle children and adults alike.

Popular tastes in public spectacle tended toward the bizarre and the fantastic. Most men and women lived in a constricted world of familiar things. Relatively few people traveled; and in the absence of film, radio, television, or even much photography, they hungered for visions of unusual phenomena that contrasted with their normal experiences. People going to the theater or the circus or the museum wanted to see things that amazed and even frightened them. Perhaps the most celebrated provider of *P. T. Barnum* such experiences was the famous and unscrupulous showman P. T. Barnum, who opened the American Museum in New York in 1842—not a showcase for art or nature, but a great freak show populated by midgets (the most famous named Tom Thumb), Siamese twins, magicians, and ventriloquists. Barnum was a genius in publicizing his ventures with garish posters and elaborate newspaper announcements. Only later, in the 1870s, did he launch the famous circus for which he is still best remembered. But he was always a pioneer in exploiting public tastes for the wild and exotic.

One of the ways Barnum tried to draw visitors to his museum was by engaging lecturers. He did so because he understood that the lecture was one of the most popular forms of entertainment in nineteenth-century America. Men and women flocked in enormous numbers to lyceums (see pp. 364–365), churches, schools, and auditoriums to hear lecturers explain the latest advances in science, or to describe their visits to exotic places, or to provide vivid historical narratives, or to rail against the evils of alcohol or slavery. Messages of social uplift and reform attracted rapt audiences, particularly among women eager for guidance as they adjusted to the often jarring changes in the character of family life in the industrializing world.

THE AGRICULTURAL NORTH

Even in the rapidly urbanizing and industrializing Northeast, and more so in what nineteenth-century Americans called the Northwest (and what Americans today call the Midwest), most people remained tied to the agricultural world. But agriculture, like industry and commerce, was becoming increasingly a part of the new capitalist economy, linked to the national *Rise of Commercial Agriculture* and international market. Where agriculture could not compete in this new commercial world—as in much of the Northeast—it declined. Where it could compete—as in most of the Northwest—it simultaneously flourished and changed.

Northeastern Agriculture

The story of agriculture in the Northeast after 1840 is one of decline and transformation. The reason for the decline was simple: the farmers of the section could no longer compete with the new and richer soil of the Northwest.

Centers of production were gradually shifting westward for many of the farm goods that had in the past been most important to northeastern agriculture: wheat, corn, grapes, cattle, sheep, and hogs. In 1840, the leading wheat-growing states were New York, Pennsylvania, Ohio, and Virginia; in 1860 they were Illinois, Indiana, Wisconsin, Ohio, and Michigan. In raising corn, Illinois, Ohio, and Missouri supplanted New York, Pennsylvania, and Virginia. In 1840 the most important cattle-raising areas in the country were New York, Pennsylvania, and New England; but by the 1850s the leading cattle states were Illinois, Indiana, Ohio, and Iowa in the West, and Texas in the South.

Some eastern farmers responded to these changes by moving west themselves and establishing new farms. Still others moved to mill towns and became laborers. Some farmers, however, remained on the land and managed to hold their own against the Northwest, and at times even

Truck Farming in the Northeast

surpass it, in certain areas of agriculture. As the eastern urban centers increased in population, many farmers turned to the task of supplying food to the cities; they raised vegetables (truck farming) or fruit and sold it in nearby towns. New York, for example, led all other states in apple production.

The rise of cities also stimulated the rise of profitable dairy farming. Supplying milk, butter, and cheese to local markets attracted many farmers in central New York, southeastern Pennsylvania, and various parts of New England. Approximately half the dairy products of the country were produced in the East; most of the rest came from the West, where Ohio was the leading dairy state. Partly because of the expansion of the dairy industry, the Northeast led other sections in the production of hay. New York was the leading hay state in the nation; Pennsylvania and New England grew large crops as well. The Northeast also exceeded other areas in producing potatoes.

But while agriculture in the region remained an important part of the economy, it was steadily becoming less important relative both to the agriculture of the Northwest and to the industrial growth of the Northeast itself. As a result, the rural population in many parts of the Northeast continued to decline.

The Old Northwest

Life was different in the states of the Northwest in the mid-nineteenth century. There was some industry in this region, more than in the South; and in the two decades before the Civil War, the section experienced steady industrial growth. By 1860, it had 36,785 manufacturing establishments employing 209,909 workers. There was a flourishing industrial and commercial area along the shore of Lake Erie, with Cleveland at its center. Another manufacturing region was in the Ohio River valley; the meatpacking city of Cincinnati was its nucleus. Farther

west, the rising city of Chicago, destined to become the great metropolis of the section, was

Industrialization in the Old Northwest

emerging as the national center of the agricultural machinery and meatpacking industries.

Most of the major industrial activities of the West either served agriculture (as in the case of farm machinery), or relied on agricultural products (as in flour milling, meatpacking, whiskey distilling, and the making of leather goods). As this suggests, industry was, on the whole, much less important in the Northwest than farming.

Some areas of the Northwest were not yet dominated by whites. Indians remained the most numerous inhabitants of large portions of most of the upper third of the Great Lakes states until after the Civil War. In those areas, hunting and fishing, along with some sedentary agriculture, remained the principal economic activities of both whites and Native Americans. But the tribes did not become integrated into the new commercialized economy that was emerging elsewhere in the Northwest.

For the white (and occasionally black) settlers who populated the lands farther south that they had by now largely wrested from the natives, the Northwest was primarily an agricultural region. Its rich and plentiful lands made farming a lucrative and expanding activity there, in contrast to the declining agrarian Northeast. Thus the typical citizen of the Northwest was not an industrial worker or poor, marginal farmer, but the owner of a reasonably prosperous family farm. The average size of western farms was 200 acres, the great majority of them owned by the people who worked them.

Rising farm prices around the world provided a strong incentive for these western farmers to engage in commercial agriculture: to concentrate on growing a single crop for market (corn, wheat, cattle, sheep, hogs, and others). In the early years of white settlement in the Northwest, farm prices rose because of the debilitation of European agriculture in the aftermath of the Napoleonic Wars and the growing urban population (and hence the growing demand for food) of industrializing areas of Europe. Europe found it necessary to import American products to feed its people. The Northwest, with good water

Agricultural Specialization

routes on the Mississippi for getting its crops to oceangoing vessels, profited from this international trade.

But industrialization, in both the United States and Europe, provided the greatest boost to agriculture. With the growth of factories and cities in the Northeast, the domestic market for farm goods increased dramatically. The growing national and worldwide demand for farm products resulted in steadily rising farm prices. For most farmers, the 1840s and early 1850s were years of increasing prosperity.

The expansion of agricultural markets had profound effects on sectional alignments in the United States. The Northwest sold most of its products to the residents of

the Northeast and was thus dependent on eastern purchasing power. Eastern indus-
try, in turn, found an important
market for its products in the
prospering West. Between the two sections a strong economic relationship was emerging that was profitable to
both—and that was increasing the isolation of the South
within the Union.

Growing Ties between Northeast and Northwest

To meet the increasing demand for its farm products,
residents of the Northwest worked strenuously, and often
frantically, to increase their productive capacities. Many
tried to take advantage of the large areas of still uncultivated land and to enlarge the area of white settlement
during the 1840s. By 1850, the growing western population was moving into the prairie regions both east and
west of the Mississippi: into areas of Indiana, Michigan,
Illinois, Missouri, Iowa, and Minnesota. They cleared forest lands or made use of fields the Indians had cleared
many years earlier. And they began to develop a timber industry to make use of the forests that remained. Wheat
was the staple crop of the region, but other crops—corn,
potatoes, and oats—and livestock were also important.

The Northwest increased production not only by expanding the area of settlement,
but also by adopting new agricultural techniques that greatly
reduced the labor necessary for producing a crop. The
new methods were also less destructive than earlier ones
and slowed the exhaustion of the region's rich soil. Farmers began to cultivate new varieties of seed, notably
Mediterranean wheat, which was hardier than the native
type; and they imported better breeds of animals, such as
hogs and sheep from England and Spain, to take the place
of native stock. Most important were improved tools and
farm machines, which American inventors and manufacturers produced in rapidly increasing numbers. During
the 1840s, more efficient grain drills, harrows, mowers,
and hay rakes came into wide use. The cast-iron plow, an
earlier innovation, remained popular because its parts
could be replaced when broken. An even better tool appeared in 1847, when John Deere established at Moline,
Illinois, a factory to manufacture steel plows, which were
more durable than those made of iron.

New Agricultural Techniques

Two new machines heralded a coming revolution in
grain production. The most important was the automatic
reaper, the invention of Cyrus H.
McCormick of Virginia. The
reaper enabled a crew of six or seven men to harvest in a
day as much wheat (or any other small grain) as fifteen men
could harvest using a sickle or other older methods.
McCormick, who had patented his device in 1834, established a factory at Chicago, in the heart of the grain belt, in
1847. By 1860, more than 100,000 reapers were in use on
western farms. Almost as important to the grain grower
was the thresher—a machine that separated the grain from
the wheat stalks. Threshers appeared in large numbers after 1840. Before that, farmers generally flailed grain by hand

McCormick Reaper

(seven bushels a day was a good average for a farm) or used
farm animals to tread it (twenty bushels a day on the average). A threshing machine could thresh twenty-five bushels
or more in an hour. The Jerome I. Case factory in Racine,
Wisconsin manufactured most of the threshers.

The Northwest considered itself the most democratic
section of the country. But its democracy was based on a
defense of economic freedom and the rights of property—
a white, middle-class vision of democracy that was becoming common in many other parts of the country as well.
Abraham Lincoln, an Illinois Whig, voiced the economic
opinions of many of the people of his section. "I take it that
it is best for all to leave each man free to acquire property
as fast as he can," said Lincoln. "Some will get wealthy. I
don't believe in a law to prevent a man from getting rich; it
would do more harm than good. . . . When one starts poor,
as most do in the race of life, free society is such that he
knows he can better his condition; he knows that there is
no fixed condition of labor for his whole life."

Rural Life

Life for farming people was very different from life in towns
and cities. It also varied greatly from one farming region to
another. In the more densely populated farm areas east of
the Appalachians and in the easternmost areas of the Northwest, farmers were usually part of relatively vibrant communities and made extensive use of the institutions of those
communities—the churches, schools, stores, and taverns.
As white settlement moved further west, farmers became
more isolated and had to struggle to find any occasions for
contact with people outside their own families.

Although the extent of social interaction differed from
one area to another, the forms of interaction—outside the
South at least—were usually very similar. Religion drew
farm communities together perhaps more than any other
force, particularly since so many farm areas were populated by people of common ethnic (and therefore
religious) backgrounds. Town
or village churches were popular meeting places, both for
services and for social events—most of them dominated
by women. Even in areas with no organized churches,
farm families—and, again, women in particular—gathered
in one another's homes for prayer meetings, Bible readings, and other religious activities. Weddings, baptisms,
and funerals also brought communities together in celebration or mourning.

Importance of Religion in Rural Communities

But religion was only one of many reasons for interaction. Farm people joined together frequently to share tasks
that a single family would have difficulty performing on its
own; barn raisings were among the most frequent. And on
those occasions, families would gather and create a festive
atmosphere of celebration. Women prepared large suppers
while the men worked on the barn and the children played.
Large numbers of families also gathered together at harvest
time to help bring in crops, husk corn, or thresh wheat.

Women came together to share domestic tasks as well, holding "bees" in which groups of women joined together to make quilts, baked goods, preserves, and other products.

Rural life was not always as isolating as it was sometimes portrayed. But despite the many social gatherings farm families managed to create, they lived in a world with much less contact with popular culture and public social life than people who lived in towns and cities. Rural people, often even more than urban ones, treasured their links to the outside world—letters from relatives and friends in distant places, newspapers and magazines from cities they had never seen, catalogs advertising merchandise that their local stores never had. Yet many also valued their separation from urban culture and cherished the relative autonomy that farm life gave them. One reason many rural Americans looked back nostalgically on country life once they moved to the city was that they sensed that in the urban world they did not have as much control over the patterns of their daily lives as they had once known.

CONCLUSION

Between the 1820s and the 1850s, the American economy experienced the beginnings of an industrial revolution—a change so profound that in the United States, as in Europe, it transformed almost every area of life in fundamental ways.

The American industrial revolution was a result of many things: population growth (through both natural increase and immigration), advances in transportation and communication, new technologies that spurred the development of factories capable of mass producing goods, the recruiting of a large industrial labor force, and the creation of corporate bodies capable of managing large enterprises. The new economy created great wealth, expanding the ranks of the wealthy and helping to create a large new middle class. It also created high levels of inequality, which was particularly visible in the growth of a large industrial working class.

Culture in the industrializing areas of the North changed too, and there were important changes in the structure and behavior of the family, in the role of women, and in the way people used their leisure time and encountered popular culture. The changes were often alluring, often disorienting, and often both. They helped widen the gap in experience and understanding between the generation of the Revolution and the generation of the mid-nineteenth century. They also helped widen the gap between North and South.

FOR FURTHER REFERENCE

Charles G. Sellers, *The Market Revolution: Jacksonian America, 1815–1846* (1991) demonstrates the overwhelming impact of the market revolution on American social and political development. George R. Taylor, *The Transportation Revolution* (1951) is a classic account of economic development in the antebellum period. Christopher Clark, *The Roots of Rural Capitalism: Western Massachusetts, 1780–1860* (1990) is an examination of the impact of emerging capitalism on a rural area. Paul Johnson, *A Shopkeeper's Millennium: Society and Revivals in Rochester, New York, 1815–1837* (1978) explores the changing character of class relations in upstate New York in an age of rapid economic development. Alice Kessler-Harris, *Out to Work: A History of Wage-Earning Women in the United States* (1982) is a broad history of women in the wage labor force. Thomas Dublin, *Transforming Women's Work: New England Lives in the Industrial Revolution* (1994) looks in particularly at the mill towns of the northeast. Mary Ryan, *Cradle of the Middle Class: The Family in Oneida County, New York, 1790–1865* (1981) demonstrates the relationship between the market revolution and the changing character of middle-class family structure. Christine Stansell, *City of Women: Sex and Class in New York, 1789–1860* (1983) explores the female world of antebellum New York City. John Bodnar, *The Transplanted: A History of Immigrants in America* (1985) is a useful survey. Paul W. Gates, *The Farmer's Age: Agriculture, 1815–1860* (1966) is an important overview. Alan Taylor, *William Cooper's Town: Power and Persuasion on the Frontier in the Early American Republic* (1995) examines the early years of Cooperstown, New York, and the impact on it of the rise of the market and of democratic politics.

THE NEW ORLEANS COTTON EXCHANGE Edgar Degas, the great French impressionist, painted this scene of cotton traders examining samples in the New Orleans cotton exchange in 1873. By this time the cotton trade was producing less impressive profits than those that had made it the driving force of the booming southern economy of the 1850s. Degas's mother came from a Creole family of cotton brokers in New Orleans, and two of the artist's brothers (depicted here reading a newspaper and leaning against a window) joined the business in America. *(Giraudon/Art Resource)*

Significant Events

1800 ·	Gabriel Prosser organizes unsuccessful slave revolt in Virginia
1808 ·	Importation of slaves to United States banned
1820s ·	Prolonged depression in tobacco prices begins
·	English market for cotton textiles boosts prices and causes explosion in cotton production in the Southwest

CHAPTER ELEVEN

COTTON, SLAVERY, AND THE OLD SOUTH

The South, like the North, experienced dramatic growth in the middle years of the nineteenth century. Southerners fanned out into the new territories of the Southwest and established new communities, new states, and new markets. The southern agricultural economy grew increasingly productive and increasingly prosperous. Trade in such staples as sugar, rice, tobacco, and above all cotton made the South a major force in international commerce and created substantial wealth within the region. It also tied the South securely to the emerging capitalist world of the United States and its European trading partners.

Southern society, southern culture, southern politics—all changed in response to these important demographic and economic changes. The South in the 1850s was a very different place from the South of the first years of the century.

Yet for all the expansion and all the changes, the South experienced a much less fundamental transformation in these years than did the North. It had begun the nineteenth century a primarily agricultural region; it remained overwhelmingly agrarian in 1860. It had begun the century with few important cities and little industry; so it remained sixty years later. In 1800, a plantation system dependent on slave labor had dominated the southern economy; by 1860, that system had only strengthened its grip on the region. One historian has written, "The South grew, but it did not develop." As a result, it became increasingly unlike the North and increasingly sensitive to what it considered to be threats to its distinctive way of life.

Growth without Development

THE COTTON ECONOMY

The most important economic development in the mid-nineteenth-century South was the shift of economic power from the "upper South" (the original southern states along the Atlantic coast) to the "lower South" (the expanding agricultural regions in the new states of the Southwest). That shift reflected above all the growing dominance of cotton in the southern economy.

The Rise of King Cotton

Much of the upper South continued in the nineteenth century to rely, as it always had, on the cultivation of tobacco. But the market for that crop was notoriously unstable. Tobacco prices were subject to frequent depressions, including a prolonged one that began in the 1820s and extended into the 1850s. Tobacco also rapidly exhausted the land on which it grew; it was difficult for most growers to remain in business in the same place for very long. By the 1830s, therefore, many farmers in the old tobacco-growing regions of Virginia, Maryland, and North Carolina were shifting to other crops—notably wheat—while the center of tobacco cultivation was moving westward, into the Piedmont area.

Decline of the Tobacco Economy

The southern regions of the coastal South—South Carolina, Georgia, and parts of Florida—continued to rely on the cultivation of rice, a more stable and lucrative crop. Rice, however, demanded substantial irrigation and needed an exceptionally long growing season (nine months), so cultivation of that staple remained restricted to a relatively small area. Sugar growers along the Gulf Coast, similarly, enjoyed a reasonably profitable market for their crop. But sugar cultivation required intensive (and debilitating) labor and a long growing time. Only relatively wealthy planters could afford to engage in it, and they faced major competition from the great sugar plantations of the Caribbean. Sugar cultivation, therefore, did not spread much beyond a small area in southern Louisiana and eastern Texas. Long-staple (Sea Island) cotton was another lucrative crop, but like rice and sugar, it could grow only in a limited area—the coastal regions of the Southeast.

The decline of the tobacco economy in the upper South, and the inherent limits of the sugar, rice, and long-staple cotton economies farther south, might have forced the region to shift its attention in the nineteenth century to other, nonagricultural pursuits, had it not been for the growing importance of a new product that soon overshadowed all else: short-staple cotton. This was a hardier and coarser strain of cotton that could grow successfully in a variety of climates and in a variety of soils. It was harder to process than the long-staple variety; its seeds were more difficult to remove from the

Short-Staple Cotton

fiber. But the invention of the cotton gin (see p. 189) had largely solved that problem.

Demand for cotton was growing rapidly. The growth of the textile industry in Britain in the 1820s and 1830s, and in New England in the 1840s and 1850s, created an enormous new demand for the crop. Existing cotton lands could not satisfy the demand, and ambitious men and women rapidly moved into previously uncultivated lands—many of them newly open to planter settlement after the relocation of the tribes in the 1820s and 1830s—to establish new cotton-growing regions.

Beginning in the 1820s, therefore, cotton production spread rapidly. From the western areas of South Carolina and Georgia, production moved steadily westward—first into Alabama and Mississippi, then into northern Louisiana, Texas, and Arkansas. By the 1850s, cotton had become the linchpin of the southern economy. In 1820, the South had produced about 500,000 bales of cotton. By 1850 it was producing nearly 3 million bales a year, and by 1860 nearly 5 million. There were periodic fluctuations in cotton prices, resulting generally from overproduction; periods of boom frequently gave way to abrupt busts. But the cotton economy continued to grow, even if in fits and starts. By the time of the Civil War, cotton constituted nearly two-thirds of the total export trade of the United States and was bringing in nearly $200 million a year. The annual value of the rice crop, in contrast, was $2 million. It was little wonder that southern politicians now proclaimed: "Cotton is king!"

Spread of Cotton Production

Cotton production dominated the more recently settled areas of what came to be known as the "lower South" (or, in a later era, the "Deep South"). Some began to call this region the "Cotton Kingdom." Settlement of the area resembled in some ways the rush of gold seekers to a new strike. The prospect of tremendous profits from growing cotton drew white settlers to the lower South by the

SLAVERY AND COTTON IN THE SOUTH, 1820 AND 1860 The two maps on the opposite page show the remarkable spread of cotton cultivation in the South in the decades before the Civil War. Both maps show the areas of cotton cultivation (the mustard-colored areas) as well as areas with large slave populations (the red-dotted areas). Note how in the top map, which represents 1820, cotton production is concentrated largely in the East, with a few areas scattered among Alabama, Mississippi, Louisiana, and Tennessee. Slavery is concentrated along the Georgia and South Carolina coast, areas in which long-staple cotton was grown, with only a few other areas of highly dense slave populations. By 1860, the South had changed dramatically. Cotton production had spread throughout the lower South, from Texas to northern Florida, and slavery had moved with it. Slavery was also much denser in the tobacco-growing regions of Virginia and North Carolina, which had also grown. ◆ *How did this economic shift affect the white South's commitment to slavery?*

 For an interactive version of this map go to ww.mhhe.com/brinkley11ch11maps

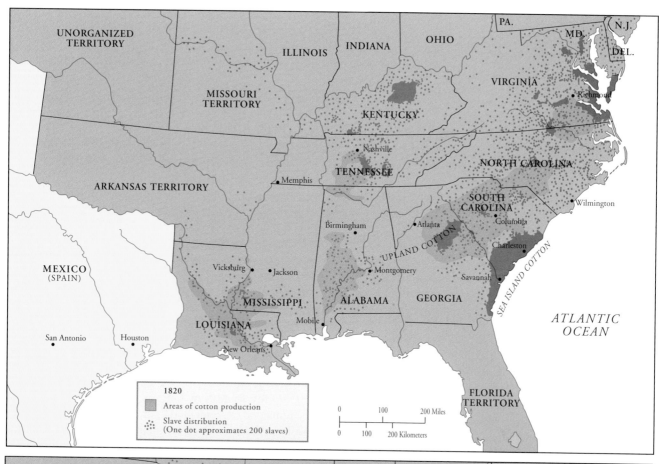

1820

Areas of cotton production

Slave distribution
(One dot approximates 200 slaves)

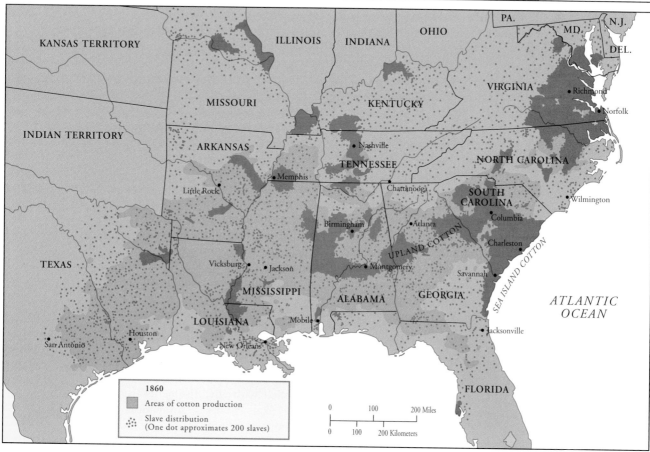

1860

Areas of cotton production

Slave distribution
(One dot approximates 200 slaves)

thousands. Some were wealthy planters from the older states who transferred their assets and slaves to a cotton plantation. Most were small slaveholders or slaveless farmers who hoped to move into the planter class.

A similar shift, if an involuntary one, occurred in the slave population. Between 1820 and 1860, the number of *Expansion of Slavery* slaves in Alabama leaped from 41,000 to 435,000, and in Mississippi from 32,000 to 436,000. In the same period, the increase in Virginia was only from 425,000 to 490,000. Between 1840 and 1860, according to some estimates, 410,000 slaves moved from the upper South to the cotton states—either accompanying masters who were themselves migrating to the Southwest, or (more often) sold to planters already there. Indeed, the sale of slaves to the Southwest became an important economic activity in the upper South and helped the troubled planters of that region compensate for the declining value of their crops.

Southern Trade and Industry

In the face of this booming agricultural expansion, other forms of economic activity developed slowly in the South. The business classes of the region—the manufacturers and merchants—were not unimportant. There was growing activity in flour milling and in textile and iron manufacturing, particularly in the upper South. The Tredegar Iron Works in Richmond, for example, compared favorably with the best iron mills in the Northeast. But industry remained an insignificant force in comparison with the agricultural economy. The total value of southern textile manufactures in 1860 was $4.5 million— a threefold increase over the value of those goods twenty years before, but only about 2 *Weak Manufacturing Sector* percent of the value of the raw cotton exported that year.

To the degree that the South developed a nonfarm commercial sector, it was largely to serve the needs of the plantation economy. Particularly important were the brokers, or "factors," who marketed the planters' crops. These merchants tended to live in such towns as New Orleans, Charleston, Mobile, and Savannah, where they worked to find buyers for cotton and other crops and where they purchased goods for the planters they served. The South had only a very rudimentary financial system, and the factors often also served the planters as bankers, providing them with credit. Planters frequently accumulated substantial debts, particularly during periods when cotton prices were in decline; and the southern merchant-bankers thus became figures of considerable influence and importance in the region. There were also substantial groups of professional people in the South— lawyers, editors, doctors, and others. In most parts of the region, however, they too were closely tied to and dependent on the plantation economy. However important

manufacturers, merchants, and professionals might have been to southern society, they were relatively unimportant in comparison with the manufacturers, merchants, and professionals of the North, on whom southerners were coming more and more (and increasingly unhappily) to depend.

The primitive character of the region's banking system matched a lack of development in other basic services and structures necessary for industrial development. Perhaps most notable was the South's inadequate transportation system. In the North in the antebellum period, enormous sums were invested in roads, canals, and above all railroads to knit the region together into an integrated market. In the South there were no such investments. Canals were almost nonexistent; most roads were crude and unsuitable for heavy transport; and railroads, although they expanded substantially in the 1840s and 1850s, failed to tie the region together effectively. Such towns as Charleston, Atlanta, Savannah, and Norfolk had direct connections with Memphis, and thus with the Northwest; and Richmond was connected, via the Virginia Central, with the Memphis and Charleston Railroad. In addition, several independent lines furnished a continuous connection between the Ohio River and New Orleans. Most of the South, however, remained unconnected to the national railroad system. Most lines in the region were short and local. The principal means of transportation was water. Planters generally shipped their crops to market along rivers or by sea; most manufacturing was in or near port towns.

Perceptive southerners recognized the economic subordination of their region to the North. "From the rattle with which the nurse tickles the ear of the child born in the South to the shroud that covers the cold form of the dead, everything comes to us from the North," the Arkansas journalist Albert Pike lamented. Perhaps the most prominent advocate of southern economic independence was James B. D. De Bow, a resident of New Orleans. He pub- *De Bow's Review* lished a magazine advocating southern commercial and agricultural expansion, *De Bow's Review*, which survived from its founding in 1846 until 1880. De Bow made his journal into a tireless advocate of southern economic independence from the North, warning constantly of the dangers of the "colonial" relationship between the sections. One writer noted in the pages of his magazine: "I think it would be safe to estimate the amount which is lost to us annually by our vassalage to the North at $100,000,000. Great God!" Yet *De Bow's Review* was itself evidence of the dependency of the South on the North. It was printed in New York, because no New Orleans printer had facilities adequate for the task; it was filled with advertisements from northern manufacturing firms; and its circulation was always modest in comparison with those of northern publications. In Charleston, for example, it sold an average of 173 copies per issue; *Harper's Magazine* of New York, in contrast, regularly sold 1,500 copies to South Carolinians.

Sources of Southern Difference

Despite this growing concern about the region's "colonial dependency," the South made few serious efforts to build an economy that might challenge that dependency. An important question about antebellum southern history, therefore, is why the region did so little to develop a larger industrial and commercial economy of its own. Why did it remain so different from the North?

Part of the reason was the great profitability of the region's agricultural system, and particularly of cotton production. In the Northeast, many people had turned to manufacturing as the agricultural economy of the region declined. In the South, the agri-

Reasons for Colonial Dependency

cultural economy was booming, and ambitious people eager to profit from the emerging capitalist economy had little

incentive to look beyond it. Another reason was that wealthy southerners had so much capital invested in their land and, particularly, their slaves that they had little left for other investments. Some historians have suggested that the southern climate—with its long, hot, steamy summers—was less suitable for industrial development than the climate of the North. Still others have gone so far as to claim that southern work habits (perhaps a reflection of the debilitating effects of the climate) impeded industrialization; some white southerners appeared—at least to many northern observers—not to work very hard, to lack the strong work ethic that fueled northern economic development.

But the southern failure to create a flourishing commercial or industrial economy was also in part the result of a set of values distinctive to the South that discouraged the growth of cities and industry. Many white southerners liked to think of themselves as representatives of a special way

The Cavalier Image

of life: one based on traditional values of chivalry, leisure,

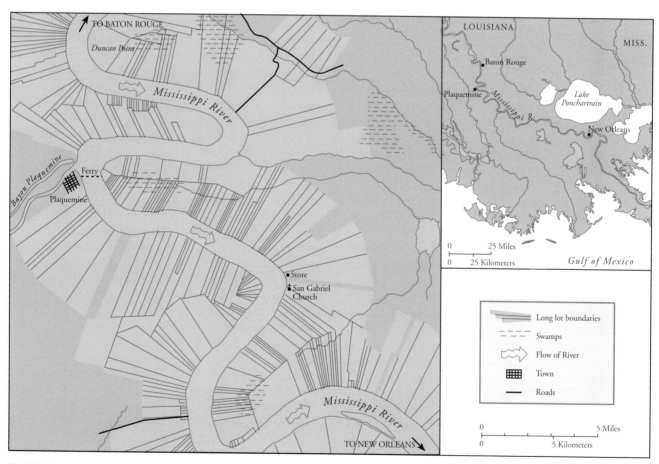

PLANTATIONS IN LOUISIANA, 1858 This map provides a detailed view of plantation lands along a stretch of the Mississippi River between New Orleans and Baton Rouge, Louisiana. Note the long, narrow shapes of these landholdings—known as "long lots." This system was designed to give as many planters as possible frontage on the river, which they needed to transport their crops to market and to receive goods in return. The river also deposited rich soil on the lands near its banks, which made cultivation of crops easier. Note how towns, stores, and churches all are near the riverbank, so planters and others living on plantations nearby could reach them easily by boat. ◆ *How is this landscape different from that of the newly opened federal lands in the West?*

and elegance. White southerners were, they argued, "cavaliers"—people happily free from the base, acquisitive instincts of the "yankees" to their north. Southern white people were, they believed, more concerned with a refined and gracious way of life than with rapid growth and development. Appealing as the "cavalier" image was to southern whites, however, it conformed to the reality of southern society in very limited ways.

WHITE SOCIETY IN THE SOUTH

Only a small minority of southern whites owned slaves. In 1850, when the total white population of the South was over 6 million, the number of slaveholders was only 347,525. In 1860, when the white population was just above 8 million, the number of slaveholders had risen to only 383,637. These figures are somewhat misleading, since each slaveholder was normally the head of a family averaging five members. But even with all members of slaveowning families included in the figures, those owning slaves still amounted to perhaps no more than one quarter of the white population. And of the minority of whites holding slaves, only a small proportion owned them in substantial numbers.

The Planter Class

How, then, did the South come to be seen—both by the outside world and by many southerners themselves— *Planter Aristocracy* as a society dominated by great plantations and wealthy landowning planters? In large part, it was because the planter aristocracy—the cotton magnates, the sugar, rice, and tobacco nabobs, the whites who owned at least forty or fifty slaves and 800 or more acres—exercised power and influence far in excess of their numbers. They stood at the apex of society, determining the political, economic, and even social life of their region. Enriched by vast annual incomes, dwelling in palatial homes, surrounded by broad acres and many black servants, they became a class to which all others deferred. The wealthiest of them maintained homes in towns or cities and spent several months of the year there, engaged in a glittering social life. Others traveled widely, especially to Europe, as an antidote to the isolation of plantation life. And many used their plantations to host opulent social events.

White southerners liked to compare their planter class to the old upper classes of England and Europe: true aristocracies, long entrenched. In fact, however, the southern upper class was in most cases not at all similar to the landed aristocracies of the Old World. In some areas of the upper South—the Tidewater region of Virginia, for example— some of the great aristocrats were indeed people whose families had occupied positions of wealth and power for generations. In most of the South, however, a longstanding landed aristocracy, although central to the "cavalier"

image, was largely a myth. Even the most important planters in the cotton-growing areas of the South were, typically, new to their wealth and power. As late as the 1850s, many of the great landowners in the lower South were still first-generation settlers, who had arrived with only modest resources, struggled for many years to clear land and develop a plantation in what was at first a rugged wilderness, and only relatively recently had started to live in the comfort and luxury for which they became famous. Large areas of the "Old South" (as Americans later called the South of the pre-Civil War era) had been settled and cultivated for less than two decades at the time of the Civil War.

Nor was the world of the planter nearly as leisured and genteel as the "cavalier" myth would suggest. Growing staple crops was a business—often a big and highly profitable business—that was in its own way just as competitive and just as risky as the industrial enterprises of the North. Planters had to supervise *Plantation Management* their operations carefully if they hoped to make a profit. They were, in many respects, just as much competitive capitalists as the industrialists of the North whose lifestyles they claimed to hold in contempt. Even many affluent planters lived rather modestly, their wealth so heavily invested in land and slaves that there was little left for personal comfort. And white planters, even some substantial ones, tended to move frequently as new and presumably more productive areas opened up to cultivation.

Indeed, it may have been the very newness and precariousness of the plantation way of life, and the differences between the reality of that life and the image of it, that made many southern planters determined to portray themselves as genteel aristocrats. Having struggled so hard to reach and maintain their positions, they were all the more determined to defend them. Perhaps that was why the defense of slavery and of the South's "rights" was stronger in the new, booming regions of the lower South and weaker in the more established and less flourishing areas of the Tidewater.

Wealthy southern whites sustained their image of themselves as aristocrats in many ways. They avoided such *Aristocratic Values* "coarse" occupations as trade and commerce; those who did not become planters often gravitated toward the military, a "suitable" career for men raised in a culture in which medieval knights (as portrayed in the novels of Walter Scott) were a powerful and popular image. The aristocratic ideal also found reflection in the definition of a special role for southern white women.

"Honor"

Above all perhaps white males adopted an elaborate code of chivalry, which obligated them to defend their "honor," often through dueling—which survived in the South long after it had largely vanished in the North. Southern white

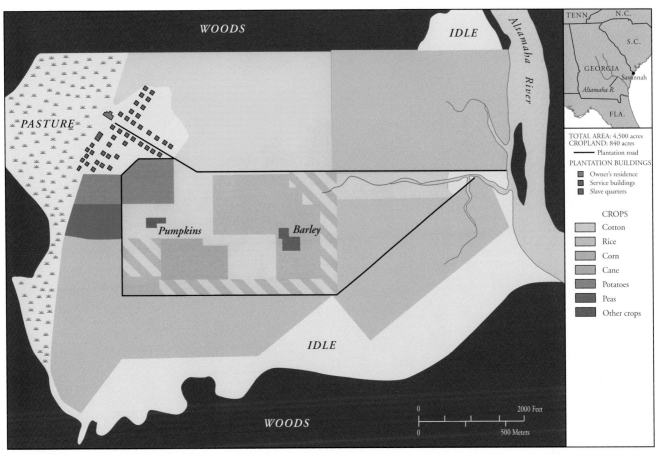

A GEORGIA PLANTATION This map of the Hopeton Plantation in South Carolina shows both how much plantations were connected to the national and world markets, and how much they tried to be self-sufficient. Note the large areas of land devoted to the growing of cotton, rice, and sugar cane, all of them crops for the market. ◆ *Why would a plantation in this part of the South be so much more diversified in the market crops it raised than the cotton plantations in the Mississippi Delta?* Note also the many crops grown for the local market or for consumption by residents of the plantation—potatoes, vegetables, corn, and others. The top left of the map shows the distribution of living quarters, with slaves' quarters grouped together very near the owner's residence. ◆ *Why would planters want their slaves living nearby? Why might slaves be unhappy about being so close to their owners?*

males placed enormous stock in conventional forms of courtesy and respect in their dealings with one another—perhaps as a way of distancing themselves from the cruelty and disrespect that were so fundamental to the slave system they controlled. Violations of such forms often brought what seemed to outsiders a disproportionately heated and even violent response.

The idea of honor in the South was only partly connected to the idea of ethical behavior and bravery. It was also tied to the importance among white males of the public appearance of dignity and authority—of saving face in the presence of others. Anything that seemed to challenge the dignity, social station, or "manhood" of a white southern male might be the occasion for a challenge to duel, or at least for a stern public rebuke. When the South Carolina congressman Preston Brooks strode into the chamber of the United States Senate and savagely beat Senator Charles Sumner of Massachusetts with a cane to retaliate for what he considered an insult to a relative, he was acting wholly in accord with the idea of

southern honor. In the North, he was reviled as a savage. In the South, he became a popular hero. But Brooks was only the most public example of a code of behavior that many white southern men followed. Avenging insults was a social necessity in many parts of southern society, and avenging insults to white southern women was perhaps the most important obligation of a white southern "gentleman."

Cult of Honor

The "Southern Lady"

In some respects, affluent white women in the South occupied roles very similar to those of middle-class white women in the North. Their lives generally centered in the home, where (according to the South's social ideal) they served as companions to and hostesses for their husbands and as nurturing mothers for their children. Even less frequently than in the North did "genteel" southern white women engage in public activities or find income-producing employment.

ST. JOHN PLANTATION, LOUISIANA This Greek Revival "big house" of the St. John Plantation in St. Martin Parish, Louisiana, still stands today. In 1861, when the artist Adrien Persac painted this view of it, it occupied the center of a 5,000-acre sugar plantation and was the setting of the self-consciously elegant life of the planter and his family. To the right is a brick sugar factory and the cabins of the plantation's slaves, who performed the arduous work of sugar harvesting and production. *(Louisiana State University Museum of Art)*

But the life of the "southern lady" was also in many ways very different from that of her northern counterpart. For

Subordinate Status of Women

one thing, the cult of honor in the region meant in theory that southern white men gave particular importance to the "defense" of women. In practice, this generally meant that white men were even more dominant and white women even more subordinate in southern culture than they were in the North. George Fitzhugh, one of the South's most important social theorists, wrote in the 1850s: "Women, like children, have but one right, and that is the right to protection. The right to protection involves the obligation to obey."

More important in determining the role of southern white women, however, were the social and economic realities in which they lived. The vast majority of females in the region lived on farms, relatively isolated from people outside their own families, with virtually no access to the "public world" and thus few opportunities to look beyond their roles as wives and mothers. Because the family was the principal economic unit on most farms, the dominance of husbands and fathers over wives and children was even greater than in those northern families in which

CLEAR STARCHING IN LOUISIANA This 1837 etching by August Hervieu offers a strikingly unromanticized view of plantation women in the South. The white plantation mistress, soberly dressed, speaks harshly to two black household servants, presumably criticizing the way they are doing the laundry. The slaves cower, carefully hiding whatever resentment they might feel behind a submissive pose. Nothing in this picture suggests anything like the kind of ease and luxury often associated with plantation life in popular mythology at the time and since. *(General Research Division, New York Public Library, Astor, Lenox and Tilden Foundations)*

income-producing activities had moved out of the home and into the factory or office. For many white women, living on farms of modest size meant a fuller engagement in the economic life of the family than was becoming typical for middle-class women in the North. These women engaged in spinning, weaving, and other production; they participated in agricultural tasks; they helped supervise the slave work force. On some of the larger plantations, however, even these limited roles were sometimes considered unsuitable for white women; and the "plantation mistress" became, in some cases, more an ornament for her husband than an active part of the economy or the society.

Southern white women also had less access to education than their northern counterparts. Nearly a quarter of all white women over twenty were completely illiterate; relatively few women had more than a rudimentary exposure to schooling. Even wealthy planters were not much interested in extensive schooling for their daughters. The few female "academies" in the South trained women primarily to be suitable wives.

Southern white women had other special burdens as well. The southern white birth *Other Burdens* rate remained nearly 20 percent higher than that of the nation as a whole, and infant mortality in the region remained higher than elsewhere; nearly half the children born in the South in 1860 died before they reached five years of age. The slave labor system had a mixed impact on white women. It helped spare many of them from certain kinds of arduous labor, but it also threatened their relationships with their husbands. Male slaveowners had frequent sexual relationships with the female slaves on their plantations; the children of those unions became part of the plantation labor force and served as a constant reminder to white women of their husbands' infidelity. Black women (and men) were obviously the most important victims of such practices. But white women suffered too.

A few southern white women rebelled against their roles and against the prevailing assumptions of their region. Some became outspoken abolitionists and joined northerners in the crusade to abolish slavery. Some agitated for other reforms within the South itself. Most white women, however, found few outlets for whatever discontent they may have felt with their lives. Instead, they generally convinced themselves of the benefits of their position and—often even more fervently than southern white men—defended the special virtues of the southern way of life. Upper-class white women in the South were particularly energetic in defending the class lines that separated them from poorer whites.

The Plain Folk

The typical white southerner was not a great planter and slaveholder, but a modest yeoman farmer. Some of these "plain folk," as they have become known, owned a few slaves, with whom they worked and lived far more closely than did the larger planters. Most (in fact, three-quarters of all white families) owned no slaves at all. Some plain folk, most of whom owned their own land, devoted themselves largely to subsistence farming; others grew cotton or other crops for the market, but usually could not produce enough to allow them to expand their operations or even get out of debt. During the 1850s, the number of nonslaveholding landowners increased much faster than the number of slaveholding landowners. While there were occasional examples of poor farmers moving into the ranks of the planter class, such cases were rare. Most yeomen knew that they had little prospect of substantially bettering their lot.

One reason was the southern educational system, which provided poor whites with few opportunities to learn and thus limited their chances of advancement. For the sons of wealthy planters, the region provided ample opportunities to gain an education. In 1860 there were 260 southern colleges and universities, public and private, with 25,000 students enrolled in them, or more than half the total number of students in the United States. But universities *Limited Educational Opportunities* were only within the reach of the upper class. The elementary and secondary schools of the South were not only fewer but also inferior to those of the Northeast (although not much worse than the crude schools of the Northwest). The South had more than 500,000 illiterate whites, or over half the country's total.

That a majority of the South's white population consisted of modest farmers largely excluded from the dominant plantation society raises another important question about the antebellum South. Why did the plain folk have so little power in the public world of the Old South? Why did they not oppose the aristocratic social system in which they shared so little? Why did they not resent the system of slavery, from which they generally did not benefit?

Some nonslaveowning whites did oppose the planter elite, but for the most part in limited ways and in a relatively few, isolated areas. These were southern highlanders, the "hill people," who lived in the Appalachian ranges east of the Mississippi, in the Ozarks to the west of the river, and in other "hill country" or "backcountry" areas cut *Hill People* off from the more commercial world of the plantation system. Of all southern whites, they were the most isolated from the mainstream of the region's life. They practiced a simple form of subsistence agriculture, owned practically no slaves, and had a proud sense of seclusion. They were, in most respects, unconnected to the new commercial economy that dominated the great cotton-planting region of the South. They produced almost no surplus for the market, had little access to money, and often bartered for the goods they could not grow themselves.

To such men and women, slavery was unattractive for many of the same reasons it was unappealing to workers and small farmers in the North: because it threatened their sense of their own independence. Upcountry farmers lived in a society of unusual individual personal freedom and unusual isolation from modern notions of property. They also held to older political ideals, which for many included the ideal of fervent loyalty to the nation as a whole.

Such whites frequently expressed animosity toward the planter aristocracy of the other regions of the South. The mountain region was the only part of the South to defy the trend toward sectional conformity, and it was the only part to resist the movement toward secession when it finally developed. Even during the Civil War itself, many refused to support the Confederacy; some went so far as to fight for the Union.

Far greater in number, however, were the nonslave-owning whites who lived in the midst of the plantation system. Many, perhaps most of them, accepted that system because they were tied to it in important ways. Small farmers depended on the local plantation aristocracy for

Close Relations with the Plantation Aristocracy

many things: access to cotton gins, markets for their modest crops and their livestock, credit or other financial assistance in time of need. In many areas, there were also extensive kinship networks linking lower- and upper-class whites. The poorest resident of a county might easily be a cousin of the richest aristocrat. Taken together, these mutual ties helped mute what might otherwise have been pronounced class tensions.

Small farmers felt tied to the plantation society in other ways as well. For white men, at least, the South was an unusually democratic society, in the sense that participation in politics—both through voting and through attending campaign meetings and barbecues—was even more widespread than in the North, where participation was also high. Just as political participation gave workers in the North a sense of connection to the social order, so it did for farmers in the South—even though officeholders in the South, even more than in the North, were almost always members of the region's elites. In the 1850s, moreover, the boom in the cotton economy allowed many small farmers to improve their economic fortunes. Some bought more land, became slaveowners, and moved into at least the fringes of plantation society. Others simply felt more secure now in their positions as independent yeomen and hence more likely to embrace the fierce regional loyalty that was spreading throughout the white South in these years.

Small farmers, even more than great planters, were also committed to a traditional, male-dominated family structure. Their household-centered economies required the participation of all family members and, they believed, a stable system of gender relations to ensure order and stability. Men were the unquestioned masters of their

Commitment to Paternalism

homes; women and children, who were both family and work force, were firmly under the master's control. As the

northern attack on slavery increased in the 1840s and 1850s, it was easy for such farmers to believe—and easy for ministers, politicians, and other propagandists for slavery to persuade them—that an assault on one hierarchical system (slavery) would open the way to an assault on another such system (patriarchy).

There were other white southerners, however, who did not share in the plantation economy in even limited ways and yet continued to accept its premises. These were the members of a particularly degraded class—numbering perhaps a half-million in 1850—known variously as "crackers," "sand hillers," or "poor white trash." Occupying the infertile lands of the pine barrens, the red hills, and the swamps, they lived in miserable cabins amid genuine squalor. Many owned no land (or owned land on which virtually nothing could be grown) and supported themselves by foraging or hunting. Others worked at times as common laborers for their neighbors, although the slave system limited their opportunities. Their degradation resulted partly from dietary deficiencies and disease. They resorted at times to eating clay (hence the tendency of more affluent whites to refer to them disparagingly as "clay eaters"); and they suffered from pellagra, hookworm, and malaria. Planters and small farmers alike held them in contempt. They formed a true underclass. In some material respects, their plight was worse than that of the African-American slaves (who themselves often looked down on the poor whites).

Even among these southerners—the true outcasts of white society in the region—there was no real opposition to the plantation system or slavery. In part, undoubtedly, this was

Limited Class Conflict

because these men and women were so benumbed by poverty that they had little strength to protest. But their relative passivity resulted also from perhaps the single greatest unifying factor among the southern white population, the one force that was most responsible for reducing tensions among the various classes. That force was their perception of race. However poor and miserable these white southerners might have been, they could still consider themselves members of a ruling race; they could still look down on the black population of the region and feel a bond with their fellow whites born of a determination to maintain their racial supremacy. As Frederick Law Olmsted, a northerner who visited the South and chronicled southern society in the 1850s, wrote: "From childhood, the one thing in their condition which has made life valuable to the mass of whites has been that the niggers are yet their inferiors."

SLAVERY: THE "PECULIAR INSTITUTION"

White southerners often referred to slavery as the "peculiar institution." By that they meant not that the institution was odd, but that it was distinctive, special. The description was apt, for American slavery was indeed distinctive. The South in the mid-nineteenth century was the only area in the Western world—except for Brazil, Cuba, and Puerto Rico—where slavery still existed. Slavery, more than any other single factor, isolated the South from the rest of American society. And as that isolation increased, so did the commitment of southerners to defend the institution. William Harper, a prominent South Carolina politician in the 1840s, wrote: "The judgment is made up. We can have no hearing before the tribunal of the civilized world. Yet, on this very account, it is more important that we, the inhabitants of the slave-holding States, insulated as we are by this institution, and cut off, in some degree, from the communion and sympathies of the world by which we are surrounded, . . . and exposed continually to their animadversions and attacks, should thoroughly understand this subject, and our strength and weakness in relation to it."

Within the South itself, the institution of slavery had paradoxical results. On the one hand, it isolated blacks from whites, drawing a sharp and inviolable racial line dividing one group of southerners from another. As a result, African Americans under slavery began to develop a society and culture of their own, one in many ways unrelated to the white civilization around them. On the other hand, slavery created a unique bond between blacks and whites—masters and slaves—in the South. The two groups may have maintained separate spheres, but each sphere was deeply influenced by, indeed dependent on, the other.

Varieties of Slavery

Slavery was an institution established and regulated in detail by law. The slave codes of the southern states forbade slaves to hold property, to leave their masters' premises without permission, to be out after dark, to congregate with other slaves except at church, to carry firearms, or to strike a white person even in self-defense. The codes prohibited whites from teaching slaves to read or write and denied to slaves the right to testify in court against white people. The laws contained no provisions to legalize slave marriages or divorces. If an owner killed a slave while punishing him, the act was generally not considered a crime. Slaves, however, faced the death penalty for killing or even resisting a white person and for inciting revolt. The codes also contained extraordinarily rigid provisions for defining a person's race. Anyone with even a trace of African ancestry was defined as black. And anyone even rumored to possess any such trace was presumed to be black unless he or she could prove otherwise—which was, of course, difficult to do.

Legal Basis of Slavery

These and dozens of other restrictions might seem to suggest that slaves lived under a uniformly harsh and dismal regime. Had the laws been rigidly enforced, that might have been the case. In fact, however, enforcement was spotty and uneven. Some slaves did acquire property, did learn to read and write, and did assemble with other slaves, in spite of laws to the contrary. Although the major slave offenses generally fell under the jurisdiction of the courts (and thus of the slave codes), white owners handled most transgressions and inflicted widely varying punishments. In other words, despite the rigid provisions of law, there was in reality considerable variety within the slave system. Some blacks lived in almost prisonlike conditions, rigidly and harshly controlled by their masters. Many (probably most) others enjoyed some flexibility and (at least in comparison to the regimen prescribed by law) a striking degree of autonomy.

Reality of Slavery

HAULING THE WHOLE WEEK'S PICKING

HAULING THE WHOLE WEEK'S PICKING This watercolor by William Henry Brown, painted in approximately 1842, portrays a slave family loading cotton onto a wagon, presumably after a hard day of picking. Even young children participate in the chores. Brown was an artist known for his silhouettes, a form popular in the nineteenth century. (One of his later subjects was Abraham Lincoln.) This picture, however, is part of a five-foot cutout he made as a gift to a family he was visiting. *(Historic New Orleans Collection)*

The nature of the relationship between masters and slaves depended in part on the size of the plantation. The typical master had a different image of slavery from that of the typical slave. Most masters possessed very few slaves, and their experience with (and image of) slavery was a reflection of the special nature of slavery on the small farm. White farmers with few slaves generally supervised their workers directly and often worked closely alongside them. On such farms, blacks and whites developed a form of intimacy unknown on larger plantations. The paternal relationship between such masters and their slaves could, like relationships between fathers and children, be warm and affectionate. It could also be tyrannical and cruel. In either case, it was a relationship based on the relative powerlessness of the slaves and the nearly absolute authority of their masters. In general, African Americans themselves preferred to live on larger plantations, where they had more privacy and a chance to build a cultural and social world of their own.

Although the majority of slaveowners were small farmers, the majority of slaves lived on plantations of medium or large size, with sizable slave work forces. Thus the relationship between master and slave was much less intimate for the typical slave than for the typical slaveowner. Substantial planters often hired overseers and even assistant overseers to represent them. "Head drivers," trusted and responsible slaves often assisted by several subdrivers, acted under the overseer as foremen.

Larger planters generally used one of two methods of assigning slave labor. One was *Task and Gang Systems* the task system (most common in rice culture), under which slaves were assigned a particular task in the morning, for example, hoeing one acre; after completing the job, they were free for the rest of the day. The other, far more common, was the gang system (employed on the cotton, sugar, and tobacco plantations), under which slaves were simply divided into groups, each of them directed by a driver, and compelled to work for as many hours as the overseer considered a reasonable workday.

Life Under Slavery

Slaves generally received at least enough necessities to enable them to live and work. Their masters usually furnished them with an adequate diet, consisting mainly of cornmeal, salt pork, molasses, and on special occasions fresh meat or poultry. Many slaves cultivated gardens for their own use. They received cheap clothing and shoes. They lived in crude cabins, called slave quarters, usually clustered together in a complex near the master's house. The plantation mistress or a doctor retained by the owner provided some medical care; but slave women themselves—as "healers" and midwives, or simply as mothers—were the more important source.

Slaves worked hard, beginning with light tasks as children; and their workdays were longest at harvest time. *Special Position of Women* Slave women worked particularly hard. They generally labored in the fields with the men, and they assumed as well the crucial chores traditionally reserved for women—cooking, cleaning, and child rearing. Because slave families were often divided, with husbands and fathers frequently living on neighboring plantations (or, at times, sold to plantation owners far away), black women often found themselves acting in effect as single parents. Within the slave family, therefore, women had special burdens but also a special authority.

Slaves were, as a group, much less healthy than southern whites. After 1808, when the importation of slaves became illegal, the proportion of blacks to whites in the nation as a whole steadily declined. In 1820, there was one African American to every four whites; in 1840, one to every *High Slave Mortality Rates* five. The slower increase of the black population was a result of its comparatively high death rate. Slave mothers had large families, but the enforced poverty in which virtually all African Americans lived ensured that fewer of their children would survive to adulthood than the children of white parents. Even those who did survive typically died at a younger age than the average white person.

Even so, according to some scholars, the actual material conditions of slavery may, in fact, have been better than those of many northern factory workers and considerably better than those of both peasants and industrial workers in nineteenth-century Europe. The conditions of American slaves were certainly less severe than those of slaves in the Caribbean and South America. That was in part because plantations in other parts of the Americas tended to grow crops that required more arduous labor; sugar production in the Caribbean islands, in particular, involved extraordinarily backbreaking work. In addition, Caribbean and South American planters continued to use the African slave trade well into the nineteenth century to replenish their labor supply, so they had less incentive than American planters (who no longer had much access to that trade) to protect their existing laborers. Working and living conditions in these other slave societies were arduous, and masters at times literally worked their slaves to death. Growing cotton, the principal activity for most slaves in the United States, was much less debilitating than growing sugar; and planters had strong economic incentives to maintain a healthy slave population. One result of this was that America became the only country where a slave population actually increased through natural reproduction (although it grew much more slowly than the white population).

Most masters did make some effort to preserve the health—and thus the usefulness—of their slaves. One example was the frequent practice of protecting slave children from hard work until early adolescence. Masters

THE CHARACTER OF SLAVERY

No issue in American history has produced a richer literature or a more spirited debate than the nature of American slavery. The debate began even before the Civil War, when abolitionists strove to expose slavery to the world as a brutal, dehumanizing institution, while southern defenders of slavery tried to depict it as a benevolent, paternalistic system. That same debate continued for a time after the Civil War; but by the late nineteenth century, with white Americans eager for sectional conciliation, both northern and southern chroniclers of slavery began to accept a romanticized and unthreatening picture of the Old South and its "peculiar institution."

The first major scholarly examination of slavery was fully within this romantic tradition. Ulrich B. Phillips's *American Negro Slavery* (1918) portrayed slavery as an essentially benign institution in which kindly masters looked after submissive, childlike, and generally contented African Americans. Phillips's apologia for slavery remained the authoritative work on the subject for nearly thirty years.

In the 1940s, as concern about racial injustice increasingly engaged the attention of white Americans, challenges to Phillips began to emerge. In 1941, Melville J. Herskovits challenged Phillips's contention that black Americans retained little of their African cultural inheritance. In 1943, Herbert Aptheker published a chronicle of

(Historic New Orleans Collection)

slave revolts as a way of challenging Phillips's claim that blacks were submissive and content.

A somewhat different challenge to Phillips emerged in the 1950s from historians who emphasized the brutality of the institution. Kenneth Stampp's *The Peculiar Institution* (1956) and, even more damningly, Stanley Elkins's *Slavery* (1959) described a labor system that did serious physical and psychological damage to its victims. Stampp and Elkins portrayed slavery as something like a prison, in which men and women had virtually no space in which to develop their own social and cultural lives. Elkins compared the system to Nazi concentration camps during World War II and likened the childlike "Sambo" personality of slavery to the distortions of character that many scholars believed the Holocaust had produced.

In the early 1970s, an explosion of new scholarship on slavery shifted the emphasis away from the damage the system inflicted on African Americans and toward the striking success of the slaves in building a culture of their own despite their enslavement. John Blassingame in 1973, echoing Herskovits's claims of thirty years earlier, argued that "the most remarkable aspect of the whole process of enslavement is the extent to which the American-born slaves were able to retain their ancestors' culture." Herbert Gutman, in *The Black Family in Slavery and Freedom* (1976) challenged the prevailing belief that slavery had weakened and even destroyed the African-American family. On the contrary, he argued, the black family survived slavery with impressive strength, although

with some significant differences from the prevailing form of the white family. Eugene Genovese's *Roll, Jordan, Roll* (1974) and other works revealed how African Americans manipulated the paternalist assumptions at the heart of slavery to build a large cultural space of their own within the system where they could develop their own family life, social traditions, and religious patterns. That same year, Robert Fogel and Stanley Engerman published their controversial *Time on the Cross,* a highly quantitative study that supported some of the claims of Gutman and Genovese about black achievement, but that went much further in portraying slavery as a successful and reasonably humane (if ultimately immoral) system. Slave workers, they argued, were better treated and lived in greater comfort than most northern industrial workers of the same era. Their conclusions produced a storm of criticism.

Some of the most important recent scholarship on slavery has focused on the role of women within it. Elizabeth Fox-Genovese's *Within the Plantation Household* (1988) examined the lives of both white and black women on the plantation. Rejecting the claims of some feminist historians that black and white women shared a common female identity born of their shared subordination to men, she portrayed slave women as defined by their dual roles as members of the plantation work force and anchors of the black family. Slave women, she argued, professed loyalty to their mistresses when forced to serve them as domestics; but their real loyalty remained to their own communities and families.

(General Research Division, New York Public Library, Astor, Lenox and Tilden Foundations)

309

believed that doing so would make young slaves more loyal and would also ensure better health as adults. Another example was the use of hired labor, when available, for the most unhealthy or dangerous tasks. A traveler in Louisiana noted, for example, that Irishmen were employed to clear malarial swamps and to handle cotton bales at the bottom of chutes extending from the river bluff down to a boat landing. If an Irish worker died of disease or in an accident, a master could hire another for a dollar a day or less. But a master would lose an investment of perhaps $1,000 or more if a prime field hand died. Still, cruel masters might forget their pocketbooks in the heat of anger. Slaves were often left to the discipline of overseers, who had less of an economic stake in their well-being; overseers were paid in proportion to the amount of work they could get out of the slaves they supervised.

Household servants had a somewhat easier life—physically at least—than did field hands. On a small plantation, the same slaves might do both field work and housework. But on a large estate, there would generally

NURSING THE MASTER'S CHILD Louisa, a slave on a Missouri plantation owned by the Hayward family in the 1850s, is photographed here holding the master's infant son. Black women typically cared for white children on plantations, sometimes with great affection and sometimes—as this photograph may suggest—dutifully and without enthusiasm. *(Missouri Historical Society)*

be a separate domestic staff: nursemaids, housemaids, cooks, butlers, coachmen. These people lived close to the master and his family, eating the leftovers from the family table *House Slaves* and in some cases even sleeping in the "big house." Between the blacks and whites of such households affectionate, almost familial relationships might sometimes develop. More often, however, house servants resented their isolation from their fellow slaves and the lack of privacy that came with living in such close proximity to the master's family. Among other things, that proximity meant that their transgressions were more visible than those of field hands, and so they received punishments more often than did other slaves. When emancipation came after the Civil War, it was often the house servants who were the first to leave the plantations of their former owners.

Female household servants were especially vulnerable to sexual abuse by their masters and white overseers, who sometimes pressured them into supposedly consensual sexual relationships and *Sexual Abuse* sometimes literally raped them. In addition to unwanted sexual attention from white men, female slaves often received vindictive treatment from white women. Plantation mistresses naturally resented the sexual liaisons between their husbands and female slaves. Punishing their husbands was not usually possible, so they often punished the slaves instead—with arbitrary beatings, increased workloads, and various forms of psychological torment.

Slavery in the Cities

The conditions of slavery in the cities differed significantly from those in the countryside. On the relatively isolated plantations, slaves had little contact with free blacks and lower-class whites, and masters maintained fairly direct and effective control; a deep and seemingly unbridgeable chasm yawned between slavery and freedom. In the city, however, a master often could not supervise his slaves closely and at the same time use them profitably. Even if they slept at night in carefully watched backyard barracks, slaves moved about during the day alone, performing errands of various kinds.

There was a considerable market in the South for common laborers, particularly since, unlike in the North, there were few European immigrants to perform menial chores. Even the poorest whites tended to prefer working on farms to doing ordinary labor, and so masters often hired out slaves for such tasks. Slaves on contract worked in mining and lumbering (often far from cities); but others worked on the docks and on construction sites, drove wagons, and performed other unskilled jobs in cities and towns. Slave women and children worked in the region's few textile mills. Particularly skilled workers such as blacksmiths or carpenters were also often hired out. After regular working hours, many of them fended for

Autonomy of Urban Slaves themselves; neither their owners nor their employers bothered to supervise them. Thus urban slaves gained numerous opportunities to mingle with free blacks and with whites. In the cities, the line between slavery and freedom became increasingly indistinct.

Indeed, white southerners generally considered slavery to be incompatible with city life, and as southern cities grew the number of slaves in them declined, relatively if not absolutely. The reasons were social rather than economic. Fearing conspiracies and insurrections, urban slaveowners sold off much of their male property to the countryside. Remaining behind in the cities was a slave population in which black women outnumbered black men. The same cities also had more white men than women—a situation that helped account for the birth of many mulattoes. Even while slavery in the cities was declining, forced segregation of urban blacks, both free and slave, from white society increased. Segregation was a means of social control intended to make up for the loosening of the discipline of slavery itself in urban areas.

Free African Americans

There were about 250,000 free African Americans in the slaveholding states by the start of the Civil War, more than half of them in Virginia and Maryland. In some cases, they were slaves who had somehow earned money with which they managed to buy their own and their families' freedom, usually by developing a skill they could market independently of their masters. It was usually urban blacks, with their greater freedom of movement and activity, who could take that route. One example was Elizabeth Keckley, a slave woman who bought freedom for herself and her son with proceeds from sewing. She later became a seamstress, personal servant, and companion to Mary Todd Lincoln in the White House. But few masters had any incentive, or inclination, to give up their slaves, so this route was open to relatively few people.

Some slaves were set free by a master who had moral qualms about slavery, or by a master's will after his death—for example, the more than 400 slaves belonging to John Randolph of Roanoke, freed in 1833. From the 1830s on, however, state laws governing slavery became more rigid. That was in part a response *Tightened Restrictions on Free Blacks* to the fears Nat Turner's revolt (see p. 312) created among white southerners: free blacks, removed from close supervision by whites, might generate more violence and rebellion than slaves. It was also in part because the community of free blacks in southern cities was becoming larger and, to whites, more threatening—a dangerous example to blacks still in slavery. The rise of abolitionist agitation in the North—and the fear that it would inspire slaves to rebel—also persuaded southern whites to tighten their system. The new laws made it more and

more difficult, and in some cases practically impossible, for owners to set free (or "manumit") their slaves; all southern states forbade free African Americans from entering. Arkansas even forced the freed slaves living there to leave.

A few free blacks (generally those on the northern fringes of the slaveholding regions) attained wealth and prominence. Some owned slaves themselves, usually relatives whom they had bought in order to ensure their ultimate emancipation. In a few cities—New Orleans, Natchez, Charleston—free black communities managed to flourish relatively unmolested by whites and with some economic stability. Most free blacks, however, lived in abject poverty, under conditions worse than those of blacks in the North. Law or custom closed many occupations to them, forbade them to assemble without white supervision, and placed numerous other restraints on them. They were only quasi-free, and yet they had all the burdens of freedom: the necessity to support themselves, to find housing, to pay taxes. Yet great as were the hardships of freedom, blacks usually preferred them to slavery.

The Slave Trade

The transfer of slaves from one part of the South to another was one of the most important consequences of the development of the Southwest. Sometimes slaves moved to the new cotton lands in the company of their original owners, who were migrating themselves. More often, however, the transfer occurred through the medium of professional slave traders. Traders transported slaves over

THE BUSINESS OF SLAVERY The offices of slave dealers were familiar sights on the streets of pre-Civil War southern cities and towns. They provide testimony to the way in which slavery was not just a social system, but a business, deeply woven into the fabric of southern economic life. *(Library of Congress)*

long distances on trains or on river or ocean steamers. On shorter journeys, the slaves moved on foot, trudging in coffles of hundreds along dusty highways—just as their

Slave Markets | ancestors had marched to the ports in Africa from which they had embarked to America. Eventually they arrived at some central market such as Natchez, New Orleans, Mobile, or Galveston, where purchasers gathered to bid for them. At the auction, the bidders checked the slaves like livestock, watching them as they were made to walk or trot, inspecting their teeth, feeling their arms and legs, looking for signs of infirmity or age. Some traders tried to deceive buyers by blacking gray hair, oiling withered skin, and concealing physical defects in other ways. A sound young field hand would fetch a price that, during the 1840s and 1850s, varied from $500 to $1,700, depending mainly on fluctuations in the price of cotton. An attractive, sexually desirable woman might bring much more.

The domestic slave trade was essential to the growth and prosperity of the whole system. It was also one of its most horrible aspects. The trade dehumanized all who were involved in it. It separated children from parents, and parents from each other. Even families kept together by scrupulous masters might be broken up in the division of the estate after the master's death. Planters might deplore the trade, but they eased their consciences by holding the traders in contempt and assigning them a low social position.

The foreign slave trade was as bad or worse. Although federal law had prohibited the importation of slaves from 1808 on, some continued to be smuggled into the United

The Foreign Slave Trade | States as late as the 1850s. The numbers can only be estimated. There were not enough such imports to satisfy all planters, and the southern commercial conventions, which met annually to consider means of making the South economically independent, began to discuss the legal reopening of the trade. "If it is right to buy slaves in Virginia and carry them to New Orleans," William L. Yancey of Alabama asked his fellow delegates at the 1858 meeting, "why is it not right to buy them in Cuba, Brazil, or Africa and carry them there?" The convention that year voted to recommend the repeal of all laws against slave imports. Within the South, only the delegates from the states of the upper South, which profited from the domestic trade, opposed the foreign competition.

Slave Resistance

Few issues have sparked as much debate among historians as the effects of slavery on the blacks themselves. (See "Where Historians Disagree," p. 309.) Slaveowners, and many white Americans after emancipation, liked to argue that the slaves were generally content, "happy with their lot." That may well have been true in some cases. But it is clear that the vast majority of southern blacks were not content with being slaves, that they yearned for freedom even though most realized there was little they could do to secure it. Evidence for that conclusion can be found, if nowhere else, from the reaction of slaves when emancipation finally came. Virtually all reacted to freedom with joy and celebration; relatively few chose to remain in the service of the whites who had owned them before the Civil War (although most blacks, of course, remained for many years subservient to whites in one way or another).

Rather than contented acceptance, the dominant response of blacks to slavery was a complex one: a combination of adaptation and resistance. At the extremes, slavery could produce two very different reactions, each of which served as the basis for a powerful stereotype in white society. One extreme was what became known as the "Sambo"—the shuffling, grinning, head-scratching, deferential slave who acted out the role that he recognized the white world expected of him. More often than not, the "Sambo" pattern of behavior was a charade, a facade assumed in the presence of whites. The other extreme was the slave rebel—the African American who could not bring himself or herself to either acceptance or accommodation but remained forever rebellious. Actual slave revolts were extremely rare, but the knowledge that they were possible struck terror into the hearts of white southerners everywhere. In 1800, Gabriel Prosser gathered 1,000 rebellious slaves outside Richmond; but two Africans gave the plot away, and the Virginia militia stymied the uprising before it could begin. Prosser and thirty-five others were executed. In 1822, the Charleston free black Denmark Vesey and his followers—rumored to total 9,000—made preparations for revolt; but again word leaked out, and suppression and retri- | *Prosser and Turner Rebellions* bution followed. In 1831, Nat Turner, a slave preacher, led a band of African Americans who armed themselves with guns and axes and, on a summer night, went from house to house in Southampton County, Virginia. They killed sixty white men, women, and children before being overpowered by state and federal troops. More than a hundred blacks were executed in the aftermath. Nat Turner's was the only actual slave insurrection in the nineteenth-century South, but fear of slave conspiracies and renewed violence pervaded the section as long as slavery lasted.

For the most part, however, resistance to slavery took other, less drastic forms. Some blacks attempted to resist by running away. A small number managed to escape to the North or to Canada, especially after sympathetic whites began organizing the so-called underground railroad to assist them in flight. But the odds against a successful escape, particularly from the Deep South, were impossibly high. The hazards of distance and the slaves' ignorance of geography were serious obstacles. So were the white "slave patrols," which stopped wandering blacks on sight throughout the South demanding to see

HARRIET TUBMAN WITH ESCAPED SLAVES Harriet Tubman (c. 1820–1913) was born into slavery in Maryland. In 1849, when her master died, she escaped to Philadelphia to avoid being sold out of state. Over the next ten years, she assisted first members of her own family and then up to 300 other slaves to escape from Maryland to freedom. During the Civil War, she served alternately as a nurse and as a spy for Union forces in South Carolina. She is shown here, on the left, with some of the slaves she had helped to free. *(Smith College Museum of Art)*

travel permits. Without such a permit, slaves were presumed to be runaways and were taken captive. Slave patrols often employed bloodhounds to track blacks who attempted to escape through the woods. Despite all the obstacles to success, however, blacks continued to run away from their masters in large numbers. Some did so repeatedly, undeterred by the whippings and other penalties inflicted on them when captured.

But perhaps the most important method of resistance was simply a pattern of everyday behavior by which blacks defied their masters. That whites so often considered blacks to be lazy and shiftless suggests one means of resistance: refusal to work hard.

Some slaves stole from their masters or from neighboring whites. Some performed isolated acts of sabotage: losing or breaking tools (southern planters gradually began to buy unusually heavy hoes because so many of the lighter ones got broken) or performing tasks improperly. In extreme cases, blacks might make themselves useless by cutting off their fingers or even committing suicide. Or, despite the terrible consequences, a few turned on their masters and killed them. The extremes, however, were very rare.

Slave Resistance

For the most part, blacks resisted by building into their normal patterns of behavior subtle methods of rebellion.

THE CULTURE OF SLAVERY

Resistance was only part of the slave response to slavery. Another was an elaborate process of adaptation—a process that did not imply contentment with bondage but a recognition that there was no realistic alternative. One of the ways blacks adapted was by developing their own, separate culture, one that enabled them to sustain a sense of racial pride and unity.

Language and Music

In many areas, slaves retained a language of their own, sometimes incorporating African speech patterns into English. Having arrived in America speaking many different African languages, the first generations of slaves had as much difficulty communicating with one another as they did with white people. To overcome these barriers, they learned a simple, common language (known to linguists as "pidgin"). It retained some African words, but

For African Americans living as slaves on southern plantations, there was little leisure time—and little opportunity for the kinds of cultural activities that were beginning to appeal to other groups of Americans. But slaves managed nevertheless to create a culture of their own. And among its most distinctive and pervasive features was music.

Indeed to white observers at least, nothing was more striking about slave life than the role music played within it. African Americans sang frequently, sometimes alone, even more often in groups. They sang while they worked together in the fields, as they shucked corn, slaughtered hogs, or repaired fences. They sang whenever they had social gatherings—on Sundays or on the rare other holidays from work. They sang when they gathered for chores in the evenings. They sang during their religious services. And they sang with a passion, at times even an ecstasy, that was completely unfamiliar to whites—and sometimes troubling to them.

Their songs were rarely written down and often seemed entirely spontaneous; but much slave music was really derived from African and Caribbean traditions passed on through generations and from snatches of other songs the performers had heard before and from which they improvised variations. In its emotionalism, its pulsing rhythms, and its lack of conventional formal structure, it resembled nothing its white listeners had ever heard before.

Slaves sang whether or not there were any musical instruments to accompany them, but they often created instruments for themselves out of whatever materials were at hand. "Us take pieces of sheep's rib or cow's jaw or a piece of iron, with an old kettle or a hollow gourd and some horsehair to make the drum," one former slave recalled years later. "They'd take the buffalo horn and scrape it out to make the flute." When they could, they would build banjos, an instrument that had originated in Africa. Their masters sometimes gave them violins and guitars. When the setting permitted it, African Americans danced to their music—dances very different from and much more spontaneous than the formal steps that nineteenth-century whites generally learned. They also used music to accompany one of their other important cultural traditions: storytelling. Black music on the plantations took a number of forms. The most common was religious songs, the precursors of modern gospel music, which expressed—in terms that their white masters, who usually did not listen to the words very carefully, usually found acceptable—a faith in their eventual freedom and salvation and often spoke of Africans as a chosen people waiting for redemption. At other times, the songs would express a bitterness toward white slaveholders. The great black abolitionist Frederick Douglass remembered one:

> We raise de wheat,
> Dey gib us de corn;
> We bake de bread,
> Dey gib us de crust;
> We sif the meal,
> Dey gib us de huss;
> We peel de meat,
> Dey gib us de skin;
> And dat's de way
> Dey take us in;
> We skim de pot,
> Dey gib us de liquor,
> And say dat's good enough for nigger.
> Your butter and the fat;
> Poor nigger, you can't ever get that.

To African Americans, in other words, music was a treasured avenue of escape from the hardships of slavery. It was also a vehicle through which they could express anger, resentment, and hope. Their masters generally tolerated their slaves' music—and even valued it, both because they often enjoyed listening to it and because the more intelligent understood that without this means of emotional and spiritual release, active resistance to slavery might be more frequent.

The powerful music that emerged from slavery helped shape the lives of African Americans on the plantations. It also helped lay the foundations for music that almost all Americans later embraced: gospel, blues, jazz, rhythm and blues, rock, and rap.

THE OLD PLANTATION This painting, by an unidentified folk artist of the early nineteenth century, suggests the importance of music in the lives of plantation slaves in America. The banjo, which the black musician at right is playing, was originally an African instrument. *(Abby Aldrich Rockefeller Folk Art Center)*

it drew primarily, if selectively, from English. And while

Pidgin slave language grew more sophisticated as blacks spent more time in America—and as new generations grew up never having known African tongues—some features of this early pidgin survived in black speech for many generations.

Music was especially important in slave society. In some ways, it was as important to African Americans as language. Again, the African heritage was an important influence. African music relied heavily on rhythm, and so did black music in America. Africans thought of music as an accompaniment to dance, and so did blacks in America. The banjo, an instrument original to Africa, became im-

Importance of Slave Spirituals portant to slave music. But most important were voices and song. Field workers often used songs to pass the time in the fields; since they sang them in the presence of whites, they usually attached relatively innocuous words to them. But African Americans also created more emotionally rich and politically challenging music in the relative privacy of their religious services. It was there that the tradition of the spiritual emerged in the early nineteenth century. And through the spiritual, Africans in America not only expressed their religious faith, but also lamented their bondage and expressed continuing hope for freedom. Similar sentiments surfaced throughout slave religion.

African-American Religion

A separate slave religion was not supposed to exist. Almost all African Americans were Christians by the early nineteenth century. Some had converted voluntarily and some after coercion by their masters and Protestant missionaries who evangelized among them. Masters expected their slaves to worship under the supervision of white ministers. Indeed, autonomous black churches were banned by law; and many slaves became members of the same denominations as their owners—usually Baptist or Methodist. In the 1840s and 1850s, as slavery expanded in the South, missionary efforts increased. Vast numbers of blacks became members of Protestant churches in those years.

Nevertheless, blacks throughout the South developed their own version of Christianity, at times incorporating into it such practices as voodoo or other polytheistic religious traditions of Africa. Or they simply bent religion to the special circumstances of bondage. Natural leaders emerging within the slave community rose to the rank of preacher.

African-American religion was more emotional than its

Slave Religion white counterparts and reflected the influence of African customs and practices. Slave prayer meetings routinely involved fervent chanting, spontaneous exclamations from the

PLANTATION RELIGION A black preacher leads his fellow slaves, as well as the family of the master, in a Sunday service in the modest plantation chapel. African-American religious services were considerably less restrained when white people were not present— one reason why blacks withdrew so quickly from white churches after the Civil War and formed their own. *(Bettmann/Corbis)*

congregation, and ecstatic conversion experiences. Black religion was also more joyful and affirming than that of many white denominations. And above all, black religion emphasized the dream of freedom and deliverance. In their prayers and songs and sermons, black Christians talked and sang of the day when the Lord would "call us home," "deliver us to freedom," "take us to the Promised Land." And while their white masters generally chose to interpret such language merely as the expression of hopes for life after death, many blacks themselves used the images of Christian salvation to express their own dream of freedom in the present world. Christian images, and biblical injunctions, were central to Gabriel Prosser, Denmark Vesey, Nat Turner, and others who planned or engaged in open resistance to slavery.

In cities and towns in the South, some African Americans had their own churches, where free blacks occasionally worshiped alongside slaves. In the countryside, however, slaves usually attended the same churches as their masters—sometimes a chapel on the plantation itself, sometimes a church serving a larger farm community. Seating in such churches was usually segregated. Blacks sat in the rear or in balconies. They held their own services later, often in secret, usually at night.

The Slave Family

The slave family was the other crucial institution of black culture in the South. Like religion, it suffered from certain legal restrictions—most notably the lack of legal marriage. Nevertheless, what we now call the "nuclear family" consistently emerged as the dominant kinship model among African Americans.

Such families did not always operate according to white customs. Black women generally began bearing children at younger ages than most whites, often as early as age fourteen or fifteen. Slave communities did not condemn premarital pregnancy in the way white society did, and black couples would often begin living together before marrying. It was customary, however, for couples to marry—in a ceremony involving formal vows—soon

Slave Marriages after conceiving a child. Often, marriages occurred between slaves living on neighboring plantations. Husbands and wives sometimes visited each other with the permission of their masters, but often such visits had to be in secret, at night. Family ties were no less strong than those of whites, and many slave marriages lasted throughout the course of long lifetimes.

When marriages did not survive, it was often because of circumstances over which blacks had no control. Up to a third of all black families were broken apart by the slave trade; an average slave might expect during a lifetime to see ten or more relatives sold. And that accounted for some of the other distinctive characteristics of the black family, which adapted itself to the cruel realities of its own

Importance of Kinship Networks uncertain future. Extended kinship networks—which grew to include not only spouses and their children, but also aunts, uncles, grandparents, even distant cousins—were strong and important and often helped compensate for the breakup of nuclear families. A slave forced suddenly to move to a new area, far from his or her family, might create fictional kinship ties and become "adopted" by a family in the new community. Even so, the impulse to maintain contact with a spouse and children remained strong long after the breakup of a family. One of the most frequent causes of flight from the plantation was a slave's desire to find a husband, wife, or child who had been sent elsewhere.

It was not only by breaking up families through sale that whites intruded on black family life. Black women, usually powerless to resist the sexual advances of their masters, often bore the children of whites—children whom the whites almost never recognized as their own and who were consigned to slavery from birth.

In addition to establishing social and cultural institutions of their own, slaves adapted themselves to slavery by forming complex relationships with their masters. However much blacks resented their lack of freedom, they often found it difficult to maintain an entirely hostile attitude toward their owners. Not only were they dependent on whites for the material means of existence—food, clothing, and shelter; they also often derived from their *Paternal Nature of Slavery* masters a sense of security and protection. There was, in short, a paternal relationship between slave and master—sometimes harsh, sometimes kindly, but almost invariably important. That paternalism, in fact, became (even if not always consciously) a vital instrument of white control. By creating a sense of mutual dependence, whites helped reduce resistance to an institution that, in essence, served only the interests of the ruling race.

CONCLUSION

While the North was creating a complex and rapidly developing commercial-industrial economy, the South was expanding its agrarian economy without making many fundamental changes in its character. Great migrations took many southern whites, and even more African-American slaves, into new agricultural areas in the Deep South, where they created a booming "cotton kingdom" that raised crops for export around the world. The cotton economy created many great fortunes, and some modest ones. It also entrenched the planter class as the dominant force within southern society—both as owners of vast numbers of slaves, and as patrons, creditors, landlords, and marketers for the large number of poor whites who lived on the edge of the planter world.

The differences between the North and the South were a result of differences in natural resources, differences in social structure, differences in climate, and differences in culture. Above all, they were the result of the existence within the South of an unfree labor system that prevented the kind of social fluidity that an industrializing society usually requires and that kept a large proportion of the southern population in debilitating bondage.

FOR FURTHER REFERENCE

Peter Kolchin, *American Slavery, 1619–1877* (1993) is an excellent recent synthesis of the history of slavery in the United States from the settlement of Virginia through Reconstruction. James Oakes, *Slavery and Freedom* (1990) provides an overview of southern politics and society in the antebellum period. Eugene Genovese's classic study, *Roll, Jordan, Roll: The World the Slaves Made* (1974) argues that masters and slaves forged a system of mutual obligations within a fundamentally coercive social system. Genovese's *The Political Economy of Slavery*

(1965) argues that slavery blocked southern economic development. James Oakes, *The Ruling Race: A History of American Slaveholders* (1982) argues that slaveowners were hardheaded businessmen and capitalists. Frederick Douglass's *Narrative of the Life of Frederick Douglass,* first published in 1845, is a classic autobiography. Elizabeth Fox-Genovese, *Within the Plantation Household* (1988) argues against the idea that black and white women shared a community of interests on southern plantations. Charles Joyner, *Down by the Riverside: A South Carolina Slave Community* (1984) is a fine study of slavery in a single community. Charles C. Bolton, *Poor Whites of the Antebellum South: Tenants and Laborers in Central North and Northeast Mississippi* (1994) is a good study of a neglected group in the southern population. Bertram Wyatt-Brown, *Southern Honor: Ethics and Behavior in the Old South* (1982) argues that concepts of honor lay at the core of southern white identity in the antebellum period. Steven Hahn, *The Roots of Southern Populism: Yeomen Farmers and the Transformation of the Georgia Upcountry, 1850–1890* (1983) argues that white farmers in upcountry regions of the antebellum South maintained economically self-sufficient communities on the periphery of the market.

For quizzes, Internet resources, references to additional books and films, and more, consult this book's Online Learning Center at www.mhhe.com/brinkley11.

GIRLS' EVENING SCHOOL (C. 1840), ANONYMOUS Schooling for women, which expanded significantly in the mid-nineteenth century, included training in domestic arts (as indicated by the sewing table at right), as well as in reading, writing, and other basic skills. *(Museum of Fine Atrs, Boston)*

Significant Events

1817 · American Colonization Society founded

1821 · New York constructs first penitentiary

1823 · Catharine Beecher founds Hartford Female Seminary

1825 · Robert Owen founds New Harmony community in Indiana

1826 · James Fenimore Cooper publishes *The Last of the Mohicans*
· American Society for the Promotion of Temperance founded

1829 · David Walker publishes *Appeal . . . to the Colored Citizens*

1830 · Joseph Smith publishes the Book of Mormon
· American Colonization Society helps create Liberia for emigrating American slaves

1831 · William Lloyd Garrison begins publishing the *Liberator*

1833 · American Antislavery Society founded

1834 · Anti-abolitionist mob burns abolitionist headquarters in Philadelphia

1837 · Horace Mann becomes first secretary of Massachusetts Board of Education
· Elijah Lovejoy killed by anti-abolitionist mob in Illinois

CHAPTER TWELVE

ANTEBELLUM CULTURE AND REFORM

*T*he United States in the mid-nineteenth century was a rapidly changing society. The nation was growing in geographical extent, in the size and diversity of its population, and in the dimensions and complexity of its economy. Like any people faced with such rapid and fundamental alterations in their surroundings, most Americans reacted with ambiguity. On the one hand, many were excited by the new possibilities that economic growth was providing. On the other hand, many were painfully aware of the dislocations that it was creating: the challenges to traditional values and institutions, the social instability, the increasing inequality, the uncertainty about the future.

One result of these conflicting attitudes was the emergence of a broad array of movements intended to adapt society to its new conditions, to "reform" the nation. These reform efforts took many different shapes, but in general they reflected one of two basic impulses, and at times elements of both. Many of these movements rested on an optimistic faith in human nature, a belief that within every individual resided a spirit that was basically good and that society should attempt to unleash.

This assumption—which spawned in both Europe and America a movement known, *Romanticism* in its artistic aspects at least, as romanticism—stood in marked contrast to traditional Protestant assumptions of original sin, which humans needed to overcome through a disciplined, virtuous life. Instead, reformers now argued, individuals should strive to give full expression to the inner spirit, should work to unleash their innate capacity to experience joy and to do good.

A second impulse, which appeared directly to contradict the first but in practice often existed alongside it, was *Order and Control* a desire for order and control. With society changing so rapidly, with traditional values and institutions under assault and often eroding, many Americans yearned above all for a restoration of stability and discipline to their nation. Often, this impulse embodied a conservative nostalgia for better, simpler times. But it also inspired forward-looking efforts to create new institutions of social control, suited to the realities of the new age.

The reforms that flowed from these two impulses came in many guises and mobilized many different groups. Reformers were far more numerous and influential in the North and Northwest than in the South, but reform activity could be found in all areas of the nation. In the course of the 1840s, however, one issue—slavery—came to overshadow all others. And one group of reformers—the abolitionists—became the most visible of all. At that point, the reform impulse, which at first had been a force that tended to unify the sections, became another wedge between the North and the South.

THE ROMANTIC IMPULSE

National Cultural Aspirations

"In the four quarters of the globe," wrote the English wit Sydney Smith in 1820, "who reads an American book? or goes to an American play? or looks at an American picture or statue?" The answer, he assumed, was obvious: no one. American intellectuals were painfully aware of the low regard in which Europeans held their artistic and intellectual life, and in the middle decades of the nineteenth century they continued to work for both an elevation and a liberation of their nation's culture—for the creation of an American artistic world independent of Europe, one that would express their nation's special virtues.

At the same time, however, some of the nation's cultural leaders were beginning to strive for another kind of liberation, one that would gradually come almost to overshadow their self-conscious nationalism. That impulse—which was, ironically, largely an import from Europe—was the spirit of romanticism. In literature, in philosophy, in art, even in politics and economics, American intellectuals were committing themselves to the liberation of the human spirit.

Nationalism and Romanticism in American Painting

When Sidney Smith asked in 1820 who looked at an American painting, he was expressing the almost universal belief among European artists that they—and they alone—stood at the center of the world of art. But in the United States, a great many people were, in fact, looking at American paintings in the antebellum era—and they were doing so not because the paintings introduced them to the great traditions of Europe, but because they believed Americans were creating important new artistic traditions of their own.

The most important and popular American paintings of the first half of the nineteenth century set out to evoke the wonder of the nation's landscape. Unlike their European counterparts, American painters did not favor gentle scenes of carefully cultivated countrysides. They sought instead to capture the undiluted power of nature by portraying some of the nation's wildest and most spectacular areas—to evoke what many nineteenth-century people called the "sublime," the feeling of awe and wonderment and even fear of the grandeur of nature. The first great school of American painters emerged in New York.

Hudson River School

Frederic Church, Thomas Cole, Thomas Doughty, and Asher Durand—who were, along with others, known as the Hudson River School—painted the spectacular vistas of the rugged and still largely unsettled Hudson Valley. Like Emerson and Thoreau, whom many of the painters read and admired, they considered nature—more than civilization—the best source of wisdom and spiritual fulfillment.

In portraying the Hudson Valley, they seemed to announce that in America, unlike in Europe, "wild nature" still existed; and that America, therefore, was a nation of greater promise than the played-out lands of the Old World. Yet there was also a sense of nostalgia in many of the Hudson River paintings, an effort to preserve and cherish a kind of nature that many Americans feared was fast disappearing.

In later years, some of the Hudson River painters traveled further west, in search of even more profound spiritual experiences in an even more rugged and spectacular natural world. Their enormous canvases of great natural wonders—the Yosemite Valley, Yellowstone, the Rocky Mountains—touched a passionate chord among the public. Some of the most famous of their paintings—particularly the works of Albert Bierstadt and Thomas Moran—traveled around the country attracting enormous crowds.

Literature and the Quest for Liberation

American readers in the first decades of the nineteenth century were relatively indifferent to the work of their nation's own writers. The most popular novelist in America in these years was the British writer Sir Walter Scott, whose swashbuckling historical novels set in eighteenth-century England and Scotland won him an impassioned readership in both Britain and America. When Americans read books written in their own country, many were more likely to turn to the large number of "sentimental novels," written mostly by and for women, than to what would ordinarily be considered serious literature. (See "Patterns of Popular Culture," pp. 338–339 [Sentimental Novels].)

But even during the heyday of Scott in the 1820s, the effort to create a distinctively American literature—which Washington Irving and others had advanced in the first decades of the century—made considerable progress with the emergence of the first great American novelist: James Fenimore Cooper. The author of over thirty novels in the space of three decades, Cooper was known to his contemporaries as a master of adventure and suspense. What most distinguished his work, however, was its evocation of the American wilderness. Cooper had grown up in central New York, at a time when the edge of white settlement was not far away; and he retained

Cooper and the American Wilderness

throughout his life a fascination with man's relationship to nature and with the challenges (and dangers) of America's expansion westward. His most important novels were known as the "Leatherstocking Tales." Among them were *The Last of the Mohicans* (1826) and *The Deerslayer* (1841). They explored the American frontiersman's experience with Indians, pioneers, violence, and the law.

Cooper's novels were a continuation, in many ways a culmination, of the early-nineteenth-century effort to produce a truly American literature. But they also served as a link to the concerns of later intellectuals. For in the

"Leatherstocking Tales" could be seen not only a celebration of the American spirit and landscape but an evocation, through the central character of Natty Bumppo, of the ideal of the independent individual with a natural inner goodness. There was also evidence of another impulse that would motivate American reform: the fear of disorder. Many of Cooper's less savory characters illustrated the vicious, grasping nature of some of the nation's western settlers and suggested a need for social discipline even in the wilderness.

Another group of important American writers emerged on the heels of Cooper. They displayed even more clearly the grip of romanticism on the nation's intellectual life. Walt Whitman, the self-proclaimed poet of American

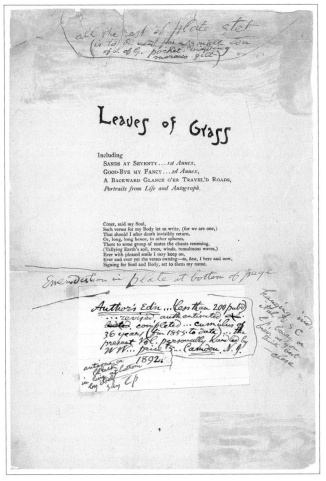

TITLE PAGE FOR WHITMAN'S *LEAVES OF GRASS* For more than thirty years after the publication of the original *Leaves of Grass* in 1855, Walt Whitman constantly revised and expanded the collection of poems and issued numerous subsequent editions. This sample title page, with notations by Whitman indicating changes and additions he wanted made, is for the final such edition, published in 1892, the year of Whitman's death. In a public announcement he prepared to announce publication, he said that "the book *Leaves of Grass,* which he has been working on at great intervals and partially issued for the past thirty-five or forty years, is now completed. . . . Faulty as it is, he decides it is by far his special and entire self-chosen poetic utterance." *(Rare Book and Special Collections Division, Library of Congress)*

democracy, was the son of a Long Island carpenter and lived for many years roaming from place to place, doing odd jobs. Finally, in 1855, he hired a printer and published a first volume of work: *Leaves of Grass.* His poems were an unrestrained celebration of democracy, of the liberation of the individual, and of the pleasures of the flesh as well as of the spirit. They also expressed Whitman's personal yearning for emotional and physical release and personal fulfillment—a yearning perhaps rooted in part in his own experience as a homosexual living in a society profoundly intolerant of unconventional sexuality. In these poems, as well as in a large body of other work spanning nearly forty more years until his death in 1892, Whitman not only helped liberate verse from traditional, restrictive conventions but also helped express the soaring spirit of individualism that characterized his age.

The new literary concern with the unleashing of human emotions did not always produce such optimistic works, *Herman Melville* as the work of Herman Melville suggests. Born in New York in 1819, Melville ran away to sea as a youth and spent years sailing the world (including the South Seas) before returning home to become the greatest American novelist of his era. The most important of his novels was *Moby Dick,* published in 1851. His portrayal of Ahab, the powerful, driven captain of a whaling vessel, was a story of courage and of the strength of individual will; but it was also a tragedy of pride and revenge. Ahab's maniacal search for Moby Dick, a great white whale that had maimed him, suggested how the search for personal fulfillment and triumph could not only liberate but destroy. The result of Ahab's great quest was the annihilation of Ahab himself, reflecting Melville's conviction that the human spirit was a troubled, often self-destructive force.

Similarly bleak were the works of one of the few southern writers of the time to embrace the search for the essence of the human spirit: Edgar Allan Poe. In the course of his short and unhappy life (he died in 1849 at the age of forty), Poe produced stories and poems that were primarily sad and macabre. His first book, *Tamerlane and Other Poems* (1827), received little recognition. But later works, including his most famous poem, "The Raven" (1845), established him as a major, if controversial, literary figure. Poe evoked images of individuals rising above the narrow confines of intellect and exploring the deeper world of the spirit and the emotions. Yet that world, he seemed to say, contained much pain and horror. Other American writers were contemptuous of Poe's work and his message, but he was ultimately to have a profound effect on European poets such as Baudelaire.

Literature in the Antebellum South

Poe, however, was something of an exception in the world of southern literature. The South experienced a literary flowering of its own in the mid-nineteenth century, and it produced writers and artists who were, like their northern counterparts, concerned with defining the nature of American society and of the American nation. But white southerners tended to produce very different images of what that society was and should be.

Southern novelists of the 1830s (among them Beverly Tucker, William Alexander Caruthers, and John Pendleton Kennedy), some of them writ-

Southern Romanticism

ers of great talent, many of them residents of Richmond, produced historical romances or romantic eulogies of the plantation system of the upper South. In the 1840s, the southern literary capital moved to Charleston, home of the most distinguished of the region's men of letters: William Gilmore Simms. For a time, his work expressed a broad nationalism that transcended his regional background; but by the 1840s he too had become a strong defender of southern institutions—especially slavery—against the encroachments of the North. There was, he believed, a unique quality to southern life that it was the duty of intellectuals to defend.

One group of southern writers, however, produced works that were more broadly American and less committed to a glorification of the peculiarities of southern life. These were writers from the fringes of plantation society, who depicted the world of the backwoods rural areas. Augustus B. Longstreet, Joseph G. Baldwin, Johnson J. Hooper, and others focused not on aristocratic "cavaliers," but on ordinary people and poor whites. Instead of romanticizing their subjects, they were deliberately and sometimes painfully realistic. And they seasoned their sketches with a robust, vulgar humor that was new to American literature. These southern realists established a tradition of American regional humor that was ultimately to find its most powerful voice in Mark Twain.

The Transcendentalists

One of the outstanding expressions of the romantic impulse in America came from a group of New England writers and philosophers known as the transcendentalists. Borrowing heavily from German philosophers such as Kant, Hegel, and Schelling, and from the English writers Coleridge and Carlyle, the transcendentalists embraced a theory of the individual that rested on a distinction (first suggested by Kant) between what they called "reason" and "understanding"—words they used in ways that seem unfamiliar, even strange, to modern ears. Reason, as they defined it, had little to do with rationality. It was, rather, the individual's innate capacity to grasp beauty and truth through giving full expression to the instincts and emotions; and as such, it was the highest human faculty. Understanding, the transcendentalists argued, was the use of intellect in the narrow, artificial ways imposed by society; it involved the repression of instinct and the victory of externally imposed learning. Every person's goal, therefore, should be liberation from the confines of "understanding" and the cultivation of "reason." Each individual should strive to "transcend" the limits of the intellect and allow the emotions, the "soul," to create an "original relation to the Universe."

Transcendentalist philosophy emerged first among a small group of intellectuals centered in Concord, Massachusetts. Their leader and most eloquent voice was Ralph Waldo Emerson. A Unitarian minister in his youth, Emerson left the church in 1832 to devote himself entirely to writing and teaching the elements of transcendentalism. He was a dazzling figure to his contemporaries—a lecturer whose public appearances drew rapturous crowds; a conversationalist who drew rapt intellectuals to his Concord home almost daily. He was the most important intellectual of his age.

Ralph Waldo Emerson

Emerson produced a significant body of poetry, but he was most renowned for his essays and lectures. In "Nature" (1836), one of his best-known essays, Emerson wrote that in the quest for self-fulfillment, individuals should work for a communion with the natural world: "in the woods, we return to reason and faith. . . . Standing on the bare ground—my head bathed by the blithe air, and uplifted into infinite space,—all mean egotism vanishes. . . . I am part and particle of God." In other essays, he was even more explicit in advocating a commitment of the individual to the full exploration of inner capacities. "Nothing is at last sacred," he wrote in "Self-Reliance" (1841), perhaps his most famous essay, "but the integrity of your own mind." The quest for self-reliance, he explained, was really a search for communion with the unity of the universe, the wholeness of God, the great spiritual force that he described as the "Oversoul." Each person's innate capacity to become, through his or her private efforts, a part of this essence was perhaps the classic expression of the romantic belief in the "divinity" of the individual.

Emerson was also a committed nationalist, an ardent proponent of American cultural independence. In a famous 1837 lecture, "The American Scholar," he boasted that "Our day of dependence, our long apprenticeship to the learning of other lands, draws to a close." His belief that truth and beauty could be derived as much from instinct as from learning suggested that Americans, lacking the rich cultural heritage of European nations, could still aspire to artistic and literary greatness. Artistic and intellectual achievement need not rely on tradition and history; it could come from the instinctive creative genius of individuals. "Let the single man plant himself indomitably on his instincts and there abide," Emerson once said, "and the huge world will come round to him."

Almost as influential as Emerson was another leading Concord transcendentalist, Henry David Thoreau. Thoreau went even further than his friend Emerson in repudiating the repressive forces of society, which produced, he said, "lives of quiet desperation." Individuals should work for self-realization by resisting pressures to conform to society's expectations and responding instead to their own instincts. Thoreau's own effort to free himself—immortalized in his most famous book, *Walden* (1854)—led him to build a small cabin in the Concord woods on the edge of Walden Pond, where he lived alone for two years as simply as he could. "I went to the woods," he explained, "because I wished to live deliberately, to front only the essential facts of life, and see if I could not learn what it had to teach, and not, when I came to die, discover that I had not lived." Living simply, he believed, was a desirable alternative to the rapidly modernizing world around him—a world, he believed, that the disruptive and intrusive railroad unhappily symbolized.

Thoreau's rejection of what he considered the artificial constraints of society extended as well to his relationship with government. In 1846, he went to jail (briefly) rather than agree to pay a poll tax. He would not, he insisted, give financial support to a government that permitted the existence of slavery. In his 1849 essay "Resistance to Civil Government," he explained his refusal by claiming that the individual's personal morality had the first claim on his or her actions, that a government which required violation of that morality had no legitimate authority. The proper response was "civil disobedience," or "passive resistance"—a public refusal to obey unjust laws.

Thoreau and Civil Disobedience

The Defense of Nature

As the tributes of Emerson and Thoreau to the power of nature suggest, a small but influential group of Americans in the mid- and late nineteenth century were uneasy with the rapid economic development of their age. They feared the impact of the new capitalist enthusiasms on the integrity of the natural world. "The mountains and cataracts, which were to have made poets and painters," wrote the essayist Oliver Wendell Holmes, "have been mined for anthracite and dammed for water power."

To the transcendentalists, as well as to others, nature was not just a setting for economic activity, as many farmers, miners, and others believed; and it was not simply a body of data to be catalogued and studied, as many scientists thought. It was the source of deep, personal human inspiration—the vehicle through which individuals could best realize the truth within their own souls. Genuine spirituality, they argued, did not come from formal religion, but through communion with the natural world. As they watched the rapid march of industrialization, and the even more rapid race to exploit natural resources for economic gain, they expressed horror at the destruction of the wilderness and began to mount a defense of preservation. "In wildness is the preservation of the world," Thoreau once wrote. Humans separated from nature, he believed, would lose a substantial part of their humanity.

In making such claims, the transcendentalists were among the first Americans to anticipate the environmental movement of the twentieth century. They had no scientific basis for their defense of the wilderness, no knowledge of modern ecology, little sense of the twentieth-century notion of the interconnectedness of species. But they did believe in, and articulate, an essential unity between humanity and nature—a spiritual unity, they believed, without which civilization would be impoverished. They looked at nature, they said, "with new eyes," and with those eyes they saw that "behind nature, throughout nature, spirit is present."

Visions of Utopia

Although transcendentalism was above all an individualistic philosophy, it helped spawn the most famous of all nineteenth-century experiments in communal living: Brook Farm, which the Boston transcendentalist George Ripley established as an experimental community in West Roxbury, Massachusetts, in 1841. There, according to Ripley, individuals would gather to create a new form of social organization, one that would permit every member of the community full opportunity for self-realization. All residents would share equally in the labor of the community so that all could share too in the leisure, for it was leisure that was the first necessity for cultivation of the self. (Ripley was one of the first Americans to attribute positive connotations to the idea of leisure; most of his contemporaries equated it with laziness and sloth.) Participation in manual labor served another purpose as well: it helped individuals bridge the gap between the world of the intellect and learning, and the world of instinct and nature. The obvious tension between the ideal of individual freedom and the demands of a communal society took their toll on Brook Farm. Increasingly, individualism gave way to a form of socialism. Many residents became disenchanted and left; when a fire destroyed the central building of the community in 1847, the experiment dissolved.

Brook Farm

Among the original residents of Brook Farm was the writer Nathaniel Hawthorne, who expressed his disillusionment with the experiment and, to some extent, with transcendentalism in a series of notable novels. In *The Blithedale Romance* (1852), he wrote scathingly of Brook Farm itself, portraying the disastrous consequences of the experiment on the individuals who submitted to it and describing the great fire that destroyed the community as a kind of liberation from oppression. In other novels—most notably *The Scarlet Letter* (1850) and *The House of Seven Gables* (1851)—he wrote equally passionately about the price individuals pay for cutting themselves off from society. Egotism, he claimed (in an indirect challenge to the transcendentalist faith in the self), was the "serpent" that lay at the heart of human misery.

NEW HARMONY New Harmony, Indiana, is best remembered as the site of a short-lived Utopian community founded by the British reformer Robert Owen in 1824. But before it became the home of Owenites, it was the site of another earlier Utopian community of German pietists, known as Rappites (after their leader George Rapp). Like the Shakers, Rappites were celibate. Unlike the Shakers, the social organization of the sect was highly authoritarian. The "community house," shown in this photograph, originally served the Rappites. But in 1824 the group sold its land and buildings to Owen, moved to Pennsylvania, and—after the death of Rapp in 1847—began a long decline. The remnants of the group finally disbanded for good in 1905. *(National Archives and Records Administration)*

The failure of Brook Farm did not, however, prevent the formation of other experimental communities. Some borrowed, as Ripley had done, from the ideas of the French philosopher Charles Fourier, whose ideas of socialist communities organized as cooperative "phalanxes" received wide attention in America. Others drew from the ideas of the Scottish industrialist and philanthropist Robert Owen. Owen himself founded an experimental community in Indiana in 1825, which he named New Harmony. It was to be a "Village of Cooperation," in which every resident worked and lived in total equality. The community was an economic failure, but the vision that had inspired it continued to enchant Americans. Dozens of other "Owenite" experiments began in other locations in the following years.

New Harmony

Redefining Gender Roles

One of the principal concerns of many of the new utopian communities (and of the new social philosophies on which they rested) was the relationship between men and women. Transcendentalism and other movements of this period fostered expressions of a kind of feminism that would not gain a secure foothold in American society until the late twentieth century.

One of those most responsible for drawing issues of gender into the larger discussion of individual liberation was Margaret Fuller. A leading transcendentalist and a close associate of Emerson, she suggested the important relationship between the discovery of the "self" that was so central to antebellum reform and the questioning of gender roles: "Many women are considering within themselves what they need and what they have not," she wrote in a famous feminist work, *Woman in the Nineteenth Century* (1844). "I would have Woman lay aside all thought, such as she habitually cherishes, of being taught and led by men." Fuller herself, before her premature death in a shipwreck in 1850, lived a life far different from the domestic ideal of her time. She had intimate relationships with many men; became a great admirer of European socialists and a great champion of the Italian revolution of 1848, which she witnessed during travels there; and established herself as an intellectual leader whose power came in part from her perspective as a woman.

A redefinition of gender roles was crucial to one of the most enduring of the utopian colonies of the nineteenth century: the Oneida Community, established in 1848 in upstate New York by John Humphrey Noyes. The Oneida "Perfectionists," as residents of the community called themselves, rejected traditional notions of family and marriage. All residents, Noyes declared, were "married" to all other residents; there were to be no permanent conjugal ties. But Oneida was not, as its horrified critics often claimed, an experiment in unrestrained "free love." It was a place where the community carefully monitored sexual behavior; where women were to be protected from unwanted childbearing; in which children were raised communally, often seeing little of their own parents. The Oneidans took special pride in what they considered the liberation of their women from the demands of male "lust" and from the traditional bonds of family.

Redefined Gender Roles at the Oneida Community

The Shakers, even more than the Oneidans, made a redefinition of traditional sexuality and gender roles central to their society. Founded by "Mother" Ann Lee in the 1770s, the society of the Shakers survived throughout the nineteenth century and into the twentieth. (A tiny remnant survives today.) But the Shakers attracted a particularly large following in the antebellum period and established more than twenty communities throughout the Northeast and Northwest in the 1840s. They derived their name from a unique religious ritual, a sort of ecstatic dance, in which members of a congregation would "shake" themselves free of sin while performing a loud chant.

The most distinctive feature of Shakerism, however, was its commitment to complete celibacy—which meant, of course, that no one could be born to Shakerism; all Shakers had to choose the faith voluntarily. Shaker communities attracted about 6,000 members in the

The Shakers

1840s, more women than men; and members lived in conditions in which contact between men and women was very limited. Shakers openly endorsed the idea of sexual equality; they even embraced the idea of a God who was not clearly male or female. Indeed, within the Shaker society as a whole, it was women who exercised the most power. Mother Ann Lee was succeeded as leader of the movement by Mother Lucy Wright. Shakerism, one observer wrote in the 1840s, was a refuge from the "perversions of marriage" and "the gross abuses which drag it down."

The Shakers were not, however, motivated only by a desire to escape the burdens of traditional gender roles. They were trying as well to create a society separated and protected from the chaos and disorder that they believed had come to characterize American life as a whole. They were less interested in personal freedom than in social discipline. And in that, they were like some other dissenting religious sects and utopian communities of their time. Another example was the Amana Community, founded by German immigrants in 1843; its members settled in Iowa in 1855. The Amanas attempted to realize Christian ideals by creating an ordered, socialist society.

The Mormons

Among the most important efforts to create a new and more ordered society within the old was that of the

Joseph Smith

Church of Jesus Christ of Latter Day Saints—the Mormons. Mormonism began in upstate New York as a result of the efforts of Joseph Smith, a young, energetic, but economically unsuccessful man, who had spent most of his twenty-four years moving restlessly through New England and the Northeast. Then, in 1830, he published a remarkable document—the Book of Mormon, named for the ancient prophet who he claimed had written it. It was, he said, a translation of a set of golden tablets he had found in the hills of New York, revealed to him by an angel of

God. The Book of Mormon told the story of an ancient and successful civilization in America, peopled by one of the lost tribes of Israel who had found their way to the New World centuries before Columbus. Its members waited patiently for the appearance of the Messiah, and they were rewarded when Jesus actually came to America after his resurrection. Subsequent generations, however, had strayed from the path of righteousness that Jesus had laid out for them. Ultimately, their civilization collapsed, and God punished the sinful by making their skin dark. These darkened people, Smith believed, were the descendants of the American Indians, although the modern tribes had no memory of their origins. But while the ancient Hebrew kingdom in America had ultimately vanished, Smith believed, its history as a righteous society could serve as a model for a new holy community in the United States.

In 1831, gathering a small group of believers around him, Smith began searching for a sanctuary for his new community of "saints," an effort that would continue unhappily for more than twenty years. Time and again, the Mormons attempted to establish their "New Jerusalem." Time and again, they met with persecution from surrounding communities suspicious of their radical religious doctrines—which included polygamy (the right of men to take several wives), a rigid form of social organization, and particularly damaging to their image, an intense secrecy, which gave rise to wild rumors among their critics of conspiracy and depravity.

Driven from their original settlements in Independence, Missouri, and Kirtland, Ohio, the Mormons moved on to the new town of Nauvoo, Illinois, which in the early 1840s became an imposing and economically successful community. In 1844, however, Joseph Smith was arrested, charged with treason (for allegedly conspiring against the government to win foreign support for a new Mormon colony in the Southwest), and imprisoned in Carthage, Illinois.

There an angry mob attacked the jail, forced Smith from his cell, and shot and killed him. The Mormons now abandoned Nauvoo and, under the leadership of Smith's successor, Brigham Young, traveled

Establishment of Salt Lake City

across the desert—a society of 12,000 people, in one of the largest single group migrations in American history—and established a new community in Utah, the present Salt Lake City. There, at last, the Mormons were able to create a permanent settlement. And although they were not long to remain as isolated from the rest of American society as they were at the beginning, never again were they to be dislodged.

Like other experiments in social organization of the era, Mormonism reflected a belief in human perfectibility. God had once been a man, the church taught, and thus every man or woman could aspire to become—as Joseph Smith had become—a god. But unlike other new communities,

JOSEPH SMITH REVIEWING HIS TROOPS After being driven from earlier homes in Missouri, Mormons under the leadership of the religion's founder Joseph Smith created a model city in Nauvoo, Illinois—where they also organized an army of over 4,000 men. This painting by the Mormon artist Carl Christensen portrays Smith, aboard the white horse in front, reviewing a vast array of troops—with the pastoral and productive landscape of Nauvoo arrayed in the background. The existence of this large private army aroused great alarm in surrounding non-Mormon communities and contributed to the clashes that led both to the murder of Smith himself and the expulsion of the Mormons from Illinois. *(Joseph Mustering the Nauvoo Legion by C.C.A. Christensen. Courtesy Brigham Young University Museum of Art. All Rights Reserved.)*

the Mormons did not embrace the doctrine of individual liberty. Instead, they created a highly organized, centrally directed, almost militarized social structure, a refuge against the disorder and uncertainty of the secular world. They placed particular emphasis on the structure of the family. Mormon religious rituals even included a process by which men and women went through a baptism ceremony in the name of a deceased ancestor; as a result, they believed, they would be reunited with those ancestors in heaven. The intense Mormon interest in genealogy, which continues today, is a reflection of this belief in the possibility of reuniting present generations with those of the past.

The original Mormons were, for the most part, men and women who felt displaced in their rapidly changing society—economically marginal people left behind by the material growth and social progress of their era. In the new religion, they found genuine faith. In the society it created, they found security and order.

REMAKING SOCIETY

The simultaneous efforts to liberate the individual and impose order on a changing world also helped create a wide range of new movements to remake society—movements in which, to a striking degree, women formed the real rank and file and often the leadership as well. By the 1830s, such movements had taken the form of organized reform societies. "In no country in the world," Tocqueville had observed, "has the principle of association been more successfully used, or more unsparingly applied to a multitude of different objects, than in America. . . . for there is no end which the human will, seconded by the collective exertions of individuals, despairs of attaining."

The new organizations did indeed work on behalf of a wide range of goals: temperance; education; peace; the care *New Reform Movements* of the poor, the handicapped, and the mentally ill; the treatment of criminals; the rights of women; and many more. Few eras in American history have witnessed as wide a range of reform efforts. And few eras have exposed more clearly the simultaneous attraction of Americans to the ideas of personal liberty and social order.

Revivalism, Morality, and Order

The philosophy of reform arose from two distinct sources. One was the optimistic vision of those who, like the transcendentalists, rejected Calvinist doctrines and preached the divinity of the individual. These included not only Emerson, Thoreau, and their followers, but a much larger group of Americans who embraced the doctrines of Unitarianism and Universalism and absorbed European romanticism.

The second, and in many respects more important, source was Protestant revivalism—the movement that had begun with the Second Great Awakening early in the century and had, by the 1820s, evolved into a powerful force for social reform. Although the New Light revivalists were theologically far removed from the transcendentalists and Unitarians, they had come to share the optimistic belief that every individual was capable of salvation. According to Charles Grandison Finney, an evangelistic Presbyterian minister who became the most influential revival leader of the 1820s and 1830s, traditional Calvinist doctrines of predestination and individual human helplessness were both obsolete and destructive. Each person, he preached, contained within himself or herself the capacity to experience spiritual rebirth and achieve salvation. A revival of faith need not depend on a miracle from God; it could be created by individual effort.

Finney enjoyed particular success in upstate New York, where he helped launch a *Revivalism in the Burned-Over District* series of passionate revivals in towns along the Erie Canal—a region so prone to religious awakenings that it was known as the "burned-over district." It was no coincidence that the new revivalism should prove so powerful there, for this region of New York was experiencing— largely as a result of the construction of the canal—a major economic transformation. And with that transformation had come changes in the social fabric so profound that many men and women felt baffled and disoriented. (It was in roughly this same area of New York that Joseph Smith first organized the Mormon church.)

Finney's doctrine of personal regeneration appealed *Finney's Doctrine of Personal Regeneration* strongly to those who felt threatened by change. In Rochester, New York, the site of his greatest success, he staged a series of emotionally wrenching religious meetings that aroused a large segment of the community. He had particular success in mobilizing women, on whom he tended to concentrate his efforts— both because women found the liberating message of revivalism particularly appealing and because, Finney dis-

covered, they provided him with access to their male relatives. Gradually, he developed a large following among the relatively prosperous citizens of the region, who were enjoying the economic benefits of the new commercial growth but who were also uneasy about some of the social changes accompanying it (among them the introduction into their community of a new, undisciplined pool of transient laborers). For them, revivalism became not only a means of personal salvation but a mandate for the reform (and control) of the larger society. Finney's revivalism became a call for a crusade against personal immorality. "The church," he maintained, "must take right ground on the subject of Temperance, the Moral Reform, and all the subjects of practical morality which come up for decision from time to time."

The Temperance Crusade

Evangelical Protestantism added major strength to one of the most influential reform movements of the era: the crusade against drunkenness. No social vice, argued some reformers (including, for example, many of Finney's converts in cities such as Rochester), was more responsible for crime, disorder, and poverty than the excessive use of alcohol. Women, who were particularly active in the temperance movement, claimed that alcoholism placed a special burden on wives: men spent money on alcohol that their families needed for basic necessities, and drunken husbands often abused their wives and children.

In fact, alcoholism was an even more serious problem in antebellum America than it has been in the twentieth century. The supply of alcohol was growing rapidly, particularly in the West; farmers there grew more grain than they could sell in the still-limited markets in this prerailroad era, so they distilled much of it into whiskey. But in the East, too, commercial distilleries and private stills were widespread. The appetite for alcohol was growing as well: in isolated western areas, where drinking provided a social pastime in small towns and helped ease the loneliness and isolation on farms; in pubs and saloons in eastern cities, where drinking was the principal leisure activity for many workers. The average male in the 1830s drank nearly three times as much alcohol as the average person does today. And as that figure suggests, many people drank habitually and excessively, with bitter consequences for themselves and others. Among the many supporters of the temperance movement were people who saw it as a way to overcome their own problems with alcoholism.

Although advocates of temperance had been active since the late eighteenth century, the new reformers gave the movement an energy and influence it had never previously known. In 1826, the American *American Society for the Promotion of Temperance* Society for the Promotion of Temperance emerged as a coordinating agency among various groups; it attempted to use many of the techniques of revivalism in preaching abstinence. Then, in 1840, six reformed alcoholics in

THE DRUNKARD'S PROGRESS This 1846 lithograph by Nathaniel Currier shows what temperance advocates argued was the inevitable consequence of alcohol consumption. Beginning with an apparently innocent "glass with a friend," the young man rises step by step to the summit of drunken revelry, then declines to desperation and suicide while his abandoned wife and child grieve. *(Library of Congress)*

Baltimore organized the Washington Temperance Society and began to draw large crowds—in which workers (many of them attempting to overcome their own alcoholism) were heavily represented—to hear their impassioned and intriguing confessions of past sins. By then, temperance advocates had grown dramatically in numbers; more than a million people had signed a formal pledge to forgo hard liquor.

As the movement gained in strength, it also became divided in purpose. Some temperance advocates now urged that abstinence include not only liquor but beer and wine; not everyone agreed. Some began to demand state legislation to restrict the sale and consumption of alcohol (Maine passed such a law in 1851); others insisted that temperance must rely on the conscience of the individual. Whatever their disagreements, however, most temperance advocates shared similar motives. By promoting abstinence, reformers were attempting to promote the moral self-improvement of individuals. They were also trying to impose discipline on society.

The latter impulse was particularly clear in the battle over prohibition laws, which pitted established Protes-

Cultural Divisions over Alcohol

tants against new Catholic immigrants, to many of whom drinking was an important social ritual and an integral part of the life of their community. The arrival of the immigrants was profoundly disturbing to

established residents of many communities, and the restriction of alcohol seemed to them a way to curb the disorder they believed the new population was creating.

Health Fads and Phrenology

For some Americans, the search for individual and social perfection led to an interest in new theories of health and knowledge. Threats to public health were critical to the sense of insecurity that underlay many reform movements, especially after the terrible cholera epidemics of the 1830s and 1840s. Cholera is a severe bacterial infection of the intestines, usually a result of consuming contaminated food or water. In the nineteenth century, long before the discovery of antibiotics, fewer than half of those who contracted the disease normally survived. Thousands of people died of cholera during its occasional outbreaks, and in certain cities—New Orleans in 1833 and St. Louis in 1849—the effects were truly catastrophic. Nearly a quarter of the population of New Orleans died in the 1833 epidemic. Many municipalities, pressured by reformers, established city health boards to try to find solutions to the problems of epidemics. But the medical profession of the time, unaware of the nature of bacterial infections, had no answers; and the boards therefore found little to do.

Instead, many Americans turned to nonscientific theories for improving health. Affluent men and, especially,

"SPOUT BATH AT WARM SPRINGS" Among the many fads and theories about human health to gain currency in the 1830s and 1840s, one of the most popular was the idea that bathing in warm, sulphurous water was restorative. Visitors to "warm springs" all over the United States and Europe "took the baths," drank the foul-smelling water, and sometimes stayed for weeks as part of a combination vacation and "cure." This 1837 drawing is by Sophie Dupont, a visitor to a popular spa. She wrote to a friend that the water, "notwithstanding its odour of half spoiled eggs and its warmth, is not very nauseous to the taste." *(Courtesy of Hagley Museum and Library)*

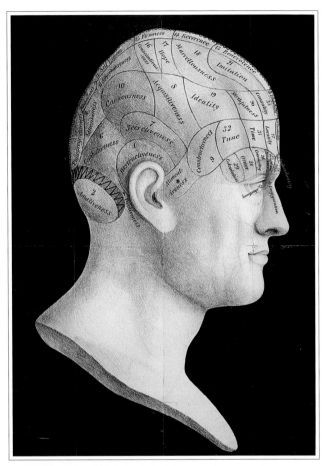

PHRENOLOGY This lithograph illustrates some of the ideas of the popular "science" of phrenology in the 1830s. Drawing from the concepts of the German writer Johann Gaspar Spurzheim, American phrenologists promoted the belief that a person's character and talents could be understood by the formation of his or her skull; that the brain was, in fact, a cluster of autonomous organs, each controlling some aspect of human thought or behavior. In this diagram, the areas of the brain that supposedly control "identity," "acquisitiveness," "secretiveness," "marvelousness," and "hope" are clearly identified. The theory has no scientific basis. *(Library of Congress)*

women flocked to health spas for the celebrated "water cure" (known to modern scientists as hydrotherapy), which purported to improve health through immersing people in hot or cold baths or wrapping them in wet sheets. Although the water cure in fact delivered few of the benefits its promoters promised, it did have some therapeutic value; some forms of hydrotherapy are still in use today. Other people adopted new dietary theories. Sylvester Graham, a Connecticut-born Presbyterian minister and committed reformer, won many followers with his prescriptions for eating fruits, vegetables, and bread made from coarsely ground flour—a prescription not unlike some dietary theories today—instead of meat. (The "Graham cracker" is made from a kind of flour named for him.) Graham accompanied his dietary prescriptions with moral warnings about the evils of excess and luxury.

Perhaps strangest of all to modern sensibilities was the *Phrenology* widespread belief in the new "science" of phrenology, which appeared first in Germany and became popular in the United States beginning in the 1830s through the efforts of Orson and Lorenzo Fowler, publishers of the *Phrenology Almanac*. Phrenologists argued that the shape of an individual's skull was an important indicator of his or her character and intelligence. They made elaborate measurements of bumps and indentations to calculate the size (and,

they claimed, the strength) of different parts of the brain, each of which, they argued, controlled a specific kind of intelligence or behavior. For a time, phrenology seemed to many Americans an important vehicle for improving society. It provided a way of measuring an individual's fitness for various positions in life and seemed to promise an end to the arbitrary process by which people matched their talents to occupations and responsibilities. The theory is now universally believed to have no scientific value at all.

Medical Science

In an age of rapid technological and scientific advances, the science of medicine sometimes seemed to lag behind. In part, that was because of the greater difficulty of experimentation in medicine, which required human subjects as compared to other areas of science and technology that relied on inanimate objects. In part, it was because of the character of the medical profession, which—in the absence of any significant regulation—attracted many poorly educated people and many quacks, in addition to trained physicians. Efforts to regulate the profession were beaten back in the 1830s and 1840s by those who considered the licensing of physicians to be a form of undemocratic monopoly. The prestige of the profession, therefore, remained low, and it was for many people a career of last resort.

The biggest problem facing American medicine, however, was the absence of basic knowledge about disease. The great medical achievement of the eighteenth century—the development of a vaccination against smallpox by Edward Jenner—came from no broad theory of infection, but from a brilliant adaptation of folk practices among country people. The development of anesthetics came not from medical doctors at first, but from a New England dentist, William Morton, who was looking for ways to help his patients endure the extraction of teeth. Beginning in 1844, Morton began experimenting with using sulphuric ether. John Warren, a Boston surgeon, soon began using ether to sedate surgical patients. Even these advances met with stiff resistance from traditional physicians, some of whom continued to believe that all medical knowledge derived from timeless truths and ancient scholars and who mistrusted innovation and experimentation. Others rejected scientific advances because they became convinced of the power of new, unorthodox, and untested "medical" techniques popularized by entrepreneurs, many of them charlatans.

In the absence of any broad acceptance of scientific methods and experimental practice in medicine, it was very difficult for even the most talented doctors to make progress in treating disease. Indeed, almost no one had any idea at all how diseases were transmitted. Even so, halting progress toward the discovery of the germ theory did occur in antebellum America. In 1843, the Boston essayist, poet, and physician Oliver Wendell Holmes published his findings from a study of large numbers of cases of "puerperal fever" (septicemia in children) and concluded that the disease could be transmitted from one person to

Discovery of Contagion

another. This discovery of contagion met with a storm of criticism, but was later vindicated by the clinical success of the Hungarian physician Ignaz Semmelweis, who noticed that the infection seemed to be spread by medical students who had been working with corpses. Once he began requiring students to wash their hands and disinfect their instruments, the infections virtually disappeared.

Reforming Education

One of the outstanding reform movements of the mid-nineteenth century was the effort to produce a system of universal public education. As of 1830, no state yet had such a system, although some states—such as Massachusetts—

had supported a limited version for many years. In the 1830s, however, interest in public education grew rapidly. It was a reflection of the new belief in the innate capacity of every person and of society's obligation to tap that capacity; but it was a reflection, too, of the desire to expose students to stable social values as a way to resist instability.

The greatest of the educational reformers was Horace Mann, the first secretary of the Massachusetts Board of Education, which was established in 1837. To Mann and his followers, education was the only way to "counterwork this

Horace Mann's Reforms

tendency to the domination of capital and the servility of labor." It was also the only way to protect democracy, for an educated electorate was essential to the workings of a free political system. Mann reorganized the Massachusetts school system, lengthened the academic year (to six months), doubled teachers' salaries (although he did nothing to eliminate the large disparities between the salaries of male and female teachers), enriched the curriculum, and introduced new methods of professional training for teachers.

Other states experienced similar expansion and development. They built new schools, created teachers' colleges, and offered vast new

Rapid Growth of Public Education

groups of children access to education. Henry Barnard helped produce a new educational system in Connecticut and Rhode Island. Pennsylvania passed a law in 1835 appropriating state funds for the support of universal education. Governor William Seward of New York extended public support of schools throughout the state in the early 1840s. By the 1850s, the principle of tax-supported elementary schools had been accepted in all the states; and all, despite continuing opposition from certain groups, were making at least a start toward putting the principle into practice.

Yet the quality of the new education continued to vary widely. In some places—Massachusetts, for example, where Mann established the first American state-supported teachers' college in 1839 and where the first professional association of teachers was created in 1845—educators were usually capable men and women, often highly trained, and with an emerging sense of themselves as career professionals. In other areas, however, teachers were often barely literate, and limited funding for education restricted opportunities severely. In the newly settled regions of the West, where the white population was highly dispersed, many children had no access to schools at all. In the South, the entire black population was barred from formal education (although approximately 10 percent of the slaves managed to achieve literacy anyway), and only about a third of all white children of school age actually enrolled in schools in 1860. In the North the percentage was 72 percent, but even there, many students attended classes only briefly and casually.

The interest in education (and, implicitly, in the unleashing of individual talents that could result from it) was visible too in the growing movement to educate American Indians in the antebellum period. Some reformers held racist assumptions about the unredeemability of nonwhite peoples; but even many who accepted that idea about African Americans continued to believe that Indians could be "civilized" if only they could be taught the ways of the white world. Efforts by missionaries and others to educate Native Americans and encourage them to assimilate were particularly prominent in such areas of the Far West as Oregon, where substantial numbers of whites were beginning to settle in the 1840s but where conflicts with the natives had not yet become acute. Nevertheless, the great majority of Native Americans remained outside the reach of educational reform, either by choice or by circumstance or both.

Despite limitations and inequities, the achievements of the school reformers were impressive by any standard. By the beginning of the Civil War, the *Achievements of Educational Reform* United States had one of the highest literacy rates of any nation of the world: 94 percent of the population of the North and 83 percent of the white population of the South (58 percent of the total southern population).

The conflicting impulses that underlay the movement for school reform were visible in some of the different educational institutions that emerged. In New England, for example, the transcendentalist Bronson Alcott established a controversial experimental school in Concord that reflected his strong belief in the importance of complete self-realization. He urged children to learn from their own inner wisdom, not from the imposition of values by the larger society. Children were to teach themselves, rather than rely on teachers.

A similar emphasis on the potential of the individual sparked the creation of new in-*The Benevolent Empire* stitutions to help the handicapped, institutions that formed part of a great network of charitable activities known as the Benevolent Empire. Among them was the Perkins School for the Blind in Boston, the first such school in America. Nothing better exemplified the romantic impulse of the era than the belief of those who founded Perkins that even society's supposedly least-favored members—the blind and otherwise handicapped—could be helped to discover inner strength and wisdom. One teacher at the school expressed such attitudes when he described to the visiting English writer Charles Dickens the case of a blind, deaf, and speechless young woman who had been taught to communicate with the world. Although the "darkness and the silence of the tomb were around her," the teacher explained, "the immortal spirit which had been implanted within her could not die, nor be maimed nor mutilated." Gradually, she had learned to deal with the world around her, even to sew and knit, and most importantly, to speak through sign language. No longer was she a "dog or parrot." She was "an immortal spirit, eagerly seizing upon a new link of union with other spirits!"

More typical of educational reform, however, were efforts to use schools to impose a set of social values on children—the values that reformers believed were appropriate for their new, industrializing society. These values included thrift, order, discipline, punctuality, and respect for authority. Horace Mann, for example, spoke frequently of the role of public schools in extending democracy and expanding individual opportunity. But he spoke, too, of their role in creating social order. "The unrestrained passions of men are not only homicidal, but suicidal," he said, suggesting a philosophy very different from that of Alcott and other transcendentalists, who emphasized instinct and emotion. "Train up a child in the way he should go, and when he is old he will not depart from it."

Rehabilitation

Similar impulses helped create another powerful movement of reform: the creation of "asylums" (as they now began *The Asylum Movement* to be called) for criminals and for the mentally ill. On the one hand, in advocating prison and hospital reform, Americans were reacting to one of society's most glaring ills. Criminals of all kinds, debtors unable to pay their debts, the mentally ill, even senile paupers—all were crowded together indiscriminately into prisons and jails, which in some cases were literally holes in the ground; one jail in Connecticut was an abandoned mine shaft. Beginning in the 1820s, numerous states replaced these antiquated facilities with new "penitentiaries" and mental institutions designed to provide a proper environment for inmates. New York built the first penitentiary at Auburn in 1821. In Massachusetts, the reformer Dorothea Dix began a national movement for new methods of treating the mentally ill. Imprisonment of debtors and paupers gradually disappeared, as did such traditional practices as legal public hangings.

But the creation of "asylums" for social deviants was not simply an effort to curb the abuses of the old system. It was *Prison Reform* also an attempt to reform and rehabilitate the inmates. New forms of rigid prison discipline were designed to rid criminals of the "laxness" that had presumably led them astray. Solitary confinement and the imposition of silence on work crews (both adopted in Pennsylvania and New York in the 1820s) were meant to give prisoners opportunities to meditate on their wrongdoings. (Hence the term "penitentiary": a place for individuals to cultivate penitence.) Some reformers argued that the discipline of the asylum could serve as a model for other potentially disordered environments—for example, factories and schools. But penitentiaries and many mental hospitals soon fell victim to overcrowding, and the original reform ideal

A PENNSYLVANIA ASYLUM In 1843 the United States had only thirteen mental hospitals. Most communities locked the mentally ill in jails with common criminals and often confined them to the worst quarters. By the 1880s, largely as a result of the work of the Massachusetts reformer Dorothea Dix, who worked tirelessly prodding states to build new facilities, there were more than 120 asylums for the insane—including this one in Berks County, Pennsylvania, which also served as an almshouse for the poor. *(Historical Society of Berks County, Reading, Pennsylvania)*

gradually faded. Many prisons ultimately degenerated into little more than warehouses for criminals, with scant emphasis on rehabilitation. The idea, in its early stages, had been more optimistic.

The "asylum" movement was not, however, restricted only to criminals and people otherwise considered "unfit." The idea that a properly structured institution could prevent moral failure or rescue individuals from failure and despair helped spawn the creation of new orphanages designed as educational institutions. Such institutions, reformers believed, would provide an environment in which children who might otherwise be drawn into criminality could be trained to become useful citizens. Similar institutions emerged to provide homes for "friendless" women—women without families or homes, but otherwise respectable, for whom the institutions might provide an opportunity to build a new life. (Such homes were in part an effort to prevent such women from turning to prostitution.) There were also new facilities for the poor: almshouses and workhouses, which created closely supervised environments for those who had failed to work their way up in society.

Such an environment, reformers believed, would train them to live more productive lives.

The Indian Reservation

Some of these same beliefs underlay the emergence in the 1840s and 1850s of a new "reform" approach to the problems of Native Americans: the idea of the reservation. For several decades, the dominant thrust of U.S. policy toward the Indians in areas of white settlement had been relocation. The principal motive behind relocation had always been a simple one: getting the tribes out of the way of white civilization. But among some whites there had also been another, if secondary, intent: to move the Indians to a place where they would be protected from whites and allowed to develop to a point where assimilation might be possible. Even Andrew Jackson, whose animus toward Indians was legendary, once described the removals as part of the nation's "moral duty . . . to protect and if possible to preserve and perpetuate the scattered remnants of the Indian race."

It was a small step from the idea of relocation to the idea of the reservation: the idea of creating an enclosed region in which Indians would live in isolation from white society. Again, the reservations served white economic purposes above all—moving Native Americans out of good lands that white settlers wanted. But they were also supposed to serve a reform purpose. Just as prisons, asylums, and orphanages would provide society with an opportunity to train and uplift misfits and unfortunates within white society, so the reservations might provide a way to undertake what one official called "the great work of regenerating the Indian race." Native Americans on reservations, reformers argued, would learn the ways of civilization in a protected setting and would progress toward (in the words of an Indian commissioner of the time) "a point at which they will be able to compete with a white population, and to sustain themselves under any probable circumstances of contact or connexion with it."

The Rise of Feminism

The reform ferment of the antebellum period had a particular meaning for American women. They played central roles in a wide range of reform movements and a particularly important role in the movements on behalf of temperance and the abolition of slavery. In the process, they expressed their awareness of the problems that women themselves faced in a male-dominated society. The result was the creation of the first important American feminist movement, one that laid the groundwork for more than a century of agitation for women's rights.

Women in the 1830s and 1840s suffered not only all the traditional restrictions imposed on members of their sex by society, but a new set of barriers that had emerged from the transformation of the family into a unit in which women were expected to focus their energies on the home and the raising of children and leave the income-producing activities to their husbands. Many women who began to involve themselves in reform movements in the 1820s and 1830s came to look on such restrictions with rising resentment. Some began to defy them.

Reform Movements and the Rise of Feminism

Sarah and Angelina Grimké, sisters born in South Carolina who had become active and outspoken abolitionists, ignored attacks by men who claimed that their activities were inappropriate for their sex. "Men and women were CREATED EQUAL," they argued. "They are both moral and accountable beings, and whatever is right for man to do, is right for women to do." Other reformers—Catharine Beecher, Harriet Beecher Stowe (her sister), Lucretia Mott, Elizabeth Cady Stanton, and Dorothea Dix—also chafing at the restrictions placed on them by men, similarly pressed at the boundaries of "acceptable" female behavior.

Finally, in 1840, the patience of several women snapped. A group of American female delegates arrived at a world antislavery convention in London, only to be turned away by the men who controlled the proceedings. Angered at the rejection, several of the delegates—notably Lucretia Mott and Elizabeth Cady Stanton—became convinced that their first duty as reformers should now be to elevate the status of women. Over the next several years, Mott, Stanton, Susan B. Anthony, and others began drawing pointed parallels between the plight of women and the plight of slaves; and in 1848, they organized a convention in Seneca Falls, New York, to discuss the question of women's *Seneca Falls* rights. Out of the meeting emerged a "Declaration of Sentiments and Resolutions" (patterned on the Declaration of Independence), which stated that "all men and women

7

FREDERICK DOUGLASS, AMY POST, CATHARINE STEBBINS, and ELIZABETH C. STANTON, and was unanimously adopted, as follows :

DECLARATION OF SENTIMENTS.

When, in the course of human events, it becomes necessary for one portion of the family of man to assume among the people of the earth a position different from that which they have hitherto occupied, but one to which the laws of nature and of nature's God entitle them, a decent respect to the opinions of mankind requires that they should declare the causes that impel them to such a course.

THE DECLARATION OF SENTIMENTS Frederick Douglass joined female abolitionists in signing the famous "Declaration of Sentiments" that emerged out of the Women's Rights Convention at Seneca Falls, New York, in 1848—one of the founding documents of American feminism. This introduction to the declaration makes clear how closely it was modeled on the 1776 Declaration of Independence. *(National Park Service, U.S. Department of the Interior)*

are created equal," that women no less than men have certain inalienable rights. Their most prominent demand was for the right to vote, thus launching a movement for woman suffrage that would continue until 1920. But the document was in many ways more important for its rejection of the whole notion that men and women should be assigned separate "spheres" in society.

It should not be surprising, perhaps, that many of the women involved in these feminist efforts were Quakers. Quakerism had long embraced the ideal of sexual equality and had tolerated, indeed encouraged, the emergence of women as preachers and community leaders. Women taught to expect the absence of gender-based restrictions in their own communities naturally resented the restrictions they encountered when they moved outside them. Quakers had also been among the leaders of the antislavery movement, and Quaker women played a leading role within those efforts.

Not all Quakers went so far as to advocate full sexual equality in American society; but enough Quaker women coalesced around such demands to cause a schism in the yearly meeting of the Society of Friends in Genesee, New York, in 1848. That dissident faction formed the core of the group that organized the Seneca Falls convention. Of the women who drafted the Declaration of Sentiments there, all but Elizabeth Cady Stanton were Quakers.

Progress toward feminist goals was limited in the antebellum years, but certain individual women did manage to break the social barriers to advancement. Elizabeth Blackwell, born in England, gained acceptance and fame as a physician. Her sister-in-law Antoinette Brown Blackwell became the first ordained woman minister in the United States; and another sister-in-law, Lucy Stone, took the revolutionary step of retaining her maiden name after marriage (as did the abolitionist Angelina Grimké). Stone became a successful and influential lecturer on women's rights. Emma Willard, founder of the Troy Female Seminary in 1821, and Catharine Beecher, who founded the Hartford Female Seminary in 1823, worked on behalf of women's education. Some women expressed their feminist sentiments even in their choice of costume—by wearing a distinctive style of dress (introduced in the 1850s) that combined a short skirt with full length pantalettes—an outfit that allowed freedom of movement without loss of modesty. Introduced by the famous actress Fanny Kemble, it came to be called the "bloomer" costume, after one of its advocates, Amelia Bloomer. (It provoked so much controversy that feminists finally abandoned it, convinced that the furor was drawing attention away from their more important demands.) Yet there was an irony in this rise of interest in the rights of women. Feminists benefited greatly from their association with other reform movements, most notably abolitionism; but they also suffered from them. For the demands of women were usually assigned—even by some women

Limited Progress for Women

themselves—a secondary position to what many considered the far greater issue of the rights of slaves.

THE CRUSADE AGAINST SLAVERY

The antislavery movement was not new to the mid-nineteenth century. There had been efforts even before the Revolution to limit, and even eliminate, the institution. Those efforts had helped remove slavery from most of the North by the end of the eighteenth century. There were powerful antislavery movements in England and Europe that cried out forcefully against human bondage. But American antislavery sentiment remained relatively muted in the first decades after independence. Not until 1830 did it begin to gather the force that would ultimately enable it to overshadow virtually all other efforts at social reform.

Early Opposition to Slavery

In the early years of the nineteenth century, those who opposed slavery were, for the most part, a calm and genteel lot, expressing moral disapproval but engaging in few overt activities. To the extent that there was an organized antislavery movement, it centered on the concept of colonization—the effort to encourage the resettlement of African Americans in Africa or the Caribbean. In 1817, a group of prominent white Virginians organized the American Colonization Society (ACS), which worked carefully to challenge slavery without challenging property rights or southern sensibilities. The ACS proposed a gradual manumission (or freeing) of slaves, with masters receiving compensation through funds raised by private charity or appropriated by state legislatures. The Society would then transport liberated slaves out of the country and help them to establish a new society of their own elsewhere.

American Colonization Society

The ACS was not without impact. It received some funding from private donors, some from Congress, some from the legislatures of Virginia and Maryland. And it arranged the shipment of several groups of African Americans out of the country, some of them to the west coast of Africa where in 1830 they established the nation of Liberia (which became an independent republic in 1846—its capital, Monrovia, was named for the American president who had presided over the initial settlement).

But the ACS was in the end a negligible force. Neither private nor public funding was nearly enough to carry out the vast projects its supporters envisioned. In the space of a decade, they managed to "colonize" fewer slaves than were born in the United States in a month. No amount of funding, in fact, would have been enough; there were far too many black men and women in America in the nineteenth

Failure of Colonization

century to be transported to Africa by any conceivable program. And in any case, the ACS met resistance from African Americans themselves, many of whom were now three or more generations removed from Africa and had no wish to move to a land of which they knew almost nothing. (The Massachusetts free black Paul Cuffe had met similar resistance from members of his race in the early 1800s when he proposed a colonization scheme of his own.)

By 1830, in other words, the early antislavery movement was rapidly losing strength. Colonization was proving not to be a viable method of attacking the institution, particularly since the cotton boom in the Deep South was increasing the commitment of planters to their "peculiar" labor system. Those opposed to slavery had reached what appeared to be a dead end.

Garrison and Abolitionism

It was at this crucial juncture, with the antislavery movement seemingly on the verge of collapse, that a new figure emerged to transform it into a dramatically different phenomenon. He was William Lloyd Garrison. Born in Massachusetts in 1805, Garrison was an assistant in the 1820s to the New Jersey Quaker Benjamin Lundy, who published the leading antislavery newspaper of the time— the *Genius of Universal Emancipation*—in Baltimore. Garrison shared Lundy's abhorrence of slavery, but he soon

Garrison and the Liberator grew impatient with his employer's moderate tone and mild proposals for reform. In 1831, therefore, he returned to Boston to found his own weekly newspaper, the *Liberator.*

Garrison's simple philosophy was genuinely revolutionary. Opponents of slavery, he said, should view the institution from the point of view of the black man, not the white slaveowner. They should not, as earlier reformers had done, talk about the evil influence of slavery on white society; they should talk about the damage the system did to blacks. And they should, therefore, reject "gradualism" and demand the immediate, unconditional, universal abolition of slavery. Garrison spoke with particular scorn about the advocates of colonization. They were not emancipationists, he argued; on the contrary, their real aim was to strengthen slavery by ridding the country of those African Americans who were already free. The true aim of foes of slavery, he insisted, must be to extend to African Americans all the rights of American citizenship. As startling as the drastic nature of his proposals was the relentless, uncompromising tone with which he promoted them. "I am aware," he wrote in the very first issue of the *Liberator,* "that many object to the severity of my language; but is there not cause for severity? I will be as harsh as truth, and as uncompromising as justice. . . . I am in earnest—I will not equivocate—I will not excuse—I will not retreat a single inch—AND I WILL BE HEARD."

Garrison soon attracted a large group of followers throughout the North, enough to enable him to found the New England Antislavery Society in 1832 and a year later, after a convention in Philadelphia, the American Antislavery Society. Membership in the new *American Antislavery Society* organizations mushroomed. By 1835, there were more than 400 chapters of the societies; by 1838, there were 1,350 chapters, with more than 250,000 members. Antislavery sentiment was developing a strength and assertiveness greater than at any point in the nation's history.

This success was in part a result of the similarity between abolitionism and other reform movements of the era. Like reformers committed to other causes, abolitionists were calling for an unleashing of the individual human spirit, the elimination of artificial social barriers to fulfillment. Who, after all, was more in need of assistance in realizing individual potential than enslaved men and women? Theodore Dwight Weld, a prominent New England abolitionist (and husband of Angelina Grimké), expressed this belief in an 1833 letter to Garrison. Slavery was a sin, Weld wrote, because "no condition of birth, no shade of color, no mere misfortune of circumstances can annul the birthright charter, which God has bequeathed to every being upon whom he has stamped his own image, by making him a free moral agent."

Black Abolitionists

Abolitionism had a particular appeal to the free blacks of the North, who in 1850 numbered about 250,000, mostly concentrated in cities. They lived in conditions of poverty and oppression often worse than those of their slave counterparts in the South. An English traveler who had visited both sections of the country wrote in 1854 that he was "utterly at a loss to imagine the source of that prejudice which subsists against [African Americans] in the Northern states, a prejudice unknown in the South, where the relations between the Africans and the European [white American] are so much more intimate." This confirmed an earlier observation by Tocqueville that "the prejudice which repels the Negroes seems to increase in proportion as they are emancipated." Northern blacks were often victimized by mob violence; they had virtually no access to education; they could vote in only a few states; and they were barred from all but the most menial of occupations. Most worked either as domestic servants or as sailors in the American merchant marine, and their wages were such that they lived, for the most part, in squalor. Some were kidnapped by whites and forced back into slavery.

For all their problems, however, northern blacks were aware of, and fiercely proud of, their freedom. And they remained acutely sensitive to the plight of those members of their race who remained in bondage, aware that their own *Free Blacks' Commitment to Abolition* position in society would remain precarious as long as slavery existed. Many in the 1830s came to support Garrison, to subscribe to his newspaper,

FUGITIVE SLAVE LAW CONVENTION
Abolitionists gathered in Cazenovia, New York, in August 1850 to consider how to respond to the law recently passed by Congress requiring northern states to return fugitive slaves to their owners. Frederick Douglass is seated just to the left of the table in this photograph of some of the participants. The gathering was unusual among abolitionist gatherings in including substantial numbers of African Americans. *(Madison County Historical Society, Oneida, NY)*

and to sell subscriptions to it in their own communities. Indeed, the majority of the *Liberator's* early subscribers were free blacks.

There were also important African-American leaders who expressed the aspirations of their race. One of the most militant was David Walker, a free black from Boston, who in 1829 published a harsh pamphlet: *Walker's Appeal . . . to the Colored Citizens.* In it he declared: "America is more our country than it is the whites'—we have enriched it with our blood and tears." He warned: "The whites want slaves, and want us for their slaves, but some of them will curse the day they ever saw us." Slaves should, he declared, cut their masters' throats, should "kill, or be killed!"

Most black critics of slavery, however, were less violent in their rhetoric. One of them was Sojourner Truth, a freed black who after spending several years involved in a strange religious cult in upstate New York, emerged as a powerful and eloquent spokeswoman for the abolition of slavery. The greatest African-American abolitionist of all—and one of the most electrifying orators of his time, black or white—was Frederick Douglass. Born a slave in Maryland, *Frederick Douglass* Douglass escaped to Massachusetts in 1838, became an outspoken leader of antislavery sentiment, and spent two years lecturing in England, where members of that country's vigorous antislavery movement lionized him. On his return to the United States in 1847, Douglass purchased his freedom from his Maryland owner and founded an antislavery newspaper, the *North Star,* in Rochester, New York. He achieved wide renown as well for his autobiography, *Narrative of the Life of Frederick Douglass* (1845), in which he presented

FREDERICK DOUGLASS Frederick Douglass, an escaped slave and active abolitionist, was one of the great orators of his age, widely admired among antislavery groups in the United States and Great Britain. So central did he become in the imaginations of antislavery men and women that he inspired tributes such as the "Fugitive's Song" published in Boston in 1845. *(Bettmann/Corbis)*

THE ABOLITION OF SLAVERY

The United States abolished slavery through the Thirteenth Amendment to the Constitution in 1865, in the aftermath of a great Civil War. But the effort to abolish slavery did not begin or end in North America. Emancipation in the United States was part of a worldwide antislavery movement that had begun in the late eighteenth century and continued through the end of the nineteenth.

The end of slavery, like the end of monarchies and aristocracies, was one of the ideals of the Enlightenment, which inspired new concepts of individual freedom and political equality. As Enlightenment ideas spread throughout the western world in the seventeenth and eighteenth centuries, introducing the idea of human rights and individual liberty to the concept of civilization, people on both sides of the Atlantic began to examine slavery anew and to ask whether it was compatible with these new ideas. Some Enlightenment thinkers, including some of the founders of the American Republic, believed that freedom was appropriate for white people, but not for people of color. But others came to believe that all human beings had an equal claim to liberty, and their views became the basis for an escalating series of antislavery movements.

Opponents of slavery first targeted the slave trade—the vast commerce in human beings that had grown up in the seventeenth and eighteenth centuries and had come to involve large parts of Europe, Africa, the Caribbean, and North and South America. In the aftermath of the revolutions in America, France, and Haiti in the late eighteenth and early nineteenth centuries, the attack on the slave trade quickly gained momentum. Its central figure was the English reformer William Wilberforce, who spent years attacking Britain's connection with the slave trade. He argued against it on moral and religious grounds, and eventually, after the Haitian revolution, he argued as well that the continuation of slavery would create more slave revolts. In 1807, he persuaded Parliament to pass a law ending the slave trade within the entire British empire. The British example—when combined with heavy political, economic, and even military pressure from London—persuaded many other nations to make the international slave trade illegal as well: the United States in 1808, France in 1814, Holland in 1817, and Spain in 1845. Trading in slaves continued within countries and colonies where slavery remained legal (including the United States), and some illegal slave trading continued throughout the Atlantic world. But the sale of slaves steadily declined after 1807. The last known shipment of slaves across the Atlantic—from Africa to Cuba—occurred in 1867.

Ending the slave trade was a great deal easier than ending slavery itself, in which many people had major investments and on which much agriculture, commerce, and industry depended. But pressure to abolish slavery grew steadily throughout the nineteenth century, with Wilberforce once more helping to lead the international outcry against the institution. In Haiti, the slave revolts that began in 1791 eventually abolished not only slavery but also French rule. In some parts of South America, slavery came to an end with the overthrow of Spanish rule in the 1820s. Simon Bolivar, the great leader of Latin American independence, considered abolishing slavery an important part of his mission. He freed those slaves who joined his armies, and he insisted on constitutional prohibitions of slavery in several of the constitutions he helped frame. In 1833, the British parliament passed a law abolishing slavery throughout the British empire and compensated slaveowners for freeing their slaves. France abolished slavery in its empire, after years of agitation from abolitionists within France, in 1848. In the Caribbean, Spain followed Britain in slowly eliminating slavery from its colonies. Puerto Rico abolished slavery in 1873 and Cuba became the last colony in the Caribbean to end slavery, in 1886, in the face of increasing slave resistance and the declining profitability of slave-based plantations. Brazil was the last nation in the Americas to end the system, in 1888. The Brazilian military began to turn against slavery after the valiant participation of slaves in Brazil's war with Paraguay in the late 1860s; eventually educated Brazilian civilians began to oppose the system too, arguing that it obstructed economic and social progress.

In the United States, the power of world opinion—and the example of Wilberforce's movement in England—became an important source of the abolitionist movement as it gained strength in the 1820s and 1830s. American abolitionism, in turn, helped reinforce the movements abroad. Frederick Douglass, the former slave turned abolitionist, became a major figure in the international antislavery movement and was a much-admired and much-sought-after speaker in England and Europe in the 1840s and 1850s. No other nation paid such a terrible price for abolishing slavery as did the United States during its Civil War, but American emancipation was nevertheless a part of a worldwide movement toward ending legalized human bondage.

"AM I NOT A MAN AND A BROTHER" This bronze medallion commemorates the victory of British antislavery activists in extinguishing slavery from throughout the British empire in 1834. It also records the close links between their movement and the American abolitionist movement led by William Lloyd Garrison. The image on this medallion of a man in chains became a popular one in American antislavery circles in the following years. *(The Art Archive)*

"America is now wholly given over to a damned mob of scribbling women," Nathaniel Hawthorne complained in 1855, "and I should have no chance of success while the public taste is occupied with their trash." Hawthorne was one of the leading novelists of his time; and what he was complaining about was the most popular form of fiction in mid-nineteenth-century America—not his own dark and serious works, but the "sentimental novel," a genre of literature written and read mostly by middle-class women.

In an age when affluent women occupied primarily domestic roles, and in which finding a favorable marriage was the most important thing many women could do to secure or improve their lots in life, the sentimental novel gave voice to both female hopes and female anxieties. The heroines in such books were almost always beautiful, and often vaguely helpless—requiring special attention from and protection by men, and using their looks and charms to get it. The plots of sentimental novels were usually filled with character-improving problems and domestic trials, but most of them ended with the heroine securely and happily married. They were phenomenally successful, as Hawthorne lamented. Many of them sold over 100,000 copies each—far more than almost any other books of the time—and the more celebrated of such novels were the subject of rapt discussion among middle-class women when they gathered for social occasions.

Sentimental heroines were not only beautiful. They were also endowed with specifically female qualities—"all the virtues," one novelist wrote, "that are founded in the sensibility of the heart: Pity, the attribute of angels, and friendship, the balm of life, delight to dwell in the female breast." Women were highly sensitive creatures, the sentimental writers believed, incapable of disguising their feelings, and subject to such emotional expressions as fainting, mysterious illnesses, trances, and, of course, tears—things rarely expected of men. But they were also capable of a kind of nurturing love and natural sincerity that was hard to find in the predominantly male public world. In Susan Warner's *The Wide, Wide World* (1850), for example, the heroine, a young girl named Ellen Montgomery, finds herself suddenly thrust into the "wide, wide world" of male competition after her father loses his fortune. She is unable to adapt to it, but she is saved in the end when she is taken in by wealthy relatives, who will undoubtedly prepare her for a successful marriage. They restore to her the security and comfort to which she had been born and without which she seemed unable to thrive.

Sentimental novels created idealized images of conventional female success. In doing so, they performed

"A SAD STORY" This nineteenth-century engraving shows a reader gazing sadly and wistfully away from a popular sentimental novel of the time. The magazine that published this picture wrote a disapproving story to accompany it, which began: "The young girl whose tender heart is so powerfully stirred with imaginative sorrow by the reading of some fictitious tale of distress might in our judgment have been provided by wise parents with a more wholesome form of entertainment." *(Culver Pictures, Inc.)*

a damning picture of slavery. Douglass demanded for African Americans not only freedom but full social and economic equality. Black abolitionists had been active for years before Douglass emerged as a leader of their cause; they had held their first national convention in 1830. But with Douglass's leadership, they became a more influential force; and they began, too, to forge alliances with white antislavery leaders such as Garrison.

Anti-Abolitionism

Abolitionism was a powerful force, but it provoked a powerful opposition as well. Almost all white southerners, of course, looked on the movement with fear and contempt. But so too did many northern whites. Indeed, even in the North, abolitionists were never more than a small, dissenting minority.

To its critics, the abolitionist crusade was a dangerous and frightening threat to the existing social system. Some whites (including many substantial businessmen) warned that it would produce a destructive war between the sections. Others feared that it might lead to a great influx of free blacks into the North. The strident, outspoken movement seemed to many northern whites a sign of the disorienting social changes their society was experiencing, yet another threat to stability and order.

The result was an escalating wave of violence directed against abolitionists in the 1830s. When Prudence Crandall attempted to admit several African-American girls to her private school in Connecticut, local citizens had her arrested, threw filth into her well, and forced her to close down the school. A mob in Philadelphia attacked the abolitionist headquarters, the "Temple of Liberty," in 1834, burned it to the ground, and began a

something of the same function that romance novels of the twentieth century perform today (although without the overt sexuality that is so central to modern romances). They accepted uncritically the popular assumptions about women's special needs and desires, and they offered stirring tales of how women satisfied them. But sentimental novels did not stop with romanticized images of female fulfillment through protection and marriage. They hinted as well at the increasing role of women in movements of social and moral reform. Many such books portrayed women dealing with problems of drunkenness, poverty, irreligion, and prostitution—and using their highly developed female sensibilities to help other women escape from their troubles. Women were particularly suitable for such reform work, the writers implied, because they were specially gifted at helping and nurturing others.

The most famous sentimental novelist of her day was Harriet Beecher Stowe. Most of her books—*The Minister's Wooing, My Wife and I, We and Our Neighbors,* and others—portrayed the travails and ultimate triumphs of women as they became wives, mothers, and hostesses. But Stowe was and remains best known for her 1852 antislavery novel *Uncle Tom's Cabin,* one of the most influential books ever published in America. As a story about slavery, and about an aging black man—Uncle Tom—who is unfailingly submissive to his white masters, it is in many ways very different from her other novels. But *Uncle*

UNCLE TOM'S CABIN *Uncle Tom's Cabin* did much to inflame public opinion in both the North and the South in the last years before the Civil War. When Abraham Lincoln was introduced to Stowe once in the White House, he reportedly said to her: "So you are the little lady that has brought this great war." At the time, however, Stowe was equally well known as one of the most successful American writers of sentimental novels. *(Bettmann/Corbis)*

Tom's Cabin is a sentimental novel, too. Stowe's critique of slavery is based on her belief in the importance of domestic values and family security. Slavery's violation of those values, and its denial of that security, is what made it so abhorrent to her. The simple, decent Uncle Tom faces many of the same dilemmas that the simple, decent female heroines of other sentimental novels encounter in their struggles to find security and tranquility in their lives.

Women were emerging from their domestic sphere in at least one other important way in the mid-nineteenth century. They were becoming consumers of the expanding products of America's industrializing economy. The female characters in sentimental novels, therefore, searched not just for love, security, and social justice. They also searched for luxury, and for the pleasure of buying some favored item. Susan Warner illustrated this aspect of the culture of the sentimental novel—and the desires of the women who read them—in *The Wide, Wide World,* in her description of the young Ellen Montgomery in an elegant bookstore, buying a Bible: "Such beautiful Bibles she had never seen; she pored in ecstasy over their varieties of type and binding, and was very evidently in love with them all."

---

bloody race riot. Another mob seized Garrison on the

Violent Reprisals

streets of Boston in 1835 and threatened to hang him. Authorities saved him from death only by locking him in jail. Elijah Lovejoy, the editor of an abolitionist newspaper in Alton, Illinois, was a repeated victim of mob violence. Three times angry whites invaded his offices and smashed his presses. Three times Lovejoy installed new machines and began publishing again. When a mob attacked his office a fourth time, late in 1837, he tried to defend his press. The attackers set fire to the building and, as Lovejoy fled, shot and killed him.

That so many men and women continued to embrace abolitionism in the face of such vicious opposition from within their own communities suggests much about the nature of the movement. Abolitionists were not people who made their political commitments lightly or casually. They were strong-willed, passionate crusaders, displaying enormous courage and moral strength, and displaying, too, at times a level of fervor that many of their contemporaries (and some later historians) found disturbing. Abolitionists were widely denounced, even by some who shared their aversion to slavery, as wild-eyed fanatics bent on social revolution. The anti-abolitionist mobs, in other words, were only the most violent expression of a sentiment that many other white Americans shared.

Abolitionism Divided

By the mid-1830s, the abolitionist crusade had become impossible to ignore. It had also begun to experience serious internal strains and divisions. One reason was the violence of the anti-abolitionists, which persuaded some members of the movement that a more moderate approach was *Moderates versus Extremists* necessary. Another reason was the growing radicalism of

William Lloyd Garrison, who shocked even many of his own allies (including Frederick Douglass) by attacking not only slavery but the government itself. The Constitution, he said, was "a covenant with death and an agreement with hell." The nation's churches, he claimed, were bulwarks of slavery. In 1840, finally, Garrison precipitated a formal division within the American Antislavery Society by insisting that women, who had always been central to the organization's work, be permitted to participate in the movement on terms of full equality. He continued after 1840 to arouse controversy with new and even more radical stands: an extreme pacifism that rejected even defensive wars; opposition to all forms of coercion—not just slavery but prisons and asylums; and finally, in 1843, a call for northern disunion from the South. The nation could, he suggested, purge itself of the sin of slavery by expelling the slave states from the Union.

From 1840 on, therefore, abolitionism moved in many channels and spoke with many different voices. The Garrisonians remained influential, with their uncompromising moral stance. Others operated in more moderate ways, arguing that abolition could be accomplished only as the result of a long, patient, peaceful struggle—"immediate abolition gradually accomplished," as they called it. At first, such moderates depended on "moral suasion." They would appeal to the conscience of the slaveholders and convince them that their institution was sinful. When that produced no results, they turned to political action, seeking to induce the northern states and the federal government to aid the cause wherever possible. They joined the Garrisonians in helping runaway slaves find refuge in the North or in Canada through the so-called underground railroad (although their efforts were never as highly organized as the term suggests). They helped fund *The Amistad Case* the legal battle over the Spanish slave vessel, *Amistad.* Africans destined for slavery in Cuba had seized the ship from its crew in 1839 and tried to return it to Africa. But the U.S. navy had seized the ship and held the Africans as pirates. But with abolitionist support, legal efforts to declare the Africans free (because the international slave trade had been illegal in the United States since 1808) finally reached the Supreme Court, where the antislavery position was argued by former president John Quincy Adams. The court declared the Africans free in 1841 and antislavery groups funded their passage back to Africa. Later, after the Supreme Court (in *Prigg* v. *Pennsylvania,* 1842) ruled that states need not aid in enforcing the 1793 law requiring the return of fugitive slaves to their owners, abolitionists secured the passage of "personal liberty laws" in several northern states. These laws forbade state officials to assist in the capture and return of runaways. Above all, the antislavery societies petitioned Congress to abolish slavery in places where the federal government had jurisdiction—in the territories and in the District of Columbia—and to prohibit the interstate slave trade. But political abolition-

ism had severe limits. Few members of the movement believed that Congress could constitutionally interfere with a "domestic" institution such as slavery within the individual states themselves.

Although the abolitionists engaged in pressure politics, they never actually formed a political party. Antislavery sentiment underlay the formation in 1840 of the Liberty Party, which offered the Kentucky antislavery leader James G. Birney as its presidential candidate. But this party, and its successors, never campaigned for outright abolition (an illustration of the important fact that "antislavery" and "abolitionism" were not always the same thing). They stood instead for "free soil," for keeping slavery out of the territories. Some free-soilers were concerned about the welfare of African Americans; others cared nothing about the slaves but simply wanted to keep the West a country for whites. Garrison dismissed free-soilism as "white-manism." But the free-soil position would ultimately do what abolitionism never could accomplish: attract the support of large numbers, even a majority, of the white population of the North.

The frustrations of political abolitionism drove some critics of slavery to embrace more drastic measures. A few began to advocate violence; it was a group of prominent abolitionists in New England, for example, who funneled money and arms to John Brown for his bloody uprisings in Kansas and Virginia (see pp. 360–361, 366–367). Others attempted to arouse widespread public anger through propaganda. Abolitionist descriptions of slavery—for example, Theodore Dwight Weld and Angelina Grimké's *American Slavery as It Is: Testimony of a Thousand Witnesses* (1839)—presented what the authors claimed were careful, factual pictures of slavery, but what were in fact highly polemical, often wildly distorted images.

The most powerful document of abolitionist propaganda, however, was a work of fiction: Harriet Beecher Stowe's *Uncle Tom's Cabin.* It appeared first, in 1851–1852, as a serial in an antislavery *Harriet Beecher Stowe* weekly. Then, in 1852, it was published as a book. It rocked the nation. It sold more than 300,000 copies within a year of publication and was later issued again and again to become one of the most remarkable best-sellers in American history.

Stowe's novel emerged not just out of abolitionist politics, but also out of a popular tradition of sentimental novels written by, and largely for, women (see "Patterns of Popular Culture," pp. 338–339). Most such novels had no political message at all. But Stowe combined the emotional conventions of the sentimental novel with the political ideas of the abolition movement, and to sensational effect. Her novel, by embedding the antislavery message within a familiar and popular literary form, succeeded in bringing the message of abolitionism to an enormous new audience—not only those who read the book but also those who watched dramatizations of its story by countless theater companies throughout the nation. The novel's emotional portrayal of good, kindly blacks victimized by a cruel system; of the loyal, trusting Uncle Tom; of the vicious overseer Simon Legree (described as a New Englander so as to prevent the book from seeming to be an attack on southern whites); of the escape of the beautiful Eliza; of the heart-rending death of Little Eva—all became a part of American popular legend. Reviled throughout the South, Stowe became a hero to many in the North. And in both regions, her novel helped to inflame sectional tensions to a new level of passion. Few books in American history have had so great an impact on the course of public events.

Even divided, therefore, abolitionism remained a powerful influence on the life of the nation. Only a relatively small number of people before the Civil War ever accepted the abolitionist position that slavery must be entirely eliminated in a single stroke. But the crusade that Garrison had launched, and that thousands of committed men and women kept alive for three decades, was a constant, visible reminder of how deeply the institution of slavery was dividing America.

Abolitionism's Enduring Influence

CONCLUSION

The rapidly changing society of antebellum America produced a remarkable upsurge of cultural nationalism and reform. Writers, artists, intellectuals, and others drew heavily from new European notions of personal liberation—a set of ideas often known as romanticism. But they also strove to create a truly American culture, unbeholden to European models. The literary and artistic life of the nation expressed the rising interest in personal liberation—in giving individuals the freedom to explore their own souls and to find in nature a full expression of their divinity. It also called attention to some of the nation's glaring social problems.

Reformers, too, made use of the romantic belief in the divinity of the individual. They flocked to religious revivals, worked on behalf of such "moral" reforms as temperance, supported education, and stirred the beginnings of feminism. Above all, in the North, they rallied against slavery. Out of this growing antislavery movement emerged a new and powerful phenomenon: abolitionism, which rejected moderate reform and insisted on nothing less than immediate emancipation of the slaves. The abolitionist crusade galvanized much of the North. It also contributed greatly to the growing schism between North and South.

FOR FURTHER REFERENCE

Steven Mintz, *Moralists and Moralizers: America's Pre-Civil War Reformers* (1995) and Ronald G. Walters, *American Reformers, 1815–1860* (1978) are good overviews. David Reynolds, *Walt Whitman's America* (1995) is both a cultural biography of Whitman and an evocation of the society Whitman celebrated. Leo Marx, *The Machine in the Garden* (1964) is an influential study of the tension between technological progress and the veneration of nature in the era of early industrialization. Nancy F. Cott, *The Bonds of Womanhood: "Woman's Sphere" in New England, 1780–1835* (1977) argues that nineteenth-century feminism emerged from the separation of home and work in the early nineteenth century. Klaus J. Hansen, *Mormonism and the American Experience* (1981) examines the emergence of the most important new religion in nineteenth-century America. Ellen C. Dubois, *Feminism and Suffrage: The Emergence of an Independent Women's Movement in America, 1848–1869* (1978) examines the origins of the suffrage movement. David Brion Davis, *The Problem of Slavery in the Age of Revolution, 1770–1823* (1975) is an influential study of the rise of antislavery sentiment in the western world. James Brewer Stewart, *Holy Warriors* (1976) is a good summary of the trajectory of abolitionism from the American Revolution through the emancipation. Ronald G. Walters, *The Antislavery Appeal: American Abolitionists After 1830* (1976) emphasizes the religious motivations of antebellum abolitionism.

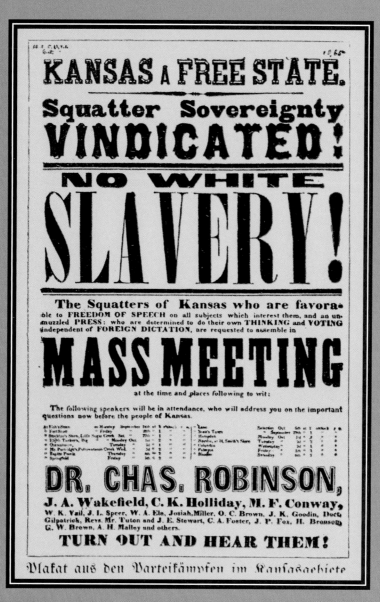

"BLEEDING KANSAS" The battle over the fate of slavery in Kansas was one of the most turbulent events of the 1850s. This 1855 poster invites antislavery forces to a meeting to protest the actions of the "bogus" pro-slavery territorial legislature, which had passed laws that, among other things, made it illegal to speak or write against slavery. "Squatter sovereignty" was another term for "popular sovereignty," the doctrine that gave residents of a prospective state the power to decide the fate of slavery there. *(Bettmann/Corbis)*

Significant Events

CHAPTER THIRTEEN

THE IMPENDING CRISIS

Until the 1840s, the tensions between the North and the South remained relatively contained. Had no new sectional controversies arisen, the United States might have avoided a civil war and the two sections might have resolved their differences peaceably over time. But new controversies did arise, all of them centered on slavery. From the North came the strident and increasingly powerful abolitionist movement, which kept the issue alive in the public mind and increased sectional animosities. From the South came an increasingly belligerent defense of slavery and a rising insistence on its expansion.

But it was the West that brought these differences to a head most forcefully. Ironically, the vigorous nationalism that was in some ways helping to keep the United States together was also producing a desire for territorial expansion that would tear the nation apart. As the nation annexed extensive new lands—Texas, the Southwest territories, California, Oregon country, and others—the question began to arise: What would be the status of *Territorial Growth* slavery in the territories? By the late 1840s, differences over this question had created a dangerous and persistent crisis. And by the end of the 1850s, that crisis had produced such bitterness, such anger, and such despair on both sides that it could no longer be contained.

LOOKING WESTWARD

The United States acquired more than a million square miles of new territory in the 1840s—the greatest wave of expansion since the Louisiana Purchase nearly forty years before. By the end of the decade, the nation possessed all the territory of the present-day United States except Alaska, Hawaii, and a few relatively small areas acquired later through border adjustments. Many factors accounted for this great new wave of expansion, the most important of which were the hopes and ambitions of the many thousands of Americans who moved into or invested in these new territories. Advocates of expansion justified their goals with a carefully articulated set of ideas—an ideology known as "Manifest Destiny," which itself became one of the factors driving white Americans to look to the West.

Manifest Destiny

Manifest Destiny reflected both the burgeoning pride that characterized American nationalism in the mid-nineteenth century and the idealistic vision of social perfec-

tion that fueled so much of the reform energy of the time. It rested on the idea that America was destined—by God and by history—to expand its boundaries over a vast area, an area that included, but was not necessarily restricted to, the continent of North America. American expansion was not selfish, its advocates insisted; it was an altruistic attempt to extend American liberty to new realms. John L. O'Sullivan, the influential Democratic editor who gave the movement its name, wrote in 1845 that the American claim to new territory

> . . . is by the right of our manifest destiny to overspread and to possess the whole of the continent which Providence has given us for the development of the great experiment of liberty and federative self government entrusted to us. It is a right such as that of the tree to the space of air and earth suitable for the full expansion of its principle and destiny of growth.

Manifest Destiny represented more than pride in the nation's political system. Running throughout many of the arguments for expansion was an explicitly racial justification.

Racial Justification

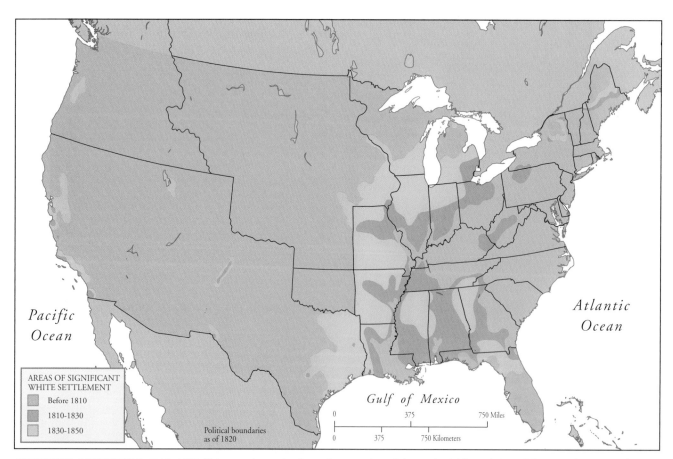

Pacific Ocean

Atlantic Ocean

Gulf of Mexico

AREAS OF SIGNIFICANT
WHITE SETTLEMENT

Before 1810

1810-1830

1830-1850

Political boundaries
as of 1820

0   375   750 Miles

0   375   750 Kilometers

EXPANDING SETTLEMENT, 1810–1850 This map shows the dramatic expansion of the territorial boundaries of the United States in the decades after the Louisiana Purchase. By 1850, the nation had reached its present boundaries (with the exception of Alaska and Hawaii, which it acquired later). Much of this acquisition occurred in the 1840s. ◆ *What events contributed to the annexation of new land to the United States in those years?*

Throughout the 1840s, many Americans defended the idea of westward expansion by citing the superiority of the "American race"—white people of northern European origins. The peoples of the territories into which American civilization was destined to spread, these advocates of Manifest Destiny argued, could not be absorbed into the republican system. The Indians, the Mexicans, and others in the western regions were racially unfit to be part of an "American" community. Westward expansion was, therefore, a movement to spread both a political system and a racially defined society.

By the 1840s, the idea of Manifest Destiny had spread throughout the nation, publicized by the new "penny press" (inexpensive newspapers aimed at a mass audience), and fanned by the rhetoric of nationalist politicians. Advocates of Manifest Destiny disagreed, however, about how far and by what means the nation should expand. Some had relatively limited territorial goals; others envisioned a vast new "empire of liberty" that would include Canada, Mexico, Caribbean and Pacific islands, and ultimately, a few dreamed, much of the rest of the world. Some believed America should use force to achieve its expansionist goals, while others felt that the nation should expand peacefully or not at all.

THE LONE STAR FLAG Almost from the moment Texas won its independence from Mexico in 1836, it sought admission to the United States as a state. Controversies over the status of slavery in the territories prevented its admission until 1845, and so for nine years it was an independent republic. The tattered banner pictured here was one of the republic's original flags. *(Frank Lerner, from Showers-Brown Collection, Star of the Republic Museum)*

Not everyone embraced the idea of Manifest Destiny. Henry Clay and other prominent politicians feared, correctly as it turned out, that territorial expansion would reopen the painful controversy over slavery and threaten the stability of the Union. But their voices were barely audible over the clamor of enthusiasm for expansion in the 1840s, which began with the issues of Texas and Oregon.

Opposition to Further Expansion

Americans in Texas

The United States had once claimed Texas—which until the 1830s was part of the Republic of Mexico—as a part of the Louisiana Purchase, but it had renounced the claim in 1819. Twice thereafter the United States had offered to buy Texas, only to meet with indignant Mexican refusals.

But in the early 1820s, the Mexican government launched an ill-advised experiment that would eventually cause it to lose its great northern province: it encouraged American immigration into Texas. The Mexicans hoped to strengthen the economy of the territory and increase their own tax revenues. They also liked the idea of the Americans sitting between Mexican settlement and the large and sometimes militant Indian tribes to the north. They convinced themselves, too, that settlers in Texas would serve as an effective buffer against United States expansion into the region; the Americans, they thought, would soon become loyal to the Mexican government. An 1824 colonization law designed to attract American settlers promised the newcomers cheap land and a four-year exemption from taxes.

Thousands of Americans, attracted by the rich soil in Texas, took advantage of Mexico's welcome. Since much of the available land was suitable for growing cotton, the great majority of the immigrants were southerners, many of whom brought slaves with them. By 1830, there were about 7,000 Americans living in Texas, more than twice the number of Mexicans there.

The Mexican government offered land directly to immigrants, but most of the settlers came to Texas through the efforts of American intermediaries, who received sizable land grants from Mexico in return for promising to bring settlers into the region. The most successful of them was Stephen F. Austin, a young immigrant from Missouri who had established the first legal American settlement in Texas in 1822. Austin and other intermediaries were effective in recruiting American immigrants to Texas, but they also created centers of power in the region that competed with the Mexican government. In 1826, one of these American intermediaries led a revolt to establish Texas as an independent nation (which he proposed

Stephen Austin

calling Fredonia). The Mexicans quickly crushed the revolt and, four years later, passed new laws barring any further American immigration into the region. They were too late. Americans kept flowing into the territory, and in 1833 Mexico dropped the futile immigration ban. By 1835 over 30,000 Americans, white and black, had settled in Texas.

Tensions Between the United States and Mexico

Friction between the American settlers and the Mexican government continued to grow. It arose, in part, from the continuing cultural and economic ties of the immigrants to the United States and their desire to create stronger bonds with their former home. It arose, too, from their desire to legalize slavery, which the Mexican government had made illegal in Texas (as it was in Mexico) in 1830. But the Americans were divided over how to address their unhappiness with Mexican rule. Austin and his followers wanted to reach a peaceful settlement that would give Texas more autonomy within the Mexican republic. Others wanted to fight for independence.

In the mid-1830s, instability in Mexico itself drove General Antonio Lopez de Santa Anna to seize power as a dictator and impose a new, more conservative and autocratic regime on the nation and its territories. A new law increased the powers of the national government of Mexico at the expense of the state governments, a measure that Texans from the United States assumed Santa Anna was aiming specifically at them. The Mexicans even imprisoned Stephen Austin in Mexico City for a time, claiming that he was encouraging revolts among his fellow Americans in Texas. Sporadic fighting between Americans and Mexicans in Texas began in 1835 and escalated as the Mexican government sent more troops into the territory. In 1836, the American settlers defiantly proclaimed their independence from Mexico.

Santa Anna led a large army into Texas, where the American settlers were having enormous difficulties organizing an effective defense of their new "nation." Several different factions claimed to be the legitimate government of Texas, and American soldiers could not even agree on who their commanders were. Mexican forces annihilated an American garrison at the Alamo mission in San Antonio after a famous, if futile, defense by a group of Texas "patriots," a group that included, among others, the renowned frontiersman and former Tennessee congressman Davy Crockett. Another garrison at Goliad suffered substantially the same fate when the Mexicans executed most of the force after it had surrendered. By the end of 1836, the rebellion appeared to have collapsed. Americans were fleeing east toward Louisiana to escape Santa Anna's army.

But General Sam Houston managed to keep a small force together. And on April 23, 1836, at the Battle of San Jacinto *San Jacinto* (near the present-day city of Houston), he defeated the Mexican army and took Santa Anna prisoner. American troops then killed many of the Mexican soldiers in retribution for the executions at Goliad. Santa Anna, under pressure from his captors, signed a treaty giving Texas independence. And while the Mexican government repudiated the treaty, there were no further military efforts to win Texas back.

A number of Mexican residents of Texas *(Tejanos)* had fought with the Americans in the revolution. But soon after Texas won its independence, their positions grew difficult. The Americans did not trust them, fearing

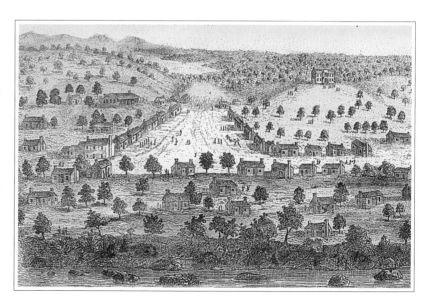

AUSTIN, TEXAS, 1840 Four years after Texas declared its independence from Mexico, the new republic's capital, Austin, was still a small village most of whose buildings were rustic cabins, as this handcolored lithograph from the time suggests. The imposing house atop the hill at right was a notable exception. It was the residence of President Mirabeau Lamar. *(The Center for the American History, The University of Texas at Austin)*

that they were agents of the Mexican government, and in effect drove many of them out of the new republic. Most of those who stayed had to settle for a politically and economically subordinate status within the fledgling nation.

Above all, American Texans hoped for annexation by the United States. One of the first acts of the new president of Texas, Sam Houston, was to send a delegation to Washington with an offer to join the Union. There were supporters of expansion in the United States who welcomed these overtures; indeed, expansionists in the United States had been supporting and encouraging the revolt against Mexico for years. But there was also opposition. Many American northerners opposed acquiring a large new slave territory, and others opposed increasing the southern votes in Congress and in the electoral college. Unfortunately for the Texans, one of the opponents was President Jackson, who feared annexation might cause a dangerous sectional controversy and even a war with Mexico. He therefore did not support annexation and even delayed recognizing the new republic until 1837. Presidents Martin Van Buren and William Henry Harrison also refrained from pressing the issue during their terms of office.

Opposition to Annexation

Spurned by the United States, Texas cast out on its own. Its leaders sought money and support from Europe. Some of them dreamed of creating a vast southwestern nation, stretching to the Pacific, that would rival the United States—a dream that appealed to European nations eager to counter the growing power of America. England and France quickly recognized and concluded trade treaties with Texas. In response, President Tyler persuaded Texas to apply for statehood again in 1844. But when Secretary of State Calhoun presented an annexation treaty to Congress as if its only purpose were to extend slavery, northern senators rebelled and defeated it. Rejection of the treaty only spurred advocates of Manifest Destiny to greater efforts toward their goal. The Texas question quickly became the central issue in the election of 1844.

Oregon

Control of what was known as Oregon country, in the Pacific Northwest, was another major political issue in the 1840s. Its half-million square miles included the present states of Oregon, Washington, and Idaho, parts of Montana and Wyoming, and half of British Columbia. Both Britain and the United States claimed sovereignty in the region—the British on the basis of explorations in the 1790s by George Vancouver, a naval officer; the Americans on the basis of simultaneous claims by Robert Gray, a fur trader. Unable to resolve their conflicting claims diplomatically, they agreed in an 1818 treaty to allow citizens of each country equal access to the territory. This

Disputed Claims

arrangement, known as "joint occupation," continued for twenty years.

In fact, by the time of the treaty neither Britain nor the United States had established much of a presence in Oregon country. White settlement in the region consisted largely of American and Canadian fur traders; and the most significant white settlements were the fur trading post established by John Jacob Astor's company at Astoria and other posts built by the British Hudson Bay Company north of the Columbia River—where residents combined fur trading with farming and recruited Indian labor to compensate for their small numbers.

But American interest in Oregon grew substantially in the 1820s and 1830s. Missionaries considered the territory an attractive target for evangelical efforts, especially after the strange appearance of four Nez Percé and Flathead Indians in St. Louis in 1831. White Americans never discovered what had brought the Indians (who spoke no English) from Oregon to Missouri, and all four died before they could find out. But some missionaries considered the visit a divinely inspired invitation to extend their efforts westward. They were also motivated by a desire to counter the Catholic missionaries from Canada, whose presence in Oregon, many believed, threatened American hopes for annexation. The missionaries had little success with the tribes they attempted to convert, and some—embittered by Indian resistance to their efforts—began encouraging white immigration into the region, arguing that by repudiating Christianity the Indians had abdicated their right to the land. "When a people refuse or neglect to fill the designs of Providence, they ought not to complain of the results," said the missionary Marcus Whitman, who, with his wife Narcissa, had established an important, if largely unsuccessful, mission among the Cayuse Indians east of the Cascade Mountains.

Significant numbers of white Americans began emigrating to Oregon in the early 1840s, and they soon substantially outnumbered the British settlers there. They also devastated much of the Indian population, in part through a measles epidemic that spread through the Cayuse. The tribe blamed the Whitman mission for the plague, and in 1847 they attacked it and killed thirteen whites, including Marcus and Narcissa. But such resistance did little to stem the white immigration. By the mid-1840s, American settlements had spread up and down the Pacific coast; and the new settlers (along with advocates of Manifest Destiny in the East) were urging the United States government to take possession of the disputed Oregon territory.

Conflict between Settlers and Indians

The Westward Migration

The migrations into Texas and Oregon were part of a larger movement that took hundreds of thousands of white and black Americans into the far western regions of

PROMOTING THE WEST Cyrus McCormick was one of many American businessmen with an interest in the peopling of the American West. The reaper he invented was crucial to the cultivation of the new agricultural regions, and the rapid settlement of those regions was, in turn, essential to the health of his company. In this poster, the McCormick Reaper Company presents a romantic, idealized image of vast, fertile lands awaiting settlement, an image that drew many settlers westward. *(Chicago Historical Society)*

the continent between 1840 and 1860. Southerners flocked mainly to Texas. But the largest number of migrants came from the Old Northwest (today's Midwest)—white men and women, and a few blacks, who undertook arduous journeys in search of new opportunities. Most traveled in family groups, until the early 1850s, when the great gold rush attracted many single men (see pp. 355–357). Most were relatively young people. Most had undertaken earlier, if usually shorter, migrations in the past. Few were wealthy, but many were relatively prosperous. Poor people could not afford the expensive trip and the cost of new land. Those without money who wished to migrate usually had to do so by joining more established families or groups as laborers—men as farm or ranch hands, women as domestic servants, teachers, or, in some cases, prostitutes. The character of the migrations varied according to the destination of the migrants. Groups headed for areas where mining or lumbering was the principal economic activity consisted mostly of men. Those heading for farming regions traveled mainly as families.

All the migrants were in search of a new life, but they harbored many different visions of what the new life would bring. Some—particularly after the discovery of gold in California in 1848—hoped for quick riches. Others planned to take advantage of the vast public lands the federal government was selling at modest prices to acquire property for farming or speculation. Still others hoped to establish themselves as merchants and serve the new white communities developing in the West. Some (among them the Mormons) were on religious missions or were attempting to escape the epidemic diseases that were plaguing many cities in the East. But the vast majority of migrants were looking for eco-

nomic opportunities. They formed a vanguard for the expanding capitalist economy of the United States. Perhaps not surprisingly, migrations were largest during boom times in the United States and dwindled during recessions.

Life on the Trail

Most migrants—about 300,000 between 1840 and 1860—traveled west along the great overland trails. They generally gathered in one of several major depots in Iowa and Missouri (Independence, St. Joseph, or Council Bluffs), joined a wagon train led by hired guides, and set off with their belongings piled in covered wagons, livestock trailing behind. The major route west was the 2,000-mile Oregon Trail, which stretched from Independence across the Great Plains and through the South Pass of the Rocky Mountains. From there, migrants moved north into Oregon or south (along the California trail) to the *Oregon Trail* northern California coast. Other migrations moved along the Santa Fe Trail, southwest from Independence into New Mexico.

However they traveled, overland migrants faced considerable hardships—although the death rate for travelers was only slightly higher than the rate for the American population as a whole. The mountain and desert terrain in the later portions of the trip were particularly difficult. Most journeys lasted five or six months (from May to November), and there was always pressure to get through the Rockies before the snows began, not always an easy task given the very slow pace of most wagon trains (about fifteen miles a day). And although some migrants were moving west at least in part to escape the epidemic

WESTERN TRAILS IN 1860 This map shows how much of western North America had little or no non-Indian population in 1800. As settlers began the long process of exploring and establishing farms and businesses in the West, major trails began to develop to facilitate travel and trade between the region and the more thickly settled areas to the East. Note how many of the trails lead to California and how few of them lead into any of the far northern regions of United States territory. Note too the important towns and cities that grew up along these trails.
◆ *What other, later forms of transportation performed the functions that these trails performed prior to the Civil War?*

diseases of eastern cities, they were not immune from plagues. Thousands of people died on the trail of cholera during the great epidemic of the early 1850s.

In the years before the Civil War, fewer than 400 migrants (about one-tenth of 1 percent) died in conflicts with the tribes. In fact, Indians were usually more helpful than dangerous to the white migrants. They often served as guides through difficult terrain or aided travelers in crossing streams or herding livestock. They maintained an

extensive trade with the white travelers in horses, clothing, and fresh food. But stories of the occasional conflicts between migrants and Indians on the trail created widespread fear among white travelers, even though more Indians than white people (and relatively few of either) died in those conflicts.

Life on the trail was obviously very different from life on a farm or in a town. But the society of the trail re-created many of the patterns of conventional American society.

CROSSING THE PLAINS A long wagon train carries migrants across the Plains toward Montana in 1866. This photograph gives some indication of the rugged condition of even some of the most well-traveled trails. *(New-York Historical Society)*

Families divided tasks along gender lines: the men driving and, when necessary, repairing the wagons or hunting game; the women cooking, washing clothes, and caring for children. Almost everyone, male or female, walked the great majority of the time, to lighten the load for the horses drawing the wagons; and so the women, many of whose chores came at the end of the day, generally worked much harder than the men, who usually rested when the caravan halted.

Life on the Trail

Despite the traditional image of westward migrants as rugged individualists, most travelers found the journey a highly collective experience. That was partly because many expeditions consisted of groups of friends, neighbors, or relatives who had decided to pull up stakes and move west together. And it was partly because of the intensity of the experience: many weeks of difficult travel with no other human contacts except, occasionally, with Indians. Indeed, one of the most frequent causes of disaster for travelers was the breakdown of the necessarily communal character of the migratory companies. Even so, it was a rare expedition in which there were not some internal conflicts before the trip was over.

EXPANSION AND WAR

The growing number of white Americans in the lands west of the Mississippi put great pressure on the government in Washington to annex Texas, Oregon, and other territory. And in the 1840s, these expansionist pressures helped push the United States into a war that—however dubious its origins—became a triumph for the advocates of Manifest Destiny.

The Democrats and Expansion

In preparing for the election of 1844, the two leading candidates—Henry Clay and the Democrat and former president Martin Van Buren—both tried to avoid taking a stand on the controversial issue of the annexation of Texas. Sentiment for expansion was mild within the Whig Party, and Clay had no difficulty securing the nomination despite his noncommittal position. But many southern Democrats supported annexation, and the party passed over Van Buren to nominate a strong supporter of annexation, the previously unheralded James K. Polk.

Polk was not as obscure as his Whig critics claimed. He had represented Tennessee in the House of Representatives for fourteen years, four of them as Speaker, and had subsequently served as governor. But by 1844, he had been out of public office—and for the most part out of the public mind—for three years. What made his victory possible was his support for the position, expressed in the Democratic platform, "that the re-occupation of Oregon and the re-annexation of Texas at the earliest practicable period are great American measures." By combining the Oregon and Texas questions, the Democrats hoped to appeal to both northern and southern expansionists. Polk carried the election by 170 electoral votes to 105, although his popular majority was less than 40,000.

James K. Polk

Polk entered office with a clear set of goals and with plans for attaining them. John Tyler accomplished the first of Polk's goals for him in the last days of his own presidency. Interpreting the election returns as a mandate for the annexation of Texas, the outgoing president won congressional approval for it in February 1845. That December, Texas became a state.

Polk himself resolved the Oregon question. The British minister in Washington brusquely rejected a compromise Polk offered that would establish the United States–Canadian border at the 49th parallel; he did not even refer the proposal to London. Incensed, Polk again asserted the American claim to all of Oregon. There was loose talk of war on both sides of the Atlantic—talk that in the United States often took the form of the bellicose slogan "Fifty-four forty or fight!" (a reference to where the Americans hoped to draw the northern boundary of their part of Oregon). But neither country really wanted war. Finally, the British government accepted Polk's original proposal to divide the territory at the 49th parallel. On June 15, 1846, the Senate approved a treaty that fixed the boundary at the 49th parallel, where it remains today.

Compromise over Oregon

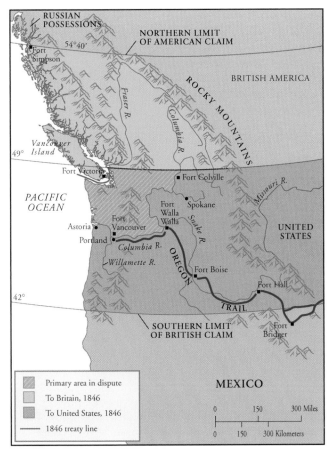

THE OREGON BOUNDARY, 1846 One of the last major boundary disputes between the United States and Great Britain involved the territory known as Oregon—the large region on the Pacific Coast north of California (which in 1846 was still part of Mexico). For years, America and Britain had overlapping claims on the territory. The British claimed land as far south as the present state of Oregon, while the Americans claimed land extending well into what is now Canada. Tensions over the Oregon border at times rose to the point that many Americans were demanding war, some using the slogan "54-40 or fight," referring to the latitude of the northernmost point of the American claim. ◆ *How did President James K. Polk defuse the crisis?*

The Southwest and California

One of the reasons the Senate and the president had agreed so readily to the British offer to settle the Oregon question was that new tensions were emerging in the Southwest—tensions that ultimately led to a war with Mexico. As soon as the United States admitted Texas to statehood in 1845, the Mexican government broke diplomatic relations with Washington. Mexican-American relations grew still worse when a dispute developed over the *Texas Boundary in Dispute* | boundary between Texas and Mexico. Texans claimed the Rio Grande as their western and southern border, a claim that would have added much of what is now New Mexico to Texas. Mexico, although still not conceding the loss of Texas, argued nevertheless that the border had always been the Nueces River, to the north of the Rio Grande.

Polk accepted the Texas claim, and in the summer of 1845 he sent a small army under General Zachary Taylor to Texas to protect it against a possible Mexican invasion.

Part of the area in dispute was New Mexico, whose Spanish and Indian residents lived in a multiracial society that had by the 1840s endured for nearly a century and a half. In the 1820s, the Mexican government had invited American traders into the region (just as it invited American settlers into Texas), hoping to speed development of the province. And New Mexico, like Texas, soon began to become more American than Mexican. A flourishing commerce soon developed between Santa Fe and Independence, Missouri.

Americans were also increasing their interest in an even more distant province of Mexico: California. In this vast region lived members of several *American Interests in California* | western Indian tribes and perhaps 7,000 Mexicans, mostly descendants of Spanish colonists. Gradually, however, white Americans began to arrive: first maritime traders and captains of Pacific whaling ships, who stopped to barter goods or buy supplies; then merchants, who established stores, imported merchandise, and developed a profitable trade with the Mexicans and Indians; and finally pioneering farmers, who entered California from the east, by land, and settled in the Sacramento Valley. Some of these new settlers began to dream of bringing California into the United States.

President Polk soon came to share their dream and committed himself to acquiring both New Mexico and California for the United States. At the same time that he dispatched the troops under Taylor to Texas, he sent secret instructions to the commander of the Pacific naval squadron to seize the California ports if Mexico declared war. Representatives of the president quietly informed Americans in California that the United States would respond sympathetically to a revolt against Mexican authority there.

The Mexican War

Having appeared to prepare for war, Polk turned to diplomacy and dispatched a special minister, John Slidell, to try to buy *Failure of the Slidell Mission* | off the Mexicans. But Mexican leaders rejected Slidell's offer to purchase the disputed territories. On January 13, 1846, as soon as he heard the news, Polk ordered Taylor's army in Texas to move across the Nueces River, where it had been stationed, to the Rio Grande. For months, the Mexicans refused to fight. But finally, according to disputed American accounts, some Mexican troops crossed the Rio Grande and attacked a unit of American soldiers. Polk now told Congress: "War exists by the act of Mexico herself." On May 13, 1846, Congress declared war by votes of 40 to 2 in the Senate and 174 to 14 in the House.

SACRAMENTO IN THE 1850S The busy river port of Sacramento served the growing agricultural and mining economies of north central California in the 1850s—years in which the new state began the dramatic population growth that a century later would make it the nation's largest. *(California State Library, Sacramento)*

The war had many opponents in the United States. Whig critics charged from the beginning (and not without

Opposition to the War

out some justification) that Polk had deliberately maneuvered the country into the conflict and had staged the border incident that had precipitated the declaration. Many argued that the hostilities with Mexico were draining resources and attention away from the more important issue of the Pacific Northwest; and when the United States finally reached its agreement with Britain on the Oregon question, opponents claimed that Polk had settled for less than he should have because he was preoccupied with Mexico. Opposition intensified as the war continued and as the public became aware of the casualties and expense.

American forces did well against the Mexicans, but victory did not come as quickly as Polk had hoped. The president ordered Taylor to cross the Rio Grande, seize parts of northeastern Mexico, beginning with the city of Monterrey, and then march on to Mexico City itself. Taylor captured Monterrey in September 1846, but he let the Mexican garrison evacuate without pursuit. Polk now began to fear that Taylor lacked the tactical skill for the planned advance against Mexico City. He also feared that, if successful, Taylor would become a powerful political rival (as, in fact, he did).

In the meantime, Polk ordered other offensives against New Mexico and California. In the summer of 1846, a small army under Colonel Stephen W. Kearny captured Santa Fe with no opposition. Then Kearny proceeded to California, where he joined a conflict already in progress that

Bear Flag Revolution

was being staged jointly by American settlers, a well-armed exploring party led by John C. Frémont, and the American navy: the so-called Bear Flag Revolution. Kearny brought the disparate American forces together under his command, and by the autumn of 1846 he had completed the conquest of California.

The United States now controlled the two territories for which it had gone to war. But Mexico still refused to concede defeat. At this point, Polk and General Winfield Scott, the commanding general of the army and its finest soldier, launched a bold new campaign. Scott assembled an army at Tampico, which the navy transported down the Mexican coast to Veracruz. With an army that never numbered more than 14,000, Scott advanced 260 miles along the Mexican National Highway toward Mexico City, kept American casualties low, and never lost a battle before finally seizing the Mexican capital. A new Mexican government took power and announced its willingness to negotiate a peace treaty.

President Polk was now growing thoroughly unclear about his objectives. He continued to encourage those who demanded that the United States annex much of Mexico itself. At the same time, concerned about the

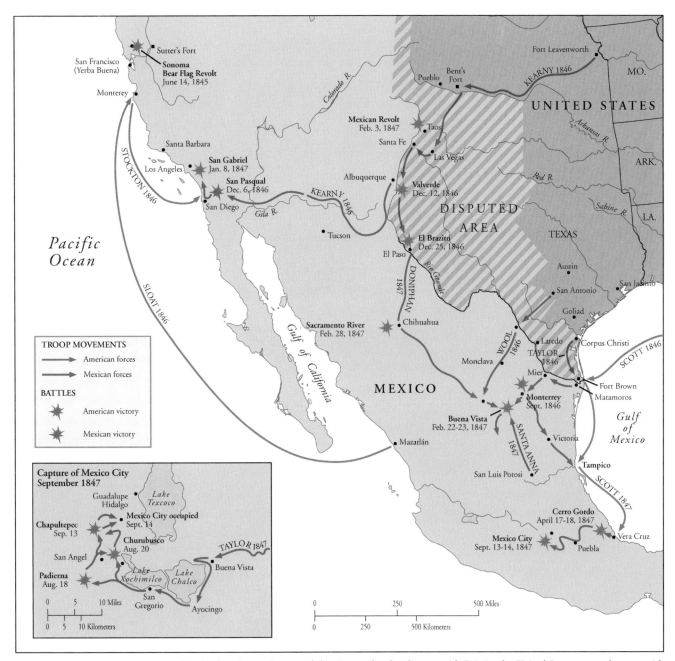

THE MEXICAN WAR, 1846–1848 Shortly after the settlement of the Oregon border dispute with Britain, the United States entered a war with Mexico over another contested border. This map shows the movement of Mexican and American troops during the fighting, which extended from the area around Santa Fe south to Mexico City and west to the coast of California. Note the American use of its naval forces to facilitate a successful assault on Mexico City, and others on the coast of California. Note, too, how unsuccessful the Mexican forces were in their battles with the United States. Mexico won only one battle—a relatively minor one at San Pasqual near San Diego—in the war. ◆ *How did President Polk deal with the popular clamor for the United States to annex much of present-day Mexico?*

For an interactive version of this map go to www.mhhe.com/brinkley11ch13maps

approaching presidential election, he was growing anxious to get the war finished quickly. Polk had sent a special presidential envoy, Nicholas Trist, to negotiate a settlement. On February 2, 1848, he reached agreement with the new Mexican government on the Treaty of Guadalupe Hidalgo, by which Mexico agreed

Treaty of Guadalupe Hidalgo

to cede California and New Mexico to the United States and acknowledge the Rio Grande as the boundary of Texas. In return, the United States promised to assume any financial claims its new citizens had against Mexico and to pay the Mexicans $15 million. Trist had obtained most of Polk's original demands, but he had not satisfied the new, more expansive dreams of acquiring additional territory in Mexico

STEPHEN KEARNY IN SANTA FE Colonel
Stephen Kearny led a small U.S. military party
to Santa Fe in 1846 and seized the town
without opposition. In this 1909 drawing
(which the artist Stephen Chapman
acknowledged was not entirely accurate),
Kearny raises the American flag over the "old
palace" in Santa Fe. The image appeared on a
U.S. postage stamp in 1946. *(Museum of New
Mexico)*

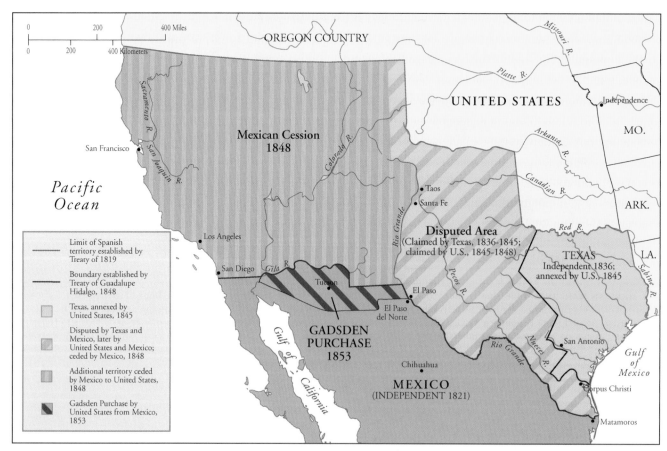

SOUTHWESTERN EXPANSION, 1845–1853 The annexation of much of what is now Texas in 1845, the much larger territorial gains won in
the Mexican War in 1848, and the purchase of additional land from Mexico in 1853 completed the present continental border of the United
States. ◆ *What great event shortly after the Mexican War contributed to a rapid settlement of California by migrants from the eastern
United States?*

 For an interactive version of this map go to www.mhhe.com/brinkley11ch13maps

itself. Polk angrily claimed that Trist had violated his instructions, but he soon realized that he had no choice but to accept the treaty to silence a bitter battle growing between ardent expansionists demanding the annexation of "All Mexico!" and antislavery leaders charging that the expansionists were conspiring to extend slavery to new realms. The president submitted the Trist treaty to the Senate, which approved it by a vote of 38 to 14. The war was over, and America had gained a vast new territory. But it had also acquired a new set of troubling and divisive issues.

THE SECTIONAL DEBATE

James Polk tried to be a president whose policies transcended sectional divisions. But conciliating the sections was becoming an ever more difficult task, and Polk gradually earned the enmity of northerners and westerners alike, who believed his policies (and particularly his enthusiasm for territorial expansion in the Southwest) favored the South at their expense.

Slavery and the Territories

In August 1846, while the Mexican War was still in progress, Polk asked Congress to appropriate $2 million for purchasing peace with Mexico. Representative David Wilmot of Pennsylvania, an antislavery Democrat, intro-

Wilmot Proviso

duced an amendment to the appropriation bill prohibiting slavery in any territory acquired from Mexico. The so-called Wilmot Proviso passed the House but failed in the Senate. It would be called up, debated, and voted on repeatedly for years. Southern militants, in the meantime, contended that all Americans had equal rights in the new territories, including the right to move their slaves (which they considered property) into them.

As the sectional debate intensified, President Polk supported a proposal to extend the Missouri Compromise

Competing Plans

line through the new territories to the Pacific coast, banning slavery north of the line and permitting it south of the line. Others supported a plan, originally known as "squatter sovereignty" and later by the more dignified phrase "popular sovereignty," which would allow the people of each territory (acting through their legislature) to decide the status of slavery there. The debate over these various proposals dragged on for many months, and the issue remained unresolved when Polk left office in 1849.

The presidential campaign of 1848 dampened the controversy for a time as both Democrats and Whigs tried to avoid the slavery question. When Polk, in poor health, declined to run again, the Democrats nominated Lewis Cass of Michigan, a dull, aging party regular. The Whigs nominated General Zachary Taylor of Louisiana, hero of the Mexican War but a man with no political experience

whatsoever. Opponents of slavery found the choice of candidates unsatisfying, and out of their discontent emerged the new Free-Soil Party, which drew from the existing Liberty Party and the antislavery wings of the Whig and Democratic Parties and which endorsed the Wilmot Proviso. Its candidate was former president Martin Van Buren.

Taylor won a narrow victory. But while Van Buren failed to carry a single state, he polled

Free-Soil Party

an impressive 291,000 votes (10 percent of the total), and the Free-Soilers elected ten members to Congress. The emergence of the Free-Soil Party as an important political force, like the emergence of the Know-Nothing and Liberty Parties before it, signaled the inability of the existing parties to contain the political passions slavery was creating. It was an important part of a process that would lead to the collapse of the second party system in the 1850s.

The California Gold Rush

By the time Taylor took office, the pressure to resolve the question of slavery in the far western territories had become more urgent as a result of dramatic events in California. In January 1848, James Marshall, a carpenter working on one of John Sutter's sawmills, found traces of gold in the foothills of the Sierra Nevadas. Sutter tried to suppress the news, fearing a gold rush would destroy his own substantial empire in the region. But by May, word of the discovery had reached San Francisco; by late summer, it had reached the east coast of the United States and much of the rest of the world. Almost immediately, hundreds of thousands of people from around the world began flocking to California in a frantic search for gold. The non-Indian population increased nearly twentyfold in four years: from 14,000 in 1848 to over 220,000 in 1852.

The atmosphere in California at the peak of the gold rush was one of almost crazed excitement and greed. For a short time San Francisco was almost completely depopulated as residents raced to the mountains to search for gold; the city's principal newspaper (which had been criticizing the gold mania) had to stop publication because it could no longer find either staff or readers. "Nothing but the introduction of insane asylums can effect a cure," one visitor remarked of the gold mania.

Most migrants to the Far West prepared carefully before making the journey. But the California migrants (known

Forty-niners

as "Forty-niners") threw caution to the winds. They abandoned farms, jobs, homes, families; they piled onto ships and flooded the overland trails—many carrying only what they could pack on their backs. The overwhelming majority of the Forty-niners (perhaps 95 percent) were men, and the society they created on their arrival in California was unusually fluid and volatile because of the almost total absence of women, children, or families.

"MINERS WITH ROCKERS AND BLUE SHIRTS" Despite its romantic image, mining for gold during the great California Gold Rush was for most people hard, discouraging, and ultimately profitless work—as this photograph of a grim band of miners with their equipment suggests. Most of those who came to California in search of gold eventually either returned home with nothing to show for their efforts or remained in California to make their way in some other occupation. *(Collection of W. Bruce Lundberg. Photograph courtesy Oakland Museum of California)*

The gold rush also attracted some of the first Chinese migrants to the western United States. News of the discoveries created great excitement in China, particularly in impoverished areas, where letters from Chinese already in California and reports from Americans visiting in China spread the word. It was, of course, extremely difficult for a poor Chinese peasant to get to America; but many young, adventurous people (mostly men) decided to go anyway—believing that they could quickly become rich and then return to China. Emigration brokers loaned many migrants money for passage to California, which the migrants paid off out of their earnings there. The migration was almost entirely voluntary (unlike the forced movement of kidnapped "coolies" to such places as Peru and Cuba at about the same time). The Chinese in California were, therefore, free laborers and merchants, looking for gold or, more often, hoping to profit from other economic opportunities the gold boom was creating.

The gold rush created a serious labor shortage in California, as many male workers left their jobs and flocked to the gold fields. This shortage created opportunities for many people who needed work (including Chinese immi-

grants). It also led to an overt exploitation of Indians that resembled slavery in all but name. At the same time that white vigilantes, who called themselves "Indian hunters," were hunting down and killing thousands of Indians (contribut-   *Indian Slavery* ing to the process by which the Native American population of California declined from 150,000 to 30,000 between the 1850s and 1870), a state law permitted the arrest of "loitering" or orphaned Indians and their assignment to a term of "indentured" labor.

The gold rush was of critical importance to the growth of California, but not for the reasons most of the migrants hoped. There was substantial gold in the hills of the Sierra Nevada, and many people got rich from it. But only a tiny fraction of the Forty-niners ever found gold, or even managed to stake a claim to land on which they could look for gold. Some disappointed migrants returned home after a while. But many stayed in California and swelled both the agricultural and urban populations of the territory. By 1856, for example, San Francisco—whose population had been 1,000 before the gold rush (and at one point declined to about 100 as people left for the mines)—was the home of over 50,000 people. By the early 1850s, California, which had always had a diverse population, had become remarkably heterogeneous. The gold rush had attracted not just white Americans, but Europeans, Chinese, South Americans, Mexicans, free blacks, and slaves who accompanied southern migrants. Conflicts over gold intersected with racial and ethnic tensions to make the territory an unusually turbulent place. As a result, pressure grew to create a more stable and effective government. The gold rush, therefore, became another factor putting pressure on the United States to resolve the status of the territories—and of slavery within them.

Rising Sectional Tensions

Zachary Taylor believed statehood could become the solution to the issue of slavery in the territories. As long as the new lands remained territories, the federal government was responsible for deciding the fate of slavery within them. But once they became states, he thought, their own governments would be able to settle the slavery question. At Taylor's urging, California quickly adopted a constitution that prohibited slavery, and in December 1849 Taylor asked Congress to admit California as a free state. New Mexico, he added, should also be granted statehood as soon as it was ready and should, like California, be permitted to decide for itself what it wanted to do about slavery.

Congress balked, in part because of several other controversies concerning slavery that were complicating the debate. One was the effort of antislavery forces to abolish slavery in the District of Columbia, a movement bitterly resisted by southerners. Another was the emergence of personal liberty laws in northern states, which barred courts and police officers from helping to return runaway slaves to their owners. In response, southerners demanded a stringent law that would require northern states to return fugitive slaves to their owners. But the biggest obstacle to the president's program was the white South's fear that two new free states would be added to the northern majority. The number of free and slave states was equal in 1849—fifteen each. But the admission of California would upset the balance; and New Mexico, Oregon, and Utah might upset it further, leaving the South in a minority in the Senate, as it already was in the House.

Tempers were now rising to dangerous levels. Even many otherwise moderate southern leaders were beginning to talk about secession from the Union. In the North, every state legislature but one adopted a resolution demanding the prohibition of slavery in the territories.

Sectional Conflict over Slavery in the Territories

The Compromise of 1850

Faced with this mounting crisis, moderates and unionists spent the winter of 1849–1850 trying to frame a great compromise. The aging Henry Clay, who was spearheading the effort, believed that no compromise could last unless it settled all the issues in dispute between the sections. As a result, he took several measures that had been proposed separately, combined them into a single piece of legislation, and presented it to the Senate on January 29, 1850. Among the bill's provisions were the admission of California as a free state; the formation of territorial governments in the rest of the lands acquired from Mexico, without restrictions on slavery; the abolition of the slave trade, but not slavery itself, in the District of Columbia; and a new and more effective fugitive slave law. These resolutions launched a debate that raged for seven months—both in Congress and throughout the nation. The debate occurred in two phases, the differences between which revealed much about how American politics was changing in the 1850s.

Clay's Proposed Solution

In the first phase of the debate, the dominant voices in Congress were those of old men—national leaders who still remembered Jefferson, Adams, and other founders—who argued for or against the compromise on the basis of broad ideals. Clay himself, seventy-three years old in 1850, appealed to shared national sentiments of nationalism. Early in March, another of the older leaders—John C. Calhoun, sixty-eight years old and so ill that he had to sit grimly in his seat while a colleague read his speech for him—joined the debate. He insisted that the North grant the South equal rights in the territories, that it agree to observe the laws concerning fugitive slaves, that it cease attacking slavery, and that it amend the Constitution to create dual presidents, one from the North and one from the South, each with a veto. Calhoun was making radical demands that had no chance of passage. But like Clay, he was offering what he considered a comprehensive, permanent solution to the sectional problem that would, he believed, save the Union. After Calhoun came the third of the elder statesmen, sixty-eight-year-old Daniel Webster, one of the great orators of his time. Still nourishing presidential ambitions, he delivered an eloquent address in the Senate, trying to rally northern moderates to support Clay's compromise.

But in July, after six months of this impassioned, nationalistic debate, Congress defeated the Clay proposal. And with that, the controversy moved into its second phase, in which a very different cast of characters predominated. Clay, ill and tired, left Washington to spend the summer resting in the mountains. Calhoun had died even before the vote in July. And Webster accepted a new appointment as secretary of state, thus removing himself from the Senate and from the debate.

In place of these leaders, a new, younger group now emerged. One spokesman was William H. Seward, forty-nine years old, of New York, a wily political operator who staunchly opposed the proposed compromise. The ideals of Union were to him less important than the issue

New Leadership

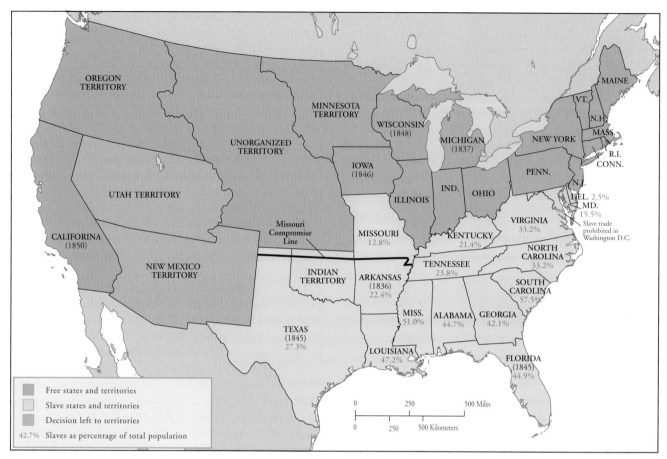

SLAVE AND FREE TERRITORIES UNDER THE COMPROMISE OF 1850 The acquisition of vast new western lands raised the question of the status of slavery in new territories organized for statehood by the United States. Tension between the North and South on this question led in 1850 to a great compromise, forged in Congress, to settle this dispute. The compromise allowed California to join the Union as a free state and introduced the concept of "popular sovereignty" for other new territories. ◆ *How well did the compromise of 1850 work?*

 For an interactive version of this map go to www.mhhe.com/brinkley11ch13maps

---

of eliminating slavery. Another was Jefferson Davis of Mississippi, forty-two years old, a representative of the new, cotton South. To him, the slavery issue was less one of principles and ideals than one of economic self-interest. Most important of all, there was Stephen A. Douglas, a thirty-seven-year-old Democratic senator from Illinois. A westerner from a rapidly growing state, he was an open spokesman for the economic needs of his section—and especially for the construction of railroads. His was a career devoted not to any broad national goals but frankly to sectional gain and personal self-promotion.

The new leaders of the Senate were able, as the old leaders had not been, to produce a compromise. One spur to the compromise was the disappearance of the most powerful obstacle to it: the president. Zachary Taylor had been adamant that only after California and possibly New Mexico were admitted as states could other measures be discussed. But on July 9, 1850, Taylor suddenly died—the victim of a violent stomach disorder. He was

succeeded by Millard Fillmore of New York—a dull, handsome, dignified man who understood the political importance of flexibility. He supported the compromise and used his powers of persuasion to swing northern Whigs into line.

The new leaders also benefited from their own pragmatic tactics. Douglas's first step, after the departure of Clay, was to break up the "omnibus bill" that Clay had envisioned as a great, comprehensive solution to the sectional crisis and to introduce instead a series of separate measures to be voted on one by one. Thus representatives of different sections could support those elements of the compromise they liked and oppose those they did not. Douglas also gained support with complicated backroom deals linking the compromise to such nonideological matters as the sale of government bonds and the construction of railroads. As a result of his efforts, by mid-September Congress had enacted and the president had signed all the components of the compromise.

Temporary Compromise

The Compromise of 1850, unlike the Missouri Compromise thirty years before, was not a product of widespread agreement on common national ideals. It was, rather, a victory of self-interest. Still, members of Congress hailed the measure as a triumph of statesmanship; and Millard Fillmore, signing it, called it a just settlement of the sectional problem, "in its character final and irrevocable."

THE CRISES OF THE 1850s

For a few years after the Compromise of 1850, the sectional conflict seemed briefly to be forgotten amid booming prosperity and growth. But the tensions between North and South remained, and the crisis continued to smolder until—in 1854—it once more burst into the open.

The Uneasy Truce

Both major parties endorsed the Compromise of 1850 in 1852, and both nominated presidential candidates unidentified with sectional passions. The Democrats chose the obscure New Hampshire politician Franklin Pierce and the Whigs the military hero General Winfield Scott, a man of entirely unknown political views. But the sectional question was a divisive influence in the election anyway, and the Whigs were the principal victims. They suffered massive defections from antislavery members angered by the party's evasiveness on the issue. Many of them flocked to the Free-Soil Party, whose antislavery presidential candidate, John P. Hale, repudiated the Compromise of 1850. The divisions among the Whigs helped produce a victory for the Democrats in 1852.

Franklin Pierce, a charming, amiable man of no particular distinction, attempted to maintain party—and national—harmony by avoiding divisive issues, and particularly by avoiding the issue of slavery. But it was an impossible task. Northern opposition to the Fugitive Slave Act intensi-*Opposition to the Fugitive Slave Act* fied quickly after 1850, when southerners began appearing occasionally in northern states to pursue people they claimed were fugitives. Mobs formed in some northern cities to prevent enforcement of the law, and several northern states also passed their own laws barring the deportation of fugitive slaves. White southerners watched with growing anger and alarm as the one element of the Compromise of 1850 that they had considered a victory seemed to become meaningless as a result of northern defiance.

"Young America"

One of the ways Franklin Pierce hoped to dampen sectional controversy was through his support of a movement in the Democratic Party known as "Young America."

Its adherents saw the expansion of American democracy throughout the world as a way to divert attention from the controversies over slavery. The great liberal and nationalist revolutions of 1848 in Europe stirred them to dream of a republican Europe with governments based on the model of the United States. They dreamed as well of expanding American commerce in the Pacific and acquiring new territories in the Western Hemisphere.

But efforts to extend the nation's domain could not avoid becoming entangled with the sectional crisis. Pierce had been pursuing un-*Ostend Manifesto* successful diplomatic attempts to buy Cuba from Spain (efforts begun in 1848 by Polk). In 1854, however, a group of his envoys sent him a private document from Ostend, Belgium, making the case for seizing Cuba by force. When the Ostend Manifesto, as it became known, was leaked to the public, it enraged many antislavery northerners, who charged the administration with conspiring to bring a new slave state into the Union.

The South, for its part, opposed all efforts to acquire new territory that would not support a slave system. The kingdom of Hawaii agreed to join the United States in 1854, but the treaty died in the Senate because it contained a clause prohibiting slavery in the islands. A powerful movement to annex Canada to the United States—a movement that had the support of many Canadians eager for access to American markets—similarly foundered, at least in part because of slavery.

Slavery, Railroads, and the West

What fully revived the sectional crisis, however, was the same issue that had produced it in the first place: slavery in the territories. By the 1850s, the line of substantial white settlement had moved beyond the boundaries of Missouri, Iowa, and what is now Minnesota into a great expanse of plains, which many white Americans had once believed was unfit for cultivation. Now it was becoming apparent that large sections of this region were, in fact, suitable for farming. In the states of the Old Northwest, therefore, prospective settlers urged the government to open the area to them, provide territorial governments, and—despite the solemn assurance the United States had earlier given the Indians of the sanctity of their reservations—dislodge the tribes located there so as to make room for white settlers. There was relatively little opposition from any segment of white society to this proposed violation of Indian rights. But the interest in further settlement raised two issues that did prove highly divisive and that gradually became entwined with each other: railroads and slavery.

As the nation expanded westward, the problem of communication between the older states and the areas west *Transcontinental Railroad and Slavery* of the Mississippi River became more and more critical. As a result, broad support began to emerge for building a transcontinental railroad. The problem was where to place it—and in particular, where to locate the railroad's eastern terminus, where the line could connect with the existing rail network east of the Mississippi. Northerners favored Chicago, the rapidly growing capital of the free states of the Northwest. Southerners supported St. Louis, Memphis, or New Orleans—all located in slave states. The transcontinental railroad, in other words, had become part of the struggle between the North and the South.

Pierce's secretary of war, Jefferson Davis of Mississippi, *Gadsden Purchase* removed one obstacle to a southern route. Surveys indicated that a railroad with a southern terminus would have to pass through an area in Mexican territory. But in 1853 Davis sent James Gadsden, a southern railroad builder, to Mexico, where he persuaded the Mexican government to accept $10 million in exchange for a strip of land that today comprises part of Arizona and New Mexico. The so-called Gadsden Purchase only accentuated the sectional rivalry.

The Kansas-Nebraska Controversy

As a senator from Illinois, a resident of Chicago, and the acknowledged leader of northwestern Democrats, Stephen A. Douglas naturally wanted the transcontinental railroad for his own city and section. He also realized the strength of the principal argument against the northern route west of the Mississippi: that it would run mostly through country with a substantial Indian population. As a result, he introduced a bill in January 1854 to organize (and thus open to white settlement) a huge new territory, known as Nebraska, west of Iowa and Missouri.

Douglas knew the South would oppose his bill because it would prepare the way for a new free state; the proposed territory was in the area of the Louisiana Purchase north of the Missouri Compromise line (36°30') and hence closed to slavery. In an effort to make the measure acceptable to southerners, Douglas inserted a provision that the status of slavery in the territory would be determined by the territorial legislature—that is, according to *Kansas-Nebraska Act* "popular sovereignty." In theory, the region could choose to open itself to slavery (although few believed it actually would). When southern Democrats demanded more, Douglas agreed to an additional clause explicitly repealing the Missouri Compromise. He also agreed to divide the area into two territories—Nebraska and Kansas—instead of one. The new, second territory (Kansas) was more likely to become a slave state. In its final form the measure was known as the Kansas-Nebraska Act. President Pierce supported the bill, and after a strenuous debate, it became law in May 1854 with the unanimous support of the South and the partial support of northern Democrats.

No piece of legislation in American history produced so many immediate, sweeping, and ominous consequences. It divided and destroyed the Whig Party, which disappeared almost entirely by 1856. It divided the northern Democrats (many of whom were appalled at the repeal of the Missouri Compromise, which they considered an almost sacred part of the fabric of the Union) and drove many of them from the party. Most important of all, it spurred the creation of a new party that was frankly sectional in composition and creed. People in both major parties *Birth of the Republican Party* who opposed Douglas's bill began to call themselves Anti-Nebraska Democrats and Anti-Nebraska Whigs. In 1854, they formed a new organization and named it the Republican Party. It instantly became a major force in American politics. In the elections of that year, the Republicans won enough seats in Congress to permit them, in combination with allies among the Know-Nothings, to organize the House of Representatives.

"Bleeding Kansas"

Events in Kansas itself in the next two years increased the political turmoil in the North. White settlers from both the North and the South began moving into the territory almost immediately after the passage of the Kansas-Nebraska Act. In the spring of 1855, elections were held for a territorial legislature. There were only about 1,500 legal voters in Kansas by then, but thousands of Missourians, some traveling in armed bands into Kansas, swelled the vote to over 6,000. The result was that pro-slavery forces elected a majority to the legislature, which immediately legalized slavery. Outraged free-staters elected their own delegates to a constitutional convention, which met at Topeka and adopted a constitution excluding slavery. They then chose their own governor and legislature and petitioned Congress for statehood. President Pierce denounced them as traitors and threw the full support of the federal government behind the pro-slavery territorial legislature. A few months later a pro-slavery federal marshal assembled a large posse, consisting mostly of Missourians, to arrest the free-state leaders, who had set up their headquarters in Lawrence. The posse sacked the town, burned the "governor's" house, and destroyed several printing presses. Retribution came quickly.

Among the most fervent abolitionists in Kansas was John Brown, a grim, fiercely committed zealot who considered him- *Pottawatomie Massacre* self an instrument of God's will to destroy slavery. He had moved to Kansas with his sons so that they could fight to make it a free state. After the events in Lawrence, he gathered six followers (including four of his sons) and in one night murdered five pro-slavery settlers, leaving their mutilated bodies to discourage other supporters of slavery from entering Kansas. This terrible episode, known as the Pottawatomie Massacre, led to more civil strife in Kansas—irregular, guerrilla warfare conducted by armed bands, some of them more interested in land claims or loot than in

"BLEEDING KANSAS" During the bitter battles over slavery in 1856, the slave state of Missouri tried to prevent antislavery emigrants from passing through their territory en route to Kansas. Free-staters responded by organizing a large emigration through Iowa, circumventing Missouri. Those who entered Kansas by that route tended to arrive armed, some of them with large cannon—among them the one pictured here, which Free-staters brought with them to Topeka that year. *(Kansas State Historical Society)*

ideologies. Northerners and southerners alike came to believe that the events in Kansas illustrated (and were caused by) the aggressive designs of the other section. "Bleeding Kansas" became a symbol of the sectional controversy.

Another symbol soon appeared, in the United States Senate. In May 1856, Charles Sumner of Massachusetts—a militant and passionately doctrinaire opponent of slavery—rose to give a speech entitled "The Crime Against Kansas." In it, he gave particular attention to Senator Andrew P. Butler of South Carolina, an outspoken defender of slavery. The South Carolinian was, Sumner claimed, the "Don Quixote" of slavery, having "chosen a mistress . . . who, though ugly to others, is always lovely to him, though polluted in the sight of the world, is chaste in his sight . . . the harlot slavery."

The pointedly sexual references and the general viciousness of the speech enraged Butler's nephew, Preston Brooks, a member of the House of Representatives from *Preston Brooks and Charles Sumner* South Carolina. Several days after the speech, Brooks approached Sumner at his desk in the Senate chamber during a recess, raised a heavy cane, and began beating him repeatedly on the head and shoulders. Sumner, trapped in his chair, rose in agony with such strength that he tore the desk from the bolts holding it to the floor. Then he collapsed, bleeding and unconscious. So severe were his injuries that he was unable to return to the Senate for four years. Throughout the North, he became a hero—a martyr to the barbarism of the South. In the South, Preston Brooks became a hero, too. Censured by the House, he resigned his seat, returned to South Carolina, and stood successfully for reelection.

The Free-Soil Ideology

What had happened to produce such deep hostility between the two sections? In part, the tensions were reflections of the two sections' differing economic and territorial interests. But they were also reflections of a hardening of ideas in both North and South. As the nation expanded and political power grew more dispersed, each section became concerned with ensuring that its vision of America's future would be the dominant one.

In the North, assumptions about the proper structure of society came to center on the belief in "free soil" and "free *"Free Soil" Ideology* labor." Although abolitionists generated some support for their argument that slavery was a moral evil and must be eliminated, most white northerners came to believe that the existence of slavery was dangerous not because of what it did to blacks but because of what it threatened to do to whites. At the heart of American democracy, they argued, was the right of all citizens to own property, to control their own labor, and to have access to opportunities for advancement.

According to this vision, the South was the antithesis of democracy—a closed, static society, in which slavery pre- *"Slave Power Conspiracy"* served an entrenched aristocracy and in which common whites had no opportunity to improve themselves. While the North was growing and prospering, the South was stagnating, rejecting the values of individualism and progress. The South was, northern free-laborites further maintained, engaged in a conspiracy to extend slavery throughout the nation and thus to destroy the openness of northern capitalism and replace it with the closed, aristocratic system of the South. The only solution to this "slave power conspiracy" was to fight the spread of slavery and extend the nation's democratic (i.e., free-labor) ideals to all sections of the country.

This ideology, which lay at the heart of the new Republican Party, also strengthened the commitment of Republicans to the Union. Since the idea of continued growth and progress was central to the free-labor vision, the prospect of

THE BATTLE FOR KANSAS The conflicts over Kansas eventually took on much of the character of a civil war, as this picture of a battle between free-soilers and pro-slavery forces at Hickory Point, Kansas, makes clear. *(Anne S. K. Brown Military Collection, Brown University Library)*

ANTI-ABOLITIONIST VIOLENCE This 1838 woodcut depicts the anti-abolitionist riot in Alton, Illinois, in which Elijah P. Lovejoy, publisher of an abolitionist newspaper, was slain on November 7, 1837. The death of Lovejoy aroused the antislavery movement throughout the United States. *(Library of Congress)*

dismemberment of the nation—a diminution of America's size and economic power—was unthinkable.

The Pro-Slavery Argument

In the South, in the meantime, a very different ideology—entirely incompatible with the free-labor ideology—was emerging out of a rapid hardening of position among southern whites on the issue of slavery. It was a result of many things: the Nat Turner uprising in 1831, which terrified southern whites and made them more determined than ever to make slavery secure; the expansion of the cotton economy into the Deep South, which made slavery unprecedentedly lucrative; and the growth of the Garrisonian abolitionist movement, with its strident attacks on southern society. The popularity of Harriet

Beecher Stowe's *Uncle Tom's Cabin* was perhaps the most glaring evidence of the success of those attacks, but other abolitionist writings had been antagonizing white southerners for years.

In response to these pressures, a number of white southerners produced a new intellectual defense of slavery. Professor Thomas R. Dew of the College of William and Mary helped begin that effort in 1832. Twenty years later, apologists for slavery summarized their views in an anthology that gave their ideology its name: *The Pro-Slavery Argument*. John C. Calhoun stated the essence of the case in 1837: Southerners should stop apologizing for slavery as a necessary evil and defend it as "a good—a positive good." It was good for the slaves, the southern apologists argued, because they enjoyed better conditions than industrial workers in the North. Slavery was good for southern society as a whole because it was the only way the two races could live together in peace. It was good for the entire country because the southern economy, based on slavery, was the key to the prosperity of the nation.

The Pro-Slavery Argument

Above all, southern apologists argued, slavery was good because it served as the basis for the southern way of life—a way of life superior to any other in the United States, perhaps in the world. White southerners looking at the North saw a spirit of greed, debauchery, and destructiveness. "The masses of the North are venal, corrupt, covetous, mean and selfish," wrote one southerner. Others wrote with horror of the factory system and the crowded, pestilential cities filled with unruly immigrants. But the South, they believed, was a stable, orderly society, operating at a slow and human pace. It was free from the feuds between capital and labor plaguing the North. It protected the welfare of its workers. And it allowed the aristocracy to enjoy a refined and accomplished cultural life. It was, in short, an ideal social order in which all elements of the population were secure and content.

The defense of slavery rested, too, on increasingly elaborate arguments about the biological inferiority of African Americans, who were, white Southerners claimed, inherently unfit to take care of themselves, let alone exercise the rights of citizenship. And just as abolitionist arguments drew strength from Protestant theology in the North, the pro-slavery defense mobilized the Protestant clergy in the South to give the institution a religious and biblical justification.

Buchanan and Depression

In this unpromising climate, the presidential campaign of 1856 began. Democratic Party leaders wanted a candidate who, unlike President Pierce, was not closely associated with the explosive question of "Bleeding Kansas." They

Election of 1856

chose James Buchanan of Pennsylvania, a reliable party stalwart who as minister to England had been safely out of the country during the recent controversies. The Republicans, participating in their first presidential contest, denounced the Kansas-Nebraska Act and the expansion of slavery but also endorsed a Whiggish program of internal improvements, thus combining the idealism of antislavery with the economic aspirations of the North. As eager as the Democrats to present a safe candidate, the Republicans nominated John C. Frémont, who had made a national reputation as an explorer of the Far West and who had no political record. The Native American, or Know-Nothing, Party was beginning to break apart, but it nominated former president Millard Fillmore, who also received the endorsement of a sad remnant of the Whig Party.

After a heated, even frenzied campaign, Buchanan won a narrow victory over Frémont and Fillmore. A slight shift of votes in Pennsylvania and Illinois would have elected the Republican candidate. Particularly ominous was that Frémont had attracted virtually no votes at all in the South while outpolling all other candidates in the North. At the time of his inauguration, Buchanan was, at age sixty-five, the oldest president, except for William Henry Harrison, ever to have taken office. Whether because of age and physical infirmities or because of a more fundamental weakness of character, he was a painfully timid and indecisive president at a critical moment in history.

In the year Buchanan took office, a financial panic struck the country, followed by a depression that lasted several years. In the North, the depression strengthened the Republican Party because distressed manufacturers, workers, and farmers came to believe that the hard times were the result of the unsound policies of southern-controlled Democratic administrations. They expressed their frustrations by moving into an alliance with antislavery elements and thus into the Republican Party.

The Dred Scott Decision

On March 6, 1857, the Supreme Court of the United States projected itself into the sectional controversy with one of the most controversial and notorious decisions in its history—its ruling in the case of *Dred Scott* v. *Sandford*, handed down two days after Buchanan was inaugurated. Dred Scott was a Missouri slave, once owned by an army surgeon who had taken Scott with him into Illinois and Wisconsin, where slavery was forbidden. In 1846, after the surgeon died, Scott sued his master's widow for freedom on the grounds that his residence in free territory had liberated him from slavery. The claim was well grounded in Missouri law, and in 1850 the circuit court in which Scott filed the suit declared him free. By now, John Sanford, the brother of the surgeon's widow, was claiming ownership of Scott, and he appealed the circuit court

Two passions of the mid-nineteenth century—education and oratory—combined in the 1830s to create a movement that was both popular and, its creators believed, educational: the lyceum.

The lyceum was not a place, although some places were given its name (which came from a building in ancient Greece where Aristotle had taught). It was an idea. It was the brainchild of Josiah Holbrook, a Yale graduate and schoolteacher who dreamed of bringing knowledge to adults. Holbrook himself gave a series of lectures in Millbury, Massachusetts, in 1826 to an audience of "farmers and mechanics," offering "instruction in the sciences and other branches of useful knowledge." From that modest experiment, the "lyceum movement" quickly spread through Massachusetts, New England, and other parts of the American North and Northwest. (The movement had only a small impact in the South.)

Making use of public libraries, vacant schools, and other existing spaces, lyceum organizers recruited some of the leading scholars, politicians, and orators of their time to provide entertainment and instruction to adult audiences. The topics of lectures were as various as the speakers. The lyceum in Salem, Massachusetts, for example, sponsored lectures in 1838 on "Causes of the American Revolution," "The Sun," "The Legal Rights of Women," and "The Satanic School of Literature and Reform." At the Lowell Institute in Boston, founded in 1830 as "a perennial source of public good—a dispensation of sound science, of useful knowledge, of truth," there were lectures by the geologist Benjamin Silliman (who spoke there ninety-six times), the naturalist Louis Aggasiz, the Russian traveler George Kennan, and the writer Oliver Wendell Holmes (who appeared many times to give a popular lecture on "The Common Law"). Organizers estimated that 13,000 people attended the Lowell lectures in the 1837–1838 season alone. Lectures were open to all (for a small admission charge), but those who attended had to be "neatly dressed and of orderly behavior," and no one could leave the hall while a lecture was in progress. Lyceums may have entertained, but their purpose was to educate. Their founders considered them serious business and expected their audiences to do the same.

As the nation became increasingly preoccupied with sectional divisions and battles over slavery, the lyceums became important forums for discussion of public controversies. In Springfield, Illinois, in 1838, Abraham Lincoln spoke at the Young Men's Lyceum to denounce the lynchings of several slaves in Mississippi and an attack on a free black man in St. Louis—examples, he said, of the "mobocratic spirit" and a challenge to the "reverence for the laws" that should be the "political religion of the nation." In the years that followed, prominent abolitionists—William Lloyd Garrison, Wendell Phillips, Frederick Douglass, and others—became among the most popular lyceum orators in the North. Douglass, a former slave turned antislavery orator, traveled widely speaking at lyceums as far-flung as central Ohio, the island of Nantucket, Massachusetts, and England (where he created a sensation within the British lyceum movement). Douglass mesmerized audiences with his scathing descriptions of life under slavery, and his lyceum lectures helped make him one of the best known and, in the North, most widely admired public figures of his time.

---

ruling to the state supreme court, which reversed the earlier decision. When Scott appealed to the federal courts, Sanford's attorneys claimed that Scott had no standing to sue because he was not a citizen, but private property.

The Supreme Court (which misspelled Sanford's name

Taney's Sweeping Opinion in its decision) was so divided that it was unable to issue a single ruling on the case. The thrust of the various rulings, however, was a stunning defeat for the antislavery movement. Chief Justice Roger Taney, who wrote one of the majority opinions, declared that Scott could not bring a suit in the federal courts because he was not a citizen. Blacks had no claim to citizenship, Taney argued, and in fact virtually no rights at all under the Constitution. Slaves were property, and the Fifth Amendment prohibited Congress from taking property without "due process of law." Consequently, Taney concluded, Congress possessed no authority to pass a law depriving persons of their slave property in the territories. The Missouri Compromise, therefore, had always been unconstitutional.

The ruling did nothing to challenge the right of an individual state to prohibit slavery within its borders, but the statement that the federal government was powerless to act on the issue was a drastic and startling one. Few judicial opinions have ever created as much controversy. Southern whites were elated: the highest tribunal in the land had sanctioned parts of the most extreme southern argument. In the North, the decision produced widespread dismay. Republicans threatened that when they won control of the national government, they would reverse the decision—by "packing" the Court with new members.

Deadlock over Kansas

President Buchanan timidly endorsed the *Dred Scott* decision. At the same time, he tried to resolve the controversy over Kansas by supporting its admission to the Union as a slave state. In response, the pro-slavery territorial legislature called an election for delegates to a constitutional convention. The free-state residents refused to participate, claiming

LYCEUM LECTURE, 1841 This drawing portrays an 1841 Lyceum lecture at Clinton Hall in New York City by James Pollard Espy, a meteorologist. "An army of men of talent," the New York *Mirror* commented at the time, observing the great popularity of the Lyceum series, "has held the town captive." *(Museum of the City of New York)*

At their heart, lyceums always remained what they had been at the start: a place for men and women to educate and improve themselves by listening to knowledgeable speakers talk about what they knew. They both reflected, and helped strengthen, the growing interest in education in mid-nineteenth-century America. They helped drive the expansion and improvement of the public school system in many areas, and they marked the beginning of many decades of efforts to extend the benefits of education to adults. They helped popularize the lecture system of instruction, which remains a staple of university education even today. In the fevered years preceding the Civil War, however, lyceums also helped spread explosive ideas about slavery, freedom, and union that fanned the popular passions of the age.

that the legislature had discriminated against them in drawing district lines. As a result, the pro-slavery forces won control of the convention, which met in 1857 at Lecompton, framed a constitution legalizing slavery, and refused to give voters a chance to reject it. When an election for a new territorial legislature was called, the antislavery groups turned out to vote and won a majority. The new legislature promptly submitted the Lecompton constitution to the voters, who rejected it by more than 10,000 votes.

Both sides had resorted to fraud and violence, but it was clear nevertheless that a majority of the people of Kansas opposed slavery. Buchanan, however, pressured Congress to admit Kansas under the Lecompton constitution. Stephen A. Douglas and other western Democrats refused to support the president's proposal, which died in the House of Representatives. Finally, in April 1858, Congress approved a compromise: The Lecompton constitution would be submitted to the voters of Kansas again. If it was approved, Kansas would be admitted to the Union; if it was rejected, statehood

Lecompton Constitution Rejected

would be postponed. Again, Kansas voters decisively rejected the Lecompton constitution. Not until the closing months of Buchanan's administration in 1861, after several southern states had already withdrawn from the Union, did Kansas enter the Union—as a free state.

The Emergence of Lincoln

Given the gravity of the sectional crisis, the congressional elections of 1858 took on a special importance. Of particular note was the United States Senate election in Illinois, which pitted Stephen A. Douglas, the most prominent northern Democrat, against Abraham Lincoln, who was largely unknown outside Illinois but who quickly emerged as one of the most skillful politicians in the Republican Party.

Lincoln was a successful lawyer who had long been involved in state politics. He had served several terms in the Illinois legislature and one undistinguished term in Congress. But he was not a national figure like Douglas, and so he tried to increase his visibility by engaging Douglas in a

Lincoln-Douglas Debates

365

series of debates. The Lincoln-Douglas debates attracted enormous crowds and received wide attention. By the time they ended, Lincoln's increasingly eloquent and passionate attacks on slavery had made him nationally prominent.

At the heart of the debates was a basic difference on the issue of slavery. Douglas appeared to have no moral position on the issue and, Lincoln claimed, did not care whether slavery was "voted up, or voted down." Lincoln's opposition to slavery was more fundamental. If the nation could accept that blacks were not entitled to basic human rights, he argued, then it could accept that other groups—immigrant laborers, for example—could be deprived of rights, too. And if slavery were to extend into the western territories, he argued, opportunities for poor white laborers to better their lots there would be lost. The nation's future, he argued (reflecting the central idea of the Republican Party), rested on the spread of free labor.

Lincoln believed slavery was morally wrong, but he *Lincoln's Position* was not an abolitionist. That was in part because he could not envision an easy alternative to slavery in the areas where it already existed. He shared the prevailing view among northern whites that the black race was not prepared (and perhaps never would be) to live on equal terms with whites. He and his party would "arrest the further spread" of slavery—that is, prevent its expansion into the territories; they would not directly challenge it where it already existed, but would trust that the institution would gradually die out there of its own accord.

Douglas's position satisfied his followers sufficiently to win him reelection to the Senate, but it aroused little enthusiasm and did nothing to enhance his national political ambitions. Lincoln, by contrast, lost the election but emerged with a growing following both in and beyond the state. And outside Illinois, the elections went heavily against the Democrats, who lost ground in almost every northern state. The party retained control of the Senate but lost its majority in the House, with the result that the congressional sessions of 1858 and 1859 were bitterly deadlocked.

John Brown's Raid

The battles in Congress, however, were almost entirely overshadowed by a spectacular event that enraged and horrified the entire South and greatly hastened the rush toward disunion. In the fall of 1859, John Brown, the antislavery zealot whose bloody actions in Kansas had inflamed the crisis there, staged an even more dramatic episode, this time in the South *John Brown's Raid* itself. With private encouragement and financial aid from some prominent eastern abolitionists, he made elaborate plans to seize a mountain

THE HARPERS FERRY ARSENAL John Brown's famous raid on Harpers Ferry in 1859 centered on this arsenal, from which he and his followers tried, in vain, to foment slave rebellion throughout the South. *(National Park Service, Harper's Ferry. U.S. Department of the Interior)*

fortress in Virginia from which, he believed, he could foment a slave insurrection in the South. On October 16, he and a group of eighteen followers attacked and seized control of a United States arsenal in Harpers Ferry, Virginia. But the slave uprising Brown hoped to inspire did not occur, and he quickly found himself besieged in the arsenal by citizens, local militia companies, and before long United States troops under the command of Robert E. Lee. After ten of his men were killed, Brown surrendered. He was promptly tried in a Virginia court for treason against the state, found guilty, and sentenced to death. He and six of his followers were hanged.

No other single event did more than the Harpers Ferry raid to convince white southerners that they could not live safely in the Union. John Brown's raid, many southerners believed (incorrectly) had the support of the Republican Party, and it suggested to them that the North was now committed to producing a slave insurrection.

The Election of Lincoln

The presidential election of 1860 had the most momentous consequences of any in American history. It was also among the most complex.

The Democratic Party was torn apart by a battle between southerners, who demanded a strong endorsement of slavery, and westerners, who supported the idea of popular sovereignty. The party convention met in April in Charleston, South Carolina. When the convention endorsed popular sovereignty, delegates from eight states in the lower South walked out. The remaining delegates could not agree on a presidential candidate and finally adjourned after agreeing to meet again in Baltimore in June. The decimated convention at Baltimore nominated Stephen Douglas for president. In the meantime, disenchanted southern Democrats met in Richmond and nominated John C. Breckinridge of Kentucky. Later, a group of conservative ex-Whigs met in Baltimore to form the Constitutional Union Party, with John Bell of Tennessee as their presidential candidate. They endorsed the Union and remained silent on slavery.

The Republican leaders, in the meantime, were trying to broaden their appeal so as to attract every major interest group in the North that feared the South was blocking its economic aspirations. The platform endorsed such traditional Whig measures as a high tariff, internal improvements, a homestead bill, and a Pacific railroad to be built with federal financial assistance. It supported the right of each state to decide the status of slavery within its borders. But it also insisted that neither Congress nor territorial legislatures could legalize slavery in the territories. The Republican convention chose Abraham Lincoln as

Divided Democrats

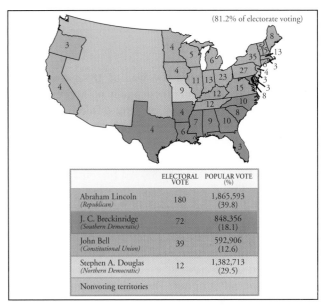

	ELECTORAL VOTE	POPULAR VOTE (%)
Abraham Lincoln *(Republican)*	180	1,865,593 (39.8)
J. C. Breckinridge *(Southern Democratic)*	72	848,356 (18.1)
John Bell *(Constitutional Union)*	39	592,906 (12.6)
Stephen A. Douglas *(Northern Democratic)*	12	1,382,713 (29.5)
Nonvoting territories		

(81.2% of electorate voting)

THE ELECTION OF 1860 The stark sectional divisions that helped produce the Civil War were clearly visible in the results of the 1860 presidential election. Abraham Lincoln, the antislavery Republican candidate, won virtually all the free states. Stephen Douglas, a northern Democrat with no strong position on the issue of slavery, won most of the border states. John Breckinridge, a strong proslavery southern Democrat, carried the entire South. Lincoln won under 40 percent of the popular vote, but because of the four-way division in the race, managed to win a slim majority of the electoral vote. ◆ *What impact did the election of Lincoln have on the sectional crisis?*

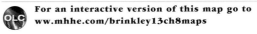 **For an interactive version of this map go to ww.mhhe.com/brinkley13ch8maps**

the party's presidential nominee. Lincoln was appealing because of his growing reputation for eloquence, because of his firm but moderate position on slavery, and because his relative obscurity ensured that he would have none of the drawbacks of other, more prominent (and therefore more controversial) Republicans. He was a representative of the West, a considerable asset in a race against Douglas.

In the November election, Lincoln won the presidency with a majority of the electoral votes but only about two-fifths of the fragmented popular vote. The Republicans, moreover, failed to win a majority in Congress. Even so, the election of Lincoln became the final signal to many white southerners that their position in the Union was hopeless. And within a few weeks of Lincoln's victory, the process of disunion began—a process that would quickly lead to a prolonged and bloody war between two groups of Americans, each heir to more than a century of struggling toward nationhood, each now convinced that it shared no common ground with the other.

Disunion

CONCLUSION

In the decades following the War of 1812, a vigorous sense of nationalism pervaded much of American life, helping to smooth over the growing differences among the very different societies emerging in the regions of the United States. During the 1850s, however, the forces that had worked to hold the nation together in the past fell victim to new and much more divisive pressures that were working to split the nation apart.

Driving the sectional tensions of the 1850s was a battle over national policy toward the western territories, which were clamoring to become states of the Union—and over the place of slavery within them. Should slavery be permitted in the new states? And who should decide whether to permit it or not? There were strenuous efforts to craft compromises and solutions to this dilemma: the Compromise of 1850, the Kansas-Nebraska Act of 1854, and others. But despite these efforts, positions on slavery continued to harden in both the North and South until ultimately each region came to consider the other its enemy. Bitter battles in the territory of Kansas over whether to permit slavery there; growing agitation by abolitionists

in the North and pro-slavery advocates in the South; the Supreme Court's controversial *Dred Scott* decision in 1857; the popularity of *Uncle Tom's Cabin* throughout the decade; and the emergence of a new political party—the Republican party—openly and centrally opposed to slavery: all worked to destroy the hopes for compromise and push the South toward secession.

In 1860, all pretense of common sentiment collapsed when no political party presented a presidential candidate capable of attracting national support. The Republicans nominated Abraham Lincoln of Illinois, a little-known politician recognized for his eloquent condemnations of slavery in a Senate race two years earlier. The Democratic party split apart, with its northern and southern wings each nominating different candidates. A third party, devoted to the Constitution and the Union, forlornly nominated a candidate of its own who found almost no constituency at all. Lincoln won the election easily, but with less than forty percent of the vote. And almost immediately after his victory, the states of the South began preparing to secede from the Union.

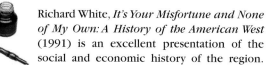

FOR FURTHER REFERENCE

Richard White, *It's Your Misfortune and None of My Own: A History of the American West* (1991) is an excellent presentation of the social and economic history of the region. Anders Stephanson, *Manifest Destiny* (1995) briefly traces the origins of American expansion ideology. Robert M. Johannsen, *To the Halls of Montezuma: The Mexican War in the American Imagination* (1985) examines public attitudes toward the conflict. Paul D. Lack, *The Texas Revolutionary Experience: A Political and Social History, 1835–1836* (1992) chronicles Texas's route to independence from Mexico. Malcolm Rorabaugh, *Days of Gold: The California Gold Rush and the American Nation* (1997) is an account of this seminal event in the history of the West. Susan Lee Johnson, *Roaring Camp: The Social World of the Gold Rush* (2000) examines the experiences of men and

women involved in the frenzy. David M. Pletcher, *The Diplomacy of Annexation: Texas, Oregon, and the Mexican War* (1973) is the standard work on war and diplomacy in the 1840s. Reginald Horsman, *Race and Manifest Destiny* (1981) is a seminal study of racial views in antebellum America. William W. Freehling, *The Road to Disunion, Vol. 1: Secessionists at Bay, 1776–1854* (1990) explores the successful containment of sectionalism prior to the 1850s. David Potter, *The Impending Crisis, 1848–1861* (1976) is a thorough summary of the decisive decade. Eric Foner, *Free Soil, Free Labor, Free Men* (1970) traces the emergence of the Republican Party. Michael Holt, *The Political Crisis of the 1850s* (1978) challenges Foner by emphasizing ethnic and religious alignment in northern politics. Don E. Fehrenbacher, *The Dred Scott Case* (1978) explains the Supreme Court's most infamous decision.

OLC

For quizzes, Internet resources, references to additional books and films, and more, consult the book's Online Learning Center at www.mhhe.com/brinkley11.

YOUNG SOLDIER This somber 1864 painting by
Winslow Homer portrays a young Union soldier—
perhaps a drummer boy. When they were not playing
music, drummers and buglers performed other functions
in camp, as barbers, valets, and members of burial teams.
Boys as young as 12 and 13 sometimes joined the army
and grew up quickly in the rough surroundings of the
camps. *(Cooper-Hewitt Museum, Smithsonian Institution.
Gift of Charles Savage Homer, 1912-12-110/Art Resource, NY)*

Significant Events

1860	South Carolina secedes from Union
1861	Ten more Southern states secede
	Confederate States of America formed
	Jefferson Davis named president of Confederacy
	Conflict at Fort Sumter, South Carolina (April 12–14), begins Civil War
	George B. McClellan appointed commander of Army of the Potomac and army chief of staff
	Union blockades Confederate coast
	Trent affair imperils U.S. relations with Britain
	First Battle of Bull Run
1862	Battle of Shiloh (April 6–7)
	Union forces capture New Orleans (April 25)
	Second Battle of Bull Run (August 29–30)
	Battle of Antietam (September 17)

CHAPTER FOURTEEN

THE CIVIL WAR

By the end of 1860, the cords that had once bound the Union together seemed to have snapped. The almost mystical veneration of the Constitution and its framers was no longer working to unite the nation; most residents of the North and South—particularly after the controversial *Dred Scott* decision—now differed fundamentally on their interpretations of the Constitution and what the framers had meant. The romantic vision of America's great national destiny had ceased to be a unifying force; the two sections now defined that destiny in different and apparently irreconcilable terms. The stable two-party system could not dampen sectional conflict any longer; that system had collapsed in the 1850s, to be replaced by a new one that accentuated, rather than muted, regional controversy. Above all, the federal government was no longer the remote, unthreatening presence it once had been; the need to resolve the status of the territories had made it necessary for Washington to deal with sectional issues in a direct and forceful way. And thus, beginning in 1860, the divisive forces that had always existed within the United States were no longer counterbalanced by unifying forces. As a result, the Union began to dissolve.

THE SECESSION CRISIS

Almost as soon as the news of Abraham Lincoln's election reached the South, the militant leaders of the region—the champions of the new concept of "Southern nationalism," men known both to their contemporaries and to history as the "fire-eaters"—began to demand an end to the Union.

"Southern Nationalism"

The Withdrawal of the South

South Carolina, long the hotbed of Southern separatism, seceded first. It called a special convention, which voted unanimously on December 20, 1860, to withdraw the state from the Union. By the time Lincoln took office, six other states—Mississippi (January 9, 1861), Florida (January 10), Alabama (January 11), Georgia (January 19), Louisiana (January 26), and Texas (February 1)—had seceded. In February 1861, representatives of the seven seceded states met at Montgomery, Alabama, and formed a new nation: the Confederate States of America. The response from the North was confused and indecisive. President James Buchanan told Congress in December 1860 that no state had the right to secede from the Union but suggested that the federal government had no authority to stop a state if it did.

Establishment of the Confederacy

The seceding states immediately seized the federal property—forts, arsenals, government offices—within their boundaries. But at first they did not have sufficient military power to seize two fortified offshore military installations: Fort Sumter, on an island in the harbor of Charleston, South Carolina, garrisoned by a small force under Major Robert Anderson; and Fort Pickens in the harbor of Pensacola, Florida. South Carolina sent commissioners to Washington to ask for the surrender of Sumter; but Buchanan, timid though he was, refused to yield it. Indeed, in January 1861 he ordered an unarmed merchant ship to proceed to Fort Sumter with additional troops and supplies. Confederate guns on shore fired at the vessel—the first shots between North and South—and turned it back. Still, neither section was yet ready to concede that war had begun. And in Washington, efforts began once more to forge a compromise.

The Failure of Compromise

Gradually, the compromise forces gathered behind a proposal first submitted by Senator John J. Crittenden of Kentucky and known as the Crittenden Compromise. It called for several constitutional amendments, which would guarantee the permanent existence of slavery in the slave states and would satisfy Southern demands on such issues as fugitive slaves and slavery in the District of Columbia. But the heart of Crittenden's plan was a proposal to reestablish the Missouri Compromise line in all present and future territory of the United States: Slavery would be prohibited north of the line and permitted south of it. The remaining southerners in the Senate seemed willing to accept the plan, but the Republicans were not. The compromise would have required the Republicans to abandon their most fundamental position: that slavery not be allowed to expand.

Crittenden Compromise

And so nothing had been resolved when Abraham Lincoln arrived in Washington for his inauguration—sneaking into the city in disguise on a night train to avoid assassination as he passed through the slave state of Maryland. In his inaugural address, which dealt directly with the secession crisis, Lincoln laid down several basic principles. Since the Union was older than the Constitution, no state could leave it. Acts of force or violence to support secession were insurrectionary. And the government would "hold, occupy, and possess" federal property in the seceded states—a clear reference to Fort Sumter.

Fort Sumter

Conditions at Fort Sumter were deteriorating quickly. Union forces were running short of supplies; unless they received fresh provisions the fort would have to be evacuated. Lincoln believed that if he surrendered Sumter, his commitment to maintaining the Union would no longer be credible. So he sent a relief expedition to the fort,

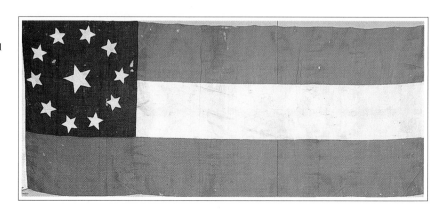

AN EARLY CONFEDERATE FLAG This early Confederate naval flag was seized by Union forces when they captured New Orleans in April 1862. *(The Museum of the Confederacy, Richmond, Virginia. Photography by Katherine Wetzel)*

FORT SUMTER DURING THE BOMBARDMENT This graphic drawing shows the interior of Fort Sumter during its bombardment by Confederate forces in April 1861. Union forces faced the dual problem of heavy artillery and cannon fire, and dwindling supplies—since the Confederates had blockaded the Charleston harbor to prevent the North from resupplying the fort. *(National Geographic Society)*

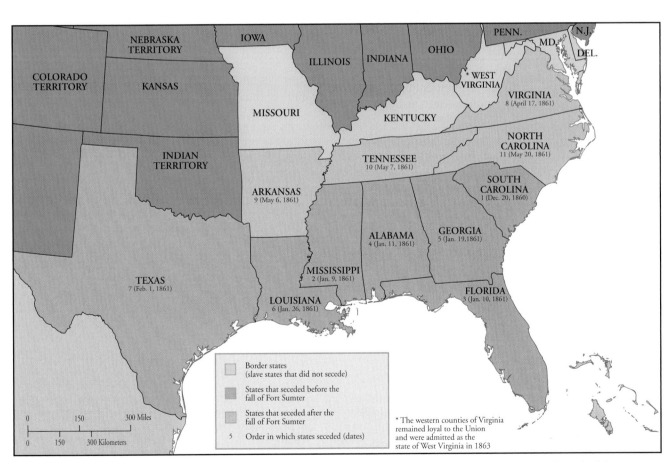

THE PROCESS OF SECESSION The election of Lincoln, the candidate of the antislavery Republican party, to the presidency had the immediate result of inspiring many of the states in the deep South to secede from the Union, beginning with South Carolina only a little more than a month after the November election. Other states nearer the northern border of the slaveholding region remained in the Union for a time, but the U.S. attempt to resupply Fort Sumter (and the bombardment of the fort by the new Confederate army) mobilized the upper South to secede as well. Only enormous pressure from the federal government kept the slaveholding states of Maryland, Kentucky, and Missouri in the Union. ◆ *What accounted for the creation of the state of West Virginia in 1861?*

 For an interactive version of this map go to www.mhhe.com/brinkley11ch14maps

carefully informing the South Carolina authorities that there would be no attempt to send troops or munitions unless the supply ships met with resistance.

The new Confederate government now faced a dilemma. Permitting the expedition to land would seem to be a tame submission to federal authority. Firing on the ships or the fort would seem (to the North at least) to be aggression. But Confederate leaders finally decided that to appear cowardly would be worse than to appear belligerent, and they ordered General P. G. T. Beauregard, com-

The War Begins | mander of Confederate forces at Charleston, to take the island, by force if necessary. When Anderson refused to surrender the fort, the Confederates bombarded it for two days, April 12–13, 1861. On April 14, Anderson surrendered. The Civil War had begun.

Almost immediately, Lincoln began mobilizing the North for war. And equally promptly, four more slave states seceded from the Union and joined the Confederacy: Virginia (April 17, 1861), Arkansas (May 6), Tennessee (June 8), and North Carolina (May 20). The four remaining slave states—Maryland, Delaware, Kentucky, and Missouri—cast their lot with the Union (under heavy political and even military pressure from Washington).

Was there anything that Lincoln (or those before him) could have done to settle the sectional conflict peaceably? That question has preoccupied historians for more than a century without resolution (see "Where Historians Disagree," pp. 376–377). There were, of course, actions that might have prevented a war: if, for example, northern leaders had decided to let the South withdraw in peace. The real question, however, is not what hypothetical situations might have reversed the trend toward war but whether the preponderance of forces in the nation were acting to hold the nation together or to drive it apart. And by 1861, it seems clear that in both the North and the South, sectional antagonisms—whether justified or not—had risen to such a point that the existing terms of union had become untenable.

People in both regions had come to believe that two distinct and incompatible civilizations had developed in the United States and that those civilizations were incapable of living together in peace. Ralph Waldo Emerson, speaking for much of the North, said at the time: "I do not see how a barbarous community and a civilized community can constitute one state." And a slaveowner, expressing the sentiments of much of the South, said shortly after the election of Lincoln: "These [Northern] people hate us, annoy us, and would have us assassinated by our slaves if they dared. They are a different people from us, whether better or worse, and there is no love between us. Why then continue together?"

That the North and the South had come to believe these things helped lead to secession and war. Whether these things were actually true—whether the North and the South were really as different and incompatible as they

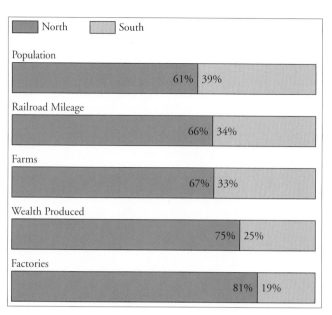

UNION AND CONFEDERATE RESOURCES Virtually all the material advantages—population, manufacturing, railroads, wealth, even agriculture—lay with the North during the Civil War, as this chart shows. ◆ *What advantages did the South have in the conflict?*

thought—is another question, one that the preparations for and conduct of the war help to answer.

The Opposing Sides

As the war began, only one thing was clear: all the important material advantages lay with the North. Its population was more than twice as large as that of the South (and *Union Advantages* nearly four times as large as the nonslave population of the South), so the Union had a much greater manpower reserve both for its armies and its work force. The North had an advanced industrial system and was able by 1862 to manufacture almost all its own war materials. The South had almost no industry at all and, despite impressive efforts to increase its manufacturing capacity, had to rely on imports from Europe throughout the war.

In addition, the North had a much better transportation system than did the South, and in particular more and better railroads: twice as much trackage as the Confederacy, and a much better integrated system of lines. During the war, moreover, the already inferior Confederate railroad system steadily deteriorated and by the beginning of 1864 had almost collapsed.

But in the beginning the North's material advantages were not as decisive as they appear in retrospect. The South was, for the most part, fighting a defensive war on its own land and thus had the advantage of local support and familiarity with the territory. The Northern armies, on the other hand, were fighting mostly within the South, with long lines of communications, amid hostile local populations, and with access only to the

WAR BY RAILROAD Union soldiers pose beside a mortar mounted on a railroad car in July 1864, during the siege of Petersburg, Virginia. Railroads played a critical role in the Civil War, and the superiority of the North's rail system was an important factor in its victory. It was appropriate, perhaps, that the battle for Petersburg, the last great struggle of the war, was over control of critical railroad lines. *(National Archives and Records Administration)*

South's own inadequate transportation system. The commitment of the white population of the South to the war was, with limited ex-

Southern Advantages

ceptions, clear and firm. In the North, opinion about the war was more divided and support for it remained shaky until very near the end. A major Southern victory at any one of several crucial moments might have proved decisive by breaking the North's will to continue the struggle. Finally, many Southerners believed that the dependence of the English and French textile industries on American cotton would require them to intervene on the side of the Confederacy.

THE MOBILIZATION OF THE NORTH

In the North, the war produced considerable discord, frustration, and suffering. But it also produced prosperity and economic growth by giving a major stimulus to both industry and agriculture.

Economic Measures

With Southern forces now gone from Congress, the Republican Party could exercise virtually unchallenged authority. During the war, it enacted an aggressively nationalistic program to promote economic development,

In his second inaugural address in March 1865, Abraham Lincoln looked back at the beginning of the Civil War four years earlier. "All knew," he said, that slavery "was somehow the cause of the war." Few historians in the decades since Lincoln spoke have doubted the basic truth of Lincoln's statement; no credible explanation of the causes of the Civil War can ignore slavery. But historians have, nevertheless, disagreed sharply about many things. Was the Civil War inevitable, or could it have been avoided? Was slavery the only, or even the principal, cause of the war? Were other factors equally or more important?

This debate began even before the war itself. In 1858, Senator William H. Seward of New York took note of two competing explanations of the sectional tensions that were then inflaming the nation. On one side, he claimed, stood those who believed the sectional hostility to be "accidental, unnecessary, the work of interested or fanatical agitators." Opposing them stood those (like Seward himself) who believed there to be "an irrepressible conflict between opposing and enduring forces." For at least a century, the division Seward described remained at the heart of scholarly debate.

The "irrepressible conflict" argument was the first to dominate historical discussion. In the first decades after the fighting, histories of the Civil War generally reflected the views of Northerners who had themselves participated in the conflict. To them, the war appeared to be a stark moral conflict in which the South was clearly to blame, a conflict that arose inevitably as a result of the militant immorality of slave society. Henry Wilson's *History of the Rise and Fall of the Slave Power* (1872–1877) was a particularly vivid version of this moral interpretation of the war, which argued that Northerners had fought to preserve the Union and a system of free labor against the aggressive designs of the South.

A more temperate interpretation, but one that reached generally the same conclusions, emerged in the 1890s, when the first serious histories of the war began to appear. Preeminent among them was the seven-volume *History of the United States from the Compromise of 1850 . . .* (1893–1900) by James Ford Rhodes. Like Wilson and others, Rhodes identified slavery as the central, indeed virtually the only, cause of the war. "If the Negro had not been brought to America," he wrote, "the Civil War could not have occurred." And because the North and South had reached positions on the issue of slavery that were both irreconcilable and unalterable, the conflict had become "inevitable."

Although Rhodes placed his greatest emphasis on the moral conflict over slavery, he suggested that the struggle also reflected fundamental differences between the Northern and Southern economic systems. In the 1920s, the idea of the war as an irrepressible economic, rather than moral, conflict received fuller expression from Charles and Mary Beard in *The Rise of American Civilization* (2 vols., 1927). Slavery, the Beards claimed, was not so much a social or cultural institution as an economic one, a labor system. There were, they insisted, "inherent antagonisms" between Northern industrialists and Southern planters. Each group sought to control the federal government so as to protect its own economic interests. Both groups used arguments over slavery and states' rights largely as smoke screens.

The economic determinism of the Beards influenced a generation of historians in important ways, but ultimately most of those who believed the Civil War to have been "irrepressible" returned to an emphasis on social and cultural factors. Allan Nevins argued as much in his great work, *The Ordeal of the Union* (8 vols., 1947–1971). The North and the South, he wrote, "were rapidly becoming separate peoples." At the root of these cultural differences was the "problem of slavery," but the "fundamental assumptions, tastes, and cultural aims" of the two regions were diverging in other ways as well.

More recent proponents of the "irrepressible conflict" argument have taken different views of the Northern and Southern positions on the conflict but have been equally insistent on the role of culture and ideology in creating them. Eric Foner, in *Free Soil, Free Labor, Free Men* (1970) and other writings, emphasized the importance of the "free-labor ideology" to Northern opponents of slavery. The moral concerns of the abolitionists were not the dominant sentiments in the North, he claimed. Instead, most Northerners (including Abraham

(*National Geographic Society*)

Lincoln) opposed slavery largely because they feared it might spread to the North and threaten the position of free white laborers. Convinced that Northern society was superior to that of the South, and increasingly persuaded of the South's intentions to extend the "slave power" beyond its existing borders, Northerners were embracing a viewpoint that made conflict almost inevitable. Eugene Genovese, writing of Southern slaveholders in *The Political Economy of Slavery* (1965), emphasized their conviction that the slave system provided a far more humane society than industrial labor, that the South had constructed "a special civilization built on the relation of master to slave." Just as Northerners were becoming convinced of a Southern threat to their economic system, so Southerners believed that the North had aggressive and hostile designs on the Southern way of life. Like Foner, therefore, Genovese saw in the cultural outlook of the section the source of an all but inevitable conflict.

Historians who argue that the conflict emerged naturally, even inevitably, out of a fundamental divergence between the sections have therefore disagreed markedly over whether moral, cultural, social, ideological, or economic issues were the primary causes of the Civil War. But they have been in general accord that the conflict between North and South was deeply embedded in the nature of the two societies, that slavery was somehow at the heart of the differences, and that the crisis that ultimately emerged was irrepressible. Other historians, however, have questioned that assumption and have argued that the Civil War might have been avoided, that the differences between North and South were not so fundamental as to have necessitated war. Like proponents of the "irrepressible conflict" school, advocates of the war as a "repressible conflict" emerged first in the nineteenth century. President James Buchanan, for example, believed that extremist agitators were to blame for the conflict, and many Southerners writing of the war in the late nineteenth century claimed

(Library of Congress)

that only the fanaticism of the Republican Party could account for the conflict.

The idea of the war as avoidable gained wide recognition among historians in the 1920s and 1930s, when a group known as the "revisionists" began to offer new accounts of the origins of the conflict. One of the leading revisionists was James G. Randall, who saw in the social and economic systems of the North and the South no differences so fundamental as to require a war. Slavery, he suggested, was an essentially benign institution; it was in any case already "crumbling in the presence of nineteenth century tendencies." Only the political ineptitude of a "blundering generation" of leaders could account for the Civil War, he claimed. Avery Craven, another leading revisionist, placed more emphasis on the issue of slavery than had Randall. But in *The Coming of the Civil War* (1942) he too argued that slave laborers were not much worse off than Northern industrial workers, that the institution was already on the road to "ultimate extinction," and that war could therefore have been averted had skillful and responsible leaders worked to produce compromise.

More recent students of the war have kept elements of the revisionist interpretation alive by emphasizing the role of political agitation and ethnocultural conflicts in the coming of the war. In 1960, for example, David Herbert Donald argued that the politicians of the 1850s were not unusually inept, but that they were operating in a society in which traditional restraints

were being eroded in the face of the rapid extension of democracy. Thus the sober, statesmanlike solution of differences was particularly difficult. Michael Holt, in *The Political Crisis of the 1850s* (1978), emphasized the role of political parties and especially the collapse of the second party system, rather than the irreconcilable differences between sections, in explaining the conflict, although he avoided placing blame on any one group.

Holt, however, also helped introduce another element to the debate. He was, along with Paul Kleppner, Joel Silbey, and William Gienapp, one of the creators of an "ethnocultural" interpretation of the war. The Civil War began, the ethnoculturalists argue, in large part because the party system—the most effective instrument for containing and mediating sectional differences—collapsed in the 1850s and produced a new Republican party that aggravated, rather than calmed, the divisions in the nation. But unlike other scholars, who saw the debate over slavery as the central factor in the collapse of the party system, the ethnoculturalists argue for other factors. For example, William Gienapp, in *The Origins of the Republican Party, 1852–1856* (1987) argues that the disintegration of the party system in the early 1850s was less a result of the debate over slavery in the territories than of such ethnocultural issues as temperance and nativism. The Republican Party itself, he argues, was less a product of antislavery fervor than of a sustained competition with the Know-Nothing Party over ethnic and cultural issues. Gienapp and the other ethnoculturalists would not entirely dispute Lincoln's claim that slavery was "somehow the cause of the war." But they do challenge the arguments of Eric Foner and others that the "free labor ideal" of the North—and the challenge slavery, and its possible expansion into the territories, posed to that ideal—was the principal reason for the conflict. Slavery became important, they suggest, less because of irreconcilable differences of attitude than because of the collapse of parties and other structures that might have contained the conflict.

particularly in the West. The Homestead Act of 1862 permitted any citizen or prospective citizen to claim 160 acres of public land and to purchase it for a small fee after living on it for five years. The Morrill Land Grant Act of the same year transferred substantial public acreage to the state governments, which were to sell the land and use the proceeds to finance public education. This act led to the creation of many new state colleges and universities, the so-called land-grant institutions. Congress also passed a series of tariff bills that by the end of the war had raised duties to the highest level in the nation's history—a great boon to domestic industries eager for protection from foreign competition.

Republican Economic Policy

Congress also moved to complete the dream of a transcontinental railroad. It created two new federally chartered corporations: the Union Pacific Railroad Company, which was to build westward from Omaha, and the Central Pacific, which was to build eastward from California. The two projects were to meet in the middle and complete the link. The government provided free public lands and generous loans to the companies.

The National Bank Acts of 1863–1864 created a new national banking system. Existing or newly formed banks could join the system if they had enough capital and were willing to invest one-third of it in government securities. In return, they could issue U.S. Treasury notes as currency. The new system eliminated much of the chaos and uncertainty in the nation's currency and created a uniform system of national bank notes.

National Bank Acts

More difficult than promoting economic growth was financing the war itself. The government tried to do so in three ways: by levying taxes, issuing paper currency, and borrowing. Congress levied new taxes on almost all goods and services; and in 1861 the government levied an income tax for the first time, with rates that eventually rose to 10 percent on incomes above $5,000. But taxation raised only a small proportion of the funds necessary for financing the war, and strong popular resistance prevented the government from raising the rates. At least equally controversial was the printing of paper currency, or "greenbacks." The new currency was backed not by gold or silver, but simply by the good faith and credit of the government (much like today's currency). The value of the greenbacks fluctuated according to the fortunes of the Northern armies. Early in 1864, with the war effort bogged down, a greenback dollar was worth only 39 percent of a gold dollar. Even at the close of the war, it was worth only 67 percent of a gold dollar. Because of the difficulty of making purchases with this uncertain currency, the government used greenbacks sparingly. The Treasury issued only $450 million worth of paper currency—a small proportion of the cost of the war but enough to produce significant inflation.

Financing the War

By far the largest source of financing for the war was loans from the American people. In previous wars, the government had sold bonds only to banks and to a few wealthy investors. Now, however, the Treasury persuaded ordinary citizens to buy over $400 million worth of bonds—the first example of mass financing of a war in American history. Still, bond purchases by individuals constituted only a small part of the government's borrowing, which in the end totaled $2.6 billion. Most of the loans came from banks and large financial interests.

Raising the Union Armies

Over 2 million men served in the Union armed forces during the course of the Civil War. But at the beginning of 1861, the regular army of the United States consisted of

SENDING THE BOYS OFF TO WAR In this painting by Thomas Nast, New York's Seventh Regiment parades down Broadway in April 1861, to the cheers of exuberant, patriotic throngs, shortly before departing to fight in what most people then assumed would be a brief war. Thomas Nast is better known for his famous political cartoons of the 1870s. *(Seventh Regiment Armory, New York City)*

only 16,000 troops, many of them stationed in the West to protect white settlers from Indians. So the Union, like the Confederacy, had to raise its army mostly from scratch. Lincoln called for an increase of 23,000 in the regular army, but the bulk of the fighting, he knew, would have to be done by volunteers in state militias. When Congress convened in July 1861, it authorized enlisting 500,000 volunteers for three-year terms (as opposed to the customary three-month terms). This voluntary system of recruitment produced adequate forces only briefly. After the first flush of enthusiasm for the war, enlistments declined. By March 1863, Congress was forced to pass a national draft law. Virtually all young adult males were eligible to be drafted; but a man could escape service by hiring someone to go in his place or by paying the government a fee of $300. Only about 46,000 men were ever actually conscripted, but the draft greatly increased voluntary enlistments.

To a people accustomed to a remote and inactive national government, conscription was strange and ominous. Opposition to the law was widespread, particularly

Draft Riots among laborers, immigrants, and Democrats opposed to the war (known as "Peace Democrats"). Occasionally it erupted into violence. Demonstrators against the draft rioted in New York City for four days in July 1863, after the first names were selected for conscription. Over 100 people died. Irish workers were at the center of the violence. They were angry because black strikebreakers had been used against them in a recent longshoremen's strike; and they blamed African Americans generally for the war, which they thought was being fought for the benefit of slaves who would soon be competing with white workers for jobs. The rioters lynched a number of African Americans, burned down homes and businesses (mostly those of free blacks), and even destroyed an orphanage for African-American children. Only the arrival of federal troops subdued the rioters.

HANGING A NEGRO IN CLARKSON STREET.

THE NEW YORK CITY DRAFT RIOT, 1863 Opposition to the Civil War draft was widespread in the North and in July 1863 produced a violent four-day uprising in New York City in which as many as 100 people died. The riot began on July 13 with a march by 4,000 men, mostly poor Irish laborers, who were protesting the provisions by which some wealthy people could be exempted from conscription. "Rich man's war, poor man's fight," the demonstrators cried (just as some critics of the war chanted at times in the South). Many New Yorkers also feared that the war would drive black workers north to compete for their jobs. The demonstration turned violent when officials began drawing names for the draft. The crowd burned the draft building and then split into factions. Some rioters attacked symbols of wealth such as exclusive shops and mansions. Others terrorized black neighborhoods and lynched some residents. This contemporary engraving depicts one such lynching. Only by transferring five regiments to the city from Gettysburg (less than two weeks after the great battle there) was the government able to restore order. *(The Granger Collection)*

Wartime Politics

When Abraham Lincoln arrived in Washington early in 1861, many politicians—noting his lack of national experience and his folksy, unpretentious manner—considered him a minor politician from the prairies, a man whom the real leaders of his party would easily control. But the new president moved quickly to establish his own authority. He assembled a cabinet representing every faction of the Republican Party and every segment of Northern opinion—men of exceptional prestige and influence and in some cases arrogance, several of whom believed that they, not Lincoln, should be president. Lincoln moved boldly as well to use the war powers of the presidency, ignoring inconvenient parts of the Constitution because, he said, it would be foolish to lose the whole by being afraid to disregard a part. He sent troops into battle without asking Congress for

a declaration of war. (Lincoln insisted on calling the conflict a domestic insurrection, which required no formal declaration of war; to ask for a declaration would, he believed, constitute implicit recognition of the Confederacy as an independent nation.) He increased the size of the regular army without receiving legislative authority to do so. He unilaterally proclaimed a naval blockade of the South.

Lincoln's greatest political problem was the widespread popular opposition to the war, mobilized by factions in the Democratic Party. The Peace Democrats (or, as their enemies called them, "Copperheads") feared that agriculture and the Northwest were losing influence to industry and the East and that Republican nationalism was eroding states' rights. Lincoln used extraordinary methods to suppress them. He ordered military arrests of civilian dissenters and suspended the right of habeas corpus (the right of an arrested person to a speedy trial). At first, Lincoln used these methods only in sensitive areas such as the border states; but in 1862, he proclaimed that all persons who discouraged enlistments or engaged in disloyal practices were subject to martial law. In all, more than 13,000 persons were arrested and imprisoned for varying periods. The most prominent Copperhead in the country—Clement L. Vallandigham, a member of Congress from Ohio—was seized by military authorities and exiled to the Confederacy after he made a speech claiming that the purpose of the war was to free the blacks and enslave the whites. Lincoln defied all efforts to curb his authority to suppress opposition. He even defied the Supreme Court. When Chief Justice Taney issued a writ (*Ex parte Merryman*) requiring him to release an imprisoned Maryland secessionist leader, Lincoln simply ignored it. (After the war, in 1866, the Supreme Court ruled in *Ex parte Milligan* that military trials in areas where the civil courts existed were unconstitutional.)

The presidential election of 1864 occurred, therefore, in the midst of considerable political dissension. The Republicans had suffered heavy losses in the congressional elections of 1862, and in response leaders of the party tried to create a broad coalition of all the groups that supported the war. They called the new organization the Union Party, but in reality it was little more than the Republican Party and a small faction of War Democrats. The Union Party nominated Lincoln for another term as president and Andrew Johnson of Tennessee, a War Democrat who had opposed his state's decision to secede, for the vice presidency.

The Democrats nominated George B. McClellan, a celebrated former Union general who had been relieved of his command by Lincoln, and adopted a platform denouncing the war and calling for a truce. McClellan repudiated that demand, but the Democrats were clearly the peace party in the campaign, trying to profit from growing war weariness and from the Union's discouraging military position in the summer of 1864.

At this crucial moment, however, several Northern military victories, particularly the capture of Atlanta, Georgia, early in September, rejuvenated Northern morale and boosted Republican prospects. *1864 Election* Lincoln won reelection comfortably, with 212 electoral votes to McClellan's 21; the president carried every state except Kentucky, New Jersey, and Delaware. But Lincoln's lead in the popular vote was a more modest 10 percent. Had Union victories not occurred when they did, and had Lincoln not made special arrangements to allow Union troops to vote, the Democrats might have won.

The Politics of Emancipation

Despite their surface unity in 1864 and their general agreement on most economic matters, the Republicans disagreed sharply on the issue of slavery. Radicals—led in Congress by such men as Representative Thaddeus Stevens of Pennsylvania and Senators Charles Sumner of Massachusetts and Benjamin Wade of Ohio—wanted to use the war to abolish slavery immediately and completely. Conservatives favored a slower, more gradual, and, they believed, less disruptive process for ending slavery; in the beginning, at least, they had the support of the president.

Despite Lincoln's cautious view of emancipation, momentum began to gather behind it early in the war. In 1861, Congress passed the Confiscation Act, which declared that all slaves used for "insurrectionary" purposes (that *Confiscation Acts* is, in support of the Confederate military effort) would be considered freed. Subsequent laws in the spring of 1862 abolished slavery in the District of Columbia and in the western territories, and compensated owners. In July 1862, the Radicals pushed through Congress the second Confiscation Act, which declared free the slaves of persons aiding and supporting the insurrection (whether or not the slaves themselves were doing so) and authorized the president to employ African Americans, including freed slaves, as soldiers. As the war progressed, much of the North seemed slowly to accept emancipation as a central war aim; nothing less, many believed, would justify the enormous sacrifices of the struggle. As a result, the Radicals increased their influence within the Republican Party—a development that did not go unnoticed by the president, who decided to seize the leadership of the rising antislavery sentiment himself.

On September 22, 1862, after the Union victory at the Battle of Antietam, the president announced his intention to use his war powers to issue an executive order freeing all *Emancipation Proclamation* slaves in the Confederacy. And on January 1, 1863, he formally signed the Emancipation Proclamation, which declared forever free slaves in all areas of the Confederacy except those already under Union control: Tennessee, western Virginia, and southern Louisiana. The proclamation did not apply to the border slave states, which had never seceded from the Union and therefore were not subject to the president's war powers.

The immediate effect of the proclamation was limited, since it applied only to slaves still under Confederate control. But the document was of great importance nevertheless, because it clearly and irrevocably established that the war was being fought not only to preserve the Union but also to eliminate slavery. Eventually, as federal armies occupied much of the South, the proclamation became a practical reality and led directly to the freeing of thousands of slaves. Even in areas not directly affected by the proclamation, the antislavery impulse gained strength. By the end of the war, slavery had been abolished in two Union slave states—Maryland and Missouri—and in three Confederate states occupied by Union forces—Tennessee, Arkansas, and Louisiana. The final step came in 1865,

AFRICAN-AMERICAN TROOPS Although most of the black soldiers who enlisted in the Union army during the Civil War performed non-combat jobs behind the lines, there were also black combat regiments—members of one of which are pictured here—who fought with great success and valor in critical battles. *(Library of Congress)*

when Congress approved and the necessary states ratified the Thirteenth Amendment, abolishing slavery as an institution in all parts of the United States. After more than two centuries, legalized slavery finally ceased to exist in the United States.

African Americans and the Union Cause

About 186,000 emancipated blacks served as soldiers, sailors, and laborers for the Union forces, joining a significant number of free blacks from the North. The services of African Americans to the Union military were significant in many ways, not least because of the substantial obstacles many blacks had to surmount in order to enlist.

In the first months of the war, African Americans were largely excluded from the military. A few black regiments *Black Enlistment* eventually took shape in some of the Union-occupied areas of the Confederacy, largely because they were a ready source of manpower in these defeated regions. But once Lincoln issued the Emancipation Proclamation, black enlistment increased rapidly and the Union military began actively to recruit African-American soldiers and sailors in both the North and, where possible, the South.

Some of these men were organized into fighting units, of which the best known was probably the Fifty-fourth Massachusetts infantry, which (like most black regiments) had a white commander: Robert Gould Shaw, a member of an aristocratic Boston family. Shaw and more than half his regiment died during a battle near Charleston, South Carolina, in the summer of 1863.

Most black soldiers, however, were assigned menial tasks behind the lines, such as digging trenches and transporting water. Even though fewer blacks than whites died in combat, the black mortality rate was actually higher than the rate for white soldiers be- *Mistreatment of Black Soldiers* cause so many black soldiers died of disease from working long, arduous hours in unsanitary conditions. Conditions for blacks and whites were unequal in other ways as well. African-American soldiers were paid a third less than were white soldiers (until Congress changed the law in mid-1864). Black fighting men captured by the Confederates were, unlike white prisoners, not returned to the North in exchange for Southern soldiers being returned to the South. They were sent back to their masters (if they were escaped slaves) or often executed. In 1864, Confederate soldiers killed over 260 African Americans after capturing them in Tennessee.

The War and Economic Development

The Civil War did not, as some historians used to claim, transform the North from an agrarian to an industrial society. Industrialization was already far advanced when the war began, and in some areas, the war actually retarded growth—by cutting manufacturers off from their Southern markets and sources of raw material, and by diverting labor and resources to military purposes.

On the whole, however, the war sped the economic development of the North. That was in part a result of the political dominance of the Republican Party and its promotion of nationalistic economic legislation. But it was also because the war itself required the expansion of certain sectors of the economy. Coal production increased by nearly 20 percent during the war. Railroad facilities improved—mainly through the adoption of a standard gauge (track width) on new lines. The loss of farm labor to the military forced many farmers to increase the mechanization of agriculture.

The war was a difficult experience for many American workers. Industrial laborers experienced a substantial loss of purchasing power, as prices in the North rose by more than 70 percent during the war while wages rose only about 40 percent. That was partly because liberalized immigration laws permitted a flood of new workers into *Hard Times for Workers* the labor market and helped keep wages low. It was also because the increasing mechanization of production eliminated the jobs of many skilled workers. One result of these hardships was a substantial increase in union membership in many industries and the creation of several national unions, for coal miners, railroad engineers, and others—organizations bitterly opposed and rigorously suppressed by employers.

Women, Nursing, and the War

Women found themselves, either by choice or by necessity, thrust into new and often unfamiliar roles during the war. They took over positions vacated by men and worked as teachers, retail sales clerks, office workers, and mill and factory hands. They were responding not only to the needs of employers for additional labor, but to their own, often desperate, need for money. With husbands and fathers away in the army, many women were left destitute—particularly since military pay was low and erratic.

Above all, women entered nursing, a field previously dominated by men. The U.S. Sanitary Commission, an organization of civilian volunteers led by Dorothea Dix, mobilized *U.S. Sanitary Commission* large numbers of female nurses to serve in field hospitals. By the end of the war, women were the dominant force in nursing; by the end of the century, nursing had become an almost entirely female profession. Female nurses not only cared for patients but performed other tasks considered appropriate for women: cooking, cleaning, and laundering.

Female nurses encountered considerable resistance from male doctors, many of whom considered women too weak for medical work and who, in any case, found the sight of women taking care of strange men inappropriate. The Sanitary Commission tried to counter such arguments by attributing to *Traditional Gender Roles Reinforced* nursing many of the domestic ideals that American society attributed to women's work in the home. Women as nurses were to play the same maternal, nurturing, instructive role they played as wives and mothers. The commission was, according to its own literature, "a great artery that bears the people's love to the army." Just as women cared for sick people at home, so they could—and must—do so in the military hospitals. "The right of woman to her sphere, which includes housekeeping, cooking, and nursing, has never been disputed," one Sanitary Commission official insisted. But not all women who worked for the commission were content with a purely maternal role; some challenged the dominance of men in the organization and even stood up against doctors whom they considered incompetent, increasing the resentment felt toward them by many men. In the end, though, the work of

THE U.S. SANITARY COMMISSION Mathew Brady took this photograph of female nurses and Union soldiers standing before an infirmary at Brandy Station, Virginia, near Petersburg, in 1864. The infirmary was run by the U.S. Sanitary Commission, the government-supported nursing corps that became indispensable to the medical care of wounded soldiers during the Civil War. *(National Archives and Records Administration)*

female nurses was so indispensable to the military that the complaints of male doctors were irrelevant.

Nurses, and many other women, found the war a liberating experience, in which (as one Sanitary Commission nurse later wrote) the American woman "had developed potencies and possibilities of which she had been unaware and which surprised her, as it did those who witnessed her marvelous achievement." Some women, especially those who had been committed to feminist causes earlier, came to see the war as an opportunity to win support for their own goals. Elizabeth Cady Stanton and Susan B. Anthony, who together founded the National Woman's Loyal League in 1863, worked simultaneously for the abolition of slavery and the awarding of suffrage to women. Clara Barton, who was active during the war in collecting and distributing medical supplies and who later became an important figure in the nursing profession (and a founder of the American Red Cross), said in 1888: "At the war's end, woman was at least fifty years in advance of the normal position which continued peace would have assigned her." That may have been a considerable exaggeration; but it captured the degree to which many women looked back on the war as a crucial moment in the redefinition of female roles and in the awakening of a sense of independence and new possibilities.

Whatever nursing may have done for the status of women, it had an enormous impact on the medical pro-

Nursing and Medicine | fession and on the treatment of wounded soldiers during the war. The U.S. Sanitary Commission not only organized women to serve at the front, it also funneled medicine and supplies to badly overtaxed field hospitals. The commission also (as its name suggests) helped spread ideas about the importance of sanitary conditions in hospitals and clinics and probably contributed to the relative decline of death by disease in the Civil War. Nevertheless, twice as many soldiers died of diseases—malaria, dysentery, typhoid, gangrene, and others—as died in combat during the war. Even minor injuries could lead to fatal infections.

THE MOBILIZATION OF THE SOUTH

Early in February 1861, representatives of the seven states that had seceded from the Union met at Montgomery, Alabama, to create a new Southern nation. When Virginia seceded several months later, the government of the Confederacy moved to Richmond—one of the few Southern cities large enough to house a national government.

Many Southerners boasted loudly of the differences between their new nation and the nation they had left. Those differences were real. But there were also important similarities between the Union and the Confederacy,

which became particularly clear as the two sides mobilized for war: similarities in their political systems, in the methods they used for financing the war and conscripting troops, and in the way they fought.

The Confederate Government

The Confederate constitution was almost identical to the Constitution of the United States, with several significant exceptions: It explicitly acknowledged the sovereignty of the individual states (although not the right of secession), and it specifically sanctioned slavery and made its abolition (even by one of the states) practically impossible.

The constitutional convention at Montgomery named a provisional president and vice president: Jefferson Davis of Mississippi and Alexander H. Stephens of Georgia, who were later chosen by the general electorate, without opposition, for six-year terms. Davis had been a moderate secessionist before the war; Stephens had argued against secession. The Confederate government, like the Union government, was dominated throughout the war by moderate leaders. Also like the Union, it was dominated less by the old aristocracy of the East than by the newer aristocrats of the West, of whom Davis was the most prominent example.

Davis was, in the end, an unsuccessful president. He was a reasonably able administrator and the dominating figure in his government, encountering little interference from the generally tame members of his unstable cabinet and serving as his own secre-

tary of war. But he rarely pro- | *Davis's Leadership* vided genuinely national leadership. He spent too much time on routine items; and unlike Lincoln, he displayed a punctiliousness about legal and constitutional niceties inappropriate to the needs of a new nation at war. One shrewd Confederate official wrote: "All the revolutionary vigor is with the enemy. . . . With us timidity-hair splitting."

There were no formal political parties in the Confederacy, but its congressional and popular politics were rife with dissension nevertheless. Some white Southerners (and of course most African Americans who were aware of the course of events) opposed secession and war altogether. Many white people in poorer "backcountry" and "upcountry" regions, where | *Southern Divisions* slavery was limited, refused to recognize the new Confederate government or to serve in the Southern army; some worked or even fought for the Union. Most white Southerners supported the war, but as in the North many were openly critical of the government and the military, particularly as the tide of battle turned against the South and the Confederate economy decayed.

Money and Manpower

Financing the Confederate war effort was a monumental and ultimately impossible task. It involved creating a national revenue system in a society unaccustomed to significant

The American Civil War was an event largely rooted in conditions particular to the United States. But it was also a part of a worldwide movement in the nineteenth century to create large, consolidated nations. America's expansion into the western regions of the continent—and its efforts to incorporate those areas into the nation—was one of the principal causes of the controversies over slavery that led to the Civil War. A commitment to preserving the Union—to consolidating, rather than dismantling, the nation—was one of the principal motives for the North's commitment to fighting a war against the seceding states. Similar efforts at expansion, consolidation, and unification were occurring in many other nations around the same time.

The consolidation of nation states was, of course, not new to the nineteenth century. Spain, Britain, Russia, and other nations had united disparate states and regions into substantial nations in the fifteenth, sixteenth, and seventeenth centuries. But nationalism took on new force in the nineteenth century. That was partly because of growing nationalist sentiment among peoples who shared language, culture, ethnicity, and tradition and who came to believe that a consolidated nation was the best vehicle for strengthening their common bonds. Nationalism was also a product of the centralization of governments in many areas of the world, and the development within them of the ability to administer large

territories from above. The revolutions in America and France in the late eighteenth century—and the subsequent strengthening of the French concept of nationhood under Napoleon in the early nineteenth century—inspired new nationalist enthusiasms in other parts of Europe.

In 1848, a wave of nationalist revolutions erupted in Italy, France, and Austria, challenging the imperial powers that many Europeans believed were subjugating national cultures. Those revolutions failed, but they helped lay the groundwork for the two most important national

THE UNIFICATION OF ITALY This painting shows a climactic moment in the history of Italian unification. Garibaldi, the great leader of independence forces in southern Italy, greets King Victor Emmanuel of the Piedmont, the leader of independence forces in the North. Garibaldi greeted him by saying, "Saluto il primo Re d'Italia" ("I hail the first king of Italy"). The moment was significant both practically—it demonstrated Garibaldi's willingness to accept Victor Emmanuel's authority—and symbolically, as the triumph of nationalist sentiment in this once decentralized country. *(Museo del Risorgimento, Milan/Index S.A.S.)*

tax burdens. It depended on a small and unstable banking system that had little capital to lend. Because most wealth in the South was invested in slaves and land, liquid assets were scarce; and the Confederacy's only specie—seized from U.S. mints located in the South—was worth only about $1 million.

The Confederate Congress tried at first not to tax the people directly but to requisition funds from the individual states. But most of the states were also unwilling to *Funding Problems* tax their citizens and paid their shares, when they paid them at all, with bonds or notes of dubious worth. In 1863, therefore, the congress enacted an income tax—which planters

384

could pay "in kind" (as a percentage of their produce). But taxation never provided the Confederacy with very much revenue; it produced only about 1 percent of the government's total income. Borrowing was not much more successful. The Confederate government issued bonds in such vast amounts that the public lost faith in them and stopped buying them, and efforts to borrow money in Europe using cotton as collateral fared no better.

As a result the Confederacy had to pay for the war through the least stable, most destructive form of financing: paper currency, which it began issuing in 1861. By 1864, the Confederacy had issued the staggering total of $1.5 billion in paper money, more than twice what the

consolidations of nineteenth-century Europe.

One of them occurred in Germany, which was divided into numerous small, independent states in the early nineteenth century but where popular sentiment for German unification had been growing for decades. It was spurred in part by new histories of the German *volk* (people) and by newly constructed images of German traditions, visible in such literature as Grimm's fairy tales—an effort to record and popularize German folk traditions and make them the basis of a shared sense of a common past. In 1862, King Wilhelm I of Prussia—the leader of one of the most powerful of the scattered German states—appointed an aristocratic landowner, Otto von Bismarck, as his prime minister. Bismarck exploited the growing nationalism throughout the various German states and helped develop a strong popular base for unification. He did so in part by launching Prussian wars against Denmark, Austria, and France—wars Prussia easily won, inspiring pride in German power that extended well beyond Prussia itself. The Franco-Prussian War of 1870 was particularly important, because Prussia fought it to take possession of the French provinces of Alsace and Lorraine—provinces the Prussians claimed were part of the German "national community" because its people, although legally French citizens, were ethnically and linguistically German. In 1871, capitalizing on the widespread nationalist sentiment the war had created throughout the German-speaking states, Bismarck persuaded the German king to proclaim himself emperor (or *Kaiser*) of a new empire that united all German peoples except those in Austria and Switzerland.

The second great European movement for national unification occurred in Italy, which had long been divided into small kingdoms, city-states, and regions controlled by the Vatican. Some areas of Italy were at one time or another dominated by the French, the Spanish, and the Austro-Hungarian empire.

Beginning in the early nineteenth century, Italian nationalists formed what became known as the Young Italy movement, under the leadership of Giuseppe Mazzini. The movement demanded an end of foreign control in Italy and the unification of the Italian people into a single nation. It promoted an idea of the nation as a kind of family, and of its territories as a family home. Peoples with common language, culture, and tradition, Mazzini believed, should be free to unite and govern themselves. More important than this growing popular nationalism as a cause of Italian unification were the efforts of powerful and ambitious leaders. The most powerful Italian state in the mid-nineteenth century was the kingdom of the Piedmont and Sardinia, in the northwestern part of the peninsula. Its king, Victor Emmanuel II, appointed his own version of Bismarck—Camillo di Cavour—as prime minister in 1852. Cavour joined forces with nationalists in other areas of Italy to drive the Spanish and the Austrians out of Italian territory. Having first won independence for northern Italy, Cavour joined forces with the southern nationalist leader Giuseppe Garibaldi, who helped win independence in the South and then agreed to a unification of the entire Italian nation under Victor Emmanuel in 1860.

Other nations in these years were also trying to create, preserve, and strengthen nation states. Some failed to do so—Russia, which despite the reform efforts of several tsars, never managed to create a stable nation-state from among its broad and diverse peoples; Austria, whose empire could never consolidate its claim over a similarly diverse group of national groups; Turkey, whose Ottoman empire (known as "the sick man of Europe") remained frail despite the efforts of leaders to strengthen it; and China, which likewise tried and failed to produce reforms that would consolidate its vast lands effectively. But others succeeded—Meiji Japan, for example, instituted a series of reforms in the 1880s and 1890s that created a powerful new Japanese nation-state.

In fighting and winning the Civil War, the nationalists of the northern parts of the United States not only preserved the unity of their nation. They also became part of a movement toward the consolidation of national cultures and national territories that extended through many areas of the globe.

Union had produced. And unlike the Union, the Confederacy did not establish a uniform currency system; the national government, states, cities, and private banks all issued their own notes, producing widespread chaos and confusion. The result was a disastrous inflation, far worse than anything the North experienced. Prices in the North rose 80 percent in the course of the war; in the South they rose 9,000 percent, with devastating effects on the new nation's morale.

Like the United States, the Confederacy first raised a military by calling for volunteers. And as in the North, by the end of 1861 voluntary enlistments were declining. In April 1862, therefore, the congress enacted a Conscription Act, which subjected all white males between the ages of eighteen and thirty-five to military service for three years. As in the North, a draftee could avoid service if he furnished a substitute. But since the price of

Raising the Confederate Army

substitutes was high, the provision aroused such opposition from poorer whites that it was repealed in 1863. Even more controversial was the exemption from the draft of one white man on each plantation with twenty or more slaves, a provision that caused smaller farmers to complain: "It's a rich man's war but a poor man's fight." Many more white Southerners were exempted from military service than Northerners.

CONFEDERATE VOLUNTEERS Young Southern soldiers posed for this photograph in 1861, shortly before the first Battle of Bull Run. The Civil War was the first major military conflict in the age of photography, and it launched the careers of many of America's early photographers. *(Cook Collection, Valentine Museum)*

Even so, conscription worked for a time. At the end of 1862, about 500,000 men were in the Confederate military. (A total of approximately 900,000 served in the course of the entire war.) That number did not include the many slave men and women recruited by the military to perform such services as cooking, laundry, and manual labor, hence freeing additional white manpower for fighting. (Only late in the war, when the military situation was becoming desperate, was there any effort to involve slaves in combat.) After 1862, however, conscription began producing fewer men—in part because the Union had by then begun to seize large areas of the Confederacy and thus had cut off much of the population from conscription or recruitment. The armed forces steadily decreased in size.

As 1864 opened, the government faced a critical manpower shortage. In a desperate move, the Confederate *Manpower Shortages* Congress began trying to draft men as young as seventeen and as old as fifty. But in a nation suffering from intense war weariness, where many had concluded that defeat was inevitable, nothing could attract or retain an adequate army any longer. In 1864–1865 there were 100,000 desertions. In a frantic final attempt to raise men, the congress authorized the conscription of 300,000 slaves, but the war ended before the government could attempt this incongruous experiment.

States' Rights versus Centralization

The greatest source of division in the South, however, was not differences of opinion over the war, but the doctrine of states' rights. States' rights had become such a cult among many white Southerners that they resisted virtually all efforts to exert national authority, even those necessary to win the war. States' rights enthusiasts obstructed the conduct of the war in many ways. They restricted Davis's ability to impose martial law and suspend habeas corpus. They obstructed conscription. Recalcitrant governors such as Joseph Brown of Georgia and Zebulon M. Vance of North Carolina tried at times to keep their own troops apart from the Confederate forces and insisted on hoarding surplus supplies for their own states' militias.

But the Confederate government did make substantial strides in centralizing power in the South. By the end of the war, the Confederate bureaucracy was larger than its counterpart in Washington. *Centralization* The national government experimented, successfully for a time, with a "food draft"—which permitted soldiers to feed themselves by seizing crops from farms in their path. The government impressed slaves, often over the objections of their owners, to work as laborers on military projects. The Confederacy seized control of the railroads and shipping; it imposed regulations on industry; it limited corporate profits. States' rights sentiment was a significant handicap, but the South nevertheless took dramatic steps in the direction of centralization—becoming in the process increasingly like the region whose institutions it was fighting to escape.

Economic and Social Effects of the War

The war had a devastating effect on the economy of the South. It cut off Southern planters and producers from the markets in the North on which they had depended; it made the sale of cotton overseas much more difficult; it robbed farms and industries that did not have large slave populations of a male work force, leaving some of them unable to function effectively. While in the North production of all goods, agricultural and industrial, increased somewhat during the war, in the South it declined by more than a third.

Most of all, perhaps, the fighting itself wreaked havoc on the Southern economy. Almost all the major battles of the war occurred within the Confederacy; both armies spent most of their time on Southern soil. As a result of the savage fighting, the South's already inadequate railroad system was nearly destroyed; much of its most valuable farmland, and many of its most successful plantations, were ruined by Union troops (especially in the last year of the war).

ATLANTA AFTER THE BURNING General Sherman captured Atlanta on September 2, 1864, evacuated most of the population, and set fire to the city. This photograph shows the extent of the devastation. The destruction of Atlanta was the beginning of Sherman's famous "March to the Sea." It also signaled the beginning of a new kind of warfare, waged not just against opposing armies but against the economies and even the populations of the enemy. *(Bettmann/Corbis)*

Once the Northern naval blockade became effective, the South experienced massive shortages of almost everything. The region was overwhelmingly agricultural, but since it had concentrated so single-mindedly on producing cotton and other export crops, it did not grow enough food to meet its own needs. And despite the efforts of women and slaves to keep farms functioning, the departure of white male workers seriously diminished the region's ability to keep up what food production there had

Economic Woes

been. Large numbers of doctors were conscripted to serve the needs of the military, leaving many communities without any medical care. Blacksmiths, carpenters, and other craftsmen were similarly in short supply.

As the war continued, the shortages, the inflation, and the suffering created increasing instability in Southern society. There were major food riots, some led by women, in Georgia, North Carolina, and Alabama in 1863, as well as a large demonstration in Richmond that quickly turned violent. Resistance to conscription, food impressment, and taxation increased throughout the Confederacy, as did hoarding and black-market commerce.

In economic terms, in other words, the war affected the South very differently from the way it affected the North. In other respects, however, the war transformed Confederate society in many of the same ways that it was changing the society of the Union. It was particularly significant for Southern women. Because so many men left the farms and plantations to fight, the task of keeping families together and maintaining agricultural production fell increasingly to women. Slaveowners' wives often became responsible for managing large slave work forces; the wives of more mod-

New Roles for Women

est farmers learned to plow fields and harvest crops. Substantial numbers of females worked in government agencies in Richmond. Even larger numbers chose nursing, both in hospitals and in temporary facilities set up to care for wounded soldiers. Others became schoolteachers.

The long-range results of the war for Southern women are more difficult to measure but equally profound. The experience of the 1860s almost certainly forced many women to question the prevailing Southern assumption that females were unsuited for certain activities, that they were not fit to participate actively in the public sphere. A

Long before the great urban stadiums, long before the lights and the cameras and the multimillion dollar salaries, long before the Little Leagues and the high school and college teams, baseball was the most popular game in America. And during the Civil War, it was a treasured pastime for soldiers, and for thousands of men (and some women) behind the lines, in both North and South.

Baseball was not invented by Abner Doubleday, who probably never even saw the game. The legend that it was came many years later from Albert G. Spalding, a patriotic sporting-goods manufacturer eager to prove that the game had purely American origins and to dispel the notion that it came from England. In fact, baseball was derived from a variety of earlier games, especially the English pastimes of cricket and rounders. American baseball took its own distinctive form beginning in the 1840s, when Alexander Cartwright, a shipping clerk, formed the New York Knickerbockers, laid out a diamond-shaped field with four bases, and declared that batters with three strikes were out and that teams with three outs were retired.

Cartwright moved west in search of gold in 1849, ultimately grew rich, and settled finally in Hawaii (where he brought the game to Americans in the Pacific). But the game did not languish in his absence. Henry Chadwick, an English-born journalist, developed his own passion for baseball in the late 1840s and spent much of the next decade popularizing the game (and regularizing its rules). "Our ambition," he said, was "that of endeavoring to establish a national game." It was also to keep baseball a sport for the "best classes," for gentlemen—a goal that was already lost before it was even uttered. By 1860, baseball was being played by college students and Irish workers, by urban elites and provincial farmers, by people of all classes and ethnic groups from New England to Louisiana. It was also attracting the attention of women. Students at Vassar College formed "ladies" teams in the 1860s. And in Philadelphia, free black men formed the first of what was to become a great network of African-American baseball teams, the Pythians. From the beginning, they were barred from playing against most white teams.

When young men donned their uniforms of blue and gray and marched off to war in 1861, some took their bats and balls with them. Almost from the start of the fighting, soldiers in both armies took advantage of idle moments to lay out baseball diamonds and organize games. There were games in prison camps; games on the White House lawn (where Union soldiers were sometimes billeted); and games on battlefields that were sometimes interrupted by gunfire and cannon. "It is astonishing how indifferent a person can become to danger," a soldier wrote home to Ohio in 1862. "The report of musketry is heard but a very little distance from us, . . . yet over there on the other side of the road is most of our company, playing Bat Ball." After a skirmish in Texas, another Union soldier lamented that, in addition to casualties, his company had lost "the only baseball in Alexandria, Texas."

An unlikely legend has it that in Hilton Head, South Carolina—occupied by Union soldiers very early in the war—two teams of New York volunteers played a game in front of more than 40,000 spectators. Far from discouraging baseball, military commanders—and the United States Sanitary Commission, the Union army's medical arm—actively encouraged the

more concrete legacy was the decimation of the male population and the creation of a major gender imbalance in the region. After the war, there were many thousands more women in the South than men. In Georgia, for example, women outnumbered men by 36,000 in 1870; in North Carolina by 25,000. The result, of course, was a large number of unmarried or widowed women who, both during and after the war, had no choice but to find employment—thus, by necessity rather than choice, expanding the number of acceptable roles for women in Southern society.

Even before emancipation, the war had far-reaching effects on the lives of slaves. Confederate leaders were even more terrified of slave revolts during the war than they had been in peacetime, and they enforced slave codes and other regulations with particular severity. Even so, many slaves—especially those near the front—found ways to escape their masters and cross behind Union lines in search of freedom. Those who had no realistic avenue for escape seemed, to their owners at least, to be particularly resistant to authority during the war. That was in part because on many plantations, the masters and overseers for

whom they were accustomed to working were away at war; they found it easier to resist the authority of the women and boys left behind to manage the farms.

STRATEGY AND DIPLOMACY

Militarily, the initiative in the Civil War lay mainly with the North, since it needed to defeat the Confederacy while the South needed only to avoid defeat. Diplomatically, however, the initiative lay with the South. It needed to enlist the recognition and support of foreign governments; the Union wanted only to preserve the status quo.

The Commanders

The most important Union military commander was Abraham Lincoln, whose previous military experience consisted only of brief service in his state militia during the Black *Lincoln's Leadership*

Hawk War. Lincoln was a successful commander in chief because he realized that numbers and resources were on

RIFLES AND BATS Union soldiers pose on the battlefield in full uniform and carrying their rifles, with a pile of baseball bats on the grass in front of them. Baseball was a popular recreation for troops on both sides of the Civil War. *(Dennis Goldstein, Atlanta)*

ten or twenty thousand. The National Association of Baseball Players (founded in 1859) had recruited ninety-one clubs in ten northern states by 1865; a North Western Association of Baseball Players, organized in Chicago in 1865, indicated that the game was becoming well established in the West as well. And in Brooklyn during the war, William Cammeyer drained a skating pond on his property, built a board fence around it, and created the first enclosed baseball field in America—the Union grounds. He charged 10 cents admission. The professionalization of the game was underway.

But for all the commercialization and spectacle that came to be associated with baseball in the years after the Civil War, the game remained for many Americans what it was to millions of young men fighting in the most savage war in the nation's history—an American passion that at times, even if briefly, erased the barriers dividing groups from one another. "Officers and men forget, for a time, the differences in rank," a Massachusetts private wrote in 1863, "and indulge in the invigorating sport with a schoolboy's ardor."

game during the war. It would, they believed, help keep up the soldiers' morale.

Away from the battlefield, baseball continued to flourish (even if diminished by the departure of so many young men to the war). In New York, still the leading baseball city in the nation, games between local teams continued to draw crowds of

his side, and because he took advantage of the North's material advantages. He realized, too, that the proper objective of his armies was the destruction of the Confederate armies and not the occupation of Southern territory. It was important that Lincoln had a good grasp of strategy, because many of his generals did not. The problem of finding adequate commanders for the troops in the field plagued him throughout the first three years of the war. From 1861 to 1864, Lincoln tried time and again to find a chief of staff capable of orchestrating the Union war effort. He turned first to General Winfield Scott, the aging hero of the Mexican War. But Scott was unprepared for the magnitude of the new conflict and retired on November 1, 1861. Lincoln replaced him with the young George B. McClellan, commander of the Union armies in the East, the Army of the Potomac; but the proud, arrogant McClellan had a wholly inadequate grasp of strategy and in any case returned to the field in March 1862. For most of the rest of the year, Lincoln had no chief of staff at all. And when he finally appointed General Henry W. Halleck to the post, he found him an ineffectual strategist who left all substantive decision making

to the president. Not until March 1864 did Lincoln finally find a general he trusted to command the war effort: Ulysses S. Grant, who shared Lincoln's belief in making enemy armies and resources, not enemy territory, the target of military efforts. Lincoln gave Grant a relatively free hand, but the general always submitted at least the broad outlines of his plans to the president for advance approval.

Lincoln's (and later Grant's) handling of the war effort faced constant scrutiny from the Committee on the Conduct of the War, a joint investigative committee of the two houses of Congress and the most powerful voice the legislative branch has ever had in formulating war policies. Established in December 1861 and chaired by Senator Benjamin F. Wade of Ohio, it complained constantly of the insufficient ruthlessness of Northern generals, which Radicals on the committee attributed (largely inaccurately) to a secret sympathy among the officers for slavery. The committee's efforts often seriously interfered with the conduct of the war.

Southern command arrangements centered on President Davis, who unlike Lincoln was a trained professional

ULYSSES S. GRANT One observer said of Grant (seen here posing for a photograph during the Wilderness campaign of 1864): "He habitually wears an expression as if he had determined to drive his head through a brick wall, and was about to do it." It was an apt metaphor for Grant's military philosophy, which relied on constant, unrelenting assault. One result was that Grant was willing to fight when other Northern generals held back. Another was that Grant presided over some of the worst carnage of the Civil War. *(Library of Congress)*

ROBERT E. LEE Lee was a moderate by the standards of Southern politics in the 1850s. He opposed secession and was ambivalent about slavery. But he could not bring himself to break with his region, and he left the U.S. army to lead Confederate forces beginning in 1861. He was (and remains) the most revered of all the white Southern leaders of the Civil War. For decades after his surrender at Appomattox, he was a symbol to white Southerners of the "Lost Cause." *(Bettmann/Corbis)*

soldier but who, also unlike Lincoln, failed ever to create an effective command system. Early in 1862, Davis named *Robert E. Lee* | General Robert E. Lee as his principal military adviser. But in fact, Davis had no intention of sharing control of strategy with anyone. After a few months, Lee left Richmond to command forces in the field, and for the next two years Davis planned strategy alone. In February 1864, he named General Braxton Bragg as a military adviser; but Bragg never provided much more than technical advice. Not until February 1865 did the Confederate Congress create the formal position of general in chief. Davis named Lee to the post but made clear that he expected to continue to make all basic decisions. In any case, the war ended before this last command structure had time to take shape.

At lower levels of command, men of markedly similar backgrounds controlled the war in both the North and the South. Many of the professional officers on both sides were graduates of the United States Military Academy at West Point and the United States Naval Academy at Annapolis, and thus had been trained in similar ways.

Many were closely acquainted, even friendly, with their counterparts on the other side. And all were imbued with the classic, eighteenth-century models of warfare that the service academies still taught. The most successful officers were those who, like Grant and William Tecumseh Sherman, were able to see beyond their academic training and envision a new kind of warfare in which destruction of resources was as important as battlefield tactics.

Amateur officers played an important role in both armies as commanders of volunteer regiments. In both North and South, such men were usually economic or social leaders in their communities who appointed themselves officers and rounded up troops to lead. This system was responsible for recruiting considerable numbers of men into the armies of the two nations. Only occasionally, however, did it produce officers of real ability.

The Role of Sea Power

The Union had an overwhelming advantage in naval power, and it gave its navy two important roles in the war. One was enforcing a blockade of the Southern coast, which the president ordered on April 19, 1861. The other was assisting the Union armies in field operations.

The blockade of the South was never fully effective, but it had a major impact on the Confederacy nevertheless. The United States Navy could gener-

The Union Blockade

ally keep oceangoing ships out of Confederate ports. For a time, small blockade runners continued to slip through. But gradually, federal forces tightened the blockade by seizing the ports themselves. The last important port in Confederate hands—Wilmington, North Carolina—fell to the Union early in 1865.

The Confederates made bold attempts to break the blockade with new weapons. Foremost among them was an ironclad warship, constructed by plating with iron a former United States frigate, the *Merrimac,* which the Yankees had scuttled in Norfolk

Ironclads

harbor when Virginia seceded. On March 8, 1862, the refitted *Merrimac,* renamed the *Virginia,* left Norfolk to attack a blockading squadron of wooden ships at nearby Hampton Roads. It destroyed two of the ships and scattered the rest. But the Union government had already built ironclads of its own. And one of them, the *Monitor,* arrived off the coast of Virginia only a few hours after the *Virginia's* dramatic foray. The next day, it met the *Virginia* in the first battle between ironclad ships. Neither vessel was able to sink the other, but the *Monitor* put an end to the *Virginia's* raids and preserved the blockade. The Confederacy experimented as well with other naval innovations, such as small torpedo boats and hand-powered submarines. But despite occasional small successes with these new weapons, the South never managed to overcome the Union's naval advantages.

As a supporter of land operations, the Union navy was particularly important in the western theater of war—the vast region between the Appalachian Mountains and the Mississippi River—where the major rivers were navigable by large vessels. The navy transported supplies and troops and joined in attacking Confederate strong points. With no significant navy of its own, the South could defend only with fixed land fortifications, which proved no match for the mobile land-and-water forces of the Union.

Europe and the Disunited States

Judah P. Benjamin, the Confederate secretary of state for most of the war, was a clever and intelligent man, but he lacked strong convictions and confined most of his energy to routine administrative tasks. William Seward, his counterpart in Washington, gradually became one of the great American secretaries of state. He had invaluable assistance from Charles Francis Adams, the American minister to London, who had inherited the considerable diplomatic talents of his father, John Quincy Adams, and his grandfather, John Adams.

At the beginning of the war, the ruling classes of England and France, the two nations whose support was most crucial to both sides, were generally sympathetic to the Confederacy, for several reasons. The two nations imported much Southern cotton for their textile industries; they were eager to weaken the United States, an increasingly powerful commercial rival; and some admired the supposedly aristocratic social order of the South, which they believed resembled the hierarchical structures of their own societies. But France was unwilling to take sides in the conflict unless England did so first. And in England, the government was reluctant to act because there was powerful popular support for the Union. Important English liberals such as John Bright and Richard Cobden considered the war a struggle between free and slave labor and urged their followers to support the Union cause. The politically conscious but largely unenfranchised workers in Britain expressed their sympathy for the North frequently and unmistakably—in mass meetings, in resolutions, and through their champions in Parliament. After Lincoln issued the Emancipation Proclamation, these groups worked particularly avidly for the Union.

Southern leaders hoped to counter the strength of the British antislavery forces by arguing that access to Southern cotton was vital to the English and French textile in-

King Cotton Diplomacy

dustries. But this "King Cotton diplomacy," on which the Confederacy had staked so many of its hopes, was a failure. English manufacturers had a surplus of both raw cotton and finished goods on hand in 1861 and could withstand a temporary loss of access to American cotton. Later, as the supply of cotton began to diminish, both England and France managed to keep at least some of their mills open by importing cotton from Egypt, India, and other sources. Equally important, English workers, the people most seriously threatened by the cotton shortage, did not clamor to have the blockade broken. Even the 500,000 English textile workers thrown out of jobs as a result of mill closings continued to support the North. In the end, therefore, no European nation offered diplomatic recognition to the Confederacy or intervened in the war. No nation wanted to antagonize the United States unless the Confederacy seemed likely to win, and the South never came close enough to victory to convince its potential allies to support it.

Even so, there was considerable tension, and on occasion near hostilities, between the United States and Britain, beginning in the first days of the war. Great Britain declared itself neutral as soon as the fighting began, followed by France and other nations. The Union government was furious. Neutrality implied that the two sides to the conflict had equal stature, but Washington was insisting that the conflict was simply a domestic insurrection, not a war between two legitimate governments.

A more serious crisis, the so-called Trent affair, began in late 1861. Two Confederate diplomats, James M. Mason and John Slidell, had slipped through the then ineffective

Trent Affair

Union blockade to Havana, Cuba, where they boarded an English steamer, the *Trent,* for England. Waiting in Cuban waters was the American frigate *San Jacinto,* commanded by the impetuous Charles Wilkes. Acting without authorization, Wilkes stopped the British vessel, arrested the diplomats, and carried them in triumph to Boston. The British government demanded the release of the prisoners, reparations, and an apology. Lincoln and Seward, aware that Wilkes had violated maritime law and unwilling to risk war with England, spun out the negotiations until American public opinion had cooled off, then released the diplomats with an indirect apology. A second diplomatic crisis produced problems that lasted for years. Unable to construct large vessels itself, the Confederacy bought six ships, known as commerce destroyers, from British shipyards. The best known of them were the *Alabama,* the *Florida,* and the *Shenandoah.* The United States protested that this sale of military equipment to a belligerent violated the laws of neutrality, and the protests became the basis, after the war, of damage claims by the United States against Great Britain (see p. 422).

The American West and the War

Most of the states and territories of the American West, about which there had been so much controversy in the years leading up to the Civil War, were far removed from the major fighting. But they played a continuing political, diplomatic, and military part in the conflict nevertheless.

Except for Texas, which joined the Confederacy, all the western states and territories remained officially loyal to the Union—but not without controversy and conflict. Southerners and Southern sympathizers were active throughout the West encouraging secession and attempting to enlist both white settlers and Indians to support the Confederacy. And in some places, there was actual combat between Unionists and secessionists.

There was particularly vicious fighting in Kansas and Missouri, the scene of so much bitterness before the war. The same pro-slavery and free-state forces who had

Guerrilla War in the West

fought one another in the 1850s continued to do so, with even more deadly results. William C. Quantrill, an Ohio native who had spent much of his youth in the West, became a captain in the Confederate army after he organized a band of guerrilla fighters (mostly teenage boys) with which he terrorized areas around the Kansas-Missouri border. Quantrill and his band were an exceptionally murderous group, notorious for killing almost everyone in their path. Their most infamous act was a siege of Lawrence, Kansas, during which they slaughtered 150 civilians, adults and children alike. Quantrill finally died at the hands of Union troops shortly after the end of the war. Union sympathizers in Kansas, organized in bands known as the Jayhawkers, were only marginally less savage, as they moved across western Missouri exacting reprisals for the actions of Quantrill and other Confederate guerrillas. One Jayhawk unit was commanded by the son of John Brown

and the brother of Susan B. Anthony, men who brought the fervor of abolitionists to their work. Even without a major battle, the border areas of Kansas and Missouri were among the bloodiest and most terrorized places in the United States during the Civil War.

Not long after the war began, Confederate agents tried to negotiate alliances with the Five Civilized Tribes living in Indian Territory (later Oklahoma), in hopes of recruiting their support against Union forces in the West. The Indians themselves were divided. Some wanted to support the South, both because they resented the way the United States government had treated them and because some tribal leaders were themselves slaveholders. But other Indians supported the North out of a general hostility to slavery (both in the South and in their own nation).

One result of these divisions was something of a civil war within Indian Territory itself. Another was that Indian regiments fought for both the Union and the Confederacy during the war. But the tribes themselves never formally allied themselves with either side.

THE COURSE OF BATTLE

In the absence of direct intervention by the European powers, the two contestants in America were left to resolve the conflict between themselves. They did so *High Casualties* in four long years of bloody combat that produced more carnage than any war in American history, before or since. More than 618,000 Americans died in the Civil War, far more than the 115,000 who perished in World War I or the 318,000 who died in World War II; more, indeed, than died in all other American wars prior to Vietnam combined. There were nearly 2,000 deaths for every 100,000 of population during the Civil War. In World War I, the comparable figure was 109 deaths; in World War II, 241 deaths.

Despite the gruesome cost, the Civil War has become the most romanticized and the most intently studied of all American wars. In part, that is because the conflict produced—in addition to terrible fatalities—a series of military campaigns of classic strategic interest and a series of military leaders who displayed unusual brilliance and daring.

The Technology of Battle

Much of what happened on the battlefield in the Civil War was a result of new technologies that transformed the nature of combat. The Civil War has often been called the first "modern" war and the first "total" war. Such descriptions are imprecise and debatable. But it is certainly true that the great conflict between the North and the South was unlike any war fought before it. It is also clear that it suggested a great deal about what warfare would be like in the future.

The most obvious change in the character of warfare in the 1860s was the nature of the armaments that both

Repeating Weapons

sides used in battle. Among the most important was the introduction of repeating weapons. Samuel Colt had patented a repeating pistol (the revolver) in 1835, but more important for military purposes was the repeating rifle, introduced in 1860 by Oliver Winchester. Two years later, Richard Gatling perfected the revolving machine gun (although it was little used during the Civil War). Also important were greatly improved cannons and artillery, a result of advances in iron and steel technology of the previous decades.

These devastating advances in the effectiveness of arms and artillery changed the way soldiers in the field fought. It was now impossibly deadly to fight battles as they had been fought for centuries, with lines of infantry soldiers standing erect in the field firing volleys at their opponents until one side withdrew. Fighting in that way now produced almost inconceivable slaughter, and soldiers quickly learned that the proper position for combat was staying low to the ground and behind cover. For the first time in the history of organized warfare, therefore, infantry did not fight in formation, and the battlefield became a more chaotic place. Gradually, the deadliness of the new weapons encouraged armies on both sides to spend a great deal of time building elaborate fortifications and trenches to protect themselves from enemy fire. The sieges of Vicksburg and Petersburg, the defense of Richmond, and many other military events all produced the construction of vast fortifications around the cities and around the attacking armies. (They became the predecessors to the great network of trenches that became so central a part of World War I.)

Other weapons technologies were less central to the fighting of the war, but important nevertheless. There was sporadic use of the relatively new technology of hot-air balloons, employed intermittently to provide a view of enemy formations in the field. (During one battle, a Union balloonist took a telegraph line aloft with him in his balloon and tapped out messages about troop movements to the commanders below.) Ironclad ships such as the *Merrimac* (or *Virginia*) and the *Monitor* suggested the dramatic changes that would soon overtake naval warfare, but did not have a great impact on the fighting of the Civil War. Torpedoes and submarine technology also made a fleeting appearance in the 1860s, showing the way to future innovations in warfare but not playing a major role in the Civil War.

Critical to the conduct of the war, however, were two other relatively new technologies: the railroad and the

Importance of the Railroad

telegraph. The railroad was particularly important in a war in which millions of soldiers were being mobilized and transferred to the front, and in which a single field army could number as many as 250,000 men. Transporting such enormous numbers of soldiers, and the supplies necessary to sustain them, by land or by horse and wagon would have been almost impossible. Railroads made it possible for these large armies to be assembled and moved from place to place. However, they also limited the mobility of the armies. Railroad lines and stations are, of course, in fixed positions. Commanders, therefore, were forced to organize their campaigns at least in part around the location of the railroads rather than on the basis of the best topography or most direct land route to a destination. The dependence on the rails—and the resulting necessity of concentrating huge numbers of men in a few places—also encouraged commanders to prefer great battles with large armies rather than smaller engagements with fewer troops.

The impact of the telegraph on the war was limited both by the scarcity of qualified telegraph operators and by the difficulty of bringing telegraph wires into the fields

The Telegraph

where battles were being fought. Things improved somewhat after the new U.S. Military Telegraph Corps, headed by Thomas Scott and Andrew Carnegie, trained and employed over 1,200 operators. Gradually, too, both the Union and Confederate armies learned to string telegraph wires along the routes of their troops (who, once they were off the railroads, generally moved slowly, on foot or horseback), so that field commanders were able to stay in close touch with one another during battles. Both the North and the South sent spies behind enemy lines who tried to tap the telegraph lines of their opponents and send important information back about troop movements and formations.

The Opening Clashes, 1861

The Union and the Confederacy fought their first major battle of the war in northern Virginia. A Union army of over 30,000 men under the command of General Irvin McDowell was stationed just outside Washington. About thirty miles away, at the town of Manassas, was a slightly smaller Confederate army under P. G. T. Beauregard. If the Northern army could destroy the Southern one, Union leaders believed, the war might end at once. In mid-July, McDowell marched his inexperienced troops toward Manassas. Beauregard moved his troops behind Bull Run, a small stream north of Manassas, and called for reinforcements, which reached him the day before the battle. The two armies were now approximately the same size.

On July 21, in the First Battle of Bull Run, or First Battle of Manassas, McDowell almost succeeded in dispersing the Confederate forces. But the Southerners stopped a last strong

First Battle of Bull Run

Union assault and then began a savage counterattack. The Union troops, exhausted after hours of hot, hard fighting, suddenly panicked. They broke ranks and retreated chaotically. McDowell was unable to reorganize them, and he had to order a retreat to Washington—a disorderly withdrawal complicated by the presence along the route of many civilians who had ridden down from the capital, picnic baskets in hand, to watch the battle from nearby hills. The Confederates, as disorganized by victory as the Union forces were by defeat, and short of supplies and transportation, did not pursue. The battle was a severe blow to Union morale and to the president's confidence in his officers. It also dispelled the illusion that the war would be a quick one.

Elsewhere in 1861, Union forces were achieving some small but significant victories. In Missouri, rebel forces gathered behind Governor Claiborne Jackson and other state officials who wanted to secede from the Union. Nathaniel Lyon, who commanded a small regular army force in St. Louis, moved his troops into southern Missouri to face the secessionists. On August 10, at the Battle of Wilson's Creek, he was defeated and killed—but not before he had seriously weakened the striking power of the Confederates. Union forces were subsequently able to hold most of the state.

Wilson's Creek

Meanwhile, a Union force under George B. McClellan moved east from Ohio into western Virginia. By the end of 1861, it had "liberated" the anti-secession mountain people of the region. They created their own state government loyal to the Union and were admitted to the Union as West Virginia in 1863. The occupation of western Virginia was of limited military value, since the mountains cut the area off from the rest of Virginia. It was, however, an important symbolic victory for the North.

The Western Theater

After the battle at Bull Run, military operations in the East settled into a long and frustrating stalemate. The first decisive operations in 1862 occurred, therefore, in the western theater. Union forces were trying to seize control of the southern part of the Mississippi River, which would divide the Confederacy and give the North easy transportation into the heart of the South. Northern soldiers advanced on the southern Mississippi from both the north and south, moving downriver from Kentucky and upriver from the Gulf of Mexico toward New Orleans.

In April, a Union squadron of ironclads and wooden vessels commanded by David G. Farragut gathered in the Gulf of Mexico, then smashed past weak Confederate forts near the mouth of the Mississippi, and from there sailed up to New Orleans, which was virtually defenseless because the Confederate high command had expected the attack to come from the north. The city surrendered on April 25—the first major Union victory and an important turning point in the war. From then on, the mouth of the Mississippi was closed to Confederate trade; and the South's largest city and most important banking center was in Union hands.

New Orleans Captured

Farther north in the western theater, Confederate troops under the command of Albert Sidney Johnston were stretched out in a long defensive line centered at two forts in Tennessee, Fort Henry and Fort Donelson, on the Tennessee and Cumberland Rivers respectively. But the forts were located well behind the main Southern flanks, a fatal weakness that Union commanders recognized and exploited. Early in 1862, Ulysses S. Grant attacked Fort Henry, whose defenders, awed by the ironclad riverboats accompanying the Union army, surrendered with almost no resistance on February 6. Grant then moved both his naval and ground forces to Fort Donelson, where the Confederates put up a stronger fight but finally, on February 16, had to surrender. By cracking the Confederate center, Grant had gained control of river communications and forced Confederate forces out of Kentucky and half of Tennessee.

With about 40,000 men, Grant now advanced south along the Tennessee River to seize control of railroad lines vital to the Confederacy. From Pittsburg Landing, he marched to nearby Shiloh, Tennessee, where a force almost equal to his own, commanded by Albert Sidney Johnston and P. G. T. Beauregard, caught him by surprise. The result was the Battle of Shiloh, April 6–7. In the first day's fighting (during which Johnston was killed), the Southerners drove Grant back to the river. But the next day, reinforced by 25,000 fresh troops, Grant recovered the lost ground and forced Beauregard to withdraw. After the narrow Union victory at Shiloh, Northern forces occupied Corinth, Mississippi, the hub of several important railroads, and established control of the Mississippi River as far south as Memphis.

Shiloh

Braxton Bragg, now in command of the Confederate army in the West, gathered his forces at Chattanooga, in eastern Tennessee, which the Confederacy still controlled. He hoped to win back the rest of the state and then move north into Kentucky. But first he had to face a Union army (commanded by Don Carlos Buell and later by William S. Rosecrans), whose assignment was to capture Chattanooga. The two armies maneuvered for advantage inconclusively in northern Tennessee and southern Kentucky for several months until they finally met, December 31–January 2, in the Battle of Murfreesboro, or Stone's River. Bragg was forced to withdraw to the south, his campaign a failure. By the end of 1862, Union forces had made considerable progress in the West. But the major conflict remained in the East, where they were having much less success.

The Virginia Front, 1862

Union operations were being directed in 1862 by George B. McClellan, commander of the Army of the Potomac and the most controversial general of the war. McClellan was a superb trainer of men, but he often appeared reluctant

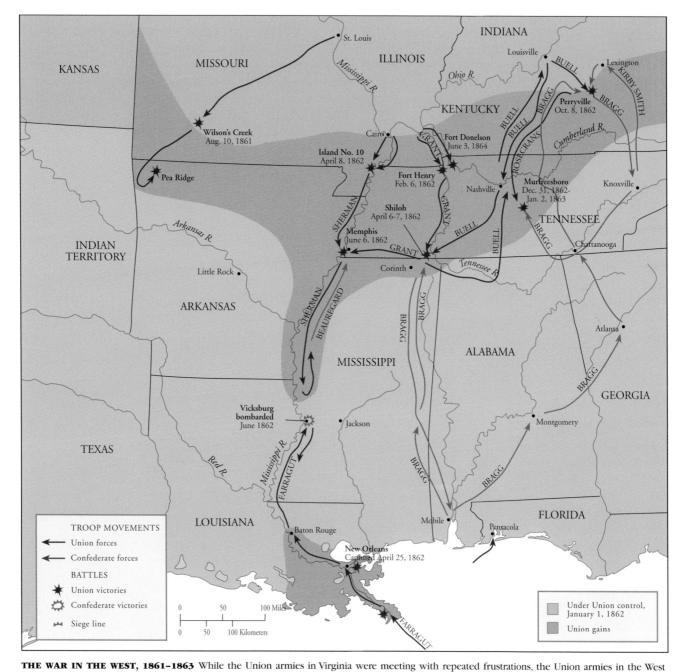

THE WAR IN THE WEST, 1861–1863 While the Union armies in Virginia were meeting with repeated frustrations, the Union armies in the West were scoring notable successes in the first two years of the war. This map shows a series of Union drives in the western Confederacy. Admiral David Farragut's ironclads led to the capture of New Orleans—a critical Confederate port—in April 1862, while forces further north under the command of Ulysses S. Grant drove the Confederate army out of Kentucky and western Tennessee. These battles culminated in the Union victory at Shiloh, which led to Union control of the upper Mississippi River. ◆ *Why was control of the Mississippi so important to both sides?*

 For an interactive version of this map go to www.mhhe.com/brinkley11ch14maps

to commit his troops to battle. Opportunities for important engagements came and went, and McClellan seemed

George McClellan | never to take advantage of them—claiming always that his preparations were not yet complete or that the moment was not right. During the winter of 1861–1862, McClellan concentrated on training his army of 150,000 men near Washington. Finally, he designed a spring campaign whose

purpose was to capture the Confederate capital at Richmond. But instead of heading overland directly toward Richmond, McClellan chose a complicated, roundabout route that he thought would circumvent the Confederate defenses. The navy would carry his troops down the Potomac to a peninsula east of Richmond, between the York and James Rivers. The army would approach the city from there. It became known as the Peninsular campaign.

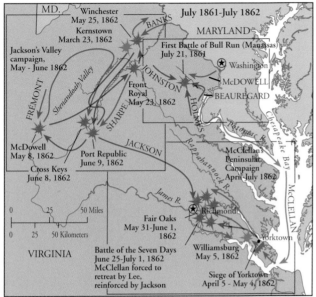

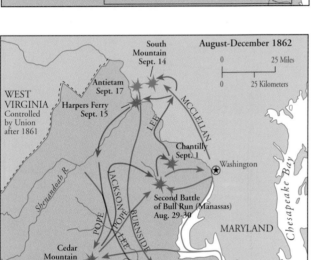

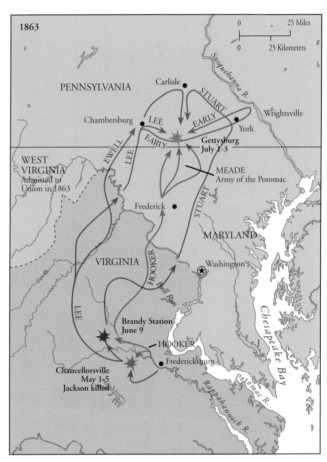

THE VIRGINIA THEATER, 1861–1863 Much of the fighting during the first two years of the Civil War took place in what became known as the Virginia theater—although the campaigns in this region eventually extended north into Maryland and Pennsylvania. The Union hoped for a quick victory over the newly created Confederate army. But as these maps show, the southern forces consistently thwarted these hopes. The map at top left shows the battles of 1861 and the first half of 1862, almost all of them won by the Confederates. The map at lower left shows the last months of 1862, during which the southerners again defeated the Union in most of their engagements—although northern forces drove the Confederates back from Maryland in September. The large map on the right shows the troop movements that led to the climactic battle of Gettysburg in 1863. ◆ *Why were the Union forces unable to profit more from material advantages during these first years of the war?*

 For an interactive version of this map go to www.mhhe.com/brinkley11ch14maps

McClellan began the campaign with only part of his army. Approximately 100,000 men accompanied him down the Potomac. Another 30,000—under General Irvin McDowell—remained behind to protect Washington. McClellan insisted that Washington was safe as long as he was threatening Richmond, and finally persuaded Lincoln to promise to send him the additional men. But before the president could do so, a Confederate army under Thomas J. ("Stonewall") Jackson changed his plans. Jackson staged a rapid march north through the Shenandoah Valley, as if he were planning to cross the Potomac and attack Washington. Alarmed, Lincoln dispatched McDowell's corps to head off Jackson. In the brilliant Valley campaign of May 4–June 9, 1862, Jackson defeated two separate Union forces and slipped away before McDowell could catch him.

Meanwhile, Confederate troops under Joseph E. Johnston were attacking McClellan's advancing army outside Richmond. But in the two-day Battle of Fair Oaks, or Seven Pines (May 31–June 1), they could not repel the Union forces. Johnston, badly wounded, was replaced by Robert E. Lee, who then recalled Stonewall Jackson from the Shenandoah Valley. With a combined force of 85,000 to face McClellan's 100,000, Lee launched a new offensive, known as the Battle of the Seven Days (June 25–July 1). Lee wanted to cut McClellan off from his base on the York River and then destroy the isolated Union army. But McClellan fought his way across the peninsula and set up a new base on the James. There, with naval support, the Army of the Potomac was safe.

Seven Pines

McClellan was now only twenty-five miles from Richmond, with a secure line of water communications, and thus in a good position to renew the campaign. Time and again, however, he found reasons for delay. Instead of replacing McClellan with a more aggressive commander, Lincoln finally ordered the army to move to northern Virginia and join a smaller force under John Pope. The president hoped to begin a new offensive against Richmond on the direct overland route that he himself had always preferred.

As the Army of the Potomac left the peninsula by water, Lee moved north with the Army of Northern Virginia to strike Pope before McClellan could join him. Pope was as rash as McClellan was cautious, and he attacked the approaching Confederates without waiting for the arrival of all of McClellan's troops. In the ensuing Second Battle of Bull Run, or Second Battle of Manassas (August 29–30), Lee threw back the assault and routed Pope's army, which fled to Washington. With hopes for an overland campaign against Richmond now in disarray, Lincoln removed Pope from command and put McClellan in charge of all the Union forces in the region.

Lee soon went on the offensive again, heading north through western Maryland, and McClellan moved out to meet him. McClellan had the good luck to get a copy of Lee's orders, which revealed that a part of the Confederate army, under Stonewall Jackson, had separated from the rest to attack Harpers Ferry. But instead of attacking quickly before the Confederates could recombine, McClellan stalled and gave Lee time to pull most of his forces together behind Antietam Creek, near the town of Sharpsburg. There, on September 17, in the bloodiest single-day engagement of the war, McClellan's 87,000-man army repeatedly attacked Lee's force of 50,000, with enormous casualties on both sides. Six thousand soldiers died, and 17,000 sustained injuries. Late in the day, just as the

Antietam

THE FIRST NEW YORK ARTILLERY
Photographed on an unidentified battlefield, the first New York artillery stands posing before its array of cannon—and the stumps of trees cut down to allow them unimpeded shots at the enemy. *(US Army Military History Institute, Carlisle PA)*

Confederate line seemed ready to break, the last of Jackson's troops arrived from Harpers Ferry to reinforce it. McClellan might have broken through with one more assault. Instead, he allowed Lee to retreat into Virginia. Technically, Antietam was a Union victory, but in reality, it was an opportunity squandered. In November, Lincoln finally removed McClellan from command for good.

McClellan's replacement, Ambrose E. Burnside, was a short-lived mediocrity. He tried to move toward Richmond by crossing the Rappahannock at Fredericksburg, the strongest defensive point on the river. There, on December 13, he launched a series of attacks against Lee, all of them bloody, all of them hopeless. After losing a large part of his army, Burnside withdrew to the north bank of the Rappahannock. He was relieved at his own request.

1863: Year of Decision

At the beginning of 1863, General Joseph Hooker was in command of the still formidable Army of the Potomac, whose 120,000 troops remained north of the Rappahannock, opposite Fredericksburg. But despite his reputation as a fighter (his popular nickname was "Fighting Joe"), Hooker showed little resolve as he launched his own campaign in the spring. Taking part of his army, Hooker crossed the river above Fredericksburg and moved toward the town and Lee's army. But at the last minute, he apparently lost his nerve and drew back to a defensive position in a desolate area of brush and scrub trees known as the Wilderness. Lee had only half as many men as Hooker did, but he boldly divided his forces for a dual assault on the Union army. In the Battle of Chancellorsville, May 1–5, Stonewall Jackson attacked the Union right and Lee himself charged the front. Hooker barely managed to escape with his

Battle of Chancellorsville army. Lee had defeated the Union objectives, but he had not destroyed the Union army. And his ablest officer, Jackson, was fatally wounded during the battle.

While the Union forces were suffering repeated frustrations in the East, they were continuing to win important victories in the West. In the

Vicksburg spring of 1863, Ulysses S. Grant was driving at Vicksburg, Mississippi, one of the Confederacy's two remaining strongholds on the southern Mississippi River. Vicksburg was well protected, surrounded by rough country on the north and low, marshy ground on the west, and with good artillery coverage of the river itself. But in May, Grant boldly moved men and supplies—overland and by water—to an area south of the city, where the terrain was better. He then attacked Vicksburg from the rear. Six weeks later, on July 4, Vicksburg—whose residents were by then literally starving as a result of a prolonged siege—surrendered. At almost the same time, the other Confederate strong point on the river, Port Hudson, Louisiana, also surrendered—to a Union force that had moved north from New Orleans.

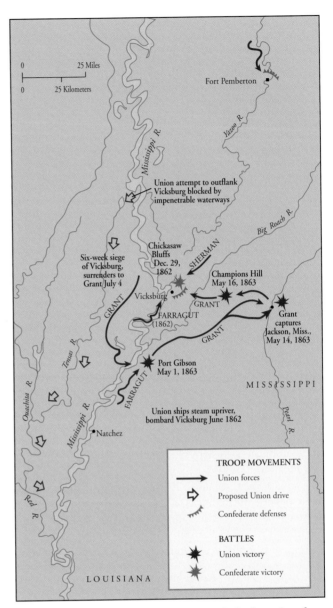

THE SIEGE OF VICKSBURG, MAY–JULY 1863 In the spring of 1863, Grant began a campaign to win control of the final piece of the Mississippi River still controlled by the Confederacy. To do that required capturing the southern stronghold at Vicksburg—a well-defended city sitting above the river. Vicksburg's main defenses were in the North, so Grant boldly moved men and supplies around the city and attacked it from the South. Eventually, he cut off the city's access to the outside world, and after a six-week siege, its residents finally surrendered. ◆ *What impact did the combined victories at Vicksburg and Gettysburg have on northern commitment to the war?*

 For an interactive version of this map go to www.mhhe.com/brinkley11ch14maps

The Union had achieved one of its basic military aims: control of the whole length of the Mississippi. The Confederacy was split in two, with Louisiana, Arkansas, and Texas cut off from the other seceded states. The victories on the Mississippi were one of the great turning points of the war.

Early in the siege of Vicksburg, Lee proposed an invasion of Pennsylvania, which would, he argued, divert Union troops north and remove the pressure on the lower Mississippi. Further, he argued, if he could win a major victory on Northern soil, England and France might come to the Confederacy's aid. The war-weary North might even quit the war before Vicksburg fell.

In June 1863, Lee moved up the Shenandoah Valley into Maryland and then entered Pennsylvania. The Union Army of the Potomac, commanded first by Hooker and then by George C. Meade, also moved north, parallel with the Confederates' movement, staying between Lee and Washington. The two armies finally encountered one another at the small town of Gettysburg, Pennsylvania. There, on July 1–3, 1863, they fought the most celebrated battle of the war.

Meade's army established a strong, well-protected position on the hills south of the town. The confident *Gettysburg* and combative Lee attacked, even though his army was outnumbered 75,000 to 90,000. His first assault on the Union forces on Cemetery Ridge failed. A day later he

ordered a second, larger effort. In what is remembered as Pickett's Charge, a force of 15,000 Confederate soldiers advanced for almost a mile across open country while being swept by Union fire. Only about 5,000 made it up the ridge, and this remnant finally had to surrender or retreat. By now Lee had lost nearly a third of his army. On July 4, the same day as the surrender of Vicksburg, he withdrew from Gettysburg—another major turning point in the war. Never again were the weakened Confederate forces able to seriously threaten Northern territory.

Before the end of the year, there was a third important turning point, this one in Tennessee. After occupying Chattanooga on September 9, Union forces under William Rosecrans began an unwise pursuit of Bragg's retreating Confederate forces. Bragg was waiting for them just across the Georgia line, with reinforcements from Lee's army. The two armies engaged in the Battle of Chickamauga (September 19–20), one of the few battles in which the Confederates enjoyed a numerical superiority (70,000 to 56,000). Union forces could not break the Confederate lines and retreated back to Chattanooga.

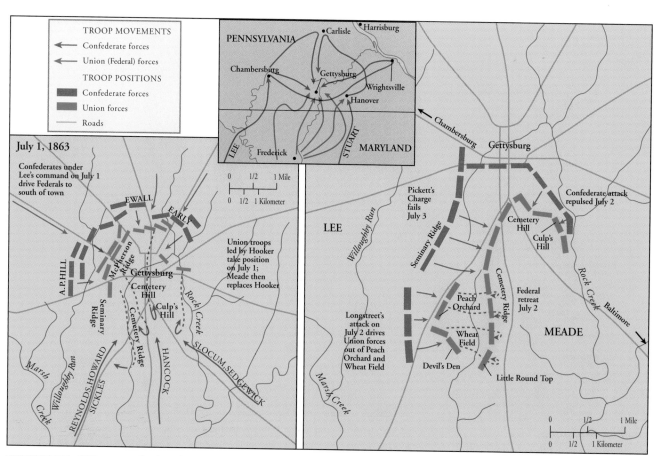

GETTYSBURG, JULY 1–3, 1863 Gettysburg was the most important single battle of the Civil War. Had Confederate forces prevailed at Gettysburg, the future course of the war might well have been very different. The map on the right shows the distribution of Union and Confederate forces at the beginning of the battle, July 1, after Lee had driven the northern forces south of town. The map on the left reveals the pattern of the attacks on July 2 and 3. Note, in particular, Pickett's bold and costly charge, whose failure on July 3 was the turning point in the battle and, some have argued, the war. ◆ *Why did Robert E. Lee believe that an invasion of Pennsylvania would advance the Confederate cause?*

Bragg now began a siege of Chattanooga itself, seizing the heights nearby and cutting off fresh supplies to the Union forces. Grant came to the rescue. In the Battle of Chattanooga (November 23–25), the reinforced Union army drove the Confederates back into Georgia. Northern troops then occupied most of eastern Tennessee. Union forces had now achieved a second important objective: control of the Tennessee River. Four of the eleven Confederate states were now effectively cut off from the Southern nation. No longer could the Confederacy hope to win independence through a decisive military victory. They could hope to win only by holding on and exhausting the Northern will to fight.

Battle of Chattanooga

The Last Stage, 1864–1865

By the beginning of 1864, Ulysses S. Grant had become general in chief of all the Union armies. At long last, the president had found a commander whom he could rely on to pursue the war doggedly and tenaciously. Grant was not a subtle strategic or tactical general; he believed in using the North's overwhelming advantage in troops and material resources to overwhelm the South. He was not afraid to absorb massive casualties as long as he was inflicting similar casualties on his opponents.

Grant planned two great offensives for 1864. In Virginia, the Army of the Potomac (technically under Meade's command, but really now under Grant's) would advance toward Richmond and force Lee into a decisive battle. In Georgia, the western army, under William T. Sherman, would advance east toward Atlanta and destroy the remaining Confederate force further south, which was now under the command of Joseph E. Johnston. The northern campaign began when the Army of the Potomac, 115,000 strong, plunged into the rough, wooded Wilderness area of northwestern Virginia in pursuit of Lee's 75,000-man army. After avoiding an engagement for several weeks, Lee turned Grant back in the Battle of the Wilderness (May

Grant's Strategy

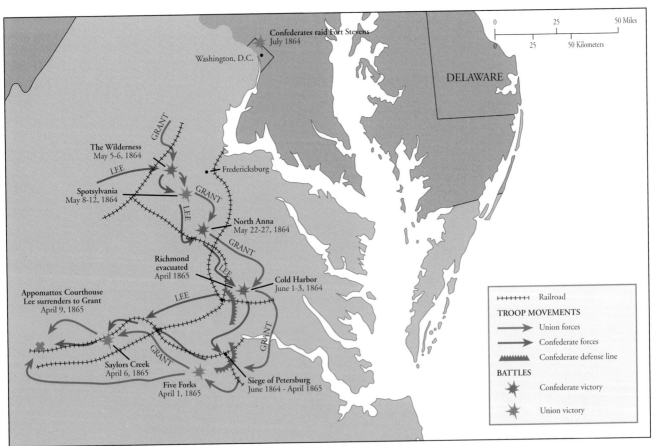

VIRGINIA CAMPAIGNS, 1864–1865 From the Confederate defeat at (and retreat from) Gettysburg until the end of the war, most of the eastern fighting took place in Virginia. By now, Ulysses S. Grant was commander of all Union forces and had taken over the Army of the Potomac. Although Confederate forces won a number of important battles during the Virginia campaign, the Union army grew steadily stronger and the southern forces steadily weaker. Grant believed that the Union strategy should reflect the North's greatest advantage: its superiority in men and equipment. ◆ *What effect did this decision have on the level of casualties?*

 For an interactive version of this map go to www.mhhe.com/brinkley11ch14maps

MOBILE BAY, 1864 This painting by Robert Weir portrays a famous naval battle at the entrance to Mobile Bay between a Union Sloop-of War, the *U.S.S. Richmond*, part of a fleet commanded by Admiral David Farragut, and a Confederate ironclad, the *C.S.S. Tennessee*. Although Confederate mines were scattered across the entrance to the harbor, Farragut ordered his ships into battle with the memorable command: "Damn the torpedoes! Full speed ahead!" The Union forces defeated the Confederate flotilla and three weeks later captured the forts defending the harbor—thus removing from Confederate control the last port on the Gulf Coast available to the blockade runners who were attempting to supply the South's war needs. *(Mariners' Museum, Newport News, Virginia)*

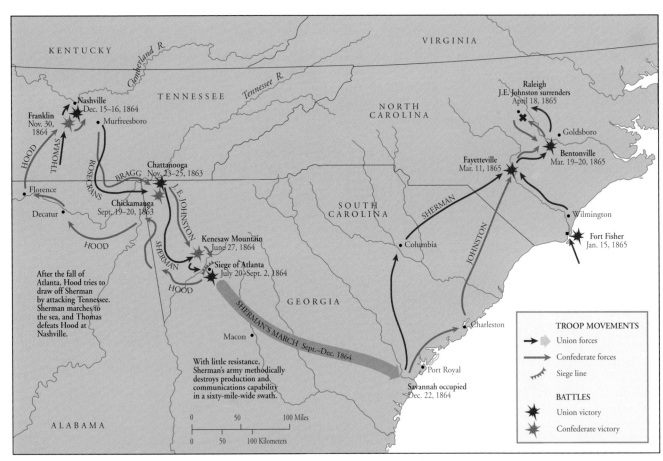

SHERMAN'S MARCH TO THE SEA, 1864–1865 While Grant was wearing Lee down in Virginia, General William Tecumseh Sherman was moving east across Georgia. After a series of battles in Tennessee and northwest Georgia, Sherman captured Atlanta and then marched unimpeded to Savannah, on the Georgia coast—deliberately devastating the towns and plantations through which his troops marched. Note that after capturing Savannah by Christmas 1864, Sherman began moving North through the Carolinas. A few days after Lee surrendered to Grant at Appomattox, Confederate forces further south surrendered to Sherman. ◆ *What did Sherman believe his devastating March to the Sea would accomplish?*

 For an interactive version of this map go to www.mhhe.com/brinkley11ch14maps

5–7). But Grant was undeterred. Without stopping to rest or reorganize, he resumed his march toward Richmond. He met Lee again in the bloody, five-day Battle of Spotsylvania Court House, in which 12,000 Union troops and a large but unknown number of Confederates died or were wounded. Despite the enormous losses, Grant kept moving. But victory continued to elude him.

Lee kept his army between Grant and the Confederate capital and on June 1–3 repulsed the Union forces again, just northeast of Richmond, at Cold Harbor. The month-long Wilderness campaign had cost Grant 55,000 men (killed, wounded, and captured) to Lee's 31,000. And Richmond still had not fallen.

Grant now changed his strategy. He moved his army east of Richmond, bypassing the capital altogether, and headed south toward the railroad center at Petersburg. If he could seize Petersburg, he could cut off the capital's communications with the rest of the Confederacy. But Petersburg had strong defenses; and once Lee came to the city's relief, the assault became a prolonged siege, which lasted nine months. In Georgia, meanwhile, Sherman was facing a less ferocious resistance. With 90,000 men, he confronted Confederate forces of 60,000 under Johnston, who was unwilling to risk a direct engagement. As Sherman advanced, Johnston tried to delay him by maneuvering. The two armies fought only one real battle— at Kennesaw Mountain, northwest of Atlanta, on June 27—where Johnston scored an impressive victory. Even

Capture of Atlanta

so, he was unable to stop the Union advance toward Atlanta. President Davis replaced Johnston with the combative John B. Hood, who twice daringly attacked Sherman's army but accomplished nothing except seriously weakening his own forces. Sherman took Atlanta on September 2. News of the victory electrified the North and helped unite the previously divided Republican Party behind President Lincoln.

Hood now tried unsuccessfully to draw Sherman out of Atlanta by moving back up through Tennessee and threatening an invasion of the North. Sherman did not take the bait. But he did send Union troops to reinforce Nashville. In the Battle of Nashville on December 15–16, 1864, Northern forces practically destroyed what was left of Hood's army.

Meanwhile, Sherman had left Atlanta to begin his soon-to-be-famous March to the Sea. Living off the land, de-

March to the Sea

stroying supplies it could not use, his army cut a sixty-mile-wide swath of desolation across Georgia. "War is all hell," Sherman had once said. By that he meant not that war is a terrible thing to be avoided, but that it should be made as horrible and costly as possible for the opponent. He sought not only to deprive the Confederate army of war materials and railroad communications but also to break the will of the Southern people, by burning towns and plantations along his route. By December 20, he had

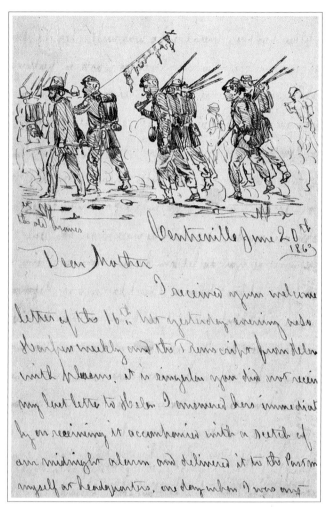

A LETTER FROM THE FRONT Charles Wellington Reed, a nineteen-year-old soldier who was also a talented artist, sent illustrated letters to the members of his family throughout the war. In this 1863 letter to his mother, he portrays the Ninth Massachusetts Battery leaving Centreville, Virginia on its way to Gettysburg. Two weeks later, Reed fought in the famous battle and eventually received the Congressional Medal of Honor for his bravery there. "Such a shrieking, hissing, seathing I never dreamed was imaginable," he wrote of the fighting at the time. *(Manuscript Division, Library of Congress)*

reached Savannah, which surrendered two days later. Sherman offered it to President Lincoln as a Christmas gift. Early in 1865, having left Savannah largely undamaged, Sherman continued his destructive march northward through South Carolina. He was virtually unopposed until he was well inside North Carolina, where a small force under Johnston could do no more than cause a brief delay.

In April 1865, Grant's Army of the Potomac—still engaged in the prolonged siege at Petersburg—finally captured a vital railroad junction southwest of the town. Without rail access to the South, cut off from other Confederate forces, Lee could no longer hope to defend Richmond. With the remnant of his army, now about

25,000 men, Lee began moving west in the forlorn hope of finding a way around the Union forces so he could head south and link up with Johnston in North Carolina. But the Union army pursued him and blocked his escape route. Finally recognizing that further blood-

Appomattox Courthouse shed was futile, Lee arranged to meet Grant at a private home in the small town of Appomattox Courthouse, Virginia. There, on April 9, he surrendered what was left of

his forces. Nine days later, near Durham, North Carolina, Johnston surrendered to Sherman.

In military terms, at least, the long war was now effectively over, even though Jefferson Davis refused to accept defeat. He fled south from Richmond and was finally captured in Georgia. A few Southern diehards continued to fight, but even their resistance collapsed before long. Well before the last shot was fired, the difficult process of re-uniting the shattered nation had begun.

CONCLUSION

The American Civil War began with high hopes and high ideals on both sides. In both the North and the South, thousands of men enthusiastically enlisted in local regiments; marched down the streets of their towns and cities dressed in uniforms of blue or gray to the cheers of family, friends, and neighbors; and went off to war. Four years later, over 600,000 of them were dead and many more maimed and traumatized for life. A fight for "principles" and "ideals"—a fight few people had thought would last more than a few months—had become one of the longest wars, and by far the bloodiest war, in American history, before or since.

During the first two years of fighting, the Confederate forces seemed to have all the advantages. They were fighting on their own soil. Their troops seemed more committed to the cause than those of the North. Their commanders were exceptionally talented, while Union forces were for a time erratically led. Gradually, however, the Union's advantages began to assert themselves. It had a stabler political system led by one of the greatest leaders in the nation's history (as opposed to the Confederacy's untested government led by a relatively weak president). It had a much larger population, a far more developed industrial economy, superior financial institutions, and a better railroad system. By the middle of 1863, the tide of war had changed; and over the next two years, Union forces gradually wore down the Confederate armies before finally triumphing in 1865.

The North's victory was not just a military one. The war strengthened the North's economy, giving a spur to industry and railroad development. It greatly weakened the South's, by destroying millions

Impact of the North's Victory

of dollars of property and depleting the region's young male population. Southerners had gone to war in part because of their fears of growing Northern dominance. The war itself, ironically, confirmed and strengthened that dominance. There was no doubt by 1865 that the future of the United States lay in the growth of industry and commerce, which would occur for many years primarily outside the South.

But most of all, the Civil War was a victory for the millions of African-American slaves, over whose plight the conflict had largely begun in the first place. The war produced Abraham Lincoln's epochal Emancipation Proclamation and, later, the Thirteenth Amendment to the Constitution, which abolished slavery altogether. It also encouraged hundreds of thousands of slaves literally to free themselves, to desert their masters and seek refuge behind Union lines—at times to fight in the Union armies. The future of the freed slaves was not to be an easy one, but three and a half million people who had once lived in bondage emerged from the war as free men and women.

FOR FURTHER REFERENCE

James McPherson, *Battle Cry of Freedom* (1988) is a fine general history of the Civil War. Shelby Foote, *The Civil War: A Narrative,* 3 vols. (1958–1974) recounts the military history of the war with great literary power. David Donald, *Lincoln* (1995) is the best modern biography of the sixteenth president. James M. McPherson, *Abraham Lincoln and the Second American Revolution* (1990) offers provocative reflections on the life and significance of Lincoln. Douglas Southall Freeman, *Robert E. Lee,* 4 vols. (1934–1935) and William McFeely, *Grant* (1981) are the leading biographies of the two most important Civil War generals. Philip Shaw Paludan, *"A People's Contest": The Union at War, 1861–1865* (1988) is a good account of the social impact of the war in the North. Iver Bernstein, *The New York City Draft Riots* (1990) examines an important event away from the battlefield. Alvin Josephy, *The Civil War in the West* (1992) remedies a long-neglected aspect of the war. Emory Thomas, *The Confederate*

Nation (1979) is a fine one-volume history of the Confederacy. Drew Gilpin Faust, *Mothers of Invention* (1996) examines the lives of elite southern women during the war. Ira Berlin et al., eds., *Free At Last: A Documentary History of Slavery, Freedom and the Civil War* (1992) is a superb compilation of primary sources from slaves and slaveowners relating to the demise of slavery during the Civil War years. Ira Berlin et al., *Slaves No More: Three Essays on Emancipation and the Civil War* (1992), the companion volume to the documents in *Free At Last,* argues that slaves and freedmen played an active role in destroying slavery and redefining freedom. Catherine Clinton and Nina Silber, *Divided Houses* (1992) is a collection of essays in the "new social history" from various historians demonstrating the importance of gender to the history of the Civil War. *The Civil War* (1989), Ken Burns's outstandingly popular and award-winning, nine-hour epic documentary has shaped the recent popular image of the conflict for many Americans.

For quizzes, Internet resources, references to additional books and films, and more, consult this book's Online Learning Center at www.mhhe.com/brinkleyll.

THE GENIUS OF FREEDOM This 1874 lithograph portrays a series of important moments in the history of African Americans in the South during Reconstruction—among them the participation of black soldiers in the Civil War, a speech by a black representative in the North Carolina legislature, and the movement of African-American workers from slavery into a system of free labor. It also portrays some of the white leaders (among them Lincoln and Charles Sumner) who had promoted the cause of the freedmen. *(Chicago Historical Society)*

Significant Events

1863 · Lincoln announces preliminary Reconstruction plan

1864 · Louisiana, Arkansas, and Tennessee readmitted to Union under Lincoln plan
· Wade-Davis Bill passed

1865 · Lincoln assassinated (April 14); Andrew Johnson becomes president
· Johnson tries to readmit rest of Confederate states to Union
· Black Codes enacted in South
· Freedmen's Bureau established
· Congress reconvenes (December) and refuses to admit Southern representatives; creates Joint Committee on Reconstruction

1866 · Freedmen's Bureau Act renewed

· Congress approves Fourteenth Amendment; most Southern states reject it
· Republicans gain in congressional elections
· *Ex parte Milligan* challenges Radicals' Reconstruction plans
· Ku Klux Klan formed in South

1867 · Military Reconstruction Act (and two supplementary acts) outlines congressional plan of Reconstruction
· Tenure of Office Act and Command of the Army Act restrict presidential power
· Southern states establish Reconstruction governments under congressional plan
· U.S. purchases Alaska

1868 · Most Southern states readmitted to Union under congressional plan

CHAPTER FIFTEEN

RECONSTRUCTION AND THE NEW SOUTH

Few periods in the history of the United States have produced as much bitterness or created such enduring controversy as the era of Reconstruction—the years following the Civil War when Americans attempted to reunite their shattered nation. Those who lived through Reconstruction viewed it in sharply different ways. To many white Southerners, it was a vicious and destructive experience—a time when vindictive Northerners inflicted humiliation and revenge on the prostrate South and unnecessarily delayed a genuine reunion of the sections. Northern defenders of Reconstruction, in contrast, argued that their policies were the only way to keep unrepentant Confederates from restoring Southern society as it had been before the war; without forceful federal intervention, it would be impossible to stop the re-emergence of a backward aristocracy and the continued subjugation of former slaves; there would be no way, in other words, to prevent the same sectional problems that had produced the Civil War in the first place.

To most African Americans at the time, and to many people of all races since, Reconstruction was notable for other reasons. Neither a vicious tyranny, as white Southerners charged, nor a thoroughgoing reform, as many Northerners claimed, it was, rather, a small but important first step in the effort by former slaves to secure civil rights and economic power. Reconstruction did not provide African Americans with either the legal protections or the material resources to assure them anything like real equality. And when it came to an end, finally, in the late 1870s—as a result of an economic crisis, a lack of political will in the North, and organized, at times violent, resistance by white Southerners—the freed slaves found themselves abandoned by the federal government to face a system of economic peonage and legal subordination alone. For the remainder of the nineteenth century, those blacks who continued to live in what came to be known as the New South were unable effectively to resist oppression. And yet for all its shortcomings, Reconstruction did help African Americans create institutions and legal precedents that they carried with them into the twentieth century and that became the basis for later efforts to win freedom and equality.

THE PROBLEMS OF PEACEMAKING

In 1865, as it became clear that the war was almost over, no one in Washington knew quite what to do. Abraham Lincoln could not negotiate a treaty with the defeated government; he continued to insist that the Confederate government had no legal right to exist. Yet neither could he simply readmit the Southern states into the Union as if nothing had happened.

The Aftermath of War and Emancipation

What happened to the South in the Civil War was a catastrophe with no parallel in America's experience as a nation. The region in 1865 was a desolate place. Towns had been gutted, plantations burned, fields neglected, bridges and railroads destroyed. Many white Southerners, stripped of their slaves through emancipation and stripped of the capital they had invested in now worthless Confederate bonds and currency, had almost no personal property.

The Devastated South

Many families had to rebuild their fortunes without the help of adult males. Some white Southerners faced starvation and homelessness.

More than 258,000 Confederate soldiers had died in the war—more than 20 percent of the adult white male population of the region; thousands more returned home wounded or sick. Almost all surviving white Southerners had lost people close to them in the fighting. A cult of ritualized mourning developed throughout the region in the late 1860s, particularly among white women—many of whom wore mourning clothes (and even special mourning jewelry) for two years or longer. At the same time, white Southerners began to romanticize the "Lost Cause" and its leaders, and to look back nostalgically at the South as it had existed before the terrible disruptions of war. Such Confederate heroes as Robert E. Lee, Stonewall Jackson, and (later) Jefferson Davis were treated with extraordinary reverence, almost as religious figures. Communities throughout the South built elaborate monuments to their war dead in town squares. The tremendous sense of loss

Myth of the "Lost Cause"

RICHMOND, 1865 By the time Union forces captured Richmond in early 1865, the Confederate capital had been under siege for months and much of the city lay in ruins, as this photograph reveals. On April 4, President Lincoln, accompanied by his son Tad, visited Richmond. As he walked through the streets of the shattered city, hundreds of former slaves emerged from the rubble to watch him pass. "No triumphal march of a conqueror could have equalled in moral sublimity the humble manner in which he entered Richmond," a black soldier serving with the Union army wrote. "It was a great deliverer among the delivered. No wonder tears came to his eyes." *(Library of Congress)*

A MONUMENT TO THE LOST CAUSE This monument in the town square of Monroe, Georgia, was typical of many such memorials erected all across the South after the Civil War. They served both to commemorate the Confederate dead and to remind white southerners of what was by the 1870s already widely known and romanticized as the "Lost Cause." *(©Lee Snider/Corbis)*

that pervaded the white South reinforced the determination of many whites to protect what remained of their now-vanished world.

If conditions were bad for many Southern whites, they were far worse for most Southern blacks—the 4 million men and women emerging from bondage. Some of them had also seen service during the war—as servants to Confederate officers or as teamsters and laborers for the Southern armies. Nearly 200,000 had fought for the Union, and 38,000 had died. Others had worked as spies or scouts for Union forces in the South. Many more had flocked to the Union lines to escape slavery. Even before Emancipation, thousands of slaves in many parts of the South had taken advantage of wartime disruptions to leave their owners and move off in search of freedom. As soon as the war ended, hundreds of thousands more former slaves—young and old, healthy and sick—left their

plantations. But most had nowhere to go. Many of them trudged to the nearest town or city, roamed the countryside camping at night on the bare ground, or gathered around Union occupation forces, hoping for assistance. Others spent months, even years, searching for relatives from whom they had been separated. Virtually none, of course, owned any land or property. Most had no possessions except the clothes they wore.

In 1865, in short, Southern society was in disarray. Blacks and whites, men and women faced a future of great uncertainty. Yet people of both races faced this future with some very clear aspirations. For both blacks and whites, Reconstruction became a struggle to define the meaning of freedom. But the former slaves and the defeated whites had very different conceptions of what freedom meant.

Competing Notions of Freedom

For African Americans, freedom meant above all an end to slavery and to all the injustices and humiliation they associated with it. But it also meant the acquisition of rights and protections that would allow them to live as free men and women in the same way white people did. "If I cannot do like a white man," one African-American man told his former master, "I am not free."

Blacks differed with one another on how to achieve that freedom. Some demanded a redistribution of economic resources, especially land, because, as a convention of Alabama freedmen put it in a formal resolution, "The property *Freedom for the Ex-slaves* which they hold was nearly all earned by the sweat of our brows." Others asked simply for legal equality, confident that given the same opportunities as white citizens they could advance successfully in American society. But whatever their particular demands, virtually all former slaves were united in their desire for independence from white control. Freed from slavery, blacks throughout the South began almost immediately to create autonomous African-American communities. They pulled out of white-controlled churches and established their own. They created fraternal, benevolent, and mutual aid societies. When they could, they began their own schools.

For most white Southerners, freedom meant something very different. It meant the ability to control their own destinies without interference from the North or the federal government. And in the immediate aftermath of the war, they attempted to exercise this version of freedom by trying to restore their society to its antebellum form. Slavery had been abolished in the former Confederacy by the Emancipation Proclamation, and everywhere else (as of December 1865) by the Thirteenth Amendment. But many white planters wanted to continue slavery in an altered form by keeping black workers legally tied to the plantations. When these white Southerners fought for what they considered freedom,

A FREEDMANS' BUREAU SCHOOL African-American students and teachers stand outside a school for former slaves, one of many run by the Freedman's Bureau throughout the defeated Confederacy in the first years after the war. *(U.S. Military History Institute, Carlisle, Pennsylvania. Photo by Jim Enos)*

they were fighting above all to preserve local and regional autonomy and white supremacy.

The federal government kept troops in the South after the war to preserve order and protect the freedmen. *The Freedman's Bureau* In March 1865, Congress established the Freedmen's Bureau, an agency of the army directed by General Oliver O. Howard. The Freedmen's Bureau distributed food to millions of former slaves. It established schools staffed by missionaries and teachers who had been sent to the South by Freedmen's Aid Societies and other private and church groups in the North. It made modest efforts to settle blacks on lands of their own. (The bureau also offered considerable assistance to poor whites, many of whom were similarly destitute and homeless after the war.) But the Freedmen's Bureau was not a permanent solution. It had authority to operate for only one year; and in any case it was far too small to deal effectively with the enormous problems facing southern society. By the time the war ended, other proposals for reconstructing the defeated South were emerging.

Issues of Reconstruction

The terms by which the southern states rejoined the Union had important implications for both major political parties. The Republican victories in 1860 and 1864 had been a result in large part of the division of the Democratic Party and, later, the removal of the South from

the electorate. Readmitting the South, leaders of both parties believed, would reunite the Democrats and weaken the Republicans. In addition, the Republican Party had taken advantage of the South's absence from Congress to pass a program of nationalistic economic legislation—railroad subsidies, protective tariffs, banking and currency reforms, and other measures to benefit northern business leaders and industrialists. Should the Democratic Party regain power with heavy southern support, these programs would be in jeopardy. Complicating these practical questions were emotional concerns. Many northerners believed the South should be punished in some way for the suffering and sacrifice its rebellion had caused. Many northerners believed, too, that the South should be transformed, made over in the North's urbanized image—its supposedly backward, feudal, undemocratic society civilized and modernized.

Even among the Republicans in Congress, there was considerable disagreement about the proper approach to Reconstruction—disagreement that reflected the same factional division (between the party's Conservatives and Radicals) that had created disputes over emancipation during the war. Conservatives insisted that the South accept the abolition of slavery, but proposed few other conditions for the readmission *Conservative and Radical Republicans* of the seceded states. The Radicals, led by Representative Thaddeus Stevens of Pennsylvania and Senator Charles Sumner of Massachusetts, urged that the civil and military leaders of the Confederacy be punished, that large numbers of Southern whites be disenfranchised, that the legal rights of blacks be protected, and that the property of wealthy white Southerners who had aided the Confederacy be confiscated and distributed among the freedmen. Some Radicals favored granting suffrage to the former slaves. Others hesitated, since few Northern states permitted blacks to vote. Between the Radicals and the Conservatives stood a faction of uncommitted Republicans, the Moderates, who rejected the punitive goals of the Radicals but supported extracting at least some concessions from the South on black rights.

Plans for Reconstruction

President Lincoln's sympathies lay with the Moderates and Conservatives of his party. He believed that a lenient Reconstruction policy would encourage southern unionists and other former Whigs to join the Republican Party and would thus prevent the readmission of the South from strengthening the Democrats. More immediately, the southern unionists could become the nucleus of new, loyal state governments in the South. Lincoln was not uninterested in the fate of the freedmen, but he was willing to defer questions about their future for the sake of rapid reunification.

Lincoln's Reconstruction plan, which he announced in December 1863, offered a general amnesty to white

Lincoln's 10% Plan

southerners—other than high officials of the Confederacy— who would pledge loyalty to the government and accept the elimination of slavery. Whenever 10 percent of the number of voters in 1860 took the oath in any state, those loyal voters could set up a state government. Lincoln also hoped to extend suffrage to those blacks who were educated, owned property, and had served in the Union army. Three southern states—Louisiana, Arkansas, and Tennessee, all under Union occupation—reestablished loyal governments under the Lincoln formula in 1864.

The Radical Republicans were astonished at the mildness of Lincoln's program. They persuaded Congress to deny seats to representatives from the three "reconstructed" states and refused to count the electoral vote of those states in the election of 1864. But for the moment, the Radicals were uncertain about what form their own

Wade-Davis Bill

Reconstruction plan should take. Their first effort to resolve that question was the Wade-Davis Bill, passed by Congress in July 1864. It authorized the president to appoint a provisional governor for each conquered state. When a majority (not Lincoln's 10 percent) of the white males of the state pledged their allegiance to the Union, the governor could summon a state constitutional convention, whose delegates were to be elected by those who would swear (through the so-called Ironclad Oath) that they had never borne arms against the United States—another departure from Lincoln's plan. The new state constitutions would have to abolish slavery, disfranchise Confederate civil and military leaders, and repudiate debts accumulated by the state governments during the war. After a state had met these conditions, Congress would readmit it to the Union. Like the president's proposal, the Wade-Davis Bill left up to the states the question of political rights for blacks. Congress passed the bill a few days before it adjourned in 1864, and Lincoln disposed of it with a pocket veto. His action enraged the Radical leaders, and the pragmatic Lincoln became convinced he would have to accept at least some of the Radical demands. He began to move toward a new approach to Reconstruction.

The Death of Lincoln

What plan he might have produced no one can say. On the night of April 14, 1865, Lincoln and his wife attended a play at Ford's Theater in Washington. As they sat in the presidential box, John Wilkes Booth, a member of a distinguished family of actors and a man obsessed with aiding the Southern cause, entered the box from the rear and shot Lincoln in the head. The president was carried unconscious to a house across the street, where early the next morning, surrounded by family, friends, and political associates (among them a tearful Charles Sumner), he died.

ABRAHAM LINCOLN This haunting photograph of Abraham Lincoln, showing clearly the weariness and aging that four years as a war president had created, was taken in Washington only four days before his assassination in 1865. *(Library of Congress)*

The circumstances of Lincoln's death earned him immediate martyrdom. It also produced something close to hysteria throughout the North. There were accusations that Booth had acted as part of a great conspiracy— accusations that contained some truth. Booth did indeed have associates, one of whom shot and wounded Secretary of State Seward the night of the assassination, another of whom abandoned at the last moment a scheme to murder Vice President Johnson. Booth himself escaped on horseback into the Virginia countryside, where, on April 26, he was cornered by Union troops and shot to death in a blazing barn. A military tribunal convicted eight other people of participating in the conspiracy (at least two of them on the basis of virtually no evidence). Four were hanged.

To many Northerners, however, the murder of the president seemed evidence of an even greater conspiracy— one masterminded and directed by the unrepentant leaders of the defeated South. Militant Republicans exploited such suspicions relentlessly for months, ensuring that Lincoln's death would help doom his plans for a relatively easy peace.

Johnson and "Restoration"

Leadership of the Moderates and Conservatives fell to Lincoln's successor, Andrew Johnson, who was not well suited, either by circumstance or personality, for the task. A

Democrat until he had joined the Union ticket with Lincoln in 1864, he became a Republican president at a moment when partisan passions were growing. Johnson himself was

Andrew Johnson's Personality

an intemperate and tactless man, filled with resentments and insecurities. He was also openly hostile to the freed slaves and unwilling to support any plans that guaranteed them civil equality or enfranchisement. He once declared, "White men alone must manage the South."

Johnson revealed his plan for Reconstruction—or "Restoration," as he preferred to call it—soon after he took office, and he implemented it during the summer of 1865 when Congress was in recess. Like Lincoln, he offered amnesty to those Southerners who would take an oath of allegiance. (High-ranking Confederate officials and any white Southerner with land worth $20,000 or more would have to apply to the president for individual pardons. Johnson, a self-made man, apparently liked the thought of the great planter aristocrats humbling themselves before him.) In most other respects, however, his plan resembled that of the Wade-Davis Bill. For each state, the president appointed a provisional governor, who was to invite qualified voters to elect delegates to a constitutional convention. Johnson did not specify how many qualified voters were necessary, but he implied that he would require a majority (as had the Wade-Davis Bill). In order to win readmission to Congress, a state had to revoke its ordinance of secession, abolish slavery, ratify the Thirteenth Amendment, and repudiate the Confederate and state war debts. The final procedure before restoration was for a state to elect a state government and send representatives to Congress.

By the end of 1865, all the seceded states had formed new governments—some under Lincoln's plan, some under Johnson's—and were prepared to rejoin the Union as soon as Congress recognized them. But Radical Republicans vowed not to recognize the Johnson governments, just as they had previously refused to recognize the Lincoln regimes; for by now, northern

Northern Attitudes Harden

opinion had become more hostile toward the South than it had been a year earlier when Congress passed the Wade-Davis Bill. Many northerners were disturbed by the apparent reluctance of some delegates to the southern conventions to abolish slavery, and by the refusal of all the conventions to grant suffrage to any blacks. They were astounded that states claiming to be "loyal" should elect prominent leaders of the recent Confederacy as state officials and representatives to Congress. Particularly hard to accept was Georgia's choice of Alexander H. Stephens, former Confederate vice president, as a United States senator.

RADICAL RECONSTRUCTION

Reconstruction under Johnson's plan—often known as "presidential Reconstruction"—continued only until Congress reconvened in December 1865. At that point, Congress refused to seat the representatives of the "restored" states and created a new Joint Committee on Reconstruction to frame a Reconstruction policy of its own. The period of "congressional" or "Radical" Reconstruction had begun.

The Black Codes

Meanwhile, events in the South were driving Northern opinion in even more radical directions. Throughout the South in 1865 and early 1866, state legislatures were enacting sets of laws known as the Black Codes, designed to give whites substantial control over the former slaves. The codes authorized local officials to apprehend unemployed blacks, fine them for vagrancy, and hire them out to private employers to satisfy the fine. Some of the codes forbade blacks to own or lease farms or to take any jobs other than as plantation workers or domestic servants.

Congress first responded to the Black Codes by passing an act extending the life of the Freedmen's Bureau and widening its powers so that it could nullify work agreements

Johnson's Vetoes

forced on freedmen under the Black Codes. Then, in April 1866, Congress passed the first Civil Rights Act, which declared blacks to be citizens of the United States and gave the federal government power to intervene in state affairs to protect the rights of citizens. Johnson vetoed both bills, but Congress overrode him on each of them.

The Fourteenth Amendment

In April 1866, the Joint Committee on Reconstruction proposed a new amendment to the Constitution, which Congress approved in early summer and sent to the states for ratification. Eventually, it became one of the most important of all the provisions in the Constitution.

The Fourteenth Amendment offered the first constitutional definition of American citizenship. Everyone born in the United States, and everyone naturalized, was automatically a citizen and entitled to all the "privileges and immunities" guaranteed by the Constitution, including equal

Citizenship for Blacks

protection of the laws by both the state and national governments. There could be no other requirements for citizenship. The amendment also imposed penalties—reduction of representation in Congress and in the electoral college—on states that denied suffrage to any adult male inhabitants. (The wording reflected the prevailing view in Congress and elsewhere that the franchise was properly restricted to men.) Finally, it prohibited former members of Congress or other former federal officials who had aided the Confederacy from holding any state or federal office unless two-thirds of Congress voted to pardon them.

Congressional Radicals offered to readmit to the Union any state whose legislature ratified the Fourteenth Amendment. Only Tennessee did so. All the other former

THE MEMPHIS RACE RIOT, 1866 Angry whites (shown here shooting down blacks) rampaged through the black neighborhoods of Memphis, Tennessee, during the first three days of May 1866, burning homes, schools, and churches and leaving forty-six people dead. Some claimed the riot was a response to strict new regulations protecting blacks that had been imposed on Tennessee by General George Stoneman, the military commander of the district; others argued that it was an attempt by whites to intimidate and control an African-American population that was trying to exercise its new freedom. Such riots were among the events that persuaded Radical Republicans in Congress to press for a harsher policy of Reconstruction. *(The Granger Collection)*

Confederate states, along with Delaware and Kentucky, refused, leaving the amendment temporarily without the necessary approval of three-fourths of the states.

But by now, the Radicals were growing more confident and determined. Bloody race riots in New Orleans and other Southern cities—riots in which African Americans were the principal victims—were among the events that strengthened their hand. In the 1866 congressional elections, Johnson actively campaigned for Conservative candidates, but he did his own cause more harm than good with his intemperate speeches. The voters returned an overwhelming majority of Republicans, most of them Radicals, to Congress. In the Senate, there were now 42 Republicans to 11 Democrats; in the House, 143 Republicans to 49 Democrats. (The South remained largely unrepresented in both chambers.) Congressional Republicans were now strong enough to enact a plan of their own even over the president's objections.

The Congressional Plan

The Radicals passed three Reconstruction bills early in 1867 and overrode Johnson's vetoes of all of them. These bills *Three Reconstruction Bills* finally established, nearly two years after the end of the war, a coherent plan for Reconstruction.

Under the congressional plan, Tennessee, which had ratified the Fourteenth Amendment, was promptly readmitted. But Congress rejected the Lincoln-Johnson governments of the other ten Confederate states and, instead, combined those states into five military districts. A military commander governed each district and had orders to register qualified voters (defined as all adult black males and those white males who had not participated in the rebellion). Once registered, voters would elect conventions to prepare new state constitutions, which had to include

AMERICAN CITIZENS (TO THE POLLS) The artist T. W. Wood painted this watercolor of voters standing in line at the polls during the 1866 elections. A prosperous Yankee, a working-class Irishman, and a Dutch coach driver stand next to the newest addition to the American electorate: an African American, whose expression conveys his excitement at being able to join the community of voters. Wood meant this painting to celebrate the democratic character of American life after the Civil War. *(T. W. Wood Art Gallery, Vermont College, Montpelier)*

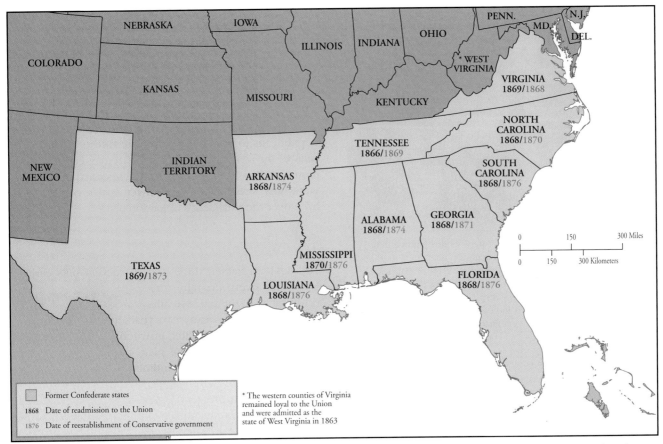

RECONSTRUCTION, 1866–1877 This map shows the former Confederate states and provides the dates when each was readmitted to the Union as well as a subsequent date when each state managed to return political power to traditional white, conservative elites—a process white southerners liked to call "redemption." ◆ *What had to happen for a state to be readmitted to the Union? What had to happen before a state could experience "redemption"?*

provisions for black suffrage. Once voters ratified the new constitutions, they could elect state governments. Congress had to approve a state's constitution, and the state legislature had to ratify the Fourteenth Amendment. Once that happened, and once enough states ratified the amendment to make it part of the Constitution, then the former Confederate states could be restored to the Union.

By 1868, seven of the ten former Confederate states (Arkansas, North Carolina, South Carolina, Louisiana, Alabama, Georgia, and Florida) had fulfilled these conditions (including ratification of the Fourteenth Amendment, which now became part of the Constitution) and were readmitted to the Union. Conservative whites held up the return of Virginia and Texas until 1869 and Mississippi until 1870. By then, Congress had added an additional requirement for readmission—ratification of another constitutional amendment, the Fifteenth, which forbade the states and the federal government to deny suffrage to any citizen on account of "race, color, or previous condition of servitude."

Fifteenth Amendment

To stop the president from interfering with their plans, the congressional Radicals passed two remarkable laws of

dubious constitutionality in 1867. One, the Tenure of Office Act, forbade the president to remove civil officials, including members of his own cabinet, without the consent of the Senate. The principal purpose of the law was to protect the job of Secretary of War Edwin M. Stanton, who was cooperating with the Radicals. The other law, the Command of the Army Act, prohibited the president from issuing military orders except through the commanding general of the army (General Grant), who could not be relieved or assigned elsewhere without the consent of the Senate.

The congressional Radicals also took action to stop the Supreme Court from interfering with their plans. In 1866, the Court had declared in the case of *Ex parte Milligan* that military tribunals were unconstitutional in places where civil courts were functioning, a decision that seemed to threaten the system of military government the Radicals were planning for the South. Radicals in Congress immediately proposed several bills that would require two-thirds of the justices to support any decision overruling a law of Congress, would deny the Court jurisdiction in Reconstruction cases, would reduce its membership to three, and would even abolish it. The justices apparently took notice. Over the next two years, the Court refused to accept jurisdiction in any cases involving Reconstruction (and the congressional bills concerning the Court never passed).

The Impeachment of the President

President Johnson had long since ceased to be a serious obstacle to the passage of Radical legislation, but he was still the official charged with administering the Reconstruction programs. As such, the Radicals believed, he remained a serious impediment to their plans. Early in 1867, they began looking for a way to impeach him and remove him from office. A search for grounds for impeachment began. Republicans found them, they believed, when Johnson dismissed Secretary of War Stanton despite Congress's refusal to agree, thus deliberately violating the

Tenure of Office Act | Tenure of Office Act in hopes of testing the law before the courts.

Elated Radicals in the House quickly impeached the president and sent the case to the Senate for trial.

The trial before the Senate lasted throughout April and May 1868. The Radicals put heavy pressure on all the Republican senators, but the Moderates (who were losing

Johnson Acquitted | faith in the Radical program) vacillated. On the first three

charges to come to a vote, seven Republicans joined the Democrats and independents to support acquittal. The vote was 35 to 19, one short of the constitutionally required two-thirds majority. After that, the Radicals dropped the impeachment effort.

THE SOUTH IN RECONSTRUCTION

When white Southerners spoke bitterly in later years of the effects of Reconstruction, they referred most frequently to the governments Congress helped impose on them—governments they claimed were both incompetent and corrupt, that saddled the region with enormous debts, and that trampled on the rights of citizens. When black Southerners and their defenders condemned Reconstruction, in contrast, they spoke of the failure of the national and state governments to go far enough to guarantee freedmen even the most elemental rights of citizenship—a failure that resulted in a harsh new system of economic subordination. (See "Where Historians Disagree," pp. 424–425).

The Reconstruction Governments

In the ten states of the South that were reorganized under the congressional plan, approximately one-fourth of the white males were at first excluded from voting or holding office. That produced black majorities among voters in South Carolina, Mississippi, and Louisiana (states where blacks were also a majority of the population), and in Alabama and Florida (where they were not). But the government soon lifted most suffrage restrictions so that nearly all white males could vote. After that, Republicans maintained control only with the support of many Southern whites.

Critics called these Southern white Republicans "scalawags." Many were former Whigs who had never felt comfortable in the Democratic Party—some of them wealthy | *"Scalawags"* (or once wealthy) planters or businessmen interested in the economic development of the region. Others were farmers who lived in remote areas where there had been little or no slavery and who hoped the Republican program of internal improvements would help end their economic isolation. Despite their diverse social positions, scalawags shared a belief that the Republican Party would serve their economic interests better than the Democrats.

White men from the North also served as Republican leaders in the South. Critics of Reconstruction referred

THE BURDENED SOUTH This Reconstruction-era cartoon expresses the South's sense of its oppression at the hands of Northern Republicans. President Grant (whose hat bears Abraham Lincoln's initials) rides in comfort in a giant carpetbag, guarded by bayonet-wielding soldiers, as the South staggers under the burden in chains. More evidence of destruction and military occupations is visible in the background. *(Culver Pictures, Inc.)*

THE LOUISIANA CONSTITUTIONAL CONVENTION, 1868 This lithograph commemorates the brief moment during which black voters actually dominated the politics of Louisiana. When the state held a constitutional convention in 1868, a majority of the delegates were African Americans (many of them freeborn blacks who had moved to Louisiana from the North). The Constitution they passed guaranteed political and civil rights to black citizens. When white conservatives regained control of the state several years later, they passed a new constitution of their own, repealing most of those guarantees. *(Library of Congress)*

to them pejoratively as "carpetbaggers," which conveyed an image of penniless adventurers who arrived with all

"Carpetbaggers"

their possessions in a carpet-bag (a common kind of cheap suitcase covered with carpeting material). In fact, most of the so-called carpetbaggers were well-educated people of middle-class origin, many of them doctors, lawyers, and teachers. Most were veterans of the Union army who looked on the South as a new frontier, more promising than the West. They had settled there at war's end as hopeful planters, or as business and professional people.

But the most numerous Republicans in the South were the black freedmen, most of whom had no previous experience in politics and who tried, therefore, to build institutions through which they could learn to exercise their power. In several states, African-American voters held their own conven-

Freedmen

tions to chart their future course. One such "colored convention," as Southern whites called them, assembled in Alabama in 1867 and announced: "We claim exactly the same rights, privileges and immunities as are enjoyed by white men—we ask nothing more and will be content with nothing less." The black churches freedmen created after emancipation, when they withdrew from the white-dominated churches they had been compelled to attend under slavery, also helped give unity and political self-confidence to the former slaves. African Americans played a significant role in the politics of the Reconstruction South. They served as delegates to the constitutional conventions. They held public offices of practically every kind. Between 1869 and 1901, twenty blacks served in the U.S. House of Representatives, two in the Senate (Hiram Revels of Mississippi and Blanche K. Bruce of Mississippi). African Americans served, too, in state legislatures and in various other state offices. Southern whites complained loudly (both at the time and for generations to come) about "Negro rule" during Reconstruction, but no such thing ever actually existed in any of the states. No black man was ever elected governor of a southern state (although Lieutenant Governor P. B. S. Pinchback briefly performed gubernatorial duties in Louisiana). Blacks never controlled any of the state legislatures, although they held a majority in the lower house in South Carolina for a time. In the South as a whole, the percentage of black officeholders was always far lower than the percentage of blacks in the population. The record of the Reconstruction governments is mixed. Critics at the time and since denounced them for corruption and financial extravagance, and there is some truth to both charges. Officeholders in many states enriched themselves through graft and other illicit activities. State budgets expanded to hitherto unknown totals, and state debts soared to previously undreamed-of heights. In South Carolina, for example, the public debt increased from $7 million to $29 million in eight years.

But the corruption in the South, real as it was, was hardly unique to the Reconstruction governments. Corruption was at least as rampant in the northern states. And in both North and South, it was a result of the same thing: a rapid economic expansion of government services (and revenues) that put new strains on (and new temptations before) elected officials everywhere. The end of Reconstruction did not end corruption in southern state governments. In many states, in fact, corruption increased.

And the state expenditures of the Reconstruction years were huge only in comparison with the meager budgets of the antebellum era. They represented an effort to provide the South with desperately needed services that antebellum governments had never offered: public education, public works programs, poor relief, and other costly new commitments. There were, to be sure, graft and extravagance in Reconstruction governments; there were also positive and permanent accomplishments.

Education

Perhaps the most important of those accomplishments was a dramatic improvement in southern education—an improvement that benefited both whites and blacks. In the first years of Reconstruction, much of the impetus for educational reform in the South came from outside groups—from the Freedmen's Bureau, from Northern private philanthropic organizations, from many Northern women, black and white, who traveled to the South to teach in freedmen's schools—and from southern blacks themselves. Over the opposition of many southern whites, who feared that education would give blacks "false notions of equality," these reformers established a large network of schools for former slaves—4,000 schools by 1870, staffed by 9,000 teachers (half of them black), teaching 200,000 students (about 12 percent of the total school-age population of the freedmen). In the 1870s, Reconstruction governments began to build a comprehensive public school system in the South. By 1876, more than half of all white children and about 40 percent of all black children were attending schools in the South. Several black "academies," offering more advanced education, also began operating. Gradually, these academies grew into an important network of black colleges and universities, which included such distinguished schools as Fisk and Atlanta Universities and Morehouse College.

Already, however, southern education was becoming divided into two separate systems, one black and one

Segregated Schools

white. Early efforts to integrate the schools of the region were a dismal failure. The Freedmen's Bureau schools, for example, were open to students of all races, but almost no whites attended them. New Orleans set up an integrated school system under the Reconstruction government; again, whites almost universally stayed away. The one federal effort to mandate school integration—the Civil Rights Act of 1875—had its provisions for educational desegregation removed before it was passed. As soon as the Republican governments of Reconstruction were replaced, the new Southern Democratic regimes quickly abandoned all efforts to promote integration.

Landownership and Tenancy

The most ambitious goal of the Freedmen's Bureau, and of some Republican Radicals in Congress, was to make Reconstruction the vehicle for a fundamental reform of landownership in the South. The effort failed. In the last years of the war and the first years of Reconstruction, the

Freedmen's Bureau did oversee the redistribution of substantial amounts of land to freedmen in a few areas—notably the Sea Islands of South Carolina and Georgia, and areas of Mississippi that had once belonged to the family of Jefferson Davis. By June 1865, the Bureau had settled nearly 10,000 black families on their own land—most of it drawn from abandoned plantations—arousing dreams among former slaves throughout the South of "forty acres and a mule." By the end of that year, however, the experiment was already collapsing. Southern plantation owners were returning and demanding the restoration of their property, and President Johnson was supporting their demands. Despite the resistance of the Freedmen's Bureau, the government eventually returned most of the confiscated land to the original white owners. Congress, moreover, never had much stomach for the idea of land redistribution. Very few Northern Republicans believed that the federal government had the right to confiscate property. Even so, distribution of landownership in the South changed considerably in the postwar years. Among whites, there was a striking decline in landownership, from 80 percent before the war to 67 percent by the end of Reconstruction. Some whites lost their land because of unpaid debt or increased taxes; some left the marginal lands they had owned to move to more fertile areas, where they rented. Among blacks, during the same period, the proportion who owned land rose from virtually none to more than 20 percent. Many black landowners acquired their property through hard work or luck or both. But some relied on assistance from white-dominated financial or philanthropic institutions. One of them was the Freedman's Bank, established in 1865 by antislavery whites in an effort to promote landownership among blacks. They persuaded thousands of freedmen to deposit their modest savings in the bank, but then invested heavily in unsuccessful enterprises. It was ill prepared, therefore, for the national depression of the 1870s and it failed in 1874.

Failure of Land Redistribution

Still, most blacks, and a growing minority of whites, did not own their own land during Reconstruction; and some who acquired land in the 1860s had lost it by the 1890s. These people worked for others in one form or another. Many black agricultural laborers—perhaps 25 percent of the total—simply worked for wages. Most, however, became tenants of white landowners—working their own plots of land and paying their landlords either a fixed rent or a share of their crop (see pp. 430–431).

Sharecropping

The new system represented a repudiation by blacks of the gang-labor system of the antebellum plantation, in which slaves had lived and worked together under the direction of a master. As tenants and sharecroppers, blacks enjoyed at least a physical independence from their landlords and had the sense of working their own land, even if in most cases they could never hope to buy it. But tenantry

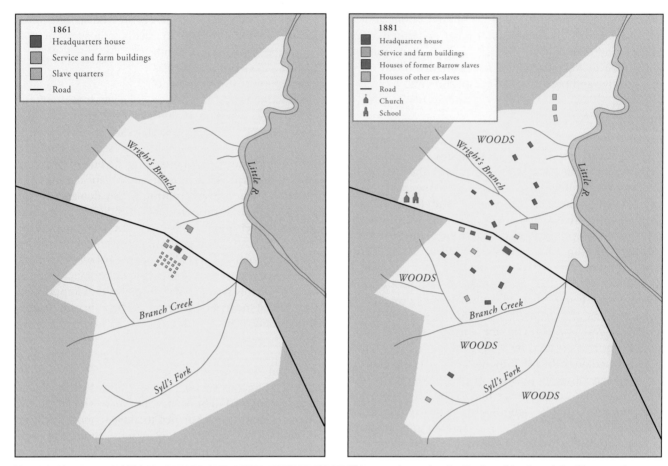

THE SOUTHERN PLANTATION BEFORE AND AFTER EMANCIPATION This map shows the distribution of lands and dwellings on the Barrow Plantation in Oglethorpe County, Georgia, before and after the emancipation of slaves at the close of the Civil War. The map on the left shows the plantation in 1861, as the war began. Like the Hopeton Plantation shown on p. 303, the Barrow plantation was highly centralized before the war, with slaves living all together in a complex of dwellings near the master's house. Twenty years later, as the map on the right shows, the same landscape was very differently divided. Housing was now widely dispersed, as former slaves became tenants or sharecroppers and began working their own small pieces of land and living more independently. Churches had sprung up away from the landowner's house as well. ◆ *Why did former slaves move so quickly to relocate their homes and churches away from their former masters?*

 For an interactive version of this map go to www.mhhe.com/brinkley11ch15maps

also benefited landlords in some ways, relieving them of any responsibility for the physical well-being of their workers.

The Crop-Lien System

In some respects, the postwar years were a period of remarkable economic progress for African Americans. If the material benefits they had received under slavery are calculated as income, then prewar blacks had earned about a 22 percent share of the profits of the plantation system. By the end of Reconstruction, they were earning 56 percent. Measured another way, the per capita income of southern blacks rose 46 percent between 1857 and 1879, while the per capita income of southern whites declined 35 percent. This represented one of the most significant redistributions of income in American history.

But these figures are somewhat misleading. For one thing, while the black share of profits was increasing, the total profits of southern agriculture were declining—a result of the dislocations of the war and a reduction in the world market for cotton. For another thing, while blacks were earning a greater return on each hour of labor than they had under slavery, they were working fewer hours. Women and children were less likely to labor in the fields than in the past. Adult men tended to work shorter days. In all, the black labor force worked about one-third fewer hours during Reconstruction than it had been compelled to work under slavery—a reduction that brought the working schedule of blacks roughly into line with that of white farm laborers. Nor did the income redistribution of the postwar years lift many blacks out of poverty. Black per capita income rose from about one-quarter of white per capita income to about one-half in the first few years after the war. And after this initial increase, it rose hardly at all.

For blacks and poor whites alike, whatever gains there might have been as a result of land and income redistribution were often overshadowed by the ravages of the crop-lien system. Few of the traditional institutions of *New System of Credit* credit in the South—the "factors" and banks—returned after the war. In their stead emerged a new system of credit, centered in large part on local country stores, some of them owned by planters, others by independent merchants. Blacks and whites, landowners and tenants—all depended on these stores for such necessities as food, clothing, seed, and farm implements. And since farmers did not have the same steady cash flow as other workers, customers usually had to rely on credit from these merchants in order to purchase what they needed. Most local stores had no competition (and went to great lengths to ensure that things stayed that way). As a result, they were able to set interest rates as high as 50 or 60 percent. Farmers had to give the merchants a lien (or claim) on their crops as collateral for the loans (thus the term "crop-lien system," generally used to describe Southern farming in this period). Farmers who suffered a few bad years in a row, as often happened, could become trapped in a cycle of debt from which they could never escape.

This burdensome credit system had a number of effects on the region, almost all of them unhealthy. One was that some blacks who had acquired land during the early years of Reconstruction gradually lost it as they fell into debt. So, to a lesser extent, did white small landowners. Another was that Southern farmers became almost wholly dependent on cash crops—and most of all on cotton—because only such marketable commodities seemed to offer any possibility of escape from debt. Thus Southern agriculture, never

sufficiently diversified even in the best of times, became more one-dimensional than ever. The relentless planting of cotton, moreover, was contributing to an exhaustion of the soil. The crop-lien system, in other words, was not only helping to impoverish small farmers; it was also contributing to a general decline in the Southern agricultural economy.

The African-American Family in Freedom

One of the most striking features of the black response to Reconstruction was the effort to build or rebuild family structures and to protect them from the interference they had experienced under slavery. A major reason for the rapid departure of so many blacks from plantations was the desire to find lost relatives and reunite families. Thousands of African Americans wandered through the South—often over vast distances—looking for husbands, wives, children, or other relatives from whom they had been separated. In the few black newspapers that circulated in the South, there were many advertisements by people searching for information about their relatives. Former slaves rushed to have marriages, previously without legal standing, sanctified by church and law. Black families resisted living in the former slave quarters and moved instead to small cabins scattered widely across the countryside, where they could enjoy at least some privacy. Within the black family, the definition of male and female roles quickly came to resemble that within white families. Many women and children ceased working in the fields. Such work, they believed, was a badge of slavery. Instead, many women restricted themselves largely to domestic tasks—cooking, cleaning, gardening, raising children, attending to the needs of their husbands. Some black husbands refused to allow their wives to work as servants in white homes. "When I married my wife I married her to

A VISIT FROM THE OLD MISTRESS Winslow Homer's 1876 painting of an imagined visit by a southern white woman to a group of her former slaves was an effort to convey something of the tension in relations between the races in the South during Reconstruction. The women, once intimately involved in one another's lives, look at each other guardedly, carefully maintaining the space between them. White southerners attacked the painting for portraying white and black women on a relatively equal footing. Some black southerners criticized it for depicting poor rural African Americans instead of the more prosperous professional blacks who were emerging in southern cities. "There were plenty of well-dressed negroes if he would but look for them," one wrote. *(National Museum of American Art, Smithsonian Institution. Gift of William T. Evans/Art Resource, NY)*

AFRICAN-AMERICAN WORK AFTER SLAVERY Black men and women engaged in a wide range of economic activities in the aftermath of slavery. But discrimination by white Southerners and the former slaves' own lack of education limited most of them to relatively menial jobs. Many black women (including this former slave) earned money for their families by working as "washer women," doing laundry for white people. *(Historic New Orleans Collection)*

wait on me," one freedman told a former master who was attempting to hire his wife as a servant. "She got all she can do right here for me and the children."

Still, middle-class notions of domesticity were often difficult to sustain in the impoverished circumstances of most *Changing Gender Roles* | former slaves. Economic necessity required many black women to engage in income-producing activities, including activities that they and their husbands resisted because they reminded them of slavery: working as domestic servants, taking in laundry, or helping in the field. By the end of Reconstruction, half of all black women over the age of sixteen were working for wages. And unlike white working women, most black female income-earners were married.

THE GRANT ADMINISTRATION

Exhausted by the political turmoil of the Johnson administration, American voters in 1868 yearned for a strong, stable figure to guide them through the troubled years of Reconstruction. They turned trustingly to General Ulysses S. Grant, the hero of the war and, by 1868, a revered national idol.

The Soldier President

Grant could have had the nomination of either party in 1868. But believing that Republican Reconstruction policies were more popular in the North, he accepted the | *U. S. Grant* Republican nomination. The Democrats nominated former governor Horatio Seymour of New York. The campaign was a bitter one, and Grant's triumph was surprisingly narrow. Without the 500,000 new black Republican voters in the South, he would have had a minority of the popular vote.

Grant entered the White House with no political experience, and his performance was clumsy and ineffectual from the start. Except for Hamilton Fish, whom Grant appointed secretary of state and who served for eight years with great distinction, most members of the cabinet were ill-equipped for their tasks. Grant relied chiefly, and increasingly, on established party leaders—the group most ardently devoted to patronage, and his administration used the spoils system even more blatantly than most of its predecessors, embittering reform-minded members of his party. Grant also alienated the many Northerners who were growing disillusioned with the Radical Reconstruction policies, which the president continued to support. Some Republicans suspected, correctly, that there was also corruption in the Grant administration itself.

By the end of Grant's first term, therefore, members of a substantial faction of the party—who referred to themselves as Liberal Republicans— | *Liberal Republicans* had come to oppose what they called "Grantism." In 1872, hoping to prevent Grant's reelection, they bolted the party and nominated their own presidential candidate: Horace Greeley, veteran editor and publisher of the *New York Tribune*. The Democrats, somewhat reluctantly, named Greeley their candidate as well, hoping that the alliance with the Liberals would enable them to defeat Grant. But the effort was in vain. Grant won a substantial victory, polling 286 electoral votes to Greeley's 66, and nearly 56 percent of the popular total.

The Grant Scandals

During the 1872 campaign, the first of a series of political scandals came to light that would plague Grant and the Republicans for the next | *Crédit Mobilier* eight years. It involved the French-owned Crédit Mobilier construction company, which had helped build the Union Pacific Railroad. The heads of Crédit Mobilier had used their positions as

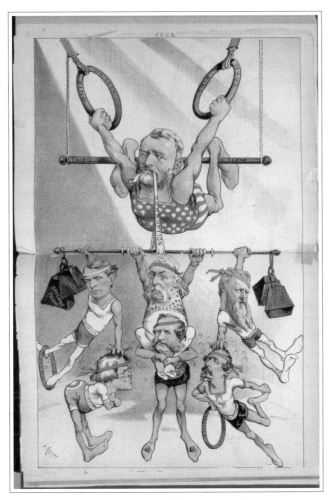

GRANT THE TRAPEZE ARTISTS This cartoon by the eminent cartoonist Joseph Keppler shows President Ulysses S. Grant swinging on a trapeze holding on the "whiskey ring" and the "Navy ring" (references to two of the many scandals that plagued his presidency). Using a strap labeled corruption, he holds aloft some of the most notorious figures in those scandals. The cartoon was published in 1880, when Grant was attempting to win the Republican nomination to run for another term as president. *(Library of Congress)*

Union Pacific stockholders to steer large fraudulent contracts to their construction company, thus bilking the Union Pacific (and the federal government, which provided large subsidies to the railroad) of millions. To prevent investigations, the directors had given Crédit Mobilier stock to key members of Congress. But in 1872, Congress did conduct an investigation, which revealed that some highly placed Republicans—including Schuyler Colfax, now Grant's vice president—had accepted stock.

One dreary episode followed another in Grant's second term. Benjamin H. Bristow, Grant's third Treasury secretary, discovered that some of his officials and a group of distillers operating as a "whiskey ring" were cheating the government out of taxes by filing false reports. Then a House investigation revealed that William W. Belknap, secretary of war, had accepted bribes to retain an Indian-post trader in office (the so-called Indian ring). Other, lesser scandals added to the growing impression that "Grantism" had brought rampant corruption to government.

The Greenback Question

Compounding Grant's, and the nation's, problems was a financial crisis, known as the Panic of 1873. It began with the failure of a leading investment banking firm, Jay Cooke *Panic of 1873* and Company, which had invested too heavily in postwar railroad building. There had been panics before—in 1819, 1837, and 1857—but this was the worst one yet. The depression it produced lasted four years.

Debtors now pressured the government to redeem federal war bonds with greenbacks, paper currency of the sort printed during the Civil War, which would increase the amount of money in circulation. But Grant and most Republicans wanted a "sound" currency— based solidly on gold reserves—which would favor the interests of banks and other creditors. There was approximately $356 million in paper currency issued during the Civil War that was still in circulation. In 1873, the Treasury issued more in response to the panic. But in 1875, Republican leaders in Congress, in an effort to crush the greenback movement for good, passed the Specie Resumption Act. It provided that after January 1, 1879, the greenback dollars, whose value constantly fluctuated, would be redeemed by the government and replaced with new certificates, firmly pegged to the price of gold. The law satisfied creditors, who had worried that debts would be repaid in paper currency of uncertain value. But "resumption" made things more difficult for debtors, because the gold-based money supply could not easily expand.

In 1875, the "greenbackers," as the inflationists were called, formed their own political organization: the National Greenback Party. It *National Greenback Party* was active in the next three presidential elections, but it failed to gain widespread support. It did, however, keep the money issue alive. The question of the proper composition of the currency was to remain one of the most controversial and enduring issues in late-nineteenth-century American politics.

Republican Diplomacy

The Johnson and Grant administrations achieved their greatest successes in foreign affairs. The accomplishments were the work not of the presidents themselves, who displayed little aptitude for diplomacy, but of two outstanding secretaries of state: William H. Seward, who had served Lincoln and who remained in office until 1869; and Hamilton Fish, who served throughout the two terms of the Grant administration.

An ardent expansionist, Seward acted with as much daring as the demands of Reconstruction politics and the Republican hatred of President Johnson would permit. Seward accepted a Russian offer to sell Alaska to the United States for $7.2 million, despite criticism from many who considered Alaska a frozen wasteland and derided it as "Seward's Folly." In 1867, Seward also engineered the American annexation of the tiny Midway Islands, west of Hawaii.

"Seward's Folly"

Hamilton Fish's first major challenge was resolving the longstanding controversy with England over the American claims that it had violated neutrality laws during the Civil War by permitting English shipyards to build ships (among them the *Alabama*) for the Confederacy. American demands that England pay for the damage these vessels had caused became known as the "*Alabama* claims." In 1871, after a number of failed efforts, Fish forged an agreement, the Treaty of Washington, which provided for international arbitration and in which Britain expressed regret for the escape of the *Alabama* from England.

Alabama Claims

THE ABANDONMENT OF RECONSTRUCTION

As the North grew increasingly preoccupied with its own political and economic problems, interest in Reconstruction began to wane. The Grant administration continued to protect Republican governments in the South, but less because of any interest in ensuring the position of freedmen than because of a desire to prevent the reemergence of a strong Democratic Party in the region. But even the presence of federal troops was not enough to prevent white Southerners from overturning the Reconstruction regimes. By the time Grant left office, Democrats had taken back (or, as white Southerners liked to put it, "redeemed") the governments of seven of the eleven former Confederate states. For three other states—South Carolina, Louisiana, and Florida—the end of Reconstruction had to wait for the withdrawal of the last federal troops in 1876, a withdrawal that was the result of a long process of political bargaining and compromise at the national level. (One former Confederate state, Tennessee, had never been part of the Reconstruction process.)

The Southern States "Redeemed"

In the states where whites constituted a majority—the states of the upper South—overthrowing Republican control was relatively simple. By 1872, all but a handful of Southern whites had regained suffrage. Now a clear majority of the electorate, they needed only to organize and vote for their candidates.

In other states, where blacks were a majority or the populations of the two races were almost equal, whites used intimidation and violence to undermine the Reconstruction regimes. Secret societies—the Ku Klux Klan, the Knights of the White Camellia, and others—used terrorism to frighten or physically bar blacks from voting or otherwise exercising citizenship. Paramilitary organizations—the Red Shirts and White Leagues—armed themselves to "police" elections and worked to force all white males to join the Democratic Party and to exclude all blacks from meaningful political activity.

The Ku Klux Klan was the largest and most effective of these organizations. Formed in 1866 and led by former Confederate General Nathan Bedford Forrest, it gradually absorbed many of the smaller terrorist organizations. Its leaders devised rituals, costumes, secret languages, and other airs of mystery to create a bond among its members and make it seem even more terrifying to those it was attempting to intimidate. The Klan's "midnight rides"—bands of men clad in white sheets and masks, their horses covered with white robes and with hooves muffled—created terror in black communities throughout the South.

Ku Klux Klan

Many white Southerners considered the Klan and the other secret societies and paramilitary groups proud, patriotic societies. Together such groups served, in effect, as a military force (even if a decentralized and poorly organized one) continuing the battle against Northern rule. They worked in particular to advance the interests of those with the most to gain from a restoration of white supremacy—above all the planter class and the Southern Democratic Party. Even stronger than the Klan in discouraging black political power, however, was the simple weapon of economic pressure. Some planters refused to rent land to Republican blacks; storekeepers refused to extend them credit; employers refused to give them work.

The Ku Klux Klan Acts

The Republican Congress tried for a time to turn back this new wave of white repression. In 1870 and 1871, they passed two Enforcement Acts, also known as the Ku Klux Klan Acts, which were in many ways the most radical measures of the era. The Enforcement Acts prohibited the states from discriminating against voters on the basis of race and gave the federal government power to supersede the state courts and prosecute violations of the law. It was the first time the federal government had ever claimed the power to prosecute crimes by individuals under federal law. Federal district attorneys were

Enforcement Acts

now empowered to take action against conspiracies to deny African Americans such rights as voting, holding office, and serving on juries. The new laws also authorized the president to use the military to protect civil rights and to suspend the right of habeas corpus (the right of individuals to be freed from jail unless they are formally charged with a crime) when violations of the rights seemed particularly egregious. In October 1871, President Grant used this provision of the law when he declared a "state of lawlessness" in nine counties in South Carolina and sent in federal troops to occupy the area. Hundreds of suspected Klan members were arrested; some were held for long periods without trial; some were eventually convicted under the law and sent to jail.

The Enforcement Acts were seldom used as severely as they were in South Carolina, but they were effective in
Decline of the Klan | the effort by blacks and Northern whites to weaken the Klan. By 1872, Klan violence against blacks was in decline throughout the region.

Waning Northern Commitment

The Ku Klux Klan Acts marked the peak of Republican commitment to enforce the new rights Reconstruction was extending to black citizens. But that commitment did not last for very long. Southern blacks were gradually losing the support of many of their former backers in the North. As early as 1870, after the adoption of the Fifteenth Amendment, some reformers convinced themselves that their long campaign on behalf of black people was now over; that with the vote, blacks ought to be able to take care of themselves. Over the next several years, former Radical leaders such as Charles Sumner and Horace Greeley now began calling themselves Liberals, cooperating with Democrats, and at times outdoing even the Democrats in denouncing what they viewed as black and carpetbag misgovernment. Within the South itself, many white Republicans joined the Liberals and eventually moved into the Democratic Party.

The Panic of 1873 further undermined support for Reconstruction. This economic crisis spurred Northern
Impact of Social Darwinism | industrialists and their allies to find an explanation for the poverty and instability around them. They found it in a new idea known as "Social Darwinism" (see p. 484), a harsh theory that argued that individuals who failed did so because of their own weakness and "unfitness." Those influenced by Social Darwinism came to view the large number of unemployed vagrants in the North as irredeemable misfits. They took the same view of poor blacks in the South. Social Darwinism also encouraged a broad critique of government intervention in social and economic life, which further weakened commitment to the Reconstruction program. Support for land redistribution,

never great, waned quickly after 1873. So did willingness to spend money from the depleted federal treasury to aid the freedmen. State and local governments also found themselves short of funds, and rushed to cut back on social services—which in the South meant the end of almost all services to the former slaves.

In the congressional elections of 1874, the Democrats won control of the House of Representatives for the first time since 1861. Grant took note of the changing temper of the North and made use of military force to prop up the Republican regimes that were still standing in the South. By the end of 1876, only three states were left in the hands of the Republicans—South Carolina, Louisiana, and Florida. In state elections that year, Democrats (after using terrorist tactics) claimed victory in all three. But the Republicans challenged the results and claimed victory as well, and they were able to remain in office because of the presence of federal troops. Without federal troops, it was now clear, the last of the Republican regimes would quickly fall.

The Compromise of 1877

Grant had hoped to run for another term in 1876, but most Republican leaders—shaken by recent Democrat successes, afraid of the scandals with which Grant was associated, and concerned about the president's failing health—resisted. Instead, they sought a candidate not associ- | *Hayes versus Tilden* ated with the problems of the Grant years, one who might entice Liberals back and unite the party again. They settled on Rutherford B. Hayes, a former Union army officer, governor, and congressman, champion of civil service reform. The Democrats united behind Samuel J. Tilden, the reform governor of New York who had been instrumental in overthrowing the corrupt Tweed Ring of New York City's Tammany Hall.

Although the campaign was a bitter one, there were few differences of principle between the candidates, both of whom were conservatives committed to moderate reform. The November election produced an apparent Democratic victory. Tilden carried the South and several large Northern states, and his popular margin over Hayes was nearly 300,000 votes. But disputed returns from Louisiana, South Carolina, Florida, and Oregon, whose total electoral vote was 20, threw the election in doubt. Tilden had undisputed claim to 184 electoral votes, only one short of a majority. But Hayes could still win if he managed to receive all 20 disputed votes.

The Constitution had established no method to determine the validity of disputed returns. It was clear that the decision lay with Congress, but it was not clear with which house or through what method. (The Senate was Republican, the House, Democratic.) Members of each party naturally supported a solution that would yield them the victory.

Debate over the nature of Reconstruction—not only among historians, but among the public at large—has created so much controversy over the decades that one scholar, writing in 1959, described the issue as a "dark and bloody ground." Among historians, the passions of the debate have to some extent subsided since then; but in the popular mind, Reconstruction continues to raise "dark and bloody" images.

For many years, a relatively uniform and highly critical view of Reconstruction prevailed among historians, a reflection of broad currents in popular thought. By the late nineteenth century, most white Americans in both the North and the South had come to believe that few real differences any longer divided the sections, that the nation should strive for a genuine reconciliation. And most white Americans believed as well in the superiority of their race, in the inherent unfitness of blacks for political or social equality. Out of this mentality was born the first major historical interpretation of Reconstruction, through the work of William A. Dunning. In *Reconstruction, Political and Economic* (1907), Dunning portrayed Reconstruction as a corrupt outrage perpetrated on the prostrate South by a vicious and vindictive cabal of Northern Republican Radicals. Reconstruction governments were based on "bayonet rule." Unscrupulous and self-aggrandizing carpetbaggers flooded the South to profit from the misery of the defeated region. Ignorant, illiterate blacks were thrust into positions of power for which they were entirely unfit. The Reconstruction experiment, a moral

abomination from its first moments, survived only because of the determination of the Republican Party to keep itself in power. (Some later writers, notably Howard K. Beale, added an economic motive—to protect Northern business interests.) Dunning and his many students (who together formed what became known as the "Dunning school") compiled state-by-state evidence to show that the legacy of Reconstruction was corruption, ruinous taxation, and astronomical increases in the public debt.

The Dunning school not only shaped the views of several generations of historians. It also reflected and helped to shape the views of much of the public. Popular depictions of Reconstruction for years to come (as first the 1915 film *The Birth of a Nation* and then the 1936 book and 1939 movie *Gone With the Wind* illustrated) portrayed the era as one of tragic exploitation of the South by the North. Even today, many white southerners and many others continue to accept the basic premises of the Dunning interpretation. Among historians, however, the old view of Reconstruction has gradually lost credibility.

The great African-American scholar W. E. B. Du Bois was among the first to challenge the Dunning view in a 1910 article and, later, in a 1935 book, *Black Reconstruction*. To him, Reconstruction politics in the Southern states had been an effort on the part of the masses, black and white, to create a more democratic society. The misdeeds of the Reconstruction governments, he claimed, had been greatly exaggerated, and their achievements overlooked. The governments had

(U.S. Military History Institute, Carlisle, Pennsylvania. Photo by Jim Enos)

been expensive, he insisted, because they had tried to provide public education and other public services on a scale never before attempted in the South. But Du Bois's use of Marxist theory in his work caused many historians to dismiss his argument; and it remained for a group of less radical, white historians to shatter the Dunning image of Reconstruction.

In the 1940s, historians such as C. Vann Woodward, David Herbert Donald, Thomas B. Alexander, and others began to reexamine the Reconstruction governments in the South and to suggest that their records were not nearly as bad as most historians had previously assumed. They also looked at the Radical Republicans in Congress and suggested that they had not been motivated by vindictiveness

---

Finally, late in January 1877, Congress tried to break the deadlock by creating a special electoral commission to judge the disputed votes. The commission was to be composed of five senators, five representatives, and five justices of the Supreme Court. The congressional delegation would consist of five Republicans and five Democrats. The Court delegation would include two Republicans, two Democrats, and an independent. But the indepen-

Special Electoral Commission

dent seat ultimately went to a justice whose real sympathies were with the Republicans. The commission voted along straight party lines, 8 to 7, awarding every disputed vote to Hayes. Congress accepted their verdict on March 2. Two days later, Hayes was inaugurated.

Behind the resolution of the deadlock however, lay a series of elaborate compromises among leaders of both parties. When a Democratic filibuster threatened to derail the commission's report, Republican Senate leaders

and partisanship alone. By the early 1960s, a new view of Reconstruction was emerging from these efforts, a view whose appeal to historians grew stronger with the emergence of the "Second Reconstruction," the civil rights movement. The revisionist approach was summarized by John Hope Franklin in *Reconstruction After the Civil War* (1961) and Kenneth Stampp in *The Era of Reconstruction* (1965), which claimed that the postwar Republicans had been engaged in a genuine, if flawed, effort to solve the problem of race in the South by providing much-needed protection to the freedmen. The Reconstruction governments, for all their faults, had been bold experiments in interracial politics. The congressional Radicals were not saints, but they had displayed a genuine concern for the rights of slaves. Andrew Johnson was not a martyred defender of the Constitution, but an inept, racist politician who resisted reasonable compromise and brought the government to a crisis. There had been no such thing as "bayonet rule" or "Negro rule" in the South. Blacks had played only a small part in Reconstruction governments and had generally acquitted themselves well. The Reconstruction regimes had, in fact, brought important progress to the South, establishing the region's first public school system and other important social changes. Corruption in the South had been no worse than corruption in the North at that time. What was tragic about Reconstruction, the revisionist view claimed, was not what it did to Southern whites but what it did not do for Southern blacks. By stopping

(Library of Congress)

short of the reforms necessary to ensure blacks genuine equality, Reconstruction had consigned them to more than a century of injustice and discrimination.

In recent years scholars have begun to question the revisionist view—not in an effort to revive the old Dunning interpretation, but in an attempt to draw attention to those things Reconstruction in fact achieved. Eric Foner, in *Nothing but Freedom* (1983) and *Reconstruction: America's Unfinished Revolution* (1988) concluded that what is striking about the American experience in this context is not how little was accomplished, but how far the former slaves moved toward freedom and independence in a short time, and how large a role

African Americans themselves played in shaping Reconstruction. During Reconstruction, blacks won a certain amount of legal and political power in the South; and even though they held that power only temporarily, they used it for a time to strengthen their economic and social positions and to win a position of limited but genuine independence. Through Reconstruction they won, if not equality, a measure of individual and community autonomy, building blocks of the freedom that emancipation alone had not guaranteed.

Historians writing from the perspective of African-American and women's history have made related arguments. Leon Litwack's *Been in the Storm So Long* (1979) maintained that former slaves used the relative latitude they enjoyed under Reconstruction to build a certain independence for themselves within Southern society. They strengthened their churches; they reunited their families; they refused to work in the "gang labor" system of the plantations and forced the creation of a new labor system in which they had more control over their own lives. Amy Dru Stanley and Jacqueline Jones have both argued that the freed slaves displayed considerable independence in constructing their households on their own terms and asserting their control over family life, reproduction, and work. Women in particular sought the opportunity, according to Jacqueline Jones in *Labor of Love, Labor of Sorrow* (1985), "to labor on behalf of their own families and kin within the protected spheres of household and community."

met secretly with Southern Democratic leaders to work out terms by which the Democrats would allow the election of Hayes. According to traditional accounts, Republicans and Southern Democrats met at Washington's Wormley Hotel. In return for a Republican pledge that Hayes would withdraw the last federal troops from the South, thus permitting the overthrow of the last Republican governments there, the Southerners agreed to abandon the filibuster.

Actually, the story behind the "Compromise of 1877" is somewhat more complex. Hayes was already on record favoring withdrawal of the troops, so Republicans needed *Compromise of 1877* to offer more than that if they hoped for Democratic support. The real agreement, the one that won over the Southern Democrats, was reached well before the Wormley meeting. As the price of their cooperation, the Southern Democrats (among them some former Whigs) exacted

425

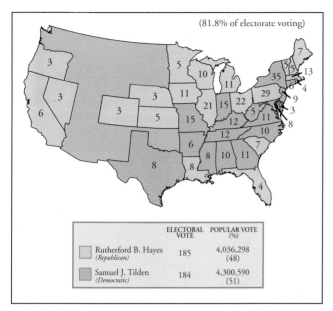

	ELECTORAL VOTE	POPULAR VOTE (%)
Rutherford B. Hayes (Republican)	185	4,036,298 (48)
Samuel J. Tilden (Democratic)	184	4,300,590 (51)

THE ELECTION OF 1876 The election of 1876 was one of the most controversial in American history. As in the elections of 1824, 1888, and 2000, the winner of the popular vote—Samuel J. Tilden—was not the winner of the electoral college, which he lost by one vote. The final decision as to who would be president was not made until the day before the official Inauguration in March. ◆ *How did the Republicans turn this apparent defeat into a victory?*

 For an interactive version of this map go to www.mhhe.com/brinkley11ch15maps

several pledges from the Republicans in addition to withdrawal of the troops: the appointment of at least one Southerner to the Hayes cabinet, control of federal patronage in their areas, generous internal improvements, and federal aid for the Texas and Pacific Railroad. Many powerful Southern Democrats supported industrializing their region. They believed Republican programs of federal support for business would aid the South more than the states' rights policies of the Democrats.

In his inaugural address, Hayes announced that the South's most pressing need was the restoration of "wise, honest, and peaceful local self-government"—a signal that he planned to withdraw federal troops and let white Democrats take over the state governments. That statement, and Hayes's subsequent actions, supported the widespread charges that he was paying off the South for acquiescing in his election and strengthened those who referred to him as "his Fraudulency." Hayes tried to counter such charges by projecting an image of stern public (and private) rectitude. But the election had already created such bitterness that even Hayes's promise to serve only one term could not mollify his critics.

The president and his party had hoped to build up a "new Republican" organization in the South drawn from Whiggish conservative white groups and committed to some modest acceptance of African-American rights. But all such efforts failed. Although many white Southern

leaders sympathized with Republican economic policies, popular resentment of Reconstruction was so deep that supporting the party was politically impossible. At the same time, the withdrawal of federal *Republican Failure in the South* troops signaled that the national government was giving up its attempts to control Southern politics and to improve the lot of blacks in Southern society.

The Legacies of Reconstruction

Reconstruction made some important contributions to the efforts of former slaves to achieve dignity and equality in American life. And it was not as disastrous an experience for Southern whites as most believed at the time. But Reconstruction was in the end largely a failure. For in those years the United States failed in its first serious effort to resolve its oldest and deepest social problem—the problem of race. What was more, the experience so disappointed, disillusioned, and embittered

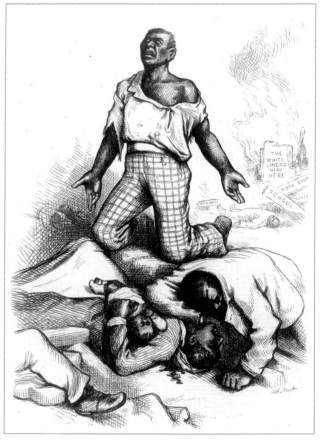

"IS *THIS* A REPUBLICAN FORM OF GOVERNMENT?" The New York artist and cartoonist Thomas Nast marked the end of Reconstruction in 1876 with this biting cartoon in *Harper's Weekly*, expressing his dismay at what he considered the nation's betrayal of the former slaves, who still had not received adequate guarantees of their rights. The caption of the cartoon continued: "Is *this* protecting life, liberty, or property? Is *this* equal protection of the laws? (*The Newberry Library, Chicago, Illinois*)

white Americans that it would be nearly a century before they would try again in any serious way.

Why did this great assault on racial injustice not achieve more? In part, it was because of the weaknesses *Ideological Limits* and errors of the people who directed it. But in greater part, it was because attempts to produce solutions ran up against conservative obstacles so deeply embedded in the nation's life that they could not be dislodged. Veneration of the Constitution sharply limited the willingness of national leaders to infringe on the rights of states and individuals. A profound respect for private property and free enterprise prevented any real assault on economic privilege in the South. Above all, perhaps, a pervasive belief among many of even the most liberal whites that African Americans were inherently inferior served as an obstacle to equality. Given the context within which Americans of the 1860s and 1870s were working, what is surprising, perhaps, is not that Reconstruction did so little, but that it did even as much as it did.

Considering the odds confronting them, therefore, African Americans had reason for pride in the gains they were able to make during Reconstruction. And future generations had reason for gratitude for two great charters of freedom—the Fourteenth and Fifteenth Amendments to the Constitution—which, although largely ignored at the time, would one day serve as the basis for a "Second Reconstruction" that would renew the drive to bring freedom and equality to all Americans.

THE NEW SOUTH

The agreement between southern Democrats and northern Republicans that helped settle the disputed election of 1876 was supposed to be the first step toward developing a stable, permanent Republican Party in the South. In that respect, at least, it failed. In the years following the end of Reconstruction, white southerners established the Democratic Party as the only viable political organization for the region's whites. Even so, the South did change in the years after Reconstruction in some of the ways the framers of the Compromise of 1877 had hoped.

The "Redeemers"

By the end of 1877—after the last withdrawal of federal troops—every southern state government had been *Bourbon Rule* "redeemed." That is, political power had been restored to white Democrats. Many white southerners rejoiced at the restoration of what they liked to call "home rule." But in reality, political power in the region was soon more restricted than at any time since the Civil War. Once again, the South fell under the control of a powerful, conservative oligarchy, whose members were known variously as the "Redeemers"

(to themselves and their supporters) or the "Bourbons" (a term for aristocrats used by some of their critics).

In a few places, this post-Reconstruction ruling class was much the same as the ruling class of the antebellum period. In Alabama, for example, the old planter elite—despite challenges from new merchant and industrial forces—retained much of its former power and continued largely to dominate the state for decades. In most areas, however, the Redeemers constituted a genuinely new ruling class. They were merchants, industrialists, railroad developers, and financiers. Some of them were former planters, some of them northern immigrants who had become absorbed into the region's life, some of them ambitious, upwardly mobile white southerners from the region's lower social tiers. They combined a commitment to "home rule" and social conservatism with a commitment to economic development.

The various Bourbon governments of the New South behaved in many respects quite similarly to one another. Conservatives had complained that the Reconstruction governments fostered widespread corruption, but the Redeemer regimes were, if anything, even more awash in waste and fraud. (In this, they were little different from governments in every region of the country.) At the same time, virtually all the new Democratic regimes lowered taxes, reduced spending, and drastically diminished state services—including many of the most important accomplishments of Reconstruction. In one state after another, for example, state support for public school systems was reduced or eliminated. "Schools are not a necessity," an economy-conscious governor of Virginia commented.

By the late 1870s, significant dissenting groups were challenging the Bourbons: protesting the cuts in services and denouncing the commitment of the Redeemer governments to paying off the prewar and Reconstruction debts in full, at the original (usually high) rates of interest. In Virginia, for example, a vigorous "Readjuster" movement emerged, demanding that the state revise its debt payment procedures so as to make more money available for state services. In 1879, the Readjusters won control of the legislature, and in the next few years they captured the governorship and a U.S. Senate seat. Other states produced similar movements, some of them adding demands as well for greenbacks, debt relief, and other economic reforms. (A few such independent movements included significant numbers of blacks in their ranks, but all consisted primarily of lower-income whites.) By the mid-1880s, however, conservative southerners—largely by exploiting racial prejudice—had effectively destroyed most of the dissenting movements.

Industrialization and the "New South"

Many white southern leaders in the post-Reconstruction era hoped to see their region become the home of a vigorous industrial economy. The South had lost the war,

planters had usually shipped their cotton out of the region to manufacturers in the North or in Europe. Now textile factories appeared in the South itself—many of them drawn to the region from New England by the abundance of water power, the ready supply of cheap labor, the low taxes, and the accommodating conservative governments. The tobacco-processing industry, similarly, established an important foothold in the region, largely through the work of James B. Duke of North Carolina, whose American Tobacco Company established for a time a virtual monopoly over the processing of raw tobacco into marketable materials. In the lower South, and particularly in Birmingham, Alabama, the iron (and, later, steel) industry grew rapidly. By 1890, the southern iron and steel industry represented nearly a fifth of the nation's total capacity.

Railroad development increased substantially in the post-Reconstruction years—at a rate far greater than that of the nation at large. Between *Railroad Development* 1880 and 1890, trackage in the South more than doubled. And the South took a major step toward integrating its transportation system with that of the rest of the country when, in 1886, it changed the gauge (width) of its trackage to correspond with the standards of the North. No longer would it be necessary for cargoes heading into the South to be transferred from one train to another at the borders of the region. Yet southern industry developed within strict limits, and its effects on the region were never even remotely comparable to the effects of industrialization on the North. The southern share of national manufacturing doubled in the last twenty years of the century, to 10 percent of the total. But that percentage was the same the South had claimed in 1860; the region, in other words, had done no more than regain what it had lost during the war and its aftermath. The region's per capita income increased 21 percent in the same period. But at the end of the century, average income in the South was only 40 percent of that in the North; in 1860 it had been more than 60 percent. And even in those areas where development had been most rapid—textiles, iron, railroads—much of the capital had come from the North. In effect, the South was developing a colonial economy.

The growth of industry in the South required the region to recruit a substantial industrial work force for the first time. From the beginning, a high percentage of the factory workers (and an especially high percentage of textile workers) were women. Heavy male casualties in the Civil War had helped create a large population of unmarried women who desperately needed employment. Factories also hired entire families, many of whom were moving into towns from failed farms. Hours were long (often as much as twelve hours a day) and wages were far below the northern equivalent; indeed one of the greatest attractions of the South to industrialists was that employers were able to pay workers there as little as one-half what

northern workers received. Life in most mill towns was rigidly controlled by the owners and managers of the factories. They rigorously suppressed attempts at protest or union organization. Company stores sold goods to workers at inflated prices and issued credit at exorbitant rates (much like country stores in agrarian areas), and mill owners ensured that no competitors were able to establish themselves in the community. At the same time, however, the conditions of the mill town helped create a strong sense of community and solidarity among workers (even if they seldom translated such feelings into militancy).

Some industries, textiles for example, offered virtually no opportunities to African-American workers. Others—tobacco, iron, and lumber, among others—did provide some employment for blacks, usually the most menial and lowest-paid positions. Some mill towns, therefore, were places where black and white culture came into close contact. That proximity contributed less to the growth of racial harmony than to the determination of white leaders to take additional measures to protect white supremacy.

At times, industrialization proceeded on the basis of no wage-paying employment at all. Through the "convict-lease" system, southern states leased gangs of convicted criminals to private interests as a cheap labor supply. The system exposed the convicts to brutal and at times fatal mistreatment. It paid them nothing (the leasing fees went to the states, not the workers). And it denied employment in railroad construction and other projects to the free labor force.

Tenants and Sharecroppers

Despite significant growth in southern industry, the region remained primarily agrarian. The most important economic reality in the post-Reconstruction South, therefore, was the impoverished state of agriculture. The 1870s and 1880s saw an acceleration of the trends that had begun in the immediate postwar years: the imposition of systems of tenantry and debt peonage on much of the region; the reliance on a few cash crops rather than on a diversified agricultural system; and increasing absentee ownership of valuable farmlands (many of them purchased by merchants and industrialists who paid little attention to whether the land was being properly used). During Reconstruction, perhaps a third or more of the farmers in the South were tenants; by 1900 the figure had increased to 70 percent. That was in large part the result of the crop-lien system that had emerged in the aftermath of the Civil War. Farmers who owned their own land often lost it as merchants seized it for payment of liens. Farmers who rented could never accumulate enough capital to buy land.

Tenancy took several forms. Farmers who owned tools, equipment, and farm animals—or who had the money to buy them—usually paid an annual cash rent for

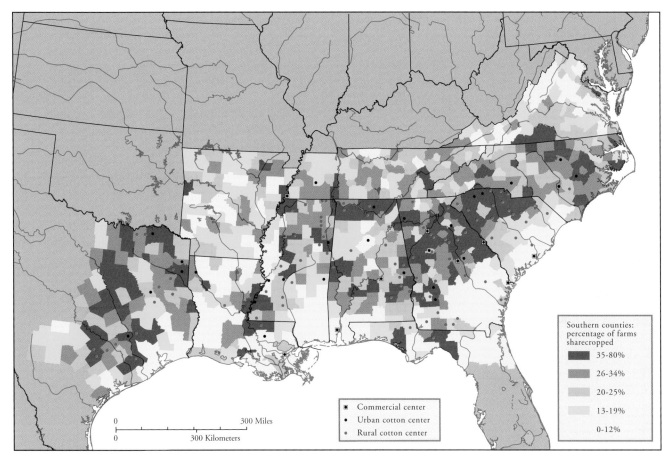

THE CROP-LIEN SYSTEM IN 1880 In the years after the Civil War, more and more southern farmers—white and black—became tenants or sharecroppers on land owned by others. This map shows the percentage of farms that were within the so-called crop-lien system, the system by which people worked their lands for someone else, who had a claim (or "lien") on a part of the farmers' crops. Note the high density of sharecropping and tenant farming in the most fertile areas of the deep South, the same areas where slaveholding had been most dominant before the Civil War. ◆ *How did the crop-lien system contribute to the shift in southern agriculture toward one-crop farming?*

 For an interactive version of this map go to www.mhhe.com/brinkley11ch15maps

their land. But many farmers (including most black ones) had no money or equipment at all. Landlords would supply them with land, a crude house, a few tools, seed, and sometimes a mule. In return, farmers would promise the landlord a large share of the annual crop—hence the term "sharecropping." After paying their landlords and their local furnishing merchants (who were often the same people), sharecroppers seldom had anything left to sell on their own. The crop-lien system was one of several factors contributing to a particularly harsh social and economic transformation of the southern backcountry,

Transformation of the Backcountry

the piney woods and mountain regions where cotton and slavery had always been rare and where farmers lived ruggedly independent lives. Subsistence agriculture had long been the norm in these areas; but as indebtedness grew, many farmers now had to grow cash crops such as cotton instead of the food crops they had traditionally cultivated in order to make enough money to pay off their loans.

But the transformation of the backcountry was a result of other factors as well. Many backcountry residents had traditionally subsisted by raising livestock, which had roamed freely across the landscape. In the 1870s, as commercial agriculture began to intrude into these regions, many communities began to pass "fence laws," which required farmers to fence in their animals (as opposed to fencing off their crops, as had once been the custom). There were widespread protests against the new laws, and at times violent efforts to resist them. But the existence of the open range (which had once been as much a part of life in the backcountry South as it was in the American West) could not survive the spread of commercial agriculture. Increasingly, therefore, opportunities for families to live largely self-sufficiently were declining. At the same time, opportunities for profiting within the market remained slim. The people of the backcountry, perhaps even more than other groups for whom agriculture had always been a business, felt the pain of losing their economic independence. They would be among the most important constituents for the populist protests of the 1880s and 1890s.

The crop-lien system was particularly devastating to southern blacks, few of whom owned their own land to begin with. These economic difficulties were compounded by social and legal discrimination, which in the post-Reconstruction era began to take new forms and to inspire new responses.

African Americans and the New South

The "New South creed" was not the property of whites alone. Many African Americans were attracted to the

Black Middle Class

vision of progress and self-improvement as well. Some blacks succeeded in elevating themselves into a distinct middle class—economically inferior to the white middle class, but nevertheless significant. These were former slaves (and, as the decades passed, their offspring) who managed to acquire property, establish small businesses,

or enter professions. A few blacks accumulated substantial fortunes by establishing banks and insurance companies for their race. One of those was Maggie Lena, a black woman who became the first female bank president in the United States when she founded the St. Luke Penny Savings Bank in Richmond in 1903. Most middle-class blacks experienced more modest gains by becoming doctors, lawyers, nurses, or teachers serving members of their own race.

A cardinal tenet of this rising group of blacks was that education was vital to the future of their race. With the support of northern missionary societies and, to a far lesser extent, a few southern state governments, they expanded the network of black colleges and institutes that had taken root during Reconstruction into an important educational system.

The chief spokesman for this commitment to education, and for a time the major spokesman for his race as a whole, was Booker T. Washington, founder and president of

Booker T. Washington

TUSKEGEE INSTITUTE, 1881 From these modest beginnings, Booker T. Washington's Tuskegee Institute in Alabama became the preeminent academy offering technical and industrial training to black men. It deliberately deemphasized the traditional liberal arts curricula of most colleges. Washington considered such training an unnecessary frill and encouraged his students to work on developing practical skills. *(Bettmann/Corbis)*

the Tuskegee Institute in Alabama. Born into slavery, Washington had worked his way out of poverty after acquiring an education (at Virginia's famous Hampton Institute). He urged other blacks to follow the same road to self-improvement.

Washington's message was both cautious and hopeful. African Americans should attend school, learn skills, and establish a solid footing in agriculture and the trades. Industrial, not classical, education should be their goal. Blacks should, moreover, refine their speech, improve their dress, and adopt habits of thrift and personal cleanliness; they should, in short, adopt the standards of the white middle class. Only thus, he claimed, could they win the respect of the white population, the prerequisite for any larger social gains. Blacks should forgo agitating for political rights, he said, and concentrate on self-improvement and preparation for equality. In a famous speech in Georgia in 1895, Washington outlined a philosophy of race relations that became

The Atlanta Compromise | widely known as the Atlanta Compromise. "The wisest among my race understand," he said, "that the agitation of questions of social equality is the extremest folly." Rather, blacks should engage in "severe and constant struggle" for economic gains; for, as he explained, "no race that has anything to contribute to the markets of the world is long in any degree ostracized." If blacks were ever to win the rights and privileges of citizenship, they must first show that they were "prepared for the exercise of these privileges." Washington offered a powerful challenge to those whites who wanted to discourage African Americans from acquiring an education or winning any economic gains. He helped awaken the interest of a new generation to the possibilities for self-advancement through self-improvement. But his message was also an implicit promise that blacks would not challenge the system of segregation that whites were then in the process of erecting.

The Birth of Jim Crow

Few white Southerners had ever accepted the idea of racial equality. That the former slaves acquired any legal and political rights at all after emancipation was in large part the result of federal support. That support all but vanished after 1877. Federal troops withdrew. Congress lost interest. And the Supreme Court effectively stripped the Fourteenth and Fifteenth Amendments of much of their significance. In the so-called civil rights cases of 1883, the Court ruled that the Fourteenth Amendment prohibited state governments from discriminating against people because of race but did not restrict private organizations or individuals from doing so. Thus railroads, hotels, theaters, and the like could legally practice segregation.

Eventually, the Court also validated state legislation that institutionalized the separation of the races. In *Plessy v. Ferguson* (1896), a case involving a Louisiana law that required separate seating arrangements for the races on railroads, the Court held that separate accommodations did not deprive blacks of equal rights if the accommodations were equal, a decision that

Plessy v. Ferguson

survived for years as part of the legal basis of segregated schools. In *Cumming* v. *County Board of Education* (1899), the Court ruled that laws establishing separate schools for whites were valid even if there were no schools for blacks comparable to the white schools from which they were excluded.

Even before these decisions, white southerners were working to strengthen white supremacy and to separate the races to the greatest extent possible. One illustration of this movement from subordination to segregation was black voting rights. In some states, disfranchisement had begun almost as soon as Reconstruction ended. But in other areas, black voting continued for some time after Reconstruction—largely because conservative whites believed they could control the black electorate and use it to beat back the attempts of poor white farmers to take control of the Democratic Party. In the 1890s, however, franchise restrictions became much more rigid. During those years, some small white farmers began to demand complete black disfranchisement—both because of racial prejudice and because they objected to the black vote being used against them by the Bourbons. At the same time, many members of the conservative elite began to fear that poor whites might unite politically with poor blacks to challenge them. They too began to support further franchise restrictions.

In devising laws to disfranchise black males (black females, like white women, had never voted), the southern states had to find ways to evade the Fifteenth Amendment, which | *Restricting the Franchise* prohibited states from denying anyone the right to vote because of race. Two devices emerged before 1900 to accomplish this goal. One was the poll tax or some form of property qualification; few blacks were prosperous enough to meet such requirements. Another was the "literacy" or "understanding" test, which required voters to demonstrate an ability to read and to interpret the Constitution. Even those African Americans who could read had difficulty passing the difficult test white officials gave them. Such restrictions were often applied unequally. Literacy tests for whites, for example, were sometimes much easier than those for blacks. Even so, the laws affected poor white voters as well as blacks. By the late 1890s, the black vote had decreased by 62 percent, the white vote by 26 percent. One result was that some states passed so-called grandfather laws, permitting men who could not meet the literacy and property qualifications to be enfranchised if their ancestors had voted before Reconstruction began, thus barring the descendants of slaves from the polls while allowing poor whites access to them. In many areas, however, ruling elites were quite content to see poor whites, a potential source of opposition to their power, barred from voting.

Not until after World War II, when the emergence of the civil rights movement forced white Americans to confront the issue of racial segregation, did historians pay much attention to the origins of the institution. Most had assumed that the separation of the races had emerged naturally and even inevitably out of the abolition of slavery. It had been a response to the failure of Reconstruction, the weakness and poverty of the African-American community, and the pervasiveness of white racism. It was (as W. J. Cash argued in his classic and controversial 1941 study, *The Mind of the South*) the way things had always been.

The first major challenge to these assumptions, indeed the first serious scholarly effort to explain the origins of segregation, was C. Vann Woodward's *The Strange Career of Jim Crow* published in 1956. Not only was it important in reshaping scholarship. It had a significant political impact as well. As a southern liberal, Woodward was eager to refute assumptions that segregation was part of an unchanging and unchangeable southern tradition. He wanted to convince scholars that the history of the South had been one of sharp discontinuities; and he wanted to convince a larger public that the racial institutions they considered part of a long, unbroken tradition were in fact the product of a particular set of historical circumstances.

In the aftermath of emancipation, and indeed for two decades after Reconstruction, Woodward argued, race relations in the South had remained relatively fluid. Blacks and whites did not often interact as equals, certainly, but black southerners enjoyed a degree of latitude in social and even political affairs that they would subsequently lose. Blacks and whites often rode together in the same railroad cars, ate in the same restaurants, used the same public facilities. African Americans voted in significant numbers. Blacks and whites considered a number of different visions of how the races should live together, and as late as 1890 it was not at all clear which of those visions would prevail. By the end of the nineteenth century, however, a great wave of racist legislation—the Jim Crow laws, which established the basis of segregation—had hardened race relations and destroyed the gentler alternatives that many whites and blacks had considered viable only a few years before. The principal reason, Woodward argued, was the Populist political insurgency of the 1890s, which mobilized blacks and whites alike and which frightened many white southerners into thinking that African Americans might soon be a major political power in the region. Southern conservatives, in particular, used the issue of white supremacy to attack the Populists and to prevent blacks from forming an alliance with them. The result was segregation and the disfranchisement of African Americans (along with many poor whites).

Woodward's argument suggested that laws are important in shaping social behavior—that laws had made segregation and, by implication, other laws could unmake it. Not all historians agreed. A more pessimistic picture of segregation emerged in 1965 from Joel Williamson's study of South Carolina, *After Slavery.* Williamson argued that the laws of the 1890s did not mean very much, that they simply ratified a set of conditions that had been firmly established by the end of Reconstruction. As early as the mid-1870s, Williamson claimed, the races had already begun to live in two separate societies. Blacks had constructed their own churches, schools, businesses, and neighborhoods; whites had begun to exclude blacks from white institutions. The separation was partly a result of pressure and coercion from whites, partly a result of the desire of blacks to develop their own, independent culture. Whatever the reasons, however, segregation was largely in place by the end of the 1870s, continuing in a different form a pattern of racial separation established under slavery. The laws of the 1890s did little more than codify an already established system.

In the same year that Williamson published his argument, Leon Litwack joined the debate, even if somewhat indirectly, with the publication of *North of Slavery.* Litwack revealed the existence of widespread segregation, supported by an early version of Jim Crow laws, in the North before the Civil War. In almost every northern state, he revealed, free blacks experienced a kind of segregation not very different from what freed slaves would experience in the South after the Civil War. A few years later, Ira Berlin argued in *Slaves Without Masters* (1974) that in the antebellum South, too, white people had created a wide range of discriminatory laws aimed at free blacks and ensuring segregation. The

---

The Supreme Court proved as compliant in ruling on the disfranchising laws as it was in dealing with the civil rights cases. The Court eventually voided the grandfather laws, but it validated the literacy test (in the 1898 case of *Williams* v. *Mississippi*) and displayed a general willingness to let the southern states define their own suffrage standards as long as evasions of the Fifteenth Amendment were not too glaring.

Laws restricting the franchise and segregating schools were only part of a network of state statutes—known as the Jim Crow laws—that by the first years of the twentieth century had institutionalized an elaborate system of segregation reaching into almost every area of southern life. Blacks and whites could not ride together in the same railroad cars, sit in the same waiting rooms, use the same *White Control Perpetuated* washrooms, eat in the same restaurants, or sit in the same theaters. Blacks had no access to many public parks, beaches, and picnic areas; they could not be patients in many hospitals. Much of the new legal structure did no more than confirm what had already been widespread social practice in the South since well before the end of Reconstruction. But the Jim Crow laws also stripped blacks of many of the modest social, economic, and political

postbellum regime of Jim Crow, such works suggested, emerged naturally out of well-established precedents from before the Civil War, in both the North and the South.

Other scholars have challenged all these interpretations by attempting to link the rise of legal segregation to changing social and economic circumstances in the South. Howard Rabinowitz's *Race Relations in the Urban South* (1978) linked the rise of segregation to the new challenge of devising a form of race relations suitable to life in the growing southern cities, into which rural blacks were moving in substantial numbers. The creation of separate public facilities—schools, parks, waiting rooms, etc.—was not so much an effort to drive blacks out of white facilities; they had never had access to those facilities, and few whites had ever been willing to consider granting them access. It was, rather, an attempt to create for a black community that virtually all whites agreed must remain essentially separate a set of facilities where none had previously existed. Without segregation, in other words, urban blacks would have had no schools or parks at all. The alternative to segregation, Rabinowitz suggested, was not integration, but exclusion.

In the early 1980s, a number of scholars began examining segregation anew in light of the rising American interest in South Africa, whose system of apartheid seemed to them to be similar in many ways to the by-then largely dismantled Jim Crow system in the South. John Cell's *The Highest Stage of White Supremacy* (1982) used the

THE NEGRO GALLERY.

(Reproduced from Every Saturday, *Gift of the Louisiana Museum Foundation)*

comparison to construct a revised explanation of how segregation emerged in the American South. Like Rabinowitz, he considered the increasing urbanization of the region the principal factor. But he ascribed different motives to those whites who promoted the rise of Jim Crow. The segregation laws, Cell argued, were a continuation of an unchanging determination by southern whites to retain control over the black population. What had shifted was not their commitment to white supremacy but the things necessary to preserve it. The emergence of large black communities in urban areas and

of a significant black labor force in factories presented a new challenge to white southerners. In the city, blacks and whites were in more direct competition than they had been in the countryside. There was more danger of social mixing. The city therefore required different, and more rigidly institutionalized, systems of control. The Jim Crow laws were a response not just to an enduring commitment to white supremacy, but to a new reality that required white supremacy to move to its "highest stage," where it would have a rigid legal and institutional basis.

gains they had made in the more fluid atmosphere of the late nineteenth century. They served, too, as a means for whites to retain control of social relations between the races in the newly growing cities and towns of the South, where traditional patterns of deference and subjugation were more difficult to preserve than in the countryside. What had been maintained by custom in the rural South was to be maintained by law in the urban South.

More than legal efforts were involved in this process. The 1890s witnessed a dramatic increase in white violence against blacks, which, along with the Jim Crow laws, served to inhibit black agitation for equal rights. The

worst such violence—lynching of blacks by white mobs, either because the victims were accused of crimes or because they had seemed somehow to violate their proper station—reached appalling levels. In the nation as a whole in the 1890s, there was an average of 187 lynchings each year, more than 80 percent of them in the South. The vast majority of victims were black.

Lynchings

The most celebrated lynchings occurred in cities and towns, where large, well-organized mobs—occasionally with the tacit cooperation of local authorities—seized black prisoners from the jails and hanged them in great

435

A LYNCH MOB, 1893 A large, almost festive crowd gathers to watch the lynching of a black man accused of the murder of a three-year-old white girl. Lynchings remained frequent in the South until as late as the 1930s, but they reached their peak in the 1890s and the first years of the twentieth century. Lynchings such as this one—published well in advance and attracting whole families who traveled great distances to see them—were relatively infrequent. Most lynchings were the work of smaller groups, operating with less visibility. *(Library of Congress)*

public rituals. Such public lynchings were often planned well in advance and elaborately organized. They attracted large audiences from surrounding regions. Entire families traveled many miles to witness the spectacles. But such great public lynchings were relatively rare. Much more frequent, and more dangerous to blacks because less visible or predictable, were lynchings performed by small vigilante mobs, often composed of friends or relatives of the victim (or supposed victim) of a crime. Those involved in lynchings often saw their actions as a legitimate form of law enforcement; and indeed, some victims of lynchings had in fact committed crimes. But lynchings were also a means by which whites controlled the black population through terror and intimidation. Thus, some lynch mobs killed blacks whose only "crime" had been presumptuousness. Others chose as victims outsiders in the community, whose presence threatened to disturb the normal pattern of race relations. Black men who had made any sexual advances toward white women (or who white men

thought had done so) were particularly vulnerable to lynchings; the fear of black sexuality, and the unspoken fear among many men that white women might be attracted to that sexuality, was always an important part of the belief system that supported segregation. Whatever the reasons or circumstances, the victims of lynch mobs were denied the protection of the laws and the opportunity to prove their innocence.

The rise of lynchings shocked the conscience of many white Americans in a way that other forms of racial injustice did not. Almost from the start there was a substantial anti-lynching movement. In 1892 Ida B. Wells, a committed black journalist, launched what became an international anti-lynching movement with a series of impassioned articles after the lynching of three of her friends in Memphis, Tennessee, her home. The movement gradually gathered strength in the first years of the twentieth century, attracting substantial support from whites in both the North and South (particularly from white women). Its goal was a federal anti-lynching law, which would allow the national government to do what state and local governments in the South were generally unwilling to do: punish those responsible for lynchings.

But the substantial white opposition to lynchings in the South stood as an exception to the general white support for suppression of African Americans. Indeed, just as in the antebellum period, the shared commitment to white supremacy helped dilute class animosities between poorer whites and the Bourbon oligarchies. Economic issues tended to play a second- *White Unity* ary role to race in southern pol- itics, distracting people from the glaring social inequali- ties that afflicted blacks and whites alike. The commitment to white supremacy, in short, was a burden for poor whites as well as for blacks.

CONCLUSION

Reconstruction, long remembered by many white Americans as a vindictive outrage or a tragic failure, was in fact a profoundly important moment in American history. Despite the bitter political battles in Washington and throughout the South, culminating in the unsuccessful effort to impeach President Andrew Johnson, the most important result of the effort to reunite the nation after its long and bloody war was a reshaping of the lives of ordinary people in all regions of the nation.

In the North, Reconstruction solidified the power of the Republican Party and ensured that public policy would support the continued growth of an advanced industrial economy. The rapid growth of the northern economy continued and accelerated, drawing more and more of its residents into an expanding commercial world.

In the South, Reconstruction did more than simply bring slavery to an end. It fundamentally rearranged the relationship between the region's white and black citizens. Only for a while did Reconstruction permit African Americans to participate actively and effectively in southern politics. After a few years of widespread black voting and significant black officeholding, the forces of white supremacy forced most African Americans to the margins of the southern political world, where they would mostly remain until the 1960s.

But in other ways, the lives of southern blacks changed dramatically. Overwhelmingly, they left the plantations. Some sought work in towns and cities. Some left the region altogether. But the great majority began farming on small farms of their own—not as landowners, except in rare cases, but as tenants and sharecroppers on land owned by whites. The result was a form of economic bondage, driven by debt, only scarcely less oppressive than the legal bondage of slavery. But within this system, African Americans managed to carve out a much larger sphere of social and cultural activity than they had ever been able to create under slavery. Black churches organized in great numbers. African-American schools emerged in some communities, and black colleges began to appear in the region. Some former slaves owned businesses and flourished. In southern cities and towns, a fledgling black middle class began to emerge.

The system of tenantry, which emerged in the course of Reconstruction, continued after its end to dominate the southern economy. Strenuous efforts by "New South" advocates to advance industry and commerce in the region produced significant results in a few areas. But the South on the whole remained what it had always been, an overwhelmingly rural society with a sharply defined class structure. It was also a region with a deep commitment among its white citizens to the subordination of African Americans—a commitment solidified in the 1890s and the early twentieth century when white southerners erected an elaborate legal system of segregation (the "Jim Crow" laws). The promise of the great Reconstruction amendments to the Constitution—the Fourteenth and Fifteenth—remained largely unfulfilled in the South as the century drew to its close.

FOR FURTHER REFERENCE

Eric Foner, *Reconstruction: America's Unfinished Revolution, 1863–1877* (1988), the most important modern synthesis of Reconstruction scholarship, emphasizes the radicalism of Reconstruction and the role of freed people in the process of political and economic renovation. Thomas Holt, *Black over White: Negro Political Leadership in South Carolina During Reconstruction* (1977) examines Reconstruction in the state where black political power reached its apex. C. Vann Woodward, *Origins of the New South* (1951), is a classic work on the history of the South after Reconstruction after forty years, and argues that a rising middle class defined the economic and political transformation of the New South. Edward Ayers, *The Promise of the New South* (1992) offers a rich portrait of social and cultural life in the New South. Jacqueline Jones, *Labor of Love, Labor of Sorrow* (1985) examines the lives of African-American women after Emancipation. Leon Litwack, *Been in the Storm So Long: The Aftermath of Slavery* (1979) is a major study of the experiences of freed slaves. C. Vann Woodward, *The Strange Career of Jim Crow* (rev. 1974) claims that segregation emerged only gradually across the South after Reconstruction. The "Woodward Thesis" has been challenged by, among others, Joel Williamson, *After Slavery: The Negro in South Carolina During Reconstruction* (1965); John W. Cell, *The Highest Stage of White Supremacy: The Origins of Segregation in South Africa and the American South* (1982); and Howard N. Rabinowitz, *Race Relations in the Urban South, 1865–1890* (1978).

For quizzes, Internet resources, references to additional books and films, and more, consult this book's Online Learning Center at www.mhhe.com/brinkley11.

AMERICAN PROGRESS, 1872 John Gast, an artist in Brooklyn, New York, painted this tribute to westward expansion—a picture of hardy pioneers marching toward the frontier, protected by the goddess of progress—at the request of a publisher of travel guides. Engravings adapted from the painting appeared in one guidebook, and color reproductions were offered to customers as a bonus for subscribing to others. It is an example of the wide-ranging promotional effort—by railroads, landowners, farm-equipment manufacturers, even guidebook publishers—designed to persuade Americans to move into the western territories in the late nineteenth century. *(Gene Autry Museum of Western Heritage, Los Angeles)*

Significant Events

1847 · Taos Indians rebel in New Mexico, killing American governor and precipitating military rule

1848–1849 · California gold rush begins

1851 · "Concentration" policy devised for western tribes

1852 · California legislature passes "foreign miners" tax to exclude Chinese from gold mining

1858 · Comstock Lode silver deposits discovered in Nevada

1859 · Colorado gold rush launches western mining bonanza
· Mexicans in Texas raid Brownsville jail

1861 · Kansas admitted to Union

1862 · Homestead Act passed

1864 · Nevada admitted to Union
· U.S. troops massacre Arapaho and Cheyenne at Sand Creek

1865–1867 · Sioux Wars

1866 · "Long drives" launch western cattle bonanza
· Chinese workers strike against Union Pacific

1867 · Nebraska admitted to Union
· Indian Peace Commission establishes "Indian Territory" (later Oklahoma)

1868 · Black Kettle and his Cheyenne warriors captured and killed by U.S. forces

1869 · Union Pacific, first transcontinental railroad, completed

1872 · Cochise, chief of Chiricahua Apaches, agrees to treaty with U.S.

1873 · Barbed wire invented
· Timber Culture Act passed

1874 · Gold rush begins in Black Hills, Dakota Territory

1875 · Sioux uprising begins
· Southern buffalo herd nearly extinguished

CHAPTER SIXTEEN

THE CONQUEST OF THE FAR WEST

*T*hrough much of the first half of the nineteenth century, relatively few English-speaking Americans considered moving into the vast lands west of the Mississippi River. For some the obstacle was distance; for others it was lack of money; for many more it was the image of much of the Far West, popularized by some early travelers, as the "Great American Desert," unfit for civilization.

By the mid-1840s, however, enough migrants from the eastern regions of the nation had settled in the West to begin to challenge that image. Some were farmers, who had found fertile land in areas once considered too arid for agriculture. Others were ranchers, who had discovered great open grasslands on which they could raise large herds of cattle or sheep for the market. Many were miners, including some of the hundreds of thousands of people who had flocked to California during the 1848–1849 gold rush. By the end of the Civil War, the West had already become legendary in the eastern states. No longer the Great American Desert, it was now the "frontier": an empty land awaiting settlement and civilization; a place of wealth, adventure, opportunity, and untrammeled individualism; a place of fresh beginnings and bold undertakings.

In fact, the real West of the mid-nineteenth century bore little resemblance to either of these images. It was a diverse land, with many different regions, many different climates, many different stores of natural resources. And it was extensively populated, with a number *Myth and Reality* of well-developed societies and cultures. The English-speaking migrants of the late nineteenth century did not find an empty, desolate land. They found Indians, Mexicans, French and British Canadians, Asians, and others, some of whose families had been living in the West for generations. The Anglo-American settlers helped create new civilizations in this vast and complicated land, but they did not do so by themselves. Although they tried, with considerable success, to conquer and disperse many of the peoples already living in the region, they were never able to make the West theirs alone. They interacted in countless ways with the existing population. Almost everything the Anglo-Americans did and built reflected the influence of these other cultures.

Most of all, however, English-speaking Americans transformed the West by connecting it with, and making it part of, the growing capitalist economy of the East. And despite their self-image as rugged individualists, they relied heavily on assistance from the federal government—land grants, subsidies, and military protection—as they developed the region.

THE SOCIETIES OF THE FAR WEST

The Far West (or what many nineteenth-century Americans called the "Great West")—the region beyond the Mississippi River into which millions of Anglo-Americans moved in the years after the Civil War—was in fact many lands. It contained some of the most arid territory in the United States, and some of the wettest and lushest. It contained the flattest plains and the highest mountains. It contained vast treeless prairies and deserts and great forests. And it contained many peoples.

The Western Tribes

The largest and most important western population group before the great Anglo-American migration was the Indian tribes. Some were members of eastern tribes—Cherokee, Creek, and others—who had been forcibly resettled west of the Mississippi to "Indian Territory" (later Oklahoma) and elsewhere before the Civil War. But most were members of tribes that had always lived in the West.

The western tribes had developed several forms of civilization. More than 300,000 Indians (among them the Serrano, Chumash, Pomo, Maidu, Yurok, and Chinook) had lived on the Pacific coast before the arrival of Spanish settlers. Disease and dislocation decimated the tribes, but in the mid-nineteenth century 150,000 remained—some living within the Hispanic society the Spanish and Mexican settlers had created, many still living within their own tribal communities. The Pueblos of the Southwest had long lived largely as farmers and had established permanent settlements there even before the Spanish arrived in the seventeenth century. The Pueblos grew corn; they built towns and cities of adobe houses; they practiced elaborate forms of irrigation; and they participated in trade and commerce. In the eighteenth and nineteenth centuries, their intimate relationship with the Spanish (later Mexicans) produced, in effect, an alliance against the Apaches, Navajos, and Comanches of the region.

The complex interaction between the Pueblos and the Spanish, and between both of them and other tribes, produced an elaborate caste system in the Southwest. At the top were the Spanish or Mexicans, who owned the largest estates and controlled the trading centers at Santa Fe and elsewhere. The Pueblos, subordinate but still largely free, were below them. Apaches, Navajos, and others—some captured in war and enslaved for a fixed time, others men and women who had voluntarily left their own tribes—were at the bottom. They were known as *genizaros,* Indians without tribes, and they had become in many ways part of Spanish society. This caste system reflected the preoccupation of the society of the Spanish Empire in America with racial ancestry; almost every group in the Southwest—not just Spanish and Indians, but several categories

Caste System

of mulattoes and mestizos (people of mixed race) had a clear place in an elaborate social hierarchy.

The most widespread Indian groups in the West were the Plains Indians, a diverse group of tribes and language groups. Some formed alliances with one another; others were in constant conflict. Some lived more or less sedentary lives as farmers; others were highly nomadic hunters. Despite their differences, however, the tribes shared some traits. Their cultures were based on close and extended family networks and on an intimate relationship with nature. Tribes (which sometimes numbered several thousand) were generally subdivided into "bands" of up to 500 men and women, usually made up of highly interrelated people. Each band had its own governing council, but the community had a decision-making process in which most members participated. Within each band, tasks were divided by gender. Women's roles were largely domestic and artistic: raising children, cooking, gathering roots and berries, preparing hides, and creating many of the impressive artworks of tribal culture. They also tended fields and gardens in those places where bands remained settled long enough to raise crops. Men worked as hunters and traders and supervised the religious and military life of the band. Most of the Plains Indians practiced a religion centered on a belief in the spiritual power of the natural world—of plants and animals and the rhythms of the days and the seasons.

Plains Indians

Many of the Plains tribes—including some of the most powerful tribes in the Sioux Nation—subsisted largely through hunting buffalo. Riding small but powerful horses, descendants of Spanish stock, the tribes moved through the grasslands following the herds. Permanent settlements were rare. When a band halted, it constructed tepees as temporary dwellings; when it departed, it left the landscape almost completely undisturbed, a reflection of the deep reverence for nature that was central to Indian culture and religion.

The magnet that drew the hunters and guided their routes was the buffalo, or bison. This huge grazing animal provided the economic basis for the Plains Indians' way of life. Its flesh was their principal source of food, and its skin supplied materials for clothing, shoes, tepees, blankets, robes, and utensils. "Buffalo chips"—dried manure—provided fuel; buffalo bones became knives and arrow tips; buffalo tendons formed the strings of bows.

Economic Importance of the Buffalo

The Plains Indians were proud and aggressive warriors, schooled in warfare from their frequent (and usually brief) skirmishes with rival tribes. The male members of each tribe were, in effect, a warrior class. They competed with one another to develop reputations for fierceness and bravery both as hunters and as soldiers. By the early nineteenth century, the Sioux had become the most powerful tribe in the Missouri River valley and had begun expanding west and south until they dominated much of the Plains and were the most important military force in the region.

BUFFALO CHASE The painter George Catlin captured this scene of Plains Indians in the 1830s hunting among the great herds of buffalo, which provided the food and materials on which many tribes relied. *(National Museum of American Art/Art Resource)*

The Plains warriors proved to be the most formidable foes white settlers encountered. But they also suffered from several serious weaknesses that in the end made it impossible for them to prevail. One weakness was the inability of the various tribes (and often even of the bands within tribes) to unite against white aggression. This was a problem that had plagued Native Americans in the East for centuries and had contributed to their ultimate undoing. The western tribes, like the eastern ones, were culturally ill-disposed toward political or military centralization. Not only were they seldom able to draw together a coalition large enough to counter white power, they were also frequently distracted from their battles with whites by conflicts among the tribes themselves. And at times, tribal warriors faced white forces who were being assisted by guides and even fighters from other, usually rival, tribes.

Even so, some tribes were able to overcome their divisions and unite effectively. By the mid-nineteenth century, *Indian Weaknesses* for example, the Sioux, Arapaho, and Cheyenne had forged a powerful alliance that dominated the northern Plains. The more important weaknesses of the western tribes in their contest with white society were, in fact, ecological and economic. Indians were tragically vulnerable to eastern infectious diseases. Smallpox epidemics, for example, decimated the Pawnees in Nebraska in the 1840s and many of the California tribes in the early 1850s. And the tribes were, of course, at a considerable disadvantage in any long-term battle with an economically and industrially advanced people. They were, in the end, outmanned and outgunned.

Hispanic New Mexico

For centuries, much of the Far West had been part of, first, the Spanish Empire and, later, the Mexican Republic. Although the lands the United States acquired in the 1840s did not include any of Mexico's most populous regions, considerable numbers of Mexicans did live in them and suddenly became residents of American territory. Most of them stayed.

Spanish-speaking communities were scattered throughout the Southwest, from Texas through New Mexico and Arizona, and into California. All of them were transformed in varying degrees by the arrival of Anglo-American migrants and, equally important, by the expansion of the American capitalist economy into the region. For some, the changes created opportunities for greater wealth. But for most it meant an end to the more communal societies and economies they had built over many generations.

In New Mexico, the centers of Spanish-speaking society were the farming and trading communities the Spanish had established in the seventeenth century (see p. 17). Descendants of the original Spanish settlers (and more recent migrants from Mexico) lived alongside the Pueblo Indians and some American traders and engaged primarily in cattle and sheep ranching. There was a small aristocracy of great landowners, whose estates radiated out from the major trading center at Santa Fe. And there was a large population of Spanish (later Mexican) peasants, who worked on the great estates, farmed small plots of their own, or otherwise scraped out a subsistence. There were also large groups of Indian laborers, some enslaved or indentured.

When the United States acquired title to New Mexico in the aftermath of the Mexican War, General Stephen Kearney—who had commanded the American troops in the region during the conflict—tried to establish a territorial government that excluded the established Mexican ruling class (the landed aristocrats from around Santa Fe and *Taos Indian Rebellion* the most influential priests). He drew most of the officials from among the approximately 1,000 Anglo-Americans in the region, ignoring the over 50,000 Hispanics. There were widespread fears among Hispanics and Indians alike that the new American rulers of the region would confiscate their lands and otherwise threaten their societies. In 1847, Taos Indians rebelled; they killed the new governor and other Anglo-American officials before being subdued by United States Army forces. New Mexico remained under military rule for three years, until the United States finally organized a territorial government there in 1850.

By the 1870s, the government of New Mexico was dominated by one of the most notorious of the many "territorial rings" that sprang up in the West in the years before statehood. These were circles of local businesspeople and ambitious politicians with access to federal money who worked together to make the territorial government mutually profitable. In Santa Fe, the ring used its influence to gain control of over 2 million acres of land, much of which had long been in the possession of the original Mexican residents of the territory. The old Hispanic elite in New Mexico had lost much of its political and economic authority.

Even without its former power, Hispanic society in New Mexico survived and even grew in the face of the expansion of Anglo-American settlement in the Southwest. The U.S. Army finally did what the Hispanic residents had been unable to accomplish for 200 years: it broke the power of the Navajo, Apache, and other tribes that had so often harassed the residents of New Mexico and had prevented them from expanding their society and commerce. The defeat of the tribes led to substantial Hispanic migration into other areas of the Southwest and as far north as Colorado. Most of the expansion involved peasants and small tradespeople who were looking for land or new opportunities for commerce. The pattern of large estates and a self-conscious aristocracy did not repeat itself in the newer Hispanic settlements.

Hispanic societies survived in the Southwest in part because they were so far from the centers of English-speaking society that Anglo-American migrants (and the rail- *Hispanic Resistance* roads that carried them) were slow to get there. But Mexican Americans in the region also fought at times to preserve control of their societies. In the late 1880s, for example, Mexican peasants in an area of what is now Nevada harassed English-speaking cattle ranchers who were attempting to move into the region and successfully fended off their encroachments.

But by then, such successes were already the exception. The Anglo-American presence in the Southwest grew rapidly once the railroads established lines into the region in the 1880s and early 1890s. With the railroads came extensive new ranching, farming, and mining. The expansion of economic activity in the region attracted a new wave of Mexican immigrants—perhaps as many as 100,000 by 1900—who moved across the border (which was unregulated until World War I) in search of work. But the new immigrants, unlike the earlier Hispanic residents of the Southwest, were coming to a society in which they were from the beginning subordinate to Anglo-Americans. The English-speaking proprietors of the new enterprises restricted most Mexicans to the lowest-paying and least stable jobs.

Hispanic California and Texas

In California, Spanish settlement began in the eighteenth century with a string of Christian missions along the Pacific coast. The missionaries and the soldiers who accompanied

THE CALIFORNIOS Before the arrival of large waves of immigrants from the United States, California was the home of a flourishing Mexican ranching and mission culture, with a wealthy aristocracy—as this 1850 painting of the Don Manuel family suggests. *(Courtesy W. Graham Arader, III, San Francisco)*

them gathered most of the coastal Indians into their communities, some forcibly and some by persuasion. The Indians were targets of the evangelizing efforts of the missionaries, who baptized over 50,000 of them. But they were also a labor force for the flourishing and largely self-sufficient economies the missionaries created; the Spanish forced most of these laborers into a state of servitude little different from slavery. The missions had enormous herds of cattle, horses, sheep, and goats, most of them tended by Indian workers; they had brickmakers, blacksmiths, weavers, and farmers, most of them Indians as well. Few of the profits of the mission economy flowed to the workers.

In the 1830s, after the new Mexican government began reducing the power of the church, the mission society largely collapsed, despite strenu-

Decline of Mission Society

ous resistance from the missionaries themselves. In its place emerged a secular Mexican aristocracy, which controlled a chain of large estates (some of them former missions) in the fertile lands west of the Sierra Nevada mountains. For them, the arrival of Anglo-Americans before and after the Civil War was disastrous. So vast were the numbers of English-speaking immigrants that the *californios* (as the Hispanic residents of the state were known) had little power to resist the onslaught. In the central and northern parts of the state, where the Anglo population growth was greatest, the *californios* experienced a series of defeats. English-speaking prospectors organized to exclude them, sometimes violently, from the mines during the gold rush. Many *californios* also lost their lands—either through corrupt business deals or through outright seizure (sometimes with the help of the courts and often through simple occupation by squatters). Years of litigation by the displaced Hispanics had very little effect on the changing distribution of landownership.

In the southern areas of California, where there were at first fewer migrants, some Mexican landowners managed to hang on for a time. The booming Anglo communities in the north of the state created a large market for the cattle that southern *rancheros* were raising. But a combination of reckless expansion, growing indebtedness, and a severe drought in the 1860s devastated the Mexican ranching culture. By the 1880s, the Hispanic aristocracy in California had largely ceased to exist. Increasingly, Mexicans and Mexican Americans became part of the lower end of the state's working class, clustered in barrios in Los Angeles or elsewhere, or becoming migrant farmworkers. Even small landowners who managed to hang on to their farms found themselves unable to raise livestock, as the once communal grazing lands fell under the control of powerful Anglo ranchers. The absence of herding destroyed many family economies and, by forcing farmers into migrant work, displaced much of the peasantry.

A similar pattern of dispossession occurred in Texas, where many Mexican landowners lost their land after the territory joined the United States (see pp. 346–347). This occurred as a result of fraud, coercion, and the inability of even the most substantial Mexican ranchers to compete with the enormous Anglo-American ranching kingdoms that were emerging. In 1859, Mexican resentments erupted in an armed challenge to American power: a raid on a jail in Brownsville, led by the

Declining Status of Hispanics

rancher Juan Cortina, who freed all the Mexican prisoners inside. But such resistance had little long-term effect. Cortina continued to harass Anglo communities in Texas until 1875, but the Mexican government finally captured and imprisoned him. As in California, Mexicans in southern Texas (who constituted nearly three-quarters of the population there) became an increasingly impoverished working class relegated largely to unskilled farm or industrial labor.

On the whole, the great Anglo-American migration was less catastrophic for the Hispanic population of the West than it was for the Indian tribes. Indeed, for some Hispanics, it created new opportunities for wealth and station. For the most part, however, the late nineteenth century saw the destruction of Mexican Americans' authority in a region they had long considered their home; and it saw the movement of large numbers of Hispanics—both longtime residents of the West and more recent immigrants—into an impoverished working class serving the expanding capitalist economy of the United States.

The Chinese Migration

At the same time that ambitious or impoverished Europeans were crossing the Atlantic in search of opportunities in the New World, many Chinese crossed the Pacific in hopes of better lives than they could expect in their own poverty-stricken land. Not all came to the United States. Many Chinese moved to Hawaii, Australia, South and Central America, South Africa, and even the Caribbean—some as "coolies" (indentured servants whose condition was close to slavery).

A few Chinese had come to California even before the gold rush (see pp. 355–357), but after 1848 the flow increased dramatically. By 1880, more than 200,000 Chinese had settled in the United States, mostly in California, where they constituted nearly a tenth of the population. Almost all came as free laborers. For a time, white Americans welcomed the Chinese as a conscientious, hardworking peo-

Racism

ple. In 1852, the governor of California called them "one of the most worthy classes of our newly adopted citizens" and called for more Chinese immigration to swell the territory's inadequate labor force. Very quickly, however, white opinion turned hostile—in part because the Chinese were so industrious and successful that some white Americans began considering them rivals, even threats. The experience of Chinese immigrants in the West became, therefore, a struggle to advance economically in the face of racism and discrimination.

In the early 1850s, large numbers of Chinese immigrants worked in the gold mines. Many of them were well-organized, hardworking prospectors, and for a time some of them enjoyed considerable success. But opportunities for Chinese to prosper in the mines were fleeting. In 1852, the California legislature began trying to exclude the Chinese from gold mining by enacting a "foreign miners" tax (which also helped exclude Mexicans).

A series of other laws in the 1850s were designed to discourage Chinese immigration into the territory. Gradually, the effect of the discriminatory laws, the hostility of white miners, and the declining profitability of the surface mines drove most Chinese out of prospecting. Those who remained in the mountains became primarily hired workers in the mines built by corporations with financing from the East. These newer mines—which extended much deeper into the mountains than individual prospectors or small, self-financed groups had been able to go—replaced the early, smaller operations.

As mining declined as a source of wealth and jobs for the Chinese, railroad employment grew. Beginning in 1865,

Building the
Transcontinental Railroad

over 12,000 Chinese found work building the transcontinental railroad. In fact, Chinese workers formed 90 percent of the labor force of the Central Pacific and were mainly responsible for construction of the western part of the new road. The company

preferred them to white workers because they had no experience of labor organization. They worked hard, made few demands, and accepted relatively low wages. Many railroad workers were recruited in China by agents for the Central Pacific. Once employed, they were organized into work gangs under Chinese supervisors.

Work on the Central Pacific was arduous and often dangerous. As the railroad moved through the mountains, the company made few concessions to the difficult conditions and provided their workers with little protection from the elements. Work continued through the winter, and many Chinese tunneled into snowbanks at night to create warm sleeping areas for themselves. The tunnels frequently collapsed, suffocating those inside; but the company allowed nothing to disrupt construction.

Chinese laborers, however, were not always as docile as their employers imagined them to be. In the spring of 1866, 5,000 Chinese railroad workers went on strike demanding higher wages and a shorter workday. The company isolated them, surrounded them with strikebreakers, and starved them into submission. The strike failed, and most of the workers returned to their jobs.

In 1869 the transcontinental railroad was completed. Thousands of Chinese were now out of work. Some hired themselves out on vast drainage and irrigation projects in the agricultural valleys of central California. Some became common agricultural laborers, picking fruit for low wages.

THE TRANSCONTINENTAL RAILROAD This complicated trestle under construction by the Union Pacific was one of many large spans necessary for the completion of the transcontinental railroad. It gives some indication of the enormous engineering challenges the railroad builders had to overcome. *(Union Pacific Railroad Museum Collection)*

A CHINESE FAMILY IN SAN FRANCISCO Like many other Americans, Chinese families liked to pose for photograph portraits in the late nineteenth century. And like many other immigrants, they often sent them back to relatives in China. This portrait of Chun Duck Chin and his seven-year-old son Chun Jan Yut was taken in a studio in San Francisco in the 1870s. Both father and son appear to have dressed up for the occasion, in traditional Chinese garb, and the studio—which likely took many such portraits of Chinese families—provided a formal Chinese backdrop. The son is holding what appears to be a chicken, perhaps to impress relatives in China with the family's prosperity. *(National Archives and Records Administration)*

Some became tenant farmers, often on marginal lands that white owners saw no profit in working themselves. Some managed to acquire land of their own and established themselves as modestly successful truck farmers.

Increasingly, however, Chinese immigrants flocked to cities. By 1900, nearly half the Chinese population of

Establishment of "Chinatowns"

California lived in urban areas. By far the largest single Chinese community was in San Francisco. Much of community life there, and in other "Chinatowns" throughout the West, revolved around powerful organizations—usually formed by people from the same clan or community in China—that functioned as something like benevolent societies and filled many of the roles that

political machines often served in immigrant communities in eastern cities. They were often led by prominent merchants. (In San Francisco, the leading merchants—known as the "Six Companies"—often worked together to advance their interests in the larger community of the city and state.) These organizations became, in effect, employment brokers, unions, arbitrators of disputes, defenders of the community against outside persecution, and dispensers of social services. They also organized the elaborate festivals and celebrations that were such a conspicuous and important part of life in Chinatowns.

Other Chinese organizations were secret societies, known as "tongs." Some of the tongs were violent criminal organizations, involved in the opium trade and prostitution. Few people outside the Chinese communities were aware of their existence, except when rival tongs engaged in violent conflict (or "tong wars"), as occurred frequently in San Francisco in the 1880s.

Life was hard for most urban Chinese, in San Francisco and elsewhere. The Chinese usually occupied the lower rungs of the employment ladder in the western cities in which most lived. Many worked as common laborers, servants, and unskilled factory hands. Some established their own small businesses, especially laundries. They moved into this business not because of experience—there were few commercial laundries in China—but because they were excluded from so many other areas of employment. Laundries could be started with very little capital, and required only limited command of English. By the 1890s, Chinese constituted over two-thirds of all the laundry workers in California, many of them in shops they themselves owned and ran.

The relatively small number of Chinese women fared even worse. During the earliest Chinese migrations to California, virtually all the women who made the journey did so because they had been sold into prostitution in China. As late as 1880, nearly half the Chinese women in California were prostitutes. Both Anglo and Chinese reformers tried to stamp out the prostitution in Chinatowns in the 1890s, but more effective than their efforts was the growing number of Chinese women in America. Once the sex ratio became more balanced, Chinese men were more likely to seek companionship in families.

Anti-Chinese Sentiments

As Chinese communities grew larger and more conspicuous in western cities, anti-Chinese sentiment among white residents became increasingly strong. In fact, next to the

Anti-Coolie Clubs

Indians, the Chinese probably suffered the most intense persecution from white Americans in the West. Anti-coolie clubs emerged in the 1860s and 1870s. They sought a ban on employing Chinese and organized boycotts of products made with Chinese labor. Some of these

AN ANTI-CHINESE RIOT White citizens of Denver attacked the Chinese community of the city in 1880, beating many of its residents and vandalizing their homes and businesses. It was one of a number of anti-Chinese riots in the cities of the West. They were a result of a combination of racism and resentment by white workers of what they considered unfair competition from Chinese laborers who were willing to work for very low wages. *(Bettmann/Corbis)*

clubs attacked Chinese workers in the streets and were suspected of setting fire to factories in which Chinese worked. These activities reflected the resentment of many white workers toward Chinese laborers for accepting low wages and thus undercutting union members.

As the political value of attacking the Chinese grew in California, the Democratic Party took up the call. So did the Workingmen's Party of California—created in 1878 by Denis Kearney, an Irish immigrant—which gained significant political power in the state in large part on the basis of its hostility to the Chinese. By the mid-1880s, anti-Chinese agitation and violence had spread up and down the Pacific coast and into other areas of the West.

But the denunciations of the Chinese did not rest on economic grounds alone. They rested on cultural and racial arguments as well. For example, the reformer Henry George, a critic of capitalism and a champion of the rights of labor (see p. 487), described the Chinese as products of a civilization that had failed to progress, that remained mired in barbarism and savagery. They were, therefore, "unassimilable" and should be excluded.

In 1882, Congress responded to the political pressure and the growing violence by passing the Chinese Exclusion Act, which banned Chinese immigration into the United States for ten years and barred Chinese already in the country from becoming naturalized citizens. Support for the act came from representatives from all regions of the country. It reflected the growing fear of unemployment and labor unrest throughout the nation and the belief that excluding "an industrial army of Asiatic laborers" would protect "American" workers and help reduce class conflict. Congress renewed the law for another ten years in 1892 and made it permanent in 1902. It had a dramatic effect on the Chinese population, which declined by more than 40 percent in the forty years after its passage.

Chinese Exclusion Act

The Chinese in America did not accept the new laws quietly. They were shocked by the anti-Chinese rhetoric that lumped them together with African Americans and Indians. They were, they insisted, descendants of a great and enlightened civilization. How could they be compared to people who knew "nothing about the relations of society"? White Americans, they said, did not protest the great waves of immigration by Italians ("the most dangerous of men," one Chinese American said) or Irish or Jews. "They are all let in, while Chinese, who are sober, are duly law abiding, clean, educated and industrious, are shut out." The Six Companies in San Francisco organized strenuous letter-writing campaigns, petitioned the president, and even filed suit in federal court. Their efforts had no significant effect.

Chinese Resistance

Migration from the East

The great wave of new settlers in the West from the eastern United States after the Civil War came on the heels of important earlier migrations. California and Oregon had substantial Anglo-American settlements and were both already states of the Union by 1860. There were large and growing Anglo- and African-American communities in Texas, which had entered the Union in 1845 and had been part of the Confederacy during the war. And from Texas and elsewhere, traders, farmers, and ranchers had begun to establish Anglo-American outposts in parts of New Mexico, Arizona, and other areas of the Southwest.

But the scale of the postwar migration dwarfed everything that had preceded it. In previous decades, the settlers had come in thousands. Now they came in millions, spreading throughout the vast western territories—into empty and inhabited lands alike. Most of the new settlers were from the established Anglo-American societies of the eastern United States, but substantial numbers—over 2 million between 1870 and 1900—were foreign-born immigrants from Europe: Scandinavians, Germans, Irish, Russians, Czechs, and others. They came for many reasons. Settlers were attracted by gold and silver deposits, by the shortgrass pastures for cattle and sheep, and ultimately by the sod of the plains and the meadowlands of the mountains, which they discovered were suitable for farming or ranching. The completion of the great transcontinental railroad line in 1869, and the construction of the many subsidiary lines that spread out from it, also encouraged settlement.

The land policies of the federal government also encouraged settlement. The Homestead Act of 1862 permit-

Homestead Act

ted settlers to buy plots of 160 acres for a small fee if they occupied the land they purchased for five years and improved it. The Homestead Act was intended as a progressive measure. It would give a free farm to any American who needed one. It would be a form of government relief to people who otherwise might have no prospects. And it would help create new markets and new outposts of commercial agriculture for the nation's growing economy.

But the Homestead Act rested on a number of misperceptions. The framers of the law had assumed that mere possession of land would be enough to sustain a farm family. They had not recognized the effects of the increasing mechanization of agriculture and the rising costs of running a farm. Moreover, they had made many of their calculations on the basis of eastern agricultural experiences that were inappropriate for the region west of the Mississippi. A unit of 160 acres was too small for the grazing and grain farming of much of the Great Plains. Although over

400,000 homesteaders stayed on Homestead Act claims long enough to gain title to their land, a much larger number abandoned the region before the end of the necessary five years, unable to cope with the bleak life on the windswept plains and the economic realities that were making it difficult for families without considerable resources to thrive.

Not for the last time, beleaguered westerners looked to the federal government for solutions to their problems. In response to their demands, Congress increased the home-

Government Assistance

stead allotments. The Timber Culture Act (1873) permitted homesteaders to receive grants of 160 additional acres if they planted 40 acres of trees on them. The Desert Land Act (1877) provided that claimants could buy 640 acres at $1.25 an acre provided they irrigated part of their holdings within three years. The Timber and Stone Act (1878), which presumably applied to nonarable land, authorized sales at $2.50 an acre. These laws ultimately made it possible for individuals to acquire as much as 1,280 acres of land at little cost. Some enterprising settlers got much more. Fraud ran rampant in the administration of the acts. Lumber, mining, and cattle companies, by employing "dummy" registrants and using other illegal devices, seized millions of acres of the public domain.

Political organization followed on the heels of settlement. After the admission of Kansas as a state in 1861, the remaining territories of Washington, New Mexico, Utah,

SODBUSTERS As farmers moved onto the Great Plains in Nebraska and other states on the agrarian frontier, their first task was to cut through the sod that covered the land to get to soil in which they could plant crops. The sod itself was so thick and solid that some settlers (including the Summers family of West Custer County, Nebraska, pictured here in 1888) used it to build their houses. The removal of the sod made cultivation of the plains possible; it also removed the soil's protective covering and contributed to the great dust storms that plagued the region in times of drought. *(Nebraska State Historical Society)*

and Nebraska were divided into smaller units that would presumably be easier to organize. By the close of the 1860s, territorial governments were in operation in the new provinces of Nevada, Colorado, Dakota, Arizona, Idaho, Montana, and Wyoming. Statehood rapidly followed. Nevada became a state in 1864, Nebraska in 1867, and Colorado in 1876. In 1889, North and South Dakota, Montana, and Washington won admission; Wyoming and Idaho entered the next year. Congress denied Utah statehood until its Mormon leaders convinced the government in 1896 that polygamy (the practice of men taking several wives) had been abandoned. At the turn of the century, only three territories remained outside the union. Arizona and New Mexico were excluded because their scanty white populations remained minorities in the territories, because their politics was predominantly Democratic in a Republican era, and because they were unwilling to accept admission as a single state. Oklahoma (formerly Indian Territory) was opened to white settlement and granted territorial status in 1889–1890.

THE CHANGING WESTERN ECONOMY

Among the many effects of the new wave of Anglo-American settlement in the Far West was a transformation of the region's economy. The new American settlers tied the West firmly to the growing industrial economy of the East (and of much of the rest of the world). Mining, timbering, ranching, commercial farming, and many other economic activities relied on the East for markets and for capital. Some of the most powerful economic institutions in the West were great eastern corporations that controlled mines, ranches, and farms.

Labor in the West

As commercial activity increased, many farmers, ranchers, and miners found it necessary to recruit a paid labor force—not an easy task for those far away from major population centers and unable or unwilling to hire Indian workers. The labor shortage of the region led to higher wages for workers than were typical in most areas of the East. But working conditions were often arduous, and job security was almost nonexistent. Once a railroad was built, a crop harvested, a herd sent to market, a mine played out, hundreds and even thousands of workers could find themselves suddenly unemployed. Competition from Chinese immigrants, whom employers could usually hire for considerably lower wages than they had to pay whites, also forced some Anglo-Americans out of work. Communities of the jobless gathered in the region's few cities, in mining camps, and elsewhere; other unemployed people moved restlessly from place to place in search of work.

Those who owned no land were highly mobile, mostly male, and seldom married. Indeed, the West had the highest percentage of single people (10 percent) of any region in the country—one reason why single women found working in dance halls and as prostitutes among the most readily available forms of employment.

Despite the enormous geographical mobility in western society, actual social mobility was limited. Many Americans thought of the West as a land of limitless opportunity, but, as in *Limited Social Mobility* the rest of the country, advancement was easiest and most rapid for those who were economically advantaged to begin with. Studies of western communities suggest that social mobility in most of them was no greater than it was in the East. And the distribution of wealth in the region was little different from that in the older states as well.

Even more than in many parts of the East, the western working class was highly multiracial. English-speaking whites worked alongside African Americans and immigrants from *Racially Stratified* southern and eastern Europe, as *Working Class* they did in the East. Even more, they worked with Chinese, Filipinos, Mexicans, and Indians. But the work force was highly stratified along racial lines. In almost every area of the western economy, white workers (whatever their ethnicity) occupied the upper tiers of employment: management and skilled labor. The lower tiers—people who did unskilled and often arduous work in the mines, on the railroads or in agriculture—consisted overwhelmingly of nonwhites.

Reinforcing this dual labor system was a set of racial assumptions developed and sustained largely by white employers. Chinese, Mexicans, and Filipinos, they argued, were genetically or culturally suited to manual labor. Because they were small, those who promoted these racist stereotypes argued, they could work better in deep mines than whites. Because they were accustomed to heat, they could withstand arduous work in the fields better than whites. Because they were unambitious and unconcerned about material comfort, they would accept low wages and live in conditions that white people would not tolerate. These racial myths served the interests of employers above all, but white workers tended to embrace them too. That was in part because the myths supported a system that reserved whatever mobility there was largely for whites. An Irish common laborer might hope in the course of a lifetime to move several rungs up the occupational ladder. A Chinese or Mexican worker in the same job had no realistic prospects of doing the same.

The Arrival of the Miners

The first economic boom in the Far West came in mining, and the first part of the area to be extensively settled by migrants was the mineral-rich region of mountains and plateaus, where settlers hoped to make quick fortunes by finding precious metals. The life span of the mining boom was relatively brief. It began in earnest around 1860 (although there had, of course, been some earlier booms, most notably in California), and flourished until the 1890s. And then it abruptly declined.

News of a gold or silver strike in an area would start a stampede reminiscent of the California gold rush of 1849, *Life Cycle of a Mining Boom* followed by several stages of settlement. Individual prospectors would exploit the first shallow deposits of ore largely by hand, with pan and placer mining. After these surface deposits dwindled, corporations moved in to engage in lode or quartz mining, which dug deeper beneath the surface. Then, as those deposits dwindled, commercial mining either disappeared or continued on a restricted basis, and ranchers and farmers moved in and established a more permanent economy.

The first great mineral strikes (other than the California gold rush) occurred just before the Civil War. In 1858, gold was discovered in the Pike's Peak district of what would soon be the territory of Colorado; the following year, 50,000 prospectors stormed in from California, the Mississippi Valley, and the East. Denver and other mining camps blossomed into "cities" overnight. Almost as rapidly as it had developed, the boom ended. After the mining frenzy died down, corporations, notably the Guggenheim interests, revived some of the profits of the gold boom, and the discovery of silver near Leadville supplied a new source of mineral wealth.

While the Colorado rush of 1859 was still in progress, news of another strike drew miners to Nevada. Gold had been found in the Washoe district, but the most valuable ore *Comstock Lode* in the great Comstock Lode (first discovered in 1858 by Henry Comstock) and other veins was silver. The first prospectors to reach the Washoe fields came from California; and from the beginning, Californians dominated the settlement and development of Nevada. In a remote desert without railroad transportation, the territory produced no supplies of its own, and everything—from food and machinery to whiskey and prostitutes—had to be shipped from California to Virginia City, Carson City,

COLORADO BOOM TOWN After a prospector discovered silver nearby in 1890, miners flocked to the town of Creede, Colorado. For a time in the early 1890s, 150 to 300 people arrived there daily. Although the town was located in a canyon so narrow that there was room for only one street, buildings sprouted rapidly to serve the growing community. Like other such boom towns, however, Creede's prosperity was short-lived. In 1893 the price of silver collapsed, and by the end of the century, Creede was almost deserted. *(Henry Ford Museum & Greenfield Village)*

and other roaring camp towns. When the first placer (or surface) deposits ran out, California and eastern capitalists bought the claims of the pioneer prospectors and began to use the more difficult process of quartz mining, which enabled them to retrieve silver from deeper veins. For a few years these outside owners reaped tremendous profits; from 1860 to 1880 the Nevada lodes yielded bullion worth $306 million. After that, the mines quickly played out.

The next important mineral discoveries came in 1874, when gold was found in the Black Hills of southwestern Dakota Territory. Prospectors swarmed into the area, then (and for years to come) accessible only by stagecoach. Like the others, the boom flared for a time, until surface resources faded and corporations took over from the miners. One enormous company, the Homestake, came to dominate the fields. Population declined, and the Dakotas, like other boom areas of the mineral empire, ultimately developed a largely agricultural economy.

Although the gold and silver discoveries generated the most popular excitement, in the long run other, less glamorous natural resources proved more important to the development of the West. The great Anaconda copper mine launched by William Clark in 1881 marked the beginning of an industry that would remain important to Montana for many decades. In other areas, mining operations had significant success with lead, tin, quartz, and zinc. Such efforts generally proved more profitable in the long run than the usually short-lived gold and silver extraction.

Life in the boomtowns had a hectic tempo and a gaudy flavor unknown in any other part of the Far West. A speculative spirit, a mood of heady optimism, gripped almost everyone and dominated every phase of community activity. And while relatively few of the prospectors and miners who flocked to the bonanzas ever "struck it rich," there was at least some truth to the popular belief that mining provided opportunities for sudden wealth. The "bonanza kings"—the miners who did become enormously wealthy off a strike—were much more likely to have come from modest or impoverished backgrounds than the industrial tycoons of the East.

Boomtown Life

The conditions of mine life in the boom period—the presence of precious minerals, the vagueness of claim boundaries, the cargoes of gold being shipped out—attracted outlaws and "bad men," operating as individuals or gangs. When the situation became intolerable in a community, those members interested in order began enforcing their own laws through vigilante committees, an unofficial system of social control used earlier in California. Vigilantes were unconstrained by the legal system, and they often imposed their notion of justice arbitrarily and without regard for any form of due process. Sometimes criminals themselves secured control of the committees. Some vigilantes continued to operate as private "law" enforcers after the creation of regular governments.

Gender Imbalance

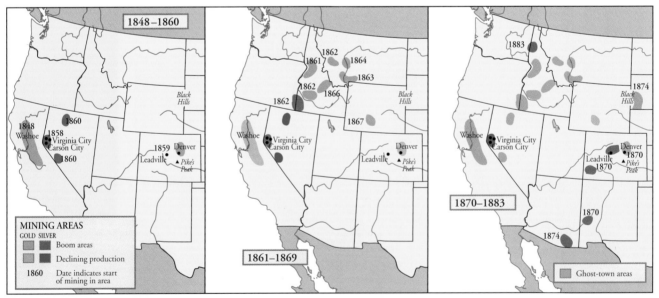

MINING TOWNS, 1848–1883 These three maps illustrate the rapid movement from boom to bust in the western mining industry in the mid-nineteenth century. Note how quickly the "boom" areas of gold and silver mining turn into places of "declining production," often in the space of less than a decade. Note, too, how mining for both metals moved from California and Nevada in the 1860s to areas further east and north in the 1870s and beyond. The map also shows the areas in which "ghost towns"—mining communities abandoned by their residents once production ceased—proliferated. • *What impact did mining have on the population of the West?*

 For an interactive version of this map go to www.mhhe.com/brinkley11ch16maps

Men greatly outnumbered women in the mining towns, and younger men in particular had difficulty finding female companions of comparable age. Those women who did gravitate to the new communities often came with their husbands, and their activities were generally (although not always) confined to the same kinds of domestic tasks that eastern women performed. Single women, or women whose husbands were earning no money, did choose (or find it necessary) to work for wages at times, as cooks, laundresses, and tavern keepers. And in the sexually imbalanced mining communities, there was always a ready market for prostitutes.

The thousands of people who flocked to the mining towns in search of quick wealth and who failed to find it often remained as wage laborers in corporate mines after the boom period. Working conditions were almost uniformly terrible. The corporate mines were deep and extremely hot, with temperatures often exceeding 100 degrees Fahrenheit. Some workers died of heatstroke (or of pneumonia, a result of experiencing sudden changes of temperature when emerging from the mines). Poor ventilation meant large accumulations of poisonous carbon dioxide, which caused dizziness, nausea, and headaches. Lethal dusts stayed in the stagnant air to be inhaled over and over by the miners, many of whom developed silicosis (a disabling disease of the lungs) as a result. There were frequent explosions, cave-ins, and fires, and there were many accidents with the heavy machinery they used to bore into the earth. In the 1870s, before technological advances eliminated some of the dangers, one worker in every thirty was disabled in the mines, and one in every eighty was killed. That rate fell later in the nineteenth century, but mining remained one of the most dangerous and arduous working environments in the United States.

The Cattle Kingdom

A second important element of the changing economy of the Far West was cattle ranching. The open range—the vast grasslands of the public domain—provided a huge area on the Great Plains where cattle raisers could graze their herds free of charge and unrestricted by the boundaries of private farms. The railroads gave birth to the range-cattle industry by giving it access to markets. Eventually, the same railroads ended it by bringing farmers to the plains and thus destroying the open range.

The western cattle industry was Mexican and Texan by ancestry. Long before citizens of the United States invaded the Southwest, Mexican ranchers had developed the techniques and equipment that the cattlemen and cowboys of the Great Plains later employed: branding (a device known in all frontier areas where stock was common), roundups, roping, and the gear of the herders—their lariats, saddles, leather chaps, and spurs. Americans in Texas adopted these methods and carried them to the northernmost ranges of

Mexican Origins

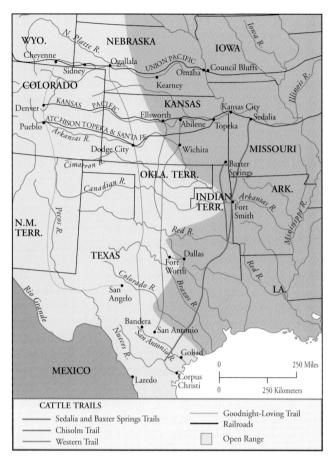

THE CATTLE KINGDOM, C. 1866–1887 Cattle ranching and cattle drives are among the most romanticized features of the nineteenth-century West. But they were also hard-headed businesses, made possible by the growing eastern market for beef and the availability of reasonably inexpensive transportation to take cattle to urban markets. This map shows two important characteristics of the "cattle kingdom" in the 1860s and 1870s. One is the vast expanse of "open range." ◆ *Why was that necessary for the great cattle drives, and what eventually ended it?* The other is the dense network of trails and railroads that together made possible the commerce in cattle.

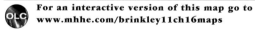 **For an interactive version of this map go to www.mhhe.com/brinkley11ch16maps**

the cattle kingdom. Texas also had the largest herds of cattle in the country; the animals were descended from imported Spanish stock—wiry, hardy longhorns—and allowed to run wild or semiwild. From Texas, too, came the horses that enabled the caretakers of the herds, the cowboys, to control them—small, muscular broncos or mustangs well suited to the requirements of cattle country.

At the end of the Civil War, an estimated 5 million cattle roamed the Texas ranges. Eastern markets were offering fat prices for steers in any condition, and the challenge facing the cattle industry was getting the animals from the range to the railroad centers. Early in 1866, some Texas cattle ranchers began driving their combined herds, some 260,000 head, north to Sedalia, Missouri, on the Missouri Pacific Railroad. Traveling over rough country and beset by outlaws, Indians, and property-conscious farmers, the caravan suffered heavy losses, and only a fraction of the animals arrived in Sedalia. But the drive was an important experiment. It proved that cattle could be driven to distant markets and pastured along the trail, and that they would even gain weight during the journey. This earliest of the "long drives," in other words, established the first, tentative link between the isolated cattle breeders of west Texas and the booming urban markets of the East. The drive laid the groundwork for the explosion of the industry—for the creation of the "cattle kingdom."

With the precedent of the long drive established, the next step was to find an easier route through more accessible country. Market facilities grew up at Abilene, Kansas, on the Kansas Pacific Railroad, and for years the town *Chisholm Trail* reigned as the railhead of the cattle kingdom. Between 1867 and 1871, cattlemen drove nearly 1.5 million head up the Chisholm Trail to Abilene—a town that, when filled with rampaging cowboys at the end of a drive, rivaled the mining towns in rowdiness. But by the mid-1870s, agricultural development in western Kansas was eating away at the open range land at the same time that the supply of animals was increasing. Cattlemen therefore had to develop other trails and other market outlets. As the railroads began to reach farther west, Dodge City and Wichita in Kansas, Ogallala and Sidney in Nebraska, Cheyenne and Laramie in Wyoming, and Miles City and Glendive in Montana all began to rival Abilene as major centers of stock herding.

A long drive was a spectacular sight, and it is perhaps unsurprising that it became the most romanticized and mythologized aspect of life in the West. It began with the spring, or calf, roundup. The cattlemen of a district met with their cowboys at a specified place to round up stock from the open range; these herds contained the stock of many different owners, with only their brands to distinguish them from one another. As the cattle were driven in, the calves were branded with the marks of their mothers. Stray calves with no identifying symbols, "mavericks," were divided on a pro-rata basis. Then the cows and calves were turned loose to pasture, while the yearling steers (year-old males) were readied for the drive to the north. The combined herds, usually numbering from 2,000 to 5,000 head, moved out. Cowboys representing each of the major ranchers accompanied them. Most of the cowboys in the early years were veterans of the Confederate army. The next largest group consisted of African Americans—over half a million of them. They were more numerous than white northerners or Mexicans and other foreigners. They were usually assigned such jobs as wrangler (herdsman) or cook.

Every cattleman had to have a permanent base from which to operate, and so the ranch emerged. A ranch consisted of the employer's dwelling, quarters for employees, and a tract of grazing land. In the early years of the cattle kingdom, most ranches were relatively small, since so much of the grazing occurred in the vast, open areas that cattlemen shared. But as farmers and sheep breeders began to compete for the open plains, ranches became

COWBOYS ON A "LONG DRIVE" The "long drive" not only provided cattle for the eastern market, it also created communities of men who spent much of their lives on the trail, working for ranchers tending cattle. These cowboys were mostly young, unmarried men, mostly white but including many African Americans. Most of them later settled down, but many agreed with the former cowboy Charles Goodknight who wrote years later, "All in all, my years on the trail were the happiest I ever lived. There were many hardships and dangers . . . but when all went well, there was no other life so pleasant. Most of the time we were solitary adventurers in a great land, . . . and we were free and full of the zest of darers." This photograph of cowboys riding here dates from the 1880s. *(Library of Congress)*

larger and more clearly defined; cattlemen gradually had to learn to raise their stock on their own fenced land. There had always been an element of risk and speculation in the open-range cattle business. At any time, "Texas fever"—a disease transmitted to cattle by parasite-carrying ticks—might decimate a herd. Rustlers and Indians frequently seized large numbers of animals.

But as settlement of the plains increased, new forms of competition joined these traditional risks. Sheep breeders *Competition with Farmers* from California and Oregon brought their flocks onto the range to compete for grass. Farmers ("nesters") from the East threw fences around their claims, blocking trails and breaking up the open range. A series of "range wars"—between sheepmen and cattlemen, between ranchers and farmers—erupted out of the tensions between these competing groups. Some of the wars resulted in significant loss of life and extensive property damage.

Accounts of the lofty profits to be made in the cattle business—it was said that an investment of $5,000 would return $45,000 in four years—tempted eastern, English, and Scottish capital to the plains. Increasingly, the structure of the cattle economy became corporate; in one year, twenty corporations with a combined capital of $12 million were chartered in Wyoming. The inevitable result of this frenzied, speculative expansion was that the ranges, already severed and shrunk by the railroads and the farmers, became overstocked. There was not enough grass to support the crowding herds or sustain the long drives. Finally nature intervened with a destructive finishing blow. Two severe winters, in 1885–1886 and 1886–1887, with a searing summer between them, stung and scorched the plains. Hundreds of thousands of cattle died, streams and grass dried up, princely ranches and costly investments disappeared in a season.

The open-range industry never recovered; the long drive disappeared for good. Railroads displaced the trail as the route to market for livestock. But the established cattle ranches—with fenced-in grazing land and stocks of hay for winter feed—survived, grew, and prospered, eventually producing more beef than ever.

Although the cattle industry was overwhelmingly male in its early years, there were always a few women involved in ranching and driving. As ranching became more sedentary, the presence of women greatly increased. By 1890, more than 250,000 women owned ranches or farms in the western states (many of them as proxies for their husbands or fathers, but some in their own right). Indeed, the region provided women with many opportunities that were closed to them in the East—including the opportunity to participate in politics. Wyoming was the first state in the Union to guarantee woman suffrage; and throughout the West, women established themselves as an important political presence (and occasionally as significant officeholders).

Women won the vote earlier in the West than they did in the rest of the nation for different reasons in different places. In Utah, the Mormons granted women suffrage in an *Political Gains for Women* effort to stave off criticism of their practice of polygamy. In some places, women won suffrage before statehood to swell the electorate to the number required by Congress; men alone were not numerous enough to qualify the territories for admission to the Union. In others, women won the vote by persuading men that they would help bring a "moral" voice into the politics of the region and strengthen the sense of community in the West. Because women were, most men (and many women) believed, more "generous and virtuous" than men, they might bring these special qualities to the raw societies of the region. (Many of the same arguments were ultimately used to justify suffrage in the East as well.)

THE ROMANCE OF THE WEST

The supposedly unsettled West had always occupied a special place in the Anglo-American imagination, beginning in the seventeenth century when the first white settlers along the Atlantic coast began to look to the interior for new opportunities and for refuge from the civilized world. The vast regions of this "last frontier" had a particularly strong romantic appeal to many whites.

The Western Landscape

The allure of the West was obvious. The Great Plains, the Rocky Mountains, the basin and plateau region beyond the Rockies, the Sierra Nevada, and the Cascade Range—all constituted a landscape of brilliant diversity and spectacular grandeur, different from anything white Americans had encountered before. It was little wonder that newcomers *"Rocky Mountain School"* looked on the West with reverence and wonder. Painters of the new "Rocky Mountain School"—of whom the best known were Albert Bierstadt and Thomas Moran—celebrated the new West in grandiose canvases, some of which were taken on tours around the eastern and midwestern states and attracted enormous crowds, eager for a vision of the Great West. Such paintings emphasized the ruggedness and dramatic variety of the region, and reflected the same awe toward the land that earlier regional painters had displayed toward the Hudson River valley and other areas.

Gradually, the interest in paintings of the West inspired a growing wave of tourism among people eager actually to see the natural wonders of the region. Travel to the most spectacular areas of the West was difficult in the first decades after the war. But increasingly in the 1880s and 1890s, as railroads extended further into the region and as the Indian wars subsided, resort hotels

THE WILD WEST SHOW

For many Americans, the "Old West" has always been a place of myth—a source of some of our culture's most romantic and exciting stories. Historians have offered a picture of the West sharply at odds with its popular image, but the image survives despite them. One reason the romantic depiction of the Old West has persisted is the astonishing popularity of the "Wild West show" in the late nineteenth and early twentieth centuries. These colorful entertainments may have had little connection with the reality of western life, but they stamped on their audiences an image of the West as a place of adventure and romance that has lasted for

generations. The Wild West show emerged out of a number of earlier entertainment traditions. The great showman P. T. Barnum had begun popularizing the "wild West" as early as the 1840s when he staged a "Grand Buffalo Hunt" for spectators in New York, and such shows continued into the 1870s, one of them featuring the famous "Wild Bill" Hickok. At about the same time, Western cowboys began staging versions of the modern rodeo when their cattle drives passed near substantial towns. But the first real Wild West show opened in Omaha, Nebraska in 1883. Its organizer was William F. Cody, better known as "Buffalo Bill."

Cody had once ridden for the Pony Express, fought in the Civil War, and been a supplier of buffalo meat to workers on the transcontinental railroad (hence his celebrated nickname). But his real fame was a result of his work as a scout for the U.S. Cavalry during the Indian wars of the 1870s, and as a guide for hunting parties of notable easterners. One of them, a dime-novel writer who published under the name Ned Buntline, wrote a series of books portraying (and greatly exaggerating) Buffalo Bill's exploits. The novels turned Cody into a national celebrity.

The Wild West show Cody began in 1883 inspired dozens of imitators, and

PROMOTING THE WEST Buffalo Bill's Wild West show was popular all over the United States, and indeed through much of the world. He was so familiar a figure that many of his posters contained only his picture with the words "He is Coming." This more conventional poster announces a visit of the show to Brooklyn. *(Culver Pictures, Inc.)*

began to spring up near some of the most spectacular landscapes in the region; and easterners began to come for visits of several weeks or more, combining residence in a comfortable hotel with hikes and excursions into the "wilderness."

The Cowboy Culture

Even more appealing than the landscape, perhaps, was the rugged, free-spirited lifestyle that many Americans associated with the West—a lifestyle that supposedly stood

in sharp contrast to the increasingly stable and ordered world of the East. Many nineteenth-century Americans came to romanticize, especially, the figure of the cowboy and transformed him remarkably quickly from the low-paid worker he actually was into a powerful and enduring figure of myth.

Myth of the Cowboy

Admiring Americans seldom thought about the many dismal aspects of the cowboy's life: the tedium, the loneliness, the physical discomforts, the relatively few opportunities for advancement. Instead, in western novels such

ANNIE OAKLEY Annie Oakley had been a vaudeville and circus entertainer for years before joining Buffalo Bill's Wild West show in 1885. She was less than five feet tall and weighed less than a hundred pounds, but her exploits with pistols, rifles, and horses earned her a reputation as a woman of unusual strength and skill. *(Bettmann/Corbis)*

reenactment of Custer's last stand. And later still, he began to include stagings of such nonwestern heroics as Theodore Roosevelt's charge up Kettle Hill during the Spanish-American War. But the effort to evoke the romance of the Old West always remained at the show's center.

Buffalo Bill was always the star performer in his own productions. But the show had other celebrities, too. A woman who used the stage name Annie Oakley became wildly popular for her shooting acts, during which she would throw small cards with her picture on them into the air, shoot a hole through their middle, and toss them into the audience as souvenirs.

Native Americans were important parts of the Wild West shows, and hundreds of them participated—showing off their martial skills and exotic costumes and customs. The great Sioux leader Sitting Bull toured with the show for four months in 1885, during which he discussed Indian affairs with President Cleveland, who was a member of one of his audiences. The famous Chiricahua Apache warrior Geronimo, who had fought against the United States until 1886, spent a season touring with one of Buffalo Bill's competitors—having previously been paraded around the country as a prisoner by the U.S. Army. He later appeared in a re-creation of an Apache village at the 1904 World's Fair in St. Louis.

Buffalo Bill's show was an immediate success and quickly began traveling across the nation and throughout Europe. Over 41,000 people saw it in

one day in Chicago in 1884. In 1886, it played for six months on Staten Island in New York, where General William T. Sherman, Mark Twain, P. T. Barnum, Thomas A. Edison, and the widow of General Custer all saw and praised it. Members of the royal family attended the show in England, and it drew large crowds as well in France, Germany, and Italy.

The Wild West shows died out not long after World War I, but many of their features survived in circuses and rodeos, and later in films, radio and television shows, and theme parks. Their popularity was evidence of the nostalgia with which late-nineteenth-century Americans looked at their own imagined past, and their eagerness to remember a "Wild West" that had never really been what they liked to believe. Buffalo Bill and his imitators confirmed the popular image of the West as a place of romance and glamor and helped keep that image alive for later generations.

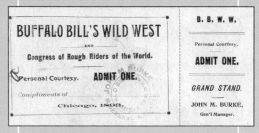

FREE ADMISSION The managers of Buffalo Bill's company were eager to attract visits from the famous and influential and gave out many complimentary tickets (like this one for a show in Chicago in 1893) to local dignitaries in an effort to entice them to appear. *(Culver Pictures, Inc.)*

almost all of them used some version of its format. Cody's shows included mock Indian attacks (by real Indians) on stage coaches and wagon trains. There were portrayals of the Pony Express. There were shooting, riding, and roping exhibitions. And there was a grand finale—"A Grand Hunt on the Plains"—that included buffalo, elk, deer, mountain sheep, longhorn cattle, and wild horses. Later, Cody added a

as Owen Wister's *The Virginian* (1902), they romanticized his freedom from traditional social constraints, his affinity with nature, even his supposed propensity for violence. Wister's character—one of the most enduring and popular in all of American literature—was a semi-educated man whose natural decency, courage, and compassion made him a powerful symbol of the supposed virtues of the frontier. But *The Virginian* was only the most famous (and one of the best) examples of a type of literature that soon swept throughout the United States: novels and stories about the West, and about the lives of

cowboys in particular, that appeared in boys' magazines, pulp novels, theater, and even serious literature. The enormous popularity of traveling Wild West Shows spread the cult of the cowboy still further. (See "Patterns of Popular Culture" above.)

The cowboy had become perhaps the most widely admired popular hero in America. He had also become a powerful and enduring symbol of what had long been an important ideal in the American mind: the ideal of the natural man (the same idea that had shaped such earlier novels as James Fenimore Cooper's *The Deerslayer* and *The*

The American West, and the process by which people of European descent settled there, has been central to the national imagination for at least two centuries. It has also, at times, been central to American historical scholarship.

Through most of the nineteenth century, the history of the West reflected the romantic and optimistic view of the region beloved by many Americans. The lands west of the Mississippi River were places of adventure and opportunity. The West was a region where life could start anew, where brave and enterprising people endured great hardships to begin building a new civilization. Francis Parkman's *The Oregon Trail* (1849), a classic of American literature, expressed many of these assumptions and in the process shaped the way in which later generations of Americans would view the West and its past. But the emergence of western history as an important field of scholarship can best be traced to the famous paper Frederick Jackson Turner delivered at a meeting of the American Historical Association in 1893. It was entitled "The Significance of the Frontier in American History." The "Turner thesis" or "frontier thesis," as his argument quickly became known, shaped both popular and scholarly views of the West (and of much else) for two generations.

Turner stated his thesis simply. The settlement of the West by white people—"the existence of an area of free land, its continuous recession, and the advance of American settlement westward"—was the central story of American history. The process of westward expansion had transformed a desolate and savage land into modern civilization. It had also continually renewed American ideas of democracy and individualism and had, therefore, shaped not just the West but the nation as a whole. "What the Mediterranean Sea was to the Greeks, breaking the bonds of custom, offering new experiences, calling out new institutions and activities, that, and more, the ever retreating frontier has been to the United States." The Turner thesis shaped the

writing of American history for a generation, and it shaped the writing of western American history for even longer. In the first half of the twentieth century, virtually all the major figures in the field echoed and elaborated at least part of Turner's argument. Ray Allen Billington's *Westward Expansion* (1949) was for decades the standard textbook in the field; his skillful revision of the Turner thesis kept the idea of what he called the "westward course of empire" (the movement of Europeans into an unsettled land) at the center of scholarship. In *The Great Plains* (1931) and *The Great Frontier* (1952), Walter Prescott Webb similarly emphasized the bravery and ingenuity of white

settlers in Texas and the Southwest in overcoming obstacles (most notably, in Webb's part of the West, aridity) to create a great new civilization.

The Turner thesis was never without its critics. But serious efforts to displace it as the explanation of western American history did not begin in earnest until after World War II. In *Virgin Land* (1950), Henry Nash Smith examined many of the same heroic images of the West that Turner and his disciples had presented; but he treated those images less as descriptions of reality than as myths, which many Americans had used to sustain an image of themselves that the actual character of the modern world contradicted. Earl Pomeroy, in an influential 1955 essay

READING THE WAR BULLETINS, SAN FRANCISCO Residents of San Francisco's Chinatown gather on a sidewalk to await a Chinese-language newspaper's posting of the reports from Asia of the progress of the Sino-Japanese War. The conflict between China and Japan in 1894–1895 left China so weakened that it could no longer effectively resist incursions from western nations. *(Library of Congress)*

and in many other works, challenged Turner's notion of the West as a place of individualism, innovation, and democratic renewal. "Conservatism, inheritance, and continuity bulked at least as large," he claimed. "The westerner has been fundamentally imitator rather than innovator. . . . He was often the most ardent of conformists." Howard Lamar, in *Dakota Territory, 1861–1889* (1956) and *The Far Southwest* (1966), emphasized the highly diverse experiences of different areas of the West and thus challenged the emphasis of the Turnerians on a distinctive western environment as the crucial determinant of western experience.

The generation of western historians who began to emerge in the late 1970s launched an even more emphatic attack on the Turner thesis and the idea of the "frontier." Echoing the interest of historians in other fields in issues of race, gender, ethnicity, and culture, "new" western historians such as Richard White, Patricia Nelson Limerick, William Cronon, Donald Worster, Peggy Pascoe, and many others challenged the Turnerians on a number of points.

Turner saw the nineteenth-century West as "free land" awaiting the expansion of Anglo-American settlement and American democracy. Pioneers settled the region by conquering the "obstacles" in the way of civilization—the "vast forests," the "mountainous ramparts," the "desolate, grass-clad prairies, barren oceans of rolling plains, arid deserts, and a fierce race of savages." The "new western historians" rejected the concept of a "frontier" and emphasized, instead, the elaborate and highly developed civilizations (Native American, Hispanic, mixed-blood, and others) that already existed in the region. White, English-speaking Americans, they have argued, did not so much settle the West as conquer it. And that conquest was never complete. Anglo-Americans in the West continue to share the region not only with the Indians and Hispanics who preceded them there, but also with African Americans, Asians, Latin Americans, and others who flowed into the West

at the same time they did. Western history, these recent scholars have claimed, is a process of cultural "convergence," a constant competition and interaction—economic, political, cultural, and linguistic—among diverse peoples.

The Turnerian West was a place of heroism, triumph, and, above all, progress, dominated by the feats of brave white men. The West the new historians describe is a less triumphant (and less masculine) place in which bravery and success coexist with oppression, greed, and failure; in which decaying ghost towns, bleak Indian reservations, impoverished barrios, and ecologically devastated landscapes are as characteristic of western development as great ranches, rich farms, and prosperous cities; and in which women are as important as men in shaping the societies that emerged. This aspect of the "new western history" has attracted particular criticism from those attached to more traditional accounts. The novelist Larry McMurtry, for example, has denounced the new scholarship as "Failure Studies." He has insisted that in rejecting the romantic

image westerners had of themselves, the revisionists omit an important part of the western experience.

To Turner and his disciples, the nineteenth-century West was a place where rugged individualism flourished and replenished American democracy. To the new scholars, western individualism is a self-serving myth. The region was inextricably tied to a national and international capitalist economy; indeed, the only thing that sustained Anglo-American settlement of the West was the demand in other places for its natural resources. Western "pioneers" were never self-sufficient. They depended on government-subsidized railroads for access to markets, federal troops for protection from Indians, and (later) government-funded dams and canals for irrigating their fields and sustaining their towns.

And while Turner defined the West as a process—a process of settlement that came to an end with the "closing of the frontier" in the late nineteenth century—the new historians see the West as a region. Its distinctive history does not end in 1890. It continues into our own time.

(Montana Historical Society, Helena)

Last of the Mohicans). That symbol has survived into the late twentieth century—in popular literature, in song, in film, and on television.

The Idea of the Frontier

Yet it was not simply the particular character of the new West that made it so important to the nation's imagina-

Romantic Image of the West

tion. It was also that many Americans considered it the last frontier. Since the earliest moments of European settlement in America, the image of uncharted territory to the west had always comforted and inspired those who dreamed of starting life anew. Now, with the last of that unsettled land being slowly absorbed into the nation's civilization, that image exercised a stronger pull than ever.

Mark Twain, one of the great American writers of the nineteenth century, gave voice to this romantic vision of the frontier in a series of brilliant novels and memoirs. In some of his writings—notably *Roughing It* (1872)—he wrote of the Far West, and of his own experience as a newspaper reporter in Nevada during the mining boom. His greatest works, however, dealt with life on an earlier frontier: the Mississippi Valley of his boyhood. In *The Adventures of Tom Sawyer* (1876) and *The Adventures of Huckleberry Finn* (1885), he produced characters who repudiated the constraints of organized society and attempted to escape into a more natural world. For Huck Finn, the vehicle of escape might be a small raft on the Mississippi, but the yearning for freedom reflected a larger vision of the West as the last refuge from the constraints of civilization.

The painter and sculptor Frederic Remington also captured the romance of the West and its image as an alternative to the settled civilization of

Frederic Remington

the East. He portrayed the cowboy as a natural aristocrat, much like Wister's Virginian, living in a natural world in which all the normal supporting structures of "civilization" were missing. The romantic quality of his work made Remington one of the most beloved and successful artists of the nineteenth century—and one whose work is still exceptionally popular today.

Theodore Roosevelt, who was, like both Wister and Remington, a man born and raised in the East, traveled to

TURN HIM LOOSE, BILL Frederic Remington is perhaps best known for his sculptures of cowboys and their horses, but he was also a popular painter of western scenes. This portrayal of a cowboy trying to break a wild bronco is typical of his adventurous and somewhat romanticized view of the West. *(Anschutz Collection)*

the Dakota Badlands in the mid-1880s to help himself recover from the sudden death of his young wife. He had long romanticized the West as a place of physical regeneration—a place where a man could gain strength through rugged activity (just as Roosevelt himself, a sickly, asthmatic boy, had hardened himself through adherence to the idea of a strenuous life). His long sojourn into the Badlands in the 1880s cemented his love of the region, which continued to the end of his life. And like Wister and Remington, he made his own fascination with the West a part of the nation's popular culture. In the 1890s, he published a four-volume history, *The Winning of the West*, with a romanticized account of the spread of white civilization into the frontier. These and other books on the West enhanced his own reputation. They also contributed to the public's fascination with the "frontier."

Frederick Jackson Turner

Perhaps the clearest and most influential statements of the romantic vision of the frontier came from the historian Frederick Jackson Turner, of the University of Wisconsin.

Turner's Frontier Thesis

In 1893, the thirty-three-year-old Turner delivered a memorable paper to a meeting of the American Historical Association in Chicago entitled "The Significance of the Frontier in American History." In it, he cited the findings of the 1890 census that the unsettled area of the West had been "so broken into by isolated bodies of settlement" that a continuous frontier line could no longer be drawn. The passing of that line, he argued, ended an era in the nation's history. For, as Turner stated, "the existence of an area of free land, its continuous recession, and the advance of settlement westward, explain American development." This experience of expansion into the frontier had stimulated individualism, nationalism, and democracy. It had kept opportunities for advancement alive. It had made Americans the distinctive people that they were. "Now," Turner concluded portentously, "four centuries from the discovery of America, at the end of a hundred years of life under the Constitution, the frontier has gone and with its going has closed the first period of American history."

In fact, Turner's assessments were both inaccurate and premature. The West had never been a "frontier" in the sense he meant the term: an empty, uncivilized land awaiting settlement. White migrants into the region had joined (or displaced) already established societies and cultures. At the same time, considerable unoccupied land remained in the West for many years to come. A vast public domain still existed in the 1890s, and during the forty years thereafter the government was to give away many more acres than it had granted as homesteads in the past. But Turner did express a growing and generally accurate sense that much of the best farming and grazing land was now taken, that in the future it would be more difficult for individuals to acquire valuable land for little or nothing.

The Loss of Utopia

In accepting the idea of the "passing of the frontier," many Americans were acknowledging the end of one of their most cherished myths. As long as it had been possible for them *Psychological Loss* to consider the West an empty, open land, it was possible to believe that there were constantly revitalizing opportunities in American life. Now there was a vague and ominous sense of opportunities foreclosed, of individuals losing their ability to control their own destinies. The psychological loss was all the greater because of what historian Henry Nash Smith would later call, in *Virgin Land* (1950), the "myth of the garden": the once widely shared belief that the West had the potential to be a virtual Garden of Eden, where a person could begin life anew and where the ideals of democracy could be restored.

That, too, was a theme in late-nineteenth-century fiction. For example, in *Ramona* (1884), the novelist Helen Hunt Jackson wrote of California before American settlement as an agrarian paradise of rugged Hispanic pioneers and saintly missionaries. The setting for utopia, once the New World as a whole, had shrunk to the West of the United States. And now even that West seemed to be vanishing.

THE DISPERSAL OF THE TRIBES

Having imagined the West as a "virgin land" awaiting civilization by white people, many Americans tried to force the region to match their image of it. That meant, above all, ensuring that the Indian tribes would not remain obstacles to the spread of white society.

White Tribal Policies

The traditional policy of the federal government was to regard the tribes simultaneously as independent nations and as wards of the president, and to negotiate treaties with them that were solemnly ratified by the Senate. This limited concept of Indian sovereignty had been responsible for the government's attempt before 1860 to erect a permanent frontier between whites and Indians, to reserve the region west of the bend of the Missouri River as permanent Indian country. However, treaties or agreements with the tribes seldom survived the pressure of white settlers eager for access to Indian lands. The history of relations between the United States and the Native Americans was, therefore, one of nearly endless broken promises.

By the early 1850s, the idea of establishing one great enclave in which many tribes could live gave way, in the face of white demands for access to lands in Indian Territory, *"Concentration" Policy* to a new reservations policy, known as "concentration." In 1851, each tribe was assigned its own defined reservation,

CHIEF GARFIELD George Curtis, one of the most accomplished photographers of tribal life in the early twentieth century, made this portrait of a Jicarilla Apache chief in 1904. By then, the Jicarilla were living in a reservation in northern New Mexico, and white officials had assigned all members of the tribe Spanish or English names. The man depicted here, the head chief, had chosen the name Garfield himself. *(Chief Garfield-Jicarilla, 1904. Edward Curtis. Reproduced by permission of Christopher Cardozo, Inc.)*

confirmed by separate treaties—treaties often illegitimately negotiated with unauthorized "representatives" chosen by whites, people known sarcastically as "treaty chiefs." The new arrangement had many benefits for whites and few for the Indians. It divided the tribes from one another and made them easier to control. It allowed the government to force tribes into scattered locations and to take over the most desirable lands for white settlement. But it did not survive as the basis of Indian policy for long.

In 1867, in the aftermath of a series of bloody conflicts, Congress established an Indian Peace Commission, composed of soldiers and civilians, to recommend a new and presumably permanent Indian policy. The commission recommended replacing the "concentration" policy with a new one. The government would move all the Plains Indians into two large reservations—one in Indian Territory (Oklahoma), the other in the Dakotas. At a series of meetings with the tribes, government agents cajoled, bribed, and tricked representatives of the Arapaho, Cheyenne,

Sioux, and other tribes into agreeing to treaties establishing the new reservations.

But this solution worked little better than previous ones. Part of the problem was the way in which the government administered the reservations it had established. White management of Indian *Poorly Administered Reservations* matters was entrusted to the Bureau of Indian Affairs, a branch of the Department of the Interior. The bureau was responsible for distributing land, making payments, and supervising the shipment of supplies. Its record was appalling. The bureau's agents in the West, products of political patronage, were often men of extraordinary incompetence and dishonesty. But even the most honest and diligent agents were generally ill-prepared for their jobs, had no understanding of tribal ways, and had little chance of success. The poor and usually corrupt administration of the reservations was one reason for the constant conflicts between the tribes and the whites who were surrounding them.

But the problem was also a result of what was, in effect, economic warfare by whites: the relentless slaughtering of the buffalo herds that supported the tribes' way of life. Even in the 1850s, whites had been killing buffalo at a rapid rate to provide food and supplies for the large bands of migrants traveling to the gold rush in California. After the Civil War the white demand for buffalo hides became a national phenomenon—partly for economic reasons and partly as a fad. (Everyone east of the Missouri seemed to want a buffalo robe from the romantic West, and there was a strong demand for buffalo leather, which was used to make machine belts in eastern factories.) Gangs of professional hunters swarmed over the Plains to shoot the huge animals. Some hunters killed merely for the sport of the chase, although the lumbering victims did not present much of a challenge. Railroad companies hired riflemen (such as Buffalo Bill Cody) and arranged large shooting expeditions to kill large numbers of buffalo, hoping to thin the herds, which were obstructions to railroad traffic. Some Indian tribes (notably the Blackfeet) also began killing large numbers of buffalo to sell in the booming new market.

It was not just the hunting that threatened the buffalo. The ecological changes that white settlement brought to the region—the reduction, and in some areas virtual disappearance, of the open plains on which the buffalo depended—also decimated the buffalo population. The southern herd was virtually exterminated by 1875, and within a few years the smaller northern herd had met the same fate. In 1865, there had been at least 15 million buffalo; a decade later, fewer than a thousand of the great beasts survived. The army and the agents of the Bureau of Indian Affairs condoned and even encouraged the killing. By destroying the buffalo herds, whites were destroying the Indians' source of food and

supplies and their ability to resist the white advance. They were also contributing to a climate in which Indian warriors felt the need to fight to preserve their way of life.

The Indian Wars

There was almost incessant fighting between whites and Indians from the 1850s to the 1880s, as Indians struggled

Indian Resistance | against the growing threats to their civilizations. Indian war-

riors, usually traveling in raiding parties of thirty to forty men, attacked wagon trains, stagecoaches, and isolated ranches, often in retaliation for earlier attacks on them by whites. As the United States Army became more deeply involved in the fighting, the tribes began to focus more of their attacks on white soldiers.

At times, this small-scale fighting escalated into something close to a war. During the Civil War, the eastern Sioux in Minnesota, cramped on an inadequate reservation and exploited by corrupt white agents, suddenly rebelled against the restrictions imposed on them by the government's policies. Led by Little Crow, they killed more than 700 whites before being subdued by a force of regulars and militiamen. Thirty-eight of the Indians were hanged, and the tribe was exiled to the Dakotas.

At the same time, fighting flared up in eastern Colorado, where the Arapaho and Cheyenne were coming into con-

Sand Creek Massacre | flict with white miners settling in the region. Bands of Indians

attacked stagecoach lines and settlements in an effort to regain territory they had lost. In response to these incidents, whites called up a large territorial militia, and the army issued dire threats of retribution. The governor urged all friendly Indians to congregate at army posts for

protection before the army began its campaign. One Arapaho and Cheyenne band under Black Kettle, apparently in response to the invitation, camped near Fort Lyon on Sand Creek in November 1864. Some members of the party were warriors, but Black Kettle believed he was under official protection and exhibited no hostile intention. Nevertheless, Colonel J. M. Chivington, apparently encouraged by the army commander of the district, led a volunteer militia force—largely consisting of unemployed miners, many of whom were apparently drunk—to the unsuspecting camp and massacred 133 people, 105 of them women and children. Black Kettle himself escaped the Sand Creek massacre. Four years later, in 1868, he and his Cheyennes, some of whom were now at war with the whites, were caught on the Washita River, near the Texas border, by Colonel George A. Custer. White troops killed the chief and slaughtered his people.

At the end of the Civil War, white troops stepped up their wars against the western Indians on several fronts. The most serious and sustained conflict was in Montana, where the army was attempting to build a road, the Bozeman Trail, to connect Fort Laramie, Wyoming, to the new mining centers. The western Sioux resented this intrusion into the heart of their buffalo range. Led by one of their great chiefs, Red Cloud, they so harried the soldiers and the construction party—among other things, burning the forts that were supposed to guard the route—that the road could not be used.

But it was not only the United States military that threatened the tribes. It was also unofficial violence by white vigilantes who engaged in what became known as | *"Indian Hunting"* "Indian hunting." In California, in particular, tracking down and killing Indians became for some whites a kind of sport. Some who did not engage in killing offered rewards (or bounties) to those who did; these bounty hunters brought back scalps and skulls as proof of their deeds. Sometimes the killing was in response to Indian raids on white communities. But often it was in service to a more basic and terrible purpose. Considerable numbers of whites were committed to the goal of literal "elimination" of the tribes, a goal that rested on the belief in the essential inhumanity of Indians and the impossibility of white society's coexisting with them. In Oregon in 1853, for example, whites who had hanged a seven-year-old Indian boy explained themselves by saying simply "nits breed lice." In California, civilians killed close to 5,000 Indians between 1850 and 1880—one of many factors (disease and poverty being the more important) that reduced the Indian population of the state from 150,000 before the Civil War to 30,000 in 1870.

The treaties negotiated in 1867 brought a temporary lull to many of the conflicts. But new forces soon shattered the peace again. In the early 1870s, more waves of white settlers, mostly miners, began to penetrate some of the lands in Dakota Territory supposedly guaranteed to the tribes in 1867. At the same time, the federal government, responding to the recommendations of a commission, decided that it would no longer recognize the tribes as independent entities and would no longer

negotiate with tribal chiefs. This step was intended to undermine the collective nature of Indian life and to force the Indians to assimilate into white culture—a goal cherished by many white reformers, who believed that only through assimilation could the Indians achieve genuine "civilization."

Indian resistance flared anew, this time with even greater strength. In the northern plains, the Sioux, in response to the entrance of miners into the Black Hills and in anger at the corrupt behavior of white agents, rose up in 1875 and left their reservation. When white officials ordered them to return, bands of warriors gathered in Montana and united under two great leaders: Crazy Horse and Sitting Bull.

Three army columns set out to round them up and force them back onto the reservation. With the expedition, as colonel of the famous Seventh Cavalry, was the colorful and *Little Bighorn* controversial George A. Custer, golden-haired romantic and glory seeker. At the Battle of the Little Bighorn in southern Montana in 1876—perhaps the most famous of all conflicts between whites and Indians—the tribal warriors surprised Custer and 264 members of his regiment, surrounded them, and killed every man. Custer has been accused of rashness, but he seems to have encountered

THE BATTLE OF THE LITTLE BIG HORN: AN INDIAN VIEW This 1898 watercolor by one of the Indian participants portrays the aftermath of the Battle of the Little Big Horn, June 25–26, 1876, in which an army unit under the command of General George Armstrong Custer was surrounded and wiped out by Sioux and Cheyenne warriors. This grisly painting shows Indians on horseback riding over the corpses of Custer and his men. Custer can be seen lying at left center, dressed in yellow buckskin with his hat beside him. The four standing men at center are Sitting Bull, Rain-in-the-Face, Crazy Horse, and Kicking Bear (the artist). At lower right, Indian women begin preparations for a ceremony to honor the returning warriors. *(Southwest Museum, Pasadena, California)*

something that no white man would likely have predicted. The chiefs had gathered as many as 2,500 warriors, one of the largest Indian armies ever assembled at one time in the United States.

But the Indians did not have the political organization or the supplies to keep their troops united. Soon the warriors drifted off in bands to elude pursuit or search for food, and the army ran them down singly and returned them to Dakota. The power of the Sioux was soon broken. The proud leaders, Crazy Horse and Sitting Bull, accepted defeat and the monotony of life on reservations. Both were later killed by reservation police after being tricked or taunted into a last pathetic show of resistance.

One of the most dramatic episodes in Indian history occurred in Idaho in 1877. The Nez Percé were a small and relatively peaceful tribe, some of whose members had managed to live unmolested in Oregon into the 1870s without ever signing a treaty with the United States. But under pressure from white settlers, the government forced them to move into a reservation that another branch of the tribe had accepted by treaty in the 1850s. With no realistic prospect of resisting, the Indians began the journey to the reservation; but on the way, several younger Indians, drunk and angry, killed four white settlers.

The leader of the band, Chief Joseph, persuaded his followers to flee from the expected retribution. American

Chief Joseph

troops pursued and attacked them, only to be driven off in a battle at White Bird Canyon. After that, the Nez Percé scattered in several directions and became part of a remarkable chase. Joseph moved with 200 men and 350 women, children, and elders in an effort to reach Canada and take refuge with the Sioux there. Pursued by four columns of American soldiers smarting from their defeat at White Bird Canyon, the Indians covered 1,321 miles in seventy-five days, repelling or evading the army time and again. They were finally caught just short of the Canadian boundary. Some escaped and slipped across the border; but Joseph and most of his followers, weary and discouraged, finally gave up. "Hear me, my chiefs," Joseph said after meeting with the American general Nelson Miles. "I am tired. My heart is sick and sad. From where the sun now stands, I will fight no more forever." He surrendered to Miles in exchange for a promise that his band could return to the Nez Percé reservation in Idaho. But the government refused to honor Miles's promise, and the Nez Percé were shipped from one place to another for several years; in the process, many of them died of disease and malnutrition (although Joseph himself lived until 1908).

The last Indians to maintain organized resistance against the whites were the Chiricahua Apaches, who fought intermittently from the 1860s to the late 1880s. The two ablest chiefs of this fierce tribe were Mangas Colorados and Cochise. Mangas was murdered during the Civil War by white soldiers who tricked him into surrendering, and in 1872 Cochise agreed to peace in exchange for a reservation that included some of the tribe's traditional land. But Cochise died in 1874, and his successor, Geronimo—unwilling to bow to white pressures to assimilate—fought on for more than a decade longer, establishing bases in the mountains of Arizona and Mexico and leading warriors in intermittent raids against white outposts. With each raid, however, the number of warring Apaches dwindled, as some warriors died and others drifted away to the reservation. By 1886, Geronimo's plight was hopeless. His band consisted of only about thirty people, including women and children, while his white pursuers numbered perhaps ten thousand. Geronimo recognized the odds and surrendered, an event that marked the end of formal warfare between Indians and whites. The Apache wars were the most violent of all the Indian conflicts, perhaps because the tribes were now the most desperate. But it was the whites who committed the most flagrant and vicious atrocities. In 1871, for example, a mob of white miners invaded an Apache camp, slaughtered over a hundred Indians, and captured children, whom they sold as slaves to rival tribes. On other occasions, white troops murdered Indians who responded to invitations to peace conferences, once killing them with poisoned food.

Nor did the atrocities end with the conclusion of the Apache wars. Another tragic encounter occurred in 1890 as a result of a religious revival among the Sioux—a revival that itself symbolized the catastrophic effects of the white assaults on Indian civilization. The Sioux were by now aware that their culture and their glories were irrevocably fading; some were also near starvation because corrupt government agents had reduced their food rations. As other tribes had done in trying times in the past, many of these Indians turned to a prophet who led them into a religious revival.

This time the prophet was Wovoka, a Paiute who inspired an ecstatic spiritual awakening that began in Nevada and spread quickly to the plains. The new revival em-

"Ghost Dance"

phasized the coming of a messiah, but its most conspicuous feature was a mass, emotional "Ghost Dance," which inspired ecstatic visions that many participants believed were genuinely mystical. Among these visions were images of a retreat of white people from the plains and a restoration of the great buffalo herds. White agents on the Sioux reservation watched the dances in bewilderment and fear; some believed they might be the preliminary to hostilities.

On December 29, 1890, the Seventh Cavalry (which had once been Custer's regiment) tried to round up a group of about 350 cold and starving Sioux at Wounded

Wounded Knee

Knee, South Dakota. Fighting broke out in which about 40 white soldiers and up to 200 of the Indians, including women and children, died. What precipitated the conflict is a matter of dispute. An Indian may well have fired the

BURIAL AT WOUNDED KNEE Soldiers bury some of the Sioux Indians killed at Wounded Knee. This mass grave held over 100 bodies, many of them women and children. The Wounded Knee massacre was the last major episode in a year-long effort by whites to suppress the Sioux religious revival known as the Ghost Dance. *(Amon Carter Museum)*

LE SABRE INDIAN SCHOOL, MONTANA Government authorities and private philanthropists tried in many ways to encourage Indians to assimilate into mainstream white American society after the end of the Indian wars of the late nineteenth century. One of the most ambitious, and controversial, was a series of boarding schools for Indian children, where white teachers worked to teach them the ways of the English-speaking world. Most such schools were for boys, but some—such as this school in Montana, run by Catholic nuns—were created for girls. *(Montana Historical Society)*

first shot, but the battle soon turned into a one-sided massacre, as the white soldiers turned their new machine guns on the Indians and mowed them down in the snow.

The Dawes Act

Even before the Ghost Dance and the Wounded Knee tragedy, the federal government had moved to destroy forever the tribal structure that had always been the cornerstone of Indian culture. Reversing its policy of nearly fifty years of creating reservations in which the tribes would be isolated from white society, Congress abolished the practice by which tribes owned reservation lands communally. Some supporters of the new policy believed they were acting for the good of the Indians, whom they considered a "vanishing race" in need of rescue by white society. But the action was frankly designed to force Indians to become landowners and farmers, to abandon their collective society and culture and become part of white civilization.

The Dawes Severalty Act of 1887 (usually known simply as the Dawes Act) provided for the gradual elimina-

Assimilation tion of tribal ownership of land and the allotment of tracts to individual owners: 160 acres to the head of a family, 80 acres to a single adult or orphan, 40 acres to each dependent child. Adult owners were given United States citizenship, but unlike other citizens, they could not gain full title to their property for twenty-five years (supposedly to prevent them from selling the land to speculators). The act applied to most of the western tribes. The Pueblo, who continued to occupy lands long ago guaranteed them, were excluded from its provisions. In applying the Dawes Act, the Bureau of Indian Affairs relentlessly promoted the idea of assimilation that lay behind it. Not only did they try to move Indian families onto their own plots of land; they also took Indian children away from their families and sent them to boarding schools run by whites, where they believed the young people could be educated to abandon tribal ways. They also moved to stop Indian religious rituals and encouraged the spread of Christianity and the creation of Christian churches on the reservations.

Few Indians were prepared for this wrenching change from their traditional collective society to capitalist individualism. In any case, white administration of the program was so corrupt and inept that ultimately the government simply abandoned it. Much of the reservation land, therefore, was never distributed to individual owners. Congress attempted to speed the transition with the Burke Act of 1906, but Indians continued to resist forced assimilation.

Neither then nor later could legislation provide a satisfactory solution to the problem of the Indians, largely because there was no entirely happy solution to be had. The interests of the Indians were not compatible with those of the expanding white civilization. Whites successfully settled the American West only at the expense of the region's indigenous peoples.

THE RISE AND DECLINE OF THE WESTERN FARMER

The arrival of the miners, the empire building of the cattle ranchers, the dispersal of the Indian tribes—all served as a prelude to the decisive phase of white settlement of the Far West. Even before the Civil War, farmers had begun moving into the plains region, challenging the dominance of the ranchers and the Indians and occasionally coming into conflict with both. By the 1870s, what was once a trickle had become a deluge. Farmers poured into the plains and beyond, enclosed land that had once been hunting territory for Indians and grazing territory for cattle, and established a new agricultural region.

For a time in the late 1870s and early 1880s, the new western farmers flourished, enjoying the fruits of an agricultural economic boom comparable in many ways to the booms that eastern industry periodically enjoyed. Beginning in the mid-1880s, however, the boom turned to bust. American agriculture—not only in the new West but in the older Middle West and the South as well—was producing more than it ever had, too much for the market to absorb. For that and other reasons, prices for agricultural goods declined. Both economically and psychologically, the agricultural economy began a long, steady decline.

Farming on the Plains

Many factors combined to produce this surge of western settlement, but the most important was the railroads. Before the Civil War, the Great Plains had been accessible only through a difficult journey by wagon. But beginning in the 1860s, a great new network of railroad lines developed, spearheaded by the transcontinental routes Congress had authorized and subsidized in 1862. They made huge new areas of settlement accessible.

The building of the transcontinental line was a dramatic and monumental achievement. Thousands of immigrant workers—mostly Irish on the eastern route, Chinese on the western—labored in what were at times unimaginably difficult conditions to penetrate mountain ranges, cross deserts, protect themselves against Indians, and—finally—connect the two lines at Promontory Point in northern Utah in the spring of 1869.

But while this first transcontinental line captured the public imagination, the construction of subsidiary lines in the following years proved of greater importance to the West. State governments, imitating Washington, encouraged railroad development by offering direct financial aid, favorable loans, and more than 50 million acres of land (on top of the 130 million acres the federal government had already provided). Although operated by private corporations, the railroads were essentially public projects.

It was not only by making access to the Great Plains easier that the railroads helped spur agricultural settlement there. The railroad companies themselves actively promoted settlement, both to provide themselves with customers for their services and to increase the value of their vast landholdings. In addition, the companies set

Key Role of the Railroad | rates so low for settlers that almost anyone could afford the trip west. And they sold much of their land at very low prices and provided liberal credit to prospective settlers.

Contributing further to the great surge of white agricultural expansion was a temporary change in the climate of the Great Plains. For several years in succession, beginning in the 1870s, rainfall in the plains states was well above average. White Americans now rejected the old idea that the region was the Great American Desert. Some even claimed that cultivation of the plains actually encouraged rainfall.

Even under the most favorable conditions, farming on the plains presented special problems. First was the problem of fencing. Farmers had to enclose their land, if for no other reason than to protect it from the herds of the open-range cattlemen. But traditional wood or stone fences were too expensive and were ineffective as barriers to cattle. In 1873, however, two Illinois farmers, Joseph H.

Barbed Wire | Glidden and I. L. Ellwood, solved this problem by developing and marketing barbed wire, which became standard equipment on the plains and revolutionized fencing practices all over the country.

The second problem was water. Much of the land west of the Mississippi was considerably more arid than the lands to the east. Some of it was literally desert. As a result, the growth of the West depended heavily on irrigation—providing water from sources other than rainfall. Water was diverted from rivers and streams and into farmlands throughout the West—in California and in the Southwest more than anywhere else. In other areas, farmers drilled wells or found other methods of channeling water onto their lands. The search for water—and the resulting battles over control of water (between different landowners and even between different states) became a central and enduring characteristic of western life.

In the Plains states, the problems of water created an epic disaster. Through much of the 1870s and 1880s, rain-

Drought | fall was above average in many agricultural regions of the plains, encouraging farmers and others to believe that a permanent change in the climate had occurred. Some even began to argue that the processes of settlement and cultivation had themselves caused the rainfall to increase. But after 1887, a series of dry seasons began, and lands that had been fertile now returned to semidesert. Some farmers dealt with the problem by using deep wells pumped by steel windmills, by turning to what was called dryland farming (a system of tillage designed to conserve moisture in the soil by covering it with a dust blanket), or by planting drought-resistant crops. In many areas of the plains, however, only large-scale irrigation could save the endangered farms. But irrigation projects of the necessary magnitude required government assistance, and neither the state nor federal governments were prepared to fund the projects.

Most of the people who moved into the region had previously been farmers in the Middle West, the East, or Europe. In the booming years of the early 1880s, with land val- | *Hard Times for Farmers* ues rising, the new farmers had no problem obtaining extensive and easy credit and had every reason to believe they would soon be able to retire their debts. But the arid years of the late 1880s—during which crop prices were falling while production was becoming more expensive—changed that prospect. Tens of thousands of farmers could not pay their debts and were forced to abandon their farms. There was, in effect, a reverse migration: white settlers moved back east, sometimes turning once flourishing communities into desolate ghost towns. Those who remained continued to suffer from falling prices (for example, wheat, which had sold for $1.60 a bushel at the end of the Civil War, dropped to 49 cents in the 1890s) and persistent indebtedness.

Commercial Agriculture

American farming by the late nineteenth century no longer bore very much relation to the comforting image many Americans continued to cherish. The sturdy, independent farmer of popular myth was being replaced by the commercial farmer—attempting to do in the agricultural economy what industrialists were doing in the manufacturing economy.

Commercial farmers were not self-sufficient and made no effort to become so. They specialized in cash crops, which they sold in national or world markets. They did not make their own household supplies or grow their own food but bought them instead at town or village stores. This kind of farming, when it was successful, raised the farmers' living standards. But it also made them dependent on bankers and interest rates, railroads and freight rates, national and European markets, world supply and demand. And unlike the capitalists of the industrial order, they could not regulate their production or influence the prices of what they sold.

Between 1865 and 1900, agriculture became an international business. Farm output increased dramatically, not only in the United States but also in Brazil, Argentina, Canada, Australia, New Zealand, Russia, and elsewhere. At the same time, modern forms of communication and transportation—the telephone, telegraph, steam navigation, railroads—were creating new markets around the world for agricultural goods. American commercial farmers, constantly opening new lands, produced much more than the domestic market could absorb; they relied on the world market to absorb their surplus, but in that market they faced major competition. Cotton farmers depended on export sales for 70 percent of their annual income, wheat farmers for 30 to 40 percent; but the volatility of the international market put them at great risk.

Beginning in the 1880s, worldwide overproduction led to a drop in prices for most agricultural goods and hence to

Consequences of Overproduction

great economic distress for many of the more than 6 million American farm families. By the 1890s, 27 percent of the farms in the country were mortgaged; by 1910, 33 percent. In 1880, 25 percent of all farms had been operated by tenants; by 1910, the proportion had grown to 37 percent. Commercial farming made some people fabulously wealthy. But the farm economy as a whole was suffering a significant decline relative to the rest of the nation.

The Farmers' Grievances

American farmers were painfully aware that something was wrong. But few yet understood the implications of national and world overproduction. Instead, they concentrated their attention and anger on more immediate, more comprehensible—and no less real—problems: inequitable freight rates, high interest charges, and an inadequate currency.

The farmers' first and most burning grievance was against the railroads. In many cases, the railroads charged higher freight rates for farm goods than for other goods, and higher rates in the South and West than in the Northeast. Railroads also controlled elevator and warehouse facilities in buying centers and charged arbitrary storage rates.

Farmers also resented the institutions controlling credit—banks, loan companies, insurance corporations. Since sources of credit in the West and South were few,

Farmers' Grievances

farmers had to take loans on whatever terms they could get, often at interest rates ranging from 10 to 25 percent. Many farmers had to pay these loans back in years when prices were dropping and currency was becoming scarce. Increasing the volume of currency eventually became an important agrarian demand.

A third grievance concerned prices—both the prices farmers received for their products and the prices they paid for goods. Farmers sold their products in a competitive world market over which they had no control and of which they had no advanced knowledge. A farmer could plant a large crop at a moment when prices were high and find that by harvesttime the price had declined. Farmers' fortunes rose and fell in response to unpredictable forces. But many farmers became convinced (often with

valid reason) that "middlemen"—speculators, bankers, regional and local agents—were combining to fix prices so as to benefit themselves at the growers' expense. Many farmers also came to believe (again, not entirely without reason) that manufacturers in the East were conspiring to keep the prices of farm goods low and the prices of industrial goods high. Although farmers sold their crops in a competitive world market, they bought manufactured goods in a domestic market protected by tariffs and dominated by trusts and corporations.

The Agrarian Malaise

These economic difficulties produced a series of social and cultural resentments. In part, this was a result of the isolation of farm life. Farm families in some parts of the country—particularly in the prairie and plains regions, where

Isolation

large farms were scattered over vast areas—were virtually cut off from the outside world and human companionship. During the winter months and spells of bad weather, the loneliness and boredom could become nearly unbearable. Many farmers lacked access to adequate education for their children, to proper medical facilities, to recreational or cultural activities, to virtually anything that might give them a sense of being members of a community. Older farmers felt the sting of watching their children leave the farm for the city. They felt the humiliation of being ridiculed as "hayseeds" by the new urban culture that was coming to dominate American life.

The result of this sense of isolation and obsolescence was a growing malaise among many farmers, a discontent that would help create a great national political movement in the 1890s. It found reflection, too, in the literature that emerged from rural America. Late-nineteenth-century writers often romanticized the rugged life of the cowboy and the western miner. For the farmer, however, the image was often different. Hamlin Garland, for example, reflected the growing disillusionment in a series of novels and short stories. In the past, Garland wrote in the introduction to his novel *Jason Edwards* (1891), the agrarian frontier had seemed to be "the Golden West, the land of wealth and freedom and happiness. All of the associations called up by the spoken word, the West, were fabulous, mythic, hopeful." Now, however, the bright promise had faded. The trials of rural life were crushing the human spirit. "So this is the reality of the dream!" a character in *Jason Edwards* exclaims. "A shanty on a barren plain, hot and lone as a desert. My God!" Once, sturdy yeoman farmers had viewed themselves as the backbone of American life. Now they were becoming painfully aware that their position was declining in relation to the rising urban-industrial society to the east.

CONCLUSION

To many Americans in the late nineteenth century, the West seemed a place utterly unlike the rest of the United States—an untamed "frontier" in which hardy pioneers were creating a new society, in which sturdy individuals still had a chance to be heroes. This image was a stark and deliberate contrast to the reality of the urbanizing, industrializing East, in which the role of the individual was being transformed by the rise of industrial life and its institutions.

The reality of the West in these years, however, was very different from the image. White Americans were moving into the vast regions west of the Mississippi at a remarkable rate in the years after the Civil War, and many of them, it is true, were settling in lands far from any civilization they had ever known. But the West was not an empty place in these years. It contained a large population of Indians, with whom the white settlers sometimes lived uneasily and sometimes battled, but almost always in the end pushed aside and (with help from the federal government) relocated onto lands whites did not want. There were significant numbers of Mexicans in some areas, small populations of Asians in others, and African Americans moving in from the South in search of land and freedom. The West was not a barren frontier, but a place of many cultures.

The West was also closely and increasingly tied to the emerging capitalist-industrial economy of the East. The miners who flooded into California, Colorado, Nevada, the Dakotas, and elsewhere were responding to the demand in the East for gold and silver, but even more for such utilitarian minerals as iron ore, copper, lead, zinc, and quartz that had industrial uses. Cattle and sheep ranchers produced meat, wool, and leather for eastern consumers and manufacturers. Farmers grew crops for sale in national and international commodities markets. The West certainly looked different from the East, and its people lived their lives in surroundings very different from those of eastern cities. But the growth of the West was very much a part of the growth of the rest of the nation. And the culture of the West, despite the romantic images of pioneering individuals embraced by easterners and westerners alike, was at its heart as much a culture of economic growth and capitalist ambition as was the culture of the rest of the nation.

FOR FURTHER REFERENCE

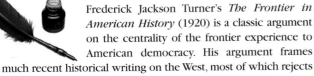

Frederick Jackson Turner's *The Frontier in American History* (1920) is a classic argument on the centrality of the frontier experience to American democracy. His argument frames much recent historical writing on the West, most of which rejects the "Turner thesis." Patricia Nelson Limerick's *The Legacy of Conquest: The Unbroken Past of the American West* (1987) argues that the West was not a frontier but rather an inhabited place conquered by Anglo-Americans. Richard White, in *"It's Your Misfortune and None of My Own": A History of the American West* (1991), is an outstanding general history of the region that revises many myths about the West. Ronald Takaki, *Strangers from a Different Shore: A History of Asian Americans* (1989), surveys the experiences of Asian Americans as immigrants to America's western shore. John Mack Faragher, *Women and Men on the Overland Trail* (1979) examines the social experience of westering migrants, and Peggy Pascoe, *Relations of Rescue: The Search for Female Authority in the American West, 1874–1939* (1990) describes the female communities of the West. William Cronon, *Nature's Metropolis and the Great West* (1991) describes the relationships among economies and environments in the West. Jon Gjerde, *The Minds of the West: Ethnocultural Evolution in the Rural Middle West, 1830–1914* (1997) examines the impact of the ethnicity on the shaping of the agrarian West. Robert Wooster, *The Military and United States Indian Policy, 1865–1902* (1988) examines the military campaigns against the Indians in the late nineteenth century. Frederick E. Hoxie, *A Final Promise: The Campaign to Assimilate the Indians, 1880–1920* (1984) examines U.S. policies toward Native Americans in the years after the end of the Indian Wars. John Mack Faragher, *Daniel Boone* (1992) is a study of one of the West's most fabled figures. Richard Slotkin, *The Fatal Environment: The Myth of the Frontier in the Age of Industrialization* (1985) and *Gunfighter Nation* (1992) are provocative cultural studies of the idea of the West. Henry Nash Smith, *Virgin Land* (1950) is a classic study of the West in American culture. *The West* (1996), a documentary film by Stephen Ives and Ken Burns, offers a broad history of the region, along with a companion book of the same title by Geoffrey C. Ward.

For quizzes, Internet resources, references to additional books and films, and more, consult this book's Online Learning Center at www.mhhe.com/brinkley11.

SOURCES OF INDUSTRIAL GROWTH

Many factors contributed to the growth of American industry: abundant raw materials; a large and growing labor supply; a surge in technological innovation; the emergence of a talented, ambitious, and often ruthless group of entrepreneurs; a federal government eager to assist the growth of business; and a great and expanding domestic market for the products of manufacturing.

Industrial Technologies

Perhaps the most important technological development in a nation whose economy rested so heavily on railroads and urban construction was the revolutionizing of iron and steel production in the late nineteenth century. Iron production had developed slowly in the United States through most of the nineteenth century, mostly driven by the demand for iron rails for railroads; steel production had developed hardly at all by the end of the Civil War. In the 1870s and 1880s, however, iron production soared as railroads added 40,000 new miles of track, and steel production made great strides toward what would soon be its dominance in the metals industry.

The story of the rise of steel is, like so many other stories of economic development, a story of technological discovery. An Englishman, Henry Bessemer, and an American, William Kelly, had developed, almost simultaneously, a process for converting iron into the much more durable and versatile steel. (The process, which took Bessemer's name, consisted of blowing air through molten iron to burn out the impurities.) The Bessemer process also relied on the discovery by the British metallurgist Robert Mushet that ingredients could be added to the iron during conversion to transform it into steel. In 1868, the New Jersey ironmaster Abram S. Hewitt introduced from Europe another method of making steel—the open-hearth process, which ultimately largely supplanted the Bessemer process. These techniques made possible the production of steel in great quantities and large dimensions, for use in the manufacture of locomotives, steel rails, and girders for the construction of tall buildings.

New Steel Production Techniques

The steel industry emerged first in western Pennsylvania and eastern Ohio. That was partly because iron ore could be found there in abundance and because there was already a flourishing iron industry there. It was also because the new forms of steel production created a demand for new kinds of fuel—and particularly for the anthracite (or hard) coal that was plentiful in Pennsylvania. Later, new techniques made it possible to use soft bituminous coal (easily mined in western Pennsylvania), which could then be converted to coke to fuel steel furnaces. As a result, Pittsburgh quickly became the center of the

Pittsburgh

steel world. But the industry was growing so fast that new sources of ore were soon necessary. The upper peninsula of Michigan, the Mesabi Range in Minnesota, and the area around Birmingham, Alabama, became important ore-producing centers by the end of the century, and new centers of steel production grew up near them: Cleveland, Detroit, Chicago, and Birmingham, among others.

Until the Civil War, iron and steel furnaces were mostly made of stone and usually built against the side of a hill to reduce construction demands. In the 1870s and after, however, furnaces were redesigned as cylindrical iron shells lined with brick. These massive new furnaces were 75 feet tall and higher and could produce over 500 tons a week.

As the steel industry spread, new transportation systems emerged to serve it. The steel production in the Great Lakes region was possible only because of the availability of steam freighters capable of carrying ore on the lakes. The demand for vessels capable of transporting oil and the development of the new and more powerful steam engine encouraged, in turn, the design of larger and heavier freighters—such as the *R. J. Hackett,* launched in 1869, which could carry 1,200 tons of ore. Shippers used new steam engines to speed the unloading of ore, a task that previously had been performed, slowly and laboriously, by men and horses.

There was even a closer relationship between the emerging steel companies and the railroads. Steel manufacturers provided rails and parts for cars to the railroads; railroads were both markets for and transporters of manufactured steel. But the relationship soon became more intimate than that. The Pennsylvania Railroad, for example, literally created the Pennsylvania Steel Company, provided it with substantial initial capital, and ensured it a market for its products with an immediate contract for steel rails. That was only one of many cases in which railroad and steel companies effectively merged or formed intimate connections.

The steel industry's need for lubrication for its machines helped create another important new industry in the late nineteenth century—oil. (Not until later did oil become important primarily for

Rise of the Petroleum Industry

its potential as a fuel.) The existence of petroleum reserves in western Pennsylvania had been common knowledge for some time. Not until the 1850s, however, after Pennsylvania businessman George Bissell showed that the substance could be burned in lamps and that it could also yield such products as paraffin, naphtha, and lubricating oil, was there any sense of its commercial value. Bissell raised money to begin drilling; and in 1859, Edwin L. Drake, one of Bissell's employees, established the first oil well near Titusville, Pennsylvania, which was soon producing 500 barrels of oil a month. Demand for petroleum grew quickly, and promoters soon developed other fields

INDUSTRIAL SUPREMACY

Writing several decades later of the remarkable expansion of America's industrial economy in the late nineteenth and early twentieth centuries, the historians Charles and Mary Beard commented: "With a stride that astonished statisticians, the conquering hosts of business enterprise swept over the continent; twenty-five years after the death of Lincoln, America had become, in the quantity and value of her products, the first manufacturing nation of the world. What England had accomplished in a hundred years, the United States had achieved in half the time." They were expressing the amazement many Americans at the time had felt as they watched the changes around them.

In fact, America's rise to industrial supremacy was not as sudden as such observers suggested. The nation had been building a manufacturing economy since early in the nineteenth century, and industry was well established before the Civil War. But Americans were clearly correct in observing that the accomplishments of the last three decades of the *Transformation of the National Economy* nineteenth century overshadowed all that had come earlier. Those years witnessed nothing less than the transformation of the national economy.

The remarkable growth did much to increase the wealth and improve the lives of many Americans. But the benefits were far from universal. While industrial titans and a growing middle class were enjoying a prosperity without precedent in the nation's history, workers, farmers, and others were experiencing a disorienting and often painful transition that slowly edged the United States toward a great economic and political crisis.

SMELTING WORKS AT DENVER The painter Thomas Moran was best known for his enormous canvases depicting the natural landscapes and rugged outdoor societies of the late-nineteenth-century West. In this 1892 watercolor, however, he captures another, less renowned feature of western life: the emergence of industrial manufacturing in the rapidly developing region. *(Smelting Works at Denver, 1892, by Thomas Moran. Watercolor and gouache over black chalk, 34.9 × 42.2 cm. © Cleveland Museum of Art, 1998, Bequest of Mrs. Henry A. Everett for the Dorothy Burnham Everett Collection, 1938.56)*

Significant Events

1851	I. M. Singer and Company, one of first modern corporations, founded
1859	First oil well drilled in Pennsylvania
1866	William H. Sylvis founds National Labor Union
	First transatlantic cable laid
1868	Open-hearth steelmaking begins in America
1869	Knights of Labor founded
1870	John D. Rockefeller founds Standard Oil
1873	Carnegie Steel founded
	Commercial and financial panic disrupts economy

PIONEER OIL RUN, 1865 The American oil industry emerged first in western Pennsylvania, where speculators built makeshift facilities almost overnight. An oil field on the other side of the hill depicted here had been producing 600 barrels a day, and the wells quickly spilled over the hill and down the slope shown in this photograph. *(Library of Congress)*

in Pennsylvania, Ohio, and West Virginia. By the 1870s, oil had advanced to fourth place among the nation's exports.

The Airplane and the Automobile

Among the technological innovations that was to have the farthest-reaching impact on the United States was the invention of the automobile. Two technologies were critical to its development. One was the creation of gasoline (or petrol), which was the result of an extraction process developed in the late nineteenth century in the United States by which lubricating oil and fuel oil were removed separately from crude oil. As early as the 1870s, designers in France, Germany, and Austria—inspired by the success of railroad engines—had begun to develop an "internal combustion engine," which used the expanding power of burning gas to drive pistons. A German, Nicolaus August Otto, created a gas-powered "four-stroke" engine in the mid-1860s, which was a precursor to automobile engines. But he did not develop a way to untether it from gas lines to be used portably in machines. One of Otto's former employees, Gottfried Daimler later perfected an engine that could be used in automobiles (including the famous early car that took Daimler's name).

The American automobile industry developed rapidly in the aftermath of these breakthroughs. Charles and Frank Duryea built the first gasoline-driven motor vehicle in America in 1903. Three years later, Henry Ford produced the *Henry Ford* first of the famous cars that would bear his name. By 1910, the industry had become a major force in the economy, and the automobile was beginning to reshape American social and cultural life, as well as the nation's landscape. In 1895, there were only four automobiles on the American highways. By 1917, there were nearly 5 million.

The search for a means of human flight was as old as civilization, and had been almost entirely futile until the late nineteenth century when engineers, scientists, and tinkerers in both the United States and Europe began to experiment with a wide range of aeronautic devices. Balloonists began to consider ways to make dirigibles useful vehicles of transportation. Others experimented with kites and gliders to see if they could somehow be used to propel humans through the air.

Among those testing gliders were two brothers in Ohio, Wilbur and Orville Wright, who owned a bicycle shop in which they began to construct a glider that could be propelled through the air by an internal-combustion

THE WRIGHT BROTHERS Orville and Wilbur Wright became closely watched celebrities after their famous flight at Kitty Hawk, North Carolina, in 1903. Although they made few additional contributions to the development of aviation technology, they were much in demand to demonstrate their "flying machine." Here they pose before a demonstration flight—Wilbur taking a reading of flight conditions and Orville watching, the struts of their plane visible in the background. *(Library of Congress)*

engine (the same kind of engine that was propelling automobiles). Four years after they began their experiments, Orville made a celebrated test flight near Kitty Hawk, North Carolina, in which an airplane took off by itself and traveled 120 feet in 12 seconds under its own power before settling back to earth. By the fall of 1904, they had improved the plane to the point where they were able to fly over 23 miles, and in the following year they began to take a few passengers on their flights with them.

Although the first working airplane was built in the United States, aviation technology was slow to gain a foothold in America. Most of the early progress in airplane design occurred in France, where there was substantial government funding for research and development. The U.S. government created the National Advisory Committee

on Aeronautics in 1915, twelve years after the Wright brothers' flight, and American airplanes became a significant presence in Europe during World War I. But the prospects for commercial flight seemed dim until the 1920s, when Charles Lindbergh's famous solo flight from New York to Paris electrified the nation and the world and helped make aviation a national obsession.

Research and Development

The rapid development of new industrial technologies, and the emergence of large integrated corporations taking advantage of those technologies, persuaded a growing number of business leaders of the need to sponsor their own research to allow them to keep up with the rapid changes in industry. General Electric, fearful of technological competition, created one of the first corporate laboratories in 1900. The emergence of corporate research and

Corporate Research and Development

development laboratories coincided with a decline in government support for research. That helped corporations to attract skilled researchers who had once worked for government agencies and were looking for new employment. It also decentralized the sources of research funding and ensured that inquiry would move in many different directions, and not just along paths determined by the government.

A rift began to emerge between scientists and engineers. Engineers—both inside and out of universities—became increasingly tied up with the research and development agendas of corporations and worked hard to be of practical use to the new economy. Many scientists continued to scorn this "commercialization" of knowledge and preferred to stick to basic research that had no immediate practical applications. Even so, American scientists were more closely connected to practical challenges than were their European counterparts, and some joined engineers in corporate research and development laboratories, which over time began to sponsor not just practical but also basic research.

American universities transformed themselves in growing numbers in the late nineteenth and early twentieth centuries. And while there were many reasons for, and many results of, these transformations, one product of the change was a growing connection between university-based research and the needs of the industrial economy.

Transformation of Higher Education

University faculty and laboratories began to receive funding from corporations for research of interest to them, and a partnership began to develop between the academic world and the commercial world that has continued into the twentieth century. No comparable partnership emerged in European universities in these years, and some have argued that America's more rapid development in the twentieth century is in part a product of the market's success in harnessing knowledge—from the academic world and elsewhere—more effectively than the nation's competitors abroad.

The Science of Production

Central to the growth of the automobile and other industries were changes in the techniques of production. By the turn of the century, many industrialists were turning to the new principles of "scientific management." Those principles were often known as "Taylorism," after their leading theoretician, Frederick Winslow Taylor. Taylor's ideas were controversial during his lifetime and have remained controversial since. Taylor himself, and his many admirers, argued that scientific management was a way to manage human labor to make it compatible with the demands of the machine age. But scientific

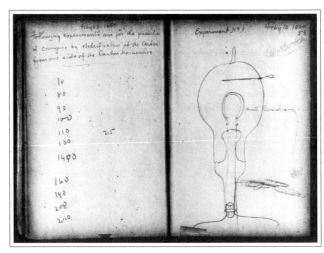

EDISON'S NOTEBOOK This page from one of Thomas Edison's notebooks shows sketches of and notes on some of his early experiments on an incandescent lamp—what we know as an electric lightbulb. Edison was not only the most celebrated inventor of his day, but by the early twentieth century one of the greatest popular heroes in American life in a time when scientific and technological progress was considered the defining feature of the age. *(U.S. Department of the Interior, National Park Service, Edison National Historic Site)*

management was also a way to increase the employer's control of the workplace, to make working people less independent.

Taylor urged employers to reorganize the production process by subdividing tasks. This would speed up production; it would also make workers more interchangeable

"Taylorism"

and thus diminish a manager's dependence on any particular employee. And it would reduce the need for highly trained skilled workers. If properly managed by trained experts, Taylor claimed, workers using modern machines could perform simple tasks at much greater speed, significantly increasing productive efficiency.

Manufacturers also began placing greater emphasis on industrial research. In part because of the phenomenal success of Thomas Edison's famous industrial laboratory in Menlo Park, New Jersey, dozens of corporations were, by the early years of the twentieth century, establishing laboratories of their own. By 1913, Bell Telephone, Du Pont, General Electric, Eastman Kodak, and about fifty other companies were budgeting hundreds of thousands of dollars each year for research by their own engineers and scientists.

The most important change in production technology in the industrial era was the emergence of mass production and, above all, the moving assembly line, which

Moving Assembly Line

Henry Ford introduced in his automobile plants in 1914. This revolutionary technique cut the time for assembling a chassis from twelve and a half hours to one and a half hours. It enabled Ford to raise the wages and

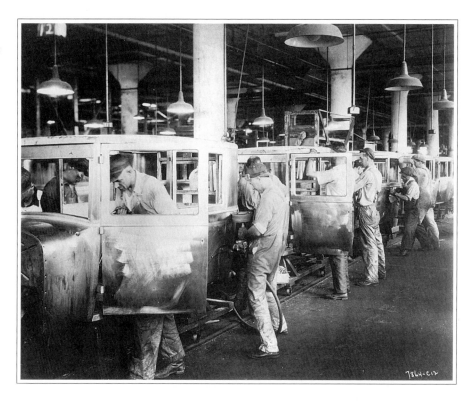

AUTOMOBILE PRODUCTION Workers labor to finish and paint automobile bodies in a Fisher Body plant in 1918, just after the end of World War I. By then, General Motors had emerged as the giant of the industry, and Fisher Body was one of many companies it had bought to consolidate its control over the entire production process. *(General Motors Corporation)*

reduce the hours of his workers while cutting the base price of his Model T from $950 in 1914 to $290 in 1929. Ford's assembly line became a standard for many other industries.

Railroad Expansion

The principal agent of industrial development in the late nineteenth century was the expansion of the railroads. Railroads promoted economic growth in many ways. They were the nation's main method of transportation and gave industrialists access to distant markets and distant sources of raw materials. They were the nation's largest businesses and created new forms of corporate organization that served as models for other industries. And they were America's biggest investors, stimulating economic growth through their own enormous expenditures on construction and equipment.

Every decade in the late nineteenth century, total railroad trackage increased dramatically: from 30,000 miles

Rapid Expansion of the Railroad

in 1860 to 52,000 miles in 1870, to 93,000 in 1880, to 163,000 in 1890, and to 193,000 by 1900. Subsidies from federal, state, and local governments—as well as investments from abroad—were vital to these vast undertakings, which required far more capital than private entrepreneurs in America could raise by themselves. Equally important was the emergence of great railroad combinations that brought most of the nation's rails under the control of a very few men. Many railroad combinations

continued to be dominated by individuals. The achievements (and excesses) of these tycoons—Cornelius Vanderbilt, James J. Hill, Collis P. Huntington, and others—became symbols to much of the nation of great economic power concentrated in individual hands. But railroad development was less significant for the individual barons it created than for its contribution to the growth of a new institution: the modern corporation.

The Corporation

There had been various forms of corporations in America since colonial times, but the modern corporation emerged as a major force only after the Civil War, when railroad magnates and other industrialists realized that no single person or group of limited partners, no matter how wealthy, could finance their great ventures.

Under the laws of incorporation passed in many states in the 1830s and 1840s, business organizations could raise money by selling stock to members of the public; after the Civil War, one industry after another began doing so. At the same time, affluent Americans began to consider the purchase of stock a good investment even if they were not themselves involved in the business whose stock they were purchasing. What made the practice appealing was that investors had only "limited liability"—that is, they risked only the amount of their investments;

Limited Liability

they were not liable for any debts the corporation might accumulate beyond that. The ability to sell stock to a

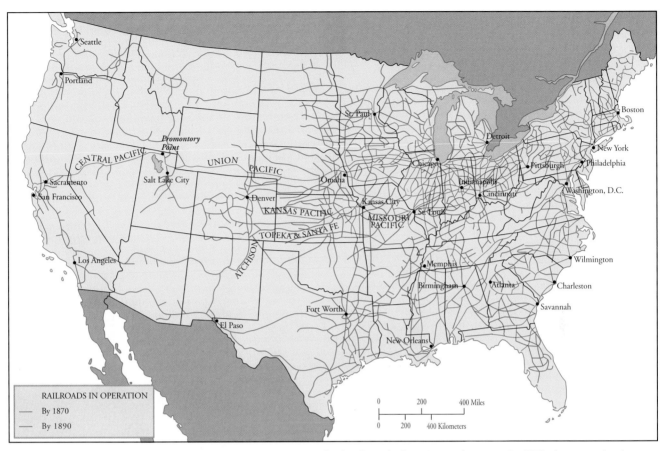

RAILROADS, 1870–1890 This map illustrates the rapid expansion of railroads in the late nineteenth century. In 1870, there was already a dense network of rail lines in the Northeast and Middle West, illustrated here by the red lines. The green lines show the further expansion of rail coverage between 1870 and 1890, much of it in the South and the areas west of the Mississippi River. ◆ *Why were railroads so essential to the nation's economic growth in these years?*

 For an interactive version of this map go to www.mhhe.com/brinkley11ch17maps

broad public made it possible for entrepreneurs to gather vast sums of capital and undertake great projects.

The Pennsylvania Railroad and others were among the first to adopt the new corporate form of organization. But it quickly spread beyond the railroad industry. In steel,

Andrew Carnegie

the central figure was Andrew Carnegie, a Scottish immigrant who had worked his way up from modest beginnings and in 1873 opened his own steelworks in Pittsburgh. Soon he dominated the industry. His methods were much like those of other industrial titans. He cut costs and prices by striking deals with the railroads and then bought out rivals who could not compete with him. With his associate Henry Clay Frick, he bought up coal mines and leased part of the Mesabi iron range in Minnesota, operated a fleet of ore ships on the Great Lakes, and acquired railroads. Ultimately, Carnegie controlled the processing of his steel from mine to market. He financed his undertakings not only out of his own profits but out of the sale of stock. Then, in 1901, he sold out for $450 million to the banker J. Pierpont Morgan, who merged the

Carnegie interests with others to create the giant United States Steel Corporation—a $1.4 billion enterprise that controlled almost two-thirds of the nation's steel production.

There were similar developments in other industries. Gustavus Swift developed a relatively small Chicago meatpacking company into a great national corporation, in part because of profits he earned selling to the military in the Civil War. Isaac Singer patented a sewing machine in 1851 and created I. M. Singer and Company, one of the first modern manufacturing corporations.

Many of the corporate organizations developed a new approach to management. Large, national business enterprises needed more systematic administrative structures than the limited, local ventures of the past. As a result, corporate leaders introduced a set of managerial techniques—the genesis of modern business administration—that relied on the division of responsibilities, a carefully designed hierarchy of control, modern cost-accounting procedures, and perhaps above all a new breed of business executive: the "middle manager," who

New Managerial Techniques

THE LOCOMOTIVE'S MAGIC WAND

The story of the building of American railroads is among the best-known narratives of American history. For contemporary observers, the locomotive was the great icon of the age, a "magic wand" that transformed city and country alike. Most saw in it the central symbol of American progress. The writer Caroline Kirkland was typical in describing the railroad as "the resistless chariot of civilization with scythed axles mowing down ignorance and prejudice as it whirls along," driving "the shadows of the past . . . into the dim woods." Among the "shadows" that fled before it were some of the most familiar features of American ecosystems.

The basic achievement of the railroad was to reduce the cost of space by increasing the speed at which one could move across it. In the 1830s, traveling from New York to Chicago by lake and canal took roughly three weeks. By railroad in the 1850s, it took less than two days. A team of horses did well to haul a wagonload of grain a dozen miles in a day, but a railroad could transport the same grain hundreds of miles in the same time. The railroad also liberated America's rural economy from the forced hibernation of winter. While roads and canals sat idle under winter ice, locomotives kept hauling goods to market no matter how cold the weather. As a result, the entire economy became more productive.

This was why the railroad seemed such a symbol of progress. Wherever it went, farms and towns sprang up in response to the new opportunities it brought, and settlers followed the railroads out onto the midwestern prairies in increasing numbers. As they plowed up the sod to raise grain, they dismantled the tallgrass prairie, so much so that it had almost disappeared by the end of the century. The same fate befell the white pine forests of northern Michigan, Wisconsin, and Minnesota. Sawed into lumber and shipped south on Lake Michigan or the Mississippi River, pine trees were delivered by rail

EARLY RAILROAD CONSTRUCTION CREW For many nineteenth-century Americans, the appearance of railroad surveyors and construction crews seemed to herald a new era. The locomotive symbolized progress, bringing in its wake a sudden growth of farms, factories, and towns. *(Bettmann/Corbis)*

formed a layer of command between workers and owners. Beginning in the railroad corporations, these new management techniques moved quickly into virtually every area of large-scale industry. Efficient administrative capabilities helped make possible another major feature of the modern corporation: consolidation.

Consolidating Corporate America

Businessmen created large, consolidated organizations primarily through two methods. One was "horizontal in-

Horizontal and Vertical Integration

tegration"—the combining of a number of firms engaged in the same enterprise into a single corporation. The consolidation of many different railroad lines into one company was an example. Another method, which became popular in the 1890s, was "vertical inte-

gration"—the taking over of all the different businesses on which a company relied for its primary function. Carnegie Steel, which came to control not only steel mills, but mines, railroads, and other enterprises, was an example of vertical integration.

The most celebrated corporate empire of the late nineteenth century was John D. Rockefeller's Standard Oil, a great combination created through both horizontal and vertical integration. Shortly after the Civil War, Rockefeller

Rockefeller's Standard Oil

launched a refining company in Cleveland and immediately began trying to eliminate his competition. Allying himself with other wealthy capitalists, he proceeded methodically to buy out competing refineries. In 1870, he formed the Standard Oil Company of Ohio; within a few years it had acquired twenty of the twenty-five refineries in Cleveland, as well as plants in Pittsburgh, Philadelphia,

to prairie farmers who used them for fences and houses. By 1900, the pines had nearly vanished from the upper Midwest, and lumber companies were moving their operations elsewhere.

Farther west, an equally dramatic fate befell the great bison (or buffalo) herds which had been the mainstay of Great Plains Indian life for generations. With the coming of the Union Pacific in the North and the Kansas Pacific in the South, bison were slaughtered at an almost unimaginable rate. A single hunting party might gun down hundreds in a day for their skins. Tourists shot from the windows of their trains without even stopping to inspect their kills. Within half a decade of the arrival of the railroads, over 4 million bison died on the southern plains alone. By 1883, the last major herd had vanished. An animal that had numbered in the tens of millions less than a quarter-century before now teetered on the brink of extinction—and with it died the ecological foundation of the Plains Indians' economy.

The railroad also introduced the herds of livestock that replaced the bison. The long drives that brought longhorn steers from Texas to the Kansas cattle towns did so for only one reason: to reach the railroad for shipment to market. By the late nineteenth century, the old shortgrass prairies of the high plains were raising range-fed cattle, their native bison having almost entirely disappeared. The tallgrass prairies of Iowa and Illinois had been converted to corn production, and much of the grain they now raised was used in feedlots where western cattle were fattened for final sale. Whether raised in Texas, Montana, or Illinois, cattle eventually made their way to Chicago's great Union Stockyard. There they were slaughtered and shipped to the eastern markets, where they were finally eaten. None of this would have occurred in the same way without the railroad.

By the end of the century, the railroads had linked the continent together in a great national market. No matter where they lived, no matter what the time of year, Americans relied on the railroad to satisfy their basic needs. Minnesota flour, Texas beef, and Washington lumber all reached their customers via the iron horse. These benefits had come at the cost of immense ecological changes, but those changes were rarely evident to customers living hundreds of miles from landscapes they never saw. Even had they seen the ties between their own lives and the slaughtered bison herds, vanished prairies, disappearing forests, and dispersed tribes, they would almost certainly have joined Caroline Kirkland in regarding them as reasonable costs of civilized progress.

Just how thoroughly the railroads altered the landscape of the United States can be suggested by one further change. Until the 1880s, every community in America had its own "local" time. People set their clocks according to the rules of astronomy: noon was the moment when the sun stood highest in the midday sky. When it was noon in Chicago, it was 11:50 A.M. in St. Louis, 11:27 A.M. in Omaha, and 12:18 P.M. in Detroit, with every possible variation in between. For the railroad companies, trying to keep track of hundreds of different times was a nightmare, since a train leaving a station at one local time arrived at its destination at an entirely different local time. Such scheduling problems could even cause train wrecks. And so, on November 18, 1883, the major railroad companies carved up the continent into four uniform time zones and declared that they intended to ignore all local times. Henceforth, for railroad purposes, every community in a time zone would have the same time. The U.S. government did not finally ratify this change until 1918, but most communities adopted railroad "standard" time very quickly. The magic wand of the locomotive had managed to change not just the many natural environments of North America, but time itself.

New York, and Baltimore. So far, Rockefeller had expanded only horizontally. But soon he began expanding vertically as well. He built his own barrel factories, terminal warehouses, and pipelines. Standard Oil owned its own freight cars and developed its own marketing organization. By the 1880s, Rockefeller had established such dominance within the petroleum industry that to much of the nation he served as the leading symbol of monopoly. He controlled access to 90 percent of the refined oil in the United States.

Rockefeller and other industrialists saw consolidation as a way to cope with what they believed was the greatest curse of the modern economy: "cutthroat competition." Most businessmen claimed to believe in free enterprise and a competitive marketplace, but in fact they feared the existence of too many competing firms, convinced that substantial competition could spell instability and ruin for all. A successful enterprise, many capitalists believed (but did not say publicly), was one that could eliminate or absorb its competitors.

As the movement toward combination accelerated, new vehicles emerged to facilitate it. The railroads began making so-called pool arrangements—informal agreements among various companies to stabilize rates and divide markets (arrangements that would in later years be known as cartels). But the pools did not work very well. If even a few firms in an industry were unwilling to cooperate (as was almost always the case), the pool arrangements collapsed.

The Trust and the Holding Company

The failure of the pools led to new techniques of consolidation resting less on cooperation than on centralized control. At first, the most successful such technique was

JOHN D. ROCKEFELLER Rockefeller's Standard Oil company became perhaps the largest and most powerful monopoly in America in the late nineteenth century, and Rockefeller himself became one of the nation's wealthiest and most controversial men. *(Culver Pictures, Inc.)*

ANDREW CARNEGIE Carnegie was one of a relatively small number of great industrialists of the late nineteenth century who genuinely rose "from rags to riches." Born in Scotland, he came to the United States in 1848, at the age of thirteen, and soon found work as a messenger in a Pittsburgh telegraph office. His skill in learning to transcribe telegraphic messages (he became one of the first telegraphers in the country able to take messages by sound) brought him to the attention of a Pennsylvania Railroad official, and before he was twenty, he had begun his ascent to the highest ranks of industry. After the Civil War, he shifted his attention to the growing iron industry; in 1873 he invested all his assets in the development of the first American steel mills. Two decades later he was one of the wealthiest men in the world. In 1901 he abruptly resigned from his businesses and spent the remaining years of his life as a philanthropist. By the time of his death in 1919, he had given away some $350 million. *(Culver Pictures, Inc.)*

the creation of the "trust"—pioneered by Standard Oil in the early 1880s and perfected by the banker J. P. Morgan. Over time, the word "trust" became a term for any great economic combination. But the trust was in fact a particular

kind of organization. Under a trust agreement, stockholders in individual corporations transferred their stocks to a small group of trustees in exchange for shares in the trust itself. Owners of trust certificates often had no direct control over the decisions of the trustees; they simply received a share of the profits of the combination. The trustees themselves, on the other hand, might literally own only a few companies but could exercise effective control over many.

The Trust Agreement

In 1889, the state of New Jersey helped produce a third form of consolidation by changing its laws of incorporation to permit companies actually to buy up other companies. Other states soon followed. That made the trust unnecessary and permitted actual corporate mergers. Rockefeller, for example, quickly relocated Standard Oil to New Jersey and created there what became known as a "holding company"—a central corporate body that would buy up the stock of various members of the Standard Oil trust and establish direct, formal ownership of the corporations in the trust.

J. PIERPONT MORGAN This arresting 1903 portrait by the great photographer Alfred Steichen captures something of the intimidating power of J. Pierpont Morgan, the most powerful financier in America. This photograph is sometimes known as the "dagger portrait," because Morgan appears to be holding a knife in his left hand. In fact, the shiny object is the arm of his chair. (*J. P. Morgan, c. 1903, Steichen Collection, The Museum of Modern Art, New York, Gift of A. Conger Goodyear*)

By the end of the nineteenth century, as a result of corporate consolidation, 1 percent of the corporations in America were able to control more than 33 percent of the manufacturing. A system of economic organization was emerging that lodged enormous power in the hands of a very few men: the great bankers of New York such as J. P. Morgan, industrial titans such as Rockefeller (who himself gained control of a major bank), and others.

Rapid Corporate Consolidation

Whether or not this relentless concentration of economic power was the only way or the best way to promote industrial expansion became a major source of debate in America in the late nineteenth century and beyond. But it is clear that, whatever else they may have done, the industrial giants of the era were responsible for substantial economic growth. They were integrating operations, cutting costs, creating a great industrial infrastructure, stimulating new markets, creating jobs for a vast new pool of unskilled workers, and opening the way to large-scale mass production. They were also creating the basis for some of the greatest public controversies of their era.

CAPITALISM AND ITS CRITICS

The rise of big business was not without its critics. Farmers and workers saw in the growth of the new corporate power centers a threat to notions of a republican society in which wealth and authority were widely distributed. Middle-class critics pointed to the corruption that the new industrial titans seemed to produce in their own enterprises and in local, state, and national politics. The growing criticisms challenged the captains of industry to defend the new corporate economy, to convince the public (and themselves) that it was compatible with the ideology of individualism and equal opportunity that had long been central to the American self-image.

The "Self-Made Man"

The rationale for modern capitalism rested squarely on the older ideology of individualism. The new industrial economy, its defenders argued, was not reducing opportunities for individual advancement, it was expanding them. It was providing every individual with a chance to succeed and attain great wealth.

There was an element of truth in such claims, but only a small one. Before the Civil War there had been few millionaires in America; by 1892 there were more than 4,000. Some were in fact what almost all millionaires claimed to be: "self-made men." Andrew Carnegie had worked as a bobbin boy in a Pittsburgh cotton mill; John D. Rockefeller had begun as a clerk in a Cleveland commission house; E. H. Harriman, a great railroad tycoon, had begun as a broker's office boy. But most of the new business tycoons had begun their careers from positions of wealth and privilege.

Myth of the Self-Made Man

Nor was their rise to power and prominence always a result simply of hard work and ingenuity, as they liked to claim. It was also a result of ruthlessness, arrogance, and, at times, rampant corruption. The railroad magnate Cornelius Vanderbilt expressed the attitude of many corporate tycoons with his belligerent question: "Can't I do what I want with my own?" So did his son William, with his oft-quoted statement: "The public be damned." Once, when the elder Vanderbilt's lawyers warned him that a move he contemplated was illegal, he bellowed: "What do I care about the law? H'aint I got the power?" Industrialists made large financial contributions to politicians, political parties, and government officials in exchange for assistance and support. And more often than not, politicians responded as they hoped. Cynics said that Standard Oil did everything to the Ohio legislature except refine it.

"MODERN COLOSSUS OF (RAIL) ROADS" Cornelius Vanderbilt, known as the "Commodore," accumulated one of America's great fortunes by consolidating several large railroad companies under his control in the 1860s. His name became a synonym not only for enormous wealth, but also (in the eyes of many Americans) for excessive corporate power—as suggested in this cartoon, showing him standing astride his empire and manipulating its parts. *(Culver Pictures, Inc.)*

A member of the Pennsylvania legislature once reportedly said: "Mr. Speaker, I move we adjourn unless the Pennsylvania Railroad has more business for us to transact." During the notorious "Erie War" of 1868, in which Cornelius Vanderbilt battled Jay Gould and Jim Fisk for control of the Erie Railroad, both sides in the dispute offered lavish bribes to members of the New York State legislature to support measures favorable to their cause. The market price of legislators during the fight was $15,000 a head. One enterprising politician collected $75,000 from Vanderbilt and $100,000 from Gould. Politicians were not innocent victims of this corruption. Many of them openly demanded bribes and in effect blackmailed businessmen.

The average industrialist of the late nineteenth century was not, however, a Rockefeller or a Vanderbilt, but a more modest entrepreneur engaged in highly risky ventures in an unstable economy. For every successful millionaire, there were dozens of aspiring businessmen whose efforts failed. Some industries fell under the monopolistic control of a single firm or a small group of large firms. But many more industries remained fragmented, with many small companies struggling to carve out a stable position for themselves in an uncertain, highly competitive environment. The annals of business did indeed include real stories of individuals rising from rags to riches. They also included stories of people moving from riches back to rags.

Survival of the Fittest

Most tycoons liked to claim that they had attained their wealth and power through hard work, acquisitiveness, and thrift—the traditional virtues of Protestant America. Those who succeeded, they argued, deserved their success. "God gave me my money," explained John D. Rockefeller, expressing the assumption that riches were a reward for worthiness. Those who failed had earned their failure—through their own laziness, stupidity, or carelessness. "Let us remember," said a prominent Protestant minister, "that there is not a poor person in the United States who was not made poor by his own shortcomings."

Such assumptions became the basis of a popular social theory of the late nineteenth century: Social Darwinism, the application of Charles Darwin's laws of evolution and natural selection among species to human society. Just as only the *Social Darwinism* fittest survived in the process of evolution, so in human society only the fittest individuals survived and flourished in the marketplace.

The English philosopher Herbert Spencer was the first and most important proponent of this theory. Society, he argued, benefited from the elimination of the unfit and the survival of the strong and talented. Spencer's books were popular in America in the 1870s and 1880s. And his teachings found prominent supporters among American intellectuals, most notably William Graham Sumner of Yale, who promoted similar ideas in lectures, articles, and a famous 1906 book, *Folkways*. Sumner did not agree with everything Spencer wrote, but he did share Spencer's belief that individuals must have absolute freedom to struggle, to compete, to succeed, or to fail. Many industrialists seized on the theories of Spencer and Sumner to justify their own power. "The growth of a large business is merely the survival of the fittest," Rockefeller proclaimed. "This is not an evil tendency in business. It is merely the working out of the law of nature and a law of God." Carnegie, who became the leading exponent of Social Darwinism among American industrialists, later described his reaction on first reading Spencer: "I remember that light came as in a flood and all was clear."

Social Darwinism appealed to businessmen because it seemed to legitimize their success and confirm their virtues. It appealed to them because it placed their activities within the context of traditional American ideas of

Justifying the Status Quo | freedom and individualism. Above all, it appealed to them

because it justified their tactics. Social Darwinists insisted that all attempts by labor to raise wages by forming unions and all endeavors by government to regulate economic activities would fail, because economic life was controlled by a natural law, the law of competition. And Social Darwinism coincided with another "law" that seemed to justify business practices and business dominance: the law of supply and demand as defined by Adam Smith and the classical economists. The economic system, they argued, was like a great and delicate machine functioning by natural and automatic rules, by the "invisible hand" of market forces. The greatest among these rules, the law of supply and demand, determined all economic values—prices, wages, rents, interest rates at a level that was just to all concerned. Supply and demand worked because human beings were essentially economic creatures who understood and pursued their own interests, and because they operated in a free market regulated only by competition.

But Social Darwinism and the ideas of classical economics did not have very much to do with the realities of the corporate economy. At the same time that businessmen were celebrating the virtues of competition and the free market, they were actively seeking to protect themselves from competition and to replace the natural workings of the marketplace with control by great combinations. Rockefeller's great Standard Oil monopoly was the clearest example of the effort to free an enterprise from competition. But many businessmen made similar attempts on a smaller scale. Vicious competitive battle—something Spencer and Sumner celebrated and called a source of healthy progress—was in fact the very thing that American businessmen most feared and tried to eliminate.

The Gospel of Wealth

Some businessmen attempted to temper the harsh philosophy of Social Darwinism with a more gentle, if in some ways equally self-serving idea: the "gospel of wealth." People of great wealth, advocates of this idea argued, had not only great power but great responsibilities. It was their duty to use their riches to advance social progress. Andrew Carnegie elaborated on the creed in his 1901 book *The Gospel of Wealth,* in which he wrote that the wealthy should consider all revenues in excess of their own needs as "trust funds" to be used for the good of the community; the person of wealth, he said, was "the mere trustee and agent for his poorer brethren." Carnegie was only one of many great industrialists who devoted large parts of their fortunes to philanthropic works—much of it to libraries and schools, institutions he believed would help the poor to help themselves.

The notion of private wealth as a public blessing existed alongside another popular concept: the notion of great wealth as something avail-

able to all. Russell H. Conwell, a | *Russell Conwell*

Baptist minister, became the most prominent spokesman for the idea by delivering one lecture, "Acres of Diamonds," more than 6,000 times between 1880 and 1900. Conwell told a series of stories, which he claimed were true, of individuals who had found opportunities for extraordinary wealth in their own backyards. (One such story involved a modest farmer who discovered a vast diamond mine in his own fields in the course of working his land.) "I say to you," he told his rapt audiences, "that you have 'acres of diamonds' beneath you right here . . . that the men and women sitting here have within their reach opportunities to get largely wealthy. . . . I say that you ought to get rich, and that it is your duty to get rich." Most of the millionaires in the country, Conwell claimed (inaccurately), had begun on the lowest rung of the economic ladder and had worked their way to success. Every industrious individual had the chance to do likewise.

Horatio Alger was the most famous promoter of the success story. (See "Patterns of Popular Culture," p. 486). Alger was originally a minister in a

small town in Massachusetts | *Horatio Alger*

but was driven from his pulpit as a result of a sexual scandal. He moved to New York, where he wrote his celebrated novels—more than 100 in all, which together sold more than 20 million copies. The titles varied: *Andy Grant's Pluck, Ragged Dick, Tom the Bootblack, Sink or Swim.* But the story and message were invariably the same: A poor boy from a small town went to the big city to seek his fortune. By work, perseverance, and luck, he became rich. Alger's name became synonymous—both in his own time and in later years—with the powerful myth that anyone could advance to great wealth through hard work. Alger himself grew very wealthy from his writings, which were among the most popular of his time, and became something of a folk hero in American culture. Few of his many fans were aware of his homosexuality. Like most other gay men of his era, he kept his private life carefully hidden, fearful that publicity would destroy his reputation and his career.

Alternative Visions

Alongside the celebrations of competition, the justifications for great wealth, and the legitimization of the existing order stood a group of alternative philosophies, challenging the corporate ethos and at times capitalism itself.

One such philosophy emerged in the work of the sociologist Lester Frank Ward. Ward was a Darwinist, but he rejected the application of

Darwinian laws to human soci- | *Lester Frank Ward*

ety. In *Dynamic Sociology* (1883) and other books, he argued that civilization was not governed by natural

A young boy, perhaps an orphan, makes his perilous way through life on the rough streets of the city by selling newspapers or peddling matches. One day, his energy and determination catches the eye of a wealthy man, who gives him a chance to improve himself. Through honesty, charm, hard work, and aggressiveness, the boy rises in the world to become a successful man.

That, in a nutshell, is the story that Horatio Alger presented to his vast public in novel after novel—over 100 of them in all—for over forty years. During his lifetime, according to rough estimates, Americans bought over 100 million copies of his novels. After his death in 1899, his books (and others written in his name) continued to sell at an astonishing rate. Even today, when the books themselves are largely forgotten, the name Horatio Alger has come to represent the idea of individual

advancement through (in a phrase Alger coined) "pluck and luck."

Alger was born in 1832 into a middle-class New England family, attended Harvard, and spent a short time as a Unitarian minister. He himself never experienced the hardships he later chronicled. In the mid-1850s, he turned to writing stories and books, and continued to do so for the rest of his life. His most famous novel, *Ragged Dick,* was published in 1868; but there were many others that were almost identical to it: *Tom, the Bootblack; Sink or Swim; Jed, the Poorhouse Boy; Phil, the Fiddler; Andy Grant's Pluck.* Most of his books were aimed at young people, and almost all of them were fables of a young man's rise "from rags to riches." The purpose of his writing, he claimed, was twofold. He wanted to "exert a salutary influence upon the class of whom [I] was writing, by setting before them inspiring examples of what energy, ambition, and an honest purpose may achieve." He also wanted to show his largely middle-class readers "the life and experiences of the friendless and vagrant children to be found in all our cities."

But Alger's intentions probably had little to do with the success of his books. Most Americans of the late nineteenth and early twentieth centuries were attracted to Alger because his stories helped them to believe in one of the most cherished of all their national myths: that it is possible for individuals to rise in the world with willpower and hard work, that anyone can become a "self-made man." That belief was all the more important in the late nineteenth century when the rise of large-scale corporate industrialization was making it increasingly difficult for individuals to control their own fates.

Alger placed great emphasis on the moral qualities of his heroes; their success was a reward for their virtue. But many of his readers ignored the moral message and clung simply to the image of sudden and dramatic success. After the author's death, his publishers responded to that yearning by abridging many of Alger's works to eliminate the parts of his stories where the heroes do good deeds. Instead, they empha-

HORATIO ALGER This photographic portrait shows Alger late in life, when he was already a celebrated writer and, to much of the public, an emblem of American opportunity and success. *(Brown Brothers)*

sized the success of Alger's heroes in rising in the world.

Alger himself had very mixed feelings about the new industrial order he described. His books were meant to reveal not just the opportunities for advancement it sometimes created, but also its cruelty. That was one reason that in almost all his books, his heroes triumphed not just because of their own virtues or efforts, but because of some amazing stroke of luck. To Alger, at least, the modern age did not guarantee success through hard work alone; there had to be some providential assistance as well. Over time, however, Alger's admirers came to ignore his own misgivings about industrialism and to portray his books purely as celebrations of (and justifications for) laissez-faire capitalism and the accumulation of wealth.

An example of the transformation of Alger into a symbol of individual achievement is the Horatio Alger Award, established in 1947 by the American Schools and Colleges Association to honor "living individuals who by their own efforts had pulled themselves up by their bootstraps in the American tradition." Among its recipients have been Presidents Dwight D. Eisenhower and Ronald Reagan, Evangelist Billy Graham, and Supreme Court Justice Clarence Thomas.

A NEWSBOY'S STORY Alger's novels were even more popular after his death in 1899 than they had been in his lifetime. This reprint of one of his many "rags-to-riches" stories—about the rise of a New York newsboy to wealth and success—includes in the background a rendering of the Woolworth building, built in 1913 and one of the first and most celebrated skyscrapers of the early twentieth century. *(Private Collection)*

selection but by human intelligence, which was capable of shaping society as it wished. Unlike Sumner, who believed that state intervention to remodel the environment was futile, Ward thought that an active government engaged in positive planning was society's best hope. The people, through their government, could intervene in the economy and adjust it to serve their needs.

Other Americans skeptical of the laissez-faire ideas of the Social Darwinists adopted more drastic approaches to reform. Some dissenters found a home in the Socialist Labor Party, founded in the 1870s and led for many years by Daniel De Leon, an immigrant from the West Indies. De Leon attracted a modest following in the industrial cities, but the party failed to become a major political force. It never polled more than 82,000 votes. De Leon's theoretical and dogmatic approach appealed to intellectuals more than to workers. A dissident faction of his party, eager to forge ties with organized labor, broke away and in 1901 formed the more enduring American Socialist Party.

Other radicals gained a wider following. One of the most influential was Henry George of California. His angrily eloquent *Progress and Poverty,* published in 1879, became one of the best-selling nonfiction works in American publishing history. George tried to explain why poverty existed amidst the wealth created by modern industry. "This association of poverty with progress is the great enigma of our times," he wrote. "So long as all the increased wealth which modern progress brings goes but to build up great fortunes, to increase luxury and make sharper the contrast between the House of Have and the House of Want, progress is not real and cannot be permanent."

Henry George

George blamed social problems on the ability of a few monopolists to grow wealthy as a result of rising land values. An increase in the value of land, he claimed, was a result not of any effort by the owner, but of the growth of society around the land. It was an "unearned increment," and it was rightfully the property of the community. And so George proposed a "single tax," to replace all other taxes, which would return the increment to the people. The tax, he argued, would destroy monopolies, distribute wealth more equally, and eliminate poverty. Single-tax societies sprang up in many cities. George himself moved east to New York; and in 1886, with the support of labor and the socialists, he narrowly missed being elected mayor.

Rivaling George in popularity was Edward Bellamy, whose utopian novel *Looking Backward,* published in 1888, sold more than 1 million copies. It described the experiences of a young Bostonian who went into a hypnotic sleep in 1887 and awoke in the year 2000 to find a new social order where want, politics, and vice were unknown. The new society had emerged from a peaceful, evolutionary process. The large trusts of the late nineteenth

Looking Backward

century had continued to grow in size and to combine with one another until ultimately they formed a single great trust, controlled by the government, which absorbed all the businesses of all the citizens and distributed the abundance of the industrial economy equally among all the people. Society had become a great machine, "so logical in its principles and direct and simple in its workings" that it almost ran itself. "Fraternal cooperation" had replaced competition. Class divisions had disappeared. Bellamy labeled the philosophy behind this vision "nationalism," and his work inspired the formation of more than 160 Nationalist Clubs to propagate his ideas.

The Problems of Monopoly

Relatively few Americans shared the views of those who questioned capitalism itself. But by the end of the century a growing number of people were becoming deeply concerned about a particular, glaring aspect of capitalism: the growth of monopoly (control of the market by large corporate combinations). A wide range of groups began to assail monopoly and economic concentration. Laborers, farmers, consumers, small manufacturers, conservative bankers and financiers, advocates of radical change—all joined the attack.

They blamed monopoly for creating artificially high prices and for producing a highly unstable economy. In the absence of competition, they argued, monopolistic industries could charge whatever prices they wished; railroads, in particular, charged very high rates along some routes because, in the absence of competition, they knew their customers had no choice but to pay them. Artificially high prices, moreover, contributed to the economy's instability, as production consistently outpaced demand. Beginning in 1873, the economy fluctuated erratically, with severe recessions creating havoc every five or six years, each recession worse than the previous one, until finally, in 1893, the system seemed on the verge of total collapse.

Adding to the resentment of monopoly was the emergence of a new class of enormously and conspicuously wealthy people, whose lifestyles became an affront to those struggling to stay afloat in the erratic economy. According to one estimate early in the century, 1 percent of the families in America controlled nearly 88 percent of the nation's assets. Some of the wealthy—Andrew Carnegie, for example—lived relatively unostentatiously and donated large sums to charities. Others, however, lived in almost grotesque luxury. Like a clan of feudal barons, the Vanderbilts maintained, in addition to many country estates, seven opulent mansions on seven blocks of New York City's Fifth Avenue. Other wealthy New Yorkers lavished vast sums on parties. The most notorious, a ball on which Mrs. Bradley Martin spent $368,000, created such a furor that she and her husband fled to England to escape public abuse.

CHILDREN OF WEALTH The children of the wealthy railroad executive George Jay Gould (son of the notorious financier Jay Gould) ride through a Paris park in *voiturettes,* miniature automobiles manufactured in France. *(Culver Pictures, Inc.)*

Observing their flagrant displays of wealth were the four-fifths of the American people who lived modestly, *Increasing Inequality* and at least 10 million people who lived below the commonly accepted poverty line. The standard of living was rising for everyone, but the gap between rich and poor was increasing. To those in difficult economic circumstances, the sense of relative deprivation could be almost as frustrating and embittering as poverty itself.

INDUSTRIAL WORKERS IN THE NEW ECONOMY

The American working class was both a beneficiary and a victim of the growth of industrial capitalism. Many workers in the late nineteenth century experienced a real rise in their standard of living. But they did so at the cost of arduous and often dangerous working conditions, diminishing control over their own work, and a growing sense of powerlessness.

The Immigrant Work Force

The industrial work force expanded dramatically in the late nineteenth century as demand for factory labor grew. The source of that expansion was a massive migration into industrial cities—migration of two sorts. The first was the continuing flow of rural Americans into factory towns and cities—people disillusioned with or bankrupted by life on the farm and eager for new economic and social opportunities.

The second was the great wave of immigration from Mexico, Asia, Canada, and above all Europe in the decades following the Civil War—an influx greater than that of any previous era. The 25 million immigrants who arrived in the United States between 1865 and 1915 were more than four times the number who had arrived in the fifty years before.

In the 1870s and 1880s, most of the immigrants to eastern industrial cities came from the nation's traditional sources: England, Ireland, and northern Europe. By the end of *New Sources of Immigration* the century, however, the major sources of immigration had shifted, with large numbers of southern and eastern Europeans (Italians, Poles, Russians, Greeks, Slavs, and others) moving to America and into the industrial work force. In the West, the major sources of immigration were Mexico and, until the Chinese Exclusion Act of 1882, Asia. No reliable figures are available for either group, but an estimated 1 million Mexicans entered the United States in the first three decades of the twentieth century, many of them swelling the industrial work force of western cities.

ELLIS ISLAND The great photographer Lewis Hine took this picture of an Italian mother with her three children arriving on Ellis Island, the processing center for the millions of immigrants who entered the United States through New York City. *(Bettmann/Corbis)*

The new immigrants were coming to America in part to escape poverty and oppression in their homelands. But they were also lured to the United States by expectations of new opportunities. Sometimes such expectations were realistic, but often they were the result of false promises. Railroads tried to lure immigrants into their western land-holdings by distributing misleading advertisements overseas. Industrial employers actively recruited immigrant workers under the Labor Contract Law, which—until its repeal in 1885—permitted them to pay for the passage of workers in advance and deduct the amount later from their wages. Even after the repeal of the law, employers continued to encourage the immigration of unskilled laborers, often with the assistance of foreign-born labor brokers, such as the Greek and Italian padrones, who recruited work gangs of their fellow nationals.

The arrival of these new groups introduced heightened ethnic tensions into the dynamic of the working

Heightened Ethnic Tensions | class. Low-paid Poles, Greeks, and French Canadians began to displace higher-paid British and Irish workers in the textile factories of New England. Italians, Slavs, and Poles emerged as a major source of labor for the mining indus-

try in the East, traditionally dominated by native workers or northern European immigrants. Chinese and Mexicans competed with Anglo-Americans and African Americans in mining, farmwork, and factory labor in California, Colorado, and Texas. Even within industries, moreover, workers tended to cluster in particular occupations (and thus, often, at particular income levels) by ethnic group.

Wages and Working Conditions

The average standard of living for workers rose in the years after the Civil War, but for many laborers, the return for their labor remained very small. At the turn of the century, the average income of the American worker was $400 to $500 a year—below the $600 figure widely considered the minimum for a reasonable level of comfort. Nor did workers have much job security. All workers were vulnerable to the boom-and-bust cycle of the industrial economy, and some lost their jobs because of technological advances or because of the cyclical or seasonal nature of their work. Even those who kept their jobs could find their wages suddenly and substantially cut in hard times. Few workers, in other words, were ever very far from poverty.

American laborers faced other hardships as well. For first-generation workers accustomed to the patterns of agrarian life, there was a difficult adjustment to the nature of modern industrial labor: the performance of routine, repetitive tasks, often requiring little skill, on a strict and monotonous schedule. To skilled artisans whose once valued tasks were now performed by machines, the new system was impersonal and demeaning. Factory laborers worked ten-hour days, six days a week; in the steel industry they worked twelve hours a day. Many worked in appallingly unsafe or unhealthy factories. Industrial accidents were frequent and severe. Compensation to the victims, either from their employers or from the government, was often limited, until many states began passing workmen's compensation laws in the early twentieth century.

For many workers, the most disturbing aspect of factory labor in the new industrial system was their loss of control over the conditions of their work. Skilled workers had been accustomed to   *Loss of Control* running their own shops. Even semiskilled workers and common laborers had managed to maintain some control over their labor in the relatively informal working conditions of the early and mid-nineteenth century. As the corporate form of organization spread, employers set out to make the factory more efficient (often in response to the principles of scientific management). That meant, they believed, centralizing control of the workplace in the hands of managers, ensuring that workers had no authority or control that might disrupt the flow of production. This loss of control, as much as the low wages and long

WEST LYNN MACHINE SHOP This machine tool shop in West Lynn, Massachusetts, photographed in the mid-1890s, suggests something of the growing scale of factory enterprise in the late nineteenth century—and also of the extraordinary dangers workers in these early manufacturing shops faced. *(Brown Brothers)*

hours, lay behind the substantial working-class militancy in the late nineteenth century.

Women and Children at Work

The decreasing need for skilled work in factories induced many employers to increase the use of women and children, whom they could hire for lower wages than adult males. By 1900, women made up 17 percent of the industrial work force, a fourfold increase since 1870; and 20 percent of all women (well over 5 million) were wage earners. Some of these working women were single and took jobs to support themselves or their parents or siblings. Many others were married and had to work to supplement the inadequate earnings of their husbands; for many working-class families, two incomes were required to support even a minimal standard of living. Even so, in some communities the aversion to seeing married women work was so strong—among both men and women—that families struggled on inadequate wages rather than see a wife and mother take a job.

Women industrial workers were overwhelmingly white and mostly young, 75 percent of them under twenty-five. The vast majority were immigrants or the daughters of immigrants. There were some women in all *Poorly Paid Women* areas of industry, even in some of the most arduous jobs. Most women, however, worked in a few industries where unskilled and semiskilled machine labor (as opposed to heavy manual labor) prevailed. The textile industry remained the largest single industrial employer of women. (Domestic service remained the most common female occupation overall.) Women worked for wages as low as $6 to $8 a week, well below the minimum necessary for survival (and well below the wages paid to men working the

same jobs). At the turn of the century, the average annual wage for a male industrial worker was $597; for a woman, it was $314. Even highly skilled women workers made about half what men doing the same job earned. Advocates of a minimum wage law for women created a sensation when they brought several women to a hearing in Chicago to testify that low wages and desperate poverty had driven them to prostitution. (The testimony was not, however, sensational enough for the Illinois legislature, which promptly defeated the bill.)

At least 1.7 million children under sixteen years of age were employed in factories and fields in 1900, more than twice the number of thirty years before. Ten percent of all girls aged ten to fifteen, and 20 percent of all boys, held jobs. Under the pressure of outraged public opinion, thirty-eight state legislatures passed child labor laws in the late nineteenth century; but these laws were of limited impact. Sixty percent of child *Ineffective Child-Labor Laws* workers were employed in agriculture, which was typically exempt from the laws; such children often worked twelve-hour days picking or hoeing in the fields. And even for children employed in factories, the laws merely set a minimum age of twelve years and a maximum workday of ten hours, standards that employers often ignored in any case. In the cotton mills of the South, children working at the looms all night were kept awake by having cold water thrown in their faces. In canneries, little girls cut fruits and vegetables sixteen hours a day. Exhausted children were particularly susceptible to injury while working at dangerous machines, and they were maimed and even killed in industrial accidents at an alarming rate.

As much as the appalling conditions of women and child workers troubled the national conscience, conditions for

SPINDLE BOYS Young boys, some of them barefoot, clamber among the great textile machines in a Georgia cotton mill adjusting spindles. Many of them were the children of women who worked in the plants. The photograph is by Lewis Hine. *(Bettmann/Corbis)*

many men were at least equally dangerous. In mills and mines, and on the railroads, the American accident rate was higher than that of any industrial nation in the world. As late as 1907, an average of twelve railroad men a week died on the job. In factories, thousands of workers faced such occupational diseases as lead or phosphorus poisoning, against which few employers took precautions.

The Struggle to Unionize

Labor attempted to fight back against such conditions by adopting some of the same tactics their employers had used so effectively: creating large combinations, or unions. But by the end of the century their efforts had met with little success.

There had been craft unions in America, representing small groups of skilled workers, since well before the Civil War. Alone, however, individual *National Labor Union* unions could not hope to exert significant power in the new corporate economy, and in the 1860s some labor leaders began to search for ways to combine the energies of the various labor organizations. The first attempt to federate separate unions into a single national organization came in 1866, when William H. Sylvis founded the National Labor Union—a polyglot association, claiming 640,000 members, that included a variety of reform groups having little direct relationship with labor. After the Panic of 1873 the National Labor Union disintegrated and disappeared.

The National Labor Union, like most of the individual unions that joined it, excluded women workers. Male workers argued (not entirely incorrectly) that women were used to drive down their wages; and they justified their hostility by invoking the ideal of domesticity. "Woman was created to be man's companion," a National Labor Union official said, "to be the presiding deity of the home circle." Most women workers agreed that "man should be the breadwinner," as one female union organizer said. But many argued that as long as conditions made it impossible for men to support their families, women should have full and equal opportunities in the workplace.

Unions faced special difficulties during the recession years of the 1870s. Not only was there widespread unemployment, which depression conditions created; there was also widespread middle-class hostility toward the unions. When labor disputes with employers turned bitter and violent, as they occasionally did, much of the public *Molly Maguires* instinctively blamed the workers (or the "radicals" and "anarchists" they believed were influencing the workers) for the trouble, rarely the employers. Particularly alarming to middle-class Americans was the emergence of the "Molly Maguires," a militant labor organization in the anthracite coal region of Pennsylvania. The Mollies operated within the Ancient Order of Hibernians, an Irish fraternal society, and sometimes used terrorist tactics. They attempted to intimidate the coal operators through violence and occasionally murder, and they added to the growing perception that labor activism was motivated by dangerous radicals. Much of the violence attributed to the Molly Maguires, however, was instigated or performed by informers and agents employed by the mine owners, who wanted a pretext for ruthless measures to suppress unionization.

A WARNING FROM THE MOLLY MAGUIRES The Molly Maguires were known for their harsh, intimidating, and at times violent tactics against the owners and managers of anthracite coal mines. In this "coffin notice" sent to a mine foreman in the early 1870s, they inform him: "You are hereby notified that if you don't leave this place right away, you will be a dead man." *(The Historical Society of Schuylkill County)*

The Great Railroad Strike

Excitement over the Molly Maguires paled beside the near hysteria that gripped the country during the railroad strike of 1877, which began when the eastern railroads announced a 10 percent wage cut and which soon expanded into something approaching a class war. Strikers

disrupted rail service from Baltimore to St. Louis, destroyed equipment, and rioted in the streets of Pittsburgh and other cities. State militias were called out, and in July *National Strike* President Hayes ordered federal troops to suppress the disorders in West Virginia. In Baltimore, eleven demonstrators died and forty were wounded in a conflict between workers and militiamen. In Philadelphia, state militia opened fire on thousands of workers and their families who were attempting to block the railroad crossings and killed twenty people. In all, over 100 people died before the strike finally collapsed several weeks after it had begun.

The great railroad strike was America's first major, national labor conflict, and it illustrated how disputes between workers and employers could no longer be localized in the increasingly national economy. It illustrated as well the depth of resentment among many American workers toward their employers (and toward the governments allied with them) and the lengths to which they were prepared to go to express that resentment. And finally, it was an indication of the frailty of the labor movement. The failure of the strike seriously weakened the railroad unions and damaged the reputation of labor organizations in other industries as well.

The Knights of Labor

The first major effort to create a genuinely national labor organization was the founding in 1869 of the Noble Order of the Knights of Labor, under the leadership of Uriah S. Stephens. Membership was open to all who "toiled," a definition that included all workers and most business and professional people. The only excluded groups were lawyers, bankers, liquor dealers, and professional gamblers.

KNIGHTS OF LABOR DELEGATES, 1886 The Knights of Labor aspired to represent everyone in America who could be considered a producer, and it was the first, and for many years the only, labor organization to welcome women unreservedly, as this portrait of delegates to the Knights 1886 convention indicates. *(Brown Brothers)*

Unlike most labor organizations of the time, the Knights welcomed women members—not just female factory workers, but domestic servants and women who worked in their own homes. Leonora Barry, an Irish immigrant who had worked in a New York hosiery factory, ran the Woman's Bureau of the Knights. Under her effective leadership, the Knights enlisted 50,000 women members (both black and white) and created over a hundred all-female locals.

The Knights were loosely organized, without much central direction. Members met in local "assemblies," which took many different forms. They were loosely affiliated with a national "general assembly." Their program was similarly vague. Although they championed an eight-hour day and the abolition of child labor, the leaders were more interested in long-range reform of the economy. Leaders of the Knights hoped to replace the "wage system" with a new "cooperative system," in which workers would themselves control a large part of the economy.

For several years, the Knights remained a secret fraternal organization. But in the late 1870s, under the leadership of Terence V. Powderly, the order moved into the *Dissolution of the Knights of Labor* open and entered a spectacular period of expansion. By 1886, it claimed a total membership of over 700,000, including some militant elements that the moderate leadership could not always control. Local unions or assemblies associated with the Knights launched a series of strikes in the 1880s in defiance of Powderly's wishes. In 1885, striking railway workers forced the Missouri Pacific, a link in the Gould system, to restore wage cuts and recognize their union. But the victory was temporary. In the following year, a strike on another Gould railroad, the Texas and Pacific, was crushed, and the power of the unions in the Gould system was broken. Their failure helped discredit the organization. By 1890, the membership of the Knights had shrunk to 100,000. A few years later, the organization disappeared altogether.

The AFL

Even before the Knights began to decline, a rival organization based on a very different organizational concept appeared. In 1881, representatives of a number of existing craft unions formed the Federation of Organized Trade and Labor Unions of the United States and Canada. Five years later, it changed its name to the American Federation of Labor (AFL), and it soon became the most important and enduring labor group in the country. Rejecting the Knights' idea of one big union for everybody, the Federation was an association of essentially autonomous craft unions and represented mainly skilled workers. It was generally hostile to organizing unskilled workers, who did not fit comfortably within the craft-based structure of existing organizations.

Toward women, the AFL adopted an apparently contradictory policy. On the one hand, the male leaders of the AFL were essentially hostile to the idea of women entering the paid work force. Because women *Opposition to Female Employment* were weak, they believed, employers could easily take advantage of them by paying them less than men. As a result, women workers drove down wages for everyone. "It is the so-called competition of the unorganized, defenseless woman worker, the girl and the wife, that often tends to reduce the wages of the father and husband," Samuel Gompers, the powerful leader of the AFL, once said. He talked often about the importance of women remaining in the home, and argued (incorrectly) that "There is no necessity of the wife contributing to the support of the family by working." More than that, female labor was, the AFL newspaper wrote, "the knife of the assassin, aimed at the family circle."

Although hostile to the idea of women workers, the AFL nevertheless sought equal pay for those women who did work and even hired some female organizers to encourage unionization in industries dominated by women. These positions were, in fact, less contradictory than they seem. By raising the pay of women, the AFL could make them less attractive to employers and, in effect, drive them out of the work force.

Gompers accepted the basic premises of capitalism; his goal was simply to secure for the workers he represented a greater share of capitalism's material rewards. Gompers rejected the idea of fundamental economic reform; *The AFL's Agenda* he opposed the creation of a worker's party; he was generally hostile to any government efforts to protect labor or improve working conditions, convinced that what government could give it could also take away. The AFL concentrated instead on the relationship between labor and management. It supported the immediate objectives of most workers: better wages, hours, and working conditions. And while it hoped to attain its goals by collective bargaining, it was ready to use strikes if necessary.

As one of its first objectives, the AFL demanded a national eight-hour day and called for a general strike if workers did not achieve the goal by May 1, 1886. On that day, strikes and demonstrations calling for a shorter workday took place all over the country, most of them staged by AFL unions but a few by more radical groups.

In Chicago, a center of labor and radical strength, a strike was already in progress at the McCormick Harvester Company when the general strike began. City police had *Haymarket Square* been harassing the strikers, and labor and radical leaders called a protest meeting at Haymarket Square. When the police ordered the crowd to disperse, someone threw a bomb that killed seven officers and injured sixty-seven other people. The police, who had killed four strikers the day before, fired into the crowd and killed four more people. Conservative, property-conscious Americans, frightened and outraged, demanded retribution, even though no one knew who had thrown the bomb. Chicago officials finally rounded up eight anarchists and charged them with murder, on the grounds that their statements had incited whoever had hurled the bomb. All eight scapegoats were found guilty after a remarkably injudicious trial. Seven were sentenced to death. One of the condemned committed suicide, four were executed, and two had their sentences commuted to life imprisonment.

To most middle-class Americans, the Haymarket bombing was an alarming symbol of social chaos and radicalism. "Anarchism" now became a code word in the public mind for terrorism and violence, even though most anarchists were relatively peaceful visionaries dreaming of a new social order. For the next thirty years, the specter of anarchism remained one of the most frightening concepts in the American middle-class imagination. It also became a constant obstacle to the goals of the AFL and other labor organizations, and it was particularly devastating to the Knights of Labor, which, as the most radical of the major labor organizations, never recovered from the post-Haymarket hysteria. However much they tried to distance themselves from radicals, unions were always vulnerable to accusations of anarchism, as the violent strikes of the 1890s occasionally illustrated.

The Homestead Strike

The Amalgamated Association of Iron and Steel Workers, which was affiliated with the American Federation of Labor, was the most powerful trade union in the country. Its members were skilled workers, in great demand by employers and thus able to exercise significant power in the workplace. Employers sometimes called such workers "little shopfloor autocrats," and they resented the substantial control over working conditions these skilled laborers often had. The union had a rulebook with fifty-six pages of what workers called "legislation" limiting the power of employers. In the emerging corporate world of the late nineteenth century, such challenges to management control were beginning to seem intolerable to many employers.

By the mid-1880s, the steel industry had introduced new production methods and new patterns of organization that were streamlining the steelmaking process and, at the same time, reducing the companies' dependence on skilled labor. In the Carnegie system, which was coming to dominate the steel industry, the union had a foothold in only one of the corporation's three major *Henry Clay Frick* | factories—the Homestead plant near Pittsburgh. By 1890, Carnegie and his chief lieutenant, Henry Clay Frick, had decided that the Amalgamated "had to go," even at Homestead. Over the next two years, they repeatedly cut wages at Homestead. At first, the union acquiesced, aware that it was not strong enough to wage a successful strike.

In 1892, the company stopped even discussing its decisions with the Amalgamated, in effect denying the union's right to negotiate at all. Finally, when Frick announced another wage cut at Homestead and gave the union two days to accept it, the Amalgamated called for a strike. Frick abruptly shut down the plant and called in 300 guards from the Pinkerton Detective Agency to enable the company to hire nonunion workers. The hated Pinkertons were well-known strikebreakers, and their mere presence was often enough to incite workers to violence.

The Pinkertons approached the plant by river on barges on July 6, 1892. The strikers prepared for them by pouring oil on the water and setting it on fire, and they met the guards at the docks with guns and dynamite. After several hours of pitched battle, during which three guards and ten strikers were killed and many others injured, the Pinkertons surrendered and were escorted roughly out of town.

But the workers' victory was temporary. The governor of Pennsylvania, at the company's request, sent the state's entire National Guard contingent, some 8,000 troops, *The Union Defeated* to Homestead. Production resumed, with strikebreakers now protected by troops. And public opinion turned against the strikers when a radical made an attempt to assassinate Frick. Slowly workers drifted back to their jobs; and finally—four months after the strike began—the Amalgamated surrendered. By 1900, every major steel plant in the Northeast had broken with the Amalgamated, which now had virtually no power to resist. Its membership shrank from a high of 24,000 in 1891 (two-thirds of all eligible steelworkers) to fewer than 7,000 a decade later. Its decline was symbolic of the general erosion of union strength in the late nineteenth century, as factory labor became increasingly unskilled and workers thus became easier to replace. The AFL unions were often powerless in the face of these changes.

The Pullman Strike

A dispute of greater magnitude and equal bitterness, if less violence, was the Pullman strike in 1894. The Pullman Palace Car Company manufactured sleeping and parlor cars for railroads, which it built and repaired at a plant near Chicago. There the company built the 600-acre town of Pullman and rented its trim, orderly houses to the employees. George M. Pullman, owner of the company, considered the town a model solution to the industrial problem; he referred to the workers as his "children." But many residents chafed at the regimentation and the high rents.

In the winter of 1893–1894, the Pullman Company slashed wages by about 25 percent, citing the declining revenues the depression was causing. At the same time, Pullman refused to reduce rents in its model town, which were 20 to 25 percent higher than rents for comparable

BREAKING THE PULLMAN STRIKE Company C of the 15th United States Infantry, called into service by President Grover Cleveland to break a widespread railroad strike in 1894, poses here before a special patrol train near Rock Island, Illinois. The strike began when workers at the Pullman Palace Car Company outside Chicago walked off the job to protest wage cuts and rent increases. Their walkout generated broad support from other railroad workers and even from the governor of Illinois, John Peter Altgeld, who refused to call out the state militia to keep the trains running. Cleveland, however, had little sympathy for striking workers and he used his authority as president to protect the delivery of the mails to call out federal troops to break the strike. *(Bettmann/Corbis)*

accommodations in surrounding areas. Workers went on strike and persuaded the militant American Railway Union, led by Eugene V. Debs, to support them by refusing to handle Pullman cars and equipment. Opposing the strikers was the General Managers' Association, a consortium of twenty-four Chicago railroads. It persuaded its member companies to discharge switchmen who refused to handle Pullman cars. Every time this happened, Debs's union instructed its members who worked for the offending companies to walk off their jobs. Within a few days thousands of railroad workers in twenty-seven states and territories were on strike, and transportation from Chicago to the Pacific coast was paralyzed.

Eugene Debs

Most state governors responded readily to appeals from strike-threatened businesses; but the governor of Illinois, John Peter Altgeld, was a man with demonstrated sympathies for workers and their grievances. Altgeld had criticized the trials of the Haymarket anarchists and had pardoned the convicted men who were still in prison when he took office. He refused to call out the militia to protect employers now. Bypassing Altgeld, railroad operators asked the federal government to send regular army troops to Illinois, on the pretext that the strike was

preventing the movement of mail on the trains. President Grover Cleveland and Attorney General Richard Olney, a former railroad lawyer and a bitter foe of unions, complied. In July 1894, over Altgeld's objections, the president ordered 2,000 troops to the Chicago area. A federal court issued an injunction forbidding the union to continue the strike. When Debs and his associates defied it, they were arrested and imprisoned. With federal troops protecting the hiring of new workers and with the union leaders in a federal jail, the strike quickly collapsed.

Sources of Labor Weakness

The last decades of the nineteenth century were years in which labor, despite its organizing efforts, made few real gains and suffered many important losses. In a rapidly expanding industrial economy, wages for workers rose hardly at all, and not nearly enough to keep up with the rising cost of living. Labor leaders won a few legislative victories: the abolition by Congress in 1885 of the Contract Labor Law; the establishment by Congress in 1868 of an eight-hour day on public works projects and in 1892 of an eight-hour day for government employees; state laws governing hours of labor and safety standards; and gradually some guaranteed compensation for workers injured on the job. But many of these laws were not enforced, and neither strikes nor protests seemed to have much effect. The end of the century found most workers with less political power and considerably less control of the workplace than they had had forty years before.

Workers failed to make greater gains for many reasons. The principal labor organizations represented only a small percentage of the industrial work force. Four percent of all workers (fewer than 1 million people) belonged to unions in 1900. The AFL, the most important, excluded unskilled workers, who were emerging as the core of the industrial work force, and along with them most women, blacks, and recent immigrants. Women responded to this exclusion in 1903 by forming their own organization, the Women's Trade Union League. But the WTUL was mostly interested in securing protective legislation for women workers, not in a general organization and mobilization of labor; and the WTUL would have found little support within the AFL or other male-dominated organizations even if its goals had been more expansive. Other divisions within the work force contributed further to union weakness. Tensions between different ethnic and racial groups kept laborers divided.

Another source of labor weakness was the shifting nature of the work force. Many immigrant workers came to

Shifting Nature of the Workshop

America intending to remain only briefly, to earn some money and return home. The assumption that they had no long-range future in the country (even though it was often a mistaken one) eroded their willingness to organize. Other workers—natives and immigrants alike—were in constant motion, moving from one job to another, one town to another, seldom in one place long enough to establish any sort of institu-tional ties or exert any real power. A study of Newbury-port, Massachusetts over a thirty-year period shows that 90 percent of the workers there vanished from the town records in those years, many of them because they moved elsewhere. Even workers who stayed put often did not remain in the same job for long. The rags-to-riches stories of the Horatio Alger novels had few counterparts in reality. But some real social mobility did exist.

Workers might move from unskilled to semiskilled or skilled jobs during their lifetimes; their children might become foremen or managers. The gains were small, but they were enough to inspire considerable (and often unrealistic) hopes and to persuade some workers that they were not part of a permanent working class.

Above all, workers made few gains in the late nineteenth century because of the strength of the forces arrayed against them. They faced corporate organizations   *Corporate Strength*
of vast wealth and power, which were generally determined to crush any efforts by workers to challenge their prerogatives—not just through brute force, but also through infiltration of unions, espionage within working-class communities, and sabotage of organizational efforts. And as the Homestead and Pullman strikes suggest, the corporations had the support of local, state, and federal authorities, who were willing to send in troops to "preserve order" and crush labor uprisings on demand.

Despite the creation of new labor unions, despite a wave of strikes and protests that in the 1880s and 1890s reached startling proportions, workers in the late nineteenth century failed on the whole to create successful organizations or to protect their interests in the way the large corporations managed to do. In the battle for power within the emerging industrial economy, almost all the advantages seemed to lie with capital.

CONCLUSION

In the four decades following the end of the Civil War, the United States propelled itself into the forefront of the industrializing nations of the world. Large areas of the nation remained overwhelmingly rural, to be sure, and the majority of the population was still engaged in activities closely tied to farming. Even so, America's economy, and along with it the nation's society and culture, were being profoundly transformed.

New technologies, new forms of corporate management, and new supplies of labor helped make possible the rapid growth of the nation's industries and the construction of its railroads. The factory system contributed to the growth of the nation's cities and at times created entirely new ones. Immigration provided a steady supply of new workers for the growing industrial economy. The result was a steady and substantial increase in national wealth, rising living standards for much of the population, and the creation of great new fortunes.

But industrialization did not spread its fruits evenly. Large areas of the country, most notably the South, and large groups in the population, most notably minorities, women, and recent immigrants, profited relatively little from economic growth. Industrial workers experienced arduous conditions of labor and wages that rose much more slowly than the profits of the corporations for which they worked. Small merchants and manufacturers found themselves overmatched by great new combinations.

Industrialists strove to create a rationale for their power and to persuade the public that everyone had something to gain from it. But many Americans remained skeptical of modern capitalism, and some—workers struggling to form unions, reformers denouncing trusts, women fighting to win protections for female laborers, socialists envisioning a new world, and many others—created broad and powerful critiques of the new economic order. Industrialization brought both progress and pain to late-nineteenth-century America. Controversies over its effects defined the era and would continue to define the first decades of the twentieth century.

FOR FURTHER REFERENCE

Robert Wiebe's *The Search for Order, 1877–1920* (1968) is a classic analysis of America's evolution from a society of what he calls island communities to a national urban society. Alfred D. Chandler, Jr., describes the new business practices that made industrialization possible in *The Visible Hand: The Managerial Revolution in American Business* (1977) and *Scale and Scope: The Dynamics of Industrial Capitalism* (1990). Olivier Zunz offers a provocative analysis of the social underpinnings of the new corporate order in *Making America Corporate, 1870–1920* (1990) and *Why the American Century?* (1998). David F. Noble, *America by Design: Science, Technology, and the Rise of Corporate Capitalism* (1977) and David Hounshell, *From the American System and to Mass Production, 1800–1932* (1984) discuss the explosion of science and technology in the era of rapid industrialization. Daniel Rodgers, *The Work Ethic in Industrial America, 1850–1920* (1978) is an important intellectual history of the way Americans viewed industrial workers. David Montgomery, *The Fall of the House of Labor: The Workplace, the State, and American Labor Activism, 1865–1925* (1987) analyzes the way industrialization shaped (and was shaped by) the workers, their expertise, and the strong cultural traditions of the shop floor. Alice Kessler-Harris documents the tremendous movement of women into the work force in the period in *Out to Work: A History of Wage-Earning Women in the United States* (1982). John L. Thomas, *Alternative America: Henry George, Edward Bellamy, Henry Demarest Lloyd, and the Adversary Tradition* (1983) examines some important critics of corporate capitalism.

For quizzes, Internet resources, references to additional books and films, and more, consult this book's Online Learning Center at www.mhhe.com/brinkley11.

MILWAUKEE, 1900 In the middle years of the nineteenth century, Americans were dazzled by large paintings of the dramatic landscape of the Far West. By the beginning of the twentieth century, they were at least as interested in the new landscape of the city—with its tall buildings, its new technologies, and its dramatic design. This painted photograph of downtown Milwaukee is typical of many images of American city centers in this period, with its focus on a particularly dramatic large building and its presentation of such urban wonders as streetcars and electric wires. Such images were often reproduced on postcards. *(Photo by William Henry Jackson/Detroit Publishing Company. Reproduced by permission of Christopher Cardozo, Inc.)*

Significant Events

1836 · Mount Holyoke College founded as seminary for women	**1872** · Tammany's Boss Tweed convicted of corruption · Montgomery Ward distributed first catalog
1840s · Modern baseball established	**1876** · Baseball's National League founded · Johns Hopkins University creates first modern graduate school
1850 · First urban tenement built in New York City	
1859 · New York City's Central Park opened	**1879** · Carlisle Indian Industrial School founded in Pennsylvania
1865 · Vassar College founded	· Salvation Army begins operations in America
1869 · Princeton and Rutgers play first intercollegiate football game	· First F. W. Woolworth store opens in Utica, New York
1870 · New York City opens elevated railroads · Wellesley College founded	**1882** · Congress restricts Chinese immigration
1871 · Great fires destroy much of Chicago and Boston · Smith College founded	**1883** · Brooklyn Bridge opened **1884** · First steel girder "skyscraper" built in Chicago

CHAPTER EIGHTEEN

THE AGE OF THE CITY

The industrialization and commercialization of America changed the face of society in countless ways. Nowhere were those changes more profound than in the growth of cities and the creation of an urban society and culture. Having begun its life as a primarily agrarian republic, the United States in the late nineteenth century was becoming an urban nation.

The change did not come easily. Cities grew so rapidly that their facilities and institutions could not keep pace. Housing, transportation, sewers, social services, governments—all lagged far behind the enormous demands the new urban population was placing on them. American sensibilities lagged behind as well. Many people rebelled at the new and intimidating pace of urban life and at the dazzling and at times uncomfortable diversity of the urban population. "Our cities," wrote the sociologist Charles Horton Cooley, "are full of the disintegrated materials of the old order looking for a place in the new."

THE URBANIZATION OF AMERICA

The great migration from the countryside to the city was not unique to the United States. It was occurring simultaneously throughout much of the Western world in response to industrialization and the factory system. But America, a society with little experience of great cities, found urbanization particularly jarring—but also particularly alluring.

The Lure of the City

"We cannot all live in cities," Horace Greeley wrote shortly after the Civil War, "yet nearly all seem determined

Rapid Urban Growth

to do so." The urban population of America increased sevenfold in the half-century after the Civil War. And in 1920, the census revealed that for the first time, a majority of the American people lived in "urban" areas—defined as communities of 2,500 people or more. New York and its environs grew from 1 million in 1860 to over 3 million in

1900. Chicago had 100,000 residents in 1860 and more than a million in 1900. Cities were experiencing similar growth in all areas of the country.

Natural increase accounted for only a small part of the urban growth. In fact, urban families experienced a high rate of infant mortality, a declining fertility rate, and a high death rate from disease. Without immigration, cities would have grown relatively slowly, if at all. The city attracted people from the countryside because it offered conveniences, entertainments, and cultural experiences unavailable in rural communities. But it attracted people most of all because it offered more and better-paying jobs than were available in rural America or in the foreign economies many immigrants were fleeing.

People moved to cities, too, because new forms of transportation made it easier for them to get there. Railroads made simple, quick, and relatively inexpensive what once might have seemed a daunting journey from parts of the American countryside to nearby cities. The development of large, steam-powered ocean liners created a highly competitive shipping industry, allowing

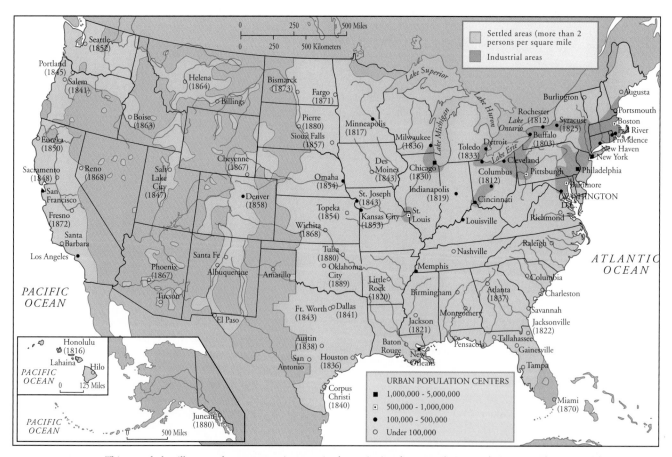

AMERICA IN 1900 This map helps illustrate the enormous increase in the nation's urban population in the nineteenth century. The map of America in 1800, on p. 193 in Chapter 7, reveals a nation with very few significant cities and with a population clustered largely along the eastern seaboard. By 1900, a much larger area of the United States had consistent areas of settlement, and many more of those areas consisted of towns and cities—including two cities (New York and Philadelphia) with populations of over a million and a considerable number of other cities with 100,000 or more people. Also striking, however, is the amount of land in the West with very light settlement or virtually no settlement at all. ◆ *Does climate and geography help explain the variable patterns of settlement?*

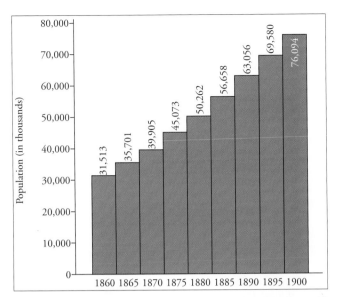

POPULATION GROWTH, 1860–1900 This chart illustrates the rapid increase in the nation's population in the last forty years of the nineteenth century. As you can see, the American population more than doubled in those years. ◆ *What were the principal factors behind this substantial population growth?*

Europeans and Asians to cross the oceans to America much more cheaply and quickly than they had in the past.

Migrations

As a result, the late nineteenth century was an age of unprecedented geographical mobility, as Americans left the

Geographic Mobility

declining agricultural regions of the East at a dramatic rate. Some who left were moving to the newly developing farmlands of the West. But almost as many were moving to the cities of the East and the Midwest.

Among those leaving rural America for industrial cities in the late nineteenth century were young rural women, for whom opportunities in the farm economy were limited. As farms grew larger, more commercial, and more mechanized, they became increasingly male preserves; and since much of the work force on many farms consisted of unskilled and often transient workers, there were fewer family units than before. Farm women had once been essential for making clothes and other household goods, but those goods were now available in stores or through catalogs. Hundreds of thousands of women moved to the cities, therefore, in search of work and community.

Southern blacks were also beginning what would be a nearly century-long exodus from the countryside into the city. Their withdrawal was a testament to the poverty, debt, violence, and oppression African Americans encountered in the late-nineteenth-century rural South, because the opportunities they found in cities were limited. Factory jobs for blacks were rare and professional opportunities almost nonexistent. Urban blacks tended to work as cooks, janitors, domestic servants, and in other low-paying service occupations. Since many such jobs were considered women's work, black women often outnumbered black men in the cities.

By the end of the nineteenth century, there were substantial African-American communities (10,000 people or more) in over thirty cities— many of them in the South, but some (New York, Chicago, Washington, Baltimore) in the North or in border states. Much more substantial African-American migration was to come during World War I and after; but the black communities established in the late nineteenth century paved the way for the great population movements of the future.

African-American Communities

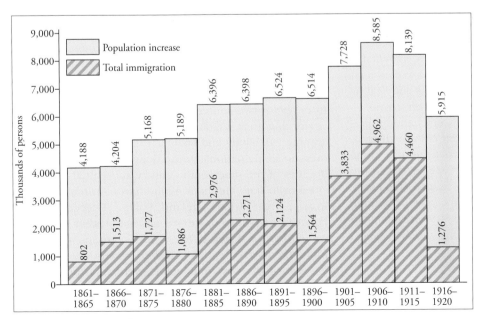

IMMIGRATION'S CONTRIBUTION TO POPULATION GROWTH, 1860–1920 Immigration, mostly from Europe, was responsible for a substantial share of the nation's population growth in the late nineteenth and early twentieth century—in some periods, as this chart shows, most of the population growth. ◆ *What factors drew so many immigrants to the United States in these years?*

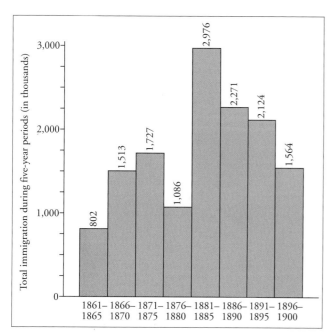

TOTAL IMMIGRATION, 1860–1900 Over 10 million immigrants from abroad entered the United States in the last forty years of the nineteenth century, with particularly high numbers arriving in the 1880s and 1890s. This chart shows the pattern of immigration in five-year intervals. ◆ *What external events might help explain some of the rises and falls in the rates of immigration in these years?*

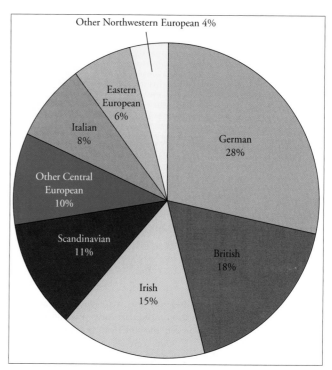

SOURCES OF IMMIGRATION FROM EUROPE, 1860–1900 This pie-chart shows the sources of European immigration in the late nineteenth century. The largest number of immigrants continued to come from traditional sources (Britain, Ireland, Germany, Scandinavia), but the beginnings of what in the early twentieth century would become a major influx of immigrants from new sources—southern and eastern Europe in particular—are already visible here. Immigration from other sources—Mexico, South and Central America, and Asia— was also significant during this period. ◆ *Why would these newer sources of European and other kinds of immigration create controversy among older-stock Americans?*

The most important source of urban population growth in the late nineteenth century, however, was the arrival of great numbers of new immigrants from abroad: 10 million between 1860 and 1890, 18 million more in the three decades after that. Some came from Canada, Mexico, Latin America, and—particularly on the West Coast—China and Japan. But by far the greatest number came from Europe. After 1880, the flow of new arrivals began for the first time to include large numbers of people from southern and eastern Europe: Italians, Greeks, Slavs, Slovaks, Russian Jews, Armenians, and others. By the 1890s, more than half of all immigrants came from these new regions, as opposed to fewer than 2 percent in the 1860s.

In earlier stages of immigration, most new immigrants from Europe (with the exception of the Irish) were at least modestly prosperous and educated. Germans and Scandinavians in particular had headed west on their arrival, either to farm or to work as businessmen, merchants, professionals, or skilled laborers in midwestern cities such as St. Louis, Cincinnati, and Milwaukee. Most of the new immigrants of the late nineteenth century, however, lacked the capital to buy farmland and lacked the education to establish themselves in professions. So, like the poor Irish immigrants before the Civil War, they settled overwhelmingly in industrial cities, where most of them took unskilled jobs.

The Ethnic City

By 1890, most of the population of some major urban areas consisted of foreign-born immigrants and their children: 87 percent of the population of Chicago, 80 percent

in New York, 84 percent in Milwaukee and Detroit. (London, the largest industrial city in Europe, by contrast, had a population that was 94 percent native.) New York had more Irish than Dublin and more Germans than Hamburg. Chicago eventually had more Poles than Warsaw.

Equally striking was the diversity of the new immigrant populations. In other countries experiencing heavy immigration in this period, most of the new arrivals were coming *The Diverse American City* from one or two sources: Argentina, for example, was experiencing great migrations too, but almost everyone was coming from Italy and Spain. In the United States, however, no single national group dominated. In the last four decades of the nineteenth century, substantial groups arrived from Italy, Germany, Scandinavia, Austria, Hungary, Russia, Great Britain, Ireland, Poland, Greece, Canada, Japan, China, Holland, Mexico, and many other nations. In some towns, a dozen different ethnic groups might have found themselves living in close proximity.

Most of the new immigrants were rural people, and their adjustment to city life was often a painful one. To help ease the transition, many national groups formed close-knit ethnic communities within the cities: Italian,

The large waves of immigration that transformed American society in the nineteenth and early twentieth centuries were not unique to the United States. They were part of a great, global movement of peoples—unprecedented in history—that affected every continent. These epic migrations were the product of two related forces: population growth and industrialization.

The population of Europe grew faster in the second half of the nineteenth century than it had ever grown before and than it has ever grown since—almost doubling between 1850 and the beginning of World War I. The population growth was a result of growing economies able to support more people and of more efficient and productive agriculture that helped end debilitating famines. But the rapid growth nevertheless strained the resources of many parts of Europe and affected, in particular, rural people who were now too numerous to live off the available land. Many decided to move to other parts of the world where land was more plentiful or jobs were available.

At the same time, industrialization drew millions of people out of the countryside and into cities—sometimes into cities in their own countries, but often into industrial cities in other, more economically advanced nations. Historians of migration speak of "push" factors (pressures on people to leave their homes) and "pull" factors (the lure of new lands) in explaining population movements. The "push" for many nineteenth-century migrants was poverty and inadequate land at home; for others it was political and religious oppression. The "pull" was the availability of land or industrial jobs in other regions or lands—and for some, the prospect of greater freedom abroad. Faster, cheaper, and easier transportation—railroads and steamships, in particular—also aided large-scale immigration.

From 1800 to the start of World War I, fifty million Europeans migrated to new lands overseas—people from almost all areas of Europe, but in the later years of the century (when migration reached its peak) mostly from poor rural areas in southern and eastern Europe. Italy, Russia, and Poland were among the biggest sources of late-nineteenth-century migrants. Almost two-thirds of these immigrants came to the United States. But nearly twenty million Europeans migrated to other lands. Migrants from England and Ireland (among others) moved in large numbers to those areas of the British empire with vast, seemingly open lands: Canada, Australia, New Zealand, and South Africa. Large numbers of Italians moved to Argentina and other parts of South America. Many of these migrants moved to vast areas of open land in these countries; established themselves as farmers, using the new mechanical farming devices made possible by industrialization; and in many places—Australia, New Zealand, Argentina, South Africa, and the United States—evicted the original residents of their territories and created societies of their own. Many others settled in the industrial cities that were growing up in all these regions and formed distinctive ethnic and national communities within them.

But it was not only Europeans who were transplanting themselves in these years. Vast numbers of migrants—usually poor, desperate people—left Asia, Africa, and the Pacific Islands in search of better lives. Most of them could not afford the journey abroad on their own. They moved instead as indentured servants (in much the same way many English migrants moved to America in the seventeenth century), agreeing to a term of servitude in their new land in exchange for food, shelter, and transportation. Recruiters of indentured servants fanned out across China, Japan, areas of Africa and the Pacific Islands, and, above all, India. French and British recruiters brought hundreds of thousands of Indian migrants to work in plantations in their own Asian and African colonies. Chinese laborers were recruited to work on plantations in Cuba and

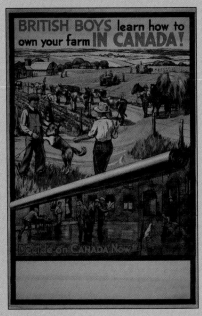

(© Bodleian Library, Univesity of Oxford, 2002)

Hawaii; mines in Malaya, Peru, South Africa, and Australia; and railroad projects in Canada, Peru, and the United States. African indentured servants moved in large numbers to the Caribbean, and Pacific Islanders tended to move to other islands or to Australia.

The migration of European peoples to new lands was largely voluntary and brought most migrants to the United States, where indentured servitude was illegal. But the migration of non-European peoples often involved an important element of coercion and brought relatively small numbers of people to the United States. This non-European migration was a function of the growth of European empires and it was made possible by the imperial system—by its labor recruiters, by its naval resources, by its laws, and by its economic needs. Together, these various forms of migration produced one of the greatest population movements in the history of the world and transformed not just the United States, but much of the globe.

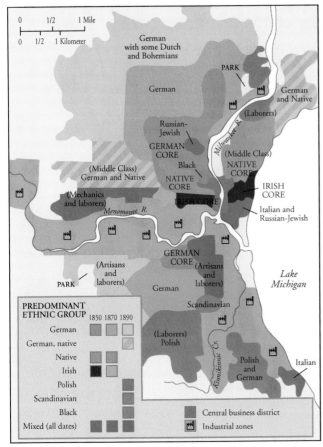

ETHNIC AND CLASS SEGREGATION IN MILWAUKEE, 1850–1890
This map illustrates the complex pattern of settlement in Milwaukee, a pattern that was in many ways typical of many industrial cities, in the late nineteenth century. Two related phenomena—industrialization and massive immigration from abroad—shaped the landscape of the city in these years. By 1890, first- and second-generation immigrants made up 84 percent of the city's population. Note the complicated distribution of ethnic groups in distinctive neighborhoods throughout the city, and note too the way in which middle-class people (especially "native-born" middle-class people, which included many people of German descent whose families had been in the United States for generations) isolated themselves from the areas in which the working class lived. ◆ *What were some of the advantages and disadvantages of this ethnic clustering to the immigrants who lived in these communities?*

Polish, Jewish, Slavic, Chinese, French-Canadian, Mexican, and other neighborhoods (often called "immigrant ghettoes") that attempted to re-create in the New World many of the features of the Old.

Some ethnic neighborhoods consisted of people who had migrated to America from the same province, town, or village. Even when the population was more diverse, however, the community offered newcomers much that was familiar. They could find newspapers and theaters in their native languages, stores selling their native foods, churches or synagogues, and fraternal organizations that provided links with their national

Benefits of Ethnic Communities

pasts. Many immigrants also maintained close ties with their native countries. They stayed in touch with relatives who had remained behind. Some (perhaps as many as a third in the early years) returned to Europe or Asia or Mexico after a relatively short time; others helped bring the rest of their families to America.

The cultural cohesiveness of the ethnic communities clearly eased the pain of separation from the immigrants' native lands. What role it played in helping immigrants become absorbed into the economic life of America is a more difficult question to answer. It is clear that some ethnic groups (Jews and Germans in particular) advanced economically more rapidly than others (for example, the Irish). One explanation is that, by huddling together in ethnic neighborhoods, immigrant groups tended to reinforce the cultural values of their previous societies. When those values were particularly well suited to economic advancement in an industrial society—as was, for example, the high value Jews placed on education—ethnic identification may have helped members of a group to improve their lots. When other values predominated—maintaining community solidarity, sustaining family ties, preserving order—progress may have been less rapid.

But other factors were at least as important in determining how well immigrants fared in the New World. Immigrants who aroused strong racial prejudice among native-born whites—most notably African Americans, Asians, and Mexicans—found it very difficult to advance whatever their talents. Among others, however, those who arrived with a valuable skill did better than those who did not. Those who arrived with at least some capital had an enormous advantage over those who were penniless. And over time, those who lived in cities where people of their own nationality came to predominate—for example, the Irish in New York and Boston, or the Germans in Milwaukee—gained a tremendous advantage as they learned to exert their political power.

Assimilation

Despite the substantial differences among the various immigrant communities, virtually all groups of the foreign-born had certain things in common. Most immigrants, of course, shared the experience of living in cities (and of adapting from a rural past to an urban present). Most were young; the majority of newcomers were between fifteen and forty-five years old. And in virtually all communities of foreign-born immigrants, the strength of ethnic ties had to compete against another powerful force: the desire for assimilation.

Many of the new arrivals from abroad had come to America with romantic visions of the New World. And however disillusioning they might find their first contact with the United States, they usually retained the dream of becoming true "Americans." Even some first-generation

Americanization

PUSHCART VENDOR Many immigrants to American cities aspired to be merchants. But many people with such aspirations could not afford to rent or buy a shop. So they set up business instead in pushcarts, which they parked along sidewalks and from which they sold a variety of wares. This pushcart was photographed with its owner on the lower east side of Manhattan at around the end of the nineteenth century. *(The Jewish Museum)*

immigrants worked hard to rid themselves of all vestiges of their old cultures, to become thoroughly Americanized. Second-generation immigrants were even more likely to attempt to break with the old ways, to try to assimilate completely into what they considered the real American culture. Some even looked with contempt on parents and grandparents who continued to preserve traditional ethnic habits and values.

The urge to assimilate put a particular strain on relations between men and women in immigrant communities. Many of the foreign-born came from cultures in *Changing Gender Roles* which women were even more subordinate to men, and even more fully lodged within the family, than women in the United States. In some immigrant cultures, parents expected to arrange their children's marriages and to control almost every moment of their daughters' lives until marriage. But either out of choice or out of economic necessity, many immigrant women (and even more of the American-born daughters of immigrants) began working outside the home and developing friendships, interests, and attachments outside the family. The result was not the collapse of the family-centered cultures of immigrant communities; those cultures proved remarkably durable. But there were important adjustments to the new and more fluid life of the American city, and often considerable tension in the process.

Assimilation was not entirely a matter of choice. Native-born Americans encouraged it, both deliberately and inadvertently, in countless ways. Public schools taught children in English, and employers often insisted that workers speak English on the job. Although there were merchants in immigrant communities who sold ethnically distinctive foods and clothing, most stores by necessity sold mainly American products, forcing immigrants to adapt their diets, wardrobes, and lifestyles to American norms. Church leaders were often native-born Americans or more assimilated immigrants who encouraged their parishioners to adopt American ways. Some even reformed their theology and liturgy to make it more compatible with the norms of the new country. Reform Judaism, imported from Germany to the United States in the mid-nineteenth century, was an effort by American Jewish leaders (as it had been among German leaders) to make their faith less "foreign" to the dominant culture of a largely Christian nation.

Exclusion

The arrival of so many new immigrants, and the way many of them clung to old ways and created culturally distinctive communities, provoked fear and resentment among some native-born Americans, *Nativism* just as earlier arrivals had done. Some people reacted against the immigrants out of generalized fears and prejudices, seeing in their "foreignness" the source of all the disorder and corruption of the urban world. "These people," a Chicago newspaper wrote shortly after the Haymarket bombing, referring to striking immigrant workers, "are not American, but the very scum and offal of Europe . . . Europe's human and inhuman rubbish." Native-born Americans on the West Coast had a

IMMIGRATION UNDER ATTACK Louis Dalrymple, one of the most famous political cartoonists of the early twentieth century, published this harsh warning in 1903 about what he called "The High Tide of Immigration." He makes no secret here of his belief that the danger lay not only in the number of immigrants, but in their origins and character as "riff raff." (*Special Collections, New York Public Library. Astor, Lenox and Tilden Foundations*)

similar cultural aversion to Mexican, Chinese, and Japanese immigrants. Others had economic concerns. Native laborers were often incensed by the willingness of the immigrants to accept lower wages and to take over the jobs of strikers.

The rising nativism provoked political responses. In 1887, Henry Bowers, a self-educated lawyer obsessed with a hatred of Catholics and foreigners, founded the American Protective Association, a group committed to stopping the immigrant tide. By 1894, membership in the organization had reportedly reached 500,000, with chapters throughout the Northeast and *Immigration Restriction League* Midwest. That same year a more genteel organization, the Immigration Restriction League, was founded in Boston by five Harvard alumni. It was dedicated to the belief that immigrants should be screened, through literacy tests and other standards designed to separate the desirable from the undesirable. The league avoided the crude conspiracy theories and the rabid xenophobia of the American Protective Association, and its more sophisticated nativism made it possible for many educated, middle-class people to support the restrictionist cause.

Even before the rise of these new organizations, politicians were struggling to find answers to the "immigration question." In 1882 Congress had responded to strong anti-Asian sentiment in California and elsewhere and restricted Chinese immigration, even though the Chinese made up only 1.2 percent of the population of the West Coast (see pp. 447–448). In the same year, Congress denied entry to "undesirables"—convicts, paupers, the mentally incompetent—and placed a tax of 50 cents on each person admitted. Later legislation of the 1890s enlarged the list of those barred from immigrating and increased the tax.

But these laws kept out only a small number of aliens, and more ambitious restriction proposals made little progress. Congress passed a literacy requirement for immigrants in 1897, but President Grover Cleveland vetoed it. The restrictions had limited success because many native-born Americans, far from fearing immigration, welcomed *Advantages of Cheap Labor* it and exerted strong political pressure against the restrictionists. Immigration was providing a rapidly growing economy with a cheap and plentiful labor supply; many argued that America's industrial (and indeed agricultural) development would be impossible without it.

THE URBAN LANDSCAPE

The city was a place of remarkable contrasts. It had homes of almost unimaginable size and grandeur, and hovels of indescribable squalor. It had conveniences unknown to earlier generations, and problems that seemed beyond society's capacity to solve. Both the attractions and the problems were a result of the stunning pace at which cities were growing. The expansion of the urban population helped spur important new technological and industrial developments. But the rapid growth also produced misgovernment, poverty, congestion, filth, epidemics, and great fires. Planning and building simply could not match the pace of growth. "The problem in America," a municipal reformer wrote, "has been to make a great city in a few years out of nothing."

The Creation of Public Space

In the eighteenth and early nineteenth centuries, cities had generally grown up haphazardly, with little central planning, in response to the individual decisions of the people who owned land and built buildings. Public authorities basically responded to private decisions and did little to affect the shape of municipalities. By the

CENTRAL PARK BAND CONCERT By the late nineteenth century, New York City's Central Park was already considered one of the great urban landscapes of the world. To New Yorkers, it was an irresistible escape from the crowded, noisy life of the rest of the city. But the park itself sometimes became enormously crowded as well, as this well-dressed audience at a band concert makes clear. *(Brown Brothers)*

mid-nineteenth century, however, reformers, planners, architects, and others began to call for a more ordered vision of the city. The result was the self-conscious creation of public spaces and public services.

Among the most important innovations of the mid-nineteenth century were great urban parks, which reflected the desire of a growing number of urban leaders to provide an antidote to the congestion of the city landscape. Parks, they argued, would allow city residents a healthy, restorative escape from the strains of urban life by reacquainting them with the *Frederick Law Olmstead and* natural world. The most suc-
Calvert Vaux cessful promoters of this notion of the park as refuge were the landscape designers Frederick Law Olmsted and Calvert Vaux, who teamed with one another in the late 1850s to design New York's Central Park. They deliberately created a public space that would look as little like the city as possible. Instead of the ordered, formal spaces common in some European cities, they created instead a space that seemed to be entirely natural—even though almost every square inch of

Central Park was carefully designed and constructed. Central Park was from the start one of the most popular and admired public spaces in the world, and as a result Olmsted and Vaux were recruited to design other great parks and public spaces in other cities: Brooklyn, Boston, Philadelphia, Chicago, and Washington, D.C.

At the same time that cities were creating great parks, they were also creating great public buildings: libraries, art galleries, natural history museums, theaters, concert and opera halls. New York's Metropolitan Museum of Art was only the largest and best known of many great museums taking shape in the late nineteenth century; others were created in such cities as Boston, Chicago, Philadelphia, and Washington. In one city after another, new and lavish public libraries appeared as if to confirm the city's role as a center of learning and knowledge.

Wealthy residents of cities were the principal force behind the creation of the great art museums, concert halls, opera houses, and at times even parks. As their own material and social aspirations grew, they wanted the public life of the city to provide them with amenities to match their expectations. Becoming an important patron of a major cultural institution was an especially effective route to social distinction. But this philanthropy, whatever the motives behind it, also produced valuable assets for the city as a whole.

As both the size and the aspirations of the great cities increased, urban leaders launched monumental projects to remake the way their cities looked. Inspired by massive city rebuilding projects in Paris, London, Berlin, and other European cities, some American *"City Beautiful Movement"* cities began to clear away older neighborhoods and streets and create grand, monumental avenues lined with new and more impressive buildings. A particularly important event in inspiring this effort to remake the city was the 1893 Columbian Exposition in Chicago, a world's fair constructed to honor the 400th anniversary of Columbus's first voyage to America. At the center of the wildly popular exposition was a cluster of neoclassical buildings—the "Great White City"—constructed in the fashionable "beaux-arts" style of the time, arranged symmetrically around a formal lagoon. It became the inspiration for what became known as the "city beautiful" movement, led by the architect of the Great White City, Daniel Burnham. The movement aimed to impose a similar order and symmetry on the disordered life of cities around the country. "Make no little plans," Burnham liked to tell city planners. Those influenced by him strove to remake cities all across the country—from Washington, D.C. to Chicago and San Francisco. Only rarely, however, were planners to overcome the obstacles of private landowners and complicated urban politics to realize more than a small portion of their dreams. There were no reconstructions of American cities to match the elaborate nineteenth-century reshaping of Paris and London.

The effort to remake the city did not just focus on redesigning the existing landscape. It occasionally led to the creation of entirely new ones. In Boston in the late 1850s, a large area of marshy tidal land was gradually filled in to create the neighborhood known as "Back Bay." The landfill project took more than forty years to complete and was one of the largest public works projects

The Back Bay

ever undertaken in America to that point. But Boston was not alone. Chicago reclaimed large areas from Lake Michigan as it expanded and at one point raised the street level for the entire city to help avoid the problems the marshy land created. In Washington, D.C., another marshy site, large areas were filled in and slated for development. In New York and other cities, the response to limited space was not so much creating new land as annexing adjacent territory. A great wave of annexations expanded the boundaries of many American cities in the 1890s and beyond.

Housing the Well-to-Do

One of the greatest problems of this precipitous growth was finding housing for the thousands of new residents who were pouring into the cities every day. For the prosperous, however, housing was seldom a worry. The availability of cheap labor and the increasing accessibility of tools and materials reduced the cost of building in the late nineteenth century and let anyone with even a moderate income afford a house.

Many of the richest urban residents lived in palatial mansions in the heart of the city and created lavish "fashionable districts"—Fifth Avenue in New York, Back Bay and Beacon Hill in Boston, Society Hill in Philadelphia, Lake Shore Drive in Chicago, Nob Hill in San Francisco, and many others.

The moderately well-to-do (and as time went on, increasing numbers of wealthy people as well) took advantage of the less expensive land on the edges of the city

Growth of Suburbs

and settled in new suburbs, linked to the downtowns by trains or streetcars or improved roads. Chicago in the 1870s, for example, boasted nearly 100 residential suburbs connected with the city by railroad and offering the joys of "pure air, peacefulness, quietude, and natural scenery." Boston, too, saw the development of some of the earliest "streetcar suburbs"—Dorchester, Brookline, and others—which catered to both the wealthy and the middle class. New Yorkers of moderate means settled in new suburbs on the northern fringes of Manhattan and commuted downtown by trolley or riverboat. Real estate developers worked to create and promote suburban communities that would appeal to the nostalgia for the countryside that many city dwellers felt. Affluent suburbs, in particular, were notable for lawns, trees, and houses designed to look manorial. Even more modest communities strove to emphasize the opportunities suburbs provided for owning land.

Housing Workers and the Poor

Most urban residents, however, could not afford either to own a house in the city or to move to the suburbs. Instead, they stayed in the city centers and rented. Because demand was so high and space so scarce, they had little bargaining power in the process. Landlords tried to squeeze as many rent-paying residents as possible into the smallest available space. In Manhattan, for example, the average population density in 1894 was 143 people per acre—a higher rate than that of the most crowded cities of Europe (Paris had 127 per acre, Berlin 101) and far higher than in any other American city then or since. In some neighborhoods—the lower East Side, for example—density was more than 700 people per acre, among the highest levels in the world.

Landlords were reluctant to invest much in immigrant housing, confident they could rent dwellings for a profit regardless of their conditions. In the cities of the South—Charleston, New Orleans, Richmond—poor blacks lived in crumbling former slave quarters. In Boston, they moved into cheap three-story wooden houses ("triple deckers"), many of them decaying fire hazards. In Baltimore and Philadelphia, they crowded into narrow brick row houses. And in New York, as in many other cities, more than a million people lived in tenements.

The word "tenement" had originally referred simply to a multiple-family rental building, but by the late nineteenth century it was being used to describe slum dwellings

Tenements

only. The first tenements, built in New York City in 1850, had been hailed as a great improvement in housing for the poor. "It is built with the design of supplying the laboring people with cheap lodgings," a local newspaper commented, "and will have many advantages over the cellars and other miserable abodes which too many are forced to inhabit." But tenements themselves soon became "miserable abodes," with many windowless rooms, little or no plumbing or central heating, and perhaps a row of privies in the basement. A New York state law of 1870 required a window in every bedroom of tenements built after that date; developers complied by adding small, sunless air shafts to their buildings. Most of all, tenements were incredibly crowded, with three, four, and, sometimes many more people crammed into each small room.

Jacob Riis, a Danish immigrant and New York newspaper reporter and photographer, shocked many middle-class Americans with his sensational (and some would say

Jacob Riis

sensationalized) descriptions and pictures of tenement life in his 1890 book *How the Other Half Lives.* Slum dwellings, he said, were almost universally sunless, practically airless, and "poisoned" by "summer stenches." "The hall is dark and you might stumble over the children

A TENEMENT LAUNDRY Immigrant families living in tenements, in New York and in many other cities, earned their livelihoods as they could. This woman, shown here with some of her children, was typical of many working-class mothers who found income-producing activities they could pursue in the home (in this case laundry). This room, dominated by large vats and piles of other people's laundry, is also the family's home, as the crib and religious pictures make clear. *(Bettmann/Corbis)*

pitching pennies back there." But the solution many reformers (including Riis) favored, and that governments sometimes adopted, was to raze slum dwellings without building any new housing to replace them.

In most working-class neighborhoods (and in many middle-class ones as well), it was common for families to take in boarders, especially when children grew up and moved out and there was extra room. Often the boarders were relatives—newly arrived immigrants staying with brothers, sisters, or cousins. Others were strangers, single men or women who could not afford lodging on their own and paid to live with a family offering a room. Perhaps half the population of the city lived in homes with boarders in the late nineteenth century.

Urban Transportation

Urban growth posed monumental transportation challenges. Old downtown streets were often too narrow for the heavy traffic that was beginning to move over them. Most were without a hard, paved surface and resembled either a sea of mud or a cloud of dust, depending on the weather. In the last decades of the century, more and more streets were paved, usually with wooden blocks, bricks, or asphalt; but paving could not keep up with the number of new thoroughfares the expanding cities were creating. By 1890, Chicago had paved only about 600 of its more than 2,000 miles of streets.

Transportation Problems

But it was not simply the conditions of the streets that impeded urban transportation. It was the numbers of people who needed to move every day from one part of the city to another, numbers that mandated the development of mass transportation. Streetcars drawn on tracks by horses had been introduced into some cities even before the Civil War. But the horsecars were not fast enough, so many communities developed new forms of mass transit.

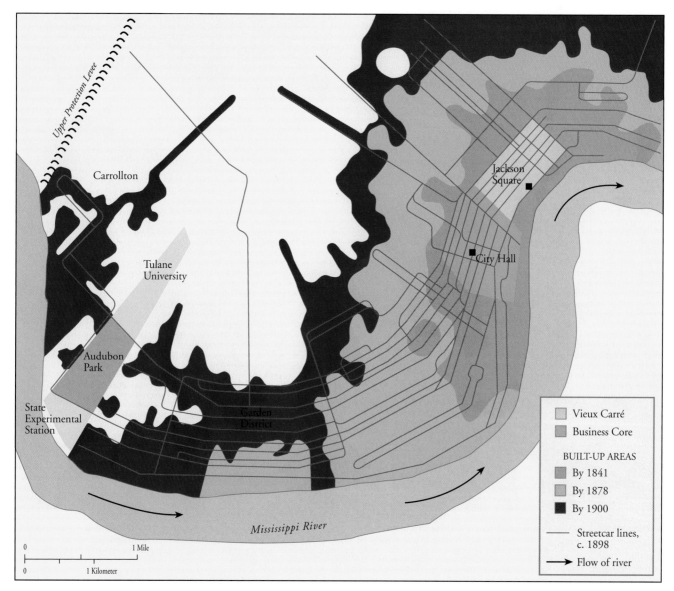

STREETCAR SUBURBS IN NINETEENTH-CENTURY NEW ORLEANS This map of streetcar lines in New Orleans reveals a pattern that repeated itself in many cities: changing residential patterns emerging in response to new forms of transportation. The map reveals the movement of population outward from the central city as streetcar lines emerged to make access to the downtown easier. Note the dramatic growth of residential suburbs in the last forty years of the nineteenth century in particular. ◆ *What other forms of mass transportation were emerging in American cities in these years?*

 For an interactive version of this map go to www.mhhe.com/brinkley11ch18maps

In 1870, New York opened its first elevated railway, whose noisy, filthy steam-powered trains moved rapidly above the city streets on massive iron structures. New

Mass Transit

York, Chicago, San Francisco, and other cities also experimented with cable cars, towed by continuously moving underground cables. Richmond, Virginia, introduced the first electric trolley line in 1888, and by 1895 such systems were operating in 850 towns and cities. In 1897, Boston opened the first American subway when it put some of its trolley lines underground. At the same time,

cities were developing new techniques of road and bridge building. One of the great technological marvels of the 1880s was the completion of the Brooklyn Bridge in New York, a dramatic steel-cable suspension span designed by John A. Roebling.

The "Skyscraper"

Cities were growing upward as well as outward. Until the mid-nineteenth century, almost no buildings more than four or five stories high could be constructed. Construction techniques were such that it was difficult and expensive to build adequate structural supports for tall buildings. There was also a limit to the number of flights of stairs the users of buildings could be expected to climb. But by the 1850s, there had been successful experiments with machine-powered passenger elevators; and by the 1870s, new methods of construction using cast iron and steel beams made it easier to build tall buildings.

Not long after the Civil War, therefore, tall buildings began to appear in the major cities. The Equitable Building in New York, completed in 1870 and rising seven and a half floors above the street, was one of the first in the nation to be built with an elevator. A few years later, even taller buildings of ten and twelve stories were appearing elsewhere in New York, in Chicago, and in other growing cities around the country. With each passing decade, both the size and the number of tall buildings increased until, by the 1890s, the term "skyscraper" began to become a popular description of them.

The modern skyscraper was made possible above all by steel girder construction. The first tall building to use *Steel-Girder Construction* this technique appeared in Chicago in 1884. It was followed a few years later by several in New York—which soon became the site of more tall buildings than any city in the world. That was in part because the location of New York's central business districts on the island of Manhattan made expansion outward difficult; instead, the city expanded upward.

The greatest figure in the early development of the skyscraper was the Chicago architect Louis Sullivan, who introduced many modern, functional elements to the genre—large windows, sheer lines, limited ornamentation—in an attempt to emphasize the soaring height of the building as its most distinctive feature. Sullivan's students, among them Frank Lloyd Wright, expanded the influence of these innovations still further and applied them to low buildings as well as tall ones.

STRAINS OF URBAN LIFE

The increasing congestion of the cities and the absence of adequate public services produced serious hazards. Crime, fire, disease, indigence, and pollution all placed strains on the capacities of metropolitan institutions, and both governments and private institutions were for a time poorly equipped to respond to them.

Fire and Disease

One serious problem was fires. In one major city after another, fires destroyed large downtown areas, where many buildings were still constructed of wood. Chicago and Boston suffered "great fires" in 1871. Other cities—among them Baltimore and San Francisco, where a tremendous earthquake produced a catastrophic fire in 1906—experienced similar disasters. The great fires were terrible and deadly experiences, but they were also important events in the development of the cities *Development of Professional Fire Departments* involved. They encouraged the construction of fireproof buildings and the development of professional fire departments. They also forced cities to rebuild at a time when new technological and architectural innovations were available. Some of the modern, high-rise downtowns of American cities arose out of the rubble of great fires.

An even greater hazard than fire was disease, especially in poor neighborhoods with inadequate sanitation facilities. But an epidemic that began in a poor neighborhood could (and often did) spread easily into other neighborhoods *Inadequate Sanitation* as well. Few municipal officials recognized the relationship of improper sewage disposal and water contamination to such epidemic diseases as typhoid fever and cholera; and many cities lacked adequate systems for disposing of human waste until well into the twentieth century. Flush toilets and sewer systems began to appear in the 1870s, but they could not solve the problem as long as sewage continued to flow into open ditches or streams, polluting cities' water supplies.

Environmental Degradation

Modern notions of environmental problems were unknown to most Americans in the late nineteenth and early twentieth centuries. But the environmental degradation of many American cities was a visible and disturbing fact of life in those years. The frequency of great fires, the dangers of disease and plague, the extraordinary crowding of working-class neighborhoods were all examples of the environmental costs of industrialization and rapid urbanization.

Improper disposal of human and industrial waste was a common feature of almost all large cities in these years. That contributed to the pollution of rivers and lakes, and also in many cases to the compromising of the city's drinking water. This was particularly true in poor neighborhoods with primitive plumbing (and sometimes no indoor plumbing at all), outdoor privies that leaked into the ground water, and overcrowded tenements. The presence of domestic animals—horses, which were the principal means of transportation until the late nineteenth century, but in poor neighborhoods also cows, pigs, and other animals—contributed as well to the environmental problems. The director of a large-scale study of conditions of life in Pittsburgh in 1914 could not contain his outrage at the conditions he found, even though the report he was supervising was a primarily academic document. "Go out on the street and scan closely the faces of the boys and girls who are growing into manhood and womanhood and see what kind of men and women these environments are producing."

CHICAGO IN FLAMES The great Chicago fire of 1871 (which legend attributes to a kerosene lantern kicked over by "Mrs. O'Leary's cow") devastated much of the central part of the city, just as great fires destroyed parts of other large cities (among them San Francisco and Boston) in the late nineteenth century. The fires were tragedies for those who lost their property or their lives; but they were opportunities for speculators and developers, who used the destruction as an opportunity to build new, "modern" city centers. *(Chicago Historical Society)*

Air quality in many cities was poor as well. Few Americans had the severe problems that London experienced in these years with its perpetual "fogs" created by the debris from the burning of soft coal. But air pollution from factories and from stoves and furnaces in offices, homes, and other buildings was constant and at times severe. The incidence of respiratory infection and related diseases was much higher in cities than it was in rural areas, and it accelerated rapidly in the late nineteenth century.

Air Pollution

By the early twentieth century, reformers were actively crusading to improve the environmental conditions of cities and were beginning to achieve some notable successes. New sewage and drainage systems were created to protect drinking water from sewage disposal. By 1910, most large American cities had constructed sewage disposal systems, often at great cost, to protect the drinking water of their inhabitants and to prevent the great bacterial plagues that impure water had helped create in the past—such as the yellow fever epidemic in Memphis that killed 5,000 people.

Alice Hamilton, a physician who became an investigator for the United States Bureau of Labor, was a pioneer in the identification of pollution in the workplace. She documented ways in which improper disposal of such potentially dangerous substances as lead (she was one of the first physicians to identify lead poisoning), chemical waste, and ceramic dust were creating widespread sickness. And despite considerable resistance from many factory owners, she did bring such problems to public attention and, in some states at least, inspired legislation to require manufacturers to solve them. In 1912, the federal government created the Public Health Service, which was charged with preventing such occupational diseases as tuberculosis and anemia and carbon dioxide poisoning, which were common in the garment industry and other trades. It attempted to create common health standards for all factories; but since the agency had few powers of enforcement, it had limited impact. It did, however, establish the protection of public health as a responsibility of the federal government and also helped bring to attention the environmental forces that endangered health. The creation of the Occupational Health and Safety Administration in 1970, which gave government the authority to require employers to

Public Health Service

create safe and healthy workplaces, was a legacy of the Public Health Service's early work.

Urban Poverty

Above all, perhaps, the expansion of the cities spawned widespread and often desperate poverty. Despite the rapid growth of urban economies, the sheer number of new residents ensured that many people would be unable to earn enough for a decent subsistence.

Public agencies and private philanthropic organizations offered very limited relief, and even they were generally dominated by middle-class people, who tended to believe that too much assistance would breed dependency and that poverty was the fault of the poor themselves—a result of laziness or alcoholism or other kinds of irresponsibility. Most tried to restrict aid to the "deserving poor"—those who truly could not help themselves (at least according to the standards of the organizations themselves, which conducted elaborate "investigations" to separate the "deserving" from the "undeserving").

Other charitable societies—for example, the Salvation Army, which began operating in America in 1879, one year after it was founded in London—concentrated more

Salvation Army | on religious revivalism than on the relief of the homeless and hungry. Tensions often arose between native Protestant philanthropists and Catholic immigrants over religious doctrine and standards of morality. Middle-class faith in the idea of self-improvement led to a widespread inattention to the structural roots of urban poverty.

Middle-class people grew particularly alarmed over the rising number of poor children in the cities, some of them orphans or runaways, living alone or in small groups scrounging for food. These "street arabs," as they were often called, attracted more attention from reformers than any other group—although that attention produced no lasting solutions to their problems.

Crime and Violence

Poverty and crowding naturally bred crime and violence. Much of it was relatively minor, the work of pickpockets,

High Crime Rates | con artists, swindlers, and petty thieves. But some was more dangerous. The American murder rate rose rapidly in the late nineteenth century (even as such rates were declining in Europe), from 25 murders for every million people in 1880 to over 100 by the end of the century—a rate slightly higher than even the highest rates of the 1980s and 1990s. That reflected in part a very high level of violence in some nonurban areas: the American South, where rates of lynching and homicide were particularly high; and the West, where the rootlessness and instability of new communities (cow towns, mining camps, and the like) created much violence. But the cities contributed their share to the increase in crime as well. Native-born

Americans liked to believe that crime was a result of the violent proclivities of immigrant groups, and they cited the rise of gangs and criminal organizations in various ethnic communities. But even in the cities, native-born Americans were as likely to commit crimes as immigrants.

The rising crime rates encouraged many cities to develop larger and more professional police forces. In the early nineteenth century, police forces had often been private and informal organizations; urban governments had resisted professionalized law enforcement. By the end of the century, however, professionalized public police departments were a part of the life of virtually every city and town. The modern police force contained uniformed officers who patrolled the streets and attempted to intervene when crimes were in progress, and plainclothes detectives, who investigated crimes after they occurred. They worked closely with district attorneys and other public prosecutors, who were also becoming more numerous and more important in city life. But police forces themselves could spawn corruption and brutality, particularly since jobs on them were often filled through political patronage. And complaints well known in recent years about police dealing differently with white and black suspects, or with rich and poor communities, were common in the late nineteenth century as well.

Some members of the middle class, fearful of urban insurrections, felt the need for even more substantial forms of protection. Urban national guard groups (many of them created and manned by middle-class elites) built imposing armories on the outskirts of affluent neighborhoods and stored large supplies of weapons and ammunition in preparation for uprisings that, in fact, virtually never occurred.

Fear of the City

Americans and Europeans alike reacted to life in the city with marked ambivalence. It was a place of strong allure and great excitement. Yet it was also a place of alienating impersonality, of a new feeling of anonymity, of a different kind of work with which the individual could feel only limited identification. To some, it was also a place of degradation and exploitation. Theodore Dreiser's novel *Sister Carrie* (1900) exposed one troubling aspect of urban life: the plight of single women (like Dreiser's heroine, Carrie) who moved from the countryside into the city and found themselves without any means of support. Carrie first took an exhausting and ill-paying job in a Chicago shoe factory, then drifted into a life of "sin," exploited by predatory men. Many women were experiencing in reality the dilemmas Carrie experienced in fiction. Living in conditions of extreme poverty and hardship, some moved into prostitution—which, degrading and dangerous as it was, also produced a livelihood and a form of community for desperate people.

The Machine and the Boss

Newly arrived immigrants, many of whom could not speak English, needed help in adjusting to American urban life: its laws, its customs, usually its language. Some ethnic communities created their own self-help organizations. But for many residents of the inner cities, the principal source of assistance was the political machine.

The urban machine was one of America's most distinctive political institutions. It owed its existence to the

Boss Rule

power vacuum that the chaotic growth of cities (and the very limited growth of governments) had created. It was also a product of the potential voting power of large immigrant communities. Any politician who could mobilize that power stood to gain enormous influence, if not public office. And so there emerged a group of urban "bosses," themselves often of foreign birth or parentage. Many were Irish, because they spoke English and because some had acquired previous political experience from the long Irish struggle against the English at home. All were men (unsurprisingly, since in most states women could not yet vote). The principal function of the political boss was simple: to win votes for his organization. That meant winning the loyalty of his constituents. To do so, a boss might provide them with occasional relief—baskets of groceries, bags of coal. He might step in to save those arrested for petty crimes from jail. When he could, he found jobs for the unemployed. Above all, he rewarded many of his followers with patronage: with jobs in city government or in such city agencies as the police (which the machine's elected officials often controlled); with jobs building or operating the new transit systems; and with opportunities to rise in the political organization itself.

Machines were also vehicles for making money. Politicians enriched themselves and their allies through various

Graft and Corruption

forms of graft and corruption. Some of it might be fairly open—what George Washington Plunkitt of New York's Tammany Hall called "honest graft." For example, a politician might discover in advance where a new road or streetcar line was to be built, buy an interest in the land near it, and profit when the city had to buy the land from him or when property values rose as a result of the construction. But there was also covert graft: kickbacks from contractors in exchange for contracts to build streets, sewers, public buildings, and other projects; the sale of franchises for the operation of such public utilities as street railways, waterworks, and electric light and power systems. The most famously corrupt city boss was William M. Tweed, boss of New York City's Tammany Hall in the 1860s and 1870s, whose excesses finally landed him in jail in 1872.

Middle-class critics saw the corrupt machines as blights on the cities and obstacles to progress. In fact, political organizations were responsible not just for corruption, but

"KEEPING TAMMANY'S BOOTS SHINED," C. 1887 This lithograph by cartoonist Joseph Keppler shows the heavy foot of New York City's Tammany Hall sitting atop City Hall, while Hugh Grant, a Tammany sheriff later elected mayor, applies the patronage polish that was the organization's lifeblood. The strap dangling from the boot bears the name of Richard Croker, who emerged as one of Tammany's principal leaders after the fall of Boss Tweed and who served as the undisputed chief of the organization from 1886 until 1901. *(Bettmann/Corbis)*

also for modernizing city infrastructures, for expanding the role of government, and for creating stability in a political and social climate that otherwise would have lacked a center. The motives of the bosses may have been largely venal, but their achievements were often greater than those of the more scrupulous reformers who challenged them.

Several factors made boss rule possible. One was the power of immigrant voters, who were less concerned with middle-class ideas of political morality than with obtaining

Reasons for Boss Rule

the services that machines provided and reformers did not. Another was the link between the political organizations and wealthy, prominent citizens who profited from their dealings with bosses and resisted efforts to overthrow them. Still another was the structural weakness of city governments. Within the municipal government, no single official usually had decisive power or responsibility. Instead, authority was generally divided among many officeholders and was limited by the state legislature. The boss, by virtue of his control over his machine, formed an "invisible government" that provided an alternative to the inadequacy of the regular government. Through his organization, he might control a majority of those who were in office even if (as was usually the case) he did not hold public office himself.

The urban machine was not without competition. Reform groups frequently mobilized public outrage at the corruption of the bosses and often succeeded in driving machine politicians from office. Tammany, for example, saw its candidates for mayor and other high city offices lose almost as often as they won in the last decades of the nineteenth century. But the reform organizations typically lacked the permanence of the machine, and more often than not, their power faded after a few years. Thus, many critics of machines began to argue for more basic reforms: for structural changes in the nature of city government.

THE RISE OF MASS CONSUMPTION

Middle-Class Culture

For urban middle-class Americans, the last decades of the nineteenth century were a time of dramatic advances. Indeed, it was in those years that a distinctive middle-class culture began to exert a powerful influence over the whole of American life. Much of the rest of American society—the majority of the population, which was neither urban nor middle class—advanced less rapidly or not at all; but almost no one was unaffected by the rise of a new urban, consumer culture.

Patterns of Income and Consumption

American industry could not have grown as it did without the expansion of markets for the goods it produced. The growth of demand occurred at almost all levels of society, a result not just of the new techniques of production and mass distribution that were making consumer goods less expensive, but also of rising incomes.

Incomes in the industrial era were rising for almost everyone, although at highly uneven rates. While the most conspicuous result of the new economy was the creation of vast fortunes, more important for society as a whole was the growth and increasing prosperity of the middle class. The salaries of clerks, accountants, middle managers, and other "white collar" workers rose on average by a third between 1890 and 1910—and in some parts of the middle class salaries rose by much more. Doctors, lawyers, and other professionals, for example, experienced a particularly dramatic increase in both the prestige and the profitability of their professions.

Rising Income

Working-class incomes rose too in those years, although from a much lower base and considerably more slowly. Iron and steel workers, despite the setbacks their unions suffered, saw their hourly wages increase by a third between 1890 and 1910; but industries with large female, African-American, or Mexican work forces—shoes, textiles, paper, laundries, many areas of commercial agriculture—saw very small increases, as did almost all industries in the South. Still, some workers in these industries experienced a rise in family income because women and children often worked to supplement the husband's and father's earnings, or because families took in boarders or laundry or otherwise supplemented their incomes.

Also important to the new mass market was the development of affordable products and the creation of new merchandising techniques, which made many consumer goods available to a broad market for the first time. A good example of such changes was the emergence of ready-made clothing. In the early nineteenth century, most Americans had made their own clothing—usually from cloth they bought from merchants, at times from fabrics they spun and wove themselves. More affluent people contracted with private tailors to make their clothes. But the invention of the sewing machine and the spur that the Civil War (and its demand for uniforms) gave to the manufacture of clothing created an enormous industry devoted to producing ready-made garments. By the end of the century, virtually all Americans bought their clothing from stores.

New Merchandising Techniques

Partly as a result, much larger numbers of people became concerned with personal style. Interest in women's fashion, for example, had once been a luxury reserved for the relatively affluent. Now middle-class and even working-class women could strive to develop a distinctive style of dress. Substantial wardrobes, once a luxury reserved for the wealthy, began to become common at other levels of society as well. New homes, even relatively modest ones, now included clothes closets. Even people in remote rural areas could develop more stylish wardrobes by ordering from the new mail-order houses.

Another example of the rise of the mass market was the way Americans bought and prepared food. The development and mass production of tin cans in the 1880s created a large new industry devoted to packaging and selling canned food and (as a result of the techniques Gail Borden discovered in the 1850s) condensed milk. Refrigerated railroad cars made it possible for perishables—meats, vegetables, dairy products, and other foodstuffs—to travel over long distances without spoiling. The development of artificially frozen ice made it possible for many more households to afford iceboxes. Among other things, the changes meant improved diets and better health; life expectancy rose six years in the first two decades of the twentieth century.

Chain Stores and Mail-Order Houses

Changes in marketing also altered the way Americans bought goods. Small local stores faced competition from new "chain stores." The Great Atlantic & Pacific Tea

Company (the A & P) began creating a national network

Chain Stores

of grocery stores as early as the 1850s and expanded it rapidly after the Civil War.

F. W. Woolworth opened his first "Five and Ten Cent Store" in Utica, New York, in 1879 and went on to build a national chain of dry goods stores. Chain stores were able to sell manufactured goods at lower prices than the local, independent stores with which they competed. From the beginning, they faced opposition from the established merchants they threatened to displace, and from others who feared that they would jeopardize the character of their communities. (Similar controversies have continued into the late twentieth century over the spread of large chains such as Wal-Mart or Barnes & Noble.) But most customers, however loyal they might feel to a local merchant, found it difficult to resist the greater variety and lower prices the chains provided them.

Chain stores were slow to reach remote, rural areas, which remained dependent on poorly stocked and often

Social Consequences of Mail-Order Catalogs

very expensive country stores. But rural people gradually gained access to the new consumer world through the great mail-order houses. In 1872, Montgomery Ward—a Chicago-based traveling salesman—distributed a catalog of consumer goods in association with the farmers' organization, the Grange (see pp. 537–538). By the 1880s, he was offering thousands of items at low prices to farmers throughout the Middle West and beyond. He soon faced stiff competition from Sears Roebuck, first established by Richard Sears in Chicago in 1887. Sears created a large market for his mail-order merchandise by distributing an enormous catalog each year, which, like Ward's, was particularly popular among people in remote rural areas. Together, the bulky catalogs from Ward and Sears changed the lives of many isolated people—introducing them to (and explaining for them) new trends of fashion and home decor as well as making available new tools, machinery, and technologies for the home.

Department Stores

In larger cities, the emergence of great department stores (which had appeared earlier in Europe) helped transform

Impact of the Department Store

buying habits and turn shopping into a more alluring and glamorous activity. Marshall Field in Chicago created one of the first American department stores. Similar stores emerged elsewhere: Macy's in New York, Abraham and Straus in Brooklyn, Jordan Marsh and Filene's in Boston, Wanamaker's in Philadelphia.

The department stores transformed the concept of shopping in several ways. First, they brought together under one roof an enormous array of products of all kinds: clothing, cosmetics, household goods, furniture, toys,

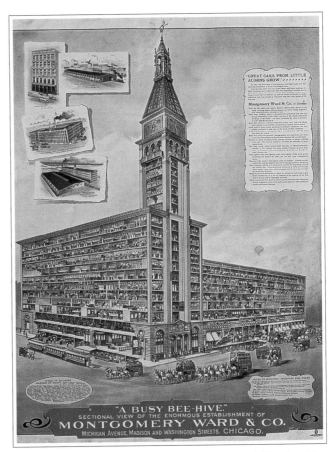

THE MONTGOMERY WARD DEPARTMENT STORE This advertising poster for the Montgomery Ward department store in downtown Chicago dates from about 1880. The designer has stripped away the outside walls to reveal the vast array of goods inside what the poster calls "the enormous establishment." *(Chicago Historical Society)*

cooking utensils, stationery, and other items that had previously been sold in separate shops. Second, they strove to create an atmosphere of wonder and excitement, to make shopping a glamorous activity. The new stores were elaborately decorated to suggest great luxury and elegance. They included restaurants and tea rooms and comfortable lounges, to suggest that shopping could be a social event as well as a practical necessity. They hired well-dressed sales clerks, mostly women, to provide attentive service to customers. Third, department stores—like mail-order houses—took advantage of economies of scale to sell merchandise at lower prices than many of the individual shops with which they competed.

Women as Consumers

The rise of mass consumption had particularly dramatic effects on American women, who were generally the primary consumers within families. Women's clothing styles changed much more rapidly and dramatically than men's, which encouraged more frequent purchases. Women generally bought and prepared food for their families, so the availability of new food products changed not only the way everyone ate, but also the way women shopped and cooked. Canning and refrigeration meant greater variety in the diet. It also meant that food did not always have to be eaten on the day it was purchased.

The consumer economy produced new employment opportunities for women as sales clerks in department
National Consumers League | stores and as waitresses in the rapidly proliferating restaurants. And it spawned the creation of a new movement in which women were to play a vital role: the consumer protection movement. The National Consumers League, formed in the 1890s under the leadership of Florence Kelley, attempted to mobilize the power of women as consumers to force retailers and manufacturers to improve wages and working conditions. By defining themselves as consumers, many middle-class women were able to find a stance from which they could become active participants in public life. Indeed, the mobilization of women behind consumer causes—and eventually many other causes—was one of the most important political developments of the late nineteenth century.

LEISURE IN THE CONSUMER SOCIETY

Closely related to the growth of consumption was an increasing interest in leisure time, in part because time away from work was expanding rapidly for many people. Members of the urban middle and professional classes had large blocks of time in which they were not at work—evenings, weekends, even vacations (previously almost unknown among salaried workers). Working hours in many factories declined, from an average of nearly seventy hours a week in 1860 to under sixty in 1900. Industrial workers might still be on the job six days a week, but many of them had more time off in the evenings. Even farmers found that the mechanization of agriculture gave them more free time. The lives of many Americans were becoming compartmentalized, with clear distinctions between work and leisure that had not existed in the past. The change produced a search for new forms of recreation and entertainment.

Redefining Leisure

It also produced a redefinition of the idea of "leisure." In earlier eras, relatively few Americans had considered
New Conceptions of Leisure | leisure a valuable thing. On the contrary, many equated it with laziness or sloth. "Rest," as in the relative inactivity many Americans considered appropriate for the Sabbath, was valued because it offered time for spiritual reflection and because it prepared people for work. But leisure—time spent amusing oneself in nonproductive

pursuits—was not only unavailable to most Americans, but faintly scorned.

The late nineteenth century saw the beginnings of a redefinition of leisure. With the rapid expansion of the economy and the increasing number of hours workers had away from work, it became possible to imagine leisure time as a normal part of the lives of many people. Industrial workers, in pursuit of shorter hours, adopted the slogan: "Eight hours for work, eight hours for rest, and eight hours for what we will." Others were equally adamant in claiming that leisure time was both a right and an important contribution to an individual's emotional and even spiritual health.

The economist Simon Patten was one of the first intellectuals to articulate this new view of leisure, which he tied closely to the rising interest in consumption. Patten, in *The Theory of Prosperity* (1902), *The New Basis of Civi-* | *Simon Patten* *lization* (1910), and other works, challenged the centuries-old assumption that the normal condition of civilization was a scarcity of goods. In earlier times, Patten argued, fear of scarcity had caused people to place a high value on thrift, self-denial, and restraint. But in modern industrial societies, the problems of scarcity had been overcome. The new economies could create enough wealth to satisfy not just the needs, but also the desires, of all. "We are now in the transition stage," he wrote, "from this pain economy [the economy of scarcity] to a pleasure economy." The principal goal of such an economy, he claimed, "should be an abundance of goods and the pursuit of pleasure."

As Americans became more accustomed to leisure as a normal part of their lives, they not only made increased use of traditional forms of recre-
ation and entertainment; they | *Public Leisure* also began to look for new experiences with which to entertain themselves. In cities, in particular, the demand for popular entertainment produced a rich mix of spectacles, recreations, and other activities. One of the most distinctive characteristics of late-nineteenth- and early-twentieth-century urban leisure was its intensely public character. In the late twentieth century, Americans spend much of their leisure time privately, in their homes. But in earlier times, entertainment meant "going out." Americans of diverse classes and backgrounds spent their leisure time in public places where they would find not only entertainment, but also other people. Thousands of working-class New Yorkers flocked to the amusement park at Coney Island, for example, not just for the rides and shows, but for the excitement of the crowds, as did the thousands who spent evenings in dance halls, vaudeville houses, and concert halls. More affluent New Yorkers enjoyed afternoons in Central Park, where a principal attraction was seeing other people (and being seen by them). Moviegoers were attracted not just by the movies themselves, but by the energy of the audiences at the lavish "movie palaces"

People who lived in the crowded cities of early-twentieth-century America yearned at times for ways to escape the noise and smells and heat and stress of the urban world. Wealthy families could travel to resorts or country houses. But most city-dwellers could not afford to venture far, and for them ambitious entrepreneurs tried to provide dazzling escapes close to home. The most celebrated such escape was Coney Island in Brooklyn, New York—which became for a time the most famous and popular urban resort in America.

POSTCARD FROM LUNA PARK Visitors to Coney Island sent postcards to friends and relatives by the millions, and those cards were among the most effective promotional devices for the amusement parks. This one shows the brightly lit entrance to Luna Park, Coney Island's most popular attraction for many years. *(Bettmann/Corbis)*

THE ELEPHANT HOTEL One of the early attractions of Coney Island as it became a popular resort was this hotel, built inside a large wooden elephant. This picture, taken in 1890, shows Coney Island at a point when development was still relatively modest. *(Bettmann/Corbis)*

Coney Island had been an attractive destination for visitors since the early nineteenth century, because it was near New York City and because it had a broad, sandy beach on the ocean. The first resort hotel was built there in 1824. In the 1870s and 1880s, investors built railroad lines from the city to the beach and began to create spectacular amusements to induce New Yorkers to visit: huge ballrooms and restaurants, a 300-foot-high iron tower, and a hotel shaped like an enormous elephant, with an observatory in its head. But the real success of Coney Island began in the 1890s, when the amusements and spectacles reached a new level. Sea Lion Park, which opened in 1895, showcased trained sea lions and exotic water rides. Two years later, Steeplechase Park began operations, attracting visitors with a mechanical steeplechase ride in which visitors could pretend to be jockeys, and stunt rooms with moving floors and powerful blasts of compressed air.

By then, Coney Island was a popular site for real horse racing, for boxing matches, and for other sports. It was also attracting gambling casinos, saloons, and brothels. From the beginning, among affluent middle-class people at least, Coney Island had a reputation as a rough and unsavory place. "If the whole horrible aggregation of shanties, low resorts, shacks masquerading as hotels, and the rest were swept off the earth," one visitor wrote in 1915, "the thanksgivings of the community would be in order." But to the working-class immigrants and lower middle-class people who were always its most numerous visitors, it was a place of wonder, excitement, and escape.

that began to appear in cities in the early twentieth century, just as sports fans were drawn by the crowds as well as by the games.

Mass entertainment did not always bridge differences of class, race, or gender. Saloons and some sporting events tended to be male preserves. Shopping (itself becoming a valued leisure-time activity) and going to tea rooms and luncheonettes was more characteristic of female leisure. Theaters, pubs, and clubs were often specific to particular

ethnic communities or particular work groups. There were, in fact, relatively few places where people of widely diverse backgrounds gathered together.

When the classes did meet in public spaces—as they did, for example, in city parks—there was often considerable conflict over what constituted appropriate public behavior. Elites in New York City, for example, tried to prohibit anything but quiet, "genteel" activities in Central Park, while working-class people wanted to use the

STEEPLECHASE PARK Steeplechase Park opened in 1897 and immediately began attracting crowds eager to ride the mechanical steeplechase shown here. *(Brown Brothers)*

The greatest of the Coney Island attractions, Luna Park, opened in 1903. It provided not just rides and stunts, but lavish reproductions of exotic places and spectacular adventures: Japanese gardens, Venetian canals with gondoliers, a Chinese theater, a simulated trip to the moon, and re-enactments of such disasters as burning buildings, earthquakes, and even the volcanic eruption that destroyed Pompeii. A year later, a competing company opened Dreamland, which tried to outdo even Luna Park with a 375-foot tower (modeled after a famous building in Spanish Seville), a three-ring circus, chariot races, and a Lilliputian village inspired by Gulliver's Travels. It also tried to create a soothing alternative to the crowded city around it, with neoclassical buildings, formal gardens, and, as the promoters promised, "avenues wide and imposing—no crowding." (A fire destroyed Dreamland in 1911.)

The popularity of Coney Island in these years was phenomenal. Thousands of people flocked to the large resort hotels that lined the beaches. Many thousands more made day trips out from the city by train and (after 1920) subway. In 1904, the average daily attendance at Luna Park alone was 90,000 people. On weekends, the Coney Island post office handled over 250,000 postcards, through which visitors helped spread the reputation of the resort throughout the region and the nation. Coney Island's popularity reflected a number of powerful impulses among urban Americans at the turn of the century. At the simplest level, it provided visitors with an escape from the heat and crowding of the vast metropolis around it. But it also offered many other things. It gave people who had

few opportunities for travel a simulated glimpse of exotic places and events that they would never be able to experience in reality. For immigrants, many of whom lived in insular ethnic communities, Coney Island provided a way of experiencing American mass culture on an equal footing with people of backgrounds different from their own. And almost everyone who found Coney Island appealing did so in part because it provided an escape from the genteel standards of behavior that governed so much of American life at the time. In the amusement parks of Coney Island, decorum was often forgotten, and people delighted in finding themselves in situations that in any other setting would have seemed embarrassing or improper: women's skirts blown above their heads with hot air; people pummeled with water and rubber paddles by clowns; hints of sexual freedom as strangers were forced to come into physical contact with one another on rides and amusements and as men and women revealed themselves to each other wearing bathing suits on the beach.

Coney Island remained popular throughout the first half of the twentieth century, and it continues to attract visitors even today (although in much smaller numbers). But its heyday was in the years before World War I, when the exotic sights and thrilling adventures it was able to offer had almost no counterparts elsewhere in American culture. In the 1920s, when radio and movies began to offer their own kind of mass escapism—and their own entry into mainstream American culture for immigrants aspiring to assimilate—Coney Island ceased to be the dazzling, unmatchable marvel it had seemed to earlier generations.

public spaces for sports and entertainments. But even divided by class, ethnicity, and gender, leisure and popular entertainment did help sustain a vigorous public culture.

Spectator Sports

Among the responses to the search for public forms of leisure was the rise of organized spectator sports, and especially baseball, which by the end of the century was

well on its way to becoming the "national pastime." A game much like baseball, known as "rounders" and derived from cricket, had enjoyed limited popularity in Great Britain in the early nineteenth century. Versions of the game began to appear in America in the early 1830s, well before Abner Doubleday supposedly "invented" baseball. (Doubleday, in fact, had little to do with the creation of baseball and actually cared little for sports. Alexander Cartwright, a member of a New York City

THE AMERICAN NATIONAL GAME Long before the modern major leagues began, local baseball clubs were active throughout much of the United States establishing the game as the "national pastime." This print of a "grand match for the championship" depicts an 1866 game at Elysian Fields, a popular park just across the river from New York City in Hoboken, New Jersey. *(National Baseball Hall of Fame and Museum, Inc.)*

baseball club in the 1840s, defined many of the rules and features of the game as we know it today.)

By the end of the Civil War, interest in baseball had grown rapidly. More than 200 amateur or semiprofes- *Major League Baseball* sional teams or clubs existed, many of which joined a national association and agreed on standard rules. As the game grew in popularity, it became a source of profit. The first salaried team, the Cincinnati Red Stockings, was formed in 1869. Other cities soon fielded professional teams, and in 1876, at the urging of Albert Spalding, they banded together in the National League. A rival league, the American Association, soon appeared. It eventually collapsed, but in 1901 the American League emerged to replace it. In 1903, the first modern World Series was played, in which the American League Boston Red Sox beat the National League Pittsburgh Pirates. By then, baseball had become an important business and a great national preoccupation (at least among men), attracting paying crowds in the thousands.

The second most popular game, football, appealed at first to a more elite segment of the male population, in part because it originated in colleges and universities. The first intercollegiate football game in America occurred between Princeton and Rutgers in 1869, and soon the game began to become entrenched as part of collegiate life. Early intercollegiate football bore only an indirect relation to the modern game; it was more similar to what is now known as rugby. By the late 1870s, however, the game was becoming standardized and was taking on the outlines of its modern form.

As college football grew in popularity, it spread to other sections of the country, notably to the midwestern state universities, which were destined soon to replace the eastern schools as the great powers of the game. It

also began to exhibit the taints of professionalism that have marked it ever since. Some schools used "ringers," tramp athletes who were not even registered as students. In *Growth of College Football* an effort to eliminate such abuses, Amos Alonzo Stagg, athletic director and coach at the University of Chicago, led in forming the Western Conference, or Big Ten, in 1896, which established rules governing eligibility.

Football also became known for a high level of violence on the field; eighteen college students died of football-related injuries and over a hundred were seriously hurt in 1905. The carnage prompted a White House conference on organized sports convened by President Theodore Roosevelt. As a result of its deliberations, a new intercollegiate association (which in 1910 became known as the National College Athletic Association, the NCAA) revised the rules of the game in an effort to make it safer and more honest.

Other popular spectator sports were emerging at about the same time. Basketball was invented in 1891 at Springfield, Massachusetts, by Dr. James A. Naismith, a Canadian working as athletic director for a local college. Boxing, which had long been a disreputable activity concentrated primarily among the urban working classes, became by the 1880s a more popular and in some places more reputable sport, particularly after the adoption of the Marquis of Queensberry rules (by which fighters wore padded gloves and fought in three-minute rounds). The first modern boxing hero, John L. Sullivan, became heavyweight champion of the world in 1882. Even so, boxing remained illegal in some states until after World War I. Horse racing, popular since colonial times, became increasingly commercialized with the construction of large tracks and the establishment of large-purse races such as the Kentucky Derby.

THE FLORADORA SEXTET The Floradora Sextet was a popular vocal group of the late nineteenth and early twentieth centuries and became fixtures on the vaudeville and burlesque stages of many cities and resorts. They are shown here in an elaborately costumed production number at the famous Weber and Fields Music Hall in New York, which opened in 1896. *(Bettmann/Corbis)*

Even in its infancy, spectator sports was closely associated with gambling. There was elaborate betting—

Gambling and Sports

some of it organized by underground gambling syndicates—on baseball and football almost from the start. One of the most famous incidents in the history of baseball was the alleged "throwing" of the 1919 World Series by the Chicago White Sox (an incident that became known as the "Black Sox Scandal"). That event resulted in the banning of some of the game's most notable figures from the sport for life and the establishment of the office of commissioner of baseball to "clean up" the game. Boxing was troubled throughout its history by the influence of gambling and the frequent efforts of managers to "fix" fights in the interests of bettors. Horse racing as it became commercialized was openly organized around betting, with the racetracks themselves establishing odds and taking bets.

The major spectator sports of the era were activities open almost exclusively to men. But a number of other sports were emerging in which women became important participants. Golf and tennis seldom attracted crowds in the late nineteenth century, but both experienced a rapid increase in participation among relatively wealthy men and women. Bicycling and croquet also enjoyed widespread popularity in the 1890s among women as well as men. Women's colleges were beginning to introduce their students to more strenuous sports as well—track, crew, swimming, and (beginning

in the late 1890s) basketball—challenging the once prevalent notion that vigorous exercise was dangerous to women.

Music and Theater

Other forms of popular entertainment developed in the cities in response to the large potential markets there. Many ethnic communities maintained their own theaters, in which immigrants listened to the music of their homelands and heard comedians making light of their experiences in the New World. Italian theaters often drew on the traditions of Italian opera to create sentimental musical events. The Yiddish theater built on the experiences of American Jews—and was the training ground for a remarkable group of musicians and playwrights who later went on to play a major role in mainstream, English-speaking theater.

Ethnic Theater

Urban theaters also introduced one of the most distinctively American entertainment forms: the musical comedy, which evolved gradually from the comic operettas of European theater. George M. Cohan, an Irish vaudeville entertainer, became the first great creator of musical comedies in the early twentieth century; in the process of creating his many shows, he wrote a series of patriotic songs—"Yankee Doodle Dandy," "Over There," and "You're a Grand Old Flag"—that remained popular many decades later. Irving Berlin, a veteran of the Yiddish theater, wrote more than 1,000 songs for the musical theater during his long career, including such popular favorites as "Alexander's Ragtime Band" and "God Bless America."

Vaudeville, a form of theater adapted from French models, was the most popular urban entertainment in *Vaudeville* the first decades of the twentieth century. Even saloons and small community theaters could afford to offer their customers vaudeville, which consisted of a variety of acts (musicians, comedians, magicians, jugglers, and others) and was, at least in the beginning, inexpensive to produce. As the economic potential of vaudeville grew, some promoters—most prominently Florenz Ziegfeld of New York—staged much more elaborate spectacles. Vaudeville was also one of the few entertainment media open to black performers. They brought to it elements of the minstrel shows they had earlier developed for black audiences in the late nineteenth century. (See "Patterns of Popular Culture," pp. 428–429.)

The Movies

The most important form of mass entertainment (until the invention of radio and television), and the one that reached most widely across the nation, was the movies. Thomas Edison and others had created the technology of the motion picture in the 1880s. Not long after, short films became available to individual viewers through "peep shows" in pool halls, penny arcades, and amusement parks. Soon larger projectors made it possible to project the images onto big screens, which permitted substantial audiences to see films in theaters.

By 1900, Americans were becoming attracted in large numbers to these early movies—usually plotless films of trains or waterfalls or other spectacles designed *Birth of a Nation* mainly to show off the technology. D. W. Griffith carried the motion picture into a new era with his silent epics—*The Birth of a Nation* (1915), *Intolerance* (1916), and others—which introduced serious plots and elaborate productions to filmmaking. Some of them—most notably *The Birth of a Nation,* with its celebration of the Ku Klux Klan and its demeaning portraits of blacks—also contained notoriously racist messages, an indication, among other things, that the audiences for these early films were overwhelmingly white. Motion pictures were the first truly mass entertainment medium, reaching all areas of the country and almost all groups in the population.

Working-Class Leisure

Leisure had a particular importance to working-class men and women—in part because it was a relatively new part of their lives and in part because it stood in such sharp

A NICKELODEON, 1905 Before the rise of the great movie palaces, urban families flocked to "nickelodeons," smaller theaters that charged five cents for admission and that showed many different films each day, including serials—dramas that drew audiences back into theaters day after day with new episodes of a running story. *(Brown Brothers)*

contrast to the grueling environments in which many industrial workers labored. More than most other groups in society, workers spent their leisure time on the streets—walking alone or in groups, watching street entertainers, meeting friends, talking and joking. For people with time but little money, the life of the street was an appealing source of camaraderie and energy.

Another important setting for the leisure time of working-class men was the neighborhood saloon, which tended to be patronized by the same people over time and be-*Importance of the Saloon* came a place where a worker could be sure of encountering a regular circle of friends. Saloons were often ethnically specific, in part because they served particular neighborhoods dominated by particular national groups. They also became political centers. Saloonkeepers were especially important figures in urban political machines, largely because they had regular contact with so many men in a neighborhood. When the Anti-Saloon League and other temperance organizations attacked the saloon, one of the reasons they cited was that eliminating saloons would weaken political machines. Saloons were also sometimes places of crime, violence, and prostitution—an entryway into the dark underworld of urban life; opponents of saloons attacked them for this reason as well.

Boxing was a particularly popular sport among working-class men. Many workers could not afford to attend the great public boxing matches pairing such popular heroes as John L. Sullivan and "Gentleman Jim" Corbett. But there were less glittering boxing matches in small rings and even in saloons—bare-knuckled fights organized by ethnic clubs and other groups that gave men an opportunity to demonstrate their strength and courage, something that the working world did not always provide them.

The Fourth of July

The Fourth of July played a large role in the lives of many working-class Americans. That was in part because in an

Importance of the Fourth of July

age of six-day workweeks and before regular vacations, it was for many decades one of the few full days of leisure—other than the Sabbath, during which activities were restricted by law—that many workers had. Fourth of July celebrations were one of the highlights of the year in many ethnic, working-class communities. In Worcester, Massachusetts, for example, the Ancient Order of Hibernians (an Irish organization) sponsored boisterous picnics for the Irish working class of the city. Competing with them were Irish temperance organizations, which offered more sober and "respectable" entertainments to those relatively few workers who wished to avoid the heavy drinking at the Hibernian affairs. Other ethnic groups organized their own Fourth of July events—picnics, games, parades—making the day not just a celebration of the nation's independence, but of the cultures of immigrant communities. The city's affluent middle class, in the meantime, tended to stay away. They remained indoors or organized family picnics at resort areas outside the city.

In southern cities such as Charleston, the Fourth of July was a more complicated affair, shaped in part by the memory of the Civil War and the continuing racial divisions within southern society. During Reconstruction, African-American workers in Charleston had exultantly celebrated the Fourth of July, seeing in it a symbol of the Union that had liberated them from slavery. Throughout the South, the Fourth was a day of celebration and self-congratulation for the Republican Party and its predominantly working-class or agrarian black constituency in the region. But white southerners slowly regained control of the Fourth, particularly once the drive toward sectional reconciliation had removed any pressure on them to change the racial culture of the region. Whites imposed ever tighter restrictions on how African Americans could celebrate the holiday. In the meantime, they themselves began once again to identify with the symbols of American patriotism, now that the idea of the nation was no longer a symbol to them of Union supremacy and the effort to achieve racial equality.

Private Pursuits

Not all popular entertainment, however, involved public events. Many Americans amused themselves privately by reading novels and poetry. The so-called dime novels, cheaply

Dime Novels

bound and widely circulated, became popular after the Civil War, with tales of the Wild West, detective stories, sagas of scientific adventure (such as the Tom Swift stories), and novels of "moral uplift" (among them those of Horatio Alger). Publishers also continued to distribute sentimental novels of romance, which developed a large audience among women, as did books about animals and about young children growing up. Louisa May Alcott's *Little Women* (1869) proved to be enduringly popular; most of its readers were women, and it sold more than 2 million copies.

Music was also a popular form of private leisure. There were, of course, public performances of music that attracted large crowds. But equally popular, and much more readily accessible, were opportunities to perform music in the home. Middle-class families in particular placed a high value on learning to play an instrument. Middle-class girls often spent years studying the piano, the harp, or some other "parlor instrument" and giving performances for family and friends in the home. Sales of sheet music soared to provide material for these domestic musicales.

Many kinds of music were popular in the home. More affluent families emphasized classical music, and many middle-class families favored traditional and usually sentimental ballads. The great popularity of ragtime—a form of music that had originated in black music halls in the South and then spread into nightclubs in other parts of the country—extended into the home as well in the 1890s when the music of Scott Joplin and other ragtime composers was published for the first time.

Mass Communications

Urban industrial society created a vast market for new vehicles for transmitting news and information. And so American publishing and journalism experienced an important change in the decades following the Civil War. Between 1870 and 1910, the circulation of daily newspapers increased nearly ninefold (from under 3 million to more than 24 million), a rate three times as great as the rate of population increase. And while standards varied widely from one paper to another, American journalism began to develop the beginnings of a professional identity. Salaries of reporters increased; many newspapers began separating the reporting of news from the expression of opinion; and newspapers themselves became important businesses.

One striking change was the emergence of national press services, which made use of the telegraph to supply news and features to papers throughout the country and which contributed as a result to the standardization of the product. By the turn of the century, important newspaper chains had emerged as well. The most powerful was

Emergence of Newspaper Chains

William Randolph Hearst's, which by 1914 controlled nine newspapers and two magazines. Hearst and rival publisher Joseph Pulitzer helped popularize what became known as "yellow journalism"—a deliberately sensational, often lurid style of reporting presented in bold graphics, designed to reach a mass audience. (See "Patterns of Popular Culture," pp. 560–561.) Another major change occurred in the nature of American magazines. Beginning in the 1880s, new kinds of magazines appeared that were designed for a mass audience. One of the pioneers was Edward W. Bok, who took over the *Ladies' Home Journal* in 1899 and, by targeting a mass female audience, built its circulation to over 700,000.

HIGH CULTURE IN THE AGE OF THE CITY

In addition to the important changes in popular culture that accompanied the rise of cities and industry, there were profound changes in the realm of "high culture"—in the ideas and activities of intellectuals and elites. Even the notion of a distinction between "highbrow" and "lowbrow" culture was relatively new to the industrial era. In the early nineteenth century, most cultural activities attracted people of widely varying backgrounds and targeted people of all classes. By the late nineteenth century, however, elites were developing a cultural and intellectual life quite separate from the popular amusements of the urban masses.

The Literature of Urban America

Many foreign observers and even some Americans in the late nineteenth century viewed the culture of the United States with contempt. Critics claimed that American life, despite its glittering surface, was essentially acquisitive and corrupt, with little cultural depth. But whatever the quality of culture and society in late-nineteenth-century America, the growth of industry and the rise of the city were having profound effects on them. Some writers and artists—the local-color writers of the South, for example, and Mark Twain, in such novels as *Huckleberry Finn* and *Tom Sawyer*—responded to the new civilization by evoking an older, more natural world. But others grappled directly with the modern order.

One of the strongest impulses in late-nineteenth- and early-twentieth-century American literature was the effort

Social Realism

to re-create urban social reality. This trend toward realism found an early voice in Stephen Crane, who—although best known for his novel of the Civil War, *The Red Badge of Courage* (1895)—was the author of an earlier, powerful indictment of the plight of the working class. Crane created a sensation in 1893 when he published *Maggie: A Girl of the Streets,* a grim picture of urban poverty and slum life. Theodore Dreiser was even more influential in encouraging writers to abandon the genteel traditions of earlier times and turn to the social dislocations and injustices of the present. He did so both in *Sister Carrie* and in other, later novels (including *An American Tragedy,* published in 1925).

Many of Dreiser's contemporaries followed him in chronicling the oppression of America's poor. In 1901 Frank Norris published *The Octopus,* an account of a struggle between oppressed wheat farmers and powerful railroad interests in California. The socialist writer Upton Sinclair published *The Jungle* in 1906, a novel designed to reveal the depravity of capitalism. It exposed abuses in the American meatpacking industry; and while it did not inspire the kind of socialist response for which Sinclair had hoped, it did produce legislative action to deal with the problem. Kate Chopin, a southern writer who explored the oppressive features of traditional marriage, encountered widespread public abuse after publication of her shocking novel *The Awakening* in 1899. It described a young wife and mother who abandoned her family in search of personal fulfillment. It was formally banned in some communities. William Dean Howells, in *The Rise of Silas Lapham* (1884) and other works, described what he considered the shallowness and corruption in ordinary American lifestyles.

Other critics of American society responded to the new civilization not by attacking it but by withdrawing from it. The historian Henry Adams published a classic autobiography in 1906, *The Education of Henry Adams,* in which he portrayed himself as a man disillusioned with and unable to relate to his society, even though he continued to live in it. The novelist Henry James lived the major part of his adult life in England and Europe and produced a series of coldly realistic novels—*The American* (1877), *Portrait of a Lady* (1881), *The Ambassadors* (1903), and others—that showed his ambivalence about the character of modern, industrial civilization—and about American civilization in particular.

Art in the Age of the City

American art through most of the nineteenth century had been overshadowed by the art of Europe. By 1900, however, a number of American artists, although some continued to study and even live in Europe, broke from the Old World traditions and experimented with new styles. Winslow Homer was vigorously American in his paintings of New England maritime life and other native subjects. James McNeil Whistler was one of the first

HAIRDRESSER'S WINDOW This 1907 painting is by John Sloan, an American artist who belonged to the so-called Ashcan School. Sloan and others revolted against what they considered the sterile formalism of academic painting and chose instead to portray realistic scenes of ordinary life. In 1913 they stirred the art world with a startling exhibition in New York, known as the Armory Show. In it they displayed not only their own work (which was relatively conventional in technique, even if sometimes daring in its choice of subjects) but also the work of innovative European artists, who were already beginning to explore wholly new artistic forms. *(Wadsworth Atheneum, Hartford)*

Western artists to appreciate the beauty of Japanese color prints and to introduce Oriental concepts into American and European art.

By the first years of the new century, some American artists were turning decisively away from the traditional

Ashcan School

academic style, a style perhaps best exemplified in America by the brilliant portraitist John Singer Sargent. Instead, many younger painters were exploring the same grim aspects of modern life that were becoming the subject of American literature. Members of the so-called Ashcan School produced work startling in its naturalism and stark in its portrayal of the social realities of the era. John Sloan portrayed the dreariness of American urban slums; George Bellows caught the vigor and violence of his time in paintings and drawings of prize fights; Edward Hopper explored the starkness and loneliness of the modern city. The Ashcan artists were also among the first Americans to appreciate expressionism and abstraction; and they showed their interest in new forms in 1913 when they helped stage the famous and controversial

"Armory Show" in New York City, which displayed works of the French Postimpressionists and of some American moderns.

The work of these and other artists marked the beginning in America of an artistic movement known as modernism, a movement that had counterparts in many other areas of cultural and intellectual life as well. Rejecting the heavy reliance on established forms that characterized the "genteel tradition" of the nineteenth-century art world, modernists rejected the past and embraced new subjects and new forms. Where the genteel tradition emphasized the "dignified" and "elevated" aspects of civilization (and glorified the achievements of gifted elites), modernism gloried in the ordinary, even the coarse. Where the genteel tradition placed great importance on respect for the past and the maintenance of "standards," modernism looked to the future and gloried in the new. Eventually, modernism developed strict orthodoxies of its own. But in its early stages, it seemed to promise an escape from rigid, formal traditions and an unleashing of individual creativity.

DEMPSEY AND FIRPO The artist George Bellows began painting fight scenes in the first years of the twentieth century, when boxing appealed primarily to working-class urban communities. By 1924, when he painted this view of the Dempsey-Firpo fight, prizefighting had become one of the most popular sports in America. *(Whitney Museum of American Art, New York; gift of Gertrude Vanderbilt Whitney)*

The Impact of Darwinism

The single most profound intellectual development in the late nineteenth century was the widespread acceptance

"Natural Selection" of the theory of evolution, associated most prominently with the English naturalist Charles Darwin. Darwinism argued that the human species had evolved from earlier forms of life (and most recently from simian creatures similar to apes) through a process of "natural selection." It challenged the biblical story of the Creation and almost every other tenet of traditional American religious faith. History, Darwinism suggested, was not the working out of a divine plan, as most Americans had always believed. It was a random process dominated by the fiercest or luckiest competitors.

The theory of evolution met widespread resistance at first from educators, theologians, and even many scientists. By the end of the century, however, the evolutionists had converted most members of the urban professional and educated classes. Even many middle-class Protestant religious leaders had accepted the doctrine, making significant alterations in theology to accommodate it. Evolution had become enshrined in schools and universities; virtually no serious scientist any longer questioned its basic validity.

Unseen by most urban Americans at the time, however, the rise of Darwinism was contributing to a deep schism between the new, cosmopolitan culture of the city—which was receptive to new ideas such as evolution—and a more traditional, provincial culture located mainly

CHARLES DARWIN Darwin's theories of natural selection, or evolution, revolutionized biological science. They also had a stunning impact on religious and even social thought. By challenging large parts of traditional religion and by suspecting that species were changeable, Darwinism opened the way for decades of theological controversy and for a series of spurious applications of his ideas to contemporary social problems. *(Bettmann/Corbis)*

(although not wholly) in rural areas—which remained wedded to more fundamentalist religious beliefs and older values. Thus the late nineteenth century saw not only the rise of a liberal Protestantism in tune with new scientific discoveries. It also saw the beginning of an organized Protestant fundamentalism, which would make its presence felt politically in the 1920s and again in the 1980s.

Darwinism helped spawn other new intellectual currents. There was the Social Darwinism of William Graham

"Pragmatism"

Sumner and others, which industrialists used so enthusiastically to justify their favored position in American life. But there were also more sophisticated philosophies, among them a doctrine that became known as "pragmatism," which seemed peculiarly a product of America's changing material civilization. William James, a Harvard psychologist and brother of the novelist Henry James, was the most prominent publicist of the new theory, although earlier intellectuals such as Charles S. Peirce and later ones such as John Dewey were also important to its development and dissemination. According to the pragmatists, modern society should rely for guidance not on inherited ideals and moral principles but on the test of scientific inquiry. No idea or institution (not even religious faith) was valid, they claimed, unless it worked and unless it stood the test of experience. "The ultimate test for us of what a truth means," James wrote, "is the conduct it dictates or inspires."

A similar concern for scientific inquiry was intruding into the social sciences and challenging traditional orthodoxies. Economists such as Richard T. Ely and Simon Patten argued for a more active and pragmatic use of scientific discipline. Sociologists such as Edward A. Ross and Lester Frank Ward urged applying the scientific method to the solution of social and political problems. Historians such as Frederick Jackson Turner and Charles Beard argued that economic factors more than spiritual ideals had been the governing force in historical development. John Dewey proposed a new approach to education that placed less emphasis on the rote learning of traditional knowledge and more on a flexible, democratic approach to schooling, one that enabled students to acquire knowledge that would help them deal with the realities of their society.

The relativistic implications of Darwinism also pro-

Growth of Anthropology

moted the growth of anthropology and encouraged some scholars to begin examining other cultures—most significantly, perhaps, the culture of American Indians—in new ways. A few white Americans began to look at Indian society as a coherent culture with its own norms and values that were worthy of respect and preservation, even though different from those of white society. But such ideas about Native Americans found very little support outside a few corners of the intellectual world until much later in the twentieth century.

Toward Universal Schooling

A society that was coming to depend increasingly on specialized skills and scientific knowledge was, of course, a society with a high demand for education. The late nineteenth century, therefore, was a time of rapid expansion and reform of American schools and universities.

One example was the spread of free public primary and secondary education. In 1860, there were only 100 public high schools in the entire United States. By 1900, the

Spread of Public Education

number had reached 6,000 and by 1914 over 12,000. By 1900, compulsory school attendance laws were in effect in thirty-one states and territories. But education was still far from universal. Rural areas lagged far behind urban-industrial ones in funding public education. And in the South, many blacks had access to no schools at all.

Educational reformers, few of whom shared the more relativistic views of anthropologists, sought to provide educational opportunities for the Indian tribes as well, in an effort to "civilize" them and help them adapt to white society. In the 1870s, reformers recruited small groups of Indians to attend Hampton Institute, a primarily black college. In 1879, Richard Henry Pratt, a former army officer, organized the Carlisle Indian Industrial School in Pennsylvania. Like many black colleges, Carlisle emphasized the kind of practical "industrial" education that Booker T. Washington had urged. Equally important, it isolated Indians from their tribes and tried to force them to assimilate to white norms. The purpose, Pratt said, was to "kill the Indian and save the man." Carlisle spawned other, similar schools in the West. The tribes themselves resisted this new approach to Indian education, both because of the hostility of the white educators to tribal culture and because the schools were often dreary and dangerous places. Ultimately, the reform efforts failed, although less because of Indian resistance than because of inadequate funding, incompetent administration, and poor teaching.

Colleges and universities were also proliferating rapidly in the late nineteenth century. They benefited particularly from the Morrill Land Grant Act of the Civil War era,

"Land-Grant" Institutions

by which the federal government had donated land to states for the establishment of colleges. After 1865, states in the South and West took particular advantage of the law. In all, sixty-nine "land-grant" institutions were established in the last decades of the century—among them the state university systems of California, Illinois, Minnesota, and Wisconsin.

Other universities benefited from millions of dollars contributed by business and financial tycoons. Rockefeller, Carnegie, and others gave generously to such schools as Columbia, the University of Chicago, Harvard, Northwestern, Princeton, Syracuse, and Yale. Other philanthropists founded new universities or reorganized and renamed older ones to perpetuate their family names—Vanderbilt, Johns Hopkins, Cornell, Duke, Tulane, and Stanford.

Education for Women

The post-Civil War era saw, too, an important expansion of educational opportunities for women, although such opportunities continued to lag far behind those available to men and were almost always denied to black women.

Most public high schools accepted women readily, but opportunities for higher education were few. At the end of the Civil War, only three American colleges were coeducational. In the years after the war,

 Women's Colleges

many of the land-grant colleges and universities in the Middle West and such private universities as Cornell and Wesleyan began to admit women along with men. But coeducation played a less crucial role in the education of women in this period than the creation of a network of women's colleges. Mount Holyoke, which had begun its life in 1836 as a "seminary" for women, became a full-fledged college in the 1880s. At about the same

time, entirely new female institutions were emerging: Vassar, Wellesley, Smith, Bryn Mawr, Wells, and Goucher. A few of the larger private universities created separate colleges for women on their campuses (Barnard at Columbia and Radcliffe at Harvard, for example). Proponents of women's colleges saw the institutions as places where female students would not be treated as "second-class citizens" by predominantly male student bodies and faculties.

The female college was part of an important phenomenon in the history of modern American women: the emergence of a distinctive women's community. Most faculty members and many administrators were women (usually unmarried). And the life of the college produced a spirit of sorority and commitment among educated women that had important effects in later years, as women became the leaders of many reform activities. Most female college graduates ultimately married, but they married at a later age than their non-college-educated counterparts and in some cases continued to pursue careers after marriage and motherhood. A significant minority, perhaps over 25 percent, did not marry at all, but devoted themselves exclusively to careers. A leader at Bryn Mawr remarked, "Our failures marry." That was surely a bit of rhetorical excess. But the growth of female higher education clearly became for some women a liberating experience, persuading them that they had roles to perform in society in addition to those of wives and mothers.

CONCLUSION

The extraordinary growth of American cities in the last decades of the nineteenth century led to both great achievements and enormous problems. Cities became centers of learning, art, and commerce. They produced great advances in technology, transportation, architecture, and communications. They provided their residents—and their many visitors—with varied and dazzling experiences, so much so that many rural people left the countryside to move to the city, and many more dreamed of doing so.

But cities were also places of congestion, filth, disease, and corruption. With populations expanding too rapidly for services to keep up, most American cities in this era struggled with makeshift governments and makeshift techniques to solve the basic problems of providing water, disposing of sewage, building roads, providing public transportation, fighting fire, stopping crime, and preventing or curing disease. City governments, many of them dominated by political machines and ruled by party bosses, were often models of inefficiency and corruption—although in their informal way they also provided substantial services to the working-class and immigrant constituencies who needed them most. They also managed, despite the administrative limitations of most

municipal governments, to oversee great public projects: the building of parks, museums, opera houses, and theaters, usually in partnership with private developers.

The city brought together races, ethnic groups, and classes of extraordinary variety—from the families of great wealth that the new industrial age was creating to the vast working class, much of it consisting of immigrants, that crowded into densely packed neighborhoods sharply divided by nationality. The city also produced new forms of popular culture. It created temples of consumerism: shops, boutiques, and, above all, the great department stores. And it created forums for public recreation and entertainment: parks, theaters, athletic fields, amusement parks, and later movie palaces.

Urban life created great anxiety among those who lived within the cities and among those who observed them from afar—so much so that in some cities middle-class people literally armed themselves to prepare for the insurrections they expected from the poor. But in fact, American cities adapted reasonably successfully over time to the great demands their growth made of them and learned to govern themselves if not entirely honestly and efficiently, at least adequately to allow them to survive and grow.

FOR FURTHER REFERENCE

Lewis Mumford, author of *The City in History* (1961), was America's foremost critic and chronicler of urbanization through the mid-twentieth century. John Bodnar provides a synthetic history of immigration in *The Transplanted: A History of Immigrants in America* (1985), which challenges an earlier classic study by Oscar Handlin, *The Uprooted: The Epic Story of the Great Migrations that Made the American People* (1973, 2nd ed.). The new urban mass culture of America's cities is the subject of William Leach, *Land of Desire: Merchants, Power, and the Rise of a New American Culture* (1993), and Kathy Peiss, *Cheap Amusements: Working Women and Leisure in Turn-of-the-Century New York* (1986). Stuart Blumin, *The Emergence of the Middle Class: Social Experience in the American City, 1760–1900* (1989) examines urban society and culture. T. J. Jackson Lears, *No Place of Grace: Antimodernism and the Transformation of American Culture, 1880–1920* (1981) chronicles patterns of resistance to the new culture. Roy Rosenzweig and Elizabeth Blackmar, *The Park and the People: A History of Central Park* (1992) studies the creation of America's most famous public park. Edwin G. Burrows and Mike Wallace, *Gotham: A History of New York City to 1898* (1998) is a thorough history of New York's remarkable growth. John F. Kasson, *Amusing the Millions: Coney Island at the Turn of the Century* (1978) is an illustrated history and interpretation of the amusement park's place in American culture. *Coney Island* (1991), a film by Ric Burns, presents a colorful history of America's favorite seaside resort. The documentary film *Baseball* (1994), by Ken Burns—and the companion book by the same name, by Geoffrey C. Ward—provide sweeping narratives of the national pastime, its origins in the age of the city, and its wider social context of race relations, immigration, and popular culture. *New York* (1999–2001), a film by Ric Burns, is a sweeping documentary history of the city, accompanied by a companion book, Ric Burns et al., *New York: An Illustrated History* (1999).

For quizzes, Internet resources, references to additional books and films, and more, consult this book's Online Learning Center at www.mhhe.com/brinkley11.

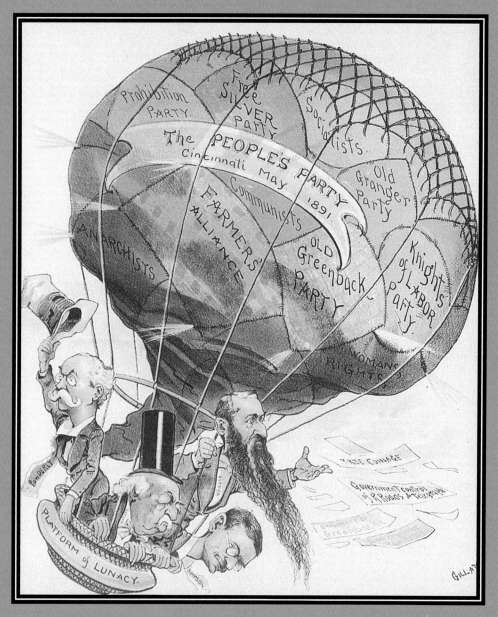

"A PARTY OF PATCHES," ***JUDGE*** **MAGAZINE, JUNE 6, 1891** This political cartoon suggests the contempt and fear with which many easterners, in particular, viewed the emergence of the People's Party in 1891. *(Kansas State Historical Society)*

Significant Events

1867 · National Grange founded

1873 · Congress discontinues coinage of silver

1875 · First Farmers' Alliances form in Texas

1880 · James A. Garfield elected president

1881 · Garfield assassinated; Chester A. Arthur succeeds him

1883 · Congress passes Pendleton Act, first national civil
        service law

1884 · Grover Cleveland elected president

1886 · Supreme Court in *Wabash* case restricts state
        regulation of commerce

1887 · Interstate Commerce Act passed

CHAPTER NINETEEN

FROM STALEMATE TO CRISIS

$\mathcal{T}$he enormous changes America was experiencing in the late nineteenth century strained not only the nation's traditional social arrangements but its political institutions as well. Economic growth brought both progress and disorder. And it was to government, gradually, that Americans began to look for leadership in their search for stability.

Yet American government during much of this period was ill equipped to deal with the new challenges confronting it. In the face of unprecedented dilemmas, it responded with apparent passivity and confusion. Its leaders, for the most part, seemed political mediocri-ties. The issues with which it was concerned were often irrelevant to the nation's most serious problems. Rather than taking active leadership of the nation's dramatic transformation, the American political system for nearly two decades after the end of Reconstruction was locked in a rigid stalemate—watching the remarkable changes that were occurring in the nation and doing little to affect them. The result was a set of problems and grievances that festered and grew without any natural outlet. And it was not surprising, under the circumstances, that in the 1890s the United States entered a period of national crisis.

THE POLITICS OF EQUILIBRIUM

To modern eyes, the nature of the American political system in the late nineteenth century appears in many ways paradoxical. The two political parties enjoyed a strength and stability during those years that neither was ever to know again. And yet the federal government, which the two parties were struggling to control, was doing relatively little of importance. In fact, most Americans in those years engaged in political activity not because of an interest in particular issues but because of broad regional, ethnic, or religious sentiments.

The Party System

The most striking feature of the late-nineteenth-century party system was its remarkable stability. From the end of Reconstruction until the late 1890s, the electorate was divided almost precisely evenly between the Republicans and the Democrats. Loyalties fluctuated almost not at all. Sixteen states were solidly and consistently Republican, and fourteen states (most of them in the South) were solidly and consistently Democratic. Only five states (the most important of them New York and Ohio) were usually in doubt, and their voters generally decided the results of national elections, often on the basis of voter turnout. The Republican Party captured the presidency in all but two of the elections of the era, but the party was not really as dominant as those victories suggest. In the five presidential elections beginning in 1876, the average popular-vote margin separating the Democratic and Republican candidates was 1.5 percent. The congressional balance was similarly stable, with the Republicans generally controlling the Senate and the Democrats generally controlling the House.

Electoral Stability

As striking as the balance between the parties was the intensity of public loyalty to them. In most of the country, Americans viewed their party affiliations with a passion and enthusiasm that is difficult for later generations to understand. Voter turnout in presidential elections between 1860 and 1900 averaged over 78 percent of all eligible voters (as compared with only about 50 percent in the 1980s and 1990s). Even in nonpresidential years, from 60 to 80 percent of the voters turned out to cast ballots for congressional and local candidates. Large groups of potential voters were disfranchised in these years: women in most states; almost all blacks and many poor whites in the South. But for adult white males outside the South, there were few franchise restrictions. The remarkable turnout represented a genuinely mass-based politics.

High Turnout

What explains this extraordinary loyalty to the two political parties? It was not, certainly, that the parties took distinct positions on important public issues. They did so rarely. Party loyalties reflected other factors. Region was perhaps the most important. To white southerners, loyalty to the Democratic Party was a matter of unquestioned faith. It was the vehicle by which they had triumphed over Reconstruction, the vehicle by which they preserved white supremacy. To many northerners, white and black, Republican loyalties were equally intense. To them, the party of Lincoln remained what it had been during the Civil War: a bulwark against slavery and treason.

Religious and ethnic differences also shaped party loyalties. The Democratic Party attracted most of the Catholic voters, most of the recent immigrants, and most of the poorer workers—groups that often overlapped. The Republican Party appealed to northern Protestants, citizens of old stock, and much of the middle class—groups that also had considerable overlap. Among the few substantive issues on which the parties took clearly different stands were matters connected with immigrants. Republicans tended to support measures restricting immigration and to favor temperance legislation, which many believed would help discipline immigrant communities. Catholics and immigrants viewed such proposals as assaults on them and their cultures and opposed them; the Democratic Party followed their lead.

Party identification, then, was usually more a reflection of cultural inclinations than a calculation of economic interest. Individuals might affiliate with a party because their parents had done so, or because it was the party of their region, their church, or their ethnic group. Most clung to their party loyalties with great persistence and passion.

Cultural Basis of Party Identification

The National Government

One reason the two parties managed to avoid substantive issues was that the federal government (and to some degree state and local governments as well) did relatively little. The government in Washington was responsible for delivering the mails, for maintaining a national military, for conducting foreign policy, and for collecting tariffs and taxes. It had few other responsibilities and few institutions with which it could have undertaken additional responsibilities even if it had chosen to do so.

There were significant exceptions. The federal government had been active for decades aiding and supporting the economic development of the nation. In the late nineteenth century, that took the form most prominently of giving tremendous subsidies to railroads, usually in the form of grants of federal land, to encourage them to extend their lines deeper into the heart of the nation. And as President Cleveland's intervention in the Pullman strike suggests, the government was also not averse to using its military and police power to protect capitalists from challenges from their workers.

In addition, from the end of the Civil War to the early twentieth century, the federal government administered a system of annual pensions for Union Civil War veterans who had retired from work and for their widows. At its peak, this pension system was making payments to a majority of the male citizens (black and white) of the North and to many women as well. Some reformers hoped to

Civil War Pension System | make the system permanent and universal; they pressured the government to create a system of old-age pensions for all Americans. But their efforts failed, in part because the Civil War pension system was awash in party patronage and corruption. Other reformers—believers in "good government"—saw elimination of the pension system as a way to fight graft, corruption, and party rule. When the Civil War generation died out, the pension system died with it.

In most other respects, however, the United States in the late nineteenth century was a society without a modern, national government. The most powerful national political institutions were the two political parties (and the bosses and machines that dominated them) and the federal courts. The national leaders of both parties were primarily concerned not with policy but with office—with winning elections and controlling patronage.

Presidents and Patronage

The power of party bosses had an important effect on the power of the presidency. The office had great symbolic importance, but its occupants were unable to do very much except distribute government appointments. A new president and his tiny staff had to make almost 100,000 appointments (most of them in the post office, the only really large government agency); and even in that function, presidents had limited latitude, since they had to avoid offending the various factions within their own parties.

Sometimes that proved impossible, as the presidency of Rutherford B. Hayes (1877–1881) demonstrated. By the

Stalwarts and Half-Breeds | end of his term, two groups—the Stalwarts, led by Roscoe Conkling of New York, and the Half-Breeds, captained by James G. Blaine of Maine—were competing for control of the Republican Party and threatening to split it. The dispute between the Stalwarts and the Half-Breeds was characteristic of the political battles of the era in having little basis in substance. Rhetorically, the Stalwarts favored traditional, professional machine politics, while the Half-Breeds favored reform. In fact, both groups were mainly interested in a larger share of the patronage pie. Hayes tried to satisfy both and ended up satisfying neither.

The battle over patronage overshadowed all else during Hayes's unhappy presidency. His one important substantive initiative—an effort to create a civil service system—attracted no support from either party. And his early announcement that he would not seek reelection only weakened him further. (His popularity with politicians in Washington was not enhanced by the unwillingness

PRESIDENT AND MRS. RUTHERFORD B. HAYES Hayes was one of a series of generally undistinguished late-nineteenth-century presidents whose subordination to the fiercely competitive party system left them with little room for independent leadership. This photograph captures the dignity and sobriety that Hayes and his wife sought to convey to the public. His wife was a temperance advocate and refused to serve alcoholic beverages in the White House, thereby earning the nickname "Lemonade Lucy." Hayes attracted less whimsical labels. Because of the disputed 1876 election that had elevated him to the presidency, critics referred to him throughout his term as "His Fraudulency." *(Library of Congress)*

of his wife, a temperance advocate widely known as "Lemonade Lucy," to permit alcoholic beverages to be served in the White House.) Hayes's presidency was a study in frustration.

The Republicans managed to retain the presidency in 1880 in part because they agreed on a ticket that included a Stalwart and a Half-Breed. After a long convention deadlock, they nominated James A. Garfield, a veteran congressman from Ohio and a Half-Breed, for president and Chester A. Arthur of New York, a Stalwart and Conkling henchman, for vice president. The Democrats nominated

General Winfield Scott Hancock, a minor Civil War commander with no national following. Benefiting from the end of the recession of 1879, Garfield won a decisive electoral victory, although his popular-vote margin was very thin. The Republicans also captured both houses of Congress.

Garfield began his presidency by trying to defy the Stalwarts in his appointments and by showing support for

Garfield Assassinated | civil service reform. He soon found himself embroiled in an ugly public quarrel with both Conkling and other Stalwarts. It was never resolved. On July 2, 1881, only four months after his inauguration, Garfield was shot twice while standing in the Washington railroad station by an apparently deranged gunman (and unsuccessful office seeker) who shouted, "I am a Stalwart and Arthur is president now!" Garfield lingered for nearly three months but finally died, a victim as much of inept medical treatment as of the wounds themselves.

Chester A. Arthur, who succeeded Garfield, had spent a political lifetime as a devoted, skilled, and open spoilsman and a close ally of Roscoe Conkling. But on becoming president, he tried—like Hayes and Garfield before

Pendleton Act | him—to follow an independent course and even to promote reform, aware no doubt that the Garfield assassination had to some degree discredited the traditional spoils system. To the dismay of the Stalwarts, Arthur kept most of Garfield's appointees in office and supported civil service reform. In 1883, Congress passed the first national civil service measure, the Pendleton Act, which required that some federal jobs be filled by competitive written examinations rather than by patronage. Relatively few offices fell under civil service at first, but its reach extended steadily so that by the mid-twentieth century most federal employees were civil servants.

Cleveland, Harrison, and the Tariff

In the unsavory election of 1884, the Republican candidate for president was Senator James G. Blaine of Maine—known to his adoring admirers as the "Plumed Knight"—but to thousands of other Americans as a symbol of seamy party politics. A group of disgruntled "liberal Republicans," known derisively by their critics as the "mugwumps," announced they would bolt the party and support an honest Democrat. Rising to the bait, the Democrats nominated Grover Cleveland, the reform governor of New York. He differed from Blaine on no substantive issues but had acquired a reputation as an enemy of corruption.

In a campaign filled with personal invective, what may have decided the election was the last-minute introduction of a religious controversy. Shortly before the election, a delegation of Protestant ministers called on Blaine in New York City; their spokesman, Dr. Samuel Burchard,

referred to the Democrats as the party of "rum, Romanism, and rebellion." Blaine was slow to repudiate Burchard's indiscretion, and Democrats

quickly spread the news that | *Election of 1884*

Blaine had tolerated a slander on the Catholic Church. Cleveland's narrow victory was probably a result of an unusually heavy Catholic vote for the Democrats in New York. Cleveland won 219 electoral votes to Blaine's 182; his popular margin was only 23,000.

Grover Cleveland was respected, if not often liked, for his stern and righteous opposition to politicians, grafters, pressure groups, and Tammany Hall. He had become famous as the "veto governor," as an official who was not afraid to say no. He was the embodiment of an era in which few Americans believed the federal government could, or should, do very much. Cleveland had always doubted the wisdom of protective tariffs (taxes on imported goods designed to protect domestic producers). The existing high rates, he believed, were responsible for the annual surplus in federal revenues, which was tempting Congress to pass "reckless" and "extravagant" legislation, which he frequently vetoed. In December 1887, therefore, he asked Congress to reduce the tariff rates. Democrats in the House approved a tariff reduction, but Senate Republicans defiantly passed a bill of their own actually raising the rates. The resulting deadlock made the tariff an issue in the election of 1888.

The Democrats renominated Cleveland and supported tariff reductions. The Republicans settled on former senator Benjamin Harrison of Indiana, who was obscure but respectable (and the grandson of President William Henry Harrison); and they endorsed protection. The campaign was the first since the Civil War to involve a clear question of economic difference between the parties. It was also one of the most corrupt (and one of the closest) elections in American history. Harrison won an electoral majority of 233 to 168, but Cleveland's popular vote exceeded Harrison's by 100,000.

New Public Issues

Benjamin Harrison's record as president was little more substantial than that of his grandfather, who had died a month after taking office. Harrison had few visible convictions, and he made no effort to influence Congress. And yet during Harrison's passive administration, public opinion was beginning to force the government to confront some of the pressing social and economic issues of the day. Most notably, perhaps, sentiment was rising in favor of legislation to curb the power of trusts.

By the mid-1880s, fifteen western and southern states had adopted laws prohibiting combinations that restrained competition. But corporations found it easy to escape limitations by incorporating in states such as New Jersey and Delaware that offered them special privileges. If antitrust legislation was to be effective, its supporters

THE TOURNAMENT OF TO-DAY.—A SET-TO BETWEEN LABOR AND MONOPOLY.

LABOR AND MONOPOLY This 1883 cartoon appeared in *Puck*, a magazine popular for its satirical treatment of American politics. It expresses a common sentiment of the Populists and many others: that ordinary men and women (portrayed here by the pathetic figure of "labor" and by the grim members of the audience) were almost hopelessly overmatched by the power of corporate monopolies. The knight's shield, labeled "corruption of the legislature," and his spear, labeled "subsidized press," make clear that—in the view of the cartoonist at least— corporations had many allies in their effort to oppress workers. *(Culver Pictures, Inc.)*

believed, it would have to come from the national government. Responding to growing popular demands, both houses of Congress passed the Sherman Antitrust Act

Sherman Antitrust Act

in July 1890, almost without dissent. Most members of Congress saw the act as a largely symbolic measure, one that would help deflect public criticism but was not likely to have any real effect on corporate power. For over a decade after its passage, the Sherman Act—indifferently enforced and steadily weakened by the courts—had virtually no impact. As of 1901, the Justice Department had instituted many antitrust suits against unions, but only fourteen against business combinations; there had been few convictions.

The Republicans were more interested, however, in the issue they believed had won them the 1888 election: the tariff. Representative William McKinley of Ohio and Senator Nelson W. Aldrich of Rhode Island drafted the

highest protective measure ever proposed to Congress. Known as the McKinley Tariff, it became law in October 1890. But Republican leaders apparently misinterpreted public sentiment, for the party suffered a stunning reversal in

McKinley Tariff

the 1890 congressional election. The Republicans' substantial Senate majority was slashed to 8; in the House, the party retained only 88 of the 323 seats. McKinley himself was among those who went down in defeat. Nor were the Republicans able to recover in the course of the next two years. In the presidential election of 1892, Benjamin Harrison once again supported protection; Grover Cleveland, renominated by the Democrats, once again opposed it. A new third party, the People's Party, with James B. Weaver as its candidate, advocated more substantial economic reform. Cleveland won 277 electoral votes to Harrison's 145 and had a popular margin of 380,000. Weaver showed some significant strength, but still ran far

SHACKLED BY THE TARIFF This 1894 cartoon by the political satirist Louis Dalrymple portrays an unhappy Uncle Sam bound hand and foot by the McKinley Tariff and by what tariff opponents considered a closely related evil—monopoly. Members of the Senate are portrayed as tools of the various industries and special interests protected by the tariff. The caption, "A Senate for Revenue Only," is a parody of the anti-tariff rallying cry, "A tariff for revenue only," meaning that duties should be designed only to raise money for the government, not to stop imports of particular goods to protect domestic industries. *(The Granger Collection)*

behind. For the first time since 1878, the Democrats won a majority of both houses of Congress.

The policies of Cleveland's second term were much like those of his first—devoted to minimal government and hostile to active efforts to deal with social or economic problems. Again, he supported a tariff reduction, which the House approved but the Senate weakened. Cleveland denounced the result but allowed it to become law as the Wilson-Gorman Tariff. It included only a few, very modest reductions.

THE STATE, WAR, AND NAVY BUILDING This sprawling Victorian office building was one of the largest in Washington when it was constructed shortly after the Civil War. It housed the State, War, and Navy Departments until not long before World War II. It suggests both the degree to which the federal government was growing in the late nineteenth century and, more importantly, the degree to which it remained a tiny entity compared to what it would later become. This building, which stands directly next door to the White House, today houses a part (but only a part) of the president's staff. *(Library of Congress)*

But public pressure was growing in the 1880s for other reforms, among them regulation of the railroads. Farm organizations in the Midwest (most notably the Grangers) had persuaded several state legislatures to pass regulatory legislation in the early 1870s. But in 1886, the Supreme Court—in *Wabash, St. Louis, and Pacific Railway Co.* v. *Illinois,* known as the *Wabash* case—ruled one of the Granger Laws in Illinois unconstitutional. According to the Court, the law was an attempt to control interstate commerce and thus infringed on the exclusive power of Congress. Later, the courts limited the powers of the states to regulate commerce even within their own boundaries.

Effective railroad regulation, it was now clear, could come only from the federal government. Congress grudg-

Interstate Commerce Act

ingly responded to public pressure in 1887 with the Interstate Commerce Act, which banned discrimination in rates between long and short hauls, required that railroads publish their rate schedules and file them with the government, and declared that all interstate rail rates must be "reasonable and just"—although the act did not define what that meant. A five-person agency, the Interstate Commerce Commission (ICC), was to administer the act. But it had to rely on the courts to enforce its rulings. For almost twenty years after its passage, the Interstate Commerce Act—which was, like the Sherman Act, haphazardly enforced and narrowly interpreted by the courts—was without much practical effect.

"THE GRANGE AWAKENING THE SLEEPERS" This 1873 cartoon illustrates the way the Grange embraced many of the same concerns that the Farmers' Alliances and their People's Party later expressed. A farmer is attempting to arouse passive citizens (lying in place of the "sleepers," or cross ties on railroad tracks), who are about to be crushed by a train. The cars bear the names of the costs of the railroads' domination of the agrarian economy. *(Culver Pictures, Inc.)*

THE AGRARIAN REVOLT

No group watched the performance of the federal government in the 1880s with more dismay than American farmers. Isolated from the urban-industrial society that was beginning to dominate national life, suffering from a long economic decline, afflicted with a painful sense of obsolescence, rural Americans were keenly aware of the problems of the modern economy and particularly eager for government assistance in dealing with them. The result of their frustrations was the emergence of one of the most powerful movements of political protest in American history: what became known as populism.

The Grangers

According to popular myth, American farmers were the most individualistic of citizens, the least likely to join together in a cooperative economic or political movement. In reality, however, farmers had been making efforts to organize for many decades. There had been occasional cooperative movements in the first decades of the nineteenth century, but the first major farm organization appeared in the 1860s: the Grange. It was less a movement of protest than a social and self-help association. The depression of 1873 turned it into an agency of political change.

The Grange had its origins shortly after the Civil War in a tour through the South by a minor Agriculture Department official, Oliver H. Kelley. Kelley was appalled by what he considered the isolation and drabness of rural life, and in 1867 he left the government and, with other department em-

Origins

ployees, founded the National Grange of the Patrons of Husbandry, to which he devoted years of labor as secretary and from which emerged a network of local organizations. At first, the Granges defined their purposes modestly. They attempted to bring farmers together to learn new scientific agricultural techniques—to keep farming "in step with the music of the age." The Granges also hoped to create a feeling of community, to relieve the loneliness of rural life. An elaborate system of initiation and ritual and a strict code of secrecy lent to the organization many of the trappings of urban fraternal organizations.

The Grange grew slowly for a time. But when the depression of 1873 caused a major decline in farm prices, membership rapidly increased. By 1875, the Grange claimed over 800,000 members and 20,000 local lodges; it had chapters in almost every state but was strongest, naturally, in the great staple-producing regions of the South and the Midwest.

As membership grew, the lodges in the Midwest began to focus less on the social benefits of organization and more on the economic possibilities. They attempted to organize marketing cooperatives to allow farmers to circumvent the hated middlemen. And they urged cooperative political action to curb the monopolistic practices

Economic Grievances of the railroads and warehouses. Throughout the Midwest on Independence Day 1873, embittered farmers assembled to hear Granger orators read "The Farmers' Declaration of Independence," which proclaimed that the time had come for farmers, "suffering from long continued systems of oppression and abuse, to rouse themselves from an apathetic indifference to their own interests." The declaration also vowed that farmers would use "all lawful and peaceful means to free [themselves] from the tyranny of monopoly."

The Grangers set up cooperative stores, creameries, elevators, warehouses, insurance companies, and factories that produced machines, stoves, and other items. Some 400 enterprises were in operation at the height of the movement, and some of them forged lucrative relationships with existing businesses. One corporation emerged specifically to meet the needs of the Grangers: the first mail-order business, Montgomery Ward and Company, founded in 1872. Eventually, however, most of the Grange enterprises failed, both because of the inexperience of their operators and because of the opposition of the middlemen whose businesses they were challenging.

The Grangers also worked to elect state legislators pledged to their program. Usually they operated through the existing parties, although occasionally they ran candidates under such independent party labels as "Antimonopoly" and "Reform." At their

Political Program peak, they managed to gain control of the legislatures in most of the midwestern states. Their purpose, openly and angrily announced, was to subject the railroads to government controls. The Granger laws of the early 1870s, by which many states imposed strict regulations on railroad rates and practices, seemed for a time to vindicate the predictions of those farmers who claimed that their new organization foretold a permanent change in the political status of agriculture.

But the new regulations were soon destroyed by the courts. That defeat, combined with the political inexperience of many Grange leaders and, above all, the temporary return of agricultural prosperity in the late 1870s, produced a dramatic decline in the power of the association. Some of the Granger cooperatives survived as effective economic vehicles for many years, but the movement as a whole dwindled rapidly. By 1880, its membership had shrunk to 100,000.

The Farmers' Alliances

The successor to the Grange as the leading vehicle of agrarian protest began to emerge even before the Granger movement had faded. As early as 1875, farmers in parts of

A POPULIST GATHERING Populism was a response to real economic and political grievances. But like most political movements of its time, it was also important as a cultural experience. For farmers in sparsely settled regions in particular, it provided an antidote to isolation and loneliness. This gathering of Populist farmers in Dickinson County, Kansas, shows how the political purposes of the movement were tightly bound up with its social purposes. *(Kansas State Historical Society)*

the South (most notably in Texas) were banding together in so-called Farmers' Alliances. By 1880, the Southern Alliance had more than 4 million members; and a comparable Northwestern Alliance was taking root in the plains states and the Midwest and developing ties with its southern counterpart.

Like the Granges, the Alliances were principally concerned with local problems. They formed cooperatives and other marketing mechanisms. They established stores, banks, processing plants, and other facilities for their members—to free them from dependence on the hated "furnishing merchants" who kept so many farmers in debt. Some Alliance leaders, however, also saw the movement in larger terms: as an effort to build a society in which economic competition might give way to cooperation. They did not advocate rigid collectivism; instead, they argued for a sense of mutual, neighborly responsibility that would enable farmers to resist oppressive outside forces. Alliance lecturers traveled throughout rural areas lambasting the concentration of power in great corporations and financial institutions and promoting cooperation as an alternative economic system.

The Alliances were notable, too, for the prominent role women played within them. From the beginning, women were full voting members in most local Alliances. Many

Mary Lease

held offices and served as lecturers. A few, most notably Mary E. Lease, went on to become fiery Populist orators. (Lease was famous for urging farmers to "raise less corn and more hell.") Most others emphasized issues of particular concern to women, especially temperance. Like women in urban areas concerned about the impact of drinking on family life, agrarian women argued that sobriety was a key to stability in rural society.

Although the Alliances quickly became far more widespread than the Granges had ever been, they suffered from similar problems. Their cooperatives did not always work well, partly because the market forces operating against them were sometimes too strong to be overcome, partly because the cooperatives themselves were often mismanaged. These economic frustrations helped push the movement into a new phase at the end of the 1880s: the creation of a national political organization.

In 1889, the Southern and Northwestern Alliances, despite continuing differences between them, agreed to a loose merger. The next year the Alliances held a national convention at Ocala, Florida, and issued the so-called Ocala Demands, which were, in effect, a party platform. In the 1890 off-year elections, candidates supported by the Alliances won partial or complete control of the legislatures in twelve states. They also won six governorships, three seats in the U.S. Senate, and approximately fifty in the U.S. House of Representatives. Many of the successful Alliance candidates were simply Democrats who had benefited—often passively—from Alliance endorsements. But dissident farmers drew enough encouragement from the results to

MARY E. LEASE The fiery Populist orator Mary E. Lease was a fixture on the Alliance lecture circuit in the 1890s. She made some 160 speeches in 1890 alone. Her critics called her the "Kansas Pythoness," but she was popular among populist farmers with her denunciations of banks, railroads, and "middlemen," and her famous advice to "raise less corn and more hell." *(Brown Brothers)*

contemplate further political action, including forming a party of their own.

Sentiment for a third party was strongest among the members of the Northwestern Alliance. But several southern leaders supported the ideas as well—among them

Birth of the People's Party

Tom Watson of Georgia, the only southern congressman elected in 1890 openly to identify with the Alliance, and Leonidas L. Polk of North Carolina, perhaps the ablest mind in the movement. Alliance leaders discussed plans for a third party at meetings in Cincinnati in May 1891 and St. Louis in February 1892—meetings attended by many Northwestern Alliance members, a smaller but still significant number of Southern Alliance leaders, and representatives of the fading Knights of Labor, whom some farm leaders hoped to bring into the coalition. Then, in July 1892, 1,300 exultant delegates poured into Omaha, Nebraska, to proclaim the creation of the new party, approve an official set of principles, and nominate candidates for the presidency and vice presidency. The new organization's official name was the People's Party, but its members were more commonly known as Populists.

The election of 1892 demonstrated the potential power of the new movement. The Populist presidential candidate

THE CHAUTAUQUAS

The Populist movement of the 1880s and 1890s revealed, in addition to a wide range of economic, political, and social grievances among American farmers, a tremendous thirst for knowledge. Men and women flocked by the hundreds, even the thousands, to hear speeches and discussions by the traveling lecturers of the Alliance movement. For many farmers, the Alliance lectures were among their only contacts with the wider world—their only access to information about events and ideas outside their own communities.

But it was not only Populist farmers who hungered for information and education in the late nineteenth and early twentieth centuries. Men and women throughout the United States were as eager for knowledge as were the people a generation earlier who had flocked to the Lyceum movement (see pp. 364–365). Out of that hunger emerged a wide range of systems for bringing lectures to otherwise isolated communities. The most famous of them were known as the Chautauquas.

The Chautauquas began in the summer of 1874, when two enterprising men in Chautauqua Lakes, New York, established a series of what they called "Assemblies" for the instruction of Sunday school teachers. A year later, the organizers persuaded President Ulysses S. Grant to attend an Assembly; his appearance brought them enormous publicity and helped ensure their success. Within a few years, the Chautauqua Assembly had expanded to include lectures on literary, scientific, theological, and practical subjects and was attracting ever larger audiences for one- or two-week "schools" throughout much of the year. In 1883, the New York State legislature granted the Assemblies a charter and gave them the name "The Chautauqua University."

So successful (and profitable) were the Chautauqua assemblies that scores of towns and villages began establishing lecture series of their own—"Little Chatauquas"—throughout the Midwest. Finally, in 1904, a Chicago promoter began organizing traveling programs under tents and sending them on tours through rural areas across the United States—to over 8,000 different communities in the space of one year at the peak of their popularity.

From 1904 through the mid-1920s, these "traveling Chautauquas" attracted

THE HALL OF CHRIST, CHAUTAUQUA
This ornate meeting hall, very different from the rustic structures of the early days of Chautauqua, was constructed after the organization became prosperous and nationally influential. Its name recalls the Christian origins of the organization and the religious character of many of its activities still. *(Brown Brothers)*

enormous crowds and great excitement almost everywhere they went. For rural men and women in particular, the Chautauquas were both sources of knowledge and great entertainments. A Chautauqua was often the only large popular amusement to visit a community in the course of a year. On the day of a Chautauqua lecture, roads were sometimes clogged for miles in every direction with buggies

was James B. Weaver of Iowa, a former Greenbacker who received the nomination after the death of Leonidas Polk, the early favorite. Weaver polled more than 1 million votes, 8.5 percent of the total, and carried six mountain and plains states for 22 electoral votes. Nearly 1,500 Populist candidates won election to seats in state legislatures. The party elected three governors, five senators, and ten congressmen. It could also claim the support of many Republicans and Democrats in Congress who had been elected by appealing to populist sentiment.

The Populist Constituency

The Populists dreamed of creating a broad political coalition that included many groups. But populism always appealed principally to farmers, and particularly to small farmers with little long-range economic security—people whose operations were only minimally mechanized, if at all, who relied on one crop, and who had access only to limited and unsatisfactory mechanisms of credit. In the Midwest, the Populists were usually family farmers struggling to hold on to their land (or to get it back if they had

lost it). In the South, there were many modest landowners too, but in addition there were significant numbers of sharecroppers and tenant farmers. Whatever their differences, however, most Populists had at least one thing in common: they were engaged in a type of farming that was becoming less viable in the face of new, mechanized, diversified, and consolidated commercial agriculture.

There is evidence, too, that Populists tended to be not only economically but also culturally marginal, that the movement appealed above all to geographically isolated farmers who felt cut off from the mainstream of national life and resented their isolation. Populism gave such people an outlet for their grievances; it also provided them with a social experience, a sense of belonging to a community that they had previously lacked.

The Populists were also notable for the groups they failed to attract. There were energetic efforts to include labor within the coalition. Representatives of the Knights of Labor attended early organizational meetings; the new party added a labor plank to its platform—calling for shorter hours for workers and restrictions on immigration, and denouncing the use of private detective agencies as

BRYAN AT CHAUTAUQUA William Jennings Bryan, the most famous orator of the early twentieth century, was a fixture at Chautauqua meetings, not only at the original Chautauqua in New York, depicted here, but in the traveling and tented Chautauquas that spread across the country. *(Brown Brothers)*

Chautauqua speakers were drawn from many walks of life, but they included some of the greatest figures of the age: William Jennings Bryan, William McKinley, Theodore Roosevelt, Booker T. Washington, Eugene V. Debs, and many others. The Chautauquas themselves also made some speakers rich and famous. The Philadelphia minister Russell Conwell, for example, made a great name (and a great fortune) with his famous lecture "Acres of Diamond," which he gave thousands of times over the course of several decades, preaching a simple and attractive message: "Get rich . . . for money is power and power ought to be in the hands of good people." Conwell's sermon was characteristic of one kind of popular Chautauqua event: lectures that stressed self-improvement. But equally popular were discussions of religion, health, current public issues, and politics. The Chautauqua circuit was one of the best ways for a reformer to reach large numbers of people and spread a message, which was one reason that so many progressive leaders and feminist reformers were eager to join it. It was, for a time, one of the nation's most powerful forms of national communication, and one of its most self-consciously serious. Its connections with the earnest lakefront "university" in New York pushed the Chautauqua circuit to keep its programs rooted in the original Assembly's desire for education and enlightenment, and not just entertainment. It reflected a continuing expression of the hunger for knowledge and uplift that had resurfaced repeatedly throughout American history. Theodore Roosevelt once called the Chautauqua movement "the most American thing in America."

The traveling Chautauquas declined during the 1920s and vanished altogether in the 1930s—victims of radio, movies, and the increased ease of travel in the age of the automobile; of the spread of public education into rural areas; and of the reckless overexpansion of the enterprise by ambitious organizers. But the original Chautauqua Assembly in upstate New York survived, although in much-diminished form, and exists today as a resort—which continues to offer lectures and other educational events to its small but dedicated clientele.

and, later, automobiles transporting farm families dressed in their best clothes, carrying picnic baskets, straining excitedly to see the tents and the posters and the crowds in the distance.

---

strikebreakers in labor disputes. On the whole, however, Populism never attracted significant labor support in part because the economic interests of labor and the interests of farmers were often at odds.

One exception was the Rocky Mountain states, where the Populists did have some significant success in attracting miners to their cause. They did so partly because local Populist leaders supported a broader platform than the national party embraced. In particular, *"Free Silver"* they endorsed a demand that the national party only later accepted: "free silver," the idea of permitting silver to become, along with gold, the basis of the currency so as to expand the money supply. In Colorado, Idaho, Nevada, and other areas of the Far West where silver mining was an important activity, the Populist constituency contained more working-class people and more immigrants than it did elsewhere; and the People's Party enjoyed substantial, if temporary, success there.

In the South (and to a lesser degree elsewhere), white Populists struggled with the question of accepting African Americans into the party. Their numbers and poverty made black farmers possibly valuable allies. And indeed there was an important black component to the movement—a network of "Colored Alliances" that by 1890 numbered over one and a quarter million members. But most white Populists were *"Colored Alliances"* willing to accept the assistance of African Americans only as long as it was clear that whites would remain indisputably in control. When southern conservatives began to attack the Populists for undermining white supremacy, the interracial character of the movement quickly faded.

Most of the Populist leaders were members of the rural middle class: professional people, editors and lawyers, or longtime politicians and agitators. Few were themselves marginal farmers. Almost all leaders were, like most of their constituents, Protestants. But beyond these basic characteristics there were wide variations. Some Populist leaders were somber, serious theoreticians; others were semihysterical rabble-rousers. In the South, in particular, Populism produced the first generation of what was to become a distinctive and enduring political breed—the "southern demagogue." Tom Watson in Georgia, Jeff Davis in Arkansas, and others attracted widespread popular support by arousing

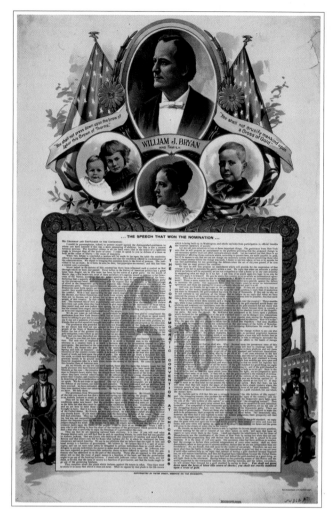

THE CULT OF BRYAN After his famous "Cross of Gold" speech at the 1896 Democratic convention, Bryan became a figure of almost cultish importance to his many followers. This campaign poster presents icons of Bryan's sudden fame: the text of his convention speech, pictures of his young family, and the slogan of the Free Silver movement that Bryan now led: 16 to 1.

the resentment of poor southerners against the entrenched planter aristocracy (often known as the "Bourbons," after the traditional royal family of France).

There were similarly flamboyant leaders in the Midwest: "Sockless" Jerry Simpson of Kansas, for example, and Ignatius Donnelly of Minnesota. Donnelly, in particular, seemed to exemplify the divided character of the movement: sincere idealism combined with crassness and opportunism. A committed, principled man who spoke eloquently on behalf of Populist ideals and appeared sincerely to believe in them, Donnelly was also at times something of a charlatan. As a member of Congress, he compiled a shabby legislative record marked, among other things, by a series of seamy, secret deals with railroad companies.

Populist Ideas

The reform program of the Populists was spelled out first in the Ocala Demands of 1890 and then, even more clearly, in the Omaha platform of 1892. It proposed a system of

"subtreasuries," which would and strengthen the cooperatives with which both the Grangers and Alliances had been experimenting for years. The government would establish a network of warehouses, where farmers could deposit their crops. Using those crops as collateral, growers could then borrow money from the government at low rates of interest and wait for the price of their goods to go up before selling them. In addition, the Populists called for the abolition of national banks, which they believed were dangerous institutions of concentrated power; the end of absentee ownership of land; the direct election of United States senators (which would weaken the power of conservative state legislatures); and other devices to improve the ability of the people to influence the political process. They called as well for regulation and (after 1892) government ownership of railroads, telephones, and telegraphs. And they demanded a system of government-operated postal savings banks, a graduated income tax, and the inflation of the currency. Eventually, the party as a whole embraced (with varying degrees of enthusiasm) the demand of its western members for the remonetization of silver.

Populist Platform

Some Populists were openly anti-Semitic, pointing to the Jews as leaders of the obscure financial forces attempting to enslave them. Others were anti-intellectual, anti-eastern, and anti-urban. A few of the leading Populists gave an impression of personal failure, brilliant instability, and brooding communion with mystic forces. Ignatius Donnelly, for example, wrote one book locating the lost isle of Atlantis, another claiming that Bacon had written Shakespeare's plays, and still another—*Caesar's Column* (1891)—presenting an almost lunatic vision of bloody revolution and the creation of a populist utopia. Tom Watson, once a champion of interracial harmony, ended his career baiting blacks and Jews.

Yet the occasional bigotry of some Populists should not be allowed to dominate the image of Populism as a whole, which was a serious and usually responsible effort to find solutions to real problems. Populists emphatically rejected the laissez-faire orthodoxies of their time, the idea that the rights of ownership are absolute. They raised one of the most overt and powerful challenges of the era to the direction in which American industrial capitalism was moving. Populism was not a challenge to industrialization or to capitalism itself, but a response to what the Populists considered the brutal and chaotic way in which the economy was developing. Progress and growth should continue, they urged, but should be more strictly defined by the needs of individuals and communities.

Populism's Ideological Challenge

THE CRISIS OF THE 1890s

The agrarian protest was only one of many indications of the national political crisis emerging in the 1890s. There was a severe depression, which began in

TAKING ARMS AGAINST THE POPULISTS Kansas was a Populist stronghold in the 1890s, but the new party faced powerful challenges. In 1893 state Republicans disputed an election that the Populists believed had given them control of the legislature. When the Populists occupied the statehouse, Republicans armed themselves, drove out the Populists, and seized control of the state government. Republican members of the legislature pose here with their weapons in a photograph perhaps intended as a warning to any Populists inclined to challenge them. *(Kansas State Historical Society)*

1893. There was widespread labor unrest and violence, culminating in the tumultuous strikes of 1894. There was the continuing failure of either major party to respond to the growing distress. And there was the rigid conservatism of Grover Cleveland, who took office for the second time just at the moment that the economy collapsed. Out of this growing sense of crisis came some of the most heated political battles in American history, culminating in the dramatic campaign of 1896, on which, many Americans came to believe, the future of the nation hung.

The Panic of 1893

The Panic of 1893 precipitated the most severe depression the nation had yet experienced. It began in March 1893, when the Philadelphia and Reading Railroad, unable to meet payments on loans it had secured from British banks, declared bankruptcy. Two months later, the National Cordage Company (a new corporation that was trying unsuccessfully to establish itself as the dominant force in its industry) failed as well. Together, the two corporate failures triggered a collapse of the stock market. And since many of the major New York banks were heavy investors in the market, a wave of bank failures soon began. That caused a contraction of credit, which meant that

many of the new, aggressive businesses that had recently begun operations soon went bankrupt because they were unable to secure the loans they needed.

There were other, longer-range causes of the financial collapse. Depressed prices in agriculture since 1887 had weakened the purchasing power of farmers, the largest group in the population. Depression conditions that had begun earlier in Europe were resulting in a loss of American markets abroad and a withdrawal by foreign investors of gold invested in the United States. Railroads and other major industries had expanded too rapidly, well beyond market demand. The depression reflected the degree to which the American economy was now interconnected, the degree to which failures in one area affected all other areas. And the depression showed how dependent the economy was on the health of the railroads, which remained the nation's most powerful corporate and financial institutions. When the railroads suffered, as they did beginning in 1893, everything suffered.

Overexpansion and Weak Demand

Once the panic began, its effects spread with startling speed. Within six months, more than 8,000 businesses, 156 railroads, and 400 banks failed. Already low agricultural prices tumbled further. Up to 1 million workers,

POPULISM

American history offers few examples of successful popular movements operating outside the two major parties. Perhaps that is why Populism, which in its brief, meteoric life became one of the few such phenomena to gain real national influence, has attracted particular attention from historians. It has also produced deep disagreements among them. Scholars have differed in many ways in their interpretations of Populism, but at the heart of most such disagreements have been disparate views of the value of popular, insurgent politics. Some historians have harbored a basic mistrust of such mass uprisings and have therefore viewed the Populists with suspicion and hostility. Others have viewed such insurgency approvingly, as evidence of

(Kansas State Historical Society)

a healthy resistance to oppression and exploitation; and to them, the Populists have appeared as essentially admirable, democratic activists.

This latter view was the basis of the first, and for many years the only, general history of Populism: John D. Hicks's *The Populist Revolt* (1931). Rejecting the then prevailing view of the Populists as misguided and unruly radicals, Hicks described them as people reacting rationally and progressively to economic misfortune. Hicks was writing in an era in which the ideas of Frederick Jackson Turner were dominating historical studies, and he brought to his analysis of populism a strong emphasis on regionalism. Populists, he argued, were part of the democratic West, resisting pressures from the more aristocratic East. (He explained southern Populism by describing the South as an "economic frontier" region—not newly settled like the West, but prey to many of the same pressures and misfortunes.) The Populists, Hicks suggested, were aware of the harsh, even brutal, impact of eastern industrial growth on rural society. They were proposing reforms that would limit the oppressive power of the new financial titans and restore a measure of control to the farmers. Populism was, he wrote, "the last phase of a long and perhaps a losing struggle—the struggle to save agricultural America from the devouring jaws of industrial America." A losing

struggle, perhaps, but not a vain one; for many of the reforms the Populists advocated, Hicks implied, became the basis of later progressive legislation.

This generally approving view of Populism prevailed among historians for more than two decades, amplified in particular by C. Vann Woodward, whose *Origins of the New South* (1951) and *The Strange Career of Jim Crow* (1955) portrayed southern Populism as a challenge to the stifling power of old elites and even, at times, to at least some elements of white supremacy. But Woodward was not typical of most scholars viewing Populism in the early 1950s. For others, the memory of European fascism and uneasiness about contemporary communism combined to create a general hostility among scholars toward mass popular politics; and a harsh new view of the Populist movement appeared in a work by one of the nation's leading historians. Richard Hofstadter, in *The Age of Reform* (1955), admitted that Populism embraced some progressive ideas and advocated some sensible reforms. But the bulk of his effort was devoted to exposing both the "soft" and the "dark" sides of the movement.

Populism was "soft," he claimed, because it rested on a nostalgic and unrealistic myth, because it romanticized the nation's agrarian past and refused to confront the realities of modern life. Farmers, he argued, were themselves fully committed to the values of the

---

20 percent of the labor force, lost their jobs—the highest level of unemployment in American history to that point, a level comparable to that of the Great Depression of the 1930s. The leading financial newspaper of the time declared in the summer of 1893: "The month of August will long remain memorable in our industrial history. Never before has there been such a sudden and striking cessation of industrial activity. Nor is any section of the country exempt from the paralysis." The depression was unprecedented not only in its severity but also in its persistence. Although there was slight improvement beginning in 1895, prosperity did not fully return until 1901.

The suffering the depression caused naturally produced social unrest, especially among the enormous numbers of unemployed workers. In 1894, Jacob S. Coxey, an Ohio

businessman and Populist, began advocating a massive public works program to create jobs for the unemployed and an inflation of the currency. When it became clear that his *"Coxey's Army"* proposals were making no progress in Congress, Coxey announced that he would "send a petition to Washington with boots on"—a march of the unemployed to the capital to present their demands to the government. "Coxey's Army," as it was known, numbered only about 500 when it reached Washington, after having marched on foot from Masillon, Ohio. Armed police barred them from the Capitol and arrested Coxey (who was later convicted—of walking on the grass). He and his followers were herded into camps because their presence supposedly endangered public health. Congress took no action on their demands.

capitalist system they claimed to abhor. And Populism was "dark," he argued, because it was permeated with bigotry and ignorance. Populists, he claimed, revealed anti-Semitic tendencies, and they displayed animosity toward intellectuals, easterners, and urbanites as well.

Almost immediately, historians more favorably disposed toward mass politics in general, and Populism in particular, began to challenge what became known as the "Hofstadter thesis." Norman Pollack argued in a 1962 study, *The Populist Response to Industrial America,* and in a number of articles that the agrarian revolt had rested not on nostalgic, romantic concepts but on a sophisticated, farsighted, and even radical vision of reform—one that recognized, and even welcomed, the realities of an industrial economy, but that sought to make that economy more equitable and democratic by challenging many of the premises of capitalism. Walter T. K. Nugent, in *Tolerant Populists* (1963), argued—as his title implies—that the Populists in Kansas were far from bigoted, that they not only tolerated but welcomed Jews and other minorities into their party, and that they offered a practical, sensible program.

Not until 1976, however, did a comprehensive study of Populism emerge that could rival Hicks and Hofstadter in influence. Lawrence Goodwyn, in *Democratic Promise* (and in an abridged version of the same work, *The Populist Moment,* published in 1978), described the Populists as members of a "cooperative crusade," battling against the "coercive potential of the emerging corporate state." Populists were more than the nostalgic bigots Hofstadter described, more even than the progressive reformers portrayed by Hicks. They offered a vision of truly radical change, widely disseminated through what Goodwyn called a "movement culture." They advocated an intelligent, and above all a democratic, alternative to the inequities of modern capitalism.

At the same time that historians were debating the question of what Populism meant, they were also arguing over who the Populists were. Hicks, Hofstadter, and Goodwyn disagreed on many things, but they shared a general view of the Populists as victims of economic distress—usually one-crop farmers in economically marginal agricultural regions victimized by drought and debt. Other scholars, however, have suggested that the problem of identifying the Populists is more complex. Sheldon Hackney, in *Populism to Progressivism in Alabama* (1969), argued that the Populists were not only economically troubled but socially rootless, "only tenuously connected to society by economic function, by personal relationships, by stable community membership, by political participation, or by psychological identification with the South's distinctive myths." Peter Argersinger, Stanley Parsons, James Turner, and others have similarly suggested that Populists were characterized by a form of social and even geographical isolation. Steven Hahn's 1983 study *The Roots of Southern Populism* identified poor white farmers in the "upcountry" as the core of populist activity in Georgia; and he argued that they were reacting not simply to the psychic distress of being "left behind," but also to a real economic threat to their way of life—to the encroachments of a new commercial order of which they had never been and could never be a part.

Finally, there has been continuing debate over the legacy of Populism. Michael Kazin, in *The Populist Persuasion* (1994), is one of a number of scholars (and others) who have argued that a Populist tradition has survived throughout much of American history, and into our own time, influencing movements as disparate as those led by Huey Long in the 1930s, both the New Left and George Wallace in the 1960s, and Ross Perot in the 1990s. Others have maintained that the term "populism" has been used (and misused) so widely as to have become virtually meaningless, that its only real value is in reference to the agrarian insurgents of the 1890s, who first gave meaning to the word in America.

There were many signs of union unrest as well during the decade—the Homestead and Pullman strikes, for example. (See above, pp. 494–495.) To many middle-class Americans, the labor turmoil was a sign of a dangerous instability, even perhaps a revolution. Labor radicalism—some of it real, more of it imagined by the frightened middle class—was of persistent concern to much of the public, heightening the general sense of crisis.

The Silver Question

The financial panic weakened the government's monetary system. President Cleveland was one of many people who believed that the instability of the currency was the primary cause of the depression. The "money question," therefore, became the basis for some of the most dramatic political conflicts of the era.

The currency issue is a complicated and confusing one, and later generations have often had difficulty understanding the enormous passions the controversy aroused. The heart of the debate was over what would form the basis of the dollar, what would lie behind it and give it value. Today, the value of the dollar rests on little more than public confidence in the government. But in the nineteenth century, many people believed that currency was worthless if there was not something concrete behind it—precious metal (specie), which holders of paper money could collect if they presented their currency to a bank or to the Treasury.

COXEY'S ARMY Jacob S. Coxey leads his "army" of unemployed men through the town of Allegheny, Pennsylvania, in 1894, en route to Washington, where he hoped to pressure Congress to approve his plans for a massive public works program to put people back to work. *(Culver Pictures, Inc.)*

During most of its existence as a nation, the United States had recognized two metals—gold and silver—as a basis for the dollar, a situation known as "bimetallism." In the 1870s, however, that had changed. The official ratio of the value of silver to the value of gold for purposes of creating currency (the "mint ratio") was 16 to 1: sixteen ounces of silver equaled one ounce of gold. But the actual commercial value of silver (the "market ratio") was much higher than that. Owners of silver could get more by selling it for manufacture into jewelry and other objects than they could by taking it to the mint for conversion to coins. So they stopped taking it to the mint, and the mint stopped coining silver.

In 1873, Congress passed a law that seemed simply to recognize the existing situation by officially discontinuing silver coinage. Few objected at the time. But in the course of the 1870s, the market value of silver fell well below the official mint ratio of 16 to 1. (Sixteen ounces of silver, in other words, were now worth less, not more, than one ounce of gold.) Silver was available for coinage again. Congress had thus foreclosed a potential method of expanding the currency and had eliminated a potential market for silver miners. Before long, many Americans concluded that a conspiracy of big bankers had been responsible for the "demonetization" of silver and referred to the law as the "Crime of '73."

Two groups of Americans were especially determined to undo the "Crime of '73." One consisted of the silver-mine owners, now understandably eager to have the government take their surplus silver and pay them much more than the market price. The other group consisted of discontented farmers, who wanted an increase in the quantity of money—an inflation of the currency—as a means of raising the prices of farm products and easing payment of the farmers' debts. The inflationists demanded that the government return at once to "free silver"—that is, to the "free and unlimited coinage of silver" at the old ratio of 16 to 1. But by the time the depression began in 1893, Congress had made no more than a token response to their demands.

"Crime of '73"

At the same time, the nation's gold reserves were steadily dropping. And the Panic of 1893 intensified the demands on those reserves. President Cleveland believed that the chief cause of the weakening gold reserves was the Sherman Silver Purchase Act of 1890, which had required the government to purchase (but not to coin) silver, and to pay for it in gold. Early in his second

administration, therefore, a special session responded to his request and repealed the Sherman Act—although only after a bitter and divisive battle that helped create a permanent split in the Democratic Party. The president's gold policy had aligned the southern and western Democrats in a solid alliance against him and his eastern followers.

By now, both sides had invested the currency question with great symbolic and emotional importance. Indeed, the issue aroused passions rarely seen in American politics, culminating in the tumultuous presidential election of 1896. Supporters of the gold standard considered its survival essential to the honor and stability of the nation. Supporters of free silver considered the gold standard an instrument of tyranny. "Free silver" became to them a symbol of liberation. Silver would be a "people's money," as opposed to gold, the money of oppression and exploitation. It would eliminate the indebtedness of farmers and of whole regions of the country. A graphic illustration of the popularity of the silver issue was the enormous success of William H. Harvey's *Coin's Financial School,* published in 1894, which became one of the great bestsellers of its age. The fictional Professor Coin ran an imaginary school specializing in finance, and the book consisted of his lectures and his dialogues with his students. The professor's brilliant discourses left even his most vehement opponents dazzled as he persuaded his listeners, with simple logic, of the almost miraculous restorative qualities of free silver: "It means the reopening of closed factories, the relighting of fires in darkened furnaces; it means hope instead of despair; comfort in place of suffering; life instead of death."

Symbolic Importance of the Currency Question

"A CROSS OF GOLD"

Most Populists did not pay much attention to the silver issue at first. But as the party developed strength, the money question became more important to its leaders. The Populists desperately needed funds to finance their campaigns. Silver-mine owners were willing to provide assistance but insisted on an elevation of the currency plank. The Populists also needed to form alliances with other political groups. The "money question" seemed a way to win the support of many people not engaged in farming but nevertheless starved for currency.

The Emergence of Bryan

As the election of 1896 approached, Republicans, watching the failure of Cleveland and the Democrats to deal effectively with the depression, were confident of success. Party leaders, led by the Ohio boss Marcus A. Hanna, settled on Governor William McKinley of Ohio, who had as a mem-

William McKinley

ber of Congress authored the 1890 tariff act, as the party's presidential candidate. The Republican platform opposed the free coinage of silver except by agreement with the leading commercial nations (which everyone realized was unlikely). Thirty-four delegates from the mountain and plains states walked out of the convention in protest and joined the Democratic Party.

The Democratic convention of 1896 was the scene of unusual drama. Southern and western delegates, eager to neutralize the challenge of the People's Party, were determined to seize control of the party from conservative easterners and incorporate some Populist demands—among them free silver—into the Democratic platform. They wanted as well to nominate a pro-silver candidate. The divided platform committee presented two reports to the convention. The majority report, the work of westerners and southerners, called for tariff reduction, an income tax, "stricter control" of trusts and railroads, and—most prominently—free silver. The minority report, the product of the party's eastern wing, echoed the Republican platform by opposing the free coinage of silver except by international agreement. The debate over the two competing platforms dominated the convention.

Defenders of the gold standard seemed to dominate the debate, until the final speech. Then William Jennings Bryan, a handsome, thirty-six-year-old congressman from Nebraska already well known as an effective orator, mounted the podium to address the convention. His great voice echoed through the hall as he delivered what became one of the most famous political speeches in American history in support of free silver. The closing passage sent his audience into something close to a frenzy: "If they dare to come out in the open and defend the gold standard as a good thing, we will fight them to the uttermost. Having behind us the producing masses of this nation and the world, supported by the commercial interests, the laboring interests and the toilers everywhere, we will answer their demand for a gold standard by saying to them: 'You shall not press down upon the brow of labor this crown of thorns; you shall not crucify mankind upon a cross of gold.'" It became known as the "Cross of Gold" speech.

"Cross of Gold" Speech

The convention voted to adopt the pro-silver platform. Perhaps more important, the agrarians found a leader. And the following day, Bryan (as he had eagerly and not entirely secretly hoped) was nominated for president on the fifth ballot. He was, and remains, the youngest person ever nominated for president by a major party. Republican and conservative Democrats attacked Bryan as a dangerous demagogue. But his many admirers hailed him as the Great Commoner. Born in Illinois of typical middle-class stock, he had attended a small sectarian college, had practiced law with only average success, and then, repeating a normal American pattern, had moved to

BRYAN WHISTLESTOPPING By long-established tradition, candidates for the presidency did not actively campaign after receiving their party's nomination. Nineteenth-century Americans considered public "stumping" to be undignified and inappropriate for a future president. But in 1896, William Jennings Bryan—a young candidate little known outside his own region, a man without broad support even among the leaders of his own party—decided that he had no choice but to go directly to the public for support. He traveled widely and incessantly in the months before the election, appearing before hundreds of crowds and hundreds of thousands of people. In this photograph, he stands (far left) on the platform of a campaign train in Ohio. His wife stands at right holding a bouquet from a well-wisher. *(Corbis)*

Nebraska, a frontier area, in search of opportunity. He served as a potent symbol of rural, Protestant, middle-class America.

The choice of Bryan and the nature of the Democratic platform created a quandary for the Populists. They had

"Fusion"

expected both major parties to adopt conservative programs and nominate conservative candidates, leaving the Populists to represent the growing forces of protest. But now the Democrats had stolen much of their thunder. The Populists faced the choice of naming their own candidate and splitting the protest vote or endorsing Bryan and losing their identity as a party. By now, the Populists had embraced the free-silver cause, but somewhat reluctantly. Most Populists still believed that other issues were more important. Many argued that "fusion" with the Democrats—who had endorsed free silver but ignored most of the other Populist demands—would destroy their party. But the majority concluded that there was no viable alternative. Amid considerable acrimony, the convention voted to support Bryan.

The Conservative Victory

The campaign of 1896 produced desperation among conservatives. The business and financial community, frightened beyond reason at the prospect of a Bryan victory, contributed lavishly to the Republican campaign, which may have spent as much as $7 million, as compared to the Democrats' $300,000. From his home at Canton, Ohio, McKinley hewed to the tradition by which candidates for president did not actively campaign for the office. He con-

ducted a dignified "front-porch" campaign by receiving pilgrimages of the Republican faithful, organized and paid for by Hanna.

Bryan showed no such restraint. He became the first presidential candidate in American history to stump every section of the country systematically, to appear in villages and hamlets, indeed the first to say frankly to the voters that he wanted to be president.

Birth of Modern Campaigning

He traveled 18,000 miles and addressed an estimated 5 million people. But Bryan may have done himself more harm than good. His revivalistic, camp-meeting style pleased old-stock Protestants; but it antagonized many of the immigrant Catholics and other ethnics who normally voted Democratic and who saw in Bryan the embodiment of a rural, Protestant morality that had often been directed against them. By violating a longstanding tradition by which presidential candidates remained aloof from their own campaigns (the tradition by which they "stood" for office rather than "running" for it), Bryan helped establish the modern form of presidential politics. But he also antagonized many voters, who considered his campaign undignified.

On election day, McKinley polled 271 electoral votes to Bryan's 176 and received 51.1 percent of the popular vote to Bryan's 47.7. Bryan carried only those areas of the South and West where miners or struggling staple farmers predominated. The Democratic program, like that of the Populists, had been too narrow to win a national election.

For the Populists and their allies, the election results were a disaster. They had gambled everything on their

	ELECTORAL VOTE	POPULAR VOTE (%)
William McKinley *(Republican)*	271	7,104,779 (51.1)
William Jennings Bryan *(Democratic)*	176	6,502,925 (47.7)

ELECTION OF 1896 The results of the presidential election of 1896 are, as this map shows, striking for the regional differentiation they reveal. William McKinley won the election by a comfortable but not enormous margin, but his victory was not broad-based. He carried all the states of the Northeast and the industrial Midwest, along with California and Oregon, but virtually nothing else. Bryan carried the entire South and almost all of the agrarian West. ◆ *What campaign issues in 1896 help account for the regional character of the results?*

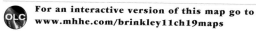

For an interactive version of this map go to www.mhhe.com/brinkley11ch19maps

"fusion" with the Democratic Party and lost. Within months of the election, the People's Party began to dissolve. Never again would American farmers unite so militantly to demand economic reform. And never again would so large a group of Americans raise so forceful a protest against the nature of the industrial economy.

End of the People's Party

McKinley and Recovery

The administration of William McKinley, which began in the aftermath of turmoil, saw a return to relative calm. One reason was the exhaustion of dissent. By 1897, when McKinley took office, the labor unrest that had so frightened many middle-class Americans and so excited working-class people had subsided. With the simultaneous decline of agrarian protest, the greatest destabilizing forces in the nation's politics were—temporarily at least—in retreat. Another reason was the character of the McKinley administration itself, which was politically shrewd and committed to reassuring stability. Most important, however, was the gradual easing of the economic crisis, a development that undercut many of those who were agitating for change.

McKinley and his allies committed themselves fully to only one issue, one on which they knew virtually all Republicans agreed: the need for higher tariff rates. Within weeks of his inauguration, the administration won approval of the Dingley Tariff, raising duties to the highest point in American history. The administration dealt more gingerly with the explosive silver question (an issue that McKinley himself had never considered very important in any case). McKinley sent a commission to Europe to explore the possibility of a silver agreement with Great Britain and France. As he and everyone else anticipated, the effort produced no agreement. The Republicans then enacted the Currency, or Gold Standard, Act of 1900, which confirmed the nation's commitment to the gold standard by assigning a specific gold value to the dollar and required all currency issued by the United States to hew to that value.

Currency Act

And so the "battle of the standards" ended in victory for the forces of conservatism. Economic developments at the time seemed to vindicate the Republicans. Prosperity began to return in 1898. Foreign crop failures sent farm prices surging upward, and American business entered another cycle of expansion. Prosperity and the gold standard, it seemed, were closely allied.

But while the free-silver movement had failed, it had raised an important question for the American economy. In the quarter-century before 1900, the countries of the Western world had experienced a spectacular growth in productive facilities and population. Yet the supply of money had not kept pace with economic progress, because the supply was tied to gold and the amount of gold had remained practically constant. Had it not been for a dramatic increase in the gold supply in the late 1890s (a result of new techniques for extracting gold from low-content ores and the discovery of huge new gold deposits in Alaska, South Africa, and Australia), Populist predictions of financial disaster might in fact have proved correct. In 1898, two and a half times as much gold was produced as in 1890, and the currency supply was soon inflated far beyond anything Bryan and the free-silver forces had anticipated.

By then, however, Bryan—like many other Americans—was becoming engaged with another major issue: a growing United States presence in world affairs and the possibility of America becoming an imperialist nation.

CONCLUSION

For nearly three decades after the battles over Reconstruction, American politics remained locked in a rigid stalemate. The electorate was relatively evenly divided between the two major parties, which differed with one another on only a few issues. The national government, never fully dominated by either party, remained small and inconsequential. Except for Indian tribes, people engaged in international trade (and thus subject to tariffs), and the many northern Civil War veterans who received federal pensions, few Americans had any direct contact with the government in Washington except to receive mail from the federal post office. A series of worthy and generally dull presidents presided over this political system as unwitting symbols of its stability and passivity.

Beneath the placid surface of national politics, however, great social issues were creating deep divisions in American life. Battles between employers and workers intensified. American farmers became increasingly resentful of their declining fortunes. Men and women throughout the country grew angry about corruption in government and excessive power in the hands of a few corporate leaders. When a great depression, the worst in the nation's history to that point, began in 1893, these social tensions exploded to the surface and reshaped national politics.

The most visible sign of the challenge to politics was the Populist movement, a great uprising of American farmers demanding far-reaching changes in the political system and the structure of the economy and the financial system. The populists created their own political party, showed impressive strength in several elections, and then—in 1896—joined with the Democrats to nominate the great Nebraska orator William Jennings Bryan for president. But the forces of insurgency were, in the end, no match for the forces of established institutions. After a campaign notable for its hysterical attacks on Bryan and on the issue with which he was identified ("free silver," making silver a basis for issuing currency in addition to gold), Bryan lost the election to William McKinley. Perhaps more important, the election became the occasion for a great electoral realignment, which left the Republicans the clear majority party for the next three decades.

The Republican victory did not, however, end the battle over power and corruption in American life. It simply redirected it into other channels. The challenges to the old politics soon made themselves felt as more conventional reform movements that became known, collectively, as progressivism.

FOR FURTHER REFERENCE

Morton Keller, *Affairs of State: Public Life in Late Nineteenth-Century America* (1977) is an important study of politics and government after Reconstruction. Nell Irvin Painter's *Standing at Armageddon: The United States, 1877–1919* (1987) explores the multicultural dimensions of industrialization, emphasizing the particularly cataclysmic effect of industrialization on minority populations and on race relations. Martin J. Sklar, *The Corporate Reconstruction of American Capitalism, 1890–1916* (1988), offers an interpretation of the evolution of American business practice and, by extension, American politics and society. Two significant books charting the growing capacities of the American state during this period are Theda Skocpol, *Protecting Soldiers and Mothers: The Political Origins of Social Policy in the United States* (1992); and Stephen Skowronek, *Building a New American State: The Expansion of National Administrative Capacities, 1877–1920* (1982). Richard Hofstadter's *The Age of Reform: From Bryan to FDR* (1955) and Lawrence Goodwyn's *The Populist Moment* (1978) offer sharply contrasting characterizations of the populist and progressive reform movements of this time. Other important studies of populism include John D. Hicks, *The Populist Revolt* (1931), a classic account, and Steven Hahn, *The Roots of Southern Populism: Yeoman Farmers and the Transformation of the Georgia Upcountry* (1983). Michael Kazin, *The Populist Persuasion: An American History* (1995) places populist ideas in a broad historical context.

For quizzes, Internet resources, references to additional books and films, and more, consult this book's Online Learning Center at www.mhhe.com/brinkley11.

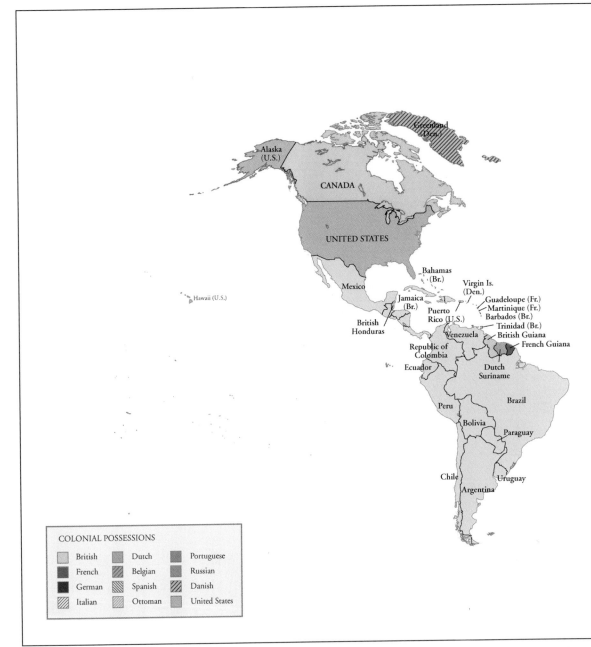

IMPERIALISM AT HIGH TIDE: 1900 The United States became a formal imperial power in 1898, when it acquired colonies in the aftermath of the Spanish-American War. But the U.S. was a decided latecomer to imperialism. During the nineteenth century, European nations dramatically expanded the reach of their empires, moving in particular in Africa and Asia. Although the British remained the world's largest imperial power by a significant margin, vast areas of the globe came under the control of other European colonizers, as this map shows. ◆ *How did the United States, and the European imperial nations, justify their acquisition of empire?*

STIRRINGS OF IMPERIALISM

For over two decades after the Civil War, the United States expanded hardly at all. By the 1890s, however, some Americans were ready—indeed, eager—to resume the course of Manifest Destiny that had inspired their ancestors to wrest an empire from Mexico in the expansionist 1840s.

The New Manifest Destiny

Several developments helped shift American attention to lands across the seas. The experience of subjugating the Indian tribes had established a precedent for exerting colonial control over dependent peoples. The concept of the "closing of the frontier," widely heralded by Frederick Jackson Turner and many others in the 1890s, produced

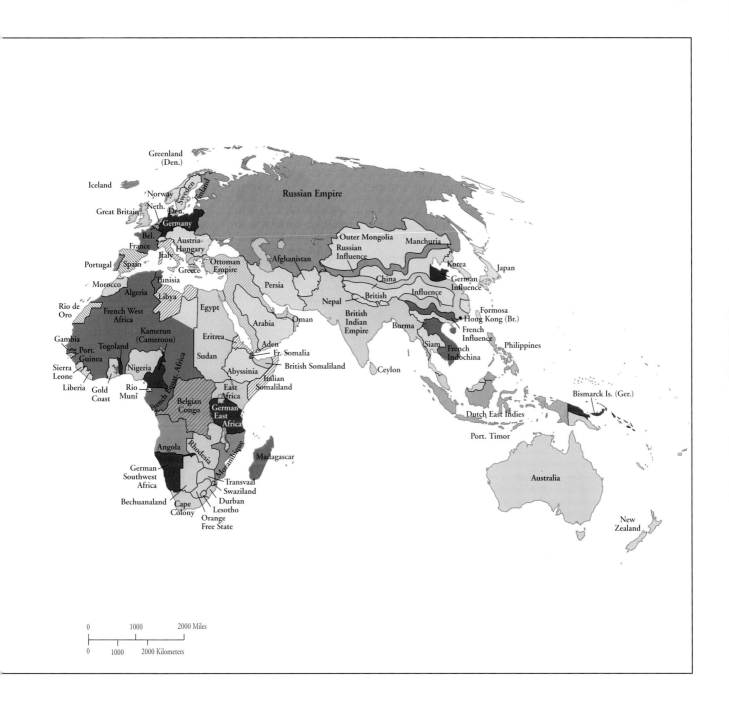

fears that natural resources would soon dwindle and that
alternative sources must be found abroad. The depression
that began in 1893 encouraged some businessmen to look
overseas for new markets. The bitter social protests of the
time—the populist movement, the free-silver crusade, the
bloody labor disputes—led some politicians to urge a
more aggressive foreign policy as an outlet for frustrations
that would otherwise destabilize domestic life.

fears that natural resources would soon dwindle and that
alternative sources must be found abroad. The depression
that began in 1893 encouraged some businessmen to look
overseas for new markets. The bitter social protests of the
time—the populist movement, the free-silver crusade, the
bloody labor disputes—led some politicians to urge a
more aggressive foreign policy as an outlet for frustrations
that would otherwise destabilize domestic life.

Foreign trade was becoming increasingly important
to the American economy in the late nineteenth century.
The nation's exports had totaled about $392 million in
1870; by 1890, the figure was $857 million; and by
1900, $1.4 billion. Many Americans began to consider

the possibility of acquiring colonies that might expand such markets further. "Today," Senator Albert J.
Beveridge of Indiana cried in
1899, "we are raising more
than we can consume. Today,
we are making more than we can use. Therefore, we
must find new markets for our produce, new occupation for our capital, new work for our labor."

Increasing Importance of Trade

Americans were, moreover, well aware of the imperialist fever that was raging through Europe and leading the
major powers to partition most of Africa among themselves and to turn eager eyes on the Far East and the feeble
Chinese Empire. Some Americans feared that their nation

Empires were not, of course, new to the nineteenth century, when the United States acquired its first overseas colonies. They have existed since the early moments of recorded history—in Greece, Rome, China, and many other parts of the world—and continued into the sixteenth and seventeenth centuries with vast imperial projects undertaken by Spain, Portugal, France, the Netherlands, and Great Britain in the Americas.

But in the mid- and late-nineteenth century, the construction of empires took on a new and different form from those of earlier eras, and the word "imperialism" emerged for the first time to describe it. In many places, European powers now created colonies not by sending large numbers of migrants to settle and populate new lands, but instead by creating military, political, and business structures that allowed them to dominate and profit from the existing populations. This new imperialism changed the character of the imperial nations themselves, enriching them greatly and producing new classes of people whose lives were shaped by the demands of imperial business and administration. It changed the character of colonized societies even more, by drawing them into the vast nexus of global industrial capitalism and by introducing European customs, institutions, and technologies to the subject peoples.

As the popularity of empire grew in the West in the late nineteenth century, efforts to justify it grew as well. Champions of imperialism argued that the acquisition of colonies was essential for the health, even the survival, of their own industrializing nations. Colonies were sources of raw materials vital to industrial production, they were markets for manufactured goods, and they could be suppliers of cheap labor. But defenders of the idea of empire also argued that imperialism was good for the colonized people. Many saw colonization as an opportunity to export Christianity to "heathen" lands, and great new missionary movements emerged in Europe and America in response. More secular apologists argued that imperialism helped bring colonized people into the modern world. The British poet Rudyard Kipling was perhaps the most famous spokesman for empire. In his celebrated poem "The White Man's Burden," he spoke of the duty of the colonizers to lift up primitive peoples, to "fill full the mouth of famine and bid the sickness cease."

The growth of empire was not simply a result of need and desire. It was also a result of the new capacities of the imperial powers. The invention of steamships, railroads, telegraphs, and other modern vehicles of transportation and communication; the construction of canals (particular the Suez Canal, completed in 1869, and the Panama Canal, completed in 1914); the birth of new military technologies (repeating rifles, machine guns, and modern artillery)—all contributed to the ability of western nations to reach, conquer, and control distant lands.

The greatest imperial power of the nineteenth century, indeed one of the greatest imperial powers in all of human history, was Great Britain. By 1800, despite its recent loss of the colonies that became the United States, it already possessed vast territory in North America, the Caribbean, and the Pacific—most notably Canada and Australia. But in the second half of the nineteenth century, Britain greatly expanded its empire. Its most important acquisition was India, one of the largest and most populous countries in the world. Britain had carried on a substantial trade with India for many years and had gradually increased its economic and military power there. In 1857, when native Indians revolted against British authority, British forces brutally crushed the rebellion and established formal colonial control over the land. British officials, backed by substantial military power, now governed India through a large civil service staffed mostly by people from England and Scotland, but with some Indians serving in minor or symbolic positions. The British invested heavily in railroads, telegraphs, canals, harbors, and

would soon be left out, that no territory would remain to be acquired. Senator Henry Cabot Lodge of Massachusetts, a leading imperialist, warned that the United States "must not fall out of the line of march." Scholars and others found a philosophic justification for expansionism in Charles Darwin's theories. They contended that nations or "races," like biological species, struggled constantly for existence and that only the fittest could survive. For strong nations to dominate weak ones was, therefore, in accordance with the laws of nature. The same distortion of Darwinism that industrialists and others had long been applying to domestic economic affairs in the form of Social Darwinism was now applied to world affairs.

One of the first to advance this argument was the popular writer John Fiske, who predicted in an 1885 article in *Harper's Magazine* that the English-speaking peoples would eventually control every land that was not already the seat of an "established civilization." The experience of white Americans in subjugating the native population of their own continent, Fiske argued, was "destined to go on" in other parts of the world. Support for Fiske's position came the same *Intellectual Justifications for Imperialism* year from Josiah Strong, a Congregational clergyman and champion of overseas missionary work. In a book entitled *Our Country: Its Possible Future and Its Present Crisis* (1885), Strong declared that the Anglo-Saxon "race," and especially its American branch, represented the great ideas of civil liberty and pure Christianity and was "divinely commissioned" to spread its institutions over the earth. John W. Burgess, founder of Columbia University's School of Political Science, gave a stamp of scholarly approval to imperialism. In his 1890 study *Political Science and Comparative Law,* he flatly stated that the Anglo-Saxon and Teutonic nations possessed the highest political talents. It was their duty, therefore, to

agricultural improvements to enhance the economic opportunities available to them. They created schools for Indian children in an effort to draw them into British culture and make them supporters of the imperial system.

In those same years, the British extended their empire into Africa and other parts of Asia. The great imperial champion Cecil Rhodes expanded a small existing British colony at Capetown into a substantial colony that included what is now South Africa. In 1895, he added new territories to the north, which he named Rhodesia (and which today are Zimbabwe and Zambia). Others spread British authority into Kenya, Uganda, Nigeria, and much of Egypt. British imperialists simultaneously extended the empire into east Asia, with the acquisition of Singapore, Hong Kong, Burma, and Malaya; and they built a substantial presence—although not formal colonial rule—in China.

Other European states, watching the vast expansion of the British empire, quickly jumped into the race for colonies. France created colonies in Indochina (Vietnam and Laos), Algeria, west Africa, and Madagascar. Belgium moved into the Congo in west Africa. Germany established colonies in the Cameroons, Taganyika, and other parts of Africa, and in the Pacific Islands north of Australia. Dutch, Italian, Portuguese, Spanish, Russian, and

THE BRITISH RAJ The Drum Corps of the Royal Fusiliers in India poses here for a formal portrait, taken in 1877. Although the drummers are British, an Indian associate is included at top left. This blending of the dominant British with subordinate Indians was characteristic of the administration of the British empire in India—a government known as the "raj," from the Indian word for "rule." *(Mansell/Timepix)*

Japanese imperialists created colonies as well in Africa, Asia, and the Pacific—driven both by a calculation of their own commercial interests and by the frenzied competition that had developed among rival imperial powers. And in 1898, the United States was drawn into the imperial race. Americans entered it in part inadvertently, as an unanticipated result of the Spanish-American War. But they also sought colonies as a result of the deliberate efforts of homegrown proponents of empire (among them Theodore Roosevelt), many of them heavily influenced by British friends and colleagues, who believed that in the modern industrial-imperial world a nation without colonies would have difficulty remaining, or becoming, a true great power.

uplift less fortunate peoples, even to force superior institutions on them if necessary. "There is," he wrote, "no human right to the status of barbarism."

The ablest and most effective apostle of imperialism was Alfred Thayer Mahan, a captain and later admiral in the United States Navy. Mahan's thesis, presented in *The Influence of Sea Power upon History* (1890) and other works, was simple: Countries with sea power were the great nations of history; the greatness of the United States, bounded by two oceans, would rest on its sea power. The prerequisites for sea power were a productive domestic economy, foreign commerce, a strong merchant marine, a navy to defend trade routes—and colonies, which would provide raw materials and markets and could serve as naval bases. Specifically, Mahan advocated that the United States construct a canal across the isthmus of Central America to join the oceans, acquire defensive bases on

Alfred Thayer Mahan

both sides of the canal in the Caribbean and the Pacific, and take possession of Hawaii and other Pacific islands. "Whether they will or no," he proclaimed, "Americans must now begin to look outward."

Mahan feared the United States did not have a large enough navy to play the great role he envisioned. But during the 1870s and 1880s, the government launched a shipbuilding program that by 1898 had moved the United States to fifth place among the world's naval powers, and by 1900 to third.

Hemispheric Hegemony

James G. Blaine, who served as secretary of state in two Republican administrations in the 1880s, led early efforts to expand American influence into Latin America, where, he believed, the United States must look for markets for its surplus goods. In October 1889, Blaine helped organize the first Pan-American Congress, which attracted delegates from nineteen nations. The delegates agreed to create the Pan-American Union, a weak international organization located in Washington that served as a clearinghouse for distributing information to the member nations. But they rejected Blaine's more substantive proposals: for an inter-American customs union and arbitration procedures for hemispheric disputes.

The Cleveland administration took a similarly active interest in Latin America. In 1895, it supported Venezuela in *Venezuelan Dispute* | a dispute with Great Britain over the boundary between Venezuela and British Guiana. When the British ignored American demands that the matter be submitted to arbitration, Secretary of State Richard Olney charged that Britain was violating the Monroe Doctrine. When Britain still did not act, Cleveland created a special commission to determine the boundary line; if Britain resisted the commission's decision, he insisted, the United States should be willing to go to war to enforce it. As war talk raged throughout the country, the British government finally realized that it had stumbled into a genuine diplomatic crisis and agreed to arbitration.

Hawaii and Samoa

The islands of Hawaii in the mid-Pacific had been an important way station for American ships in the China trade since the early nineteenth century. By the 1880s, officers of the expanding American navy were looking covetously at Pearl Harbor on the island of Oahu as a possible permanent base for United States ships. Pressure for an increased American presence in Hawaii was emerging from another source as well: the growing number of Americans who had settled on the islands and who had gradually come to dominate their economic and political life.

In doing so, the Americans were wresting authority away from the leaders of an ancient civilization. Settled *Self-Sufficient Societies* | by Polynesian people beginning in about 1500 B.C., Hawaii had developed an agricultural and fishing society in which different islands (and different communities on the same islands), each with its own chieftain, lived more or less self-sufficiently. When the first Americans arrived in Hawaii in the 1790s on merchant ships from New England, there were perhaps a half-million people living there. Battles among rival communities were frequent, as ambitious chieftains tried to consolidate power over their neighbors. In 1810, after a series of such battles, King Kamehameha I established his dominance over the other chieftains on Hawaii. He welcomed American traders and helped them develop a thriving trade between Hawaii and China, from which the natives profited along with the merchants. But Americans soon wanted more than trade. Missionaries began settling there in the early nineteenth century; and in the 1830s, William

Hooper, a Boston trader, became the first of many Americans to buy land and establish a sugar plantation on the islands.

The arrival of these merchants, missionaries, and planters was devastating to Hawaiian society. The newcomers inadvertently brought infectious diseases to which the Hawaiians, like the American Indians before them, were tragically vulnerable. By the mid-nineteenth century, more than half the native population had died. By the turn of the century, disease had cut the population by more than half again. But the Americans brought other incursions as well. Missionaries worked to undermine native religion. Other white settlers introduced liquor, firearms, and a commercial economy, all of which eroded the traditional character of Hawaiian society. By the 1840s, American planters had spread throughout the islands; and an American settler, G. P. Judd, had become prime minister of Hawaii under King Kamehameha III, who had agreed to establish a constitutional monarchy. Judd governed Hawaii for over a decade.

In 1887, the United States negotiated a treaty with Hawaii that permitted it to open a naval base at Pearl Harbor. By then, growing sugar for export to America had become the basis of the Hawaiian economy—as a result of an 1875 agreement allowing Hawaiian sugar to enter the United States duty-free. The American-dominated sugar plantation system not only displaced native Hawaiians from their lands but relied heavily on Asian immigrants for workers, whom the Americans considered more reliable and more docile than the natives. Indeed, finding adequate labor, and keeping it under control, was the principal concern of many planters. Some deliberately sought to create a mixed-race work force (Chinese, Japanese, native Hawaiian, Filipinos, Portuguese, and others) as a way to keep the workers divided and unlikely to challenge them.

Native Hawaiians did not accept their subordination without protest. In 1891, they elevated a powerful nationalist to the throne: Queen Liliuokalani, who set out to chal- | *Queen Lilinokalani* lenge the growing American control of the islands. But she remained in power only two years. In 1890, the United States had eliminated the privileged position of Hawaiian sugar in international trade. The result was devastating to the economy of the islands, and American planters concluded that the only way for them to recover was to become part of the United States (and hence exempt from its tariffs). In 1893 they staged a revolution and called on the United States for protection. After the American minister ordered marines from a warship in Honolulu harbor to go ashore to aid the rebels, the queen yielded her authority.

A provisional government, dominated by Americans (who constituted less than 5 percent of the population of the islands), immediately sent a delegation to Washington to negotiate a treaty of annexation. President Harrison

HAWAIIAN SUGAR CANE PLANTATION The sugar cane plantations of nineteenth-century Hawaii (like the sugar plantations of Barbados in the seventeenth and eighteenth centuries) required a vast labor force that the island's native population could not provide. The mostly American owners of the plantations imported over 300,000 Asian workers from China, Japan, and Korea to work in the fields between 1850 and 1920. The work was arduous, as the words of a song by Japanese sugar workers suggests: "Hawaii, Hawaii, But when I came what I saw was Hell. The boss was Satan, The lunas [overseers] his helpers." *(Hawaii State Archives)*

signed an annexation agreement in February 1893, just before leaving office. But the Senate, controlled by Democrats after the 1892 election, refused to ratify the treaty, and Grover Cleveland, the new president, refused to support it. Debate over the annexation of Hawaii continued until 1898, when the Republicans returned to power and approved the agreement.

Three thousand miles south of Hawaii, the Samoan islands had also long served as a way station for American ships in the Pacific trade. As American commerce with Asia increased, business groups in the United States regarded Samoa with new interest, and the American navy began eyeing the Samoan harbor at Pago Pago. In 1878, the Hayes administration extracted a treaty from Samoan leaders for an American naval station at Pago Pago. It bound the United States to arbitrate any differences between Samoa and other nations. Clearly, the United States now expected to have a voice in Samoan affairs.

But Great Britain and Germany were also interested in the islands, and they too secured treaty rights from the na-

Acquisition of Samoa

tive princes. For the next ten years the three powers jockeyed for dominance in Samoa, playing off one native ruler against another and coming dangerously close to war. Finally, the three nations agreed to share power over Samoa. They created a protectorate, under which the native chiefs survived

but exercised only nominal authority. The three-way arrangement failed to halt the intrigues and rivalries of its members; and in 1899, the United States and Germany divided the islands between them, compensating Britain with territories elsewhere in the Pacific. The United States retained the harbor at Pago Pago.

WAR WITH SPAIN

Imperial ambitions had thus begun to stir within the United States well before the late 1890s. But a war with Spain in 1898 turned those stirrings into overt expansionism. The war transformed America's relationship to the rest of the world, and left the nation with a far-flung overseas empire.

Controversy Over Cuba

The Spanish-American War emerged out of events in Cuba, which along with Puerto Rico represented virtually all that remained of Spain's once extensive American empire. Cubans had been resisting Spanish rule since at least 1868, when they began a long but ultimately unsuccessful fight for independence. Many Americans had sympathized with the Cubans during that ten-year struggle, but the United States did not intervene.

Joseph Pulitzer was a Hungarian immigrant, a Civil War veteran, and a successful newspaper publisher in St. Louis, Missouri, when he traveled to New York City in 1883 to buy a struggling paper, the *World*. "There is room in this great and growing city," he wrote in one of his first editorials, "for a journal that is not only cheap, but bright, not only bright but large, not only large but truly democratic . . . that will serve and battle for the people with earnest sincerity." Within a year, the *World*'s daily circulation had soared from 10,000 to over 60,000. By 1886, it had reached 250,000 and was making enormous profits.

The success of Pulitzer's *World* marked the birth of what came to be known as "yellow journalism," a phrase that reportedly derived from a character in one of the *World*'s comic strips: "the Yellow Kid." Color printing in newspapers was relatively new, and yellow was the most difficult color to print; so in the beginning, the term "yellow journalism" was probably a comment on the new technological possibilities that Pulitzer was so eagerly embracing. Eventually, however, it came to mean something else. It referred to a sensationalist style of reporting and writing, and a self-conscious effort to reach a mass market, that spread quickly through urban America and changed the character of newspapers forever.

Sensationalism was not new to journalism in the late nineteenth century, of course. Political scandal sheets had been publishing lurid stories since before the American Revolution, and the penny press that had emerged in the 1820s and 1830s (see pp. 256–257) incorporated scandal, crime, and intrigue into mainstream journals. But the yellow journalism of the 1880s and 1890s took the search for a mass audience to new levels. The *World* created one of the first Sunday editions, with lavishly colored special sections, comics, and illustrated features. It

expanded coverage of sports, fashion, literature, and theater. It pioneered large, glaring, overheated headlines that captured the eyes of those passing newsstands. It published exposes of political corruption. It made considerable efforts to bring drama and energy to its coverage of crime. It tried to involve readers directly in its stories (as

when a *World* campaign helped raise $300,000 to build a base for the Statue of Liberty, with much of the money coming in donations of five or ten cents from working-class readers). And it introduced a self-consciously populist style of writing that appealed to working-class readers. "The American people want something terse, forcible,

THE YELLOW PRESS AND THE WRECK OF THE *MAINE* No evidence was ever found tying the Spanish to the explosion in Havana harbor that destroyed the American battleship *Maine* in February 1898. Indeed, most evidence indicated that the blast came from inside the ship, a fact that suggests an accident rather than sabotage. Nevertheless, the newspapers of Joseph Pulitzer and William Randolph Hearst ran sensational stories about the incident that were designed to arouse public sentiment in support of a war against the Spanish. This front page from Pulitzer's *New York World* is an example of the lurid coverage the event received. Circulation figures at the top of the page indicate, too, how successful the coverage was in selling newspapers. *(The Granger Collection)*

picturesque, striking," Pulitzer said. His reporters wrote short, forceful sentences. They did not shy away from expressing sympathy or outrage. And they were not always constrained by the truth.

Pulitzer very quickly spawned imitators, the most important of them the California publisher William Randolph Hearst, who in 1895 bought the *New York Journal*, cut its price to one cent (Pulitzer quickly followed suit), copied many of the *World*'s techniques, and within a year raised its circulation to 400,000. Hearst used color even more lavishly than Pulitzer, recruited such notable writers as Stephen Crane, and committed the paper to an active role in civic affairs. The "new journalism," Hearst boasted in 1897, was not content simply to report news of crime, for example. It "strives to apprehend the criminal, to bring him to the bar of justice." He soon made the *Journal* the largest-circulation paper in the country—selling over a million copies a day. Pulitzer, whose own circulation was not far behind, accused him of "pandering to the worst tastes of the prurient and the horror-loving" and "dealing in bogus news." But the *World* wasted no time imitating the *Journal*. The competition between these two great "yellow" journals soon drove both to new levels of sensationalism. Their success drove newspapers in other cities around the nation to copy their techniques.

The civil war in Cuba in the 1890s between native rebels and the Spanish colonial regime gave both papers their best opportunities yet for combining sensational reporting with shameless appeals to patriotism and moral outrage. They avidly published exaggerated reports of Spanish atrocities toward the Cuban rebels, fanning popular anger toward Spain. When the American battleship *Maine* mysteriously exploded in Havana harbor in 1898, both papers immediately blamed Spanish authorities (without any evidence). The *Journal* of-

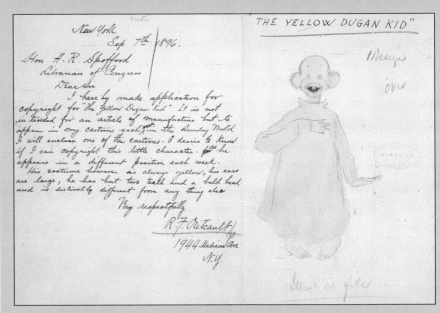

"THE YELLOW DUGAN KID"   *Hogan's Alley*, one of the most popular cartoons of the late nineteenth and early twentieth centuries, debuted in the *New York World* in 1895. Perhaps its best known character was Mickey Dugan, the goofy-looking creation of cartoonist Richard Outcault, known as "the Yellow Kid," whose nickname very likely was the source of the term "yellow journalism." *Hogan's Alley* was the forerunner of modern serial cartoons—not least because it was one of the first newspaper features to make elaborate use of color. [The drawing above accompanied Outcault's letter requesting copyright registration for the character of what he called "the yellow Dugan kid."]   *(Library of Congress)*

fered a $50,000 reward for information leading to the conviction of those responsible for the explosion, and it crowded all other stories off its front page ("There is no other news," Hearst told his editors) to make room for such screaming headlines as THE WHOLE COUNTRY THRILLS WITH WAR FEVER and HAVANA POPULACE INSULTS THE MEMORY OF THE *MAINE* VICTIMS. In the three days following the *Maine* explosion, the *Journal* sold over 3 million copies, a new world's record for newspaper circulation. The *World* exploited the destruction of the *Maine* less successfully (although not for lack of trying), but it soon made up for it in its highly sensationalized coverage of the Spanish-American War, which soon followed.

In the aftermath of the *Maine* episode, the more conservative press launched a spirited attack on yellow journalism. That was partly in response to Hearst's boast that the conflict in Cuba was "the *Journal*'s war" and to the publicity surrounding a cable he sent to one of his reporters in Cuba saying: "You furnish the pictures, and I'll furnish the war." But it was also an effort to discourage a kind of journalism that more "respectable" editors both deplored and feared. Some schools, libraries, and clubs began to banish the papers from their premises. But the techniques the "yellow" press pioneered in the 1890s helped map the way for a tradition of colorful, popular journalism—later embodied in "tabloids," some elements of which eventually found their way into television news—that has endured into the present day.

THE DUTY OF THE HOUR:—TO SAVE HER NOT ONLY FROM SPAIN BUT FROM A WORSE FATE.

"THE DUTY OF THE HOUR" This 1892 lithograph was no doubt inspired by the saying "Out of the frying pan and into the fire." A despairing Cuba, struggling to escape from the frying pan of Spanish misrule, contemplates an even more dangerous alternative: "anarchy" (or home rule). Cartoonist Louis Dalrymple here suggests that the only real solution to Cuba's problems is control by the United States, whose "duty" to Cuba is "To Save Her Not Only from Spain but from a Worse Fate." *(The Granger Collection)*

In 1895, the Cubans rose up again. (Although their goal was an end to Spanish misrule, the island's problems were *Cuban Revolt* now in part a result of the Wilson-Gorman Tariff of 1894, whose high duties on sugar had devastated Cuba's important sugar economy by cutting off exports to the United States, the island's principal market.) This rebellion produced a ferocity on both sides that horrified Americans. The Cubans deliberately devastated the island to force the Spaniards to leave. The Spanish, commanded by General Valeriano Weyler, confined civilians in some areas to hastily prepared concentration camps, where they died by the thousands, victims of disease and malnutrition. The American press took to calling the general "Butcher Weyler." The Spanish had used some of these same savage methods during the earlier struggle in Cuba without shocking American sensibilities. But the revolt of 1895 was reported more fully and sensationally by the American press, which helped create the impression that the Spaniards were committing all the atrocities, when in fact there was considerable brutality on both sides.

The conflict in Cuba came at a particularly opportune moment for the publishers of some American newspapers. Joseph Pulitzer with his *New York World* and William Randolph Hearst with his *New York Journal* were revolutionizing American journalism in the late nineteenth century by creating a new kind of newspaper, which catered openly to a broad popular audience lower *"Yellow Journalism"* in economic status than the readership of the traditional press. Like the "penny press" of the mid-nineteenth century, their papers specialized in lurid and sensational news; when such news did not exist, editors were not above creating it. But they fused the sensationalism of the old penny press with a much more aggressive style and broader ambitions. More traditional journalists referred to the new form as "yellow journalism." (See "Patterns of Popular Culture," pp. 560–561.) In the 1890s, Hearst and Pulitzer were engaged in a ruthless circulation war, and they saw the struggle in Cuba as a great opportunity. Both sent batteries of reporters and illustrators to the island with orders to provide accounts of Spanish atrocities. "You furnish the pictures," Hearst supposedly told an overly scrupulous artist, "and I'll furnish the war." A growing population of Cuban emigres in the United States—centered in Florida, New York, Philadelphia, and Trenton, New Jersey—gave extensive support to the Cuban Revolutionary Party (whose headquarters was in New York) and helped publicize its leader, Jose Marti, who was killed in

Cuba in 1895. Later, Cuban Americans formed other clubs and associations to support the cause of *Cuba Libre*. In some areas of the country, their efforts were as important as those of the yellow journalists in generating popular support for the revolution.

The mounting storm of indignation against Spain did not persuade President Cleveland to support American intervention in Cuba. He proclaimed American neutrality, and he urged authorities in New York City to try to stop the agitation by Cuban refugees there. But when McKinley became president in 1897, he took a stronger stand. He formally protested Spain's "uncivilized and inhuman" conduct, causing the Spanish government (fearful of American intervention) to recall Weyler, modify the concentration policy, and grant the island a qualified autonomy. At the end of 1897, with the insurrection losing ground, it seemed that American involvement in the war might be averted.

But whatever chances there were for a peaceful settlement vanished as a result of two dramatic incidents in February 1898. The first occurred when a Cuban agent in Havana stole a private letter written by Dupuy de Lôme, the Spanish minister in Washington, and turned it over to the American press. The letter described McKinley as a weak man and "a bidder for the admiration of the crowd." This was no more than many Americans, including some Republicans, were saying about their president. (Theodore Roosevelt described McKinley as having "no more backbone than a chocolate eclair.") But coming from a foreigner, it created intense popular anger. Dupuy de Lôme promptly resigned.

While excitement over the de Lôme letter was still high, the American battleship *Maine* blew up in Havana

The Maine

harbor with a loss of more than 260 people. The ship had been ordered to Cuba in January to protect American lives and property against possible attacks by Spanish loyalists. Many Americans assumed that the Spanish had sunk the ship, particularly when a naval court of inquiry hastily and inaccurately reported that an external explosion by a submarine mine had caused the disaster. (Later evidence suggested that the disaster was actually the result of an accidental explosion inside one of the engine rooms.) War hysteria swept the country, and Congress unanimously appropriated $50 million for military preparations. "Remember the *Maine*!" became a national chant for revenge.

McKinley still hoped to avoid a conflict. But others in his administration (including Assistant Secretary of the Navy Theodore Roosevelt) were clamoring for war. In March 1898, the president asked Spain to agree to an armistice, negotiations for a permanent peace, and an end to the concentration camps. Spain agreed to stop the fighting and eliminate the concentration camps but refused to negotiate with the rebels and reserved the right to resume hostilities at its discretion. That satisfied neither public opinion nor the Congress; and a few days later

McKinley asked for and, on April 25, received a congressional declaration of war.

"A Splendid Little War"

Secretary of State John Hay called the Spanish-American conflict "a splendid little war," an opinion that most Americans—with the exception of many of the enlisted men who fought in it—seemed to share. Declared in April, it was over in August. That was in part because Cuban rebels had already greatly weakened the Spanish resistance, which made the American intervention in many respects little more than a "mopping up" exercise. Only 460 Americans were killed in battle or died of wounds, although some 5,200 others perished of disease: malaria, dysentery, and typhoid, among others. Casualties among Cuban insurgents, who continued to bear the brunt of the fighting, were much higher.

And yet the American war effort was not without difficulties. United States soldiers faced serious supply problems: a shortage of modern rifles and ammunition, uniforms too heavy for the warm Caribbean *Supply and Mobilization Problems* weather, inadequate medical services, and skimpy, almost indigestible food. The regular army numbered only 28,000 troops and officers, most of whom had experience in quelling Indian outbreaks but none in larger-scale warfare. That meant that, as in the Civil War, the United States had to rely heavily on National Guard units, organized by local communities and commanded for the most part by local leaders without military experience. The entire mobilization process was conducted with remarkable inefficiency.

There were also racial conflicts. A significant proportion of the American invasion force consisted of black soldiers. Some were volunteer troops put together by African-American communities (although some governors refused to allow the formation of such units). Others were members of the four black regiments in the regular army, who had been stationed on the frontier to defend white settlements against Indians and were now transferred east to fight in Cuba. As the black soldiers traveled through the South toward the training camps, they chafed at the rigid segregation to which they were subjected and occasionally resisted the restrictions openly. Black soldiers in Georgia deliberately made use of a "whites only" park; in Florida, they beat a soda-fountain operator for refusing to serve them; in Tampa, white provocations and black retaliation led to a nightlong riot that left thirty wounded.

Racial tensions continued in Cuba itself, where American blacks played crucial roles in some of the important battles of the war (including the famous charge at San Juan Hill) and won many medals. Nearly half the Cuban insurgents fighting with the Americans were black, and unlike their American counterparts they were fully integrated into the rebel army. (Indeed, one of the leading

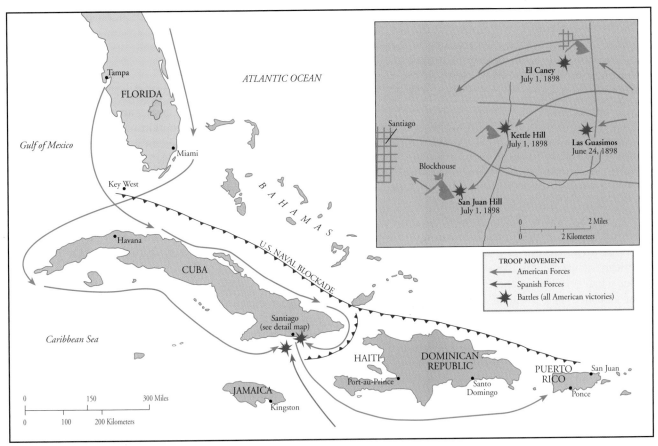

THE SPANISH-AMERICAN WAR IN CUBA, 1898 The military conflict between the United States and Spain in Cuba was a brief affair. The Cuban rebels and an American naval blockade had already brought the Spanish to the brink of defeat. The arrival of American troops was simply the final blow. In the space of about a week, U.S. troops won four decisive battles in the area around Santiago in southeast Cuba—one of them (the Battle of Kettle Hill) the scene of Theodore Roosevelt's famous charge up the adjacent San Juan Hill. This map shows the extent of the American naval blockade, the path of American troops from Florida to Cuba, and the location of the actual fighting. ◆ *What were the implications of the war in Cuba for Puerto Rico?*

 For an interactive version of this map go to www.mhhe.com/brinkley11ch20maps

insurgent generals, Antonio Maceo, was a black man.) The sight of black Cuban soldiers fighting alongside whites as equals gave American blacks a stronger sense of the injustice of their own position.

Seizing the Philippines

No agency in the American military had clear authority over strategic planning. Only the navy had worked out an objective, and its objective had little to do with freeing Cuba. Assistant Secretary of the Navy Theodore Roosevelt was an ardent imperialist, active proponent of war, and a man uninhibited by the knowledge that he was a relatively minor figure in the military hierarchy. Roosevelt strengthened the navy's Pacific squadron and instructed its commander, Commodore George Dewey, to attack Spanish naval forces in the Philippines, a colony of Spain, in the event of war.

Immediately after war was declared, Dewey sailed for Manila. On May 1, 1898, he steamed into Manila Bay and completely destroyed the aging Spanish fleet stationed there. Only one American sailor died in the battle (of heatstroke), and George Dewey, immediately promoted to admiral, *Dewey's Victory* had become the first hero of the war. Several months later, after the arrival of an American expeditionary force, the Spanish surrendered the city of Manila itself. In the rejoicing over Dewey's victory, few Americans paused to note that the character of the war was changing. What had begun as a war to free Cuba was becoming a war to strip Spain of its colonies. There had not yet been any decision about what the United States would do with the Spanish possessions it was suddenly acquiring.

The Battle for Cuba

But Cuba remained the principal focus of American military efforts. At first, the American commanders planned a long period of training before actually sending troops into

AFRICAN-AMERICAN CAVALRY Substantial numbers of African Americans fought in the United States Army during the Spanish-American War. Although confined to all-black units, they engaged in combat alongside white units and fought bravely and effectively. This photograph shows a troop of African-American cavalry in formation in Cuba. *(Corbis)*

combat. But when a Spanish fleet under Admiral Pascual Cervera slipped past the American navy into Santiago harbor on the southern coast of Cuba, plans changed quickly. The American Atlantic fleet quickly bottled Cervera up in the harbor. And the U.S. Army's commanding general, Nelson A. Miles, hastily altered his strategy and left Tampa in June with a force of 17,000 to attack Santiago. Both the departure from Florida and the landing in Cuba were scenes of fantastic incompetence. It took five days for this relatively small army to be put ashore, and that with the enemy offering no opposition.

General William R. Shafter, the American commander, moved toward Santiago, which he planned to surround

The Rough Riders

and capture. On the way he met and defeated Spanish forces at Las Guasimos and, a week later, in two simultaneous battles, El Caney and San Juan Hill. At the center of the fighting (and on the front pages of the newspapers) during most of these engagements was a cavalry unit known as the Rough Riders. Nominally commanded by General Leonard Wood, its real leader was Colonel Theodore Roosevelt, who had resigned from the Navy Department to get into the war and who had struggled with an almost desperate fury to ensure that his regiment made it to the front before the fighting ended. Roosevelt rapidly emerged as a hero of the conflict. His fame rested in large part on his role in leading a bold, if perhaps reckless, charge up Kettle Hill (a charge that was a minor part of the larger battle for the adjacent San Juan Hill) directly into the face of Spanish guns. Roosevelt himself emerged

unscathed, but nearly a hundred of his soldiers were killed or wounded. To the end of his life, he remembered the battle as "the great day of my life."

Although Shafter was now in position to assault Santiago, his army was so weakened by sickness that he feared he might have to abandon his position, particularly once the commander of the American naval force blockading Santiago refused to enter the harbor because of mines. Disaster seemed imminent. But unknown to the Americans, the Spanish government had by now decided that Santiago was lost and had ordered Cervera to evacuate. On July 3, believing the effort to defend the port was hopeless, Cervera tried to escape the harbor. The waiting American squadron destroyed his entire fleet. On July 16, the commander of Spanish ground forces in Santiago surrendered. At about the same time, an American army landed in Puerto Rico and occupied it against virtually no opposition. On August 12, an armistice ended the war.

Under the terms of the armistice, Spain recognized the independence of Cuba. It ceded Puerto Rico (now occupied by American troops) and the Pacific island of Guam to the United States. And it accepted continued American occupation of Manila pending the final disposition of the Philippines.

Puerto Rico and the United States

The annexation of Puerto Rico produced relatively little controversy in the United States—ironically, since of all the territory America acquired as a result of the Spanish-

THE ROUGH RIDERS Theodore Roosevelt resigned as assistant secretary of the navy to lead a volunteer regiment in the Spanish-American War. They were known as the Rough Riders, and their bold charge during the battle of San Juan Hill made Roosevelt a national hero. Roosevelt is shown here (at center with hat and glasses) posing with the other members of the regiment. *(Bettmann/Corbis)*

American war, Puerto Rico would be the most important to the nation's future. The island of Puerto Rico had been

Annexation of Puerto Rico | a part of the Spanish Empire since Ponce de León arrived there in 1508, and it had contained Spanish settlements since the founding of San Juan in 1521. The native people of the island, the Arawaks, disappeared almost entirely as a result of infectious diseases, Spanish brutality, and poverty. Puerto Rican society developed, therefore, with a Spanish ruling class and a large African work force for the coffee and sugar plantations that came to dominate its economy.

As Puerto Rican society became increasingly distinctive, resistance to Spanish rule began to emerge, just as it had emerged in Cuba. Uprisings occurred intermittently beginning in the 1820s; the most important of them—the so-called Lares Rebellion—was, like the others, effectively crushed

by the Spanish in 1868. But the growing resistance did prompt some reforms: the abolition of slavery in 1873, representation in the Spanish parliament, and other changes. Demands for independence continued to grow, and in 1898, in response to political pressure organized by Luis Muñoz Rivera, Spain granted the island a degree of independence. But before the changes had any chance to take effect, control of Puerto Rico shifted to the United States. American military forces occupied the island during the war. They remained in control until 1900, when the Foraker Act ended military rule and established a formal colonial government: an American governor and a two-chamber legislature (the members of the upper chamber appointed by the United States, the members of the lower elected by the Puerto Rican people). The United States could amend or veto any legislation the Puerto Ricans passed. Agitation for independence continued. And in 1917, under pressure to clarify the relationship between Puerto Rico and America, Congress passed the Jones Act, which declared Puerto Rico to be United States territory and made all Puerto Ricans American citizens.

The Puerto Rican sugar industry flourished as it took advantage of the American market that was now open to it without tariffs. As in Hawaii, *Sugar Economy* Americans began establishing large sugar plantations on the island and hired natives to work them; many of the planters did not even live in Puerto Rico. The growing emphasis on sugar as a cash crop, and the transformation of many Puerto Rican farmers into paid laborers led to a reduction in the growing of food for the island. Puerto Ricans became increasingly dependent on imported food and hence increasingly a part of the international commercial economy. When international sugar prices were high, Puerto Rico did well. When they dropped, the island's economy sagged, pushing the many plantation workers—already desperately poor—into destitution. Unhappy with the instability, the poverty among natives, and the American threat to Hispanic culture, many Puerto Ricans continued to agitate for independence. Others, however, began to envision closer relations with the United States, even statehood.

The Debate over the Philippines

Although the annexation of Puerto Rico produced relatively little controversy, the annexation of the Philippines occasioned a long and impassioned debate. Controlling a nearby Caribbean island fit reasonably comfortably into America's sense of itself as the dominant power in the Western Hemisphere. Controlling a large and densely populated territory thousands of miles away seemed different, and to many Americans more ominous.

McKinley claimed to be reluctant to support annexation. But, according to his own accounts, he came to believe *The Philippines Question* there were no acceptable alternatives. Emerging from what he described as an "agonizing night of prayer," he claimed divine guidance for his decision to accept responsibility for the islands. Returning them to Spain would be "cowardly and dishonorable," he claimed. Turning them over to another imperialist power (France, Germany, or Britain) would be "bad business and discreditable." Granting the islands independence would be irresponsible; the Filipinos were "unfit for self government." The only solution was "to take them all and to educate the Filipinos, and uplift and Christianize them, and by God's grace do the very best we could by them." Growing popular support for annexation and the pressure of the imperialist leaders of his party undoubtedly helped him reach this decision of conscience.

The Treaty of Paris, signed in December 1898, brought a formal end to the war. It confirmed the terms of the armistice concerning Cuba, Puerto Rico, and Guam. But American negotiators startled the Spanish by demanding that they cede the Philippines to the United States, something the original armistice had not included. The Spanish objected briefly, but an American offer of $20 million for the islands softened their resistance. They accepted all the American terms.

In the United States Senate, however, resistance was fierce. During debate over ratification of the treaty, a powerful anti-imperialist movement arose around the country to oppose acquisition of the Philippines. The anti-imperialists *Anti-Imperialist League* included some of the nation's wealthiest and most powerful figures: Andrew Carnegie, Mark Twain, Samuel Gompers, Senator John Sherman, and others. Their motives were various. Some believed simply that imperialism was immoral, a repudiation of America's commitment to human freedom. Some feared "polluting" the American population by introducing "inferior" Asian races into it. Industrial workers feared being undercut by a flood of cheap laborers from the new colonies. Conservatives feared the large standing army and entangling foreign alliances that they believed imperialism would require and that they feared would threaten American liberties. Sugar growers and others feared unwelcome competition from the new territories. The Anti-Imperialist League, established by upper-class Bostonians, New Yorkers, and others late in 1898 to fight against annexation, attracted a widespread following in the Northeast and waged a vigorous campaign against ratification of the Paris treaty.

Favoring ratification was an equally varied group. There were the exuberant imperialists such as Theodore Roosevelt, who saw the acquisition of empire as a way to reinvigorate the nation, and keep alive what they considered the healthy, restorative influence of the war. Some businessmen saw opportunities to profit in the Philippines and believed annexation would position the United States to dominate the Oriental trade. And most Republicans saw partisan advantages in acquiring valuable new territories through a war fought and won by a Republican administration. Perhaps the strongest argument in favor of annexation, however, was the apparent ease with which it could be accomplished. After all, the United States already possessed the islands.

When anti-imperialists warned of the danger of acquiring territories with large populations who might have to become citizens, the imperialists had a ready answer. The nation's longstanding policies toward Indians—treating them as dependents rather than as citizens—had created a precedent for annexing land without absorbing people. Senator Henry Cabot Lodge of Massachusetts, one of the leading imperialists in Congress, made the point explicitly:

> The other day . . . a great Democratic thinker announced that a Republic can have no subjects. He seems to have forgotten that this Republic not only has held subjects from the beginning, . . . but [that we have] acquired them by purchase. . . . [We] denied to the Indian tribes even the right to choose their allegiance, or to become citizens.

Other supporters of annexation argued that the "uncivilized" Filipinos "would occupy the same status precisely as our Indians. . . . They are, in fact, 'Indians'—and the Fourteenth Amendment does not make citizens of Indians."

The fate of the treaty remained in doubt for weeks, until it received the unexpected support of William Jennings Bryan, a fervent anti-imperialist. He backed ratification not because he approved of annexation but because he hoped to move the issue out of the Senate and make it the subject of a national referendum in 1900, when he expected to be the Democratic presidential candidate again. Bryan persuaded a number of anti-imperialist Democrats to support the treaty so as to set up the 1900 debate. The Senate ratified it finally on February 6, 1899.

But Bryan miscalculated. If the election of 1900 was in fact a referendum on the Philippines, as Bryan tried to

Election of 1900

make it, it proved beyond doubt that the nation had decided in favor of imperialism. Once again Bryan ran against McKinley; and once again McKinley won—even more decisively than in 1896. It was not only the issue of the colonies, however, that ensured McKinley's victory. The Republicans were the beneficiaries of growing national prosperity—and also of the colorful personality of their vice presidential candidate, Colonel Theodore Roosevelt, the hero of San Juan Hill.

THE REPUBLIC AS EMPIRE

The new American empire was small by the standards of the great imperial powers of Europe. But it created large challenges. It embroiled the United States in the politics of both Europe and the Far East in ways the nation had always tried to avoid in the past. It also drew Americans into a brutal war in the Philippines.

Governing the Colonies

Three of the American dependencies—Hawaii, Alaska (acquired from Russia in 1867), and Puerto Rico—presented relatively few problems. They received territorial status (and their residents American citizenship) relatively quickly: Hawaii in 1900, Alaska in 1912, and Puerto Rico in 1917. The navy took control of the Pacific islands of Guam and Tutuila. And some of the smallest, least populated Pacific islands now under American control the United States simply left alone. Cuba was a thornier problem. American military forces, commanded by General Leonard Wood, remained there until 1902 to prepare the island for independence. They built roads, schools, and hospitals, reorganized the legal, financial, and administrative systems, and introduced medical and sanitation reforms. But the United States also laid the basis for years of American economic domination of the island.

When Cuba drew up a constitution that made no reference to the United States, Congress responded by passing the Platt Amendment in 1901 and pressuring Cuba into incorporating its terms into its constitution. The Platt Amend-

Platt Amendment

ment barred Cuba from making treaties with other nations (thus, in effect, giving the United States control of Cuban foreign policy); gave the United States the right to intervene in Cuba to preserve independence, life, and property; and required Cuba to permit American naval stations on its territory. The amendment left Cuba with only nominal political independence.

American capital, which quickly took over the island's economy, made the new nation an American economic appendage as well. American investors poured into Cuba, buying up plantations, factories, railroads, and refineries. Absentee American ownership of many

American Economic Dominance

of the island's most important resources was the source of resentment and agitation for decades. Resistance to "Yankee imperialism" produced intermittent revolts against the Cuban government—revolts that at times prompted U.S. military intervention. American troops occupied the island from 1906 to 1909 after one such rebellion; they returned again in 1912, to suppress a revolt by black plantation workers. As in Puerto Rico and Hawaii, sugar production—spurred by access to the American market—increasingly dominated the island's economy and subjected it to the same cycle of booms and busts that so plagued other sugar-producing appendages of the United States economy.

The Philippine War

Americans did not like to think of themselves as imperial rulers in the European mold. Yet like other imperial powers, the United States soon discovered—as it had discovered at home in its relations with the Indians—that subjugating another people required more than ideals; it also required strength and brutality. That, at least, was the lesson of the American experience in the Philippines, where American forces soon became engaged in a long and bloody war with insurgent forces fighting for independence.

The conflict in the Philippines is the least remembered of all American wars. It was also one of the longest (it lasted from 1898 to 1902) and one of the most vicious. It involved 200,000 American troops and resulted in 4,300 American deaths, nearly ten times the number who had died in combat in the Spanish-American War. The number of Filipinos killed in the conflict has long been a matter of dispute, but it seems likely that at least 50,000 natives (and perhaps many more) died. The American occupiers faced brutal guerrilla tactics in the Philippines very similar to those the Spanish occupiers had faced prior to 1898 in Cuba. And they soon found themselves drawn into the same pattern of brutality that had outraged so many Americans when Weyler had used them in the Caribbean.

FILIPINO PRISONERS American troops guard captured Filipino guerrillas in Manila. The suppression of the Filipino insurrection was a much longer and costlier military undertaking than the Spanish-American War, by which the United States first gained possession of the islands. By mid-1900 there were 70,000 American troops in the Philippines, under the command of General Arthur MacArthur (whose son, Douglas, won fame in the Philippines during World War II). *(Library of Congress)*

The Filipinos had been rebelling against Spanish rule even before 1898. And as soon as they realized the Americans had come to stay, they rebelled against them as well. Ably led by Emilio Aguinaldo, who claimed to head the legitimate government of the nation, Filipinos harried the American army of occupation from island to island for more than three years. At first, American commanders believed the rebels had only a small popular following. But by early 1900, General Arthur MacArthur (father of General Douglas MacArthur), an American commander in the islands, was writing: "I have been reluctantly compelled to believe that the Filipino masses are loyal to Aguinaldo and the government which he heads."

Emilio Aguinaldo

To MacArthur and others, that realization was not a reason to moderate American tactics or conciliate the rebels. It was a reason to adopt much more severe measures. Gradually, faced with the harsh tactics of the rebels, the American military effort became more systematically vicious and brutal. Captured Filipino guerrillas were treated not as prisoners of war, but as murderers. Most were summarily executed. On some islands, entire communities were evacuated—the residents forced into concentration camps while American troops destroyed their villages, farms, crops, and livestock. A spirit of savagery grew among some American soldiers, who came to view the Filipinos as almost subhuman and at times seemed to take pleasure in killing almost arbitrarily. One American commander ordered his troops "to kill and burn, the more you kill and burn the better it will please me. . . . Shoot everyone over the age of 10." Over fifteen Filipinos were killed for every one wounded; in the American Civil War—the bloodiest conflict in U.S. history to that point—one person had died for every five wounded.

By 1902, reports of the brutality and of the American casualties had soured the American public on the war. But by then, the rebellion had largely exhausted itself and the occupiers had established control over most of the islands. The key to their victory was the March 1901 capture of Aguinaldo, who later signed a document urging his followers to stop fighting and declaring his own allegiance to the United States. (Aguinaldo then retired from public life and lived quietly until 1964.) Fighting continued in some places for another year, and the war revived intermittently until as late as 1906; but American possession of the Philippines was now secure. In the summer of 1901, the military transferred authority over the islands to William Howard Taft, who became their first civilian governor. Taft announced that the

Growing Economic Dependence

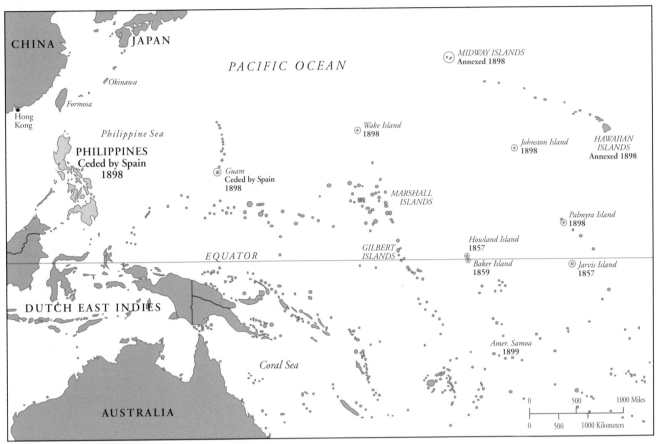

THE AMERICAN SOUTH PACIFIC EMPIRE, 1900 Except for Puerto Rico, all of the colonial acquisitions of the United States in the wake of the Spanish-American War occurred in the Pacific. The new attraction of imperialism persuaded the United States to annex Hawaii in 1898. The war itself gave America control of the Philippines, Guam, and other, smaller Spanish possessions in the Pacific. When added to the small, scattered islands that the United States had acquired as naval bases earlier in the nineteenth century, these new possessions gave the nation a highly far-flung Pacific empire, even if one whose total territory and population remained small by the standards of the other great empires of the age. ◆ *What was the reaction in the United States to the acquisition of this new empire?*

American mission in the Philippines was to prepare the islands for independence, and he gave the Filipinos broad local autonomy. The Americans also built roads, schools, bridges, and sewers; instituted major administrative and financial reforms; and established a public health system. The Philippine economy—dominated by fishing, agriculture, timber, and mining—also became increasingly linked to the economy of the United States. Americans did not make many investments in the Philippines, and few Americans moved there. But trade with the United States grew to the point that the islands were almost completely dependent on American markets.

In the meantime, a succession of American governors gradually increased Filipino political autonomy. But not until July 4, 1946, did the islands finally gain their independence.

The Open Door

The acquisition of the Philippines greatly increased the already strong American interest in Asia. Americans were particularly concerned about the future of China, with which the United States already had an important trade and which was now so enfeebled that it provided a tempting target for exploitation by stronger countries. By 1900, England, France, Germany, Russia, and Japan were beginning to carve up China among themselves. They pressured the Chinese government for "concessions," which gave them effective control over various regions of China. In some cases, they simply seized Chinese territory and claimed it as their own. Many Americans feared the process would soon cut them out of the China trade altogether.

Eager for a way to protect American interests in China without risking war, McKinley issued a statement in September 1898 saying the United States wanted access to China, but no special advantages there. "Asking only the open door for ourselves, we are ready to accord the open door *Hay's "Open Door Notes"* to others." The next year, Secretary of State John Hay translated those words into policy when he addressed identical messages—which became known as the "Open Door notes"—to England, Germany, Russia, France, Japan, and Italy. He asked them to approve three principles: Each nation with a sphere of influence in China was to respect the rights and privileges of other nations in its sphere; Chinese officials were to continue to collect tariff duties in all spheres (the existing tariff favored the United States); and nations were not to discriminate against other nations in levying port dues and railroad rates within their own spheres. Together, these principles would allow the United States to trade freely with the Chinese without fear of interference and without having to become militarily involved in the region. They would also retain the illusion of Chinese sovereignty and thus prevent formal colonial dismemberment of China, which might also create obstacles to American trade.

But Europe and Japan received the Open Door proposals coolly. Russia openly rejected them; the other powers claimed to accept them in principle but to be unable to act unless all the other powers agreed. Hay refused to consider this a rebuff. He boldly announced that all the powers had accepted the principles of the Open Door in "final and definitive" form and that the United States expected them to observe those principles. But unless the United States was willing to go to war, it could not prevent any nation that wanted to violate the Open Door from doing so.

No sooner had the diplomatic maneuvering over the Open Door ended than the Boxers, a secret Chinese martial-arts society with highly nationalist convictions, launched a revolt against foreigners in China. The climax of the Boxer Rebellion was a siege of the entire foreign diplomatic corps, which took refuge in the British embassy in Peking. The imperial powers (including the United States) sent an international expeditionary force into China to rescue the diplomats. In August 1900, it fought its way into Peking and broke the siege.

Boxer Rebellion

McKinley and Hay had agreed to American participation in quelling the Boxer Rebellion so as to secure a voice in the settlement of the uprising and to prevent the partition of China by the European powers. Hay now won support for his Open Door approach from England and Germany and induced the other participating powers to accept compensation from the Chinese for the damages the Boxer Rebellion had caused. Chinese territorial integrity survived at least in name, and the United States retained access to its lucrative trade.

A Modern Military System

The war with Spain had revealed glaring deficiencies in the American military system. The army had exhibited the greatest weaknesses, but the entire military organization had demonstrated problems of supply, training, and coordination. Had the United States been fighting a more powerful nation, disaster might have resulted. After the war, McKinley appointed Elihu Root, an able corporate lawyer in New York, as secretary of war to supervise a major overhaul of the armed forces. (Root was one of the first of several generations of attorney-statesmen who moved easily between public and private roles and constituted much of what has often been called the American "foreign policy establishment.") Between 1900 and 1903, Root created a new military system.

The Root reforms enlarged the regular army from 25,000 to a maximum of 100,000. They established federal army standards for the National Guard, ensuring that never again would the nation fight a war with volunteer regiments trained *Root's Military Reforms* and equipped differently from the regular army. They sparked the creation of a system of officer training schools, including the Army Staff College (later the Command and General Staff School) at Fort Leavenworth, Kansas, and the Army War College at Washington. And in 1903, a general staff (named the Joint Chiefs of Staff) was established to act as military advisers to the secretary of war. It was this last reform that Root considered most important: the creation of a central planning agency modeled on the example of European general staffs. The Joint Chiefs were charged with many functions. They were to "supervise" and "coordinate" the entire army establishment, and they were to establish an office that would plan for possible wars. An Army and Navy Board, on which both services were represented, was to foster interservice cooperation. As a result of the new reforms, the United States entered the twentieth century with something resembling a modern military system.

THE BOXER REBELLION American troops scale the walls surrounding the compound in Beijing where the Chinese Boxers held American and European diplomats hostage during the 1900 Boxer Rebellion. The Americans were part of an international force dispatched to crush the rebellion and rescue the diplomats. *(Brown Brothers)*

CONCLUSION

After more than a century of continual national expansion on the North American continent, the United States joined the community of colonial nations in the 1890s and acquired a substantial empire far from its own shores. But the rise of American imperialism was a halting and contested process, whose purposes were never wholly clear.

In the beginning, America's new internationalism took the form of a supposedly humanitarian intervention in a civil war in Spanish Cuba. The American public, inflamed by lurid journalistic accounts of Spanish atrocities supposedly inflicted on innocent Cubans, helped push the United States into a short, victorious war with Spain, fought in theory to secure Cuban independence. But through the efforts of some committed internationalists in the McKinley administration, among them Theodore Roosevelt, the Spanish-American War was soon transformed from a fight to free Cuba into a fight to wrest important colonies from Spain. At its end, the United States found itself in possession of new territories in the Caribbean (including Puerto Rico) and an important territory in the Pacific—the Philippines. A vigorous domestic anti-imperialist movement failed to stop the annexationist drive, and by 1899 the United States found itself in possession of colonies.

Taking the colonies proved easier than holding them. In the Philippines, American forces became bogged down in a four-year war with Filipino rebels, a war that dragged the American forces into the same kinds of brutal tactics that had so outraged Americans when the Spanish had used them in Cuba. The new colonial rulers soon pacified the Philippines, but not before souring much of the American public on the effort. In part as a result, the territories the United States acquired in the aftermath of the Spanish-American War marked not only the beginning but also the end of American territorial imperialism.

FOR FURTHER REFERENCE

Walter LaFeber, *The New Empire: An Interpretation of American Expansion, 1860–1898* (1963) and Ernest May, *Imperial Democracy* (1961) are important introductions to the subject. David F. Healy, *U.S. Expansionism: Imperialist Urge in the 1890s* (1970), is a contrasting view. Walter LaFeber, *The Cambridge History of American Foreign Policy, Vol. 2: The Search for Opportunity, 1865–1913* (1993) is an important overview. William Appleman Williams, *The Tragedy of American Diplomacy*, rev. ed. (1972), is a classic revisionist work on the origins and tragic consequences of American imperialism, supplemented by his *Empire as a Way of Life: An Essay on the Causes and Character of America's Present Predicament* (1982). Anders Stephanson, *Manifest Destiny: American Expansionism and the Empire of Right* (1995) is a short and provocative history of Americans' ideology of expansionism. Robert L. Beisner's *Twelve Against Empire* (1968) chronicles the careers of the leading opponents of imperial expansion. Emily S. Rosenberg, *Spreading the American Dream: American Economic and Cultural Expansion, 1890–1945* (1982) is a provocative cultural interpretation. Gerald F. Linderman, *The Mirror of War: American Society and the Spanish-American War* (1974) examines the social meaning of the war within the United States. Stuart Creighton Miller, *"Benevolent Assimilation": The American Conquest of the Philippines, 1899–1903* (1982) describes the American war in the Philippines. Michael Hunt, *The Making of a Special Relationship: The United States and China to 1914* (1983) is a good introduction to the subject.

For quizzes, Internet resources, references to additional books and films, and more, consult this book's Online Learning Center at www.mhhe.com/brinkley11.

"VOTES FOR WOMEN," BY B. M. BOYE This striking poster was the prize-winning entry in a 1911 contest sponsored by the College Equal Suffrage League of Northern California. *(Schlesinger Library, Radcliffe College)*

Significant Events

CHAPTER TWENTY-ONE

THE RISE OF PROGRESSIVISM

*W*ell before the turn of the century, many Americans had become convinced that the rapid industrialization and urbanization of their society had created intolerable problems, that the nation's most pressing need was to impose order on the growing chaos and to curb industrial society's most glaring injustices. In the early years of the new century, that outlook acquired a name: progressivism.

Not even the progressives themselves could always agree on what the word really meant. Indeed, more than one historian has suggested that the word "progressive" ultimately came to mean so many different things to so many different people that it ceased to mean anything at all (see "Where Historians Disagree," pp. 578–579). Yet if progressivism was a phenomenon of great scope and diversity, it was also one that rested on an identifiable set of central assumptions.

1899 ·	Thorstein Veblen publishes *A Theory of the Leisure Class*
1900 ·	Galveston, Texas, establishes commission government
·	Robert La Follette elected governor of Wisconsin
1901 ·	American Medical Association reorganized
1902 ·	Oregon adopts initiative and referendum
·	Mississippi adopts direct primary
1903 ·	Women's Trade Union League founded
1904 ·	Ida Tarbell publishes exposé of Standard Oil trust
1909 ·	Herbert Croly publishes *The Promise of American Life*

·	NAACP formed
1911 ·	Fire kills 146 workers at Triangle Shirtwaist Company in New York City
1912 ·	United States Chamber of Commerce founded
1913 ·	Louis D. Brandeis publishes *Other People's Money*
1914 ·	Walter Lippmann publishes *Drift and Mastery*
1916 ·	Madison Grant publishes *The Passing of the Great Race*
1919 ·	Eighteenth Amendment (prohibition) ratified
1920 ·	Nineteenth Amendment (woman suffrage) ratified

THE PROGRESSIVE IMPULSE

Progressivism was, first, an optimistic vision. Progressives believed, as their name implies, in the idea of progress. They believed that so-

Belief in Progress

ciety was capable of improvement and that continued growth and advancement were the nation's destiny.

But progressives believed, too, that growth and progress could not continue to occur recklessly, as they had in the late nineteenth century. The "natural laws" of the marketplace, and the doctrines of laissez faire and Social Darwinism that celebrated those laws, were not sufficient to create the order, stability, and justice their growing society required. Direct, purposeful human intervention in social and economic affairs was essential to ordering and bettering society.

Varieties of Progressivism

Progressives did not always agree on the form their intervention should take, and the result was a variety of reform impulses that sometimes seemed to have little in common. One powerful impulse was the spirit of "antimonop-

"Antimonopoly"

oly," the fear of concentrated power and the urge to limit and disperse authority and wealth. This impulse, which had much in common with populism, appealed not only to many workers and farmers but to some middle-class Americans as well. And it helped empower government to regulate or break up trusts at both the state and national level.

Another progressive impulse was a belief in the importance of social cohesion: the belief that individuals are not autonomous but part of a great web of social relationships, that the welfare of any single person is dependent on the welfare of society as a whole. That assumption produced a concern about the "victims" of industrialization. A large number of progressive initiatives and reforms involved efforts to help women, children, industrial workers, immigrants, and—to a lesser extent—African Americans.

Still another impulse was a deep faith in knowledge—in the possibilities of applying to society the principles of natural and social sciences. To some, those principles seemed a route to organization and efficiency. Many re-

Faith in Knowledge

formers believed that social order was a result of intelligent social organization and rational procedures for guiding social and economic life. To others, knowledge was more important as a vehicle for making society more equitable and humane. Most progressives believed, too, that a modernized government could—and must—play an important role in the process of improving and stabilizing society. Modern life was too complex to be left in the hands of party bosses, untrained amateurs, and antiquated institutions. It required new and enhanced institutions of government, and a new breed of leaders and experts.

These varied reform impulses were not always as mutually incompatible as they seemed. Many progressives made use of all these ideas (and others), separately or in combination, as they tried to bring order and progress to their turbulent society.

The Muckrakers

Among the first people to articulate the new spirit of reform were crusading journalists who began in the late nineteenth and early twentieth centuries to direct public attention toward social, economic, and political injustices. They became known as the "muckrakers," after Theodore Roosevelt accused one of them of raking up muck through his writings. They were committed to exposing scandal, corruption, and injustice to public view.

At first, their major targets were the trusts and particularly the railroads, which the muckrakers considered dangerously powerful and deeply corrupt. Exposés of the great corporate organizations began to appear as early as the 1860s, when Charles Francis Adams, Jr., and others uncovered corruption among the railroad barons. Such inquiries continued into the twentieth century. The most no-

Ida Tarbell and Lincoln Steffens

table of them was Ida Tarbell's enormous and influential study of the Standard Oil trust (published first in magazines and then as a two-volume book in 1904). By the turn of the century, many muckrakers were turning their attention to government and particularly to the urban political machines. The most influential, perhaps, was Lincoln Steffens, a reporter for *McClure's* magazine. His portraits of "machine government" and "boss rule"; his exposure of "boodlers" in cities as diverse as St. Louis, Minneapolis, Cleveland, Cincinnati, Chicago, Philadelphia, and New York; his tone of studied moral outrage (as reflected in the title of his series and of the book that emerged from it, *The Shame of the Cities*)—all helped arouse sentiment for urban political reform. The alternative to leaving government in the hands of corrupt party leaders, the muckrakers argued, was for the people themselves to take a greater interest in public life. Indeed, some journalists seemed less outraged at the bosses themselves than at the apathetic public that seemed not to care about the corruption occurring in their midst.

The muckrakers reached the peak of their influence in the first decade of the twentieth century. They investigated governments, labor unions, and corporations. They explored the problems of child labor, immigrant ghettoes, prostitution, and family disorganization. They denounced the waste and destruction of natural resources, the subjugation of women, even occasionally the oppression of blacks. By presenting social problems to the public with indignation and moral fervor, they helped inspire other Americans to take action. In the process they expressed some of the most basic progressive impulses: the opposition

"THE BOSSES OF THE SENATE" (1889), BY JOSEPH KEPPLER Keppler was a popular political cartoonist of the late nineteenth century who shared the growing concern about the power of the trusts—portrayed here as bloated, almost reptilian figures standing menacingly over the members of the U.S. Senate, to whose chamber the "people's entrance" is "closed." *(The Granger Collection)*

to monopoly, the belief in the need for social unity in the face of corruption and injustice, even at times the cry for efficiency and organization.

The Social Gospel

The moralistic tone of the muckrakers' exposés reflected one important aspect of emerging progressive sentiment: a sense of outrage at social and economic injustice. That outrage, combined with a humanitarian sense of social responsibility, helped produce many reformers committed to the pursuit of social justice. A clear expression of that concern was the rise of what became known as the "Social Gospel." By the early twentieth century, it had become a powerful movement within American Protestantism (and, to a lesser extent, within American Catholicism and Judaism). It was chiefly concerned with redeeming the nation's cities.

The Salvation Army, which began in England but soon spread to the United States, was one example of the fusion of religion with reform. A Christian social welfare organization with a vaguely military structure, by 1900 it had recruited 3,000 "officers" and 20,000 "privates" and

was offering both material aid and spiritual service to the urban poor. In addition, many ministers, priests, and rabbis left traditional parish work to serve in the troubled cities. Charles Sheldon's *In His Steps* (1898), the story of a young minister who abandoned a comfortable post to work among the needy, sold more than 15 million copies and established itself as the most successful novel of the era.

Walter Rauschenbusch, a Protestant theologian with socialist inclinations from Rochester, New York, published a series of influential discourses on the possibilities for human salvation through Christian reform. To him, the message of Darwinism was not that the individual was engaged in a brutal struggle for survival of the fittest, but that all individuals should work to ensure a humanitarian evolution of the social fabric. "Translate the evolutionary themes into religious faith," he wrote, "and you have the doctrine of the Kingdom of God." Some American Catholics seized on the 1893 publication of Pope *Father John Ryan* Leo XIII's encyclical *Rerum Novarum* ("New Things") as justification for their own crusade for social justice. Catholic liberals such as Father John A. Ryan took to

Few issues in the history of twentieth-century America have inspired more disagreement, even confusion, than the nature of progressivism. Until about 1950, most historians were in general accord about the nature of the progressive "movement." It was, they generally agreed, just what it purported to be: a movement by the "people" to curb the power of the "special interests."

In the early 1950s, however, a new interpretation emerged to challenge the traditional view. It offered a new explanation of who the progressives were and what they were trying to do. George Mowry, in *The California Progressives* (1951), described the reform movement in the state not as a protest by the mass of the people, but as an effort by a relatively small and privileged group of business and professional men to limit the overbearing power of large new corporations and labor unions. Richard Hofstadter expanded on this idea in *The Age of Reform* (1955), in which he described progressives throughout the country as people suffering from "status anxiety"—old, formerly influential, upper-middle-class families seeking to restore their fading prestige by challenging the powerful new institutions that had begun to displace them. Like the Populists, Hofstadter suggested, the progressives were suffering from psychological, not economic, discontent.

The Mowry-Hofstadter thesis was never without critics. In its wake, a bewildering array of new interpretations emerged. Perhaps the harshest challenge to earlier views came from Gabriel Kolko, whose influential 1963 study *The Triumph of Conservatism* dismissed the supposedly "democratic" features of progressivism as meaningless rhetoric. But he also rejected the Mowry-Hofstadter idea that it represented the efforts of a displaced elite. Progressivism, he argued, was an effort to regulate business. But it was not the "people" or "displaced elites" who were responsible for this regulation. It was corporate leaders themselves, who saw in government supervision a way to protect themselves from competition. Regulation, Kolko claimed, was "invariably controlled by the leaders of the regulated industry and directed towards ends they deemed acceptable or desirable." Martin Sklar, *The Corporate Reconstruction of American Capitalism* (1988) is a more recent and more sophisticated version of a similar argument.

A somewhat more moderate challenge to the "psychological" interpretation of progressivism came from historians embracing a new "organizational" view of history. Particularly influential was a 1967 study by Robert Wiebe, *The Search for Order, 1877–1920*. Wiebe presented progressivism as a response to dislocations in

(Brown Brothers)

American life. There had been rapid changes in the nature of the economy, but there had been no corresponding changes in social and political institutions. Economic power had moved to large, national organizations, while social and political life remained centered primarily in local communities. The result was widespread disorder and unrest, culminating in the turbulent 1890s. Progressivism, Wiebe argued, was the effort of a "new middle class"—a class tied to the emerging national economy—to stabilize and enhance their position in society by

---

heart the pope's warning that "a small number of very rich men have been able to lay upon the masses of the poor a yoke little better than slavery itself. . . . No practical solution of this question will ever be found without the assistance of religion and the church." For decades, he worked to expand the scope of Catholic social welfare organizations.

The Social Gospel was never the dominant element in the movement for urban reform. Some progressives dismissed it as irrelevant moralization; others viewed it as little more than a useful complement to their own work. But the engagement of religion with reform helped bring to progressivism a powerful moral component and a commitment to redeem the lives of even the least favored citizens. Walter Rauschenbusch captured some of both the optimism and the spirituality of the Social Gospel with his

proud comment, after a visit to a New York slum known as Hell's Kitchen, where Christian reformers were hard at work: "One could hear human virtue cracking and crashing all around."

The Settlement House Movement

One of the strongest elements of much progressive thought was the belief in the influence of the environment on individual development. Social Darwinists such as William Graham Sumner had argued that people's fortunes reflected their inherent "fitness" for survival. Many progressive theorists disagreed. Ignorance, poverty, even criminality, they argued, were not the result of inherent moral or genetic failings or of the workings of providence; they were, rather, the effects of an unhealthy environment.

creating national institutions suitable for the new national economy.

Despite the influences of these interpretations, some historians continued to argue that the reform phenomenon was indeed a movement of the people against the special interests, although some identified the "people" somewhat differently from earlier such interpretations. J. Joseph Huthmacher argued in 1962 that much of the force behind progressivism came from members of the working class, especially immigrants, who pressed for such reforms as workmen's compensation and wage and hour laws. John Buenker strengthened this argument in *Urban Liberalism and Progressive Reform* (1973), claiming that political machines and urban "bosses" were important sources of reform energy and helped create twentieth-century liberalism. David P. Thelen, in a 1972 study of progressivism in Wisconsin, *The New Citizenship,* pointed to a real clash between the "public interest" and "corporate privilege" in Wisconsin. The depression of the 1890s had mobilized a broad coalition of citizens of highly diverse backgrounds behind efforts to make both business and government responsible to the popular will. It marked the emergence of a new "consumer" consciousness that crossed boundaries of class and community, religion and ethnicity.

(Brown Brothers)

Other historians writing in the 1970s and 1980s attempted to link reform to some of the broad processes of political change that had created the public battles of the era. Richard L. McCormick's *From Realignment to Reform* (1981), for example, studied political change in New York State and argued that the crucial change in this era was the decline of the political parties as the vital players in public life and the rise of interest groups working for particular social and economic goals.

At the same time, many historians were focusing on the role of women (and the vast network of voluntary associations they created) in shaping and promoting progressive reform and were seeing in these efforts concerns rooted in gender. Some progressive battles, such historians as

Kathryn Sklar, Linda Gordon, Ruth Rosen, Elaine Tyler May, and others argued, were part of an effort by women to protect their interests within the domestic sphere in the face of jarring challenges from the new industrial world. This protective urge drew women reformers to such issues as temperance, divorce, and prostitution. Many women mobilized behind protective legislation for female and children workers. Other women worked to expand their own roles in the public world. Progressivism cannot be understood, historians of women contend, without understanding the role of women and the importance of issues involving the family and the private world within it.

Given the range of disagreement over the nature of the progressive movement, it is hardly surprising that some historians have despaired of finding any coherent definition for the term at all. Peter Filene, for one, suggested in 1970 that the concept of progressivism as a "movement" had outlived its usefulness. But Daniel Rodgers, in an important 1982 article, "In Search of Progressivism," disagreed. The very diversity of progressivism, he argued, accounted both for its enormous impact on its time and for its capacity to reveal to us today the "noise and tumult" of an age of rapid social change.

To elevate the distressed, therefore, required an improvement of the conditions in which they lived.

Nothing produced more distress, many reformers believed, than the crowded immigrant neighborhoods of American cities, which publicists such as Jacob Riis were exposing through vivid photographs and lurid descriptions. One response to the problems of such communities, borrowed from England, was the settlement house.

Jane Addams and Hull House

The most famous, and one of the first, was Hull House, which opened in 1889 in Chicago as a result of the efforts of Jane Addams. It became a model for more than 400 similar institutions throughout the nation. Staffed by members of the educated middle class, imbued with ideas derived from the social sciences, settlement houses sought to help immigrant families adapt to the language and customs of their new country. Settlement houses avoided the condescension and moral disapproval of earlier philanthropic efforts. But they generally embraced a belief that middle-class Americans had a responsibility to impart their own values to immigrants and to teach them how to create middle-class lifestyles. Even the word "settlement" suggested as much: middle-class people "settling" in the inner city and bringing civilization to the urban frontier.

Central to the settlement houses were the efforts of college women. Indeed, the movement became a training ground for many important female leaders of the twentieth century, including Eleanor Roosevelt. The settlement houses provided these women with an environment and a role that society considered "appropriate" for unmarried women: urban "homes" where settlement workers helped

TENEMENT FAMILY, 1899 Jacob Riis, an indefatigable chronicler of the lives of tenant-dwelling immigrants, became one of the most influential photographers, and reformers, of his day. His book *How the Other Half Lives* became one of the classics of his era. In this photograph, he shows a grim-looking immigrant family crowded into a cramped tenement room—the kind of scene characteristic of his work. *(Jacob Riis/Museum of the City of New York)*

TENEMENT CIGARMAKERS Among the social problems Jacob Riis attempted to illuminate were those of working conditions in immigrant communities. In this photograph from *How the Other Half Lives,* a cigarmaker works in his already crowded home surrounded by his children. Such home workers—many, perhaps most, of whom were women—were normally paid by the "piece," that is, by the amount of work they performed rather than the number of hours; the result was very long hours of labor (often with the help of the young children in the home) and very low pay. *(Museum of the City of New York)*

THE INFANT WELFARE SOCIETY, CHICAGO The Infant Welfare Society was one of many "helping" organizations in Chicago and other large cities—many of them closely tied to the settlement houses—that strove to help immigrants adapt to American life and create safe and healthy living conditions. Here, a volunteer helps an immigrant mother learn to bathe her baby sometime around 1910. *(Chicago Historical Society)*

immigrants to become better members of society. (The settlement house was "home" only to some of the reformers; their immigrant constituents did not live there.) The settlement houses also helped spawn another important institution of reform: the profession of social work—a profession in which women were also to play a vital role. Workers at Hull House, for example, maintained a close relationship with the University of Chicago's pioneering work in the field of sociology. A growing number of programs for the professional training of social workers began to appear in the nation's leading universities, partly in response to the activities of the settlements. The professional social worker combined a compassion for the poor with a commitment to the values of bureaucratic progressivism: scientific study, efficient organization, reliance on experts. The new profession produced elaborate surveys and reports, collected statistics, and published scholarly tracts on the need for urban reform.

The Allure of Expertise

As the emergence of the social work profession suggests, progressives involved in humanitarian efforts placed a high value on knowledge and expertise. Even nonscientific problems, they believed, could be analyzed and solved scientifically. Many reformers came to believe that only enlightened experts and well-designed bureaucracies could create the stability and order America needed.

This belief found expression in many ways, among them in the writings of a new group of scholars and intellectuals. Unlike the Social Darwinists of the nineteenth century, these theorists were no longer content with merely justifying the existing industrial system. They spoke instead of the creation of a new civilization, in which the expertise of scientists and engineers could be

brought to bear on the problems of the economy and society. Among the most influential was the social scientist Thorstein Veblen. Harshly critical of the industrial tycoons of the late nineteenth century—the "leisure class" as he satirically described them in his first major work, *A Theory of the Leisure Class* (1899)—Veblen proposed a new economic system in which power would reside in the hands of highly trained engineers. Only they, he argued, could fully understand the "machine process" by which modern society must be governed.

In practical terms, the impulse toward expertise and organization helped produce the idea of scientific management, or "Taylorism" (see p. 477). It encouraged the development of modern mass-production techniques and, above all, the assembly line. But it also inspired a revolution in American education and the creation of a new area ┃ *Rise of Social Sciences* of inquiry: social science, the use of scientific techniques in the study of society and its institutions. It produced a generation of bureaucratic reformers concerned with the structure of organizations and committed to building new political and economic institutions capable of managing a modern society. It also helped create a movement toward organization among the expanding new group of middle-class professionals.

The Professions

The late nineteenth century saw a dramatic expansion in the number of Americans engaged in administrative and professional tasks. Industries needed managers, technicians, and accountants as well as workers. Cities required commercial, medical, legal, and educational services. New technology required scientists and engineers who, in turn, required institutions and instructors to train them.

By the turn of the century, those performing these services had come to constitute a distinct social group—what some have called a new middle class.

The new middle class placed a high value on education and individual accomplishment. By the early twentieth century, its millions of members were building organizations and establishing standards to secure their position in society. As their principal vehicle, they created the modern, organized professions. The idea of professionalism had been a frail one in America even as late as 1880. When every patent-medicine salesman could claim to be a doctor, when every frustrated politician could set up shop as a lawyer, when anyone who could read and write could pose as a teacher, a professional label by itself carried little weight. There were, of course, skilled and responsible doctors, lawyers, teachers, and others; but they had no way of controlling or distinguishing themselves clearly from the amateurs, charlatans, and incompetents who presumed to practice their trades. As the demand for professional services increased, so did the pressures for reform.

Among the first to respond was the medical profession. Throughout the 1890s, doctors who considered themselves trained professionals began forming local associations and societies. In 1901, they reorganized the

American Medical Association into a national professional society. By 1920, nearly two-thirds of all American doctors were members. The AMA quickly called for strict, scientific standards for admission to the practice of medicine, with doctors themselves serving as protectors of the standards. State and local governments responded by passing new laws requiring the licensing of all physicians and granting licenses only to those practitioners approved by the profession.

Accompanying the emphasis on strict regulation of the profession came a concern for rigorous scientific training and research. By 1900, medical education at a few medical schools—notably Johns Hopkins in Baltimore (founded in 1893)—compared favorably with that in the leading institutions of Europe. Doctors such as William H. Welch at Hopkins revolutionized the teaching of medicine by moving students out of the classrooms and into laboratories and clinics. Rigorous new standards forced many inadequate medical schools out of existence, and those that remained were obliged to adopt a strict scientific approach.

There was similar movement in other professions. By 1916, lawyers in all forty-eight states had established professional bar associations; and virtually all of them had succeeded in creating central examining boards, composed of lawyers, to regulate admission to the profession. Increasingly, aspiring lawyers found it necessary to enroll in graduate programs, and the nation's law schools accordingly expanded greatly, both in numbers and in the rigor of their curricula. Businessmen supported the creation of schools of business administration and created

their own national organizations: the National Association of Manufacturers in 1895 and the United States Chamber of Commerce in 1912. Even farmers, long the symbol of the romantic spirit of individualism, *National Association of Manufacturers* responded to the new order by forming, through the National Farm Bureau Federation, a network of agricultural organizations designed to spread scientific farming methods, teach sound marketing techniques, and lobby for the interests of their members.

Among the purposes of the new professionalism was guarding entry into the professions. This was only partly an effort to defend the professions from the untrained and incompetent. The admission requirements also protected those already in the professions from excessive competition and lent prestige and status to the professional level. Some professionals used their entrance requirements to exclude blacks, women, immigrants, and other "undesirables" from their ranks. (Among the victims of professionalization, for example, were many of the female midwives who profited from many generations of experience in helping women give birth.) Others used them simply to keep the numbers down, to ensure that demand for the services of existing members would remain high.

Women and the Professions

Both by custom and by active barriers of law and prejudice, American women found themselves excluded from most of the emerging professions. But a substantial number of middle-class women—particularly those emerging from the new women's colleges and from the coeducational state universities—entered professional careers nevertheless.

A few women managed to establish themselves as physicians, lawyers, engineers, scientists, and corporate managers. Several leading medical schools admitted women, and in 1900 about 5 percent of all American physicians were female (a proportion that remained unchanged until the 1960s). Most, however, turned by necessity to those professions that society considered suitable for women. Settlement houses and social work provided two "appropriate" professional outlets for women. The most important, however, was teaching. Indeed, in the late *Female-Dominated Professions* nineteenth century, more than two-thirds of all grammar school teachers were women, and perhaps 90 percent of all professional women were teachers. For educated black women, in particular, teaching was often the only professional opportunity they could hope to find. The existence of segregated black schools in the South created a substantial market for African-American teachers.

Women also dominated other professional activities. Nursing had become primarily a women's field during and after the Civil War, when it was still considered a menial occupation, akin to domestic service. But by the early twentieth century, it was adopting professional standards. Prospective nurses generally needed certification from schools of nursing and could not simply learn on the job. Women also found opportunities as librarians, another field beginning to define itself in professional terms. And many women entered academia—often receiving advanced degrees at such predominantly male institutions as the University of Chicago, MIT, or Columbia, and finding professional opportunities in the new and expanding women's colleges.

The "women's professions" had much in common with other professions: the value they placed on training and expertise, the creation of professional organizations and a professional "identity," the monitoring of admission to professional work. But they also had distinctive qualities. Teaching, nursing, library work, and others were "helping" professions. They usually involved working primarily with other women or with children. Their activities occurred in places that seemed different from the offices that dominated the predominantly male business and professional worlds; such places as schools, hospitals, and libraries had a vaguely "domestic" image.

WOMEN AND REFORM

The prominence of women in reform movements is one of the most striking features of progressivism.

Key Role of Women in Reform Causes

In most states in the early twentieth century, women could not vote. They almost never held public office. They had footholds in only a few (and usually primarily female) professions. They lived in a culture in which most people, male and female, believed that women were not suited for the male-dominated public world, that they did, and should, inhabit their own sphere. What, then, explains the prominent role so many women played in the reform activities of the period? In fact, female activism in the progressive era represented both an expansion of women's separate sphere and a confirmation of it.

The "New Woman"

The phenomenon of the "new woman," widely remarked upon at the time, was a product of social and economic

Socioeconomic Origins of the New Woman

changes that affected the private world as much as the public one. By the end of the nineteenth century, almost all income-producing activity had moved out of the home and into the factory or the office. At the same time, children were beginning school at earlier ages and spending more time there. For wives and mothers who did not work for wages, the home was a less all-consuming place. Most women still oversaw the domestic functions of the home. Technological innovations such as running water, electricity, and eventually household appliances made housework less onerous (even if higher standards of cleanliness counterbalanced many of these gains); and for middle-class women with domestic help, housework occupied only a small part of the day. It was not surprising, perhaps, that more and more women were looking for activities outside the home.

Declining family size also changed the lives of many women. Middle-class white women in the late nineteenth century had fewer children than their mothers and grandmothers had borne. They also lived longer than previous generations. Many women thus now spent fewer years with young children in the home and lived more years after their children were grown.

There were also many more women who lived outside traditional families altogether. Some educated women shunned marriage entirely, believing that only by remaining single could they play the roles they envisioned in the public world; approximately 10 percent of all American women in the last decades of the nineteenth century never married—a high proportion of them middle-class women. Single women were among the most prominent female reformers of the time: Jane Addams and Lillian Wald in the settlement house movement, Frances Willard in the temperance movement, Anna Howard Shaw in the suffrage movement, and many others. Some of these women lived alone. Others lived with other women, often in long-term relationships—some of them secretly romantic—that were known at the time as "Boston marriages." The divorce rate also rose rapidly in the late nineteenth century, from one divorce for every twenty-one marriages in 1880 to one in nine by 1916; women initiated the great majority of them.

"Boston Marriages"

Higher levels of education also contributed to the prominence of women in reform activities. The proliferation of women's colleges and of coeducational public universities in the late nineteenth century produced the first generation of women in which significant numbers had education above the high-school level (see p. 528). The new colleges also helped create female communities, within which women could find support for their ambitions and companionship for their activities.

There was, in the end, no single profile for the "new woman." But a growing number of American women at the beginning of the twentieth century were defining their lives in ways that included a substantial amount of activity outside the home, and they were deriving from their identity as women a set of distinctive concerns that defined—and limited—their public activities.

The Clubwomen

Among the most visible signs of the increasing public roles of women in the late nineteenth and early twentieth centuries were the women's clubs—a large network of

THE COLORED WOMEN'S LEAGUE OF WASHINGTON The women's club movement spread widely through American life and produced a number of organizations through which African-American women gathered to improve social and political conditions. The Colored Women's League of Washington, D.C., members of which appear in this 1894 photograph, was founded in 1892 by Sara Iredell Fleetwood, a registered nurse who married Christian Iredell, one of the first African-American soldiers to receive the Congressional Medal of Honor for his heroism in the Civil War. The League she founded was committed to "racial uplift," and it consisted mostly of teachers, who created nurseries and evening schools for adults. They are shown here gathered on the steps of Frederick Douglass's home on Capitol Hill. Sara Fleetwood is in the second row on the far right. *(Manuscript Division, Library of Congress)*

women's associations that proliferated rapidly beginning in the 1880s and 1890s and that became the vanguard of many important reforms.

The women's clubs began largely as cultural organizations to provide middle- and upper-class women with an outlet for their intellectual energies. In 1892, when women formed the General Federation of Women's Clubs to coordinate the activities of local organizations, there were more than 100,000 members in nearly 500 clubs. Eight years later, there were 160,000 members; and by 1917, over 1 million.

By the early twentieth century, the clubs were becoming less concerned with cultural activities and more concerned with contributing to social betterment. Because many club members were from wealthy families, some organizations had substantial funds at their disposal to make their influence felt. And ironically, because women

could not vote, the clubs had a nonpartisan image that made them more difficult for politicians to dismiss.

Black women occasionally joined clubs dominated by whites. But most such clubs excluded blacks, and so African Americans formed clubs of their own, some of which affiliated with the General Federation, but more of which became part of the independent National Association of Colored Women. They modeled themselves primarily on their white counterparts, but some black clubs also took positions on issues of particular concern to blacks. Some crusaded against lynching and called for congressional legislation to make lynching a federal crime. Others protested aspects of segregation.

The women's club movement raised few overt challenges to prevailing assumptions about the proper role of women in society. But it did represent an important effort by women to extend their influence beyond the traditional female sphere within the home and the family. Few

SHIRTWAIST WORKERS ON STRIKE The Women's Trade Union League was notable for bringing educated, middle-class women together with workers in efforts to improve factory and labor conditions. The parade shown here was part of the shirtwaist workers' strike shortly before World War I. Fannie Horowitz, counsel to the strikers, is shown here driving her own automobile in the parade. *(Brown Brothers)*

clubwomen were willing to accept the arguments of such committed feminists as Charlotte Perkins Gilman, who in

A Public Space for Women her 1898 book *Women and Economics* argued that the traditional definition of gender roles was exploitive and obsolete. The club movement, rather, allowed women to define a space for themselves in the public world without openly challenging the existing, male-dominated order. And it gave many women access to a female community in which they were able to act and express themselves in ways usually impossible in male-dominated institutions. As one Boston clubwoman said, "We need to feel the cheer and inspiration of meeting each other, we gain the courage and fresh life that comes from the mingling of congenial souls, of those working for the same ends."

But the importance of the club movement did not lie simply in what it did for middle-class women. It lay also in what those women accomplished for the working-class people they attempted to help. Much of what the clubs did was uncontroversial: planting trees; supporting schools, libraries, and settlement houses; building hospitals and parks. But clubwomen also supported measures that attracted significant opposition. They were an important force in winning passage of state (and ultimately federal) laws that regulated the conditions of woman and child labor, that established government inspection of workplaces, that regulated the food and drug industries,

that reformed policies toward the Indian tribes, that applied new standards to urban housing, and perhaps most notably that outlawed the manufacture and sale of alcohol. They were instrumental in pressuring state legislatures in most states to provide pensions to widowed or abandoned mothers with small children—a system known as "mother's pensions," which ultimately became absorbed into the Social Security system. In 1912, they pressured Congress into establishing the Children's Bureau in the Labor Department, an agency directed to develop policies to protect children.

In many of these efforts, the clubwomen formed alliances with other women's groups, such as the Women's Trade Union League, founded in 1903 by female union members and upper-class reformers and *Women's Trade Union League* committed to persuading women to join unions. In addition to working on behalf of protective legislation for women, WTUL members held public meetings on behalf of female workers, raised money to support strikes, marched on picket lines, and bailed striking women out of jail.

Women reformers often worked closely with men; and of course the success of most of their efforts depended on the support of male voters, legislators, and public officials. What made their crusades palatable to men was also what made them appealing to many women:

their self-consciously "maternal" character. In campaigning for measures to protect women and children workers and to assist the most powerless members of society, women's clubs emphasized the "nurturing" and "protective" features of their work and fought for "moral uplift." In doing so, they were reflecting contemporary ideas about the natural inclinations of women.

Woman Suffrage

Perhaps the largest single reform movement of the progressive era, indeed one of the largest in American history, was the fight for woman suffrage—a movement that attracted support from both women and men but whose most important leaders were women.

It is sometimes difficult for today's Americans to understand why the suffrage issue could have become the source of such enormous controversy. But at the time,

Radical Challenge of Women's Suffrage

suffrage seemed to many of its critics a very radical demand, in part because of the rationale some of its early supporters used to advance it. Throughout the late nineteenth century, many suffrage advocates presented their views in terms of "natural rights," arguing that women deserved the same rights as men—including, first and foremost, the right to vote. Elizabeth Cady Stanton, for example, wrote in 1892 of woman as "the arbiter of her own destiny . . . if we are to consider her as a citizen, as a member of a great nation, she must have the same rights as all other members." A woman's role as "mother, wife, sister, daughter" was "incidental" to her larger role as a part of society. This was an argument that boldly challenged the views of the many men (and even many women) who believed that society required a distinctive female "sphere" in which women would serve first and foremost as wives and mothers. And so a powerful antisuffrage movement emerged, dominated by men but with the active support of many women. The movement defended existing social norms, by which women's roles were largely defined by their places within families. There were antisuffrage organizations, some with substantial memberships; antisuffrage newspapers; rallies; petitions to legislatures; and widely circulated tracts. Opponents railed against the threat suffrage posed to the "natural order" of civilization. Woman, said one opponent, "was made man's helper, was given a servient place (not necessarily inferior) and man the dominant place (not necessarily superior) in the division of labor." Antisuffragists associated suffrage with divorce (not without some reason, since many suffrage advocates also supported revising the laws to make it easier for women to obtain a divorce). They linked suffrage with promiscuity, looseness, and neglect of children.

In the first years of the twentieth century, the suffrage movement began to overcome this opposition and win some substantial victories, in part because suffragists were becoming better organized and more politically sophisticated than their opponents. Under the leadership of Anna Howard Shaw, a Boston social worker, and Carrie Chapman Catt, a journalist from Iowa, membership in

NAWSA

the National American Woman Suffrage Association grew from about 13,000 in 1893 to over 2 million in 1917. The involvement of such well-known and widely admired women as Jane Addams gave added respectability to the cause. But the movement also gained strength because many of its most prominent leaders began to justify suffrage in "safer," less threatening ways. Suffrage, some supporters began to argue, would not challenge the "separate sphere" in which women resided. It would allow women to bring their special and distinct virtues more widely to bear on society's problems. It was, they claimed, precisely because women occupied a distinct sphere—because as mothers and wives and homemakers they had special experiences and special sensitivities to bring to public life—that woman suffrage could make such an important contribution to politics. Jane Addams expressed this more maternalist justification for suffrage in a 1909 article: "If women would effectively continue their old avocations, they must take part in the slow upbuilding of that code of legislation which is alone sufficient to protect the home from its dangers incident to modern life."

In particular, many suffragists argued that enfranchising women would help the temperance movement, by giving its largest group of supporters a political voice. Some suffrage advocates claimed that once women had the vote, war would become a thing of the past, since women would—by their calming, maternal influence—help curb the belligerence of men. That was one reason why World War I gave a final, decisive push to the movement for suffrage.

Suffrage also attracted support for other, less optimistic reasons. Many middle-class people found persuasive the argument that if blacks, immigrants, and other "base" groups had access to the franchise, then it was not only a matter of justice but of common

Conservative Arguments for Suffrage

sense to allow educated, "well-born" women to vote. Some people, in fact, supported woman suffrage because they believed that it would add to the constituency that supported immigration restriction and racial disfranchisement. Florence Kelley, a prominent social reformer who was later to help organize the NAACP, remarked unhappily in 1906 on this aspect of the suffrage movement: "I have rarely heard a ringing suffrage speech which did not refer to the 'ignorant and degraded' men, or the 'ignorant immigrants' as our masters. This is habitually spoken with more or less bitterness."

Not all suffragists abandoned the more radical rationales. Among working-class, immigrant, and black women in particular, suffrage continued to generate substantial support precisely because it seemed so radical, because it promised to reshape the role of women and reform the social order. But among members of the middle class, the separation of the suffrage movement from more radical feminist goals, and its association with other reform causes of concern to many Americans, helped it gain widespread support.

The principal triumphs of the suffrage movement began in 1910. That year, Washington became the first state in fourteen years to extend suffrage to women. California followed a year later, and four other western states in 1912. This impressive early strength of the suffrage movement in the western states was a result, in part, of the absence of large Catholic communities in the region. In the East, battles over suffrage seemed inevitably to become linked to ethnic battles over cultural issues—most notably temperance—that divided Catholics and Protestants. In the West, the suffrage fight only rarely intersected with other, more divisive issues.

In 1913, Illinois became the first state east of the Mississippi to embrace woman suffrage. And in 1917 and 1918, New York and Michigan—two of the most populous states in the Union—gave women the vote. By 1919, thirty-nine states had granted women the right to vote in

Nineteenth Amendment | at least some elections; fifteen had allowed them full participation. In 1920, finally, suffragists won ratification of the Nineteenth Amendment, which guaranteed political rights to women throughout the nation.

To some feminists, however, the victory seemed less than complete. Alice Paul, head of the militant National Woman's Party (founded in 1916), never accepted the relatively conservative "separate sphere" justification for suffrage. She argued that the Nineteenth Amendment alone would not be sufficient to protect women's rights. Women needed more: a constitutional amendment that would provide clear, legal protection for their rights and

Equal Rights Amendment | would prohibit all discrimination on the basis of sex. But Alice Paul's argument found limited favor even among many of the most important leaders of the recently triumphant suffrage crusade. Jane Addams, Florence Kelley, Carrie Chapman Catt, and others showed no interest in the Equal Rights Amendment. Some, such as Addams, denounced it bitterly, fearing it would invalidate the special protective legislation for women that they had fought so hard to have enacted. It would be many years before the divisions between these two wings of American feminism were healed.

As the controversy over the Equal Rights Amendment suggests, the suffrage movement did not, in the end, produce a coherent movement behind any issue other than securing women the vote. On most other questions, in fact, women were generally no more in agreement than men. Once enfranchised, the new voters did little to support the arguments of those suffragists who had claimed that women would operate in politics as a coherent force for reform.

SUFFRAGISTS Suffrage activists hang posters along the boardwalk in the beachfront town of Long Beach, New Jersey. Thirty-nine states had permitted women at least some access to the ballot before ratification of the Nineteenth Amendment in 1920. New Jersey was not one of them. *(Culver Pictures, Inc.)*

THE ASSAULT ON THE PARTIES

Sooner or later, most progressive goals required the involvement of government. Only government, reformers agreed, could effectively counter the many powerful private interests that threatened the nation. But American government at the dawn of the new century was, progressives believed, poorly adapted to perform their ambitious tasks. At every level political institutions were outmoded, inefficient, and *Reforming Government* corrupt. Before they could reform society effectively, they would have to reform government itself. In the beginning, at least, many reformers believed the first step must be an assault on the dominant role the political parties played in the life of the state. They considered the parties corrupt, undemocratic, and reactionary.

Early Attacks

Attacks on party dominance had been frequent in the late nineteenth century. Greenbackism and populism, for example, had been efforts to break the hammerlock with which the Republicans and Democrats controlled public life. The Independent Republicans (or mugwumps) had attempted to challenge the grip of partisanship; and former mugwumps became important supporters of progressive political reform activity in the 1890s and later.

The early assaults enjoyed some success. In the 1880s and 1890s, for example, most states adopted the secret ballot. Prior to that, the political parties themselves had printed ballots (or "tickets"), with the names of the party's candidates, and no others. They distributed the tickets to their supporters, who then simply went to the polls to deposit them in the ballot box. The old system had made it possible for bosses to monitor the voting behavior of their constituents; it had also made it difficult for voters to "split" their tickets—to vote for candidates of different parties for different offices. The new secret ballot—printed by the government and distributed at the polls to be filled out and deposited in secret—helped chip away at the power of the parties over the voters.

By the late 1890s, critics of the parties were expanding their goals. Party rule could be broken, they believed, in one of two ways. It could be broken by increasing the *Attacking Party Rule* power of the people, by permitting them to circumvent partisan institutions and express their will directly at the polls. Or it could be broken by placing more power in the hands of nonpartisan, nonelective officials, insulated from political life. Reformers promoted measures that moved along both those paths.

Municipal Reform

Many progressives believed the impact of party rule was most damaging in the cities. Municipal government therefore became the first target of those working for political reform. Muckraking journalists such as Lincoln Steffens were especially successful in arousing public outrage at corruption and incompetence in city politics.

The muckrakers struck a responsive chord among a powerful group of urban middle-class progressives. For several decades after the Civil War, "respectable" citizens of the nation's large cities had avoided participation in municipal government. Viewing politics as a debased and de-*Middle-class Progressives* meaning activity, they shrank from contact with the "vulgar" elements who were coming to dominate public life. By the end of the century, however, a new generation of activists—some of them members of old aristocratic families, others a part of the new middle class—were taking a growing interest in government.

They faced a formidable array of opponents. In addition to challenging the powerful city bosses and their entrenched political organizations, they were attacking a large group of special interests: saloon owners, brothel keepers, and, perhaps most significantly, those businessmen who had established lucrative relationships with the urban machines and who viewed reform as a threat to their profits. Allied with these interests were many influential newspapers, which ridiculed the reformers as naive do-gooders. Finally, there was the great constituency of urban working people, many of them recent immigrants, to whom the machines were a source of needed jobs and services. Gradually, however, the reformers gained in political strength—in part because of their own growing numbers, in part because of the failures of the existing political leadership. And in the first years of the twentieth century, they began to score some important victories.

New Forms of Governance

One of the first major successes came in Galveston, Texas, where the old city government proved completely unable to deal with the effects of a destructive tidal wave in 1900. Capitalizing on public dismay, reformers, many of them local businessmen, won approval of a new city charter. The mayor and council *Commission Plan* were replaced by an elected, nonpartisan commission. In 1907, Des Moines, Iowa, adopted its own version of the commission plan, and other cities soon followed.

Another approach to municipal reform, similarly motivated by the desire to remove city government from the hands of the parties, was the city-manager plan, by which elected officials hired an outside expert—often a profes-*City-Manager Plan* sionally trained business manager or engineer—to take charge of the government. The city manager would presumably remain untainted by the corrupting influence of politics. By the end of the progressive era, almost 400 cities were operating under commissions, and another 45 employed city managers.

In most urban areas, and in the larger cities in particular, the enemies of party had to settle for less absolute victories. Some cities made the election of mayors nonpartisan (so that the parties could not choose the candidates) or moved them to years when no presidential or

TOM JOHNSON As sentiment for municipal reform grew in intensity in the late nineteenth century, it became possible for progressive mayors committed to ending "boss rule" to win election over machine candidates in some of America's largest cities. One of the most prominent was Tom Johnson, the reform mayor of Cleveland. Johnson made a fortune in the steel and streetcar business, and then entered politics, partly as a result of reading Henry George's *Poverty and Progress*. He became mayor in 1901 and in his four terms waged strenuous battles against party bosses and corporate interests. He won many fights, but he lost what he considered his most important one: the struggle for municipal ownership of public utilities. *(Western Reserve Historical Society)*

congressional races were in progress (to reduce the influence of the large turnouts that party organizations produced on such occasions). Reformers tried to make city councilors run at large, to limit the influence of ward leaders and district bosses. They tried to strengthen the power of the mayor at the expense of the city council, on the assumption that reformers were more likely to succeed in getting a sympathetic mayor elected than they were to win control of the entire council.

Indeed, some of the most successful reformers emerged not from the new commission and city-manager systems but from conventional political structures that progressives *Tom Johnson* came to control. Tom Johnson, the celebrated reform mayor of Cleveland, waged a long and difficult war against the powerful streetcar interests in his city, fighting to raise the ridiculously low assessments on railroad and utilities properties, to lower streetcar fares to 3 cents, and ultimately to impose municipal ownership on certain basic utilities. After Johnson's defeat and death, his talented aide Newton D. Baker won election as mayor and helped maintain Cleveland's reputation as the best-governed city in America. Hazen Pingree of Detroit, Samuel "Golden Rule" Jones of Toledo, and other mayors effectively challenged local party bosses to bring the spirit of reform into city government.

Statehouse Progressivism

The assault on boss rule in the cities did not, however, always produce results satisfying to reformers. As a result, many progressives turned to state government as an agent for reform. These state-level progressives, like their municipal counterparts, considered existing state governments unfit to answer society's needs. They looked with particular scorn on state legislatures, whose ill-paid, relatively undistinguished members they believed were generally incompetent, often corrupt, and totally controlled by party bosses. Many reformers began looking for ways to circumvent the legislatures (and the party bosses that controlled them) by increasing the power of the electorate.

Two of the most important changes were innovations first proposed by Populists in the 1890s: the initiative and the referendum. The initiative *Initiative and Referendum* allowed reformers to circumvent state legislatures altogether by submitting new legislation directly to the voters in general elections. The referendum provided a method by which actions of the legislature could be returned to the electorate for approval. By 1918, more than twenty states had enacted one or both of these reforms.

Similarly, the direct primary and the recall were efforts to limit the power of party and improve the quality of elected officials. The primary *Direct Primary and Recall* election was an attempt to take the selection of candidates away from the bosses and give it to the people. In the South, it was also an effort to limit black voting—since primary voting, many white southerners believed, would be easier to control than general elections. The recall gave voters the right to remove a public official from office at a special election, which could be called after a sufficient number of citizens had

ROBERT LA FOLLETTE CAMPAIGNING IN WISCONSIN After three terms as governor of Wisconsin, La Follette began a long career in the United States Senate in 1906 during which he worked uncompromisingly for advanced progressive reforms—so uncompromisingly, in fact, that he was often almost completely isolated. He entitled a chapter of his autobiography "Alone in the Senate." La Follette had a greater impact on his own state, whose politics he and his sons dominated for nearly forty years and where he was able to win passage of many reforms that the federal government resisted. *(State Historical Society of Wisconsin)*

signed a petition. By 1915 every state in the nation had instituted primary elections for at least some offices. The recall encountered more strenuous opposition, but a few states adopted it as well.

Other reform measures attempted to clean up the legislatures themselves by limiting the influence of corporations on their activities and on the behavior of the parties. Between 1903 and 1908, twelve states passed laws restricting lobbying by business interests in state legislatures. In those same years, twenty-two states banned campaign contributions by corporations, and twenty-four states forbade public officials from accepting free passes from railroads.

Reform efforts proved most effective in states that elevated vigorous and committed politicians to positions of leadership. In New York, Governor Charles Evans Hughes exploited progressive sentiment to create a commission to regulate public utilities. In California, Governor Hiram Johnson used the new reforms to limit the political power of the Southern Pacific Railroad. In New Jersey, Woodrow Wilson, the Princeton University president elected governor in 1910, used executive leadership to win reforms designed to end New Jersey's widely denounced position as the "mother of trusts."

But the most celebrated state-level reformer was Robert M. La Follette of Wisconsin. Elected governor in *Robert La Follette* | 1900, he helped turn his state | into what reformers across the nation described as a "laboratory of progressivism." Under his leadership the Wisconsin progressives won approval of direct primaries, initiatives, and referendums. They regulated railroads and utilities. They passed laws to regulate the workplace and provide compensation for laborers in-

jured on the job. They instituted graduated taxes on inherited fortunes, and they nearly doubled state levies on railroads and other corporate interests. La Follette brought to progressivism his own fervent, almost evangelical, commitment to reform; and he used his personal magnetism to widen public awareness of progressive goals and to mobilize the energies of many previously passive groups. Reform was not simply the responsibility of politicians, he argued, but of newspapers, citizens' groups, educational institutions, and business and professional organizations. Ultimately, La Follette would be overshadowed by other national progressive leaders. In the early years of the century, however, few men were as effective in publicizing the message of reform. None was as successful in bending state government to that goal.

Parties and Interest Groups

The reformers did not, of course, eliminate parties from American political life. But they did contribute to a decline in party influence. Evidence of their impact came from, among other things, the | *Decline of Party Influence* decline in voter turnout. In the | late nineteenth century, up to 81 percent of eligible voters routinely turned out for national elections. In the early twentieth century, while turnout remained very high by today's standards, the figure declined markedly. In the presidential election of 1900, 73 percent of the electorate voted. By 1912, it had declined to about 59 percent. Never again did voter turnout reach as high as 70 percent.

At the same time that parties were declining, other power centers were beginning to replace them: what

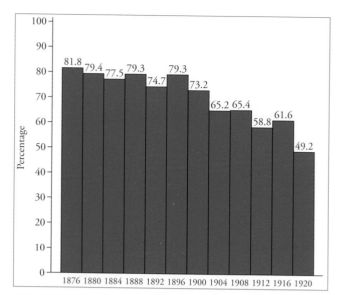

VOTER PARTICIPATION IN PRESIDENTIAL ELECTIONS, 1876–1920 One of the striking developments of early twentieth-century politics was the significant decline in popular participation in politics. This chart shows the steady downward progression of voter turnout in presidential elections from 1876 to 1920. Turnout remained high by modern standards (except for the aberrant election of 1920, in which turnout dropped sharply because women had recently received the vote but had not yet begun to participate in elections in large numbers). But from an average rate of participation of about 79 percent in the last quarter of the nineteenth century, turnout dropped to an average of about 65 percent between 1900 and 1916. ◆ *What were some of the reasons for this decline?*

have become known as "interest groups." Beginning late in the nineteenth century and accelerating rapidly in the twentieth, new organizations emerged outside the party system, designed to pressure government to do their members' bidding: professional organizations, trade associations representing particular businesses and industries, labor organizations, farm lobbies, and many others. Social workers, the settlement house movement, women's clubs, and others learned to operate as interest groups to advance their demands. A new pattern of politics, in which many individual interests organized to influence government directly rather than through party structures, was emerging. It would become the characteristic form of American politics in the twentieth century.

SOURCES OF PROGRESSIVE REFORM

Middle-class reformers, most of them from the East, dominated the public image and much of the substance of progressivism in the late nineteenth and early twentieth centuries. But they were not alone in seeking to improve social conditions. Working-class Americans, African Americans, westerners, and even party bosses also played crucial roles in advancing some of the important reforms of the era.

Labor, the Machine, and Reform

Although the American Federation of Labor, and its leader Samuel Gompers, remained largely aloof from many of the reform efforts of the time (reflecting Gompers's firm belief that workers should not rely on government to improve their lot), some unions nevertheless played important roles in reform battles. In San Francisco, for example, workers in the Building Trades Council spearheaded the formation of the new Union Labor Party, committed to a program of reform almost indistinguishable from that of middle-class and elite progressives in the city. Corruption and ineptitude within the new party's leadership limited its effectiveness, but the party did manage to elect two of its candidates mayor. Although the workers never controlled enough votes in the state legislature to have much direct influence, other Bay Area politicians supported pro-labor legislation in an effort to appeal to the party's constituency. Between 1911 and 1913, California passed a child labor law, a workmen's compensation law, and a limitation on working hours for women. Union pressures contributed to the passage of similar laws in many other states as well.

One result of the assault on the parties was a change in the party organizations themselves, which attempted to adapt to the new realities so as to preserve their influence. Some party machines emerged from the progressive era almost as powerful as they had entered it. In large part, this was because bosses themselves recognized that they must change in order to survive. Thus they sometimes allowed their machines to become vehicles of social reform. One example was New York's Tammany Hall, the nation's oldest and most notorious city machine. Its astute leader, Charles Francis Murphy, began in the early years of the century to fuse the techniques of boss rule with some of the concerns of social reformers. Murphy did nothing to challenge the fundamental workings of Tammany Hall. But Tammany began to take an increased interest in state and national politics, which it had traditionally scorned; and it used its political power on behalf of legislation to improve working conditions, protect child laborers, and eliminate the worst abuses of the industrial economy.

In 1911, a terrible fire swept through the factory of the Triangle Shirtwaist Company in New York; 146 workers, most of them women, died. Many of them had been trapped *Triangle Shirtwaist Fire* inside the burning building because management had locked the emergency exits to prevent malingering. For the next three years, a state commission studied not only the background of the fire but the general condition of the industrial workplace. It was responding to intense public pressure from women's groups and New York City labor unions—and to less public pressure from Tammany Hall. By 1914, the commission had issued a series of

VICTIMS OF THE TRIANGLE FIRE In this bleak photograph, victims of the fire in the Triangle Shirtwaist Factory are laid out on the sidewalk near the building, as police and passersby look up at the scene of the blaze. The tragedy of the Triangle Fire galvanized New York legislators into passing laws to protect women workers. *(Brown Brothers)*

reports calling for major reforms in the conditions of modern labor. The report itself was a classic progressive document, based on the testimony of experts, filled with statistics and technical data.

Yet when its recommendations reached the New York legislature, its most effective supporters were not middle-class progressives but two Tammany Democrats from working-class backgrounds: Senator Robert F. Wagner and Assemblyman Alfred E. Smith. With the support of Murphy and the backing of other Tammany legislators, they steered through a series of pioneering labor laws that imposed strict regulations on factory owners and established effective mechanisms for enforcement.

Western Progressives

The American West produced some of the most notable progressive leaders of the time: Hiram Johnson of California, George Norris of Nebraska, William Borah of Idaho, and others—almost all of whom spent at least some of their political careers in the United States Senate. For western states, the most important target of reform energies was not state or local governments, which had relatively little power, but the federal government, which exercised a kind of authority in the West that it had never possessed in the East. That was in part because some of the most important issues to the future of the West required action above the state level. Disputes over water, for example, almost always involved rivers and streams that crossed state lines. The question of who had the rights to the waters of the Colorado River created a political battle that no state government could resolve; the federal government had to arbitrate. More significant, perhaps, the federal government exercised enormous power over the lands and resources of the western states and provided substantial subsidies to the region in the form of land grants and support for railroad and water projects. Huge areas of the West remained (and still remain) public lands, controlled by Washington—a far greater proportion than in any states east of the Mississippi; and much of the growth of the West was (and continues to be) a result of federally funded dams and water projects.

Because so much authority in the region rested in federal bureaucracies that state and local governments could

Sources of Western Progressivism

not control, political parties in most of the West were relatively weak. That was one reason why western states could move so quickly and decisively to embrace reforms that parties did not like: the initiative, the referendum, the recall, direct primaries. It is also why aspiring politicians were much quicker to look to Washington as a place from which they could influence the future of their region.

African Americans and Reform

One social question that received relatively little attention from white progressives was race. But among African Americans themselves, the progressive era produced some significant challenges to existing racial norms.

African Americans faced greater obstacles—legal, economic, social, and political—than any other group in challenging their own oppressed status and seeking reform. Thus it was not surprising, perhaps, that so many embraced the message of Booker T. Washington in the late nineteenth century, to "put down your bucket where you are," to work for immediate self-improvement rather than long-range social change. Not all blacks, however, were content with this approach. And by the turn of the century a powerful challenge was emerging—to the philosophy of Washington and, more important, to the entire structure of race relations. The chief spokesman for this new approach was W. E. B. Du Bois.

Du Bois, unlike Washington, had never known slavery. Born in Massachusetts, educated at Fisk University in

W. E. B. Du Bois

Atlanta and at Harvard, he grew to maturity with a more expansive view than Washington of the goals of his race and the responsibilities of white society to eliminate prejudice and injustice. In *The Souls of Black Folk* (1903), he launched an open attack on the philosophy of the Atlanta Compromise, accusing Washington of encouraging white efforts to impose segregation and of unnecessarily limiting the aspirations of his race. "Is it possible and probable," he asked, "that nine millions of men can make effective progress in economic lines if they are deprived of political rights, made a servile caste, and allowed only the most meager chance for developing their exceptional men? If history and reason give any distinct answer to these questions, it is an emphatic No."

Rather than content themselves with education at the trade and agricultural schools, Du Bois advocated, talented blacks should accept nothing less than a full university education. They should aspire to the professions. They should, above all, fight for the immediate restoration

THE YOUNG W. E. B. DU BOIS This formal photograph of W. E. B. Du Bois was taken in 1899, when he was thirty-one years old and a professor at Atlanta University. He had just published *The Philadelphia Negro,* a classic sociological study of an urban community, which startled many readers with its description of the complex class system among African Americans in the city. *(Hulton/Archive/Getty Images)*

of their civil rights, not simply wait for them to be granted as a reward for patient striving. In 1905, Du Bois and a group of his supporters met at Niagara Falls—on the Canadian

NAACP Founded

side of the border because no hotel on the American side of the Falls would have them—and launched what became known as the Niagara Movement. Four years later, after a race riot in Springfield, Illinois, they joined with white progressives sympathetic to their cause to form the National Association for the Advancement of Colored People (NAACP). Whites held most of the offices at first, but Du Bois, its director of publicity and research, was the guiding spirit. In the ensuing years, the new organization led the drive for equal rights, using as its principal weapon lawsuits in the federal courts.

Within less than a decade, the NAACP had begun to win some important victories. In *Guinn* v. *United States* (1915), the Supreme Court supported their position that the grandfather clause in an Oklahoma law was unconstitutional. (The statute denied the vote to any citizen whose ancestors had not been enfranchised in 1860.) In *Buchanan* v. *Worley* (1917), the Court struck down a Louisville, Kentucky, law requiring residential segregation. Disfranchisement and segregation would survive through other methods for many decades to come, but the NAACP had established a pattern of black resistance that would ultimately bear important fruits. It had also established itself, particularly after Booker T. Washington's death in 1915, as one of the nation's leading black organizations, a position it would maintain for many years.

The NAACP was not a radical, or even an egalitarian, organization. It relied, rather, on the efforts of the most intelligent and educated members of the black race, the "talented tenth" as Du Bois called them. And it stressed

The NAACP's Strategy | not so much the elevation of all blacks from poverty and oppression as the opportunity for exceptional blacks to gain positions of full equality. Ultimately, its members believed, such efforts would benefit all blacks. By creating a trained elite, blacks would in effect be creating a leadership group capable of fighting for the rights of the race as a whole.

CRUSADE FOR SOCIAL ORDER AND REFORM

Reformers directed many of their energies at the political process. But they also crusaded on behalf of what they considered moral issues. There were campaigns to eliminate alcohol from national life, to curb prostitution, to limit divorce, and to restrict immigration. Proponents of each of those reforms believed that success would help regenerate society as a whole.

The Temperance Crusade

Many progressives considered the elimination of alcohol from American life a necessary step in restoring order to society. Workers in settlement houses and social agencies abhorred the effects of drinking on working-class families: Scarce wages vanished as workers spent hours in the saloons. Drunkenness spawned violence, and occasionally murder, within urban families. Women, in particular, saw alcohol as a source of some of the greatest problems of working-class wives and mothers, and hoped through temperance to reform male behavior and thus improve women's lives. Employers, too, regarded alcohol as an impediment to industrial efficiency; workers often missed time on the job because of drunkenness or, worse, came

CRUSADING FOR TEMPERANCE This unflattering painting by Ben Shahn portrays late-nineteenth-century women demonstrating grimly in front of a saloon. It suggests the degree to which temperance and prohibition had fallen out of favor with liberals and progressives by the 1930s, when Shahn was working. In earlier years, however, temperance attracted the support of some of the most advanced American reformers. (*©Estate of Ben Shahn/Licensed by VAGA, New York, NY/Museum of the City of New York*)

to the factory intoxicated and performed their tasks sloppily and dangerously. Critics of economic privilege denounced the liquor industry as one of the nation's most sinister trusts. And political reformers, who (correctly) looked on the saloon as one of the central institutions of the urban machine, saw an attack on drinking as part of an attack on the bosses. Out of such sentiments emerged the temperance movement.

Temperance had been a major reform movement before the Civil War, mobilizing large numbers of people (and particularly large numbers of women) in a crusade

WCTU

with strong evangelical overtones. Beginning in the 1870s, it experienced a major resurgence. As in the antebellum years, the movement was led and supported primarily by women. In 1873, temperance advocates formed the Women's Christian Temperance Union (WCTU), led after 1879 by Frances Willard. By 1911, it had 245,000 members and had become the single largest women's organization in American history to that point. The WCTU publicized the evils of alcohol and the connection between drunkenness and family violence, unemployment, poverty, and disease. In 1893, the Anti-Saloon League joined the temperance movement and, along with the WCTU, began to press for a specific legislative solution: the legal abolition of saloons. Gradually, that demand grew to include the complete prohibition of the sale and manufacture of alcoholic beverages.

Despite substantial opposition from immigrant and working-class voters, pressure for prohibition grew steadily through the first decades of the new century. By 1916, nineteen states had passed prohibition laws. But since the consumption of alcohol was actually increasing in many unregulated areas, temperance advocates were beginning to advocate a national prohibition law. America's entry

Eighteenth Amendment

into World War I, and the moral fervor it unleashed, provided the last push to the advocates of prohibition. In 1917, with the support of rural fundamentalists who opposed alcohol on moral and religious grounds, progressive advocates of prohibition steered through Congress a constitutional amendment embodying their demands. Two years later, after ratification by every state in the nation except Connecticut and Rhode Island (bastions of Catholic immigrants), the Eighteenth Amendment became law, to take effect in January 1920.

Immigration Restriction

Virtually all reformers agreed that the growing immigrant population had created social problems, but there was wide disagreement on how to best respond. Some progressives believed that the proper approach was to help the new residents adapt to American society. Others argued that efforts at assimilation had failed and that the only solution was to limit the flow of new arrivals.

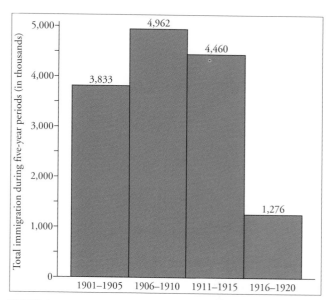

TOTAL IMMIGRATION, 1900–1920 Immigration into the United States reached the highest level in the nation's history to that point in the first fifteen years of the twentieth century. In the nineteenth century, there was no five-year period when as many as 3 million immigrants arrived in America. In the first fifteen years of the twentieth century, more than 3 million newcomers arrived in every five-year period—and in one of them, as this chart reveals, the number reached almost 5 million. ◆ *Why did the flow of immigrants drop so sharply in the period 1916–1920?*

In the first decades of the century, therefore, pressure grew to close the nation's gates. New scholarly theories, appealing to the progressive respect for expertise, argued that the introduction of immigrants into American society was polluting the nation's racial stock. Among the theories created to support this argument was eugenics. (Eugenics is the science of altering the reproductive processes of plants and animals to produce new hybrids or breeds.) In the early twentieth century, there was an effort, funded by the Carnegie Foundation, to turn eugenics into a method of altering human reproduction as well.

But the eugenics movement

Eugenics and Nativism

when applied to humans was not an effort to "breed" new people, an effort for which no scientific tools existed. It was, rather, an effort to grade races and ethnic groups according to their genetic qualities. Eugenicists advocated the forced sterilization of the mentally retarded, criminals, and others. But they also spread the belief that human inequalities were hereditary and that immigration was contributing to the multiplication of the unfit. Skillful publicists such as Madison Grant, whose *The Passing of the Great Race* (1916) established him as the nation's most effective nativist, warned of the dangers of racial "mongrelization" and of the importance of protecting the purity of Anglo-Saxon and other Nordic stock from pollution by eastern Europeans, Hispanics, and Asians.

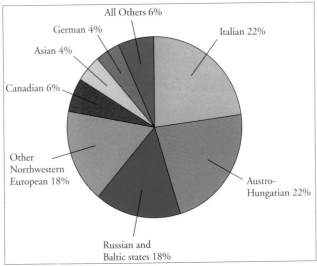

SOURCES OF IMMIGRATION, 1900–1920 At least as striking as the increase in immigration in the early twentieth century was the change in its sources. In the nineteenth century, the vast majority of immigrants to the United States had come from northern and western Europe (especially Britain, Ireland, Germany, and Scandinavia). Now, as this chart shows, the major sources were southern and eastern Europe, with over sixty percent coming from Italy, Russia, and the eastern European regions of the Austro-Hungarian empire. ♦ *What impact did these changing sources have on attitudes toward immigration in the United States?*

A special federal commission of "experts," chaired by Senator William P. Dillingham of Vermont, issued an elaborate study filled with statistics and scholarly testimony. The Dillingham Report argued that the newer immigrant groups—largely southern and eastern Europeans—had proven themselves less assimilable than earlier immigrants. Immigration, the report implied, should be restricted by nationality. Many people who rejected these racial arguments nevertheless supported limiting immigration as a way to solve such urban problems as overcrowding, unemployment, strained social services, and social unrest.

The combination of these concerns gradually won for the nativists the support of some of the nation's leading progressives: Theodore Roosevelt, Henry Cabot Lodge, and others. Powerful opponents—employers who saw immigration as a source of cheap labor, immigrants themselves, and their political representatives—managed to block the restriction movement for a time. But by the beginning of World War I (which itself effectively blocked immigration temporarily), the nativist tide was clearly gaining strength.

CHALLENGING THE CAPITALIST ORDER

One of the things that makes "progressivism" so difficult to identify is the wide range of issues and concerns that attracted the attention of reformers in the late nineteenth and early twentieth centuries. There were efforts to limit the power of the political parties; efforts to reform state, local, and national governments; efforts to enhance the role of women in American life; efforts to impose moral reform on society; efforts to protect industrial workers; and efforts to restrict immigration. But if there was one issue that overshadowed, and helped to shape, all others in the minds of reformers, it was the character of the dramatically growing modern industrial economy. Most of the problems that concerned progressives could be traced back, directly or indirectly, to the growing power and influence—and also, reformers believed, corruption—of corporate America. So it is not surprising that prominent among progressive concerns was reshaping or reforming the behavior of the capitalist world. The challenges to the structure of capitalism took many different forms.

The Dream of Socialism

At no time in the history of the United States to that point, and seldom after, did radical critiques of the capitalist system attract more support than in the period between 1900 and 1914. Although never a force to rival or even seriously threaten the two major parties, the Socialist Party of America grew during the progressive era into a force of considerable strength. In the election of 1900, it had attracted the support of fewer than 100,000 voters; in 1912, its durable leader and perennial presidential candidate, Eugene V. Debs, received nearly 1 million ballots. Strongest in urban immigrant communities, particularly among Germans and Jews, it also attracted the loyalties of a substantial number of Protestant farmers in the South and Midwest. Socialists won election to over 1,000 state and local offices. And they had the support at times of such intellectuals as Lincoln Steffens, the crusader against municipal corruption, and Walter Lippmann, the brilliant young journalist and social critic. Florence Kelley, Frances Willard, and other women reformers were attracted to socialism, too, in part because of its support for pacifism and labor militancy.

Eugene Debs

Virtually all socialists agreed on the need for basic structural changes in the economy, but they differed widely on the extent of those changes and the tactics necessary to achieve them. Some endorsed the radical goals of European Marxists; others envisioned a more moderate reform that would allow small-scale private enterprise to survive but would nationalize major industries. Some believed in working for reform through electoral politics; others favored militant direct action. Most conspicuous among the militants was the radical labor union the Industrial Workers of the World (IWW), known to opponents as the "Wobblies." Under the leadership of William ("Big Bill") Haywood, the IWW advocated a sin-

"Wobblies"

MAY DAY, 1900 The American Socialist Party staged this vast rally in New York City's Union Square to celebrate May Day in 1900. The Second Socialist International had designated May Day as the official holiday for radical labor in 1899. *(Brown Brothers)*

gle union for all workers and abolition of the "wage slave" system; it rejected political action in favor of strikes—especially the general strike. The Wobblies were widely believed to have been responsible for the dynamiting of railroad lines and power stations and other acts of terror, although the popular image of their use of violence was undoubtedly exaggerated.

The IWW was one of the few labor organizations of the time to champion the cause of unskilled workers, and it had particular strength in the West—where a large group of migratory laborers (miners, timbermen, and others) found it very difficult to organize or sustain conventional unions. The Wobblies created not just a union, but a far-flung social network that became something of a home to workers who were otherwise largely rootless.

In 1917, a strike by IWW timber workers in Washington and Idaho virtually shut down production in the industry. That brought down upon the union the wrath of the federal government, which had just begun mobilizing for war and needed timber for war production. Federal authori-

ties imprisoned the leaders of the union, and state governments between 1917 and 1919 passed a series of laws that effectively outlawed the IWW. The organization survived for a time, but never fully recovered.

More moderate socialists who advocated peaceful change through political struggle dominated the party. They emphasized a gradual education of the public to the need for change and patient efforts within the system to enact it. But by the end of World War I, because the party had refused to support the war effort and because of a growing wave of antiradicalism that subjected the socialists to *Socialism's Demise* enormous harassment and persecution, socialism was in decline as a significant political force.

Decentralization and Regulation

Many reformers agreed with the socialists that the greatest threat to the nation's economy was excessive corporate centralization and consolidation, but most progressives retained a faith in the possibilities of reform within a capitalist system. Rather than nationalize basic industries, many reformers hoped to restore the economy to a more human scale. Few envisioned a return to a society of small, local enterprises; some consolidation, they recognized, was inevitable. They did, however, argue that the federal government should work to break up the largest combinations and enforce a balance between the need for bigness and the need for competition.

This viewpoint came to be identified particularly closely with Louis D. Brandeis, a brilliant lawyer and later justice of the Supreme Court, who spoke and wrote widely (most notably in his 1913 book *Other People's Money*) about the "curse of bigness." "If the Lord had intended things to be big," Brandeis once wrote, "he would have made man bigger—in brains and character."

Brandeis and his supporters opposed bigness in part because they considered it inefficient. But their opposition had a moral basis as well.

The Problem of Corporate Centralization

Bigness was a threat not just to efficiency but to freedom. It limited the ability of individuals to control their own destinies. It encouraged abuses of power. Government must, Brandeis insisted, regulate competition in such a way as to ensure that large combinations did not emerge.

Other progressives were less enthusiastic about the virtues of competition. More important to them was efficiency, which they believed economic concentration usually encouraged. What government should do, they argued, was not to fight "bigness,"

"Good Trusts" and "Bad Trusts"

but to guard against abuses of power by large institutions. It should distinguish between "good trusts" and "bad trusts," encouraging the good while disciplining the bad. Since economic consolidation was destined to remain a permanent feature of American society, continuing oversight by a strong, modernized government was essential. One of the most influential spokesmen for this emerging "nationalist" position was Herbert Croly, whose 1909 book *The Promise of American Life* became one of the most influential progressive documents.

Increasingly, the attention of nationalists such as Croly focused on some form of coordination of the industrial economy. Society must act, Walter Lippmann wrote in a notable 1914 book, *Drift and Mastery,* "to introduce plan where there has been clash, and purpose into the jungles of disordered growth." To some, that meant businesses themselves learning new ways of cooperation and self-regulation; some of the most energetic "progressive" reformers of the period, in fact, were businessmen searching for ways to bring order to their own troubled world. To others, the solution was for

LOUIS BRANDEIS Brandeis graduated from Harvard Law School in 1877 with the best academic record of any student in the school's previous or subsequent history. His success in his Boston law practice was such that by the early twentieth century he was able to spend much of his time in unpaid work for public causes. His investigations of monopoly power soon made him a major figure in the emerging progressive movement. Woodrow Wilson nominated him for the United States Supreme Court in January 1916. He was one of the few nominees in the Court's history never to have held prior public office, and he was the first Jew ever to have been nominated. The appointment aroused five months of bitter controversy in the Senate before Brandeis was finally confirmed. For the next twenty years, he was one of the Court's most powerful members—all the while lobbying behind the scenes on behalf of the many political causes (preeminent among them Zionism, the founding of a Jewish state) to which he remained committed. *(Bettmann/Corbis)*

government to play a more active role in regulating and planning economic life. One of those who came to endorse that position (although not fully until after 1910) was Theodore Roosevelt, who once said: "We should enter upon a course of supervision, control, and regulation of those great corporations—a regulation which we should not fear, if necessary, to bring to the point of control of monopoly prices." Roosevelt became for a time the most powerful symbol of the reform impulse at the national level.

CONCLUSION

A powerful surge of reform efforts emerged in the last years of the nineteenth century and the first years of the twentieth—reforms intended to help the United States deal with the extraordinary changes and vexing problems that the rise of the modern industrial economy had caused. American reformers at the time thought of themselves as "progressives." But neither then nor since has there ever been wide agreement on what the term "progressive" meant in those years.

The reforms themselves were of a bewildering variety—efforts to improve the moral fabric of families and communities; efforts to make politics more efficient and less corrupt; efforts to tame or discipline the great industrial combinations of the time; efforts to empower some groups and restrict or control others. The ideas that lay behind these re-forms were similarly various, and the constituencies supporting them included at times representatives of almost every group in the population. "Progressivism" was a re-markably heterogeneous movement, united—if it was united at all—by the common belief among reformers that progress was indeed possible, even necessary; and that laissez-faire orthodoxy was inadequate to the needs of the nation, that purposeful human intervention in the life of society and its economy was necessary. The reform crusades gained strength steadily from the 1880s onward, driven in large part by the energy and commitment of millions of women organized in clubs and other organizations. By the early years of the twentieth century, reform was beginning to transform the character of society and the nature of American politics.

FOR FURTHER REFERENCE

Richard Hofstadter, *The Age of Reform: From Bryan to FDR* (1955) is a classic, and now con-troversial, analysis of the partly psychological origins of the populist and progressive move-ments. Robert Wiebe, *The Search for Order, 1877–1920* (1967) is an important organizational interpretation of the era. Gabriel Kolko makes a distinctly revisionist argument that business con-servatism was at the heart of the progressive movement in *The Triumph of Conservatism* (1963). Alan Dawley, *Struggles for Justice: Social Responsibility and the Liberal State* (1991) is a sophisticated synthetic account of progressive movements and their ideas. John Milton Cooper, *The Pivotal Decade: The United States, 1900–1920* (1990) is a good narrative history of the pe-riod. Arthur S. Link and Richard L. McCormick, *Progressivism* (1983) is a brief interpretation. For powerful insights into prag-matism, an important philosophical underpinning to much re-form, see Robert Westbrook, *John Dewey and American Democracy* (1991) and Louis Menand, *The Metaphysical Club: A Story of Ideas* (2001). Thomas L. Haskell, *The Emergence of Professional Social Science* (1977) is an important study of the social sciences and professionalism. Paul Starr, *The Social Trans-formation of American Medicine* (1982) is a pathbreaking study of the emergence of modern systems of health care. Morton J. Horwitz, *The Transformation of American Law, 1870–1960: The Challenge to Legal Orthodoxy* (1992) is an important, controversial study of the way the legal world responded to economic and social change. Nancy Cott, *The Grounding of American Feminism* (1987) studies the shifting roles and be-liefs of women. Kathryn Kish Sklar, *Florence Kelley and the Nation's Work: The Rise of Women's Political Culture, 1830–1900* (1995) examines the impact of female reformers on the progressive movement and the nation's political culture as a whole. Paula Giddings. *When and Where I Enter: The Impact of Black Women on Race and Sex in America* (1984) is a good in-troduction to the intersection of gender and race. Glenda Gilmore, *Gender and Jim Crow: Women and the Politics of White Supremacy in North Carolina, 1896–1920* (1996) ex-amines the role of gender in the construction of segregation. Louis Harlan, *Booker T. Washington: The Making of a Black Leader* (1956) and *Booker T. Washington: The Wizard of Tuskegee* (1983) are parts of an outstanding multi-volume biog-raphy, as are David Levering Lewis, *W. E. B. Du Bois: Biography of a Race* (1993) and *W. E. B. Du Bois: The Fight for Equality and the American Century* (2000).

For quizzes, Internet resources, references to additional books and films, and more, consult this book's Online Learning Center at www.mhhe.com/brinkley11.

THEODORE ROOSEVELT This heroic portrait of Theodore Roosevelt is by the great American portraitist John Singer Sargent. It hangs today in the White House. *(John Singer Sargent/White House Historical Association)*

Significant Events

1898 · Theodore Roosevelt elected governor of New York	· Roosevelt mediates settlement of Russo-Japanese War
1900 · Roosevelt elected vice president	
1901 · McKinley assassinated; Roosevelt becomes president	1906 · Hepburn Railroad Regulation Act passed
· Hay-Pauncefote Treaty ratified	· Upton Sinclair publishes *The Jungle*
1902 · Northern Securities antitrust case filed	· Meat Inspection Act passed
· Roosevelt intervenes in anthracite coal strike	· American troops intervene in Cuba
· National Reclamation Act (Newlands Act) passed	1907 · Financial panic and recession
1903 · Department of Commerce and Labor created	1908 · William Howard Taft elected president
· United States orchestrates Panamanian independence; new government signs treaty allowing United States to build Panama Canal	1909 · Payne-Aldrich Tariff passed
	· Pinchot-Ballinger dispute begins
	· U.S. troops intervene in Nicaragua
1904 · "Roosevelt corollary" announced	1910 · Roosevelt's Osawatomie speech outlines "New Nationalism"
1905 · Roosevelt elected president	

CHAPTER TWENTY-TWO

THE BATTLE FOR NATIONAL REFORM

Efforts to reform the industrial economy encountered repeated frustrations at the state and local levels. The great combinations were national in scope, and reformers gradually concluded that only national action could effectively control their power. Beginning early in the twentieth century, they began to look to the federal government.

But like state and local government, the national government—bureaucratically weak and mired in partisan politics—seemed poorly suited to serve as an agent of reform. Progressives attempted to make it more responsive to their demands. Some reformers, for example, urged an end to the

Reforming the National Government

system by which United States senators were elected by the members of their state legislatures; they proposed instead a direct popular election, which they believed would force the Senate to react to public demands. The Seventeenth Amendment, passed by Congress in 1912 and ratified by the states in 1913, brought about that change.

Even a reformed Congress, however, could not provide the kind of coherent leadership the progressive agenda required. If the federal government was truly to fulfill its mission, most reformers agreed, it would require leadership from the one office capable of providing it: the presidency.

THEODORE ROOSEVELT AND THE MODERN PRESIDENCY

"Presidents in general are not lovable," the writer Walter Lippmann, who had known many, said near the end of his life. "They've had to do too much to get where they are. But there was one President who was lovable— Teddy Roosevelt—and I loved him."

Lippmann was not alone. To a generation of progressive reformers, Theodore Roosevelt was more than an admired public figure; he was an idol. No president before, and few since, attracted such attention and devotion. Yet for all his popularity among reformers, Roosevelt was in many respects decidedly conservative. He earned his extraordinary popularity less because of the extent of the reforms he championed than because he brought to his office a broad conception of its powers and invested the presidency with something of its modern status as the center of national political life.

The Accidental President

When President William McKinley suddenly died in September 1901, the victim of an assassination, Roosevelt (who had been elected vice president less than a year before) was only forty-two years old, the youngest man ever to assume the presidency. Already, however, he had achieved a considerable reputation within the Republican Party as something of a wild man. Party leaders sensed his independence and despaired of controlling him. "I told William McKinley that it was a mistake to nominate that wild man at Philadelphia," party boss Mark Hanna was reported to have exclaimed. "I asked him if he realized what would happen if he should die. Now look, that damned cowboy is President of the United States!"

Roosevelt's reputation as a wild man was a result less of the substance of his early political career than of its style. As *Roosevelt's Background* a young member of the New York legislature, he had displayed an energy seldom seen in that lethargic body. As a rancher in the Dakota Badlands (where he retired briefly after the sudden death of his first wife), he had helped capture outlaws. As New York City police commissioner, he had been a flamboyant battler against crime and vice. As assistant secretary of the navy, he had been a bold proponent of American expansion. As commander of the Rough Riders, he had led a heroic, if militarily useless, charge in the battle of San Juan Hill in Cuba during the Spanish-American War.

But Roosevelt as president never openly rebelled against the leaders of his party. He became, rather, a champion of cautious, moderate change. Reform, he believed, was less a vehicle for remaking American society than for protecting it against more radical challenges.

Government, Capital, and Labor

Roosevelt envisioned the federal government not as the agent of any particular interest but as a mediator of the public good, with the president at its center. These attitudes found expression in Roosevelt's policies toward the great industrial combinations. He was not opposed to the principle of economic concentration, but he acknowledged that consolidation produced dangerous abuses of power. He allied himself, therefore, with those progressives who urged regulation (but not destruction) of the trusts.

Roosevelt's Vision of Federal Power

At the heart of Roosevelt's policy was his desire to win for government the power to investigate the activities of corporations and publicize the results. The pressure of educated public opinion, he believed, would alone eliminate most corporate abuses. Government could legislate solutions for those that remained. The new Department of Commerce and Labor, established in 1903 (later to be divided into two separate departments), was to assist in this task through its investigatory arm, the Bureau of Corporations.

Although Roosevelt was not a trustbuster at heart, he made a few highly publicized efforts to break up combinations. In 1902, he ordered the Justice Department to invoke the Sherman Antitrust Act against a great new railroad monopoly in the Northwest, the Northern Securities Company, a $400 million enterprise pieced together by J. P. Morgan, E. H. Harriman, and James J. Hill. To Morgan, accustomed to a warm, supportive relationship with Republican administrations, the action was baffling. Hurrying to the White House with two conservative senators in tow, he told the president, "If we have done anything wrong, send your man to my man and they can fix it up." Roosevelt proceeded with the case nonetheless, and in 1904 the Supreme Court ruled that the Northern Securities Company must be dissolved. At the same time, however, he assured Morgan and others that the suit did not signal a general campaign to dissolve trusts. Although he filed more than forty additional antitrust suits during the remainder of his presidency, Roosevelt had no serious commitment to reverse the prevailing trend toward economic concentration.

Northern Securities Company

A similar commitment to establishing the government as an impartial regulatory mechanism shaped Roosevelt's policy toward labor. In the past, federal intervention in industrial disputes had almost always meant action on behalf of employers. Roosevelt was willing to consider labor's position as well. When a bitter 1902 strike by the United Mine Workers against the anthracite coal industry dragged on long enough to endanger coal supplies for the coming winter, Roosevelt asked both the operators and the miners to accept impartial federal arbitration. When the mine owners balked, Roosevelt threatened to send federal troops to seize the mines and resume coal production. The operators finally relented. Arbitrators awarded the strikers a 10 percent wage increase and a nine-hour day, although no recognition of their union— less than they had wanted but more than they would likely have won without Roosevelt's intervention. Despite

BOYS IN THE MINES These young boys, covered in grime and no more than twelve years old, pose for the noted photographer Lewis Hine at the entrance to the coal mine in Pennsylvania where they worked—most likely as "breaker boys," crawling into newly blasted areas and breaking up the loose coal. The rugged conditions in the mines were one cause of the great strike of 1902, in which Theodore Roosevelt intervened. *(Lewis Hine/Corbis)*

such episodes, Roosevelt viewed himself as no more the champion of labor than of management. On several occasions, he ordered federal troops to intervene in strikes on behalf of employers.

"The Square Deal"

Reform was not Roosevelt's top priority during his first years as president. He was principally concerned with winning reelection, which required that he not antagonize the conservative Republican Old Guard. By skillfully dispensing patronage to conservatives and progressives alike, by reshuffling the leadership of unstable Republican organizations in the South, by winning the support of northern businessmen while making adroit gestures to reformers, Roosevelt had all but neutralized his opposition within the party by early 1904. He won its presidential nomination with ease. And in the general election, where he faced a pallid conservative Democrat, Alton B. Parker, he captured over 57 percent of the popular vote and lost no states outside the South. Now, relieved of immediate political concerns, he was free to display the extent—and the limits—of his commitment to reform.

During the 1904 campaign, Roosevelt boasted that he had worked in the anthracite coal strike to provide everyone with a "square deal." In his second term, he tried to extend his square deal further. One of his first targets was the powerful railroad industry. The Interstate Commerce Act of 1887, establishing the Interstate Commerce Commission (ICC), had been an early effort to regulate the industry; but over the years, the courts had sharply limited its influence. Roosevelt asked Congress for legislation to increase the government's power to oversee railroad rates. The Hepburn Railroad Regulation Act of 1906 sought to restore some regulatory authority to the government, although the bill was so cautious that it *Hepburn Act* satisfied few progressives. Some reformers were enraged. Robert La Follette, now a U.S. senator, never forgave Roosevelt for the concessions he made.

Roosevelt also pressured Congress to enact the Pure Food and Drug Act, which, despite weaknesses in its enforcement mechanisms, restricted the sale of dangerous or *Pure Food and Drug Act* ineffective medicines. When Upton Sinclair's powerful novel *The Jungle* appeared in 1906, featuring appalling descriptions of conditions in the meatpacking industry, Roosevelt pushed for passage of the Meat Inspection Act, which ultimately helped eliminate many diseases once transmitted in impure meat. Starting in 1907, he proposed even more stringent measures: an eight-hour day for workers, broader compensation for victims of industrial accidents, inheritance and income taxes, regulation of the stock market, and others. He also started openly to criticize conservatives in Congress and the judiciary who were obstructing these programs. The result was not only a general stalemate in Roosevelt's reform agenda, but also a widening gulf between the president and the conservative wing of his party.

Roosevelt and Conservation

Roosevelt's aggressive policies on behalf of conservation contributed to that gulf. An ardent sportsman and naturalist, he had long been concerned about the unregulated exploitation of America's natural resources and its remaining wilderness. And as a man who had often found

ADVERTISING *THE JUNGLE* Doubleday, Page & Co., the publishers of Upton Sinclair's sensational novel describing the terrible conditions in the meatpacking industry, distributed this poster in 1906 to advertise the book. The lion sitting atop a steer suggests both the title of the book and its subject. *(Library of Congress)*

the Far West a source of solace and reinvigoration, he had an almost romantic regard for the wilderness. Using executive powers, he restricted private development on millions of acres of undeveloped government land—most of it in the West—by adding them to the previously modest national forest system. When conservatives in Congress restricted his authority over public lands in 1907, Roosevelt and his chief forester, Gifford Pinchot, worked furiously to seize all the forests and many of the water power sites still in the public domain before the bill became law.

Roosevelt was the first president to take an active interest in the new and struggling American conservation movement, and his policies had a lasting effect on national environmental policies. Many of his policies would not seem compatible today to modern environmental sensibilities. In the early twentieth century, the idea of preserving the natural world for ecological reasons was not well established. Instead, many people who considered themselves "conservationists" promoted policies to protect land for carefully managed development. That was in part a result of the influence of Pinchot, the first director

of the National Forest Service (which he had helped create), who supported rational and efficient human use of the wilderness. Some conservationists argued for the "aesthetic" value of the forests; Pinchot insisted, in contrast, that "the whole question is a practical one." He and Roosevelt both believed that trained experts in forestry and resource management, such men as Pinchot himself, should apply to the landscape the same scientific standards that others were applying to the management of cities and industries. As a result, the most important legacy of Roosevelt's conservation policy was to establish the government's role as manager of the continuing development of the wilderness.

The Old Guard may have opposed Roosevelt's efforts to extend government control over vast new lands. But they eagerly supported another important aspect of Roosevelt's *Federal Aid to the West* natural resource policy: public reclamation and irrigation projects. In 1902, the president backed the National Reclamation Act, better known as the Newlands Act (named for its sponsor, Nevada senator Francis Newlands). It was the culmination of years of lobbying by businessmen and others from the West (through the National Irrigation Association). Frustrated by the failure of private capital and state governments to develop their water resources, they wanted the federal government to take over such projects. The Newlands Act provided federal funds for the construction of dams, reservoirs, and canals in the West—projects that would open new lands for cultivation and (years later) provide cheap electric power. It was the beginning of many years of critical federal aid for irrigation and power development in the western states, even though the Newlands Act (and the Bureau of Reclamation it created) had relatively little impact for more than twenty years after passage.

Roosevelt and Preservation

Despite his sympathy with Pinchot's vision of conservation as a method for ensuring rational human use of nature, Roosevelt also shared some of the concerns of the naturalists—those within the conservation movement committed to protecting the natural beauty of the land and the health of its wildlife from human intrusion. Early in his presidency, Roosevelt even spent four days camping in the Sierras with John Muir, the nation's leading preservationist and the founder of the Sierra Club.

Roosevelt may have championed the expansion of the National Forest System as a way to protect the landscape for continued, rational lumbering. But he also added significantly to the still-young National Park System, whose purpose was to protect public land from any exploitation or development at all. Congress had created the first national park—Yellowstone, in Wyoming, in 1872—and had authorized others in the 1890s: Yosemite and Sequoia in California, and Mount Rainier in Washington State.

WILLIAM HOWARD TAFT Taft could be a jovial companion in small groups, but his public image was of a dull, stolid man who stood in sharp and unfortunate contrast to his dynamic predecessor, Theodore Roosevelt. Taft also suffered public ridicule for his enormous size. He weighed as much as 350 pounds at times, and wide publicity accompanied his installation of a special oversized bathtub in the White House. *(Bettmann/Corbis)*

separation of powers if he were to intervene in legislative matters. The result was the feeble Payne-Aldrich Tariff, which reduced tariff rates scarcely at all and in some areas actually raised them. Progressives resented the president's passivity.

A sensational controversy broke out late in 1909 that helped destroy Taft's popularity with reformers for good. Many progressives had been unhappy when Taft replaced Roosevelt's secretary of the interior, James R. Garfield, an aggressive conservationist, with Richard A. Ballinger, a more conservative corporate lawyer. Suspicion of Ballinger grew when he attempted to invalidate Roosevelt's removal of nearly 1 million acres of forests and mineral reserves from the public lands available for private development.

In the midst of this mounting concern, Louis Glavis, an Interior Department investigator, charged the new secretary with having once connived to turn over valuable public coal lands in Alaska to a private syndicate for personal profit. Glavis took the evidence to Gifford Pinchot, still head of *Ballinger-Pinchot Dispute* the Forest Service and a critic of Ballinger's policies. Pinchot took the charges to the president. Taft investigated them and decided they were groundless. But Pinchot was not satisfied, particularly after Taft fired Glavis for his part in the episode. He leaked the story to the press and asked Congress to investigate the scandal. The president discharged him for insubordination, and the congressional committee appointed to study the controversy, dominated by Old Guard Republicans, exonerated Ballinger. But progressives throughout the country supported Pinchot. The controversy aroused as much public passion as any dispute of its time; and when it was over, Taft had alienated the supporters of Roosevelt completely and, it seemed, irrevocably.

The Return of Roosevelt

During most of these controversies, Theodore Roosevelt was far away: on a long hunting safari in Africa and an extended tour of Europe. To the American public, however, Roosevelt remained a formidable presence. His return to New York in the spring of 1910 was a major public event. Roosevelt insisted that he had no plans to reenter politics, but within a month he announced that he would embark on a national speaking tour before the end of the summer. Furious with Taft, he was becoming convinced that he alone was capable of reuniting the Republican Party.

The real signal of Roosevelt's decision to assume leadership of Republican reformers came in a speech he gave on *"New Nationalism"* September 1, 1910, in Osawatomie, Kansas. In it he outlined a set of principles, which he labeled the "New Nationalism," that made clear he had moved a considerable way from the cautious conservatism of the first years of his presidency. He argued that social justice was possible only through the vigorous efforts of a strong federal government whose executive acted as the "steward of the public welfare." Those who thought primarily of property rights and personal profit "must now give way to the advocate of human welfare." He supported graduated income and inheritance taxes, workers' compensation for industrial accidents, regulation of the labor of women and children, tariff revision, and firmer regulation of corporations.

Spreading Insurgency

The congressional elections of 1910 provided further evidence of how far the progressive revolt had spread. In primary elections, conservative Republicans suffered defeat after defeat while almost all the progressive

ROOSEVELT AT OSAWATOMIE Roosevelt's famous speech at Osawatomie, Kansas, in 1910 was the most radical of his career and openly marked his break with the Taft administration and the Republican leadership. "The essence of any struggle for liberty," he told his largely conservative audience, "has always been, and must always be to take from some one man or class of men the right to enjoy power, or wealth, or position or immunity, which has not been earned by service to his or their fellows." *(Brown Brothers)*

incumbents were reelected. In the general election, the Democrats, who were now offering progressive candidates of their own, won control of the House of Representatives for the first time in sixteen years and gained strength in the Senate. Reform sentiment seemed clearly on the rise. But Roosevelt still denied any presidential ambitions and claimed that his real purpose was to pressure Taft to return to progressive policies. Two events, however, changed his mind. The first, on October 27, 1911, was the announcement by the administration of a suit against U.S. Steel, which charged, among other things, that the 1907 acquisition of the Tennessee Coal and Iron Company had been illegal. Roosevelt had approved that acquisition in the midst of the 1907 panic, and he was enraged by the implication that he had acted improperly.

Roosevelt was still reluctant to become a candidate for president, because Senator Robert La Follette, the great Wisconsin progressive, had been working since 1911 to secure the presidential nomination for himself. But La Follette's candidacy stumbled in February 1912 when, exhausted, and distraught over the illness of a daughter, he appeared to suffer a nervous breakdown during a speech

in Philadelphia. Roosevelt announced his candidacy on February 22.

Roosevelt versus Taft

La Follette retained some diehard support. But for all practical purposes, the campaign for the Republican nomination had now become a battle between Roosevelt, the champion of the progressives, and Taft, the candidate of the conservatives. Roosevelt scored overwhelming victories in all thirteen presidential primaries. Taft, however, remained the choice of most party leaders, who controlled the nominating process.

The battle for the nomination at the Chicago convention revolved around an unusually large number of contested delegates: 254 in all. Roosevelt needed fewer than half the disputed seats to clinch the nomination. But the Republican National Committee, controlled by the Old Guard, awarded all but 19 of them to Taft. At a rally the night before the convention opened, Roosevelt addressed 5,000 cheering supporters and announced that if the party refused to seat his delegates, he would continue his own candidacy outside the party. "We stand at Armageddon," he told the roaring crowd, "and we battle for the Lord." The next day, he led his supporters out of the convention, and out of the party. The convention then quietly nominated Taft on the first ballot.

Roosevelt summoned his supporters back to Chicago in August for another convention, this one to launch the new Progressive Party and nominate himself as its presidential candidate. Roosevelt approached the battle feeling, as he put it, "fit as a bull moose" (thus giving his new party an enduring nickname). But by then, he was aware that his cause was virtually hopeless. That was partly because many of the insurgents who had supported him during the primaries refused to follow him out of the Republican Party. It was also because of the man the Democrats had nominated for president.

The Progressive Party

WOODROW WILSON AND THE NEW FREEDOM

The 1912 presidential contest was not simply one between conservatives and reformers. It was also one between two brands of progressivism, expressing two different views of America's future. And it matched the two most important national leaders of the early twentieth century in unequal contest.

Woodrow Wilson

Reform sentiment had been gaining strength within the Democratic as well as the Republican Party in the first years of the century. At the 1912 Democratic Convention in Baltimore in June, Champ Clark, the conservative Speaker of the House, was unable to assemble the two-thirds majority necessary for nomination because of progressive opposition. Finally, on the forty-sixth ballot, Woodrow Wilson, the governor of New Jersey and the only genuinely progressive candidate in the race, emerged as the party's nominee.

Wilson had risen to political prominence by an unusual path. He had been a professor of political science at Princeton until 1902, when he was named president of the university. Elected governor of New Jersey in 1910, he demonstrated a commitment to reform that he had already displayed as a university president, and during his two years in the statehouse, he earned a national reputation for winning passage of progressive legislation. As a presidential candidate in 1912, Wilson presented a progressive program that came to be called the "New Freedom." Wilson's New Freedom differed from Roosevelt's New Nationalism most clearly in its approach to economic policy and the trusts. Roosevelt believed in accepting economic concentration and using government to regulate

Wilson's "New Freedom"

WILSON IN PARIS One of the great moments in Woodrow Wilson's life was his arrival in Paris in 1918, just after the close of World War I. There he was greeted by adoring crowds, who considered him not only the leader of the nation that had helped France win the war, but the spokesman for a new world order that would bring lasting peace. He is shown here riding through the streets, tipping his hat to the rapturous crowds. *(Hulton/Archive/Getty Images)*

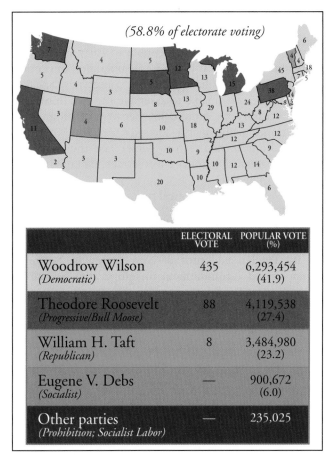

(58.8% of electorate voting)

	ELECTORAL VOTE	POPULAR VOTE (%)
Woodrow Wilson (Democratic)	435	6,293,454 (41.9)
Theodore Roosevelt (Progressive/Bull Moose)	88	4,119,538 (27.4)
William H. Taft (Republican)	8	3,484,980 (23.2)
Eugene V. Debs (Socialist)	—	900,672 (6.0)
Other parties (Prohibition; Socialist Labor)	—	235,025

ELECTION OF 1912 The election of 1912 was one of the most unusual in American history because of the dramatic schism within the Republican party. Two Republican presidents—William Howard Taft, the incumbent, and Theodore Roosevelt, his predecessor—ran against each other in 1912, opening the way for a victory by the Democratic candidate Woodrow Wilson, who won with only about 42 percent of the popular vote. A fourth candidate, the socialist Eugene V. Debs, received a significant 6 percent of the vote. ◆ *What events caused the schism between Taft and Roosevelt?*

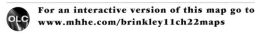 **For an interactive version of this map go to www.mhhe.com/brinkley11ch22maps**

and control it. Wilson seemed to side with those who (like Brandeis) believed that bigness was both unjust and inefficient, that the proper response to monopoly was not to regulate it but to destroy it.

The 1912 presidential campaign was something of an anticlimax. William Howard Taft, resigned to defeat, barely campaigned at all. Roosevelt campaigned energetically (until a gunshot wound from a would-be assassin forced him to the sidelines during the last weeks before the election), but he failed to draw any significant numbers of Democratic progressives away from Wilson. In November, Roosevelt and Taft split the Republican vote; Wilson held onto most Democrats and won. He polled only a plurality of the popular vote: 42 percent, compared with 27 percent for Roosevelt, 23 percent for Taft, and 6 percent for the socialist Eugene Debs. But in the electoral college,

Wilson won 435 of the 531 votes. Roosevelt had carried only six states, Taft two, Debs none.

The Scholar as President

Wilson was a bold and forceful president. More than William Howard Taft, more even than Theodore Roosevelt, he concentrated the powers of the executive branch in his own hands. He exerted firm control over his cabinet, and he delegated real authority only to those whose loyalty to him was beyond question. Perhaps the clearest indication of his style of leadership was the identity of his most powerful adviser: Colonel Edward M. House, an intelligent and ambitious Texan who held no office and whose only claim to authority was his personal intimacy with the president.

In legislative matters, Wilson skillfully used his position as party leader to weld together a coalition that would support his program. Democratic majorities in both houses of Congress made his task easier. Wilson's first triumph as president was the fulfillment of an old Democratic (and progressive) goal: a substantial lowering of the protective tariff. The Underwood-Simmons Tariff, passed in a special session of Congress that Wilson summoned shortly after his inauguration, provided cuts substantial enough, progressives believed, to introduce real competition into American markets and thus to help break the power of trusts. To make up for the loss of revenue under the new tariff, Congress approved a graduated income tax, which the recently adopted Sixteenth Amendment to the Constitution now permitted. This first modern income tax imposed a 1 percent tax on individuals and corporations earning over $4,000, with rates ranging up to 6 percent on incomes over $500,000.

Lowering the Tariff

Wilson held Congress in session through the summer to work on a major reform of the American banking system: the Federal Reserve Act, which Congress passed and which the president signed on December 23, 1913. It created twelve regional banks, each to be owned and controlled by the individual banks of its district. The regional Federal Reserve banks would hold a certain percentage of the assets of their member banks in reserve; they would use those reserves to support loans to private banks at an interest (or "discount") rate that the Federal Reserve system would set; they would issue a new type of paper currency—Federal Reserve notes—that would become the nation's basic medium of trade and would be backed by the government. Most important, perhaps, they would be able to shift funds quickly to troubled areas—to meet increased demands for credit or to protect imperiled banks. Supervising and regulating the entire system was a national Federal Reserve Board, whose members were appointed by the president. Nearly half the nation's banking resources were represented in the system within a year, and 80 percent by the late 1920s.

Federal Reserve Act

In 1914, turning to the central issue of his 1912 campaign, Wilson proposed two measures to deal with the problem of monopoly. In the process he revealed how his own approach to the issue was beginning to change. There was a proposal to create a federal agency through which the government would help business police itself—a regulatory commission of the type Roosevelt had advocated in 1912. There were also proposals to strengthen the government's ability actually to break up trusts—a decentralizing approach more characteristic of Wilson's 1912 campaign. The two measures took shape as the Federal Trade Commission Act and the Clayton Antitrust Act. The Federal Trade Commission Act created a regulatory agency that would help businesses determine in advance whether their actions would be acceptable to the government. The agency would also have authority to launch prosecutions against "unfair trade practices," which the law did not define, and it would have wide power to investigate corporate behavior. The act, in short, increased the government's regulatory authority significantly. Wilson signed it happily. But he seemed to lose interest in the Clayton Antitrust Bill and did little to protect it from conservative assaults, which greatly weakened it. The vigorous legal pursuit of monopoly that Wilson had promised in 1912 never materialized. The future, he had apparently decided, lay with government supervision.

Retreat and Advance

By the fall of 1914, Wilson believed that the program of the New Freedom was essentially complete and that agitation for reform would now subside. He refused to support the movement for national woman suffrage. Deferring to southern Democrats, and reflecting his own southern background, he condoned the reimposition of segregation in the agencies of the federal government (in contrast to Theodore Roosevelt, who had ordered the elimination of many such barriers). When congressional progressives attempted to enlist his support for new reform legislation, he dismissed their proposals as unconstitutional or unnecessary.

The congressional elections of 1914, however, shattered the president's complacency. Democrats suffered major losses in the House of Representatives, and voters who in 1912 had supported the Progressive Party began returning to the Republicans. Wilson would not be able to rely on a divided opposition when he ran for reelection in 1916. By the end of 1915, therefore, Wilson had begun to support a second flurry of reforms. In January 1916, he appointed Louis Brandeis to the Supreme Court, making him not only the first Jew but the most advanced progressive to serve there. Later, he supported a measure to make it easier for farmers to receive credit and one creating a system of workers' compensation for federal employees.

Wilson was sponsoring measures that expanded the role of the national government in important ways. In 1916, for example, Wilson supported the Keating-Owen Act, the first federal law regulating child labor. The measure prohibited the shipment of goods produced by underage *Child Labor Laws* children across state lines, thus giving an expanded importance to the constitutional clause assigning Congress the task of regulating interstate commerce. (It would be some years before the Supreme Court would uphold this interpretation of the clause; the Court invalidated the Keating-Owen Act in 1918.) The president similarly supported measures that used federal taxing authority as a vehicle for legislating social change. After the Court struck down Keating-Owen, a new law attempted to achieve the same goal by imposing a heavy tax on the products of child labor. (The Court later struck it down, too.) And the Smith-Lever Act of 1914 demonstrated another way in which the federal government could influence local behavior; it offered matching federal grants to states that agreed to support agricultural extension education.

THE "BIG STICK": AMERICA AND THE WORLD, 1901–1917

American foreign policy during the progressive years reflected many of the same impulses that were motivating domestic reform. But more than that, it reflected the nation's new sense of itself as a world power with far-flung economic and political interests. To the general public, foreign affairs remained largely remote. Walter Lippmann once wrote: "I cannot remember taking any interest whatsoever in foreign affairs until after the outbreak of the First World War." But to Theodore Roosevelt and later presidents, that made foreign affairs even more appealing. There the president could act with less regard for the Congress or the courts. There he could free himself from concerns about public opinion. Overseas, the president could exercise power unfettered and alone.

Roosevelt and "Civilization"

Theodore Roosevelt was well suited, both by temperament and by ideology, for an activist foreign policy. He believed in the value and importance of using American power in the world (a conviction he once described by citing the proverb, "Speak softly, but carry a big stick"). But he had two different standards for using that power.

Roosevelt believed that an important distinction existed between the "civilized" and "uncivilized" nations of the world. "Civilized" nations, as he defined them, were predominantly white and Anglo-Saxon *Racial and Economic Basis of Roosevelt's Diplomacy* or Teutonic; "uncivilized" nations were generally nonwhite, Latin, or Slavic. But racism was only partly the basis of the distinction. Equally important was economic development. He believed, therefore, that Japan, a rapidly

"THE NEW DIPLOMACY" This 1904 drawing by the famous *Puck* cartoonist Louis Dalrymple conveys the new image of America as a great power that Theodore Roosevelt was attempting to project to the world. Roosevelt the world policeman deals effectively with "less civilized" peoples (Asians and Latin Americans, seen clamoring at left) by using the "big stick" and deals equally effectively with the "civilized" nations (at right) by offering arbitration. *(Culver Pictures, Inc.)*

industrializing society, had earned admission to the ranks of the civilized.

Civilized nations were, by Roosevelt's definition, producers of industrial goods; uncivilized nations were suppliers of raw materials and markets. There was, he believed, an economic relationship between the two parts that was vital to both of them. A civilized society, therefore, had the right and duty to intervene in the affairs of a "backward" nation to preserve order and stability—for the sake of both nations. That belief was one important reason for Roosevelt's early support of the development of American sea power. By 1906, the American navy had attained a size and strength surpassed only by that of Great Britain (although Germany was fast gaining ground).

Protecting the "Open Door" in Asia

In 1904 the Japanese staged a surprise attack on the Russian fleet at Port Arthur in southern Manchuria, a province of China that both Russia and Japan hoped to control. Roosevelt, hoping to prevent either nation from

becoming dominant there, agreed to a Japanese request to mediate an end to the conflict. Russia, faring badly in the war, had no choice but to agree. At a peace conference in Portsmouth, New Hampshire, in 1905, Roosevelt extracted from the embattled Russians a recognition of Japan's territorial gains and from the Japanese an agreement to cease the fighting and expand no further. At the same time, he negotiated a secret agreement with the Japanese to ensure that the United States could continue to trade freely in the region. Roosevelt won the Nobel Peace Prize in 1906 for his work in ending the Russo-Japanese War. But in the years that followed, relations between the United States and Japan steadily deteriorated. Having destroyed the Russian fleet at Port Arthur, Japan now emerged as the pre-   *"Great White Fleet"*
eminent naval power in the Pacific and soon began to exclude American trade from many of the territories it controlled. Roosevelt took no direct action against Japan, but to be sure the Japanese government recognized the power of the United States, he sent sixteen battleships of the new American navy (known as the "Great White Fleet" because the ships were temporarily painted white for the voyage)

on an unprecedented journey around the world that included a call on Japan—to remind the Japanese of the potential might of the United States.

The Iron-Fisted Neighbor

Roosevelt took a particular interest in events in what he (and most other Americans) considered the nation's special sphere of interest: Latin America. Unwilling to share trading rights, let alone military control, with any other nation, Roosevelt embarked on a series of ventures in the Caribbean and South America. He established a pattern of American intervention in the region that would long survive his presidency.

Crucial to Roosevelt's thinking was an incident early in his administration. In 1902, the financially troubled government of Venezuela began to renege on debts to European bankers. Naval forces of Britain, Italy, and Germany blockaded the Venezuelan coast in response. Then German ships began to bombard a Venezuelan port amid rumors that Germany planned to establish a permanent base in the region. Roosevelt used the threat of American naval power to pressure the German navy to withdraw.

The incident helped persuade Roosevelt that European intrusions into Latin America could result not only from aggression but from instability or irresponsibility (such as defaulting on debts) within the Latin American nations themselves. As a result, in 1904 he announced what came to be known as the "Roosevelt Corollary" to the Monroe Doctrine. The United States, he claimed, had the right not only to oppose European intervention in the Western Hemisphere but also to intervene itself in the domestic affairs of its neighbors if those neighbors proved unable to maintain order and national sovereignty on their own.

"Roosevelt Corollary"

The immediate motivation for the Roosevelt Corollary, and the first opportunity for using it, was a crisis in the Dominican Republic. A revolution had toppled its corrupt

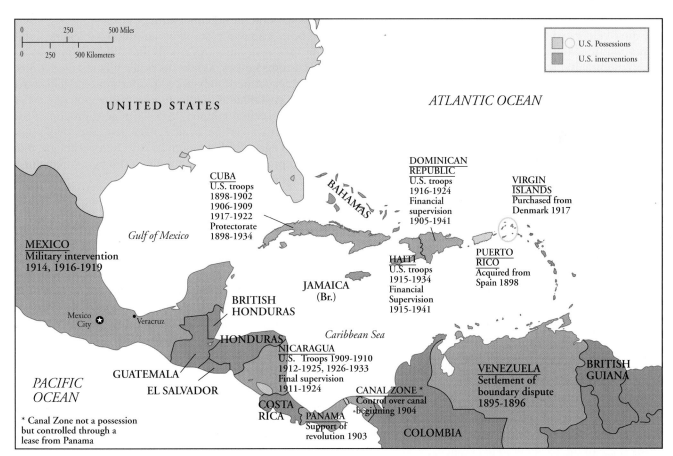

THE UNITED STATES AND LATIN AMERICA, 1895–1941 Except for Puerto Rico, the Virgin Islands, and the Canal Zone, the United States had no formal possessions in Latin America and the Caribbean in the late nineteenth century and the first half of the twentieth. But as this map reveals, the U.S. exercised considerable influence in these regions throughout this period—political and economic influence, augmented at times by military intervention. Note the particularly intrusive presence of the United States in the affairs of Cuba, Haiti, and the Dominican Republic—as well as the canal-related interventions in Colombia and Panama. ◆ *What were some of the most frequent reasons for American intervention in Latin America?*

 For an interactive version of this map go to www.mhhe.com/brinkley11ch22maps

and bankrupt government in 1903, but the new regime proved no better able than the old to make good on the country's $22 million in debts to European nations. Using the rationale provided by the Roosevelt Corollary, Roosevelt established, in effect, an American receivership, assuming control of Dominican customs and distributing 45 percent of the revenues to the Dominicans and the rest to foreign creditors. This arrangement lasted, in one form or another, for more than three decades.

In 1902, the United States granted political independence to Cuba, but only after the new government had

Platt Amendment

agreed to the so-called Platt Amendment (named after Senator Thomas Platt of Pennsylvania) to its constitution. The amendment gave the United States the right to prevent any foreign power from intruding into the new nation. In 1906, when domestic uprisings seemed to threaten the internal stability of the island, American troops landed in Cuba, quelled the fighting, and remained there for three years.

The Panama Canal

The most celebrated accomplishment of Roosevelt's presidency was the construction of the Panama Canal, which linked the Atlantic and the Pacific by creating a channel through Central America. At first, Roosevelt and many others favored a route across Nicaragua, which would permit a sea-level canal requiring no locks. But they soon turned instead to the narrow Isthmus of Panama in Colombia, the site of an earlier, failed effort by a French company to construct a channel. Although the Panama route was not at sea level (and would thus require locks), it was shorter than the one in Nicaragua. And construction was already about 40 percent complete. When the French company lowered the price for its holdings from $109 million to $40 million, the United States chose Panama.

Roosevelt dispatched John Hay, his secretary of state, to negotiate an agreement with Colombian diplomats in Washington that would allow construction to begin without delay. Under heavy American pressure, the Colombian chargé d'affaires, Tomas Herrén, unwisely signed an agreement giving the United States perpetual rights to a six-mile-wide "canal zone" across Colombia; in return, the United States would pay Colombia $10 million and an annual rental of $250,000. The treaty produced outrage in the Colombian senate, which refused to ratify it. Colombia then sent a new representative to Washington with instructions to demand at least $20 million from the Americans plus a share of the payment to the French.

Roosevelt was furious and began to look for ways to circumvent the Colombian government. Philippe Bunau-Varilla, chief engineer of the French canal project, was a

Panamanian Revolt

ready ally. In November 1903, he helped organize and finance a revolution in Panama. There had been many previous revolts, all of them failures, but this one had the support of

the United States. Roosevelt landed troops from the U.S.S. *Nashville* in Panama to "maintain order." Their presence prevented Colombian forces from suppressing the rebellion, and three days later Roosevelt recognized Panama as an independent nation. The new Panamanian government quickly agreed to the terms the Colombian senate had rejected. Work on the canal proceeded rapidly, and it opened in 1914.

Taft and "Dollar Diplomacy"

Like his predecessor, William Howard Taft worked to advance the nation's economic interests overseas. But he showed little interest in Roosevelt's larger vision of world stability. Taft's secretary of state, the corporate attorney Philander C. Knox, worked aggressively to extend American investments into less-developed regions. Critics called his policies "Dollar Diplomacy."

It was particularly visible in American policy in the Caribbean. When a revolution broke out in Nicaragua in 1909, the administration quickly

Intervention in Nicaragua

sided with the insurgents (who had been inspired to revolt by an American mining company) and sent American troops into the country to seize the customs houses. As soon as peace was restored, Knox encouraged American bankers to offer substantial loans to the new government, thus increasing Washington's financial leverage over the country. When the new pro-American government faced an insurrection less than two years later, Taft again landed American troops in Nicaragua, this time to protect the existing regime. The troops remained there for more than a decade.

Diplomacy and Morality

Woodrow Wilson entered the presidency with relatively little interest or experience in international affairs. Yet he faced international challenges of a scope and gravity unmatched by those of any president before him. Although the greatest test of Wilsonian diplomacy did not occur until World War I, many of the qualities that he would bring to that ordeal were evident in his foreign policy from his first moments in office, and particularly in his dealings with Latin America.

Having already seized control of the finances of the Dominican Republic in 1905, the United States established a military government there in 1916 when the Dominicans refused to accept a treaty that would have made the country a virtual American protectorate. The military occupation lasted eight years. In Haiti, which shares the island of Hispaniola with the Dominican Republic, Wilson landed the marines in 1915 to quell a revolution in the course of which a mob had murdered an unpopular president. American military forces remained in the country until 1934, and American officers drafted the new Haitian constitution adopted in 1918. When Wilson began

OPENING THE PANAMA CANAL The great Miraflores locks of the Panama Canal open in October 1914 to admit the first ship to pass through the channel. The construction of the canal was one of the great engineering feats of the early twentieth century. But the heavy-handed political efforts of Theodore Roosevelt were at least equally important to its completion. *(Bettmann/Corbis)*

to fear that the Danish West Indies might be about to fall into the hands of Germany, he bought the colony from Denmark and renamed it the Virgin Islands. Concerned about the possibility of European influence in Nicaragua, he signed a treaty with that country's government ensuring that no other nation would build a canal there and winning for the United States the right to intervene in Nicaragua's internal affairs to protect American interests. In all of these actions, Wilson was displaying an approach to Latin America very similar to the approaches of Roosevelt and Taft.

But Wilson's view of America's role in the Western Hemisphere (and the world) was not entirely similar to the views of his predecessors. That became clear in his *Wilson's Moral Diplomacy* dealings with Mexico. For many years, under the friendly auspices of the corrupt dictator Porfirio Díaz, American businessmen had been establishing an enormous economic presence in Mexico. In 1910, however, Díaz had been overthrown by the popular leader Francisco Madero, who promised democratic reform but who also seemed hostile to American businesses in Mexico. The United States quietly encouraged a reactionary general, Victoriano Huerta, to depose Madero early in 1913, and the Taft administration, in its last weeks in office, prepared to recognize the new Huerta regime and welcome back a receptive

environment for American investments in Mexico. Before it could do so, however, the new government murdered Madero, and Woodrow Wilson took office in Washington. The new president instantly announced that he would never recognize Huerta's "government of butchers."

The conflict dragged on for years. At first, Wilson hoped that simply by refusing to recognize Huerta he could help topple the regime and bring to power the opposing Constitutionalists, led by Venustiano Carranza. But when Huerta, with the support of American business interests, established a full military dictatorship in October 1913, the president became more assertive. In April 1914, a minor naval incident provided the president with an excuse for open intervention. An officer in Huerta's army briefly arrested several American sailors from the U.S.S. *Dolphin* who had gone ashore in Tampico. The men were immediately released, but the American admiral—unsatisfied with the apology he received—demanded that the Huerta forces fire a twenty-one-gun salute to the American flag as a public display of penance. The Mexicans refused. Wilson used the trivial incident as a pretext for seizing the Mexican port of Veracruz.

Wilson had envisioned a bloodless action, but in a clash with Mexican troops in Veracruz, the Americans killed 126   *Veracruz*

PANCHO VILLA AND HIS TROOPS Pancho Villa (fourth from left) poses with some of the leaders of his army, whose members Americans came to consider bandits once they began staging raids across the U.S. border. He was a national hero in Mexico. *(Brown Brothers)*

of the defenders and suffered 19 casualties of their own. Now at the brink of war, Wilson began to look for a way out. His show of force, however, had helped strengthen the position of the Carranza faction, which captured Mexico City in August and forced Huerta to flee the country. At last, it seemed, the crisis might be over.

But Wilson was not yet satisfied. He reacted angrily when Carranza refused to accept American guidelines for the creation of a new government, and he briefly considered throwing his support to still another aspirant to leadership: Carranza's erstwhile lieutenant Pancho Villa, who was now leading a rebel army of his own. When Villa's military position deteriorated, however, Wilson abandoned him and finally, in October 1915, granted preliminary recognition to the Carranza government. By now, however, he had created yet another crisis. Villa, angry at what he considered an American betrayal, retaliated in January 1916 by taking sixteen American mining engineers from

a train in northern Mexico and shooting them. Two months later, he led his soldiers (or "bandits," as the United States called them) across the border into Columbus, New Mexico, where they killed seventeen more Americans.

With the permission of the Carranza government, Wilson ordered General John J. Pershing to lead an American expeditionary force across the Mexican border in pursuit of Villa. The American troops never found Villa, but they did engage in two ugly skirmishes with Carranza's army, in which forty Mexicans and twelve Americans died. Again, the United States and Mexico stood at the brink of war. But at the last minute, Wilson drew back. He quietly withdrew American troops from Mexico, and in March 1917, he at last granted formal recognition to the Carranza regime. By now, however, Wilson's attention was turning elsewhere—to the far greater international crisis engulfing the European continent and ultimately much of the world.

Intervention in Mexico

CONCLUSION

Driven by the great surge of reform energies emerging throughout the United States, American national politics in the early twentieth century itself became an im-

portant battleground for progressives. The rise of national reform was a result of many things, but two in particular.

First, many of the reform efforts that had been gaining strength outside of politics, or within states and localities, eventually discovered that success required the engagement of the federal government in their efforts. Progressives themselves increasingly turned to Washington as a potential ally in their efforts. Second, two national leaders helped transform both the image and the reality of the federal government from the inconspicuous ally of business interests it had been in the late nineteenth century into a visible and muscular vehicle of reform. Theodore Roosevelt's eight years as president transformed popular expectations of the office and launched a significant reform agenda. Woodrow Wilson, who defeated not only Roosevelt's ill-fated successor William Howard Taft in 1912, but also Roosevelt himself, running as a third-party challenger, became the most successful legislative president of the early twentieth century by winning passage of a broad and ambitious reform agenda of his own.

Roosevelt, Taft, and Wilson—despite considerable disagreements among them—also contributed to a continuation, and indeed an expansion, of America's active role in international affairs in the first years of the century, in part as an effort to abet the growth of American capitalism and in part as an attempt to impose American standards of morality and democracy on other parts of the world. Similar mixtures of ideals and self-interest would soon guide the United States into a great world war.

FOR FURTHER REFERENCE

John Milton Cooper, Jr., compares the lives and ideas of the progressive movement's leading national politicians in *The Warrior and the Priest: Woodrow Wilson and Theodore Roosevelt* (1983). John Morton Blum, *The Republican Roosevelt* (1954) is a long-popular brief study. Donald E. Anderson, *William Howard Taft* (1973) is a useful account of this unhappy presidency. Arthur S. Link is Wilson's most important biographer and the author of *Woodrow Wilson*, 5 vols. (1947–1965). Kendrick A. Clements, *The Presidency of Woodrow Wilson* (1992) is a more recent study. Thomas K. McCraw, *Prophets of Regulation* (1984) is an excellent examination of important figures in the making of modern state capacity. Michael McGerr, *The Decline of Popular Politics* (1986) is a perceptive examination of the decline of public enthusiasm for parties in the North in the late nineteenth and early twentieth centuries. Samuel P. Hays, *The Gospel of Efficiency: The Progressive Conservation Movement, 1890–1920* (1962) makes a pioneering argument about the organizational imperatives behind the conservation movement, and Stephen R. Fox, *The American Conservation Movement: John Muir and His Legacy* (1981) is another valuable study. John Opie, *Nature's Nation: An Environmental History of the United States* (1998) is an ambitious synthesis of environmental history. The effects of America's interventionist policies in Latin America are described in John Womack's arresting account of the revolution in *Mexico, Zapata and the Mexican Revolution* (1968).

Theodore Roosevelt, by David Grubin (1997), is a fine biographical film. *The Battle for the Wilderness* (1990) is a documentary film about the conservation movement and two of its rival leaders, Gifford Pinchot and John Muir.

OLC

For quizzes, Internet sources, references to additional books and films, and more, consult this book's Online Learning Center at www.mhhe.com/brinkley11.

AN APPEAL TO DUTY This most famous of all American war posters, by the artist James Montgomery Flagg, shows a fierce-looking Uncle Sam requesting, almost demanding, Americans to join the army to fight in World War I. With the nation very divided over the wisdom of entering the war, the Wilson administration believed it needed to persuade Americans not only to support the struggle but also—something unusual for Americans—to feel a sense of obligation to the government and its overseas commitments. *(National Archives and Records Administration)*

Significant Events

1914 · Austria invades Serbia
· World War I begins
· Wilson declares American neutrality
· Coalminers' strike in Ludlow, Colorado, ends in massacre of thirty-nine people

1915 · Wartime economic boom begins
· Great Migration of blacks to the North begins
· Woman's Peace Party founded
· Germany begins submarine warfare
· *Lusitania* torpedoed
· Wilson launches preparedness program

1916 · *Sussex* attacked
· Wilson reelected president

1917 · Germany announces unrestricted submarine warfare
· Germans launch major offensive in France
· Zimmermann telegram disclosed
· Russian czar overthrown
· United States declares war on Central Powers
· Selective Service Act passed
· War Industries Board created
· Espionage Act passed
· Race riot in East St. Louis, Illinois
· Racial tensions lead to violence among soldiers based in Houston
· Bolshevik Revolution in Russia

1918 · Bernard Baruch takes over War Industries Board
· Wilson announces Fourteen Points

CHAPTER TWENTY-THREE

AMERICA AND THE GREAT WAR

The Great War, as it was known to a generation unaware that another, greater war would soon follow, began relatively inconspicuously in August 1914 when forces of the Austro-Hungarian Empire invaded the tiny Balkan nation of Serbia. Within weeks, however, it had grown into a widespread conflagration, engaging the armies of almost all the major nations of Europe and shattering forever the delicate balance of power that had maintained a general peace on the Continent since the early nineteenth century. Most Americans looked on with horror as the war became the most savage in history, but also at first with a conviction that the conflict had little to do with them.

After nearly three years of attempting to affect the outcome of the conflict without becoming embroiled in it, the United States formally entered the war in April 1917. In doing so, it joined the most savage conflict in history. The fighting had already dragged on for two and a half years, inconclusive, almost inconceivably murderous, engaging not only the armies of the contending nations but their civilian populations as well. Although the American Civil War had greatly increased the ferocity and extent of *Total War* combat, World War I was the first war to pit entire societies against one another. By 1917 it had left Europe exhausted and on the brink of utter collapse. By the time it ended late in 1918, Germany had lost nearly 2 million soldiers in battle,

Russia 1.7 million, France 1.4 million, Great Britain 900,000. A generation of European youth was decimated; centuries of political, social, and economic traditions were damaged and all but destroyed.

For America, however, the war was the source of a very different experience. As a military struggle, it was brief, decisive, and—in relative terms—without great cost. Only 112,000 American soldiers died in the conflict, half of them from influenza and other diseases rather than in combat. Economically, it was the source of a great industrial boom, which helped spark the years of prosperity that would follow. And the war propelled the United States into a position of international preeminence.

In other respects, World War I was a painful, even traumatic experience for the American people. At home, the nation became preoccupied with a search not just for victory but also for social unity—a search that continued and even intensified in the troubled years following the armistice, and that helped shatter many of the progressive ideals of the first years of the century. And abroad, once the conflict ended, the United States encountered frustration and disillusionment. The "war to end all wars," the war "to make the world safe for democracy," became neither. Instead, it led directly to twenty years of international instability that would ultimately generate another great conflict.

THE ROAD TO WAR

The causes of the war in Europe—indeed the question of whether there were any significant causes at all, or whether the entire conflict was the result of a tragic series of blunders—have been the subject of continued debate for nearly eighty years. What is clear is that the European nations had by 1914 created an unusually precarious international system that careened into war very quickly on the basis of what most historians agree was a minor series of provocations.

The Collapse of the European Peace

The major powers of Europe were organized by 1914 in two great, competing alliances. The "Triple Entente"

Competing Alliances | linked Britain, France, and Russia. The "Triple Alliance" united Germany, the Austro-Hungarian Empire, and Italy. The chief rivalry, however, was not between the two alliances, but between the great powers that dominated them: Great Britain and Germany—the former long established as the world's most powerful colonial and commercial nation, the latter ambitious to expand its own empire and become at least Britain's equal. The Anglo-German rivalry may have been the most important underlying source of the tensions that led to World War I, but it was not the immediate cause of its outbreak. The conflict emerged most directly out of a controversy involving nationalist movements within the Austro-Hungarian Empire. On June 28, 1914, the Archduke Franz Ferdinand, heir to the throne of the tottering empire, was assassinated while paying a state visit to Sarajevo. Sarajevo was the capital of Bosnia, a province of Austria-Hungary that Slavic nationalists wished to annex to neighboring Serbia; the Archduke's assassin was a Serbian nationalist.

This local controversy quickly escalated through the workings of the system of alliances that the great powers had constructed. With support from Germany, Austria-Hungary launched a punitive assault on Serbia. The Serbians called on Russia to help with their defense. The Russians began mobilizing their army on July 30. Things quickly careened out of control. By August 3, Germany had declared war on both Russia and France and had invaded Belgium in preparation for a thrust across the French border. On August 4, Great Britain—ostensibly to honor its alliance with France, but more importantly to blunt the advance of its principal rival—declared war on Germany. Russia and the Austro-Hungarian Empire formally began hostilities on August 6. Italy, although an ally of Germany in 1914, remained neutral at first and later entered the war on the side of the British and French. The Ottoman Empire (Turkey) and other, smaller nations all joined the fighting later in 1914 or in 1915. Within less than a year, virtually the entire European continent and part of Asia were embroiled in a major war.

PROMOTING THE WAR IN AUSTRALIA The government of Australia at times had difficulty persuading men to sign up to fight in World War I, which some Australians believed was being fought to aid the British and had nothing to do with them. This poster was part of a drive to recruit volunteers in 1915. *(Private Collection)*

Wilson's Neutrality

Wilson called on his fellow citizens in 1914 to remain "impartial in thought as well as deed." But that was impossible, for several reasons. For one thing, many Americans were not, in fact, genuinely impartial. Some sympathized with the German cause (German Americans because of affection for Germany, Irish Americans because of hatred of Britain). Many more (including Wilson himself) sympathized with Britain. Wilson himself was only one of many Americans who fervently admired England—its traditions, its culture, its political system; almost instinctively, these Americans attributed to the cause of the Allies (Britain, France, Italy, Russia) a moral quality that they denied to the Central Powers (Germany, the Austro-Hungarian Empire, and the Ottoman Empire). Lurid reports of German atrocities in Belgium and France, skillfully exaggerated by British propagandists, strengthened the hostility of many Americans toward Germany.

Economic realities also made it impossible for the United States to deal with the belligerents on equal terms. The British had imposed a naval blockade on Germany to prevent munitions and supplies from reaching the enemy. As a *Economic Ties to Britain* neutral, the United States had the right, in theory, to trade with Germany. A truly neutral response to the blockade would have been to stop trading with Britain as well. But while the United States could survive an interruption of its relatively modest trade with the Central Powers, it could not easily weather an embargo on its much more extensive trade with the Allies, particularly when war orders from Britain and France soared after 1914, helping to produce one of the greatest economic booms in the nation's history. So America tacitly ignored the blockade of Germany and continued trading with Britain. By 1915, the United States had gradually transformed itself from a neutral power into the arsenal of the Allies.

The Germans, in the meantime, were resorting to a new and, in American eyes, barbaric tactic: submarine warfare. Unable to challenge British domination on the ocean's surface, Germany began early in 1915 to use the newly improved submarine to try to stem the flow of supplies to England. Enemy vessels, the Germans announced, *Lusitania* would be sunk on sight. Months later, on May 7, 1915, a German submarine sank the British passenger liner *Lusitania* without warning, causing the deaths of 1,198 people, 128 of them Americans. The ship was, it later became clear, carrying not only passengers but munitions; but most Americans considered the attack what Theodore Roosevelt called it: "an act of piracy."

Wilson angrily demanded that Germany promise not to repeat such outrages and that the Central Powers affirm their commitment to neutral rights (among which, he implausibly insisted, was the right of American citizens to travel on the nonmilitary vessels of belligerents). The Germans finally agreed to Wilson's demands, but tensions between the nations continued to grow. Early in 1916, in response to an announcement that the Allies were now arming merchant ships to sink submarines, Germany proclaimed that it would fire on such vessels without warning. A few weeks later it attacked the unarmed French steamer *Sussex,* injuring several American passengers. Again Wilson demanded that Germany abandon its "unlawful" tactics; again the German government relented. Lacking sufficient naval power to enforce an effective blockade against Britain, the Germans decided that the marginal advantages of unrestricted submarine warfare did not yet justify the possibility of drawing America into the war.

Preparedness versus Pacifism

Despite the president's increasing bellicosity in 1916, he was still far from ready to commit the United States to war. One obstacle was American domestic politics. Facing a difficult battle for reelection, Wilson could not ignore the powerful factions that continued to oppose intervention. His policies, therefore, represented an effort to balance the demands of those who, like Theodore Roosevelt, insisted that the nation defend its "honor" and economic interests against the demands of those who, like Bryan,

La Follette, and others (including many German Americans and Irish Americans hostile to Britain), denounced any action that seemed to increase the chance of war.

The question of whether America should make military and economic preparations for war provided the first issue over which pacifists and interventionists could openly debate. Wilson at first sided with the anti-preparedness forces, denouncing the idea of an American military buildup as needless and provocative. As tensions between the United States and Germany grew, however, he changed his mind. In the fall of 1915, he endorsed an ambitious proposal by American military leaders for a large and rapid increase in the nation's armed forces. Amid expressions of outrage from pacifists in Congress and elsewhere, he worked hard to win approval of it. He even embarked on a national speaking tour early in 1916 to arouse support for the proposal. By midsummer 1916, armament for a possible conflict was well under way.

Still, the peace faction wielded considerable political strength, as became clear at the Democratic Convention in the summer of 1916. The convention became almost hysterically enthusiastic when the keynote speaker, enumerating Wilson's accomplishments, punctuated his list of the president's diplomatic achievements with the chant, *1916 Election* "What did we do? What did we do? . . . We didn't go to war! We didn't go to war!" That speech helped produce one of the most prominent slogans of Wilson's reelection campaign (although one the president himself never used or entirely approved): "He kept us out of war." During the campaign, Wilson did nothing to discourage those who argued that the Republican candidate, the progressive New York governor Charles Evans Hughes (supported by the bellicose Theodore Roosevelt), was more likely than he to lead the nation into war. And when pro-war rhetoric became particularly heated, Wilson spoke defiantly of the nation being "too proud to fight." He ultimately won reelection by one of the smallest margins for an incumbent in American history: fewer than 600,000 popular votes and only 23 electoral votes. The Democrats retained a precarious control over Congress.

A War for Democracy

The election was behind him, and tensions between the United States and Germany were unabated. But Wilson still required a justification for American intervention that would unite public opinion and satisfy his own sense of morality. In the end, he created that rationale himself. The United States, Wilson insisted, had no material aims in the conflict. Rather, the nation was committed to using the war as a vehicle for constructing a new world order, one based on the same progressive ideals that had motivated reform in America. In a speech before Congress in January 1917, he presented a plan for a postwar order in which the United States would help maintain peace through a

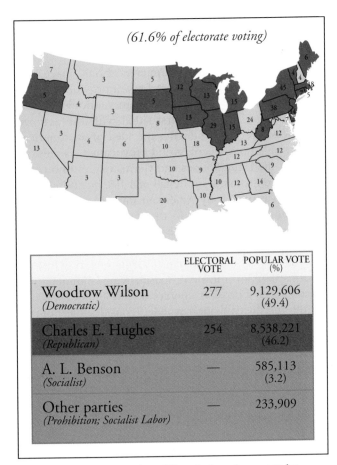

(61.6% of electorate voting)

	ELECTORAL VOTE	POPULAR VOTE (%)
Woodrow Wilson *(Democratic)*	277	9,129,606 (49.4)
Charles E. Hughes *(Republican)*	254	8,538,221 (46.2)
A. L. Benson *(Socialist)*	—	585,113 (3.2)
Other parties *(Prohibition; Socialist Labor)*	—	233,909

ELECTION OF 1916 Woodrow Wilson had good reason to be concerned about his re-election prospects in 1916. He had won only about 42 percent of the vote in 1912, and the Republican party—which had been divided four years earlier—was now reunited around the popular Charles Evans Hughes. In the end, Wilson won a narrow victory over Hughes with just under 50 percent of the vote and an even narrower margin in the electoral college. Note the striking regional character of his victory. ◆ *How did Wilson use the war in Europe to bolster his election prospects?*

permanent league of nations—a peace that would ensure self-determination for all nations, a "peace without victory." These were, Wilson believed, goals worth fighting for if there was sufficient provocation. Provocation came quickly.

In January, after months of inconclusive warfare in the trenches of France, the military leaders of Germany decided on one last dramatic gamble to achieve victory. They would launch a series of major assaults on the enemy's lines in France. At the same time, they would begin unrestricted submarine warfare (against American as well as Allied ships) to cut Britain off from vital supplies. The Allied defenses would collapse, they hoped, before the United States could intervene. The new German policy made American *Zimmermann Telegram* entry into the war virtually inevitable. Two additional events helped clear the way. On February 25, the British gave Wilson a telegram they had intercepted from the German foreign minister, Arthur Zimmermann, to the government of Mexico. It proposed that in the event of war between

Germany and the United States, the Mexicans should join with Germany against the Americans. In return, they would regain their "lost provinces" (Texas and much of the rest of the American Southwest) to the north when the war was over. (The Germans understood that anti-American sentiment was still high in Mexico after the interventions of the previous few years.) Widely publicized by British propagandists and in the American press, the Zimmermann telegram inflamed public opinion and helped build popular sentiment for war. A few weeks later, in March 1917, a revolution in Russia toppled the reactionary czarist regime and replaced it with a new, republican government. The United States would now be spared the embarrassment of allying itself with a despotic monarchy. The war for a progressive world order could proceed untainted.

On the rainy evening of April 2, two weeks after German submarines had torpedoed three American ships, Wilson appeared before a joint session of Congress and asked for a declaration of war:

> It is a fearful thing to lead this great peaceful people into war, into the most terrible and disastrous of all wars, civilization itself seeming to be in the balance. But the right is more precious than peace, and we shall fight for the things which we have always carried nearest our hearts—for democracy, for the right of those who submit to authority to have a voice in their own Governments, for the rights and liberties of small nations, for a universal dominion of right by such a concert of free peoples as shall bring peace and safety to all nations and make the world itself at last free.

Even then, opposition remained. For four days, pacifists in Congress carried on their futile struggle. When the declaration of war finally passed on April 6, fifty representatives and six senators voted against it.

"WAR WITHOUT STINT"

Armies on both sides in Europe were decimated and exhausted by the time of Woodrow Wilson's declaration of war. The German offensives of early 1917 had failed to *Stalemate* produce an end to the struggle, and French and British counteroffensives had accomplished little beyond adding to the appalling number of casualties. The Allies looked desperately to the United States for help. Wilson, who had called on the nation to wage war "without stint or limit," was eager to oblige.

Entering the War

American intervention had its most immediate effect on the conflict at sea. By the spring of 1917, Great Britain was suffering such vast losses from attacks by German submarines—one of every four ships setting sail from British ports never returned—that its ability to continue receiving vital supplies from across the Atlantic was in

THE WARTIME DRAFT This office in New York handled hundreds of men every day who arrived to enlist in response to draft notices. Although both the Union and the Confederacy had tried (and often failed) to use the draft during the Civil War, the World War I draft was the first centrally organized effort by the federal government to require military service from its citizens. Although some Americans evaded the draft in 1917 and 1918 (and were reviled by others as "shirkers"), most of those drafted complied with the law. *(Brown Brothers)*

question. Within weeks of joining the war, the United States had begun to alter the balance. A fleet of American destroyers aided the British navy in its assault on the U-boats. Other American warships escorted merchant vessels across the Atlantic. Americans also helped sow antisubmarine mines in the North Sea. The results were dramatic. Sinkings of Allied ships had totaled nearly 900,000 tons in the month of April 1917; by December, the figure had dropped to 350,000; by October 1918, it had declined to 112,000. The convoys also helped the United States protect its own soldiers en route to Europe. No American troop ship was lost at sea in World War I.

Many Americans had hoped that providing naval assistance alone would be enough to turn the tide in the war, but it quickly became clear that a major commitment of American ground forces would also be necessary to shore

Russian Revolution

up the tottering Allies. Britain and France had few remaining reserves. By early 1918, Russia had withdrawn from the war altogether. After the Bolshevik Revolution in November 1917, the new government, led by V. I. Lenin, negotiated a hasty and costly peace with the Central Powers, thus freeing additional German troops to fight on the western front.

The American Expeditionary Force

But the United States did not have a large enough standing army to provide the necessary ground forces in 1917. There were only about 120,000 soldiers in the army and perhaps 80,000 more in the National Guard. Neither group had any combat experience; and except for the small number of officers who had participated in the Spanish-American War two decades before and the Mexican intervention of 1916, few commanders had any experience in battle either.

Some urged a voluntary recruitment process to raise the needed additional forces. Among the advocates of this approach was Theodore Roosevelt, now old and ill, who swallowed his hatred of Wilson and called on him at the White House with an offer to raise a regiment to fight in Europe. But the president and his secretary of war, Newton D. Baker, decided that only a national draft could provide the needed men; and despite the protests of those who agreed with House Speaker Champ Clark that "there is precious little difference between a conscript and a convict," he won passage of the Selective Service Act in

Selective Service Act

mid-May. The draft brought nearly 3 million men into the army; another 2 million joined various branches of the armed services voluntarily. Together, they formed what became known as the American Expeditionary Force (AEF).

It was the first time in American history that any substantial number of soldiers and sailors had fought overseas for an extended period. The military did its best to keep up morale among men who spent most of their time living in the appalling conditions of the trenches. They were frequently shelled and even when calm were muddy,

A WOMEN'S MOTOR CORPS Although the most important new role that women performed during World War I was probably working in factories that male workers had left, many women also enlisted in auxiliary branches of the military—among them these uniformed women who served as drivers for the army. *(Culver Pictures, Inc.)*

polluted, and infested with rats. But when soldiers had time away from the front, they were usually less interested in the facilities the Red Cross tried to make available for them than in exploring the bars and brothels of local towns. More than one in every ten American soldiers in Europe contracted venereal disease during World War I, which inspired elaborate official efforts to prevent infection and to treat it when it occurred. (The Secretary of War declined an offer from the French president, Georges Clemenceau, to provide officially inspected houses of prostitution where women would be inspected regularly for disease.)

In some respects, the AEF was the most diverse fighting force the United States had ever assembled. For the first time, women were permitted to enlist in the military—over ten thousand in the navy and a few hundred in the marines. They were not allowed to participate in combat, but they served crucial auxiliary roles in hospitals and offices.

Nearly 400,000 black soldiers enlisted in or were drafted into the army and navy as well. (The marines would not accept them.) And while most of them performed rela-

African-American Soldiers tively menial tasks on military bases in the United States, more than 50,000 went to France. African-American soldiers served in segregated, all-black units under white commanders; and even in Europe, most of them were assigned to noncombat duty. But some black units fought valiantly in the great offensives of 1918. Most African-American soldiers learned to live with the racism they encountered—in part because they hoped their military service would ultimately improve their status. But a few responded to provocations violently. In August 1917, a group of black soldiers in Houston, subjected to continuing abuse by people in the community, used military weapons to kill seventeen whites. Retribution was quick. Thirteen black

soldiers were hanged, and another forty were sentenced to life terms in military jails.

Having assembled this first genuinely national army, the War Department permitted the American Psychological Association to study it. The psychologists gave thousands of soldiers new tests designed to measure intelligence: the "Intelligence Quotient" or "IQ" test and other newly designed aptitude tests. In fact, the tests were less effective in measuring intelligence than in measuring education; and they reflected the educational expectations of the white middle-class people who had devised them. It is not surprising, therefore, that the largely working-class and racially mixed group of soldiers the psychologists examined performed poorly. Half the whites and the vast majority of the African Americans taking the test scored at levels that classified them as "morons." In reality, most of them were simply people who had not had very much access to education.

The Military Struggle

The engagement of these forces in combat was intense but brief. In the first months after entering the war, the United States had its biggest impact on the seas. Not until the spring of 1918 were significant numbers of American ground troops available for battle. Eight months later, the war   *General John Pershing*
was over. Under the command of General John J. Pershing, who had only recently been leading the unsuccessful American pursuit of Pancho Villa in Texas and northern Mexico, the American Expeditionary Force—although it retained a command structure independent of the other Allies—joined the existing Allied forces.

The experience of American troops during World War I was very different from those of other nations, which had already been fighting for nearly four years by the time

the trenches were places of extraordinary physical stress and discomfort. They were also places of intense boredom, laced with fear. By the time the Americans arrived, morale on both sides was declining, and many soldiers had come to believe that the war would be virtually endless.

Although the American forces had trench experiences of their own, they were very brief compared to those of the European armies. Instead, the United States tipped the balance of power in the battle and made it possible for the Allies at last to break out of their entrenched positions and advance against the Germans. In early June 1918, American forces at Château-Thierry assisted the French in *Château-Thierry* repelling a bitter German offensive that had brought German forces within fifty miles of Paris. Six weeks later, after over a million American troops had flooded into France, the Americans helped turn away another assault, at Rheims, farther south. By July 18, the Allies had halted the German advance and were beginning a successful offensive of their own.

On September 26, the American fighting force advanced against the Germans in the Argonne Forest in the southern part of a 200-mile attack (the Meuse-Argonne offen- *Meuse-Argonne Offensive* sive) that lasted nearly seven weeks. By the end of October, despite terrible weather, they had helped push the Germans back toward their own border and had cut the enemy's major supply lines to the front. It was a measure of how different warfare had become from a generation earlier that the American forces used more ammunition in this seven-week offensive than they had used in the entire four years of the Civil War.

Faced with an invasion of their own country, German military leaders now began to seek an armistice—an immediate cease-fire that would, they hoped, serve as a prelude to negotiations among the belligerents. Pershing wanted to drive on into Germany itself; but other Allied leaders, after first insisting on terms that made the agreement little different from a surrender, accepted the German proposal. On November 11, 1918, the Great War shuddered to a close.

The New Technology of Warfare

World War I was a proving ground for a range of military and other technologies that came into use on a large scale for the first time during the fighting in France. The trench warfare that characterized the conflict was necessary because of the enormous destructive power of newly improved machine guns and higher-powered artillery. It was no longer feasible to send troops out into an open field, or even to allow them to camp in the open. The new weaponry would slaughter them in an instant. Trenches sheltered troops while allowing limited, and usually inconclusive, fighting. But technology overtook

LIFE IN THE TRENCHES For most British, French, German, and ultimately American troops in France, the most debilitating part of World War I was the seeming endlessness of life in the trenches. Some young men lived in these cold, wet, muddy dugouts for months, even years, surrounded by filth, sharing their space with vermin, eating mostly rotten food. Occasional attacks to try to dislodge the enemy from its trenches usually ended in failure and became the scenes of terrible slaughters. *(National Archives and Records Administration)*

the U.S. forces arrived in significant numbers. British, French, German, and other troops had by then spent years living in the vast network of trenches that had been dug into the French countryside. Modern weapons made conventional, frontal battles a recipe for mass suicide. Instead, the two sides relied on heavy shelling of each other's trenches and occasional, usually inconclusive, and always murderous assaults across the "no-man's land" dividing them. Life in the trenches was almost indescribably terrible. Muddy, wet, cold, swarming with lice and rats,

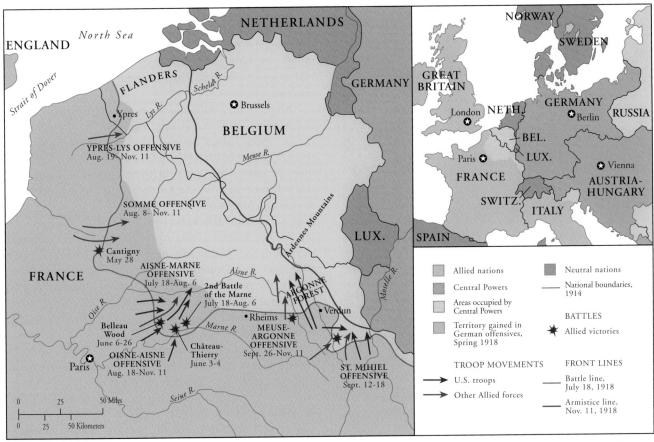

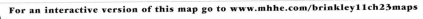

AMERICA IN WORLD WAR I: THE WESTERN FRONT, 1918 These maps show the principal battles in which the United States participated in the last year of World War I. The small map on the upper right helps locate the area of conflict within the larger European landscape. The larger map at left shows the long, snaking red line of the western front in France—stretching from the border between France and southwest Germany all the way to the northeast border between Belgium and France. Along that vast line, the two sides had been engaged in murderous, inconclusive warfare for over three years by the time the Americans arrived. Beginning in the spring and summer of 1918, bolstered by reinforcements from the United States, the Allies began to win a series of important victories that finally enabled them to begin pushing the Germans back. American troops, as this map makes clear, were decisive along the southern part of the front. ◆ *At what point did the Germans begin to consider putting an end to the war?*

For an interactive version of this map go to www.mhhe.com/brinkley11ch23maps

the trenches, too, as mobile weapons—tanks and flamethrowers—proved capable of piercing entrenched positions. Most terrible of all, perhaps, new chemical weapons—poisonous mustard gas, which required troops to carry gas masks at all times—made it possible to attack entrenched soldiers without direct combat.

The new forms of technological warfare required elaborate maintenance. Faster machine guns required more ammunition. Motorized vehicles required fuel and spare parts and mechanics capable of servicing them. The logistical difficulties of supplying so many supplies became a major factor in planning tactics and strategy. Once supplies were unloaded and stored, the process of repacking and moving them forward when troops broke through lines and advanced forward was hopelessly time-consuming. Late in the war, when Allied armies were advancing toward Germany, they frequently had to

stop for days at a time to wait for their equipment to catch up with them.

World War I was the first conflict in which airplanes played a significant role. The planes themselves were relatively simple and not very maneuverable; but anti-aircraft technology was not yet highly developed either, so their effectiveness was still considerable. Planes began to be constructed to serve various functions: bombers, fighters (planes that would engage in "dogfights" with other planes), and reconaissance aircraft.

The most "modern" part of the military during World War I was the navy. New battleships emerged—of which the British *Dreadnought* was perhaps the most visible example—that made use of new technologies such as turbine propulsion, hydraulic gun controls, electric light and power, wireless telegraphy, and advanced navigational aids. Submarines, which had made a brief appearance in the American Civil War, now became significant weapons (as the German U-boat campaign in 1915 and 1916 made clear). The new submarines were driven by diesel engines, which had the advantage of being more compact than a steam engine and whose fuel was less explosive than that of a gasoline engine. The diesel engine also had a much greater range than ships powered by other fuels.

The new technologies were to a large degree responsible for the most stunning and horrible characteristic of World War I—its appalling level of casualties. A million men representing the British Empire (Britain, Canada, *High Casualty Rates* Australia, India, and others) died. France lost 1.7 million men; Germany 2 million; the former Austro-Hungarian Empire 1.5 million; Italy 460,000; and Russia 1.7 million. The number of Turkish dead, which was surely large, was never counted. In Britain, one third of the men born between 1892 and 1895 died in the war. Similarly terrible percentages could be calculated for other warring nations. Even greater numbers of men returned home with injuries, some of them permanently crippling. The United States, which entered the war near its end and became engaged only in the last successful offensives, suffered very light casualties in contrast—112,000 dead, half of them victims of influenza, not battle. But the American casualties were very high in the battles in which U.S. troops were centrally involved. One of the reasons that World War I became so reviled in the 1920s and 1930s, even by the victors, was that the enormous number of deaths—and the terrible grief those deaths created—afflicted all of Europe in profound ways. But that did not stop the development of new and deadlier military technologies that, a generation later, would make World War II the source of even more terrible carnage.

THE WAR AND AMERICAN SOCIETY

The American experience in World War I was brief, but it had profound effects on the government, on the economy, and on society. Mobilizing an industrial economy for total war required an unprecedented degree of government involvement in industry, agriculture, and other areas. It also required, many believed, a strenuous effort to ensure the loyalty and commitment of the people.

Organizing the Economy for War

By the time the war ended, the United States government had appropriated $32 billion for expenses directly related *Financing the War* to the conflict. This was a staggering sum by the standards of the time. The entire federal budget had seldom exceeded $1 billion before 1915, and as recently as 1910 the nation's

entire gross national product had been only $35 billion. To raise the money, the government relied on two devices. First, it launched a major drive to solicit loans from the American people by selling "Liberty Bonds" to the public. By 1920, the sale of bonds, accompanied by elaborate patriotic appeals, had produced $23 billion. At the same time, new taxes were bringing in an additional sum of nearly $10 billion—some from levies on the "excess profits" of corporations, much from new, steeply graduated income and inheritance taxes that ultimately rose as high as 70 percent in some brackets.

An even greater challenge was organizing the economy to meet war needs. The administration tried two very different approaches. In 1916, Wilson established a Council of National Defense, composed of members of his cabinet, and a Civilian Advisory Commission, which set up local defense councils in every state and locality. Economic mobilization, according to this first plan, was to rest on a large-scale dispersal of power to local communities.

But this early administrative structure soon proved completely unworkable. Some members of the Council of National Defense, many of them disciples of the social engineering gospel of Thorstein Veblen and the "scientific management" principles of Frederick Winslow Taylor, urged a more centralized approach. Instead of dividing the economy geographically, they proposed dividing it functionally by organizing a series of planning bodies, each to supervise a specific sector of the economy. Thus one agency would control transportation, another agriculture, another manufacturing. The administrative structure that slowly emerged from such proposals was dominated by a series of "war boards," one to oversee the railroads, one to supervise fuel supplies (largely coal), another to handle food (a board that helped elevate to prominence the brilliant young engineer and business executive Herbert Hoover). The boards were not without weaknesses, but they generally succeeded in meeting essential war needs without paralyzing the domestic economy.

At the center of the effort to rationalize the economy was the War Industries Board, an agency created in July 1917 to coordinate government purchases of military supplies. *War Industries Board* Casually organized at first, it stumbled badly until March 1918, when Wilson restructured it and placed it under the control of the Wall Street financier Bernard Baruch. From then on, the board wielded powers greater (in theory at least) than any government agency had ever possessed. Baruch decided which factories would convert to the production of which war materials and set prices for the goods they produced. When materials were scarce, Baruch decided to whom they should go. When corporations were competing for government contracts, he chose among them. He was, it seemed, providing the centralized regulation of the economy that some progressives had long urged.

SELLING LIBERTY BONDS A nurse, a matron, and a soldier pose before the entrance of a station selling war bonds, illustrating the range of groups in society that were working together to support the American commitment to the struggle. *(National Archives and Records Administration)*

In reality, the vaunted efficiency of the WIB was something of a myth. The agency was, in fact, plagued by mismanagement and inefficiency. It was less important to the nation's ability to meet its war needs than the sheer extent of American resources and productive capacities. Nor was the WIB in any real sense an example of state control of the economy. Baruch viewed himself, openly and explicitly, as the partner of business; and within the WIB, businessmen themselves—the so-called dollar-a-year men, who took paid leave from their corporate jobs and worked for the government for a token salary–supervised the affairs of the private economy. Baruch ensured that manufacturers who coordinated their efforts in accord with his goals would be exempt from antitrust laws. He helped major industries earn enormous profits from their efforts.

Rather than working to restrict private power and limit corporate profits, as many progressives had urged, the government was working to enhance the private sector through a mutually beneficial alliance.

The effort to organize the economy for war produced some spectacular accomplishments: Hoover's efficient organization of domestic food supplies, William McAdoo's success in untangling the railroads, and others. In some areas, however, progress *Lessons of the Managed Economy* was so slow that the war was over before many of the supplies ordered for it were ready. Even so, many leaders of both government and industry emerged from the experience convinced of the advantages of a close, cooperative relationship between the public and private sectors. Some hoped to continue the wartime experiments in peacetime.

Labor and the War

This growing link between the public and private sectors extended, although in greatly different form, to labor. The National War Labor Board, established in April 1918 to resolve labor disputes, pressured industry to grant important concessions to workers: an eight-hour day, the maintenance of minimal living standards, equal pay for women doing equal work, recognition of the right of unions to organize and bargain collectively. In return, it insisted that workers forgo all strikes and that employers not engage in lockouts. Membership in labor unions increased by more than 1.5 million between 1917 and 1919.

The war provided workers with important, if usually temporary, gains. But it did not stop labor militancy. That was particularly clear in the West, where the Western Federation of Miners staged a series of strikes to improve the terrible conditions in the underground mines. The bloodiest of them occurred just before the war. In Ludlow, Colorado, in 1914, workers (mostly Italians, Greeks, and Slavs) walked out of coal mines owned by John D. Rockefeller. Joined by their wives and daughters, they continued the strike even after they had been evicted from company housing and had moved into hastily erected tents. The state militia was called into the town to protect the mines, but in fact (as was often the case in labor actions), it actually worked to help employers defeat the strikers.

Joined by strikebreakers and others, the militia attacked the workers' tent colony; and in the battle that followed, thirty-nine people died, among them eleven children.
Ludlow Massacre
The episode became known as the Ludlow Massacre. But the events in Ludlow were precursors to continued conflict in the mines that the war itself did little to discourage.

Economic and Social Results of the War

Whatever its other effects, the war helped produce a remarkable period of economic growth in the United States—a boom that began in 1914 (when European demands for American products began to increase) and accelerated after 1917 (when demand from the United States war effort fueled production). Industrial production soared, and manufacturing activity expanded in regions that had previously had relatively little of it. The shipbuilding industry, for example, grew rapidly on the West Coast. Employment increased dramatically; and because so many men were away at war, new opportunities for female, African-American, Mexican, and Asian workers appeared. Some workers experienced a significant growth in income, but inflation cut into the wage increases many workers won from employers and often produced a net loss in purchasing power. The agricultural economy profited from the war as well. Farm prices rose to their highest levels in decades, and agricultural production increased dramatically as a result.

One of the most important social changes of the war years was the migration of hundreds of thousands of African Americans from the rural South into northern industrial cities. It became known as the "Great Migration." Like most migrations, it was a result of both a "push" and a "pull." The push was the poverty, indebtedness, racism, and violence most blacks experienced in the South. The pull was the prospect of factory jobs in the urban North and the opportunity to live in communities where blacks could enjoy more freedom and autonomy. In the labor-scarce economy of the war years, northern factory owners dispatched agents to the South to recruit African-American workers. Black newspapers advertised the prospects for employment in the North. And perhaps most important, those who migrated first sent word back to friends and families of the opportunities they encountered—one reason for the heavy concentration of migrants from a single area of the South in certain cities in the North. In Chicago, for example, the more than 70,000 new black residents came disproportionately from a few areas of Alabama and Mississippi.

The result was a dramatic growth in black communities in northern industrial cities such as New York, Chicago, Cleveland, and Detroit. Older, more established black residents of these cities were unsettled by these new arrivals, with their country ways and their revivalistic religion; the existing African-American communities considered the newcomers coarse and feared that their presence would increase their own vulnerability to white racism. But the movement could not be stopped. New churches sprang up in black neighborhoods (many of them simple storefronts, from which self-proclaimed preachers searched for congregations). Low-paid black workers crowded into inadequate housing—small apartments known as kitchenettes, in which several families sometimes lived together. As the black communities expanded, they inevitably began to rub up against white neighborhoods,
Race Riots
with occasionally violent results. In East St. Louis, Illinois, a white mob attacked a black neighborhood on July 2, 1917, burned down many houses, and shot the residents of some of them as they fled. As many as forty African Americans died.

For American women, black and white, the war meant new opportunities for employment. A million or more women worked in a wide range of industrial jobs that, in peacetime, were considered male preserves: steel, munitions, trucking, public transportation. Most of them had been working in other, less well-paying jobs earlier. Among some feminists, the war inspired hopes of a lasting change in the role of women in the economy and the society. Margaret Dreier Robins, an official of the Women's

WOMEN INDUSTRIAL WORKERS In World War II, such women were often called "Rosie the Riveter." Their presence in these previously all-male work environments was no less startling to Americans during World War I. These women are shown working with pneumatic hammers in the Midvale Steel and Ordnance factory in Philadelphia in 1918. (*National Archives and Records Administration*)

Trade Union League, said in 1918: "The war has created new values. Men and women are conscious that as citizens they must . . . share in the management of industry and the administration of government." But whatever changes the war brought were temporary ones. As soon as the war was over, almost all of the women working in previously male industrial jobs quit or were fired; in fact, the percentage of women working for wages actually declined between 1910 and 1920.

THE SEARCH FOR SOCIAL UNITY

The idea of unity—not only in the direction of the economy but in the nation's social purpose—had been the dream of many progressives for decades. To them, the war seemed to offer an unmatched opportunity for America to close ranks behind a great common cause. In the process, they hoped, society could achieve a lasting sense of collective purpose. In fact, however, the search for unity produced considerable repression.

The Peace Movement

Government leaders, and many others, realized that public sentiment about American involvement in the war had been deeply divided before April 1917 and remained so even after the declaration of war.

The peace movement in the United States before 1917 had many constituencies: German Americans, who opposed American intervention against Germany; Irish Americans, who opposed any support for the British; religious pacifists (Quakers, Mennonites, and others); intellectuals

such as Randolph Bourne and groups on the left such as the Socialist Party and the Industrial Workers of the World, all of whom considered the war a meaningless battle among capitalist nations for commercial supremacy—an opinion many others, in America and Europe, later came to share. But the most active and widespread peace activism came from the women's move- *Women's Peace Party* ment. In 1915, Carrie Chapman Catt, a leader of the fight for woman suffrage, helped create the Woman's Peace Party, with a small but active membership. As the war in Europe intensified, the party's efforts to keep the United States from intervening grew.

Women peace activists were sharply divided once America entered the war in 1917. The National American Woman Suffrage Association, the single largest women's organization, supported the war and, more than that, presented itself as a patriotic organization dedicated to advancing the war effort. Its membership grew dramatically as a result. Catt, who was among those who abandoned the peace cause, now began calling for woman suffrage as a "war measure," to ensure that women (whose work was essential to the war effort) would feel fully a part of the nation. But many other women refused to support the war even after April 1917. Among them were Jane Addams, who was widely reviled as a result, and Charlotte Perkins Gilman, a leading feminist activist.

Women peace activists shared many of the political and economic objections to the war of the Socialist Party (to which some of them be- *Maternal Opposition* longed). But some criticized the *to War* war on other grounds as well, arguing that as wives and mothers they had a special moral basis for their pacifism. The Woman's Peace Party had claimed to represent the "mother half of humanity," and a similarly maternal opposition to war shaped the position of the many women who remained in opposition after 1917.

Selling the War and Suppressing Dissent

World War I was not as popular among the American people as World War II would be, but most of the country supported the intervention once it began. That support was most clearly visible in the voluntary, even spontaneous decision of millions of Americans to back the government, the president, and the American "boys" overseas in 1917 and 1918. In communities all across the nation, there were outbursts of fervent patriotism, floods of voluntary enlistments in the military, and greatly increased displays of patriotism. Women joined local Red Crosses in an effort to contribute to the war effort. Children raised money for war bonds in their schools. Churches included prayers for the president and the troops in their services. Indeed, the war gave a large boost to the wave of religious revivalism that had been growing already for a decade before 1917; and revivalism, in turn, became a source of support for the war. Billy Sunday, the leading revivalist of his time, dropped his early opposition to intervention in 1917 and became a fervent champion of the American military effort.

Nevertheless, government leaders (and many others) remained deeply concerned about the significant minorities who continued to oppose the war even after the United States entered it. Many believed that a crucial prerequisite for victory was an energetic, even coercive, effort to unite public opinion behind the military effort.

The most conspicuous government effort to rally public support was a vast propaganda campaign orchestrated by the new Committee *CPI* on Public Information (CPI). It was directed by the Denver journalist George Creel, who spoke openly of the importance of achieving social unity:

> When I think of the many voices that were heard before the war and are still heard, interpreting America from a class or sectional or selfish standpoint, I am not sure that, if the war had to come, it did not come at the right time for the preservation and reinterpretation of American ideals.

The CPI supervised the distribution of innumerable tons of pro-war literature (75 million pieces of printed material in all). War posters plastered the walls of offices, shops, theaters, schools, churches, and homes. Newspapers dutifully printed official government accounts of the reasons for the war and the prospects for quick victory. Creel encouraged reporters to exercise "self-censorship" when reporting news about the struggle; and although many people in the press resented the suggestion, the veiled threats that accompanied it persuaded most of them to comply.

A WARNING The fear of disloyalty—and the belief that there were many spies circulating through American society gathering information to pass to the enemy—inspired a series of posters such as this one warning citizens not to trust the people around them. *(Library of Congress)*

The CPI attempted at first to distribute only the "facts," believing that the truth would speak for itself. As the war continued, however, their tactics became increasingly crude. Government-promoted posters and films, at first relatively mild in tone, were by 1918 becoming lurid portrayals of the savagery of the Germans, bearing such titles as *The Prussian Cur* and *The Kaiser: Beast of Berlin,* encouraging Americans to think of the German people as something close to savages.

The government soon began more coercive efforts to suppress dissent. The CPI ran full-page advertisements in popular magazines like the *Saturday Evening Post* urging citizens to notify the Justice Department when they encountered "the man who spreads the pessimistic stories . . . , cries for peace, or belittles our efforts to win the war." The Espionage Act of 1917 gave the government new tools with which to respond to such reports. It created stiff penalties for spying, sabotage, or obstruction of the war effort (crimes that were often broadly defined); and it empowered the post office to ban "seditious" material from the mails, a responsibility Postmaster General Albert Sidney Burleson accepted with great relish. Sedition, he said, *Espionage Act*

BILLY SUNDAY AND MODERN REVIVALISM

Billy Sunday was a farm boy from Iowa who attended school only until the eighth grade, became a professional baseball player in his teens, and then, in 1886, at the age of 24, experienced a conversion to evangelical Christianity. Over the next decade, he rose to become the most successful revivalist in America in an era when revivalism was spreading rapidly through rural and urban communities alike.

The great revival of the early twentieth century was not the first or the last in American history. But that revival—which reached something close to its peak during the anxious years of World War I—stirred vast numbers of Americans and both reflected and helped to create a deep and lasting schism in the nation's Christian community.

The new revivalism was, among other things, an effort by conservative Christians to fight off the influence of Darwin and his theory of evolution. Conservatives deplored the impact of Darwin on science. But even more alarming to them was the impact of Darwin on religion. A great many American Protestants in the late nineteenth century—people known as modernists—had revised their faith to incorporate Darwin's teaching. In the process, they had discarded from religion some of the beliefs that many conservative Christians considered critically important: the literal truth of the Bible (including the story of Creation), the faith in personal conversion, the factuality of miracles, the strong belief in the existence of heaven and hell, and many others. Faith in these religious "fundamentals" was important to conservatives (who began to be known as "fundamentalists") because without them, they believed, religion would no longer be a vibrant, central presence in their lives.

And in an age of rapid and often disorienting social change, many Americans found traditional religious belief an important source of solidity and stability.

Billy Sunday combined an instinctive feel for fundamentalist belief with an eager and skillful understanding of modern techniques of marketing and publicity and a genius for making religion entertaining. In the process, he became a prototype for the great revivalists of the later twentieth century: Aimee Semple McPherson, Billy Graham, Oral Roberts, and many others. In his own time, Sunday was as popular and successful as any of them.

Sunday enlisted the support of advertisers and public relations experts to publicize his crusades, and he developed sophisticated methods of measuring the success of his mission. He raised enormous sums of money from eager worshipers (and, at times, wealthy patrons). But while he used some of it to live and travel comfortably, most of it went to publicizing his revival meetings and constructing the elaborate, if temporary, "tabernacles" in which he spoke before up to 20,000 people at a time. Established churches canceled their services when Sunday was in town and sent their congregants to hear him. Newspapers devoted enormous attention to his sermons and their impact. People lined the streets to catch a glimpse of him as he walked or rode through towns.

Part of Sunday's success was a result of his previous career as a baseball player, which he used to create a bond with male members of his audience. And part was a result of his flamboyant oratorical style. He leaped around his platform like the athlete he was, told jokes, waved the American flag, raised and lowered his voice to create a sense of intimacy and then a sense of passion. He was a natural showman, and he had no inhibitions about using the

BILLY SUNDAY IN ILLINOIS, 1908 This photograph shows one of the many temporary tabernacles erected to house the enormous crowds—in this case over 5,000 people—whom Billy Sunday regularly attracted. He is shown here in Bloomington, Illinois, in January 1908, but the scene repeated itself in many places through the first decades of the twentieth century. *(C. U. Williams, Bloomington, Illinois/Archives of the Billy Graham Center, Wheaton, Illinois)*

included statements that might "impugn the motives of the government and thus encourage insubordination," anything that suggested "that the government is controlled by Wall Street or munitions manufacturers, or any other special interests." He included in that category all publications of the Socialist Party.

More repressive were two measures of 1918: the Sabotage Act of April 20 and the Sedition Act of May 16. These bills expanded the meaning of the Espionage Act to make illegal any public expression of opposition to the war; in practice, it allowed officials to prosecute anyone who criticized the

Sedition Act

BILLY SUNDAY ON THE PULPIT   The artist George Bellows based this 1925 lithograph of Sunday preaching on an earlier painting of the same scene. It reveals something of the enormous energy Sunday brought to his sermons. *(Bettmann/Corbis)*

POSING WITH THE BIBLE   Sunday was almost never photographed in conventional portrait style. Even posed pictures usually showed him in some animated form—gesticulating, lunging, or (as here) holding up the Bible. *(Culver Pictures, Inc.)*

techniques of showmanship to manipulate his audiences. But he was successful, too, because he combined fundamentalist religious themes with outspoken positions on social issues.

He was a highly effective advocate of prohibition and sometimes seemed to convert an entire community to temperance in a single stroke. "BURLINGTON IS DRY," an Iowa newspaper headline announced after one of his visits. "BILLY SUNDAY HAS MADE GRAVEYARD OF ONCE FAST TOWN." Sunday also spoke, at times with great fervor, about other reforms: cleaning up corrupt city governments, attacking the great trusts, fighting poverty. "I believe," he once said, "if society permits any considerable proportion of people to live in foul, unlighted rooms . . . if society allows deserving men to stagger along with less than a living wage . . . if society . . . throws the unripe strength of children into the hopper of corporate greed to be ground down into dividends, then society must share the responsibility if these people become criminals, thieves, cutthroats, drunkards, and prostitutes."

Yet he also insisted that individuals were not simply victims of society. "A man is not supposed to be the victim of his environment," he argued. Society could not explain the failures of "the individual who's got a rotten heart." Most of all, he argued, even the most degraded individuals could save themselves through Christ. An active faith would not only give them spiritual peace; it would also help them rise in the world. Religion, as Sunday presented it, was a form of self-help in a time when many Americans were searching desperately for ways to gain control over their lives and their fates.

Sunday opposed American involvement in World War I in the first years of fighting in Europe. "A lot of fools over there are murdering each other to satisfy the damnable ambitions of a few mutts who sit on thrones," he once said. But when the United States entered the fighting, he took second place to no one in the fervor of his support and the passion of his patriotism. By then, the surge of revivalism he had helped create had spread widely through America—partly because of the ambitions of Sunday's many imitators (over a thousand of them, according to some estimates), who hoped to achieve something like his fame and

fortune; and partly because of the eagerness of established congregations to bring revivalists into their communities to get people back into their churches. The war increased the appetite for revivalism in many communities, and it brought Sunday—and many others—a last great burst of success.

One of the things that made the war so important to revivalists, and their critics, was the hatred of Germany that became so powerful in American culture in those years. That hatred took several very different forms. To fundamentalists like Sunday, Germany was a source of evil because it had abandoned religion and embraced the new secular, scientific values of the modern world. To critics of fundamentalists, the problem with Germany was that it was not modern enough, that it was trapped in an older, discredited world of tribalism and savagery. This disagreement became the source of harsh charges and counter-charges between fundamentalists and modernists during the war and contributed to lasting bitterness between the two groups. It also increased the fervor with which fundamentalists responded to charismatic leaders like Sunday.

Sunday's popularity faded after 1920, as he became a harsh critic of "radicalism" and "foreignness" and as the popularity of revivals declined in the face of a beckoning new consumer culture. When he died in 1935, he was attracting crowds only in scattered, rural communities of deeply conservative views. But in his heyday, Sunday provided millions of Americans with a combination of dazzling entertainment and prescriptions for renewing their religious faith. In the process, he helped sustain their belief in the possibility of personal success through a combination of faith and hard work even as the new industrial society was rapidly eroding the reality of the "self-made man."

president or the government. Senator Hiram Johnson of California offered a bitter description of the provisions of the law. He said: "You shall not criticize anything or anybody in the Government any longer or you shall go to jail."

The most frequent targets of the new legislation (and one of the reasons for its enactment in the first place) were such anticapitalist groups (and now antiwar) groups as the Socialist Party and the Industrial Workers of the World. Many Americans had favored the repression of socialists and radicals even before the war; the wartime policies now made it possible to move against them with full legal sanction. Eugene V. Debs, the humane leader of the party and an opponent of the war, was sentenced to ten years in prison in 1918. Only a pardon by President Warren G. Harding ultimately won his release in 1921. Big Bill Haywood and members of the IWW were especially energetically prosecuted. Only by fleeing to the Soviet Union did Haywood avoid long imprisonment. In all, more than 1,500 people were arrested in 1918 for the crime of criticizing the government.

State and local governments, corporations, universities, and private citizens contributed as well to the climate of repression. Vigilante mobs sprang up to "discipline" those who dared challenge the war. A dissident Protestant clergyman in Cincinnati was pulled from his bed

Repressing Dissent

one night by a mob, dragged to a nearby hillside, and whipped "in the name of the women and children of Belgium." An IWW organizer in Montana was seized by a mob and hanged from a railroad bridge.

A cluster of citizens' groups emerged to mobilize "respectable" members of their communities to root out disloyalty. The American Protective League, probably the largest of such groups, enlisted the services of 250,000 people, who served as "agents"—prying into the activities and thoughts of their neighbors, opening mail, tapping telephones, and in general attempting to impose unity of opinion on their communities. It received government funds to support its work. Attorney General Thomas W. Gregory, a particularly avid supporter of repressing dissent, described the league and other, similar organizations approvingly as "patriotic organizations." Other vigilante organizations—the National Security League, the Boy Spies of America, the American Defense Society—performed much the same function.

There were many victims of such activities: socialists, labor activists, female pacifists (some of whom were arrested and imprisoned simply for criticizing the government or capitalism). But the most frequent targets of repression were immigrants: Irish Americans because of their historic

"100 Percent Americanism"

animosity toward the British and because some had, before 1917, expressed hopes for a German victory; Jews because many had expressed opposition to the anti-Semitic policies of the Russian government, until 1917 one of the Allies; and others. "Loyalist" citizens' groups policed immigrant neighborhoods. They monitored meetings and even conversations for signs of disloyalty. Even some settlement house workers, many of whom had once championed ethnic diversity, contributed to such efforts. The director of the National Security League described the origins of the anti-immigrant sentiment, which was producing growing support for what many were now calling "100 percent Americanism":

> . . . the melting pot has not melted. . . . there are vast communities in the nation thinking today not in terms of America, but in terms of Old World prejudices, theories, and animosities. . . . In the bottom of the melting pot there lie heaps of unfused metal.

The greatest target of abuse was the German-American community. Its members had unwittingly contributed to their plight. In the first years of the war in Europe, some had openly advocated American assistance to the Central Powers, and many had opposed United States intervention on behalf of the Allies. But while most German Americans supported the American war effort once it began, public opinion turned bitterly hostile. A campaign to purge society of all things German quickly gathered speed, at times assuming ludicrous forms. Sauerkraut was renamed "liberty cabbage." Hamburger became "liberty sausage." Performances of German music were frequently banned. German books were removed from the shelves of libraries. Courses in the German language were removed from school curricula; the California Board of Education called it "a language that disseminates the ideals of autocracy, brutality, and hatred." Germans were routinely fired from jobs in war industries, lest they "sabotage" important tasks. Some were fired from positions entirely unrelated to the war—for example Karl Muck, the German-born conductor of the Boston Symphony Orchestra. Vigilante groups routinely subjected Germans to harassment and beatings, including a lynching in southern Illinois in 1918. Relatively few Americans favored such extremes, but many came to agree with the belief of the eminent psychologist G. Stanley Hall that "there is something fundamentally wrong with the Teutonic soul."

THE SEARCH FOR A NEW WORLD ORDER

Woodrow Wilson had led the nation into war promising a more just and stable peace at its conclusion. Well before the armistice, he was preparing to lead the fight for what he considered a democratic postwar settlement. That settlement, he believed, must rest on a set of war aims reflecting a philosophy of internationalist relations that became known as Wilsonianism.

The Fourteen Points

On January 8, 1918, Wilson appeared before Congress to present the principles for which he claimed the nation was fighting. The war aims had fourteen distinct provisions, widely known as the Fourteen Points; but they fell into three broad categories. First, Wilson's proposals contained eight specific recommendations for adjusting postwar boundaries and for establishing new nations to replace the defunct Austro-Hungarian and Ottoman Empires. Those recommendations reflected his belief in the right of

Wilson's Idealistic Vision

all peoples to self-determination. Second, there were five general principles to govern international conduct in the future: freedom of the seas, open covenants instead of secret treaties, reductions in armaments, free trade, and impartial mediation of colonial claims. Finally, there was a proposal for a league of nations that would help implement these new principles and territorial adjustments and resolve future controversies.

There were serious flaws in Wilson's proposals. He provided no formula for deciding how to implement the "national self-determination" he promised for subjugated peoples. He said little about economic rivalries and their effect on international relations, even though such economic tensions had been in large part responsible for the war. Nevertheless, Wilson's international vision quickly came to enchant not only much of his own generation (in both America and Europe), but also members of generations to come. It reflected his belief, strongly rooted in the ideas of progressivism, that the world was as capable of just and efficient government as were individual nations; that once the international community accepted certain basic principles of conduct, and once it constructed modern institutions to implement them, the human race could live in peace.

The Fourteen Points were also an answer to the new Bolshevik government in Russia. In December 1917, Lenin issued his own statement of war aims strikingly similar to Wilson's. Wilson's announcement, which came just three weeks later, was, among other things, a last-minute (and unsuccessful) effort to persuade the Bolshevik regime to keep Russia in the war. But Wilson also realized that Lenin was now a competitor in the effort to lead the postwar order. And he announced the Fourteen Points in part to ensure that the world looked to the United States, and not Russia, for guidance. "Liberalism," he said, referring to his own ideals, "is the only thing that can save civilization from chaos—from a flood of ultra-radicalism that will swamp the world. . . . Liberalism must be more liberal than ever before, it must even be radical, if civilization is to escape the typhoon."

Lenin's Challenge

Early Obstacles

Wilson was confident, as the war neared its end, that popular support would enable him to win Allied approval of his peace plan. But there were ominous signs both at home and abroad that his path might be more difficult than he expected. In Europe, leaders of the Allied powers were preparing to resist him even before the armistice was signed. Most of them resented what they considered Wilson's tone of moral superiority. They had reacted unhappily when Wilson refused to make the United States their "ally" but had kept his distance as an "associate" of his European partners. They had been offended by his insistence on keeping American military forces separate from the Allied armies they were joining.

Most of all, however, Britain and France, having suffered incalculable losses in their long years of war, and having stored up an enormous reserve of bitterness toward Germany as a result, were in no mood for a benign and generous peace. The British prime minister, David Lloyd George, insisted for a time that the German kaiser be captured and executed. He and Georges Clemenceau, president of France, remained determined to the end to gain something from the struggle to compensate them for the catastrophe they had suffered.

Allied Intransigence

At the same time, Wilson was encountering problems at home. In 1918, with the war almost over, Wilson unwisely appealed to the American voters to support his peace plans by electing Democrats to Congress in the November elections. A Republican victory, he declared, would be "interpreted on the other side of the water as a repudiation of my leadership." Days later, the Republicans captured majorities in both houses. Domestic economic troubles, more than international issues, had been the most important factor in the voting; but because of the president's ill-timed appeal, the results damaged his ability to claim broad popular support for his peace plans.

The leaders of the Republican Party, in the meantime, were developing their own reasons for opposing Wilson. Some were angry that he had tried to make the 1918 balloting a referendum on his war aims, especially since many Republicans had been supporting the Fourteen Points. Wilson further antagonized them when he refused to appoint any important Republicans to the negotiating team that would represent the United States at the peace conference in Paris. But the president considered such matters unimportant. Only one member of the American negotiating party would have any real authority: Wilson himself. And once he had produced a just and moral treaty, he believed, the weight of world and American opinion would compel his enemies to support him. As he sailed for Paris late in 1918, he said:

> In the name of the people of the United States, I have uttered as the objects of this great war ideals and nothing but ideals, and the war has been won by that inspiration. . . . There is a great wind of moral force moving through the world, and every man who opposes that wind will go down in disgrace.

The Paris Peace Conference

Wilson arrived in Europe to a welcome such as few men in history have experienced. To the war-weary people of the Continent, he was nothing less than a savior, the man who would create a new and better world. When he entered Paris on December 13, 1918, he was greeted, some claimed, by the largest crowd in the history of France. The negotiations themselves, however, proved less satisfying.

The principal figures in the negotiations were the leaders of the victorious Allied nations: Lloyd George representing Great Britain; Clemenceau representing France; Vittorio Orlando, the prime minister of Italy; and Wilson, who hoped to dominate them all. Some of Wilson's advisers

THE BIG FOUR IN PARIS Surface cordiality during the Paris Peace Conference disguised serious tensions among the so-called Big Four, the leaders of the victorious nations in World War I. As the conference progressed, the European leaders developed increasing resentment of Woodrow Wilson's high (and some thought sanctimonious) moral posture in the negotiations. Shown here in the library of the Hotel Crillon are, from left to right, Vittorio Orlando of Italy, David Lloyd George of Great Britain, Georges Clemenceau of France, and Wilson. *(Bettmann/Corbis)*

had warned him that if agreement could not be reached at the "summit," there would be nowhere else to go, and that

The Big Four

it would therefore be better to begin negotiations at a lower level. Wilson, however, was adamant; he alone would represent the United States.

From the beginning, the atmosphere of idealism Wilson had sought to create was competing with a spirit of national aggrandizement. There was, moreover, a pervasive sense of unease about the unstable situation in eastern Europe and the threat of communism. Russia, whose new Bolshevik government was still fighting "White" counter-revolutionaries, was unrepresented in Paris; but the radical threat it seemed to pose to Western governments was never far from the minds of any of the delegates, least of all Wilson himself.

Indeed, not long before he came to Paris, Wilson ordered the landing of American troops in the Soviet Union. They were there, he claimed, to help a group of 60,000 Czech soldiers trapped in Russia to escape. But the Americans soon became involved, at least indirectly, in assisting the White Russians (the anti-Bolsheviks) in their fight against the new regime. Some American troops remained as late as April 1920. Lenin's regime survived these challenges, but Wilson refused to recognize his new government nevertheless. Diplomatic relations between the United States and the Soviet Union were not restored until 1933.

In the tense and often vindictive atmosphere these competing concerns produced in Paris, Wilson was unable to win approval of many of the broad principles he had espoused: freedom of the seas, which the British re-

Wilson's Retreat

fused even to discuss; free trade; "open covenants openly arrived at" (the Paris negotiations themselves were often conducted in secret). Despite his support for "impartial

mediation" of colonial claims, he was forced to accept a transfer of German colonies in the Pacific to Japan, to whom the British had promised them in exchange for Japanese assistance in the war. His pledge of "national self-determination" for all peoples suffered numerous assaults. Economic and strategic demands were constantly coming into conflict with the principle of cultural nationalism.

Where the treaty departed most conspicuously from Wilson's ideals was on the question of reparations. As the conference began, the president opposed demanding compensa-

Reparations

tion from the defeated Central Powers. The other Allied leaders, however, were intransigent, and slowly Wilson gave way and accepted the principle of reparations, the specific sum to be set later by a commission. That figure, established in 1921, was $56 billion, supposedly to pay for damages to civilians and for military pensions.

There were continued negotiations for a decade, which scaled the sum back considerably. In the end, Germany paid only $9 billion, which was still more than its crippled economy could afford. The reparations, combined with other territorial and economic penalties, constituted an effort to keep Germany not only weak but prostrate for the indefinite future. Never again, the Allied leaders believed, should the Germans be allowed to become powerful enough to threaten the peace of Europe.

Wilson did manage to win some important victories in Paris in setting boundaries and dealing with former colonies. He secured approval of a plan to place many former colonies and imperial possessions (among them Palestine) in "trusteeship" under the League of Nations—the so-called mandate system. He blocked a French proposal to break up western Germany into a group of smaller states. He helped design the creation of two new nations: Yugoslavia and Czechoslovakia, which were welded together out of, among other territories, pieces of the former Austro-Hungarian Empire. Each contained an uneasy collection of ethnic groups that had frequently battled one another in the past.

But Wilson's most visible triumph, and the one most important to him, was the creation of a permanent inter-

League of Nations national organization to oversee world affairs and prevent future wars. On January 25, 1919, the Allies voted to accept the "covenant" of the League of Nations; and with that, Wilson believed, the peace treaty was transformed from a disappointment into a success. Whatever mistakes and inequities had emerged from the peace conference, he was convinced, could be corrected later by the League.

The covenant provided for an assembly of nations that would meet regularly to debate means of resolving disputes and protecting the peace. Authority to implement League decisions would rest with a nine-member Executive Council; the United States would be one of five permanent members of the council, along with Britain, France, Italy, and Japan. The covenant left many questions unanswered, most notably how the League would enforce its decisions. Wilson, however, was confident that once established, the new organization would find suitable answers.

The Ratification Battle

Wilson was well aware of the political obstacles awaiting him at home. Many Americans, accustomed to their nation's isolation from Europe, questioned the wisdom of this major new commitment to internationalism. Others had serious reservations about the specific features of the treaty and the covenant. After a brief trip to Washington in February 1919, during which he listened to harsh objections to the treaty from members of the Senate and others, he returned to Europe and insisted on several modifications in the covenant to satisfy his critics. The revisions limited America's obligations to the League by ensuring that the United States would not be obliged to accept a League mandate to oversee a territory and that the League would not challenge the Monroe Doctrine. But the changes were not enough to mollify his opponents, and Wilson refused to go further. When Colonel House, his close friend and trusted adviser, told him he must be prepared to compromise more, the president retorted sharply: "I have found that you get nothing in this world that is worthwhile without fighting for it." His long friendship with House ended abruptly.

Wilson presented the Treaty of Versailles (which took its name from the palace outside Paris where the final negotiating sessions had taken place) to the Senate on July

Wilson's Intransigence 10, 1919, asking, "Dare we reject it and break the heart of the world?" In the weeks that followed, he refused to consider even the most innocuous compromise. His deteriorating physical condition—he was suffering from hardening of the arteries and had apparently experienced something like a mild stroke (undiagnosed) in Paris—may have contributed to his intransigence.

The Senate, in the meantime, was raising many objections. Some senators—the fourteen so-called irreconcilables, many of them western isolationists—opposed the agreement on principle. But other opponents, with less fervent convictions, were principally concerned with constructing a winning issue for the Republicans in 1920 and with weakening a president

whom they had come to de- *Henry Cabot Lodge* spise. Most notable of these was Senator Henry Cabot Lodge of Massachusetts, the powerful chairman of the Foreign Relations Committee. A man of stunning arrogance and a close friend of Theodore Roosevelt (who had died early in 1919, spouting hatred of Wilson to the end), Lodge loathed the president with genuine passion. "I never thought I could hate a man as I hate Wilson," he once admitted. He used every possible tactic to obstruct, delay, and amend the treaty. Wilson, for his part, despised Lodge as much as Lodge despised him. He made his feelings clear when he described his opponents in the Senate (obviously thinking primarily of Lodge) as "contemptible, narrow, selfish, poor little minds that never get anywhere."

Public sentiment clearly favored ratification, so at first Lodge could do little more than play for time. When the document reached his committee, he spent two weeks slowly reading aloud each word of its 300 pages; then he held six weeks of public hearings to air the complaints of every disgruntled minority (Irish Americans, for example, angry that the settlement made no provision for an independent Ireland). Gradually, Lodge's general opposition to the treaty crystallized into a series of "reservations"— amendments to the League covenant limiting American obligations to the organization.

At this point Wilson might still have won approval if he had agreed to some relatively minor changes in the language of the treaty. But the president refused to yield. The United States had a moral obligation, he claimed, to respect the terms of the agreement precisely as they stood. When he realized the Senate would not budge, he decided to appeal to the public.

Wilson's Ordeal

What followed was a political disaster and a personal tragedy. Wilson embarked on a grueling, cross-country speaking tour to arouse public support for the treaty. In a little more than three weeks, he traveled over 8,000 miles by train, speaking as often as four times a day, resting hardly at all. Finally, he reached the end of his strength. After speaking at Pueblo, Colorado, on September 25, he collapsed with severe headaches. Canceling the rest of his itinerary, he rushed back to Washington, where, a few days later, he suffered a major stroke. For two weeks he was close to death; for six weeks more, he was so seriously ill that he could conduct virtually no public business. His wife and his doctor formed an almost impenetrable barrier around him, shielding him from any official pressures that might impede his recovery, preventing the public from receiving any accurate information about the gravity of his condition.

Wilson ultimately recovered enough to resume a limited official schedule, but he was essentially an invalid for the remaining eighteen months of his presidency. His left side was partially paralyzed; more important, like many stroke victims, he had only partial control of his mental and emotional state. His condition only intensified what had already been his strong tendency to view public issues in moral terms and to resist any attempts at compromise. When the Senate Foreign Relations Committee finally sent the treaty to the full Senate for ratification, recommending nearly fifty amendments and reservations, Wilson refused to consider any of them. When the full Senate voted in November to accept fourteen of the reservations, Wilson gave stern directions to his Democratic allies: They must vote only for a treaty with no changes whatsoever; any other version must be defeated. On November 19, 1919, forty-two Democrats, following

League Membership Rejected

the president's instructions, joined with the thirteen Republican "irreconcilables" to reject the amended treaty. When the Senate voted on the original version without any reservations, thirty-eight senators, all but one a Democrat, voted to approve it; fifty-five senators (some Democrats among them) voted no.

There were sporadic efforts to revive the treaty over the next few months. But Wilson's opposition to anything but the precise settlement he had negotiated in Paris remained too formidable an obstacle to surmount. He was, moreover, becoming convinced that the 1920 national election would serve as a "solemn referendum" on the League. By now, however, public interest in the peace process had begun to fade—partly as a reaction against the tragic bitterness of the ratification fight, but more in response to a series of other crises.

A SOCIETY IN TURMOIL

Even during the Paris Peace Conference, many Americans were less concerned about international matters than about turbulent events at home. In the aftermath of the war, various groups of Americans set out to claim the social advances that the idealistic justifications

New Social Environment

of the conflict seemed to have promised them. But the social environment after 1918 was no longer receptive to progressive reform. The American economy experienced a severe postwar recession. And much of middle-class America responded to demands for change with a fearful,

conservative hostility. The aftermath of war brought not the age of liberal reform that progressives had predicted, but a period of repression and reaction.

Industry and Labor

Citizens of Washington, on the day after the armistice, found it impossible to place long-distance telephone calls: the lines were jammed with officials of the war agencies canceling government contracts. The fighting had ended sooner than anyone had anticipated, and without warning, without planning, the nation was launched into the difficult task of economic reconversion.

At first, the wartime boom continued. But the postwar prosperity rested largely on the lingering effects of the war (government deficit spending continued for some months after the armistice) and on sudden, temporary demands (a booming market for scarce consumer goods at home and a strong market for American products in the war-ravaged nations of Europe). The postwar boom was accompanied, moreover, by raging inflation, a result in part of the precipitous abandonment of wartime price controls. Through most of 1919 and 1920, prices rose at an average of more than 15 percent a year.

Finally, late in 1920, the economic bubble burst, as many of the temporary forces that had created it disappeared and as inflation began killing the market for consumer goods. Between 1920 and 1921, the gross national product (GNP) declined nearly 10 percent; 100,000

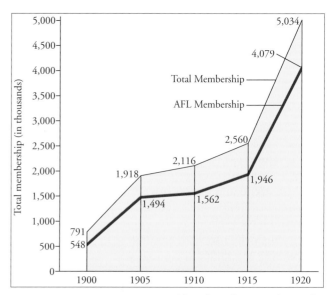

UNION MEMBERSHIP, 1900–1920 This chart illustrates the steady increase in union membership in the first half of the twentieth century—a membership dominated by unions associated with the AFL. Note the particularly sharp increase between 1915 and 1920, the years of World War I. ◆ *Why did the war years see such an expansion of union labor?*

THE BOSTON POLICE STRIKE National guardsmen stand guard in front of a sporting goods store, where broken windows suggest looting has already occurred, during the Boston Police Strike of 1919. *(Bettmann/Corbis)*

businesses went bankrupt; 453,000 farmers lost their land; nearly 5 million Americans lost their jobs. In this un-

Postwar Recession

promising economic environment, leaders of organized labor set out to consolidate the advances they had made in the war, which now seemed in danger of being lost. The raging inflation of 1919 wiped out the modest wage gains workers had achieved during the war; many laborers worried about job security as hundreds of thousands of veterans returned to the work force; arduous working conditions—such as the twelve-hour day in the steel industry—continued to be a source of discontent. Employers aggravated the resentment by using the end of the war (and the end of government controls) to rescind benefits they had been forced to concede to workers in 1917 and 1918—most notably recognition of unions. The year 1919, therefore, saw an unprecedented wave of strikes— more than 3,600 in all, involving over 4 million workers. In January, a walkout by shipyard workers in Seattle, Washington, evolved into a general strike that brought the entire city to a virtual standstill. The mayor requested and received the assistance of U.S. Marines to keep the city running, and eventually the strike failed. But the brief success

of a general strike, something Americans associated with European radicals, made the Seattle incident reverberate loudly throughout the country.

In September, there was a strike by the Boston police force, which was responding to layoffs and wage cuts by demanding recognition of its union. Seattle had remained

Boston Police Strike

generally calm during its strike; but with its police off the job, Boston erupted in violence and looting. Efforts by local businessmen, veterans, and college students to patrol the streets proved ineffective; and finally Governor Calvin Coolidge called in the National Guard to restore order. (His public statement that "there is no right to strike against the public safety by anybody, anywhere, any time" attracted national acclaim.) Eventually, Boston officials dismissed the entire police force and hired a new one.

In September 1919, the greatest strike in American history began, when 350,000 steelworkers in several eastern and midwestern cities walked off the job, demanding an eight-hour day and recognition of their union. The steel strike was long, bitter, and violent—most of the violence coming from employers, who hired armed guards to disperse picket lines and escort strikebreakers into factories.

It climaxed in a riot in Gary, Indiana, in which eighteen strikers were killed. Steel executives managed to keep most plants running with non-union labor, and public

Steel Workers' Strike Defeated

opinion was so hostile to the strikers that the AFL—having at first endorsed the strike—soon timidly repudiated it. By January, the strike had collapsed. It was a setback from which organized labor would not recover for more than a decade.

The wave of strikes was a reflection of the high expectations workers had in the aftermath of a war they believed had been fought, in part, to secure their rights. It was also a reflection of the power of the forces arrayed against them. An official of the War Labor Board, observing the dismal postwar experience of unions, said in 1919: "The workers of the Allied world have been told that they were engaged in a democracy. . . . They are asking now, 'Where is that democracy for which we fought?'"

The Demands of African Americans

The black men who had served in the armed forces during the war (almost 400,000 of them) came home in 1919 and marched down the main streets of the industrial cities with other returning troops. And then (in New York and other cities), they marched again through the streets of black neighborhoods such as Harlem, led by jazz bands, cheered by thousands of African Americans, worshiped as heroes. The black soldiers were an inspiration to thousands of urban African Americans, a sign, they thought, that a new age had come, that the glory of black heroism in the war would make it impossible for white society ever again to treat African Americans as less than equal citizens.

In fact, that black soldiers had fought in the war had almost no impact at all on white attitudes. But it did have a profound effect on black attitudes: it accentuated African-American bitterness—and increased black determination to fight for their rights. For soldiers, there was an

New Black Attitudes

expectation of some social reward for their service. For many other American blacks, the war had raised economic expectations, as they moved into industrial and other jobs vacated by white workers, jobs to which they had previously had no access. Just as black soldiers expected their military service to enhance their social status, so black factory workers regarded their move north as an escape from racial prejudice and an opportunity for economic gain.

By 1919, however, the racial climate had become savage and murderous. In the South, there was a sudden increase in lynchings: more than seventy blacks, some of them war veterans, died at the hands of white mobs in 1919 alone. In the North, black factory workers faced widespread layoffs as returning white veterans displaced them from their jobs. Black veterans found no significant

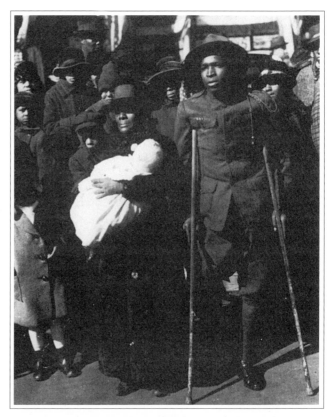

A BLACK VETERAN Residents of Harlem watch the 309th Colored Infantry parading through New York on the occasion of their return from Europe in March 1919. A disabled veteran, still in uniform, is standing somberly among the crowd—as if already aware of the disappointments awaiting other black veterans as they reentered civilian life. *(Bettmann/Corbis)*

new opportunities for advancement. Rural black migrants to northern cities encountered white communities unfamiliar with and generally hostile to them; and as whites became convinced that black workers with lower wage demands were hurting them economically, animosity grew rapidly.

The wartime riots in East St. Louis and elsewhere were a prelude to a summer of much worse racial violence in 1919. In Chicago, a black teenager swimming in Lake Michigan on a hot July day happened to drift toward a white beach. Whites on shore allegedly stoned him uncon-

Chicago Race Riots

scious; he sank and drowned. Angry blacks gathered in crowds and marched into white neighborhoods to retaliate; whites formed even larger crowds and roamed into black neighborhoods shooting, stabbing, and beating passersby, destroying homes and properties. For more than a week, Chicago was virtually at war. In the end, 38 people died—15 whites and 23 blacks—and 537 were injured; over 1,000 people were left homeless. The Chicago riot was the worst but not the only racial violence during the so-called red summer of 1919; in all, 120 people died

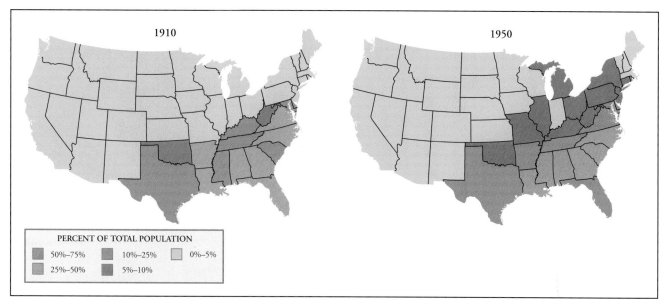

AFRICAN-AMERICAN MIGRATION, 1910–1950 Two great waves of migration produced a dramatic redistribution of the African-American population in the first half of the twentieth century—one around the time of World War I, the other during and after World War II. The map on the left shows the almost exclusive concentration of African Americans in the South as late as 1910. The map on the right shows both the tremendous increase of black populations in northern states by 1950, and the relative decline of black populations in parts of the South. Note in particular the changes in Mississippi and South Carolina. ◆ *Why did the wars produce such significant migration out of the South?*

in such racial outbreaks in the space of little more than three months.

Racial violence, and even racially motivated urban riots, were not new. The deadliest race riot in American history had occurred in New York during the Civil War. But the 1919 riots were different in one respect: they did not just involve white people attacking blacks; they also involved blacks fighting back. The NAACP signaled this change by urging blacks not just to demand government protection, but also to retaliate, to defend themselves. The poet Claude McKay, one of the major figures of what would shortly be known as the Harlem Renaissance, wrote a poem after the Chicago riot called "If We Must Die":

> Like men we'll face the murderous cowardly pack.
> Pressed to the wall, dying, but fighting back.

At the same time, a black Jamaican, Marcus Garvey, began to attract a wide American following—mostly among

Marcus Garvey's Black Nationalism

poor urban blacks—with an ideology of black nationalism. Garvey encouraged African Americans to take pride in their own achievements and to develop an awareness of their African heritage—to reject assimilation into white society and develop pride in their own race and culture (which was, he claimed, superior to that of white society). His United Negro Improvement Association (UNIA) launched a chain of black-owned grocery stores and pressed for the creation of other black businesses. Eventually, Garvey began urging his supporters to leave America and return to Africa,

where they could create a new society of their own. In the 1920s, the Garvey movement experienced explosive growth for a time; and the UNIA became notable for its mass rallies and parades, for the opulent uniforms of its members, and for the growth of its enterprises. It began to decline, however, after Garvey was indicted in 1923 on charges of business fraud. He was deported to Jamaica two years later. But the allure of black nationalism, which he helped make visible to millions of African Americans, survived in black culture long after Garvey himself was gone.

The Red Scare

To much of the white middle class at the time, the industrial warfare, the racial violence, and other forms of dissent all appeared to be frightening omens of instability and radicalism. This was in part because other evidence emerging at the same time seemed likewise to suggest the existence of a radical menace. The Russian Revolution of November 1917 made it clear that communism was no longer simply a theory, but now an important regime.

Concerns about the communist threat grew in 1919 when the Soviet government announced the formation of the Communist International (or Comintern), whose purpose was to export revolution around the world. And in America itself, there were, in addition to the great number of imagined radicals, a modest number of real ones. The American Communist Party began its life in 1919, and

MARCUS GARVEY Marcus Garvey can be seen here enthroned on an opulent stage set for the 1924 convention of his United Negro Improvement Association. He is surrounded by uniformed guards and delegates from his organization. At the organization's peak, these annual meetings attracted thousands of people from around the world and lasted for weeks. *(Marcus Garvey at Liberty Hall, 1924. Photograph by James VanDerZee. © Donna Mussendem VanDerZee.)*

there were other radical groups (many of them dominated by immigrants from Europe who had been involved in radical politics before coming to America). Some of these radicals were presumably responsible for a series of bombings in the spring of 1919 that produced great national alarm. In April, the post office intercepted several dozen parcels addressed to leading businessmen and politicians that were triggered to explode when opened. Several of them reached their destinations, and one of them exploded, severely injuring a domestic servant of a public official in Georgia. Two months later, eight bombs exploded in eight cities within minutes of one another, suggesting a nationwide conspiracy. One of them damaged the facade of Attorney General A. Mitchell Palmer's home in Washington. In 1920, there was a terrible explosion in front of the Morgan bank on Wall Street, which killed thirty people (although only one person in the bank itself—a clerk).

The bombings crystallized what was already a growing determination among many middle-class Americans (and some government officials) to fight back against radicalism—a determination steeled by the repressive at-

mosphere of the war years. This antiradicalism accompanied, and reinforced, the already strong commitment among old-stock Protestants to the idea of "100 Percent Americanism." And it produced what became known as the Red Scare.

Popular Antiradicalism

Antiradical newspapers and politicians now began to portray almost every form of instability or protest as a sign of a radical threat. Race riots, one newspaper claimed, were the work of "armed revolutionaries running rampant through our cities." The steel strike, the *Philadelphia Inquirer* claimed, was "penetrated with the Bolshevik idea . . . steeped in the doctrines of the class struggle and social overthrow." Nearly thirty states enacted new peacetime sedition laws imposing harsh penalties on those who promoted revolution; some 300 people went to jail as a result—many of them people whose "crime" had been nothing more than opposition to the war. There were spontaneous acts of violence against supposed radicals in some communities. A mob of off-duty soldiers in New York City ransacked the offices of a socialist newspaper and beat up its staff. Another mob, in Centralia, Washington,

SEARCHING FOR RADICALS During the period of the notorious Palmer Raids, federal agents raided the homes and offices of thousands of suspected radicals in search of weapons and other evidence of impending violence. They rarely found anything incriminating. Here, agents search the Brooklyn offices of a Lithuanian newspaper thought to be editorially radical. *(Bettmann/Corbis)*

dragged an IWW agitator from jail and castrated him before hanging him from a bridge. Citizens in many communities removed "subversive" books from the shelves of libraries; administrators in some universities dismissed "radical" members from their faculties. Women's groups such as the National Consumers' League came under attack by antiradicals because so many feminists had opposed American intervention in the fighting in Europe.

Perhaps the greatest contribution to the Red Scare came from the federal government. On New Year's Day, 1920, Attorney General A. Mitchell Palmer and his ambitious assistant, J. Edgar Hoover, orchestrated a series of raids on alleged radical centers throughout the country and arrested more than 6,000 people.

The Palmer Raids had been intended to uncover huge caches of weapons and explosives; they netted a total of three pistols and no dynamite. *Palmer Raids* Most of those arrested were ultimately released, but about 500 who were not American citizens were summarily deported.

The ferocity of the Red Scare soon abated, but its effects lingered well into the 1920s, most notably in the celebrated case of Sacco and Vanzetti. In May of 1920, two Italian immigrants, Nicola Sacco and Bartolomeo Vanzetti, *Sacco and Vanzetti* were charged with the murder of a paymaster in Braintree, Massachusetts. The evidence against them was questionable; but because both men were confessed anarchists, they faced a widespread public presumption of guilt. They were convicted in a trial of extraordinary injudiciousness, before an openly bigoted judge, Webster Thayer, and were sentenced to death. Over the next several years, public support for Sacco and Vanzetti grew to formidable proportions. But all requests for a new trial

SACCO AND VANZETTI The artist Ben Shahn painted this view of the anarchists Nicola Sacco and Bartolomeo Vanzetti, handcuffed together in a courtroom in 1927 waiting to hear if the appeal of their 1921 verdicts for murdering a Boston paymaster would succeed. It did not, and the two men were executed later that year. Just before his execution, Vanzetti said: "Never in our full life can we hope to do such work for tolerance, for man's understanding of man, as now we do by an accident. Our words— our lives—our pains—nothing! The taking of our lives—lives of a good shoemaker and a poor fish-peddler—all! That last moment belongs to us—that agony is our triumph." *(©Estate of Ben Shahn/Licensed by VAGA, New York, NY. Photo courtesy Museum of Modern Art)*

or a pardon were denied. On August 23, 1927, amid widespread protests around the world, Sacco and Vanzetti, still proclaiming their innocence, died in the electric chair. Theirs was a cause that a generation of Americans never forgot. Fifty years later, the writer Katherine Anne Porter, who had demonstrated on their behalf, described the case as the "Never-Ending Wrong." It kept the bitter legacy of the Red Scare alive for many years.

The Retreat from Idealism

On August 26, 1920, the Nineteenth Amendment, guaranteeing women the right to vote, became part of the Constitution. To the woman suffrage movement, this was the culmination of nearly a century of struggle. To many progressives, who had seen the inclusion of women in the electorate as a way of bolstering their political strength, it seemed to promise new support for reform. Yet the passage of the Nineteenth Amendment marked not the beginning of an era of reform, but the end of one. Economic problems, feminist demands, labor unrest, racial tensions, and the intensity of the antiradicalism they helped create—all combined in the years immediately following the war to produce a general sense of disillusionment.

That became particularly apparent in the election of 1920. Woodrow Wilson wanted the campaign to be a referendum on the League of Nations, and the Democratic candidates, Ohio Governor James M. Cox and Assistant Secretary of the Navy Franklin D. Roosevelt, tried to keep Wilson's ideals alive. The Republican presidential nominee, however, offered a different vision. He was Warren Gamaliel Harding, an obscure Ohio senator whom party leaders had chosen as their nominee confident that he would do their bidding once in office. Harding offered no ideals, only a vague promise of a return, as he later phrased it, to "normalcy." He won in a land- *Return to "Normalcy"* slide. The Republican ticket received 61 percent of the popular vote and carried every state outside the South. The party made major gains in Congress as well. Woodrow Wilson, who had tried and failed to create a postwar order based on democratic ideals, stood repudiated. Early in 1921, he retired to a house on S Street in Washington, where he lived quietly until his death in 1924. In the meantime, for most Americans, a new era had begun.

CONCLUSION

The greatest and most terrible war in human history to that point was also an important moment in the rise of the United States to global pre-eminence. The powers of Europe emerged from more than four years of carnage with their societies and economies in disarray. The United States emerged from its own, much briefer, involvement in the war poised to become the most important political and economic force in the world.

For a time after the outbreak of war in Europe in 1914, most Americans—President Wilson among them—wanted nothing so much as to stay out of the conflict. Gradually, however, as the war dragged on and the tactics of Britain and Germany began to impinge on American trade and on freedom of the seas, the United States found itself drawn slowly into the conflict. In April 1917, finally, Congress agreed (although not without considerable dissent) to the president's request that the United States enter the war as an ally of Britain.

American forces quickly broke the stalemate that had bogged the European forces down in years of inconclusive trench warfare. Within a few months after the arrival of substantial numbers of American troops in Europe, Germany agreed to an armistice and the war shuddered to a close. American casualties, although not inconsiderable, were negligible compared to the millions suffered by the European combatants. In the meantime, the American economy experienced an enormous industrial boom as a result of the war.

The social experience of the war in the United States was, on the whole, dismaying to reformers. Although the war enhanced some reform efforts—most notably prohibition and woman suffrage—it also introduced an atmosphere of intolerance and repression into American life, an atmosphere assisted by policies of the federal government designed to suppress dissent. The aftermath of the war was even more disheartening to progressives, both because of a brief but highly destabilizing recession, and because of a wave of repression directed against labor, radicals, African Americans, and immigrants in 1919 and 1920.

At the same time, Woodrow Wilson's bold and idealistic dream of a peace based on the principles of democracy and justice suffered a painful death. The Treaty of Versailles, which he helped to draft, was itself far from what Wilson had hoped. It did, however, contain a provision for a League of Nations, which Wilson believed could transform the international order. But the League quickly became controversial in the United States; and despite strenuous efforts by the president—efforts that hastened his own physical collapse—the treaty was defeated in the Senate. In the aftermath of that traumatic battle, the American people seemed to turn away from Wilson and his ideals and entered a very different era.

FOR FURTHER REFERENCE

Ernest R. May, *The World War and American Isolation* (1959), is an authoritative account of America's slow and controversial entry into the Great War. Frank Freidel provides a sweeping account of the American soldier's battlefield experience during World War I in *Over There: The Story of America's First Great Overseas Crusade* (1964). David Kennedy, *Over Here: The First World War and American Society* (1980) is an important study of the domestic impact of the war. Robert D. Cuff, *The War Industries Board: Business-Government Relations During World War II* (1973) is a good account of mobilization for war in the United States. Ronald Schaffer, *America in the Great War: The Rise of the War Welfare State* (1991) examines the ways in which mobilization for war created new public benefits for various groups, including labor. Maureen Greenwald, *Women, War, and Work* (1980) describes the impact of World War I on women workers. John Keegan, *The First World War* (1998) is a superb military history. Thomas Knock, *To End All Wars:*

Woodrow Wilson and the Quest for a New World Order (1992) is a valuable study of the battle for the peace. Arno Mayer, *Wilson vs. Lenin* (1959) and *Politics and Diplomacy of Peacemaking: Containment and Counterrevolution* (1965) are important revisionist accounts of the peacemaking process. America's stormy debate over immigration and national identity before, during, and after World War I is best captured by John Higham, *Strangers in the Land: Patterns of American Nativism* (1955). William M. Tuttle, Jr., in *Race Riot: Chicago in the Red Summer of 1919* (1970), recounts the terrible riots of 1919 that showed America violently divided along racial and ideological lines. Paul L. Murphy, *World War I and the Origins of Civil Liberties* (1979) shows how wartime efforts to quell dissent created new support for civil liberties. *The Great War—1918* (1997) is a documentary film chronicling the experiences of American soldiers in the closing battles of World War I through their letters and diaries.

For quizzes, Internet resources, references to additional books and films, and more, consult this book's Online Learning Center at www.mhhe.com/brinkley11.

THE FLAPPER, 1927 The popular Condé Nast fashion magazine, Vogue, portrayed a fashionably dressed "flapper" on its cover in 1927. The short hair and the cap pulled down low over the forehead were both part of the flapper style. What had begun as a fashion among working-class women had by 1927 moved into stylish high society. *(Georges Lepape/©Vogue, The Condé Nast Publications Inc.)*

Significant Events

CHAPTER TWENTY-FOUR

"THE NEW ERA"

*T*he image of the 1920s in the American popular imagination is of an era of affluence, conservatism, and cultural frivolity: the "Roaring Twenties"; what Warren G. Harding once called the age of "normalcy." In reality, the decade was a time of significant, even dramatic social, economic, and political change. It was an era in which the American economy not only enjoyed spectacular growth but developed new forms of organization. It was a time in which American popular culture reshaped itself in response to the urban, industrial, consumer-oriented society America was becoming. And it was a decade in which American government, for all its apparent conservatism, experimented with new approaches

Myth and Reality

to public policy that helped pave the way for the important period of reform that was to follow. Contemporaries liked to refer to the 1920s as the "New Era"—an age in which America was becoming a modern nation.

At the same time, however, the decade saw the rise of a series of spirited and at times effective rebellions against the modern developments that were transforming American life. The intense cultural conflicts that characterized the 1920s were evidence of how many Americans remained outside the reach of the new, affluent consumer culture; and evidence, too, of how some of those inside it remained unreconciled to the modernizing currents of the New Era.

1923 · Nation experiences mild recession
· Harding dies; Calvin Coolidge becomes president
· Teapot Dome and other scandals revealed
· *Time* magazine founded

1924 · National Origins Act passed
· Ku Klux Klan reaches peak membership
· Coolidge elected president

1925 · F. Scott Fitzgerald publishes *The Great Gatsby*
· Scopes trial in Dayton, Tennessee
· A. Philip Randolph founds Brotherhood of Sleeping Car Porters

1926 · Congress passes McNary-Haugen bill; Coolidge vetoes it

1927 · First feature-length sound motion picture, *The Jazz Singer*, released
· Charles Lindbergh makes solo transatlantic flight

1928 · Congress passes, and Coolidge vetoes, McNary-Haugen bill again
· Herbert Hoover elected president

1929 · Sheppard-Towner program terminated
· Ernest Hemingway publishes *A Farewell to Arms*

THE NEW ECONOMY

After the recession of 1921–1922, the United States began a long period of almost uninterrupted prosperity and economic expansion. Less visible at the time, but equally significant, was the survival (and even the growth) of serious inequalities and imbalances.

Technology and Economic Growth

No one could deny the remarkable, some believed miraculous, feats of the American economy in the 1920s. The nation's manufacturing output rose by more than 60 percent during the decade. Per capita income grew by a third. Inflation was negligible. A mild recession in 1923 interrupted the pattern of growth, but when it subsided early in 1924, the economy expanded with even greater vigor than before.

The economic boom was a result of many things. An immediate cause was the debilitation of European industry in the aftermath of World War I, which left the United States for a short time the only truly healthy industrial power in the world. More important in the long run was technology, and the great industrial expansion it made possible. The automobile industry, as a result of the development of the assembly line and other innovations, now became one of the most important industries in the nation. It stimulated growth in many related industries as well. Auto manufacturers purchased the products of steel, rubber, glass, and tool companies. Auto owners bought gasoline from the oil corporations. Road construction in response to the proliferation of motor vehicles became an important industry. The increased mobility that the automobile made possible increased the demand for suburban housing, fueling a boom in the construction industry.

Sources of the Boom

Other new industries benefiting from technological innovations contributed as well to the economic growth. Radio began to become a popular technology even before commercial broadcasting began in 1920. Early radio had been able to broadcast little beside pulses, which meant that radio communication could occur only through the Morse Code. But with the discovery of the theory of modulation, pioneered by the Canadian scientist Reginald Fessenden, it became possible to transmit speech and music. (Modulation also eventually made possible the transmission of video signals and later helped create radar and television.) Many people built their own radio sets at home for very little money, benefiting from the discovery that inexpensive crystals could receive signals over long distances (but not very well over short ones). These "short wave" radios, which allowed individual owners to establish contact with each other, marked the beginning of an enduring passion among millions of people around the world, who talked with one another over what later became known to many people as "ham radio." Once commercial broadcasting began, families flocked to buy more conventional radio sets, which could receive high-quality signals over short and medium distances. They were powered by vacuum tubes that were much more reliable than earlier models. By 1925, there were two million sets in American homes, and by the end of the 1920s almost every family had one.

Radio

Commercial aviation developed slowly in the 1920s, beginning with the use of planes to deliver mail. On the whole, airplanes remained curiosities and sources of entertainment. But technological advances—the development of the radial engine and the creation of pressurized cabins—were laying the groundwork for the great increase in commercial travel in the 1930s and beyond. Trains became faster and more efficient as well with the development of the diesel-electric engine. Electronics, home appliances, plastics and synthetic fibers such as nylon (both pioneered by researchers at DuPont), aluminum, magnesium, oil, electric power, and other industries fueled by technological advances—all grew

THE STEAMFITTER Lewis Hine was among the first American photographers to recognize his craft as an art. In this photograph from the mid-1920s, Hine made a point that many other artists were making in other media: The rise of the machine could serve human beings, but might also bend them to its own needs. The steamfitter (carefully posed by the photographer) is forced to shape his body to the contours of his machine in order to complete his task.
(International Museum of Photography at George Eastman House)

dramatically and spurred the economic boom. Telephones continued to proliferate. By the late 1930s, there were approximately 25 million telephones in the United States, approximately one for every six people.

The seeds of future widespread technologies were also visible in the 1920s and 1930s. In both England and America, scientists and engineers were working to transform prim-

Early Computers

itive calculating machines into devices capable of performing more complicated tasks. By the early 1930s, researchers at MIT, led by Vannevar Bush, had created an instrument capable of performing a variety of complicated tasks—the first analog computer, which became the starting point for dramatic progress over the next several decades. A few years later, Howard Aiken, with financial assistance from Harvard and MIT, built a much more complex computer with memory, capable of multiplying eleven-digit numbers in three seconds.

Genetic research had begun in Austria in the mid-nineteenth century through the work of Gregor Mendel, a Catholic monk who performed experiments on the hybridization of vegetables in the garden of his monastery. His findings attracted little attention during his lifetime, but in the early twentieth century they were discovered by several investigators and helped shape modern genetic research. Among the American pioneers was Thomas Hunt Morgan of Columbia University and later Cal Tech, whose experiments with fruit flies revealed how several genes could be transmitted together (as opposed to Mendel's belief that they could only be transferred separately). He also revealed the way in which genes were arranged along the chromosome. His work helped open the path to understanding how genes could recombine—a critical discovery that led to more advanced experiments in hybridization and genetics.

Economic Organization

Large sectors of American business were accelerating their drive toward national organization and consolidation. Certain industries—notably those, such as steel, dependent on large-scale mass production—seemed naturally to move toward concentrating production in a few large firms; U.S. Steel, the nation's largest corporation, was so dominant that almost everyone used the term "Little Steel" to refer to all of its competitors. Other industries, such as textiles, that were less dependent on technology and less susceptible to great economies of scale, proved more resistant to consolidation, despite the efforts of many businessmen to promote it.

In those areas where industry did consolidate, new forms of corporate organization emerged to advance the

Modern Administrative Systems

trend. General Motors, which by 1920 was not only the largest automobile manufacturer but the fifth largest American corporation, was a classic example.

GM's founder, William Durant, had expanded the company dramatically but had never replaced the informal, personal management style with which he began. When GM foundered in the 1920 recession, leadership of the company fell to Alfred P. Sloan, who created a modern administrative system with an efficient divisional organization. The new system not only made it easier for GM to control its many subsidiaries; it also made it simpler for it—and for the many other corporations that adopted similar administrative systems—to expand further.

Some industries less susceptible to domination by a few great corporations attempted to stabilize themselves not through consolidation but through cooperation. An important vehicle was the trade association—a national organization created by various members of an industry to en-

Trade Associations

courage coordination in production and marketing techniques. Trade associations worked reasonably well in the mass-production industries that had already succeeded in limiting competition through consolidation. But in more decentralized industries, such as cotton textiles, their effectiveness was limited.

The strenuous efforts by industrialists throughout the economy to find ways to curb competition through consolidation or cooperation reflected a strong fear of overproduction. Even in the booming 1920s, industrialists remembered how too-rapid expansion had helped produce recessions in 1893, 1907, and 1920. The great, unrealized dream of the New Era was to find a way to stabilize the economy so that such collapses would never occur again.

Labor in the New Era

The remarkable economic growth was accompanied by a continuing, and in some areas even increasing, maldistribution of wealth and purchasing power. More than two-thirds of the American people in 1929 lived at no better than what one major study described as the "minimum comfort level." Half of those languished at or below the level of "subsistence and poverty." Large segments of society, unable to organize, were without power to protect their economic interests.

American industrial workers experienced both the successes and the failures of the 1920s as much as any other group. On the one hand, most workers saw their standard of living rise during the decade; many enjoyed greatly improved working conditions and other benefits. Some employers in the 1920s, eager to avoid disruptive labor unrest and forestall the growth of independent trade unions, adopted paternal-

"Welfare Capitalism"

istic techniques that came to be known as "welfare capitalism." Henry Ford, for example, shortened the workweek, raised wages, and instituted paid vacations. U.S. Steel made conspicuous efforts to improve safety and sanitation in its factories. For the first time, some workers became eligible for pensions on retirement—nearly 3 million by 1926. When labor grievances surfaced despite these efforts, workers could voice them through the so-called company unions that were emerging in many industries. These were workers' councils and shop committees, organized by the corporations themselves and thus without the independence unions usually require.

Welfare capitalism brought many workers important economic benefits, but it did not help them gain any real control over their own fates. Company unions were feeble vehicles, forbidden in most industries from raising the issues most important to workers. And welfare capitalism survived only as long as industry prospered. After 1929, with the economy in crisis, the entire system quickly collapsed.

Welfare capitalism affected only a relatively small number of workers, in any case. Most laborers worked for employers interested primarily in keeping their labor costs to a minimum. Workers as a whole, therefore, received wage increases that were proportionately far below increases in production and profits. Unskilled workers, in particular, saw their wages increase almost imperceptibly—by only a little over 2 percent between 1920 and 1926. In the end, American workers in the 1920s remained a relatively impoverished and powerless group. Their wages rose; but the average annual income of a worker remained below $1,500 a year when $1,800 was considered necessary to maintain a minimally decent standard of living. Only by relying on the earnings of several family members at once could many working-class families make ends meet. And almost all such families had to live with the very real possibility of one or more members losing their jobs. Unemployment was lower in the 1920s than it had been in the previous two decades, and much lower than it would be in the 1930s. But a large proportion of the work force was out of work for at least some period during the decade—in part because the rapid growth of industrial technology made many jobs obsolete. The unemployment rate for the 1920s is difficult to calculate, but scholars estimate that an average of 5 to 7 percent of the work force was without a job at any given time.

Many laborers continued to regard an effective, independent union movement as their best hope. But the New Era was a bleak time for labor organization, in part because the unions themselves were generally conservative and failed to adapt to the realities of the modern economy. The American Federation of Labor remained wedded to the concept of the craft union, in which workers were organized on the basis of particular skills. It continued to make no provision for the fastest-growing area of the work force: unskilled industrial workers, many of them immigrants from southern or eastern Europe. Ignored by the craft unions, they had few organizations of their own. William Green, who became

Hard Times for Organized Labor

president of the AFL in 1924, was committed to peaceful cooperation with employers and to strident opposition to communism and socialism. He frowned on strikes.

Women and Minorities in the Work Force

A growing proportion of the work force consisted of women, who were concentrated in what have since become known as "pink-collar" jobs—low-paying service occupations with many of the same problems as manufacturing employment. Large numbers of women worked as secretaries, salesclerks, telephone operators, and other, similarly underpaid jobs. Because technically such positions were not industrial jobs, the AFL and other labor organizations were generally uninterested in organizing these workers.

"Pink-collar" Jobs

Similarly, the half-million African Americans who had migrated from the rural South to the cities during the Great Migration after 1914 had few opportunities for union representation. The skilled crafts represented in the AFL often worked actively to exclude blacks from their

PREPARING WOMEN FOR WORK This school was established during World War I by the Northern Pacific Telegraph Company to train new women employees to be telephone operators. Both during and after the war, telephone companies were among the largest employers of women. *(Bettmann/Corbis)*

A SLEEPING CAR PORTER The Brotherhood of Sleeping Car Porters was one of the first unions to represent a group of workers (such as the Pullman porter shown here) who were mostly black. *(Culver Pictures, Inc.)*

trades and organizations. Most blacks worked in jobs in which the AFL took no interest at all —as janitors, dishwashers, garbage collectors, commercial laundry attendants, domestics, and in other types of service jobs. The Brotherhood of Sleeping Car Porters, founded in 1925 and led for years by A. Philip Randolph, was a notable exception: a vigorous union, led by an African American, and representing a virtually all-black work force. Over time, Randolph won some significant gains for his members—increased wages, shorter working hours, and other benefits. He also enlisted the union in battles for civil rights for African Americans.

A. Philip Randolph

In the West and the Southwest, the ranks of the unskilled included considerable numbers of Asians and Hispanics, few of them organized, most actively excluded from white-dominated unions. In the wake of the Chinese Exclusion Acts, Japanese immigrants increasingly took the place of the Chinese in menial jobs in California, despite the continuing hostility of the white population. They worked on railroads, construction sites, farms, and in many other low-paying workplaces. Some Japanese managed to escape the ranks of the unskilled by forming their

own small businesses or setting themselves up as truck farmers; and many of the *Issei* (Japanese immigrants) and *Nisei* (their American-born children) enjoyed significant economic success—so much so that California passed laws in 1913 and 1920 to make it more difficult for them to buy land. Other Asians—most notably Filipinos—also swelled the unskilled work force and generated considerable hostility. Anti-Filipino riots in California beginning in 1929 helped produce legislation in 1934 virtually eliminating immigration from the Philippines.

Mexican immigrants formed a major part of the unskilled work force throughout the Southwest and California. Nearly half a million Mexicans entered the United States in the 1920s, more than any other national group, increasing the total Mexican population to over a million. Most lived in California, Texas, Arizona, and New Mexico; and by 1930, most lived in cities. Large Mexican barrios— usually raw urban communities, often without even such basic services as plumbing and sewage—grew up in Los Angeles, El Paso, San Antonio, Denver, and many other cities and towns. Some of the residents found work locally in factories and shops; others traveled to mines or did migratory labor on farms, but returned to the cities between jobs. Mexican workers, too, faced hostility and discrimination from the Anglo population of the region; but there were few efforts actually to exclude them. Employers in the relatively underpopulated West needed this ready pool of low-paid, unskilled, and unorganized workers.

The "American Plan"

Whatever the weaknesses of the unions and of unorganized, unskilled workers, the strength of the corporations was the principal reason for the absence of effective labor organization. After the turmoil of 1919, corporate leaders worked hard to spread the doctrine that unionism was somehow subversive, that a crucial element of democratic capitalism was the protection of the open shop (a shop in which no worker could be required to join a union). The crusade for the open shop, euphemistically titled the "American Plan," received the endorsement of the National Association of Manufacturers in 1920 and became a pretext for a harsh campaign of union busting across the country.

Protecting the Open Shop

When such tactics proved insufficient to counter union power, government assistance often made the difference. In 1921, the Supreme Court upheld a lower-court ruling that declared picketing illegal and supported the right of courts to issue injunctions against strikers. In 1922, the Justice Department intervened to quell a strike by 400,000 railroad workers. In 1924, the courts refused protection to members of the United Mine Workers Union when mine owners launched a violent campaign in western Pennsylvania to drive the union from the coal

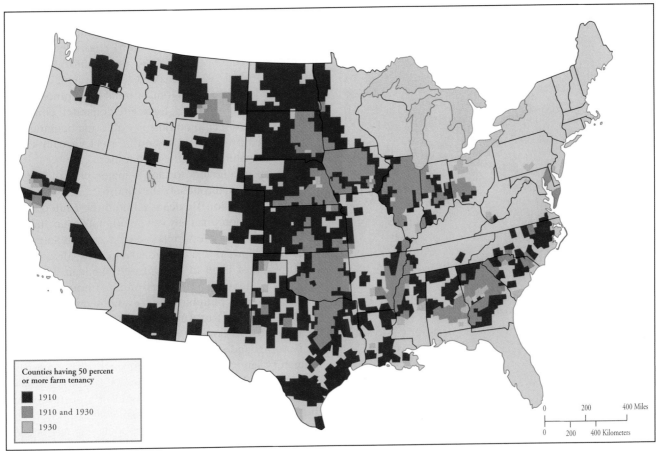

FARM TENANCY, 1910–1930 This map illustrates the significant increase in farm tenancy—that is, the number of farmers who did not own their land but worked as tenants for others—between 1910 and 1930. The dark green areas of the map show how extensive tenancy was even in 1910; over fifty percent of the land in those areas was farmed by tenants. The light brown and light green parts of the map show the significant expansion of tenancy between 1910 and 1930—creating many new areas in which more than half the farmers were tenants.

◆ *How did the increasing efficiency and technological progress of agriculture in these years contribute to the growth of tenancy?*

fields. As a result of these developments, union membership fell from more than 5 million in 1920 to under 3 million in 1929.

Agricultural Technology and the Plight of the Farmer

Like industry, American agriculture in the 1920s was embracing new technologies for increasing production. The number of tractors on American farms, for example, quadrupled during the 1920s, especially after they began

Mechanized Farming | to be powered by internal combustion engines (like automobiles) rather than by the cumbersome steam engines of the past. They helped to open 35 million new acres to cultivation. Increasingly sophisticated combines and harvesters were proliferating, helping to make it possible to produce more crops with fewer workers.

Agricultural researchers were already at work on other advances that would later transform food production in America and around the world: the invention of hybrid

corn (made possible by advances in genetic research), which became available to farmers in 1921 but was not grown in great quantities for a decade or more; and the creation of chemical fertilizers and pesticides, which also began to have limited use in the 1920s but which proliferated quickly in the 1930s and 1940s.

The new technologies greatly increased agricultural productivity, both in the United States and in other parts of the world. But the demand for agricultural goods was not rising as fast as production. The results were substantial surpluses, a disastrous decline in food prices, and a severe drop in farmers' income beginning early in the 1920s. More than 3 million people left agriculture altogether in the course of the decade. Of those who remained, many lost ownership of their lands and had to rent instead from banks or other landlords.

In response, some farmers began to demand relief in the form of government price supports. One price-raising scheme in particular came to dominate agrarian demands: the idea of "parity." Parity was a complicated formula for setting an adequate price for farm goods and ensuring that farmers would earn back at least their production costs no matter how the national or world agricultural market might fluctuate. Champions of parity urged high tariffs against foreign agricultural goods and a government commitment to buy surplus domestic crops at parity and sell them abroad at whatever the market would bring.

"Parity"

The legislative expression of the demand for parity was the McNary-Haugen Bill, named after its two principal sponsors in Congress and introduced repeatedly between 1924 and 1928. In 1926 and again in 1928, Congress (where farm interests enjoyed disproportionate influence) approved a bill requiring parity for grain, cotton, tobacco, and rice, but President Coolidge vetoed it both times.

McNary-Haugen Bill

THE NEW CULTURE

The increasingly urban and consumer-oriented culture of the 1920s helped many Americans in all regions live their lives and perceive their world in increasingly similar ways. That same culture exposed them to a new set of values that reflected the prosperity and complexity of the modern economy. But the new culture could not, of course, erase the continuing, and indeed increasing, diversity of the United States. The relatively uniform mass culture reached Americans divided by region, race, religion, gender, and class, and those characteristics shaped the way individuals responded to national cultural messages.

Consumerism

Among the many changes industrialization produced in the United States was the creation of a mass consumer culture. By the 1920s, America was a society in which many men and women (although not, of course, all) could afford not merely the means of subsistence, but a considerable measure of additional, discretionary goods and services; a society in which people could buy items not just because of need but for pleasure. Middle-class families purchased such new appliances as electric refrigerators, washing machines, electric irons, and vacuum cleaners, which revolutionized housework and had a particularly dramatic impact on the lives of women. Men and women wore wristwatches and smoked cigarettes. Women purchased cosmetics and mass-produced fashions. Above all, Americans bought automobiles. By the end of the decade, there were more than 30 million cars on American roads.

Growing Mass Consumption

The automobile affected American life in countless ways. It greatly expanded the geographical horizons of millions of people who had previously seldom ventured very far from their homes. Rural men and women, in

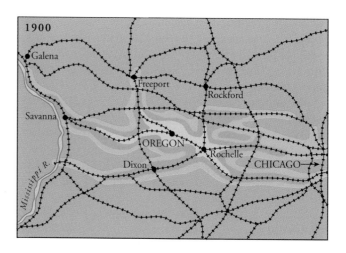

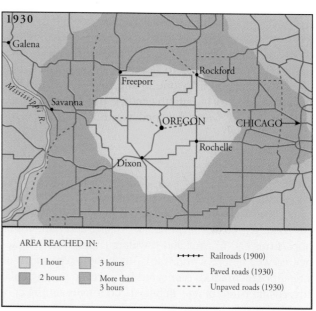

AREA REACHED IN:

1 hour	3 hours
2 hours	More than 3 hours

⊢⊢⊢⊢ Railroads (1900)
——— Paved roads (1930)
- - - - - Unpaved roads (1930)

BREAKING DOWN RURAL ISOLATION: THE EXPANSION OF TRAVEL HORIZONS IN OREGON, ILLINOIS This map uses the small town of Oregon, Illinois—west of Chicago—to illustrate the way in which first railroads and then automobiles reduced the isolation of rural areas in the first decades of the twentieth century. The gold and purple areas of the two maps show the territory that residents of Oregon could reach within two hours. Note how small that area was in 1900 and how much larger it was in 1930, by which time an area of over a hundred square miles had become easily accessible to the town. Note, too, the significant network of paved roads in the region by 1930, few of which had existed in 1900. ◆ *Why did automobile travel do so much more than railroads to expand the travel horizons of small towns?*

 For an interactive version of this map go to www.mhhe.com/brinkley11ch24maps

particular, found in the automobile a means of escaping the isolation of farm life; now they could visit friends or drive into town quickly and more or less at will, rather than spending hours traveling by horse or foot. City dwellers found in the automobile an escape from the congestion of urban life. Weekend drives

Social Impact of the Automobile

through the countryside became a staple of urban leisure. Many families escaped the city in a more permanent sense: by moving to the new suburbs that were rapidly growing up around large cities in response to the ease of access the automobile had created.

The automobile also transformed the idea of vacations. In the past, the idea of traveling for pleasure had been a luxury largely reserved for the wealthy. Now many middle-class and even working-class people could aspire to travel considerable distances for vacations, which were themselves a relatively new concept for most men and women in this era. Many businesses and industries began to include paid vacations among their employee benefits; and many employers encouraged their vacationing workers to travel, on the assumption that a change of scene would help restore their energy and vigor at work.

For young people in families affluent enough to afford a car, the automobile was often a means of a different kind of escape. It allowed them to move easily away from parents and family and to develop social lives of their own. It contributed to one of the distinctive developments of the early twentieth century: the emergence of a distinctive and well-developed youth culture in many communities.

Advertising

No group was more aware of the emergence of consumerism (or more responsible for creating it) than the advertising industry. The first advertising and public relations firms (N. W. Ayer and J. Walter Thompson) had appeared well before World War I; but in the 1920s, partly as a result of techniques pioneered by wartime propaganda, advertising came of age. Publicists no longer simply conveyed information; they sought to identify products with a particular lifestyle, to invest them with glamour and prestige, and to persuade potential consumers that purchasing a commodity could be a personally fulfilling and enriching experience.

Advertisers also encouraged the public to absorb the values of promotion and salesmanship and to admire

The Man Nobody Knows | those who were effective "boosters" and publicists. One of the most successful books of the 1920s was *The Man Nobody Knows,* by advertising executive Bruce Barton. It portrayed Jesus Christ as not only a religious prophet but also a "super salesman," who "picked up twelve men from the bottom ranks of business and forged them into an organization that conquered the world." The parables, Barton claimed, were "the most powerful advertisements of all time." Barton's message was fully in tune with the new spirit of the consumer culture. Jesus had been a man concerned with living a full and rewarding life in this world; twentieth-century men and women should do the same. ("Life is meant to live and enjoy as you go along," Barton once wrote.) Jesus had succeeded because he knew how

to make friends, to become popular, to please others; that talent was a prescription for success in the modern era as well.

The advertising industry could never have had the impact it did without the emergence of new vehicles of communication that made it possible to reach large audiences quickly and easily. Newspapers were being absorbed into national chains, and wire services were making it possible even for independent newspapers to carry nationally syndicated material.

New or expanded mass-circulation magazines also attracted broad, national audiences. *The Saturday Evening Post,* which began publication | *Mass-Circulation Magazines* as a magazine in 1871, appealed to rural and small-town families in particular with its homey stories and its conspicuous traditionalism; its popularity was, in some respects, evidence of a yearning for an earlier time. But other magazines responded directly to the realities of modern, urban life. *The Reader's Digest,* founded in 1921 by DeWitt and Lila Wallace, condensed stories and even books originally published in other places in an effort to make the expanding world of knowledge and information available in a brief, efficient form for people who would otherwise have no access to it. *Time* magazine, founded in 1923 by Henry Luce and Briton Hadden, set out to condense the news of the week into a brief, accessible, lively format for busy people who did not have time to read newspapers (which they considered stuffy and tedious) in detail. Luce thought of the magazine's name while riding a New York subway one night and imagining the "time" that reading such a magazine would save.

The Movies and Broadcasting

At the same time, movies were becoming an ever more popular and powerful form of mass communication. Over 100 million people saw films in 1930, as compared to 40 million in 1922. The addition of sound to motion pictures—beginning in 1927 with the first feature-length "talkie," *The Jazz Singer* with Al Jolson—created nationwide excitement. An embarrassing scandal in 1921 involving the popular comedian | *Hollywood* Fatty Arbuckle produced public outrage and political pressure to "clean up" Hollywood. In response, the film industry introduced "standards" to its films. Studio owners created the Motion Picture Association, a new trade association, and hired former postmaster general Will Hays to head it. More important, they gave Hays broad powers to review films and to ban anything likely to offend viewers (or politicians). Hays exercised his powers broadly and imposed on the film industry a safe, sanctimonious conformity for many years.

The most important communications vehicle was the only one truly new to the 1920s: radio. The first commercial radio station in America, KDKA in Pittsburgh, began

VALENTINO The popularity of the film star Rudolph Valentino among American women was one of the most striking cultural phenomena of the 1920s. Valentino was slight and delicate, not at all like the conventional image of "manliness." But he developed an enormous following among women, in part—as this poster is obviously intended to suggest—by baring his body on screen. Valentino was Italian, which made him seem somehow strange and foreign to many older-stock Americans, and he was almost always cast in exotic roles, never as an American. His sudden death in 1926 (at the age of 31) created enormous outpourings of grief among American women. *(George Kleiman/Bettmann/Corbis)*

"RADIO GAME" In the early 1920s, when radio was still new, many people considered it a "hobby," appropriate to people interested in technology. By the end of the decade, radio was a normal part of the everyday lives of almost everyone. But the boxed "Radio Game," whose cover is shown here and which remained popular well into the 1930s, reminded the public of radio's early days. *(Henry Ford Museum & Greenfield Village)*

broadcasting in 1920; and the first national radio network, the National Broadcasting Company, was formed in 1927. By 1923, there were more than 500 radio stations, covering virtually every area of the country; by 1929, more than 12 million families owned radio sets. The radio industry, too, feared government regulation and control; the national networks, and most radio stations, monitored program content carefully and excluded controversial or provocative material. But radio was much less centralized than filmmaking. Individual stations had considerable autonomy, and even carefully monitored stations and networks could not control the countless hours of programming as effectively as the Hays office could control films.

Radio programming, therefore, was more diverse—and at times more controversial and even subversive—than film.

Modernist Religion

The influence of the consumer culture, and its increasing emphasis on immediate, personal fulfillment, was visible even in religion. Theological modernists taught their followers to abandon some of the traditional tenets of evangelical Christianity (literal interpretation of the Bible, belief in the Trinity, attribution of human traits to the deity) and to accept a faith that would help individuals to live more fulfilling lives in the present world.

The most influential spokesman for liberal Protestantism in the 1920s was Harry Emerson Fosdick, the pastor of Riverside Church in New York. The basis of Christian religion, *Harry Emerson Fosdick* he claimed, was not unexamined faith, but a fully developed personality: "not an outward temple, but the inward shrine of man's personality, with all its possibilities and powers, is . . . infinitely sacred." In his 1926 book *Abundant Religion*, he argued that Christianity would "furnish an inward spiritual dynamic for radiant and triumphant living."

Most Americans, even most middle-class Americans, stopped well short of this view of religion as a vehicle for advancing "man's abundant life" and remained faithful to more traditional religious messages. But many other middle-class Americans were gradually devaluing religion altogether, assigning it a secondary role or (at times) no role at all in their lives. When the sociologists Robert and Helen Merrell Lynd studied the society of Muncie, Indiana, in the mid-1920s, they were struck by how many people there claimed that they paid less attention to religion than their parents had. They no longer devoted much time to teaching their children the tenets of their faith; they seldom prayed at home or attended church on any day but Sunday. Even the Sabbath was becoming not a day of rest and reflection, but a holiday filled with activities and entertainments.

Professional Women

In the 1920s college-educated women were no longer pioneers. There were now two and even three generations of graduates of women's or coeducational colleges and universities; and some were making their presence felt in professional areas that in the past they had rarely penetrated. Some middle-class women now combined marriage and careers, but most still had to choose between work and family. The majority of the 25 percent of married women who worked outside the home in the 1920s were working class.

Professional opportunities for women remained limited by society's assumptions (assumptions prevalent among many women as well as among most men) about what were suitable female occupations. Although there were notable success stories about female business executives, journalists, doctors, and lawyers, most professional women remained confined to such traditionally "feminine" fields as fashion, education, social work, and nursing, or to the lower levels of business management. The "new professional woman" was a vivid and widely publicized image in the 1920s. In reality, however, most middle-class married women remained in the home.

Limited Opportunities for Women

Changing Ideas of Motherhood

Yet the 1920s constituted a new era for middle-class women nonetheless. In particular, the decade saw a redefinition of the idea of motherhood. Shortly after World War I, an influential group of psychologists—the "behaviorists," led by John B. Watson—began to challenge the long-held assumption that women had an instinctive capacity for motherhood. Maternal affection was not, they claimed, sufficient preparation for child rearing. Instead, mothers should rely on the advice and assistance of experts and professionals: doctors, nurses, and trained educators in nursery schools and kindergartens.

For many middle-class women, these changes helped redefine what had been an all-consuming activity. Motherhood was no less important in behaviorist theory than it had been before; if anything it was more so. But for many women it was less emotionally fulfilling, less connected to their instinctive lives, more dependent on (and tied to) people and institutions outside the family. Many attempted to compensate by devoting new attention to their roles as wives and companions, to developing what became known as the "companionate marriage." The middle-class wife shared increasingly in her husband's social life; she devoted more attention to cosmetics and clothing; she was less willing to allow children to interfere with the development of the marital relationship. Most of all, many women now found support for thinking of their sexual relationships with their husbands not simply as a means of procreation, as earlier generations had been taught to do, but as an important and pleasurable experience in its own right, as the culmination of romantic love.

"Companionate Marriages"

Progress in the development of birth control was both a cause and a result of this change. The pioneer of the American birth-control movement was Margaret Sanger, who had become committed to the cause in part because of the influence of Emma Goldman—a Russian immigrant and political radical who had agitated for birth control before World War I. Sanger began her career promoting the diaphragm and other birth-control devices out of a concern for working-class women, believing that large families were among the major causes of poverty and distress in poor communities. By the 1920s, partly because she had limited success in persuading working-class women to accept her teachings, she was becoming more concerned with persuading middle-class women of the benefits of birth control. Women, she argued, should be free to enjoy the pleasures of sexual activity without any connection to procreation. Birth-control devices began to find a large market among middle-class women, even though some techniques remained illegal in many states (and abortion remained illegal nearly everywhere).

Birth Control

The "Flapper": Image and Reality

The new, more secular view of womanhood had effects on women beyond the middle class as well. Some women concluded that in the "New Era" it was no longer necessary to maintain a rigid, Victorian female "respectability." They could smoke, drink, dance, wear seductive clothes and makeup, and attend lively parties. They could strive for physical and emotional fulfillment, for release from repression and inhibition. (The wide popularity of Freudian ideas in the 1920s—often simplified and distorted for mass consumption—contributed to the growth of these impulses.)

Such assumptions became the basis of the "flapper"—the modern woman whose liberated lifestyle found expression in dress, hairstyle, speech, and behavior. The "flapper" lifestyle had a particular impact on lower-middle-class and working-class single women, who were flocking to new jobs in industry and the service sector. (The young, affluent, upper-class "Bohemian" women most often

THE FLAPPER By the mid-1920s, the "flapper"—the young woman who challenged traditional expectations—had become not only a social type but a movement in fashion. This drawing was one of many efforts by fashion designers to create clothes that reflected the liberated spirit that the flappers had introduced into popular culture. *(Culver Pictures, Inc.)*

associated with the "flapper" image were, in fact, imitating a style that emerged first among this larger working-class group.) At night, such women flocked, often alone, to clubs and dance halls in search of excitement and companionship.

Despite the image of liberation the "flapper" evoked in popular culture, most women remained highly dependent on men—both in the workplace, where they were usually poorly paid, and in the home—and relatively powerless when men exploited that dependence.

Pressing for Women's Rights

The realization that the "new woman" was as much myth as reality inspired some American feminists to continue their crusade for reform. The National Woman's Party, under the leadership of Alice Paul, pressed on with its campaign for the Equal Rights Amendment, although it found little support in Congress (and met continued resistance from other feminist groups). Nevertheless, women's organizations and female political activities grew in *League of Women Voters* many ways in the 1920s. Responding to the suffrage victory, women organized the League of Women Voters and the women's auxiliaries of both the Democratic and Republican Parties. Female-dominated consumer groups grew rapidly and increased the range and energy of their efforts.

Women activists won a significant triumph in 1921, when they helped secure passage in Congress of a measure in keeping with the traditional feminist goal of securing *Sheppard-Towner Act* "protective" legislation for women: the Sheppard-Towner Act. It provided federal funds to states to establish prenatal and child healthcare programs. From the start, however, the bill produced controversy. Alice Paul and her supporters opposed the measure, complaining that it classified all women as mothers. Margaret Sanger complained that the new programs would discourage birth-control efforts. More important, the American Medical Association fought Sheppard-Towner, warning that it would introduce untrained outsiders into the health-care field. In 1929, Congress terminated the program. The demise of Sheppard-Towner illustrated the power of the medical profession. It also revealed how little woman suffrage had done to sustain the hopes of many of its supporters (and the fears of many of its foes). When Congress passed Sheppard-Towner in 1921, its members did so in part because they assumed the new female electorate would become a potent political force, generating substantial pressure on behalf of "female" issues. By 1929, it was clear that women voters changed electoral outcomes hardly at all; the female vote distributed itself almost precisely the same as the male vote. As a result, male politicians, in Congress and elsewhere, felt less concern about the consequences of opposing the demands of female reformers.

Education and Youth

The growing secularism of American culture and its expanding emphasis on training and expertise found reflection in the increasingly important role of education in the lives of American youth. The changes were evident in numerous ways. First, more people were going to school in the 1920s than ever before. High-school attendance more than doubled during the decade: from 2.2 million to over 5 million. Enrollment in colleges and universities increased threefold between 1900 and 1930, with much of that increase occurring after World War I. In 1918, there had been 600,000 college students; in 1930, there were 1.2 million, nearly 20 percent of the college-age population. Attendance was increasing as well at trade and vocational schools and in other institutions

In the booming, boisterous, consumerist world struggling to be born in the 1920s, many Americans—especially those living in urban areas—challenged the rules and inhibitions of traditional public culture. They looked instead for freedom, excitement, and release. Nowhere did they do so more vigorously and visibly than in the great dance halls that were proliferating in cities across the nation in these years.

The dance craze that swept urban America in the 1920s and 1930s was a result of many things. The great African-American migration during World War I had helped bring new forms of jazz out of the South and into the urban North—where the phonograph and the radio popularized it. The growth of a distinctive youth culture—and the increasing tendency of men and women to socialize together in public—created an audience for uninhibited, sexually titillating entertainment. The relative prosperity of the 1920s enabled many young working-class people to afford to spend evenings

THE SAVOY The Savoy ballroom in New York's Harlem was one of the largest and most popular dance halls in America, and a regular home to many of the most noted dance bands in the 1920s and 1930s. *(Hulton/Archive/Getty Images)*

out. And prohibition, by closing down most saloons and taverns, limited their other options.

And so, night after night, in big cities and small, young people flocked to dance halls to hear the powerful, pulsing new music; to revel in dazzling lights and ornate surroundings; to show off new clothes and hairstyles; and, of course, most of all, to dance. Some of the larger dance halls in the big cities—Roseland and the Savoy in New York, the Trianon and the Aragon in Chicago, the Raymor in Boston, the Greystone in Detroit, the Hollywood Paladium, and many others—were truly cavernous, capable of accommodating thousands of couples at once. Some were outdoors and, in warm weather, attracted even larger crowds. Many gave off some of the same sense of grandiosity and glamor that the new movie palaces, which were being built at the same time, provided. (Indeed, it was not unusual for couples to combine an evening at the movies with a visit to a dance hall.) Many of the great ballrooms became the sites of regular radio programs—and thus enabled even isolated, rural people to experience something of the excitement of an evening of dance. In 1924, in New York City alone, 6 million people attended dance halls. Over 10 percent of the men and women between the ages of 17 and 40 in New York went dancing at least once a week, and the numbers were almost certainly comparable in other large cities.

What drew so many people to the dance halls? In large part, it was the music, which both its defenders and critics alike recognized as something very new in mainstream American culture. Dancing was "moral ruin," the *Ladies Home Journal* primly warned in 1921, prompting "carelessness, recklessness, and laxity of moral responsibility" with its "direct appeal to

JITTERBUGGERS As dance halls became more popular, dancing became more exuberant—perhaps never more so than when the "jitterbug" became popular in the 1930s. This photograph shows an acrobatic pair of dancers during a huge dance event in Los Angeles designed to raise money for the Salvation Army. More than 10,000 people attended the event and the police on hand to keep order had to call for reinforcements as the crowd became more and more frenzied and enthusiastic. *(Bettmann/Corbis)*

the body's sensory centers." Many young dancers might have agreed with the description, if not with the moral judgment. Jazz encouraged a kind of uninhibited, even frenetic dancing—expressive, athletic, sensual—that young couples, in particular, found extraordinarily exciting, a welcome release from the often staid worlds of family, school, or work. The larger dance halls also attracted crowds by showcasing the most famous bands of the day. Performances by Paul Whiteman, Ben Pollack, Fletcher Henderson, Bix Beiderbecke, Louis Armstrong, or Duke Ellington—musicians already

providing the specialized training that the modern economy demanded. Schools were also beginning to perform new and more varied functions. Instead of offering instruction only in the traditional disciplines, they were providing training in modern technical skills: engineering, management, economics.

The growing importance of education contributed to the emergence of a separate youth culture. The idea of adolescence as a distinct period in the life of an individual was for *Youth Culture* the most part new to the twentieth century. In some measure it was a result of the influence of Freudian psychology.

DANCING AT THE SAVOY   This photograph of the interior of the famous Savoy ballroom shows the hundreds of men and women who typically flocked there to dance to the great black jazz bands of the 1920s and 1930s.   *(Hulton/Archive/Getty Images)*

familiar to everyone through radio performances and recordings—drew enormous crowds.

Some of the less savory halls also attracted dancers for more illicit reasons—as sources of bootleg liquor or as places to buy drugs. The popular "taxi-dance" ballrooms—which allowed men without their own partners to buy tickets to dance with "hostesses" and "instructresses"—were sometimes closed by municipal authorities for "lewd" dancing and prostitution. At least sixty city governments passed regulations in the 1920s restricting the styles of public dancing; and the managers of the larger ballrooms tried to distance themselves from the unsavory image of the taxidance halls by imposing dress codes and making at least some efforts,

usually futile, to require "decorum" among their patrons.

Dance halls were particularly popular with young men and women from working-class, immigrant communities. For them, going dancing was part of becoming American, a way to escape— even if momentarily—the insular world of the immigrant neighborhood. (Their parents saw it that way too, and often tried to stop their children from going because they feared the dance halls would pull them out of the family and the community.) Going dancing was a chance to mingle with hundreds, sometimes thousands of strangers of diverse backgrounds, and to participate in a cultural ritual that had no counterpart in ethnic cultures.

But dance halls were not melting pots. African Americans—who flocked

to ballrooms at least as eagerly as whites—usually gathered at clubs in black neighborhoods, where there were only occasional white patrons. White working-class people might encounter a large number of different ethnic groups in a great hall at once, but the groups did not usually mix very much. In Chicago's Dreamland, for example, Italians congregated near the door, Poles near the band, and Jews in the middle of the floor. Still, the experience of the dance hall— like the experience of the movie palace or the amusement park— drew people into the growing mass culture that was competing with and beginning to overwhelm the close-knit ethnic cultures into which many young Americans had been born.

But it was a result, too, of society's recognition that a more extended period of training and preparation was necessary before a young person was ready to move into the workplace. Schools and colleges provided adolescents with a setting in which they could develop their own social patterns, their own hobbies, their own interests and

activities. An increasing number of students saw school as a place not just for academic training but for organized athletics, other extracurricular activities, clubs, and fraternities and sororities—that is, as an institution that allowed them to define themselves less in terms of their families and more in terms of their peer group.

VASSAR STUDENTS, 1920 Although a few prominent women's colleges, Vassar among them, had been educating women since the late nineteenth century, the number of colleges and universities willing to accept women, and hence the number of women enrolled in higher education, soared in the 1920s. *(Bettmann/Corbis)*

The Decline of the "Self-Made Man"

The increasing importance of education and the changing nature of adolescence underscored one of the most important changes in American society: the gradual disappearance of the reality, and to some degree even of the ideal, of the "self-made man." The belief that any person could, simply through hard work and innate talent, achieve wealth and renown had always been largely a myth; but it had had enough basis in reality to remain a convincing myth for generations. The ideal of sturdy independence had long been central to the identities of many men, in particular.

Beginning in the late nineteenth century and accelerating in the early twentieth century, it became more difficult to believe any longer that success was possible without education and training. "The self-made manager in business," wrote *Century* magazine in 1925, "is nearing the end of his road. He cannot escape the relentless pursuit of the same forces that have eliminated self-made lawyers and doctors and admirals."

That sense of losing control, of becoming ever more dependent on rules and norms established by large, impersonal bureaucracies, created a crisis of self-identification among many American men. Robbed of the independence and control that had once defined "masculinity," many men looked for other means to do so. Theodore Roosevelt, for example, had glorified warfare and the "strenuous life" as a route to "manhood." Other men turned to fraternal societies, to athletics, and to other settings where they found confirmation of their masculinity.

The "Doom of the Self-Made Man," as *Century* described it, produced marked ambivalence. These mixed feelings were reflected in the identity of three men who became the most widely admired heroes of the New Era: Thomas Edison, the inventor of the electric lightbulb and many other technological marvels; Henry Ford, the creator of the assembly line and one of the founders of the automobile industry; and Charles Lindbergh, the first aviator to make a solo flight across the Atlantic Ocean. All received the adulation of much of the American public. Lindbergh, in particular, became a national hero the like of which the country had never seen before.

Charles Lindbergh

The reasons for their popularity indicated much about how Americans viewed the new epoch in which they were living. On the one hand, all three men represented the triumphs of the modern technological and industrial society. On the other hand, all three had risen to success without the benefit of formal education and at least in part through their own efforts. They were, their admirers liked to believe, genuinely self-made men. Even many Americans who were happily embracing a new society and a new culture were doing so without entirely diverting their gaze from a simpler past.

The Disenchanted

The generation of artists and intellectuals coming of age in the 1920s found the new society in which they lived especially disturbing. Many were experiencing a disenchantment with modern America so fundamental that they were often able to view it only with contempt. As a result, they adopted a role sharply different from that of most intellectuals of most earlier eras. Rather than trying to influence and reform their society, they isolated themselves from it and embarked on a restless search for personal fulfillment. Gertrude Stein once referred to the young Americans emerging from World War I as a "Lost Generation." For some writers and intellectuals, at least, it was an apt description.

At the heart of the Lost Generation's critique of modern society was a sense of personal alienation, a belief that contemporary America no longer provided individu-

Lost Generation's Critique

als with avenues by which they could achieve personal fulfillment. This disillusionment had its roots in many things, but in nothing so deeply as the experience of World War I. To those who had fought in the conflict, and even to many who had not, the aftermath of the war was shattering. The repudiation of Wilsonian idealism, the restoration of "business as usual," the growing emphasis on materialism and consumerism suggested that nothing had been gained. The war had been a fraud; the suffering and the dying had been in vain. Ernest Hemingway, one of the most celebrated (and most commercially successful) of the new breed of writers, expressed the generation's contempt for the war in his novel *A Farewell to Arms* (1929). Its protagonist, an American officer fighting in Europe, decides that there is no justification for his participation in the conflict and deserts the army with a nurse with whom he has fallen in love. Hemingway made it clear that the officer was to be admired for doing so.

But however disillusioning intellectuals found the war, they were equally disturbed by the character of American society in peacetime. To many, it was a society and culture utterly devoid of idealism or vision, steeped in outmoded and priggish morality, obsessed with materialism and consumerism, alienating and dehumanizing.

One result of this alienation was a series of savage critiques of modern society by a wide range of writers, some

H. L. Mencken

of whom were known as the "debunkers." Among them was the Baltimore journalist H. L. Mencken. His magazines—first the *Smart Set* and later the *American Mercury*—ridiculed everything most middle-class Americans held dear: religion, politics, the arts, even democracy itself. Mencken could not believe, he claimed, that "civilized life was possible under a democracy," because it was a form of government that placed power in the hands of the common people, whom he ridiculed as the "booboisie." When someone asked Mencken why he continued to live in a society he found so loathsome, he replied: "Why do people go to the zoo?" Echoing Mencken's contempt was the novelist Sinclair Lewis, the first American to win a Nobel Prize in literature. In a series of savage novels—*Main Street* (1920), *Babbitt* (1922), *Arrowsmith* (1925), and others—he lashed out at one aspect of modern society

after another: the small town, the modern city, the medical profession, popular religion.

Intellectuals of the 1920s claimed to reject the "success ethic" that they believed dominated American life (even though many of them hoped for—and a few achieved—

Rejecting Success

commercial and critical success). The novelist F. Scott Fitzgerald, for example, ridiculed the American obsession with material success in *The Great Gatsby* (1925). The novel's title character, Jay Gatsby, spends his life accumulating wealth and social prestige in order to win the woman he loves. The world to which he has aspired, however, turns out to be one of pretension, fraud, and cruelty, and it ultimately destroys him.

Some artists and intellectuals responded to their disillusionment by leaving America to live in France, making Paris for a time a center of American artistic life. Others moved to supposedly more isolated and "natural" communities in the American West; colonies of artists and writers settled in Taos and Santa Fe, New Mexico. Some adopted hedonistic lifestyles, involving drinking, drugs, casual sex, and wild parties. For most of these young men and women, however, the only real refuge from the travails of modern society was art. Only art, they argued, could allow them full individual expression; only the act of creation could offer them fulfillment. The result of this quest for fulfillment through art was not, for the most part, personal satisfaction for the writers and artists involved. They did, however, produce a body of work that made the decade one of the great eras of American literature. The roster of important American writers who produced significant work in the 1920s may have no equal in any other period: Hemingway, Fitzgerald, Lewis, Thomas Wolfe, John Dos Passos, Ezra Pound, T. S. Eliot, Gertrude Stein, Edna Ferber, Willa Cather, William Faulkner, Eugene O'Neill.

Not all intellectuals of the 1920s expressed alienation and despair. Some expressed reservations about their society not by withdrawing from it but by advocating reform. John Dewey, for example, kept alive the philosophical tradition of pragmatism and appealed for "practical" educa-

Charles and Mary Beard

tion and experimentation in social policy. Charles and Mary Beard, perhaps the most influential historians of their day, stressed economic factors in tracing the development of modern society and, like other progressive reformers, emphasized the clash of economic interests as central to American history.

The Harlem Renaissance

To other groups of intellectuals, the solution to contemporary problems lay in an exploration of their own cultural or regional origins. Nowhere was that clearer than in New York City's Harlem, once an affluent white suburb in northern Manhattan that had, by the end of World War I,

AARON
DOUGLAS

Weary As I Can Be

"WEARY AS I CAN BE" Aaron Douglas was one of the most accomplished artists of the era of the Harlem Renaissance. This illustration accompanied publication of a poem by Langston Hughes, "Lonesome Place," published in *Opportunity* magazine in 1926. *(Aaron Douglas,* As Weary As I Can Be, *1926, offset lithograph, 16 × 11 1/2 inches. The Schomburg Center for Research in Black Culture, Art and Artifacts Division, The New York Public Library, Astor, Lenox and Tilden Foundations)*

become one of the nation's largest and most influential African-American communities.

In postwar Harlem, a new generation of black artists and intellectuals created a flourishing African-American culture widely described as the "Harlem Renaissance." There was a thriving popular culture in the community. There were nightclubs (among them the famous Cotton Club) featuring many of the great jazz musicians who would later become staples of national popular culture: Duke Ellington, Jelly Roll Morton, Fletcher Henderson, and others. There were theaters featuring ribald musical comedies and vaudeville acts. Many white New Yorkers traveled up to Harlem for the music and theater, but the audiences were largely black.

Harlem in the 1920s was above all a center of literature, poetry, and art that drew heavily from African roots. Black artists were trying in part to demonstrate the richness of their own racial heritage (and not incidentally, to prove to whites that their race was worthy of respect).

The poet Langston Hughes captured much of the spirit of the movement in a single sentence: "I am a Negro—and beautiful." One of the leaders of the Harlem Renaissance was *African-American Pride* Alain Locke, who assembled a notable collection of black writings published in 1925 as *The New Negro*. Gradually, white publishers began to notice and take an interest in the writers Locke helped launch. Hughes, Zora Neale Hurston, Countee Cullen, Claude McKay, James Weldon Johnson, and others gradually found readerships well beyond the black community. The painter Aaron Douglas, talented chronicler of the African-American experience, eventually found himself commissioned to create important murals in universities and public buildings. The Harlem Renaissance, in other words, not only helped advance African-American art and culture, but brought its products to the attention of the larger society in ways that had tremendous impact on both whites and blacks.

Some writers of the Harlem Renaissance—perhaps most prominently Claude McKay—were notable for the way they fused their writing with radical politics. But on the whole, the creative ferment in Harlem was not directly political. Alain Locke, for example, saw the turn to art and literature as a welcome escape from the "arid fields" of politics and saw culture as a more promising vehicle for increasing the self-respect and raising the status of African Americans. The Harlem Renaissance may have had few immediate effects on the lives of ordinary black men and women, few of whom were aware of its work. But it had a deep and lasting effect on the development of some of America's most important cultural and artistic traditions.

The Southern Agrarians

Another effort to retrieve a cultural past was under way among an influential group of white southern intellectuals. These young poets, novelists, and critics sought to counter the depersonalization of industrial society by evoking the strong rural traditions of their own region. The effort grew out of a small circle of poets centered at Vanderbilt University in the early 1920s, who had then called *The Fugitives* themselves the Fugitives. They included, among many others, Robert Penn Warren, John Crowe Ransom, and Allen Tate. The Fugitives were not at first particularly interested in their identity as southerners. But by the late 1920s, they had become so disillusioned by what they considered the crass, dehumanizing materialism of modern industrial society that they began looking to the South—what most people considered the backward, underdeveloped, benighted South—as an alternative. The South, they said, had managed to maintain a nonindustrial, agrarian way of life (which led them to choose a new name for themselves: the "Agrarians"). Southern life was not based on the harsh, crass values of material gain, but on the more rewarding and enduring human values. It was a society in tune not with the unnatural discipline of the machine, but with the natural rhythms of life.

In 1930, they published a collection of essays, an agrarian manifesto, called (from a phrase in the song "Dixie") *I'll Take My Stand*. It was often denounced as reactionary, which in many respects it was (particularly in its justifications for segregation and white supremacy). But it was above all a critique of industrialization and the society it was creating. They wrote in their preface, their "statement of principles," that "the theory of agrarianism is that the culture of the soil is the best and most sensitive of vocations." They added, "If a community, or a section, or a race, or an age, is groaning under industrialism and well aware that it is an evil dispensation, it must find the way to throw it off." Donald Davidson, one of the leaders of the group, wrote:

> Suddenly we realized to the full what we had long been dimly feeling, that the Lost Cause might not be wholly lost after all. In its very backwardness, the South had clung to some secret which embodied, it seemed, the elements out of which its own reconstruction—and possibly even the reconstruction of America—might be achieved.

The supposedly "backward" South, in other words, could serve as a model for a nation drunk with visions of limitless growth and modernization.

A CONFLICT OF CULTURES

The modern, secular culture of the 1920s was not unchallenged. It grew up alongside older, more traditional cultures, with which it continually and often bitterly competed. The older cultures expressed the outlook of generally less affluent, less urban, more provincial Americans—men and women who continued to revere traditional values and customs and who feared and resented the modernist threats to their way of life. Their convictions and their fears resulted in a series of harsh cultural controversies.

Prohibition

When the prohibition of the sale and manufacture of alcohol went into effect in January 1920, it had the support of most members of the middle class and most of those who considered themselves progressives. Within a year, however, it had become clear that the "noble experiment," as its defenders called it, was not working well.

Failure of Prohibition | Prohibition did substantially reduce drinking, at least in some regions of the country. But it also produced conspicuous and growing violations that made the law an almost immediate source of disillusionment and controversy. The federal government hired only 1,500 agents to enforce the prohibition laws, and in many places they received little help from local police. Before long, it was almost as easy to acquire illegal alcohol in much of the country as it had once been to acquire legal alcohol. And since an enormous, lucrative industry was now barred to legitimate businessmen, organized crime figures took it over. In Chicago, Al Capone built a criminal empire based largely on illegal alcohol. He guarded it against interlopers with an army of as many as 1,000 gunmen, whose zealousness contributed to the violent deaths of more than 250 people in the city between 1920 and 1927. Other regions produced gangsters and gang wars of their own.

Alcohol and Organized Crime

Many middle-class progressives who had originally supported prohibition soon soured on the experiment. But an enormous constituency of provincial, largely rural, Protestant Americans continued vehemently to defend it. To them, prohibition had always carried implications far beyond the issue of drinking itself. It represented the effort of an older America to maintain its dominance in a society in which they were becoming relatively less powerful. Drinking, which they associated with the modern city and with Catholic immigrants, became a symbol of the new culture they believed was displacing them.

As the decade proceeded, opponents of prohibition (or "wets," as they came to be known) gained steadily in influence. Not until 1933, however, when the Great Depression added weight to their appeals, were they finally able effectively to challenge the "drys" and win repeal of the Eighteenth Amendment.

Nativism and the Klan

Like prohibition (which was itself in part a result of old-stock Americans trying to discipline the new immigrant population), agitation for a curb on foreign immigration to the United States had begun in the nineteenth century; and like prohibition, it had gathered strength in the years before the war largely because of the support of middle-class progressives. Such concerns had not been sufficient in the first years of the century to win passage of curbs on immigration; but in the troubled and repressive years immediately following the war, many old-stock Americans began to associate immigration with radicalism.

Sentiment on behalf of restriction grew rapidly as a result. In 1921, Congress passed an emergency immigration act, establishing a quota system by which annual immigration from any country could not exceed 3 percent of the number of persons of that nationality who had been in the United States in 1910. The new law cut immigration from 800,000 to 300,000 in any single year, but the nativists remained unsatisfied and pushed for a harsher law. The National Origins Act of 1924 banned immigration from east Asia entirely. That provision deeply angered Japan, which understood that the

National Origins Act of 1924

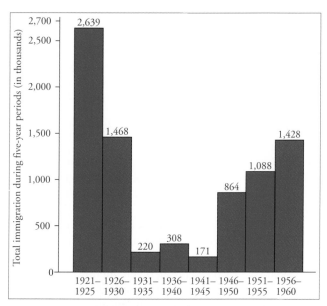

TOTAL IMMIGRATION, 1920–1960 After many years of enormous immigration from Europe and elsewhere, the United States experienced several decades of much lower immigration beginning in the 1920s. Immigration restriction legislation passed in 1921 and 1924 was one important reason for the decline. ◆ *What other factors depressed immigration in the 1930s and 1940s?*

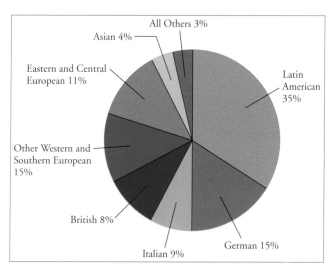

SOURCES OF IMMIGRATION, 1920–1960 This chart shows a dramatic change in the sources of immigration between 1920 and 1960, a direct result of the National Origins Act of 1924, which established national quotas for immigrants to the United States based on the number of such immigrants who had been in the country in 1890. Note the shift back toward northern and western Europe and away from Italy and other southern and eastern European nations (which had not been heavily represented in the immigration of the 1890s). But the most dramatic change was the enormous increase in the proportion of immigrants from Latin America, a region explicitly exempted from the quota system established in 1924. ◆ *Why were Latin Americans treated differently from Europeans in immigration law in these years?*

Japanese were the principal target; Chinese immigration had been illegal since 1892. The law also reduced the quota for Europeans from 3 percent to 2 percent. The quota would be based, moreover, not on the 1910 census, but on the census of 1890, a year in which there had been many fewer southern and eastern Europeans in the country. What immigration there was, in other words, would heavily favor northwestern Europeans—people of "Nordic" or "Teutonic" stock. Five years later, a further restriction set a rigid limit of 150,000 immigrants a year. In the years that followed, immigration officials seldom permitted even half that number actually to enter the country.

But the nativism of the 1920s extended well beyond restricting immigration. To defenders of an older, more homogeneous America, the growth of large communities of foreign peoples, alien in their speech, their habits, and their values, came to seem a direct threat to their own embattled way of life. Among other things, this provincial nativism helped instigate the rebirth of the Ku Klux Klan as a major force in American society.

The first Klan, founded during Reconstruction, had died in the 1870s. But in 1915, another group of white

The New Klan southerners met on Stone Mountain near Atlanta and established a modern version of the society. Nativist passions had swelled in Georgia and elsewhere in response to the case of Leo Frank, a Jewish factory manager in Atlanta convicted in 1914 (on very flimsy evidence) of murdering a female employee; a mob stormed Frank's jail and lynched him. The premiere (also in Atlanta) of

D. W. Griffith's film *The Birth of a Nation,* which glorified the early Klan, also helped inspire white southerners to join a new one. At first the new Klan, like the old, was largely concerned with intimidating blacks, who according to Klan leader William J. Simmons were becoming insubordinate. And at first it remained small, obscure, and almost entirely southern. After World War I, however, concern about blacks became secondary to concern about Catholics, Jews, and foreigners. The Klan, its organizers proclaimed, would devote itself to purging American life of impure, alien influences. At that point, membership in the Klan expanded rapidly and dramatically, not just in the small towns and rural areas of the South, but in industrial cities in the North and Midwest. Indiana had the largest membership of any state, and there were substantial Klans in Chicago, Detroit, and other northern industrial cities as well. The Klan was also strong in the West, with particularly large and active chapters in Oregon and Colorado. By 1923, there were reportedly 3 million members; by 1924, 4 million.

In some communities, where Klan leaders came from the most "respectable" segments of society, the organization operated much like a fraternal society, engaging in nothing more dangerous than occasional political pronouncements. Many Klan units (or "klaverns") tried to present themselves as patriots and defenders of morality. Many established women's and even children's auxiliaries

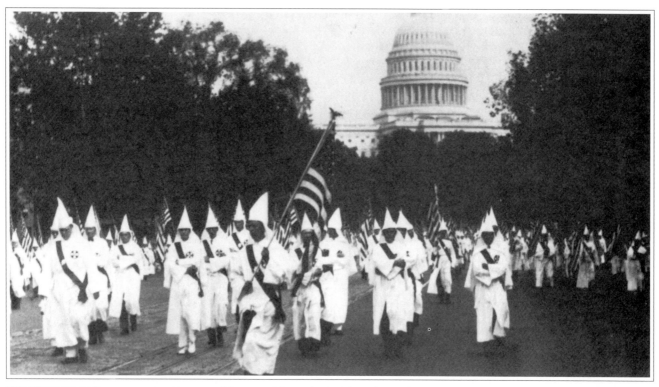

THE KU KLUX KLAN IN WASHINGTON, 1926 So powerful was the Ku Klux Klan in the mid-1920s that its members felt emboldened to march openly and defiantly down the streets of major cities—even down Pennsylvania Avenue in Washington, in the shadow of the Capitol of the United States. *(Culver Pictures, Inc.)*

to demonstrate their commitment to the family. Often, however, the Klan also operated as a brutal, even violent, opponent of "alien" groups and as a defender of traditional, fundamentalist morality. Some Klansmen systematically terrorized blacks, Jews, Catholics, and foreigners: boycotting their businesses, threatening their families, and attempting to drive them out of their communities. Occasionally, they resorted to violence: public whipping, tarring and feathering, arson, and lynching.

What the Klan feared, it soon became clear, was not simply "foreign" or "racially impure" groups; it was anyone who posed a challenge to "traditional values," as the Klan

Defending "Traditional Values"

defined them. Klansmen persecuted not only immigrants and blacks but those white Protestants they considered guilty of irreligion, sexual promiscuity, or drunkenness. The Klan worked to enforce prohibition; it attempted to institute compulsory Bible reading in schools; it worked to punish divorce. The Ku Klux Klan, in short, was fighting not just to preserve racial homogeneity but to defend its definition of a traditional culture against the values and morals of modernity.

It also provided its members, many of them people of modest means with little real power in society, with a sense of community and seeming authority. Its bizarre costumes, its elaborate rituals, its "secret" language, its burning crosses—all helped produce a sense of excitement

and cohesion. For the many women who joined Klan auxiliaries, the organization served important social functions. The Klan was as committed to defending traditional gender roles as it was to defending white supremacy and Protestant morality, but women found in the Klan opportunities for activism and involvement within the confines of conventional female "spheres."

The organization itself declined quickly after 1925, when a series of internal power struggles and several sordid scandals discredited some of its most important leaders. The most damaging episode involved David Stephenson, *David Stephenson* head of the Indiana Klan, who raped a young secretary, kidnapped her, and watched her die rather than call a doctor after she swallowed poison. The Klan staggered on in some areas into the 1930s, but by World War II it was effectively dead. (The postwar Ku Klux Klan, which still survives, is modeled on but has no direct connection to the Klan of the 1920s and 1930s.)

Religious Fundamentalism

Another cultural controversy of the 1920s was the result of a bitter conflict over the place of religion in contemporary society, a conflict that had its roots in nineteenth-century controversies. By 1921, American Protestantism was already divided into two warring camps. On one side

BRYAN AND DARROW IN DAYTON Clarence Darrow (left) and William Jennings Bryan pose for photographers during the 1925 Scopes trial. Both men had removed their jackets because of the intense heat, and Bryan had shocked many of his admirers by revealing that he was not wearing suspenders (as most country people did), but a belt—which in rural Tennessee was a symbol of urban culture. *(Brown Brothers)*

stood the modernists: mostly urban, middle-class people who had attempted to adapt religion to the teachings of modern science and to the realities of their modern, secular society. On the other side stood the defenders of traditional faith: provincial, largely (although not exclusively) rural men and women, fighting to maintain the centrality of religion in American life. They became known as "fundamentalists," a term derived from an influential set of pamphlets, *The Fundamentals,* published just before World War I. The fundamentalists were outraged at the abandonment of traditional beliefs in the face of scientific discoveries. They insisted the Bible was to be interpreted literally. Above all, they opposed the teachings of Charles Darwin, who had openly challenged the biblical story of the Creation. Human beings had not evolved from lower orders of animals, the fundamentalists insisted; they had been created by God, as described in Genesis.

Fundamentalism was a highly evangelical movement, interested in spreading the doctrine to new groups. Fundamentalist evangelists, among them the celebrated Billy Sunday, a former professional baseball player, traveled from state to state (particularly in the South and parts of the West) attracting huge crowds to their revival meetings. (See "Patterns of Popular Culture," pp. 634–635.) Protestant modernists looked on much of this activity with condescension and amusement. But by the mid-1920s, to their great alarm, evangelical fundamentalism was gaining political strength in some states with its demands for legislation to forbid the teaching of evolution in the public schools. In Tennessee in March 1925, the legislature actually adopted a measure making it illegal for any public school teacher "to teach any theory that denies the story of the divine creation of man as taught in the Bible."

The Tennessee law attracted the attention of the fledgling American Civil Liberties Union, which had been founded in 1920 by Jane Addams, Norman Thomas, Helen Keller, and others alarmed by the repressive legal and social climate of the war and its aftermath; they had felt the need for an organization to defend (among other things) freedom of speech and belief. The ACLU offered free counsel to any Tennessee educator willing to defy the law and become the defendant in a test case. A twenty-four-year-old biology teacher in the town of Dayton, John T. Scopes, *Scopes Monkey Trial* agreed to have himself arrested. And when the ACLU decided to send the famous attorney Clarence Darrow to defend Scopes, the aging William Jennings Bryan (now an important fundamentalist spokesman) announced that he would travel to Dayton to assist the prosecution. Journalists from across the country, among them H. L. Mencken, flocked to Tennessee to cover the trial, which opened in an almost circuslike atmosphere. Scopes had, of course, clearly violated the law; and a verdict of guilty was a foregone conclusion, especially when the judge refused to permit "expert" testimony by evolution scholars. Scopes was fined $100, and the case was ultimately dismissed in a higher court because of a technicality. Nevertheless, Darrow scored an important victory for the modernists by calling Bryan himself to the stand to testify as an "expert on the Bible." In the course of the cross-examination, which was broadcast by radio to much of the nation, Darrow made Bryan's stubborn defense of biblical truths appear foolish and finally tricked him into admitting the possibility that not all religious dogma was subject to only one interpretation.

The Scopes trial was a traumatic experience for many fundamentalists. It isolated and ultimately excluded them from many mainstream Protestant denominations. It helped put an end to much of their political activism. But it did not, of course, change their religious convictions. Even without connection to traditional denominations, fundamentalists continued to congregate in independent churches or new denominations of their own.

The Democrats' Ordeal

The anguish of provincial Americans attempting to defend an embattled way of life proved particularly troubling to the Democratic Party, which suffered during the 1920s as a result of tensions between its urban and rural factions. More than the Republicans, the Democrats were a diverse coalition of interest groups, linked to the party more by local tradition than common commitment. Among those interest groups were prohibitionists, Klansmen, and fundamentalists on one side and Catholics, urban workers, and immigrants on the other.

In 1924, the tensions between them proved devastating. At the Democratic National Convention in New York that summer, bitter conflict broke out over the platform when the party's urban wing attempted to win approval of planks calling for the repeal of prohibition and a denunciation of the Klan. Both planks narrowly failed. More damaging to the party was a deadlock in the balloting for a presidential candidate. Urban Democrats supported Alfred E. Smith, the Irish Catholic Tammanyite who had risen to become a progressive governor of New York. Rural Democrats backed William McAdoo, Woodrow Wilson's Treasury secretary (and son-in-law), later to become a senator from California; he had skillfully positioned himself to win the support of southern and western delegates suspicious of Tammany Hall and modern urban life. The convention dragged on for 103 ballots, until finally, after both Smith and McAdoo withdrew, the party settled on a compromise: the bland corporate lawyer John W. Davis, who had served as solicitor general and ambassador to Britain under Wilson.

A similar schism plagued the Democrats again in 1928, when Al Smith finally secured his party's nomination for president after a much shorter and less acrimonious battle. *Al Smith* Smith was not, however, able to unite his divided party—largely because of widespread anti-Catholic sentiment, especially in the South. He was the first Democrat since the Civil War not to carry the entire South. Elsewhere, although he did well in the large cities, he carried no states at all except Massachusetts and Rhode Island. Smith's opponent, and the victor in the presidential election, was a man who perhaps more than any other contemporary politician seemed to personify the modern, prosperous, middle-class society of the New Era: Herbert Hoover. The business civilization of the 1920s, with its new institutions, fashions, and values, continued to arouse the animosity of large portions of the population; but the majority of the American people appeared to have accepted and approved it.

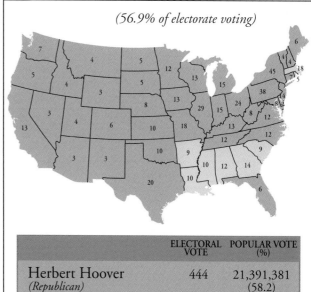

(56.9% of electorate voting)

	ELECTORAL VOTE	POPULAR VOTE (%)
Herbert Hoover (Republican)	444	21,391,381 (58.2)
Alfred E. Smith (Democratic)	87	15,016,443 (40.9)
Norman Thomas (Socialist)	—	267,835 (0.7)
Other parties (Socialist Workers, Prohibition)	—	62,890

ELECTION OF 1928 The election of 1928 was, by almost any measure highly one-sided. Herbert Hoover won over 58 percent of the vote to Alfred Smith's 41. Smith carried only Massachusetts and some traditionally Democratic states in the South. ◆ *Why did Smith do so poorly even in traditionally Democratic areas of the country in 1928?*

For an interactive version of this map go to www.mhhe.com/brinkley11ch24maps

REPUBLICAN GOVERNMENT

For twelve years, beginning in 1921, both the presidency and the Congress rested securely in the hands of the Republican Party—a party in which the power of reformers had greatly dwindled since the heyday of progressivism before the war. For most of those years, the federal government enjoyed a warm and supportive relationship with the American business community. Yet the government of the New Era was more than the passive, pliant instrument that critics often described. It also attempted to serve as an active agent of economic change.

Harding and Coolidge

Nothing seemed more clearly to illustrate the unadventurous character of 1920s politics than the characters of the two men who served as president during most of the decade: Warren G. Harding and Calvin Coolidge.

HARDING AND FRIENDS President Warren G. Harding (center left, holding a rod) poses with companions during a fishing trip to Miami in 1921. He enjoyed these social and sporting events with wealthy friends and political cronies. Two of his companions here, Attorney General Harry Daugherty (to the left of Harding) and Interior Secretary Albert Fall (at far right) were later principal figures in the scandals that rocked the administration before and after Harding's death. *(Bettmann/Corbis)*

Harding was elected to the presidency in 1920, having spent many years in public life doing little of note. An undistinguished senator from Ohio, he had received the Republican presidential nomination as a result of an agreement among leaders of his party, who considered him, as one noted, a "good second-rater." Harding appointed capable men to the most important cabinet offices, and he attempted to stabilize the nation's troubled foreign policy. But even as he attempted to rise to his office, he seemed baffled by his responsibilities, as if he recognized his own unfitness. "I am a man of limited talents from a small town," he reportedly told friends on one occasion. "I don't seem to grasp that I am President." Harding's intellectual limits were compounded by personal weaknesses: his penchant for gambling, illegal alcohol, and attractive women.

Harding lacked the strength to abandon the party hacks who had helped create his political success. One of them, Harry Daugherty, the Ohio party boss principally responsible for his meteoric political ascent, he appointed attorney general. Another, New Mexico Senator Albert B. Fall, he made secretary of the interior. Members of the so-called Ohio Gang filled important offices throughout the administration. Unknown to the public (and perhaps also to Harding), Daugherty, Fall, and others were engaged in fraud and corruption. The most spectacular scandal involved the rich naval oil reserves at Teapot Dome, Wyoming, and Elk Hills, California. At the urging of Fall, Harding transferred control of those reserves from the Navy Department to the Interior Department. Fall then secretly leased them to two wealthy businessmen and received in return nearly half a million dollars in "loans" to ease his private financial troubles. Fall was ultimately convicted of bribery and sentenced

Teapot Dome

to a year in prison; Harry Daugherty barely avoided a similar fate for his part in another scandal.

In the summer of 1923, only months before Senate investigations and press revelations brought the scandals to light, a tired and depressed Harding left Washington for a speaking tour in the West. In Seattle late in July, he suffered severe pain, which his doctors wrongly diagnosed as food poisoning. A few days later, in San Francisco, he died. He had suffered two major heart attacks.

In many ways, Calvin Coolidge, who succeeded Harding in the presidency, was utterly different from his predecessor. Where Harding was genial, garrulous, and debauched, Coolidge was dour, silent, even puritanical. And while Harding was, if not perhaps personally corrupt, then at least tolerant of corruption in others, Coolidge seemed honest beyond reproach. In other ways, however, Harding and Coolidge were similar figures. Both took an essentially passive approach to their office.

Calvin Coolidge

Like Harding, Coolidge had risen to the presidency on the basis of few substantive accomplishments. Elected governor of Massachusetts in 1919, he had won national attention with his laconic response to the Boston police strike that year: "There is no right to strike against the public safety." That was enough to make him his party's vice presidential nominee in 1920. Three years later, after Harding's death, he took the oath of office from his father, a justice of the peace, by the light of a kerosene lamp.

If anything, Coolidge was even less active as president than Harding, partly as a result of his conviction that government should interfere as little as possible in the life of the nation. In 1924, he received his party's presidential nomination virtually unopposed. Running against John W. Davis, he won a comfortable victory: 54 percent of the

CALVIN COOLIDGE AT LEISURE Coolidge was a silent man of simple tastes. But he was not really an outdoorsman, despite his efforts to appear so. He is shown here fishing in Simsbury, Connecticut, carefully attired in suit, tie, hat, and rubber boots. *(Bettmann/Corbis)*

popular vote and 382 of the 531 electoral votes. Robert La Follette, the candidate of the reincarnated Progressive Party, received 16 percent of the popular vote but carried only his home state of Wisconsin. Coolidge probably could have won renomination and reelection in 1928. Instead, in characteristically laconic fashion, he walked into a press room one day and handed each reporter a slip of paper containing a single sentence: "I do not choose to run for president in 1928."

Government and Business

The story of Harding and Coolidge themselves, however, is only a part—and by no means the most important part—of the story of their administrations. However passive the New Era presidents may have been, much of the federal government was working effectively and efficiently during the 1920s to adapt public policy to the widely accepted goal of the time: helping business and industry operate with maximum efficiency and productivity. The close relationship between the private sector and the federal government that had been forged during *Andrew Mellon* World War I continued. Secretary of the Treasury Andrew Mellon, a wealthy steel and aluminum tycoon, devoted himself to working for substantial reductions in taxes on corporate profits and personal incomes and inheritances.

Largely because of his efforts, Congress cut them all by more than half. Mellon also worked closely with President Coolidge after 1924 on a series of measures to trim dramatically the already modest federal budget. The administration even managed to retire half the nation's World War I debt.

The most prominent member of the cabinet was Commerce Secretary Herbert Hoover, who considered himself, and was considered by others, a notable progressive. During his eight years in the Commerce Department, Hoover constantly encouraged voluntary cooperation in the private sector as the best avenue to stability. But the idea of voluntarism did not require that the government remain passive; on the contrary, public institutions, Hoover believed, had a duty to play an active role in creating the new, cooperative order. Above all, Hoover became the champion of the concept of business "associationalism"—a *Hoover's "Associationalism"* concept that envisioned the creation of national organizations of businessmen in particular industries. Through these trade associations, private entrepreneurs could, Hoover believed, stabilize their industries and promote efficiency in production and marketing.

Some progressives derived encouragement from the election of Herbert Hoover—widely regarded as the most progressive member of the Harding and Coolidge administrations—to the presidency in 1928. Hoover easily defeated Al Smith, the Democratic candidate. And he entered office promising bold new efforts to solve the nation's remaining economic problems. But Hoover had few opportunities to prove himself. Less than a year after his inauguration, the nation plunged into the severest and most prolonged economic crisis in its history—a crisis that brought many of the optimistic assumptions of the New Era crashing down and launched the nation into a period of unprecedented social innovation and reform.

CONCLUSION

The remarkable prosperity of the 1920s—a prosperity without parallel in the previous history of the United States—shaped much of what exuberant contemporaries liked to call the "New Era." In the years after World War I, America created a vibrant and extensive national culture. Its middle class moved increasingly to embrace consumerism. Its politics reorganized itself around the needs of a booming, interdependent industrial economy—rejecting many of the reform crusades of the previous generation, but also creating new institutions to help promote economic growth and stability.

Beneath the glittering surface of the New Era, however, were roiling controversies and timeless injustices clamoring for redress. Although the prosperity of the 1920s was more widely shared than at any time in the nation's industrial history, more than half the population failed to achieve any real benefits from the growth. A new, optimistic, secular culture was attracting millions of urban, middle-class people. But many other Americans looked at it with alarm and fought against it with great fervor. The unprepossessing conservative presidents of the era suggested a time with few political challenges, but in fact few eras in modern American history have seen so much political and cultural conflict.

The 1920s ended in a catastrophic economic crash that has colored the image of those years ever since. The crises of the 1930s should not obscure the real achievements of the New Era economy. Neither, however, should the prosperity of the 1920s obscure the inequity and instability in those years that helped produce the difficult years to come.

FOR FURTHER REFERENCE

Frederick Lewis Allen, *Only Yesterday* (1931) is a classic popular history of the 1920s. Michael Parrish, *Anxious Decades: America in Prosperity and Depression, 1920–1941* (1992) is a good recent survey. Ellis Hawley, *The Great War and the Search for a Modern Order* (1979) describes the effect of World War I on American ideas, culture, and society. William E. Leuchtenburg, *The Perils of Prosperity* (rev. ed. 1994) reveals the class divisions and culture dislocation that accompanied economic prosperity in the 1920s. David Brody, *Workers in Industrial America* (1980) includes important essays on welfare capitalism and other labor systems of the 1920s. T. J. Jackson Lears, *Fables of Abudance: A Cultural History of Advertising in America* (1994) and Roland Marchand, *Advertising the American Dream* (1985) are valuable inquiries into the role of advertising in the new consumer culture. James J. Flink, *The Car Culture* (1975) examines ways in which the automobile transformed American life. Susan Smulyan, *Selling Radio: The Commercialization of American Broadcasting, 1920–1934* (1994) chronicles the emergence of commercial radio. Robert Lynd and Helen Merrell Lynd, *Middletown* (1929) is a classic sociological study of how an American city encountered the consumer culture and economy of the 1920s. Ann Douglas's *Terrible Honesty: Mongrel Manhattan in the 1920s* (1995) examines the cultural and political history of the New Era in New York City. Lynn Dumenil, *The Modern Temper: America in the 1920s* (1995) examines the reactions of Americans to modern culture. George Chauncey, *Gay New York: Gender, Urban Culture, and the Making of the Gay Male World, 1890–1940* (1994) is an excellent work in a relatively new field of history. The decline of the feminist movement in the 1920s is explored in Nancy Cott, *The Grounding of American Feminism* (1987). Gary Gerstle, *American Crucible* (2000) is an important study of the changing role of race and ethnicity in defining American nationhood in the twentieth century. Nathan I. Huggins chronicles the cultural and political efflorescence of black Harlem during these years in *Harlem Renaissance* (1971). George Marsden, *Fundamentalism and American Culture* (1980) is good study of some of the religious battles that came to a head in the 1920s. Edward J. Larson, *Summer for the Gods: The Scopes Trial and America's Continuing Debate over Science and Religion* (1997) is a valuable analysis of the Scopes Trial. Leonard Moore, *Citizen Klansmen: The Ku Klux Klan in Indiana, 1921–1928* (1991) is a challenging view of the Klan. Kathleen M. Blee, *Women and the Klan: Racism and Gender in the 1920s* (1991) recreates the female world of the Klan. David Burner, *The Politics of Provincialism* (1967) is a good study of the ordeal of the Democratic party in the 1920s. Morton Keller, *Regulating a New Economy: Public Policy and Economic Change in America, 1900–1933* (1990), and *Regulating a New Society: Public Policy and Social Change in*

America, 1900–1933 (1994) are important studies of New Era public policy.

Coney Island (1990) is a documentary film recreating the drama and fantasy of Coney Island. *That Rhythm, Those Blues* (1997) is a film documenting the one-night stands, makeshift housing, and poor transportation that were all a step toward the big time at the famed Apollo Theatre on Harlem's 125th Street. *Mr. Sears' Catalogue* (1997) is a film exploring how the Sears catalog became a symbol for the ambitions and dreams of a sprawling, fast developing America.

For quizzes, Internet resources, references to additional books and films, and more, consult this book's Online Learning Center at www.mhhe.com/brinkley11.

DETAIL FROM *PRIVATE CAR* (1932), BY LECONTE STEWART Thousands of men (and some women) left their homes during the Great Depression and traveled from city to city looking for work, often hopping freight trains for a free, if illegal, ride. *(Museum of Church History & Art, Salt Lake City, Utah)*

Significant Events

1929 · Stock market crash signals onset of Great Depression
· Agricultural Marketing Act passed

1930 · Hawley-Smoot Tariff enacted
· Ten-year drought begins in South and Midwest (the Dust Bowl)
· White workers in Atlanta organize Black Shirts to fight African-American competition for jobs
· Nisei form Japanese-American Citizens League
· John Dos Passos publishes *U.S.A.* trilogy

1931 · Federal Reserve raises interest rates
· Depression spreads to Europe and deepens in United States
· Scottsboro defendants arrested

CHAPTER TWENTY-FIVE

THE GREAT DEPRESSION

In August 1928, not long before his election to the presidency, Herbert Hoover proclaimed: "We in America today are nearer to the final triumph over poverty than ever before in the history of any land. The poorhouse is vanishing from among us." Only fifteen months later those words would return to haunt him, as the nation plunged into the severest and most prolonged economic depression in its history—a depression that continued in one form or another for a full decade, not only in the United States but throughout much of the rest of the world. The Depression was a traumatic experience for individual Americans, who faced unemployment, the loss of land and other property, and in some cases homelessness and starvation. It also placed great strains on the political and social fabric of the nation.

THE COMING OF THE GREAT DEPRESSION

The sudden economic decline that began in 1929 came as an especially severe shock because it followed so closely a period in which the New Era seemed to be performing another series of economic miracles.

The Great Crash

In February 1928, stock prices began a steady rise that continued, with only a few temporary lapses, for a year

Stock Market Boom

and a half. Between May 1928 and September 1929, the average price of stocks increased over 40 percent. The stocks of the major industrials—the stocks that are used to determine the Dow Jones Industrial Average—doubled in value in that same period. Trading mushroomed from 2 or 3 million shares a day to over 5 million, and at times to as many as 10 or 12 million. There was, in short, a widespread speculative fever that grew steadily more intense, particularly once brokerage firms began encouraging the mania by recklessly offering easy credit to those buying stocks.

In the autumn of 1929, the great bull market began to fall apart. On October 21 and again on October 23, there were alarming declines in stock prices, in both cases followed by temporary recoveries (the second of them

"Black Tuesday"

engineered by J. P. Morgan and Company and other big bankers, who conspicuously bought up stocks to restore public confidence). But on October 29, "Black Tuesday," all

AFTERMATH OF THE CRASH Walter Thornton, shown here in October 1929 next to an expensive roadster he had bought not long before, was one of the relatively affluent Americans who suffered substantial losses in the crash of the stock market in the fall of 1929. In popular mythology, many such people committed suicide in despair. In reality, very few people did. Much more common were efforts such as this to sell off assets to make up for the losses. Thornton was more fortunate than many victims of the Depression. Most had few assets to sell. *(Bettmann/Corbis)*

efforts to save the market failed. Sixteen million shares of stock were traded; the industrial index dropped 43 points; stocks in many companies became virtually worthless. In the months that followed, the market continued to decline. It remained deeply depressed for more than four years and did not fully recover for over a decade.

Many people believed that the stock market crash was the beginning, and even the cause, of the Great Depression. But although October 1929 might have been the first visible sign of the crisis, the Depression had earlier beginnings and more important causes.

Causes of the Depression

Economists, historians, and others have argued for decades about the causes of the Great Depression without reaching any consensus. But most agree on several things. They agree, first, that what is remarkable about the crisis is not that it occurred; periodic recessions are a normal feature of capitalist economies. What is remarkable is that it was so severe and that it lasted so long. The important question, therefore, is not so much why there was a depression, but why it was such a bad one. Most observers agree, too, that a number of different factors account for the severity of the crisis, even if there is considerable disagreement about which was the most important.

One of those factors was a lack of diversification in the American economy in the 1920s. Prosperity had depended excessively on a few basic industries, notably construc- *Lack of Diversification* tion and automobiles. In the late 1920s, those industries began to decline. Expenditures on construction fell from $11 billion to under $9 billion between 1926 and 1929. Automobile sales fell by more than a third in the first nine months of 1929. Newer industries were emerging to take up the slack—among them petroleum, chemicals, plastics, and others oriented toward the expanding market for consumer goods—but had not yet developed enough strength to compensate for the decline in other sectors.

A second important factor was the maldistribution of purchasing power and, as a result, a weakness in consumer demand. As industrial and agricultural production increased, the proportion of the profits going to farmers, workers, and other potential consumers was too small to cre- *Maldistribution of Wealth* ate an adequate market for the goods the economy was producing. Demand was not keeping up with supply. Even in 1929, after nearly a decade of economic growth, more than half the families in America lived on the edge of or below the minimum subsistence level— too poor to buy the goods the industrial economy was producing.

As long as corporations had continued to expand their capital facilities (factories, warehouses, heavy equipment,

THE UNEMPLOYED, 1930 Thousands of unemployed men wait to be fed outside the Muncipal Lodgers House in New York City. *(Library of Congress)*

and other investments), the economy had flourished. By 1929, however, capital investment had created more plant space than could profitably be used, and factories were producing more goods than consumers could purchase. Industries that were experiencing declining demand (construction, autos, coal, and others) began laying off workers, depleting mass purchasing power further. Even expanding industries often reduced their work forces because of new, less labor-intensive technologies; and in the sluggish economic atmosphere of 1929 and beyond, such workers had difficulty finding employment elsewhere.

A third major problem was the credit structure of the economy. Farmers were deeply in debt—their land mortgaged, crop prices too low to allow them to pay off what they owed. Small banks, especially those tied to the agricultural economy, were in constant trouble in the 1920s as their customers defaulted on loans; many of them failed. Large banks were in trouble, too. Although most American bankers were very conservative, some of the nation's biggest banks were investing recklessly in the

stock market or making unwise loans. When the stock market crashed, many of these banks suffered losses greater than they could absorb.

A fourth factor contributing to the coming of the Depression was America's position in international trade. Late in the 1920s, European demand for American goods began to decline. That was partly because European industry and agriculture were becoming more productive, and partly because some European nations (most notably Germany, under the Weimar Republic) were having financial difficulties and could not afford to buy goods from overseas. But it was also because the European economy was being destabilized by the international debt structure that had emerged in the aftermath of World War I.

Declining Exports

The international debt structure, therefore, was a fifth factor contributing to the Depression. When the war came to an end in 1918, all the European nations that had been allied with the United States owed large sums of money to American banks, sums much too large to be

CAUSES OF THE GREAT DEPRESSION

What were the causes of the Great Depression? Economists and historians have debated this question since the economic collapse began and still have not reached anything close to agreement on an answer to it. In the process, however, they have produced several very different theories about how a modern economy works.

During the Depression itself, different groups offered interpretations of the crisis that fit comfortably with their own self-interests and ideologies. Some corporate leaders claimed that the Depression was the result of a lack of "business confidence," that businessmen were reluctant to invest because they feared government regulation and high taxes. The Hoover administration, unable to solve the crisis with the tools it considered acceptable, blamed international economic forces and sought, therefore, to stabilize world currencies and debt structures. New Dealers, determined to find a domestic solution to the crisis and ideologically inclined to place limits on corporate power, argued that the Depression was a crisis of "underconsumption," that low wages and high prices had made it too difficult to buy the products of the industrial economy; and that a lack of demand had led to the economic collapse. Other groups offered equally self-serving explanations.

Scholars in the years since the Great Depression have also created interpretations that fit their views of how the economy works and which public policies are appropriate for it. One of the first important postwar interpretations came from the economists Milton Friedman and Anna Schwartz, in their *Monetary History of the United States* (1963). In a chapter entitled "The Great Contraction," they argued for what has become known as the "monetary" interpretation. The Depression, they claimed, was a result of a drastic contraction of the currency (a result of mistaken decisions by the Federal Reserve Board, which raised interest rates when it should

(Library of Congress)

repaid out of their shattered economies. That was one reason why the Allies had insisted (over Woodrow Wilson's objections) on reparation payments from Germany and Austria. Reparations, they believed, would provide them with a way to pay off their own debts. But Germany and Austria were themselves in economic trouble after the war; they were no more able to pay the reparations than the Allies were able to pay their debts.

Unstable International Debt Structure

The American government refused to forgive or reduce the debts. Instead, American banks began making large loans to European governments, with which they paid off their earlier loans. Thus debts (and reparations) were being paid only by piling up new and greater debts. In the late 1920s, and particularly after the American economy began to weaken in 1929, the European nations found it much more difficult to borrow money from the United States. At the same time, high American protective tariffs were making it difficult for them to sell their goods in American markets. Without any source of foreign exchange with which to repay their loans, they began to default. The collapse of the international credit structure was one of the reasons the Depression spread to Europe (and grew much worse in America) after 1931. (See "America in the World," p. 681.)

Progress of the Depression

The stock market crash of 1929 did not so much cause the Depression, then, as help trigger a chain of events that exposed longstanding weaknesses in the American economy. During the next three years, the crisis steadily worsened.

have lowered them). These deflationary measures turned an ordinary recession into the Great Depression. The monetary argument fits comfortably with the ideas that Milton Friedman, in particular, advocated for many years: that sound monetary policy is the best way to solve economic problems—as opposed to fiscal policies, such as taxation and spending.

A second, very different argument, known as the "spending" interpretation, is identified with, among others, the economist Peter Temin, and his book *Did Monetary Forces Cause the Great Depression?* (1976). Temin's answer to his own question is "no." The cause of the crisis was not monetary contraction (although the contraction made it worse), but a drop in investment and consumer spending, which preceded the decline in the money supply and helped to cause it. Here again, there are obvious political implications. If a decline in spending was the cause of the Depression, then the proper response was an effort to stimulate demand—raising government spending, increasing purchasing power, redistributing wealth. According to this theory, the New Deal never ended the Depression because it did not spend enough. World War II did end it because it pumped so much public money into the economy. This

is a liberal, Keynesian explanation, just as the "monetary hypothesis" is a more conservative explanation.

Another important explanation comes from the historian Michael Bernstein. In *The Great Depression* (1987) he avoids trying to explain why the economic downturn occurred and asks, instead, why it lasted so long. The reason the recession of 1929 became the Depression of the 1930s, he argues, was the timing of the collapse. The recession began as an ordinary cyclical downturn. Had it begun a few years earlier, the basic strength of the automobile and construction industries in the 1920s would have led to a reasonably speedy recovery. Had it begun a few years later, a group of newer, emerging industries would have helped produce a recovery in a reasonably short time. But the recession began in 1929, too late for the automobile and construction industries to help (since they had already experienced a serious, long-term relative decline) and too soon for emerging new industries—aviation, petrochemicals and plastics, aluminum, electronics and electrical appliances, processed foods, and others—to help, since they were still in their infancies.

The political implications of this argument are less obvious than those

for some other interpretations. But one possible conclusion is that if economic growth depends on the successful development of new industries to replace declining ones, then the most sensible economic policy for government is to target investment and other policies toward the growth of new economic sectors. One of the reasons World War II was so important to the long-term recovery of the U.S. economy, Bernstein's argument suggests, was not just that it pumped money into the economy, but that much of that money contributed to developing new industries that would help sustain prosperity after the war. This is, in other words, an explanation of the Depression that seems to support some of the economic ideas that became popular in the 1970s and 1980s calling for a more direct government role in stimulating the growth of new industries.

In the end, however, no single explanation of the Great Depression has ever seemed adequate to most scholars. The event, the economist Robert Lucas once argued, is simply "inexplicable" by any rational calculation. There is no one wholly persuasive answer—at least no answer that an economist or historian has produced—to the question of what caused it.

A collapse of much of the banking system followed the stock market crash. Over 9,000 American banks either

Banking Collapse

went bankrupt or closed their doors to avoid bankruptcy between 1930 and 1933. Depositors lost over $2.5 billion in deposits. Partly as a result of these banking closures, the nation's money supply greatly decreased. The total money supply, according to some measurements, fell by more than a third between 1930 and 1933. The declining money supply meant a decline in purchasing power, and thus deflation. Manufacturers and merchants began reducing prices, cutting back on production, and laying off workers. Some economists argue that a severe depression could have been avoided if the Federal Reserve system had acted more responsibly. But the members of the Federal Reserve Board, concerned about protecting the

Fed's own solvency in a dangerous economic environment, raised interest rates in 1931, which contracted the money supply even further.

The collapse was so rapid and so devastating that at the time it created only bewilderment among many of those who attempted to explain it.

Severe Contraction

The American gross national product plummeted from over $104 billion in 1929 to $76.4 billion in 1932—a 25 percent decline in three years. In 1929, Americans had spent $16.2 billion in capital investment; in 1933, they invested only a third of a billion. The consumer price index declined 25 percent between 1929 and 1933, the wholesale price index 32 percent. Gross farm income dropped from $12 billion to $5 billion in four years. By 1932, according to the relatively crude estimates of the time, 25 percent of the

American work force was unemployed (some believe the figure was even higher); another third of the work force experienced cuts in wages or hours or both. For the rest of the decade, unemployment averaged nearly 20 percent, never dropping below 15 percent.

THE AMERICAN PEOPLE IN HARD TIMES

Someone asked the British economist John Maynard Keynes in the 1930s whether he was aware of any historical era comparable to the Great Depression. "Yes," Keynes replied. "It was called the Dark Ages, and it lasted 400 years." The Depression did not last 400 years, but it did bring unprecedented despair to the economies of the United States and much of the Western world. And it had far-reaching effects on American society and culture.

Unemployment and Relief

The suffering extended into every area of society. In the industrial Northeast and Midwest, cities were becoming virtually paralyzed by unemployment. For example, Cleveland, Ohio, in 1932 had an unemployment rate of 50 percent; Akron, 60 percent; Toledo, 80 percent. Many industrial workers were accustomed to periods of unemployment, but no one was prepared for the scale and duration of the joblessness of the 1930s.

Most Americans had been taught to believe that every individual was responsible for his or her own fate, that unemployment and poverty were signs of personal failure;

and even in the face of national distress, many continued to believe it. Many adult men, in particular, felt deeply ashamed of their joblessness; the helplessness of unemployment was a challenge to traditional notions of masculinity. Unemployed workers walked through the streets day after day looking for jobs that did not exist.

Belief in Personal Responsibility

An increasing number of families were turning to state and local public relief systems, just to be able to eat. But that system, which in the 1920s had served only a small number of indigents, was totally unequipped to handle the new demands being placed on it. In many places, relief simply collapsed. Private charities attempted to supplement the public relief efforts, but the problem was far beyond their capabilities as well. State governments felt pressure to expand their own assistance to the unemployed; but tax revenues were declining along with everything else, and state leaders balked at placing additional strains on already tight budgets. Moreover, many public officials believed that an extensive welfare system would undermine the moral fiber of its clients.

As a result, American cities experienced scenes that a few years earlier would have seemed almost inconceivable. Breadlines stretched for blocks outside Red Cross and Salvation Army kitchens. Thousands of people sifted through garbage cans for scraps of food or waited outside restaurant kitchens in hopes of receiving plate scrapings. Nearly 2 million men, most of them young (and a much smaller number of women), simply took to the roads, riding freight trains from city to city, living as nomads.

SOUP KITCHEN IN CHICAGO This soup kitchen offered free food and coffee to about 3,500 unemployed people a day in Chicago, one of many local efforts to deal with the ravages of the Depression. Unlike some such efforts, however, this one had substantial resources behind it. It was run by the famous Chicago gangster Al Capone. *(Bettmann/Corbis)*

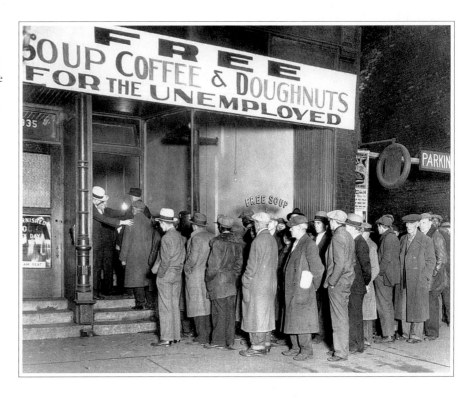

The Great Depression began in the United States. But it did not end there. The American economy was the largest in the world, and its collapse sent shock waves across the globe. By 1931, the American Depression had become a world Depression, with important implications for the course of global history.

The origins of the worldwide depression lay in the pattern of debts that had emerged during and after World War I, when the United States loaned billions of dollars to European nations. In 1931, with American banks staggering and in many cases collapsing, large banks in New York began desperately calling in their loans from Germany and Austria. That precipitated the failure of one of Austria's largest banks, which in turn created panic through much of central Europe. The economic collapse in Germany and Austria meant that those nations could not continue paying reparations to Britain and France (required by the Treaty of Versailles of 1919), which meant in turn that Britain and France could not continue paying off their loans to the United States. This spreading financial crisis was accompanied by a dramatic contraction of international trade, precipitated in part by the Smoot-Hawley Tariff in the United States, which established the highest import duties in history and stifled much global commerce. Depressed agricultural prices—a result of worldwide overproduction—also contributed to the downturn. By 1932, worldwide industrial production had declined by more than a third, and world trade had plummeted by nearly two thirds. By 1933, thirty million people in industrial nations were unemployed, five times the number of four years before.

But the Depression was not confined to industrial nations. Imperialism and industrialization had drawn almost all regions of the world into the international industrial economy. Colonies and nations in Africa, Asia, and South America—critically dependent on exporting raw materials and agricultural goods to industrial countries—experienced a decline in demand for their products, which led to rising levels of

LOOKING FOR WORK IN LONDON, 1935
An unemployed London man wears a sign that seems designed to convince passersby that he is an educated, respectable person despite his present circumstances. *(Hulton/Archive/Getty Images)*

poverty and unemployment. Some nations—among them the Soviet Union and China—remained relatively unconnected to the global economy and suffered relatively little from the Great Depression. But in most parts of the world, the Depression caused tremendous social and economic hardship.

It also created political turmoil. Among the countries hardest hit by the Depression was Germany, where industrial production declined by 50 percent and unemployment reached 35 percent in the early 1930s. The desperate economic conditions there contributed greatly to the rise of the Nazi party and its leader Adolf Hitler, who became chancellor in 1932. Japan suffered greatly as well, dependent as it was on world trade to sustain its growing industrial economy and purchase essential commodities for its needs at home. And in Japan, as in Germany, economic troubles produced political turmoil and aided the rise of a new militaristic regime. In Italy, the fascist government of Benito Mussolini, which had first taken power in the 1920s, also saw militarization and territorial expansion as a way out of economic difficulties.

In other nations, governments sought solutions to the Depression through reform of their domestic economies. The most prominent example of that was the New Deal in the United States. But there were important experiments in other nations as well. Among the most common responses to the Depression around the world was substantial government investment in public works. In the United States, Britain, France, Germany, Italy, the Soviet Union, and other countries, there was substantial investment in roads, bridges, dams, public buildings, and other large projects. Another response was the expansion of government-funded relief for the unemployed. All the industrial countries of the world experimented with one or another form of relief, often borrowing ideas from one another in the process. And the Depression helped create new approaches to economics, in the face of the apparent failure of classical models of economic behavior to explain, or provide solutions to, the crisis. The great British economist John Maynard Keynes revolutionized economic thought in much of the world. His 1936 book *The General Theory of Employment, Interest, and Money,* despite its bland title, created a sensation by arguing that the Depression was a result not of declining production, but of inadequate consumer demand. Governments, he said, could stimulate their economies by increasing the money supply and creating investment—through a combination of lowering interest rates and public spending. Keynesianism, as Keynes's theories became known, began to have an impact in the United States in 1938, and in much of the rest of the world in subsequent years.

The Great Depression was an important turning point not only in American history, but in the history of the twentieth-century world. It transformed ideas of public policy and economics in many nations. It toppled old regimes and created new ones. And perhaps above all, it was a major factor—maybe the single most important factor—in the coming of World War II.

DUST BOWL

The Dust Bowl of the 1930s was one of the great environmental disasters of American history. Although historians have often attributed it solely to an especially severe natural drought, it was in fact a much more complicated event that had as much to do with people as with nature.

The origins of the Dust Bowl stretched back more than half a century. As American settlers moved out onto the western plains after the Civil War, they encountered a more arid climate than they had known before, a climate to which the farming techniques they had known in the East were poorly suited.

To deal with the problems of too little rain, farmers experimented with new ways of farming. By plowing the soil deeply, stirring up a fine layer of dust on the surface, and leaving fields bare to gather moisture when not being cropped, they sought to conserve water as best they could. At the same time, they grew less corn and introduced winter wheats from central Europe that were especially well adapted to dry conditions. These techniques worked well enough to encourage farmers to expand into new areas.

The great period of expansion for plains farmers came during World War I. European demand and government subsidies sent the price of wheat soaring past $2 per bushel, and other grains rose as well. Farmers responded by planting as never before. By 1919, Colorado, Nebraska, Kansas, Oklahoma, and Texas had expanded their wheat acreage by 13.5 million acres—11 million of which had previously been covered with native grasses. To handle this vast new cropland, farmers invested in new mechanical equipment: disk plows, combines, and tractors. In 1915, there had been approximately 3,000 tractors in all of Kansas. By 1930 the number had risen to more than 66,000.

The new machinery enabled farm families to produce more grain per capita than ever before, but because the equipment was expensive it led them to take on new debt. They also planted larger acreages to take advantage of the new equipment, and incurred additional debts for their new land. Paying off debts was no problem during good years, but it could become a nightmare if economic or climatic conditions became unfavorable. Unfortunately, both went bad simultaneously during the 1920s.

By 1930, the world wheat market was in deep trouble, and farmers had no choice but to plant as many acres as possible in a desperate effort to earn enough to pay their debts. At the same time, rain failed up and down the plains. Starting in 1931, areas in the southern plains that ordinarily received eighteen inches of rain each year—the bare minimum for many types of farming—had annual deficits of three to seven inches. Crops died. The parched soil baked and cracked in the sun as thermometers rose above 100 degrees each day for weeks on end. Even many native grasses eventually succumbed. The region was entering its worst drought in recorded history, and it would be a decade before rainfall became abundant once again. The drought of the 1930s was unprecedented not just in its severity, but also in its human costs. The

DUST STORM, SOUTHWEST PLAINS, 1937 The dust storms of the 1930s were a terrifying experience for all who lived through them. Resembling a black wall sweeping in from the western horizon, such a storm engulfed farms and towns alike, blotting out the light of the sun and covering everything with fine dirt. *(Bettmann/Corbis)*

In rural areas conditions were in many ways worse. Farm income declined by 60 percent between 1929 and 1932. A third of all American farmers lost their land. In addition, a large area of agricultural settlement in the Great Plains of the South and West was suffering from a catastrophic natural disaster: one of the worst droughts in the history of the nation. Beginning in 1930, a large area of the nation, which came to be known as the "Dust Bowl," stretching north from Texas into the Dakotas, began to experience a steady decline in rainfall and an accompanying increase in heat. The drought continued for a decade, turning what had once been fertile farm regions into virtual deserts. In Kansas, the soil in some places was completely without moisture as far as three feet below the surface. In Nebraska, Iowa, and other states, summer temperatures were averaging over 100 degrees. Swarms of grasshoppers were moving from region to region, devouring what meager crops farmers were able to raise, often even devouring fenceposts or clothes hanging out to dry. Great

"Dust Bowl"

collapse of crop prices meant that thousands of acres, now uncultivated, stood naked in the sun. The native grasses of the plains had once formed a tight natural sod that could withstand a drought even if many individual plants died. Now the sod was gone and nothing remained to protect soil from the wind.

Dust storms had been part of life on the plains for centuries, especially in western Kansas, Oklahoma, and the Texas Panhandle, where the soil was sandy and especially susceptible to blowing. Now, however, with more acres plowed and vulnerable to erosion than ever before, they reached unprecedented severity. A single famous storm in May 1934 carried 300 million tons of Great Plains soil all the way to the Atlantic Ocean, dropping dust in New York and Washington and even on ships 300 miles at sea. On the southern plains, such storms became a regular occurrence for the better part of the 1930s. They darkened the sky at midday, seeped dust into houses, blew drifts along fencerows, even killed animals and people who were unlucky enough to be caught in their midst. "Three little words," wrote a reporter for the Associated Press in 1935, "achingly familiar on a Western farmer's tongue—rule life today in the dust bowl of the continent. . . . If it rains." And so the southern plains gained a new name: Dust Bowl. There were 22 dust storms in 1934, 40 in 1935, 68 in 1936, 72 in 1937, 61 in 1938, 30 in 1939, and 17 in both 1940 and 1941. Unplanted soil made conditions perfect for dust storms when the drought finally hit, and the combined force of economic depression

CONTOUR PLOWING Farmers responded to the dust storms by adopting new cultivation practices designed to prevent soil from blowing away in the wind. Among the most important techniques was contour plowing, which adjusted furrows to the contours of the land to break the wind's velocity as it moved across the surface. Contour plowing also discouraged water erosion. *(Bettmann/Corbis)*

and too little rain left farmers with few defenses once the cycle got going. Many families eventually abandoned their farms and took to the road, becoming the "Okies" who migrated to California in search of a better life. A number of New Deal agencies stepped in to try to help with a variety of programs. The Resettlement Administration sought to buy up farms on soils that were too marginal for safe agricultural production. The Forest Service planted over 200 million trees as "shelter belts" designed to slow the dusty winds. And the Soil Conservation Service promoted new forms of tillage that held the soil better.

All these things helped, but it was not until 1941, when the rains returned in earnest and World War II began to generate massive new demand for crops, that the Dust Bowl came to an end. New farming techniques, including irrigation systems that tapped underground water supplies, have prevented the return of dust storms on anything like the scale of the 1930s, although lesser storms have from time to time blown through the region. Whether they return in the future depends on whether farmers remember the lessons of the Dust Bowl and adapt their methods to the special needs of their land.

dust storms—"black blizzards," as they were called—swept across the plains, blotting out the sun and suffocating livestock as well as any people unfortunate or foolish enough to stay outside. (See "The American Environment," above.)

It is a measure of how productive American farmers were and how depressed the market for agricultural goods had become that even with these disastrous conditions, the farm economy continued through the 1930s to produce far more than American consumers could afford

to buy. Farm prices fell so low that few growers made any profit at all on their crops. As a result, many farmers, like many urban unemployed, left their homes in search of work. In the South, in particular, many dispossessed farmers—black and white—wandered from town to town, hoping to find jobs or handouts. Hundreds of thousands of families from the Dust Bowl (often known as "Okies," *"Okies"* since many came from Oklahoma) traveled to California and other states, where they found conditions little better than those they had left. Owning no land of their own, many worked as agricultural migrants, traveling from farm to farm picking fruit and other crops at starvation wages.

Throughout the nation, problems of malnutrition and homelessness grew at an alarming rate. Hospitals pointed to a striking increase in deaths from starvation. On the outskirts of cities, large shantytowns sprang up in which families lived in makeshift shacks constructed of flattened tin cans, scraps of wood, abandoned crates, and other debris. Many homeless Americans simply kept moving—sleeping in freight cars, in city parks, in subways, or in unused sewer ducts.

African Americans and the Depression

African Americans for the most part had not shared very much in the prosperity of the previous decade. But the Depression was devastating for them nevertheless. They experienced more unemployment, homelessness, malnutrition, and disease than they had in the past, and considerably more than most whites.

African-American Suffering

As the Depression began, over half of all black Americans still lived in the South. Most were farmers. The collapse of prices for cotton and other staple crops left some with no income at all. Many left the land altogether—either by choice or forced by landlords who no longer found the sharecropping system profitable. Some migrated to southern cities. But unemployed whites in the urban South believed they had first claim to all work. Some of them now began to take positions as janitors, street cleaners, and domestic servants, displacing the blacks who formerly had occupied such jobs.

As the Depression deepened, whites in many southern cities began to demand that all blacks be dismissed from their jobs. In Atlanta in 1930, an organization calling itself the Black Shirts organized a campaign with the slogan "No Jobs for Niggers Until Every White Man Has a Job!" In other areas, whites used intimidation and violence to drive blacks from jobs. By 1932, over half the blacks in the South were without employment. And what limited relief there was went almost invariably to whites first.

Unsurprisingly, therefore, many black southerners—perhaps 400,000 in all—left the South in the 1930s and journeyed to the cities of the North. There they generally found less blatant discrimination. But conditions were in most respects little better than in the South. In New York, black unemployment was nearly 50 percent. In other

BLACK MIGRANTS The Great Migration of blacks from the rural South into the cities had begun before World War I. But in the 1930s and 1940s the movement accelerated. Jacob Lawrence, an eminent African-American artist, created a series of paintings entitled, collectively, *The Migration of the Negro*, to illustrate this major event in the history of African Americans. *(The Phillips Collection, Washington, D.C.)*

cities, it was higher. Two million African Americans were on some form of relief by 1932.

Traditional patterns of segregation and disfranchisement in the South survived the Depression largely unchallenged. But a few particularly notorious examples of *Scottsboro Case* racism did attract national attention. The most celebrated was the Scottsboro case. In March 1931, nine black teenagers were taken off a freight train in Alabama (in a small town near Scottsboro) and arrested for vagrancy and disorder. Later, two white women who had also been riding the train accused them of rape. In fact, there was overwhelming evidence, medical and otherwise, that the women had not been raped at all; they may have made their accusations out of fear of being arrested themselves. Nevertheless, an all-white jury in Alabama quickly convicted all nine of the "Scottsboro boys" (as they were known to both friends and foes) and sentenced eight of them to death.

The Supreme Court overturned the convictions in 1932, and a series of new trials began that attracted increasing national attention. The International Labor Defense, an organization associated with the Communist Party, came to the aid of the accused youths and began to publicize the case. Later, the NAACP provided assistance as well. The trials continued throughout the 1930s. Although the white southern juries who sat on the case never acquitted any of the defendants, all of them eventually gained their freedom—four because the charges were dropped, four because of early paroles, and one because he escaped. But the last of the Scottsboro defendants did not leave prison until 1950.

The Depression was a time of important changes in the role and behavior of leading black organizations. The *NAACP's Changing Role* NAACP, for example, began to work diligently to win a position for blacks within the emerging labor movement, supporting the formation of the Congress of Industrial Organizations and helping to break down racial barriers within labor unions. Walter White, secretary of the NAACP, once even made a personal appearance at an auto plant to implore blacks not to work as strikebreakers. Partly as a result of such efforts, more than half a million blacks were able to join the labor movement. In the Steelworkers Union, for example, African Americans constituted about 20 percent of the membership.

Mexican Americans in Depression America

Similar patterns of discrimination confronted Mexicans and Mexican Americans. The Mexican population of the United States had been growing steadily since early in the century, largely in California and other areas of the Southwest through massive immigration from Mexico (which was specifically excluded from the immigration restriction laws of the 1920s). In the 1930s, there were approximately 2 million Latinos (or Hispanics) in the United States.

Chicanos (as Mexican Americans are often known) filled many of the same menial jobs in the West and elsewhere that blacks filled in other regions. Some farmed small, marginal tracts. Some became agricultural migrants, traveling from region to region harvesting fruit, lettuce, and other crops. But most lived in urban areas—in California, New Mexico, and Arizona, but also in Detroit, Chicago, New York, and other eastern industrial cities—and occupied the lower ranks of the unskilled labor force in such industries as steel, automobiles, and meatpacking.

Even during the prosperous 1920s, theirs had been a precarious existence. The Depression made things significantly worse. As in the South, unemployed white Anglos in the Southwest demanded jobs held by Hispanics, jobs that the Anglos had previously considered beneath them. Thus Mexican unemployment rose quickly to levels far higher than those for Anglos. Some Mexicans were, in effect, forced to leave the country by officials who arbitrarily removed them from relief rolls or simply rounded them up and transported them across the border. Perhaps half a million Chicanos left the United States for Mexico in the first years of the Depression.

Those who remained faced persistent discrimination. Most relief programs excluded Mexicans from their rolls or offered them benefits far below those available to whites. Hispanics generally had no access to American schools. *Discrimination against Hispanics* Many hospitals refused them admission. American blacks had established educational and social facilities of their own in response to discrimination, but Hispanics generally had fewer institutional supports. Some joined the American Communist Party. Some turned to the Mexican consulates or to the social and economic leaders of Mexican-American communities, but with little effect. Even many who possessed American citizenship found themselves treated like foreigners.

Occasionally, there were signs of organized resistance by Mexican Americans themselves, most notably in California, where some formed a union of migrant farmworkers. But harsh repression by local growers and the public authorities allied with them prevented such organizations from having much impact. Like African-American farmworkers, many Mexicans began as a result to migrate to cities such as Los Angeles, where they lived in a poverty comparable to that of urban blacks in the South and Northeast.

Asian Americans in Hard Times

For Asian Americans, too, the Depression reinforced longstanding patterns of discrimination and economic marginalization. In California, where the largest Japanese-American and Chinese-American populations resided, even educated Asians had always found it difficult, if not impossible, to move into mainstream professions. Japanese-American college graduates often found themselves working in family fruit stands; 20 percent of all Nisei in

CHINATOWN, NEW YORK A Chinese man carries a "sandwich board" through the streets of New York's Chinatown bearing the latest news of the war between China and Japan, which in 1938 was already well under way. Chinese Americans had the dual challenge in the 1930s of dealing both with large-scale unemployment and with continuing news of catastrophe from China, where most still had many family members. *(Hulton/Archive/Getty Images)*

Chinese Americans fared no better. The overwhelming majority continued to work in Chinese-owned laundries and restaurants. Those who moved outside the Asian community could rarely find jobs above the entry level. Chinese women, for example, might find work as stock girls in department stores, but almost never as salesclerks. Educated Chinese men and women could hope for virtually no professional opportunities outside the world of the Chinatowns.

Women and the Workplace in the Great Depression

The economic crisis served in many ways to strengthen the widespread belief that a woman's proper place was in the home. Most men and many women believed that with employment so scarce, what work there was should go to men. There was a particularly strong belief that no woman whose husband was employed should accept a job. Indeed, from 1932 until 1937, it was illegal for more than one member of a family to hold a federal civil service job, and such jobs went overwhelmingly to men.

Popular Disapproval of Women's Employment

But the widespread assumption that married women, at least, should not work outside the home did not stop them from doing so. Both single and married women worked in the 1930s, despite public condemnation of the practice, because they or their families needed the money. In fact, the largest new group of female workers consisted of precisely those people who, according to popular attitudes, were supposed to be leaving the labor market: wives and mothers. By the end of the Depression, 20 percent more women were working than had been doing so at the beginning.

Increased Female Employment

The increase occurred despite considerable obstacles. Professional opportunities for women declined because unemployed men began moving into professions such as teaching and social work that had previously been considered women's fields. Female industrial workers were more likely to be laid off or to experience wage reductions than their male counterparts. But white women also had certain advantages in the workplace. The nonprofessional jobs that women traditionally held—as salesclerks and stenographers, and in other service positions—were less likely to disappear than the predominantly male jobs in heavy industry. Nor were many men, even unemployed men, likely to ask for such jobs.

Black women, however, enjoyed few such advantages. Particularly in the South, they suffered massive unemployment because of a great reduction of domestic service jobs. As many as half of all black working women lost their jobs in the 1930s. Even so, at the end of the 1930s, 38 percent of black women were employed, as compared to 24 percent of white women. That was because black

Los Angeles worked at such stands at the end of the 1930s. For those who found jobs (usually poorly paid) in the industrial or service economy, employment was precarious; like blacks and Hispanics, they often lost jobs to white Americans desperate for work that a few years earlier they would not have considered. Japanese farmworkers, like Chicano farmworkers, suffered from the increasing competition for even these low-paying jobs from white migrants from the Great Plains.

In California, younger Nisei tried to challenge the obstacles facing them through politics. They organized Japanese American Democratic Clubs in several cities, which worked for, among other things, laws protecting racial and ethnic minorities from discrimination. At the same time, some Japanese-American businessmen and professionals tried to overcome obstacles by changing the Nisei themselves, by encouraging them to become more assimilated, more "American." They formed the Japanese American Citizens League in 1930 to promote their goals. By 1940, it had nearly 6,000 members.

Japanese American Citizens League

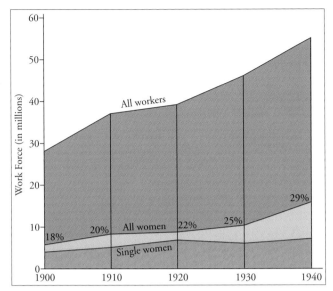

WOMEN IN THE PAID WORK FORCE, 1900–1940 The participation of women in the paid work force increased slowly but steadily in the first forty years of the twentieth century. Note, however, the general leveling off of the participation of single women—who traditionally accounted for the vast majority of women workers—after 1920, at the same time that the total number of women in the paid work force was rising. Many more married women began entering the paid work force in these years, particularly in the 1930s. ◆ *Why did so many married women begin doing paid work during the Great Depression?*

women—both married and unmarried—had always been more likely to work than white women, less out of preference than out of economic necessity.

For American feminists, the Depression years were, on the whole, a time of frustration. Although economic pressures pushed more women into the work force, those same pressures helped to erode the frail support that feminists had won in the 1920s for the idea of women becoming economically and professionally independent. In the difficult years of the 1930s, such aspirations seemed to many to be less important than dealing with economic hardship. The Depression saw the virtual extinction of the

Demise of the National Woman's Party

National Woman's Party, which had fought throughout the 1920s for the Equal Rights Amendment and other egalitarian goals. Even more moderate feminists, committed to "protective" legislation for women, saw their influence decline—although they did achieve some significant gains in the early years of the New Deal. By the end of the 1930s, American feminism had reached its lowest ebb in nearly a century.

Depression Families

The economic hardships of the Depression years placed great strains on American families. Middle-class families that had become accustomed in the 1920s to a steadily

rising standard of living now found themselves plunged suddenly into uncertainty, because of unemployment or the reduction of incomes among those who remained employed. Some working-class families, too, had achieved a precarious prosperity in the 1920s and saw their gains disappear in the 1930s.

Such circumstances forced many families to retreat from the consumer patterns they had developed in the 1920s. Women often returned to sewing clothes for them-

Retreat from Consumerism

selves and their families and to preserving their own food rather than buying such products in stores. Others engaged in home businesses—taking in laundry, selling baked goods, accepting boarders. Many households expanded to include more distant relatives. Parents often moved in with their children and grandparents with their grandchildren, or vice versa.

But the Depression also eroded the strength of many family units. There was a decline in the divorce rate, but largely because divorce was now too expensive for some. More common was the informal breakup of families, particularly the desertion of families by unemployed men bent on escaping the humiliation of being unable to earn a living. The marriage and birth rates declined simultaneously for the first time since the early nineteenth century.

THE DEPRESSION AND AMERICAN CULTURE

The Great Depression was a traumatic experience for millions of Americans, and it shook the confidence of many people in themselves or in their nation or both. Out of the crisis emerged some of the most probing criticisms of American society and the American economic system of the industrial age. At the same time, the Depression produced powerful confirmations of more traditional values and reinforced many traditional goals. There was not one Depression culture, but many.

Depression Values

Prosperity and industrial growth had done much to shape American values in the 1920s. Mainstream culture, at least, had celebrated affluence and consumerism and had stressed the importance of personal gratification through both. Many Americans assumed, therefore, that the experience of hard times would have profound effects on the nation's social values. In general, however, American social values seemed to change relatively little in response to the Depression. Rather, many people responded to hard times by redoubling their commitment to familiar ideas and goals. The sociologists Robert and Helen Merrell Lynd, who had published a celebrated study of Muncie, Indiana, *Middletown,* in 1929, returned there in the mid-1930s to see how the city had changed. They described their findings in their 1937 book, *Middletown in Transition,* and they concluded that in most respects "the texture of Middletown's culture has not changed. . . . Middletown is overwhelmingly living by the values by which it lived in 1925." Above all, the men and women of "Middletown"—and by implication many other Americans—remained committed to the traditional American emphasis on the individual.

No assumption would seem to have been more vulnerable to erosion during the Depression than the belief that the individual was in control of his or her own fate, that anyone displaying sufficient talent and industry could become a success. And in some respects, the economic crisis did work to undermine the traditional "success ethic"

Persistence of the "Success Ethic"

in America. Many people began to look to government for assistance; many blamed corporate moguls, international bankers, "economic royalists," and others for their distress. Yet the Depression did not, in the end, seriously erode the success ethic.

The survival of the ideals of work and individual advancement was evident in many ways, not least in the reactions of those most traumatized by the Depression: conscientious working people who suddenly found themselves without employment. Some expressed anger and struck out at the economic system. Many, however,

Self Blame

seemed to blame themselves. Nothing so surprised foreign observers of America in the 1930s as the apparent passivity of the unemployed, many of whom were so ashamed of their joblessness that they refused to leave their homes. Perhaps that was why people who continued in the 1930s to work and to live more or less as they always had sometimes found it easy to forget that there was an economic crisis. The Depression was sometimes hard to see, because the unemployed tended to hide themselves, unwilling to display to the world what many of them considered their own personal failure.

At the same time, millions responded eagerly to reassurances that they could, through their own efforts, restore themselves to prosperity and success. Dale Carnegie's *How to Win Friends and Influence People* (1936), a self-help manual preaching individual initiative, was one of the best-selling books of the decade. Carnegie's message was not only that personal initiative was the route to success; it was also that the best way for people to make something of themselves was to adapt to the world in which they lived, to understand the values and expectations of others and mold themselves accordingly. The way to get ahead, Carnegie taught, was to fit in and make other people feel important. Similarly, Harry Emerson Fosdick, a Protestant theologian who preached the virtues of positive thinking and individual initiative, attracted large audiences with his radio addresses.

Not all Americans, of course, responded to the crisis of the Depression so self-reflectively. Many men and women believed that the economic problems of their time were the fault of society, not of individuals, and that some collective social response was necessary. American artistic and intellectual life gave expression to such beliefs.

Artists and Intellectuals in the Great Depression

Just as many progressives had become alarmed when, early in the twentieth century, they "discovered" the existence of widespread poverty in the cities, so many Americans were shocked during the 1930s at their discovery of debilitating rural poverty. Perhaps most effective in conveying the dimensions of this poverty was a

"Discovery" of Rural Poverty

group of documentary photographers, many of them employed by the federal Farm Security Administration in the late 1930s, who traveled through the South recording the nature of agricultural life. Men such as Roy Stryker, Walker Evans, Arthur Rothstein, and Ben Shahn and women such as Margaret Bourke-White and Dorothea Lange produced memorable studies of farm families and their surroundings, studies designed to reveal the savage impact of a hostile environment on its victims.

Many writers, similarly, turned away from the personal concerns of the 1920s and devoted themselves to exposés of social injustice. Erskine Caldwell's *Tobacco Road* (1932), which later became a long-running Broadway play, was an exposé of poverty in the rural South. Richard Wright, a major African-American novelist, exposed the plight

Depression Literature

of residents of the urban ghetto in *Native Son* (1940). John Steinbeck's novels portrayed the trials of workers and migrants in California. John Dos Passos's trilogy *U.S.A.* (1930) attacked modern capitalism outright. Playwright Clifford Odets provided an explicit demonstration of the appeal of political radicalism in *Waiting for Lefty* (1935).

But the cultural products of the 1930s that attracted the widest popular audiences were those that diverted attention away from the Depression. And they came to Americans primarily through the two most powerful instruments of popular culture in the 1930s—radio and the movies.

Radio

Almost every American family had a radio in the 1930s. In cities and towns, radio consoles were now as familiar a part of the furnishing of parlors and kitchens as tables and chairs. Even in remote rural areas without access to electricity, many families purchased radios and hooked them up to car batteries when they wished to listen.

Listening to radio is generally considered a private experience—something people do alone or with their families in their homes, rather than out in public with others. But in some communities, radio was often a community experience. Young people would place radios on their front porches and invite friends over to sit, talk, or dance. In poor urban neighborhoods, many people who could not afford other kinds of social activities would gather on a street or in a backyard to listen to sporting events or concerts. Within families, the radio often drew parents and children together in the evening to listen to favorite programs.

What did Americans hear on the radio? Although radio stations occasionally carried socially and politically provocative programs, the staple of broadcasting was escapism: comedies such as *Amos 'n Andy* (with its humorous, if demeaning, picture of urban blacks); adventures such as *Superman, Dick Tracy,* and *The Lone Ranger;* and other entertainment programs. Radio brought a new kind of comedy—previously limited to vaudeville or to ethnic theaters—to a wide audience. Jack Benny, George Burns and Gracie Allen, and other masters of elaborately timed jokes and repartee began to develop broad followings (that they would later take with them to television).

Escapist Programming

Soap operas, also later to become staples of television programming, were enormously popular as well in the 1930s, especially with women who were alone in the house during the day. (That was one reason they became known as soap operas; soap companies—whose advertising was targeted at women—generally sponsored them.) Soap operas were complicated stories of romance, intrigue, and betrayal, usually without overt social or political messages.

Almost invariably, radio programs were broadcast live; and as a result, radio spawned an enormous number of public performances. Radio comedies and dramas were often performed before audiences in theaters or studios. Band concerts were broadcast from dance halls, helping jazz and swing bands to achieve broad popularity. Classical music, too, was broadcast live from studios. NBC, the premier network in the 1930s, created a major symphony orchestra of its own under the direction of the great Italian conductor Arturo Toscanini; its concerts were a regular feature of the network's schedule.

Radio provided Americans with their first direct access to important public events, and radio news and sports divisions grew rapidly to meet the demand. Some of the most dramatic moments of the 1930s were a result of radio coverage of celebrated events: the World Series, major college football games, the Academy Awards, political conventions, presidential inaugurations. When the German dirigible the *Hindenburg* crashed in flames in Lakehurst, New Jersey, in 1937 after a transatlantic voyage, it produced an enormous national reaction largely because of the live radio account by a broadcaster overcome with emotion who cried out, as he watched the terrible crash, "Oh the humanity! Oh the humanity!" The actor/director Orson Welles created another memorable event in 1938 when he broadcast a radio play on Halloween about aliens whose spaceship had landed in central New Jersey and who had set off toward New York armed with terrible weapons. The play took the form of a fictional news broadcast, and it created panic among millions of people who believed for a while that the events it described were real.

Radio's Impact

Radio was important for the way it drew the nation together by creating the possibility of shared experiences and common access to culture and information. It was

A RADIO PLAY Among the most popular entertainments of the 1930s were live dramatic readings of plays over the radio—many of them mysteries or romances written specifically for the new medium. Here, a group of actors performs a radio drama over WNBC in New York in the mid-1930s. *(Hulton/Archive/Getty Images)*

also significant for the way it helped reshape the social life of the nation, for the way it encouraged many families and individuals to center their lives more around the home than they had in the past.

The Movies

Moviegoing would seem particularly vulnerable to hard times. Families struggling to pay the rent or buy food could easily decide to forgo an evening at the movies. In the first years of the Depression, movie attendance did drop significantly. By the mid-1930s, however, most Americans had resumed their movie-going habits—in part because movies were a less expensive entertainment option than many other possibilities, and in part because the movies themselves (all of them now with sound, and by the end of the decade many of them in color) were becoming more appealing.

Continuing Popularity of Movies

In many ways, movies were as safely conventional in the 1930s as they had been in the late 1920s. Hollywood continued to exercise tight control over its products in the 1930s through its resilient censor Will Hays, who ensured that most movies carried no sensational or controversial messages. The studio system—through which a few large movie companies exercised iron control over actors, writers, and directors, and through which a few great moguls such as Louis B. Mayer or Jack Warner could single-handedly decide the fate of most projects—also worked to ensure that Hollywood films avoided controversy.

But neither the censor nor the studio system could (or wished to) prevent films from exploring social questions altogether. A few films, such as King Vidor's *Our Daily Bread* (1932) and John Ford's adaptation of *The Grapes of Wrath* (1940), did explore political themes. The director Frank Capra provided a muted social message in several of his comedies—*Mr. Deeds Goes to Town* (1936), *Mr. Smith Goes to Washington* (1939), and *Meet John Doe* (1941)— which celebrated the virtues of the small town and the decency of the common people in contrast to the selfish, corrupt values of the city and the urban rich. (See "Patterns of Popular Culture," pp. 692–693.) Gangster movies such as *Little Caesar* (1930) and *The Public Enemy* (1931) portrayed a dark, gritty, violent world with which few Americans were familiar, but their desperate stories were popular nevertheless with those engaged in their own difficult struggles; and they made stars out of such otherwise unlikely actors as James Cagney and Edward G. Robinson.

More often, however, the commercial films of the 1930s were deliberately and explicitly escapist: lavish musicals such as *Gold Diggers of 1933* (whose theme song was "We're in the Money"), "screwball" comedies such as Capra's *It Happened One Night* or the many films of the Marx Brothers—films designed to divert audiences from their troubles and, often, indulge their fantasies about quick and easy wealth.

The 1930s saw the beginning of Walt Disney's long reign as the champion of animation and children's entertainment. After producing cartoon shorts for theaters in the late 1920s—many of them starring the newly created character of Mickey Mouse who made his debut in the 1928 cartoon *Steamboat Willie*—Disney began to produce feature-length animated films, starting in 1937 with *Snow White*. Other enormously popular films of the 1930s were adaptations of popular novels: *The Wizard of Oz* and *Gone With the Wind*, both released in 1939.

Walt Disney

A NIGHT AT THE OPERA The antic comedy of the Marx Brothers provided a popular and welcome escape from the rigors of the Great Depression. The Marx Brothers, shown here in a poster for one of their most famous films, effectively lampooned dilemmas that many Americans faced in their ceaseless, and usually unsuccessful, efforts to find an easy route to wealth and comfort. *(Everett Collection)*

Hollywood did little to challenge the conventions of popular culture on issues of gender and race. Women in movies were portrayed overwhelmingly as wives and mothers, or if not, as sexually attractive people engaged in elaborate flirtations (although seldom more than that) with men. Mae West portrayed herself in a series of successful films as an overtly sexual woman manipulating men through her attractiveness (although in her own life West was a successful, wealthy, and independent producer of films, her own and others). Few films included important African-American characters. Most of the black men and women who did appear in movies were portrayed as servants or farmhands.

Popular Literature and Journalism

The social and political strains of the Great Depression found voice much more successfully in print than they did on the airwaves or the screen. Much literature and journalism in the 1930s dealt directly or indirectly with the tremendous disillusionment, and the increasing radicalism, of the time.

Not all literature, of course, was challenging or controversial. The most popular books and magazines of the time, in fact, were as escapist and romantic as the most popular radio shows and movies. Two of the best-selling novels of the decade were romantic sagas set in earlier eras: Margaret Mitchell's *Gone With the Wind* (1936) and Hervey Allen's *Anthony Adverse* (1933). Leading maga-

Life Magazine

zines focused more on fashions, stunts, scenery, and the arts than on the social conditions of the nation. The enormously popular new photographic journal *Life,* which began publication in 1936 and quickly became the most successful magazine in American history, had the largest readership of any publication in the United States. It devoted some attention to politics and to the economic conditions of the Depression, more, in fact, than did many of its competitors. But it was best known for stunning photographs of sporting and theater events, natural landscapes, and impressive public projects. Its first cover was a striking picture by Margaret Bourke-White of a New Deal hydroelectric project. One of its most popular features was "*Life* Goes to a Party," which took the chatty social columns of daily newspapers and turned them into glossy photographic glimpses of the rich and famous.

Other Depression writing, however, was frankly and openly challenging to the dominant values of American popular culture. In the first years of the Depression, some of the most significant literature offered corrosive portraits of the harshness and emptiness of American life: John Dos Passos's *U.S.A.* trilogy (1930–1936), which at-

John Dos Passos

tacked what he considered the materialistic madness of American culture; Nathanael West's *Miss Lonelyhearts* (1933), the story of an advice columnist overwhelmed by the

sadness he encounters in the lives of those who consult him; Jack Conroy's *The Disinherited* (1933), a harsh portrait of the lives of coal miners; and James T. Farrell's *Studs Lonigan* (1932), a portrait of a lost, hardened working-class youth.

The Popular Front and the Left

In the later 1930s, much of the political literature adopted a more optimistic, although often no less radical, approach to society. This was in part a result of the rise of the Popular Front, a broad coalition of "antifascist" groups on the left, of which the most important was the American Communist Party. The party had long been a harsh and unrelenting critic of American capitalism and the government it claimed was controlled by it. But in 1935, under instructions from the Soviet Union, the party softened its attitude toward Franklin Roosevelt (whom Stalin now saw as a potential ally in the coming battle against Hitler) and formed loose alliances with many other "progressive" groups. The party began to praise the New Deal and John L. Lewis, a powerful (and strongly anticommunist) labor leader, and it adopted the slogan "Communism is twentieth-century Americanism." In its heyday, the Popular Front did much to enhance the reputation and influence of the Communist party, whose formal membership grew to perhaps 100,000 in the mid-1930s, the highest it had ever been or ever would be again. But it also helped mobilize writers, artists, and intellectuals—many of them unconnected with (and many of them uninterested in) the Communist Party—behind a pattern of social criticism.

For some intellectuals, the Popular Front offered an escape from the lonely and difficult stance of detachment and alienation many had embraced in the 1920s. The importance to many American in-

Spanish Civil War

tellectuals of the Spanish Civil War of the mid-1930s was a good example of how the left helped give meaning and purpose to individual lives. The war in Spain pitted the fascists of Francisco Franco (who was receiving support from Hitler and Mussolini) against the existing republican government. It attracted a substantial group of young Americans—more than 3,000 in all—who formed the Abraham Lincoln Brigade and traveled to Spain to join in the fight against the fascists. About a third of its members died in combat; but those who survived remembered the experience with pride, as one of the great moments of their lives. Ernest Hemingway, who spent time as a correspondent in Spain during the conflict, wrote in his novel *For Whom the Bell Tolls* (1940) of how the war provided those Americans who fought in it with "a part in something which you could believe in wholly and completely and in which you felt an absolute brotherhood with others who were engaged in it." The American Communist Party was instrumental in creating the Lincoln Brigade, and directed many of its activities.

Frank Capra is probably best remembered today for his last successful film, *It's a Wonderful Life* (1946), widely re-played every year at Christmas (sometimes in a new "colorized" version, but usually in its original black and white). In it, George Bailey, a kind and compassionate small-town savings-and-loan operator (played by Jimmy Stewart) is almost destroyed by a wealthy, greedy, and malicious banker. In despair and contemplating suicide, Bailey receives a visit from an angel who shows him what life in his community, Bedford Falls, would have been like had George never been born. After a few hours of wandering through a coarse, corrupt,

degraded version of the town he knew, Bailey comes to understand the value of his own life. He returns to the real Bedford Falls to find that his family, friends, and neighbors have rallied together to rescue him from his financial difficulties and affirm his value to them, and theirs to him.

By the time *It's a Wonderful Life* appeared, Frank Capra had been the most famous and successful director in Hollywood for more than a decade. His films during those years had almost all been great commercial and critical successes. They had won two Academy Awards for best picture (and Capra himself had won an award as best

director). Capra's popularity was a result in part of his tremendous talent as a director. But it was also a result of his vision. Most of his films expressed a vision of society, and of politics, that resonated clearly with the concerns of millions of Americans as they struggled through the years of the Great Depression.

Capra was born in 1897 in a small village in Sicily and moved with his family to America six years later. After working his way through college, he found a job in the still-young movie industry in California and eventually became a director of feature films. His great breakthrough came in 1934 with *It Happened One Night,* a now-classic comedy that won five major Academy Awards including best picture and best director. Over the next seven years, he built on that success by making a series of more pointed films through which he established himself as a powerful voice of an old-fashioned vision of democracy and American life.

Capra made no secret of his romantic image of the small town and the common man, his distaste for cities, his contempt for opportunistic politicians, and his condemnation of what he considered the amoral (and often immoral) capitalist marketplace. In *Mr. Deeds Goes to Town* (1936), a simple man from a small town inherits a large fortune, moves to the city, and—not liking the greed and dishonesty he finds there—gives the money away and moves back home. In *Mr. Smith Goes to Washington* (1939), a decent man from a western state is elected to the United States Senate, refuses to join in the self-interested politics of Washington, and dramatically exposes the corruption and selfishness of his

MR. DEEDS GOES TO TOWN Gary Cooper, playing the newly wealthy Longfellow Deeds, leaves the friendly, virtuous small town of Mandrake Falls en route to New York to receive the fortune he has inherited. Capra's evocation of the warmth and generosity of Mandrake Falls was part of his effort to contrast the decent America of ordinary people with the grasping and corrupt America of the wealthy and the city. *(Photofest)*

The Communist Party was active as well in organizing the unemployed in the early 1930s and staged a hunger march in Washington, D.C., in 1931. Party members were among the most effective union organizers in some industries. And the party was virtually alone among political organizations in taking a firm stand in favor of racial justice; its active defense of the Scottsboro defendants was but one example of its efforts to ally itself with the aspirations of African Americans. It also helped organize a

union of black sharecroppers in Alabama, which resisted—in several instances violently—efforts of white landowners and authorities to displace them from their farms.

The American Communist Party was not, however, the open, patriotic organization it tried to appear. It was always under the close and rigid supervision of the Soviet Union. Its leaders took their orders from the Comintern in Moscow. Most members obediently followed the

PROMOTING CAPRA Capra was unusual among directors of the 1930s in having a distinct following of his own. Most films attempted to attract audiences by highlighting their stars. Capra films highlighted Capra himself. *(Photofest)*

colleagues. (The rugged western actor Gary Cooper portrayed Mr. Deeds, and Jimmy Stewart played Mr. Smith.) In *Meet John Doe* (1941), released on the brink of American entry into World War II, an ordinary man—played again by Gary Cooper—is manipulated by a fascist cartel to dupe the public on their behalf. He comes to his senses just in time and, by threatening suicide, rallies ordinary people to turn against the malign plans of the fascists. He then disappears into the night.

Capra was entirely conscious of the romantic populism that he brought to

his films. "I would sing the songs of the working stiffs, of the short-changed Joes, the born poor, the afflicted," he once wrote (in an apparent allusion to Walt Whitman). "I would fight for their causes on the screens of the world." He was intensely patriotic, in a way characteristic of many successful immigrants, and he believed fervently that America stood for individual opportunity and was defined by the decency of ordinary people. He was not, he said (in an effort to distance himself from the communists), a "bleeding-heart with an Olympian call to 'free the masses.'" He did not like the term "masses," and found it "insulting, degrading." He saw the people, rather, as a "collection of free individuals . . . each an island of human dignity."

When America entered World War II, Capra collaborated with the government (and the Walt Disney studios) to make a series of films designed to explain to new soldiers what the war was about—a series known as *Why We Fight.* They contrasted the individualistic democracy of the American small town with the dark collectivism of the Nazis and Fascists. Capra poured into them all his skills as a filmmaker and all his romantic, patriotic images. *It's a Wonderful Life,* released a year after the war, continued his evocation of the decency of ordinary people.

In the decades that followed, Capra—although he was still a relatively young man and although he continued to work—ceased to be an important force in American cinema. The sentimental populism and comic optimism that had been so appealing to audiences during the hard years of the Depression and the war gave way

CAPRA ON THE SET Frank Capra, seated, poses with members of his camera crew and the relatively simple cameras available to filmmakers in the 1930s. *(Culver Pictures, Inc.)*

to a harder, more realistic style of filmmaking in the 1950s and 1960s; and Capra—a romantic to the end—was never fully able to adjust. But in a time of crisis, Capra had helped his audiences find solace in his romantic vision of the American past—in the warmth and goodness of small towns and the decency of ordinary people.

"party line" (although there were many areas in which Communists were active for which there was no party line, areas in which members acted independently). The subordination of the party leadership to the Soviet Union was most clearly demonstrated in 1939, when Stalin signed a nonaggression pact with Nazi Germany. Moscow then sent orders to the American Communist Party to abandon the Popular Front and return to its old stance of harsh criticism of American liberals; and Communist

Party leaders in the United States immediately obeyed—although thousands of disillusioned members left the party as a result.

The Socialist Party of America, now under the leadership of Norman Thomas, also cited the economic crisis as evidence of the failure of capitalism and sought vigorously to win public support for its own political program. Among other things, it attempted to mobilize support among the rural poor. The Southern Tenant Farmers

Union, supported by the party and organized by a young socialist, H. L. Mitchell, attempted to create a biracial coalition of sharecroppers, tenant farmers, and others to demand economic reform. Neither the STFU nor the party itself, however, made any real progress toward establishing socialism as a major force in American politics. By 1936, in fact, membership in the Socialist Party had fallen below 20,000.

Southern Tenant Farmers Union

Antiradicalism was a powerful force in the 1930s, just as it had been during and after World War I and would be again in the 1940s and 1950s. Hostility toward the Communist Party, in particular, was intense at many levels of government. Congressional committees chaired by Hamilton Fish of New York and Martin Dies of Texas investigated communist influence wherever they could find it (or imagine it). State and local governments harried and sometimes imprisoned communist organizers. White southerners tried to drive communist organizers out of the countryside, just as growers in California and elsewhere tried (unsuccessfully) to keep communists from organizing Mexican-American and other workers.

Even so, at few times before (and few since) in American history did being part of the left seem so respectable and even conventional among workers, intellectuals, and others. Thus the 1930s witnessed an impressive, if temporary, widening of the ideological range of mainstream art and politics. The New Deal, for example, sponsored artistic work through the Works Projects Administration that was frankly challenging to the

The Left's Newfound Respectability

capitalist norms of the 1920s. The filmmaker Pare Lorentz, with funding from New Deal agencies, made a series of powerful and polemical documentaries—*The Plow that Broke the Plains* (1936), *The River* (1937)—that combined a celebration of New Deal programs with a harsh critique of the exploitation of people and the environment that industrial capitalism had produced.

A less confrontational grappling with the social misery of the 1930s was a remarkable book by the novelist James Agee and the photographer Walker Evans, *Let Us Now Praise Famous Men* (1941). Agee and Walker had traveled to rural Alabama in the mid-1930s on an assignment from *Fortune* magazine, a business-oriented periodical published by Henry Luce (who was also the founder and publisher of *Time* and *Life*). Luce was in most respects a conservative defender of capitalism and its leaders; but he was also insatiably curious, and he used *Fortune* at times to explore distressed areas of the nation's economic life. He had asked Agee and Walker to produce an article on sharecropping and rural poverty. The long, rambling, highly emotional text that Agee produced, accompanied by extraordinary photographs of three families of white southern sharecroppers, was much too long and unconventional for *Fortune*. But the book that eventually appeared, although it attracted little attention at the time, was an enduring portrait of a distressed area of what Agee called "human existence," but also a passionate tribute to the strength and even nobility of the struggling people he had come to know.

Perhaps the most successful chronicler of social conditions in the 1930s was the novelist John Steinbeck, particularly in his celebrated novel *The Grapes of Wrath*,

THE GRAPES OF WRATH This still from John Ford's 1940 film adaptation of John Steinbeck's *The Grapes of Wrath* shows the Joad family climbing into their truck to begin their difficult journey from Oklahoma to California. Ma Joad (portrayed by Jane Darwell) stands at left taking a last anguished look at her home. Tom Joad (Henry Fonda) says good-bye to some friends. The Joad family became symbols to many Americans of the hundreds of thousands of farmers who left their lands in the "Dust Bowl" in the 1930s in search of greater opportunities in California. *(Everett Collection)*

published in 1939. In telling the story of the Joad family, migrants from the Dust Bowl to California who encounter *The Grapes of Wrath* an unending string of calamities and failures, he offered a harsh portrait of the exploitive features of agrarian life in the West, but also a tribute to the endurance of his main characters—and to the spirit of community they represent.

THE ORDEAL OF HERBERT HOOVER

Herbert Hoover began his presidency in March 1929 believing, like most Americans, that the nation faced a bright and prosperous future. For the first six months of his administration, he attempted to expand the policies he had advocated during his eight years as secretary of commerce, policies that would, he believed, complete a stable system of cooperative individualism and sustain a successful economy. The economic crisis that began before the year was out forced the president to deal with a new set of problems, but for most of the rest of his term, he continued to rely on the principles that had always governed his public life.

The Hoover Program

Hoover's first response to the Depression was to attempt to restore public confidence in the economy. "The fundamental business of this country, that is, production and distribution of commodities," he said in 1930, "is on a sound and prosperous basis." He then summoned leaders of business, labor, and agriculture to the White House and urged them to adopt a program of voluntary cooperation for recovery. He implored businessmen not to cut production or lay off workers; he talked labor leaders into forgo- *Failure of Voluntarism* ing demands for higher wages or better hours. But by mid-1931, economic conditions had deteriorated so much that the structure of voluntary cooperation he had erected collapsed.

Hoover also attempted to use government spending as a tool for fighting the Depression. The president proposed to Congress an increase of $423 million—a significant sum by the standards of the time—in federal public works programs, and he exhorted state and local governments to fund public construction. But the spending was not nearly enough in the face of such devastating problems. And when economic conditions worsened, he became less willing to increase spending, worrying instead about keeping the budget balanced. In 1932, at the depth of the Depression, he proposed a tax increase to help the government avoid a deficit.

Even before the stock market crash, Hoover had begun to construct a program to assist the already troubled agricultural economy. In April 1929, he proposed the Agricultural *Agricultural Marketing Act* Marketing Act, which established the first major government program to help farmers maintain prices. A federally sponsored Farm Board would make loans to national marketing cooperatives or establish corporations to buy surpluses and thus raise prices. At the same time, Hoover attempted to protect

HOOVER THE PATRICIAN Although Herbert Hoover grew up in a family of modest means in a small town in Iowa, his critics in the 1930s delighted in portraying him as an aloof aristocrat, fond of fancy dinners and cigars. As this photograph of a formal banquet suggests, Hoover gave them many opportunities to strengthen that image.

American farmers from international competition by rais-ing agricultural tariffs. The Hawley-Smoot Tariff of 1930 contained increased protection on seventy-five farm products. But neither the Agricultural Marketing Act nor the Hawley-Smoot Tariff ultimately helped American farm-ers significantly.

By the spring of 1931, Herbert Hoover's political posi-tion had deteriorated considerably. In the 1930 congres-sional elections, Democrats won control of the House and made substantial inroads in the Senate by promising in-creased government assistance to the economy. Many

Hoover's Declining Popularity

Americans held the president personally to blame for the cri-sis and began calling the shanty-towns that unemployed people established on the out-skirts of cities "Hoovervilles." Democrats urged the president to support more vigorous programs of relief and public spending. Hoover, instead, seized on a slight improvement in economic conditions early in 1931 as proof that his policies were working.

The international financial panic of the spring of 1931 destroyed the illusion that the economic crisis was coming to an end. Throughout the 1920s, European na-tions had depended on loans from American banks to al-low them to make payments on their debts. After 1929, when they could no longer get such loans, the financial fabric of several European nations began to unravel. In May 1931, the largest bank in Austria collapsed. Over the next several months, panic gripped the financial institu-tions of neighboring countries. The American economy rapidly declined to new lows.

By the time Congress convened in December 1931, conditions had grown so desperate that Hoover supported a series of measures designed to keep endangered banks afloat and protect homeowners from foreclosure on their mortgages. More important was a bill passed in January 1932 establishing the Reconstruction

Reconstruction Finance Corporation

Finance Corporation (RFC), a government agency whose purpose was to provide federal loans to troubled banks, railroads, and other businesses. It even made funds avail-able to local governments to support public works projects and assist relief efforts. Unlike some earlier Hoover pro-grams, it operated on a large scale. In 1932, the RFC had a budget of $1.5 billion for public works alone.

Nevertheless, the new agency failed to deal directly or forcefully enough with the real problems of the economy to produce any significant recovery. The RFC lent funds only to financial institutions with sufficient collateral; much of its money went to large banks and corporations. At Hoover's insistence, it helped finance only those public works projects that promised ultimately to pay for them-selves (toll bridges, public housing, and others). Above all, the RFC did not have enough money to make any real im-pact on the Depression, and it did not even spend all the money it had. Of the $300 million available to support lo-cal relief efforts, the RFC lent out only $30 million in 1932. Of the $1.5 billion public works budget, it released only about 20 percent.

Popular Protest

For the first several years of the Depression, most Americans were either too stunned or too confused to raise any effective protest. By the middle of 1932, however, dissident voices began to be heard.

HOOVERTOWN, NEVADA, 1937 Even in 1937, more than four years after he left office, Herbert Hoover remained a symbol to many Americans of the despair of the Great Depression. This shantytown for otherwise homeless people in Nevada was still known as Hoovertown by its residents and their neighbors. *(Bettmann/Corbis)*

In the summer of 1932, a group of unhappy farm owners gathered in Des Moines, Iowa, to establish a new organization: the Farmers' Holiday Association, which endorsed the withholding of farm products from the market—in effect a farmers' strike. The strike began in August in western Iowa, spread briefly to a few neighboring areas, and succeeded in blockading several markets, but in the end it dissolved in failure.

Farmers' Holiday Association

A more celebrated protest movement emerged from American veterans. In 1924, Congress had approved the payment of a $1,000 bonus to all those who had served in World War I, the money to be paid beginning in 1945. By 1932, however, many veterans were demanding that the bonus be paid immediately. Hoover, concerned about balancing the budget, rejected their appeal. In June, more than 20,000 veterans, members of the self-proclaimed Bonus Expeditionary Force, or "Bonus Army," marched into Washington, built crude camps around the city, and promised to stay until Congress approved legislation to pay the bonus. Some of the veterans departed in July, after Congress had voted down their proposal. Many, however, remained where they were.

Their continued presence in Washington embarrassed President Hoover. Finally, in mid-July, he ordered police to clear the marchers out of several abandoned federal buildings in which they had been staying. A few marchers threw rocks at the police, and someone opened fire; two veterans fell dead. Hoover called the incident evidence of uncontrolled violence and radicalism, and he ordered the United States Army to assist the police in clearing out the buildings.

General Douglas MacArthur, the army chief of staff, carried out the mission himself (with the assistance of his aide, Dwight D. Eisenhower) and greatly exceeded the president's orders. He led the Third Cavalry (under the command of George S. Patton), two infantry regiments, a machine-gun detachment, and six tanks down Pennsylvania Avenue in pursuit of the Bonus Army. The veterans fled in terror. MacArthur followed them across the Anacostia River, where he ordered the soldiers to burn their tent city to the ground. More than 100 marchers were injured.

Demise of the Bonus Army

The incident served as perhaps the final blow to Hoover's already battered political standing. Hoover's own cold and gloomy personality reinforced the public image of

CLEARING OUT THE BONUS MARCHERS In July 1932, President Hoover ordered the Washington, D.C., police to evict the Bonus Marchers from some of the public buildings and land they had been occupying. The result was a series of pitched battles (one of them visible here), in which both veterans and police sustained injuries. Such skirmishes persuaded Hoover to call out the army to finish the job. *(Bettmann/Corbis)*

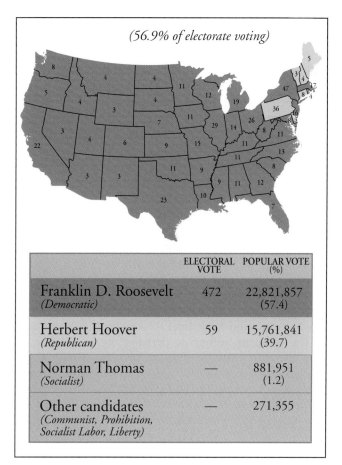

(56.9% of electorate voting)

	ELECTORAL VOTE	POPULAR VOTE (%)
Franklin D. Roosevelt *(Democratic)*	472	22,821,857 (57.4)
Herbert Hoover *(Republican)*	59	15,761,841 (39.7)
Norman Thomas *(Socialist)*	—	881,951 (1.2)
Other candidates *(Communist, Prohibition, Socialist Labor, Liberty)*	—	271,355

ELECTION OF 1932 Like the election of 1928, the election of 1932 was exceptionally one-sided. But this time, the landslide favored the Democratic candidate, Franklin Roosevelt, who overwhelmed Herbert Hoover in all regions of the country except New England. Roosevelt obviously benefited primarily from popular disillusionment with Hoover's response to the Great Depression.   ◆ *But what characteristics of Roosevelt himself contributed to his victory?*

 For an interactive version of this map go to www.mhhe.com/brinkley11ch25maps

THE CHANGING OF THE GUARD Long before the event actually occurred, Peter Arno of the *New Yorker* magazine drew this image of Franklin D. Roosevelt and Herbert Hoover traveling together to the Capitol for Roosevelt's inauguration. It predicted with remarkable accuracy the mood of the uncomfortable ride—Hoover glum and uncommunicative, Roosevelt buoyant and smiling. This was to have been the magazine's cover for the week of the inauguration, but after an attempted assassination of the president-elect several weeks earlier in Florida (in which the mayor of Chicago was killed), the editors decided to substitute a more subdued drawing. *(Franklin Delano Roosevelt Library)*

him as aloof and unsympathetic to distressed people. The Great Engineer, the personification of the optimistic days of the 1920s, had become a symbol of the nation's failure to deal effectively with its startling reversal of fortune.

The Election of 1932

As the 1932 presidential election approached, few people doubted the outcome. The Republican Party dutifully *FDR Nominated* renominated Herbert Hoover for a second term of office, but the gloomy atmosphere of the convention made it clear that few delegates believed he could win. The Democrats, in the meantime, gathered jubilantly in Chicago to nominate the governor of New York, Franklin Delano Roosevelt.

Roosevelt had been a well-known figure in the party for many years already. A Hudson Valley aristocrat, a distant cousin of Theodore Roosevelt (a connection strengthened by his marriage in 1904 to the president's niece, Eleanor), and a handsome, charming young man, he progressed rapidly: from a seat in the New York State legislature to a position as assistant secretary of the navy under Woodrow Wilson during World War I to his party's vice presidential nomination in 1920 on the ill-fated ticket with James M. Cox. Less than a year later, he was stricken with polio. Although he never regained use of his legs (and could walk only by using crutches and braces), he built up sufficient physical strength to return to politics in 1928. When Al Smith received the Democratic nomination for president that year, Roosevelt was elected to succeed him as governor. In 1930, he easily won reelection.

Roosevelt worked no miracles in New York, but he did initiate enough positive programs of government assistance to be able to present himself as a more energetic and imaginative leader than Hoover. In national politics, he avoided such divisive cultural issues as religion and prohibition and emphasized the economic grievances that most Democrats shared. He was able as a result to assemble a broad coalition within the party and win his party's nomination. In a dramatic break with tradition, he flew to Chicago to address the convention in person and accept the nomination. In the course of his acceptance speech, Roosevelt aroused the delegates with his ringing promise:"I pledge you, I pledge myself, to a new deal for the American people," giving his future program a name that would long endure. Neither then nor in the subsequent campaign did Roosevelt give much indication of what that program would be. But Herbert Hoover's unpopularity virtually ensured Roosevelt's election.

In November, to the surprise of no one, Roosevelt won by a landslide. He received 57.4 percent of the popular *1932 Election* vote to Hoover's 39.7. In the electoral college, the result was even more overwhelming. Hoover carried Pennsylvania, Connecticut, Vermont, New Hampshire, and Maine. Roosevelt won everything else. Democrats won majorities in both houses of Congress. It was a broad and convincing mandate, but it was not yet clear what Roosevelt intended to do with it.

The "Interregnum"

The period between the election and the inauguration (which in the early 1930s lasted more than four months) was a season of growing economic crisis. Presidents-elect traditionally do not involve themselves directly in government. But in a series of brittle exchanges with Roosevelt in the months following the election, Hoover tried to exact from the president-elect a pledge to maintain policies of economic orthodoxy. Roosevelt genially refused.

In February, only a month before the inauguration, a new crisis developed when the collapse of the American banking system suddenly and rapidly accelerated. Public confidence in the banks was ebbing; depositors were withdrawing their money in panic; and one bank after another was closing its doors and declaring bankruptcy. Hoover again asked Roosevelt to give prompt public assurances that there would be no tinkering with the currency, no heavy borrowing, no unbalancing of the budget. Roosevelt again refused. *Banking Crisis*

March 4, 1933, was, therefore, a day of both economic crisis and considerable personal bitterness. On that morning, Herbert Hoover, convinced that the United States was headed for disaster, rode glumly down Pennsylvania Avenue with a beaming, buoyant Franklin Roosevelt, who would shortly be sworn in as the thirty-second president of the United States

CONCLUSION

The Great Depression, which began so unexpectedly and spread so quickly and widely, changed many things in American life. It created unemployment on a scale never before experienced in the nation's history. It put enormous pressures on families, on communities, on state and local governments, and ultimately on Washington—which during the innovative but ultimately failed presidency of Herbert Hoover was unable to produce policies capable of dealing effectively with the crisis. In the nation's politics and culture, the Depression provoked strong currents of radicalism and protest; and many middle-class Americans came to fear (and many less affluent people to hope) that a revolution might be approaching.

In reality, while the Great Depression shook much of American society and culture, it actually toppled very little. The capitalist system survived, damaged for a time but never truly threatened. The widely shared values of materialism and personal responsibility were shaken, but never overturned. The American people in the 1930s were more receptive than they had been in the 1920s to evocations of community, generosity, and the dignity of common people. They were more open to experiments in government and business and even private lives than they had been in earlier years. But for most Americans, belief in the "American way of life"—a phrase that became widely resonant in the 1930s for the first time—remained strong throughout the long years of economic despair.

FOR FURTHER REFERENCE

Donald Worster scathingly indicts agricultural capitalism for its destruction of the plains environment in *Dust Bowl: The Southern Plains in the 1930s* (1979). In *The Great Depression: Delayed Recovery and Economic Change in America, 1929–1939* (1987), Michael Bernstein argues that we should ask not so much why the economy crashed in 1929 but rather why the expected recovery from the crash was so slow. Richard Pells, *Radical Visions and American Dreams: Culture and Social Thought in the Depression Years* (1973) is an important survey of the cultural and intellectual history of the 1930s. Studs Terkel, *Hard Times* (1970) is an excellent oral history of the Depression. Susan Ware analyzes the effect of the Great Depression on women in *Holding Their Own: American Women in the 1930s* (1982). The Communist Party's most popular period in the United States is the subject of Harvey Klehr's *The Heyday of American Communism: The Depression Decade* (1984) and, from quite different viewpoints, Robin D. G. Kelley, *Hammer and Hoe: Alabama Communists During the Great Depression* (1990) and Michael Denning, *The Cultural Front: The Laboring of American Culture in the Twentieth Century* (1997). Joan Hoff Wilson, *Herbert Hoover: Forgotten Progressive* (1975) argues that President Hoover was in many ways a surprisingly progressive thinker about the American social order.

The Great Depression (1993), a multipart film by Blackside Productions, is an eloquent picture of many aspects of the depression decade. *Union Maids* (1997) is a vivid film history of women organizing in the 1930s. *The Lemon Grove Incident* (1985) is a film providing a rare glimpse of Mexican-American civil rights activism over school integration in the early 1930s.

For quizzes, Internet resources, references to additional books and films, and more, consult the book's Online Learning Center at www.mhhe.com/brinkley 11.

WPA POSTER, 1930S The Works Progress Administration, which this striking poster celebrates, was the New Deal's most prominent experiment in work relief. In addition to providing jobs for unemployed farmers and industrial workers (as depicted here), it created programs to assist writers, artists, actors, and others. *(Library of Congress)*

Significant Events

1933 · Franklin Roosevelt inaugurated
· "First New Deal" legislation enacted (see p. 725)
· United States officially abandons gold standard
· Twenty-first Amendment ends prohibition with repeal of Eighteenth Amendment
· Dr. Francis Townsend begins campaign for old-age pensions

1934 · Conservatives create American Liberty League
· Huey Long establishes Share-Our-Wealth Society
· Labor militancy increases
· Indian Reorganization Act passed

1935 · Supreme Court invalidates NRA

CHAPTER TWENTY-SIX

THE NEW DEAL

*F*ranklin Roosevelt served longer as president than anyone else before or since, and during his twelve years in office he became more central to the life of the nation than any chief executive before him. Most important, his administration constructed a series of programs that permanently altered the federal government and its relationship to society.

By the end of the 1930s, the New Deal (as the Roosevelt program was called) had created many of the broad outlines of the political world we know today. It had constructed the foundations of the federal welfare system. It had extended national regulation over new areas of the economy. It had presided over the birth of the modern labor movement. It had made the government a major force in the agricultural economy. It had created a powerful coalition within the Democratic Party that would dominate American politics for most of the next thirty years. And it had produced the beginnings of a new liberal ideology that would govern reform efforts for several decades after the war.

One thing the New Deal had not done, however, was end the Great Depression. It had helped stop the disastrous downward spiral in 1933, and there had been a limited, if erratic, recovery in some areas after that. But by the end of 1939, many of the basic problems of the Depression remained unsolved. An estimated 15 percent of the work force remained unemployed. The gross national product was no larger than it had been ten years before.

LAUNCHING THE NEW DEAL

Roosevelt's first task upon taking office was to alleviate the panic that was threatening to create chaos in the financial system. He did so in part by force of personality and in part by constructing very rapidly an ambitious and diverse program of legislation.

Restoring Confidence

Much of Roosevelt's success was a result of his ebullient personality. Beginning with his inaugural address—in which he assured the American people that "the only thing we have to fear is fear itself," and promised to take drastic, even warlike, action against the emergency. He projected an infectious optimism that helped alleviate the growing despair. He was the first president to make regular use of the radio, and his friendly "fireside chats," during which he explained his programs and plans to the people, helped build public confidence in the administration. Roosevelt held frequent informal press conferences and won the respect and the friendship of most reporters. Their regard for him was such that by unwritten agreement, no journalist ever photographed the president getting into or out of his car or being wheeled in his wheelchair. Much of the American public remained unaware throughout the Roosevelt years that the president's legs were completely paralyzed.

Roosevelt's Personality

But Roosevelt could not rely on image alone. On March 6, two days after taking office, he issued a proclamation closing all American banks for four days until Congress could meet in special session to consider banking-reform legislation. So great was the panic about bank failures that

THE RADIO PRESIDENT Franklin D. Roosevelt was the first American president to master the use of radio. Beginning in his first days in office, he regularly bypassed the newspapers (many of which were hostile to him) and communicated directly with the people through his famous "fireside chats." He is shown here speaking in 1938, urging communities to continue to provide work relief for the unemployed. *(Franklin D. Roosevelt Library)*

the "bank holiday," as the president euphemistically described it, created a general sense of relief. Three days later, Roosevelt sent to Congress the Emergency Banking Act, a generally conservative bill (much of it drafted by holdovers from the Hoover administration) designed primarily to protect the larger banks from being dragged down by the weakness of smaller ones. The bill provided for Treasury Department inspection of all banks before they would be allowed to reopen, for federal assistance to some troubled institutions, and for a thorough reorganization of those in the greatest difficulty. A confused and frightened Congress passed the bill within four hours of its introduction. "I can assure you," Roosevelt told the public on March 12, in his first fireside chat, "that it is safer to keep your money in a reopened bank than under the mattress." Whatever else the new law accomplished, it helped dispel the panic. Three quarters of the banks in the Federal Reserve system reopened within the next three days, and $1 billion in hoarded currency and gold flowed back into them within a month. The immediate banking crisis was over.

"Bank Holiday"

On the morning after passage of the Emergency Banking Act, Roosevelt sent to Congress another measure—the Economy Act—designed to convince fiscally conservative Americans (and especially the business community) that the federal government was in safe, responsible hands. The act proposed to balance the federal budget by cutting the salaries of government employees and reducing pensions to veterans by as much as 15 percent. Otherwise, the president warned, the nation faced a $1 billion deficit. Like the banking bill, this one passed through Congress almost instantly—despite heated protests from some congressional progressives.

Roosevelt also moved in his first days in office to put to rest one of the divisive issues of the 1920s. He supported and then signed a bill to legalize the manufacture and sale of beer with a 3.2 percent alcohol content—an interim measure pending the repeal of prohibition, for which a constitutional amendment (the Twenty-first) was already in process. The amendment was ratified later in 1933.

Prohibition Repealed

Agricultural Adjustment

These initial actions were largely stopgaps, to buy time for more comprehensive programs. The first was the Agricultural Adjustment Act, which Congress passed in May 1933. Its most important feature was its provision for reducing crop production to end agricultural surpluses and halt the downward spiral of farm prices.

Under the provisions of the act, producers of seven basic commodities (wheat, cotton, corn, hogs, rice, tobacco, and dairy products) would decide on production limits for their crops. The government, through the Agricultural

Adjustment Administration (AAA), would then tell individual farmers how much they should produce and *AAA* would pay them subsidies for leaving some of their land idle. A tax on food processing (for example, the milling of wheat) would provide the funds for the new payments. Farm prices were to be subsidized up to the point of parity.

The AAA helped bring about a rise in prices for farm commodities in the years after 1933. Gross farm income increased by half in the first three years of the New Deal, and the agricultural economy as a whole emerged from the 1930s much more stable and prosperous than it had been in many years. The AAA did, however, favor larger farmers over smaller ones, particularly since local administration of its programs often fell into the hands of the most powerful producers in a community. By distributing payments to landowners, not those who worked the land, the government did little to discourage planters who were reducing their acreage from evicting tenants and sharecroppers and firing field hands.

In January 1936, the Supreme Court struck down the crucial provisions of the Agricultural Adjustment Act, arguing that the government had no constitutional authority to require farmers to limit production. But within a few weeks the administration had secured passage of new legislation (the Soil Conservation and Domestic Allotment Act), which permitted the government to pay farmers to reduce production so as to "conserve soil," prevent erosion, and accomplish other secondary goals. The Court did not interfere with the new laws.

The administration launched several efforts to assist poor farmers as well. The Resettlement Administration, established in 1935, and its successor, the Farm Security Administration, created in 1937, provided loans to help farmers cultivating submarginal soil to relocate to better lands. But the programs never moved more than a few thousand farmers. More effective was the Rural Electrification Administration, created in 1935, which worked to make *Rural Electrification* electric power available for the first time to thousands of farmers through utility cooperatives.

Industrial Recovery

Ever since 1931, leaders of the United States Chamber of Commerce and many others had been urging the government to adopt an antideflation scheme that would permit trade associations to cooperate in stabilizing prices within their industries. Existing antitrust laws clearly forbade such practices, and Herbert Hoover had refused to endorse suspension of the laws. The Roosevelt administration was more receptive. In exchange for relaxing antitrust provisions, however, New Dealers insisted on other provisions. Business leaders would have to make important concessions to labor—recognize the workers' right to bargain collectively through unions—to ensure that the incomes of workers would rise along with prices. And to help create jobs and increase consumer buying power, the administration added a major program of public works spending. The result of these and many other impulses was the National Industrial Recovery Act, which Congress passed in June 1933.

At first, the new program appeared to work miracles. At its center was a new federal agency, the National Recovery Administration (NRA), under the direction of the flam- *NRA* boyant and energetic Hugh S. Johnson. Johnson called on every business establishment in the nation to accept a temporary "blanket code": a minimum wage of between 30 and 40 cents an hour, a maximum workweek of thirty-five

SALUTING THE BLUE EAGLE Several thousand San Francisco schoolchildren assembled on a baseball field in 1933 to form the symbol of the National Recovery Administration: an eagle clutching a cogwheel (to symbolize industry) and a thunderbolt (to symbolize energy). This display is evidence of the widespread (if brief) popular enthusiasm the NRA produced. NRA administrators drew from their memories of World War I Liberty Loan drives and tried to establish the Blue Eagle as a symbol of patriotic commitment to recovery. *(Bettmann/Corbis)*

to forty hours, and the abolition of child labor. Adherence to the code, he claimed, would raise consumer purchasing power and increase employment. At the same time, Johnson negotiated another, more specific set of codes with leaders of the nation's major industries. These industrial codes set floors below which no company would lower prices or wages in its search for a competitive advantage, and they included provisions for maintaining employment and production. He quickly won agreements from almost every major industry in the country.

From the beginning, however, the NRA encountered serious difficulties. The codes themselves were hastily and often poorly written. Administering them was beyond the capacities of federal officials with no prior experience in running so vast a program. Large producers consistently dominated the code-writing process and ensured that the new regulations would work to their advantage and to the disadvantage of smaller firms. And the codes at times did more than simply set floors under prices; they actively

and artificially raised them—sometimes to levels higher than the market could sustain.

Other NRA goals did not progress as quickly as the efforts to raise prices. Section 7(a) of the National Industrial Recovery Act promised workers the right to form unions and *Section 7(a)* engage in collective bargaining and encouraged many workers to join unions for the first time. But Section 7(a) contained no enforcement mechanisms. Hence recognition of unions by employers (and thus the significant wage increases the unions were committed to winning) did not follow. The Public Works Administration (PWA), established to administer the National Industrial Recovery Act's spending programs, only gradually allowed the $3.3 billion in public works funds to trickle out. Not until 1938 was the PWA budget pumping an appreciable amount of money into the economy.

Perhaps the clearest evidence of the NRA's failure was that industrial production actually declined in the months

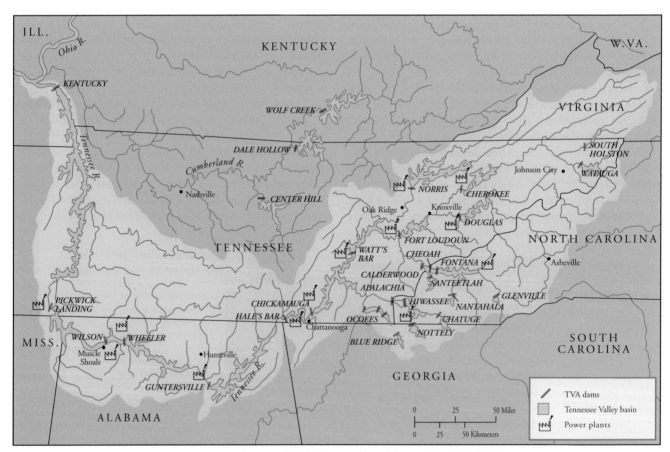

THE TENNESSEE VALLEY AUTHORITY The Tennessee Valley Authority was one of the largest experiments in government-funded public works and regional planning in American history to that point. The federal government had helped fund many projects in its history—canals, turnpikes, railroads, bridges, dams, and others. But never before had it undertaken a project of such great scope, and never before had it maintained such close control and ownership over the public works it helped create. This map illustrates the broad reach of the TVA within the Tennessee Valley region, which spanned seven states. TVA dams throughout the region helped control floods and also provided a source for hydroelectric power, which the government sold to consumers. Note the dam near Muscle Shoals, Alabama, in the bottom left of the map. It was begun during World War I, and efforts to revive it in the 1920s helped create the momentum that produced the TVA. ◆ *Why were progressives so eager to see the government enter the business of hydroelectric power in the 1920s?*

after the agency's establishment—from an index of 101 in July 1933 to 71 in November—despite the rise in prices that the codes had helped to create. By the spring of 1934, the NRA was besieged by criticism, and businessmen were flaunting many of its provisions. That fall, Roosevelt pressured Johnson to resign and established a new board of directors to oversee the NRA. Then in 1935, the Supreme Court intervened.

In 1935, a case came before the Court involving alleged NRA code violations by the Schechter brothers, who operated a wholesale poultry business confined to Brooklyn, New York. The Court ruled unanimously that the Schechters were not engaged in interstate commerce (and thus not subject to federal regulation) and, further, that Congress had unconstitutionally delegated legislative power to the president to draft the NRA codes. The justices struck down the legislation establishing the agency. Roosevelt denounced the justices for their "horse-and-buggy" interpretation of the interstate commerce clause. He was rightly concerned, for the reasoning in the Schechter case threatened many other New Deal programs as well. But the Court's destruction of the NRA itself gave the New Deal a convenient excuse for ending a failed experiment.

Regional Planning

The AAA and the NRA largely reflected the beliefs of New Dealers who favored economic planning but wanted private interests (farmers or business leaders) to dominate the planning process. Other reformers believed that the government itself should be the chief planning agent in the economy. Their most conspicuous success, and one of the most celebrated accomplishments of the New Deal, was an unprecedented experiment in regional planning: the Tennessee Valley Authority (TVA).

The TVA had its roots in a political controversy of the 1920s. Progressive reformers had agitated for years for public development of the na-

TVA

tion's water resources as a source of cheap electric power. In particular, they had urged completion of a great dam at Muscle Shoals on the Tennessee River in Alabama—a dam begun during World War I but left unfinished when the war ended. But opposition from the utilities companies had been too powerful to overcome.

In 1932, however, one of the great utility empires—that of the electricity magnate Samuel Insull—collapsed spectacularly, amid widely publicized exposés of corruption. Hostility to the utilities soon grew so intense that the companies were no longer able to block the public power movement. The result was legislation supported by the president and enacted by Congress in May 1933 creating the Tennessee Valley Authority. The TVA was authorized to complete the dam at Muscle Shoals and build others in the region, and to generate and sell electricity from them

to the public at reasonable rates. It was also intended to be an agent for a comprehensive redevelopment of the entire region: for stopping the disastrous flooding that had plagued the Tennessee Valley for centuries, for encouraging the development of local industries, for supervising a substantial program of reforestation, and for helping farmers improve productivity.

Opposition by conservatives within the administration ultimately blocked many of the ambitious social planning projects proposed by the more visionary TVA administrators, but the Authority revitalized the region in numerous ways. It improved water transportation. It virtually eliminated flooding in the region. It provided electricity to thousands who had never before had it. Throughout the country, largely because of the "yardstick" provided by the TVA's cheap production of electricity, private power rates declined. Even so, the Tennessee Valley remained a generally impoverished region despite the TVA's efforts. And

PUBLIC WORKS Among the most visible products of the New Deal was a vast network of public works in almost all areas of the country, but concentrated particularly in the South and the West. The great dams that the government built in the Tennessee Valley and elsewhere were particularly effective at capturing the public imagination. This dramatic picture by the renowned photographer Margaret Bourke White appeared on the cover of the very first issue of *Life* in 1936, which very quickly became the most popular and successful magazine in America. It shows the Fort Peck Dam on the Missouri River. *(Margaret Bourke White/Life MAGAZINE, Copyright TIME, Inc.)*

like many other New Deal programs, it made no serious effort to challenge local customs and racial prejudices.

Currency, Banks, and the Stock Market

Roosevelt was not an inflationist at heart, but he soon came to consider the gold standard a major obstacle to the restoration of adequate prices. On April 18, 1933, the president made the shift off the gold standard official with an executive order. A few weeks later, Congress passed legislation confirming his decision. By itself, the repudiation of the gold standard meant relatively little. But both before and after the April decision, the administration experimented in various ways with manipulating the value of the dollar—by making substantial purchases of gold and silver and later by establishing a new, fixed standard for the dollar (reducing its gold content substantially from the 1932 amount). The resort to government-managed currency—that is, to a dollar whose value could be raised or lowered by government policy according to economic circumstances—created an important precedent for future federal policies and permanently altered the relationship between the public and private sectors. It did not, however, have any immediate impact on the depressed American economy.

Through other legislation, the early New Deal increased federal authority over previously unregulated or

Glass-Steagall Act

weakly regulated areas of the economy. The Glass-Steagall Act of June 1933 gave the government authority to curb irresponsible speculation by banks. More important, perhaps, it established the Federal Deposit Insurance Corporation, which guaranteed all bank deposits up to $2,500. In other words, even should a bank fail, small depositors would be able to recover their money. Finally, in 1935, Congress passed a major banking act that transferred much of the authority once wielded by the regional Federal Reserve banks to the Federal Reserve Board in Washington.

To protect investors in the stock market, Congress passed the so-called Truth in Securities Act of 1933, requiring corporations issuing new securities to provide full and accurate information about them to the public. Another act of June 1934 established the Securities and

SEC

Exchange Commission (SEC) to police the stock market. Among other things, the establishment of the SEC was an indication of how far the financial establishment had fallen in public estimation. In earlier years, J. P. Morgan and other important financiers could have wielded enough influence to stop such government interference in the financial world. Now Morgan's son and successor could not even get a respectful hearing on Capitol Hill. The criminal trials of a number of once-respected Wall Street figures for grand larceny and fraud (including the conviction and imprisonment of Richard Whitney, onetime head of the New York Stock Exchange and a close

Morgan associate) eroded the public stature of the financial community still further.

The Growth of Federal Relief

The Roosevelt administration did not consider relief to the unemployed its most important task, but it recognized the necessity of doing something to help impoverished Americans survive until the government could revive the economy to the point where relief might not be necessary. Among Roosevelt's first acts as president was the establishment of the Federal Emergency Relief Administration (FERA), which provided cash grants to states to prop up bankrupt relief agencies. To administer the program, he chose the director of the New York State relief agency, Harry Hopkins, who disbursed the FERA grants widely and rapidly. But both Hopkins and Roosevelt had misgivings about establishing a government "dole."

They felt somewhat more comfortable with another form of government assistance: work relief. Thus when it became clear that the FERA grants were not enough, the administration established a second program: the Civil Works Administration (CWA). Between November 1933 and

CWA

April 1934, it put more than 4 million people to work on temporary projects. Some of the projects were of lasting value, such as the construction of roads, schools, and parks; others were little more than make-work. To Hopkins, however, the important thing was pumping money into an economy badly in need of it and providing assistance to people with nowhere else to turn.

Roosevelt's favorite relief project was the Civilian Conservation Corps (CCC). Established in the first weeks of the new administration, the CCC was designed to provide employ-

CCC

ment to the millions of young men who could find no jobs in the cities. The CCC created camps in national parks and forests and in other rural and wilderness settings. There young men (women were excluded from the program) worked in a semimilitary environment on such projects as planting trees, building reservoirs, developing parks, and improving agricultural irrigation. CCC camps were segregated by race. The vast majority of them were restricted to whites, but a few were reserved for blacks, Mexicans, and Indians.

Mortgage relief was a pressing need for millions of farm owners and homeowners. The Farm Credit Administration, which within two years refinanced one-fifth of all farm mortgages in the United States, was one response to that problem. The Frazier-Lemke Farm Bankruptcy Act of 1933 was another. It enabled some farmers to regain their land even after the foreclosure of their mortgages. Despite such efforts, however, 25 percent of all American farm owners had lost their land by 1934. Homeowners were similarly troubled, and in June 1933 the administration established the Home Owners' Loan Corporation, which by 1936 had refinanced the mortgages of more than 1 million householders. A year later, Congress established the Federal Housing Administration to insure mortgages for new construction and home repairs.

THE NEW DEAL IN TRANSITION

Seldom has an American president enjoyed such remarkable popularity as Franklin Roosevelt did during his first two years in office. But by early 1935, with no end to the Depression yet in sight, the New Deal found itself the target of fierce public criticism. In the spring of 1935, partly in response to these growing attacks, Roosevelt launched an ambitious new program of legislation that has often been called the "Second New Deal."

Critics of the New Deal

Some of the most strident attacks on the New Deal came from critics on the right. Roosevelt had tried for a time to conciliate conservatives and business leaders. By the end of 1934, however, it was clear that the American right in general, and much of the corporate world in particular, *American Liberty League* had become irreconcilably hostile to the New Deal. In August 1934, a group of the most fervent (and wealthiest) Roosevelt opponents, led by members of the Du Pont family, formed the American Liberty League, designed specifically to arouse public opposition to the New Deal's "dictatorial" policies and its supposed attacks on free enterprise. But the new organization was never able to expand its constituency much beyond the northern industrialists who had founded it.

Roosevelt's critics on the far left also managed to produce alarm among some supporters of the administration, but like the conservatives, they proved to have only limited strength. The Communist Party, the Socialist Party, and other radical and semiradical organizations were at times harshly critical of the New Deal. But they too failed ever to attract genuine mass support.

More menacing to the New Deal than either the far right or the far left was a group of dissident political movements that defied easy ideological classification. Some gained substantial public support within particular states and regions. And three men succeeded in mobilizing genuinely national followings. Dr. Francis E. Townsend, an elderly California physician, rose from obscurity to lead a movement of more than 5 million members with his plan for federal pensions for the elderly. According to the Townsend Plan, all Americans *Townsend Plan* over the age of sixty would receive monthly government pensions of $200, provided they retired (thus freeing jobs for younger, unemployed Americans) and spent the money in full each month (which would pump needed funds into the economy). By 1935, the Townsend Plan had attracted the support of many older men and women. And while the plan itself made little progress in Congress, the public sentiment behind it helped build support for the Social Security system, which Congress did approve in 1935.

Father Charles E. Coughlin, a Catholic priest in the Detroit suburb of Royal Oak, Michigan, achieved even greater renown through his weekly sermons broadcast nationally over the radio. In later years, Coughlin became notorious for his sympathy for fascism and his outspoken

"AN ATTACK ON THE NEW DEAL" This cartoon by William Gropper appeared in *Vanity Fair* in 1935 to illustrate a long excerpt from an anti-New Deal editorial that had appeared a few weeks before in the Republican newspaper, the New York *Herald Tribune.* The cartoon echoes the newspaper's references to Jonathan Swift's famous satire, *Gulliver's Travels.* In this case, Gulliver is Uncle Sam, and the Lilliputians who tie him down with a thousand tiny cords are New Deal agencies and laws. "Here is a giant if there ever was one," the *Herald Tribune* wrote, "the most powerful nation the world has ever seen. It has the makings of good times, [but] it does not make them. Why? Because the Lilliputians of the New Deal will not let it. These busy little folk cannot bear the thought of letting the great giant, America, escape." *(Courtesy* Vanity Fair ©*1935 (renewed 1963, 1991) by The Condé Nast Publications, Inc.)*

HUEY LONG Few public speakers could arouse a crowd more effectively than Huey Long of Louisiana, known to many as "the Kingfish" (a nickname borrowed from the popular radio show *Amos 'n Andy*). It was Long's effective use of radio, however, that contributed most directly to his spreading national popularity in the early 1930s. *(Culver Pictures, Inc.)*

and on the conservative political oligarchy allied with them. Elected governor in 1928, he launched an assault on his opponents so thorough and forceful that they were soon left *Huey Long* with virtually no political power whatsoever. Many claimed that he had, in effect, become a dictator. But he also maintained the overwhelming support of the Louisiana electorate, in part because of his flamboyant personality and in part because of his solid record of conventional progressive accomplishments: building roads, schools, and hospitals; revising the tax codes; distributing free textbooks; lowering utility rates. Barred by law from succeeding himself as governor, he ran in 1930 for a seat in the United States Senate and won easily.

Long, like Coughlin, supported Franklin Roosevelt for president in 1932. But within six months of Roosevelt's inauguration he had broken with the president. As an alternative to the New Deal, he advocated a drastic program of wealth redistribution, a program he ultimately named the Share-Our-Wealth Plan. The government, he claimed, could end the Depression easily by using the tax system to confiscate the surplus riches of the wealthiest men and women in America and distribute these surpluses to the rest of the population. That would, he claimed, allow the government to guarantee every family a minimum "homestead" of $5,000 and an annual wage of $2,500. In 1934, Long established his own national organization: the Share-Our-Wealth Society, which soon attracted a large following through much of the nation. A poll by the Democratic National Committee in the spring of 1935 disclosed that Long might attract more than 10 percent of the vote if he ran as a third-party candidate, possibly enough to tip a *Share-Our-Wealth Society* close election to the Republicans. Members of the Roosevelt administration considered dissident movements—and the broad popular discontent they represented—a genuine threat to the president. An increasing number of advisers were warning Roosevelt that he would have to do something dramatic to counter their strength.

The "Second New Deal"

Roosevelt launched the so-called Second New Deal in the spring of 1935 in response both to the growing political pressures and to the continuing economic crisis. The new proposals represented, if not a new direction, at least a shift in the emphasis of New Deal policy. Perhaps the most conspicuous change was in the administration's attitude toward big business. Symbolically at least, the president was now willing to attack corporate interests openly. In March, for example, he proposed to Congress an act designed to break up the great utility holding companies, and he spoke harshly of monopolistic control of their industry. The Holding Company Act of 1935 was the result, although furious lobbying by the utilities led to amendments that sharply limited its effects.

anti-semitism. But until at least 1937, he was known primarily as an advocate for changing the banking and currency systems. He proposed a series of monetary reforms—remonetization of silver, issuing of greenbacks, and nationalization of the banking system—that he insisted would restore prosperity and ensure economic justice. At first a warm supporter of Franklin Roosevelt, by late 1934 Coughlin had become disheartened by what he claimed was the president's failure to deal harshly enough with the "money powers." In the spring of 1935, he established his own political organization, the National Union for Social Justice. He was widely believed to have one of the largest regular radio audiences of anyone in America.

Most alarming of all to the administration was the growing national popularity of Senator Huey P. Long of Louisiana. Long had risen to power in his home state through his strident attacks on the banks, oil companies, and utilities

Equally alarming to affluent Americans was a series of tax reforms proposed by the president in 1935, a program conservatives quickly labeled a "soak-the-rich" scheme. Apparently designed to undercut the appeal of Huey Long's Share-Our-Wealth Plan, the Roosevelt proposals called for establishing the highest and most progressive peacetime tax rates in history—although the actual impact of these rates was limited.

The Supreme Court decision in 1935 to strike down the National Industrial Recovery Act also invalidated Section 7(a) of the act, which had guaranteed workers the right to organize and bargain collectively. A group of progressives in Congress led by Senator Robert E. Wagner of

National Labor Relations Board

New York introduced what became the National Labor Relations Act of 1935. The new law, popularly known as the Wagner Act, provided workers with a crucial enforcement mechanism missing from the 1933 law: the National Labor Relations Board (NLRB), which would have power to compel employers to recognize and bargain with legitimate unions. The president was not entirely happy with the bill, but he signed it anyway. That was in large part because American workers themselves had by 1935 become so important and vigorous a force that Roosevelt realized his own political future would depend in part on responding to their demands.

Labor Militancy

The emergence of a powerful trade union movement in the 1930s was one of the most important social and political developments of the decade. It occurred partly in response to government efforts to enhance the power of unions, but it was also a result of the increased militancy of American workers and their leaders. During the 1920s, most workers had displayed relatively little militancy in challenging employers or demanding recognition of their unions. In the 1930s, however, many of the factors that had impeded militancy vanished or grew weaker. Business leaders and industrialists lost (at least temporarily) the ability to control government policies. Equally important, new and more militant labor organizations emerged to challenge the established, relatively conservative unions.

The growing militancy first became obvious in 1934, when newly organized workers (many of them inspired by the collective bargaining provisions of the National Industrial Recovery Act) demonstrated an assertiveness and at times radicalism seldom seen in recent years. Despite the new militancy, however, it was clear that without stronger legal protection, most organizing drives would end in frustration. Once the Wagner Act became law, the search for more effective forms of organization rapidly gained strength in labor ranks.

The American Federation of Labor remained committed to the idea of the craft union: organizing workers on the basis of their skills. But that concept had little to offer unskilled laborers, who now constituted the bulk of the industrial work force. During the 1930s, therefore, a newer

Industrial Unionism

concept of labor organization challenged the craft union ideal: industrial unionism. Advocates of this approach argued that all workers in a particular industry should be organized in a single union, regardless of what functions the workers performed. All autoworkers should be in a single automobile union; all steelworkers should be in a single steel union. United in this way, workers would greatly increase their power.

Leaders of the AFL craft unions for the most part opposed the new concept. But industrial unionism found a number of important advocates, most prominent among them John L. Lewis, the talented, flamboyant, and eloquent leader of the United Mine Workers. At first, Lewis and his allies attempted to work within the AFL, but friction between the new industrial organizations Lewis was promoting and the older craft unions grew rapidly. At the 1935 AFL convention, Lewis became embroiled in a series of angry confrontations (and one celebrated fistfight) with craft union leaders before finally walking out. A few weeks later, he created the Committee on Industrial Organization. When the AFL expelled the new committee and all the industrial unions it represented, Lewis renamed the

CIO

committee the Congress of Industrial Organizations (CIO), established it in 1936 as an organization directly rivaling the AFL, and became its first president.

The CIO expanded the constituency of the labor movement. It was more receptive to women and to blacks than the AFL had been, in part because women and blacks were more likely to be relegated to unskilled jobs and in part because CIO organizing drives targeted previously unorganized industries (textiles, laundries, tobacco factories, and others) where women and minorities constituted much of the work force. The CIO was also a more militant organization than the AFL. By the time of the 1936 schism, it was already engaged in major organizing battles in the automobile and steel industries.

Organizing Battles

Out of several competing auto unions, the United Auto Workers (UAW) was gradually emerging preeminent in the early and mid-1930s. But although it was gaining recruits, it was making little progress in winning recognition from the corporations. In December 1936, however, autoworkers employed a controversial and effective new

Sit-Down Strike

technique for challenging corporate opposition: the sit-down strike. Employees in several General Motors plants in Detroit simply sat down inside the plants, refusing either to work or to leave, thus preventing the company

THE "MEMORIAL DAY MASSACRE" The bitterness of the labor struggles of the 1930s was nowhere more evident than in Chicago in 1937, when striking workers attempting to march on a Republic Steel Plant were brutally attacked by Chicago police, who used clubs, tear gas, and guns to turn the marchers away. Four strikers were killed and many others were injured. *(AP/Wide World Photos)*

from using strikebreakers. The tactic spread to other locations, and by February 1937 strikers had occupied seventeen GM plants. The strikers ignored court orders and local police efforts to force them to vacate the buildings. When Michigan's governor, Frank Murphy, a liberal Democrat, refused to call up the National Guard to clear out the strikers, and when the federal government also refused to intervene on behalf of employers, General Motors relented. In February 1937 it became the first major manufacturer to recognize the UAW; other automobile companies soon did the same. The sit-down strike proved effective for rubber workers and others as well, but it survived only briefly as a labor technique. Its apparent illegality aroused so much public opposition that labor leaders soon abandoned it.

In the steel industry, the battle for unionization was less easily won. In 1936, the Steel Workers' Organizing Committee (SWOC; later the United Steelworkers of America) began a major organizing drive involving thousands of workers and frequent, at times bitter, strikes. In March 1937, to the surprise of almost everyone, United States Steel, the giant of the industry, recognized the union rather than risk a costly strike at a time when it sensed itself on the verge of recovery from the Depression. But the smaller companies (known collectively as "Little Steel") were less accommodating. On Memorial Day 1937, a group of striking workers from Republic Steel gathered with their families for a picnic and demonstration in South Chicago. When they attempted to march peacefully (and legally) toward the steel plant, police opened fire on them. Ten demonstrators were killed; another ninety were wounded. Despite a public outcry against the "Memorial Day Massacre," the harsh tactics of Little Steel companies succeeded. The 1937 strike failed.

But the victory of Little Steel was one of the last gasps of the kind of brutal strikebreaking that had proved so effective in the past. In 1937 alone, there were 4,720 strikes—over 80 percent of them settled in favor of the

Organized Labor's Rapid Growth

unions. By the end of the year, more than 8 million workers were members of unions recognized as official bargaining units by employers (as compared with 3 million in 1932). By 1941, that number had expanded to 10 million and included the workers of Little Steel, whose employers had finally recognized the SWOC.

Social Security

From the first moments of the New Deal, important members of the administration, most notably Secretary of Labor Frances Perkins, had been lobbying for a system of federally sponsored social insurance for the elderly and the unemployed. In 1935, Roosevelt gave public support to what became the Social Security Act, which Congress passed the same year. It established several distinct programs. For the elderly, there were two types of assistance. Those who were presently destitute could receive up to $15 a month in federal assistance. More important for the future, many Americans presently working were incorporated into a pension system, to which they and their employers would contribute by paying a payroll tax; it would provide them with an income on retirement. Pension payments would not begin until 1942 and even then would provide only $10 to $85 a month to recipients. And broad categories of workers (including domestic servants and agricultural laborers, occupations with disproportionate numbers of blacks and women) were excluded from the program. But the act was a crucial first step in building the nation's most important social program for the elderly.

In addition, the Social Security Act created a system of unemployment insurance, which employers alone

Unemployment Insurance

would finance and which made it possible for workers laid off from their jobs to receive temporary government assistance. It also established a system of federal aid to people with disabilities and a program of aid to dependent children.

The framers of the Social Security Act wanted to create a system of "insurance," not "welfare." And the largest programs (old-age pensions and unemployment insurance) were in many ways similar to private insurance programs, with contributions from participants and benefits available to all. But the act also provided considerable direct assistance based on need—to the elderly poor, to those with disabilities, to dependent children and their mothers. These groups were widely perceived to be small and genuinely unable to support themselves. But in later generations the programs

SOCIAL SECURITY POSTER, 1935 Within months of the passage of the Social Security Act of 1935, the new Social Security Board began publicizing the benefits the new system offered to working Americans—the most dramatic of which was a monthly pension to retired Americans who had paid into the system. *(Library of Congress)*

for these groups would expand until they assumed dimensions that the planners of Social Security had neither foreseen nor desired.

New Directions in Relief

Social Security was designed primarily to fulfill long-range goals. But millions of unemployed Americans had immediate needs. To help them, the Roosevelt administration established in 1935 the Works Progress Administration (WPA).

WPA

Like the Civil Works Administration and other earlier efforts, the WPA established a system of work relief for the unemployed. But it was much bigger than the earlier agencies, both in the size of its budget ($5 billion at first) and in the energy and imagination of its operations.

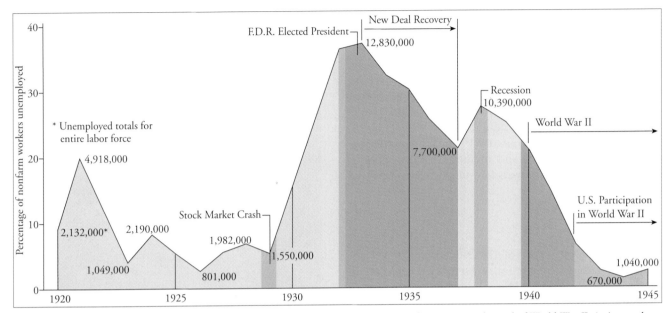

UNEMPLOYMENT, 1920–1945 This chart shows the shifting patterns of unemployment from 1920 to the end of World War II. As it reveals, unemployment was very high in the early 1920s, in the last year of the postwar recession, but remained relatively low from 1923 to 1929. The beginning of the Great Depression sent unemployment soaring—to a peak of nearly 13 million people in early 1933. The New Deal helped create a partial recovery from the Depression over the next four years, but unemployment remained very high throughout the 1930s, and spiked sharply higher again during the recession of 1937–1938, before falling rapidly after war began in Europe. ◆ *Why was the war so much more successful than the New Deal in ending unemployment?*

Under the direction of Harry Hopkins, the WPA was responsible for building or renovating 110,000 public buildings (schools, post offices, government office buildings) and for constructing almost 600 airports, more than 500,000 miles of roads, and over 100,000 bridges. In the process, the WPA kept an average of 2.1 million workers employed and pumped needed money into the economy.

The WPA also displayed remarkable flexibility and imagination in offering assistance to those whose occupations did not fit into any traditional category of relief. The Federal Writers Project of the WPA, for example, gave unemployed writers a chance to do their work and receive a government salary. The Federal Arts Project, similarly, helped painters, sculptors, and others to continue their careers. The Federal Music Project and the Federal Theater Project oversaw the production of concerts and plays, creating work for unemployed musicians, actors, and directors. Other relief agencies emerged alongside the WPA. The National Youth Administration (NYA) provided work and scholarship assistance to high-school and college-age men and women. The Emergency Housing Division of the Public Works Administration began federal sponsorship of public housing.

Men and women alike were in distress in the 1930s (as in all difficult times). But the new welfare system dealt with members of the two sexes in very different ways. For men, the government concentrated mainly on work relief—on such programs as the CCC, the CWA, and the WPA, all of which were overwhelmingly male. The principal government aid to women was not work relief but cash assistance—most notably through the Aid to Dependent Children program of Social Security, which was designed largely to assist single mothers. This disparity in treatment reflected a widespread assumption that men constituted the bulk of the paid work force and that women needed to be treated within the context of the family. In fact, millions of women were already employed by the 1930s.

The 1936 "Referendum"

For a time in 1935 there had seemed reason to question the president's prospects for reelection. But by the middle of 1936—with the economy visibly reviving—there could be little doubt that he would win a second term. The Republican Party nominated the moderate governor of Kansas, Alf M. Landon, who waged a generally pallid campaign. Roosevelt's dissident challengers now appeared powerless. One reason was the violent death of their most effective leader, Huey Long, who was assassinated in Louisiana in September 1935. Another reason was the ill-fated alliance among Father Coughlin, Dr. Townsend, and Gerald L. K. Smith (an intemperate henchman of Huey Long), who joined forces that summer to establish a new

Alf Landon

WPA WORKERS ON THE JOB The Works Progress Administration funded an enormous variety of work projects to provide jobs for the unemployed. But most WPA employees worked on construction sites of one kind or another. Here, WPA workers labor on a bridge project in the Bronx, in New York City. *(Bettmann/Corbis)*

WPA MURAL ART The Federal Arts Project of the Works Progress Administration commissioned an impressive series of public murals from the artists it employed. Many of these murals adorned post offices, libraries, and other public buildings constructed by the WPA. William Gropper's *Construction of a Dam,* a detail of which is seen here, is typical of much of the mural art of the 1930s in its celebration of the workingman. Workers are depicted in heroic poses, laboring in unison to complete a great public project. *(Library of Congress)*

THE GOLDEN AGE OF COMIC BOOKS

In the troubled years of the Great Depression and World War II, many Americans sought release from their anxieties in fantasy. Those who produced America's popular culture eagerly obliged them, with movies, plays, books, radio shows, and other diversions that drew people out of their own lives and into a safer or more glamorous or more exciting world. Beginning in 1938, one of the most popular forms of escape for many young Americans became the comic book. For decades after that, comic books remained a powerful force in American culture.

The modern comics began on the "funny pages" of American newspapers in the 1890s. In the first years of the twentieth century, publishers collected previously published strips and began selling them in books. Seldom did these early comics make any effort

SUPERMAN The most popular action figure in the history of comic books was Superman, whose superhuman powers were particularly appealing fantasies to Americans suffering through the Depression and, later, World War II. *(Superman No. 1 © 1939 DC Comics. All Rights Reserved. Used with Permission.)*

to develop continuing plots or complex characters—although the popular character Dick Tracy did serve as the hero of some continuing detective stories. In the 1930s, however, some artists and businessmen began to see new and greater possibilities in the comics. In February 1935, Malcolm Wheeler-Nicholson founded the first comics magazine—what we now know as the "comic book"—entitled *New Fun,* which published entirely original material. Wheeler had little success with *New Fun,* but he continued to believe in the potential of original comic books. He founded a new company, Detective Comics, and began in 1937 to design a new magazine called *Action Comics.* Wheeler himself ran out of money before he could publish anything, but the company continued without him. In 1938, the first issue of *Action Comics* appeared with a startling and controversial cover—a powerful man in a skin-tight suit lifting a car over his head. His name was Superman, and he became the most popular cartoon character of all time.

Within a year, Superman had a comic book named after him, which was selling over 1.2 million copies each issue. By 1940, there was a popular Superman radio show—introduced by a breathless announcer crying "It's a bird! It's a plane! It's . . . Superman!" And very soon, other publishers—and even Detective Comics itself—began developing new "superheroes" (a term invented by the creators of Superman) to capitalize on this growing new popular appetite. In 1939, a second great comic-book publisher appeared— Marvel Comics. By the early 1940s, Superman had been joined by such other supernatural heroes as the Human Torch, the Sub-Mariner, Batman, and the Flash. None proved as popular as Superman, but many were commercially successful nevertheless.

It is not hard to imagine why superheroes would be so appealing to Americans—and particularly to the teenage boys who were the largest single purchasers of comic books— in the 1930s and 1940s. Superman and other superheroes were idealized versions of the ideal boy— smart, good, "the perfect Boy Scout," as one fan put it. But they were also all-powerful, capable of righting wrong and preventing catastrophe. In a world where catastrophe was an ever-present possibility—in the lives of many families in the 1930s, and in the reality of the world at large in the 1940s—superheroes were a comforting escape from fear. Jerry Siegel and Joe Shuster, who drew and wrote the Superman comics, were themselves very young men in the late 1930s, not far removed from their own teenage fantasies. And indeed many of the early comic book writers were men in their late teens or early twenties.

Many of the creators of comic books were also Jewish, young men conscious of their outsider status in an American culture not yet wholly open to them. The characters they created almost all had alter-egos, identities they used while living within the normal world. Superman was Clark Kent, a "mild-mannered reporter." Batman was Bruce Wayne, a wealthy heir. All were wholly a part of mainstream American society, and they expressed in part the outsider's dream of assimilation. At the same time, the characters as superheroes were outsiders themselves—but outsiders endowed with special powers and abilities unavailable to ordinary people.

Even before America entered World War II, the comic books went to war with the Axis. Marvel's the Human Torch and the Sub-Mariner joined forces against the German navy. Superman fought spies and saboteurs

political movement—the Union Party, which nominated an undistinguished North Dakota congressman, William Lemke, for president.

The result was the greatest landslide in American history to that point. Roosevelt polled just under 61 percent

of the vote to Landon's 36 percent and carried every state except Maine and Vermont. The Democrats increased their already large majorities in both houses of Congress. The Union Party received fewer than 900,000 votes.

CAPTAIN AMERICA   Captain America made his comic book debut in 1941 and immediately established himself as both super-hero and super-patriot. Even before Pearl Harbor, Captain America was portrayed as a powerful foe of the Nazis and the Japanese, and as a particularly deadly enemy of spies and saboteurs who had infiltrated the United States—as in this strip where he throttles an "enemy agent." *(CAPTAIN AMERICA: TM © 2002 Marvel Characters, Inc. Used with permission.)*

THE INDUSTRY CODE   Beginning in 1955, under pressure from government officials and others who charged comic books with being vulgar and dangerous, the comic book industry established its own code authority, much like the organization created to police movies that had been created in the 1920s. This stamp was the code authority's seal of approval, designed to reassure readers (and their parents) that the contents were wholesome.

at home. A new character created in March 1941, Captain America, was a frail young man rejected by the army who, after being given a secret serum by a military doctor, became extraordinarily powerful. Joining the army at last, he posed as an ordinary private but managed to perform extraordinary deeds. On the cover of the first issue of *Captain America,* the title character could be seen punching Hitler in his headquarters in Germany. The war also expanded the readership of the comic books. They became enormously popular among soldiers and sailors—many of whom had been reading them, as teenagers, before joining the military.

The end of the war was also the end of this first "Golden Age" of American comic books. Many superhero magazines—including *Captain America*—ceased publication as peacetime reduced the popular ap-

petite for fantasy. In their place emerged new comic books, which emphasized romance and even mild sexuality. A new company, Entertainment Comics, began publishing lurid horror and science-fiction comics, with levels of violence and cruelty far higher than the earlier superhero books had ever displayed. None ever reached the levels of popularity that the superhero comics had enjoyed during the Depression and war.

In the late 1940s and early 1950s, comic books began to come under attack from educators, psychiatrists, journalists, and even the federal government. In 1954, members of the United States Senate held hearings in New York to hear testimony from comic book writers and publishers. The senators seemed unpersuaded by the claims they heard that comics were, in fact, healthy and decent. Congress took no legal action against

them, but the comic book industry itself created a trade association, which produced a "Comics Code" to prevent indecency in the industry.

Comic books experienced an unexpected revival in the late 1950s and 1960s. Old superheroes—Captain America, the Human Torch, and others—reappeared. New ones—Spiderman, Iron Man, the Silver Surfer—joined them. Superman, who had never disappeared, enjoyed newfound popularity and became the hero for a time of a popular television show. But these new or revised heroes were not entirely like those of the 1930s and 1940s—not the rock-solid Boy Scouts certain of the difference between right and wrong. They were more complicated characters, plagued at times by doubt and weakness and thwarted desire. They reflected the realities of an increasingly complex and complicated world, which their characters—like their mostly young readers—were struggling to understand.

Electoral Realignment

The election results demonstrated the party realignment that the New Deal had produced. The Democrats now controlled a broad coalition of western and southern farmers, the urban working classes, the poor and unemployed, and the black communities of northern cities, as well as traditional progressives and committed new liberals—a coalition that constituted a substantial majority of the electorate. It would be decades before the Republican Party could again create a lasting majority coalition of its own.

THE NEW DEAL IN DISARRAY

Roosevelt emerged from the 1936 election at the zenith of his popularity. Within months, however, the New Deal was mired in serious new difficulties—a result of continuing opposition, the president's own political errors, and major economic setbacks.

The Court Fight

The 1936 mandate, Franklin Roosevelt believed, made it possible for him to do something about the problem of the Supreme Court. No program of reform, he had become convinced, could long survive the conservative justices, who had already struck down the NRA and the AAA and threatened to invalidate even more legislation.

In February 1937, Roosevelt sent a surprise message to Capitol Hill proposing a general overhaul of the federal *Court Packing* court system; included among the many provisions was one to add up to six new justices to the Supreme Court. The courts were "overworked," he claimed, and needed additional manpower and younger blood to enable them to cope with their increasing burdens. But Roosevelt's real purpose was to give himself the opportunity to appoint new, liberal justices and change the ideological balance of the Court.

Conservatives were outraged at the "Court-packing plan," and even many Roosevelt supporters were disturbed by what they considered evidence of the president's hunger for power. Still, Roosevelt might well have persuaded Congress to approve at least a compromise measure had not the Supreme Court itself intervened. Of the nine justices, three reliably supported the New Deal, and four reliably opposed it. Of the remaining two, Chief Justice Charles Evans Hughes often sided with the progressives and Associate Justice Owen J. Roberts usually voted with the conservatives. On March 29, 1937, Roberts, Hughes, and the three progressive justices voted together to uphold a state minimum-wage law—in the case of *West Coast Hotel* v. *Parrish*—thus reversing a 5-to-4 decision of the previous year invalidating a similar law. Two weeks later, again by a 5-to-4 margin, the Court upheld the Wagner Act, and in May it validated the Social Security Act. Whether or not for that reason, the Court's newly moderate position made the Court-packing bill seem unnecessary. Congress ultimately defeated it.

On one level, the affair was a significant victory for Franklin Roosevelt. The Court was no longer an obstacle to New Deal reforms, particularly after the older justices began to retire, to be replaced by Roosevelt appointees. But the Court-packing episode did lasting political damage to the administration. From 1937 on, southern Democrats and other conservatives voted against Roosevelt's measures much more often than they had in the past.

Retrenchment and Recession

By the summer of 1937, the national income, which had dropped from $82 billion in 1929 to $40 billion in 1932, had risen to nearly $72 billion. Other economic indices showed similar advances. Roosevelt seized on these improvements as an excuse to try to balance the federal budget, convinced by Treasury secretary Henry Morgenthau and many economists that the real danger now was no longer depression but inflation. Between January and August 1937, for example, he cut the WPA in half, laying off 1.5 million relief workers. A few weeks later, the fragile boom collapsed. The index of industrial production dropped from 117 in August 1937 to 76 in May 1938. Four million additional workers lost their jobs. Economic conditions were soon almost as bad as they had been in the bleak days of 1932–1933.

The recession of 1937, known to the president's critics as the "Roosevelt recession," was a result of many factors. But to many observers at the time (including, apparently, the *Roosevelt Recession* president himself), it seemed to be a direct result of the administration's unwise decision to reduce spending. And so in April 1938, the president asked Congress for an emergency appropriation of $5 billion for public works and relief programs, and government funds soon began pouring into the economy once again. Within a few months, another tentative recovery seemed to be under way, and the advocates of spending pointed to it as proof of the validity of their approach.

At about the same time, at the urging of a group of younger, antimonopolist liberals in the administration, Roosevelt sent a stinging message to Congress, vehemently denouncing what he called an "unjustifiable concentration of economic power" and asking for the creation of a commission to examine that concentration with an eye to major reforms in the antitrust laws. In response, Congress established the Temporary National Economic Committee (TNEC), whose members included representatives of both houses of Congress and officials from several executive agencies. Also that spring, Roosevelt appointed a new head of the antitrust division of the Justice Department: Thurman Arnold, a Yale Law School professor who soon proved to be the most vigorous director ever to serve in that office.

Later in 1938, the administration successfully supported one of its most ambitious pieces of labor legislation, the Fair Labor Standards Act, which for the first time established a national minimum wage and a forty-hour work week, and which also placed strict limits on child labor.

Despite these achievements, however, by the end of 1938 the New Deal had essentially come to an end. Congressional opposition now *End of the New Deal* made it difficult for the president to enact any major new programs. But more important, perhaps, the threat of world crisis hung heavy

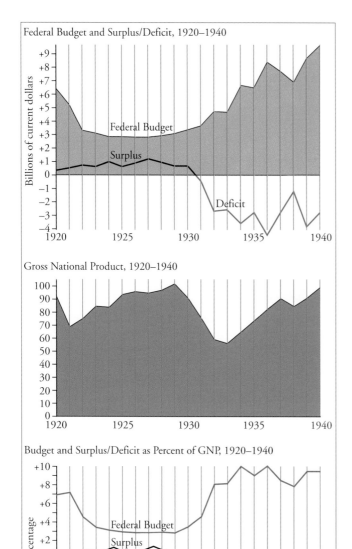

Federal Budget and Surplus/Deficit, 1920–1940

Gross National Product, 1920–1940

Budget and Surplus/Deficit as Percent of GNP, 1920–1940

FEDERAL BUDGET SURPLUS/DEFICIT AND GNP, 1920–1940
Among its many other effects, the Great Depression produced dramatic changes in the fiscal condition of the federal government. In the first of these three charts, note the sharp decline in federal spending in the early 1920s (as the nation demobilized from World War I) and the appearance of significant budget surpluses. Note, too, the dramatic increase in government spending (and the appearance of significant deficits) once the Depression began and, particularly, once Franklin Roosevelt became president. The second chart illustrates the varying fortunes of the nation's economy by showing the rise and fall of Gross National Product—the total of goods and services produced by the economy. GNP fell sharply in the first years of the Depression, but by the end of the 1930s was nearing its 1929 levels again. The final chart gives some perspective on these figures by illustrating the relationship between federal spending (and federal surpluses and deficits) and the total size of the economy. At its peak in these years, federal spending was never more than about nine percent of GNP and the deficit never more than about 5 percent. In the late twentieth century, the federal budget has often exceeded twenty percent of GNP, while deficits—much higher in absolute numbers than those of the 1930s—were rarely higher as a percentage of GNP than those of the 1930s. ◆ *Why did government deficits increase so sharply during the Great Depression?*

in the political atmosphere, and Roosevelt was gradually growing more concerned with persuading a reluctant nation to prepare for war than with pursuing new avenues of reform.

LIMITS AND LEGACIES OF THE NEW DEAL

In the 1930s, Roosevelt's principal critics were conservatives, who accused him of abandoning the Constitution and establishing a menacing, even tyrannical state. In more recent years, the New Deal's most visible critics have attacked it from the left, pointing to the major problems it left unsolved and the important groups it failed to represent. A full understanding of the New Deal requires coming to terms with the sources of both critiques, by examining both its achievements and its limits.

The Idea of the "Broker State"

In 1933, many New Dealers dreamed of using their new popularity and authority somehow to remake American capitalism—to produce new forms of cooperation and control that would create a genuinely harmonious, ordered economic world. By 1939, it was clear that what they had created was in fact something quite different. But rather than bemoan the gap between their original intentions and their ultimate achievements, New Deal liberals, both in 1939 and in later years, chose to accept what they had produced and to celebrate it—to use it as a model for future reform efforts.

What they had created was something that in later years would become known as the "broker state." Instead of forging all elements of society into a single, harmonious unit, as some reformers had *Establishment of the "Broker State"* once hoped to do, the real achievement of the New Deal was to elevate and strengthen new interest groups so as to allow them to compete more effectively in the national marketplace. The New Deal made the federal government a mediator in that continuous competition—a force that could intervene when necessary to help some groups and limit the power of others. In 1933, there had been only one great interest group (albeit a varied and divided one) with genuine power in the national economy: the corporate world. By the end of the 1930s, American business found itself competing for influence with an increasingly powerful labor movement, with an organized agricultural economy, and with aroused consumers. In later years, the "broker state" idea would expand to embrace other groups as well: racial, ethnic, and religious minorities; women; and many others. Thus, one of the enduring legacies of the New Deal was to make the federal government a protector of interest groups and a supervisor of the competition among them, rather than an instrument attempting to create a universal harmony of interests.

What determines which interest groups receive government assistance in a "broker state"? The experience of the New Deal suggests that such assistance goes largely to those groups able to exercise enough political or economic power to demand it. Thus in the 1930s, farmers—after decades of organization and agitation—and workers—as the result of militant action and mass mobilization—won from the government new and important protections. Other groups, less well organized perhaps but politically important because so numerous and visible, won more limited assistance as well: imperiled homeowners, the unemployed, the elderly.

By the same token, the interest-group democracy that the New Deal came to represent offered much less to those groups either too weak to demand assistance or not visible enough to arouse widespread public support. And yet those same groups were often the ones most in need of help from their government. One of the important limits of the New Deal, therefore, was its very modest record on behalf of several important social groups.

African Americans and the New Deal

One group the New Deal did relatively little to assist was African Americans. The administration was not hostile to black aspirations. On the contrary, the New Deal was probably more sympathetic to them than any previous government of the twentieth century. Eleanor Roosevelt spoke throughout the 1930s on behalf of racial justice and put continuing pressure on her husband and others in the federal government to ease discrimination against blacks. She was also partially responsible for what was, symbolically at least, one of the most important events of the decade for African Americans. When the black singer Marian Anderson was refused permission in the spring of 1939 to give a concert in the auditorium of the Daughters of the American Revolution (Washington's only concert hall), Eleanor Roosevelt resigned from the organization and then (along with Interior Secretary Harold Ickes, another champion of racial equality) helped secure government permission for her to sing on the steps of the Lincoln Memorial. Anderson's Easter Sunday concert attracted 75,000 people and became, in effect, one of the first modern civil rights demonstrations.

The president himself appointed a number of blacks to significant second-level positions in his administration.

"Black Cabinet" Roosevelt appointees such as Robert Weaver, William Hastie, and Mary McLeod Bethune created an informal network of officeholders who consulted frequently with one another and who became known as the "Black Cabinet." Eleanor Roosevelt, Harold Ickes, and Harry Hopkins all made efforts to ensure that New Deal relief programs did

ELEANOR ROOSEVELT AND MARY MCLEOD BETHUNE Mary McLeod Bethune was one of a small but energetic group of African-American officeholders in the Roosevelt administration. Together they formed an informal network known as the "Black Cabinet." Among their most important allies was Eleanor Roosevelt, who is shown here appearing with Bethune at a 1937 "National Conference on Problems of the Negro and Negro Youth," organized by the National Youth Administration. Bethune was the NYA's Director of Negro Activities. *(Bettmann/Corbis)*

not exclude blacks; and by 1935, perhaps a quarter of all African Americans were receiving some form of government assistance. One result was a historic change in black electoral behavior. As late as 1932, most American blacks were voting Republican, as they had since the Civil War. By 1936, more than 90 percent of them were voting Democratic—the beginnings of a political alliance that would endure for decades.

Blacks supported Franklin Roosevelt because they knew he was not their enemy. But they had few illusions that the New Deal represented a millennium in American race relations. For example, the president was never willing to risk losing the support of southern Democrats by supporting legislation to make lynching a federal crime. Nor would he endorse efforts in Congress to ban the poll tax, one of the most potent tools by which white southerners kept blacks from voting.

New Deal relief agencies did not challenge, and indeed reinforced, existing patterns of discrimination. The Civilian Conservation Corps established separate black camps. The NRA codes tolerated paying blacks *Existing Discrimination Reinforced* less than whites doing the same jobs. Blacks were largely excluded from employment in the TVA. The Federal Housing Administration refused to provide mortgages to blacks moving into white neighborhoods, and the first public housing projects financed by the federal government

HARLEM GROCERY STORE, 1940 The photographer Aaron Siskind took this picture of a community grocery store in Harlem, its manager standing proudly in the doorway. It was part of a project designed to document life in what *Look* magazine that same year called "the Negro capital of America." Siskind and other photographers worked from 1938 to 1940 to produce a series they called *The Harlem Document*. *(Print and Photographs Division, Library of Congress. Courtesy of The Aaron Siskind Foundation.)*

were racially segregated. The WPA routinely relegated black, Hispanic, and Asian workers to the least-skilled and lowest-paying jobs, or excluded them altogether; when funding ebbed, nonwhites, like women, were among the first to be dismissed.

The New Deal was not hostile to black Americans, and it did much to help them advance. But it refused to make the issue of race a significant part of its agenda.

The New Deal and the "Indian Problem"

In many respects, government policies toward the Indian tribes in the 1930s were simply a continuation of the long-established effort to encourage Native Americans to assimilate. Senator Burton K. Wheeler of Montana expressed the sentiments of many members of Congress (and many other white Americans) when he said in 1934, in the midst of a hearing on an Indian reform bill, "What we are trying to do is get rid of the Indian problem rather than add to it." By that he meant that the purpose of reforms should be to reduce the numbers of Native Americans who identified themselves as members of tribes and increase the number of those who attempted to become part of the larger society and culture.

But the principal elements of federal policy in the New Deal years worked to advance a very different goal, largely because of the efforts of the extraordinary commissioner of *John Collier* Indian affairs in those years, John Collier. Collier was a former social worker who had become committed to the cause of the Indians after exposure to tribal cultures in New Mexico in the 1920s. More important, he was greatly influenced by the work of twentieth-century anthropologists who promoted the idea of cultural relativism—the idea that every culture should be accepted and respected on its own terms and that no culture was inherently superior to another. Cultural relativism was a challenge to the three-centuries-old assumption among white Americans that Indians were "savages" and that white society was inherently superior and more "civilized."

Collier promoted legislation that would, he hoped, reverse the pressures on Native Americans to assimilate and would allow them the right to live in traditional Indian ways. Not all tribal leaders agreed with Collier; indeed, his belief in the importance of preserving Indian culture would not find its broadest support among the tribes until the 1960s. Nevertheless, Collier effectively promoted legislation—which became the Indian Reorganization Act of *Indian Reorganization Act* 1934—to advance his goals. Among other things it restored to the tribes the right to own land collectively (reversing the allotment policy adopted in 1887, which encouraged the breaking up of tribal lands into individually owned plots—a policy that had led to the loss of over 90 million acres of tribal land to white speculators and others). In the thirteen years after passage of the 1934 bill, tribal land increased by nearly 4 million acres, and Indian agricultural income increased dramatically (from under $2 million in 1934 to over $49 million in 1947).

Even with the redistribution of lands under the 1934 act, however, Indians continued to possess, for the most part, only territory whites did not want—much of it arid, some of it desert. And as a group, they continued to constitute the poorest segment of the population. The efforts of the 1930s did not solve what some called the "Indian problem." They did, however, provide Indians with some tools for rebuilding the viability of the tribes.

Women and the New Deal

The New Deal was not hostile to feminist aspirations, but neither did it do a great deal to advance them. That was largely because such aspirations did not have sufficiently widespread support (even among women) to make it politically advantageous for the administration to back them.

There were, to be sure, important symbolic gestures on behalf of women. Roosevelt appointed the first female cabinet member in the nation's history, Secretary of Labor Frances Perkins. He also named more than 100 other

THE NEW DEAL

For many years, debate among historians over the nature of the New Deal mirrored the debate among Americans in the 1930s over the achievements of the Roosevelt administration. Historians struggled, just as contemporaries had done, to decide whether the New Deal was a good thing or a bad thing.

The conservative critique of the New Deal has received relatively little scholarly expression. Edgar Robinson, in *The Roosevelt Leadership* (1955), and John T. Flynn, in *The Roosevelt Myth* (1956), attacked Roosevelt as both a radical and a despot; but few other historians have taken such charges very seriously. By far the

(Franklin D. Roosevelt Library)

dominant view of the New Deal among scholars has been an approving, liberal interpretation.

The first important voice of the liberal view was Arthur M. Schlesinger, Jr., who argued in the three volumes of *The Age of Roosevelt* (1957–1960) that the New Deal marked a continuation of the long struggle between public power and private interests, but that Roosevelt moved that struggle to a new level. The unrestrained power of the business community was finally confronted with an effective challenge, and what emerged was a system of reformed capitalism, with far more protection for workers, farmers, consumers, and others than in the past.

The first systematic "revisionist" interpretation of the New Deal came in 1963, in William Leuchtenburg's *Franklin D. Roosevelt and the New Deal*. Leuchtenburg was a sympathetic critic, arguing that most of the limitations of the New Deal were a result of the restrictions imposed on Roosevelt by the political and ideological realities of his time—that the New Deal probably could not have done much more than it did. Nevertheless,

Leuchtenburg challenged earlier views of the New Deal as a revolution in social policy and was able to muster only enough enthusiasm to call it a "halfway revolution," one that enhanced the positions of some previously disadvantaged groups (notably farmers and factory workers) but did little or nothing for many others (including blacks, sharecroppers, and the urban poor). Ellis Hawley augmented these moderate criticisms of the Roosevelt record in *The New Deal and the Problem of Monopoly* (1966). In examining 1930s economic policies, Hawley challenged liberal assumptions that the New Deal acted as the foe of private business interests. On the contrary, he argued, New Deal efforts were in many cases designed to enhance the position of private entrepreneurs—even, at times, at the expense of some of the liberal reform goals that administration officials espoused.

Other historians in the 1960s and later, writing from the left, expressed much harsher criticisms of the New Deal. Barton Bernstein, in a notable 1968 essay, compiled a dreary chronicle of missed opportunities,

women to positions at lower levels of the federal bureaucracy. They created an active female network within the

Symbolic Gains for Women

government and cooperated with one another in advancing causes of interest to women. Such appointments were in part a response to pressure from Eleanor Roosevelt, who was a committed advocate of women's rights and a champion of humanitarian causes. Molly Dewson, head of the Women's Division of the Democratic National Committee, was also influential in securing federal appointments for women as well as in increasing their role within the Democratic Party. Several women received appointments to the federal judiciary. And one, Hattie Caraway of Arkansas, became in 1934 the first woman ever elected to a full term in the U.S. Senate. (She was running to succeed her husband, who had died in office.)

But New Deal support for women operated within limits, partly because New Deal women themselves had limited views of what their aims should be. Frances Perkins and many others in the administration emerged out of the feminist tradition of the progressive era,

which emphasized not so much sexual equality as special protections for women. Perkins herself had been instrumental in fighting for passage of various state laws safeguarding female workers. She opposed the National Woman's Party and its goal of securing the Equal Rights Amendment because she feared the amendment would threaten the protective mechanisms that she had helped to establish. Perkins and other women reformers were instrumental in creating support for, and shaping the character of, the Social Security Act of 1935. But they built into that bill their own notion of women's special place in a male-dominated economy. The principal provision of the bill specifically designed for women—the Aid to Dependent Children program—was modeled on the state-level mothers' pensions that generations of progressive women had worked to pass earlier in the century.

The New Deal generally supported the prevailing belief that in hard times women should withdraw from the workplace to open up more jobs for men. Even Frances Perkins spoke out against what she called the "pin-

inadequate responses to problems, and damaging New Deal initiatives. The Roosevelt administration may have saved capitalism, Bernstein charged, but it failed to help—and in many ways actually harmed—those groups most in need of assistance. Ronald Radosh, also in 1968, portrayed the New Deal as an effective agent for the consolidation of modern corporate capitalism. Several essays by Thomas Ferguson in the 1980s and Colin Gordon's 1994 book *New Deals* took such arguments further. They cited the close ties between the New Deal and internationalist financiers and industrialists; the liberalism of the 1930s was a product of their shared interest in protecting capitalists and stabilizing capitalism.

Except for the work of Ferguson and Gordon, the attack on the New Deal from the left has not developed very far beyond its preliminary statements in the 1960s. Instead, by the 1970s and 1980s, most scholars seemed less interested in the question of whether the New Deal was a "conservative" or "revolutionary" phenomenon than in the question of the constraints within which it was operating. The sociologist Theda Skocpol, in an important series of articles, has emphasized (along with others) the issue of "state capacity" as an important New Deal constraint; ambitious reform ideas often foundered, she argued, because of the absence of a government bureaucracy with sufficient strength and expertise to shape or administer them. James T. Patterson, Barry Karl, Mark Leff, and others have emphasized the political constraints the New Deal encountered. Both in Congress and among the public, conservative inhibitions about government remained strong; the New Deal was as much a product of the pressures of its conservative opponents as of its liberal supporters. Frank Freidel, Ellis Hawley, Herbert Stein, and many others point as well to the ideological constraints affecting Franklin Roosevelt and his supporters. Alan Brinkley, in *The End of Reform* (1995), described a transition in New Deal thinking from a regulatory view of government to one that envisioned relatively little direct interference by government in the corporate world; a movement—driven in part by the need to adapt to a conservative political climate—toward an essentially "compensatory" state centered on Keynesian welfare state programs. David Kennedy, in *Freedom from Fear* (1999), argues by contrast that the more aggressive strands of early New Deal liberalism actually hampered the search for recovery, that Roosevelt's embrace of measures that unleashed the power of the market was the most effective approach to prosperity.

The phrase "New Deal liberalism" has come in the postwar era to seem synonymous with modern ideas of aggressive federal management of the economy, elaborate welfare systems, a powerful bureaucracy, and large-scale government spending. The "Reagan Revolution" of the 1980s often portrayed itself as a reaction to the "legacy of the New Deal." Many historians of the New Deal, however, would argue that the modern idea of "New Deal liberalism" bears only a limited relationship to the ideas that New Dealers themselves embraced. The liberal accomplishments of the 1930s can only be understood in the context of their own time; later liberal efforts drew from that legacy but also altered it to fit the needs and assumptions of very different eras.

money worker"—the married woman working to earn extra money for the household. New Deal relief agencies offered relatively little employment for women. The NRA sanctioned sexually discriminatory wage practices. The Social Security program at first excluded domestic servants, waitresses, and other predominantly female occupations. As with African Americans, so also with women: the New Deal was not actively hostile; in many ways, it was unprecedentedly supportive. It did, however, accept prevailing cultural norms. There was not yet sufficient political pressure from women themselves to persuade the administration to do otherwise.

Prevailing Gender Norms Buttressed

The New Deal in the West and the South

Two regions of the United States that did receive special attention from the New Deal were the West and the South, both of which benefited disproportionately from New Deal relief and public works programs. The West received more federal funds per capita through New Deal relief programs than any other region, and parts of the South were not far behind.

Most westerners were eager for the assistance New Deal agencies provided, but their political leaders were not always as supportive. In Colorado, for example, the state legislature refused to provide the required matching funds for FERA relief in 1933. When, in response, Harry Hopkins cut Colorado off from the program, unemployed people rioted in Denver and looted food stores. Only then did the legislature reverse course and provide funding.

In the South, locally administered New Deal relief programs did not challenge prevailing racial norms. In the West, too, New Deal programs accepted existing racial and ethnic prejudices. In several states, relief agencies paid different groups at different rates: white Anglos received the most generous aid; blacks, Indians, and Mexican Americans received lower levels of support. In the CCC camps in New Mexico,

Failure to Challenge Jim Crow

Hispanics and Anglos sometimes worked in the same camps, but there were frequent tensions and occasional conflicts between them. But the main reason for the New Deal's particular impact on the West was that conditions in the region made the government's programs especially important. Federal agricultural programs had an enormous impact on the West because farming remained so much more central to the economy of the region than it did in much of the East. The largest New Deal public works programs—the great dams and power stations—were mainly in the West, both because the best locations for such facilities were there and because the West had the most need for new sources of water and power. The Grand Coulee Dam on the Columbia River was the largest public works project in American history to that point, and it provided cheap electric power for much of the Northwest. Its construction, and the construction of other, smaller dams and water projects in the region, created a basis for economic development in the region.

Without this enormous public investment by the federal government, much of the economic development

New Deal's Legacy in the West

that transformed the West after World War II would have been much more difficult, if not impossible, to achieve. But the region paid a price for the government's beneficence. For generations after the Great Depression, the federal government maintained a much greater and more visible bureaucratic presence in the West than in any other region.

The New Deal located fewer great infrastructure projects in the South than it did in the West—although the largest of them all, the TVA, was an entirely southern venture. But much of the economic development efforts the Roosevelt administration undertook were of disproportionate benefit to the South, in large part because the South was the least economically developed region of the nation in the 1930s. One example was rural electrification, which had a large impact on many agrarian areas of the nation but a particular impact on the South, where vast parts of the countryside remained without access to power lines until the REA provided them.

The New Deal also directed national attention toward the economic condition of the South in a way that no previous administration had done. Many Americans outside the South had long believed the South to be somehow "backward," but they tended to attribute that backwardness to racism, segregation, and prejudice. In a 1938 economic report sponsored by the federal government, a group of social scientists and others called the South "the nation's number one economic problem." Although the report made some reference to the South's racial customs, it spoke mostly about its lack of sufficiently developed economic institutions and facilities. Some southerners objected to the report, claiming that it reinforced anti-southern prejudices outside the region. But others saw it as an opportunity to win national support for efforts to modernize and develop the region.

The New Deal and the National Economy

The most frequent criticisms of the New Deal involve its failure genuinely to revive or reform the American economy. New Dealers never fully recognized the value of government spending as a vehicle for recovery, and their efforts along other lines never succeeded in ending the Depression. The economic boom sparked by World War II, not the New Deal, finally ended the crisis. Nor did the New Deal substantially alter the

Failure to Achieve Recovery

distribution of power within American capitalism; and it had only a small impact on the distribution of wealth among the American people.

Nevertheless, the New Deal did have a number of important and lasting effects on both the behavior and the structure of the American economy. It helped elevate new groups—workers, farmers, and others—to positions from which they could at times effectively challenge the power of the corporations. It contributed to the economic development of the West and, to a lesser degree, the South. It increased the regulatory functions of the federal government in ways that helped stabilize previously troubled areas of the economy: the stock market, the banking system, and others. And the administration helped establish the basis for new forms of federal fiscal policy, which in the postwar years would give the government tools for promoting and regulating economic growth.

The New Deal also created the basis of the federal welfare state, through its many relief programs and above all through the Social Security system. The conservative inhibitions New Dealers

Federal Welfare State Established

brought to this task ensured that the welfare system that ultimately emerged would be limited in its impact (at least in comparison with those of other industrial nations), would reinforce some traditional patterns of gender and racial discrimination, and would be expensive and cumbersome to administer. But for all its limits, the new system marked a historic break with the federal government's traditional reluctance to offer public assistance to its neediest citizens.

The New Deal and American Politics

Perhaps the most dramatic effect of the New Deal was on the structure and behavior of American government itself and on the character of American politics. Franklin Roosevelt helped enhance the power of the federal government as a whole. By the end of the 1930s, state and local governments were clearly of secondary importance

MAJOR LEGISLATION OF THE NEW DEAL

1933	Emergency Banking Act	1935	Works Progress Administration
	Economy Act		National Youth Administration
	Civilian Conservation Corps		Social Security Act
	Agricultural Adjustment Act		National Labor Relations Act
	Tennessee Valley Authority		Public Utilities Holding Company Act
	National Industrial Recovery Act		Resettlement Administration
	Banking Act		Rural Electrification Administration
	Federal Emergency Relief Act		Revenue Act ("wealth tax")
	Home Owners' Refinancing Act	1936	Soil Conservation and Domestic Allotment Act
	Civil Works Administration	1937	Farm Security Administration
	Federal Securities Act		National Housing Act
1934	National Housing Act	1938	Second Agricultural Adjustment Act
	Securities and Exchange Act		Fair Labor Standards Act
	Home Owners' Loan Act	1939	Executive Reorganization Act

to the government in Washington; in the past, that had not always been clear. Roosevelt also established the presidency as the preeminent center of authority within the federal government. Never again would Congress be able to wield as much independent power as it had in the years before the New Deal. And never again would it have the same control over presidential authority.

Finally, the New Deal had a profound impact on how the American people defined themselves politically. It took a weak, divided Democratic Party, which had been a minority force in American politics for many decades, and turned it into a mighty coalition that would dominate national party competition for more than forty years. It turned the attention of many voters away from some of the cultural issues that had preoccupied them in the 1920s and awakened in them an interest in *New Expectations of Government* economic matters of direct importance to their lives. And it created among the American people greatly increased expectations of government—expectations that the New Deal itself did not always fulfill but that survived to become the basis of new liberal crusades in the postwar era.

CONCLUSION

The New Deal was the most dramatic and important moment in the modern history of American government. From the time of Franklin Roosevelt's inauguration in 1933 to the beginning of World War II eight years later, the federal government engaged in a broad and diverse series of experiments designed to relieve the distress of unemployment and poverty, to reform the economy to prevent future crises, and to bring the Great Depression itself to an end. It had only partial success in all those efforts.

Unemployment and poverty remained high throughout the New Deal, although many federal programs provided assistance to millions of people who would otherwise have had none. The structure of the American economy remained essentially the same as it had been in earlier years, although there were by the end of the New Deal some

important new regulatory agencies in Washington—and an important new role for organized labor, enforced by a new federal law. Nothing the New Deal did ended the Great Depression, but some of its policies kept it from getting worse—and some of them pointed the way toward more effective economic policies in the future.

Perhaps the most important legacy of the New Deal was to create a sense of possibilities among many Americans, to persuade them that the fortunes of individuals need not be left entirely to chance or to the workings of the market. Many Americans emerged from the 1930s convinced that individuals deserved some protections from the unpredictability and instability of the modern economy, and that the New Deal—for all its limitations—had demonstrated the value of enlisting government in the effort to provide those protections.

FOR FURTHER REFERENCE

William E. Leuchtenburg, *Franklin D. Roosevelt and the New Deal* (1963) is a classic short history of the New Deal. Anthony Badger, *The New Deal: The Depression Years* (1989) is another fine overview. David Kennedy, *Freedom from Fear: The American People in Depresion and War, 1929–1945* (1999) is an important narrative history, a volume in the Oxford History of the United States. Geoffrey Ward, *Before the Trumpet: Young Franklin Roosevelt, 1882–1905* (1985) and *A First-Class Temperament: The Emergence of Franklin Roosevelt* (1989) are superb biographical accounts of the pre-presidential FDR. Frank Freidel, *Franklin D. Roosevelt: A Rendezvous with Destiny* (1990) is a one-volume biography by one of FDR's most important biographers. Ellis Hawley, *The New Deal and the Problem of Monopoly* (1967) is a classic examination of the economic policies of the Roosevelt administration in its first five years. Colin Gordon, *New Deals: Business, Labor, and Politics in America, 1920–1935* (1994) is a challenging reinterpretation of the early New Deal years. The transformation of liberalism after 1937 is the subject of Alan Brinkley, *The End of Reform: New Deal Liberalism in Recession and War* (1995). Linda Gordon, *Pitied But Not Entitled: Single Mothers and the History of Welfare* (1994) is a pioneering work on women as the recipients and also the authors of government welfare policies. The efforts of Chicago workers to protest and organize is the subject of Lizabeth Cohen,

Making a New Deal: Industrial Workers in Chicago, 1919–1939 (1990). Nelson Lichtenstein, *The Most Dangerous Man in Detroit: Walter Reuther and the Fate of American Labor* (1995) is a valuable study of one of the early leaders of the CIO. Richard Lowitt, *The New Deal and the West* (1984) pays particular attention to water policy and agriculture in the New Deal years. Jordan Schwarz, *The New Dealers: Power Politics in the Age of Roosevelt* (1993) examines the proponents of state-funded economic development of the South and West. Alan Brinkley, *Voices of Protest: Huey Long, Father Coughlin, and the Great Depression* (1982) examines some of the most powerful challenges to the New Deal. Bruce Shulman, *From Cotton Belt to Sunbelt* (1991) explores the New Deal's effort to transform the region Roosevelt and others considered the nation's number one economic problem, the American South. Harvard Sitkoff, *A New Deal for Blacks* (1978) and Nancy J. Weiss, *Farewell to the Party of Lincoln: Black Politics in the Age of FDR* (1983) take contrasting positions on what the New Deal did for African Americans.

FDR (1994), a documentary by David Grubin, gives viewers a fine view of the private and public life of Franklin D. Roosevelt. One of the president's most vocal and powerful critics is featured in another film, by Ken Burns, *Huey Long* (1986). *The World of Tomorrow* (1984) is a provocative documentary on the 1939 World's Fair.

For quizzes, Internet resources, references to additional books and films, and more, consult the book's Online Learning Center at www.mhhe.com/brinkley11.

"DEFENDING MADRID" The Spanish Civil War, in which fascist forces led by Francisco Franco overturned the existing republican government, was an early signal to many Americans of the dangers of fascism and the threat to democracy. Although the United States government remained aloof from the conflict, several thousand Americans volunteered to fight on behalf of the republican forces. This 1938 Spanish war poster contains the words "Defending Madrid is Defending Catalonia," an effort by the government in Madrid to enlist the support of the surrounding regions in the effort to defend the capital against the fascists. *(Hulton/Archive/Getty Images)*

Significant Events

CHAPTER TWENTY-SEVEN

THE GLOBAL CRISIS, 1921–1941

Henry Cabot Lodge of Massachusetts, chairman of the Senate Foreign Relations Committee and one of the most powerful figures in the Republican Party, led the fight against ratification of the Treaty of Versailles in 1918 and 1919. In part because of his efforts, the Senate defeated the treaty; the United States failed to join the League of Nations; and American foreign policy embarked on an independent course that for the next two decades would attempt, but ultimately fail, to expand American influence and maintain international stability without committing the United States to any lasting relationships with other nations.

Lodge was not an isolationist. He recognized that America had emerged from World War I the most powerful nation in the world. He believed the United States should use that power and should exert its influence internationally. But he believed, too, that America's expanded role in the world should reflect the nation's own interests and its own special virtues; it should leave the nation unfettered with obligations to anyone else. He said in 1919:

> We are a great moral asset of Christian civilization. . . . How did we get there? By our own efforts. Nobody led

us, nobody guided us, nobody controlled us. . . . I would keep America as she has been—not isolated, not prevent her from joining other nations for . . . great purposes—but I wish her to be master of her own fate.

Lodge was not alone in voicing such sentiments. Throughout the 1920s, those controlling American foreign policy attempted to increase America's role in the world while at the same time keeping the nation free of burdensome commitments that might limit its own freedom of action. In 1933, Franklin Roosevelt became president, and brought his own legacy as a leading Wilsonian internationalist and erstwhile supporter of the League of Nations. But for more than six years, Roosevelt also attempted to keep America the "master of her own fate," to avoid important global commitments that might reduce the nation's ability to pursue its own ends.

In the end, the cautious, limited American internationalism of the interwar years proved insufficient to protect the interests of the United States, to create global stability, or to keep the nation from becoming involved in the greatest war in human history.

- Munich Conference
- 1939 · Nazi-Soviet nonaggression pact signed
- Germany invades Czechoslovakia
- Germany invades Poland
- World War II begins
- 1939–1940 · Soviet Union invades Baltic nations, Finland
- 1940 · German blitzkrieg conquers most of western Europe
- Germany, Italy, Japan sign Tripartite Pact
- Fight for Freedom Committee founded
- America First Committee founded
- Roosevelt reelected president

- United States makes destroyers-for-bases deal with Britain
- 1941 · Lend-lease plan provides aid to Britain
- American ships confront German submarines in North Atlantic
- Germany invades Soviet Union
- Atlantic Charter signed
- Japan attacks Pearl Harbor
- United States declares war on Japan
- Germany declares war on United States
- United States declares war on Germany

THE DIPLOMACY OF THE NEW ERA

Critics of American foreign policy in the 1920s often used a single word to describe the cause of their disenchantment: isolationism. Having rejected the Wilsonian vision of a new world order, they claimed, the nation had turned its back on the rest of the globe and repudiated its international responsibilities. In fact, the United States played a more active role in world affairs in the 1920s than it had at almost any previous time in its history—even if not the role the Wilsonians had prescribed.

Myth of Isolationism

Replacing the League

It was clear when the Harding administration took office in 1921 that American membership in the League of Nations was no longer a realistic possibility. As if finally to bury the issue, Secretary of State Charles Evans Hughes secured legislation from Congress in 1921 declaring the war with Germany at an end, and then proceeded to negotiate separate peace treaties with the former Central Powers. Through these treaties, American policymakers believed, the United States would receive all the advantages of the Versailles Treaty with none of the burdensome responsibilities. But Hughes was committed to finding something to replace the League as a guarantor of world peace and stability. He embarked, therefore, on a series of efforts to build safeguards against future wars—but safeguards that would not hamper American freedom of action in the world.

The most important such effort was the Washington Conference of 1921—an attempt to prevent what was threatening to become a costly and destabilizing naval armaments race between America, Britain, and Japan. In his opening speech Hughes startled the delegates by proposing a plan for dramatic reductions in the fleets of all three nations and a ten-year moratorium on the construction of large warships. He called for the actual scrapping of nearly 2 million tons of existing shipping. Far more surprising than that proposal was the fact that the conference ultimately agreed to accept most of its terms, something that Hughes himself apparently had not anticipated. The Five-Power Pact of February 1922 established both limits for total naval tonnage and a ratio of armaments among the signatories. For every 5 tons of American and British warships, Japan would maintain 3 and France and Italy 1.75 each. (Although the treaty seemed to confirm the military inferiority of Japan, in fact it sanctioned Japanese dominance in East Asia. America and Britain had to spread their fleets across the globe; Japan was concerned only with the Pacific.) The Washington Conference also produced two other, related treaties: the Nine-Power Pact, pledging a continuation of the Open Door policy in China, and the Four-Power Pact, by which

Washington Conference of 1921

the United States, Britain, France, and Japan promised to respect one another's Pacific territories and cooperate to prevent aggression.

The Washington Conference began the New Era effort to protect the peace (and to protect the international economic interests of the United States) without accepting active international duties. The Kellogg-Briand Pact of 1928 concluded it. When the French foreign minister, Aristide Briand, asked the United States in 1927 to join an alliance against Germany, Secretary of State Frank Kellogg (who had replaced Hughes in 1925) instead proposed a multilateral treaty outlawing war as an instrument of national policy. Fourteen nations signed the agreement in Paris on August 27, 1928, amid great solemnity and wide international acclaim. Forty-eight other nations later joined the pact. It contained no instruments of enforcement but rested, as Kellogg put it, on the "moral force" of world opinion.

Kellogg-Briand Pact

Debts and Diplomacy

The first responsibility of diplomacy, Hughes, Kellogg, and others agreed, was to ensure that American overseas trade faced no obstacles to expansion and that, once established, it would remain free of interference. Preventing a dangerous armaments race and reducing the possibility of war were steps to that end. So were new financial arrangements that emerged at the same time.

The United States was most concerned about Europe, on whose economic health American prosperity in large part depended. Not only were the major European industrial powers suffering from the devastation World War I had produced; they were also staggering under a heavy burden of debt. The Allied powers were struggling to repay $11 billion in loans they had contracted with the United States during and shortly after the war, loans that the Republican administrations were unwilling to reduce or forgive. "They hired the money, didn't they?" Calvin Coolidge once replied when asked if he favored offering Europe relief from their debts. At the same time, an even more debilitated Germany was attempting to pay the reparations levied against it by the Allies. With the financial structure of Europe on the brink of collapse, the United States stepped in with a solution.

In 1924 Charles G. Dawes, an American banker and diplomat, negotiated an agreement among France, Britain, Germany, and the United States under which American banks would provide enormous loans to the Germans, enabling them to meet their reparations payments; in return, Britain and France would agree to reduce the amount of those payments. Dawes won the Nobel Peace Prize for his efforts, but in fact the Dawes Plan did little to solve the problems it addressed. It was responsible for a growing American economic presence in Germany. It was also the source of a troubling circular pattern in international

Circular Loans

A FORD PLANT IN RUSSIA The success of Henry Ford in creating affordable, mass-produced automobiles made him famous around the world, and particularly popular in the Soviet Union in the 1920s and early 1930s, as the communist regime strove to push the nation into the industrial future. Russians called the system of large-scale factory production "Fordism," and they welcomed assistance from the Ford Motor Company itself, which sent engineers and workers over to Russia to help build large automobile plants such as this one. *(Bettmann/Corbis)*

finance. America would lend money to Germany, which would use that money to pay reparations to France and England, which would in turn use those funds (as well as large loans they themselves were receiving from American banks) to repay war debts to the United States. The flow was able to continue only by virtue of the enormous debts Germany and the other European nations were accumulating to American banks and corporations.

Those banks and corporations were doing more than providing loans. They were becoming a daily presence in the economic life of Europe. American automobile manufacturers were opening European factories, capturing a large share of the overseas market. Other industries in the 1920s were establishing subsidiaries worth more than $10 billion throughout the Continent, taking advantage of the devastation of European industry and the inability of domestic corporations to recover. Some groups within the American government warned that the reckless expansion of overseas loans and investments, many in enterprises of dubious value, threatened disaster; that the United States was becoming too dependent on unstable European economies.

The high tariff barriers that the Republican Congress had erected (through the Fordney-McCumber Act of 1922) were creating additional problems, such skeptics warned. European nations, unable to export their goods to the United States, were finding it difficult to earn the money necessary to repay their loans. Such warnings fell for the most part on deaf ears, and American economic expansion in Europe continued until disaster struck in 1931.

The United States government felt even fewer reservations about assisting American economic expansion in Latin America. After all, the United States had long considered that region its exclusive

Economic Expansion in Latin America

sphere of influence; and its investments there had been large even before World War I. During the 1920s, American military forces maintained a presence in numerous countries in the region. United States investments in Latin America more than doubled between 1924 and 1929; American corporations built roads and other facilities in many areas—partly, they argued, to weaken the appeal of revolutionary forces in the region, but at least equally to increase their own access to Latin America's rich natural resources. American banks were offering large loans to Latin American governments, just as they were in Europe; and just as in Europe, the Latin Americans were having great difficulty earning the money to repay them in the face of the formidable United States tariff barrier. By the end of the 1920s, resentment of "Yankee imperialism" was growing rapidly. The economic troubles after 1929 would only accentuate such problems.

Hoover and the World Crisis

After the relatively placid international climate of the 1920s, the diplomatic challenges facing the Hoover administration must have seemed ominous and bewildering. The world financial crisis that began in 1929 and greatly intensified after 1931 was not only creating economic distress, it was producing a dangerous nationalism that threatened the weak international agreements established during the previous decade. Above all, the Depression was toppling some existing political leaders and replacing them with powerful, belligerent governments bent on expansion as a solution to their economic problems. Hoover was confronted, therefore, with the beginning of a process that would ultimately lead to war. He lacked sufficient tools for dealing with it.

In Latin America, Hoover worked studiously to repair some of the damage created by earlier American policies. He made a ten-week goodwill tour through the region before his inauguration. Once in office, he tried to abstain from intervening in the internal affairs of neighboring nations and moved to withdraw American troops from Haiti. When economic distress led to the collapse of one Latin American regime after another, Hoover announced a new policy: America would grant diplomatic recognition to any sitting government in the region without questioning the means it had used to obtain power. He even repudiated the Roosevelt corollary to the Monroe Doctrine by refusing to permit American intervention when several Latin American countries defaulted on debt obligations to the United States in October 1931.

In Europe, the administration enjoyed few successes in its efforts to promote economic stability. When Hoover's

HITLER AND MUSSOLINI IN BERLIN The German and Italian dictators (shown here reviewing Nazi troops in Berlin in the mid-1930s) acted publicly as if they were equals. Privately, Hitler treated Mussolini with contempt, and Mussolini complained constantly of being a junior partner in the relationship. *(Bettmann/Corbis)*

proposed moratorium on debts in 1931 failed to attract broad support or produce financial stability (see p. 678), many economists and political leaders appealed to the president to cancel all war debts to the United States. Like his predecessors, Hoover refused; and several European nations promptly went into default, severely damaging an already tense international climate. American efforts to extend the disarmament agreements of the 1920s met with similar frustration. At a conference in London in January 1930, American negotiators reached agreement with European and Japanese delegates on extending the limits on naval construction established at the Washington Conference of 1921. But France and England, fearful of German resurgence and Japanese expansionism, insisted on so many loopholes as to make the treaty virtually meaningless. The increasing irrelevance of the New Era approach to diplomacy became even clearer at the World Disarmament Conference that opened in Geneva in January 1932. France rejected the idea of disarmament entirely and called for the creation of an international army to counter the growing power of Germany. Hoover continued to urge major reductions in armaments, including an immediate abolition of all "offensive"

World Disarmament Conference

weapons (tanks, bombers) and a 30 percent reduction in all land and naval forces. The conference ultimately dissolved in failure.

The ineffectiveness of diplomacy in Europe was particularly troubling in view of some of the new governments coming to power on the Continent. Benito Mussolini's Fascist Party had been in control of Italy since the early 1920s; by the 1930s, the regime was growing increasingly nationalistic and militaristic, and Fascist leaders were loudly threatening an active campaign of imperial expansion. Even more ominous was the growing power of the National Socialist (or Nazi) Party in Germany. By the late 1920s, the Weimar Republic, the nation's government since the end of World War I, had lost virtually all popular support, discredited by, among other things, a ruinous inflation. Adolf Hitler, the stridently nationalistic leader of the Nazis, was rapidly growing in popular favor. Although he lost a 1932 election for chancellor, Hitler would sweep into power less than a year later. His belief in the racial superiority of the Aryan (German) people, his commitment to providing *Lebensraum* (living space) for his "master race," his pathological anti-Semitism, and his passionate militarism—all posed a threat to European peace.

THE BOMBING OF CHUNGKING, 1940 Chungking (now Chongqing) was the capital of China under the Nationalist government of Chiang Kai-Shek during World War II. It was also the site of some of the most savage fighting of the Sino-Japanese War. This photograph shows buildings in Chungking burning after Japanese bombing in 1940. *(Hulton/Archive/Getty Images)*

More immediately alarming to the Hoover administration was a major crisis in Asia—another early step toward World War II. The Japanese, reeling from an economic depression of their own, were concerned about the increasing strength of the Soviet Union and of Chiang Kai-shek's nationalist China. In particular, they were alarmed at Chiang's insistence on expanding his government's power in Manchuria, which remained officially a part of China but over which the Japanese had maintained effective economic control since 1905. When the moderate government of Japan failed to take forceful steps to counter Chiang's ambitions, Japan's military leaders staged what was, in effect, a coup in the autumn of 1931—seizing control of foreign policy from the weakened liberals. Weeks later, they launched a major invasion of northern Manchuria.

Manchuria

The American government had few options. For a while, Secretary of State Henry Stimson (who had served as secretary of war under Taft) continued to hope that Japanese moderates would regain control of the Tokyo government and halt the invasion. The militarists, however, remained in command; and by the beginning of 1932, the conquest of Manchuria was complete. Stimson issued stern (but essentially toothless) warnings to Japan and tried to use moral suasion to end the crisis. But Hoover forbade him to cooperate with the League of Nations in imposing economic sanctions against the Japanese. Stimson's only real tool in dealing with the Manchurian invasion was a refusal to grant diplomatic recognition to the new Japanese territories. Japan was unconcerned and early in 1932 expanded its aggression farther into China, attacking the city of Shanghai and killing thousands of civilians.

By the time Hoover left office early in 1933, it was clear that the international system the United States had attempted to create in the 1920s—a system based on voluntary cooperation among nations and on an American refusal to commit itself to the interests of other countries—had collapsed. The United States faced a choice. It could adopt a more energetic form of internationalism and enter into firmer and more meaningful associations with other nations. Or it could resort to nationalism and rely on its own devices for dealing with its (and the world's) problems. For the next six years, it experimented with elements of both approaches.

Failure of America's Interwar Diplomacy

ISOLATIONISM AND INTERNATIONALISM

The administration of Franklin Roosevelt faced a dual challenge as it entered office in 1933. It had to deal with the worst economic crisis in the nation's history, and it had to deal with the effects of a decaying international structure. The two problems were not unrelated. It was the worldwide Depression itself that was producing much of the political chaos throughout the globe.

Through most of the 1930s, however, the United States was unwilling to make more than the faintest of gestures toward restoring stability to the world. Like many other peoples suffering economic hardship, most Americans were turning inward. Yet the realities of world affairs were not to allow the nation to remain isolated for very long—as Franklin Roosevelt realized earlier than many other Americans.

Depression Diplomacy

Roosevelt inherited from Herbert Hoover a foreign policy less concerned with issues of war and peace than with matters of economic policy. And although the New Deal rejected some of the initiatives the Republicans had begun, it continued for several years to base its foreign policy almost entirely on the nation's immediate economic needs.

Perhaps Roosevelt's sharpest break with the policies of his predecessor was on the question of American economic relations with Europe. Hoover had argued that only by resolving the question of war debts and reinforcing the gold standard could the American economy hope to recover. He had therefore, agreed to participate in the World Economic Conference, to be held in London in June 1933, to try to resolve these issues. By the time the conference assembled, however, Roosevelt had already decided to allow the gold value of the dollar to fall to enable American goods to compete in world markets. Shortly after the conference convened, Roosevelt released a famous "bombshell" message repudiating the orthodox views of most of the delegates and rejecting any agreement on currency stabilization. The conference quickly dissolved without reaching agreement, and not until 1936 did the administration finally agree to new negotiations to stabilize Western currencies.

FDR's "Bombshell"

At the same time, Roosevelt abandoned the commitments of the Hoover administration to settle the issue of war debts through international agreement. In effect, he simply let the issue die. Not only did he decline to negotiate a solution at the London Conference, but in April 1934 he signed a bill to forbid American banks from making loans to any nation in default on its debts. The result was to stop the old, circular system by which debt payments continued only by virtue of increasing American loans; within months, war-debt payments from every nation except Finland stopped for good.

Although the new administration had no interest in international currency stabilization or settlement of war debts, it did have an active interest in improving America's position in world trade. Roosevelt approved the Reciprocal Trade Agreement Act of 1934, authorizing the administration to negotiate treaties lowering tariffs by as much as 50 percent in return for reciprocal reductions by other nations. By 1939, Secretary of State Cordell Hull, a devoted free-trader, had negotiated new treaties with twenty-one countries. The result was an increase in American exports to them of nearly 40 percent. But most of the agreements admitted only products not competitive with American industry and agriculture, so imports into the United States continued to lag. Thus other nations were not obtaining the American currency needed to buy American products or pay off debts to American banks.

Reciprocal Trade Agreement Act

America and the Soviet Union

America's hopes of expanding its foreign trade helped produce efforts by the Roosevelt administration to improve relations with the Soviet Union. The United States and Russia had viewed each other with mistrust and even hostility since the Bolshevik Revolution of 1917, and the American government still had not officially recognized the Soviet regime by 1933. But powerful voices within the United States were urging a change in policy—less because the revulsion with which most Americans viewed communism had diminished than because the Soviet Union appeared to be a possible source of trade. The Russians, too, were eager for a new relationship. They were hoping in particular for American cooperation in containing the power of Japan, which Soviet leaders feared as a threat to Russia from the southeast. In November 1933, therefore, Soviet Foreign Minister Maxim Litvinov reached an agreement with the president in Washington. The Soviets would cease their propaganda efforts in the United States and protect American citizens in Russia; in return, the United States would recognize the communist regime.

Despite this promising beginning, however, relations with the Soviet Union soon soured once again. American trade failed to establish much of a foothold in Russia; and the Soviets received no reassurance from the United States that it was interested in stopping Japanese expansion in Asia. By the end of 1934, as a result of these disappointed hopes on both sides, the Soviet Union and the United States were once again viewing each other with considerable mistrust.

The Good Neighbor Policy

Somewhat more successful were American efforts to enhance both diplomatic and economic relations with Latin America through what became known as the "Good

Neighbor Policy." Latin America was one of the most important targets of the new policy of trade reciprocity. During the 1930s, the United States succeeded in increasing both exports to and imports from the other nations of the Western Hemisphere by over 100 percent. Closely tied to these new economic relationships was a new American attitude toward intervention in Latin America. The Hoover administration had unofficially abandoned the earlier American practice of using military force to compel Latin American governments to repay debts, respect foreign investments, or otherwise behave "responsibly." The Roosevelt administration went further. At the Inter-American Conference in Montevideo in December 1933,

Inter-American Conference | Secretary of State Hull signed a formal convention declaring: "No state has the right to intervene in the internal or external affairs of another." Roosevelt respected that pledge throughout his years in office. The Good Neighbor Policy did not mean, however, that the United States had abandoned its influence in Latin America. On the contrary, it had simply replaced one form of leverage with another. Instead of military force, Americans now tried to use economic influence. The new reliance on economic pressures eased tensions between the United States and its neighbors considerably, eliminating the most abrasive and conspicuous irritants in the relationship. It did nothing to stem the growing American domination of the Latin American economies.

The Rise of Isolationism

The first years of the Roosevelt administration marked not only the death of Hoover's hopes for international economic agreements, but the end of any hopes for world peace through treaties and disarmament as well. That the international arrangements of the 1920s were no longer suitable for the world of the 1930s became obvious in the first months of the Roosevelt presidency, when the new administration attempted to stimulate movement toward world disarmament.

The arms control conference in Geneva had been meeting, without result, since 1932; and in May 1933, Roosevelt attempted to spur it to action by submitting a new American proposal for arms reductions. Negotiations stalled and then broke down on the Roosevelt proposal; and only a few months later, first Hitler and then Mussolini withdrew from the talks altogether. The Geneva Conference, it was clear, was a failure. Two years later, Japan withdrew from the London Naval Conference, which was attempting to draw up an agreement to continue the limitations on naval armaments negotiated at the Washington Conference of 1921.

Faced with a choice between more active efforts to stabilize the world or more energetic attempts to isolate the nation from it, most Americans unhesitatingly chose the latter. Support for isolationism emerged from many quarters.

Old Wilsonian internationalists had grown disillusioned with the League of Nations and its inability to stop Japanese aggression in Asia; international-ism, they were beginning to argue, had failed. Other Americans were listening to the argument (popular among populist-minded politicians in the Midwest and West) that powerful business interests—Wall Street, munitions makers, and others—had tricked the United States into participating in World War I. An investigation by a Senate committee chaired by Senator Gerald Nye of North Dakota revealed exorbitant profiteering and blatant tax evasion by many corporations during the war, and it suggested (on the basis of little evidence) that bankers had pressured Wilson to intervene in the war so as to protect their loans abroad. Roosevelt himself shared some of the suspicions voiced by the isolationists and claimed to be impressed by the findings of the Nye investigation. Nevertheless, he continued to hope for at least a modest American role in maintaining world peace. In 1935, he asked the Senate to ratify a treaty to make the United States a member of the World Court—a treaty that would have expanded America's symbolic commitment to internationalism without increasing its actual responsibilities in any important way. Nevertheless, isolationist opposition (spurred by unrelenting hostility from the Hearst newspapers and a passionate broadcast by Father Charles Coughlin on the eve of the Senate vote) resulted in the defeat of the treaty. It was a devastating political blow to the president, and he did not soon again attempt to challenge the isolationist tide.

That tide seemed to grow stronger in the following months. Through the summer of 1935, it became clear that Mussolini's Italy was preparing to invade Ethiopia in an effort to expand its colonial holdings in Africa. Fearing that a general European war would result, American legislators began to design legal safeguards to prevent the United States from being dragged into the conflict. The result was the Neutrality Act of 1935.

The 1935 act, and the Neutrality Acts of 1936 and 1937 that followed, were designed to prevent a recurrence of the events that many Americans now believed had pressured the *Neutrality Acts* United States into World War I. The 1935 law established a mandatory arms embargo against both victim and aggressor in any military conflict and empowered the president to warn American citizens that they might travel on the ships of warring nations only at their own risk. Thus, isolationists believed, the "protection of neutral rights" could not again become an excuse for American intervention in war. The 1936 Neutrality Act renewed these provisions. And in 1937, with world conditions growing even more precarious, Congress passed a still more stringent measure. The new Neutrality Act established the so-called cash-and-carry policy, by which belligerents could purchase only nonmilitary goods from the United States and had to pay cash and carry the goods away on their own vessels.

Long before Pearl Harbor, well before war broke out in Europe in 1939, the first shots of what would become World War II had been fired in the Pacific in a conflict between Japan and China.

Having lived in almost complete isolation from the world until the nineteenth century, Japan had emerged from World War I as one of the world's great powers, with a proud and powerful military and growing global trade. But the Great Depression created severe economic problems for the Japanese (in part because of stiff new American tariffs on silk imports); and as in other parts of the world, the crisis strengthened the political influence of highly nationalistic armed forces. Out of the military emerged dreams of a new Japanese empire in the Pacific. Such an empire would, its proponents believed, give the nation access to fuel, raw material, and markets for its industries, and land for its agricultural needs and its rapidly increasing population. Such an empire, they argued, would free Asia from its exploitation by Europe and America and would create a "new world order based on moral principles."

During World War I, Japan had seized territory and economic concessions in China, and had created a particularly strong presence in the northern Chinese region of Manchuria. There, in September 1931, a group of militant young army officers seized on a railway explosion to justify a military campaign through which they conquered the entire province. Both the United States government and the League of Nations demanded that Japan evacuate Manchuria. The Japanese ignored them, and for the next six years consolidated their control over their new territory.

On July 7, 1937, Japan began a wider war when it attacked Chinese troops at the Marco Polo Bridge outside Beijing. Over the next few weeks, Japanese forces overran a large part of southern China, including most of the port cities, killing many Chinese soldiers and civilians in the process. Particularly notorious was the Japanese annihilation of many thousands of civilians in the city of Nanjing (the number has long been in dispute, but estimates range from 80,000 to over

ENTERING MANCHURIA, 1931 Japanese troops pour into Mukden (now Shenyang), the capital of the Chinese province of Manchuria, in 1931—following a staged incident that allowed Japan to claim that its troops had been attacked. The so-called "Mukden Incident" marked the beginning of the long Sino-Japanese War. *(Hulton/Archive/Getty Images)*

300,000) in an event that became known in China and the West as the Nanjing Massacre. The Chinese government fled to the mountains. As in 1931, the United States and the League of Nations protested in vain.

The China that the Japanese had invaded was a nation in turmoil. It was engaged in a civil war of its own—between the so-called Kuomintang, a Nationalist party led by Chiang Kai-Shek, and the Chinese Communist Party, led by Mao Zedong; and this internal struggle weakened China's capacity to resist invasion. But beginning in 1937, the two Chinese rivals agreed to an uneasy truce and began fighting the Japanese together, with some success—bogging the Japanese military down in a seemingly endless war and imposing hardships on the Japanese people at home. The Japanese government and the military, however, remained determined to continue the war against China, whatever the sacrifices.

One result of the costs of the war in China was a growing Japanese dependence on the United States for steel and oil to meet civilian and military needs. In July 1941, in an effort to pressure the Japanese to stop their expansion, the Roosevelt administration made it impossible for the Japanese to continue buying American oil. Japan now faced a choice between ending its war in China or finding other sources of fuel to keep its war effort (and its civilian economy) going. They chose to extend the war beyond China in a search for oil. The best available sources were in the Dutch East Indies; but the only way to secure that European colony, they believed, would be to neutralize the increasingly hostile United States in Asia. Visionary military planners in Japan began advocating a daring move to immobilize the Americans in the Pacific before expanding the war elsewhere—with an attack on the American naval base at Pearl Harbor. The first blow of World War II in America, therefore, was the culmination of more than a decade of Japanese efforts to conquer China.

The American stance of militant neutrality gained support in October 1935 when Mussolini finally launched

Ethiopia

his long-anticipated attack on Ethiopia. When the League of Nations protested, Italy simply resigned from the organization, completed its conquest of Ethiopia, and formed an alliance (the "Axis") with Nazi Germany. Most Americans responded to the news with renewed determination to isolate themselves from European instability. Two-thirds of those responding to public opinion polls at the time opposed any American action to deter aggression. Isolationist sentiment showed its strength once again in 1936–1937 in response to the civil war in Spain. The Falangists, a group much like the Italian fascists, revolted in July 1936 against the existing republican government. Hitler and Mussolini supported General Francisco Franco, who became the leader of the Falangists in 1937, both vocally and with weapons and supplies. Some individual Americans traveled to Spain to assist the republican cause (see p. 691); but the United States government joined with Britain and France in an agreement to offer no assistance to either side—although all three governments were sympathetic to the republicans.

Alarmed by the events of 1935 and 1936, Roosevelt began moving slowly and cautiously to challenge the grip of the isolationists on the nation's foreign policy. For a time, it seemed to be a hopeless cause. The United States was unable to do much more than watch as a series of new dangers emerged that brought the world closer to war.

Particularly disturbing was the deteriorating situation in Asia. Japan's aggressive designs against China had been clear since the invasion of Manchuria in 1931. In the summer of 1937, Tokyo launched an even broader assault, attacking China's five northern provinces. The United States, Roosevelt believed, could not allow the Japanese aggression to go unremarked or unpunished. In a speech in Chicago in October 1937, therefore, the president warned forcefully of the dangers that Japanese aggression posed to world peace. Aggressors, he proclaimed, should be "quarantined" by the international community to pre-

"Quarantine" Speech

vent the contagion of war from spreading. The president was deliberately vague about what such a "quarantine" would mean, and there is evidence that he was contemplating nothing more drastic than a break in diplomatic relations with Japan, that he was not considering economic or military sanctions. Nevertheless, public response to the speech was disturbingly hostile. As a result, Roosevelt drew back. Although his strong words encouraged the British government to call a conference in Brussels to discuss the crisis in Asia, the United States refused to make any commitments to collective action, and the conference produced no agreement.

Only months later, another episode provided renewed evidence of how formidable the obstacles to Roosevelt's efforts remained. On December 12, 1937, Japanese aviators bombed and sank the U.S. gunboat *Panay* as it sailed the Yangtze River in China. The attack was almost undoubtedly deliberate. It occurred in broad daylight, with clear visibility, and a large American flag had been painted conspicuously on the *Panay's* deck. Even so, isolationists seized eagerly on Japanese protestations that the bombing had been an accident and pressured the administration into accepting Japan's apologies and overlooking the attack.

The Failure of Munich

Hitler's determination to expand German power became fully visible in 1936, when he moved the revived German army into the Rhineland, violating the Versailles Treaty and rearming an area that France had, in effect, controlled since World War I. In March 1938, German forces marched into Austria, and Hitler proclaimed a union (or *Anschluss*) between Austria, his native land, and Germany, his adopted one—thus fulfilling his longtime dream of uniting the German-speaking peoples in one great nation. Neither in America nor in most of Europe was there much more than a murmur of opposition. The Austrian invasion, however, soon created another crisis; for Hitler had by now occupied territory surrounding three sides of western Czechoslovakia, a region he dreamed of annexing to provide Germany with the *Lebensraum* he believed it needed. In September 1938, he demanded that Czechoslovakia cede to him part of that region, the Sudetenland, an area on the Austro-German border in which many ethnic Germans lived. Czechoslovakia, which possessed substantial military power of its own, was prepared to fight rather than submit. But it realized it could not hope for success without help from other European nations. It got none. Most Western nations were appalled at the prospect of another war and were willing to pay almost any price to settle the crisis peacefully. Anxiety ran almost as high in the United States as it did in Europe during and after the crisis, and helped produce such strange expressions of fear as the hysterical response to the famous "War of the Worlds" radio broadcast in October. (See "Patterns of Popular Culture," pp. 738–739.)

On September 29, Hitler met with the leaders of France and Great Britain at Munich in an effort to resolve the crisis. The French and British

Munich Conference

agreed to accept the German demands in Czechoslovakia in return for Hitler's promise to expand no farther. "This is the last territorial claim I have to make in Europe," the Fuhrer solemnly declared. And Prime Minister Neville Chamberlain returned to England to a hero's welcome, assuring his people that the agreement ensured "peace in our time." Among those who had cabled him with encouragement at Munich was Franklin Roosevelt.

ORSON WELLES AND THE WAR OF THE WORLDS

On the evening of October 30, 1938, about 6 million Americans were listening to the weekly radio program *The Mercury Theater of the Air,* produced by the actor/filmmaker Orson Welles and broadcast over the CBS network. A few minutes into the show, an announcer broke in and interrupted some dance music with a terrifying report:

> At least forty people, including six state troopers, lie dead in a field east of Grover's Mill [New Jersey], their bodies burned and distorted beyond recognition. . . . Good heavens, something's wriggling out of the shadow like a gray snake! Now it's another one and

another. . . . It's large as a bear and it glistens like black leather. But that face . . . it's indescribable! I can hardly force myself to keep looking at it.

The panicky announcer was describing the beginning of an alien invasion of earth and the appearance of Martians armed with "death rays," determined to destroy the planet. Later in the evening, an announcer claiming to be broadcasting from Times Square reported the destruction of New York City before falling dead at the microphone. Other statements advised citizens of surrounding areas to flee.

The dramatic "news bulletins" were part of a radio play by Howard Koch, loosely adapted from H. G. Wells's 1898 novel *The War of the Worlds.* Announcers reminded the audience repeatedly throughout the broadcast that they were listening to a play, not reality. But many people either did not hear or did not notice the disclaimers. By the end of the hour, according to some estimates, as many as a million Americans were flying into panics, convinced that the end of the world was imminent.

Thousands of listeners in New York and New Jersey actually fled their

THE MERCURY THEATER OF THE AIR
Orson Welles, the founder and director of the Mercury Theater of the Air, directs a corps of actors during a rehearsal for one of the show's radio plays. *(Culver Pictures, Inc.)*

WELLES ON THE AIR   Welles is shown here during the broadcast of the "War of the Worlds" in 1938. Although he was careful to note that the broadcast was fiction, he came under intense criticism in following days for the panic it caused among many listeners.   *(Bettmann/Corbis)*

The Munich accords were the most prominent element of a policy that came to be known as "appeasement" and that came to be identified (not altogether fairly) almost exclusively with Chamberlain. Whoever was to blame, however, it became clear almost immediately that the policy was a failure. In March 1939, Hitler occupied the remaining areas of Czechoslovakia, violating the Munich agreement unashamedly. And in April, he began issuing threats against Poland. At that point, both Britain and France gave assurances to the Polish government that they would come to its assistance in case of an invasion; they even

Failure of "Appeasement"

flirted, too late, with the Stalinist regime in Russia, attempting to draw it into a mutual defense agreement. Stalin, however, had already decided that he could expect no protection from the West; after all, he had not even been invited to attend the Munich Conference. Accordingly, he signed a nonaggression pact with Hitler in August 1939, freeing the Germans for the moment from the danger of a two-front war. For a few months, Hitler had been trying to frighten the Poles into submitting to German demands. When that failed, he staged an incident on the border to allow him to claim that Germany had been attacked; and on September 1, 1939, he launched a full-scale

homes and tried to drive along clogged highways into the hills or the country-side. Others rushed into the streets, huddled in parks, or hid under bridges. In Newark, people ran from their buildings with wet towels wrapped around their faces or wearing gas masks—as if defending themselves against the chemical warfare that many remembered from the trenches in World War I. In cities across the country, people flocked into churches to pray; called police and hospitals for help; flooded the switchboards of newspapers, magazines, and radio stations desperate for information. "I never hugged my radio so closely as I did last night," one woman later explained. "I held a crucifix in my hand and prayed while looking out of my open window for falling meteors." The *New York Times* described it the next day as "a wave of mass hysteria." Other papers wrote of a "tidal wave of terror that swept the nation." For weeks thereafter Orson Welles and other producers of the show were the focus of a barrage of criticism for what many believed had been a deliberate effort to create public fear. For years, sociologists and other scholars studied the episode for clues about mass behavior.

Welles and his colleagues claimed to be surprised by the reaction their show created. It had never occurred to them, they insisted, that anyone would consider it real. But the broadcast proved more effective than they had expected because it touched on a cluster of anxieties and assumptions that

MASS HYSTERIA A *New York Times* headline the morning after the famous "War of the Worlds" Broadcast of the Mercury Theater of the Air reports on the panic the radio show had caused the night before. "A wave of mass hysteria seized thousands of radio listeners throughout the nation between 8:15 and 9:30 o'clock last night," the paper reported, "when a broadcast of H. G. Wells fantasy 'The War of the Worlds,' led thousands to believe that an interplanetary conflict had started with invading Martians spreading wide death and destruction in New Jersey and New York. *(Copyright © 1938 by the New York Times Co. Reprinted by Permission)*

ran deep in American life at the time—anxieties similar to those that run deep again today in the aftermath of the September 2001 attacks on New York and Washington. The show aired only a few weeks after the war fever that had preceded the Munich pact among Germany, Britain, and France; Americans already jittery about the possibility of war proved easy prey to fears of another kind of invasion. The show also tapped longer-standing anxieties about the fragility of life that afflicted many Americans during the long Depression of the 1930s, and it seemed to frighten working-class people—those most vulnerable to unexpected catastrophes—in particular.

Most of all, however, *The War of the Worlds* unintentionally exploited the enormous power radio had come to exercise in American life, and the great trust many people had developed in what they heard over the air. Over 85 percent of American families had radios in 1938. For many of them, the broadcasts they received had become their principal, even their only, source

of information about the outside world. When the actors from the Mercury Theater began to use the familiar phrases and cadences of radio news announcers, it was all too easy for members of their audience to assume that they were hearing the truth.

Welles concluded the broadcast by describing the play as "the Mercury Theater's own radio version of dressing up in a sheet and jumping out of a bush and saying Boo! . . . So good-bye everybody, and remember, please, for the next day or so, the terrible lesson you learned tonight. The grinning, glowing, globular invader of your living room is an inhabitant of the pumpkin patch, and if your doorbell rings and there's no one there, that was no Martian . . . it's Halloween." But the real lesson of *The War of the Worlds* was not Welles's jocular one. It was the lesson of the enormous, and at times frightening, power of the medium of broadcasting.

From *War of the Worlds* by Howard Koch. Copyright © 1938 Howard Koch. Reprinted by permission from International Creative Management, Inc.

invasion of Poland. Britain and France, true to their pledges, declared war on Germany two days later. World War II had begun.

FROM NEUTRALITY TO INTERVENTION

"This nation will remain a neutral nation," the president declared shortly after the hostilities began in Europe, "but I cannot ask that every American remain neutral in thought as well." It was a statement that stood in stark and deliberate contrast to Woodrow Wilson's 1914 plea that the nation remain neutral in both deed and thought; and it was clear from the start that among those whose opinions were decidedly unneutral in 1939 was the president himself.

Neutrality Tested

There was never any question that both the president and the majority of the American people favored Britain, France, and the other Allied nations in the contest. The question was how much the United States was prepared

739

THE OCCUPATION OF POLAND, 1939 A German motorized detachment enters a Polish town that has already been battered by heavy bombing from the German air force (the *Luftwaffe*). The German invasion of Poland, which began on September 1, 1939, sparked the formal beginning of World War II. *(Bettmann/Corbis)*

the situation in the West, the Soviet Union overran and annexed the small Baltic republics of Latvia, Estonia, and Lithuania and then, in late November, invaded Finland. Most Americans were outraged, but neither Congress nor the president was willing to do more than impose an ineffective "moral embargo" on the shipment of armaments to Russia. By March 1940, the Soviet advance was complete.

Whatever illusions anyone may have had about the reality of the war in Western Europe were shattered in the spring of 1940 when Germany launched an invasion to the west—first attacking Denmark and Norway, sweeping next across the Netherlands and Belgium, and driving finally deep into the heart of France. Allied efforts proved futile against the Nazi blitzkrieg. One western European stronghold after another fell into German hands. On June 10, Mussolini brought Italy into the war, invading France from the south as Hitler was attacking from the north. On June 22, finally, France fell to the German onslaught. Nazi troops *Fall of France* marched into Paris; a new collaborationist regime assembled in Vichy; and in all Europe, only the shattered remnants of the British army, rescued from the beaches of Dunkirk by a flotilla of military and civilian vessels assembled miraculously quickly, remained to oppose the Axis forces.

Roosevelt had already begun to increase American aid to the Allies. He also began preparations to resist a possible Nazi invasion of the United States. On May 16, he asked Congress for an additional $1 billion for defense (much of it for the construction of an enormous new fleet of warplanes) and received it quickly. With France tottering a few weeks later, he proclaimed that the United States would "extend to the opponents of force the material resources of this nation." And on May 15, Winston Churchill, the new British prime minister, sent Roosevelt the first of many long lists of requests for ships, armaments, and other assistance without which, he insisted, England could not long survive. Many Americans (including the United States ambassador to London, Joseph P. Kennedy) argued that the British plight was already hopeless, that any aid to the English was a wasted effort. The president, however, made the politically dangerous decision to "scrape the bottom of the barrel" to make war materials available to Churchill. He even circumvented the cash-and-carry provisions of the Neutrality Act by trading fifty American destroyers (most of them left over from World War I) to England in return for the right to build American bases on British territory in the Western Hemisphere; and he returned to the factories a number of new airplanes purchased by the American government so that the British could buy them instead.

Roosevelt was able to take such steps in part because of a major shift in American public opinion. Before the invasion of France, most Americans had believed that a German victory in the war would not be a threat to the

to do to assist them. At the very least, Roosevelt believed, the United States should make armaments available to the Allied armies to help them counter the highly productive German munitions industry. In September 1939, he asked Congress for a revision of the Neutrality Acts. The original measures had forbidden the sale of American weapons to any nation engaged in war; Roosevelt wanted the arms embargo lifted. Powerful isolationist opposition forced him to accept a weaker revision than he would have liked; as passed by Congress, the 1939 measure maintained the prohibition on American ships entering war zones. It *Cash-and-Carry* did, however, permit belligerents to purchase arms on the same cash-and-carry basis that the earlier Neutrality Acts had established for the sale of nonmilitary materials.

For a time, it was possible to believe that little more would be necessary. After the German armies had quickly subdued Poland, the war in Europe settled into a long, quiet lull that lasted through the winter and spring—a "phony war," some called it. The only real fighting during this period occurred not between the Allies and the Axis, but between Russia and its neighbors. Taking advantage of

THE BLITZ, LONDON The German Luftwaffe terrorized London and other British cities in 1940–1941 and again late in the war by bombing civilian areas indiscriminately in an effort to break the spirit of the English people. The effort failed, and the fortitude of the British in the face of the attack did much to arouse support for their cause in the United States. St. Paul's Cathedral, largely undamaged throughout the raids, looms in the background of this photograph, as other buildings crumble under the force of German bombs. *(Brown Brothers)*

United States. By July, with France defeated and Britain threatened, more than 66 percent of the public (according to opinion polls) believed that Germany posed a direct threat to the United States. Congress was aware of the change and was becoming more willing to permit expanded American assistance to the Allies. It was also becoming more concerned about the need for internal preparations for war, and in September it approved the Burke-Wadsworth Act, inaugurating the first peacetime military draft in American history.

Shifting Public Opinion

But while the forces of isolation may have weakened, they were far from dead. On the contrary, a spirited and at times vicious debate began in the spring of 1940 between those who advocated expanded American involvement in the war (who were termed, often inaccurately, "interventionists") and those who continued to insist on neutrality. The celebrated journalist William Allen White served as chairman of a new Committee to Defend America, whose members lobbied actively for increased American assistance to the Allies but opposed actual intervention. Others went so far as to urge an immediate declaration of war (a position that as yet had little public support) and in April 1940 created an organization of their own, the Fight for Freedom Committee.

Opposing them was a powerful new lobby called the America First Committee, which attracted some of America's most prominent leaders. Its chairman was General Robert E. Wood, until recently the president of Sears Roebuck; and its membership included Charles Lindbergh, General Hugh Johnson, Senator Gerald Nye, and Senator Burton Wheeler. It won the editorial support of the Hearst chain and other influential newspapers, and it had at least the indirect support of a large proportion of the Republican Party. (It also, inevitably, attracted a fringe of Nazi sympathizers and anti-Semites.) The debate between the two sides was loud and bitter. Through the summer and fall of 1940, moreover, it was complicated by a presidential campaign.

America First Committee

The Third-Term Campaign

For many months, the politics of 1940 revolved around the question of Franklin Roosevelt's intentions. Would he break with tradition and run for an unprecedented third term? The president himself was deliberately coy and never publicly revealed his own wishes. But by refusing to withdraw from the contest, he made it virtually impossible for any rival Democrat to establish a foothold within the party. Just before the Democratic Convention in July, he let it be known that he would accept a "draft" from his party. The Democrats quickly renominated him and even reluctantly swallowed his choice for vice president: Agriculture secretary Henry A. Wallace, a man too liberal for the taste of many party leaders.

The Republicans, again, faced a far more difficult task. With Roosevelt effectively straddling the center of the defense debate, favoring neither the extreme isolationists nor the extreme interventionists, the Republicans had few viable alternatives. Their solution was to compete with the president on his own ground. Succumbing to a remarkable popular movement (carefully orchestrated by, among others, Henry Luce, the *Wendell Willkie* publisher of *Time* and *Life* magazines), they nominated a dynamic and attractive but politically inexperienced businessman, Wendell Willkie.

Both the candidate and the party platform took positions little different from Roosevelt's: they would keep the country out of war but would extend generous assistance to the Allies. Willkie was left, therefore, with the unenviable task of defeating Roosevelt by outmatching him in personal magnetism and by trying to arouse public fears of the dangers of an unprecedented third term. An appealing figure and a vigorous campaigner, he managed to evoke more public enthusiasm than any Republican candidate in decades. In the end, however, he was no match for Franklin Roosevelt. The election was closer than it had been in either 1932 or 1936, but Roosevelt nevertheless won decisively. He received 55 percent of the popular vote to Willkie's 45 percent, and won 449 electoral votes to Willkie's 82.

Neutrality Abandoned

In the last weeks of 1940, with the election behind him, Roosevelt began to make subtle but profound changes in the American role in the war. To the public, he claimed that he was simply continuing the now established policy of providing aid to the embattled Allies. In fact, that aid was taking new and more decisive forms.

In December 1940, Great Britain was virtually bankrupt. No longer could the British meet the cash-and-carry requirements imposed by the Neutrality Acts; yet England's needs, Churchill insisted, were greater than ever. The president therefore, suggested a method that would "eliminate the dollar sign" from all arms transactions while still, he hoped, pacifying those who opposed blatant American intervention in the war. The new system was labeled "lend-lease." It would allow the government not only to sell but to lend or lease armaments to any nation deemed *Lend-lease* "vital to the defense of the United States." In other words, America could funnel weapons to England on the basis of no more than Britain's promise to return or pay for them when the war was over. Isolationists attacked the measure bitterly, arguing (correctly) that it was simply a device to tie the United States more closely to the Allies; but Congress enacted the bill by wide margins.

With lend-lease established, Roosevelt soon faced another serious problem: ensuring that the American supplies would actually reach Great Britain. Shipping lanes in the Atlantic had become extremely dangerous; German submarines destroyed as much as a half-million tons of shipping each month. The British navy was losing ships more rapidly than it could replace them and was finding it difficult to transport materials across the Atlantic from America. Secretary of War Henry Stimson (who had been Hoover's secretary of state and who returned to the cabinet at Roosevelt's request in 1940) argued that the United States should itself convoy vessels to England; but Roosevelt decided to rely instead on the concept of "hemispheric defense," by which the United States navy would defend transport ships only in the western Atlantic—which he argued was a neutral zone and the responsibility of the American nations. By July 1941, American ships were patrolling the ocean as far east as Iceland, escorting convoys of merchant ships, and radioing information to British vessels about the location of Nazi submarines.

At first, Germany did little to challenge these obviously hostile American actions. By the fall of 1941, however, events in Europe changed its position. German forces had invaded the Soviet Union in June *Germany Invades the USSR* of that year, shattering the 1939 Nazi-Soviet pact. The Germans drove quickly and forcefully deep into Russian territory. When the Soviets did not surrender, as many had predicted they would, Roosevelt persuaded Congress to extend lend-lease privileges to them—the first step toward creating a new relationship with Stalin that would ultimately lead to a formal Soviet-American alliance. Now American industry was providing crucial assistance to Hitler's foes on two fronts, and the navy was playing a more active role than ever in protecting the flow of goods to Europe.

In September, Nazi submarines began a concerted campaign against American vessels. Early that month, a German U-boat fired on the American destroyer *Greer* (which was radioing the U-boat's position to the British at the time). Roosevelt responded by ordering American ships to fire on German submarines "on sight." In October, Nazi submarines actually hit two American destroyers and sank one of them, the *Reuben James,* killing many American sailors in the process. Enraged members of Congress now voted approval of a measure allowing the United States to arm its merchant vessels and to sail all the way into belligerent ports. The United States had, in effect, launched a naval war against Germany.

At the same time, a series of meetings, some private and one public, were tying the United States and Great Britain more closely together. In April 1941, senior military officers of the two nations met in secret and agreed on the joint strategy they would follow were the United States to enter the war. In August, Roosevelt met with Churchill aboard a British vessel anchored off the coast of Newfoundland. The president made no military com-

Atlantic Charter

mitments, but he did join the prime minister in releasing a document that became known as the Atlantic Charter, in which the two nations set out "certain common principles" on which to base "a better future for the world." It was, in only vaguely disguised form, a statement of war aims that called openly for, among other things, "the final destruction of the Nazi tyranny."

By the fall of 1941, it seemed only a matter of time before the United States became an official belligerent. Roosevelt remained convinced that public opinion would support a declaration of war only in the event of an actual enemy attack. But an attack seemed certain to come, if not in the Atlantic, then in the Pacific.

The Road to Pearl Harbor

In the meantime, Japan was taking advantage of the crisis (which had preoccupied the Soviet Union and the two

Tripartite Pact

most powerful colonial powers in Asia, Britain and France) to extend its empire in the Pacific. In September 1940, Japan signed the Tripartite Pact, a loose defensive alliance with Germany and Italy that seemed to extend the Axis into Asia. (In reality, the European Axis powers never developed a very strong relationship with Japan, and the wars in Europe and the Pacific were largely separate conflicts.)

Roosevelt had already displayed his animosity toward Japanese policies by harshly denouncing their continuing assault on China and by terminating a longstanding American commercial treaty with the Tokyo government. Still the Japanese drive continued. In July 1941, imperial troops moved into Indochina and seized the capital of Vietnam, a colony of France (after having demanded and received a base there a year before). The United States, having broken the Japanese codes, knew that Japan's next target would be the Dutch East Indies; and when Tokyo failed to respond to Roosevelt's stern warnings, the president froze all Japanese assets in the United States and established a complete trade embargo, severely limiting Japan's ability to purchase essential supplies (including oil). American public opinion, shaped by strong anti-Japanese prejudices developed over several decades, generally supported these hostile actions.

Tokyo now faced a choice. It would either have to repair relations with the United States to restore the flow of supplies, or it would have to find those supplies elsewhere, most notably by seizing British and Dutch possessions in the Pacific. At first the Tokyo government seemed willing to compromise. The Japanese prime minister, Prince Konoye, had begun negotiations with the United States even before the freezing of his country's assets, and in August he increased the pace by requesting a personal meeting with President Roosevelt. But the United States rebuffed these overtures. Secretary of State Hull feared that Konoye lacked sufficient power within his own government to be able to enforce any agreement, and he persuaded Roosevelt to say that he would meet with the prime minister only if Japan would give guarantees in advance that it would respect the territorial integrity of China. Konoye could give no such assurances, as Roosevelt and Hull knew, and the negotiations collapsed. In October, militants in Tokyo forced Konoye out of office and replaced him with the leader of the war party, General Hideki Tojo. With Japan's need for new sources of fuel becoming desperate, there now seemed little alternative to war.

For several weeks, the Tojo government kept up a pretense of wanting to continue negotiations. On November 20, 1941, Tokyo proposed a modus vivendi highly favorable to itself and sent its diplomats in Washington to the State Department to discuss it. But Tokyo had already decided that it would not yield on the question of China, and Washington had made clear that it would accept nothing less than a reversal of that policy. Hull rejected the Japanese overtures out of hand; on November 27, he told Secretary of War Henry Stimson, "I have washed my hands of the Japanese situation, and it is now in the hands of you and [Secretary of the

Tokyo's Decision for War

Navy Frank] Knox, the Army and Navy." He was not merely speculating. American intelligence had already decoded Japanese messages, which made clear that war was imminent, that after November 29 an attack would be only a matter of days.

But Washington did not know where the attack would take place. Most officials were convinced that the Japanese would move first not against American territory but against British or Dutch possessions to the south. American intelligence took note of a Japanese naval task force that began sailing east from the Kurile Islands in the general direction of Hawaii on November 25, and radioed a routine warning to the United States naval facility at Pearl Harbor, near Honolulu. But officials were paying more attention to a large Japanese convoy moving southward through the China Sea. A combination of confusion and miscalculation led the government to overlook indications that Japan intended a direct attack on American forces—partly because Hawaii was so far from Japan that few believed such an attack possible.

At 7:55 A.M. on Sunday, December 7, 1941, a wave of Japanese bombers—taking off from aircraft carriers

The phrase "Remember Pearl Harbor!" became a rallying cry during World War II—reminding Americans of the surprise Japanese attack on the American naval base in Hawaii and arousing the nation to exact revenge. But within a few years of the end of hostilities, some Americans remembered Pearl Harbor for very different reasons. They began to challenge the official version of the attack on December 7, 1941, and their charges sparked a debate that has never fully subsided. Was the Japanese attack on Pearl Harbor unprovoked, and did it come without warning, as the Roosevelt administration claimed at the time? Or was it part of a deliberate plan by the president to make the Japanese force a reluctant United States into the war? Most controversial of all, did the administration know of the attack in advance? Did Roosevelt deliberately refrain from warning the commanders in Hawaii so that the air raid's effect on the American public would be more profound?

Among the first to challenge the official version of Pearl Harbor was the historian Charles A. Beard, who maintained in *President Roosevelt and the Coming of the War* (1948) that the United States had deliberately forced the Japanese into a position where they had no choice but to attack. By cutting off Japan's access to the raw materials it needed for its military adventure in China, by stubbornly refusing to compromise, the United States ensured that the Japanese would strike out into the southwest Pacific to take the needed supplies by force—even at the risk of war with the United States. Not only was American policy provocative in effect, Beard suggested, it was deliberately provocative. More than that, the administration, which had some time before cracked the Japanese code, must have known weeks in advance of Japan's plan to attack—although he did not claim that officials knew the attack would come at Pearl Harbor. Beard supported his argument by citing Secretary of War Henry Stimson's comment in his diary: "The question was how we should maneuver them into the position of firing the first shot." This view has

PEARL HARBOR, DECEMBER 7, 1941 The destroyer U.S.S. *Shaw*, immobilized in a floating drydock in Pearl Harbor in December 1941, survived the first wave of Japanese bombers unscathed. But in the second attack, the Japanese scored a direct hit and produced this spectacular explosion, which blew off the ship's bow. Damage to the rest of the ship, however, was slight. Just a few months later the *Shaw* was fitted with a new bow and rejoined the fleet. (*U.S. Navy Photo*)

hundreds of miles away—attacked the United States naval base at Pearl Harbor. A second wave came an hour later.

Pearl Harbor

Military commanders in Hawaii had taken no precautions against such an attack and had allowed ships to remain bunched up defenselessly in the harbor and airplanes to remain parked in rows on airstrips. The consequences of the raid were disastrous for America. Within two hours, the United States lost 8 battleships, 3 cruisers, 4 other vessels, 188 airplanes, and several vital shore installations. More than 2,000 soldiers and sailors died, and another 1,000 were injured. The Japanese suffered only light losses.

American forces were now greatly diminished in the Pacific (although by a fortunate accident, none of the American aircraft carriers—the heart of the Pacific fleet—had been at Pearl Harbor on December 7). Nevertheless, the raid on Pearl Harbor did virtually overnight what

more than two years of effort by Roosevelt and others had been unable to do: it unified the American people in a fervent commitment to war. On December 8, the president traveled to Capitol Hill, where he grimly addressed a joint session of Congress: "Yesterday, December 7, 1941—a date which will live in infamy—the United States of America was suddenly and deliberately attacked by the naval and air forces of the Empire of Japan." Within four hours, the Senate unanimously and the House 388 to 1 (the lone dissenter being Jeanette Rankin of Montana, who had voted against war in 1917 as well) approved a declaration of war against Japan. Three days later, Germany and Italy, Japan's European allies, declared war on the United States; and on the same day, December 11, Congress reciprocated without a dissenting vote. For the second time in twenty-five years, the United States was engaged in a world war.

reappeared more recently in Thomas Fleming, *The New Dealers's War,* which also argues that Roosevelt deliberately (and duplicitously) maneuvered the United States into war with Japan.

A partial refutation of the Beard argument appeared in 1950 in Basil Rauch's *Roosevelt from Munich to Pearl Harbor.* The administration did not know in advance of the planned attack on Pearl Harbor, he argued. It did, however, expect an attack somewhere; and it made subtle efforts to "maneuver" Japan into firing the first shot in the conflict. But Richard N. Current, in *Secretary Stimson: A Study in Statecraft* (1954), offered an even stronger challenge to Beard. Stimson did indeed anticipate an attack, Current argued, but not an attack on American territory; rather, he anticipated an assault on British or Dutch possessions in the Pacific. The problem confronting the administration was not how to maneuver the Japanese into attacking the United States, but how to find a way to make a Japanese attack on British or Dutch territory appear to be an attack on America. Only thus, Stimson believed, could Congress be persuaded to approve a declaration of war.

Roberta Wohlstetter took a different approach to the question in *Pearl Harbor: Warning and Decision* (1962), the most thorough scholarly study to appear to that point. De-emphasizing the question of whether the American government wanted a Japanese attack, she undertook to answer the question of whether the administration knew of the attack in advance. Wohlstetter concluded that the United States had ample warning of Japanese intentions and should have realized that the Pearl Harbor raid was imminent. But government officials failed to interpret the evidence correctly, largely because their preconceptions about Japanese intentions were at odds with the evidence they confronted. Admiral Edwin T. Layton, who had been a staff officer at Pearl Harbor in 1941, also blamed political and bureaucratic failures for the absence of advance warning of the attack. In a 1985 memoir, *And I Was There,* he argued that the Japanese attack was not only a result of "audacious planning and skillful execution" by the Japanese, but of "a dramatic breakdown in our intelligence process . . . related directly to feuding among high-level naval officers in Washington."

The most thorough study of Pearl Harbor to date appeared in 1981: Gordon W. Prange's *At Dawn We Slept.* Like Wohlstetter, Prange concluded that the Roosevelt administration was guilty of a series of disastrous blunders in interpreting Japanese strategy; the American government had possession of enough information to predict the attack, but failed to do so. But Prange dismissed the arguments of the "revisionists" (Beard and his successors) that the president had deliberately maneuvered the nation into the war by permitting the Japanese to attack. Instead, he emphasized the enormous daring and great skill with which the Japanese orchestrated an ambitious operation that few Americans believed possible.

But the revisionist claims have not been laid to rest. John Toland revived the charges of a Roosevelt betrayal in 1982, in *Infamy: Pearl Harbor and Its Aftermath,* claiming to have discovered new evidence (the testimony of an unidentified seaman) that proves the navy knew at least five days in advance that Japanese aircraft carriers were heading toward Hawaii. From that, Toland concluded that Roosevelt must have known that an attack was forthcoming and that he allowed it to occur in the belief that a surprise attack would arouse the nation. But like the many previous writers who have made the same argument, Toland was unable to produce any direct evidence of Roosevelt's knowledge of the planned attack. Nor could he offer any plausible explanation of why an American leader would deliberately allow his nation to enter a war with its Pacific fleet badly crippled and its navy humiliated.

CONCLUSION

American foreign policy in the years after World War I attempted something that ultimately proved impossible. The United States was determined to be a major power in the world, to extend its trade broadly around the globe, and to influence other nations in ways Americans believed would be beneficial to their own, and the world's, interests. But the United States was also determined to do nothing that would limit its own freedom of action. It would not join the League of Nations. It would not join the World Court. It would not form alliances with other nations. It would operate powerfully—and alone.

But ominous forces were at work in the world that would gradually push the United States into greater engagement with other nations. The economic disarray that the Great Depression created all around the world; the rise of totalitarian regimes in Europe and Asia; the expansionist ambitions of powerful new leaders—all worked to destroy the uneasy stability of the post-World War I international system. America's own interests, economic and otherwise, were now imperiled. And America's go-it-alone foreign policy seemed powerless to change the course of events.

Franklin Roosevelt tried throughout the later years of the 1930s to push the American people slowly into a greater involvement in international affairs. In particular, he tried to nudge the United States toward taking a more forceful stand against dictatorship and aggression. A powerful isolationist movement helped stymie him for a time, even after war broke out in Europe. Gradually, however, public opinion shifted toward support of the Allies (Britain, France, and eventually Russia) and against the Axis (Germany, Italy, and Japan). The nation began to mobilize for war, to supply ships and munitions to Britain, even to engage in naval combat with German forces in the Atlantic. Finally, on December 7, 1941, a surprise Japanese attack on the American base at Pearl Harbor in Hawaii ended the last elements of uncertainty and drove the United States—now united behind the war effort—into the greatest conflict in human history.

FOR FURTHER REFERENCE

Robert Dallek, *Franklin D. Roosevelt and American Foreign Policy, 1932–1945* (1979) is a comprehensive study of Roosevelt's foreign policy. Akira Iriye, *The Cambridge History of American Foreign Relations, vol. 3: The Globalizing of America, 1913–1945* (1993) is another important study. In *Inevitable Revolutions* (1983), Walter LaFeber recounts America's attempts to halt revolutionary movements throughout the world. James MacGregor Burns, *Roosevelt: the Soldier of Freedom* (1970) and Warren F. Kimball, *The Juggler: Franklin Roosevelt as Wartime Statesman* (1991) are two important studies of the president. Wayne S. Cole, *Charles A. Lindbergh and the Battle Against American Intervention in World War II* (1974), and *Roosevelt and the Isolationists, 1932–1945* (1983) examine prewar isolationism. A. Scott Berg, *Lindbergh* (1998) is an excellent biography of the aviation hero who became such a controversial figure in the 1930s. Charles DeBenedetti, *Origins of the Modern American Peace Movement, 1915–1929* (1978) and *The Peace Reform in American History* (1980) examine antiwar movements in American history, including prior to World War II. Joseph Lash's *Roosevelt and Churchill* (1976) explores the dynamic relationship between the two leaders of the United States and England. Akira Iriye, *The Origins of the Second World War in Asia and the Pacific* (1988) examines the conflict between China and Japan that preceded American intervention in the Pacific War. Gordon Prange, *At Dawn We Slept* (1981) examines the controversial attack on Pearl Harbor from both the Japanese and American sides.

OLC

For quizzes, Internet resources, references to additional books and films, and more, consult the book's Online Learning Center at www.mhhe.com/brinkley11.

"STEP ON 'EM" This government poster distributed during World War II suggests the dual character of the American war effort: on the one hand, a military assault on the Axis powers; on the other, the effort at home to expand the nation's industrial capacity and supply the war effort. American production was at least as important to the Allied victory in the war as the successes of American troops in the field. (*National Archives and Records Administration*)

Significant Events

CHAPTER TWENTY-EIGHT

AMERICA IN A WORLD AT WAR

𝒯he attack on Pearl Harbor thrust the United States into the greatest and most terrible war in the history of humanity. World War I had cost many lives and had destroyed centuries-old European social and political institutions. But World War II created even greater carnage and horror in Europe and in much of the rest of the globe. And in the end, it changed the world as profoundly as any event of the twentieth century, perhaps of any century.

Less readily apparent is how profoundly the war changed America—its society, its politics, and its image of itself. Except for the combatants themselves, most Americans experienced the war at a remove of several thousand miles. They endured no bombing, no invasion, no massive dislocations, no serious material shortages. Veterans returning home in 1945 and 1946 found a country that looked very much like the one they had left—something that clearly could not be said of veterans returning home to Britain, France, Germany, Russia, or Japan.

But World War II did transform the United States in profound, if not always in readily visible, ways. As the poet Archibald MacLeish said in 1943: "The great majority of the American people understand very well that this war is not a war only, but an end and a beginning—an end to things known and a beginning of things unknown. We have smelled the wind in the streets that changes weather. We know that whatever the world will be when the war ends, the world will be different." The story of American involvement in the war is not just the story of how the military forces and the industrial might of the United States helped defeat Germany, Italy, and Japan. It is also the story of the creation of a new world, both abroad and at home.

1943 · Americans capture Guadalcanal
· Soviets defeat Germans at Stalingrad
· Allies launch invasion of Italy
· Smith-Connally Act passed
· Race riot breaks out in Detroit
· Sailors battle Mexican Americans in "zoot suit" riots in Los Angeles
· Chinese Exclusion Act repealed
1944 · Allies invade Normandy
· Roosevelt reelected president
· Americans recapture Philippines
· Demonstrators force restaurant in Washington, D.C., to desegregate
1945 · Roosevelt dies; Truman becomes president
· Hitler kills himself
· Allies capture Berlin
· Germany surrenders
· Americans capture Okinawa
· Atomic bomb tested in New Mexico
· United States drops atomic bombs on Hiroshima and Nagasaki
· Japan surrenders

WAR ON TWO FRONTS

Whatever political disagreements and social tensions may have existed among the American people during World War II, there was striking unity of opinion about the conflict itself—"a unity," as one member of Congress proclaimed shortly after Pearl Harbor, "never before witnessed in this country." America's unity and confidence were severely tested in the first, troubled months of 1942. Despite the impressive display of patriotism and the dramatic flurry of activity, the war was going very badly. Britain appeared ready to collapse. The Soviet Union was staggering. One after another, Allied strongholds in the Pacific were falling to the forces of Japan. The first task facing the United States, therefore, was less to achieve victory than to stave off defeat.

America Unified

Containing the Japanese

Ten hours after the strike at Pearl Harbor, Japanese airplanes attacked the American airfields at Manila in the Philippines, destroying much of America's remaining air power in the Pacific. Three days later Guam, an American possession, fell to Japan; then Wake Island and the British colony, Hong Kong. The great British fortress of Singapore surrendered in February 1942, the Dutch East Indies in March, Burma in April. In the Philippines, exhausted Filipino and American troops gave up their defense of the islands on May 6.

American strategists planned two broad offensives to turn the tide against the Japanese. One, under the command of General Douglas MacArthur, would move north from Australia, through New Guinea, and eventually back to the Philippines. The other, under Admiral Chester Nimitz, would move west from Hawaii toward major Japanese island outposts in the central Pacific. Ultimately, the two offensives would come together to invade Japan itself.

The Allies achieved their first important victory in the Battle of Coral Sea, just northwest of Australia, on May 7–8, 1942, when American forces turned back the previously unstoppable Japanese fleet. A month later, there was an even more important turning point northwest of Hawaii. An enormous battle raged for four days, June 3–6, 1942, near the small American outpost at Midway Island, at the end of which the United States, despite great losses, was clearly victorious. The American navy destroyed four Japanese aircraft carriers while losing only one, and regained control of the central Pacific for the United States.

Midway

The Americans took the offensive for the first time several months later in the southern Solomon Islands, to the east of New Guinea. In August 1942, American forces assaulted three of the islands: Gavutu, Tulagi, and Guadalcanal. A struggle of terrible ferocity (and, before it was over, terrible savagery) developed at Guadalcanal and continued for six months, inflicting heavy losses on both sides. In the end, however, the Japanese were forced to abandon the island—and with it their last chance of launching an effective offensive to the south.

Guadalcanal

Thus in both the southern and central Pacific, the initiative had shifted to the United States by mid-1943. The Japanese advance had come to a stop. With aid from the Australians and the New Zealanders, the Americans now began the slow, arduous process of moving toward the Philippines and Japan itself.

Holding Off the Germans

In the European war, the United States had less control over military operations. It was fighting in cooperation with Britain and with the exiled "Free French" forces in the west; and it was trying also to conciliate its new ally, the Soviet Union, which was fighting Hitler in the east. The army chief of staff, General George C. Marshall, supported a plan for a major Allied invasion of France across the English Channel in the spring of 1943. But the American plan faced challenges from the Allies. The Soviet Union, which was absorbing (as it would throughout the war) the brunt of the German war effort, wanted the Allied invasion to proceed at the earliest possible moment. The British, on the other hand, wanted first to launch a series of Allied offensives around the edges of the Nazi empire—in northern Africa and southern Europe—before undertaking the major invasion of France.

Roosevelt was torn. He realized that to support the British plan would antagonize the Soviets and might delay the important cross-channel invasion. But he also knew that the invasion of Europe would take a long time to prepare, and he was reluctant to wait so long before getting American forces into combat. He was also eager to maintain good relations with Churchill. And so, over the objections of some of his most important advisers, he decided to support the British plan. At the end of October 1942, the British opened a counteroffensive against Nazi forces in North Africa under General Erwin Rommel, who was threatening the Suez Canal at El Alamein, and forced the Germans to retreat from Egypt. On November 8, Anglo-American forces landed at Oran and Algiers in Algeria and at Casablanca in Morocco—areas under the Nazi-controlled French government at Vichy—and began moving east toward Rommel.

The Germans threw the full weight of their forces in Africa against the inexperienced Americans and

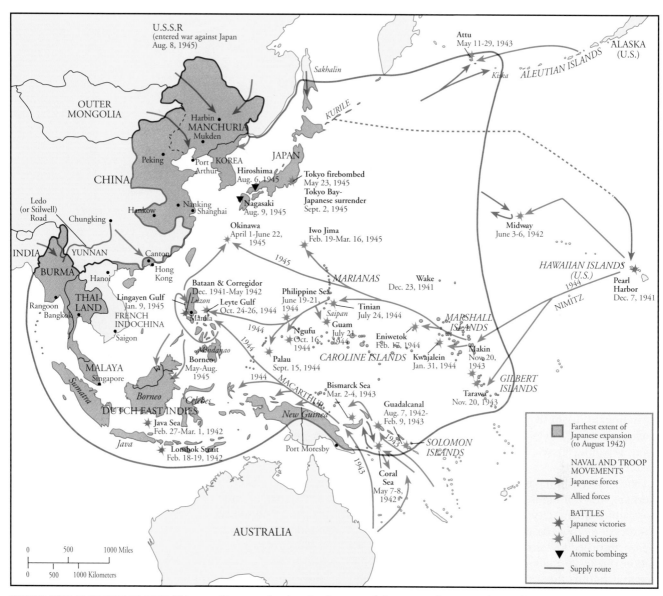

WORLD WAR II IN THE PACIFIC This map illustrates the changing fortunes of the two combatants in the Pacific phase of World War II. The long red line stretching from Burma around to Manchuria represents the eastern boundary of the vast areas of the Pacific that had fallen under Japanese control by the summer of 1942. The blue lines illustrate the advance of American forces back into the Pacific beginning in May 1942 and accelerating in 1943 and after, which drove the Japanese forces back. The American advance was a result of two separate offensives—one in the central Pacific, under the command of Chester Nimitz, which moved west from Hawaii; the other, under the command of Douglas MacArthur, which moved north from Australia. By the summer of 1945, American forces were approaching the Japanese mainland and were bombing Tokyo itself. The dropping of two American atomic bombs, on Hiroshima and Nagasaki, finally brought the war to an end. ◆ *Why did the Soviet Union enter the Pacific War in August 1945, as shown in the upper left corner of the map?*

inflicted a serious defeat on them at the Kasserine Pass in Tunisia. General George S. Patton, however, regrouped the American troops and began an effective counteroffensive. With the help of Allied air and naval power and of British forces attacking from the east under General Bernard Montgomery (the hero of El Alamein), the American offensive finally drove the last Germans from Africa in May 1943. The North Africa campaign

had tied up a large proportion of the Allied resources and contributed to the postponement of the planned May 1943 cross-channel invasion of France. That produced angry complaints from the Soviet Union. By now, however, the threat of a Soviet collapse seemed much diminished, for during the winter of 1942–1943 the Red Army had successfully held off a major German assault

Stalingrad

AMERICAN TROOPS IN TUNISIA An American field artillery unit in the Tunisian desert practices loading artillery in March 1943 shortly after having launched a heavy barrage against German positions nearby. The North Africa campaign was the first effort in which American forces played a significant role in the war against Germany and Italy. The capture of Tunis in May 1943 was the last step toward the Allied invasion of Italy that began in July. *(Hulton/Archive/Getty Images)*

at Stalingrad in southern Russia. Hitler had committed such enormous forces to the battle, and had suffered such appalling losses, that he could not continue his eastern offensive.

The Soviet victory had come at a terrible cost. The German siege of Stalingrad had decimated the civilian population of the city and devastated the surrounding countryside. Indeed, throughout the war, the Soviet Union absorbed losses far greater than any other warring nation (up to 20 million casualties)—a fact that continued to haunt the Russian memory and affect Soviet policy generations later. But the Soviet success in beating back the German offensive persuaded Roosevelt to agree, in a January 1943 meeting with Churchill in Casablanca, to a British plan for an Allied invasion of Sicily. General Marshall opposed the plan, arguing that it would further delay the vital invasion of France. But Churchill prevailed with the argument that the operation in Sicily might knock Italy out of the war and tie up German divisions that might otherwise be stationed in France. On the night of July 9, 1943, American and British armies landed in southeast Sicily; thirty-eight days later they had conquered the island and were moving onto the Italian mainland. In the face of these setbacks, Mussolini's government collapsed and the dictator himself fled north to Germany. But although Mussolini's successor, Pietro Badoglio, quickly committed Italy to the Allies, Germany moved eight divisions into the country and established a powerful defensive line south of Rome. The Allied offensive on the Italian peninsula, which began on September 3, 1943, soon bogged down, especially after a serious setback at Monte

Cassino that winter. Not until May 1944 did the Allies resume their northward advance. On June 4, 1944, they captured Rome.

The invasion of Italy contributed to the Allied war effort in several important ways. But it postponed the invasion of France by as much as a year, deeply embittering the Soviet Union, many of whose leaders *Dispute over the Second Front* believed that the United States and Britain were deliberately delaying the cross-channel invasion in order to allow the Russians to absorb the brunt of the fighting. The postponement also gave the Soviets time to begin moving toward the countries of eastern Europe.

America and the Holocaust

In the midst of this intensive fighting, the leaders of the American government were confronted with one of history's great horrors: the Nazi campaign to exterminate the Jews of Europe—the Holocaust. As early as 1942, high officials in Washington had incontrovertible evidence that Hitler's forces were rounding up Jews and others (including non-Jewish Poles, gypsies, homosexuals, and communists) from all over Europe, transporting them to concentration camps in eastern Germany and Poland, and systematically murdering them. (The death toll would ultimately reach 6 million Jews and approximately 4 million others.) News of the atrocities was reaching the public as well, and public pressure began to build for an Allied effort to end the killing or at least to rescue some of the surviving Jews.

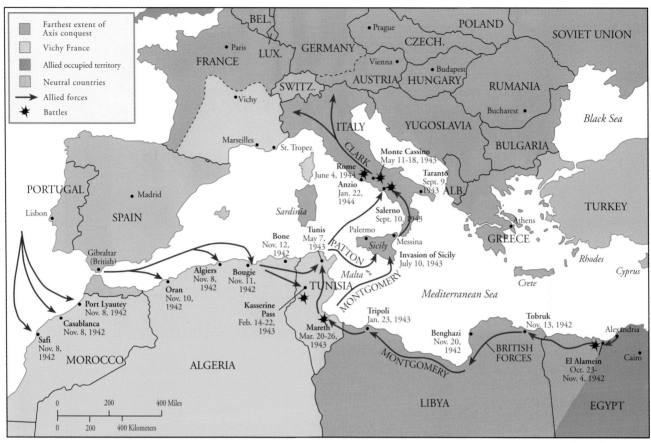

WORLD WAR II IN NORTH AFRICA AND ITALY: THE ALLIED COUNTEROFFENSIVE, 1942–1943 The United States and Great Britain understood from the beginning that an invasion of France across the English Channel would eventually be necessary for a victory in the European war. In the meantime, however, they began a campaign against Axis forces in North Africa, and in the spring of 1943 they began an invasion across the Mediterranean into Italy. This map shows the points along the coast of North Africa where Allied forces landed in 1942—with American forces moving east from Morocco and Algeria, and British forces moving west from Egypt. The two armies met in Tunisia and moved into Italy from there. ◆ *Why were America and Britain reluctant to launch the cross-channel invasion in 1942 or 1943?*

For an interactive version of this map go to www.mhhe.com/brinkley11ch28maps

The American government consistently resisted almost all such entreaties. Although Allied bombers were flying missions within a few miles of the most notorious death camp at Auschwitz in Poland, pleas that the planes try to destroy the crematoria at the camp were rejected as militarily unfeasible. So were similar requests that the Allies try to destroy railroad lines leading to the camp.

The United States also resisted entreaties that it admit large numbers of the Jewish refugees attempting to escape Europe—a pattern established well before Pearl Harbor. One ship, the *St. Louis,* had arrived off Miami in 1939 (after having already been turned away from Havana, Cuba) carrying nearly 1,000 escaped German Jews, only to be refused entry and forced to return to Europe. Both before and during the war, the State Department did not even use up the number of visas permitted by law; almost 90 percent of the quota remained untouched. This disgraceful record was not a result of inadvertence. There was, it seems clear, a deliberate effort

by officials in the State Department—spearheaded by Assistant Secretary Breckinridge Long, a genteel anti-Semite—to prevent Jews from entering the United States in large numbers. One opportunity after another to assist imperiled Jews was either ignored or rejected.

Official Anti-Semitism

After 1941, there was probably little American leaders could have done, other than defeat Germany, to save most of Hitler's victims. But more forceful action by the United States (and Britain, which was even less amenable than America to Jewish requests for assistance) before and even during the war might well have saved some lives. Policymakers at the time justified their inaction by arguing that most of the proposed actions—bombing the railroads and the death camps, for example—would have had little effect. They insisted that the most effective thing they could do for the victims of the Holocaust was to concentrate their attention solely on the larger goal of winning the war.

THE *ST. LOUIS* Many people consider the fate of the German liner *St. Louis* to be a powerful symbol of the indifference of the United States and other nations to the fate of European Jews during the Holocaust, even though its forlorn journey preceded both the beginning of World War II and the beginning of systematic extermination of Jews by the Nazi regime. The *St. Louis* carried a group of over 900 Jews fleeing from Germany in 1939, carrying exit visas of dubious legality cynically sold to them by members of Hitler's Gestapo. It became a ship without a port as it sailed from country to country—Mexico, Paraguay, Argentina, Costa Rica, and Cuba—where its passengers were refused entry time and again. Most of the passengers were hoping for a haven in the United States, but the American State Department refused to allow the ship even to dock as it sailed up the American eastern seaboard. Eventually, the *St. Louis* returned to Europe and distributed its passengers among Britain, France, Holland, and Belgium (where this photograph was taken showing refugees smiling and waving as they prepared to disembark in Antwerp in June 1939). Less than a year later, all those nations except Britain fell under Nazi control. *(Bettmann/Corbis)*

THE AMERICAN PEOPLE IN WARTIME

"War is no longer simply a battle between armed forces in the field," an American government report of 1939 concluded. "It is a struggle in which each side strives to bring to bear against the enemy the coordinated power of every individual and of every material resource at its command. The conflict extends from the soldier in the front line to the citizen in the remotest hamlet in the rear." The United States had experienced many wars before. But not since the Civil War had the nation undergone so consuming a military experience as World War II. American armed forces engaged in combat around the globe for nearly four years. American society, in the meantime, underwent changes that reached into virtually every corner of the nation.

Prosperity

World War II had its most profound impact on American domestic life by at last ending the Great Depression. By

War-Induced Economic Recovery

the middle of 1941, the economic problems of the 1930s—unemployment, deflation, industrial sluggishness —had virtually vanished before the great wave of wartime industrial expansion.

The most important agent of the new prosperity was federal spending, which after 1939 was pumping more money into the economy each year than all the New Deal relief agencies combined had done. In 1939, the federal budget had been $9 billion, the highest level it had ever reached in peacetime; by 1945, it had risen to $100 billion. Largely as a result, the gross national product soared: from $91 billion in 1939 to $166 billion in 1945. Personal incomes in some areas grew by as much as 100 percent or more. The demands of wartime production created a shortage of consumer goods, so many wage earners diverted much of their new affluence into savings, which would later help keep the economic boom alive in the postwar years.

The War and the West

The impact of government spending was perhaps most dramatic in the West, which had long relied on federal largesse more than other regions. The West Coast, naturally, became the launching point for most of the naval war against Japan; and the government created large manufacturing facilities in California and elsewhere to serve the needs of its military. Altogether, the government made almost $40 billion worth of capital investments (factories, military and transportation facilities, highways, power plants) in the West during the war, more than in any other region. Ten percent of all the money the federal government spent between 1940 and 1945 went to California alone. Other western states also shared disproportionately in war contracts and government-funded capital investments.

Henry J. Kaiser, whose construction companies had built some of the great western dams in the 1930s and

Henry Kaiser

who in the process had become a great favorite of many members of the Roosevelt administration, single-handedly steered billions of federal dollars into vast capital projects in the West. He then used the infrastructure he had helped build to create major centers for shipbuilding, steel, magnesium, and aluminum production. By the end of the war, the economy of the Pacific Coast and, to a lesser extent, other areas of the West had been transformed. The Pacific Coast had become the center of the growing American aircraft industry. New yards in southern California, Washington State, and elsewhere made the West a center of the shipbuilding industry. Los Angeles, formerly a medium-sized city notable chiefly for its film industry, now became a major industrial center as well.

Once a lightly industrialized region, parts of the West were now among the most important manufacturing areas in the country. Once a region without adequate facilities to support substantial economic growth, the West now stood poised to become the fastest-growing region in the nation after the war.

Labor and the War

Instead of the prolonged and debilitating unemployment that had been the most troubling feature of the Depression economy, the war created a serious labor shortage. The armed forces took more than 15 million men and women out of the civilian work force at the same time that the demand for labor was rising rapidly. Nevertheless, the civilian work force increased by almost 20 percent during the war. The 7 million who had previously been unemployed accounted for some of the increase; the employment of many people previously

Union Gains

considered inappropriate for the work force—the very young, the elderly, and most important, several million women— accounted for the rest. The war gave an enormous boost to union membership, which rose from about 10.5 million in 1941 to over 13 million in 1945. But it also created important new restrictions on the ability of unions to fight for their members' demands. The government was principally interested in preventing inflation and in keeping production moving without disruption. It managed to win important concessions from union leaders on both scores. One was the so-called Little Steel formula, which set a 15 percent limit on wartime wage increases. Another was the "no-strike" pledge, by which

unions agreed not to stop production in wartime. In return, the government provided labor with a "maintenance-of-membership" agreement, which ensured that the thousands of new workers pouring into unionized defense plants would be automatically enrolled in the unions. The agreement ensured the continued health of the union organizations, but in return workers had to give up the right to demand major economic gains during the war.

Many rank-and-file union members, and some local union leaders, resented the restrictions imposed on them by the government and the labor movement hierarchy. Despite the no-strike pledge, there were nearly 15,000 work stoppages during the war, mostly wildcat strikes (strikes unauthorized by the union leadership). When the United Mine Workers defied the government by striking in May 1943, Congress reacted by passing, over Roosevelt's veto, the Smith-Connally Act (War Labor Disputes Act), which required unions to wait thirty days before striking and empowered the president to seize a struck war plant. In the meantime, public animosity toward labor rose rapidly, and many states passed laws to limit union power.

Stabilizing the Boom

The fear of deflation, the central concern of the 1930s, gave way during the war to a fear of inflation, particularly after prices rose 25 percent in the two years before Pearl Harbor. In October 1942, Congress grudgingly responded to the president's request and passed the Anti-Inflation Act, which gave the administration authority to freeze agricultural prices, wages, salaries, and rents throughout the country. Enforcement of these provisions was the task of the Office of Price Administration (OPA), led first by Leon Henderson and then by Chester

Office of Price Administration

Bowles. In part because of its success, inflation was a much less serious problem during World War II than it had been during World War I.

Even so, the OPA was never popular. There was widespread resentment of its controls over wages and prices. And there was only grudging acquiescence in its complicated system of rationing scarce consumer goods: coffee, sugar, meat, butter, canned goods, shoes, tires, gasoline, and fuel oil. Black-marketing and overcharging grew to proportions far beyond OPA policing capacity.

From 1941 to 1945, the federal government spent a total of $321 billion—twice as much as it had spent in the entire 150 years of its existence to that point, and ten times as much as the cost of World War I. The national debt rose from $49 billion in 1941 to $259 billion in 1945. The government borrowed about half the revenues it needed by selling $100 billion worth of bonds. Much of the rest it raised by radically increasing income taxes through the Revenue Act of 1942, which established a 94 percent rate for the highest brackets and, for the first time, imposed taxes on the lowest-income families as well. To simplify collection, Congress enacted a withholding system of payroll deductions in 1943.

Mobilizing Production

The search for an effective mechanism to mobilize the economy for war began as early as 1939 and continued for nearly four years. One failed agency after another attempted to bring order to the mobilization effort. Finally, in January 1942, the president responded to widespread criticism by creating the War Production Board (WPB),

War Production Board | under the direction of former Sears Roebuck executive Donald Nelson. In theory, the WPB was to be a "superagency," with broad powers over the economy. In fact, it never had as much authority as its World War I equivalent, the War Industries Board. And the genial Donald Nelson never displayed the administrative or political strength of his 1918 counterpart, Bernard Baruch.

Throughout its troubled history, therefore, the WPB found itself constantly outmaneuvered and frustrated. It was never able to win control over military purchases; the army and navy often circumvented the board entirely in negotiating contracts with producers. It was never able to satisfy the complaints of small business, which charged (correctly) that most contracts were going to large corporations. Gradually, the president transferred much of the WPB's authority to a new office located within the White House: the Office of War Mobilization, directed by former Supreme Court justice and South Carolina senator James F. Byrnes. But the OWM was only slightly more successful than the WPB.

Despite the administrative problems, the war economy managed to meet almost all the nation's critical war needs. Enormous new factory complexes sprang up in the space of a few months, many of them funded by the federal government's Defense Plants Corporation. An entire new industry producing synthetic rubber emerged, to make up for the loss of access to natural rubber in the Pacific. By the beginning of 1944, American factories were, in fact, producing more than the government needed. Their output was twice that of all the Axis countries combined. There were even complaints late in the war that military production was becoming excessive, that a limited resumption of civilian production should begin before the fighting ended. The military staunchly and successfully opposed almost all such demands.

Wartime Science and Technology

More than any previous American war, World War II was a watershed for technological and scientific innovation. That was partly because the American government—in its urgent efforts to overcome the effects of the 1920s and 1930s, during which few new military technologies had been developed—poured substantial funds into research

and development beginning in 1940. In that year the government created the National Defense Research Committee, headed by the MIT scientist Vannevar Bush, who had been a pioneer in the early | *National Defense Research Committee* | development of the computer. (It later became the Office of Scientific Research and Development.) By the end of the war, the new agency had spent more that $100 million on research, more than four times the amount spent by the government on military research and development in the previous forty years.

In the first years of the war, all the technological advantages seemed to lie with the Germans and Japanese. Germany had made great advances in tanks and other mechanized armor in the 1930s, particularly during the Spanish Civil War, when it had helped arm Franco's fascist forces. It used its armor effectively during its blitzkrieg in Europe in 1940 and again in North Africa in 1942. German submarine technology was significantly advanced compared to British and American capabilities in 1940, and German U-boats were, for a time, devastatingly effective in disrupting Allied shipping. Japan had developed extraordinary capacity in its naval-air technology. Its highly sophisticated fighter planes, launched from distant aircraft carriers, conducted the successful raid on Pearl Harbor in December 1941.

But Britain and America had advantages of their own, which quickly helped redress these imbalances. American techniques of mass production—the great automotive assembly lines in particular—were converted efficiently to military production in 1941 and 1942 and soon began producing airplanes, ships, tanks, and other armaments in much greater numbers than the Germans and Japanese could produce. Allied scientists and engineers moved quickly as well to improve Anglo-American aviation and naval technology, and particularly to improve the performance of submarines and tanks. By late 1942, Allied weaponry was at least as advanced, and coming to be more plentiful, than that of the enemy.

In addition, each technological innovation by the enemy produced a corresponding innovation to limit the damage of the new techniques. | *Radar and Sonar* | American and British physicists made rapid advances in improving radar and sonar technology—taking advantage of advances in radio technology in the 1920s and beyond—which helped Allied naval forces decimate German U-boats in 1943 and effectively end their effectiveness in the naval war. Particularly important was the creation in 1940 of "centimetric radar," which used narrow beams of short wavelength that made radar more efficient and effective than ever before—as the British navy discovered in April 1941 when the instruments on one of its ships detected a surfaced submarine 10 miles away at night and, on another occasion, spotted a periscope at three-quarters of a mile range. With earlier technologies, both things would have been undetectable.

RADAR SCOPE, 1944 Navy technicians are shown here demonstrating the new radar scopes that revolutionized the tracking of ships and planes during World War II. *(National Archives and Records Administration)*

This new radar could also be effectively miniaturized, which was critical to its use on airplanes and submarines in particular. It required only a small rotating aerial, and it used newly advanced cavity magnetron valves of great power. These innovations put the Allies far in advance of Germany and Japan in radar technology. The Allies also learned early how to detect and disable German naval mines; and when the Germans tried to counter this progress by introducing an "acoustic" mine, which detonated when a ship came near it, not necessarily just on contact, the Allies developed acoustical countermeasures of their own, which transmitted sounds through the water to detonate mines before ships came near them.

Anglo-American antiaircraft technology—both on land and on sea—also improved, although never to the point where it could stop bombing raids altogether. Germany made substantial advances in the development of rocket technology in the early years of the war, and it managed to launch some rocket-propelled bombs (the V1s and

V2s) across the English Channel, aimed at London. The psychological effects of the rockets on the British people were considerable. But the Germans were never able to create a production technology capable of building enough such rockets to make a real difference in the balance of military power.

Beginning in 1942, British and American forces seized the advantage in the air war by producing new and powerful four-engine bombers in great numbers—among them the British Lancaster B1 and the American Boeing B17F, capable of flying a bomb load of 6,000 pounds for 1,300 miles, and capable of reaching 37,500 feet. Because they were able to fly higher and longer than the German equivalents, they were able to conduct extensive bombing missions over Germany (and later Japan) with much less danger of being shot down. But the success of the bombers rested heavily as well on new electronic devices capable of guiding their bombs to their targets. The Gee navigation system, which was also valuable to the navy, used electronic pulses to help pilots plot their exact location, something that in the past only a highly skilled navigator could do, and then only in good weather. In March 1942, eighty Allied bombers fitted with Gee systems staged a devastatingly effective bombing raid on German industrial and military installations in the Ruhr Valley. In the past, studies had shown that night-bombing raids were at best 30 percent accurate. The Gee system doubled the accuracy rate. Also effective was the Oboe system, a radio device that sent a sonic message to airplanes to tell them when they were within 20 yards of their targets, first introduced in December 1942.

The area in which the Allies had perhaps the greatest advantages in technology and knowledge was the gathering of intelligence, much of it

Ultra

through Britain's top-secret Ultra project. Some of the advantages the Allies enjoyed came from successful efforts to capture or steal German and Japanese intelligence devices. More important, however, were the efforts of cryptologists to puzzle out the enemy's systems, and advances in computer technology that helped the Allies decipher coded messages sent by the Japanese and the Germans. Much of Germany's coded communication made use of the so-called Enigma machine, which was effective because it constantly changed the coding systems it used. In the first months of the war, Polish intelligence had developed an electro-mechanical computer, which it called the "Bombe," which could decipher some Enigma messages. After the fall of Poland, British scientists, led by the brilliant computer pioneer Alan Turing, took the Bombe, which was too slow to keep up with the increasingly frequent changes of coding the Germans were using, and greatly improved it. Among other things, they developed a punched-hole technology related to the punch cards that were for a time so central to computer technology of the postwar era. On April 15, 1940, the new, improved, high-speed Bombe broke the coding of a series of German messages within hours (not days, as had previously been the case). A few weeks later, it began decrypting German messages at the rate of 1,000 a day, providing the British (and later the Americans) with a constant flow of information about enemy operations that continued—completely unknown to the Germans— until the end of the war. Later in the war, British scientists working for the intelligence services built the first real programmable, digital computer—the Colossus II, which became operational less than a week before the beginning of the Normandy invasion and which was able to decipher an enormous number of intercepted German messages almost instantly.

The United States also had some important intelligence breakthroughs, including, in 1941, a dramatic success by

Magic

the American Magic operation (the counterpart to the British Ultra) in breaking a Japanese coding system not unlike the German Enigma, a mechanical device known to the Allies

as Purple. The result was that Americans had access to intercepted information that, if properly interpreted, could have alerted them to the Japanese raid on Pearl Harbor in December 1941. But because such a raid had seemed entirely inconceivable to most American officials prior to its occurrence, those who received the information failed to understand or disseminate it in time.

African Americans and the War

During World War I, many African Americans had eagerly seized the chance to serve in the armed forces, believing that their patriotic efforts would win them an enhanced position in postwar society. They had been cruelly disappointed. As World War II approached, blacks were again determined to use the conflict to improve their position in society—this time, however, not by currying favor but by making demands.

In the summer of 1941, A. Philip Randolph, president of the Brotherhood of Sleeping Car Porters (a union with a predominantly black membership), began to insist that the government require companies receiving defense contracts to integrate their work forces. To mobilize support for the demand, Randolph planned a massive march on Washington, which would, he promised, bring over 100,000 demonstrators to the capital. Roosevelt was afraid of both the possibility of violence and the certainty of political embarrassment. He finally persuaded Randolph to cancel the march in return for a promise to establish a Fair Employment Practices Commission to investigate discrimination against blacks in war industries. The FEPC's en-

FEPC

forcement powers, and thus its effectiveness, were limited, but its creation was a rare symbolic victory for African Americans making demands of the government.

The demand for labor in war plants greatly increased the migration of blacks from the rural areas of the South into industrial cities—a migration that continued for more than a decade after the war and brought many more African Americans into northern cities than the first Great Migration of 1914–1919 had brought. The migration bettered the economic condition of many African Americans, but it also created urban tensions. On a hot June day in Detroit in 1943, a series of altercations between blacks and whites at a city park led to two days of racial violence in which thirty-four people died, twenty-five of them blacks.

Despite such tensions, the leading black organizations redoubled their efforts during the war to challenge the system of segregation. The Congress of Racial Equality (CORE), or-

CORE

ganized in 1942, mobilized mass popular resistance to discrimination in a way that the older, more conservative organizations had never done. Randolph, Bayard Rustin, James Farmer, and other, younger black leaders helped organize sit-ins and demonstrations in segregated theaters and restaurants. In 1944, they won a much-publicized victory by forcing a Washington, D.C., restaurant to agree to serve blacks. Their defiant spirit would survive into the 1950s and help produce the civil rights movement.

Pressure for change was also growing within the military. At first, the armed forces maintained their traditional practice of limiting blacks to the most menial assignments, keeping them in segregated training camps and units, and barring them entirely from the Marine Corps and the Army Air Forces. Gradually, however, military leaders were forced to make adjustments—in part because of public and political pressures, but also because they recognized that these forms of segregation were wasting manpower. By the end of the war, the number of black servicemen had increased sevenfold, to 700,000; some training camps were being at least partially integrated; blacks were beginning to serve on ships with white sailors; and more black units were being sent into combat. But tensions remained. In some of the partially integrated army bases—Fort Dix, New Jersey, for example—riots occasionally broke out when African Americans protested having to serve in segregated divisions. Substantial discrimination survived in all the services until well after the war. But within the military, as within the society at large, the traditional pattern of race relations was slowly eroding.

Native Americans and the War

Approximately 25,000 Native Americans performed military service during World War II. Many of them served in combat (among them Ira Hayes, one of the men who raised the American flag at Iwo Jima and became part of a legendary photograph and, later, war memorial). Others

"Code Talkers" worked as "code-talkers," working in military communications and speaking their own languages (which enemy forces would be unlikely to understand) over the radio and the telephones.

The war had important effects, too, on those Native Americans who remained civilians. Little war work reached the tribes, and government subsidies dwindled. Many talented young people left the reservations, some to serve in the military, even more (more than 70,000) to work in war plants. This brought many Indians into intimate contact with white society for the first time, and awakened in some of them a taste for the material benefits of life in capitalist America that they would retain after the war. Some never returned to the reservations, but chose to remain in the non-Indian world and assimilate to its ways. Others found that after the war, employment opportunities that had been available to them during the fighting became unavailable once again, leaving them little alternative but to return to the reservations.

The wartime emphasis on national unity undermined support for the revitalization of tribal autonomy that the Indian Reorganization Act of 1934 had launched. New pressures emerged to eliminate the reservation system and require the tribes to assimilate into white society—pressures so severe that John Collier, the energetic director of the Bureau of Indian Affairs who had done so much to promote the reinvigoration of the reservations, resigned in 1945.

Mexican-American War Workers

Large numbers of Mexican workers entered the United States during the war in response to labor shortages on the Pacific Coast, in the Southwest, and eventually in almost all areas of the nation. The American and Mexican governments agreed in 1942 to a program by which *braceros* (contract laborers) would be admitted to the United States for a limited time to work at specific jobs, and American employers in some parts of the Southwest began actively recruiting Hispanic workers.

During the Depression, many Mexican farmworkers had been deported to make room for desperate white workers. The wartime labor shortage caused farm owners to begin hiring them again. More important, however, Mexicans were able for the first time to *Employment Gains for Mexican Americans* find significant numbers of factory jobs. They formed the second largest group of migrants (after blacks) to American cities in the 1940s. Over 300,000 of them served in the United States military.

The sudden expansion of Mexican-American neighborhoods created tensions and occasionally conflict in some American cities. White residents of Los Angeles became alarmed at the activities of Mexican-American teenagers, many of whom were joining street gangs *(pachucos)*. The *pachucos* were particularly distinctive because of their members' style of dress, which whites considered outrageous. They wore long, loose jackets with padded shoulders, baggy pants tied at the ankles, long watch chains, broad-brimmed hats, and greased, ducktail hairstyles. (It was a style borrowed in part from fashions in Harlem.) The outfit was known as a "zoot suit." For those who wore them, as for many adolescents, the style of dress became a symbol of rebellion against and defiance toward conventional white, middle-class society. For oustiders who observed the "zoot-suiters," these unconventional styles often seemed hostile and threatening.

In June 1943, animosity toward the zoot-suiters produced a four-day riot in Los Angeles, during which white sailors stationed at a base in Long Beach invaded Mexican- *Zoot-Suit Riots* American communities and attacked zoot-suiters (in response to alleged attacks by them on servicemen). The city police did little to restrain the sailors, who grabbed Hispanic teenagers, tore off and burned their clothes, cut off their ducktails, and beat them. But when Hispanics tried to fight back, the police moved in and arrested them. In the aftermath of the "zoot suit riots," Los Angeles passed a law prohibiting the wearing of zoot suits.

ZOOT-SUITER The baggy pants, the long, loose jacket, the big collar, the exaggerated watch chain, the slicked-back hair—all were features of the outfit known as the zoot suit and popular in the 1940s among young Mexican-Americans in Los Angeles and elsewhere. The "zoot-suit riots" in Los Angeles in June 1943 were a product of the suspicion with which Anglos (in this case servicemen stationed nearby) looked at the culture of the Chicano communities that were growing rapidly throughout the Southwest. *(Bettmann/Corbis)*

Women and Children at War

The war drew increasing numbers of women into roles from which, either by custom or law, they had been largely barred. The number of women in the work force increased

Dramatic Increase in Female Employment

by nearly 60 percent, and women accounted for a third of paid workers in 1945 (as opposed to a quarter in 1940). These wage-earning women were more likely to be married and were on the whole older than most women who had entered the work force in the past.

Many women entered the industrial work force to replace male workers serving in the military. But while economic and military necessity eroded some of the popular objections to women in the workplace, obstacles remained. Many factory owners continued to categorize jobs by gender. (Female work, like male work, was also categorized by race: black women were usually assigned

more menial tasks, and paid at a lower rate, than their white counterparts.) Employers also made substantial investments in automated assembly lines to reduce the need for heavy labor. Special recruiting materials presented factory work to women through domestic analogies that male employers assumed females would find easily comprehensible: cutting airplane wings was compared to making a dress pattern, mixing chemicals to making a cake.

Many employers treated women in the war plants with a combination of solicitude and patronization, which was also an obstacle to winning genuine equality within the work force. Still, women did make important inroads in industrial employment during the war. Women had been working in industry for over a century, but some began now to take on heavy industrial jobs that had long been considered "men's work." The famous wartime image of "Rosie the Riveter" symbolized the new importance of the female industrial   *"Rosie the Riveter"* work force. Women workers joined unions in substantial numbers, and they helped erode at least some of the prejudice, including the prejudice against working mothers, that had previously kept many of them from paid employment.

Most women workers during the war were employed not in factories but in service-sector jobs. Above all, they worked for the government, whose bureaucratic needs expanded dramatically alongside its military and industrial needs. Washington, D.C., in particular, was flooded with young female clerks, secretaries, and typists—known as "government girls"—most of whom lived in cramped quarters in boardinghouses, private homes, and government dormitories and worked long hours in the war agencies. Public and private clerical employment for women expanded in other urban areas as well, creating high concentrations of young women in places largely depleted of young men. The result was the development of distinctively female communities, in which women, often separated for the first time from home and family, adjusted to life in the work force through their association with other female workers. Even within the military, which enlisted substantial numbers of women as WACs (army) and WAVEs (navy), most female work was clerical.

The new opportunities produced new problems. Many mothers whose husbands were in the military had to combine working with caring   *Limited Child Care* for their children. The scarcity of child-care facilities or other community services meant that some women had no choice but to leave young children—often known as "latchkey children" or "eight-hour orphans"—at home alone (or sometimes locked in cars in factory parking lots) while they worked.

Perhaps in part because of the family dislocations the war produced, juvenile crime rose markedly in the war years. Young boys were arrested at rapidly increasing rates for car theft and other burglary, vandalism, and vagrancy. The arrest rate for prostitutes, many of whom were teenage girls, rose too, as did the incidence of sexually

U. S. ARMY
OFFICIAL POSTER

SOLDIERS *without guns*

WOMEN AT WAR Many American women enlisted in the army and navy women's corps during World War II, but an equally important contribution of women to the war effort was their work in factories and offices—often in jobs that would have been considered inappropriate for them in peacetime but that they were now encouraged to assume because of the absence of so many men. *(Library of Congress)*

transmitted disease. For many children, however, the distinctive experience of the war years was not crime but work. More than a third of all teenagers between the ages of fourteen and eighteen were employed late in the war, causing some reduction in high-school enrollments.

The return of prosperity during the war helped increase the rate and lower the age of marriage, but many of these

Beginning of the "Baby Boom"

young marriages were unable to survive the pressures of wartime separation. The divorce rate rose rapidly. The rise in the birth rate that accompanied the increase in marriages was the first sign of what would become the great postwar "baby boom."

Wartime Life and Culture

The war created considerable anxiety in American life. Families worried about loved ones at the front and struggled to adjust to the absence of husbands, fathers, brothers, sons—and to the new mobility of women, which also drew family members away from home. Businesses and communities struggled to compensate for shortages of goods and the absence of men.

But the abundance of the war years also created a striking buoyancy in American life that the conflict itself only partially subdued. Suddenly, people had money to spend again and—despite the many shortages of consumer goods—

Economic Good Times

at least some things to spend it on. The book, theater, and movie industries did record business. Audiences equal to about half the population attended movies each week, often to watch heroic war films (including some—such as *Mission to Moscow*—that glorified America's murderous wartime ally, Josef Stalin). Magazines, particularly pictorial ones such as *Life,* reached the peak of their popularity, satisfying the seemingly insatiable hunger of readers for pictures of and stories about the war. Radio ownership and listening also increased, for the same reason.

To many young Americans during World War II—both those who went off to the front and those who stayed at home—nothing more strongly evoked the image of life as they remembered it and wished it to be

STARS OF THE AGE OF SWING This record-company promotional poster shows some of the most popular band leaders of the Swing Era—among them the man now widely considered the greatest of them all, Duke Ellington. *(Jon Hammer/Hulton/Archive/Getty Images)*

again than the big bands, the most popular musical groups of the era. The smooth, romantic sound of brass and woodwinds, the sultry voices of the mostly female singers, the swaying bodies of hundreds—in some places thousands—of dancers moving to the music: that, in wartime, represented what the good life was all about.

The big bands always played several different kinds of jazz, but from the mid-1930s to the mid-1940s, they played "swing" above all—a new form of jazz that, as its name implied, seemed made for dancing. And although swing quickly became wildly popular with white, middle-class audiences, it had its origins—like other kinds of jazz and like the rock music that would later help displace it—in the African-American musical world. The black musician Fletcher Henderson began experimenting with swing in Harlem in the 1920s; he called it "hot jazz." In 1934, he began working with the white jazz musician Benny Goodman, arranging numbers for Goodman's own band. And in 1935, when Goodman played several of Henderson's arrangements to a wildly enthusiastic crowd of dancers in the Palomar Ballroom in Los Angeles, the "swing era"—the era of the new music's popularity among a broad,

THE KING OF SWING Benny Goodman's orchestra—the most celebrated swing band of its time—attracted enormous crowds both before and during World War II, including at this engagement at the massive Steel Pier in Atlantic City in 1938. *(From the collection of Martin and Joyce Morley)*

multiracial public—began. After his success at the Palomar, Goodman—soon to be known as the "King of Swing"—began playing more and

Resort hotels, casinos, and racetracks were jammed with customers. Dance halls were packed with young people drawn to the seductive music of swing bands; soldiers and sailors home on leave, or awaiting shipment overseas, were especially attracted to the dances and the big bands, which became to many of them a symbol of the life they were leaving and that they believed they were fighting to defend. (See "Patterns of Popular Culture," pp. 762–763.)

Advertisers, and at times even the government, exhorted Americans to support the war effort to ensure a future of material comfort and consumer choice for themselves and their children. "Your people are giving their lives in useless sacrifice," the *Saturday Evening Post* wrote in a mock letter to the leaders of wartime Japan. "Ours are fighting for a glorious future of mass employment, mass production and mass distribution and ownership." Even troops at the front seemed at times to

justify their efforts with reference to the comforts of home more than to the character of the enemy or the ideals America claimed to be defending. "They are fighting for home," the writer John Hersey once wrote from Guadalcanal (with at least a trace of dismay), because "Home is where the good things are—the generosity, the good pay, the comforts, the democracy, the pie."

Fighting for Future Prosperity

For men at the front, the image of home was a powerful antidote to the rigors of wartime. That image became increasingly romanticized in the minds of many soldiers, often in direct relation to the amount of time they were away from America. They dreamed of music, food, movies, material comforts. Many also dreamed of women—wives and girlfriends, but also movie stars and others who became the source of one of the most popular icons of the front: the pinup. Sailors pasted pinups

more often on the radio, spreading the popularity of the music. And soon new big bands were springing up, both black and white, seizing the style, modifying it at times, and spreading it further: Count Basie ("One O'Clock Jump"), who emerged from the relative obscurity of the Kansas City jazz scene in 1936 and became one of the great innovators in modern jazz; Tommy Dorsey ("Marie"); Artie Shaw ("Begin the Beguine"); the incomparable Duke Ellington ("In a Mellotone"), probably the most gifted and inventive jazz musician of his era; and—perhaps the performer etched most vividly in the memory of fighting men during World War II—Glenn Miller, whose "In the Mood" was one of the most popular songs of the 1940s, and whose early death while traveling to entertain troops made him something of a national hero.

During the heyday of swing, band leaders were among the most recognized and popular figures in American popular culture, rivaling movie stars in their celebrity. Swing dominated the radio. It drew huge audiences to dance halls everywhere. It sold more records than any other kind of music. And it became one of the first forms of popular music to challenge racial taboos. Benny Goodman hired the black pi-

SWINGERS Exuberant dancers move to the music of Benny Goodman's band in this picture of a 1938 appearance at a ballroom in New York. *(Charles Peterson/Hulton/Archive/Getty Images)*

anist Teddy Wilson to play with his band in 1935; other white band leaders followed.

Swing was not without its critics: people who recoiled at its black roots and at its interracial culture; and others who abhorred its openly sensual style and the romantic, at times overtly sexual, dancing it inspired. It had a "dangerously hypnotic influence," the *New York Times* complained in 1938 (in a critique that echoed earlier attacks on jazz in the 1920s and resembled later ones

on rock and rap music in the postwar years) and led dancers toward "moral weakness" and "the breakdown of conventions." But young men and women in the anxious years of depression and war found in swing an avenue to escape, romance, and excitement. "It don't mean a thing if it ain't got that swing," the lyrics of a celebrated 1932 Duke Ellington song said. Until at least 1945, when swing began to give way to other forms of jazz, millions of Americans agreed.

inside their lockers, and infantrymen carried them (along with pictures of wives, mothers, and girlfriends) in their knapsacks. Fighter pilots gave their planes female names and painted bathing beauties on their nosecones. The most popular pinup was of Betty Grable, whose picture found its way into the hands of over 5 million fighting men by the end of the war. Grable was popular not just because she was sexually attractive, but also because she symbolized the modest, genteel girlfriend or wife many servicemen dreamed of finding on their return. In her films, she generally played wholesome, innocent young women, the kind many servicemen dreamed of marrying. Thousands of servicemen sent letters to her.

For the servicemen who remained in America during the war, and for soldiers and sailors in cities far from home in particular, the company of friendly, "wholesome" women was, the military believed, critical to

maintaining morale. USOs recruited thousands of young women to serve as hostesses in their clubs—women who were expected to dress nicely, dance well, and chat *USO* happily with lonely men, to give them a healthy outlet for heterosexual impulses. Other women joined "dance brigades" and travelled by bus to military bases for social evenings with servicemen. They, too, were expected to be pretty, to dress attractively (and conservatively), and to interact comfortably with men they had never met before and would likely never see again. The USO actually forbade women to have dates with soldiers after parties in the clubs, and the members of the "dance brigades" were expected to have no contact with servicemen except during the dances. Clearly, such regulations were sometimes violated. But while the military took elaborate measures to root out homosexuals and lesbians from their ranks (unceremoniously

763

dismissing many of them with undesirable discharges), it quietly tolerated other relationships. "Healthy" heterosexuality was more important than chastity.

Schools, colleges, and universities experienced major disruptions because of the war. Hundreds of thousands of male teachers and professors left the educational system for the military, creating a serious teacher shortage in many communities. Male students themselves (and some female students too) left school in droves when they were old enough, either to enlist in the military or to accept the new, lucrative jobs that the wartime economic boom was making available. Major universities, almost emptied of traditional students, turned themselves, in effect, into training camps for military officers—with lavish funding from the federal government (the beginning of what would be an increasing dependency on federal funds among most universities in the postwar era).

The Internment of Japanese Americans

World War I had produced widespread hatred, vindictiveness, and hysteria in America, as well as widespread and flagrant violations of civil liberties. World War II did not. The government barred from the mails a few papers it considered seditious, among them Father Coughlin's anti-Semitic and pro-fascist *Social Justice*, but there was no general censorship of dissident publications. A few Nazi agents and American fascists were jailed, but there was no major assault on people suspected of sympathizing with the Axis. The most ambitious effort to punish domestic fascists, a sedition trial of twenty-eight people, ended in a mistrial, and the defendants went free. Unlike during World War I, the government generally left socialists and communists (most of whom strongly supported the war effort) alone.

Nor was there much of the ethnic or cultural animosity that had shaped the social climate of the United States during World War I. The "zoot-suit" riots in Los Angeles and occasional racial conflicts in American cities and on military bases made clear that traditional racial and ethnic hostilities had not disappeared. *Ethnic Distinctions Blurred* So did wartime restrictions imposed on some Italian Americans—including provisions forbidding many of them to travel and the actual imprisonment of several hundred, including the great opera singer Ezio Pinza, as "enemy aliens." But on the whole, the war worked more to blur ethnic distinctions than to heighten them. Americans continued to eat sauerkraut without calling it "liberty cabbage." They displayed little hostility toward German Americans. Instead, they seemed on the whole to share the view of their government's propaganda: that the enemy was less the German and Italian people than the vicious political systems to which they had succumbed. In popular culture, and in everyday interactions, ethnicity began to seem less a source of menacing difference—as it often had in the past—than

evidence of healthy diversity. The participation of, and frequent heroism from, American soldiers of many ethnic backgrounds encouraged this change.

But there was a glaring exception to the general rule of tolerance: the treatment of the small, politically powerless group of Japanese Americans. From the beginning, Americans adopted a different attitude toward their Asian enemy than they did toward their European foes. They attributed to the Japanese people certain racial and cultural characteristics that made it easier to hold them in contempt. The Japanese, both government and private propaganda encouraged Americans to believe, were a devious, malign, and cruel people. The infamous attack on Pearl Harbor seemed to many to confirm that assessment.

This racial animosity soon extended to Americans of Japanese descent. There were not many Japanese Americans in the United States—only about 127,000, most of them concentrated in a few areas in California. About a third of them were unnaturalized, first-generation immigrants (Issei); two-thirds were naturalized or native-born citizens of the United States (Nisei). The Japanese in America, like the Chinese, had long been the target of ethnic and racial animosity; and unlike members of European ethnic groups, who had encountered similar resentment, *Anti-Japanese Prejudice* Asians seemed unable to dispel prejudice against them no matter how assimilated they became. Many white Americans continued to consider Asians (even native-born citizens) so "foreign" that they could never become "real" Americans. Partly as a result, much of the Japanese-American population in the West continued to live in close-knit, to some degree even insular, communities, which simply reinforced the belief that they were somehow alien and potentially menacing.

Pearl Harbor inflamed these longstanding suspicions and turned them into active animosity. Wild stories circulated about how the Japanese in Hawaii had helped sabotage Pearl Harbor and how Japanese Americans in California were conspiring to aid an enemy landing on the Pacific coast. There was no evidence to support any of these charges; but according to Earl Warren, then attorney general of California, the apparent passivity of the Japanese Americans was more evidence of the danger they posed. Because they did nothing to allow officials to gauge their intentions, Warren claimed, it was all the more important to take precautions against conspiracies.

Although there was some public pressure in California to remove the Japanese "threat," on the whole popular sentiment was more tolerant of the Nisei and Issei (and more willing to make distinctions between them and the Japanese in Japan) than was official sentiment. The real impetus for taking action came from the government. Secretary of the Navy Frank Knox, for example, said shortly after Pearl Harbor that "the most effective fifth column [a term for internal sabotage] work of the entire war was done in Hawaii," a statement that later investigations proved to be entirely false. General John L. DeWitt, the senior military commander on the West Coast, claimed to have "no confidence in [Japanese-American] loyalty whatsoever." When asked about the distinction between unnaturalized Japanese immigrants and American citizens, he said, "A Jap is a Jap. It makes no difference whether he is an American citizen or not."

In February 1942, in response to pressure from military officials like DeWitt and Knox and West Coast political leaders like Warren (and over the objections of the attorney general and J. Edgar Hoover, the director of the FBI), the president authorized the army to "intern" the Japanese Americans. He created the War Relocation Authority (WRA) to oversee the project. More than 100,000 people (Issei and Nisei alike) were rounded up, told to dispose of their property however they could (which often

"Relocation Centers" meant simply abandoning it), and taken to what the government euphemistically termed "relocation centers" in the "interior." In fact, they were facilities little different from prisons, many of them located in the western mountains and the desert. Conditions in the internment camps were

not brutal, but they were harsh and uncomfortable. Government officials talked of them as places where the Japanese could be socialized and "Americanized," much as many officials had at times considered Indian reservations as places for training Native Americans to become more like whites.

But like Indian reservations, the internment camps were more a target of white economic aspirations than of missionary work. The governor of Utah, where many of the internees were located, wanted the federal government to turn over thousands of Japanese Americans to serve as forced laborers. Washington did not comply, but the WRA did hire out many inmates as agricultural laborers.

The internment never produced significant popular opposition. For the most part, once the Japanese were in the camps, other Americans (including their former neighbors on the West Coast) largely forgot about them—except to make strenuous efforts to acquire the property they had abandoned. Even so, beginning in 1943 conditions slowly improved. Some young Japanese Americans left the camps to attend colleges and universities (mostly in the East—the WRA continued to be wary of letting Japanese return to the Pacific Coast). Others were permitted to move to cities to take factory and service jobs (although again, not on the West Coast). Some young men joined and others were drafted into the American military; a Nisei army unit fought with distinction in Europe.

In 1944, the Supreme Court ruled in *Korematsu* v. *U.S.* that the relocation was constitutionally permissible. In another case the same year, it barred the internment of "loyal" citizens, but left the interpretation of "loyal" to the discretion of the government. Nevertheless, by the end of 1944 most of the internees had been released; and in early 1945, they were finally permitted to return to the West Coast—where they faced continuing harassment and persecution, and where many found their property and businesses irretrievably lost. In 1988 they won some compensation for their losses, when, after years of agitation by survivors of the camps and their descendants, Congress voted to award them reparations. But by then, many of the internees had died.

Korematsu v. U.S.

INTERNEES A Japanese-American family waits in Seattle for evacuation by the army to the internment camps where most would spend the rest of the war. This mother appears to be fighting back tears as she keeps her daughters together while they wait for their train. *(Bettmann/Corbis)*

Chinese Americans and the War

Just as America's conflict with Japan undermined the position of Japanese Americans, the American alliance with China during World War II significantly enhanced both the legal and social status of Chinese Americans. In 1943, partly to improve relations with the government of China, Congress finally repealed the Chinese Exclusion Acts, which had barred almost all Chinese immigration since 1892. The new quota for Chinese immigrants was minuscule (105 a year), but a

Chinese Exclusion Acts Repealed

substantial number of Chinese women managed to gain entry into the country through other provisions covering war brides and fiancees. Over 4,000 Chinese women entered the United States in the first three years after the war. Permanent residents of the United States of Chinese descent were finally permitted to become citizens.

Racial animosity toward the Chinese did not disappear, but it did decline—in part because government propaganda and popular culture both began presenting positive images of the Chinese (partly to contrast them with the Japanese); in part because Chinese Americans (like African Americans and other previously marginal groups) began taking jobs in war plants and other booming areas suffering from labor shortages and hence moving out of the relatively isolated world of the Chinatowns. A higher proportion of Chinese Americans (22 percent of all adult males) were drafted than of any other national group, and the entire Chinese community in most cities worked hard and conspicuously for the war effort.

The Retreat from Reform

Late in 1943, Franklin Roosevelt publicly suggested that "Dr. New Deal," as he called it, had served its purpose and should now give way to "Dr. Win-the-War." The statement reflected the president's own genuine shift in concern: that victory was now more important than reform. But it also reflected the political reality that had emerged during the first two years of war. Liberals in government were finding themselves unable to enact new programs. They were even finding it difficult to protect existing ones from conservative assault.

Within the administration itself, many liberals found themselves displaced by the new managers of the wartime agencies, who came overwhelmingly from large corpora-

Dismantling the New Deal | tions and conservative Wall Street law firms. But the greatest assault on New Deal reforms came from conservatives in Congress, who seized on the war as an excuse to do what many had wanted to do in peacetime: dismantle many of the achievements of the New Deal. They were assisted by the end of mass unemployment, which decreased the need for such relief programs as the Civilian Conservation Corps and the Works Progress Administration (both of which were abolished). They were assisted, too, by their own increasing numbers. In the congressional elections of 1942, Republicans gained 47 seats in the House and 10 in the Senate. Roosevelt continued to talk bravely at times about his commitment to social progress and liberal reform, in part to bolster the flagging spirits of his traditional supporters. But increasingly, the president quietly accepted the defeat or erosion of New Deal measures in order to win support for his war policies and peace plans. He also accepted the changes because he realized that his chances for reelection in 1944

depended on his ability to identify himself less with domestic issues than with world peace.

Republicans approached the 1944 election determined to exploit what they believed was resentment of wartime regimentation and privation and unhappiness with Democratic reform. They nominated as their candidate the young and vigorous governor of New York, Thomas E. Dewey. Roosevelt was unopposed within his party, but Democratic leaders pressured him to abandon the controversial Vice President Henry Wallace, an outspoken liberal and hero of the CIO. They wanted Roosevelt to replace Wallace with a more moderate figure acceptable to all factions of the party. Roosevelt, tired and ill, seemed to take little interest in the matter and passively acquiesced in the selection of Senator Harry S. Truman of Missouri, a man he barely knew. Truman was not a prominent figure in the party, but he had won acclaim as chairman of the Senate War Investigating Committee (known as the Truman Committee), which had compiled an impressive record uncovering waste and corruption in wartime production.

The conduct of the war was not an issue in the campaign. Instead, the election revolved around domestic economic issues and, indirectly, the president's health. The pres- *1944 Election* ident was in fact gravely ill, suffering from, among other things, arteriosclerosis. It may not be too much to say that he was dying. But the campaign seemed momentarily to revive him. He made several strenuous public appearances late in October, which dispelled popular doubts about his health and ensured his reelection. He captured 53.5 percent of the popular vote to Dewey's 46 percent, and won 432 electoral votes to Dewey's 99. Democrats lost 1 seat in the Senate, gained 20 in the House, and maintained control of both.

THE DEFEAT OF THE AXIS

By the middle of 1943, America and its allies had succeeded in stopping the Axis advance both in Europe and in the Pacific. In the next two years, the Allies themselves seized the offensive and launched a series of powerful drives that rapidly led the way to victory.

The Liberation of France

By early 1944, American and British bombers were attacking German industrial installations and other targets almost round the clock, drastically cutting production and impeding transportation. Especially devastating was the massive bombing of such German cities as Leipzig, Dresden, *Strategic Bombing* and Berlin. A February 1945 incendiary raid on Dresden created a great firestorm that destroyed three-fourths of the previously undamaged city and killed approximately 135,000 people, almost all civilians.

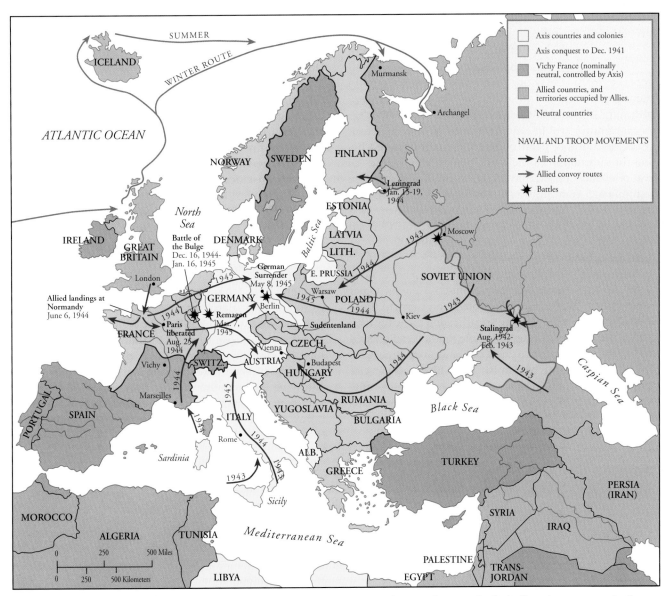

WORLD WAR II IN EUROPE: THE ALLIED COUNTEROFFENSIVE, 1943–1945 This map illustrates the final, climactic movements in the war in Europe—the two great offensives against Germany that began in 1943 and culminated in 1945. From the east, the armies of the Soviet Union, having halted the Germans at Stalingrad and Moscow, swept across eastern Europe toward Germany. From the west and the south, American, British, and other Allied forces moved toward Germany through Italy and—after the Normandy invasion in June 1944—through France. The two offensives met in Berlin in May 1945. Note, too, the northern routes that America and Britain used to supply the Soviet Union during the war. ◆ *What problems did the position of the Allied forces at the end of the war help to produce?*

 For an interactive version of this map go to www.mhhe.com/brinkley11ch28maps

Military leaders claimed that the bombing destroyed industrial facilities, demoralized the population, and cleared the way for the great Allied invasion of France in the late spring. In fact, the greatest contribution of the bombing to the military struggle was to force the German air force (the *Luftwaffe*) to relocate much of its strength in Germany itself and to engage Allied forces in the air. The air battles over Germany considerably weakened the *Luftwaffe* and made it a less formidable obstacle to the Allied invasion than it might once have been.

Preparations for the invasion were also assisted by the success of the Allies in breaking the most secret German codes—a success made possible by the acquisition of an "Ultra" machine, a sophisticated German coding device.

An enormous invasion force had been gathering in England for two years: almost 3 million troops, and perhaps the greatest array of naval vessels and armaments ever assembled in one place. On the morning of June 6, 1944, D-Day, General Dwight D. Eisenhower, the Supreme

Commander of the Allied forces, sent this vast armada into action. The landing came not at the narrowest part

D-Day

of the English Channel, where the Germans had expected and prepared for it, but along sixty miles of the Cotentin Peninsula on the coast of Normandy. While airplanes and battleships offshore bombarded the Nazi defenses, 4,000 vessels landed troops and supplies on the beaches. (Three divisions of paratroopers had been dropped behind the German lines the night before, amid scenes of great confusion, to seize critical roads and bridges for the push inland.) Fighting was intense along the beach, but the superior manpower and equipment of the Allied forces gradually prevailed. Within a week, the German forces had been dislodged from virtually the entire Normandy coast.

For the next month, further progress remained slow. But in late July in the Battle of Saint-Lô, General Omar Bradley's First Army smashed through the German lines. George S. Patton's Third Army, spearheaded by heavy tank attacks, then moved through the hole Bradley had created and began a drive into the heart of France. On August 25, Free French forces arrived in Paris and liberated the city from four years of German occupation. And by mid-September the Allied armies had driven the Germans almost entirely out of France and Belgium.

The great Allied drive came to a halt, however, at the Rhine River in the face of a firm line of German defenses and a period of cold weather, rain, and floods. In mid-December, German forces struck in desperation along fifty miles of front in the Ardennes Forest. In the Battle of

Battle of the Bulge

the Bulge (named for a large bulge that appeared in the American lines as the Germans pressed forward), they drove fifty-five miles toward Antwerp before they were finally stopped at Bastogne. The battle ended serious German resistance in the west.

While the Allies were fighting their way through France, Soviet forces were sweeping westward into central Europe and the Balkans. In late January 1945, the Russians launched a great offensive toward the Oder River inside Germany. In early spring, they were ready to launch a final assault against Berlin. By then, Omar Bradley's First Army was pushing into Germany from the west. Early in March, his forces captured the city of Cologne, on the west bank of the Rhine. The next day, in a remarkable stroke of good fortune, he discovered and seized an undamaged bridge over the river at Remagen; Allied troops were soon pouring across the Rhine. In the following weeks the British Field Marshal Bernard Montgomery, commander of Allied ground operations on D-Day and after, pushed into northern Germany with a

AMERICANS IN PARIS, 1944 American troop transports roll into Paris in August 1944 to a delirious welcome from French citizens, who had by then lived under Nazi occupation for more than four years. They had given an even warmer greeting to the Free French forces under General Charles De Gaulle, which had arrived in the city a few days earlier. *(Bettmann/Corbis)*

million troops, while Bradley's army, sweeping through central Germany, completed the encirclement of 300,000 German soldiers in the Ruhr.

The German resistance was now broken on both fronts. American forces were moving eastward faster than they had anticipated and could have beaten the Russians to Berlin and Prague. Instead, the American and British high commands decided to halt the advance along the Elbe River in central Germany to await the Russians. That decision enabled the Soviets to occupy eastern Germany and Czechoslovakia.

On April 30, with Soviet forces on the outskirts of Berlin, Adolf Hitler killed himself in his bunker in the capital. And on May 8, 1945, the remaining German forces surrendered unconditionally. V-E (Victory in Europe) Day prompted great celebrations in western Europe and in the United States, tempered by the knowledge of the continuing war against Japan.

Germany Defeated

The Pacific Offensive

In February 1944, American naval forces under Admiral Chester Nimitz won a series of victories in the Marshall Islands and cracked the outer perimeter of the Japanese Empire. Within a month, the navy had destroyed other vital Japanese bastions. American submarines, in the meantime, were decimating Japanese shipping and crippling the nation's domestic economy. By the summer of 1944, the already skimpy food rations for the Japanese people had been reduced by nearly a quarter; there was also a critical gasoline shortage.

Meanwhile, a frustrating struggle was in progress on the Asian mainland. In 1942, the Japanese had forced General Joseph W. Stilwell of the United States out of Burma and had moved their own troops as far west as the mountains bordering India. For a time, Stilwell supplied the isolated Chinese forces continuing to resist Japan with an aerial ferry over the Himalayas. In 1943, finally, he led Chinese, Indian, and a few American troops back through northern Burma, constructing a road and pipeline across the mountains into China (the Burma Road, also known as the Ledo Road or Stilwell Road), which finally opened in the fall of 1944. By then, however, the Japanese had launched a major counteroffensive and had driven so deep into the Chinese interior that they threatened the terminus of the Burma Road and the center of Chinese government at Chungking. The Japanese offensive precipitated a long-simmering feud between General Stilwell and Premier Chiang Kai-shek of China. Stilwell was indignant because Chiang (whom he called, contemptuously, the "Peanut") was using many of his troops to maintain an armed frontier against the Chinese communists and would not deploy those troops against the Japanese.

The decisive battles of the Pacific war, however, occurred in the Pacific. In mid-June 1944, an enormous American armada struck the heavily fortified Mariana Islands and, after some of the bloodiest operations of the war, captured Tinian, Guam, and Saipan, 1,350 miles from Tokyo. In September, American forces landed on the western Carolines. And on October 20, General MacArthur's troops landed on Leyte Island in the Philippines. The Japanese now used virtually their entire fleet against the Allied invaders in three major encounters—which together constituted the decisive Battle of Leyte Gulf, the largest naval engagement in history. American forces held off the Japanese onslaught and sank four Japanese carriers, all but destroying Japan's capacity to continue a serious naval war.

Battle of Leyte Gulf

Nevertheless, as American forces advanced closer to the Japanese mainland early in 1945, the imperial forces seemed only to increase their resistance. In February 1945, American marines seized the tiny volcanic island of Iwo Jima, only 750 miles from Tokyo, but only after the costliest single battle in the history of the Marine Corps. The marines suffered over 20,000 casualties.

The battle for Okinawa, an island only 370 miles south of Japan, was further evidence of the strength of the Japanese resistance in those last desperate months. Week after week, the Japanese sent kamikaze (suicide) planes against American and British ships, sacrificing 3,500 of them while inflicting great damage. Japanese troops on shore launched desperate nighttime attacks on the American lines. The United States and its allies suffered nearly 50,000 casualties before finally capturing Okinawa in late June 1945. Over 100,000 Japanese died in the siege.

Okinawa

Many believed that the same kind of bitter fighting awaited the Americans in Japan itself. But there were signs early in 1945 that such an invasion might not be necessary. The Japanese had almost no ships or planes left with which to fight. In July 1945, for example, American warships stood off the shore of Japan and shelled industrial targets (many already in ruins from aerial bombings) with impunity. A brutal firebombing of Tokyo in March, in which American bombers dropped napalm on the city and created a firestorm in which over 80,000 people died, further weakened the Japanese will to resist. Moderate Japanese leaders, who had long since decided that the war was lost, were struggling for power within the government and were looking for ways to bring the war to an end. After the invasion of Okinawa, Emperor Hirohito appointed a new premier and gave him instructions to sue for peace; but the new leader could not persuade military leaders to give up the fight. He did try, along with the emperor himself, to obtain mediation through the Soviet Union. The Russians, however, showed little interest in playing the role of arbitrator.

Whether the moderates could ultimately have prevailed is a question about which historians and others

OKINAWA The invasion of Okinawa, an island near Japan, was one of the last major battles of World War II. In this photograph, taken June 18, 1945, a bullet-scarred monument provides shelter to members of the 7th Infantry of the U.S. 10th Army as they look ahead at Japanese action. Over 11,000 Americans (and more than 80,000 Japanese) died in the rugged battle for the island, which consumed nearly three months. It ended three days after this photograph was taken. Two months later—after the bombing of Hiroshima and Nagasaki—Japan surrendered. *(Bettmann/Corbis)*

continue to disagree. In any case, the question eventually became moot. In mid-July, American scientists conducted a successful test of a new atomic bomb, which led to a major event in world history, significant only in part because it ended World War II.

The Manhattan Project

Reports had reached the United States in 1939 that Nazi scientists had taken the first step toward the creation of an atomic bomb, a weapon more powerful than any ever previously devised. The United States and Britain immediately began a race to develop the weapon before the Germans did.

The search for the new weapon emerged from theories developed by atomic physicists, beginning early in the century, and particularly from some of the founding ideas of modern science developed by Albert Einstein. Einstein's famous theory of relativity had revealed the relationships between mass and energy. More precisely, he had argued that, in theory at least, matter could be converted into a tremendous force of energy. It was Einstein himself, who was by then living in the United States, who warned Franklin Roosevelt that the Germans were developing atomic weapons and that the United States must begin trying to do the same. The

effort to build atomic weapons centered on the use of uranium, whose atomic structure made possible the creation of a nuclear chain reaction. A nuclear chain reaction occurs when the atomic nuclei in radioactive matter are split (a process known as nuclear fission) by neutrons. Each fission creates new neutrons that produce fissions in additional atoms at an ever increasing and self-sustaining pace.

The construction of atomic weapons had become feasible by the 1940s because of the discovery of the radioactivity of uranium in the 1930s by Enrico Fermi in Italy. *Enrico Fermi* In 1939, the great Danish physicist Niels Bohr sent news of German experiments in radioactivity to the United States, where experiments began in many places. In 1940, scientists at Columbia began chain-reaction experiments with uranium and produced persuasive evidence of the feasibility of using uranium as fuel for a weapon. The Columbia experiments stalled in 1941, and the work moved to Berkeley and the University of Chicago, where Enrico Fermi (who had emigrated to the United States in 1938) achieved the first controlled fission chain reaction in December 1942.

By then, the army had taken control of the research and appointed General Leslie Groves to reorganize the project—which soon became known as the Manhattan

THE MANHATTAN PROJECT J. Robert Oppenheimer, wearing the broad-brimmed hat, was one of the scientific leaders of the Manhattan Project, which developed the atomic bomb during World War II. The military commander of the project was General Leslie Groves. The two men are shown here after the war, examining the charred landscape of the Trinity site in New Mexico, where the first successful detonation of the new weapon occurred in July 1945. *(Bettmann/Corbis)*

Project, because it was devised in the Manhattan Engineer District Office of the Army Corps of Engineers. Over the next three years, the government secretly poured nearly $2 billion into the Manhattan Project—a massive scientific and technological effort conducted at hidden laboratories in Oak Ridge, Tennessee; Los Alamos, New Mexico; Hanford, Washington; and other sites. Scientists in Oak Ridge, who were charged with finding a way to create a nuclear chain reaction that could be feasibly replicated within the confined space of a bomb, began experimenting with plutonium—a derivative of uranium first discovered by scientists at Berkeley. Plutonium proved capable of providing a practical fuel for the weapon. Scientists in Los Alamos, under the direction of J. Robert Oppenheimer, were charged with the construction of the actual atomic bomb.

By 1944, the government was secretly funneling over $1 billion a year to the Manhattan Project, and despite many unforeseen problems, the scientists pushed ahead

much faster than anyone had predicted. Even so, the war in Europe ended before they were ready to test the first weapon. Just before dawn on July 16, 1945, in the desert near Alamogordo, New Mexico, the scientists gathered to witness the first atomic explosion in history: the detonation of a plutonium-fueled bomb that its creators had named *Trinity.* The explosion—a blinding flash of light, probably brighter than any ever seen on earth, followed by a huge, billowing mushroom cloud—created a vast crater in the barren desert.

The Trinity Bomb

Atomic Warfare

News of the explosion reached President Harry S. Truman (who had taken office in April on the death of Roosevelt) in Potsdam, Germany, where he was attending a conference of Allied leaders. He issued an ultimatum to the Japanese (signed jointly by the British) demanding that they surrender by August 3 or face complete devastation. The Japanese premier wanted to accept the Allied demand, but he could not persuade the military leaders to agree. There was a hint from Tokyo that the government might agree to surrender, in return for a promise that the Japanese could retain their emperor. The American government, firmly committed to the idea of "unconditional surrender," dismissed those proposals, convinced (perhaps correctly) that the moderates who were making them did not have the power to deliver them. When the deadline passed with no surrender, Truman ordered the air force to use the new atomic weapons against Japan.

Controversy has raged for decades over whether Truman's decision to use the bomb was justified and what his motives were. (See "Where Historians Disagree," pp. 772–773.) Some have argued that the atomic attack was unnecessary, that had the United States agreed to the survival of the emperor (which it ultimately did agree to in any case), or waited only a few more weeks, the Japanese would have surrendered. Others argue that nothing less than the atomic bombs could have persuaded the hard-line military leaders of Japan to surrender without a costly American invasion. Some critics of the decision, including some of the scientists involved in the Manhattan Project, have argued that whatever Japanese intentions, the United States, as a matter of morality, should not have used the terrible new weapon. One horrified physicist wrote the president shortly before the attack: "This thing must not be permitted to exist on this earth. We must not be the most hated and feared people in the world."

Debating the Bomb's Use

The nation's military and political leaders, however, showed little concern about such matters. Truman, who had not even known of the existence of the Manhattan Project until he became president, was apparently making

THE DECISION TO DROP THE ATOMIC BOMB

In the fall of 1994, the Air and Space Museum of the Smithsonian Institution in Washington installed in its main hall the fuselage of the *Enola Gay,* the airplane that dropped the first atomic bomb ever used in warfare on Hiroshima in 1945. Originally, the airplane was to have been accompanied by an exhibit that would include discussions of the many popular and academic controversies over whether the United States should have used the bomb. But a powerful group of critics—led by veterans' groups and aided by many members of Congress—organized to demand that the exhibit be altered and that it reflect only the "official" explanation of the decision. In the end, the museum decided to mount no exhibit at all. The *Enola Gay* hangs in the Smithsonian today entirely without explanation for the millions of tourists who see it each year.

The furor that surrounded the Air and Space Museum installation reflects the passions that the bombing of Hiroshima and Nagasaki continue to arouse among people around the world, and people in the United States and Japan in particular. It also reflects the continuing debate among historians about how to explain, and evaluate, President Truman's decision to use the atomic bomb in the war against Japan.

Truman himself, both at the time and in his 1955 memoirs, insisted that the decision was a simple and

HIROSHIMA, SEPTEMBER 1945 This photograph, taken by a U.S. Navy photographer, shows a Japanese soldier walking through what remained of Hiroshima a few weeks after his nation surrendered, bringing World War II to an end. The atomic bomb that the United States dropped on August 6, 1945, left little evidence of the crowded, bustling city that had stood there only a few weeks before. *(National Archives and Records Administration)*

straightforward one. The alternative to using atomic weapons, he claimed, was an American invasion of mainland Japan that might have cost as many as a million lives. Given that choice, he said, the decision was easy. "I regarded the bomb as a military weapon and never had any doubt that

what he believed to be a simple military decision. A weapon was available that would end the war quickly; he could see no reason not to use it.

Still more controversy has existed over whether there were other motives at work behind Truman's decision. With the Soviet Union poised to enter the war in the Pacific, did the United States want to end the conflict quickly to forestall an expanded communist presence in Asia? Did Truman use the bomb as a weapon to intimidate Stalin, with whom he was engaged in difficult negotiations, so the Soviet leader would accept American demands? Little direct evidence

is available to support (or definitively refute) either of these accusations.

On August 6, 1945, an American B-29, the *Enola Gay,* dropped an atomic weapon on the Japanese industrial center at Hiroshima. With a single bomb, the United States *Hiroshima* completely incinerated a four-square-mile area at the center of the previously undamaged city. More than 80,000 civilians died, according to later American estimates. Many more survived to suffer the crippling effects of radioactive fallout or to pass those effects on to their children in the form of birth defects.

it should be used." Truman's explanation of his decision has been supported by the accounts of many of his contemporaries: by Secretary of War Henry Stimson, in his 1950 memoir, *On Active Service in Peace and War;* by Winston Churchill; by Truman's senior military advisers. It has also received considerable support from historians. Herbert Feis argued in *The Atomic Bomb and the End of World War II* (1966) that Truman had made his decision on purely military grounds—to ensure a speedy American victory. David McCullough, the author of an enormously popular biography of Truman published in 1992, also accepted Truman's own account of his actions largely uncritically, as did Alonzo L. Hamby in *Man of the People* (1995), an important scholarly study of Truman. "One consideration weighed most heavily on Truman," Hamby concluded. "The longer the war lasted, the more Americans killed." Robert J. Donovan, author of an extensive history of the Truman presidency, *Conflict and Crisis* (1977), reached almost precisely the same conclusion: "The simple reason Truman made the decision to drop the bomb was to end the war quickly and save lives."

Others have strongly disagreed. As early as 1948, a British physicist, P. M. S. Blackett, wrote in *Fear, War, and the Bomb* that the destruction of Hiroshima and Nagasaki was "not so much the last military act of the second World War as the first major

operation of the cold diplomatic war with Russia." The most important critic of Truman's decision is the historian Gar Alperovitz, the author of two influential books on the subject: *Atomic Diplomacy: Hiroshima and Potsdam* (1965) and *The Decision to Use the Atomic Bomb and the Architecture of an American Myth* (1995). Alperovitz dismisses the argument that the bomb was used to shorten the war and save lives. Japan was likely to have surrendered soon even if the bomb had not been used, he claims; large numbers of American lives were not at stake in the decision. Instead, he argues, the United States used the bomb less to influence Japan than to intimidate the Soviet Union. Truman made his decision to bomb Hiroshima in the immediate aftermath of a discouraging meeting with Stalin at Potsdam. He was heavily influenced, therefore, by his belief that America needed a new way to force Stalin to change his behavior, that, as Alperovitz has argued, "the bomb would make Russia more manageable in Europe." Martin J. Sherwin, in *A World Destroyed* (1975), is somewhat more restrained in his criticism of American policymakers. But he too argues that a rapidly growing awareness of the danger Stalin posed to the peace made leaders aware that atomic weapons—and their effective use—could help strengthen the American hand in the nation's critical relationship with the Soviet Union. Truman, he said,

"increasingly came to believe that America's possession of the atomic bomb would, by itself, convince Stalin to be more cooperative."

John W. Dower's *War Without Mercy* (1986) contributed, by implication at least, to another controversial explanation of the American decision: racism. Throughout World War II, most Americans considered the Germans and the Italians to be largely military and political adversaries. They looked at the Japanese very differently: as members of a very different and almost bestial race. They were, many Americans came to believe, almost a subhuman species. And while Dower himself stops short of saying so, others have suggested that this racialized image of Japan contributed to American willingness to drop atomic bombs on Japanese cities. Even many of Truman's harshest critics, however, note that it is, as Alperovitz has written, "all but impossible to find specific evidence that racism was an important factor in the decision to attack Hiroshima and Nagasaki."

The debate over the decision to drop the atomic bomb is an unusually emotional one—driven in part by the tremendous moral questions that the destruction of so many lives raises, and it has inspired bitter professional and personal attacks on advocates of almost every position. It illustrates clearly how history has often been, and remains, a powerful force in the way societies define their politics, their values, and their character.

The Japanese government, stunned by the attack, was at first unable to agree on a response. Two days later, on August 8, the Soviet Union declared war on Japan. And the following day, the United States sent another American plane to drop another atomic weapon—this time on the city of Nagasaki—inflicting horrible damage and over 100,000 deaths on another unfortunate community. Finally, the emperor intervened to break the stalemate in the cabinet, and on August 14 the government announced that it was ready to give up. On September 2, 1945, on board the American battleship

Missouri, anchored in Tokyo Bay, Japanese officials signed the articles of surrender.

The greatest war in the history of mankind had come to an end, and the United States had emerged not only victorious but in a position of unprecedented power, influence, and prestige. It was a victory, however, that few could greet with unambiguous joy. Fourteen million combatants had died in the struggle. Many more civilians had perished, from bombings, from disease and starvation, from genocidal campaigns of extermination. The United States had suffered only light casualties in comparison with many other nations, but the cost had still been high:

Nagasaki

HIROSHIMA Long after the city was destroyed by the first atomic bomb ever used in warfare, Hiroshima remained a ghostly landscape—an incongruous backdrop for a Japanese couple strolling along the street. *(Bettmann/Corbis)*

322,000 dead, another 800,000 injured. And despite the sacrifices, the world continued to face an uncertain future, menaced by the threat of nuclear warfare and by the emerging antagonism between the world's two strongest nations—the United States and the Soviet Union—that would darken the peace for many decades to come.

CONCLUSION

The United States played a critical, indeed decisive, role in the war against Germany and Italy; and it defeated Imperial Japan in the Pacific largely alone. But America's sacrifices in the war paled next to those of the nation's most important allies. Britain, France, and, above all, the Soviet Union paid a staggering price—in lives, treasure, and social unity—that had no counterpart in the United States, most of whose citizens experienced a booming prosperity and only modest privations during the four years of American involvement in the conflict. There were, of course, jarring social changes during the war that even prosperity could not entirely offset: shortages, restrictions, regulations, family dislocations, and perhaps most of all the absence of millions of men, and considerable numbers of women, who went overseas to work and fight.

American fighting men and women, of course, had very different experiences from those Americans who remained at home. They endured tremendous hardships, substantial casualties, and great loneliness. They fought effectively and bravely. They helped liberate North Africa and Italy from German occupation. And in June 1944, finally, they joined British, French, and other forces in a great and successful invasion of France, which led less than a year later to the destruction of the Nazi regime and the end of the European war. In the Pacific, they turned back the Japanese offensive through a series of difficult naval and land battles. But in the end, it was not the American army and navy that brought the war against Japan to a close. It was the unleashing of the most destructive weapon mankind had ever created—the atomic bomb—on the people of Japan that finally persuaded the leaders of that nation to surrender.

FOR FURTHER REFERENCE

John Morton Blum, *V Was for Victory: Politics and American Culture During World War II* (1976) and Richard Polenberg, *War and Society* (1972) are important studies of the home front during World War II. David Kennedy, *Freedom from Fear: The American People in Depression and War, 1929–1945* (1999) is an important narrative of both the American military experience in the war and the war's impact on American politics and society. Alan Brinkley, *The End of Reform: New Deal Liberalism in Recession and War* (1995) examines the impact of the war on liberal ideology and political economy. Doris Kearns Goodwin, *No Ordinary Time: Franklin and Eleanor Roosevelt: The Home Front in World War II* (1994) is an engaging portrait of the Roosevelts during the war. Susan Hartmann examines the transformation in women's work and family roles during and after the war in *The Homefront and Beyond: American Women in the 1940s* (1982). Richard M. Dalfiume, *Desegregation of the U.S. Armed Forces: Fighting on Two Fronts, 1939–1953* (1969) discusses race relations in the military during World War II and beyond. Maurice Isserman, *Which Side Were You On? The American Communist Party During World War II* (1982) portrays the dramatic shifts in Communist Party strategy and status during the war. John W. Dower, *War Without Mercy: Race and Power in the Pacific War* (1986) examines the intense racism that shaped both sides of the war between the United States and Japan. Peter Irons, *Justice at War* (1983) and Roger Daniels, *Concentration Camps USA: Japanese-Americans and World War II* (1981) examine the internment of Japanese Americans. John Keegan, *Six Armies in Normandy: From D-Day to the Liberation of Paris, June 6–August 25, 1944* (1982) is a superb account of the Normandy Invasion. David S. Wyman, *The Abandonment of the Jews: America and the Holocaust, 1941–1945* (1984) is sharply critical of American policy toward the victims of the Holocaust. Richard Rhodes, *The Making of the Atomic Bomb* (1987) is an excellent account of one of the great scientific projects of the twentieth century. Gar Alperovitz, *The Decision to Use the Atomic Bomb and the Architecture of an American Myth* (1995) is an exhaustive and highly critical study of why the United States used atomic weapons in 1945. A sharply different view is visible in Herbert Feis, *The Atomic Bomb and the End of World War II* (1966). John Hersey's *Hiroshima* (1946) reconstructs in minute detail the terrifying experience of the American atomic bomb attack on that Japanese city.

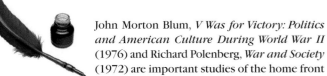

For quizzes, Internet resources, references to additional books and films, and more, consult the book's Online Learning Center at www.mhhe.com/brinkley11.

THE AMERICAN NIGHTMARE Nightmarish visions of what life would be like under communism were staples of American anticommunist propaganda in the early years of the Cold War. This is the cover of a comic book widely distributed beginning in 1947 by Christian groups concerned about inadequate popular awareness of the threat. *(From RED SCARED! by Michael Barson and Steven Heller)*

Significant Events

CHAPTER TWENTY-NINE

THE COLD WAR

*E*ven before the end of World War II, in which the United States and the Soviet Union had fought together as allies, there were signs of tension between the two nations. Once the hostilities were over, those tensions quickly grew to create what became known as a "Cold War"—a tense and dangerous rivalry that would cast its shadow over international affairs for decades. The Cold War also had profound effects on American domestic life. Among other things, it helped produce the most corrosive outbreak of antiradical hysteria of the century. America in the postwar years was both powerful and prosperous; but it was also for a time troubled and uncertain about the future.

- National Security Act passed
- Taft-Hartley Act passed
- HUAC begins investigating Hollywood
- Federal employee loyalty program launched
- 1948 · Communists stage coup in Czechoslovakia
- Economic Cooperation Administration established
- Selective Service System restored
- Berlin blockade prompts U.S. airlift
- Truman elected president
- Hiss case begins
- 1949 · NATO established
- Soviet Union explodes atomic bomb
- Communists seize power in China
- 1950 · NSC-68 outlines new U.S. policy toward communism

- Korean War begins
- American troops enter North Korea
- Chinese troops enter Korean War
- McCarran Act passed
- Fuchs-Rosenberg case begins
- Joseph McCarthy begins campaign against communists in government
- 1951 · Truman removes MacArthur from command in Korea
- Railroad workers strike
- Negotiations begin in Korea
- 1952 · American occupation of Japan ends
- Steelworkers strike
- Dwight D. Eisenhower elected president

ORIGINS OF THE COLD WAR

No issue in twentieth-century American history has aroused more debate than the question of the origins of the Cold War. Some have claimed that Soviet duplicity and expansionism created the international tensions, while others have proposed that American provocations and imperial ambitions were at least equally to blame. Most historians agree, however, that wherever the preponderance of blame may lie, both the United States and the Soviet Union contributed to the atmosphere of hostility and suspicion that quickly clouded the peace. (See "Where Historians Disagree," pp. 780–781.)

Sources of Soviet-American Tension

At the heart of the rivalry between the United States and the Soviet Union in the 1940s was a fundamental differ-

America's Postwar Vision | ence in the ways the great powers envisioned the postwar world. One vision, first openly outlined in the Atlantic Charter in 1941, was of a world in which nations abandoned their traditional beliefs in military alliances and spheres of influence and governed their relations with one another through democratic processes, with an international organization serving as the arbiter of disputes and the protector of every nation's right of self-determination. That vision appealed to many Americans, including Franklin Roosevelt.

The other vision was that of the Soviet Union and to some extent, it gradually became clear, of Great Britain. Both Stalin and Churchill had signed the Atlantic Charter. But Britain had always been uneasy about the implica-

Spheres of Influence | tions of the self-determination ideal for its own enormous empire. And the Soviet Union was determined to create a secure sphere for itself in Central and Eastern Europe as protection against possible future aggression from the West. Both Churchill and Stalin, therefore, tended to envision a postwar structure in which the great powers would control areas of strategic interest to them, in which something vaguely similar to the traditional European balance of power would reemerge. Gradually, the differences between these two positions would turn the peacemaking process into a form of warfare.

Wartime Diplomacy

Serious strains had already begun to develop in the alliance with the Soviet Union in January 1943, when Roosevelt and Churchill met in Casablanca, Morocco, to discuss Allied strategy. (Stalin had declined Roosevelt's invitation to attend.) The two leaders could not accept Stalin's most important demand—the immediate opening of a second front in western Europe. But they tried to reassure Stalin by announcing that they would accept nothing less than the unconditional surrender of the Axis powers, thus indicating

that they would not negotiate a separate peace with Hitler and leave the Soviets to fight on alone.

In November 1943, Roosevelt and Churchill traveled to Teheran, Iran, for their first meeting with Stalin. By now, however, Roosevelt's most effective bargaining tool—Stalin's need for American assistance in his struggle against Germany—had been largely removed. The German advance against Russia had been halted; Soviet forces were now launching their own westward offensive. Nevertheless, the Teheran Conference seemed in most respects a success. Roosevelt and Stalin established a cordial personal relationship. Stalin agreed to an American request that the Soviet Union enter the war in the Pacific soon after the end of hostilities in Europe. Roosevelt, in turn, promised that an Anglo-American second front would be established within six months.

On other matters, however, the origins of future disagreements were already visible. Most important was the question of the future of Poland.

Roosevelt and Churchill were | *Dispute over Poland* willing to agree to a movement of the Soviet border westward, allowing Stalin to annex some historically Polish territory. But on the nature of the postwar government in the portion of Poland that would remain independent, there were sharp differences. Roosevelt and Churchill supported the claims of the Polish government-in-exile that had been functioning in London since 1940; Stalin wished to install another, pro-communist exiled government that had spent the war in Lublin, in the Soviet Union. The three leaders avoided a bitter conclusion to the Teheran Conference only by leaving the issue unresolved.

Yalta

More than a year later, in February 1945, Roosevelt joined Churchill and Stalin for a great peace conference in the Soviet city of Yalta. On a number of issues, the Big Three reached agreements. In return for Stalin's renewed promise to enter the Pacific war, Roosevelt agreed that the Soviet Union should receive some of the territory in the Pacific that Russia had lost in the 1904 Russo-Japanese War.

The negotiators also agreed to a plan for a new international organization, a plan that had been hammered out the previous summer at a conference in Washington, D.C., at the Dumbarton Oaks estate.

The new United Nations would | *United Nations* contain a General Assembly, in which every member would be represented, and a Security Council, with permanent representatives of the five major powers (the United States, Britain, France, the Soviet Union, and China), each of which would have veto power. The Security Council would also have temporary delegates from several other nations. These agreements became the basis of the United Nations charter, drafted at a conference of fifty nations beginning April 25, 1945, in San Francisco. The United States Senate ratified the charter in July by a vote

Outline

tensions b/w Soviets and Americans created the Cold War

nor things, it produced antiradical hysteria.

origins are debatable

nor the Soviets save to blame the US

of American-Soviet Tension

are b/w both countries' visions of the post war worlds

- American vision: a post-war world in which nations abandoned their traditional beliefs in military alliances and spheres of influence, and governed themselves through democracy. Creating an international organizations serving as an arbitrator of disputes and ~~creating~~ the protector of every nations right of self-determination.

- Soviet vision:

15 pages

NAME: Kevin Brinig Chapter: 24 The cold War.

MAIN THEMES

LIST OF TERMS

QUESTIONS ON READING

NAME: Kevin Brinig **Chapter:** 28

MAIN THEMES

LIST OF TERMS

QUESTIONS ON READING

YALTA Churchill, Roosevelt, and Stalin (known during the war as the "Big Three") meet at Yalta in the Crimea in February 1945 to try to agree on the outlines of the peace that they knew was soon to come. Instead, they settled on a series of vague compromises that ultimately left all parties feeling betrayed. *(Bettmann/Corbis)*

of 80 to 2 (a striking contrast to the slow and painful defeat it had administered to the charter of the League of Nations twenty-five years before).

On other issues, however, the Yalta Conference produced no real accord. Basic disagreement remained about the postwar Polish government. Stalin, whose armies now occupied Poland, had already installed a government composed of the pro-communist "Lublin" Poles. Roosevelt and Churchill insisted that the pro-Western "London" Poles must be allowed a place in the Warsaw regime. Roosevelt envisioned a government based on free, democratic elections—which both he and Stalin recognized the pro-Western forces would win. Stalin agreed only to a vague compromise by which an unspecified number of pro-Western Poles would be granted a place in the government. He reluctantly consented to hold "free and unfettered elections" in Poland on an unspecified future date. They did not take place for more than forty years.

Nor was there agreement about the future of Germany. Roosevelt seemed to want a reconstructed and reunited Germany. Stalin wanted to impose heavy reparations on Germany and to ensure a permanent dismemberment of the nation. The final agreement was, like the Polish accord, vague and unstable. The decision on reparations would be referred to a future commission. The United States, Great Britain, France, and the Soviet Union would each control its own "zone of occupation" in Germany—the zones to be determined by

Disagreements over Germany

the position of troops at the end of the war. Berlin, the German capital, was already well inside the Soviet zone, but because of its symbolic importance it would itself be divided into four sectors, one for each nation to occupy. At an unspecified date, Germany would be reunited; but there was no agreement on how the reunification would occur. As for the rest of Europe, the conference produced a murky accord on the establishment of governments "broadly representative of all democratic elements" and "responsible to the will of the people."

The Yalta accords, in other words, were less a settlement of postwar issues than a set of loose principles that sidestepped the most difficult questions. Roosevelt, Churchill, and Stalin returned home from the conference each apparently convinced that he had signed an important agreement. But the Soviet interpretation of the accords differed so sharply from the Anglo-American interpretation that the illusion endured only briefly. In the weeks following the Yalta Conference, Roosevelt watched with growing alarm as the Soviet Union moved systematically to establish pro-communist governments in one Central or Eastern European nation after another and as Stalin refused to make the changes in Poland that the president believed he had promised.

But Roosevelt did not abandon hope. Still believing the differences could be settled, he left Washington early in the spring for a vacation at his retreat in Warm Springs, Georgia. There, on April 12, 1945, he suffered a sudden, massive stroke and died.

ORIGINS OF THE COLD WAR

No issue in recent American history has produced more controversy than that of the origins of the Cold War between the United States and the Soviet Union. Historians have disagreed, often sharply, over the question of who was responsible for the breakdown of American-Soviet relations, and on whether the conflict between the two superpowers was inevitable or could

(National Archives and Records Administration)

have been avoided. The Cold War may now be over, but the debate over its origins is not.

For more than a decade after the end of World War II, few historians in the United States saw any reason to challenge the official American interpretation of the beginnings of the Cold War. Thomas A. Bailey spoke for most students of the conflict when he argued, in *America Faces Russia* (1950), that the breakdown of relations was a direct result of aggressive Soviet policies of expansion in the immediate postwar years. Stalin's government violated its solemn promises in the Yalta accords, imposed Soviet-dominated governments on the unwilling nations of Eastern Europe, and schemed to spread communism throughout the world. American policy was the logical and necessary response.

The American involvement in Vietnam disillusioned many historians with the premises of the containment policy and, thus, with the traditional view of the origins of the Cold War. But even before the conflict in Asia had reached major proportions, the first works in what would become known as the "revisionist" interpretation began to appear. William

Appleman Williams challenged the accepted wisdom in 1959 in *The Tragedy of American Diplomacy*. The United States had operated in world affairs, Williams argued, in response to one overriding concern: its commitment to maintaining an "open door" for American trade in world markets. The confrontation with the Soviet Union, therefore, was less a response to Russian aggressive designs than an expression of the American belief in the necessity of capitalist expansion.

Later revisionists modified many of Williams's claims, but most accepted some of the basic outlines of his thesis: that the United States had been primarily to blame for the Cold War; that the Soviet Union had displayed no aggressive designs toward the West (and was too weak and exhausted at the end of World War II to be able to pose a serious threat to America in any case); that the United States had used its nuclear monopoly to attempt to threaten and intimidate Stalin; that Harry Truman had recklessly abandoned the conciliatory policies of Franklin Roosevelt and taken a provocative hard line against the Russians; and that the Soviet response had reflected a legitimate fear

THE COLLAPSE OF THE PEACE

Harry S. Truman, who succeeded Roosevelt in the presidency, had almost no familiarity with international issues. Nor did he share Roosevelt's apparent faith in the flexibility of the Soviet Union. Roosevelt had apparently believed that Stalin was, essentially, a reasonable man with whom an ultimate accord might be reached. Truman, in contrast, sided with those in the government (and there were many) who considered the Soviet Union fundamentally untrustworthy and viewed Stalin himself with suspicion and even loathing.

The Failure of Potsdam

Truman had been in office only a few days before he decided to "get tough" with the Soviet Union. Stalin had made what the new president considered solemn agreements with the United States at Yalta. The United States should insist that the Soviets honor them. Truman met on

780

April 23 with Soviet Foreign Minister Molotov and sharply chastised him for violations of the Yalta accords.

In fact, Truman had only limited leverage by which to compel the Soviet Union to carry out its agreements. Russian forces already occupied Poland and much of the rest of Central and Eastern Europe. Germany was already divided among the conquering nations. The United States was still engaged in a war in the Pacific and was neither able nor willing to enter into a second conflict in Europe. Truman insisted that the United States should be able to get "85 percent" of what it wanted, but he was ultimately forced to settle for much less.

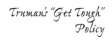

Truman's "Get Tough" Policy

He conceded first on Poland. When Stalin made a few minor concessions to the pro-Western exiles, Truman recognized the Warsaw government, hoping that non-communist forces might gradually expand their influence there. Until the 1980s, they did not. Other questions remained, above all the question of Germany. To

of capitalist encirclement. Walter LaFeber, in *America, Russia, and the Cold War, 1945–1967* (1967 and many later editions), maintained that America's supposedly idealistic internationalism at the close of the war—its vision of "One World," with every nation in control of its own destiny—was in reality an effort to ensure a world shaped in the American image, with every nation open to American influence (and American trade).

Ultimately, the revisionist interpretation began to produce a reaction of its own, what some have called the "post-revisionist" view of the conflict. Some manifestations of this reaction have consisted of little more than a reaffirmation of the traditional view of the Cold War. Arthur M. Schlesinger, Jr., for example, admitted in a 1967 article that the Soviets may not have been committed to world conquest, as most earlier accounts had claimed. Nevertheless, the Soviets (and Stalin in particular) were motivated by a deep-seated paranoia about the West, which made them insistent on dominating Eastern Europe and rendered any amicable relationship between them and the United States impossible.

But the dominant works of post-revisionist scholarship have attempted to strike a balance between the two camps, to identify areas of blame and misperception on both sides of the conflict. Thomas G. Paterson, in *Soviet-American Confrontation* (1973), viewed Russian hostility and American efforts to dominate the postwar world as equally responsible for the Cold War. John Lewis Gaddis, in *The United States and the Origins of the Cold War, 1941–1947* (1972) and other works, similarly maintained that "neither side can bear sole responsibility for the onset of the Cold War." American policymakers, he argued, had only limited options because of the pressures of domestic politics. And Stalin was immobilized by his obsessive concern with maintaining his own power and ensuring absolute security for the Soviet Union. But if neither side was entirely to blame, Gaddis concluded, the Soviets must be held at least slightly more accountable for the problems, for Stalin was in a much better position to compromise, given his broader power within his own government, than the politically hamstrung Truman. Melvyn Leffler's *Preponderance of Power* (1991) argued similarly that American

policymakers genuinely believed in the existence of a Soviet threat and were determined to remain consistently stronger than the Soviets in response.

Out of the post-revisionist literature has begun to emerge a more complex view of the Cold War, which de-emphasizes the question of who was to blame and adopts a more detached view of the conflict. The Cold War, recent historians suggest, was not so much the fault of one side or the other as it was the natural, perhaps inevitable, result of tensions between the world's two most powerful nations—nations that had been suspicious of, if not hostile toward, one another for nearly a century. As Ernest May wrote in a 1984 essay:

> After the Second World War, the United States and the Soviet Union were doomed to be antagonists. . . . There probably was never any real possibility that the post-1945 relationship could be anything but hostility verging on conflict. . . . Traditions, belief systems, propinquity, and convenience . . . all combined to stimulate antagonism, and almost no factor operated in either country to hold it back.

---

settle them, Truman met in July at Potsdam, in Russian-occupied Germany, with Churchill (who, after elections in Britain in the midst of the talks, was replaced as prime minister by Clement Attlee) and Stalin. Truman reluctantly accepted the adjustments of the Polish-German border that Stalin had long demanded; he refused, however, to permit the Russians to claim any reparations from the American, French, and British zones of Germany. This stance effectively confirmed that Germany would remain divided, with the western zones united into one nation, friendly to the United States, and the Russian zone surviving as another nation, with a pro-Soviet, communist government.

The China Problem

Central to American hopes for an open, peaceful world "policed" by the great powers was a strong, independent China. But even before the war ended, the American government was aware that those hopes faced a major,

perhaps insurmountable obstacle: the Chinese government of Chiang Kai-shek. Chiang was generally friendly to the United States, but his government was corrupt and incompetent with feeble popular support. Chiang himself lived in a world of almost surreal isolation, unable or unwilling to face the problems that were threatening to engulf him. Ever since 1927, the nationalist government he headed had been engaged in a prolonged and bitter rivalry with the communist armies of Mao Zedong. So successful had the communist challenge grown that Mao was in control of one-fourth of the population by 1945.

Chiang Kai-shek

Some Americans urged the government to try to find a "third force" to support as an alternative to either Chiang or Mao. A few argued that the United States should try to reach some accommodation with Mao. Truman, however, decided reluctantly that he had no choice but to continue supporting Chiang. For the next several years, as the long struggle between the nationalists and the communists erupted into a full-scale civil war, the United States continued to pump money and weapons to Chiang, even as it was becoming clear that the cause was lost. But Truman was not prepared to intervene militarily to save the nationalist regime.

Instead, the American government was beginning to consider an alternative to China as the strong, pro-Western *Restoring Japan* force in Asia: a revived Japan. Abandoning the strict occupation policies of the first years after the war (when General Douglas MacArthur had governed the nation), the United States lifted all restrictions on industrial development and encouraged rapid economic growth in Japan. The vision of an open, united world was giving way in Asia, as it was in Europe, to an acceptance of a divided world with a strong, pro-American sphere of influence.

The Containment Doctrine

By the end of 1945, the Grand Alliance was a shambles. With its passing went any realistic hope of a postwar world constructed according to the Atlantic Charter ideals Roosevelt and others had supported. Instead, a new American policy was slowly emerging. It became known as containment. Rather than attempting to create a unified, "open" world, the United States and its allies would work to "contain" the threat of further Soviet expansion.

The new doctrine emerged in part as a response to events in Europe in 1946. In Turkey, Stalin was trying to win control over the vital sea lanes to the Mediterranean. In Greece, communist forces were threatening the pro-Western government; the British had announced they could no longer provide assistance. Faced with these *Truman Doctrine* challenges, Truman decided to enunciate a firm new policy. In doing so, he drew from the ideas of the influential American diplomat George F. Kennan, who had warned not long after the war that in the Soviet Union the United States faced "a political force committed fanatically to the belief that with the U.S. there can be no permanent modus vivendi," and that the only answer was "a long-term, patient but firm and vigilant containment of Russian expansive tendencies." On March 12, 1947, Truman appeared before Congress and used Kennan's warnings as the basis of what became known as the Truman Doctrine. "I believe," he argued, "that it must be the policy of the United States to support free peoples who are resisting attempted subjugation by armed minorities or by outside pressures." In the same speech he requested $400 million—part of it to bolster the armed forces of Greece and Turkey, another part to provide economic assistance to Greece. Congress quickly approved the measure.

The American commitment ultimately helped ease Soviet pressure on Turkey and helped the Greek government defeat the communist insurgents. More important, it established a basis for American foreign policy that would survive for more than thirty years.

GEORGE F. KENNAN Kennan was one of the architects of the policy of containment, which became the basis of American foreign policy for over forty years. But almost from the start, he was critical of the United States government's sweeping view of containment. Americans needed, he argued, to define their vital interests more narrowly, to focus their defensive efforts on nations of direct strategic importance to them. That meant, in his view, mainly the industrialized nations of Europe and Japan. In later years, he was outspoken in his attacks on the war in Vietnam. *(Library of Congress)*

The Marshall Plan

An integral part of the containment policy was a proposal to aid in the economic reconstruction of Western Europe. There were many motives: humanitarian concern for the *Rebuilding Europe* European people; a fear that Europe would remain an economic drain on the United States if it could not quickly rebuild and begin to feed itself; a desire for a strong European market for American goods. But above all, American policymakers believed that unless something could be done to strengthen the shaky pro-American governments in Western Europe, those governments might fall under the control of rapidly growing domestic communist parties.

In June 1947, therefore, Secretary of State George C. Marshall announced a plan to provide economic assistance to all European nations (including the Soviet Union) that would join in drafting a program for recovery. Although Russia and its Eastern satellites quickly and

predictably rejected the plan, sixteen Western European nations eagerly participated. Whatever domestic opposition there was in the United States largely vanished after a sudden coup in Czechoslovakia in February 1948 that established a Soviet-dominated communist government there. In April, Congress approved the creation of the Economic Cooperation Administration, the agency that would administer the Marshall Plan, as it became known. Over the next three years, the Marshall Plan channeled over $12 billion of American aid into Europe, helping to spark a substantial economic revival. By the end of 1950, European industrial production had risen 64 percent, communist strength in the member nations had declined, and opportunities for American trade had revived.

Mobilization at Home

That the United States had fully accepted a continuing commitment to the containment policy became clear in 1947 and 1948 through a series of measures designed to maintain American military power at near wartime levels. In 1948, at the president's request, Congress approved a new military draft and revived the Selective Service System. In the meantime, the United States, having failed to reach agreement with the Soviet Union on international control of nuclear

weapons, redoubled its own efforts in atomic research, elevating nuclear weaponry to a central place in its military arsenal. The Atomic Energy Commission, established in 1946, became the supervisory body charged with overseeing all nuclear research, civilian and military alike. And in 1950, the Truman administration approved the development of the new hydrogen bomb, a nuclear weapon far more powerful than the bombs the United States had used in 1945.

Particularly important was the National Security Act of 1947, which reshaped the nation's major military and diplomatic institutions. A new Department of Defense would oversee all branches of the armed services, combining functions previously performed separately by the War and Navy departments. A National Security Council (NSC), operating out of the White House, would govern foreign and military policy. A Central Intelligence Agency (CIA) would replace the wartime Office of Strategic Services and would be responsible for collecting information through both open and covert methods; as the Cold War continued, the CIA would also engage secretly in political and military operations on behalf of American goals. The National Security Act, in other words, gave the president expanded powers with which to pursue the nation's international goals.

National Security Act of 1947

The Road to NATO

At about the same time, the United States was moving to strengthen the military capabilities of Western Europe. Convinced that a reconstructed Germany was essential to the hopes of the West, Truman reached an agreement with England and France to merge the three western zones of occupation into a new West German republic (which would include the American, British, and French sectors of Berlin, even though that city lay well within the Soviet zone). Stalin responded quickly. On June 24, 1948, he imposed a tight blockade around the western sectors of Berlin. If Germany was to be officially divided, he was implying, then the country's Western government would have to abandon its outpost in the heart of the Soviet-controlled eastern zone. Truman refused to do so. Unwilling to risk war through a military challenge to the blockade, he ordered a massive airlift to supply the city with food, fuel, and other needed goods. The airlift continued for more than ten months, transporting nearly 2.5 million tons of material, keeping a city of 2 million people alive, and transforming West Berlin into a symbol of the West's resolve to resist communist expansion. In the spring of 1949,

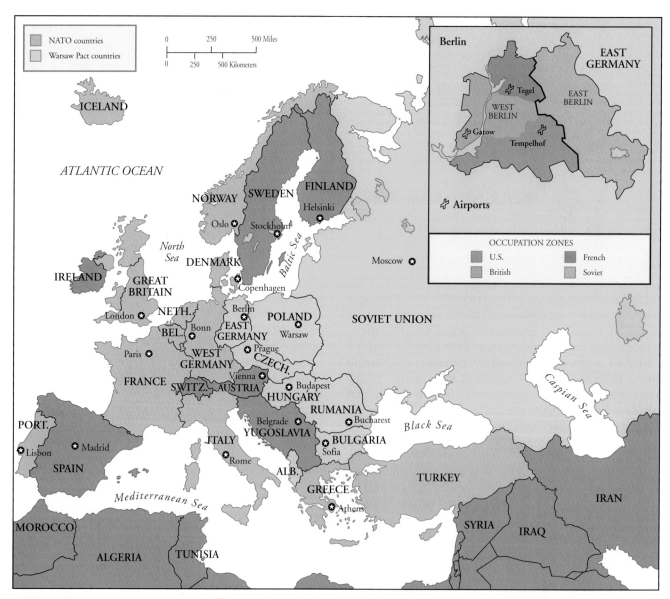

DIVIDED EUROPE AFTER WORLD WAR II This map shows the sharp division that emerged in Europe after World War II between the area under the control of the Soviet Union, and the area allied with the United States. In the east, Soviet control or influence extended into all the nations shaded gold—including the eastern half of Germany. In the west and south, the green-shaded nations were allied with the United States as members of the North Atlantic Treaty Organization (NATO). The countries shaded brown were aligned with neither of the two superpowers. The small map in the upper right shows the division of Berlin among the various occupying powers at the end of the war. Eventually, the American, British, and French sectors were combined to create West Berlin, a city governed by West Germany but entirely surrounded by communist East Germany. ◆ *How did the West prevent East Germany from absorbing West Berlin?*

Stalin lifted the now ineffective blockade. And in October, the division of Germany into two nations—the Federal Republic in the west and the Democratic Republic in the East—became official.

The crisis in Berlin accelerated the consolidation of what was already in effect an alliance among the United States and the countries of Western Europe. On April 4, *NATO* 1949, twelve nations signed an agreement establishing the North Atlantic Treaty Organization (NATO) and declaring that an armed attack against one member would be considered an attack against all. The NATO countries would, moreover, maintain a standing military force in Europe to defend against what many believed was the threat of a Soviet invasion. The formation of NATO eventually spurred the Soviet Union to create an alliance of its own with the communist governments in Eastern Europe—an alliance formalized in 1955 by the Warsaw Pact.

Reevaluating Cold War Policy

A series of events in 1949 propelled the Cold War in new directions. An announcement in September that the Soviet Union had successfully exploded its first atomic weapon, years earlier than predicted, shocked and frightened many Americans. So did the collapse of Chiang Kai-shek's nationalist government in China, which occurred with startling speed in the last months of 1949. Chiang fled with his political allies and the remnants of his army to the offshore island of Formosa (Taiwan), and the entire Chinese mainland came under the control of a communist government that many Americans believed to be an extension of the Soviet Union. The United States refused to recognize the new communist regime, and instead devoted increased attention to the revitalization of Japan as a buffer against Asian communism, ending the American occupation in 1952.

In this atmosphere of escalating crisis, Truman called for a thorough review of American foreign policy. The *NSC-68* result was a National Security Council report, issued in 1950 and commonly known as NSC-68, which outlined a shift in the American position. The first statements of the containment doctrine—the writings of George Kennan, the Truman Doctrine speech—had made at least some distinctions between areas of vital interest to the United States and areas of less importance to the nation's foreign policy and called on America to share the burden of containment with its allies. But the April 1950 document argued that the United States could no longer rely on other nations to take the initiative in resisting communism. It must itself establish firm and active leadership of the noncommunist world. And it must move to stop communist expansion virtually anywhere it occurred, regardless of the intrinsic strategic or economic value of the lands in question. Among other things, the

THE CHINESE REVOLUTION This poster celebrates the victory of Chinese communist forces in 1949. Like most communist images in these years, this one is dominated by likenesses of Mao Zedong, shown here both hovering almost godlike over jubilant citizens, and shown again in a portrait hung on the gates of the Forbidden City in the heart of Beijing—the traditional Chinese capital city that Mao's forces now controlled. *(The Art Archive)*

report called for a major expansion of American military power, with a defense budget almost four times the previously projected figure.

AMERICAN SOCIETY AND POLITICS AFTER THE WAR

The crises overseas were not the only frustrations the American people encountered after the war. The nation also faced serious economic difficulties in adapting to the peace. The resulting instability contributed to an increasingly heated political climate.

The Problems of Reconversion

The bombs that destroyed Hiroshima and Nagasaki ended the war months earlier than almost anyone had predicted and propelled the nation precipitously into a process of reconversion. The lack of planning was soon compounded by a growing popular impatience for a return to normal economic conditions. Under intense public pressure, the Truman administration attempted to hasten that return, despite dire warnings by some planners and economists. The result was a period of economic problems.

They were not, however, the problems that most Americans had feared. There had been many predictions that peace would bring a return of Depression unemployment, as war production ceased and returning soldiers flooded the labor market. But there was no general economic collapse in 1946—for several reasons. Government spending dropped sharply and abruptly, to be sure; $35 billion of war contracts were canceled at a stroke within weeks of the Japanese surrender. But increased consumer demand soon compensated. Consumer goods had been generally unavailable during the war, so many workers had saved a substantial portion of their wages and were now ready to spend. A $6 billion tax cut pumped additional money into general circula-

GI Bill

tion. The Servicemen's Readjustment Act of 1944, better known as the GI Bill of Rights, provided economic and educational assistance to veterans, increasing spending even further.

This flood of consumer demand ensured that there would be no new depression, but it contributed to more than two years of serious inflation, during which prices rose at rates of 14 to 15 percent annually. In the summer of 1946, the president vetoed an extension of the authority of the wartime Office of Price Administration, thus eliminating price controls. (He was not opposed to the controls, but to congressional amendments that had weakened the OPA.) Inflation soared to 25 percent before he relented a month later and signed a bill little different from the one he had rejected.

Compounding the economic difficulties was a sharp rise in labor unrest, driven in part by the impact of inflation. By the end of 1945, there had already been major strikes in the automobile, elec-

Postwar Labor Unrest

trical, and steel industries. In April 1946, John L. Lewis led the United Mine Workers out on strike, shutting down the coal fields for forty days. Fears grew rapidly that without vital coal supplies, the entire nation might virtually grind to a halt. Truman finally forced the miners to return to work by ordering government seizure of the mines. But in the process, he pressured mine owners to grant the union most of its demands, which he had earlier denounced as inflationary. Almost simultaneously, the nation's railroads suffered a total shutdown—the first in the nation's history—as two major unions walked out on strike. By threatening to use the army to run the trains, Truman pressured the workers back to work after only a few days.

Reconversion was particularly difficult for the millions of women and minorities who had entered the work force during the war. With veterans returning home and looking for jobs in the industrial economy, employers tended to push women, blacks, Hispanics, Chinese, and others out of the plants to make room for white males. Some of the war workers, particularly women, left the work force voluntarily, out of a desire to return to their former domestic lives. But as many as 80 percent of women workers, and virtually all black, Hispanic, and Asian males, wanted to continue working. The postwar inflation, the pressure to meet the rising expectations of a high-consumption society, the rising divorce rate, which left many women responsible for their own economic well-being—all combined to create among women a high demand for paid employment. As they found themselves excluded from industrial jobs, therefore, women workers moved increasingly into other areas of the economy (above all, the service sector).

The Fair Deal Rejected

Days after the Japanese surrender, Truman submitted to Congress a twenty-one-point domestic program outlining what he later termed the "Fair Deal." It called for expansion of

Truman's "Fair Deal"

Social Security benefits, the raising of the legal minimum wage from 40 to 65 cents an hour, a program to ensure full employment through aggressive use of federal spending and investment, a permanent Fair Employment Practices Act, public housing and slum clearance, long-range environmental and public works planning, and government promotion of scientific research. Weeks later he

A GI BILL STUDENT Joe Heinrich, recently returned from service in World War II, was an aspiring artist and used the benefits available to him under the GI Bill to enroll in art classes in San Francisco in 1946. Heinrich had not yet benefited from one of the other provisions of the GI Bill—housing assistance. Unable to find housing in San Francisco, he hitchhiked 100 miles each way every day from Sacramento to school. *(Bettmann/Corbis)*

added other proposals: federal aid to funding for the St. Lawrence Seaway, nationalization of atomic energy, and perhaps most important, national health insurance—a dream of welfare-state liberals for decades, but one deferred in 1935 when the Social Security Act was written. The president was declaring an end to the wartime moratorium on liberal reform. He was also symbolizing, as he later wrote, "my assumption of the office of President in my own right."

But the Fair Deal programs fell victim to the same public and congressional conservatism that had crippled the last years of the New Deal. Indeed, that conservatism seemed to be intensifying, as the November 1946 congressional elections suggested. Using the simple but devastating slogan "Had Enough?", the Republican Party won control of both houses of Congress.

The new Republican Congress quickly moved to reduce government spending and chip away at New Deal reforms. The president bowed to what he claimed was the popular mandate to lift most remaining wage and price controls, and Congress moved further to deregulate the economy. Inflation rapidly increased. When a public outcry arose over the soaring prices for meat, Senator Robert Taft, perhaps the most influential Republican conservative in Congress, advised consumers to "Eat less," and added, "We have got to break with the corrupting idea that we can legislate prosperity, legislate equality, legislate opportunity." True to the spirit of Taft's words, the Republican Congress quickly applied what one congressman described as a "meat-axe to government frills." It refused to appropriate funds to aid education, increase Social Security, or support reclamation and power projects in the West. It defeated a proposal to raise the minimum wage. It passed tax measures that cut rates dramatically for high-income families and moderately for those with lower incomes. Only vetoes by the president finally forced a more progressive bill.

The most notable action of the new Congress was its assault on the Wagner Act of 1935. Conservatives had always resented the new powers the legislation had granted unions; and in the light of the labor difficulties during and after the war, such resentments intensified sharply. The result was the Labor-Management Relations Act of 1947, better known as the Taft-Hartley Act. It made *Taft-Hartley Act* illegal the so-called closed shop (a workplace in which no one can be hired without first being a member of a union). And although it continued to permit the creation of so-called union shops (in which workers must join a union after being hired), it permitted states to pass "right-to-work" laws prohibiting even that. Repealing this provision, the controversial Section 14(b), would remain a goal of the labor movement for decades. The Taft-Hartley Act also empowered the president to call for a "cooling-off" period before a strike by issuing an injunction against any work stoppage that endangered national safety or health. Outraged workers and union leaders denounced the measure as a "slave labor bill." Truman vetoed it, but both houses easily overruled him the same day.

The Taft-Hartley Act did not destroy the labor movement, as many union leaders had predicted. But it did damage weaker unions in relatively lightly organized industries such as chemicals and textiles; and it made more difficult the organizing of workers who had never been union members at all, especially women, minorities, and most workers in the South.

The Election of 1948

Truman and his advisers believed the American public was not ready to abandon the achievements of the New Deal, despite the 1946 election results. As they planned strategy for the 1948 campaign, therefore, they placed their hopes in an appeal to enduring Democratic loyalties. Throughout 1948, Truman proposed one reform measure after another (including, on February 2, the first major civil rights bill of the century). Although Congress ignored or defeated them all, the president was building campaign issues for the fall.

There remained, however, the problem of Truman's personal unpopularity—the assumption among much of the electorate that he lacked stature, that his administration was weak and inept—and *Democratic Defections* the deep divisions within the Democratic Party. At the Democratic Convention that summer, two factions abandoned the party altogether. Southern conservatives reacted angrily to Truman's proposed civil rights bill and to the approval at the convention of a civil rights plank in the platform (engineered by Hubert Humphrey, the mayor of Minneapolis). They walked out and formed the States' Rights (or "Dixiecrat") Party, with Governor Strom Thurmond of South Carolina as its presidential nominee. At the same time, the party's left wing formed a new Progressive Party, with Henry A. Wallace as its candidate. Wallace supporters objected to what they considered the slow and ineffective domestic policies of the Truman administration, but they resented even more the president's confrontational stance toward the Soviet Union.

In addition, many Democratic liberals unwilling to leave the party attempted to dump the president in 1948. The Americans for Democratic Action (ADA), a coalition of liberals, tried to entice Dwight D. Eisenhower, the popular war hero, to contest the nomination. Only after Eisenhower had refused did liberals bow to the inevitable and concede the nomination to Truman. The Republicans, in the meantime, had once again nominated Governor Thomas E. Dewey of New York, whose substantial reelection victory in 1946 had made him one of the nation's leading political figures. Austere, dignified, and competent, he seemed to offer an unbeatable alternative to the president. Polls showed Dewey with an apparently insurmountable lead in September, so much so that some opinion analysts stopped taking surveys. Dewey conducted a subdued, statesmanlike campaign and tried to avoid antagonizing anyone. Only Truman, it seemed, believed he could win. As the campaign gathered momentum, he became ever more aggressive, turning the fire away from himself and toward Dewey and the "do-nothing,

good-for-nothing" Republican Congress, which was, he told the voters, responsible for fueling inflation and abandoning workers and common people. To dramatize his point, he called Congress into a special session in July to give it a chance, he said, to enact the liberal measures the Republicans had recently written into their platform. Congress met for two weeks and, predictably, did almost nothing.

The president traveled nearly 32,000 miles and made 356 speeches, delivering blunt, extemporaneous attacks. He had told Senator Alben Barkley of Kentucky, his running mate, "I'm going to fight hard. I'm going to give them hell." He called for repeal of the Taft-Hartley Act, increased price supports for farmers, and strong civil rights protection for blacks. (He was the first president to campaign in Harlem.) He sought, in short, to re-create much of Franklin Roosevelt's New Deal coalition. To the surprise of virtually everyone, he succeeded. On election night, he won a narrow but decisive victory: 49.5 percent of the popular vote to Dewey's 45.1 percent *Truman's Surprising Victory* (with the two splinter parties dividing the small remainder between them), and an electoral vote margin of 303 to 189. Democrats, in the meantime, had regained both houses of Congress by substantial margins. It was the most dramatic upset in the history of presidential elections.

The Fair Deal Revived

Despite the Democratic victories, the Eighty-first Congress was no more hospitable to Truman's Fair Deal reform than its Republican predecessor. Truman did win some important victories, to be sure. Congress raised the legal minimum wage from 40 cents to 75 cents an hour. It approved an important expansion of the Social Security system, increasing benefits by 75 percent and extending them to 10 million additional people. And it passed the National Housing Act of 1949, which provided for the construction of 810,000 units of low-income housing, accompanied by long-term rent subsidies. (Inadequate funding plagued the program for years, and it reached its initial goal only in 1972.)

But on other issues—among them national health insurance and aid to education—he made no progress. Nor was he able to persuade Congress to accept the civil *Truman Stymied* rights legislation he proposed in 1949, which would have made lynching a federal crime, provided federal protection of black voting rights, abolished the poll tax, and established a new Fair Employment Practices Commission to curb discrimination in hiring (to replace the wartime commission Roosevelt had established in 1941). Southern Democrats filibustered to kill the bill.

Truman did proceed on his own to battle several forms of racial discrimination. He ordered an end to discrimination in the hiring of government employees. He began to dismantle segregation within the armed forces. And he

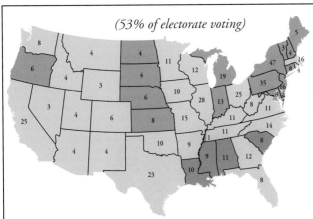

(53% of electorate voting)

	ELECTORAL VOTE	POPULAR VOTE (%)
Harry S. Truman *(Democratic)*	303	24,105,695 (49.5)
Thomas E. Dewey *(Republican)*	189	21,969,170 (45.1)
Strom Thurmond *(States' Rights)*	39	1,169,021 (2.4)
Henry A. Wallace *(Progressive)*	—	1,156,103 (2.4)
Other Candidates *(Prohibition; Socialist Labor, Socialist, Socialist Workers)*	—	272,713

ELECTION OF 1948 Despite the widespread expectation that the Republican candidate, Thomas Dewey, would easily defeat Truman in 1948, the president in fact won a substantial re-election victory that year. This map shows the broad geographic reach of Truman's victory. Dewey swept most of the Northeast, but Truman dominated almost everywhere else. Strom Thurmond, the States Rights candidate, carried four states in the South. ◆ *What had prompted Thurmond to desert the Democratic party and run for president on his own?*

 For an interactive version of this map go to www.mhhe.com/brinkley11ch29maps

allowed the Justice Department to become actively involved in court battles against discriminatory statutes. In the meantime, the Supreme Court signaled its own growing awareness of the issue by ruling, in *Shelley* v. *Kraemer* (1948), that the courts could not be used to enforce private "covenants" meant to bar blacks from residential neighborhoods. The achievements of the Truman years made only minor dents in the structure of segregation, but they were the tentative beginnings of a federal commitment to confront the problem of race.

The Nuclear Age

Looming over the political, economic, and diplomatic struggles of the postwar years was the image of the great and terrible mushroom cloud that had risen over Alamogordo in July 1945 and the ruined Japanese cities of Hiroshima and Nagasaki that atomic weapons had destroyed. Americans greeted the introduction of these terrible new instruments of destruction with fear and awe, but also with expectation. Postwar culture, therefore, was torn in many ways between a dark image of the nuclear war that many Americans feared would be a result of the rivalry with the Soviet Union, and the bright image of a dazzling technological future that atomic power might help to produce.

Conflicting Views of Nuclear Power

The fear of nuclear weapons was not hard to find in popular culture, even if it was often disguised in other ways. The late 1940s and early 1950s were the heyday of the *film noir,* a kind of filmmaking that had originated in France and had been named for the dark lighting that was characteristic of the genre. American *film noir* movies portrayed the loneliness of individuals in an impersonal world—a staple of American culture for many decades—but also suggested the menacing character of the age, the looming possibility of vast destruction. Sometimes, films and television programs addressed nuclear fear explicitly—for example, the celebrated television show of the 1950s and early 1960s, *The Twilight Zone,* which frequently featured dramatic portrayals of the aftermath of nuclear war; or postwar comic books, which depicted powerful superheroes saving the world from destruction.

Such images resonated with the public because awareness of nuclear weapons was increasingly built into their daily lives. Schools and office buildings had regular air raid drills, to prepare people for the possibility of nuclear attack. Radio stations regularly tested the emergency broadcast systems, which listeners understood to be in readiness for war. Fallout shelters sprang up in public buildings and private homes, stocked with water and canned goods, to protect citizens in case of war. America was a nation filled with anxiety.

And yet at the same time, the United States was also an exuberant nation, dazzled by its own prosperity and excited by the technological innovations that were transforming the world. Among those innovations was nuclear power—which offered the possibility that the same scientific knowledge that could destroy the world might also lead it into a dazzling future. The *New York Times,* only days after Hiroshima, expressed its own rosy view of the nuclear future:

> The atomic bomb was perfected for war, but the knowledge which made it possible came out of . . . the deathless yearning to know and to use the gifts of nature for the common good. . . . This new knowledge . . . can bring to this earth not death but life, not tyranny and cruelty, but a divine freedom.

That kind of optimism soon became widespread. The "secret of the atom," many Americans soon predicted, would bring "prosperity and a more complete life." It would create "an era of unparalleled richness and opportunities for all." It would be the "gateway to a new world" and would "set man on the road to the millennium." A Gallup poll late in 1948 revealed that approximately two-thirds of those who had an opinion on the subject believed that, "in the long run," atomic energy would "do more good than harm." Nuclear power plants began to spring up in many areas of the country, welcomed as the source of cheap and unlimited electricity, their potential dangers scarcely even discussed by those who celebrated their creation.

Promise of Cheap Nuclear Power

THE KOREAN WAR

From the beginning, the normal patterns of politics and culture had a difficult time competing against the growing national obsession with the Soviet threat in Europe. In 1950, a new and more dangerous element of the Cold War emerged and all but killed hopes for further Fair Deal reform. On June 24, 1950, the armies of communist North Korea swept across their southern border in an invasion of the pro-Western half of the Korean peninsula to the south. Within days, they had occupied much of South Korea, including Seoul, its capital. Almost immediately, the United States committed itself to the conflict. It was the nation's first military engagement of the Cold War.

The Divided Peninsula

By the end of 1945, both the United States and the Soviet Union had sent troops into Korea, and neither was willing to leave. Instead, they had divided the nation, supposedly temporarily, along the 38th parallel. The Russians finally departed in 1949, leaving behind a communist government in the north with a strong, Soviet-equipped army. The Americans left a few months later, handing control to the pro-Western government of Syngman Rhee, anticommunist but only nominally democratic. He had a relatively small military, which he used primarily to suppress internal opposition.

Syngman Rhee

The relative weakness of the south offered a strong temptation to nationalists in the North Korean government who wanted to reunite the country. The temptation to invade grew stronger when the American government implied that it did not consider South Korea within its own "defense perimeter." The role of the Soviet Union in North Korea's calculations prior to the 1950 invasion remains unclear; there is some reason to believe that the North Koreans acted without Stalin's prior approval. But the Soviets supported the offensive once it began.

The Truman administration responded quickly to the invasion. On June 27, 1950, the president ordered limited American military assistance to South Korea, and on the

WINTER IN KOREA, 1950 An American soldier trudges to the crest of an icy and embattled ridge during the bitter fighting in North Korea between American divisions and Chinese communist forces, who had entered the war as the United Nations forces approached the Korean-Chinese border. *(National Archives and Records Administration)*

same day he appealed to the United Nations to intervene. The Soviet Union was boycotting the Security Council at the time (to protest the council's refusal to recognize the new communist government of China) and thus was unable to exercise its veto power. As a result, American delegates were able to win UN agreement to a resolution calling for international assistance to the Rhee government. On June 30, the United States ordered its own ground forces into Korea, and Truman appointed General Douglas MacArthur to command the UN operations there. (Several other nations provided assistance and troops, but the "UN" armies were, in fact, overwhelmingly American.)

The intervention in Korea was the first expression of the newly expansive American foreign policy outlined in NSC-68. But the administration quickly went beyond NSC-68 and decided that the war would be an effort not simply at containment but also at "liberation." After a surprise American invasion at Inchon in September had routed the North

"Liberation"

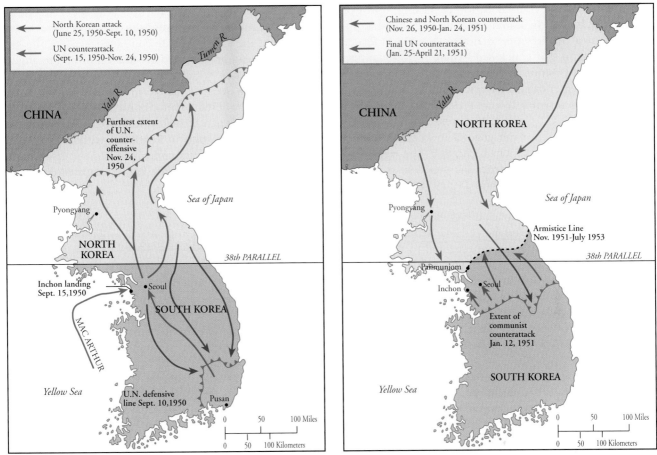

THE KOREAN WAR, 1950–1953 These two maps illustrate the changing fortunes of UN forces (which were mostly American) in Korea during the 1950–1953 war. The map at the left shows the extent of the North Korean invasion of the South in 1950; communist forces for a time controlled all of Korea except a small area around Pusan in the southeast. On September 15, 1950, UN troops under Douglas MacArthur landed in force at Inchon and soon drove the North Koreans back across the border. MacArthur then pursued the North Koreans well into their own territory. The map at right shows the very different circumstances once the Chinese entered the war in November 1950. Chinese forces drove the UN army back below the 38th parallel and, briefly, deep into South Korea, below Seoul. The UN fought troops back to the prewar border between North and South Korea late in 1951, but the war then bogged down into a stalemate that continued for a year and a half. ◆ *What impact did the Korean War have on American politics in the early 1950s?*

Korean forces from the south and sent them fleeing back across the 38th parallel, Truman gave MacArthur permission to pursue the communists into their own territory. His aim, as an American-sponsored UN resolution proclaimed in October, was to create "a unified, independent and democratic Korea."

From Invasion to Stalemate

For several weeks, MacArthur's invasion of North Korea proceeded smoothly. On October 19, the capital, Pyongyang, fell to the UN forces. Victory seemed near—until the new communist government of China, alarmed by the movement of American forces toward its border, intervened. By November 4, eight divisions of the Chinese army had entered the war. The UN offensive stalled and then collapsed. Through December 1950, outnumbered American forces fought a bitter, losing battle against the Chinese

divisions, retreating at almost every juncture. Within weeks, communist forces had pushed the Americans back below the 38th parallel once again and had captured the South Korean capital of Seoul a second time. By mid-January 1951 the rout had ceased; and by March the UN armies had managed to regain much of the territory they had recently lost, taking back Seoul and pushing the communists north of the 38th parallel once more. But with that, the war degenerated into a protracted stalemate.

From the start, Truman was determined to avoid a direct conflict with China, which he feared might lead to a new world war. Once China entered the war, he began seeking a negotiated solution to the struggle, and for the next two years he insisted that there be no wider war. But he faced a formidable opponent in General MacArthur, who resisted any limits on his military discretion. The United States was fighting the Chinese, he argued. It should therefore attack China itself, if not through an actual invasion, then at least by bombing communist forces massing north of the Chinese border. In March 1951, he indicated his unhappiness in a public letter to House Republican leader Joseph W. Martin that concluded: "There is no substitute for victory." His position had wide popular support.

The Martin letter came after nine months during which MacArthur had resisted Truman's decisions. More than

Truman-MacArthur Controversy

once, the president had warned the general to keep his objections to himself. The release of the Martin letter, therefore, struck the president as intolerable insubordination. On April 11, 1951, he relieved MacArthur of his command.

There was a storm of public outrage. Sixty-nine percent of the American people supported MacArthur, a Gallup poll reported. When the general returned to the United States later in 1951, he was greeted with wild enthusiasm. His televised farewell appearance before a joint session of Congress—which he concluded by saying "Old soldiers never die, they just fade away"—attracted an audience of millions. Public criticism of Truman finally abated somewhat when a number of prominent military figures, including General Omar Bradley, publicly supported the president's decision. But substantial hostility toward Truman remained. In the meantime, the Korean stalemate continued. Negotiations between the opposing forces began at Panmunjom in July 1951, but the talks—and the war—dragged on until 1953.

Limited Mobilization

Just as the war in Korea produced only a limited American military commitment abroad, so it created only a limited

Wartime Economic Regulation

economic mobilization at home. Still, the government did try to control the wartime economy in several important ways.

First, Truman set up the Office of Defense Mobilization to fight inflation by holding down prices and discouraging high union wage demands. When these cautious regulatory efforts failed, the president took more drastic action. Railroad workers walked off the job in 1951, and Truman ordered the government to seize control of the railroads. That helped keep the trains running, but it had no effect on union demands. Workers ultimately got most of what they had demanded. In 1952, during a nationwide steel strike, Truman seized the steel mills, citing his powers as commander in chief. But in a 6-to-3 decision, the Supreme Court ruled that the president had exceeded his authority, and Truman was forced to relent. A long and costly strike followed, and the president's drastic actions appeared to many to have been both rash and ineffective.

The Korean War gave a significant boost to economic growth by pumping new government funds into the economy at a point when many believed a recession was about to begin. But the war had other, less welcome

effects. It came at a time of rising insecurity about America's position in the world and intensified anxiety about communism. As the long stalemate continued, leaving 140,000 Americans dead or wounded, frustration turned to anger. The United States, which had recently won the greatest war in history, seemed unable to conclude what many Americans considered a minor border skirmish in a small country. Many began to believe that something must be deeply wrong—not only in Korea but within the United States as well. Such fears contributed to the rise of the second major campaign of the century against domestic communism.

THE CRUSADE AGAINST SUBVERSION

Why did the American people develop a growing fear of internal communist subversion that by the early 1950s had reached the point of near hysteria? There are many possible answers, but no single definitive explanation.

One factor was obvious. Communism was not an imagined enemy in the 1950s. It had tangible shape, in Joseph Stalin and the Soviet Union. In addition, America had encoun-

Sources of the Red Scare

tered setbacks in its battle against communism: the Korean stalemate, the "loss" of China, the Soviet development of an atomic bomb. Searching for someone to blame, many people were attracted to the idea of a communist conspiracy within American borders. But there were other factors as well, rooted in events in American domestic politics.

HUAC and Alger Hiss

Much of the anticommunist furor emerged out of the Republican Party's search for an issue with which to attack the Democrats, and out of the Democrats' efforts to stifle that issue. Beginning in 1947 (with Republicans temporarily in control of Congress), the House Un-American Activities Committee (HUAC) held widely publicized investigations to prove that, under Democratic rule, the government had tolerated (if not actually encouraged) communist subversion. The committee turned first to the movie industry, arguing that communists had infiltrated Hollywood and had tainted America with propaganda. Writers and producers, some of them former communists, were called to testify; and when some of them ("the Hollywood Ten") refused to answer questions about their own political beliefs and those of their colleagues, they were jailed for contempt. Others were barred from employment in the industry when Hollywood, attempting to protect its public image, adopted a blacklist of those of "suspicious loyalty."

More alarming to the public was HUAC's investigation into charges of disloyalty leveled against a former high-ranking member of the State Department: Alger Hiss. In 1948, Whittaker Chambers, a self-avowed former *Alger Hiss* communist agent who had turned vehemently against the party and become an editor at *Time* magazine, told the committee that Hiss had passed classified State Department documents through him to the Soviet Union in 1937 and 1938. When Hiss sued him for slander, Chambers produced microfilms of the documents (called the "pumpkin papers," because Chambers had kept them hidden in a pumpkin in his garden). Hiss could not be tried for espionage because of the statute of limitations (a law that protects individuals from prosecution for most crimes after seven years have passed). But largely because of the relentless efforts of Richard M. Nixon, a freshman Republican congressman from California and a member of HUAC, Hiss was convicted of perjury and served several years in prison. The Hiss case not only discredited a prominent young diplomat; it cast suspicion on a generation of liberal Democrats and made it possible for many Americans to believe that communists had actually infiltrated the government.

The Federal Loyalty Program and the Rosenberg Case

Partly to protect itself against Republican attacks, partly to encourage support for the president's foreign policy initiatives, the Truman administration in 1947 initiated a widely publicized program to review the "loyalty" of federal employees. In August 1950, the president authorized sensitive agencies to fire people deemed no more than "bad security risks." By 1951, more than 2,000 government employees had resigned under pressure and 212 had been dismissed.

The employee loyalty program became a signal throughout the executive branch to launch a major assault on subversion. The attorney general established a widely cited list of supposedly subversive organizations. The director of the Federal Bureau of Investigation (FBI), J. Edgar Hoover, investigated and harassed alleged radicals. The anticommunist frenzy quickly grew so intense that even a Democratic Congress felt obliged to bow to it. In 1950, Congress passed the McCarran Internal Security Act, requiring all communist organizations to *The McCarran Internal Security Act* register with the government and to publish their records, and creating other restrictions on "subversive" activity. Truman vetoed the bill. Congress easily overrode his veto.

The successful Soviet detonation of a nuclear weapon in 1949, earlier than generally expected, convinced many people that there had been a conspiracy to pass American atomic secrets to the Russians. In 1950, Klaus Fuchs, a young British scientist, seemed to confirm those fears when he testified that he had delivered to the Russians details of the manufacture of the bomb. The case ultimately settled on an obscure New York couple, Julius and Ethel Rosenberg, members of the Communist Party, whom the government claimed had been the masterminds of the conspiracy. The case against them rested in large part on testimony by Ethel's brother, David Greenglass, a machinist who had worked on the Manhattan Project. Greenglass admitted to channeling secret information to the Soviet Union through other agents (including Fuchs). His sister and brother-in-law

THE ROSENBERGS Julius and Ethel Rosenberg leave federal court in a police van after being convicted in March 1951 of transmitting atomic secrets to the Soviet Union. A week later, Judge Irving Kaufman sentenced them to death. *(Bettmann/Corbis)*

MCCARTHYISM

When the American Civil Liberties Union warned in the early 1950s, at the peak of the anticommunist fervor that is now known as McCarthyism, that "the threat to civil liberties today is the most serious in the history of our country," it was expressing a view with which many Americans wholeheartedly agreed. But while almost everyone accepts that there were unusually powerful challenges to freedom of speech and association in the late 1940s and early 1950s, there is wide disagreement about the causes and meaning of those challenges.

The simplest argument—and one that continues to attract scholarly support—is that the postwar Red Scare expressed real and legitimate concerns about communist subversion in the United States. William O'Neill, in *A Better World* (1982), and Richard Gid Powers, in *Not Without Honor* (1995) have both argued that anticommunism was a serious, intelligent, and patriotic movement, despite its excesses. The American Communist Party, according to this view, was an agent of Stalin and

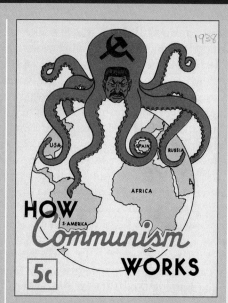

(Rare Book and Special Collections Division, Library of Congress)

the Soviet Union within the United States, actively engaged in espionage and subversion. The effort to root communists out of public life was both understandable and justifiable—and the hysteria it sometimes produced was an

unhappy but predictable byproduct of an essentially rational and justifiable effort. "Anticommunism," Powers wrote, "expressed the essential American determination to stand against attacks on human freedom and foster the growth of democracy throughout the world. . . . To superimpose on this rich history the cartoon features of Joe McCarthy is to reject history for the easy comforts of moralism."

Most interpretations, however, have been much less charitable. In the 1950s, in the midst of the Red Scare itself, an influential group of historians and social scientists began to portray the anticommunist fervor of their time as an expression of deep social maladjustment—an argument perhaps most closely associated with a famous essay by Richard Hofstadter, "The Paranoid Style in American Politics." There was, they argued, no logical connection between the modest power of actual communists in the United States and the hysterical form these scholars believed anticommunism was assuming. The explanation,

had, he claimed, planned and orchestrated the espionage. The Rosenbergs were convicted and, on April 5, 1951, sentenced to death. After two years of appeals and protests by sympathizers, they died in the electric chair on June 19, 1953, proclaiming their innocence to the end.

All these factors—the HUAC investigations, the Hiss trial, the loyalty investigations, the McCarran Act, the Rosenberg case—combined with concern about international events to create a fear of communist subversion that by the early 1950s seemed to have gripped virtually the entire country. State and local governments, the judiciary, schools and universities, labor unions—all sought to purge themselves of real or imagined subversives. A pervasive fear settled on the country—not only the fear of communist infiltration but also the fear of being suspected of communism. It was a climate that made possible the rise of an extraordinary public figure, whose behavior at any other time might have been dismissed as preposterous.

Anticommunist Hysteria

McCarthyism

Joseph McCarthy was an undistinguished first-term Republican senator from Wisconsin when, in February 1950, he suddenly burst into national prominence. In the

midst of a speech in Wheeling, West Virginia, he raised a sheet of paper and claimed to "hold in my hand" a list of 205 known communists currently working in the American State Department. No person of comparable stature had ever made so bold a charge against the federal government; and in the weeks to come, as McCarthy repeated and expanded on his accusations, he emerged as the nation's most prominent leader of the crusade against domestic subversion.

Within weeks of his charges against the State Department, McCarthy was leveling accusations at other agencies. After 1952, with the Republicans in control of the Senate and McCarthy the chairman of a special subcommittee, he conducted highly publicized investigations of subversion in many areas of the government. His unprincipled assistants, Roy Cohn and David Schine, sauntered arrogantly through federal offices and American embassies overseas looking for evidence of communist influence. One hapless government official after another appeared before McCarthy's subcommittee, where the senator belligerently and often cruelly badgered witnesses and destroyed public careers. McCarthy never produced solid evidence that any federal employee had communist ties. But a growing constituency adored him nevertheless for his coarse, "fearless" assaults on a government establishment that many considered arrogant, ef-

therefore, had to lie in something other than reality, in a deeper set of social and cultural anxieties that had only an indirect connection with the political world as it existed. Extreme anticommunism, they claimed, was something close to a pathology; it expressed fear of and alienation from the modern world. A person afflicted with the "paranoid style," Hofstadter wrote:

> . . . believes himself to be living in a world in which he is spied upon, plotted against, betrayed, and very likely destined for total ruin. He feels that his liberties have been arbitrarily and outrageously invaded. He is opposed to almost everything that has happened in American politics in the past twenty years.

Other scholars, writing not long after the decline of McCarthyism, rejected the sociocultural arguments of Hofstadter and others but shared the belief that the crusade against subversion was a distortion of normal public life. They saw the anticommunist crusade as an example of party politics run amok. Richard Freeland, in *The Truman Doctrine and the Origins of McCarthyism* (1971), argued that the Democrats began the effort to purge the government of radicals to protect themselves from attacks by the Republicans. Nelson Polsby, Robert Griffith, and others have noted how Republicans seized on the issue of communism in government in the late 1940s to reverse their nearly twenty-year exclusion from power. With each party trying to outdo the other in its effort to demonstrate its anticommunist credentials, it was hardly surprising that the crusade reached extraordinarily intense proportions.

Still other historians have emphasized the role of powerful government officials and agencies with a strong commitment to anticommunism—most notably J. Edgar Hoover and the FBI. Athan Theoharis and Kenneth O'Reilly introduced the idea of an anticommunist bureaucracy in work published in the 1970s and 1980s. Ellen Schrecker's *Many Are the Crimes* (1998) offers the fullest argument that the Red Scare was, at its heart, directed largely against communists (and not very often against people without any connection to the Communist Party) and that it was orchestrated by an interlocking cluster of official agencies with a deep commitment to the project.

Several scholars, finally, have presented an argument that does not so much challenge other interpretations as complement them. Anticommunist zealots were not alone to blame for the excesses of McCarthyism, they argue. It was also the fault of liberals—in politics, in academia, and perhaps above all in the media—who were so intimidated by the political climate, or so imprisoned within the conventions of their professions, that they found themselves unable to respond effectively to the distortions and excesses that they recognized around them.

---

fete, even traitorous. Republicans, in particular, rallied to his claims that the Democrats had been responsible for "twenty

McCarthyism's Appeal

years of treason," that only a change of parties could rid the country of subversion. McCarthy, in short, provided his followers with an issue into which they could channel a wide range of resentments: fear of communism, animosity toward the country's "eastern establishment," and frustrated partisan ambitions.

For a time, McCarthy intimidated all but a few people from opposing him. Even the highly popular Dwight D. Eisenhower, running for president in 1952, did not speak out against him, even though he disliked McCarthy's tactics and was outraged at, among other things, McCarthy's attacks on General George Marshall.

The Republican Revival

Public frustration over the stalemate in Korea and popular fears of internal subversion combined to make 1952 a bad year for the Democratic Party. Truman, whose own popularity had diminished almost to the vanishing point, wisely withdrew from the presidential contest. The party united instead behind Governor Adlai E. Stevenson of Illinois. Stevenson's dignity, wit, and eloquence made him a beloved figure to many liberals and intellectuals. But those same qualities seemed only to fuel Republican charges that Stevenson lacked the strength or the will to combat communism sufficiently. McCarthy described him as "soft" and took delight in deliberately confusing him with Alger Hiss.

Stevenson's greatest problem, however, was the Republican candidate opposing him. Rejecting the efforts of conservatives to nominate Robert Taft or Douglas MacArthur, the Republicans turned to a man who had no previous identification with the party: General Dwight D. Eisenhower, military hero, commander of NATO, president of Columbia University in New York, who won nomination on

Dwight Eisenhower

the first ballot. He chose as his running mate the young California senator who had gained national prominence through his crusade against Alger Hiss: Richard M. Nixon. Eisenhower and Nixon were a powerful combination in the autumn campaign. While Eisenhower attracted support through his geniality and his statesmanlike pledges to settle the Korean conflict (at one point dramatically promising to "go to Korea" himself), Nixon effectively exploited the issue of domestic subversion. After surviving early accusations of financial improprieties (which he effectively neutralized in a famous television address, the "Checkers speech"), Nixon went on to launch harsh attacks on Democratic "cowardice," "appeasement," and "treason." He spoke derisively of "Adlai the appeaser" and ridiculed Secretary of State Dean Acheson for running a "cowardly college of communist containment." And Nixon missed no opportunity to publicize Stevenson's early support for Alger Hiss as opposed to his own role in exposing Hiss. Eisenhower and Nixon both made effective use of allegations of corruption in the Truman administration and pledged repeatedly to "clean up the mess in Washington."

The response at the polls was overwhelming. Eisenhower won both a popular and an electoral landslide: 55 percent of the popular vote to Stevenson's 44 percent, 442 electoral votes to Stevenson's 89. Republicans gained control of both houses of Congress for only the second time in two decades. The election of 1952 ended twenty years of Democratic government. And while it might not have seemed so at the time, it also signaled the end of some of the worst turbulence of the postwar era.

CONCLUSION

Even during World War II itself, when the United States and the Soviet Union were allies, it was evident to leaders in both nations that America and Russia had quite different visions of what the postwar world should look like. Very quickly after the war ended, those differences became visible to almost everyone, and the once fruitful relationship between the world's two greatest powers quickly soured. Americans came to believe that the Soviet Union was an expansionist tyranny little different from Hitler's Germany, that Josef Stalin, the Soviet leader, was bent on world conquest. Soviets came to believe that the United States was trying to protect its own dominance in the world by encircling the Soviet Union and trying to limit its ability to operate as a great power. The result of these tensions was what became known by the end of the 1940s as the Cold War.

Actual conflicts in the early years of the Cold War were relatively few. Instead, the United States engaged in a series of policies designed to prevent both war and Soviet aggression. It helped rebuild the shattered nations of Western Europe with substantial economic aid, through the Marshall Plan, to stabilize those nations and prevent them from becoming communist. America announced a new foreign policy—known as containment—that committed it to an effort to keep the Soviet Union from expanding its influence further into the world. The United States and Western Europe formed a strong and enduring alliance, NATO, to defend Europe against possible Soviet advances.

In 1950, however, the armed forces of communist North Korea launched an invasion of the noncommunist South; and to most Americans—including, most importantly, President Truman—the conflict quickly came to be seen as a test of American resolve in the Cold War. The Korean War was long, costly, and unpopular, with many military setbacks and frustrations. In the end, however, the United States—working through the United Nations—managed to drive the North Koreans out of the south and stabilize the original division of the peninsula.

The Korean War had other effects on the domestic life of the United States. It hardened American foreign policy into a much more rigidly anticommunist form. It undermined the Truman administration, and the Democratic Party, and helped strengthen conservatives and Republicans. It greatly strengthened an already powerful crusade against communists, and those believed to be communists, within the United States—a crusade often known as McCarthyism, because of the notoriety of Senator Joseph McCarthy of Wisconsin, the most celebrated leader of the effort.

America after World War II was indisputably the wealthiest and most powerful nation in the world. But in the harsh climate of the Cold War, neither wealth nor power could prevent deep anxieties and bitter divisions.

FOR FURTHER REFERENCE

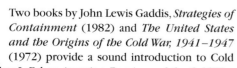

Two books by John Lewis Gaddis, *Strategies of Containment* (1982) and *The United States and the Origins of the Cold War, 1941–1947* (1972) provide a sound introduction to Cold War history. Walter LaFeber, *America, Russia, and the Cold War, 1945–1967* (7th ed. 1993) is a classic survey of American-Soviet

relations. Melvyn P. Leffler, *A Preponderance of Power: National Security, the Truman Administration, and the Cold War* (1992) is a superb, densely researched history of the policies of the 1940s. Warren I. Cohen, *The Cambridge History of American Foreign Relations, Vol. 4: America in the Age of Soviet Power, 1945–1991* (1991) is a good general history. Michael Hogan,

The Marshall Plan (1987) is a provocative interpretation of one of the pillars of the early containment doctrine. David McCullough, *Truman* (1992) is an elegant popular biography, while Alonzo Hamby, *Man of the People: A Life of Harry S. Truman* (1995) is a fine scholarly one. Bruce Cumings, *The Origins of the Korean War* (1980) is an important study of the context for America's first armed conflict of the Cold War. Ellen Schrecker, *Many Are the Crimes: McCarthyism in America* (1998) is an important recent interpretation of McCarthyism, and David Oshinsky, *A Conspiracy So Immense: The World of Joe McCarthy* (1983) is a fine biography. Richard Fried, *Nightmare in Red* (1990) is a good, short overview of the Red Scare. Richard Pells, *The Liberal Mind in a Conservative Age: American Intellectuals in the 1940s and 1950s* (1985) is a valuable survey of postwar intellectual life.

The Spy in the Sky (1996) is a documentary film that tells the story of a team of engineers and pilots racing to design, perfect, and deploy the high-flying U2 spy plane in the 1950s. *Truman* (1997) is an excellent documentary about the 33rd president.

For quizzes, Internet resources, references to additional books and films, and more, consult this book's Online Learning Center at www.mhhe.com/brinkley11.

"THE NEW TELEVISION SET" Norman Rockwell was one of the best-known American illustrators of the 1930s, 1940s, and 1950s—the creator of countless covers for the popular magazine the *Saturday Evening Post* and of some of the most beloved images of his era. In the 1930s and 1940s, most of his pictures evoked life in small-town America. By the late 1940s, however, he was beginning to portray as well the rise of the new suburban and consumer culture—as this 1949 illustration suggests. The new television antenna rises against the sky almost as if to compete with the older church steeple in the background. *(The New Television Set. By Norman Rockwell. Los Angeles County Museum of Art. Gift of Mrs. Ned Crowell. Printed by permission of the Norman Rockwell Family Trust. ©1949 The Norman Rockwell Family Trust)*

Significant Events

1946 · Dr. Benjamin Spock publishes *Baby and Child Care*

1947 · Jackie Robinson becomes first black to play in Major Leagues
· Construction begins on Levittown, New York

1948 · UAW and General Motors agree to automatic cost-of-living increases for auto workers
· United Nations votes to partition Palestine and create state of Israel

1950 · David Riesman publishes *The Lonely Crowd*

1951 · J. D. Salinger publishes *The Catcher in the Rye*

1952 · Eisenhower elected president

1953 · Economic recession begins
· Saul Bellow publishes *The Adventures of Augie March*

· Earl Warren becomes chief justice
· Truce ends Korean War
· CIA helps engineer coup in Iran
· Oppenheimer denied security clearance
· Stalin dies

1954 · Supreme Court rules in *Brown v. Board of Education*
· Democrats regain control of Congress
· Army-McCarthy hearings; Senate censures McCarthy
· France surrenders at Dien Bien Phu; Geneva agreement partitions Vietnam
· United States helps topple Arbenz regime in Guatemala

1955 · Labor organizations reconcile and form AFL-CIO
· Supreme Court announces "Brown II" decision

CHAPTER THIRTY

THE AFFLUENT SOCIETY

*I*f America was experiencing a golden age in the 1950s and early 1960s, as many Americans believed at the time and many continue to believe today, it was largely a result of two developments. One was a booming national prosperity, which profoundly altered the social, economic, and even physical landscape of the United States as well as the way many Americans thought about their lives and their world. The other was the continuing struggle against communism, a struggle that created considerable anxiety but that also encouraged some Americans to look even more approvingly at their own society.

But if these two powerful forces created a widespread sense of national purpose and self-satisfaction, they also helped blind many Americans to serious problems plaguing much of their society. More than 30 million Americans (20 percent of the population) continued to live in poverty in the 1950s, according to some measurements. Significant minorities—most prominently the 10 percent of the American people who were black, but also Latinos, Asians, Indians, gays and lesbians, and others—continued to suffer social, political, and economic discrimination. Many American women were beginning to chafe at the obstacles to their personal and professional fulfillment. The very things that made America seem so successful in the 1950s also contributed, in the end, to bringing the nation's social problems more sharply into focus. Gunnar Myrdal, a Swedish sociologist who had spent years studying life in the United States, wrote in 1944: "American affluence is heavily mortgaged. America carries a tremendous burden of debt to its poor people." The efforts to pay that debt, and others, would ultimately help move the nation into the more turbulent era of the 1960s.

Affluence and Inequality

"THE ECONOMIC MIRACLE"

Among the most striking features of American society in the 1950s and early 1960s was a booming economic growth that made even the heady 1920s seem pale by comparison. It was a better balanced and more widely distributed prosperity than that of thirty years earlier, but it was not as universal as some Americans liked to believe.

Sources of Economic Growth

By 1949, despite the continuing problems of postwar reconversion, an economic expansion had begun that would continue with only brief interruptions for almost twenty years. Between 1945 and 1960, the gross national product grew by 250 percent, from $200 billion to over $500 billion—a striking refutation of the widespread predictions in 1945 that GNP would decline once the demands of war production ended. Unemployment, which during the Depression had averaged between 15 and 25 percent, remained throughout the 1950s and early 1960s at about 5 percent or lower. Inflation, in the meantime, hovered around 3 percent a year or less.

The causes of this growth were varied. Government spending, which had ended the Depression in the 1940s, continued to stimulate growth through public funding of schools, housing, veterans' benefits, welfare, and the $100 billion interstate highway program, which began in 1956. Above all, there was military spending. Economic growth was at its peak (averaging 4.7 percent a year) during the first half of the 1950s, when military spending was highest because of the Korean War. In the late 1950s, with spending on armaments in decline, the annual rate of growth declined by more than half, to 2.25 percent.

Government Spending

The national birth rate reversed a long pattern of decline with the so-called baby boom, which had begun during the war and peaked in 1957. The nation's population rose almost 20 percent in the decade, from 150 million in 1950 to 179 million in 1960. The baby boom meant increased consumer demand and expanding economic growth.

The rapid expansion of suburbs—the suburban population grew 47 percent in the 1950s, more than twice as fast as the population as a whole—helped stimulate growth in several important sectors of the economy. The number of privately owned cars (more essential for suburban than for urban living) more than doubled in a decade, sparking a great boom in the automobile industry. Demand for new homes helped sustain a vigorous housing industry. The construction of roads, which was both a cause and a result of the growth of suburbs, stimulated the economy as well.

Suburban Growth

Because of this unprecedented growth, the economy grew nearly ten times as fast as the population in the thirty

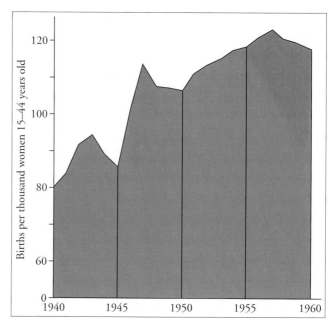

THE AMERICAN BIRTH RATE, 1940–1960 This chart shows how the American birth rate grew rapidly during and after World War II (after a long period of decline in the 1930s) to produce what became known as the "baby boom." At the peak of the baby boom, during the 1950s, the nation's population grew by 20 percent. ◆ *What impact did the baby boom have on the nation's economy?*

years after the war. And while that growth was far from equally distributed, it affected most of society. The average American in 1960 had over 20 percent more purchasing power than in 1945, and more than twice as much as during the prosperous 1920s. By 1960, per capita income (the average income for every individual man, woman, and child) was over $1,800. That was $500 more than it had been fifteen years before. Family incomes had risen even more. The American people had achieved the highest standard of living of any society in the history of the world.

The Rise of the Modern West

No region of the country experienced more dramatic changes as a result of the new economic growth than the American West. Its population expanded dramatically; its cities boomed; its industrial economy flourished. Before World War II, most of the West had been, economically at least, an appendage of the great industrial economy of the East—providing it with raw materials and agricultural goods. By the 1960s, some parts of the West were among the most important (and populous) industrial and cultural centers of the nation in their own right. As during World War II, much of the growth of the West was a result of federal spending and investment—on the dams, power stations, highways, and other infrastructure projects that made economic development possible; and on the military contracts that continued to flow disproportionately to factories in California and Texas, many of them built with government funds during the war. But other factors played a role as well. The enormous increase in automobile use after World War II—a result, among other things, of suburbanization and improved highway systems—gave a large stimulus to the petroleum industry and contributed to the rapid growth of oil fields in Texas and Colorado, and also to the metropolitan centers serving them: Houston, Dallas, and Denver. State governments in the West invested heavily in their universities. The University of Texas and University of California systems, in particular, became among the nation's largest and best; as centers of research, they helped attract technology-intensive industries to the region.

Climate also contributed. Once they had the infrastructure (and, most important, the water supplies) to sustain large populations, southern

Favorable Climate

California, Nevada, and Arizona, in particular, attracted many migrants from the East because of their warm, dry climates. The growth of Los Angeles after World War II was a particularly remarkable phenomenon. More than 10 percent of all new businesses in the United States between 1945 and 1950 began in Los Angeles. Its population rose by over 50 percent between 1940 and 1960.

The New Economics

The exciting (and to some, surprising) discovery of the power of the American economic system was a major cause of the confident, even arrogant tone of much American political life in the 1950s. During the Depression, politicians, intellectuals, and others had often questioned the viability of capitalism. In the 1950s, such doubt virtually vanished. Two features in particular made the postwar economy a source of national confidence.

First was the belief that Keynesian economics made it possible for government to regulate and stabilize the

Keynesian Economics

economy without intruding directly into the private sector. The British economist John Maynard Keynes had argued as early as the 1920s that by varying the flow of government spending and taxation (fiscal policy) and managing the supply of currency (monetary policy), the government could stimulate the economy to cure recession, and dampen growth to prevent inflation. The experience of the last years of the Depression and the first years of the war had seemed to confirm this argument. And by the mid-1950s, Keynesian theory was rapidly becoming a fundamental article of faith—not only among professional economists but also among much of the public. The most popular economics textbook of the 1950s and 1960s, Paul Samuelson's *Economics,* acquainted a generation of college students with Keynesian ideas. Armed with these fiscal and monetary tools, many economists now believed, it

was possible for the government to maintain a permanent prosperity. The dispiriting boom-and-bust cycle long considered a permanent feature of industrial capitalism could now be banished forever. Never again would it be necessary for the nation to experience another Depression.

If any doubters remained, there was ample evidence to dispel their misgivings during the brief recessions the economy experienced during the era. When the economy slackened in late 1953, Secretary of the Treasury George M. Humphrey and the Federal Reserve Board worked to ease credit and make money more readily available. The economy quickly recovered, seeming to confirm the value of Keynesian tactics (even though Humphrey and the Board did not explicitly endorse them). A far more serious recession began late in 1957 and lasted more than a year. This time, the Eisenhower administration ignored the Keynesians and adopted such deflationary tactics as cutting the budget. The slow, halting pace of the recovery, in contrast with the rapid revival in 1954, seemed further to support the Keynesian philosophy. The new economics finally won official acceptance in 1963, when John Kennedy proposed a tax cut to stimulate economic growth. Although it took Kennedy's death and the political skills of Lyndon Johnson to win passage of the measure in 1964, the result seemed to be all that the Keynesians had predicted: an increase in private demand, which stimulated economic growth and reduced unemployment.

Accompanying the belief in the possibility of permanent economic stability was the equally exhilarating belief in permanent economic growth. As the economy continued to expand far beyond what any observer had predicted was possible only a few years before, more and more Americans assumed that such growth was now without bounds—that there were few effective limits to the abundance available to the nation. This was not only a comforting thought in itself; it also made possible a new outlook on social and economic problems. In the 1930s, many Americans had argued that the elimination of poverty and injustice would require a redistribution of wealth—a limitation on the fortunes of the rich and a distribution of wealth to the

poor. By the mid-1950s, reformers concerned about economic

Ending Poverty through Economic Growth

deprivation were arguing that the solution lay in increased production. The affluent would not have to sacrifice in order to eliminate poverty; the nation would simply have to produce more abundance, thus raising the quality of life of even the poorest citizens to a level of comfort and decency.

The Keynesians never managed to remake federal economic policy entirely to their liking. Political obstacles consistently limited the ability of Keynesians to use fiscal and monetary policies as they wished; and the increasingly complex modern economy did not always respond as quickly to Keynesian policies as the theory behind them suggested it should. Still, the new economics gave many Americans a confidence in their ability to solve economic problems that previous generations had never developed.

Capital and Labor

Over 4,000 corporate mergers took place in the 1950s; and more than ever before, a relatively small number of large-scale organizations controlled an enormous proportion of the nation's economic activity. This was particularly true in industries benefiting from government defense spending. As during World War II, the federal government tended to award military contracts to large corporations. In 1959, for example, half of all defense contracts went to only twenty firms. But the same pattern repeated itself in many other areas of the economy, as corporations changed from single-industry firms to diversified *Corporate Consolidation* conglomerates. By the end of the decade, half the net corporate income in the nation was going to only slightly more than 500 firms, or one-tenth of 1 percent of the total number of corporations.

A similar consolidation was occurring in the agricultural economy. As increasing mechanization reduced the need for farm labor, the agricultural work force declined by more than half in the two decades after the war. Mechanization also endangered one of the most cherished American institutions: the family farm. By the 1960s, relatively few individuals could any longer afford to buy and equip a modern farm, and much of the nation's most productive land had been purchased by financial institutions and corporations.

Corporations enjoying booming growth were reluctant to allow strikes to interfere with their operations, and since the most important labor unions were now so large and entrenched that they could not easily be suppressed or intimidated, business leaders made important concessions to them. As early as 1948, Walter Reuther, president of the United Automobile Workers, obtained a contract from General Motors that included a built-in "escalator clause"—an automatic cost-of-living increase pegged to the consumer price index. In 1955, Reuther received a guarantee from Ford Motor Company of continuing wages to auto workers even during layoffs. A few months later, steelworkers in several corporations won guarantees of an annual salary. By the mid-1950s, factory wages in all industries had risen substantially, to an average of $80 per week.

By the early 1950s, in other words, large labor unions had developed a new kind of relationship with employers, a relationship sometimes *The "Postwar Contract"* known as the "postwar contract." Workers in steel, automobiles, and other large unionized industries were receiving generous increases in wages and benefits; in return, the unions tacitly agreed

to refrain from raising other issues—issues involving control of the workplace and a voice for workers in the planning of production. The postwar "contract" had the support of the National Labor Relations Board, whose mediators (many drawing from their experience in World War II) believed the purpose of labor relations was to maintain industrial peace and promote the general health of the economy, not to defend or expand the "rights" of workers.

The contract served the corporations and the union leadership well, but many rank-and-file workers resented the abandonment of efforts to give them more control over the conditions of their labor. By the late 1960s and 1970s, workers in some unions (Teamsters, Mine Workers, and others) were forming dissident organizations in an effort to democratize the unions and increase the scope of their demands. In the meantime, the number of industrial jobs in some major industries was beginning to diminish as a result of new technologies that automated production. Even as the labor movement was enjoying impressive successes in winning better wages for its members, its share of the labor force dropped—from an all-time high of 36 percent in 1953 to 31 percent by the end of the decade.

The economic successes of the 1950s helped pave the way for a reunification of the labor movement. In December 1955, the American Federation of Labor and the Congress of Industrial Organizations ended their twenty-year rivalry and *AFL-CIO* merged to create the AFL-CIO, under the leadership of George Meany. Relations between the leaders of the former AFL and the former CIO were not always comfortable, and at times openly antagonistic, within the joint organization. CIO leaders believed (correctly) that the AFL hierarchy was dominating the relationship. AFL leaders were suspicious of what they considered the radical pasts of the CIO leadership. Even so, the union of the two great labor movements of the 1930s survived; and gradually tensions subsided.

But success also bred stagnation and corruption in some union bureaucracies. In 1957, the powerful Teamsters Union became the subject of a congressional investigation, and its president, David Beck, was charged with misappropriation of union funds. Beck ultimately stepped down to be replaced by Jimmy Hoffa, whom government investigators pursued for nearly a decade before finally winning a conviction against him (for tax evasion) in 1967. The United Mine Workers, the union that had spearheaded the industrial movement in the 1930s, similarly became tainted by suspicions of corruption and by violence. John L. Lewis's last years as head of the union were plagued with scandals and dissent within the organization. His successor, Tony Boyle, was ultimately convicted of complicity in the 1969 murder of Joseph ("Jock") Yablonski, the leader of a dissident faction within the union.

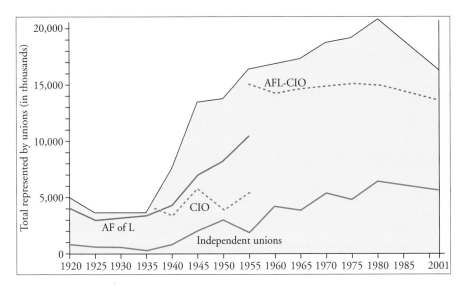

WORKERS REPRESENTED BY UNIONS, 1920–2001 This chart shows the number of workers represented by unions over an eighty–year period. Note the dramatic rise in the unionized work force during the 1930s and 1940s, the slower but still significant rise in the 1960s and 1970s, and the steady decline that began in the 1980s. The chart, in fact, understates the decline of unionized labor in the postwar era, since it shows union membership in absolute numbers and not as a percentage of the rapidly growing work force. Measured in that way, even a consistent number of union members would represent a relative decline for unions. ◆ *Why did unions cease recruiting new members successfully in the 1970s, and why did they begin actually losing members in the 1980s?*

While the labor movement enjoyed significant success in winning better wages and benefits for workers already

Limited Gains for Unorganized Workers

organized in strong unions, the majority of laborers who were as yet unorganized made fewer advances. Total union membership remained relatively stable throughout the 1950s, at about 16 million; and while this was in part a result of a shift in the work force from blue-collar to white-collar jobs, it was also a result of new obstacles to organization. The Taft-Hartley Act and the state right-to-work laws that it spawned made the creation of new unions powerful enough to demand recognition from employers more difficult. In the American South, in particular, impediments to unionization were enormous. The CIO had launched a major organizing drive in the South shortly after World War II, targeting the poorly paid workers in textile mills in particular. But "Operation Dixie," as it was called, was a failure—as were most other organizing drives for at least thirty years after World War II. Antiunion sentiment was so powerful in the South—not just among employers, but also among politicians, the press, local police, and many others—that almost all organizing drives encountered crushing and usually fatal resistance.

THE EXPLOSION OF SCIENCE AND TECHNOLOGY

In 1961, *Time* magazine selected as its "man of the year" not a specific person but "the American Scientist." The choice was an indication of the widespread fascination with which Americans in the age of atomic weapons viewed science and technology. But it was also a sign of the remarkable, and remarkably rapid, scientific and technological advances in many areas during the postwar years.

Medical Breakthroughs

The twentieth century saw more progress in the development of medical science than had occurred in all the centuries before it. A very large proportion of that progress occurred during and after World War II. Particularly important was the development of new antibacterial drugs capable of fighting infections that in the past had been all but untreatable.

The development of antibiotics had its origins in the discoveries of Louis Pasteur and Jules-Francois Joubert. Working in France in the 1870s, they produced the first conclu-

Antibiotics

sive evidence that virulent bacterial infections could be defeated by other, more ordinary bacteria. Using their discoveries, the English physician Joseph Lister revealed the value of antiseptic solutions to prevent infection during surgery.

But the practical use of antibacterial agents to combat disease did not begin until many decades later. In the 1930s, scientists in Germany, France, and England demonstrated the power of so-called sulfa drugs—drugs derived from an antibacterial agent known as sulfanilamide—which could be used effectively to treat streptococcal blood infections. New sulfa drugs were soon being developed at an astonishing rate, and were frequently improved, with dramatic results in treating what had once been a major cause of death.

In 1928, in the meantime, Alexander Fleming, an English medical researcher, accidentally discovered the antibacterial properties of an organism that he named penicillin. There was little progress in using penicillin to treat human illness, however, until a group of researchers at Oxford University, directed by Howard Florey and Ernest

Penicillin

Chain, learned how to produce stable, potent penicillin in sizable enough quantities to make it a practical weapon against bacterial disease. The first human trials of the new drug, in 1941, were dramatically successful, but progress toward the mass availability of penicillin was stalled in England because of World War II. American laboratories took the next crucial steps in developing methods for the mass production and commercial distribution of penicillin, which became widely available to doctors and hospitals around the world by 1948. Since then, a wide range of new antibiotics of highly specific character have been developed so that bacterial infections are now among the most successfully treated of all human illnesses.

There was also dramatic progress in immunization—the development of vaccines that can protect humans from contracting both bacterial and viral diseases. The first great triumph was the development of the smallpox vaccine by the English researcher Edward Jenner in the late eighteenth century. A vaccine effective against typhoid was developed by an English bacteriologist, Almorth Wright, in 1897, and was in wide use by World War I. Vaccination against tetanus became widespread just before and during World War II. Medical scientists also developed a vaccine, BCG, against another major killer, tuberculosis, in the 1920s; but controversy over its safety stalled its adoption, especially in the United States, for many years. It was not widely used in the United States until after World War II, when it largely eliminated tuberculosis—until a limited recurrence began in the 1990s.

Viruses are much more difficult to prevent and treat than bacterial infections, and progress toward vaccines against viral infections—except for smallpox—was relatively slow. Not until the 1930s, when scientists discovered how to grow viruses in laboratories in tissue cultures, could researchers study them with any real effectiveness. Gradually, they discovered how to produce forms of a virus incapable of causing disease but capable of triggering antibodies in vaccinated people that would protect them from contracting the disease. An effective vaccine against yellow fever was developed in the late 1930s, and one against influenza—one of the great killers of the first half of the twentieth century—appeared in 1945.

A particularly dramatic postwar triumph was the development of a vaccine against polio. In 1954, the American

Salk Vaccine

scientist Jonas Salk introduced an effective vaccine against the disease that had killed and crippled thousands of children and adults (among them Franklin Roosevelt). It was provided free to the public by the federal government beginning in 1955. After 1960, an oral vaccine developed by Albert Sabin—usually administered in a sugar cube—made widespread vaccination even easier. By the early 1960s, these vaccines had virtually eliminated polio from American life and much of the rest of the world.

As a result of these and many other medical advances, both infant mortality and the death rate among young children declined significantly in the first twenty-five years after the war (although not by as much as in Western Europe). Average life expectancy in that same period rose by five years, to seventy-one.

Pesticides

At the same time that medical researchers were finding cures for and vaccines against infectious diseases, other scientists were developing new kinds of chemical pesticides, which they hoped would protect crops from destruction by insects and protect humans from such insect-carried diseases as typhus and malaria. Perhaps the most famous of the new pesticides was dichlorodiphenyltrichloroethane, generally known as DDT, a compound discovered in 1939 by a Swiss chemist named Paul Muller. He had discovered that although DDT seemed harmless to human beings and other mammals, it was extremely toxic to insects. American scientists learned of Muller's discovery in 1942, just as the army was grappling with the insect-borne tropical diseases—especially malaria and typhus—that threatened American soldiers.

DDT

Under these circumstances, DDT seemed a godsend. It was first used on a large scale in Italy in 1943–1944 during a typhus outbreak, which it quickly helped end. Soon it was being sprayed in mosquito-infested areas of Pacific islands where American troops were fighting the Japanese. No soldiers suffered any apparent ill effects from the sprayings, and the incidence of malaria dropped precipitously. DDT quickly gained a reputation as a miraculous tool for controlling insects, and it undoubtedly saved thousands of lives. Only later did it become evident that DDT had long-term toxic effects on animals and humans. (See "The American Environment," pp. 876–877.)

Postwar Electronic Research

The 1940s and 1950s saw dramatic new developments in electronic technology. Researchers in the 1940s produced the first commercially viable televisions and created a technology that made it possible to broadcast programming over large areas. Later, in the late 1950s, scientists at RCA's David Sarnoff Laboratories in New Jersey developed the technology for color television, which first became widely available in the early 1960s.

Invention of Television

In 1948 Bell Labs, the research arm of AT&T, produced the first transistor, a solid-state device capable of amplifying

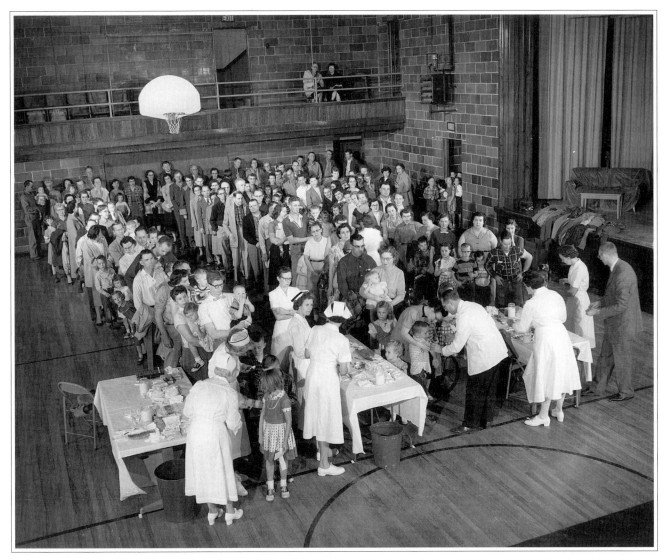

THE SALK VACCINE Dr. Jonas Salk, a medical researcher at the University of Pittsburgh, developed in the mid-1950s the first vaccine that proved effective in preventing polio. In its aftermath, scenes similar to this one—a mass inoculation of families in a school gymnasium in Kansas—repeated themselves all over the country. A few years later, Dr. Albert Sabin of the University of Cincinnati created a vaccine that could be administered more easily, through sugar cubes. *(March of Dimes Birth Defects Foundation)*

electrical signals, which was much smaller and more efficient than the cumbersome vacuum tubes that had powered most electronic equipment in the past. Transistors made possible the miniaturization of many devices (radios, televisions, audio equipment, hearing aids) and were also important in aviation, weaponry, and satellites. They contributed as well to another major breakthrough in electronics: the development of integrated circuitry in the late 1950s.

Integrated circuits combined a number of once-separate electronic elements (transistors, resistors, diodes, and others) and embedded them into a single, microscopically small device. They made it possible to create increasingly complex electronic devices requiring complicated circuitry

that would have been impractical to produce through other means. Most of all, integrated circuits helped advance the development of the computer.

Postwar Computer Technology

Prior to the 1950s, computers had been constructed mainly to perform complicated mathematical tasks, such as those required to break military codes. In the 1950s, they began to perform commercial functions for the first time, as data-processing devices used by businesses and other organizations.

The first significant computer of the 1950s was the Universal Automatic Computer (or UNIVAC), which was

THE DAWN OF THE COMPUTER AGE This massive computer, powered by tubes, was part of the first generation of mainframes developed after World War II and serving mostly government agencies and large corporations. By the 1990s, a small desktop could perform all the functions of this huge computer at much greater speed. *(Hagley Museum and Library)*

developed initially for the U.S. Bureau of the Census by the Remington Rand Company. It was the first computer *UNIVAC* able to handle both alphabetical and numerical information easily. It used tape storage and could perform calculations and other functions much faster than its predecessor, the ENIAC, developed in 1946 by the same researchers at the University of Pennsylvania who were responsible for the UNIVAC. Searching for a larger market than the census for their very expensive new device, Remington Rand arranged to use a UNIVAC to predict the results of the 1952 election for CBS television news. It would, they believed, produce valuable publicity for the machine. Analyzing early voting results, the UNIVAC accurately predicted an enormous landslide victory for Eisenhower over Stevenson. Few Americans had ever heard of a computer before that night, and the UNIVAC's television

debut became, therefore, a critical breakthrough in public awareness of computer technology.

Remington Rand had limited success in marketing the UNIVAC, but in the mid-1950s the International Business Machines Company (IBM) introduced its first major data-processing computers and began to find a wide market for them among businesses in the United States and abroad. These early successes, combined with the enormous amount of money IBM invested in research and development, made the company the worldwide leader in computers for many years.

Bombs, Rockets, and Missiles

In 1952, the United States successfully detonated the first hydrogen bomb. (The Soviet Union tested its first H-bomb a year later.) Unlike the plutonium and uranium bombs

LAUNCHING A SATELLITE, 1961 Four years after the successful Russian launching of the satellite Sputnik in 1957 threw Americans into something close to a panic, a Thor-Able Star rocket takes off from Cape Canaveral, Florida, carrying an American satellite. The satellite contained a nuclear generator capable of providing it with continuous power for its radio transmitters. *(National Archives and Records Administration)*

developed during World War II, the hydrogen bomb derives its power not from fission (the splitting of atoms)

The Hydrogen Bomb

but fusion (the joining together of lighter atomic elements with heavier ones). It is capable of producing explosions of vastly greater power than the earlier fission bombs.

The development of the hydrogen bomb gave considerable impetus to a stalled scientific project in both the United States and the Soviet Union—the effort to develop unmanned rockets and missiles capable of traveling the new weapons—not suitable for delivery by airplanes—to their targets. Both nations began to put tremendous resources into their development. The United States, in particular, benefited from the emigration to America of some of the German scientists who had helped develop rocketry for Germany during World War II.

In the United States, early missile research was conducted almost entirely by the Air Force, and there were significant early successes in developing rockets capable of traveling several hundred miles. But American and Soviet leaders were both struggling to build longer-range missiles that could cross oceans and continents—

intercontinental ballistic missiles, or ICBMs, capable of traveling through space to distant targets. American scientists experimented in the 1950s first with the Atlas and then the Titan ICBM. There were some early successes, but there were also many setbacks, particularly because of the difficulty of massing sufficient, stable fuel to provide the tremendous power needed to launch missiles beyond the atmosphere. By 1958, scientists had created a solid fuel to replace the volatile liquid fuels of the early missiles; and they had also produced miniaturized guidance systems capable of ensuring that missiles could travel to reasonably precise destinations. Within a few years, a new generation of missile, known as the Minuteman, became the basis of the American atomic weapons arsenal. It was capable of traveling several thousand miles. American scientists also developed a nuclear missile capable of being carried and fired by submarines—the Polaris, which is launched from below the surface of the ocean by compressed air and fires its engines only once it is above the surface. A Polaris was first successfully fired from underwater in 1960.

The Space Program

The American space program eventually developed a rationale of its own. In the beginning, however, it was a byproduct of the rivalry with the Soviet Union and the effort to develop effective military uses for weapons. Its origins can perhaps be traced most directly to a dramatic event in 1957, when the Soviet Union announced that it had launched an earth-orbiting satellite—*Sputnik*—into outer

The Shock of Sputnik

space. The United States had yet to perform any similar feats, and the American government (and much of American society) reacted to the announcement with alarm, as if the Soviet achievement was also a massive American failure. Federal policy began encouraging (and funding) strenuous efforts to improve scientific education in the schools, to create more research laboratories, and, above all, to speed the development of America's own exploration of outer space. The United States launched its own first satellite, *Explorer I,* in January 1958.

The centerpiece of space exploration, however, soon became the manned space program, established in 1958 through the creation of a new agency, the National Aeronautics and Space Administration (NASA) and through the selection of the first American space pilots, or "astronauts." They quickly became the nation's most revered heroes. NASA's initial effort, the Mercury Project, was designed to launch manned vehicles into space to orbit the earth. On May 5, 1961, Alan Shepard became the first American launched into space. But his short, suborbital flight came several months after a Soviet "cosmonaut," Yuri Gagarin, had made a flight in which he had actually orbited the earth. On February 2, 1962, John Glenn (later a United States senator) became the first American to orbit

APOLLO 11 Edwin ("Buzz") Aldrin is photographed by his fellow astronaut Neil Armstrong in August 1969, when they became the first humans ever to set foot on the surface of the moon. They traveled into orbit around the moon in the spaceship Apollo 11, and then traveled from the spaceship to the moon itself in a "lunar module," which they then used to return to the ship for the journey home. *(NASA)*

the globe. (Thirty-six years later, at the age of seventy-seven, Glenn traveled in space again, as a member of the crew of a space shuttle mission—the oldest man ever to have done so.) NASA later introduced the Gemini program, whose spacecraft could carry two astronauts at once.

Mercury and Gemini were followed by the Apollo program, whose purpose was to land men on the moon. It *The Apollo Program* had some catastrophic setbacks, most notably a fire in January 1967 that killed three astronauts as they sat in a capsule on the launch pad during a training session in Cape Canaveral, Florida. But on July 20, 1969, Neil Armstrong, Edwin Aldrin, and Michael Collins successfully traveled in a space capsule into orbit around the moon. Armstrong and Aldrin then detached a smaller craft from the capsule, landed on the surface of the moon, and became the first men to walk on a body other than earth. Six more lunar missions followed, the last in 1972. Not long after that, however, the government began to cut the funding for missions, and popular enthusiasm for the program began to wane.

The future of the manned space program did not lie primarily in efforts to reach distant planets, as originally envisioned. Instead, the program became a more modest effort to make travel in near-space easier and more practical through the development of the "space shuttle," an airplane-like device launched by a missile but capable both of navigating in space and landing on earth much like a conventional aircraft. The first space shuttle was successfully launched in 1982. The explosion of one shuttle, *Challenger,* in January 1986 shortly after takeoff, killing all seven astronauts, stalled the program for two years. But missions resumed in the late 1980s and have continued ever since, driven in part by commercial purposes. The space shuttle has been used to launch and repair communications satellites, to insert the Hubble Space Telescope into orbit in 1990 (and later to repair its flawed lens), and to service the orbiting *Spacelab.*

The space program, like the military development of missiles, gave a tremendous boost to the American aeronautics industry and was responsible for the development of many technologies that proved valuable in other areas.

PEOPLE OF PLENTY

Among the most striking social developments of the postwar era was the rapid extension of a middle-class lifestyle and outlook to large groups of the population previously insulated from it. The new prosperity of social groups that had previously lived on the margins; the growing availability of consumer products at affordable prices and the rising public fascination with such products; and perhaps above all, the massive population movement from the cities to the suburbs—all helped make the American middle class a larger, more powerful, more homogeneous, and more dominant force than it had ever been before.

The new prosperity, in fact, inspired some Americans to see abundance as the key to understanding the American past and the American charac- *"Consensus"* ter. Leading intellectuals argued that American history had been characterized by a broad "consensus" about the value and necessity of competitive, capitalist growth. "However much at odds on specific issues," the historian Richard Hofstadter wrote in *The American Political Tradition* (1948), Americans have "shared a belief in the rights of property, the philosophy of economic individualism, the value of competition; they have accepted the economic virtues of capitalist culture as necessary qualities of man." David Potter, another leading American historian of the era, published an influential examination of "economic abundance and American character" in 1954. He called it *People of Plenty.* For the American middle class in the 1950s, at least, it seemed an appropriate label.

The Consumer Culture

At the center of middle-class culture in the 1950s, as it had been for many decades before, was a growing absorption with consumer goods. That was a result of increased prosperity, of the increasing variety and availability of products, and of advertisers' adeptness in creating a demand for those products. It was also a result of the growth of consumer credit, which increased by 800 percent between 1945 and 1957 through the development of credit cards, revolving charge accounts, and easy-payment plans. Prosperity fueled such long-time consumer crazes as the automobile, and Detroit responded to the boom with ever-flashier styling and accessories. Consumers also responded eagerly to the development of such new products as dishwashers, garbage disposals, televisions, hi-fis, and stereos. To a striking degree, the prosperity of the 1950s and 1960s was consumer driven (as opposed to investment driven).

Because consumer goods were so often marketed (and advertised) nationally, the 1950s were notable for the *Consumer Crazes* rapid spread of great national consumer crazes. For example, children, adolescents, and even some adults became entranced in the late 1950s with the hula hoop—a large plastic ring kept spinning around the waist. The popularity of the Walt Disney–produced children's television show *The Mickey Mouse Club* created a national demand for related products such as Mickey Mouse watches and hats. It also helped produce the stunning success of Disneyland, an amusement park near Los Angeles that recreated many of the characters and events of Disney entertainment programs. The Disney technique of turning an entertainment success into an effective tool for marketing consumer goods was not an isolated event. Many other entertainers and producers took note and did the same.

The Suburban Nation

By 1960 a third of the nation's population was living in suburbs—part of a demographic shift almost without precedent in American history. The growth of suburbs was a result not only of increased affluence, which made it possible for more Americans to buy homes and land. It was also a result of desire. People moved from the cities to the suburbs for many reasons: to escape crowding, crime, pollution, and high costs; to find better schools for their children; and sometimes to escape racial and ethnic diversity—to find a more homogeneous community in which to live. The suburbs were attractive too because they seemed to many Americans to offer a fundamentally different environment—to fulfill the quiet yearning of many urban people for a greater contact with nature. Suburbs were not usually much like the countryside, of course. Most people who lived in them had small lots and many neighbors, and over time suburban communities

THE FIFTIES FAMILY This advertisement for a combination television and record player presents a popular image of the middle-class family of the 1950s—a professional father relaxing in front of the television with two well-dressed children, his glamorous wife serving drinks and presiding happily and benignly over the evening. Television marketing stressed the power of the new medium to bring families together for shared entertainment experiences. *(Gaslight Archives)*

developed many of the same environmental problems that plagued cities—traffic, pollution, crowding, crime. But moving to the suburbs did offer at least a partial connection to the natural world—grass, trees, gardens, cleaner air, less noise.

Suburbanization was also a result of important innovations in home-building, which made single-family houses affordable to millions of new people. The most famous of the postwar suburban developers, William Levitt, came to symbolize the new suburban growth with his use of mass-production techniques to construct a large housing development on Long Island, near New York City. This first "Levittown" (there would later *"Levittown"* be others in New Jersey and Pennsylvania) consisted of several thousand two-bedroom Cape Cod-style houses, with identical interiors and only slightly varied facades, each perched on its own concrete slab (to eliminate excavation costs), facing curving, treeless streets. Levittown houses sold for under $10,000, and they helped meet an enormous demand for housing that had been growing for more than a decade.

In the nineteenth century, it was the railroads that transformed notions of distance and time and reshaped the American landscape. In the twentieth century, it was the automobile. Automobiles first became widely popular in the years preceding World War I, and throughout the first half of the twentieth century they had a profound effect on the nation's built environment. But automobiles and trucks had their most dramatic impact on the American landscape (and on the nation's culture) in the years after World War II. Between 1950 and 1980, the nation's population increased by 50 percent, but the number of automobiles owned by Americans quadrupled. In 1956—responding to pressure from the automobile and trucking industries and from oil companies, among others—the government passed the Federal Highway Act, the largest public works program in American history to that

AN EARLY MCDONALD'S The new automobile-centered landscape of postwar America transformed many patterns of life, including eating, as this early McDonald's in Des Plaines, Illinois, suggests. Ray Kroc bought the company in 1955 from the McDonald brothers, who had founded it several years earlier, and expanded it to create fast, convenient restaurants for people moving from place to place by automobile. (The early competition was the older drive-ins.) Today, McDonald's operates over 23,000 restaurants in 109 countries, many of them in cities, but it remains a fixture of American car culture as well. *(Used with permission from McDonald's Corporation)*

INTERSTATES The interstate highway system changed the physical landscape of the United States. Its great, sprawling ribbons of concrete—such as this one on Long Island—sliced through cities, towns, and rural areas. But its biggest impact was in facilitating the movement of urban populations out of cities and into increasingly distant suburbs. *(Ewing Galloway)*

point. It appropriated $25 billion for a ten-year effort to construct more than 40,000 miles of interstate highways. Broad ribbons of concrete, spanned by bridges and linked to smaller roads by spiraling ramps, spread out across the nation, traversing every state, providing links to every major city (and between cities and their suburbs), and dramatically reducing the time necessary to travel from one place to another. The interstate highway system made trucking a more economically efficient means of transporting goods to markets than railroads. It made travel by automobile and bus as fast or faster than travel by passenger trains. One result of the new highway system, therefore, was the long and steady decline of the nation's railroads.

But the proliferation of automobiles and the construction of highways had many other effects on the American landscape. It now became possible for millions of people—including many with modest incomes—to move from city centers to new suburbs, which stretched out for many miles outside major cities, devouring what had once been farmland or forest. The growth of suburbs, in turn, forced the construction of vast new water and sewer systems to service the new communities; and in the arid areas of the West—in particular—it intensified the long battle for scarce water between farmers and urban areas.

The highways also encouraged the movement of economic activities—manufacturing in particular—out of

Young couples—often newly married war veterans eager to start a family, assisted by low-cost, government-subsidized mortgages provided by the GI Bill (see p. 786)—rushed to purchase the inexpensive homes, not only in the Levittowns but in similar developments that soon began appearing throughout the country.

Why did so many Americans want to move to the suburbs? One reason was the enormous importance postwar Americans placed on family life after five years of war in which families had often been separated or otherwise disrupted. Suburbs provided families with larger homes than they could find (or afford) in the cities, and thus

cities and into suburban and rural areas where land was cheaper. The decline of traditional downtowns followed. The desolate, decaying urban landscapes of the 1960s and 1970s—landscapes in which stores, factories, hotels, schools, and theaters were closing as their patrons shifted to driving-centered sites away from city centers—were a direct result of the automobile. So was the growth of what eventually became known as "edge cities" and other new centers of industry and commerce well outside traditional city centers.

The automobile made equally dramatic changes in the way millions of Americans experienced their immediate landscapes. The ability to move into homes that were significant distances from towns and cities enabled many people to live in places where they could have larger houses and lots than they previously could have afforded. Garages began to be built onto houses in great numbers after World War II; and such suburban amenities as swing-sets, barbecues, and private swimming pools became more common as backyards became more the norm. The shift of travel from train to automobile helped spawn a tremendous proliferation of motels—26,000 by 1948, 60,000 by 1960, well over 100,000 by 1970. The first Holiday Inn (launching what would soon become the largest motel chain in America) opened along a highway connecting Memphis and Nashville, Tennessee, in 1952. In the meantime, older hotels in urban downtowns were closing virtually every day. Drive-in theaters—a distinctively American phenomenon that had begun to appear in the 1930s—spread rapidly after the war. There were 4,000 drive-ins by 1958, most of them featuring movies that appealed to teenagers, their largest audience.

DRIVE-IN THEATER This drive-in theater, photographed in 1951 near New York City, was one of thousands across the country that became popular before World War II and remained so into the 1970s. *(Hulton/Archive/Getty Images)*

The automobile also transformed the landscape of retailing. It encouraged the creation of fast-food chains, many of which began with drive-in restaurants, where customers could be served and eat in their cars. The first drive-in restaurant (Royce Hailey's Pig Stand) opened in Dallas in 1921, followed later in the decade by White Tower, the first fast-food company to create franchises. Ray Kroc's McDonald's opened its first outlets in Des Plaines, Illinois, and southern California in 1955. Five years later, there were 228 McDonald's outlets; and over the decades that followed, McDonald's franchises spread throughout the nation and abroad—making the "golden arches" the most recognizable symbol of food in the world. Large supermarket chains—catering to customers with automobiles—replaced smaller, family-owned markets in town centers. Large shopping centers and malls moved the center of retailing out of cities and into widely separate complexes surrounded by large parking lots.

The automobile's impact was, of course, not limited to the built environment alone. It was one of the principal causes of the enormous increase in the demand for oil and thus of the depletion of American oil reserves; the energy crises of the 1970s and 1980s were in large part a product of the proliferation of cars. It was also one of the principal causes of air pollution and created the dank clouds of smog that blighted the landscapes (and endangered the health) of millions of urban Americans, although new pollution-control devices, first introduced in the 1970s, reduced (but did not wholly eliminate) automobile emissions.

made it easier to raise larger numbers of children. They provided privacy. They provided security from the noise and dangers of urban living. They offered space for the new consumer goods—the cars, boats, appliances, outdoor furniture, and other products—that advertisers had helped persuade many middle-class Americans to crave.

For many Americans, suburban life also helped provide a sense of community that was sometimes difficult to develop in large, crowded, impersonal urban areas. In later years, the suburbs would come under attack for their supposed conformity, homogeneity, and isolation. But in the 1950s,

Appeal of Suburban Living

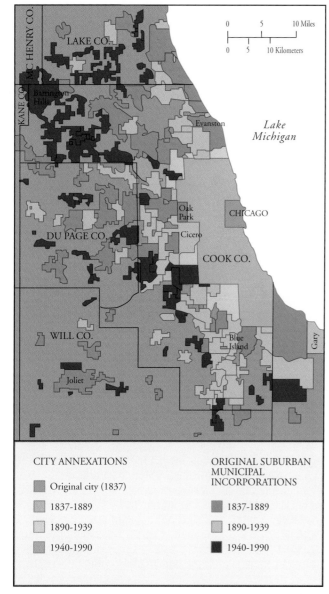

CITY ANNEXATIONS

Original city (1837)

1837–1889

1890–1939

1940–1990

ORIGINAL SUBURBAN MUNICIPAL INCORPORATIONS

1837–1889

1890–1939

1940–1990

CHICAGO'S ANNEXATIONS AND THE SUBURBAN NOOSE This map uses Chicago as an example of two important processes in the growth of American cities—municipal consolidation and suburbanization. In 1837, Chicago consisted of a small area on the shore of Lake Michigan (represented by the small shaded area on the right center of the map. Over the next fifty years, Chicago annexed an enormous amount of additional land around its original borders, followed by a few, smaller annexations in the twentieth century. At the same time, however, many of the areas around Chicago were separating themselves from the city by incorporating as independent communities—suburbs—with a particular wave of such incorporations in the first decades of the twentieth century, continuing into the 1990s. A map of New York, and of many other cities, would reveal a similar pattern. ◆ *What were the consequences for the city of its legal and financial separation from so many suburban communities?*

many people were attracted by the idea of living in a community populated largely by people of similar age and background, and found it easier to form friendships and social circles there than in the city. Women in particular often valued the presence of other nonworking mothers living nearby to share the tasks of child raising. Another factor motivating white Americans to move to the suburbs was race. There were some African-American suburbs, but most suburbs were restricted to whites—both because relatively few blacks could afford to live in them and because formal and informal barriers kept out even prosperous blacks. In an era when the black population of most cities was rapidly growing, many white families fled to the suburbs to escape the integration of urban neighborhoods and schools.

Suburban neighborhoods had many things in common with one another. But they were not uniform. A famous study of one Levittown revealed a striking variety of occupations, ethnic backgrounds, and incomes there. Still, the Levittowns and inexpensive developments like them ultimately became the homes of mainly lower-middle-class people one step removed from the inner city. Other, more affluent suburbs became enclaves of wealthy families. In virtually every city, a clear hierarchy emerged of upper-class suburban neighborhoods and more modest ones, just as such gradations had emerged years earlier among urban neighborhoods.

The Suburban Family

For professional men (who tended to work in the city, at some distance from their homes), suburban life generally meant a rigid division between their working and personal worlds. For many middle-class, married women, it meant an increased isolation from the workplace. The enormous cultural emphasis on family life in the 1950s strengthened popular prejudices against women entering the professions, or occupying any *Prevailing Gender Roles Reinforced* paid job at all. Many middle-class husbands considered it demeaning for their wives to be employed. And many women themselves shied away from the workplace when they could afford to, in part because of prevailing ideas about motherhood that seemed to require women to stay at home full-time with their children.

One of the most influential books in postwar American life was a famous guide to child rearing: Dr. Benjamin Spock's *Baby and Child Care,* first published in 1946 and reis- *Dr. Benjamin Spock* sued (and revised) repeatedly for decades thereafter. Dr. Spock's approach to raising babies was child-centered, as opposed to the parent-centered theories of many previous child-care experts. The purpose of motherhood, he taught, was to help children learn and grow and realize their potential. All other considerations, including the mother's own physical and emotional requirements, must be subordinated to the needs of the child. Dr. Spock at first envisioned only a very modest role for fathers in the process of child rearing, although he changed his views on this (and on many other issues) over time.

Thus, women who could afford not to work faced heavy pressures—both externally and internally imposed—to remain in the home and concentrate on raising their children. Some women, however, had to balance these pressures against other, contradictory ones. As expectations of material comfort rose, many middle-class families needed a second income to maintain the standard of living they desired. As a result, the number of married women working outside the home actually increased in the postwar years—even as the social pressure for them to stay out of the workplace grew. By 1960, nearly a third of all married women were part of the paid work force.

The experiences of the 1950s worked in some ways to diminish the power of feminism, which for a time ebbed

Feminism Weakened

to its lowest point in nearly a century. But they also helped create conditions that only a decade later would create the most powerful feminist movement in American history. The increasing numbers of women in the workplace laid the groundwork for demands for equal treatment by employers that became an important part of the feminist crusades of the 1960s and 1970s. Some middle-class women who were not employed became deeply involved in the public world through work in such organizations as the League of Women Voters, the Red Cross, YWCAs, and PTAs, where they gained organizational and political skills that they would later be able to use in more explicitly feminist causes. And the growing frustrations of other women, who remained in the home, heightened the demand for female professional opportunities, a demand that would also soon help fuel the women's liberation movement.

The Birth of Television

Television is perhaps the most powerful medium of mass communication in history. It was central to the culture of the postwar era. Experiments in broadcasting pictures (along with sound) had begun as early as the 1920s, but commercial television began only shortly after World War II. Its growth was phenomenally rapid. In 1946, there were only 17,000 sets in the country; by 1957, there were 40 million television sets in use—almost as many sets as there were families. More people had television sets, according to one report, than had refrigerators (a statistic strikingly similar to one in the 1920s that had revealed more people owning radios than bathtubs).

The television industry emerged directly out of the radio industry, and all three of the major networks—The National Broadcasting Company, the Columbia Broadcasting System, and the American Broadcasting Company—had started as radio companies. Like radio, the television business was driven by advertising. The need to attract advertisers determined most programming decisions; and in the early days of television, sponsors often played a direct, powerful, and continuing role in determining the content of the programs they chose to sponsor. Many early television shows bore the names of the corporations that were paying for them: the GE Television Theater, the Chrysler Playhouse, the Camel News Caravan, and others. Some daytime serials (known as "soap operas," because their sponsors were almost always companies making household goods targeted at women) were actually written and produced by Procter & Gamble and other companies.

The impact of television on American life was rapid, pervasive, and profound. By the late 1950s, television news had replaced newspapers, magazines, and radios as the nation's most important vehicle of information. Television advertising helped create a vast market for new fashions and products. Televised athletic events gradually made professional and college sports one of the most important sources of entertainment (and one of the biggest businesses) in America. Television entertainment programming—almost all of it controlled by the three national networks and their corporate sponsors—replaced movies and radio as the principal source of diversion for American families.

Social Consequences of Television

Much of the programming of the 1950s and early 1960s created a common image of American life—an image that was predominantly white, middle-class, and suburban, and that was epitomized by such popular situation comedies as *Ozzie and Harriet* and *Leave It to Beaver.* Programming also reinforced the concept of gender roles that most men (and many women) unthinkingly embraced. Most situation comedies, in particular, showed families in which, as the title of one of the most popular put it, *Father Knows Best,* and in which most women were mothers and housewives striving to serve their children and please their husbands. But television also conveyed other images: the gritty, urban working-class families in Jackie Gleason's *The Honeymooners;* the childless show-business family of the early *I Love Lucy;* the unmarried professional women in *Our Miss Brooks* and *My Little Margie;* the hapless African Americans in *Amos 'n Andy.* Television not only sought to create an idealized image of a homogeneous suburban America. It also sought to convey experiences at odds with that image—but to convey them in warm, unthreatening terms, taking social diversity and cultural conflict and domesticating them, turning them into something benign and even comic.

Television's Homogenizing Message

Yet television also, inadvertently, created conditions that could accentuate social conflict. Even those unable to share in the affluence of the era could, through television, acquire a vivid picture of how the rest of their society lived. Thus at the same time that television was reinforcing the homogeneity of the white middle class, it was also contributing to the sense of alienation and powerlessness among groups excluded from the world it portrayed. And television news conveyed with unprecedented power the social upheavals that gradually spread beginning in the

The most popular show in the history of television began as an effort by a young comedian to strengthen a difficult marriage. In 1950, 38-year-old Lucille Ball—whose fifteen-year movie career had never quite launched her to stardom—was performing in a popular weekly CBS radio comedy, *My Favorite Husband,* in which she portrayed a slightly zany housewife who tangled frequently with her banker husband, played by Richard Denning. The network proposed to transfer the show from radio to television. Lucy said she would only do it if she could replace Denning with her real-life husband of

LUCY AT HOME Although Lucy and Desi at first portrayed a childless, ethnically mixed couple living in a Manhattan apartment, many of the comic situations in the early years of the show were purely domestic. Here, Lucy, wearing an apron, deals with one of her many household predicaments with the extraordinary physical comedy that was part of her great success. Desi, watching skeptically, was a talented straight man to Lucy's zaniness. *(Photofest)*

VITAMEATAVEGAMIN One of the most popular episodes of *I Love Lucy* portrayed Lucy at a trade show promoting a new health product called "Vitameatavegamin." In the course of the show, she herself drank a great deal of the concoction, which had a high alcohol content and left her hilariously drunk. *(Photofest)*

ten years, Desi Arnaz—a celebrated, Cuban-born bandleader whose almost constant traveling was putting a strain on their marriage. Network officials tried in vain to talk her out of the idea. Arnaz had no acting experience, they told her. Lucy herself recognized another reason for their reluctance: the radicalism of portraying an ethnically mixed marriage on the air. Her radio show, she later said, had "firmly established my type of man . . . as a nice gent from Minneapolis . . . a typical Midwestern American . . . not—great heavens—Desi Arnaz from Cuba." But she held her ground.

On Monday, October 15, 1951, in the 9 P.M. time slot that Lucille Ball would dominate for years, the first episode of *I Love Lucy* was broadcast over CBS. Desi Arnaz played Ricky Ricardo, a Cuban bandleader and singer who spoke, at times, with a comically exaggerated Latin accent. Lucille Ball was Lucy Ricardo, his stage-struck and slightly dizzy wife. Performing with them were William Frawley and Vivian Vance, who played their neighbors and close friends, Fred and Ethel Mertz. In the premiere episode, "The Girls Want to Go to a Nightclub," Ricky and Fred want to go

late 1950s, and in conveying them helped make more such upheavals likely.

Travel, Outdoor Recreation, and Environmentalism

Although the idea of a paid vacation for American workers, and the association of that idea with travel, had entered American culture beginning in the 1920s, it was not

until the postwar years that vacation travel became truly widespread among middle-income Americans. The construction of the interstate highway system contributed dramatically to the growth of travel. So did the increasing affluence of workers, which made it possible for them to buy cars and to live in suburban areas that made it easier for them to garage vehicles. Even in the 1950s, there was a healthy market for vacation vehicles—trailers and small vans—that some families used while traveling, and that

to a boxing match on the night of Fred and Ethel's anniversary, while the wives are arranging an evening at a nightclub. The men and women battle each other ridiculously, but no one really wins.

The opening episode contained many of the elements that characterized the show throughout its long run and ensured its extraordinary success: the remarkable chemistry among the four principal actors, the unexpected comedic talent of Desi Arnaz, and most of all the brilliance of Lucille Ball—who proved herself one of the great comic actors of her time. She was a master of physical comedy, and many of her funniest moments involved scenes of absurdly incongruous situations (Lucy working an assembly line, Lucy stomping grapes in Italy). She had a remarkably variable voice, and her characteristic yowl of frustration became one of the most familiar sounds in American culture. She was an exceptionally beautiful woman, but she never hesitated to make herself look ridiculous. "She was everywoman," her long-time writer Jess Oppenheim once wrote; "her little expressions and inflections stimulated the shock of recognition in the audience."

But it was not just the great talents of its cast that made *I Love Lucy* such a phenomenon. It was the skill of its writers in evoking some of the most common experiences and desires of television viewers in the 1950s. The wives demanded more attention from their husbands and more glamor in their lives. Lucy, in particular, mined the frustrations of domestic life for all they were worth, constantly engaging in zany and hilarious schemes to break into show business or somehow

PROMOTING THE SHOW   The marriage of Lucille Ball and Desi Arnaz, which paralleled the television marriage of Lucy and Ricky Ricardo, was one of the most effective promotional devices for *I Love Lucy*. Here, Lucy and Desi pose for a promotional still—one of many they made for advertisements, magazine covers, and posters until their marriage (and the show) dissolved in 1960.   *(Photofest)*

expand her world. The level-headed husbands wanted calm and conventional domestic lives—and time to themselves for conspicuously male activities: boxing, fishing, baseball. In the first seasons, the fictional couples lived as neighbors, without children, in a Manhattan apartment building. Later, like so many of the show's viewers, Lucy had a child and they all moved to the suburbs. (The show used Lucy's real-life pregnancy on the air; and on January 19, 1953—only hours after Lucille Ball gave birth to her real son and second child—CBS aired a

previously filmed episode of the fictional Lucy giving birth to a fictional son, "Little Ricky" Ricardo, before one of the largest audiences in television history. "Little Ricky" became a continuing character in the show.)

I Love Lucy (and its successor, *The Lucille Ball-Desi Arnaz Comedy Hour*) was the most-watched show on television from its first weeks in 1951 until the final episode in 1960. Organizations rescheduled meetings, politicians postponed speeches, taxi drivers and other workers changed their shifts to avoid competing with Lucy. The great Marshall Field department store in Chicago posted a sign in its window stating: "We love Lucy, too, so we're closing on Monday nights." During a typical broadcast, up to two-thirds of the televisions in America were tuned to Lucy.

Lucille Ball remained a major television star for nearly twenty years after *I Love Lucy* left the air. She died in 1989. Desi Arnaz, whom Lucy divorced in 1960, remained for a time one of Hollywood's most powerful and successful studio executives as the head of Desilu Productions. And nearly half a century after the first episode of *I Love Lucy* aired, the series remains extraordinarily popular all over the world—shown so frequently in reruns that in some American cities it is sometimes possible to see six Lucy episodes in a single evening. "People identified with the Ricardos," Lucille Ball once said, "because we had the same problems they had. We just took ordinary situations and exaggerated them." In the process, *I Love Lucy* revealed many of the dilemmas of 1950s domestic life and established the pattern for the long and popular history of television situation comedies.

market grew steadily larger in subsequent decades. But the urge to travel was also an expression of some of the same impulses that produced the move to suburbs: a desire to escape the crowding and stress of densely populated areas and find a place where it was possible to experience the natural world.

Nowhere was this surge in travel and recreation more visible than in the nation's national parks, which experienced the beginnings of what became a permanent surge

in attendance in the 1950s. People who traveled to national parks did so for many reasons—some to hike and camp; some to fish and hunt (activities that themselves grew dramatcially in the 1950s and spawned a large number of clubs), some simply to look in awe at the landscape. But whatever their motives, most visitors came in search *Echo Park* less of conventional recreation than of wilderness. The importance of that search became clear in the early 1950s in the first of many battles over development of wilderness areas: the fight to preserve Echo Park.

Echo Park is a spectacular valley in the Dinosaur National Monument, on the border between Utah and Colorado, near the southern border of Wyoming. In the early 1950s, the federal government's Bureau of Reclamation—which had been created early in the century to encourage irrigation, develop electric power, and increase water supplies—proposed building a dam across the Green River, which runs through Echo Valley, so as to create a lake for recreation and a source of hydroelectric power. The American environmental movement had been relatively quiet since its searing defeat early in the century in its effort to stop a similar dam in the Hetch Hetchy Valley at Yosemite National Park. (See pp. 606–608.) But the Echo Park proposal helped rouse it from its slumber.

In 1950, Bernard DeVoto—a well-known writer and a great champion of the American West—published an essay in *The Saturday Evening Post* entitled "Shall We Let Them Ruin Our National Parks?" It had a sensational impact, arousing opposition to the Echo Valley dam from many areas of the country. The Sierra Club, relatively obscure in previous decades, was roused into action; the controversy helped elevate a new and aggressive leader, David Brower, who even-

Sierra Club Reborn

tually transformed the Club into the nation's leading environmental organization. By the mid-1950s, a large coalition of environmentalists, naturalists, and wilderness vacationers had been mobilized in opposition to the dam, and in 1956 Congress—bowing to the public pressure—blocked the project and preserved Echo Park in its natural state. The controversy was a major victory for those who wished to preserve the sanctity of the national parks, and it was an important impetus to the dawning environmental consciousness that would become so important a decade and more later.

Organized Society and Its Detractors

Large-scale organizations and bureaucracies increased their influence over American life in the postwar era, as they had been doing for many decades before. White-collar workers came to outnumber blue-collar laborers for the first time, and an increasing proportion of them worked in corporate settings with rigid hierarchical structures. Industrial workers also confronted large bureaucracies, both in the workplace and in their own unions. Consumers discovered the frustrations of bureaucracy in dealing with the large national companies from whom they bought goods and services. More and more Americans were becoming convinced that the key to a successful future lay in acquiring the specialized training and skills necessary for work in large organizations, where every worker performed a particular, well-defined function.

The American educational system responded to the demands of this increasingly organized society by experimenting with changes in curriculum and philosophy. Elementary and secondary schools gave increased attention to the teaching of science, mathematics, and foreign languages—all of which educators considered important for the development of skilled, specialized professionals. The National Defense Education Act

Growth of Specialized Education

of 1958 (passed in response to the Soviet Union's *Sputnik* success) provided federal funding for development of programs in those areas. Universities in the meantime were expanding their curricula to provide more opportunities for students to develop specialized skills. The idea of the "multiversity"—a phrase first coined by the chancellor of the University of California at Berkeley to describe his institution's diversity—represented a commitment to making higher education a training ground for specialists in a wide variety of fields.

As in earlier eras, many Americans reacted to these developments with ambivalence, even hostility. The debilitating impact of bureaucratic life on the individual slowly became a central theme of popular and scholarly debate. William H. Whyte, Jr., produced one of the most widely discussed books of the decade: *The Organization Man* (1956), which attempted to describe the special mentality of the worker in a large, bureaucratic setting. Self-reliance, Whyte claimed, was losing place to the ability to "get along" and "work as a team" as the most valued trait in the modern character. Sociologist David Riesman had made similar observations in *The Lonely Crowd* (1950), in which he argued that the traditional "inner-directed" man, who judged himself on the basis of his own values and the esteem of his family, was giving way to a new "other-directed" man, more concerned with winning the approval of the larger organization or community.

Novelists, too, expressed misgivings in their work about the enormity and impersonality of modern society. Saul Bellow produced a series of novels—*The Adventures of Augie March* (1953), *Seize the Day* (1956), *Herzog* (1964), and many others—that chronicled the difficulties American Jewish men had in finding fulfillment in modern urban America. J. D. Salinger wrote in *The Catcher in the Rye* (1951) of a prep-school student, Holden Caulfield, who was unable to find any area of society—school, family, friends, city—in which he could feel secure or committed.

The Beats and the Restless Culture of Youth

The most caustic critics of bureaucracy, and of middle-class society in general, were a group of young poets, writers, and artists generally known as the "beats" (or, derisively, as "beatniks"). They wrote harsh

The Beat Generation's Critiques

critiques of what they considered the sterility and conformity of American life, the meaninglessness of American politics, and the banality of popular culture. Allen Ginsberg's dark, bitter poem "Howl" (1955) decried the "Robot apartments! invincible suburbs! skeleton treasuries! blind capitals! demonic industries!" of modern life. Jack Kerouac produced what may have been the bible of the Beat Generation in his novel *On the Road* (1957)—an account of a cross-country automobile trip that depicted the rootless, iconoclastic lifestyle of Kerouac and his friends.

The beats were the most visible evidence of a widespread restlessness among young Americans in the 1950s. In part, that restlessness was a result of prosperity itself—of a growing sense among young people of limitless possibilities, and of the declining power of such traditional values as thrift, discipline, and self-restraint. Young middle-class Americans were growing up in a culture that encouraged them to expect wholly fulfilling lives; but of course they were living in a world in which almost all of them experienced obstacles to complete fulfillment. Youth in the 1950s never staged rebellions as widespread or as bitter as those of the 1960s.

Tremendous public attention was directed at the phenomenon of "juvenile delinquency," and in both politics and popular culture there were dire warnings about the growing criminality of American youth. The 1955 film *Blackboard Jungle,* for example, was a frightening depiction of crime and violence in city schools. Scholarly studies, presidential commissions, and journalistic exposés all contributed to the sense of alarm about the spread of delinquency—although in fact youth crime did not dramatically increase in the 1950s.

Also disturbing to many older Americans was the style of youth culture. Many young people began to wear clothes and adopt hairstyles that mimicked popular images of juvenile criminal gangs. The culture of alienation that the beats so vividly represented had counterparts even in ordinary middle-class behavior: teenage rebelliousness toward parents, youthful fascination with fast cars and motorcycles, and an increasing visibility of teenage sex, assisted by the greater availability of birth-control devices and the spreading automobile culture that came to dominate the social lives of teenagers in much of the nation. The popularity of James Dean, in such movies as *Rebel Without a Cause* (1955), *East of Eden* (1955), and *Giant* (1956), was a particularly vivid sign of this aspect of youth culture in the 1950s. Both in the roles he played (moody, alienated teenagers and young men with a streak of self-destructive violence) and in the way he lived his own life (he died in 1955, at the age of 24, in a car accident), Dean became an icon of the unfocused rebelliousness of American youth in his time.

Rock 'n' Roll

One of the most powerful signs of the restiveness of American youth was the enormous popularity of rock 'n' roll—and of the greatest early rock star, Elvis Presley.

Presley became a symbol of a youthful determination to push at the borders of the conventional and acceptable. Presley's sultry good looks; his self-conscious effort to dress in *Elvis Presley* the vaguely rebellious style of urban gangs (motorcycle jackets and slicked-back hair, even though Presley himself was a product of the rural South); and most of all, the open sexuality of his music and his public performances made him wildly popular among young Americans in the 1950s. His first great hit, "Heartbreak Hotel," established him as a national phenomenon in 1956, and he remained a powerful figure in American popular culture until—and indeed beyond—his death in 1977.

Presley's music, like that of most early white rock musicians, drew heavily from black rhythm and blues traditions, which appealed to some white youths in the early 1950s *Rock 'n' Roll's Black Roots* because of their pulsing, sensual rhythms and their hard-edged lyrics. Sam Phillips, a local record promoter who had recorded some of the important black rhythm and blues musicians of his time (among them B. B. King), reportedly said in the early 1950s: "If I could find a white man with a Negro sound, I could make a billion dollars." Soon after that, he found Presley. But there were others as well: among them Buddy Holly and Bill Haley (whose 1955 song "Rock Around the Clock"—used in the film *Blackboard Jungle*—served to announce the arrival of rock 'n' roll to millions of young people) who were closely connected to African-American musical traditions. Rock drew from other sources too: from country western music (another strong influence on Presley), from gospel music, even from jazz. But its most important influence was its roots in rhythm and blues.

The rise of such white rock musicians as Presley was a result in part (as Phillips's comment suggests) of the limited willingness of white audiences to accept black musicians. But the 1950s did see a growth in the popularity of African-American bands and singers among both black and white audiences. Chuck Berry, Little Richard, B. B. King, Chubby Checker, the Temptations, and others—many of them recorded by the black producer Barry Gordy, the founder and president of Motown Records in Detroit—never rivaled Presley in their popularity among white youths but did develop a significant multiracial audience of their own.

The rapid rise and enormous popularity of rock owed a great deal to innovations in radio and television programming. By the 1950s, radio stations no longer felt obliged to present mostly live programming—especially once television took over many of the entertainment functions radio had once performed. Instead, many radio stations devoted themselves almost entirely to playing recorded music. Early in the 1950s, a new breed of radio announcers, known now as "disk jockeys," began to create programming aimed specifically at young fans of rock music; and when those programs became wildly successful,

AMERICAN BANDSTAND One of the most popular television programs among young people in the 1950s (and into the 1960s) was *American Bandstand,* which combined the new popularity of television with the new popularity of rock 'n' roll. Dick Clark, the engaging host of the show, shown here holding a microphone and sitting among members of his audience, became one of the best-known promoters of rock music in America. *(Hulton/Archive/Getty Images)*

other stations followed suit. *American Bandstand,* a televised showcase for rock 'n' roll hits that began in 1957 featured a live audience dancing to recorded music. The show helped spread the popularity of rock—and made its host, Dick Clark, one of the best-known figures in America among young Americans.

Radio and television were important to the recording industry, of course, because they encouraged the sale of records, which was increasing rapidly in the mid- and late 1950s, especially in the inexpensive and popular 45 rpm format—small disks that contained one song on each side. Also important were jukeboxes, which played individual songs on 45s and which proliferated in soda fountains, diners, bars, and almost every other place where young people were likely to congregate. It usually cost 5 cents to play a song on the jukebox, and teenagers tended to make use of them whenever they could—thus promoting rock music further. Sales of records increased threefold—from $182 million to $521 million—between 1954 and 1960. The popularity of rock music was the driving force behind that increase. So eager were record promoters to get their songs on the air that they routinely made secret payments to station owners and disk jockeys to encourage them to showcase their artists. These payments, which became known as "payola," produced a briefly sensational series of scandals when they were exposed in the late 1950s and early 1960s.

"Payola" Scandals

Rock music began in the 1950s to do what jazz and swing had done in the 1920s, 1930s, and 1940s—to define both youth culture as a whole and the experiences of

a generation. People who grew up in the 1950s defined their era, and to some degree themselves, by the music they knew as teenagers and young people, just as people who grew up in later decades defined their experiences in part by their own generations' versions of rock. Rock music in the 1950s worked, therefore, both to transform popular music in America and to give at least indirect voice to some of the anxieties and pent-up impulses of young people.

THE "OTHER AMERICA"

It was relatively easy for white, middle-class Americans in the 1950s to believe that the world they knew—a world of economic growth, personal affluence, and cultural homogeneity—was the world virtually all Americans knew; that the values and assumptions they shared were ones that most other Americans shared too. But such assumptions were false. Even within the middle class, there was considerable restiveness—among women, intellectuals, young people, and others who found the middle-class consumer culture somehow unsatisfying, even stultifying. More importantly, large groups of Americans remained outside the circle of abundance and shared in neither the affluence of the middle class nor its values.

On the Margins of the Affluent Society

In 1962, the socialist writer Michael Harrington created a sensation by publishing a book called *The Other America,* in

The Other America

which he chronicled the continuing existence of poverty in America. The conditions he described were not new. Only the attention he was bringing to them was.

The great economic expansion of the postwar years reduced poverty dramatically but did not eliminate it. In 1960, at any given moment, more than a fifth of all American families (over 30 million people) continued to live below what the government defined as the poverty line (down from a third of all families fifteen years before). Many millions more lived just above the official poverty line, but with incomes that gave them little comfort and no security.

Most of the poor experienced poverty intermittently and temporarily. Eighty percent of those classified as poor at any particular moment were likely to have moved into poverty relatively recently and might move out of it again as soon as they found a job—an indication of how unstable employment could be at the lower levels of the job market. But approximately 20 percent of the poor were people for whom poverty was a continuous, debilitating *Persistent Poverty* reality, from which there was no easy escape. That included approximately half the nation's elderly and a large proportion of African Americans and Hispanics. Native Americans constituted the single poorest group in the country, a result of government policies that undermined the economies of the reservations and drove many Indians into cities, where some lived in a poverty worse than that they had left. These were the people Harrington had written about in particular in *The Other America,* people who suffered from what he called "a system designed to be impervious to hope." He explained:

> The other America does not contain the adventurous seeking a new life and land. It is populated by failures, by those driven from the land and bewildered by the city, by old people suddenly confronted with the torments of loneliness and poverty, and by minorities facing a wall of prejudice. . . . The entire invisible land of the other Americans became a ghetto, a modern poor farm for the rejects of society and of the economy.

This "hard-core" poverty rebuked the assumptions of those who argued that economic growth would eventually lead everyone into prosperity; that, as many claimed, "a rising tide lifts all boats." It was a poverty that the growing prosperity of the postwar era seemed to affect hardly at all, a poverty, as Harrington observed, that appeared "impervious to hope."

Rural Poverty

Among those on the margins of the affluent society were many rural Americans. In 1948, farmers had received 8.9 percent of the national income; in 1956, they received only 4.1 percent. In part, this decline reflected the steadily shrinking farm population; in 1956 alone, nearly 10 percent of the rural population moved into or was absorbed by cities. But it also reflected declining farm prices. Because of enormous surpluses in basic staples, prices fell 33 percent in those years, even though national income as a whole rose 50 percent at the same time. Even most farmers who managed to survive experienced substantial losses of income at the same time that the prices of many consumer goods rose.

Declining Agricultural Prices

Not all farmers were poor. Some substantial landowners weathered, and even managed to profit from, the changes in American agriculture. Others moved from considerable to only modest affluence. But the agrarian economy did produce substantial numbers of genuinely impoverished people. Black sharecroppers and tenant farmers continued to live at or below subsistence level throughout the rural South—in part because of the mechanization of cotton picking beginning in 1944, in part because of the development of synthetic fibers that reduced demand for cotton. (Two-thirds of the cotton acreage of the South went out of production between 1930 and 1960.) Migrant farmworkers, a group concentrated especially in the West and Southwest and containing many Mexican-American and Asian-American workers, lived in similarly dire circumstances. In rural areas without much commercial agriculture—such as the Appalachian region in the East, where the decline of the coal economy reduced the one significant source of support for the region—whole communities lived in desperate poverty, increasingly cut off from the market economy. All these groups were vulnerable to malnutrition and even starvation.

The Inner Cities

As white families moved from cities to suburbs in vast numbers, more and more inner-city neighborhoods became vast repositories for the poor, "ghettos" from which there was no easy escape. The growth of these neighborhoods owed much to a vast migration of African Americans out of the countryside (where the cotton economy was in decline) and into industrial cities. More than 3 million black men and women moved from the South to northern cities between 1940 and 1960, *Black Urban Migration* many more than had made the same journey during the Great Migration during and after World War I. Chicago, Detroit, Cleveland, New York, and other eastern and midwestern industrial cities experienced a great expansion of their black populations—both in absolute numbers and, even more, as a percentage of the whole, since so many whites were leaving at the same time.

Similar migrations from Mexico and Puerto Rico expanded poor Hispanic neighborhoods in many American cities at the same time. Between 1940 and 1960, nearly a million Puerto Ricans moved into American cities (the largest group to New York). Mexican workers crossed the border in Texas and California and swelled the already

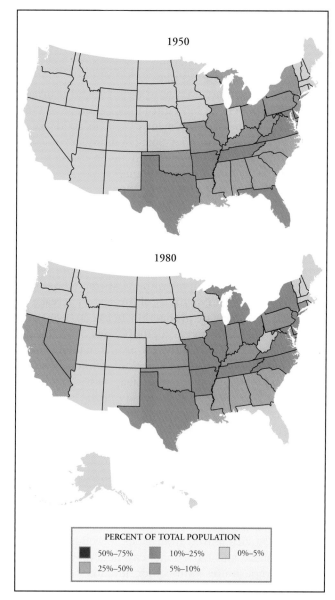

AFRICAN-AMERICAN MIGRATION, 1950–1980 Although there had been a substantial migration of African Americans out of the South and into northern industrial cities around the time of World War I and again during World War II, that process accelerated in the thirty years after 1950. By 1980, fewer southern states any longer had black populations that accounted for 25 percent or more of their total population. In the rest of the country, the number of states whose black populations exceeded 5 and 10 percent (the states shaded gold and orange) greatly increased. ◆ *What were some of the factors that produced the African-American migration in this period?*

substantial Latino communities of such cities as San Antonio, Houston, San Diego, and Los Angeles (which by 1960 had the largest Mexican-American population of any city, approximately 500,000 people).

Why these inner-city communities, populated largely by racial and ethnic minorities, remained so poor in the midst of growing affluence has been the subject of considerable,

and very heated, debate. Some critics have argued that the new migrants were victims, in part, of their own pasts, that the work habits, values, and family structures they brought with them from their rural homes were poorly adapted to the needs of the modern industrial city. Others have argued that the inner city itself—its crippling poverty, its lack of strong educational or service institutions, its crime, its violence, its apparent hopelessness—created a "culture of poverty" that made it more difficult for individuals to advance.

Many others argue that a combination of declining blue-collar jobs, inadequate support for minority-dominated public schools, and barriers to advancement rooted in racism—and not the culture and values of the poor themselves—were the source of inner-city poverty. It is indisputable that inner cities were filling up with poor minority residents at the same time that the unskilled industrial jobs they were seeking were diminishing. Employers were relocating factories and mills from old industrial cities to new locations in suburbs, smaller cities, and even abroad—places where the cost of labor or other things were lower. Even in the factories that remained, automation was reducing the number of unskilled jobs. The economic opportunities that had helped earlier immigrant groups to rise up from poverty were unavailable to most of the postwar migrants. Nor can there be any doubt that historic patterns of racial discrimination in hiring, education, and housing doomed many members of these communities to continuing, and in some cases increasing, poverty.

For many years, the principal policy response to the poverty of inner cities was "urban renewal": the effort to tear down buildings in the poorest and most degraded areas. In *"Urban Renewal"* the twenty years after World War II, urban renewal projects destroyed over 400,000 buildings, among them the homes of nearly 1.5 million people. In some cases, urban renewal provided new public housing for poor city residents. Some of it was considerably better than the housing they left; some of it was poorly designed and constructed, and deteriorated rapidly into dismal and dangerous slums. Urban renewal was, on the whole, better at eliminating "blights" than at helping the people who lived in them. In many cases, urban renewal projects replaced "slums" with middle-and upper-income housing (part of an often futile attempt to keep middle-class people from leaving), office towers, or commercial buildings; in Los Angeles, a baseball stadium for the Los Angeles Dodgers, recently relocated from Brooklyn, was erected on the site of a Mexican barrio.

One result of inner-city poverty was a rising rate of juvenile crime. Indeed, "juvenile delinquency" was one of the few results of poverty that middle-class Americans discussed and worried about with any consistency. A 1955 book, *One Million Delinquents,* called juvenile crime a "national epidemic" and described a troubling subculture of inner-city youth—embittered, rebellious adolescents with no hope of advancement and no sense of having a stake in the structure of their society.

THE RISE OF THE CIVIL RIGHTS MOVEMENT

After decades of skirmishes, an open battle began in the 1950s against racial segregation and discrimination, a battle that would prove to be one of the longest and most difficult of the century. Although white Americans played an important role in the civil rights movement, pressure from African Americans themselves was the crucial element in raising the issue of race to prominence.

The Brown Decision and "Massive Resistance"

On May 17, 1954, the Supreme Court announced its decision in the case of *Brown* v. *Board of Education of Topeka*. In considering the legal segregation of a Kansas public school system, the Court rejected its own 1896 *Plessy* v. *Ferguson* decision, which had ruled that communities could provide blacks with separate facilities as long as the facilities were equal to those of whites.

Brown v. Board of Education

The *Brown* decision was the culmination of many decades of effort by black opponents of segregation, and particularly by a group of talented NAACP lawyers, many of them trained at Howard University in Washington by the great legal educator Charles Houston. Thurgood Marshall, William Hastie, James Nabrit, and others spent years filing legal challenges to segregation in one state after another, nibbling at the edges of the system, and accumulating precedents to support their assault on the "separate but equal" doctrine itself. The same lawyers filed the suits against the school boards of Topeka, Kansas, and several other cities that became the basis for the *Brown* decision.

The Topeka suit involved the case of an African-American girl who had to travel several miles to a segregated public school every day even though she lived virtually next door to a white elementary school. When the case arrived before the Supreme Court, the justices examined it not simply in terms of legal precedent but in terms of history, sociology, and psychology. They concluded that school segregation inflicted unacceptable damage on those it affected, regardless of the relative quality of the separate schools. Chief Justice Earl Warren explained the unanimous opinion of his colleagues: "We conclude that in the field of public education the doctrine of 'separate but equal' has no place. Separate educational facilities are inherently unequal." The follow-

"Separate but Equal" Doctrine Overturned

ing year, the Court issued another decision (known as "Brown II") to provide rules for implementing the 1954 order. It ruled that communities must work to desegregate their schools "with all deliberate speed," but it set no timetable and left specific decisions up to lower courts.

In some communities—for example Washington, D.C.—compliance came relatively quickly and quietly. More often, however, strong local opposition (what came to be known in the South as "massive resistance") produced long delays and bitter conflicts. Some school districts ignored the ruling altogether. Others attempted to circumvent it with purely token efforts to integrate. More than 100 southern members of Congress signed a "manifesto" in 1956 denouncing the *Brown* decision and urging their constituents to defy it. Southern governors, mayors, local school boards, and nongovernmental pressure groups (including hundreds of "White Citizens' Councils") all worked to obstruct desegregation. Many school districts enacted "pupil placement laws" allowing school officials to place students in schools according to their scholastic abilities and social behavior. Such laws were transparent devices for maintaining segregation; but in 1958, the Supreme Court (in *Shuttlesworth* v. *Birmingham Board of Education*) refused to declare them unconstitutional.

"Massive Resistance"

By the fall of 1957, only 684 of 3,000 affected school districts in the South had even begun to desegregate their schools. In those that had complied, white resistance often produced angry mob actions and other violence. Many white parents simply withdrew their children from the public schools and enrolled them in all-white "segregation academies"; some state and local governments diverted money from newly integrated public schools and used it to fund the new, all-white academies. The *Brown* decision, far from ending segregation, had launched a prolonged battle between federal authority and state and local governments, and between those who believed in racial equality and those who did not.

The Eisenhower administration was not eager to commit itself to that battle. The president himself had greeted the *Brown* decision with skepticism (and once said it had set back progress on race relations "at least fifteen years"). But in September 1957, he faced a case of direct state defiance of federal authority and felt compelled to act.

Little Rock

Federal courts had ordered the desegregation of Central High School in Little Rock, Arkansas. An angry white mob tried to prevent implementation of the order by blockading the entrances to the school, and Governor Orval Faubus refused to do anything to stop the obstruction. President Eisenhower finally responded by federalizing the National Guard and sending troops to Little Rock to restore order and ensure that the court orders would be obeyed. Only then did Central High School admit its first black students.

LITTLE ROCK An African-American student passes by jeering whites in Arkansas on her way to Little Rock High School, newly integrated by federal court order. The black students later admitted that they had been terrified during the first difficult weeks of integration. But in public, most of them acted with remarkable calm and dignity. *(Bettmann/Corbis)*

The Expanding Movement

The *Brown* decision helped spark a growing number of popular challenges to segregation in the South. On December 1, 1955, Rosa Parks, a black woman, was arrested in Montgomery, Alabama, when she refused to give up her seat on a Montgomery bus to a white passenger (as required by the Jim Crow laws that regulated race relations in the city and throughout most of the South). Parks, an active civil rights leader in the community, had apparently decided spontaneously to resist the order to move. Her feet were tired, she later explained. But black leaders in Montgomery had been waiting for such an incident, which they wanted to use to challenge the segregation of the buses. The arrest of this admired woman produced outrage in the city's African-American community and helped local leaders organize a successful boycott of the bus system to demand an end to segregated seating.

The bus boycott owed much of its success to the prior existence of well-organized black citizens' groups. A black women's political caucus had, in fact, been developing plans for a boycott of the segregated buses for some time. They seized on Rosa Parks as a symbol of the movement. Once *Montgomery Bus Boycott* launched, the boycott was almost completely effective. Black workers who needed to commute to their jobs (of whom the largest group consisted of female domestic servants) formed car pools to ride back and forth to work, or simply walked, even at times over long distances. The boycott put economic pressure not only on the bus company (a private concern) but on many Montgomery merchants. The bus boycotters found it difficult to get to downtown stores and tended to shop instead in their own neighborhoods. Still the boycott might well have failed had it not been for a Supreme Court decision late in 1956, inspired in part by the protest, that declared segregation in public transportation to be illegal. The buses in Montgomery abandoned their discriminatory seating policies, and the boycott came to a close.

More important than the immediate victories of the Montgomery boycott was its success in establishing a new form of racial protest and in elevating to prominence a new figure in the movement for civil rights. The man chosen to head the boycott movement after its launching was a local Baptist pastor, Martin Luther King, Jr., the son of a prominent Atlanta minister, a powerful orator, and a gifted leader. At first King was reluctant to accept responsibility for the movement. But once he accepted the role, he became consumed by it.

King's approach to black protest was based on the doctrine of nonviolence—that is, of passive resistance even in the face of direct attack. He drew from the teachings of Mahatma Gandhi, the Indian nationalist leader; from Henry David Thoreau and his doctrine of civil disobedience; and from Christian doctrine. And he produced an approach to racial struggle that captured the moral high ground for his supporters. He urged African Americans to engage in peaceful demonstrations; to allow themselves to be arrested, even beaten, if necessary; and to respond to hate with love. For the next thirteen years—as leader of the Southern Christian Leadership Conference, an interracial group he founded shortly after the bus boycott—he was the most influential and most widely admired black leader in the country. The popular movement he came to represent soon spread throughout the South and throughout the country.

Pressure from the courts, from northern liberals, and from blacks themselves also speeded the pace of racial change in other areas. One important color line had been breached as early as 1947, when the Brooklyn Dodgers signed the great Jackie Robinson as the first African American to play Major League Baseball. By the mid-1950s, blacks had established themselves as a powerful force in almost all professional sports. Within the government, President Eisenhower completed the integration of the armed forces, attempted to desegregate the federal work force, and in 1957 signed a civil rights act (passed, without active support from the White House, by a Democratic Congress) providing federal protection for blacks who wished to register to vote. It was a weak bill, with few mechanisms for enforcement, but it was the first civil rights bill of any kind to win passage since the end of Reconstruction, and it served as a signal that the executive and legislative branches were beginning to join the judiciary in the federal commitment to the "Second Reconstruction."

Causes of the Civil Rights Movement

Why did a civil rights movement begin to emerge at this particular moment? The injustices it challenged and the goals it promoted were hardly new; in theory, African Americans could have launched the same movement fifty or a hundred years earlier, or decades later. Why did they do so in the 1950s and 1960s?

Several factors contributed to the rise of African-American protest in these years. The legacy of World War II was one of the most impor-

Legacy of World War II

tant. Millions of black men and women had served in the military or worked in war plants during the war and had derived from the experience a broader view of the world, and of their place in it, than they had been able to develop in their relatively isolated lives prior to the 1940s.

Another factor was the growth of an urban black middle class, which had been developing for decades but which

Urban Black Middle Class

began to flourish after the war. Much of the impetus for the civil rights movement came from the leaders of urban black communities—ministers, educators, professionals—and much of it came as well from students at black colleges and universities, which had expanded significantly in the previous decades. Men and women with education and a stake in society were often more aware of the obstacles to their advancement than poorer and more oppressed people, to whom the possibility of advancement may have seemed too remote even to consider. And urban blacks had considerably more freedom to associate with one another and to develop independent institutions than did rural blacks, who were often under the very direct supervision of white landowners.

Television and other forms of popular culture were another factor in the rising consciousness of racism among blacks. More than any previous generation, postwar blacks had constant, vivid reminders of how the white majority lived—of the world from which they were effectively excluded. Television also conveyed the activities of demonstrators to a national audience, ensuring that activism in one community would inspire similar protests in others. In addition to the forces that were inspiring African Americans to mobilize, other forces were at work

mobilizing many white Americans to support the movement once it began. One was the Cold War, which made racial injustice an embarrassment to Americans trying to present their nation as a model to the world. Another was the political mobilization of northern blacks, who were now a substantial voting bloc within the Democratic Party; politicians from northern industrial states could not ignore their views. Labor unions with substantial black memberships also played an important part in supporting (and funding) the civil rights movement. This great and largely spontaneous social movement emerged, in short, out of an unpredictable combination of broad social changes and specific local grievances. Whatever its causes, it quickly took on a momentum that, by the early 1960s, had made it one of the most powerful forces in America.

EISENHOWER REPUBLICANISM

Dwight D. Eisenhower was the least experienced politician to serve in the White House in the twentieth century. He was also among the most popular and politically successful presidents of the postwar era. At home, he pursued essentially moderate policies, avoiding most new initiatives but accepting the work of earlier reformers. Abroad, he continued and even intensified American commitments to oppose communism but brought to some of those commitments a measure of restraint that his successors did not always match.

"What Was Good for ... General Motors"

The first Republican administration in twenty years staffed itself with men drawn from the same quarter as those who had staffed Republican administrations in the 1920s: the business community. But by the 1950s, many business leaders had acquired a social and political outlook very different from that of their predecessors of earlier decades. Above all, many of the nation's leading business ex-

Business Leaders' New Outlook

ecutives and financiers had reconciled themselves to at least the broad outlines of the Keynesian welfare state the New Deal had launched. Indeed, some corporate leaders had come to see it as something that actually benefited them—by helping maintain social order, by increasing mass purchasing power, and by stabilizing labor relations.

To his cabinet, Eisenhower appointed wealthy corporate lawyers and business executives who were not apologetic about their backgrounds. Charles Wilson, president of General Motors, assured senators considering his nomination for secretary of defense that he foresaw no conflict of interest because he was certain that "what was good for our country was good for General Motors, and vice versa."

Eisenhower's consistent inclination was to limit federal activities and encourage private enterprise. He supported the private rather than public development of natural resources. To the chagrin of farmers, he lowered federal support for farm prices. He also removed the last limited wage and price controls maintained by the Truman administration. He opposed the creation of new social service programs such as national health insurance. He strove constantly to reduce federal expenditures (even during the recession of 1958) and balance the budget. He ended 1960, his last full year in office, with a $1 billion budget surplus.

The Survival of the Welfare State

The president took few new initiatives in domestic policy, but he resisted pressure from the right wing of his party to dismantle those welfare policies of the New Deal that had survived the conservative assaults of the war years and after. Indeed, during his term, he agreed to extend the Social Security system to an additional 10 million people and unemployment compensation to an additional 4 million, and he agreed to increase the minimum hourly wage from 75 cents to $1. Perhaps the most significant legislative accomplishment of the Eisenhower administration was the Federal Highway Act of 1956, which authorized $25 billion for a ten-year proj-

Federal Highway Act of 1956

ect that built over 40,000 miles of interstate highways—the largest public works project in American history. The program was to be funded through a highway "trust fund," whose revenues would come from new taxes on the purchase of fuel, automobiles, trucks, and tires.

In 1956, Eisenhower ran for a second term, even though he had suffered a serious heart attack the previous year. With Adlai Stevenson opposing him once again, he won by another, even greater landslide, receiving nearly 57 percent of the popular vote and 457 electoral votes to Stevenson's 73. Democrats retained the control of both houses of Congress they had won back in 1954. And in 1958—during a serious recession—they increased that control by substantial margins.

The Decline of McCarthyism

The Eisenhower administration did little in its first years in office to discourage the anticommunist furor that had gripped the nation. By 1954, however, the crusade against subversion was beginning to produce significant popular opposition—an indication that the anticommunist passion of several years earlier was beginning to abate. The clearest signal of that change was the political demise of Senator Joseph McCarthy.

THE ARMY-MCCARTHY HEARINGS Senator Joseph McCarthy uses a map to show the supposed distribution of communists throughout the United States during the televised 1954 Senate hearings to mediate the dispute between McCarthy and the U.S. Army. Joseph Welch, chief counsel for the army, remains conspicuously unimpressed. *(Bettmann/Corbis)*

During the first year of the Eisenhower administration, McCarthy continued to operate with impunity. But in January 1954 he overreached himself when he attacked Secretary of the Army Robert Stevens and the armed services in general. At that point, the administration and influential members of Congress organized a special investigation of the charges, which became known as the

Army-McCarthy Hearings | Army-McCarthy hearings. They were among the first congressional hearings to be nationally televised. The result was devastating to McCarthy. Watching McCarthy in action— bullying witnesses, hurling groundless (and often cruel) accusations, evading issues—much of the public began to see him as a villain, and even a buffoon. In December 1954, the Senate voted 67 to 22 to condemn him for "conduct unbecoming a senator." Three years later, with little public support left, he died—a victim, apparently, of complications arising from alcoholism.

EISENHOWER, DULLES, AND THE COLD WAR

The threat of nuclear war with the Soviet Union created a sense of high anxiety in international relations in the 1950s. But the nuclear threat had another effect as well. With the potential devastation of an atomic war so enormous, both superpowers began to edge away from direct confrontations. The attention of both the United States and the Soviet Union began to turn to the rapidly escalating instability in the nations of the Third World.

Dulles and "Massive Retaliation"

Eisenhower's secretary of state, and (except for the president himself) the dominant figure in the nation's foreign policy in the 1950s, was John Foster Dulles, an aristocratic corporate lawyer with a stern moral revulsion to communism. He entered office denouncing the containment policies of the Truman years as excessively passive, arguing that the United States should pursue an active program of "liberation," which would lead to a "rollback" of communist expansion. Once in power, however, he had to defer to the more moderate views of the president himself.

The most prominent of Dulles's innovations was the policy of "massive retaliation," which Dulles announced early in 1954. The United States would, he explained, respond to communist threats to its allies not by using conventional forces in local conflicts (a policy that had led to so much frustration in Korea) but by relying on "the deterrent of massive retaliatory power" (by which he clearly meant nuclear weapons). In part, the new doctrines reflected Dulles's inclination for tense confrontations, an approach he once defined as "brinksmanship"—pushing

EISENHOWER AND DULLES Although President Eisenhower himself was a somewhat colorless television personality, his was the first administration to make extensive use of the new medium to promote its policies and dramatize its actions. The president's press conferences were frequently televised, and on several occasions Secretary of State John Foster Dulles reported to the president in front of the cameras. Dulles is shown here in the Oval Office on May 17, 1955, reporting after his return from Europe, where he had signed the treaty restoring sovereignty to Austria. *(AP/Wide World Photos)*

the Soviet Union to the brink of war in order to exact concessions. But the real force behind the massive-retaliation

Economic Benefits of "Massive Retaliation" policy was economics. With pressure growing both in and out of government for a reduction in American military expenditures, an increasing reliance on atomic weapons seemed to promise, as some advocates put it, "more bang for the buck."

France, America, and Vietnam

What had been the most troubling foreign policy concern of the Truman years—the war in Korea—plagued the Eisenhower administration only briefly. On July 27, 1953, negotiators at Panmunjom finally signed an agreement ending the hostilities. Each antagonist was to withdraw its troops a mile and a half from the existing battle line, which ran roughly along the 38th parallel, the prewar border between North and South Korea. A conference in Geneva was to consider means by which to reunite the nation peacefully—although in fact the 1954 meeting produced no agreement and left the cease-fire line as the apparently permanent border between the two countries.

Almost simultaneously, however, the United States was being drawn into a long, bitter struggle in Southeast Asia. Ever since 1945, France had been attempting to restore its authority over Vietnam, its one-time colony, which it had been forced to abandon to the Japanese toward the end of World War II. Opposing the French, however, were the powerful nationalist forces of Ho Chi Minh, determined to win independence for their nation. Ho had hoped for American support in 1945, on the basis of the anticolonial rhetoric of the Atlantic Charter and Franklin Roosevelt's speeches, and also because he had received support from American intelligence forces during World War II while he was fighting the Japanese. But he was then, as he had been for many years, not only a committed nationalist but a committed communist. The Truman administration ignored him and supported the French, one of America's most important Cold War allies.

By 1954, Ho was receiving aid from communist China and the Soviet Union. America, in the meantime, had been paying most of the costs of France's ineffective military

Dien Bien Phu campaign in Vietnam since 1950. Early in 1954, 12,000 French troops became surrounded in a disastrous siege at the village of Dien Bien Phu. Only American intervention, it was clear, could prevent the total collapse of the French military effort. Yet despite the urgings of Secretary of State Dulles, Vice President Nixon, and others, Eisenhower refused to permit direct American military intervention in Vietnam, claiming that neither Congress nor America's other allies would support such action.

Without American aid, the French defense of Dien Bien Phu finally collapsed on May 7, 1954, and France quickly agreed to a settlement of the conflict at the same international conference in Geneva that summer that was considering the Korean settlement. The Geneva accords on Vietnam of July 1954, to which the United States was not a direct party, established a supposedly temporary division of Vietnam along the 17th parallel. The north would be governed by Ho Chi Minh, the south by a pro-Western regime. Democratic elections would be the basis for uniting the nation in 1956. The agreement marked the end of the French commitment to Vietnam and the beginning of an expanded American presence there. The United States helped establish a pro- *Ngo Dinh Diem* American government in the south, headed by Ngo Dinh Diem, a member of his country's Roman Catholic minority. Diem, it was clear, would not permit the 1956 elections, which he knew he would lose. He felt secure in his refusal because the United States had promised to provide him with ample military assistance against any attack from the north.

Cold War Crises

American foreign policy in the 1950s rested on a reasonably consistent foundation: the containment policy, as revised by the Eisenhower administration. But the nation's leaders spent much of their time reacting to both real and imagined crises in far-flung areas of the world. Among them were a series of crises in the Middle East, a region in which the United States had been little involved until after World War II.

On May 14, 1948, after years of Zionist efforts and a dramatic decision by the new United Nations, the nation of Israel proclaimed its independence. President Truman *Recognizing Israel* recognized the new Jewish homeland the next day. But the creation of Israel, while it resolved some conflicts, created others. Palestinian Arabs, unwilling to accept being displaced from what they considered their own country, joined with Israel's Arab neighbors and fought determinedly against the new state in 1948—the first of several Arab-Israeli wars.

Committed as the American government was to Israel, it was also concerned about the stability and friendliness of the Arab regimes in the oil-rich Middle East, in which American petroleum companies had major investments. Thus the United States reacted with alarm as it watched Muhammad Mossadegh, the nationalist prime minister of Iran, begin to resist the presence of Western corporations in his nation in the early 1950s. In 1953, the American CIA joined forces with conservative Iranian military leaders to engineer a coup that drove Mossadegh from office. To replace him, the CIA helped elevate the young Shah of Iran, Muhammad Reza Pahlevi, from his position as token constitutional monarch to that of virtually absolute ruler. The Shah remained closely tied to the United States for the next twenty-five years.

THE STATE OF ISRAEL The prime minister of Israel, David Ben-Gurion (left), watches the departure of the last British troops from Palestine shortly after the United Nations approved (and the United States recognized) the existence of a new Jewish state in part of the region. *(Bettmann/Corbis)*

American policy was less effective in dealing with the nationalist government of Egypt, under the leadership of General Gamal Abdel Nasser, which began to develop a trade relationship with the Soviet Union in the early 1950s. In 1956, to punish Nasser for his friendliness toward the communists, Dulles withdrew American offers *Suez Crisis* to assist in building the great Aswan Dam across the Nile. A week later, Nasser retaliated by seizing control of the Suez Canal from the British, saying that he would use the income from it to build the dam himself.

On October 29, 1956, Israeli forces attacked Egypt. The next day the British and French landed troops in the Suez to drive the Egyptians from the canal. Dulles and Eisenhower feared that the Suez crisis would drive the Arab states toward the Soviet Union and precipitate a new world war. By refusing to support the invasion, and by joining in a United Nations denunciation of it, the United States helped pressure the French and British to withdraw and helped persuade Israel to agree to a truce with Egypt.

Cold War concerns affected American relations in Latin America as well. In 1954, the Eisenhower administration ordered the CIA to help topple the new, leftist government of Jacobo Arbenz Guzmán in Guatemala, a regime that Dulles (responding to the entreaties of the United Fruit Company, a major investor in Guatemala fearful of Arbenz) argued was potentially communist.

No nation in the region had been more closely tied to America than Cuba. Its leader, Fulgencio Batista, had ruled as a military dictator since 1952, when with American assistance he had toppled a more moderate government. Cuba's relatively prosperous economy had become a virtual fiefdom of American corporations, which controlled almost all the island's natural resources and had cornered over half the vital sugar crop. American organized-crime syndicates controlled much of Havana's lucrative hotel and nightlife business. In 1957, *Fidel Castro* a popular movement of resistance to the Batista regime began to gather strength under the leadership of Fidel Castro. On January 1, 1959, with Batista having fled to exile in Spain, Castro marched into Havana and established a new government.

Castro soon began implementing drastic policies of land reform and expropriating foreign-owned businesses and resources. Cuban-American relations deteriorated rapidly as a result. When Castro began accepting assistance from the Soviet Union in 1960, the United States cut back the "quota" by which Cuba could export sugar to America at a favored price. Early in 1961, as one of its last acts, the Eisenhower administration severed diplomatic relations with Castro. Isolated by the United States, Castro soon cemented an alliance with the Soviet Union.

Europe and the Soviet Union

Although the problems of the Third World were moving slowly toward the center of American foreign policy, the direct relationship with the Soviet Union and the effort to resist communist expansion in Europe remained the principal concerns of the Eisenhower administration. In 1955, Eisenhower and other NATO leaders met with the Soviet premier, Nikolai Bulganin, at a cordial summit conference in Geneva. But when a subsequent conference of foreign ministers met to try to resolve specific issues, they could find no basis for agreement. Relations between the Soviet Union and the West soured further in 1956 in response to the Hungarian Revolution. Hungarian dissidents had launched

THE CUBAN REVOLUTION Fidel Castro is shown here in the Cuban jungle in 1957 with a small group of his staff and their revolutionary forces. Kneeling in the foreground is Castro's brother Raoul. Only two years later, Castro's forces toppled the existing government and elevated Fidel to the nation's leadership, where he has remained for over forty years. *(Bettmann/Corbis)*

a popular uprising in November to demand democratic reforms. Before the month was out, Soviet tanks and

Hungarian Revolution of 1956

troops entered Budapest to crush the uprising and restore an orthodox, pro-Soviet regime. The Eisenhower administration refused to intervene. But the suppression of the uprising convinced many American leaders that Soviet policies had not softened.

The U-2 Crisis

In November 1958, Nikita Khrushchev, who had succeeded Bulganin as Soviet premier and Communist Party chief earlier that year, renewed the demands of his predecessors that the NATO powers abandon West Berlin. When the United States and its allies predictably refused, Khrushchev suggested that he and Eisenhower discuss the issue personally, both in visits to each other's countries and at a summit meeting in Paris in 1960. The United States agreed. Khrushchev's 1959 visit to America produced a cool but polite public response. Plans proceeded

for the summit conference and for Eisenhower's visit to Moscow shortly thereafter. Only days before the scheduled beginning of the Paris meeting, however, the Soviet Union announced that it had shot down an American U-2, a high-altitude spy plane, over Russian territory. Its pilot, Francis Gary Powers, was in captivity. Khrushchev lashed out angrily at the American incursion into Soviet air space, breaking up the Paris summit almost before it could begin and withdrawing his invitation to Eisenhower to visit the Soviet Union.

The events of 1960 provided a somber backdrop for the end of the Eisenhower administration. After eight years in office, Eisenhower had failed to eliminate, and in some respects had actually increased, the tensions between the United States and the Soviet Union. Yet Eisenhower had brought to the Cold War his own sense of the limits of American power. He had resisted military interven-

Eisenhower's Restraint

tion in Vietnam. And he had placed a measure of restraint on those who urged the creation of an enormous American military establishment. In his farewell address in January 1961, he warned of the "unwarranted influence" of a vast "military-industrial complex." His caution, in both domestic and international affairs, stood in marked contrast to the attitudes of his successors, who argued that the United States must act more boldly and aggressively on behalf of its goals at home and abroad.

CONCLUSION

The booming economic growth of the 1950s—and the anxiety over the Cold War that formed a backdrop to it—shaped the politics and the culture of the decade. For most Americans, the 1950s were years of increasing personal prosperity. Sales of private homes increased dramatically; suburbs grew precipitously; young families had children at an astounding rate—creating what came to be known as the postwar "baby boom." After the end of the divisive Korean War, the nation's politics entered a period of relative calm, symbolized by the genial presence in the White House of Dwight D. Eisenhower, who provided moderate and undemanding leadership through most of the decade.

The nation's culture, too, helped create a broad sense of stability and calm. Television, which emerged in the 1950s as the most powerful medium of mass culture, presented largely uncontroversial programming dominated by middle-class images and traditional values. Movies, theater, popular magazines, and newspapers all generally contributed to a broad sense of well-being.

But the 1950s were not, in the end, as calm and contented as the politics and popular culture of the time suggested. A powerful youth culture emerged in these years that displayed a considerable level of restiveness and even disillusionment. African Americans began to escalate their protests against segregation and inequality. The continuing existence of widespread poverty among large groups of Americans attracted increasing attention as the decade progressed. These pulsing anxieties, combined with frustration over the continuing tensions of the Cold War, produced by the late 1950s a growing sense of impatience with the calm, placid public culture of the time. That was one reason for the growing desire for action and innovation as the 1960s began.

FOR FURTHER REFERENCE

James T. Patterson, *Grand Expectations: Postwar America, 1945–1974* (1996), a volume in the Oxford History of the United States, is an important general history of the postwar era. John P. Diggins, *The Proud Decades: America in War and Peace, 1941–1960* (1989) and Godfrey Hodgson, *America in Our Time* (1976) are other important surveys. Kenneth T. Jackson, *The Crabgrass Frontier: The Suburbanization of the United States* (1985) is a classic history of a major social movement. Eric Barnouw, *Tube of Plenty* (1982) and Karal Ann Marling, *As Seen on TV: The Visual Culture of Everyday Life in the 1950s* (1995) are good studies of the new medium. Elaine Tyler May, *Homeward Bound: American Families in the Cold War* (1988) is a challenging cultural history. Paul Boyer, *By the Bomb's Early Light: American Thought and Culture at the Dawn of the Atomic Age* (1985) examines the impact of the atomic bomb on American social thought. Stephen Ambrose, *Eisenhower the President* (1984) is a good biography, and Fred Greenstein, *The Hidden-Hand Presidency* (1982) is a challenge to earlier, dismissive views of Eisenhower's leadership style. Taylor Branch, *Parting the Waters: America in the King Years* (1988) is a superb narrative of the early years of the civil rights movement, and Richard Kluger, *Simple Justice* (1975) is a classic history of the *Brown* decision. John Egerton, *Speak Now Against the Day: The Generation Before the Civil Rights Movement in the South* (1994) is a history of struggles over white supremacy in the first years after World War II.

The stunning effect of the first Soviet satellite launch in 1957 is vividly portrayed in the documentary film *The Satellite Sky* (1990). *Eisenhower* (1993) is an extensive film portrait, offering a fresh reassessment of his legacy. *An Age of Conformity* (1991) is a film portraying domestic life in the 1940s and 1950s.

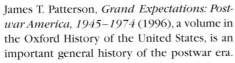

For quizzes, Internet resources, references to additional books and films, and more, consult the book's Online Learning Center at www.mhhe.com/brinkley11.

KHE SANH, VIETNAM, 1968 A beleaguered American soldier shows his exhaustion during the 76-day siege of the American marine base at Khe Sanh, which began shortly before the 1968 Tet offensive in Vietnam. American forces sustained record casualties in the fierce fighting at Khe Sanh; the Vietnamese communist forces suffered far more. *(Robert Ellison/Black Star)*

Significant Events

1959 · Soviet Comintern urges wars of "national liberation" in the Third World
· National Liberation Front (Viet Cong) created in Vietnam

1960 · John F. Kennedy elected president
· Greensboro sit-ins
· War resumes in Vietnam

1961 · Freedom rides
· United States supports failed invasion of Bay of Pigs
· Kennedy meets Khrushchev in Vienna
· Berlin Wall erected
· Peace Corps established
· Alliance for Progress established

1962 · Steel price increase provokes controversy
· Kennedy proposes tax cut to stimulate economy

· Desegregation crisis at University of Mississippi
· Cuban missile crisis

1963 · Martin Luther King, Jr., begins Birmingham campaign
· Desegregation crisis at University of Alabama
· Kennedy proposes civil rights bill
· March on Washington; King gives "I have a dream" speech
· Test ban treaty signed
· Buddhist crisis in Vietnam; Diem toppled by coup
· Kennedy assassinated; Lyndon B. Johnson becomes president

1964 · Johnson launches war on poverty
· Congress passes tax cut
· "Freedom summer" campaign in Mississippi
· Congress passes Civil Rights Act

CHAPTER THIRTY-ONE

THE ORDEAL OF LIBERALISM

*B*y the late 1950s, a growing restlessness was becoming apparent beneath the placid surface of American society. Anxiety about America's position in the world, growing pressures from African Americans and other minorities, the increasing visibility of poverty, the rising frustrations of women, and other long-suppressed discontents were beginning to shake the nation's public life. Ultimately, that restlessness would make the 1960s one of the most turbulent eras of the twentieth century. But at first, it contributed to a bold and confident effort by political leaders and popular movements to attack social and international problems within the framework of conventional liberal politics.

- Gulf of Tonkin Resolution passed
- United States bombs North Vietnam for first time
- Johnson elected president by record margin
- 1965 Medicare enacted
- Elementary and Secondary Education Act passed
- Selma campaign for voting rights
- Race riot breaks out in Watts, Los Angeles
- Malcolm X assassinated
- *Autobiography of Malcolm X* published
- Congress passes Voting Rights Act
- United States intervenes in Dominican Republic
- American combat troops sent to Vietnam
- Antiwar activities begin on university campuses
- Immigration Reform Act passed
- 1966 Medicaid enacted
- King leads Chicago campaign

- Senate Foreign Relations Committee holds hearings on Vietnam
- 1967 Johnson requests tax increase
- Race riot breaks out in Detroit
- Antiwar movement intensifies
- 1968 Viet Cong launch Tet offensive
- Johnson withdraws from presidential contest
- Martin Luther King, Jr., assassinated
- Racial violence breaks out in American cities
- Robert Kennedy assassinated
- Demonstrators clash with police at Democratic National Convention
- George Wallace launches third-party presidential campaign
- Richard M. Nixon elected president

EXPANDING THE LIBERAL STATE

Those who yearned for a more active government in the late 1950s, and who accused the Eisenhower administration of allowing the nation to "drift," looked above all to the presidency for leadership. The political scientist Richard Neustadt, for example, published an influential book in 1960 entitled *Presidential Power*, which stressed the importance of presidential action in confronting national problems. Presidents faced many constraints, he argued, but effective presidents must learn to break free of them. The two men who served in the White House through most of the 1960s—John Kennedy and Lyndon Johnson—seemed for a time to be the embodiment of these liberal hopes.

John Kennedy

The campaign of 1960 produced two young candidates who claimed to offer the nation active leadership. The Republican nomination went almost uncontested to Vice President Richard Nixon, who promised moderate reform. The Democrats, in the meantime, emerged from a spirited primary campaign united, somewhat uneasily, behind John Fitzgerald Kennedy, an attractive and articulate senator from Massachusetts who had narrowly missed being the party's vice presidential candidate in 1956.

John Kennedy was the son of the wealthy, powerful, and highly controversial Joseph P. Kennedy, former American ambassador to Britain. But while he had grown up in a world of ease and privilege, he became a spokesman for energy and sacrifice. He premised his campaign, he said, "on the single assumption that the American people are uneasy at the present drift in our national course." But his

Election of 1960

appealing public image was at least as important as his political positions in attracting popular support. He overcame doubts about his youth (he turned forty-three in 1960) and religion (he was Catholic) to win with a tiny plurality of the popular vote (49.9 percent to Nixon's 49.6 percent) and only a slightly more comfortable electoral majority (303 to 219).

Kennedy had campaigned promising a set of domestic reforms more ambitious than any since the New Deal, a program he described as the "New Frontier." But his thin popular mandate and a Congress dominated by a coalition of Republicans and conservative Democrats frustrated many of his hopes. Kennedy did manage to win approval of tariff reductions his administration had negotiated, and he began to build an ambitious legislative agenda that he hoped he might eventually see enacted—including a call for a significant tax cut to promote economic growth.

More than any other president of the century (except perhaps the two Roosevelts and, later, Ronald Reagan), Kennedy made his own personality an integral part of his presidency and a central focus of national attention. Nothing illustrated that more clearly than the popular reaction

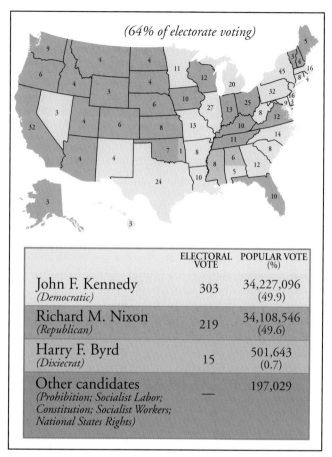

(64% of electorate voting)

	ELECTORAL VOTE	POPULAR VOTE (%)
John F. Kennedy *(Democratic)*	303	34,227,096 (49.9)
Richard M. Nixon *(Republican)*	219	34,108,546 (49.6)
Harry F. Byrd *(Dixiecrat)*	15	501,643 (0.7)
Other candidates *(Prohibition; Socialist Labor; Constitution; Socialist Workers; National States Rights)*	—	197,029

THE ELECTION OF 1960 The election of 1960 was, in the popular vote at least, one of the closest in American history. John Kennedy's margin over Richard Nixon was less than one-third of one percent of the total national vote, but greater in the electoral college. Note the distribution of electoral strength of the two candidates. Kennedy was strong in the industrial northeast and the largest industrial states of the Midwest, and he retained at least a portion of his party's traditional strength in the South and Southwest. But Nixon made significant inroads into the upper South, carried Florida, and swept most of the Plains and Mountain states. ◆ *What was the significance of this distribution of strength to the future of the two parties?*

 For an interactive version of this map go to www.mhhe.com/brinkley11ch31maps

to the tragedy of November 22, 1963. Kennedy had traveled to Texas with his wife and Vice President Lyndon Johnson for a series of political appearances. While the presi-

Kennedy Assassinated

dential motorcade rode slowly through the streets of Dallas, shots rang out. Two bullets struck the president—one in the throat, the other in the head. He was sped to a nearby hospital, where minutes later he was pronounced dead. Lee Harvey Oswald, who appeared to be a confused and embittered Marxist, was arrested for the crime later that day, and then mysteriously murdered by a Dallas nightclub owner, Jack Ruby, two days later as he was being moved from one jail to another. Most Americans at the time accepted the conclusions of a federal commission, chaired by Chief Justice Earl Warren, appointed by

JOHN KENNEDY The new president and his wife, Jacqueline, attend one of the five balls in Washington marking Kennedy's inauguration in 1961. *(Paul Schutzer/TimePix)*

President Johnson to investigate the assassination. The commission found that both Oswald and Ruby had acted alone, that there was no larger conspiracy. In later years, however, many Americans came to believe that the Warren Commission report had ignored evidence of a wider conspiracy behind the murders. Controversy over the truth about the assassination continues today.

Lyndon Johnson

The Kennedy assassination was a national trauma—a defining event for almost everyone old enough to be aware of it. At the time, however, much of the nation took comfort in the personality and performance of Kennedy's successor in the White House, Lyndon Baines Johnson. Johnson was a native of the poor "hill country" of west Texas and had risen to become majority leader of the U.S. Senate by dint of extraordinary, even obsessive, effort and ambition. Having failed to win the Democratic nomination

for president in 1960, he surprised many who knew him by agreeing to accept the second position on the ticket with Kennedy. The events in Dallas thrust him into the White House.

Johnson's rough-edged, even crude personality could hardly have been more different from Kennedy's. But like Kennedy, Johnson was a man who believed in the active use of power. Between 1963 and 1966, he compiled the most impressive legislative record of any president since Franklin Roosevelt. He was aided by the tidal wave of emotion that followed the death of President Kennedy, which helped win support for many New Frontier proposals. But Johnson also con-structed a remarkable reform *The "Great Society"* program of his own, one that he ultimately labeled the "Great Society." And he won approval of much of it through the same sort of skillful lobbying in Congress that had made him an effective majority leader.

Johnson envisioned himself as a great "coalition builder." He wanted the support of everyone, and for a time he very nearly got it. His first year in office was, by necessity, dominated by the campaign for reelection. There was little doubt that he would win—particularly after the Republican Party fell under the sway of its right wing and nominated the conservative Senator Barry Goldwater of Arizona. In the November 1964 election, the president received a larger plurality, over 61 percent, than any candidate before or since. Goldwater managed to carry only his home state of Arizona and five states in the Deep South. Record Democratic majorities in both houses of Congress, many of whose members had been swept into office only because of the margin of Johnson's victory, ensured that the president would be able to fulfill many of his goals.

The Assault on Poverty

For the first time since the 1930s, the federal government took steps in the 1960s to create important new social welfare programs. The most important of these, perhaps, was Medicare: a program to pro-vide federal aid to the elderly *Medicare and Medicaid* for medical expenses. Its enactment in 1965 came at the end of a bitter, twenty-year debate between those who believed in the concept of national health assistance and those who denounced it as "socialized medicine." But the program as it went into effect pacified many critics. For one thing, it avoided the stigma of "welfare" by making Medicare benefits available to all elderly Americans, regardless of need (just as Social Security had done with pensions). That created a large middle-class constituency for the program. The program also defused the opposition of the medical community by allowing doctors serving Medicare patients to practice privately and to charge their normal fees; Medicare simply shifted responsibility for paying those fees from the patient to the government. In

RETROACTIVE I, **1964** Within months of his death, John Kennedy had become transformed in the American imagination to a figure larger than life, a symbol of the nation's thwarted aspirations. The artist Robert Rauschenberg gave evidence of Kennedy's new mythological importance by making him the centerpiece of this evocation of contemporary American society. *(© Robert Rauschenberg/Licensed by VAGA, New York, NY. Photo Courtesy Wadsworth Atheneum)*

1966, Johnson steered to passage the Medicaid program, which extended federal medical assistance to welfare recipients and other indigent people of all ages.

Medicare and Medicaid were early steps in a much larger assault on poverty—one that Kennedy had been planning in the last months of his life and that Johnson launched only weeks after taking office. The centerpiece of this "war on poverty," as Johnson called it, was the Office of Economic Opportunity (OEO), which created an array of new educational, employment, housing, and health-care programs. But the OEO was controversial from the start, in part because of its commitment to the idea of "Community Action."

Community Action was an effort to involve members of poor communities themselves in the planning and administration of the programs designed to help them. The Community Action programs provided jobs for many poor people and gave them valuable experience in administrative and political work. Many men and women who went on to significant careers in politics or community *Community Action Program* organizing, including many black and Hispanic politicians, as well as many Indians, got their start in Community Action programs. But despite its achievements, the Community Action approach proved impossible to sustain, both because of administrative failures and because the apparent excesses of a few agencies damaged the popular image of the Community Action programs, and indeed the war on poverty, as a whole.

The OEO spent nearly $3 billion during its first two years of existence, and it helped reduce poverty in some areas. But it fell far short of eliminating poverty altogether. That was in part because of the weaknesses of the programs themselves and in part because funding for them,

THE JOHNSON TREATMENT Lyndon Johnson was legendary for his powers of persuasion—for a combination of charm and intimidation that often worked on even the most experienced politicians. He is shown here in the Oval Office meeting with his old friend, Senator Richard Russell of Georgia, and demonstrating one of his most powerful and unsettling techniques of persuasion: moving so close to the person with whom he was talking as to be almost touching him. *(LBJ Library Photo by Yoichi Okamoto)*

inadequate from the beginning, dwindled as the years passed and a costly war in Southeast Asia became the nation's first priority.

Cities, Schools, and Immigration

Closely tied to the antipoverty program were federal efforts to promote the revitalization of decaying cities and to strengthen the nation's schools. The Housing Act of 1961 offered $4.9 billion in federal grants to cities for the preservation of open spaces, the development of mass-transit systems, and the subsidization of middle-income *Housing and Urban Development* housing. In 1966, Johnson established a new cabinet agency, the Department of Housing and Urban Development (whose first secretary, Robert Weaver, was the first African American ever to serve in the cabinet). Johnson also inaugurated the Model Cities program, which offered federal subsidies for urban redevelopment pilot programs.

Kennedy had long fought for federal aid to public education, but he had failed to overcome two important obstacles: Many Americans feared that aid to education was the first step toward federal control of the schools, and Catholics insisted that federal assistance must extend to parochial as well as public schools. Johnson managed to circumvent both objections with the Elementary and Secondary Education Act of 1965 and a series of subsequent measures. The bills extended aid to both private and parochial schools and based the aid on the economic conditions of the students, not on the needs of the schools themselves. Total federal expenditures for education and technical training rose from $5 billion to $12 billion between 1964 and 1967.

The Johnson administration also supported the Immigration Act of 1965, one of the most important pieces of legislation of the 1960s. The law maintained a *Immigration Act of 1965* strict limit on the number of newcomers admitted to the country each year (170,000), but it eliminated the "national origins" system established in the 1920s, which gave preference to immigrants from northern Europe over those from other parts of the world. It continued to restrict immigration from some parts of Latin America, but it allowed people from all parts of Europe, Asia, and Africa to enter the United States on an equal basis. By the early 1970s, the character of American immigration had changed, with members of new national groups—and particularly large groups of Asians—entering the United States and changing the character of the American population.

Legacies of the Great Society

Taken together, the Great Society reforms meant a significant increase in federal spending. For a time, rising tax revenues from the growing economy nearly compensated for the new expenditures. In 1964, Johnson managed to win passage of the $11.5 billion tax cut that Kennedy had first proposed in 1962. The cut increased the federal deficit, but substantial economic growth over the next several years made up for much of the revenue initially lost. As Great Society programs began to multiply, however, and particularly as they began to compete with the escalating costs of America's military ventures, the federal budget rapidly outpaced increases in revenues. In 1961, the federal government had spent $94.4 billion. By 1970, that sum had risen to $196.6 billion.

The high costs of the Great Society programs, the deficiencies and failures of many of them, and the inability of the government to find the revenues to pay for them contributed to a growing disillusionment in later years with the idea of federal efforts to solve social problems. By the 1980s, many Americans had become convinced that the Great Society experiments had not worked and that, indeed, government programs to solve social problems could not work. But the

Failures and Achievements of the Great Society

Great Society, despite many failures, was also responsible for some significant achievements. It significantly reduced hunger in America. It made medical care available to millions of elderly and poor people who would otherwise have had great difficulty affording it. It contributed to the greatest reduction in poverty in American history. In 1959, according to the most widely accepted estimates, 21 percent of the American people lived below the officially established poverty line. By 1969, only 12 percent remained below that line. The improvements affected blacks and whites in about the same proportion: 56 percent of the black population had lived in poverty in 1959, while only 32 percent did so ten years later—a 42 percent reduction; 18 percent of all whites had been poor in 1959, but only 10 percent were poor a decade later—a 44 percent reduction. Much of that progress was a result of economic growth, but some of it was a result of Great Society programs.

THE BATTLE FOR RACIAL EQUALITY

The nation's most important domestic initiative in the 1960s was the effort to provide justice and equality to African Americans. It was the most difficult commitment, the one that produced the severest strains on American society. It was also unavoidable. Black Americans were themselves ensuring that the nation would have to deal with the problem of race.

Expanding Protests

John Kennedy had long been vaguely sympathetic to the cause of racial justice, but he was hardly a committed crusader. His intervention during the 1960 campaign to help win the release of Martin Luther King, Jr., from a Georgia prison won him a large plurality of the black vote. But like many presidents before him, he feared alienating southern Democratic voters and powerful southern Democrats in Congress. His administration set out to contain the racial problem by expanding enforcement of existing laws and supporting litigation to overturn existing segregation statutes, hoping to make modest progress without creating politically damaging divisions.

But the pressure for more fundamental change could not be contained. In February 1960, black college students

in Greensboro, North Carolina, staged a sit-in at a segregated Woolworth's lunch counter; and in the following weeks, similar demonstrations spread throughout the South, forcing many merchants to integrate their facilities. In the fall of 1960, some of those who had participated in the sit-ins formed the Student Nonviolent Coordinating Committee (SNCC), which worked to keep the spirit of resistance alive.

SNCC

In 1961, an interracial group of students, working with the Congress of Racial Equality (CORE), began what they called "freedom rides" (reviving a tactic CORE had tried, without

"Freedom Rides"

much success, in the 1940s). Traveling by bus throughout the South, the freedom riders tried to force the desegregation of bus stations. In some places, they met with such savage violence at the hands of enraged whites that the president finally dispatched federal marshals to help keep the peace. Kennedy also ordered the integration of all bus and train stations. In the meantime, SNCC workers began fanning out through black communities and even into remote rural areas to encourage blacks to challenge the obstacles to voting that the Jim Crow laws had created and that powerful social custom sustained. The Southern Christian Leadership Conference (SCLC) also created citizen-education and other programs—many of them organized by the remarkable Ella Baker, one of the great grassroots leaders of the movement—to mobilize black workers, farmers, housewives, and others to challenge segregation, disenfranchisement, and discrimination.

Continuing judicial efforts to enforce the integration of public education increased the pressure on national leaders to respond to the civil rights movement. In October 1962, a federal court ordered the University of Mississippi to enroll its first black student, James Meredith; Governor Ross Barnett, a strident segregationist, refused to enforce the order. When angry whites in Oxford, Mississippi, began rioting to protest the court decree, President Kennedy sent federal troops to the city to restore order and protect Meredith's right to attend the university.

Events in Alabama in 1963 helped bring the growing movement to something of a climax. In April, Martin Luther King, Jr., helped launch a series of nonviolent demonstrations in Birmingham, Alabama, a city unsurpassed in the strength of its commitment to segregation. Police Commissioner Eugene "Bull" Connor personally supervised a brutal effort to break up the peaceful marches, arresting hundreds of demonstrators and using attack dogs, tear gas, electric cattle prods, and fire hoses—at times

Birmingham

even against small children—as much of the nation watched televised reports in horror. Two months later, Governor George Wallace—who had won election in 1962 pledging staunch resistance to integration—pledged to stand in the doorway of a building at the University of Alabama to prevent the court-ordered

BIRMINGHAM, 1963 In one of the scenes that horrified many Americans watching on television, police in Birmingham, Alabama, turn firehoses full force on civil-rights demonstrators, knocking many of them to the ground. *(Bill Hudson/AP/Wide World Photos)*

enrollment of several black students. Only after the arrival of federal marshals and a visit from Attorney General Robert Kennedy did Wallace give way. His stand won him wide popularity among whites throughout the nation who were growing uncomfortable with the pace of integration. That same night, NAACP official Medgar Evers was murdered in Mississippi.

A National Commitment

The events in Alabama and Mississippi were a warning to the president that he could no longer contain or avoid the issue of race. In an important television address the night of the University of Alabama confrontation (and the murder of Evers), Kennedy spoke eloquently of the "moral issue" facing the nation. "If an American," he asked, "because his skin is dark, . . . cannot enjoy the full and free life which all of us want, then who among us would be

content to have the color of his skin changed and stand in his place? Who among us would then be content with the counsels of patience and delay?" Days later, he introduced a series of new legislative proposals prohibiting segregation in "public accommodations" (stores, restaurants, theaters, hotels), barring discrimination in employment, and increasing the power of the government to file suits on behalf of school integration.

To generate support for the legislation, and to dramatize the power of the growing movement, more than 200,000 demonstrators marched down *March on Washington* the Mall in Washington, D.C., in August 1963 and gathered before the Lincoln Memorial for the greatest civil rights demonstration in the nation's history. President Kennedy, who had at first opposed the idea of the march, in the end gave it his open support after receiving pledges from organizers that speakers would not criticize the administration. Martin Luther

King, Jr., in one of the greatest speeches of his distinguished oratorical career, roused the crowd with a litany of images prefaced again and again by the phrase "I have a dream." The march was the high-water mark of the peaceful, interracial civil rights movement.

The assassination of President Kennedy three months later gave new impetus to the battle for civil rights legislation. The ambitious measure that Kennedy had proposed in June 1963 had stalled in the Senate after having passed through the House of Representatives with relative ease. Early in 1964, after Johnson applied both public and private pressure, supporters of the measure finally mustered the two-thirds majority necessary to close debate and end a filibuster by southern senators; and the Senate passed the most comprehensive civil rights bill in the nation's history.

The Battle for Voting Rights

Having won a significant victory in one area, the civil rights movement shifted its focus to another: voting rights. During the summer of 1964, thousands of civil rights workers, black and white, northern and southern, spread out through the South, but primarily in Mississippi,

"Freedom Summer" to work on behalf of black voter registration and participation. The campaign was known as "freedom summer," and it produced a violent response from some southern whites. Three of the first freedom workers to arrive in the South—two whites, Andrew Goodman and Michael Schwerner, and one black, James Chaney—were brutally murdered by Ku Klux Klan members with the support of local police and others.

The "freedom summer" also produced the Mississippi Freedom Democratic Party (MFDP), an integrated alternative to the regular state party organization. Under the leadership of Fannie Lou Hamer and others, the MFDP challenged the regular party's right to its seats at the Democratic National Convention that summer. President Johnson, eager to avoid antagonizing anyone (even southern white Democrats who seemed likely to support his Republican opponent), enlisted King's help to broker a compromise. It permitted the MFDP to be seated as observers, with promises of party reforms later on, while the regular party retained its official standing. Both sides grudgingly accepted the agreement. Both were embittered by it.

A year later, in March 1965, King helped organize a major demonstration in Selma, Alabama, to press the demand for the right of blacks to register to vote. Selma sheriff Jim Clark led local police in a brutal attack on the demonstrators—which, as in Birmingham, received graphic television coverage and horrified many viewers across the nation. Two northern whites participating in the Selma march were murdered in the course of the effort there—one, a minister, beaten to death in the streets of the town;

MARTIN LUTHER KING, JR., IN WASHINGTON Moments after completing his memorable speech during the August 1963 March on Washington, King waves to the vast and enthusiastic crowd that had gathered in front of the Lincoln Memorial to demand "equality and jobs." *(AP/Wide World Photos)*

the other, a Detroit housewife, shot as she drove along a highway at night with a black passenger in her car. The national outrage that followed the events in Alabama helped push Lyndon Johnson to propose and win passage of the Civil Rights Act of 1965, better known as the Voting Rights Act, *Voting Rights Act* which provided federal protection to blacks attempting to exercise their right to vote. But important as such gains were, they failed to satisfy the rapidly rising expectations of African Americans as the focus of the movement began to move from political to economic issues.

The Changing Movement

For decades, the nation's African-American population had been undergoing a major demographic shift; and by the 1960s, the problem of racial injustice was no longer primarily southern and rural, as it had been earlier in the century. By 1966, 69 percent of American blacks were living in metropolitan areas and 45 percent outside the South. Although the economic condition of much of American society was improving, in the poor urban communities in which the black population was concentrated, things were getting significantly worse. Well over half of all American nonwhites lived in poverty at the beginning of the 1960s; black unemployment was twice that of whites.

By the mid-1960s, therefore, the issue of race was moving out of the South and into the rest of the nation. The battle against school desegregation had moved beyond the initial assault on de jure seg-

De jure and De facto Segregation

regation (segregation by law) to an attack on de facto segregation (segregation in practice, as through residential patterns), thus carrying the fight into northern cities. Many African-American leaders (and their white supporters) were demanding, similarly, that the battle against job discrimination move to a new level. Employers should not only abandon negative measures to deny jobs to blacks; they should adopt positive measures to recruit minorities, thus compensating for past injustices. Lyndon Johnson gave his tentative support to the concept of "affirmative action" in 1965. Over the next decade, affirmative action

guidelines gradually extended to virtually all institutions doing business with or receiving funds from the federal government (including schools and universities)—and to many others as well.

A symbol of the movement's new direction, and of the problems it would cause, was a major campaign in the summer of 1966 in Chicago, in which King played a prominent role. Organizers of the Chicago campaign hoped to direct national attention to housing and employment discrimination in northern industrial cities in much the same way similar campaigns had exposed legal racism in the South. But the Chicago campaign not only evoked vicious and at times violent opposition from white residents of that city; it failed to arouse the national conscience in the way events in the South had. It did produce a weak agreement with the city government to end housing discrimination, but little changed as a result. The Chicago campaign was, on the whole, an exercise in frustration.

Urban Violence

Well before the Chicago campaign, the problem of urban poverty had thrust itself into national attention when violence broke out in black neighborhoods in

"TURN LEFT OR GET SHOT" This chilling sign, erected at an intersection in the Watts neighborhood in Los Angeles during the 1965 riot there, illustrates the escalating racial tensions that were beginning to explode in American cities in the mid-1960s. *(Bettmann/Corbis)*

major cities. There were a few scattered disturbances in the summer of 1964, most notably in New York City's

Watts Riot

Harlem. The first large race riot since the end of World War II occurred the following summer in the Watts section of Los Angeles. In the midst of a seemingly routine traffic arrest, a white police officer struck a protesting black bystander with his club. The incident triggered a storm of anger and a week of violence (and revealed how deeply blacks in Los Angeles, and in other cities, resented their treatment at the hands of local police). As many as 10,000 people were estimated to have participated in the violence—attacking white motorists, burning buildings, looting stores, and sniping at policemen. Thirty-four people died during the Watts uprising, which was eventually quelled by the National Guard; twenty-eight of the dead were black. In the summer of 1966, there were forty-three additional outbreaks, the most serious of them in Chicago and Cleveland. And in the summer of 1967, there were eight major outbreaks, including the largest of them all—a racial clash in Detroit in which forty-three people (thirty-three of them black) died.

Televised reports of the violence alarmed millions of Americans and created both a new sense of urgency and a growing sense of doubt among many of those whites who had embraced the cause of racial justice only a few years before. A special Commission on Civil Disorders, created by the president in response to the disturbances, issued a celebrated report in the spring of 1968 recommending massive spending to eliminate the abysmal conditions of the ghettoes. "Only a commitment to national action on an unprecedented scale," the commission concluded, "can shape a future compatible with the historic ideals of American society." To many white Americans, however, the lesson of the riots was the need for stern measures to stop violence and lawlessness.

Black Power

Disillusioned with the ideal of peaceful change in cooperation with whites, an increasing number of African Americans were turning to a new approach to the racial

Shift from Integration to Racial Distinction

issue: the philosophy of "black power." Black power could mean many different things. But in all its forms, it suggested a move away from interracial cooperation and toward increased awareness of racial distinctiveness. It was part of a long nationalist tradition among African Americans that extended back into slavery and that had its most visible twentieth-century expression in the Garvey movement.

Perhaps the most enduring impact of the black-power ideology was a social and psychological one: instilling racial pride in African Americans, who lived in a society whose dominant culture generally portrayed blacks as inferior to whites. It encouraged the growth of black studies in schools and universities. It helped stimulate important black literary and artistic movements. It produced a new interest among many blacks in their African roots. It led to a rejection by some blacks of certain cultural practices borrowed from white society: "Afro" hairstyles began to replace artificially straightened hair; some blacks began to adopt African styles of dress, even to change their names.

But black power had political manifestations as well, most notably in creating a deep schism within the civil rights movement. Traditional

An Increasingly Divided Civil Rights Movement

black organizations that had emphasized cooperation with sympathetic whites—groups such as the NAACP, the Urban League, and King's Southern Christian Leadership Conference—now faced competition from more radical groups. The Student Nonviolent Coordinating Committee and the Congress of Racial Equality had both begun as relatively moderate, interracial organizations; SNCC, in fact, was originally a student branch of the SCLC. By the mid-1960s, however, these and other groups were calling for more radical and occasionally even violent action against the racism of white society and were openly rejecting the approaches of older, more established black leaders.

Particularly alarming to many whites (and to some African Americans as well) were organizations that existed entirely outside the mainstream civil rights movement. In Oakland, California, the Black Panther Party (founded by Huey Newton and Bobby Seale) promised to defend black rights even if that required violence. Black Panthers organized along semimilitary lines and wore weapons openly and proudly. They were, in fact, more the victims of violence from the police than they were practitioners of violence themselves. But they created an image, quite deliberately, of militant blacks willing to fight for justice, in Newton's words, "through the barrel of a gun."

Malcolm X

In Detroit, a once-obscure black nationalist group, the Nation of Islam, gained new prominence. Founded in 1931 by Elijah Poole (who converted to Islam and renamed

Nation of Islam

himself Elijah Muhammed), the movement taught blacks to take responsibility for their own lives, to be disciplined, to live by strict codes of behavior, and to reject any dependence on whites. The most celebrated of the Black Muslims, as whites often termed them, was Malcolm Little, a former drug addict and pimp who had spent time in prison and had rebuilt his life after joining the movement. He adopted the name Malcolm X ("X" to denote his lost African surname).

MALCOLM X Malcolm X, a leader of the militant Nation of Islam, arrives in Washington, D.C., in May 1963 to set up a headquarters for the organization there. Malcolm was hated and feared by many whites during his lifetime. After he was assassinated in 1965, he became a widely revered hero among African Americans. *(Bettmann/Corbis)*

Malcolm became one of the movement's most influential spokesmen, particularly among younger blacks, as a result of his intelligence, his oratorical skills, and his harsh, uncompromising opposition to all forms of racism and oppression. He did not advocate violence, as his critics often claimed; but he insisted that black people had the right to defend themselves, violently if necessary, from those who assaulted them. Malcolm died in 1965 when black gunmen, presumably under orders from rivals within the Nation of Islam, assassinated him in New York.

But Malcolm's influence did not die with him. A book he had been working on before his death with the writer Alex Haley *(The Autobiography of Malcolm X)* attracted wide attention after its publication in 1965 and spread his reputation broadly through the nation. Over time,

Malcolm became one of the most influential figures in black America. Years after his death, he was to many African Americans as important and revered a symbol as Martin Luther King, Jr.

"FLEXIBLE RESPONSE AND THE COLD WAR"

In international affairs as much as in domestic reform, the optimistic liberalism of the Kennedy and Johnson administrations dictated a more positive, more active approach to dealing with the nation's problems than in the past. And just as the new activism in domestic reform proved more difficult and divisive than liberals had imagined, so too it created frustrations and failures in foreign policy.

Diversifying Foreign Policy

The Kennedy administration entered office convinced that the United States needed to be able to counter communist aggression in more flexible ways than the atomic-weapons-oriented defense strategy of the Eisenhower years permitted. In particular, Kennedy was unsatisfied with the nation's ability to meet communist threats in "emerging areas" of the Third World—the areas in which, Kennedy believed, the real struggle against communism would be waged in the future. He gave enthusiastic support to the expansion of the Special Forces (or "Green Berets," as they were soon known)—soldiers trained specifically to fight guerrilla conflicts and other limited wars.

Flexible Response

Kennedy also favored expanding American influence through peaceful means. To repair the badly deteriorating relationship with Latin America, he proposed an "Alliance for Progress": a series of projects for peaceful development and stabilization of the nations of that region. Kennedy also inaugurated the Agency for International Development (AID) to coordinate foreign aid. And he established what became one of his most popular innovations: the Peace Corps, which sent young American volunteers abroad to work in developing areas.

Among the first foreign policy ventures of the Kennedy administration was a disastrous assault on the Castro government in Cuba. The Eisenhower administration had started the project; and by the time Kennedy took office, the CIA had been working for months to train a small army of anti-Castro Cuban exiles in Central America. On April 17, 1961, with the approval of the new president, 2,000 of the armed exiles landed at the Bay of Pigs in Cuba, expecting first American air support and then a spontaneous uprising by the Cuban people on their behalf. They

Bay of Pigs

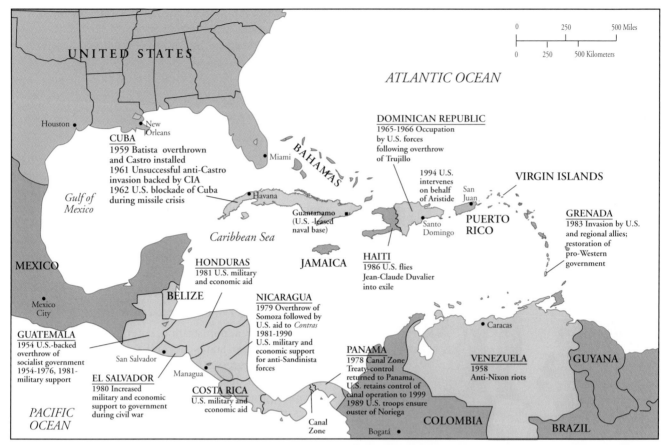

THE UNITED STATES IN LATIN AMERICA, 1954–2001 The Cold War greatly increased the readiness of the United States to intervene in the affairs of its Latin American neighbors. This map presents the many times and ways in which Washington ordered interventions in Central America, the Caribbean, and the northern nations of South America. During much of this period, the interventions were driven by Cold War concerns—by fears that communists might take over nations near the United States as they had taken over Cuba in the early 1960s. ◆ *What other interests motivated the U.S. to exert influence in Latin America, even after the end of the Cold War?*

received neither. At the last minute, as it became clear that things were going badly, Kennedy withdrew the air support, fearful of involving the United States too directly in the invasion. The expected uprising did not occur. Instead, well-armed Castro forces easily crushed the invaders, and within two days the entire mission had collapsed.

Confrontations with the Soviet Union

In the grim aftermath of the Bay of Pigs, Kennedy traveled to Vienna in June 1961 for his first meeting with Soviet Premier Nikita Khrushchev. Their frosty exchange of views did little to reduce tensions between the two nations— nor did Khrushchev's veiled threat of war unless the United States ceased to support a noncommunist West Berlin in the heart of East Germany.

Khrushchev was particularly unhappy about the mass exodus of residents of East Germany to the West through the easily traversed border in the center of Berlin. But he ultimately found a method short of war to stop it. Before dawn on August 13, 1961, the East German government, complying with directives from Moscow, constructed a

wall between East and West Berlin. Guards fired on those who continued to try to escape. For nearly thirty years, the Berlin Wall served as the most potent physical symbol of the conflict between the communist and noncommunist worlds.

The rising tensions culminated the following October in the most dangerous and dramatic crisis of the Cold War. During the summer of 1962, American intelligence agencies had become aware of the arrival of a new wave of Soviet technicians and equipment in Cuba and of military construction in progress. On October 14, aerial reconnaissance photos produced clear evidence that the Soviets were constructing sites on the island for offensive nuclear weapons. To the Soviets, placing missiles in Cuba probably seemed a reasonable—and relatively inexpensive—way to counter the presence of American missiles in Turkey (and a way to deter any future American invasion of Cuba). But to Kennedy and most other Americans, the missile sites represented an act of aggression by the Soviets toward the United States. Almost immediately, the president decided that the weapons could not be

Cuban Missile Crisis

REPAIRING THE BERLIN WALL First erected in 1961, the Berlin Wall became steadily higher and more elaborately fortified over the next several years. This 1963 photograph shows West Germans, at right, watching East German workers repair a section of wall after an East German mechanic rammed into it with an armored car as he escaped into West Berlin. He was shot by East German police but survived. *(Bettmann/Corbis)*

allowed to remain. On October 22, he ordered a naval and air blockade around Cuba, a "quarantine" against all offensive weapons. Preparations were under way for an American air attack on the missile sites when, late in the evening of October 26, Kennedy received a message from Khrushchev implying that the Soviet Union would remove the missile bases in exchange for an American pledge not to invade Cuba. Ignoring other, tougher Soviet messages, the president agreed. The crisis was over.

Johnson and the World

Lyndon Johnson entered the presidency lacking even John Kennedy's limited prior experience with international affairs. He was eager, therefore, not only to continue the policies of his predecessor but to prove quickly that he too was a strong and forceful leader.

An internal rebellion in the Dominican Republic gave him an early opportunity to do so. A 1961 assassination had toppled the repressive dictatorship of General Rafael Trujillo, and for the next four years various factions in the country had struggled for dominance. In the spring of 1965, a conservative military regime began to

Intervention in the Dominican Republic

collapse in the face of a revolt by a broad range of groups on behalf of the left-wing nationalist Juan Bosch. Arguing (without any evidence) that Bosch planned to establish a pro-Castro, communist regime, Johnson dispatched 30,000 American troops to quell the disorder. Only after a conservative candidate defeated Bosch in a 1966 election were the forces withdrawn.

From Johnson's first moments in office, however, his foreign policy was almost totally dominated by the bitter civil war in Vietnam and by the expanding involvement of the United States there.

THE AGONY OF VIETNAM

George Kennan, who helped devise the containment doctrine that drew America into war in Vietnam, once called the conflict "the most disastrous of all America's undertakings over the whole 200 years of its history." In retrospect, few would now disagree. Yet at first, the Vietnam War seemed simply one more Third World struggle on the periphery of the Cold War, a struggle in which the United States would try to tip the balance against communism without becoming too deeply or directly engaged. No president really decided to go to war in Vietnam. Rather, the American involvement there emerged from years of gradually increasing commitments that slowly and imperceptibly expanded.

The First Indochina War

Vietnam had a long history both as an independent kingdom and major power in its region, and as a subjugated province of China; its people were both proud of their past glory and painfully aware of their many years of subjugation. In the mid-nineteenth century, Vietnam became a colony of France. And like other European possessions in Asia, it fell under the control of Japan during World War II. After the defeat of Japan, the question arose of what was to happen to Vietnam in the postwar world. There were two opposing forces attempting to answer that question, both of them appealing to the United States for help. The French wanted to reassert their control over Vietnam. Challenging them was a powerful nationalist movement within Vietnam committed to creating an independent nation. The nationalists were organized into a *The Vietminh* political party, the Vietminh, which had been created in 1941 and led ever since by Ho Chi Minh, a communist educated in Paris and Moscow, and a fervent Vietnamese nationalist. The Vietminh had fought against Japan throughout World War II (unlike the French colonial officials who had remained in Vietnam during the war—as representatives of the Vichy regime—and had collaborated with the Japanese). In the fall of 1945, after the collapse of Japan and before the Western powers had time to return, the Vietminh declared Vietnam an independent nation and set up a nationalist government under Ho Chi Minh in Hanoi.

Ho had worked closely during the war with American intelligence forces in Indochina in fighting the Japanese; he apparently considered the United States something like an ally. When the war ended in 1945, he began writing President Truman asking for support in his struggle against the French. He received no reply to his letters, probably because no one in the State Department had heard of him. At the same time, Truman was under heavy pressure from both the British and the French to support France in its effort to reassert its control over Vietnam. The French argued that without Vietnam, their domestic economy would collapse. And since the economic revival of Western Europe was quickly becoming one of the Truman administration's top priorities, the United States did nothing to stop (although, at first, also relatively little to encourage) the French as they moved back into Vietnam in 1946 and began a struggle with the Vietminh to reestablish control over the country.

At first, the French had little difficulty reestablishing control. They drove Ho Chi Minh out of Hanoi and into hiding in the countryside; and in 1949, they established a nominally independent national government under the leadership of the former emperor, Bao Dai—an ineffectual, westernized playboy unable to assert any real independent authority. The real power remained in the hands of the French. But the Vietminh continued to challenge the French-dominated regime and slowly increased its control over large areas of the countryside. The French appealed to the United States for support; and in February 1950, the Truman administration formally recognized the Bao Dai regime and agreed to provide it with direct military and economic aid.

For the next four years, during what has become known as the First Indochina War, Truman and then Eisenhower continued to support the French military campaign against the Vietminh; by 1954, by some calculations, the United States was paying 80 percent of France's war costs. But the war went badly for the French in spite of the American support. Finally, late in 1953, Vietminh forces engaged the French in a major battle in the far northwest corner of the country, at Dien Bien Phu, an isolated and almost indefensible site. The French were surrounded, and the battle turned into a prolonged and horrible siege, with the French position steadily deteriorating. It was at this point that the Eisenhower administration decided not to intervene to save the French (see p. 826). The defense of Dien Bien Phu collapsed and the French government decided the time had come to get out. The First Indochina War had come to an end.

Geneva and the Two Vietnams

An international conference at Geneva, planned many months before to settle the Korean dispute and other controversies, now took up the fate of Vietnam as well. The United *Geneva Conference* States was only indirectly involved in the Vietnam phase of the Geneva Conference. Secretary of State Dulles, who did not really believe in negotiating with communists, reluctantly attended (described by one observer as a "puritan in a house of ill repute") but left early; the United States was not a party to the accords. Even so, the Geneva Conference produced an agreement to end the Vietnam conflict. There would be an immediate cease-fire in the war; Vietnam would be temporarily partitioned along the 17th parallel, with the Vietminh in control of North Vietnam, and a pro-Western regime in control of the South. In 1956, elections would be held to reunite the country under a single government.

The partition of Vietnam was, therefore, an essentially artificial one. But there were, in fact, real and important differences between North and South Vietnam. North Vietnam, the area now to be controlled by the Vietminh, was the heart of traditional Vietnamese society, the area where French influence had been the weakest. The North had remained a reasonably stable, reasonably homogeneous culture, most of whose people lived in very close-knit, traditional villages. Northern Vietnam was also the poorest region of the country—overpopulated, plagued by a serious maldistribution of scarce land, and hit by a serious famine at the end of the war. The Vietminh had worked effectively to alleviate the great famine and had won strong popular allegiance to the regime as a result. (Later, in the early 1950s, it launched a disastrous land reform policy, which it soon repudiated.) The Hanoi government was also strengthened by the mass exodus—in 1954, at the time of the partition—of many Catholics and others in the north who might have opposed them had they stayed. The North Vietnamese were passionately committed to the unification of the nation, a commitment with deep roots in Vietnamese history.

South Vietnam, by contrast, was a much more recently settled area. Until the early nineteenth century, in fact, very few Vietnamese had lived there; most of the sparse population had consisted of Khmer (Cambodians). Even

South Vietnamese Society

in the 1950s, most of its people had been there only three generations or less. For many years it had been something like the American West in the nineteenth century—the place where adventurous, or opportunistic, or disenchanted people from the poor, overpopulated North would move in search of a new beginning, and in search of land (which was scarce in the north but plentiful in the south). It was a looser, more heterogeneous, more individualistic society. It was highly factionalized—religiously, politically, and ethnically—with powerful sects (and even a powerful mafia) all competing for power. It was also more prosperous and fertile than the North. It was not overpopulated. It had experienced no famine. It was the only region of the country producing a surplus for export.

South Vietnam had no legacy of strong commitment to the Vietminh and much less fervent commitment to national unification. It was the area where the influence of the French (their language, culture, and values) had been strongest and where there was a substantial, westernized middle class. It was, in other words, a society much more difficult to unite and to govern than the society of the North.

America and Diem

As soon as the Geneva accords established the partition, the French finally left Vietnam altogether. The United States almost immediately stepped into the vacuum and became the principal benefactor of the new government

Ngo Dinh Diem

in the South, led by Ngo Dinh Diem. Diem was an aristocratic Catholic from central Vietnam, an outsider in the South. But he was also a nationalist, uncontaminated by collaboration with the French. And he was, for a time, apparently successful. With the help of the American CIA, Diem waged an effective campaign against some of the powerful religious sects and the South Vietnamese mafia, which had challenged the authority of the central government. As a result, the United States came to regard Diem as a powerful and impressive alternative to Ho Chi Minh. Lyndon Johnson once called him the "Churchill of Southeast Asia."

The American government supported Diem's refusal in 1956 to permit the elections called for by the Geneva accords, reasoning, almost certainly correctly, that Ho Chi Minh would easily win any such election. Ho could count on 100 percent of the vote in the north, with its much larger population, and at least some support in the south. In the meantime, the United States poured military and economic aid into South Vietnam. By 1956, it was the second largest recipient of American military aid in the world, after Korea.

Diem's early successes in suppressing the sects in Vietnam led him in 1959 to begin a similar campaign to eliminate the Vietminh supporters who had stayed behind in the south after the partition. He was quite successful for a time, so successful in fact that the North Vietnamese found it necessary to respond. A new policy emanating from Moscow beginning in 1959, emphasizing communist wars of national liberation (as opposed to direct Soviet confrontations with the United States and NATO), also encouraged Ho Chi Minh to resume his armed struggle for national unification. In 1959, the Vietminh cadres in the south created the National Liberation Front (NLF), known

The NLF

to many Americans as the Viet Cong—an organization closely allied with the North Vietnamese government. It was committed to overthrowing the "puppet regime" of Diem and reuniting the nation. In 1960, under orders from Hanoi, and with both material and manpower support from North Vietnam, the NLF began military operations in the South. This marked the beginning of the Second Indochina War.

By 1961, NLF forces were very successfully destabilizing the Diem regime. They were killing over 4,000 government officials a year (mostly village leaders) and establishing effective control over many areas of the countryside. Diem was also by now losing the support of many other groups in South Vietnam, and he was even losing support within his own military. In 1963, the Diem regime precipitated a major crisis by trying to discipline and repress the South Vietnamese Buddhists in an effort to make Catholicism the dominant religion of the country. The Buddhists began to stage enormous antigovernment demonstrations; and after Diem launched a series of heavy-handed military and police actions against them—which included several massacres of demonstrators and violent government raids on their sacred pagodas—the demonstrations grew much larger. Several Buddhist monks doused themselves with gasoline, sat cross-legged in the streets of downtown Saigon, and set themselves on fire—in view of photographers and television cameras.

The Buddhist crisis was alarming and embarrassing to the Kennedy administration. It caused the American government to reconsider its commitment to Diem—although not to the survival of South Vietnam. Kennedy had

Diem Overthrown

greatly increased the number of American personnel and the level of American assistance to the anticommunist regime, and he was unwilling to permit South Vietnam to fall. American officials pressured Diem to reform his government, but Diem made no significant concessions. As a result, in the fall of 1963, Kennedy gave his tacit approval to a plot by a group of South Vietnamese generals to topple Diem. In early November 1963, the generals staged the coup, assassinated Diem and his brother and principal adviser, Ngo Dinh Nhu (killings the United States had not wanted or expected), and established the first of a series of new governments, which were, for over three years, even less stable than the one

In 1965 the Department of Defense released a film intended for American soldiers about to embark for service in Vietnam and designed to explain why the United States had found it necessary to commit so many lives and resources to the defense of a small and distant land. The film was entitled *Why Vietnam?*—a question many Americans have pondered and debated in the three decades since. The debate has proceeded on two levels. At one level is an effort to assess the broad objectives Americans believed they were pursuing in Vietnam. At another is an effort to explain how and why policymakers made the specific decisions that led to the American commitment.

The Defense Department film itself offered one answer to the question of America's broad objectives, an answer

(Jim Pickerell/Black Star)

that for a time most Americans tended to accept: The United States was fighting in Vietnam to defend freedom and stop aggression; and it was fighting in Vietnam to prevent the spread of communism into a new area of the world, to protect not only Vietnam but also the other nations of the Pacific that would soon be threatened if Vietnam itself were to fall. This explanation—that America intervened in Vietnam to defend its ideals and its legitimate interests—continued to attract support well after the war ended. Political scientist Guenter Lewy contended, in *America in Vietnam* (1978), that the United States entered Vietnam to help an ally combat "foreign aggression." R. B. Smith argued that Vietnam was a vital American interest, that the global concerns of the United States required a commitment there. And historian Ernest R. May stated: "The paradox is that the Vietnam War, so often condemned by its opponents as hideously immoral, may well have been the most moral or at least the most selfless war in all of American history. For the impulse guiding it was not to defeat an enemy or to serve a national interest; it was simply not to abandon friends."

Other scholars have taken a starkly different view: that America's broad objectives in Vietnam were not altruistic, that the intervention was a form of imperialism—part of a larger effort by the United States after World War II to impose a particular political and economic order on the world. "The Vietnam War," historian Gabriel Kolko wrote in

Anatomy of a War (1985), "was for the United States the culmination of its frustrating postwar effort to merge its arms and politics to halt and reverse the emergence of states and social systems opposed to the international order Washington sought to establish." Economist Robert Heilbroner, writing in 1967, saw the American intent as somewhat more defensive; the intervention in Vietnam was a response to "a fear of losing our place in the sun," to a fear that a communist victory "would signal the end of capitalism as the dominant world order and would force the acknowledgment that America no longer constituted the model on which the future of world civilization would be mainly based." And Marilyn Young, in *The Vietnam Wars, 1945–1990* (1991), argues that the United States intervened in Vietnam as part of a broad and continuing effort to organize the post-World War II world along lines compatible with American interests and ideals.

Those who looked less at the nation's broad objectives than at the internal workings of the policymaking process likewise produced competing explanations. Journalist David Halberstam's *The Best and the Brightest* (1972) argued that policymakers deluded themselves into thinking they could achieve their goals in Vietnam by ignoring, suppressing, or dismissing the information that might have suggested otherwise. The foreign policy leaders of the Kennedy and Johnson administrations were so committed to the idea of American activism and success that

they had overthrown. A few weeks after the coup, John Kennedy too was dead.

From Aid to Intervention

Lyndon Johnson thus inherited what was already a substantial American commitment to the survival of an anticommunist South Vietnam. During his first two years in office, he expanded that commitment into a full-scale American war. Why he did so has long been a subject of debate. (See "Where Historians Disagree," above.)

Many factors played a role in Johnson's decision. But the most obvious explanation is that the new president faced many pressures to expand the American involvement and

very few to limit it. As the untested successor to a revered and martyred president, he felt obliged to prove his worthiness for the office by continuing the policies of his predecessor. Aid to South Vietnam had

Pressure for American Intervention

been one of the most prominent of those policies. Johnson also felt it necessary to retain in his administration many of the important figures of the Kennedy years. In doing so, he surrounded himself with a group of foreign policy advisers—Secretary of State Dean Rusk, Secretary of Defense Robert McNamara, National Security Adviser McGeorge Bundy, and others—who firmly believed that the United States had an obligation to resist communism in Vietnam. A compliant Congress raised little protest to, and indeed at

they refused to consider the possibility of failure; the Vietnam disaster was thus, at least in part, a result of the arrogance of the nation's leaders.

Larry Berman, a political scientist, offered a somewhat different view in *Planning a Tragedy* (1982) and *Lyndon Johnson's War* (1989). Lyndon Johnson never believed that American prospects in Vietnam were bright or that a real victory was within sight, Berman argued. Johnson was not misled by his advisers. He committed American troops to the war in Vietnam in 1965 not because he expected to win but because he feared that allowing Vietnam to fall would ruin him politically. To do otherwise, Johnson believed, would destroy his hopes for winning approval of his Great Society legislation at home.

Leslie H. Gelb and Richard K. Betts produced another, related explanation for American intervention, which saw the roots of the involvement in the larger imperatives of the American foreign policy system. In *The Irony of Vietnam: The System Worked,* published in 1979 and written in collaboration with political scientist Richard K. Betts, Gelb argued that intervention in Vietnam was the logical, perhaps even inevitable, result of a political and bureaucratic order shaped by the doctrine of containment. American foreign policy operated in response to a single, overriding imperative: the need to prevent the expansion of communism. However high the costs of intervention, policymakers believed, the costs of not intervening, of allowing South

CHICAGO '68 Although many young people traveled to Chicago during the 1968 Democratic Convention to demonstrate against the party's stance on the Vietnam War, the most radical of the protesters were the so-called Yippies, whose purpose was to create enough disruption to evoke a violent response from authorities. They succeeded in that effort. Here a group of Yippies demonstrates in Chicago's Grant Park demanding the release of the activist Tom Hayden, who had been arrested earlier in the week. *(Dennis Brack/Black Star)*

Vietnam to fall, would be higher. Only when the national and international political situation had shifted to the point where it was possible for American policymakers to reassess the costs of the commitment—to conclude that the costs of allowing Vietnam to fall were less than the costs of continuing the commitment (a shift that began to occur in the early 1970s)—was it possible for the United States to begin disengaging.

More recent studies have questioned the idea that intervention was inevitable or that there were no viable alternatives. David Kaiser, in *American Tragedy* (2000), argues that John Kennedy was not, in fact, the hawkish supporter of escalation that he has often been portrayed as, but a man whose deep skepticism about the judgment of his military advisors had led him to believe that the United States should find a negotiated settlement to the war. His successor, Lyndon Johnson, harbored no such skepticism and sided with those who favored a military solution. The death of John Kennedy, therefore, becomes a vital event in the history of America in Vietnam. Fredrik Logevall, in *Choosing War: The Lost Chance for Peace and the Escalation of the War in Vietnam* (1999), argues that there were significant opportunities for a negotiated settlement of the war in the early 1960s, but that American leaders (including both Kennedy and Johnson) chose a military response instead—in part to protect themselves politically from charges of weakness.

That the debate over the Vietnam War has been so continuous over the past quarter century is a reflection of the enormous role the United States' failure there has played in shaping the way Americans have thought about politics and policy ever since. Because the "lessons of Vietnam" remain a subject of intense popular concern, the debate over the history of Vietnam is likely to continue.

---

one point openly endorsed, Johnson's use of executive powers to lead the nation into war. And for several years at least, public opinion remained firmly behind him—in part because Barry Goldwater's bellicose remarks about the war during the 1964 campaign made Johnson seem by comparison to be a moderate on the issue.

Above all, intervention in South Vietnam was fully consistent with nearly twenty years of American foreign policy. An anticommunist ally was appealing to the United States for assistance; all the assumptions of the containment doctrine, as it had come to be defined by the 1960s, seemed to require the nation to oblige. Vietnam, Johnson believed, was a test of American willingness to fight communist aggression, a test he was determined not to fail.

During his first months in office, Johnson expanded the American involvement in Vietnam only slightly, sending an additional 5,000 military advisers there and preparing to send 5,000 more. Then, early in August 1964, the president announced that American destroyers on patrol in international waters in the Gulf of Tonkin had been attacked by North Vietnamese torpedo boats. Later information raised serious doubts as to whether the administration reported the attacks accurately. At the time, however, virtually no one questioned Johnson's portrayal of the incident as a serious act of aggression, or his insistence that the United *Gulf of Tonkin Resolution* States must respond. By a vote of 416 to 0 in the House and 88 to 2 in the Senate, Congress hurriedly passed the

THE WAR IN VIETNAM AND INDOCHINA, 1964–1975 Much of the Vietnam War was fought in small engagements in widely scattered areas and did not conform to traditional notions of combat. But as this map shows, there were traditional battles and invasions and supply routes as well. The red arrows in the middle of the map show the general path of the Ho Chi Minh Trail, the main supply route by which North Vietnam supplied its troops and allies in the South. The black arrow in southern South Vietnam indicates the point at which American troops invaded Cambodia in 1970. ♦ *What is there in the geography of Indochina, as presented on this map, that helps to explain the great difficulty the American military had in securing South Vietnam against communist attacks?*

Gulf of Tonkin Resolution, which authorized the president to "take all necessary measures" to protect American forces and "prevent further aggression" in Southeast Asia. The resolution became, in Johnson's view at least, an open-ended legal authorization for escalation of the conflict.

With the South Vietnamese leadership still in disarray, more and more of the burden of opposition to the Viet Cong fell on the United States. In February 1965, seven marines died when communist forces attacked an American military base at Pleiku. Johnson retaliated by

ordering the first American bombings of the north since the 1964 Tonkin crisis in an attempt to destroy the depots and transportation lines responsible for the flow of North Vietnamese soldiers and supplies into South Vietnam. The bombing continued intermittently until 1972. A month later, in March 1965, two battalions of American marines landed at Da Nang in South Vietnam. There were now more than 100,000 American troops in Vietnam.

Four months later, the president finally admitted that the character of the war had changed. American soldiers would now, he announced, begin playing an active combat role in the conflict. By the end of the year, there were more than 180,000 American combat troops in Vietnam; in 1966, that number doubled; and by the end of 1967, there *Mounting Casualties* were over 500,000 American soldiers there—along with a considerable number of civilian personnel working in various capacities and many American women (some enlisted, some not) who worked as nurses in military hospitals. In the meantime, the air war had intensified; ultimately the tonnage of bombs dropped on North Vietnam would exceed that in all theaters during World War II. And American casualties were mounting. In 1961, 14 Americans had died in Vietnam. By the spring of 1966, more than 4,000 Americans had been killed.

Yet the gains resulting from the carnage were negligible. The United States had finally succeeded in 1965 in creating a reasonably stable government in the south under General Nguyen Van Thieu. But the new regime was hardly less corrupt or brutal than its predecessors, and no more able than they to establish its authority in its own countryside. The Viet Cong, not the Thieu regime, controlled the majority of South Vietnam's villages and hamlets.

The Quagmire

For more than seven years, American combat forces remained bogged down in a war that the United States was never able either to win or fully to understand. Combating a foe whose strength lay less in weaponry than in its infiltration of the population, the United States responded with heavy-handed technological warfare designed for conventional battles against conventional armies. American forces succeeded in winning most of the major battles in which they became engaged. There were astounding (if not always reliable) weekly casualty figures showing that far more communists than Americans were dying in combat. There was a continuous stream of optimistic reports from American military commanders, government officials, and others—including a famous statement of Secretary of Defense McNamara that he could see "the light at the end of the tunnel." But if the war was not actually being lost, neither was it being won.

Central to the American war effort was a commitment to what the military called "attrition," a strategy premised on the belief that the United States could inflict so many casualties and so much damage on the enemy that eventually *Strategy of "Attrition"*

SEARCH AND DESTROY U.S. troops in Vietnam, often unable to distinguish enemy forces from the civilian population, increasingly sought to destroy places they considered possible enemy sanctuaries. Here an American soldier watches the burning of a village, one of many U.S. troops destroyed. *(Topham/The Image Works)*

Two impulses of the 1960s—the renewed interest among young people in the politics of the left, and the search for an "authentic" alternative to what many considered the artificial, consumerist culture of modern America—helped produce the revived popularity of folk music in that turbulent era. Although the harder, harsher, and more sensual music of rock 'n' roll was more visible and more popular in the 1960s, folk music more clearly expressed many of the political ideas and aspirations that were welling up in the youth culture of the time.

The folk-music tradition, like most American musical traditions, had many roots. It drew from some of the black musical traditions of the South, from the white country music of Appalachia. And it drew most immediately from a style of music developed by musicians associated with the Communist Party's Popular Front in the 1930s. Woody Guthrie, Pete Seeger, and others whose music would become popular again in the 1960s, began their careers singing in Popular Front and union rallies during the Great Depression. Their music, like the Popular Front itself, set out to seem entirely American, rooted in the nation's folk traditions.

Folk music remained alive in the 1940s and 1950s, but it had only a modest popular following. Pete Seeger and the Weavers continued to perform and to attract attention on college

DYLAN AND BAEZ This poster, created by the artist Eric Von Schmidt for a concert in 1961 by Joan Baez and Bob Dylan, evokes the gentle, vaguely spiritual character of folk music, which both differentiated it from rock and made it an appropriate vehicle for the idealistic political impulses that were emerging among many young people in the early 1960s. *(Hulton/Archive/ Getty Images)*

campuses. Harry Belafonte and the Kingston Trio recorded slick, pop versions of folk songs in an effort to bring them to mass audiences. In 1952, Folkway Records released the *Anthol-*

ogy of American Folk Music, a collection of eighty-four performances recorded in the 1920s and 1930s that became an inspiration and an important source of material to many younger folk musicians. Folk-music festivals—at Berkeley, Newport, and Chicago—began to proliferate beginning in 1959. And an important community of folk musicians lived and performed together in the 1950s and early 1960s in New York's Greenwich Village.

As the politics of the 1960s became more heated, and as young people in particular became politically aroused, it was folk music that most directly reflected their new values and concerns. Peter, Paul, and Mary—although only intermittently political—became icons to much of the New Left, beginning with their 1962 recording of "If I Had a Hammer," a song first performed at Communist Party rallies in the 1940s by Pete Seeger and the Weavers. Bob Dylan, whose own politics were never wholly clear to the public, had a large impact on the 1960s left, even inadvertently providing a name to the most radical offshoot of Students for a Democratic Society (SDS), the Weathermen, who named themselves after a line from one of his songs: "You don't need a weatherman to know which way the wind blows."* Joan Baez, whose politics were no secret to anyone, was actively engaged in the antiwar movement and was arrested

they would be unable and unwilling to continue the struggle. But the attrition strategy failed because the North Vietnamese proved willing to commit many more soldiers to the conflict than the United States had expected (and many more than America itself was willing to send).

It failed, too, because the United States relied heavily on its bombing of the north to eliminate the communists' war-making capacity. American bombers struck at strategic targets (factories, bridges, railroads, shipyards, oil storage depots, etc.) in North Vietnam to weaken the material capacity of the communists to continue the war; and they bombed jungle areas of Vietnam, Laos, and Cambodia to cut off the "Ho Chi Minh Trail," the infiltration routes by which Hanoi sent troops and supplies into the south. In

addition, the Americans hoped bombing would weaken the will of North Vietnam to continue the war.

By the end of 1967, virtually every identifiable target of any strategic importance in North Vietnam had been destroyed. The bombing had badly damaged the North Vietnamese economy, killed many soldiers and civilians, and made life difficult for those who survived, but it had produced none of the effects that the United States had expected. North Vietnam was not a modern, industrial society; it had few of the sorts of targets against which bombing is effective. And in any case, the North Vietnamese responded to the air raids with enormous ingenuity: They created a great network of underground tunnels, shops, and factories. They also secured increased aid from the Soviet Union and China. Infiltration of the south was

COFFEE HOUSE MUSIC The Feejon Coffee House in Manhattan was popular among young writers, poets, and others in the late 1950s, in part because it was a gathering place for folk musicians, two of whom are shown here performing at right. *(Hulton/Archive/Getty Images)*

PETE SEEGER Pete Seeger was one of several folk musicians who provided a link between the Popular Front-labor movement folk music of the 1930s and the folk revival of the 1960s. He is shown here in concert in 1966. *(Hulton/Archive/Getty Images)*

several times for participating in militant protests.

But it was not just the overt political messages of folk musicians that made them so important to young Americans in the 1960s. It was also that folk was a kind of music that seemed to reflect the "authenticity" that youth culture was attempting to find. In truth, neither the musicians themselves nor the young Americans attracted to them had much real connection with the traditions they were trying to evoke. The audiences for folk music—a product of rural and working-class traditions—were overwhelmingly urban, middle-class people. But the message of folk music—that there is a "real" America rooted in values of sharing and community, hidden beneath the crass commercialism of modern culture—resonated with the yearnings of many people in the 1960s (and beyond) for an alternative to their own troubled world. When young audiences responded to Woody Guthrie's famous ballad "This Land Is Your Land," they were expressing a hope for a different America—more democratic, more honest, and more natural than the land they knew.

unaffected; the North Vietnamese just kept moving the Ho Chi Minh Trail. Nor did the bombing weaken North Vietnam's will to continue fighting. On the contrary, it seemed to increase the nation's resolve and strengthen its hatred of the United States. As one North Vietnamese leader later explained: "There was extraordinary fervor then. The Americans thought that the more bombs they dropped, the quicker we would fall to our knees and surrender. But the bombs heightened rather than dampened our spirit."

Another crucial part of the American strategy was the "pacification" program, which was intended to push the

"Hearts and Minds"

Viet Cong from particular regions and then "pacify" those regions by winning the "hearts and minds" of the people. Routing the Viet Cong was often possible, but the subsequent pacification was more difficult. American forces were not adept at establishing the same kind of rapport with provincial Vietnamese that the Viet Cong had created; and the American military never gave that part of the program a very high priority in any case.

Gradually, the pacification program gave way to a more heavy-handed relocation strategy, through which American troops uprooted villagers from their homes, sent them fleeing to refugee camps or into the cities (producing by 1967 more than 3 million refugees), and then destroyed the vacated villages and surrounding countryside. Saturation bombings (using conventional weapons and such incendiary devices as napalm), bulldozing of settlements, chemical defoliation of fields and jungles—all were designed to eliminate possible Viet Cong sanctuaries. But the Viet Cong responded by moving to new sanctuaries elsewhere. The futility of the United States effort was suggested by the statement of an American officer after flattening one such hamlet that it had been "necessary to destroy [the village] in order to save it."

As the war dragged on and victory remained elusive, some American officers and officials began to urge the president to expand the military efforts. Some argued for heavier bombing and increased troop strength; others insisted that the United States attack communist enclaves in surrounding countries; a few began to urge the use of nuclear weapons. The Johnson administration, however, resisted. Unwilling to abandon its commitment to South Vietnam for fear of destroying American "credibility" in the world, the government was also unwilling to expand the war too far, for fear of provoking direct intervention by the Chinese, the Soviets, or both. In the meantime, the president began to encounter additional obstacles and frustrations at home.

The War at Home

As late as the end of 1965, few Americans, and even fewer influential ones, had protested the American involvement in Vietnam. But as the war dragged on and its futility began to become apparent, political support for it began to erode. A series of "teach-ins" on university campuses, beginning at the University of Michigan in 1965, sparked a national debate over the war before such debate developed inside the government itself. Such pacifist organizations as the American Friends Service Committee and the Women's International League for Peace and Freedom organized early protests. By the end of 1967, American students opposed to the war had become a significant political force. Enormous peace marches in New York, Washington, D.C., and other cities drew broad public attention to the antiwar movement. Opposition to the war had become a central issue in left-wing politics and in the culture of colleges and universities. It had penetrated popular cultures as well—most visibly in the rising popularity of folk musicians, many of whom actively opposed the war. In the meantime, a growing number of journalists, particularly reporters who had spent time in Vietnam, helped sustain the movement with their frank revelations about the brutality and apparent futility of the war. The growing chorus of popular protest soon began to stimulate opposition to the war from within the government.

Growing Opposition to the War

Senator J. William Fulbright of Arkansas, chairman of the powerful Senate Foreign Relations Committee, turned against the war and in January 1966 began to stage highly publicized and occasionally televised congressional hearings to air criticisms of it. Distinguished figures such as George F. Kennan and retired General James Gavin testified against the conflict, giving opposition to the war greater respectability in the minds of many Americans generally unwilling to question the government or the military. Other members of Congress joined Fulbright in opposing

Johnson's policies—including, in 1967, Robert F. Kennedy, brother of the slain president, now a senator from New York. Even within the administration, the consensus seemed to be crumbling. Robert McNamara, who had done much to help extend the American involvement in Vietnam, quietly left the government, disillusioned, in 1968. His successor as secretary of defense, Clark Clifford, became a quiet but powerful voice within the administration on behalf of a cautious scaling down of the commitment.

In the meantime, the American economy was beginning to suffer. Johnson's commitment to fighting the war while continuing his Great Society reforms—his promise of "guns and butter"—proved impossible to maintain. The inflation rate, which had remained at 2 percent through most of the early 1960s, rose to 3 percent in 1967, 4 percent in 1968, and 6 percent in 1969. In August 1967, Johnson asked Congress for a tax increase—a 10 percent surcharge that was widely labeled a "war tax"—which he knew was necessary if the nation was to avoid even more ruinous inflation. In return, congressional conservatives demanded and received a $6 billion reduction in the funding for Great Society programs.

War-Induced Inflation

THE TRAUMAS OF 1968

By the end of 1967, the twin crises of the war in Vietnam and the deteriorating racial situation at home—crises that fed upon and inflamed each other—had produced profound social and political tensions. In the course of 1968, those tensions seemed suddenly to burst to the surface and to threaten the nation with genuine chaos. Not since World War II had the United States experienced so profound a sense of crisis.

The Tet Offensive

On January 31, 1968, the first day of the Vietnamese New Year (Tet), communist forces launched an enormous, concerted attack on American strongholds throughout South Vietnam. A few cities, most notably Hue, fell to the communists—who, during their occupation of the city, rounded up large numbers of supporters of the Saigon regime and massacred them. Others suffered major disruptions.

Few Americans were aware of the events in Hue. But they did see vivid reports on television of communist forces in the heart of Saigon, setting off bombs, shooting down South Vietnamese officials and troops, and holding down fortified areas (including, briefly, the grounds of the American embassy). Such images shocked many Americans and proved devastating to popular support for the war. The Tet offensive suggested to the American public something of the brutality of the struggle in Vietnam. In the midst of the fighting, television cameras recorded the sight of a captured Viet Cong soldier being led up to a South Vietnamese officer in the streets of Saigon. Without a word, the officer pulled out his pistol and shot the young man in the head, leaving him lying dead in the street, his blood pouring onto the pavement. No single event, perhaps, did more to undermine support for the war in the United States.

American forces soon dislodged the Viet Cong from most of the positions they had seized, and the Tet offensive in the end cost the communists such appalling casualties that they were significantly weakened for months to come. Indeed, the Tet defeats permanently depleted the ranks of the NLF and forced North Vietnamese troops to take on a *Political and Psychological Defeat* much larger share of the subsequent fighting. But all that had little impact on American opinion. Tet may have been a military victory for the United States, but it was a political defeat for the administration, a defeat from which it would never fully recover.

In the following weeks, opposition to the war grew substantially. Leading newspapers and magazines, television commentators, and mainstream politicians began taking public stands in favor of de-escalation of the conflict. Within weeks of the Tet offensive, public opposition to the war had almost doubled. And Johnson's personal popularity rating had slid to 35 percent, the lowest of any president since Harry Truman.

The Political Challenge

Beginning in the summer of 1967, dissident Democrats (led by the talented activist Allard Lowenstein) tried to mobilize support behind an antiwar candidate who would challenge Lyndon Johnson in the 1968 primaries. When Robert Kennedy declined their invitation, they turned to Senator Eugene McCarthy of Minnesota. A brilliantly orchestrated campaign by Lowenstein and thousands of young volunteers in the New Hampshire primary produced a startling showing by McCarthy in March; he nearly defeated the president.

A few days later, Robert Kennedy finally entered the campaign, embittering many McCarthy supporters, but bringing his own substantial strength among blacks, the poor, and workers to the antiwar cause. Polls showed the president trailing badly in the next scheduled primary, in *Robert Kennedy* Wisconsin. Indeed, public animosity toward the president was now so intense that Johnson did not even dare leave the White House to campaign. On March 31, Johnson went on television to announce a limited halt in the bombing of North Vietnam—his first major concession to the antiwar forces—and, much more surprising, his withdrawal from the presidential contest.

For a moment, it seemed as though the antiwar forces had won. Robert Kennedy quickly established himself as the champion of the Democratic primaries, winning one election after another. In the meantime, however, Vice President Hubert Humphrey, with the support of President Johnson, entered the contest and began to attract the support of party leaders and of the many delegations that were selected not by popular primaries but by state party organizations. He soon appeared to be the front-runner in the race.

The King and Kennedy Assassinations

In the midst of this bitter political battle, in which the war had been the dominant issue, attention suddenly turned back to the nation's bitter racial conflicts. On April 4, Martin Luther King, Jr., who had traveled to Memphis, Tennessee, to lend his support to striking black sanitation workers in the city, was shot and killed while standing on the balcony of his motel. The assassin, James Earl Ray, who was captured days later in London and eventually convicted, had no apparent motive. Later evidence suggested that he had been hired by others to do the killing, but he himself has never revealed the identity of his employers.

King's tragic death produced an outpouring of grief matched in recent memory only by the reaction to the death of John Kennedy. Among American blacks, it also produced anger. In the days after the assassination, major riots *Riots* broke out in more than sixty American cities. Forty-three people died; more than 3,000 suffered injuries; as many as 27,000 people were arrested.

For two months following the death of King, Robert Kennedy continued his campaign for the presidential nomination. Late in the night of June 6, he appeared in the ballroom of a Los Angeles hotel to acknowledge his victory in that day's California primary. As he left the ballroom after his victory statement, Sirhan Sirhan, a young Palestinian apparently enraged by pro-Israeli remarks Kennedy had recently made, emerged from a crowd and shot him in the head. Early the next morning, Kennedy died.

By the time of his death, Robert Kennedy—who earlier in his career had been widely considered a cold, ruthless agent of his more appealing brother—had emerged as a figure of enormous popular appeal. More than John Kennedy, Robert identified his hopes with the American "underclass"—with blacks, Hispanics, Native Americans, the poor—and with the many American liberals who were coming to believe that the problems of such groups demanded attention. Indeed, Robert Kennedy, much more than John, shaped what some would later call the "Kennedy legacy," a set of ideas that would for a time become central to American liberalism: the fervent commitment to using government to help the powerless. In *The "Kennedy Legacy"* addition, Robert had an impassioned following among many people who saw in him (and his family) the kind of glamour and hopefulness they had come, at least in retrospect, to identify with the martyred president. His campaign appearances inspired outbursts of public enthusiasm rarely seen in political life. The passions Kennedy had aroused made his violent death a particularly shattering experience for many Americans.

The presidential campaign continued gloomily during the last weeks before the convention. Hubert Humphrey, who had seemed likely to win the nomination even before Robert Kennedy's death, now faced only minor

The year 1968 was one of the most turbulent in the postwar history of the United States. Much of what caused these upheavals were specifically American events—the growing controversy over the war in Vietnam, the assassinations of Martin Luther King, Jr., and Robert Kennedy, racial unrest across the nation's cities, student protests on campuses throughout America. But the turmoil of 1968 was not confined to the United States. There were tremendous upheavals in many parts of the world that year.

The most common form of turbulence around the world in 1968 was student unrest. In France, in May 1968, there was a student uprising that far exceeded in size and ferocity anything that occurred in the United States. It attracted the support of French workers, briefly paralyzed Paris and other cities, and contributed to the downfall of the government of Charles de Gaulle a year later. In England, Ireland, Germany, Italy, the Netherlands, Mexico, Canada, Japan, and South Korea, students and other young people also demonstrated in great numbers, and at times with some violence, against governments and universities and other structures

PRAGUE SPRING Czech demonstrators march through Wenceslaus Square in Prague following a radio address by their reform president, Alexander Dubcek, in August 1968. By this time, the great hopes awakened by Dubcek's reforms during the "Prague Spring" of several months ago had been crushed by Soviet pressure, including the arrival of Soviet tanks in the streets of Prague. These demonstrators are demanding the "brutal truth" from their leaders about the price Czechoslovakia paid to keep Dubcek in power. *(Bettmann/Corbis)*

opposition—despite the embittered claims of many Democrats that Humphrey would simply continue the bankrupt policies of the Johnson administration. The approaching Democratic Convention, therefore, began to take on the appearance of an exercise in futility; and antiwar activists, despairing of winning any victories within the convention, began to plan major demonstrations outside it.

When the Democrats finally gathered in Chicago in August, even the most optimistic observers were predicting a turbulent convention. Inside the hall, delegates bitterly debated an antiwar plank in the party platform that both Kennedy and McCarthy supporters favored. Miles away, in a downtown park, thousands of antiwar protesters were staging demonstrations. On the third night of the convention, as the delegates were beginning their balloting on the now virtually inevitable nomination of Hubert Humphrey, demonstrators and police clashed in a bloody riot in the streets of Chicago. Hundreds of protesters were injured as police attempted

Democratic National Convention

to disperse them with tear gas and billy clubs. Aware that the violence was being televised to the nation, the demonstrators taunted the authorities with the chant, "The whole world is watching!" And Hubert Humphrey, who had spent years dreaming of becoming his party's candidate for president, received a nomination that appeared at the time to be almost worthless.

The Conservative Response

The turbulent events of 1968 persuaded many observers that American society was in the throes of revolutionary change. In fact, however, the response of most Americans to the turmoil was a conservative one.

The most visible sign of the conservative backlash was the surprising success of the campaign of George Wallace for the presidency. Wallace had established himself in 1963 as one of the nation's leading spokesmen for the defense of segregation when, as governor of Alabama, he had attempted to block the admission of black students to

of authority. Elsewhere, 1968 created more widespread protest, as in Czechoslovakia, where hundreds of thousands of citizens took to the streets in support of what became known as "Prague spring"—a demand for greater democracy and a repudiation of many of the oppressive rules and structures imposed on the nation by its Soviet-dominated communist regimes—until Russian tanks rolled into the city to crush the uprising. For over thirty years, many people have tried to explain why so much instability emerged in so many nations at the same time.

One factor that contributed to the worldwide turbulence of 1968 was simple numbers. The postwar baby boom, which occurred in many nations, had created a very large age cohort that by the late 1960s was reaching adulthood. In western industrial nations, in particular, this rising generation was a powerful new social force. The sheer size of the new generation produced a tripling of the number of people attending colleges and universities in fewer than twenty years, and a heightened sense of the power of youth. The long period of postwar prosperity and relative peace in which this generation had grown up contributed to heightened expectations of what the world should offer them—and a greater level of impatience than previous generations had demonstrated with the obstacles that stood in the way of their hopes. A new global youth culture emerged that was in many ways at odds with the dominant culture of older generations. It valued nonconformity, personal freedom, and even rebellion.

A second force contributing to the widespread turbulence of 1968 was the power of global media. Satellite technology introduced in the early 1960s made it possible to transmit live news instantly across the world. Videotape technology and the creation of lightweight portable television cameras enabled media organizations to respond to events much more quickly and flexibly than in the past. And the audience for these televised images was by now global and enormous, particularly in industrial nations but even in the poorest areas of the world. Protests in one country were suddenly capable of inspiring protests in others. Demonstrators in Paris, for example, spoke openly of how campus protests in the United States in 1968—for ex- ample, the student uprising at Columbia University in New York—had helped motivate French students to rise up as well. Just as American students were protesting against what they considered the antiquated paternalistic features of their universities, French students demanded an end to the rigid, autocratic character of their own academic world.

In most parts of the world, the 1968 uprisings came and went without fundamentally altering the institutions and systems they were attacking. But many changes came in the wake of these protests. Universities around the globe undertook significant reforms. Religious observance in mainstream churches and synagogues in the West declined dramatically after 1968. New concepts of personal freedom gained legitimacy, helping to inspire new social movements in the years that followed—among them the dramatic growth of feminism in many parts of the world. The events of 1968 did not produce a revolution, in the United States or in most of the rest of the world, but they did help launch a period of dramatic social, cultural, and political change that affected the peoples of many nations.

the University of Alabama. In 1964, he had run in a few Democratic presidential primaries and had done surprisingly well, even in several states *George Wallace* outside the South. In 1968, he became a third-party candidate for president, basing his campaign on a host of conservative grievances, not all of them connected to race. He denounced the forced busing of students, the proliferation of government regulations and social programs, and the permissiveness of authorities toward race riots and antiwar demonstrations. There was never any serious chance that Wallace would win the election; but his standing in the polls at times rose to over 20 percent.

A more effective effort to mobilize the "silent majority" in favor of order and stability was under way within the Republican Party. Richard Nixon, whose political career had seemed at an end after his losses in the presidential race of 1960 and a California gubernatorial campaign two years later, reemerged as the preeminent spokesman for what he called "Middle America." Nixon recognized that many Americans were tired of hearing about their obligations to the poor, tired of hearing about the sacrifices necessary to achieve racial justice, tired of judicial reforms that seemed designed to help criminals. By offering a vision of stability, law and order, government retrenchment, and "peace with honor" in Vietnam, he easily captured the Republican presidential nomination. And after the spectacle of the Democratic Convention, he enjoyed a commanding lead in the polls as the November election approached.

That lead diminished greatly in the last weeks before the voting. Old doubts about Nixon's character continued to haunt the Republican candidate. A skillful last-minute surge by Hubert Humphrey, who managed to restore a tenuous unity to the Democratic Party, narrowed the gap further. And the Wallace campaign appeared to be hurting the Republicans more than the Democrats. In the end, however, Nixon eked out a victory almost as narrow as his defeat in 1960. He received 43.4 percent of the popular vote to Humphrey's 42.7 percent (a margin of only about 500,000 *Nixon Victorious*

CHICAGO, 1968 Demonstrators climb on a statue in a Chicago park during the 1968 Democratic National Convention, protesting both the Vietnam War and the harsh treatment they themselves had received from Mayor Richard Daley's Chicago police. *(Dennis Brack/Black Star)*

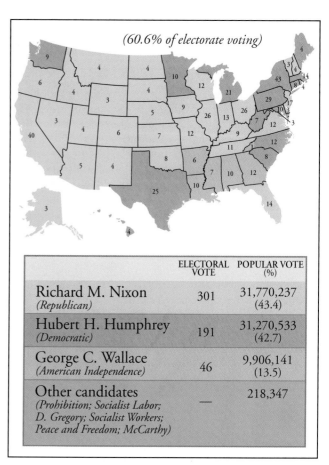

(60.6% of electorate voting)

	ELECTORAL VOTE	POPULAR VOTE (%)
Richard M. Nixon *(Republican)*	301	31,770,237 (43.4)
Hubert H. Humphrey *(Democratic)*	191	31,270,533 (42.7)
George C. Wallace *(American Independence)*	46	9,906,141 (13.5)
Other candidates *(Prohibition; Socialist Labor; D. Gregory; Socialist Workers; Peace and Freedom; McCarthy)*	—	218,347

THE ELECTION OF 1968 The 1968 presidential election, which Richard Nixon won, was almost as close as the election of 1960, which he lost. Nixon might have won a more substantial victory had it not been for the independent candidacy of Governor George C. Wallace, who attracted many of the same conservative voters to whom Nixon appealed. ◆ *How does the distribution of Democratic and Republican strength in this election compare to that in 1960?*

 For an interactive version of this map go to www.mhhe.com/brinkley11ch31maps

votes), and 301 electoral votes to Humphrey's 191. George Wallace, who like most third-party candidates faded in the last weeks of the campaign, still managed to poll 13.5 percent of the popular vote and to carry five southern states with a total of 46 electoral ballots—the best showing by a third-party candidate since the 1920s. Nixon had not won a decisive personal mandate. But the election made clear that a majority of the American electorate was more interested in restoring stability than in promoting social change.

CONCLUSION

No decade of the twentieth century has created more powerful and enduring images than the 1960s. It began with the election—and then the traumatic assassination— of an attractive and energetic young president, John Kennedy, who captured the imagination of millions and seemed to symbolize the rising idealism of the time. It produced a dramatic period of political innovation, christened the "Great Society" by President Lyndon Johnson, which greatly expanded the size and functions of the federal government and its responsibility for the welfare of the nation's citizens. It saw the emergence of a sustained, national, and enormously powerful civil rights movement that won a series of important legal victories, including two civil rights acts that dismantled the Jim Crow system so painstakingly constructed in the late nineteenth and early twentieth centuries.

The very spirit of dynamism and optimism that shaped the early 1960s also helped bring to the surface problems and grievances that had no easy solutions. The civil rights movement ended legalized segregation and disfranchisement, but it also awakened expectations of social and economic equality that laws alone could not meet and that remained in many respects unfulfilled. The peaceful, interracial crusade of the early 1960s gradually turned into a much more militant, confrontational, divided, and increasingly separatist movement toward the decade's end. The idealism among white youths that began the 1960s, and played an important role in the political success of John Kennedy, evolved into an angry rebellion against many aspects of American culture and politics and produced a large upsurge of student protest that rocked the nation at the decade's end. Perhaps most of all, a small and largely unnoticed Cold War commitment to defend South Vietnam against communist aggression from the north led to a large and disastrous American military commitment that destroyed the presidency of Lyndon Johnson, shook the faith of millions in their leaders and their political system, sent thousands of young American men to their deaths, and showed no signs of producing a victory. A decade that began with high hopes and soaring ideals ended with ugly and at times violent division, and deep disillusionment.

FOR FURTHER REFERENCE

Allen J. Matusow, *The Unraveling of America: A History of Liberalism in the 1960s* (1984) is a provocative history of this turbulent decade. David Farber, *The Age of Great Dreams: America in the 1960s* (1994) is an intelligent and lively general history. Arthur M. Schlesinger, Jr., *A Thousand Days* (1965) is a celebrated and celebratory memoir of the Kennedy years. Garry Wills, *The Kennedy Imprisonment* (1982) is an important demystification. Robert Dallek, *Lone Star Rising: Lyndon Johnson and His Times, 1908–1960* (1991) and *Flawed Giant: Lyndon B. Johnson, 1960–1973* (1998) are an important biography. Robert Weisbrot, *Freedom Bound: A History of America's Civil Rights Movement* (1990) is a good synthetic history of the movement. John Dittmer, *Local People: The Struggle for Civil Rights in Mississippi* (1994) is an excellent study of the grass-roots origins of the movement. William Chafe, *Civilities and Civil Rights: Greensboro, North Carolina, and the Black Struggle for Freedom* (1980) is an excellent study of the southern civil rights movement and the white reaction to it. Taylor Branch, *Parting the Waters: America in the King Years, 1959–1963* (1988) and *Pillar of Fire: America in the King Years, 1963–1965* are good narrative histories of the movement (1998). Nicholas Lemann, *The Promised Land: The Great Black Migration and How It Changed America* (1991) is a challenging study of the postwar African-American migration to northern cities and of the Great Society's response to it. Graham T. Allison, *The Essence of Decision: Explaining the Cuban Missile Crisis* (1971) is an important interpretation of the greatest crisis of the Cold War. Ernest R. May and Philip D. Zelikow, *The Kennedy Tapes: Inside the White House During the Cuban Missile Crisis* (1997) provides the annotated transcripts of the taped meetings of Kennedy's inner circle during the crisis. Robert D. Schulzinger, *A Time for War: The United States and Vietnam, 1945–1975* (1997) is a good general history of the war. Neil Sheehan, *A Bright Shining Lie: John Paul Vann and America in Vietnam* (1988) is a compelling picture of the war as experienced by a significant military figure of the 1960s. Christian J. Appy, *Working-Class War: American Combat Soldiers and Vietnam* (1993) examines the class basis of the army that fought in Vietnam. Larry Berman, *Planning a Tragedy* (1982) and *Lyndon Johnson's War* (1989); Leslie Gelb and Richard Betts, *The Irony of Vietnam: The System Worked* (1979); and David Halberstam, *The Best and the Brightest* (1972) are important interpretations of the American decision to intervene and stay in Vietnam. Dan T. Carter, *The Politics of Rage: George Wallace, The Origins of the New Conservatism, and the Transformation of American Politics* (1995) is a good study of the career of George Wallace. David Farber, *Chicago '68* (1988) examines the turbulent Democratic Convention and, through it, the passions that shaped a traumatic year in recent American history.

Berkeley in the Sixties (1990) is a documentary film portraying the tumultuous student politics at the University of California, Berkeley, and through them larger themes of the decade. *Eyes on the Prize: The American Civil Rights Struggle, 1954–1965* (1986–1987) is a six-part film series by Blackside Productions on the history of the civil rights movement. *Malcolm X: Make It Plain* (1994) is the definitive film biography of Malcolm X. *The Kennedys* (1992) is a film presentation of the lives of President John F. Kennedy and various members of his powerful family. *LBJ* (1991), a film by David Grubin, is a biographical treatment of President Lyndon Johnson. *America's War on Poverty* (1995) is a five-part series on the Kennedy and Johnson administrations' most dramatic welfare initiative.

For quizzes, Internet resources, references to additional books and films, and more, consult this book's Online Learning Center at www.mhhe.com/brinkley11.

THIRTY-FIVE CENTS

TIME
THE WEEKLY NEWSMAGAZINE

JANUARY 29, 1965

Today's Teen-Agers

VOL. 85 NO. 5
(REG. U.S. PAT. OFF.)

"TODAY'S TEENAGERS" The coming of age of the "baby-boom" generation, and the rise of youthful activism, led *Time* magazine to devote a 1965 cover story to "Today's Teen-Agers." As notable as the choice of subject was the choice of artist for the cover image: Andy Warhol, the great pop artist whose serial portraits of both famous and unknown people helped define his era. Warhol's work was instrumental in breaking down barriers between serious art and popular culture, both in its subject matter (celebrities, commercial products) and in its techniques, which drew heavily from commercial art. This series of silk-screened photographs made use of one of his trademark media. *(TIME Magazine, copyright TIME Inc.)*

Significant Events

1961 · Representatives of sixty-seven tribes draft
Declaration of Indian Purpose

1962 · Students for a Democratic Society formed at Port
Huron, Michigan
· Supreme Court decides *Baker v. Carr*

1963 · Betty Friedan publishes *The Feminine Mystique*

1964 · Free Speech Movement begins at UC Berkeley
· Beatles come to America

1965 · United Farm Workers strike

1966 · National Organization for Women (NOW) formed
· *Miranda* v. *Arizona* expands rights of criminal suspects

1967 · Antiwar protesters march on Pentagon
· Israel and Arabs clash in Six-Day War

1968 · Campus riots break out at Columbia University and
elsewhere
· Antiwar "mobilization" day

· American Indian Movement (AIM) launched

1969 · Antiwar movement stages Vietnam "moratorium"
· Theodore Roszak publishes *The Making of a
Counter Culture*
· People's Park uprising at Berkeley
· Nixon orders secret bombing of Cambodia
· Nixon begins withdrawing American troops from
Vietnam
· "Stonewall Riot" in New York City launches gay
liberation movement
· 400,000 people attend rock concert in Woodstock, N.Y.

1970 · American troops enter Cambodia
· Antiwar protests increase
· Students killed at Kent State and Jackson State
universities
· Palestinians expelled from Jordan
· Charles Reich publishes *The Greening of America*

CHAPTER THIRTY-TWO

THE CRISIS OF AUTHORITY

Richard Nixon's election in 1968 was the result of more than the unpopularity of Lyndon Johnson and the war. It was the result, too, of a strong popular reaction against what many Americans considered a frontal assault on the foundations of their culture. Throughout the late 1960s and early 1970s, new interest groups were mobilizing to demand protections and benefits. New values and assumptions were emerging to challenge traditional patterns of thought and behavior. The United States was in the throes, some believed, of a cultural revolution. Some Americans welcomed the changes. But the 1968 election returns suggested that more feared them. There was growing resentment against the attention directed toward minorities and the poor, against the federal social programs that were funneling billions of dollars into the inner cities to help the poor and unemployed, against the increasing tax burden on the middle class, against the "hippies" and radicals who were dominating public discourse with their bitter critiques of values many middle-class Americans held dear. It was time, their critics believed, for a restoration of stability and a relegitimation of traditional centers of authority.

In Richard Nixon they found a man who seemed perfectly to match their mood. Himself a product of a hardworking, middle-class family, he had risen to prominence on the basis of his own unrelenting efforts, and he projected an image of stern dedication to traditional values. Yet the presidency of Richard Nixon, far from returning calm and stability to American politics, coincided with, and in many ways helped to produce, more years of crisis.

THE YOUTH CULTURE

Perhaps most alarming to conservative Americans in the 1960s and 1970s was a pattern of social and cultural protest that was emerging from younger Americans, who were giving vent to two related impulses. One was the impulse, originating with the political left, to create a great new community of "the people," which would rise up to break the power of elites and force the nation to end the war, pursue racial and economic justice, and transform its political life. The other at least equally powerful impulse was related to, but not entirely compatible with, the first: the vision of "liberation." It found expression, in part, through the efforts

"Liberation"

of particular groups—African Americans, Native Americans, Hispanics, women, gays and lesbians, and others—to define and assert themselves and make demands on the larger society. It also found expression through the efforts of individuals to create a new culture—one that would allow them to escape from what they considered the dehumanizing pressures of what some called the modern "technocracy."

The New Left

In retrospect, it seems unsurprising that young Americans became so assertive and powerful in American culture and politics in the 1960s. The postwar baby-boom generation, the unprecedented number of people born in a few years just after World War II, was growing up. By 1970, more than half the American population was under thirty years old; more than 8 million Americans—eight times the number in 1950—were attending college. This was the largest generation of youth in American history, and it was coming to maturity in a time of unprecedented affluence, opportunity, and—for many—frustration. Relatively few of these young people embraced radical political causes or rebelled in any fundamental way against their culture. But those who did were numerous enough, and assertive enough, to have a disproportionate impact on both the cultural and the political climate.

One of the most visible results of the increasingly assertive youth movement was a radicalization of many American college and university students, who in the course of the 1960s formed what became known as the New Left—a large, diverse group of men and women energized by the polarizing developments of their time to challenge the political system. The New Left embraced the cause of African Americans and other minorities, but its own ranks consisted overwhelmingly of white people. Blacks and minorities formed political movements of their own.

The New Left drew from many sources. Some of its members were the children of radical parents (members of the

Sources of the New Left

so-called Old Left of the 1930s and 1940s), and had grown up with a critical view of society and politics. Indeed, the New Left drew considerable support, and guidance, from groups and individuals from the Old Left; it was not as entirely "new" as its champions liked to claim. The New Left drew as well from the writings of some of the important social critics of the 1950s—among them C. Wright Mills, a sociologist at Columbia University who wrote a series of scathing and brilliant critiques of modern bureaucracies.

Relatively few members of the New Left were communists, but many were drawn to the writings of Karl Marx and of contemporary Marxist theorists. Some came to revere Third World Marxists such as Che Guevara, the South American revolutionary and guerrilla leader; Mao Zedong; and Ho Chi Minh. For a while, left-leaning figures in the labor movement helped nurture the New Left—although relations between the two movements soon deteriorated beyond repair over the New Left's unwillingness to embrace the anticommunism of the AFL-CIO.

The New Left drew its inspiration above all from the civil rights movement, in which many idealistic young white Americans had become involved in the early 1960s. Racism, oppression, and violence were nothing new to the many African Americans fighting for civil rights. But to white college students from middle-class backgrounds, the exposure to social injustice (and, for some, personal danger) in the South was shocking and disillusioning, and it led many of them to question their assumptions about the basic values and institutions of American life. Within a few years, some white civil rights activists were beginning to consider broader political commitments.

In 1962, a group of students, most of them from prestigious universities, gathered in Michigan (at a conference center owned by the United Auto Workers) to form an organization to give voice to their demands: Students for a

SDS

Democratic Society (SDS). Their declaration of beliefs, the Port Huron Statement, expressed their disillusionment with the society they had inherited and their determination to build a new politics. "Many of us began maturing in complacency," the statement (most of it the work of student activist Tom Hayden) declared. "As we grew, however, our comfort was penetrated by events too troubling to dismiss." In the following years, SDS became the principal organization of student radicalism.

Some members of SDS moved into inner-city neighborhoods and tried for a time, without notable success, to mobilize poor, working-class people politically. But most members of the New Left were students, and their radicalism centered for a time on issues related to the modern university. A 1964 dispute at the University of California at Berkeley over the rights of students to engage in political activities on campus gained national attention. The Free Speech Movement, as it called itself, created turmoil at Berke-

Free Speech Movement

ley as students challenged campus police, occupied administrative offices, and produced a strike in which nearly three quarters of the Berkeley students participated. The immediate issue was the right of students to pass out literature and recruit volunteers for political causes on campus. But the protest quickly became as well an expression of a more basic critique of the university, and the society it seemed to represent. Mario Savio, a Berkeley graduate student and one of the leaders of the Free Speech Movement, captured something of the political anguish in a famous speech on campus, in which he said:

> There is a time when the operation of the machine becomes so odious, makes you so sick at heart, that you can't take part; you can't even passively take part, and you've got to put your bodies upon the gears and upon the wheels, upon the levers, upon all the apparatus and you've got to make it stop. And you've got to indicate to the people who run it, to the people who own it, that unless you're free, the machine will be prevented from working at all.

The revolt at Berkeley was the first outburst of what was to be nearly a decade of campus turmoil. Students at Berkeley and elsewhere protested the impersonal character of the modern university, and they denounced the role of educational institutions in sustaining what they considered corrupt or immoral public policies. The antiwar movement greatly inflamed and expanded the challenge to the universities; and beginning in 1968, campus demonstrations, riots, and building seizures became almost commonplace. At Columbia University in New York, students seized the offices of the president and other members of the administration and occupied them for days

until local police forcibly ejected them. Harvard University had a similar, and even more violent, experience a year later.

Also in 1969, Berkeley became the scene of perhaps the most prolonged and traumatic conflict of any American college campus in the 1960s: a battle over the efforts of a few students to build a "People's Park" on a vacant lot the university planned to use to build a parking garage. This seemingly minor event precipitated weeks of impassioned and often violent conflicts between the university administration, which sought to evict the intruders from the land, and the students, many of whom supported the advocates of the park and who saw the university's efforts to close it as a symbol of the struggle between liberation and oppression.

By the end of the People's Park battle, which lasted for more than a week, the Berkeley campus was completely polarized; even students who had not initially supported or even noticed the People's Park (the great majority) were, *People's Park* by the end, committed to its defense; 85 percent of the 15,000 students voted in a referendum to leave the park alone. Student radicals were, for the first time, winning large audiences for their extravagant rhetoric linking together university administrators, the police, and the larger political and economic system, describing them all as part of one united, oppressive force. As one Berkeley activist said in the midst of the battle: "You've pushed us to the end of your civilization here, against the sea in Berkeley.

BERKELEY, 1969 The People's Park controversy at the University of California at Berkeley turned the campus and the town into something close to a war zone. In this photograph, National Guardsmen with fixed bayonets stand in the way of a planned march to protest the closing of People's Park on May 30, 1969, more than two weeks after they first arrived to keep peace in Berkeley. *(AP/Wide World Photos)*

While folk music often expressed the ideals of young people in the 1960s, rock music expressed their desires. The rock music of the late 1960s and 1970s, even more than the rock 'n' roll of the 1950s and early 1960s, emphasized release. It gave vent to impulse and instinct, to physical and emotional (as opposed to intellectual) urges. That was one reason why it was so enormously popular among young people in an age of cultural and sexual revolution. It was also why it seemed so menacing and dangerous to many more conservative Americans seeking to defend more traditional values and behavior.

Rock in the late 1960s seemed simultaneously subversive and liberating. That was partly because of the behavior and lifestyles of rock musicians. They were no longer clean-cut young men wearing red blazers, as many rock performers had been in the 1950s, but men and women whose appearance and behavior was often deliberately outrageous. Rock musicians were connected at times to the drug culture of the 1960s (especially through the so-called psychedelic-rock groups inspired by experiences with the hallucinogen LSD). They had links to mystical eastern religions (most notably the Beatles, who had spent time in India studying Transcendental Meditation and who, beginning in 1967 with their album *Sergeant Pepper's Lonely Hearts Club Band,* incorporated those themes into their music). And they often reveled in flouting social conventions, beginning with the Rolling Stones and culminating, perhaps, in the extreme and self-destructive

ADVERTISING WOODSTOCK Even before the thousands of spectators gathered for the famous rock concert at Woodstock in 1969, organizers envisioned it as something more than a performance. It would, this poster claims, be a search for peace as well as for music. *(Hulton/Archive/Getty Images)*

behavior of Jimi Hendrix, Jim Morrison, and Janis Joplin, all of whom died very young of drug-related causes.

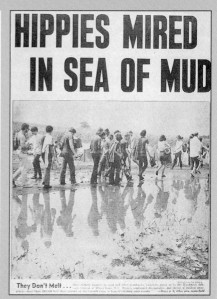

REPORTING WOODSTOCK The *New York Daily News,* whose largely working-class readership was not notably sympathetic toward the young people at Woodstock, ran this slightly derisive front-page story on the concert as heavy rains turned the concert site into a sea of mud. ["They Don't Melt," the caption said.] *(Hulton/Archive/Getty Images)*

Late Sixties rock was among many expressions of the impulses that came to be known as the counterculture; and like the counterculture itself, it inspired widely varying reactions. To its defenders, the new rock, with its emphasis on emotional release, was a healthy rebuke to the repressive norms of mainstream culture. To them, its virtues were symbolized by the great rock festival at Woodstock, New York, in August 1969, where over 400,000 young people gathered on a

Then you pushed us into a square-block area called People's Park. It was the last thing we had to defend, this square block of sanity amid all your madness. . . . We are now homeless in your civilized world. We have become the great American gypsies, with only our mythology for a culture." Over the next several years, hardly any major university was immune to some level of disruption.

Most campus radicals were rarely if ever violent (except at times in their rhetoric). But the image of student radicalism in mainstream culture was one of chaos and disorder, based in part on the disruptive actions of relatively small groups of militants. As time went on, moreover, the

student fringe groups became increasingly militant. Small numbers of especially dogmatic radicals—among them the "Weathermen," a violent offshoot of SDS—were responsible for a few cases of arson and bombing that destroyed campus buildings and claimed several lives. Not many people, not even many students, ever accepted the radical political views that lay at the heart of the New Left. But many supported the position of SDS and other groups on particular issues, and above all on the Vietnam War. Student activists tried to drive out training programs for military officers (ROTC) and bar military recruiters from college campuses. They attacked the laboratories and corporations

remote piece of farmland for several days to hear performances by such artists as the Who, Jimi Hendrix, the Grateful Dead, Janis Joplin, Joe Cocker, the Jefferson Airplane, and many others. The festival was marred by heavy rains that produced a sea of mud, and by supplies and facilities completely inadequate for the unexpectedly large crowd. Drugs were everywhere in evidence, as was a kind of open sexual freedom that a decade earlier would have seemed unthinkable to all but a few Americans. But Woodstock remained through it all peaceful, friendly, and harmonious. There was rhapsodic talk at the time of how Woodstock represented the birth of a new youth culture, the "Woodstock nation."

Critics of the new rock, and the counterculture with which they associated it, were less impressed with the idea of the "Woodstock nation." To them, the essence of the counterculture was a kind of numbing hopelessness and despair, with a menacing and violent underside. To them, the appropriate symbol was not Woodstock, but another great rock concert, which more than 300,000 people attended only four months after Woodstock, at the Altamont Speedway east of San Francisco. The concert featured many of the groups that had been at Woodstock, but the Rolling Stones, who had organized the event, were the main attraction. As at Woodstock, drugs were plentiful and sexual exhibitionism was frequent. But unlike Woodstock, Altamont was far from peaceful. Instead, it became ugly, brutal, and vio-

ALTAMONT Hell's Angels "security guards" club a spectator near the stage during the rock concert at Altamont as other concertgoers—some curious, some aghast—watch. One spectator died as a result of the beatings. *(Photofest)*

lent, and resulted in the deaths of four people. Several of them died accidentally, one, for example, from a bad drug trip, during which he fell into a stream and drowned. But numerous people were brutally beaten by members of the Hell's Angels motorcycle gang, who had been hired by the Rolling Stones as security guards. One man was beaten and stabbed to death immediately in front of the stage while the Stones were playing "Sympathy for the Devil."

Woodstock and Altamont, then, became symbols of two aspects of the counterculture of the late 1960s and early 1970s, and of the rock music that created its anthems. The Beat poet Allen Ginsberg wrote an ecstatic poem proclaiming that at Woodstock "a new kind of man has come to his bliss/to

end the cold war he has borne/against his own kind of flesh." The festival and its music, many claimed, had shown the path to an age of love and peace and justice. Altamont, however, suggested a dark underside of the rock culture, its potential for destruction and violence. "As far as I was concerned," one participant said, "Altamont was the death knell of all those things that we thought would last forever. I personally felt like the sixties had been an extravagant stage show and I had been a spectator in the audience. Altamont had rung down the curtain to no applause."*

*Allen Ginsberg's estate is affiliated with the Naropa Institute, Boulder, CO.

that were producing weapons for the war. And between 1967 and 1969, they organized some of the largest political demonstrations in American history. The October 1967 march on the Pentagon, where demonstrators were met by a solid line of armed troops; the "spring mobilization" of April 1968, which attracted hundreds of thousands of demonstrators in cities around the country; the Vietnam "moratorium" of the fall of 1969, during which millions of opponents of the war gathered in major rallies across the nation; and countless other demonstrations, large and small—all helped thrust the issue of the war into the center of American politics.

Closely related to opposition to the war—and another issue that helped fuel the New Left—was opposition to the military draft. The gradual abolition of many traditional deferments—for graduate students, teachers, husbands, fathers, and others—swelled the ranks of those faced with conscription (and thus of those likely to oppose it). Draft card burnings became common features of antiwar rallies on college campuses. Many draft-age Americans simply refused induction, accepting what occasionally were long terms in jail as a result. Thousands of others fled to Canada, Sweden, and elsewhere (where they were joined by many deserters from the armed forces) to escape conscription.

Not until 1977, when President Jimmy Carter issued a general pardon to draft resisters and a far more limited amnesty for deserters, did the Vietnam exiles begin to return to the country in substantial numbers.

The Counterculture

Closely related to the New Left was a new youth culture openly scornful of the values and conventions of middle-class society. The most visible characteristic of the counterculture, as it became known, was a change in lifestyle. As if to display their contempt for conventional standards, young Americans flaunted long *"Hippies"* hair, shabby or flamboyant clothing, and a rebellious disdain for traditional speech and decorum, which they replaced with their own "hippie" idiom. Also central to the counterculture were drugs: marijuana smoking—which after 1966 became almost as common a youthful diversion as beer drinking—and the less widespread but still substantial use of other, more potent hallucinogens, such as LSD.

There was also a new, more permissive view of sexual behavior—the beginnings of what came to be known as a sexual revolution. To some degree, the emergence of more relaxed approaches to sexuality was a result less of the counterculture than of the new accessibility of effective contraceptives, most notably the birth-control pill and, after 1973, legalized abortion. Fear of unwanted pregnancy, a powerful force inhibiting female sexuality, declined. But the new sexuality also reflected the counterculture's belief that individuals should strive for release from inhibitions and give vent to their instincts—including the instinct for sensual pleasure.

The counterculture's rejection of traditional values and its open embrace of sensual pleasure sometimes masked its philosophy, which offered a fundamental challenge to the American middle-class mainstream. Like the New Left, with which it in many ways overlapped, the counterculture challenged the structure of modern American society, attacking its banality, its hollowness, its artificiality, its materialism, its isolation from nature. The most committed adherents of the counterculture—the *Haight-Ashbury* hippies, who came to dominate the Haight-Ashbury neighborhood of San Francisco and other places, and the social dropouts, many of whom retreated to rural communes—rejected modern society altogether and attempted to find refuge in a simpler, more "natural" existence. But even those whose commitment to the counterculture was less dramatic shared a commitment to the idea of personal fulfillment through rejecting the inhibitions and conventions of middle-class culture. In a corrupt and alienating society, the new creed seemed to suggest, the first responsibility of the individual is cultivation of the self, the unleashing of one's own full potential for pleasure and fulfillment.

Theodore Roszak, whose book *The Making of a Counter Culture* (1969) became a significant document of the era, captured much of the spirit of the movement in his frank admission that "the primary project of our counterculture is to proclaim a new heaven and a new earth so vast, so marvelous that the inordinate claims of technical expertise must of necessity withdraw to a subordinate and marginal status in the lives of men." Charles Reich's *The Greening of America* (1970) created a short-lived sensation with its argument that the individual should strive for a new form of consciousness—"Consciousness III," as he called it—in which the self would be the only reality. The effects of the counterculture reached out to the larger society and helped create a new set of social norms that many young people (and some adults) chose to imitate. Long hair and freakish clothing became the badge not only of hippies and radicals but of an entire generation. The use of marijuana, the freer attitudes toward sex, the iconoclastic (and sometimes obscene) language—all spread far beyond the realm of the true devotees of the counterculture. And perhaps the most pervasive element of the new youth society was one that even the least radical members of the generation embraced: rock music.

Rock 'n' roll first achieved wide popularity in the 1950s, on the strength of such early performers as Buddy Holly and, above all, Elvis Presley. Early in the 1960s, its influence began to spread, a result in large part of the phenomenal popularity of the Beatles, the English group whose first visit to the United States in 1964 created a remarkable sensation, "Beatlemania." For a time, most rock musicians—like most popular musicians before them— *Growing Influence of Rock 'n' Roll* concentrated largely on uncontroversial, romantic themes. One of the first great hits of the Beatles was a song with the innocuous title "I Want to Hold Your Hand." By the late 1960s, however, rock had begun to reflect many of the new iconoclastic values of its time. The Beatles, for example, abandoned their once simple and seemingly innocent style for a new, experimental, even mystical approach that reflected the growing popular fascination with drugs and Eastern religions. Other groups, such as the Rolling Stones, turned even more openly to themes of anger, frustration, and rebelliousness. Many popular musicians used their music to express explicit political radicalism as well—especially some of the leading folk singers of the era, such as Bob Dylan and Joan Baez. Rock's driving rhythms, its undisguised sensuality, its often harsh and angry tone—all made it an appropriate vehicle for expressing the themes of the social and political unrest of the late 1960s. A powerful symbol of the fusion of rock music and the counterculture was the great music festival at Woodstock, New York, in the summer of 1969. (See "Patterns of Popular Culture," pp. 862–863.)

Virtually no Americans could avoid seeing how rapidly the norms of their society were changing in the late

WOODSTOCK In the summer of 1969, more than 400,000 people gathered for a rock concert on a farm near Woodstock, New York. Despite mostly terrible weather, the gathering was remarkably peaceful—sparking rapturous talk among some enthusiasts of the new youth culture about the "Woodstock nation." *(Shelly Rustin/Black Star)*

1960s. Those who attended movies saw a gradual disappearance of the banal, conventional messages that had dominated films since the 1920s. Instead, they saw explorations of political issues, of new sexual mores, of violence, of social conflict. Television too began to turn (even if more slowly than the other media) to programming that reflected social and cultural conflict—as exemplified by the enormously popular *All in the Family,* whose protagonist, Archie Bunker, was a lower-middle-class bigot.

THE MOBILIZATION OF MINORITIES

The growth of African-American protest, and of a significant white response to it, both preceded the political and cultural upheavals of the 1960s and helped produce them. It also encouraged other minorities to assert themselves and demand redress of their grievances. For Native Americans, Hispanic Americans, gay men and women, and others, the late 1960s and the 1970s were a time of growing self-expression and political activism.

Seeds of Indian Militancy

Few minorities had deeper or more justifiable grievances against the prevailing culture than American Indians—or Native Americans, as some began to call themselves in the 1960s. Indians were the least prosperous, least healthy, and least stable group in the nation. They were also one of the smallest. They constituted less than one percent of the population. Average annual family income for Indians was $1,000 less than that for blacks. The Native American unemployment rate was ten times the national rate. Joblessness was particularly high on the reservations, where nearly half the Indians lived. But even most Indians living in cities suffered from their limited education and training and could find only menial jobs. Life expectancy among Indians was more than twenty years less than the national average. Suicides among Indian youths were a hundred times more frequent than among white youths. And while black Americans attracted the attention (for good or for ill) of many whites, Indians for many years remained largely ignored.

Native American Grievances

For much of the postwar era, and particularly after the resignation of John Collier as commissioner of Indian Affairs in 1946, federal policy toward the tribes had been shaped by a determination to incorporate Indians into mainstream American society, whether Indians wanted to assimilate or not. Two laws passed in 1953 established the basis of a new policy, which became known as "termination." Through termination, the federal government withdrew all official recognition of the tribes as legal entities, administratively separate from state governments, and made them subject to the same local jurisdictions as white residents. At the same time, the government encouraged Indians to assimilate into the larger society and worked to funnel Native Americans into cities, where, presumably, they would adapt themselves to the white world and lose their cultural distinctiveness.

To some degree, the termination and assimilation policies achieved their objectives. The tribes grew weaker as legal and political entities. Many Native Americans adapted to life in the cities, at least to a degree. On the whole, however, the new policies were a disaster for the

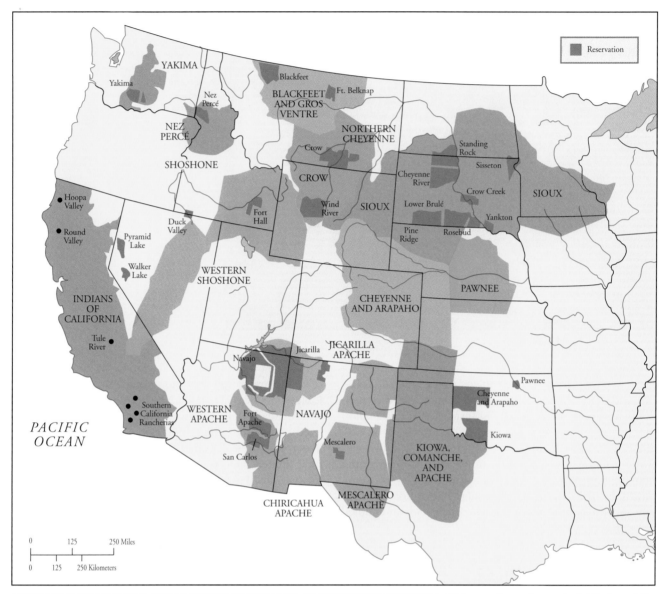

ABORIGINAL TERRITORIES AND MODERN RESERVATIONS OF WESTERN INDIAN TRIBES This map shows the rough distribution of the Native American population in the western United States before the establishment of reservations by the federal government in the nineteenth century. The large shaded regions in colors other than yellow represent the areas in which the various tribes were dominant a century and more ago. The blue shaded areas show the much smaller areas set aside for them as reservations after the Indian wars of the late nineteenth century. ◆ *What impact did life on the reservations have on the rise of Indian activism in the 1960s and 1970s?*

tribes and a failure for the reformers who had promoted them. Termination led to widespread corruption and abuse. And Indians themselves fought so bitterly against it that in 1958 the Eisenhower administration barred further "terminations" without the consent of the affected tribes. In the meantime, the struggle against termination had mobilized a new generation of Indian militants and had breathed life into the principal Native American organization, the National Congress of American Indians (NCAI), which had been created in 1944.

Failure of "Termination"

The Democratic administrations of the 1960s, though they did not disavow the termination policy, made no

effort to revive it. Instead, they made modest efforts to restore at least some degree of tribal autonomy. The funneling of war on poverty money to tribal organizations through the community-action program was one prominent example. In the meantime, the tribes themselves were beginning to fight for self-determination—partly because of the inspiration they drew from the black civil rights movement and partly in response to other social and cultural changes (among them, the expanding mobility and rising educational levels of younger Indians, who were becoming more aware of the world around them and of their own anomalous place within it). The new militancy also benefited from the rapid increase in the Indian population, which was growing much faster than that of the rest of the nation (nearly doubling between 1950 and 1970, to a total of about 800,000).

The Indian Civil Rights Movement

In 1961, more than 400 members of 67 tribes gathered in Chicago to discuss ways of bringing all Indians together in an effort to redress common wrongs. The manifesto they issued, the Declaration of Indian Purpose, stressed the "right to choose our own way of life." The 1961 meeting was only one example of a growing Indian self-consciousness. Indians and others began writing books (for example, Vine Deloria, Jr.'s *Custer Died for Your Sins* and Dee Brown's *Bury My Heart at Wounded Knee*) and otherwise drawing renewed attention to the wrongs inflicted on the tribes by white people in past generations. One result was a gradual change in the way popular culture depicted Indians. By the 1970s, almost no films or television westerns any longer portrayed Indians as brutal savages attacking peaceful white people. And Indian activists even persuaded some white institutions to abandon what they considered demeaning references to them; Dartmouth College, for example, ceased referring to its athletic teams as the "Indians." The National Indian Youth Council, created in the aftermath of the 1961 Chicago meeting, promoted the idea of Indian nationalism and intertribal unity. In 1968, a group of young militant Indians established the American Indian Movement (AIM), which drew its greatest support from those Indians who lived in urban areas but soon established a significant presence on the reservations as well.

AIM

The new activism had some immediate political results. In 1968, Congress passed the Indian Civil Rights Act, which guaranteed reservation Indians many of the protections accorded other citizens by the Bill of Rights, but which also recognized the legitimacy of tribal laws within the reservations. But leaders of AIM and other insurgent groups were not satisfied and turned increasingly to direct action. In 1968, Indian fishermen clashed with Washington State officials on the Columbia River and in Puget Sound. The Indians claimed that treaties gave them the exclusive right to fish in the area; state authorities rejected the claim and sought to keep the waters open to non-Indian fishing boats. The following year, members of several tribes made a symbolic protest by occupying the abandoned federal prison on Alcatraz Island in San Francisco Bay and claiming the site "by right of discovery."

In response to the growing pressure, the new Nixon administration appointed a Mohawk-Sioux to the position of commissioner of Indian Affairs in 1969; and in 1970, the president promised both increased tribal self-determination and an increase in federal aid. But the protests continued. In November 1972, nearly a thousand demonstrators, most of them Sioux, forcibly occupied the building of the Bureau of Indian Affairs in Washington, D.C., for six days. A more celebrated protest occurred later that winter at Wounded Knee, South Dakota, the site of the 1890 massacre of Sioux by federal troops.

In the early 1970s, Wounded Knee was part of a large Sioux reservation, two-thirds of which had been leased to white ranchers for generations as an outgrowth of the Dawes Act. Conditions for the Indian residents were desperate, and passions grew quickly in 1972 in response to the murder of a Sioux by a group of whites, who were not, many Indians believed, adequately punished. In February 1973, members of AIM seized and occupied the town of Wounded Knee for two months, demanding radical changes in the administration of the reservation and insisting that the government honor its long-forgotten treaty obligations. A brief clash between the occupiers and federal forces left one Indian dead and another wounded. Shortly thereafter the siege came to an end.

Occupation of Wounded Knee

More immediately effective than these militant protests were the victories that various tribes were achieving in the 1970s in the federal courts. In *United States* v. *Wheeler* (1978), the Supreme Court confirmed that tribes had independent legal standing and could not be "terminated" by Congress. Other decisions ratified the authority of tribes to impose taxes on businesses within their reservations and to perform other sovereign functions. In 1985, the U.S. Supreme Court, in *County of Oneida* v. *Oneida Indian Nation,* supported Indian claims to 100,000 acres in upstate New York that the Oneida tribe claimed by virtue of treaty rights long forgotten by whites.

The Indian civil rights movement, like other civil rights movements of the same time, fell far short of winning full justice and equality for its constituents. Nor did it ever resolve its own internal conflicts—conflicts similar to those facing other minority groups at the same time. To some Indians, the principal goal was to defend tribal autonomy, to protect the right of Indians (and, more to the point, individual tribal groups) to remain separate and distinct. To others, the goal was equality—to win for Indians a place in society equal to that of other groups of Americans. This latter goal helped produce a new spirit of "pan-Indianism," an effort to persuade Indians to transcend tribal divisions and work together as "a Greater Indian America." But because there was no single Indian culture or tradition in America, pan-Indianism did not flourish.

For all its limits, however, the Indian civil rights movement helped the tribes win a series of new legal rights and protections that gave them a stronger position than they had enjoyed at any previous time in the twentieth century. It helped many Indians gain a renewed awareness of and pride in their identity as Indians and as part of distinct communities within the larger United States. And it challenged

Important Legal Victories

THE OCCUPATION OF ALCATRAZ Alcatraz is an island in San Francisco Bay that once housed a large federal prison that by the late 1960s had been abandoned. In 1969, a group of Indian activists occupied the island and claimed it as Indian land—precipitating a long standoff with authorities. *(AP/Wide World Photos)*

patterns of discrimination that had prevented many Native Americans from advancing in the world outside the tribes.

Latino Activism

More numerous and more visible than Indians were Latinos (or Hispanic Americans), the fastest-growing minority group in the United States. They were no more a single, cohesive group than the Indians were. Some—including the descendants of early Spanish settlers in New Mexico—had roots as deep in American history as those of any other group. Others were men and women who had immigrated since World War II.

Large numbers of Puerto Ricans had migrated to eastern cities, particularly New York. South Florida's substantial Cuban population began with a wave of middle-class refugees fleeing the Castro regime in the early 1960s. These first Cuban migrants quickly established themselves as a successful and increasingly assimilated part of Miami's middle class. In 1980, a second, much poorer wave of Cuban immigrants—the so-called *Marielitos,* named for the port from which they left Cuba—arrived in

Florida when Castro temporarily relaxed exit restrictions. (This group included a large number of criminals, whom Castro had, in effect, expelled from the country.) This second wave was less easily assimilated. Later in the 1980s, large numbers of immigrants (both legal and illegal) began to arrive from the troubled nations of Central and South America—from Guatemala, Nicaragua, El Salvador, Peru, and others. But the most numerous and important Latino group in the United States was Mexican Americans.

There had been a significant Mexican-American population in the West throughout the nineteenth and early twentieth centuries—descendants of Spanish and Mexican people who had settled in lands that once belonged to the Spanish Empire and the Republic of Mexico. But their numbers grew rapidly and substantially during and after World War II. Large numbers of Mexican Americans had entered the country during the war in response to the labor shortage, and many had remained in the cities of the Southwest and the Pacific Coast. After the war, when the legal agreements that had allowed Mexican contract workers to enter the country expired, large numbers of immigrants continued to move to the United States illegally.

In 1953, the government launched what it called Operation Wetback to deport the illegals, but the effort failed to stem the flow of new arrivals. By 1960, there were substantial Mexican-American neighborhoods (barrios) in American cities from El Paso to Detroit. The largest (with more than 500,000 people, according to census figures) was in Los Angeles, which by then had a bigger Mexican population than any place except Mexico City.

But the greatest expansion in the Mexican-American population was yet to come. In 1960, the census reported slightly more than 3 million Latinos living in the United *Surging Latino Immigration* States (the great majority of them Mexican Americans). In 1970, that number had grown to 9 million, and by 1990 to 20 million. Latinos constituted more than a third of all legal immigrants to the United States after 1960. Since there was also an uncounted but very large number of illegal immigrants in those years (estimates ranged from 7 million to 12 million), the real percentage of Latino immigrants was undoubtedly much larger.

By the late 1960s, therefore, Mexican Americans were one of the largest population groups in the West—outnumbering African Americans—and had established communities in most other parts of the nation as well. They were also among the most urbanized groups in the population; almost 90 percent lived and worked in cities. Many of them (particularly members of the oldest and most assimilated families of Mexican descent) were affluent and successful people. Wealthy Cubans in Miami filled influential positions in the professions and local government; in the Southwest, Mexican Americans elected their own leaders to seats in Congress and to governorships.

But most newly arrived Mexican Americans and other Hispanics were less well educated than either "Anglo" or black Americans and hence less well prepared for high-paying jobs. The fact that many spoke English poorly or not at all further limited their employment prospects. Some of them found good industrial jobs in unionized industries, and some Mexican Americans became important labor organizers in the AFL-CIO. But many more (including the great majority of illegal immigrants) worked in low-paying service jobs, with few if any benefits and no job security. And like African Americans and other minorities, Mexican Americans encountered almost impossible obstacles when they attempted to move out of blue-collar or low-status service jobs. Almost nowhere were they able to establish themselves as managers or executives in the companies in which they worked; few were able to pursue successful professional careers.

Partly because of language barriers, partly because the family-centered culture of many Latino communities discouraged effective organization, and partly because of discrimination, Mexican Americans and others were slower to develop political influence than some other minorities. But some did respond to the highly charged climate of the 1960s by strengthening their ethnic identification and organizing for political and economic power. Young Mexican-American activists began to call themselves "Chicanos" (once a term of derision used by whites) as a way of *"Chicano" Activism* emphasizing the shared culture of Spanish-speaking Americans; and the term quickly moved into widespread (although never universal) use among Mexican Americans. Some Chicanos advocated a form of nationalism not unlike the ideas of black power advocates. The Texas leaders of La Raza Unida, a Chicano political party in the Southwest, called for the creation of something like an autonomous Mexican-American state within a state; it demonstrated significant strength at the polls in the 1970s.

One of the most visible efforts to organize Mexican Americans occurred in California, where an Arizona-born Chicano farmworker, Cesar Chavez, created an effective *Cesar Chavez* union of itinerant farmworkers. In 1965, his United Farm Workers (UFW), a largely Chicano organization, launched a prolonged strike against growers to demand, first, recognition of their union and, second, increased wages and benefits. When employers resisted, Chavez enlisted the cooperation of college students, churches, and civil rights groups (including CORE and SNCC) and organized a nationwide boycott, first of table grapes and then of lettuce. In 1968, Chavez campaigned openly for Robert Kennedy. Two years later, he won a substantial victory when the growers of half of California's table grapes signed contracts with his union.

Latino Americans were at the center of another controversy of the 1970s and beyond: the issue of bilingualism. It was a question that aroused the opposition not only of many whites but of some Hispanics as well. Supporters of bilingualism in education (which included not just Latinos, but Asians and others as well) argued that non-English-speaking Americans were entitled to schooling in their own language, that otherwise they would be at a grave disadvantage in comparison with native English speakers. Bilingualism, they argued, was the only way to overcome the language barrier that kept many students from making even minimal academic progress. The United States Supreme Court confirmed the right of non-English-speaking students to schooling in their native language in 1974. Opponents cited not only the cost and difficulty of bilingualism but the dangers it posed to students' ability to assimilate into the mainstream of American culture. Even many Latinos feared that bilingualism might isolate their communities further from the rest of America and increase resentments toward them.

Challenging the "Melting Pot" Ideal

The efforts of blacks, Latinos, Indians, Asians, and others to forge a clearer group identity challenged a longstanding premise of American political thought: the idea of

KENNEDY AND CHAVEZ Cesar Chavez, the magnetic leader of the largely Mexican-American United Farm Workers Union, which represented mostly migrant workers, staged a hunger strike in 1968 to demand that union members receive better treatment by growers. Robert F. Kennedy, just beginning his campaign for the presidency, paid him a visit in Delano, California, to show his support. Chavez, who had by then been fasting for many weeks, looks visibly weak here. Kennedy's visit helped persuade him to end the fast. *(Michael Rougier/TimePix)*

the "melting pot." Older, European immigrant groups liked to believe that they had advanced in American society by adopting the values and accepting the rules of the country to which they had moved and by advancing within it on its own terms. The newly assertive ethnic groups of the 1960s and after appeared less willing to accept the standards of the larger society and more likely to demand recognition of their own ethnic identities. Some, but far from all, African Americans, Indians, Latinos, and Asians challenged the assimilationist idea. They advocated instead a culturally pluralistic society, in which racial and ethnic groups would preserve a sense of their own heritage and their own social and cultural norms.

To a considerable degree, the advocates of cultural pluralism succeeded. Recognition of the special character of particular groups was embedded in federal law through a wide range of affirmative action programs, which extended not only to blacks, but to Indians, Latinos, *Cultural Pluralism* Asians, and others as well. Ethnic studies programs proliferated in schools and universities. Eventually, this impulse led to an even more assertive (and highly controversial) cultural movement that in the 1980s and 1990s became known as "multiculturalism," which, among other things, challenged the "Eurocentric" basis of American education and culture and demanded that non-European civilizations be accorded equal attention.

Gay Liberation

The last important liberation movement to make major gains in the 1960s, and the most surprising to many Americans, was the effort by homosexuals to win political and economic rights and, equally important, social acceptance. Homosexuality had been an unacknowledged reality throughout American history; not until many years after their deaths did many Americans know, for example, that revered cultural figures such as Walt Whitman and Horatio Alger were homosexuals. Nonheterosexual men and women had long been forced either to suppress their sexual preferences, to express them surreptitiously, or to live within isolated and often persecuted communities. But by the late 1960s, the liberating impulses that had affected other groups helped mobilize gay men and lesbians to fight for their own rights.

On June 27, 1969, police officers raided the Stonewall Inn, a gay nightclub in New York City's Greenwich Village, and began arresting patrons simply for frequenting the place. The raid was not unusual; police had been harassing gay bars (and homosexual men and women) for years. It was, in fact, the accumulated resentment of this long history of assaults and humiliations that caused the extraordinary response that summer night. Gay onlookers taunted the police, then attacked them. Someone started a blaze in the Stonewall Inn itself, almost trapping the police- *"Stonewall Riot"* men inside. Rioting continued throughout Greenwich Village (the center of New York's gay community) through much of the night.

The "Stonewall Riot" marked the beginning of the gay liberation movement—one of the most controversial challenges to traditional values and assumptions of its time. New organizations—among them the Gay Liberation Front, founded in New York in 1969—sprang up around the country. Public discussion and media coverage of homosexuality, long subject to an unofficial taboo, quickly and dramatically increased. Gay and lesbian activists had some

THE QUILT In the early years of gay liberation, the movement focused mostly on ending discrimination and harassment. By the 1990s, however, with the AIDS epidemic sweeping through large numbers of gay men, activists shifted much of their attention to pressing for a cure and to remembering those who had died. One of the most remarkable results of that effort was the AIDS Quilt. Friends and relatives of victims of the disease made individual patches in memory of those they had lost. Then, in many different cities, thousands of quilters would join their pieces together to create a vast testament to bereavement and memory. The enormity of the project was most visible in October 1996, when hundreds of thousands of pieces of the quilt were laid out on the Mall in Washington, stretching from the Washington Monument to the Capitol. *(Ron Edmunds /AP/Wide World Photos)*

success in challenging the longstanding assumption that homosexuality was "aberrant" behavior and argued that no sexual preference was any more "normal" than another.

Most of all, however, the gay liberation movement transformed the outlook of gay men and lesbians them-

Impact of the Gay Liberation Movement

selves. It helped them to "come out," to express their preferences openly and unapologeti-

cally, and to demand from society a recognition that gay relationships could be as significant and worthy of respect as heterosexual ones. Some gays advocated not only an acceptance of homosexuality as a valid and "normal" preference, but also a change in the larger society as well: a redefinition of personal identity to give much greater

importance to erotic impulses. There was much resistance to such efforts. But by the early 1980s, the gay liberation movement had made remarkable strides. Even the ravages of the AIDS epidemic (see pp. 937–939), which affected the gay community more disastrously than it affected any other group, failed to halt the growth of gay liberation. In many ways, it strengthened it.

By the early 1990s, gay men and lesbians were achieving some of the same milestones that other oppressed minorities had attained in earlier decades. Some openly gay politicians won election to public office. Universities were establishing gay and lesbian studies programs. And laws prohibiting discrimination on the basis of sexual preference were making slow, halting progress at the local level. But gay liberation produced a powerful backlash as well, as became evident when President Bill Clinton's 1993 effort to lift the ban on gays and lesbians serving in the military met a storm of criticism from members of Congress and from within the military itself—a backlash so strong that it forced the administration to retreat from its position and settle for an unsatisfactory compromise instead.

THE NEW FEMINISM

American women constitute 51 percent of the population. But during the 1960s and 1970s, many women began to identify with minority groups and to demand a liberation of their own. Sexual discrimination was so deeply embedded in the fabric of society, and so unnoticed by many of those who practiced it, that when feminists began to denounce it, many men (and even many women) responded with bafflement and anger. By the 1970s, however, public awareness of the issue had increased significantly, and the role of women in American life had changed more dramatically than that of any other group in the nation.

The Rebirth

Feminism had been a weak and often embattled force in American life for more than forty years after the adoption of the woman suffrage amendment in 1920. A few determined women kept feminist political demands alive in the National Woman's Party and other organizations. Many more women expanded the acceptable bounds of female activity by entering new areas of the workplace or engaging in political activities. Nevertheless, through the 1950s and early 1960s, active feminism was often difficult to detect. Yet within a very few years, it evolved from an almost invisible remnant to one of the most powerful social movements in American history.

The 1963 publication of Betty Friedan's *The Feminine Mystique* is often cited as the first event of contemporary women's liberation. Friedan had traveled around the country interviewing the women who had graduated with her from Smith College in 1947. Most of these women were living out the dream that postwar American

The Feminine Mystique

society had created for them: they were affluent wives and mothers living in comfortable suburbs. And yet many of them were deeply frustrated and unhappy. The suburbs, Friedan claimed, had become a "comfortable concentration camp," providing the women who inhabited them with no outlets for their intelligence, talent, and education. The "feminine mystique" was responsible for "burying millions of women alive." The only escape was for them to begin to fulfill "their unique possibilities as separate human beings." By chronicling their unhappiness and frustration, Friedan's book had a powerful impact. But it did not so much cause the revival of feminism as help give voice to a movement that was already stirring.

By the time *The Feminine Mystique* appeared, John Kennedy had established the President's Commission on the Status of Women; and although the president's motives in creating it probably had more to do with deflecting more substantive feminist demands than with real commitment to women's goals, the commission brought national attention to sexual discrimination and helped create important networks of feminist activists who would lobby for legislative redress. Also in 1963, the Kennedy administration helped win passage of the Equal Pay Act, which barred the pervasive practice of paying women less than men for equal work. A year later, Congress incorporated into the Civil Rights Act of 1964 an amendment—Title VII—that extended to women many of the same legal protections against discrimination that were being extended to blacks.

The events of the early 1960s helped expose a contradiction that had been developing for decades between the image and the reality of women's roles in America. The image was what Friedan had called the "feminine mystique"—the ideal of women living happy, fulfilled lives in purely domestic roles. The reality was that increasing numbers of women (including, by 1963, over a third of all married women) had already entered the workplace and were encountering widespread discrimination there; and that many other women were finding their domestic lives suffocating and frustrating. The conflict between the ideal and the reality was crucial to the rebirth of feminism.

In 1966, Friedan joined with other feminists to create the National Organization for Women (NOW), which was to become the nation's largest and most influential feminist organization. "The time has

NOW Founded

come," the founders of NOW maintained, "to confront with concrete action the conditions which now prevent women from enjoying the equality of opportunity and freedom of choice which is their right as individual Americans and as human beings." Like other movements for liberation, feminism drew much of its inspiration from the black struggle for freedom.

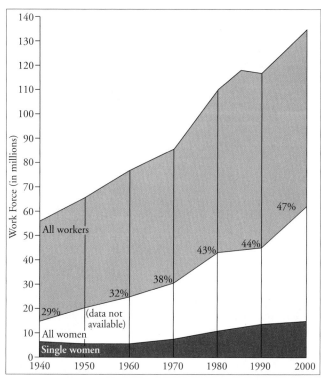

WOMEN IN THE PAID WORK FORCE, 1940–2000 The number of women working for wages steadily expanded from 1940 on, to the point that in 2000, they constituted just under half the total work force. ◆ *What role did this growing participation in the paid work force have on the rise of feminism in the 1960s and beyond?*

"There is no civil rights movement to speak for women," the NOW organizers claimed, "as there has been for Negroes and other victims of discrimination."*

The new organization reflected the varying constituencies of the emerging feminist movement. It responded to the complaints of the women Friedan's book had examined—affluent suburbanites with no outlet for their interests—by demanding greater educational opportunities for women and denouncing the domestic ideal and the traditional concept of marriage. But the heart of the movement, at least in the beginning, was directed toward the needs of women in the workplace. NOW denounced the exclusion of women from professions, from politics, and from countless other areas of American life because of prejudices about women's proper role. It decried legal and economic discrimination, including the practice of paying women less than men for equal work (a practice the Equal Pay Act had not eliminated). The organization called for "a fully equal partnership of the sexes, as part of the worldwide revolution of human rights." By the end of the decade, its membership had expanded to 15,000.

*Published by National Organization for Women.

Women's Liberation

By the late 1960s, new and more radical feminist demands were also attracting a large following, especially among younger, affluent, white, educated women—although gen-

New Directions in the Women's Movement

erally not among the older women whose lives Friedan had studied. The new feminists were mostly younger, the vanguard of the baby-boom generation. Many of them drew inspiration from the New Left and the counterculture. Some were involved in the civil rights movement, others in the antiwar crusade. Many had found that even within those movements, they faced discrimination and exclusion or subordination to male leaders.

By the early 1970s, a significant change was visible in the tone and direction of the organization and of the women's movement as a whole. New books by younger feminists expressed a harsher critique of American society than Friedan had offered. Kate Millett's *Sexual Politics* (1969) signaled the new direction by complaining that "every avenue of power within the society is entirely within male hands." The answer to women's problems, in other words, was not, as Friedan had suggested, for individual women to search for greater personal fulfillment; it was for women to band together to assault the male power structure. Shulamith Firestone's *The Dialectic of Sex* (1970) was subtitled "The Case for Feminist Revolution."

In its most radical form, the new feminism rejected the whole notion of marriage, family, and even heterosexual intercourse (a vehicle, some women claimed, of male domination). Not many women, not even many feminists, embraced such extremes. But by the early 1970s large numbers of women were coming to see themselves as an exploited group organizing against oppression and developing a culture and communities of their own. The women's liberation movement inspired the creation of grassroots organizations and activities through which women not only challenged sexism and discrimination but created communities of their own. In cities and towns across the country, feminists opened women's bookstores, bars, and coffee shops. They founded feminist newspapers and magazines. They created centers to assist victims of rape and abuse, women's health clinics (and, particularly after 1973, abortion clinics), and day-care centers.

Expanding Achievements

By the early 1970s, the public and private achievements of the women's movement were already substantial. In 1971, the government extended its affirmative action guidelines to include women—linking sexism with racism as an officially acknowledged social problem. In the meantime, women were making rapid progress in their efforts to move into the economic and political mainstream. The nation's major all-male educational institutions began to open their doors to women. (Princeton and Yale did so in 1969, and most other all-male colleges and universities soon followed.) Some women's colleges, in the meantime, began accepting male students—although some others remained committed to single-sex education, arguing for the value of the women's communities their campuses created.

Women were also becoming an important force in business and the professions. Nearly half of all married women held jobs by the mid-1970s, and almost nine-tenths of all women with college degrees worked.

Political and Economic Success

The two-career family, in which both husband and wife maintained active professional lives, was becoming a widely accepted norm; many women were postponing marriage or motherhood for the sake of their careers. There were also important symbolic changes, such as the refusal of many women to adopt their husbands' names when they married and the use of the term "Ms." in place of "Mrs." or "Miss" to denote the irrelevance of a woman's marital status in the public world. In politics, women were beginning to compete effectively with men by the early 1970s for both elected and appointive positions. By the early 1990s, considerable numbers of women were serving in both houses of Congress, in numerous federal cabinet positions, as governors of several states, and in many other positions. Ronald Reagan named the first female Supreme Court justice, Sandra Day O'Connor, in 1981; in 1993, Bill Clinton named the second, Ruth Bader Ginsburg. In 1984, the Democratic Party chose a woman, Representative Geraldine Ferraro of New York, as its vice presidential candidate. In academia, women were expanding their presence in traditional scholarly fields; they were also creating a field of their own—women's studies, which in the 1980s and early 1990s was the fastest-growing area of American scholarship.

MARCHING FOR WOMEN'S RIGHTS By the end of the 1960s, the struggle for individual rights—which the African-American civil rights movement had helped push to the center of national consciousness—had inspired a broad range of movements. Perhaps the most important in the long run was the drive for women's rights, which was already formidable in the summer of 1970, when thousands of women joined this march through New York City. *(Werner Wolff/Black Star)*

In professional athletics, in the meantime, women were beginning to compete with men both for attention and for an equal share of prize money. Billie Jean King spearheaded the most effective female challenge to male domination of sports. Under her leadership, professional women tennis players established their own successful tours and demanded equal financial incentives when they played in the same tournaments as men. By the late 1970s, the federal government was pressuring colleges and universities to provide women with athletic programs equal to those available to men. Women even joined what had previously been the most celebrated all-male fraternity in American culture: the space program. Sally Ride became the first woman astronaut to travel in space in 1983.

In 1972, Congress approved the Equal Rights Amendment to the Constitution, which some feminists had been promoting since the 1920s, and sent it to the states. For a while ratification seemed almost certain. By the late 1970s,

Failure of ERA

however, the momentum behind the amendment had died. The ERA was in trouble not because of indifference but because of a rising chorus of objections to it from people (including many antifeminist women) who feared it would disrupt traditional social patterns. In 1982, the amendment finally died when the time allotted for ratification expired.

The Abortion Controversy

A vital element of American feminism since the 1920s has been women's effort to win greater control of their own sexual and reproductive lives. In its least controversial form, this impulse helped produce an increasing awareness in the 1960s and 1970s of the problems of rape, sexual abuse, and wife beating. There continued to be some controversy over the dissemination of contraceptives and birth-control information; but that issue, at least, seemed to have lost much of the explosive character it had had in the 1920s, when Margaret Sanger had become a heroine to some and a figure of public scorn to others for her efforts on its behalf. A related issue, however, stimulated as much popular passion as any question of its time: abortion.

Abortion had once been legal in much of the United States, but by the beginning of the twentieth century it was banned by statute in most of the country and remained so into the 1960s (although many abortions continued to be performed quietly, and often dangerously, out of sight of the law). But the women's movement created strong new pressures on behalf of legalizing abortion. Several states had abandoned restrictions on abortion by the end of the 1960s. And in 1973, the Supreme Court's decision in *Roe* v.

Roe v. Wade

Wade, based on a relatively new theory of a constitutional "right to privacy" first recognized by the Court only a few years earlier in *Griswold* v. *Connecticut* (1965), invalidated all laws prohibiting abortion during the "first trimester"—the first three months of pregnancy. The issue seemed to be settled. But it soon became clear that it was not.

Although in many ways feminism was much like other liberation movements of the 1960s and 1970s, it differed from them in one fundamental respect: its success. The women's movement may not have fulfilled all its goals. But it achieved fundamental and permanent changes in the position of women in American life and promised to do much more.

ENVIRONMENTALISM IN A TURBULENT SOCIETY

Like feminism, environmentalism entered the 1960s with a long history and relatively little public support. Also like feminism, environmentalism both profited from and transcended the turbulence of the era and emerged by the 1970s as a powerful and enduring force in American life.

The rise of this new movement was in part a result of the environmental degradation that had become increasingly evident in the advanced industrial society of the late twentieth century. It was a result, too, of the growth of the science of ecology, which provided environmentalists with new and powerful arguments. And it was a product as well of some of the other social movements of the time: movements that rejected aspects of the modern, industrial, consumer society and called for a return to a more natural existence. A reverence for nature, and a desire to preserve it, contributed to the growing power of the environmental movement.

The New Science of Ecology

Until the mid-twentieth century, most people who considered themselves environmentalists (or, to use the more traditional term, conservationists) based their commitment on aesthetic or moral grounds. They wanted to preserve nature because it was too beautiful to despoil, or because it was a mark of divinity on the world, or because it permitted humans a spiritual experience that would otherwise be unavailable to them. In the course of the twentieth century, however, scientists in the United States and other nations—drawing from early, relatively obscure scientific writings—began to create a new rationale for environmentalism. They called it ecology.

Ecology is the science of the inter-relatedness of the natural world. It rests on an assumption—as the American zoologist Stephan A. Forbes wrote as early as 1880—that "Primeval nature . . . presents a settled harmony of interaction among organic groups," and that this harmony "is in strong contrast with the many serious maladjustments of plants and animals found in countries occupied by man." Such problems as air and water

Idea of an Interrelated World

pollution, the destruction of forests, the extinction of species, and toxic wastes are not, ecology teaches, separate, isolated problems. All elements of the earth's environment are intimately and delicately linked. Damaging any one of those elements, therefore, risks damaging all the others.

A number of American scientists built on Forbes's ideas in the early twentieth century, but perhaps the greatest early contribution to popular knowledge of ecology came not from a scientist at all, but from the writer and naturalist Aldo Leopold. During a career in forest management, Leopold sought to apply the new scientific findings on ecology to his interactions with the natural world. And in 1949, he published a classic of environmental literature, *The Sand County Almanac,* in which he argued that humans had a responsibility to understand and maintain the balance of nature, that they should behave in the natural world according to a code that he called the "land ethic." By then, the science of ecology was spreading widely in the scientific community. Among the findings of ecologists were such now-common ideas as the "food chain," the "ecosystem," "biodiversity," and "endangered species." Rachel Carson's sensational 1962 book, *Silent Spring,* which revealed the dangers of pesticides, was based solidly on the idea of ecologists and did at least as much as Leopold's work to introduce those ideas to a larger public.

Between 1945 and 1960, the number of ecologists in the United States grew threefold, and that number doubled again between 1960 and 1970. Funded by government agencies, by universities, by foundations, and eventually even by some corporations, ecological science gradually *Ecology's Postwar Growth* established itself as a significant field of its own—not, perhaps, with the same stature as such traditional fields as physics, chemistry, and biology, but certainly a field whose importance and appeal grew rapidly in the last decades of the twentieth century. By century's end, there were programs in and departments of ecological science in major universities throughout the United States and in many other nations.

Much more than other scientists, however, ecologists tend to fuse their commitment to research and testing with a commitment to publicizing their work and working for responsible public action to deal with environmental crises. Many ecologists argue that environmental problems must be addressed energetically even if firm scientific proof is not yet available to sustain their diagnosis of the problem. To wait for absolute proof, they insist, would be to invite irreversible damage to the environment.

Environmental Advocacy

Academic ecologists often have close ties to environmental organizations committed to public action and political lobbying. The emergence or redefinition of such organizations in the 1960s and 1970s was among the most important developments in the growth of an environmental movement. Most of them were nongovernmental agencies operating on a not-for-profit basis. The professionalized environmental advocacy they provided gave the movement a political strength it had never enjoyed in the past. Among the most important environmental organizations were the Wilderness Society, the Sierra Club, the National Audubon Society, the Nature Conservancy, the National Wildlife Federation, and the National Parks and Conservation Association. All of these organizations predated the rise of modern ecological science, but all of them entered the last decades of the twentieth century re-energized and committed to the new concepts of environmentalism. They found allies among other not-for-profit organizations that had no previous experience with environmentalism but now chose to join the battle—among them such groups as the American Civil Liberties Union, the League of Women Voters, the National Council of Churches, and even the AFL-CIO.

Out of these organizations emerged a new generation of professional environmental activists able to contribute to the legal and political battles of the movement. Scientists provided the necessary data. Lawyers *New Professional Environmental Activists* fought battles with government agencies and in the courts. Lobbyists used traditional techniques of political persuasion with legislators and other officials—knowing

FIGHTING FOR THE ENVIRONMENT As political parties declined in popular importance in the last decades of the twentieth century, new movements emerged to take their place. Perhaps the most important was environmentalism, which adopted many of the styles and tactics of political parties—rallies, marches, and, as this photograph shows, "campaign" buttons. These promote efforts in the Pacific Northwest to keep the waters in which salmon spawn clean. *(Joel W. Rogers/Corbis)*

SILENT SPRING

One summer day in 1957, a small plane flew over the nature sanctuary behind Olga Huckins's house in Duxbury, Massachusetts. It sprayed the land below with an oily mist and then vanished. The next day, Huckins found seven dead songbirds, their beaks gaping in apparent agony. She was so furious that she wrote an angry letter to a local paper; as an afterthought, she sent a copy to her friend Rachel Carson. It was one of those small events that alters the course of history.

Carson was a biologist and a gifted writer. Educated at Johns Hopkins University at a time when few women became scientists, she had gone to work for the government as an aquatic biologist, where—despite her painful shyness—she distinguished herself as a writer able to explain scientific issues to a wider public. In the meantime, she began to write popular essays about her special love, the ocean. In 1951 she published *The Sea Around Us.* It became an international bestseller, bringing Carson a fame she never imagined and enough income to retire from government. By 1957, when she received Huckins's letter, she was one of the most popular nature writers of her generation.

The mist that the plane had sprayed behind Huckins's house was a mixture

PESTICIDE SPRAYING   When pesticides first became available to farmers, they proved so effective against agricultural pests that soon they were being sprayed on most crops. Although scientists and consumers have raised many questions about the safety of such chemicals, they continue to play an important role in the farm economy. Most foods grown in the United States are still treated with pesticides to some degree, although the growing popularity of organic foods (cultivated without artificial fertilizers or pesticides) testifies to the durability of the concerns Carson raised.   *(Bettmann/Corbis)*

of ordinary fuel oil and a chemical called dichlorodiphenyltrichloroethane: DDT. In 1939, a Swiss chemist named Paul Muller had discovered that although DDT seemed harmless to human beings and other mammals, it was extremely toxic to insects. American scientists learned of Muller's discovery in 1942, just as the army was grappling with the insect-borne tropical diseases—

especially malaria and typhus—that threatened American soldiers.

Under these circumstances, DDT seemed a godsend. It was first used on a large scale in Italy in 1942–1944 during a typhus outbreak, which it quickly helped end. Soon it was being sprayed in mosquito-infested areas of Pacific Islands where American troops were fighting the Japanese. No soldiers suffered any apparent ill effects from the sprayings, and the incidence of malaria dropped precipitously. DDT quickly gained a reputation as a miraculous tool for controlling insects, and it undoubtedly saved thousands of lives. For its discovery, Paul Muller was awarded the Nobel Prize in medicine in 1948. With so many benefits and no obvious drawbacks, the new chemical was released for public use in 1945. DDT entered the marketplace billed as an extraordinarily safe and effective poison, the ultimate weapon against destructive insects.

For the next decade, the new chemical continued to live up to its early billing. It helped farmers eliminate chronic pests and was widely used to control mosquitoes. One of its most impressive successes was in virtually eliminating the gypsy moth, a voracious insect that had been stripping the leaves from northeastern

that corporations and other opponents of environmental efforts would be doing the same in opposition to their goals. When Congress or state legislatures considered environmental legislation, more often than not the environmental organizations played a critical role in drafting it. And when the same organizations became convinced that corporate or public policy threatened the environment, they mounted political and legal challenges with increasing effectiveness. But perhaps most of all, these organizations learned how to mobilize public opinion on their behalf—an effort much aided by the rise of a popular movement beginning in the early 1970s.

Environmental Degradation

Not all the impetus for environmental consciousness came from scientists and professional activists. Many other forces contributed as well in the 1960s and 1970s to create what became the environmental movement.

Lady Bird Johnson, the wife of the president, helped raise public awareness of the landscape with her energetic "beautification" campaign in the mid-1960s—a campaign unconnected to any ecological concepts, but one that reflected a growing popular dismay at the despoliation of the landscape by rapid economic growth. Members of the counterculture contributed to environmental awareness with their romanticization of the natural world and their repudiation of the "technocracy."

But perhaps the greatest force behind environmentalism was the condition of the environment itself. By the 1960s, the damage to the natural world from the dramatic economic growth of the postwar era was becoming impossible to ignore. Water pollution—which had been a problem in some areas of the country for many decades—was becoming so widespread that almost every major city was dealing with the unpleasant sight and odor, as well as the very real health risks, of polluted rivers and lakes. In Cleveland, Ohio, for example, the

forests ever since being accidentally introduced to the Boston area in 1868.

By the time Rachel Carson received Olga Huckins's letter, however, signs of trouble were beginning to appear in areas that had been sprayed with the chemical. For one, its effectiveness against certain insects declined as they developed resistance to its effects, so that higher doses were needed to produce the same lethal effect. A resistant housefly had appeared as early as 1948, and a resistant mosquito by 1949.

More worrisome were the chemical's effects on larger animals. Some were killed outright, like the birds in Olga Huckins's back yard. But DDT also seemed to inhibit some animals' ability to reproduce. It would later be learned that the eggshells of certain birds were so thinned by the chemical that young birds were crushed in their nests even before they hatched. The extraordinary persistence of DDT in the environment, and its tendency to accumulate in fatty tissues, meant that animals could concentrate surprising quantities in their flesh. This was especially true of those at the top of food chains—eagles, trout, and, not least, people. Many bird lovers were noting a general reduction in bird populations, and people who fished were catching fewer fish. As the woods

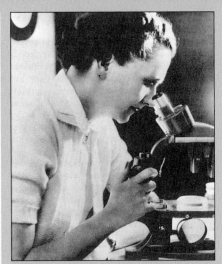

RACHEL CARSON Rachel Carson, who began her career as a marine biologist, wrote the world's best-selling book about the ocean environment in the 1950s. Carson's abiding love for the creatures of shore and surf led to her concern about the harm pesticides might do them. *(Bettmann/Corbis)*

became emptier and more silent, DDT seemed the most likely culprit. Rachel Carson had worried about pesticides for years, but it was not until reading Olga Huckins's letter that she decided to do something about them. Meticulously gathering the best available data, she wrote a book that was published in 1962, *Silent Spring*. In it, she warned that the indiscriminate use of pesticides was wreaking havoc with the web of life, destroying wildlife populations and threatening human health. She wrote of a landscape in which sickness and death threatened animals and people alike, in which "a strange stillness" had replaced the familiar songs of birds. Her eloquence was made all the more urgent by her private knowledge as she finished the book that she herself was dying of cancer.

Silent Spring became one of the most controversial books of the 1960s. It sold nearly half a million copies within six months of its publication and was discussed everywhere. The chemical industry was outraged. After first trying to suppress the book's publication altogether and threatening lawsuits against its author and publisher, pesticide manufacturers began a long campaign to discredit Carson and repair the damage her book had done. In the end, though, Carson won at least a partial victory: the U.S. finally banned the sale of DDT in 1972. More important, her book raised public awareness about the threats human activities pose to the natural environment. Although she died in 1964, no single person would be more important in shaping environmental policies over the next thirty years.

Cuyahoga River actually burst into flame from time to time from the petroleum waste being dumped into it; the city declared the river an official fire hazard.

Perhaps more alarming was the growing awareness that the air itself was becoming unhealthy, that toxic fumes from factories and power plants and, most of all, automobiles were poisoning the atmosphere. Weather forecasts and official atmospheric information began to refer to "smog" levels—using a relatively new word formed from a combination of smoke and fog. In some large cities—

Air and Water Pollution Los Angeles and Denver among them—smog became an almost perpetual fact of life, rising steadily through the day, blotting out the sun, and creating respiratory difficulties for many citizens. In 1969, an oil-well platform off Santa Barbara, California, had a blowout that spewed hundreds of thousands of gallons of crude oil into the ocean just off the popular beaches of an affluent city. This oil spill—affecting what had once seemed an idyllic place—had a tremendous impact on the environmental consciousness of millions of Americans. Another, much larger spill—indeed, the largest in American history—occurred off the coast of Alaska in 1989 when the giant tanker *Exxon Valdez* hit a reef in Prince William Sound. The damage it caused to the nearby shoreline, and to the wildlife that inhabited it, greatly increased environmental consciousness.

Environmentalists also brought to public attention some longer-term dangers of unchecked industrial development: the rapid depletion of oil and other irreplaceable fossil fuels; the destruction of lakes and forests as a result of "acid rain" (rainfall polluted by chemical contaminants); the rapid destruction of vast rain forests, in Brazil and elsewhere, which limited the earth's capacity to replenish its oxygen supply; the depletion of the ozone layer as a result of the release of chloroflurocarbons into the atmosphere, which threatened to limit the earth's protection from dangerous ultraviolet rays from the sun; and global warming, which—if unchecked—would create

STARTING YOUNG One of the greatest successes of the environmental movement has been its ability to attract the attention and support of children and young people—as this photograph of a young Massachusetts girl suggests. *(Todd Gipstein/Corbis)*

dramatic changes in the earth's climate and would threaten existing cities and settlements in coastal areas all over the world by causing a rise in ocean levels. Many of these claims became—and remain—controversial, with skeptics arguing that environmentalists have not conclusively proven their cases. But most environmentalists—and many others—came to believe that while much remained to be learned about all of these developments, the problems were real and deserving of immediate attention.

Earth Day and Beyond

On April 22, 1970, people all over the United States gathered in schools and universities, in churches and clubs, in parks and auditoria, for the first "Earth Day." Originally proposed by Wisconsin Senator Gaylord Nelson as a series of teach-ins on college campuses, Earth Day gradually

The First "Earth Day"

took on a much larger life. Carefully managed by people who wanted to avoid associations with the radical left, it had an unthreatening quality that made it appealing to many people for whom antiwar demonstrations and civil-rights rallies seemed somehow threatening. According to some estimates, over 20 million Americans participated in some part of the Earth Day observances, which may have made it the largest single demonstration in the nation's history.

The cautious, centrist character of Earth Day and related efforts to popularize environmentalism helped create a movement that had little of the danger and divisiveness of other, more controversial causes. Gradually, environmentalism became more than simply a series of demonstrations and protests. It became part of the consciousness of the vast majority of Americans—absorbed into popular culture, built into primary and secondary education, endorsed by almost all politicians (even if many of them actually opposed some environmental goals).

It also became part of the fabric of public policy. In 1970, Congress passed and President Nixon signed the National Environmental Protection Act, which created a new agency—the Environmental Protection Agency—to enforce antipollution standards on businesses and consumers.

EPA Established

The Clean Air Act, also passed in 1970, and the Clean Water Act, passed in 1972, added additional tools to the government's arsenal of weapons against environmental degradation. The actions of the federal government—and of state and local governments that soon followed its lead—had a measurable, even at times dramatic, impact on many kinds of pollution. Many lakes and rivers that had long been serious environmental hazards became markedly cleaner; restrictions on auto emissions and other air pollutants substantially improved air quality in many cities; industries found it much more difficult to dump toxic wastes in unsafe ways.

But the enlistment of the government behind many of the goals of environmentalists did not put an end to the movement. Different administrations displayed varying levels of support for environmental goals, and advocacy groups remained ready to spring into action to force them to change their positions. And of course new environmental problems continued to emerge even as older ones sometimes found solutions. Environmentalism was a movement, a set of public policies, and a broad national ideal—and it was the combination of all those aspects that made it such a continually powerful force in American life.

NIXON, KISSINGER, AND THE WAR

Richard Nixon assumed office in 1969 committed not only to restoring stability at home but to creating a new and more stable order in the world. Central to Nixon's hopes for international stability was a resolution of the stalemate in Vietnam. Yet the new president felt no freer than his predecessor to abandon the American commitment there. He realized that the endless war was undermining both the nation's domestic stability and its position in the world. But he feared that a precipitous retreat would destroy American honor and "credibility." During the 1968 campaign, Nixon claimed to have for-

"Credibility" | mulated a plan to bring "peace with honor" in Vietnam. He had refused to disclose its details. Once in office, however, he soon made clear that the plan consisted of little more than a vague set of general principles, not of any concrete measures to extricate the United States from the quagmire. American involvement in Indochina continued for four more years, during which the war expanded both in its geographic scope and in its bloodiness. And when a settlement finally emerged early in 1973, it produced neither peace nor honor. It succeeded only in removing the United States from the wreckage.

Vietnamization

Despite Nixon's own passionate interest in international affairs, he brought with him into government a man who ultimately seemed to overshadow him in the conduct of diplomacy: Henry Kissinger, a Harvard professor whom the

Henry Kissinger | president appointed as his special assistant for national security affairs. Kissinger quickly established dominance over both the secretary of state, William Rogers, and the secretary of defense, Melvin Laird, who were both more experienced in public life. That was in part a result of Nixon's passion for concentrating decision making in the White House. But Kissinger's keen intelligence, his bureaucratic skills, and his success in handling the press were at least equally important. Together, Nixon and Kissinger set out to find an acceptable solution to the stalemate in Vietnam.

The new Vietnam policy moved along several fronts. One was an effort to limit domestic opposition to the war so as to permit the administration more political space in which to maneuver. Aware that the military draft was one of the most visible targets of dissent, the administration devised a new "lottery" system, through which only a limited group—those nineteen-year-olds with low lottery numbers—would be subject to conscription. Later, the president urged the creation of an all-volunteer army. By 1973, the Selective Service System was on its way to at least temporary extinction.

More important in stifling dissent, however, was the new policy of "Vietnamization" of the war—the training

and equipping of the South Vietnamese military to assume the burden of combat in place of American forces. In the fall of 1969, Nixon announced reduction of American ground troops from Vietnam by 60,000, | *Consequences of "Vietnamization"* the first reduction in U.S. troop strength since the beginning of the war. The reductions continued steadily for more than three years, so that by the fall of 1972 relatively few American soldiers remained in Indochina. From a peak of more than 540,000 in 1969, the number had dwindled to about 60,000.

Vietnamization did help quiet domestic opposition to the war. But it did nothing to break the stalemate in the negotiations with the North Vietnamese in Paris. The new administration quickly decided that new military pressures would be necessary to do that.

Escalation

By the end of their first year in office, Nixon and Kissinger had concluded that the most effective way to tip the military balance in America's favor was to destroy the bases in Cambodia from which the American military believed the North Vietnamese were launching many of their attacks. Very early in his presidency, Nixon ordered the air force to begin bombing Cambodian territory to destroy the enemy sanctuaries. He kept the raids secret from Congress and the public. In the spring of 1970, possibly with U.S. encouragement and support, conservative military leaders overthrew the neutral government of Cambodia and established a new, pro-American regime under General Lon Nol. Lon Nol quickly gave his approval to American incursions into his territory; and on April 30, Nixon went on television to announce that he was ordering American troops across the border into Cambodia to "clean out" the bases that the enemy had been using for its "increased military aggression."

Literally overnight, the Cambodian invasion restored the dwindling antiwar movement to vigorous life. The first days of May saw the most widespread and vocal antiwar demonstrations ever. Hundreds of thousands of protesters gathered in Washington to denounce the president's policies. Millions, perhaps, participated in countless smaller demonstrations on campuses nationwide. Antiwar frenzy was reaching so high a level that it was possible briefly for some Americans to believe (incorrectly) that a genuine revolution was imminent. The mood of crisis intensified greatly on May 4, when four college students were killed and nine others injured when members of the National Guard opened fire on antiwar demonstrators at Kent State University in Ohio. Ten days later, | *Kent State* police killed two black students at Jackson State University in Mississippi during a demonstration there.

The clamor against the war quickly spread into the government and the press. Congress angrily repealed the

ANTIWAR POSTER Much of the antiwar movement was hard and angry, charging the United States with genocide and imperialism and advocating militant, even violent resistance. But there was also a gentler side to the movement, more rooted in pacifist traditions, that this poster—with its image of doves alighting on a heavily armed soldier—suggests. The image is reminiscent of a famous Picasso drawing of Don Quixote. *(Library of Congress)*

Gulf of Tonkin Resolution in December, stripping the president of what had long served as the legal basis for the war. Nixon ignored the action. Then, in June 1971, first the *New York Times* and later other newspapers began publishing excerpts from a secret study of the war prepared by the Defense Department during the Johnson administration. What came to be known as the Pentagon Papers, leaked to the press by former Defense official Daniel Ellsberg, provided confirmation of what many had long believed: that the government had been dishonest, both in reporting the military progress of the war and in explaining its own motives for American involvement. Despite public claims that the war was being fought to protect the South Vietnamese, the Pentagon Papers revealed, American officials were justifying the war to themselves as a way to protect American prestige—and America's

"reputation as a guarantor"—in other parts of the world. The administration went to court to suppress the documents, but the Supreme Court finally ruled that the press had the right to publish them.

Particularly troubling, both to the public and to the government itself, were signs of decay within the American military. Morale and discipline among U.S. troops in Vietnam, who had been fighting a savage and inconclusive war for more than five years, were rapidly deteriorating. The trial and conviction in 1971 of Lieutenant William Calley, who was charged with overseeing a massacre of more than 300 unarmed South Vietnamese civilians, attracted wide public attention. Many Americans believed that the My Lai tragedy was not an isolated incident, that it suggested the dehumanizing impact of the war on those who fought it—and the terrible consequences for the Vietnamese people of that dehumanization. Less publicized were other, more widespread problems among American troops in Vietnam: desertion, drug addiction, racial hostilities, refusal to obey orders, even the killing of unpopular officers by enlisted men.

My Lai Massacre

The continuing carnage, the increasing savagery, and the social distress at home had largely destroyed public support for the war. By 1971, nearly two-thirds of those interviewed in public opinion polls were urging American withdrawal from Vietnam. But from Richard Nixon there came no sign of retreat. On the contrary, the events of the spring of 1970 left him more convinced than ever of the importance of resisting those who opposed his military policies. With the approval of the White House, both the FBI and the CIA intensified their surveillance and infiltration of antiwar and radical groups, often resorting to blatant illegalities. Administration officials sought to discredit prominent critics of the war by leaking damaging personal information about them. At one point, White House agents broke into the office of a psychiatrist in an unsuccessful effort to steal files on Daniel Ellsberg, the former Defense Department official who had leaked a secret study of the origins of the war (the Pentagon Papers) to the press in 1971. During the congressional campaign of 1970, Vice President Spiro Agnew, using the acid rhetoric that had already made him the hero of many conservatives, stepped up his attack on the "effete" and "impudent" critics of the administration. The president himself once climbed on top of an automobile to taunt a crowd of angry demonstrators.

Meanwhile, the fighting in Indochina raged on. In February 1971, the president ordered the air force to assist the South Vietnamese army in an invasion of Laos—a test, as he saw it, of his Vietnamization program. Within weeks, the South Vietnamese scrambled back across the border in defeat. American bombing in Vietnam and Cambodia increased, despite its apparent ineffectiveness. In March 1972, the North Vietnamese mounted their biggest offensive since 1968 (the so-called Easter Offensive).

Easter Offensive

American and South Vietnamese forces managed to halt the communist advance, but it was clear that without American support the offensive would have succeeded. At the same time, Nixon ordered American planes to bomb targets near Hanoi, the capital of North Vietnam, and Haiphong, its principal port, and called for the mining of seven North Vietnamese harbors (including Haiphong) to stop the flow of supplies from China and the Soviet Union.

"Peace with Honor"

As the 1972 presidential election approached, the administration stepped up its efforts to produce a breakthrough in negotiations with the North Vietnamese. In April 1972, the president dropped his longtime insistence on a removal of North Vietnamese troops from the south before any American withdrawal. Meanwhile, Henry Kissinger was meeting privately in Paris with the North Vietnamese foreign secretary, Le Duc Tho, to work out terms for a cease-fire. On October 26, only days before the presidential election, Kissinger announced that "peace is at hand." Several weeks later (after the election), negotiations broke down once again. Although both the American and the North Vietnamese governments were ready to accept the Kissinger-Tho plan for a cease-fire, the Thieu regime balked, still insisting on a full withdrawal of North Vietnamese forces from the south. Kissinger tried to win additional concessions from the communists to meet Thieu's objections, but on December 16 talks broke off.

The next day, December 17, American B-52s began the heaviest and most destructive air raids of the entire war on Hanoi, Haiphong, and other North Vietnamese targets.

"Christmas Bombing" Civilian casualties were high. And fifteen American B-52s were shot down by the North Vietnamese; in the entire war to that point, the United States had lost only one of the giant bombers. On December 30, Nixon terminated the "Christmas bombing." The United States and the North Vietnamese returned to the conference table. And on January 27, 1973, they signed an "agreement on ending the war and restoring peace in Vietnam." Nixon claimed that the Christmas bombing had forced the North Vietnamese to relent. At least equally important, however, was the enormous American pressure on Thieu to accept the cease-fire.

The terms of the Paris accords were little different from those Kissinger and Tho had accepted in principle a few months before. There would be an immediate cease-fire. The North Vietnamese would release several hundred American prisoners of war, whose fate had become an emotional issue of great importance within the United States. After that the agreement descended into murky and plainly unworkable arrangements. The Thieu regime would survive for the moment—the principal North Vietnamese concession to the United States—but North Vietnamese forces already in the south would remain there. An undefined committee would work out a permanent settlement.

Defeat in Indochina

American forces were hardly out of Indochina before the Paris accords collapsed. During the first year after the cease-fire, the contending Vietnamese armies suffered greater battle losses than the Americans had absorbed during ten years of fighting. Finally, in March 1975, the North Vietnamese launched a full-scale offensive against the now greatly weakened forces of the south. Thieu appealed to Washington for assistance; the president (now Gerald Ford) appealed to Congress for additional funding; Congress refused. Late in April 1975, communist forces marched into Saigon, shortly after officials of the Thieu regime and the staff of *Fall of Saigon* the American embassy had fled the country in humiliating

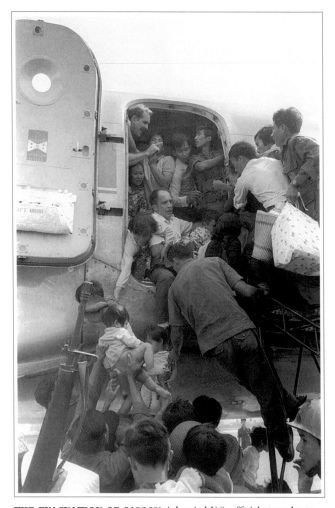

THE EVACUATION OF SAIGON A harried U.S. official struggles to keep panicking Vietnamese from boarding an already overburdened helicopter on the roof of the American embassy in Saigon. The hurried evacuation of Americans took place only hours before the arrival of North Vietnamese troops, signaling the final defeat of South Vietnam. *(AP/Wide World Photos)*

disarray. Communist forces quickly occupied the capital, renamed it Ho Chi Minh City, and began the process of re-uniting Vietnam under the harsh rule of Hanoi. At about the same time, the Lon Nol regime in Cambodia fell to the murderous communists of Pol Pot and the Khmer Rouge—whose genocidal policies led to the deaths of more than a third of the country's people over the next several years. That was the dismal end of over a decade of direct American military involvement in Vietnam. More than 1.2 million Vietnamese soldiers had died in combat, along with countless civilians throughout the region. A beautiful land had been ravaged, its agrarian economy left in ruins; for many years after, Vietnam remained one of the poorest and most politically oppressive nations in the world. The United States had paid a heavy price as well. The war had cost the nation almost $150 billion in direct costs and much more indirectly. It had resulted in the deaths of over 55,000 young Americans and the injury of 300,000 more. And the nation had suffered a blow to its confidence and self-esteem from which it would not soon recover.

NIXON, KISSINGER, AND THE WORLD

The continuing war in Vietnam provided a dismal backdrop to what Nixon considered his larger mission in world affairs: the construction of a new international order. The president had become convinced that old assumptions of a "bipolar" world—in which the United States and the Soviet Union were the only truly great powers—were now obsolete. America must adapt to the new *Toward a "Multipolar" World* "multipolar" international structure, in which China, Japan, and Western Europe were becoming major, independent forces. "It will be a safer world and a better world," he said in 1971, "if we have a strong, healthy United States, Europe, Soviet Union, China, Japan—each balancing the other, not playing one against the other, an even balance."

Nixon and Kissinger believed it was possible to construct something like the "balance of power" that had permitted nineteenth-century Europe to experience nearly a century of relative stability. To do so, however, required a major change in several longstanding assumptions of American foreign policy.

China and the Soviet Union

For more than twenty years, ever since the fall of Chiang Kai-shek in 1949, the United States had treated China, the second largest nation on earth, as if it did not exist. Instead, America recognized the forlorn regime-in-exile on Taiwan as the legitimate government of mainland China. Nixon and Kissinger wanted to forge a new relationship with the Chinese communists—in part to strengthen them as a counterbalance to the Soviet Union. The

Chinese, for their part, were eager to forestall the possibility of a Soviet-American alliance against China and to end China's own isolation from the international arena.

In July 1971, Nixon sent Henry Kissinger on a secret mission to Beijing. When Kissinger returned, the president made the startling announcement that he would visit China himself within the next few months. That fall, with American approval, the United Nations admitted the communist government of China and expelled the representatives of the Taiwan regime, whose claim to be the legitimate government of all China had been a major obstacle to western recognition of the communist regime. Finally, in February 1972, Nixon paid a formal visit to China and, in a *Nixon's China Visit* single stroke, erased much of the deep American animosity toward the Chinese communists. Nixon did not yet formally recognize the communist regime, but in 1972 the United States and China began low-level diplomatic relations.

The initiatives in China coincided with (and probably assisted) an effort by the Nixon administration to improve relations with the Soviet Union. In 1969, American and Soviet diplomats met in Helsinki, Finland, to begin talks on limiting nuclear weapons. In 1972, they produced the first Strategic Arms Limitation Treaty (SALT I), *SALT I* which froze the nuclear missiles (ICBMs) of both sides at present levels. In May of that year, the president traveled to Moscow to sign the agreement. The next year, the Soviet premier, Leonid Brezhnev, visited Washington, and the two leaders pledged renewed efforts to speed the next phase of arms control negotiations.

The Problems of Multipolarity

The policies of rapprochement with communist China and détente with the Soviet Union reflected Nixon's and Kissinger's belief in the importance of stable relationships among the great powers. But great-power relationships could not alone ensure international stability, for the "Third World" remained the most volatile and dangerous source of international tension.

Central to the Nixon-Kissinger policy toward the Third World was the effort to maintain a stable status quo without involving the United States too deeply in local disputes. In 1969 and 1970, the president described what became known as *Nixon Doctrine* the Nixon Doctrine, by which the United States would "participate in the defense and development of allies and friends" but would leave the "basic responsibility" for the future of those "friends" to the nations themselves. In practice, the Nixon Doctrine meant a declining American interest in contributing to Third World development; a growing contempt for the United Nations, where less-developed nations were gaining influence through their sheer numbers; and increasing support to authoritarian regimes attempting to withstand radical challenges from within.

DÉTENTE AT HIGH TIDE The visit of Soviet Premier Leonid Brezhnev to Washington in 1973 was a high-water mark in the search for détente between the two nations, a search that had begun as early as 1962, that continued through parts of five presidential administrations, and that collapsed in disarray in the late 1970s. Here, Brezhnev and Nixon share friendly words while standing on the White House balcony. *(J. P. Laffont/Corbis Sygma)*

In 1970, for example, the CIA poured substantial funds into Chile to help support the established government against a communist challenge. When the Marxist candidate for president, Salvador Allende, came to power through an honest election, the United States began funneling more money to opposition forces in Chile to help "destabilize" the new government. In 1973, a military junta seized power from Allende, who was subsequently murdered. The United States developed a friendly relationship with the new, repressive military government of General Augusto Pinochet.

In the Middle East, conditions were growing more volatile in the aftermath of the 1967 "Six-Day War," in *"Six-Day War"* which Israel routed Egyptian, Syrian, and Jordanian forces, gained control of the whole of the long-divided city of

Jerusalem, and occupied substantial new territories: on the west bank of the Jordan River, the Gaza Strip, the Golan Heights, and elsewhere. The war also increased the number of refugee Palestinians—Arabs who claimed the lands now controlled by Israel and who, dislodged from their homes, became a source of considerable instability in Jordan, Lebanon, and the other surrounding countries into which they now moved. Jordan's ruler, King Hussein, was particularly alarmed by the influx of Palestinians and by the activities of the Palestinian Liberation Organization (PLO) and other radical groups, which he feared would threaten Jordan's important relationship with the United States. After a series of uprisings in 1970, Hussein ordered the Jordanian army to expel the Palestinians. Many of them moved to Lebanon, where they became part of many years of instability and civil war.

In October 1973, on the Jewish High Holy Day of Yom Kippur, Egyptian and Syrian forces attacked Israel. For ten days, the Israelis struggled to recover from the surprise attack; finally, they launched an effective counteroffensive against Egyptian forces in the Sinai. At that point, the United States intervened, placing heavy pressure on Israel to accept a cease-fire rather than press its advantage.

The imposed settlement of the Yom Kippur War demonstrated the growing dependence of the United States and its allies on Arab oil. Permitting Israel to continue its drive into Egypt might have jeopardized the ability of the United States to purchase needed petroleum from the Arab states. A brief but painful embargo by the Arab governments on the sale of oil to supporters of Israel (in- *Arab Oil Embargo* cluding America) in 1973 provided an ominous warning of the costs of losing access to the region's resources. The lesson of the Yom Kippur War, therefore, was that the United States could not ignore the interests of the Arab nations in its efforts on behalf of Israel.

A larger lesson of 1973 was that the nations of the Third World could no longer be expected to act as passive, cooperative "client states." The United States could no longer depend on cheap, easy access to raw materials as it had in the past.

POLITICS AND ECONOMICS UNDER NIXON

For a time in the late 1960s, it had seemed to many Americans that the forces of chaos and radicalism were taking control of the nation. The domestic policy of the Nixon administration was an attempt to restore balance: between the needs of the poor and the desires of the middle class, between the power of the federal government and the interests of local communities. In the end, however, economic and political crises—some beyond the administration's control, some of its own making—sharply limited Nixon's ability to fulfill his domestic goals.

Domestic Initiatives

Many of Nixon's domestic policies were a response to what he believed to be the demands of his own constituency—conservative, middle-class people whom he liked to call the "silent majority" and who wanted to reduce federal "interference" in local affairs. He tried, unsuccessfully, to persuade Congress to pass legislation prohibiting the use of forced busing to achieve school desegregation. He forbade the Department of Health, Education, and Welfare to cut off federal funds from school districts that had failed to comply with court orders to integrate. At the same time, he began

Dismantling the Great Society

to reduce or dismantle many of the social programs of the Great Society and the New Frontier. In 1973, for example, he abolished the Office of Economic Opportunity, the centerpiece of the antipoverty program of the Johnson years.

Yet Nixon's domestic efforts were not entirely conservative. One of the administration's boldest efforts was an attempt to overhaul the nation's enormous welfare system. Nixon proposed replacing the existing system, which almost everyone agreed was cumbersome, expensive, and inefficient, with what he called the Family Assistance Plan. It would in effect have created a guaranteed annual income for all Americans: $1,600 in federal grants, which could be supplemented by outside earnings up to $4,000. Even many liberals applauded the proposal as an important step toward expanding federal responsibility for the poor. Nixon, however, presented the plan in conservative terms: as something that would reduce the supervisory functions of the federal government and transfer to welfare recipients themselves daily responsibility for their own lives. Although the FAP won approval in the House in 1970, concerted attacks by welfare recipients (who considered the benefits inadequate), members of the welfare bureaucracy (whose own influence stood to be sharply diminished by the bill), and conservatives (who opposed a guaranteed income on principle) helped kill it in the Senate.

From the Warren Court to the Nixon Court

Of all the liberal institutions that had aroused the enmity of the "silent majority" in the 1950s and 1960s, none had evoked more anger and bitterness than the Supreme Court. Not only had its rulings on racial matters disrupted traditional social patterns in both the North and the South, but its staunch defense of civil liberties had, in the eyes of many Americans, contributed to the increase in crime, disorder, and moral decay. In *Engel* v. *Vitale* (1962), the Court had ruled that prayers in public schools were unconstitutional, sparking outrage among religious fundamentalists and others. In *Roth* v. *United States* (1957), the Court had sharply limited the authority of local governments to curb pornography. In a series of other decisions, the Court had greatly strengthened the civil rights of criminal defendants and, in the eyes of many Americans, had greatly weakened the power of law enforcement officials to do their jobs. For example, in *Gideon* v. *Wainwright* (1963), the Court had ruled that every felony defendant was entitled to a lawyer regardless of his or her ability to pay. In *Escobedo* v. *Illinois* (1964), it had ruled that a defendant must be allowed access to a lawyer before questioning by police. In *Miranda* v. *Arizona* (1966), the Court had confirmed the obligation of authorities to inform a criminal suspect of his or her rights. By 1968, the Warren Court had become the target of Americans of all kinds who felt the balance of power in the United States had shifted too far toward the poor and dispossessed at the expense of the middle class, and toward criminals at the expense of law-abiding citizens.

One of the most important decisions of the Warren Court in the 1960s was *Baker* v. *Carr* (1962), which required state legislatures to apportion electoral districts so

Baker v. Carr

that all citizens' votes would have equal weight. In dozens of states, systems of legislative districting had given disproportionate representation to sparsely populated rural areas, hence diminishing the voting power of urban residents. The reapportionment that the decision required greatly strengthened the voting power of African Americans, Hispanics, and other groups concentrated in cities. Nixon was determined to use his judicial appointments to give the Court a more conservative cast. His first opportunity came almost as soon as he entered office. When Chief Justice Earl Warren resigned early in 1969, Nixon replaced him with a federal appeals court judge of known conservative leanings, Warren Burger. A few months later, Associate Justice Abe Fortas resigned after allegations of financial improprieties. To replace him, Nixon named Clement F. Haynsworth, a respected federal circuit court judge from South Carolina. But Haynsworth came under fire from Senate liberals, black organizations, and labor unions for his conservative record on civil rights and for what some claimed was a conflict of interest in several of the cases on which he had sat. The Senate rejected him. Nixon's next choice was G. Harrold Carswell, a judge of the Florida federal appeals court almost entirely lacking in distinction and widely considered unfit for the Supreme Court. The Senate rejected his nomination too.

Nixon angrily denounced the votes, calling them expressions of prejudice against the South. But he was careful thereafter to choose men of standing within the legal community to fill vacancies on the Supreme Court: Harry Blackmun, a moderate jurist from Minnesota; Lewis F. Powell, Jr., a respected judge from Virginia; and William Rehnquist, a member of the Nixon Justice Department. In the process, he transformed the Warren Court into what some called the "Nixon Court" and others the "Burger Court."

The new Court, however, fell short of what many conservatives had expected. Rather than retreating from its commitment to social reform, the Court in many areas actually moved further. In *Swann* v. *Charlotte-Mecklenburg Board of Education* (1971), it ruled in favor of the use of forced busing to achieve racial balance in schools. Not even the intense and occasionally violent opposition of local communities such as Boston and Louisville, Kentucky, was able to weaken the judicial commitment to integration. In *Furman* v. *Georgia* (1972), the Court overturned existing capital punishment statutes and established strict new guidelines for such laws in the future. In *Roe* v. *Wade* (1973), it struck down laws forbidding abortions. In other decisions, however, the Burger Court was more moderate. Although the justices approved busing as a tool for achieving integration, they rejected, in *Milliken* v. *Bradley* (1974), a plan to transfer students across district lines (in this case, between Detroit and its suburbs) to achieve racial balance. While the Court

Bakke v. Board of Regents of California

upheld the principle of affirmative action in its celebrated 1978 decision *Bakke* v. *Board of Regents of California,* it established restrictive new guidelines for such programs in the future. In *Stone* v. *Powell* (1976), the Court agreed to certain limits on the right of a defendant to appeal a state conviction to the federal judiciary.

The Election of 1972

However unsuccessful his administration may have been in achieving some of its specific goals, Nixon entered the presidential race in 1972 with a substantial reserve of strength. The events of that year improved his position immeasurably. His energetic reelection committee collected enormous sums of money to support the campaign. The president himself used the powers of incumbency with great effect, refraining from campaigning and concentrating on highly publicized international decisions and state visits. Agencies of the federal government dispensed funds and favors to strengthen Nixon's political standing in critical areas.

Nixon was most fortunate in 1972, however, in his opposition. The return of George Wallace to the presidential fray caused some early concern. Nixon was delighted to see Wallace run in the Democratic primaries and quietly encouraged him to do so. But he feared that Wallace would again launch a third-party campaign; Nixon's own reelection strategy rested on the same appeals to the troubled middle class that Wallace was expressing. The possibility of such a campaign vanished in May, when a would-be assassin shot the Alabama governor during a rally at a Maryland shopping center. Paralyzed from the waist down, Wallace was unable to continue campaigning.

The Democrats, in the meantime, were making their own contributions to the Nixon cause by nominating for president a representative of their most liberal wing: Senator George S. McGovern of South Dakota. An outspoken critic of the war, a forceful

George McGovern

advocate of advanced liberal positions on most social and economic issues, McGovern seemed to embody those aspects of the turbulent 1960s that middle-class Americans were most eager to reject. McGovern profited greatly from party reforms (which he himself had helped to draft) that reduced the power of party leaders and gave increased influence to women, blacks, and young people in the selection of the Democratic ticket. But those same reforms helped make the Democratic Convention of 1972 an unappealing spectacle to much of the public. McGovern then disillusioned even some of his own supporters by his indecisive reaction to revelations that his running mate, Senator Thomas Eagleton of Missouri, had undergone treatment for an emotional disturbance. Eagleton finally withdrew from the ticket. The remainder of the Democratic presidential campaign was an exercise in futility.

On election day, Nixon won reelection by one of the largest margins in history: 60.7 percent of the popular vote compared with 37.5 percent for the forlorn McGovern, and an

Nixon's Landslide

electoral margin of 520 to 17. The Democratic candidate had carried only Massachusetts and the District of Columbia. The new commitments that Nixon had so effectively expressed—to restraint in social reform, to decentralization of political power, to the defense of traditional values, and to a new balance in international relations—had clearly won the approval of the American people. But other problems were already lurking in the wings.

The Troubled Economy

Although it was political scandal that would ultimately destroy the Nixon presidency, the most important national crisis of the early 1970s was the troubled transformation of the American economy. For three decades, the American economy had been the envy of the world. It had produced as much as a third of the world's industrial goods and had dominated international trade. The American dollar had been the strongest currency in the world, and the American standard of living had risen steadily from its already substantial heights. Many Americans assumed that this remarkable prosperity was the normal condition of their society. In fact, however, it rested in part on several artificial conditions that were rapidly disappearing by the late 1960s: above all, the absence of significant foreign competition and easy access to raw materials in the Third World.

Inflation, which had been creeping upward for several years when Richard Nixon took office, soon began to soar; it would be the most disturbing economic problem of

Inflation

the 1970s. Its most visible cause was a significant increase in federal deficit spending in the 1960s, when the Johnson administration tried to fund the war in Vietnam and

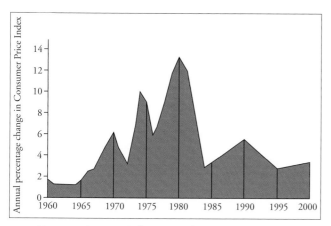

INFLATION, 1960–2000 Inflation was the biggest economic worry of most Americans in the 1970s and early 1980s, and this chart shows why. Having remained very low through the early 1960s, inflation rose slowly in the second half of the decade and then dramatically in the mid- and late 1970s, before beginning a long and reasonably steady decline in the early 1980s. ◆ *What caused the great spike in inflation in the 1970s?*

its ambitious social programs without raising taxes. But there were other, equally important causes of the inflation and of the economic problems that lay behind it. No longer did the United States have exclusive access to cheap raw materials around the globe; not only were other industrial nations now competing for increasingly scarce raw materials, but Third World suppliers of those materials were beginning to realize their value and to demand higher prices for them.

The greatest immediate blow to the American economy was the increasing cost of energy. More than any nation on earth, the United States based its economy on the easy availability of cheap and plentiful fossil fuels. No society was more dependent on the automobile; none was more wasteful in its use of oil and gas in its homes, schools, and factories. Domestic petroleum reserves were no longer sufficient to meet this demand, and the nation was heavily dependent on imports from the Middle East and Africa.

For many years, the Organization of Petroleum Exporting Countries (OPEC) had operated as an informal bargaining *OPEC* unit for the sale of oil by Third World nations, but had seldom managed to exercise any real strength. But in the early 1970s, OPEC began to assert itself, to use its oil both as an economic tool and as a political weapon. In 1973, in the midst of the Yom Kippur War, Arab members of OPEC announced that they would no longer ship petroleum to nations supporting Israel—which meant the United States and its allies in Western Europe. At about the same time, the OPEC nations agreed to raise their prices 400 percent. These twin shocks produced momentary economic chaos in the West. The United States suffered its first fuel shortage since World War II. And although the boycott ended a few months later, the price of energy continued to skyrocket both because of OPEC's new militant policies and

because of the weakening competitive position of the dollar in world markets. No single factor did more to produce the soaring inflation of the 1970s.

But inflation was only one of the new problems facing the American economy. The other, and more important in the long run, was the decline of the nation's manufacturing sector. American industry had flourished in the immediate aftermath of World War II, in part because of the new plant capacity the war had created, in part because the country faced almost no competition from other industrial nations. American workers in unionized industries had profited from this postwar success by winning some of the most generous wage and benefits packages in the world.

By the 1970s, however, the climate for American manufacturing had changed significantly. Many of the great industrial plants were now many decades old, much less efficient than the newer plants that Japan and European industrial nations had constructed after the war. In some industries (notably steel and automobiles), management had become complacent and stultifyingly bureaucratic. Most important, U.S. manufacturing now faced major competition from abroad—not only in world trade (which still constituted only a small part of the American economy) but also at home. Automobiles, steel, and many other manufactured goods from Japan and Europe established major footholds in the United States markets. Some of America's new competitors benefited from lower labor costs than their U.S. counterparts; but that was only one of many reasons for their success.

Thus the 1970s marked the beginning of a long, painful process of deindustrialization, during which thousands of factories across the country closed their gates and millions *Deindustrialization* of workers lost their jobs. New employment opportunities were becoming available in other, growing areas of the economy: technology, information systems, and many other more "knowledge-based" industries that would ultimately drive an extraordinary (if unbalanced) economic revival in the 1980s and 1990s. But many industrial workers were poorly equipped to move into those jobs. The result was a growing pool of unemployed and underemployed workers; the virtual disappearance of industrial jobs from many inner cities, where large numbers of minorities lived; and the impoverishment of communities dependent on particular industries. Some of the nation's manufacturing sectors ultimately revived, but few regained the size and dominance they had enjoyed in the 1950s and 1960s; and few employed a work force as large or as relatively well paid as they once had.

The Nixon Response

The Nixon administration responded to these mounting economic problems by focusing on the one thing it thought it could control: inflation. The government moved first to reduce spending and raise taxes. But those policies produced both congressional and popular protest, and Nixon turned increasingly to an economic tool more readily available to him: control of the currency. Placing conservative economists at the head of the Federal Reserve Board, he ensured sharply higher interest rates and a contraction of the money supply. But the tight money policy did little to curb inflation: the cost of living rose a cumulative 15 percent during Nixon's first two and a half years in office. Economic growth, in the meantime,

"Stagflation" | declined. The United States was encountering a new and puzzling dilemma: "stagflation," a combination of rising prices and general economic stagnation.

In the summer of 1971, Nixon imposed a ninety-day freeze on all wages and prices at their existing levels. Then, in November, he launched what he called Phase II of his economic plan: mandatory guidelines for wage and price increases, to be administered by a federal agency. Inflation subsided temporarily, but the recession continued. Fearful that the recession would be more damaging than inflation in an election year, the administration reversed itself late in 1971: interest rates were allowed to drop sharply, and government spending was increased—producing the largest budget deficit since World War II. The new tactics helped revive the economy in the short term, but inflation rose substantially—particularly after the administration abandoned the strict Phase II controls and replaced them with a set of voluntary, and almost entirely ineffective, guidelines.

In 1973, prices rose 9 percent; in 1974, after the Arab oil embargo and the OPEC price increases, they rose 12 percent—the highest rate since the relaxation of price controls shortly after World War II. The value of the dollar continued to slide, and the nation's international trade continued to decline. In the meantime, the energy crisis was quickly becoming a national preoccupation. But while Nixon talked often about the need to achieve "energy independence," he offered few concrete proposals.

The erratic economic programs of the Nixon administration were a sign of a broader national confusion about the prospects for American prosperity. The Nixon pattern—of lurching from a tight money policy to curb inflation at one moment, to a spending policy to cure recession at the next—repeated itself during the two administrations that followed.

THE WATERGATE CRISIS

Although economic problems greatly concerned the American people in the 1970s, another stunning development almost entirely preoccupied the nation beginning early in 1973: the fall of Richard Nixon. The president's demise was a result, in part, of his own personality. Defensive, secretive, resentful of his critics, he brought to his office an element of mean-spiritedness that helped undermine even his most important accomplishments. But the larger explanation lay in Nixon's view of American society and the world, and of his own role in both. The president believed the United States faced grave dangers from the radicals and dissidents who were challenging his policies. He came increasingly to consider any challenge to his policies a threat to "national security." By identifying his own political fortunes with those of the nation, Nixon was creating a climate in which he and those who served him could justify almost any tactics to stifle dissent and undermine opposition.

The Scandals

Nixon's outlook was in part a culmination of long-term changes in the presidency. Public expectations of the president had increased dramatically in the years since *The Changing Presidency* World War II; yet the constraints placed on the authority of the office by Congress, the courts, interest groups, the media, and elsewhere had grown as well. In response, a succession of presidents had sought new methods for the exercise of power, often stretching the law, occasionally breaking it. Nixon not only continued but greatly accelerated these trends. Facing a Democratic Congress hostile to his goals, he attempted to find ways to circumvent the legislature whenever possible. Saddled with a federal bureaucracy unresponsive to his wishes, he constructed a hierarchy of command in which virtually all executive power became concentrated in the White House. Operating within a rigid, even autocratic staff structure, the president became a solitary, at times brooding figure, whose contempt for his opponents and impatience with obstacles to his policies festered and grew. Unknown to all but a few intimates, he also became mired in a pattern of illegalities and abuses of power that in late 1972 began to break through to the surface.

Early on the morning of June 17, 1972, police arrested five men who had broken into the offices of the Democratic National Committee in the Watergate office building in *The Watergate Break-in* Washington, D.C. Two others were seized a short time later and charged with supervising the break-in. When reporters for the *Washington Post* began researching the backgrounds of the culprits, they discovered that among those involved in the burglary were former employees of the Committee for the Re-Election of the President (CRP). One of them had worked in the White House itself. Moreover, they had been paid to execute the break-in from a secret fund of the reelection committee, a fund controlled by members of the White House staff.

Public interest in the disclosures grew slowly in the last months of 1972. Few Americans questioned the president's assurances that neither he nor his staff had any connection with what he called "this very bizarre incident." Early in 1973, however, the Watergate burglars

Twenty-five years after Watergate—one of the most famous political scandals in American history—historians and others continue to argue about its causes and significance. Their interpretations tend to fall into several broad categories.

One argument emphasizes the evolution of the institution of the presidency over time and sees Watergate as the result of a much larger pattern of presidential usurpations of power that stretched back at least several decades. Arthur Schlesinger, Jr., helped develop this argument in his 1973 book *The Imperial Presidency*, which argues that ever since World War II, Americans have believed that the nation was in a state of permanent crisis, threatened from abroad by the menace of communism, threatened from within by the danger of insufficient will. The belief of a succession of presidents in the urgency of this crisis, and in their duty

(Bettmann/Corbis)

to take whatever measures might be necessary to combat it, led them gradually to usurp more and more power from Congress, from the courts, and from the public. Initially, this expansion of presidential power came

in the realm of international affairs: covert and at times illegal activities overseas. But in the postwar world, domestic politics began to seem inseparable from international politics. Gradually, presidents began to look for ways to circumvent constraints in domestic matters as well. Nixon's actions in the Watergate crisis were, in other words, a culmination of this long and steady expansion of covert presidential power. Jonathan Schell, in *The Time of Illusion* (1975), offers a variation of this argument, tying the crisis of the presidency to the pressure that nuclear weapons place on presidents to protect the nation's—and their own—"credibility." Other commentators (but not any serious historical studies) go even further and argue that what happened to produce the Watergate scandals was not substantively different from the normal patterns of presidential behavior, that Nixon simply got caught

went on trial; and under relentless prodding from federal judge John J. Sirica, one of the defendants, James W. McCord, agreed to cooperate both with the grand jury and with a special Senate investigating committee recently established under Senator Sam J. Ervin of North Carolina. McCord's testimony opened a floodgate of confessions, and for months a parade of White House and campaign officials exposed one illegality after another. Foremost among them was a member of the inner circle of the White House, counsel to the president John Dean, who leveled allegations against Nixon himself.

Two different sets of scandals were emerging from the investigations. One was a general pattern of abuses of power involving both the White House and the Nixon campaign committee, which included, but was not limited to, the Watergate break-in. The other scandal, and the one that became the major focus of public attention for nearly two years, was the way in which the administration tried to manage the investigations of the Watergate break-in and other abuses—a pattern of behavior that became *"Cover-up"* known as the "cover-up." There was never any conclusive evidence that the president had planned or approved the burglary in advance. But there was mounting evidence that he had been involved in illegal efforts to obstruct investigations of and withhold information about the episode. Testimony before the Ervin committee provided

evidence of the complicity of Dean, Attorney General John Mitchell, top White House assistants H. R. Haldeman and John Ehrlichman, and others. As interest in the case grew to something approaching a national obsession, the investigation focused increasingly on a single question: in the words of Senator Howard Baker of Tennessee, a member of the Ervin committee, "What did the President know and when did he know it?"

Nixon accepted the departure of those members of his administration implicated in the scandals. But he continued to insist that he himself was innocent. There the matter might have rested, had it not been for the disclosure during the Senate hearings of a White House taping system that had recorded virtually every conversation in the president's office during the period in question. All the groups investigating the scandals sought access to the tapes; Nixon, pleading "executive privilege," refused to release them. A special prosecutor appointed by the president to handle the Watergate cases, Harvard law professor Archibald Cox, took Nixon to court in October 1973 in an effort to force him to relinquish the recordings. Nixon, clearly growing desperate, then fired Cox and suffered the humiliation of watching both Attorney General Elliot Richardson and his deputy resign in protest. This "Saturday night massacre" made the president's predicament *"Saturday Night Massacre"* infinitely worse. Not only did public pressure force him to

where others had not, and that a long-standing liberal hostility toward Nixon ensured that he would pay a higher price for his behavior than other presidents would.

A second explanation of Watergate emphasizes the difficult social and political environment of the late 1960s and early 1970s. Nixon entered office, according to this view, facing an unprecedentedly radical opposition that would stop at nothing to discredit the war and destroy his authority. He found himself, therefore, drawn into taking similarly desperate measures of his own to defend himself from these extraordinary challenges. Nixon made this argument in his own 1975 memoirs:

> Now that this season of mindless terror has fortunately passed, it is difficult—perhaps impossible—to convey a sense of the pressures that were influencing my actions and reactions during this period, but it was this epidemic of unprecedented domestic terrorism that prompted our efforts to discover the best means by which to deal with this new phenomenon of highly organized and highly skilled revolutionaries dedicated to the violent destruction of our democratic system.*

The historian Herbert Parmet echoes parts of this argument in *Richard Nixon and His America* (1990). Stephen Ambrose offers a more muted version of the same view in *Richard Nixon* (1989).

Most of those who have written about Watergate, however, search for the explanation not in institutional or social forces, but in the personalities of the people involved, and most notably in the personality of Richard Nixon. Even many of those who have developed structural explanations (Schlesinger, Schell, and Ambrose, for example) return eventually to Nixon himself as the most important explanation for Watergate. Others begin there, perhaps most notably Stanley I. Kutler, in *The Wars of Watergate* (1990) and, later, *Abuse of Power* (1997), in which he presents extensive excerpts from conversations about Watergate taped in the Nixon White House. Kutler emphasizes Nixon's lifelong resort to vicious political tactics and his longstanding belief that he was a special target of unscrupulous enemies and had to "get" them before they got him. Watergate was rooted, Kutler argues, "in the personality and history of Nixon himself." A "corrosive hatred," he claims, "decisively shaped Nixon's own behavior, his career, and eventually his historical standing."

appoint a new special prosecutor, Texas attorney Leon Jaworski, who proved just as determined as Cox to subpoena the tapes; but the episode precipitated an investigation by the House of Representatives into the possibility of impeachment.

The Fall of Richard Nixon

Nixon's situation deteriorated further in the following months. Late in 1973, Vice President Spiro Agnew became embroiled in a scandal of his own when evidence surfaced that he had accepted bribes and kickbacks while serving as governor of Maryland and even as vice president. In return for a Justice Department agreement not to press the case, Agnew pleaded no contest to a lesser charge of income-tax evasion and resigned from the government. With the controversial Agnew no longer in line to succeed to the presidency, the prospect of removing Nixon from the White House became less worrisome to his opponents. The new vice president (the first appointed under the terms of the Twenty-fifth Amendment, which had been adopted in 1967) was House Minority Leader Gerald Ford, an amiable and popular Michigan congressman.

The impeachment investigation quickly gathered pace. In April 1974, in an effort to head off further subpoenas of the tapes, the president released transcripts of a number of relevant conversations, claiming that they proved his innocence. Investigators and much of the public felt otherwise. Even these edited tapes seemed to suggest Nixon's complicity in the cover-up. In July, the crisis reached a climax. First the Supreme Court ruled unanimously, in *United States* v. *Richard M. Nixon,* that the president must relinquish the tapes to Special Prosecutor *U.S. v. Richard Nixon* Jaworski. Days later, the House Judiciary Committee voted to recommend three articles of impeachment, charging that Nixon had, first, obstructed justice in the Watergate cover-up; second, misused federal agencies to violate the rights of citizens; and third, defied the authority of Congress by refusing to deliver tapes and other materials subpoenaed by the committee.

Even without additional evidence, Nixon might well have been impeached by the full House and convicted by the Senate. Early in August, however, he provided at last what many wavering members of Congress had begun to call the "smoking gun"—the concrete proof of his guilt that his defenders had long contended was missing from the case against him. Among the tapes that the Supreme Court compelled Nixon to relinquish were several that offered apparently incontrovertible evidence of his involvement in the Watergate cover-up. Only days after the burglary, the recordings disclosed, the president had ordered the FBI to stop investigating the break-in. Impeachment and conviction now seemed inevitable.

NIXON'S FAREWELL Only moments before, Nixon had been in tears saying goodbye to his staff in the East Room of the White House. But as he boarded a helicopter to begin his trip home to California shortly after resigning as president, he flashed his trademark "victory" sign to the crowd on the White House Lawn. *(Bettmann/Corbis)*

For several days, Nixon brooded in the White House, on the verge, some claimed, of a breakdown. Finally, on August 8, 1974, he announced his resignation—the first president in American history ever to do so. At noon the next day, while Nixon and his family were flying west to their home in California, Gerald Ford took the oath of office as president.

Nixon Resigns

Many Americans expressed relief and exhilaration that, as the new president put it, "Our long national nightmare is over." Many were relieved to be rid of Richard Nixon, who had lost virtually all the wide popularity that had won him his landslide reelection victory only two years before. And many were also exhilarated that, as some boasted, "the system had worked." But the wave of good feeling could not obscure the deeper and more lasting damage of the Watergate crisis. In a society in which distrust of leaders and institutions of authority was already widespread, the fall of Richard Nixon seemed to confirm the most cynical assumptions about the character of American public life.

CONCLUSION

The victory of Richard Nixon in the 1968 presidential election represented a popular repudiation of turbulence and radicalism. It was a call for a restoration of order and stability. But order and stability were not the dominant characteristics of Nixon's troubled years in office. Nixon entered office, rather, when the forces of the left and the counterculture were approaching the peak of their influence. American culture and society in the late 1960s and early 1970s were shaped decisively by, and were deeply divided over, the challenges of young people to the norms by which most Americans had lived. Also in those years, a host of new liberation movements joined the drive for racial equality and women mobilized effectively and powerfully to demand changes in the way their society treated gender differences.

Nixon had run for office attacking the failure of his predecessor to end the war in Vietnam. But during the four years of his presidency, the war—and the protests against it—continued and even in some respects escalated. The division of opinion over the war was as deep as any of the many other divisions in national life. It continued to poison the nation's politics and social fabric until the American role in the conflict finally shuddered to a close in 1973.

But much of the controversy and division in the 1970s was a product of the Nixon presidency itself. Nixon was in many ways a dynamic and even visionary leader, who proposed (but rarely succeeded in enacting) some important domestic reforms and who made important changes in American foreign policy, most notably making overtures to communist China and forging détente with the Soviet Union. He was also, however, a devious, secretive, and embittered man whose White House staff became engaged in a series of covert activities—many of them connected with the president's reelection campaign in 1972—that produced the most dramatic political scandal in American history. Watergate, as it was called, preoccupied much of the nation for nearly two years beginning in 1972; and ultimately, in the summer of 1974, the scandal forced Richard Nixon—who had been reelected to office only two years before by one of the largest majorities in modern history—to become the first president in American history to resign. He was a victim in part of the passions and divisions of his time and of the Vietnam War, which he had inherited but had not been able to end quickly. He was a victim as well of his own insecurities and resentments. Whatever the causes of his fall, however, the greatest cost of Watergate was not what it did to Nixon himself, but how it damaged the faith of the American people in their leaders and their government. That faith would remain weak through the remainder of the century.

FOR FURTHER REFERENCE

John Morton Blum, *Years of Discord: American Politics and Society, 1961–1974* (1991) is a good overview. James Miller, *"Democracy in the Streets": From Port Huron to the Siege of Chicago* (1987) is a perceptive history of the New Left through its leading organization, SDS. Kristin Luker, *Abortion and the Politics of Motherhood* (1984) is an excellent account of this central battle over the nature of feminism. Margaret Cruikshank, *The Rise of a Gay and Lesbian Liberation Movement* (1992) recounts another important struggle of the 1960s and beyond. Ronald Takaki, *Strangers from a Distant Shore: A History of Asian Americans* (1989) examines the growing Asian community in postwar America. Stephen Ambrose, *Nixon: The Triumph of a Politician, 1962–1972* (1989), and *Nixon, Ruin and Recovery, 1973–1990* (1992) provides a thorough chronicle of this important presidency. Joan Hoff, *Nixon Reconsidered* (1994) is a more sympathetic account of Nixon's presidency before Watergate. Stanley J. Kutler, *The Wars of Watergate* (1990) is a scholarly study of the great scandal, and Jonathan Schell, *The Time of Illusion* (1975) is a perceptive contemporary account. Marilyn Young, *The Vietnam Wars, 1945–1990* (1991) provides, among other things, a full account of the last years of American involvement in Vietnam and of the conflicts in the region that followed the American withdrawal.

Chicago 1968 (1995) is a complex and riveting film portrait of the dramatic events around the Democratic National Convention of 1968. The three-part film series *America in 1968* (1979) examines the political, cultural, and international events of that pivotal year. *Nixon* (1990) is a three-hour film biography of one of the most powerful and controversial figures in modern American history. *Watergate* (1994) is a documentary film on the unmaking of the Nixon presidency, including recent interviews with major participants. *In the Spirit of Crazy Horse* (1990) relates the history of the Lakota Indians on the centennial of the Wounded Knee massacre. *Chicano! History of the Mexican-American Civil Rights Movement* (1996) is a four-part series on the Mexican-American movement from 1967.

For quizzes, Internet resources, references to additional books and films, and more, consult this book's Online Learning Center at www.mhhe.com/brinkley11.

DEMONSTRATING AGAINST BILINGUALISM Among the many divisive issues that sparked controversy in the 1970s and 1980s, and helped fuel the rise of a powerful conservative movement, was the growing number of residents of the United States for whom English was a second language. In California and a few other states educators responded by introducing "bilingualism" into the public school system, to ensure that students whose command of English was poor could receive instruction in their own language—usually Spanish, since the largest number of immigrants in the Southwest came from Mexico. Hostility to bilingualism grew rapidly among mostly conservative Americans, who feared that the movement would not stop in the schools. This woman demonstrates in favor of one of the prized causes of the right—the campaign to make English the "official" language of the United States. *(Nathan Benn/Corbis)*

Significant Events

1965 · Richard Viguerie launches conservative direct-mail operations

1966 · Ronald Reagan elected governor of California

1974 · OPEC raises oil prices
· "Stagflation" (recession and inflation together) begins
· Ford pardons Nixon
· Ford meets Brezhnev at Vladivostok summit

1976 · Reagan challenges Ford in Republican presidential primaries
· Jimmy Carter elected president
· Mao Zedong dies

1977 · Panama Canal treaties signed

1978 · Panama Canal treaties ratified
· Voters in California approve Proposition 13, launching tax revolt
· U.S. and China restore diplomatic relations

· Camp David accords signed

1979 · Energy crisis jolts United States
· Iranian revolution overthrows Shah
· American diplomats taken hostage in Iran
· Soviet Union invades Afghanistan
· Sandinista revolution triumphs in Nicaragua
· SALT II signed

1980 · U.S. boycotts Moscow Olympics
· Edward Kennedy challenges Carter in Democratic primaries
· Ronald Reagan elected president

1981 · American hostages in Iran released
· Reagan wins major tax and budget cuts
· U.S. military buildup begins
· Soviet Union forces imposition of martial law in Poland
· United States begins supporting contra rebellion in Nicaragua

CHAPTER THIRTY-THREE

FROM "THE AGE OF LIMITS" TO THE AGE OF REAGAN

*T*he frustrations of the early 1970s—the defeat in Vietnam, the Watergate crisis, the decay of the American economy—inflicted damaging blows to the confident, optimistic nationalism that had characterized so much of the postwar era. Some Americans responded to these problems by announcing the arrival of an "age of limits," in which America would have to learn to live with increasingly constricted expectations. By the end of the decade, however, another response to the challenges was beginning to dominate both American culture and American politics. It was a response that combined a conservative retreat from some of the heady visions of the 1960s with a reinforced commitment to the idea of economic growth, international power, and American virtue.

· Reagan survives assassination attempt	1988 · US and USSR sign INF treaty
1982 · Severe recession begins	· George H. W. Bush defeats Michael Dukakis in presidential election
· Unemployment reaches 11 percent	
· United States invades Grenada	1989 · Berlin Wall dismantled and Germany reunifies
· Israel invades Lebanon	· Eastern European states overthrow communist regimes
· U.S. Marines killed in terrorist attack in Beirut	· China suppresses student uprisings with massacre in Tiananmen Square, Beijing
· Nuclear freeze movement expands in United States	
· Inflation and interest rates decline	· American forces overthrow Noriega in Panama
· Economic recovery begins	1990 · South Africa begins to eliminate apartheid
1984 · Jesse Jackson campaigns for Democratic presidential nomination	· Bush agrees to tax increase
	· Iraq invades Kuwait
· Democrats nominate Geraldine Ferraro for vice president	1991 · Soviet Union dissolves after failed coup attempt
· Reagan defeats Walter Mondale in presidential election	· Economy enters recession
	· U.S. leads multinational force in Gulf War against Iraq
1985 · Mikhail Gorbachev becomes leader of Soviet Union	1992 · Clinton defeats Bush in presidential election
1986 · Iran-contra scandal revealed	1994 · Nelson Mandela elected president of South Africa
· Democrats regain control of U.S. Senate	

POLITICS AND DIPLOMACY AFTER WATERGATE

In the aftermath of Richard Nixon's ignominious departure from office, many wondered whether faith in the presidency, and in the government as a whole, could easily be restored. The administrations of the two presidents who succeeded Nixon did little to answer those questions.

The Ford Custodianship

Gerald Ford inherited the presidency under unenviable circumstances. He had to try to rebuild confidence in government in the face of the widespread cynicism the Watergate scandals had produced. And he had to try to restore prosperity in the face of major domestic and international challenges to the American economy. He enjoyed some success in the first of these efforts but very little in the second.

The new president's effort to establish himself as a symbol of political integrity suffered a setback only a

Nixon Pardoned

month after he took office, when he granted Richard Nixon "a full, free, and absolute pardon" for any crimes he may have committed during his presidency. Ford explained that he was attempting to spare the nation the ordeal of years of litigation and to spare Nixon himself any further suffering. But much of the public suspected a secret deal with the former president. The pardon caused a decline in Ford's popularity from which he never fully recovered. Nevertheless, most Americans considered him a decent man; his honesty and amiability did much to reduce the bitterness and acrimony of the Watergate years.

The Ford administration enjoyed less success in its effort to solve the problems of the American economy. In his efforts to curb inflation, the president rejected the idea of wage and price controls and called instead for largely ineffective voluntary efforts. After supporting high interest rates, opposing increased federal spending (through liberal use of his veto power), and resisting pressures for a tax reduction, Ford had to deal with a serious recession in 1974 and 1975. Central to the economic problems was the continuing energy crisis. In the aftermath of the Arab oil embargo of 1973, the OPEC cartel began to raise the price of oil—by 400 percent in 1974 alone. Even so, American dependence on OPEC supplies continued to grow—one of the principal reasons why inflation reached 11 percent in 1976.

At first it seemed that the new administration's foreign policy would differ little from that of its predecessor. Ford retained Henry Kissinger as secretary of state and contin-

Ford's Diplomatic Successes

ued the general policies of the Nixon years. Late in 1974, Ford met with Leonid Brezhnev at Vladivostok in Siberia and signed an arms control accord that was to serve as the basis for SALT II, thus achieving a goal the Nixon administration

had long sought. The following summer, after a European security conference in Helsinki, Finland, the Soviet Union and Western nations agreed to ratify the borders that had divided Europe since 1945; and the Soviets pledged to increase respect for human rights within their own country. Meanwhile, in the Middle East, Henry Kissinger helped produce a new accord by which Israel agreed to return large portions of the occupied Sinai to Egypt, and the two nations pledged not to resolve future differences by force. In China, finally, the death of Mao Zedong in 1976 brought to power a new, apparently more moderate government eager to expand its ties with the United States.

Nevertheless, as the 1976 presidential election approached, Ford's policies were coming under attack from both the right and the left. In the Republican primary campaign, Ford faced a powerful challenge from former California governor Ronald Reagan, leader of the party's conservative wing, who spoke for many on the right who were unhappy with any conciliation of communists. The

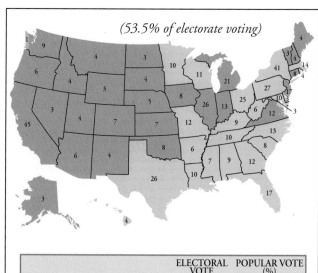

(53.5% of electorate voting)

	ELECTORAL VOTE	POPULAR VOTE (%)
Jimmy Carter *(Democratic)*	297	40,828,587 (50.0)
Gerald R. Ford *(Republican)*	240	39,147,613 (47.9)
Ronald Reagan *(Independent Republican)*	1	—
Other candidates *(McCarthy [Ind.], Libertarian)*	—	1,575,459 (2.1)

THE ELECTION OF 1976 Jimmy Carter, a former governor of Georgia, swept the South in the 1976 election and carried enough of the industrial states of the Northeast and Midwest to win a narrow victory over President Gerald R. Ford. His showing indicated the importance to the Democratic party of having a candidate capable of attracting support in the South, which was becoming increasingly Republican by the 1970s. ◆ *What drove so many southerners into the Republican party?*

president only barely survived the assault to win his party's nomination. The Democrats, in the meantime, were gradually uniting behind a new and, before 1976, almost entirely unknown candidate: Jimmy Carter, a former governor of Georgia who organized a brilliant primary campaign and appealed to the general unhappiness with Washington by offering honesty, piety, and an outsider's skepticism of the federal government. And while Carter's mammoth lead in opinion polls dwindled to almost nothing by election day, unhappiness with the economy and a general disenchantment with Ford enabled the Democrat to hold on for a narrow victory. Carter emerged with 50 percent of the popular vote to Ford's 47.9 percent and 297 electoral votes to Ford's 240.

The Trials of Jimmy Carter

Like Ford, Jimmy Carter assumed the presidency at a moment when the nation faced problems of staggering complexity and difficulty. Perhaps no leader could have thrived in such inhospitable circumstances. But Carter seemed at times to make his predicament worse by a style of leadership that many considered self-righteous and inflexible. He left office in 1981 one of the least popular presidents of the century.

Carter had campaigned for the presidency as an "outsider," representing Americans suspicious of entrenched bureaucracies and complacent public officials. He carried much of that suspiciousness with him to Washington. He surrounded himself in the White House with a group of close-knit associates from Georgia; and in the beginning, at least, he seemed deliberately to spurn assistance from more experienced political figures. Carter was among the

Carter's Lack of Direction

most intelligent men ever to serve in the White House, but his critics charged that he provided no overall vision or direction to his government. His ambitious legislative agenda included major reforms of the tax and welfare systems; Congress passed virtually none of it.

Carter devoted much of his time to the problems of energy and the economy. Entering office in the midst of a recession, he moved first to reduce unemployment by raising public spending and cutting federal taxes. Unemployment declined, but inflation soared—less because of the fiscal policies he implemented than because of the continuing, sharp increases in energy prices imposed on the West by OPEC. During Carter's last two years in office, prices rose at well over a 10 percent annual rate. Like Nixon and Ford before him, Carter responded with a combination of tight money and calls for voluntary restraint. He appointed first G. William Miller and then Paul Volcker,

High Interest Rates

both conservative economists, to head the Federal Reserve Board, thus ensuring a policy of high interest rates and reduced currency supplies. By 1980, interest rates had risen to the highest levels in American history; at times, they

exceeded 20 percent. The problem of energy also grew steadily more troublesome in the Carter years. In the summer of 1979, instability in the Middle East produced a second major fuel shortage in the United States. In the midst of the crisis, OPEC announced another major price increase, clouding the economic picture still further. Faced with increasing pressure to act (and with public opinion polls showing his approval rating at a dismal 26 percent, lower than Richard Nixon's lowest figures), Carter retreated to Camp David, the presidential retreat in the Maryland mountains. Ten days later, he emerged to deliver a remarkable television address. It included a series of proposals for resolving the energy crisis. But it was most notable for Carter's bleak assessment of the national condition. Speaking with unusual fervor, he complained of a

CARTER IN THE WHITE HOUSE Jimmy Carter made a strenuous effort to bring a sense of informality to the presidency, in contrast to the "imperial" style many had complained about during the Nixon years. He began on his Inauguration Day, when he and his family walked down Pennsylvania Avenue from the Capitol to the White House instead of riding in the traditional limousines. Here, Carter sits in a room in the White House preparing for a television address. He is sitting in front of a fire wearing a cardigan sweater, with his notes in his lap rather than on a desk. *(Bettmann/Corbis)*

"crisis of confidence" that had struck "at the very heart and soul of our national will." The address became known as the "malaise" speech (although Carter himself had never used that word), and it helped fuel charges that the president was trying to blame his own problems on the American people. Carter's sudden firing of several members of his cabinet a few days later deepened his political problems.

Human Rights and National Interests

Among Jimmy Carter's most frequent campaign promises was a pledge to build a new basis for American foreign policy, one in which the defense of "human rights" would replace the pursuit of "selfish interests." Carter spoke out sharply and often about violations of human rights in many countries (including, most prominently, the Soviet Union). Beyond that general commitment, the Carter administration focused on several more traditional concerns. Carter completed negotiations begun several years earlier on a pair of treaties to turn over control of the Panama Canal to the government of Panama. Domestic opposition to the treaties was intense, especially among conservatives who viewed the new arrangements as part of a general American retreat from international power. But the administration argued that relinquishing the canal was the best way to improve relations with Latin America and avoid violence in Panama. After an acrimonious debate, the Senate ratified the treaties by 68 to 32, only one vote more than the necessary two-thirds majority.

Less controversial, within the United States at least, was Carter's stunning success in arranging a peace treaty between Egypt and Israel—the crowning accomplishment of his presidency. Middle East negotiations had seemed hopelessly stalled when a dramatic breakthrough occurred in November 1977. The Egyptian president, Anwar Sadat, accepted an invitation from Prime Minister Menachem Begin to visit Israel. In Tel Aviv, he announced that Egypt was now willing to accept the state of Israel as a legitimate political entity. But translating these good feelings into an actual peace treaty proved more difficult.

When talks between Israeli and Egyptian negotiators stalled, Carter invited Sadat and Begin to a summit conference at Camp David in September 1978, and persuaded them to remain there for two weeks while he and others helped mediate the disputes between them. On September 17, Carter escorted the two leaders into the White House to announce agreement on a "framework" for an Egyptian-Israeli peace treaty. Carter intervened again several months later, when talks stalled once more, and helped produce a compromise on the most sensitive issue between the two parties: the Palestinian refugee issue. On March 26, 1979, Begin and Sadat returned together to the White House to sign a formal peace treaty—known as the Camp David accords—between their two nations.

Camp David Accords

In the meantime, Carter continued trying to improve relations with China and the Soviet Union and to complete a new arms agreement. He responded eagerly to the overtures of Deng Xiaoping, the new Chinese leader who was attempting to open his nation to the outside world. On December 15, 1978, Washington and Beijing announced the resumption of formal diplomatic relations between the two nations. A few months later, Carter traveled to Vienna to meet with the aging and visibly ailing Brezhnev to finish drafting the new SALT II arms control agreement. The treaty set limits on the number of long-range missiles, bombers, and nuclear warheads on each

SIGNING THE CAMP DAVID ACCORDS
Jimmy Carter experienced many frustrations during his presidency, but his successful efforts in 1978 to negotiate a peace treaty between Israel and Egypt was undoubtedly his finest hour. Egyptian President Anwar Sadat and Israeli Prime Minister Menachem Begin join Carter here in the East Room of the White House in March 1979 to sign the accords they had begun to hammer out during two weeks at the president's retreat at Camp David several months before. *(D. B. Owen/Black Star)*

side. Almost immediately, however, SALT II met with fierce conservative opposition in the United States. Central to the arguments was a fundamental distrust of the Soviet Union that nearly a decade of détente had failed to destroy; but specific provisions of the treaty—which even some supporters of détente felt were too favorable to the Soviets—also fueled the opposition. By the fall of 1979, with the Senate scheduled to begin debate over the treaty shortly, ratification was already in jeopardy. Events in the following months would provide a final blow, both to the treaty and to the larger framework of détente.

The Year of the Hostages

Ever since the early 1950s, the United States had provided political support and, more recently, massive military assistance to the government of the Shah of Iran, hoping to make his nation a bulwark against Soviet expansion in the Middle East. By 1979, however, the Shah was in deep trouble with his own people. Many Iranians resented the re-

Iranian Revolution

pressive, authoritarian tactics through which the Shah had maintained his autocratic rule. At the same time, Islamic clergy (and much of the fiercely religious populace) opposed his efforts to modernize and westernize a fundamentalist society. The combination of resentments produced a powerful revolutionary movement. In January 1979, the Shah fled the country.

The United States made cautious efforts in the first months after the Shah's abdication to establish cordial relations with the succession of increasingly militant regimes that followed. By late 1979, however, revolutionary chaos in Iran was making any normal relations impossible. What power there was resided with a zealous religious leader, the Ayatollah Ruhollah Khomeini, whose hatred of the West in general and the United States in particular was intense. In late October 1979, the deposed Shah arrived in New York to be treated for cancer. Days later, on November 4, an armed mob invaded the American embassy in Teheran, seized the diplomats and military personnel inside, and demanded the return of the Shah to Iran in exchange for their freedom. Fifty-three Americans remained hostages in the embassy for over a year. Coming after years of international humiliations and defeats, the hostage seizure released a deep well of anger and emotion in the United States.

Only weeks after the hostage seizure, on December 27, 1979, Soviet troops invaded Afghanistan, the mountainous Islamic nation lying between the USSR and Iran. The Soviet Union had in fact been a power in Afghanistan for years, and the dominant force since April 1978, when a coup had established a Marxist government there with close ties to the Kremlin. But while some observers claimed that the Soviet invasion was a Russian attempt to secure the status quo, others—most notably the president—claimed it was a Russian "stepping stone to their possible control over much of the world's oil supplies." It was also the "gravest threat to world peace since World War II." Carter angrily imposed a series of economic sanctions on the Russians, canceled American participation in the 1980 summer Olympic Games in Moscow, and announced the withdrawal of SALT II from Senate consideration.

The combination of domestic economic troubles and international crises created widespread anxiety, frustration, and anger in the United States— damaging President Carter's al- *Carter's Falling Popularity* ready low standing with the public, and giving added strength to an alternative political force that had already made great strides.

WAITING FOR KHOMEINI Iranian women, dressed in traditional Islamic garb, stand in a crowd in Teheran waiting for a glimpse of the Ayatollah Khomeini, the spiritual and eventually also political leader of the Iranian Revolution that created so many difficulties for the United States. *(David Burnett/Contact Press Images)*

In the late nineteenth century, it was the department store that tried to create a magical world, attracting patrons by arousing consumer fantasies. By the late twentieth century, it was the mall that was fusing consumption, entertainment, and desire. In cities and towns in every part of America, malls became not just places for shopping, but often centers of a much-altered community life as well.

The modern mall is the direct descendant of an earlier retail innovation,

the automobile-oriented shopping center, which strove to combine a number of different shops in a single structure, with parking for customers. The first modern shopping center, the Country Club Plaza, opened in Kansas City in 1924. By the mid-1950s, shopping centers—ranging from small "strips" to large integrated complexes—had proliferated throughout the country and were challenging traditional downtown shopping districts, which suffered from lack of parking and from the movement of middle-class residents to the suburbs.

In 1956, the first enclosed, climate-controlled shopping mall—the Southdale Shopping Center—opened in Minneapolis, followed quickly by similar ventures in New York, New Jersey, Illinois, North Carolina, and Tennessee. As the malls spread, they grew larger and more elaborate. They also began self-consciously to emulate some aspects of the older downtowns that they were rapidly displacing. At the same time, they tried to insulate customers from the dangers and aggravations of traditional urban shopping. By the 1970s, vast "regional malls" were emerging—Tyson's Corner in Fairfax, Virginia; Roosevelt Field on Long Island; the

SHOPPING CENTER, NORTHERN VIRGINIA This small shopping center near Washington, D.C., was characteristic of the new "strip malls" that were emerging in the 1950s to serve suburban customers who travelled almost entirely by automobile. *(Hulton/Archive/Getty Images)*

Galleria in Houston, and many others—that drew customers from great distances and dazzled them not only with acres of varied retail space, but also with restaurants, movie theaters, skating rinks, bowling alleys, hotels, video arcades, and large public spaces with fountains, benches, trees, gardens, and concert spaces. "The more needs you fulfill, the longer people stay," one developer observed.

Malls had become self-contained imitations of cities—but in a setting from which many of the more troubling and abrasive features of

MAIN STREET This photograph of the Main Street of Henderson, Kentucky in the 1940s was a popular image for advertisers and others trying to evoke the character of urban shopping in small cities—a kind of shopping soon to be displaced by shopping centers and malls outside the center of town. *(Ewing Galloway, N.Y.)*

THE RISE OF THE NEW AMERICAN RIGHT

Much of the anxiety that pervaded American life in the 1970s was a result of jarring public events that left many men and women shaken and uncertain about their leaders and their government. But much of it was a result, too, of significant changes in the character of America's economy, society, and culture. Together these changes disillusioned many liberals, perplexed the already weakened left, and provided the right with its most important opportunity in generations to seize a position of authority in American life.

The Sunbelt and Its Politics

The most widely discussed demographic phenomenon of the 1970s was the rise of what became known as the "Sunbelt"—a term coined by the political analyst Kevin Phillips to describe a collection of regions that emerged together in the postwar era to become the most dynamically

growing parts of the country. The Sunbelt included the Southeast (particularly Florida), the Southwest (particularly Texas), and above all, California, which became the nation's most populous state, surpassing New York, in 1964, and continued to grow dramatically in the years that followed. By 1980, the population of the Sunbelt had risen to exceed that of the older industrial regions of the North and the East.

Rise of the "Sunbelt"

In addition to shifting the nation's economic focus from one region to another, the rise of the Sunbelt helped produce a change in the political climate. The strong populist traditions in the South and the West were capable of producing progressive and even radical politics; but more often in the late twentieth century, they produced a strong opposition to the growth of government and a resentment of the proliferating regulations and restrictions that the liberal state was producing. Many of those regulations and restrictions—environmental laws, land-use restrictions, even the fifty-five-mile-per-hour speed limit

downtowns had been carefully and systematically eliminated. Malls were insulated from the elements. They were policed by private security forces, who (unlike real police) could and usually did keep "undesirable" customers off the premises. They were purged of bars, pornography shops, and unsavory businesses. They were off limits to beggars, vagrants, the homeless, and anyone else the managers considered unattractive to their customers. Malls set out to "perfect" urban space, recasting the city as a protected, controlled, and so-cially homogeneous site attractive to, and in most cases largely limited to, white middle-class people.

Some malls also sought to become community centers in sprawling sub-urban areas that had few real commu-nity spaces of their own. A few malls built explicitly civic spaces—meeting halls and conference centers, where community groups could gather. Some published their own newspa-pers. Many staged concerts, plays, and dances. But civic activities had a difficult time competing with the principal attraction of the malls: consumption.

Malls were designed with women, the principal consumers in most fami-

THE NORTHLAND MALL   Constructed in 1960, and designed by architect Victor Gruen who was one of the pioneers in designing indoor shopping malls, this vast shopping center in Northland, near Detroit, immediately attracted enormous crowds.   *(Courtesy of Victor Gruen Collection, American Heritage Center, University of Wyoming)*

lies, mainly in mind. "I wouldn't know how to design a center for a man," one architect said of the complexes he built. They catered to the concerns of mothers about their own and their children's safety, and they offered products of particular interest to them. (Male-oriented stores—men's clothing, sporting goods, hardware stores— were much less visible in most malls than shops marketing women's and children's clothing, jewelry, lingerie, and household goods.)

Malls also became important to teenagers, who flocked to them in the way that earlier generations had flocked to streetcorners and squares in traditional downtowns. The malls were places for teenagers to meet friends, go to movies, avoid parents, hang out. They were places to buy records, clothes, or personal items. And they were places to work. Low-paying retail jobs, plentiful in malls, were typical first working experiences for many teens.

The proliferation of malls has dis-mayed many people, who see in them a threat to the sense of community in America. By insulating people from the diversity and conflict of urban life, they argue, malls divide groups from one another and erode the bonds that make it possible for those groups to understand one another. But malls, like the suburbs they usu-ally serve, also serve to create a kind of community. They are homoge-neous and protected, to be sure, but they are also social gathering places in many areas where the alternative is not the rich, diverse life of the down-town but the even more isolated ex-perience of shopping in isolated strips—or through catalogs, tele-phone, and the Internet.

created during the energy crisis to force motorists to con-serve fuel—affected the West more than any other re-gion. Both the South and the West, moreover, embraced myths about their own pasts that reinforced the hostility to the liberal government of the mid- and late twentieth century. White southerners equated the federal govern-ment's effort to change racial norms in the region with what they believed was the tyranny of Reconstruction. Westerners embraced an image of their region as a refuge of "rugged individualism" and resisted what they consid-ered efforts by the government to impose new standards of behavior on them. Thus, the same impulses and rheto-ric that populists had once used to denounce banks and corporations, the new conservative populists of the post-war era used to attack the government—and the liberals, radicals, and minorities whom they believed were driving its growth.

If anything, the growth of the Sunbelt seemed to make the politics of the regions even more hostile to govern-ment. In the 1970s and early 1980s, the boom mentality of

some of these rapidly growing areas (especially south Florida, Texas, and southern California) conflicted sharply with the concerns of the older industrial states of the Northeast and Midwest. Saddled with declining industrial centers, suffering from crowding and congestion, and home to large, impoverished minority groups, they re-mained more committed to social programs and more in-terested in regulated growth than the relatively wide-open areas of the Sunbelt.

The so-called Sagebrush Rebellion, which emerged in parts of the West in the late 1970s, mobilized conserva-tive opposition to environmen-tal laws and restrictions on de-velopment. It also sought to portray the West (which had probably benefited more than any other region from federal investment) as a victim of government control. Its members complained about the very large amounts of land the federal government owned in many western states and demanded that the land be opened for development.

Sagebrush Rebellion

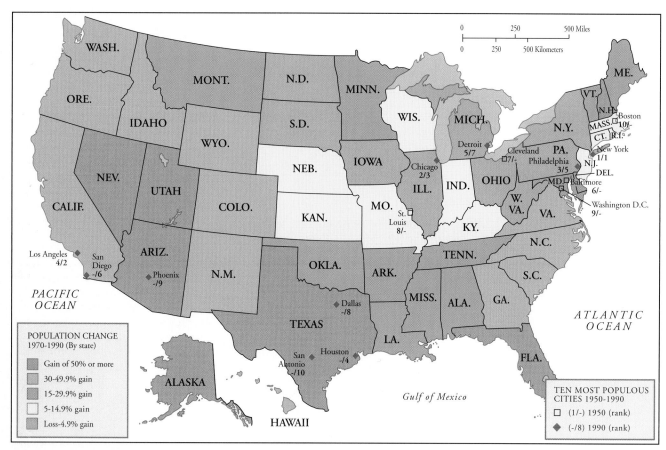

GROWTH OF THE SUNBELT, 1970–1990 One of the most important demographic changes of the last decades of the twentieth century was the shift of population out of traditional population centers in the Northeast and Midwest and toward the states of the so-called "Sunbelt"— most notably the Southwest and the Pacific coast. This map gives a dramatic illustration of the changing concentration of population between 1970 and 1990. The pale green states are those that lost population, while the purple and dark green states are those that made very significant gains (30 percent or more). ◆ *What was the impact of this population shift on the politics of the 1980s?*

The South as a whole was considerably more conservative than other parts of the nation, and its growth served to increase the power of the right in the 1960s and 1970s. The West was not, on the whole, a more conservative region than others in its political behavior; but the conservatives it produced seemed at times particularly fervent, and its rise in the postwar period helped create some of the most numerous and powerful conservative movements in the nation—particularly in southern California, where Orange County emerged as one of the most important centers of right-wing politics in the country. When the right rose to power in the 1970s and 1980s, westerners were among its most important leaders and constituents.

Suburbanization also fueled the rise of the right. Not all suburbs bred conservative politics, of course; but the most militantly conserva-

Suburban Conservatism

tive communities in America— among them Orange County—were mostly suburbs. Suburbs tended to attract people who wished to flee the problems and the jarring diversity of cities, who preferred

stable, homogeneous surroundings. Many suburbs insulated their residents from contact with different groups— through the relative homogeneity of the population, through the transferring of retail and even work space into suburban office parks and shopping malls. The seemingly tranquil life of the suburb reinforced the conservative view that other parts of the nation—cities in particular—were abandoning the values and norms that society required.

Religious Revivalism

In the 1960s, many social critics had predicted the virtual extinction of religious influence in American life. *Time* magazine had reported such assumptions in 1966 with a celebrated cover emblazoned with the question, "Is God Dead?" But religion in America was far from dead. Indeed, in the 1970s the United States experienced the beginning of a major religious revival, perhaps the most powerful since the Second Great Awakening of the early nineteenth century. It continued in various forms into the 1990s.

Some of the new religious enthusiasm found expression in the rise of various cults and pseudo-faiths: the Church of Scientology; the Unification Church of the Reverend Sun Myung Moon; even the tragic People's Temple, whose

Evangelical Christianity — members committed mass suicide in their jungle retreat in Guyana in 1978. But the most important impulse of the religious revival was the growth of evangelical Christianity.

Evangelicalism is the basis of many forms of Christian faith, but evangelicals have in common a belief in personal conversion (being "born again") through direct communication with God. Evangelical religion had been the dominant form of Christianity in America through much of its history, and a substantial subculture since the late nineteenth century. In its modern form, it became increasingly visible during the early 1950s, when evangelicals such as Billy Graham and Pentecostals such as Oral Roberts began to attract huge national (and international) followings for their energetic revivalism.

For many years, the evangelicals had gone largely unnoted by much of the media and the secular public, which had dismissed them as a limited, provincial phenomenon. By the early 1980s, it was no longer possible to ignore them. Earlier in the century, many (although never all) evangelicals had been relatively poor rural people, largely isolated from the mainstream of American culture. But the great capitalist expansion after World War II had lifted many of these people out of poverty and into the middle class, where they were more visible and more assertive. More than 70 million Americans now described themselves as "born-again" Christians—men and women who had established a "direct personal relationship with Jesus." Christian evangelicals owned their own newspapers, magazines, radio stations, and television networks. They operated their own schools and universities. They occupied positions of eminence in the worlds of entertainment and professional sports. And one of their number ultimately occupied the White House itself—Jimmy Carter, who during the 1976 campaign had talked proudly of his own "conversion experience" and who continued openly to proclaim his "born-again" Christian faith during his years in office.

For Jimmy Carter and for some others, evangelical Christianity had formed the basis for a commitment to racial and economic justice and to world peace. For many evangelicals, however, the message of the new religion was very different—but no less political. In the 1970s, some Christian evangelicals became active on the political and cultural right. They were alarmed by what they considered the spread of immorality and disorder in American life; and they were concerned about the way a secular and, as they saw it, godless culture was intruding into their communities and families—through popular culture, through the schools, and through government policies. Many evangelical men and women feared the growth of feminism and the threat they believed it posed to the traditional family, and they resented the way in which government policies advanced the goals of the women's movement. Particularly alarming to them were Supreme Court decisions eliminating all religious observance from schools and, later, the decision guaranteeing women the right to an abortion.

By the late 1970s, the "Christian right" had become a visible and increasingly powerful political force. Jerry Falwell, a fundamentalist minister in Virginia with a substantial television audience, launched a movement he called the Moral Majority, which attacked the rise of "secular humanism"—a term many conservative evangelicals used to describe the rejection of religion in American culture. The Pentecostal minister Pat

Moral Majority and the Christian Coalition

Robertson began a political movement of his own and, in the 1990s, launched an organization known as the Christian Coalition. The Moral Majority, the Christian Coalition, and other organizations of similar inclination opposed federal interference in local affairs; denounced abortion, divorce, feminism, and homosexuality; defended unrestricted free enterprise; and supported a strong American posture in the world. Some evangelicals reopened issues that had long seemed closed. For example, many fundamentalist Christians denied the scientific doctrine of evolution and instead urged the teaching in schools of the biblical story of the Creation. Others demanded various forms of censorship or control of television, movies, rock music, books, magazines, and newspapers. Their goal was a new era in which Christian values once again dominated American life.

The Emergence of the New Right

Evangelical Christians were an important part, but only a part, of what became known as the new right—a diverse but powerful movement that enjoyed rapid growth in the 1970s and early 1980s. It had begun to take shape after the 1964 election, in which Barry Goldwater had suffered his shattering defeat. Richard Viguerie, a remarkable conservative activist and organizer, took a list of 12,000 contributors to the Goldwater campaign and used it to develop a formidable conservative communications and fund-raising organization. By the mid-1970s, he had gathered a list of 4 million contributors and 15 million supporters. Conservative campaigns had for many years been less well funded and organized than those of their rivals. Beginning in the 1970s, largely because of these and other organizational advances, conservatives found themselves almost always better funded and organized than their opponents. Gradually these direct-mail operations helped create a much larger conservative infrastructure, designed to match and even exceed what the right saw as the powerful liberal infrastructure. By the late 1970s, there were right-wing think tanks, consulting firms, lobbyists, foundations, and scholarly centers.

Another factor in the revival of the right was the emergence of a credible right-wing leadership in the late 1960s and early 1970s to replace the discredited conservative hero of the 1950s, Barry Goldwater. Chief among this new generation of conservative leaders was Ronald Reagan. Reagan had grown up in modest circumstances in the Midwest and attended a small college in Illinois. In 1937, at the age of 26, he went to Hollywood and became a moderately successful actor, in westerns at times, but mostly in light romantic comedies. A liberal and a fervent admirer of Franklin Roosevelt as a young man, he moved decisively to the right. That was after his second marriage, to Nancy Davis, a woman of strong conservative convictions; and it was also after he became embroiled, as president of the Screen Actors Guild, in battles with communists in the union. In the early 1950s, he became a corporate spokesman for General Electric and won a wide following on the right with his smooth, eloquent speeches in defense of individual freedom and private enterprise.

Ronald Reagan

In 1964, Reagan delivered a memorable television speech on behalf of Goldwater. After Goldwater's defeat, he worked quickly not only to seize the leadership of the conservative wing of the party but to denounce those Republicans who had repudiated Goldwater. "I don't think we should turn the high command over to leaders who were traitors during the battle just ended," Reagan said in 1965, when other Republicans were trying to push anti-Goldwater moderates into positions of leadership in the party. In 1966, with the support of a group of wealthy conservatives, he won the first of two terms as governor of California—which gave him a much more visible platform for promoting himself and his ideas.

The presidency of Gerald Ford also played an important role in the rise of the right, by destroying the fragile equilibrium that had enabled the right wing and the moderate wing of the Republican Party to coexist. Ford, probably without realizing it, touched on some of the right's rawest nerves. He appointed as vice president Nelson Rockefeller, the liberal Republican governor of New York and an heir to one of America's great fortunes; many conservatives had been demonizing Rockefeller and his family for more than twenty years. (Viguerie attributed the birth of the new right to this event alone.) Ford proposed an amnesty program for draft resisters, embraced and even extended the hated Nixon-Kissinger policies of détente, presided over the fall of Vietnam, and agreed to cede the Panama Canal to Panama. When Reagan challenged Ford in the 1976 Republican primaries, the president survived, barely, only by dumping Nelson Rockefeller from the ticket, replacing him with Senator Robert Dole of Kansas, and agreeing to a platform largely written by one of Reagan's principal allies, Senator Jesse Helms of North Carolina. Reagan hailed that platform by saying that the party "must raise a banner of no pale pastels, but bold colors which make it unmistakably clear where we stand on all the issues troubling the people."

The Tax Revolt

At least equally important to the success of the new right was a new and potent conservative issue: the tax revolt. It had its public beginnings in 1978, when Howard Jarvis, a conservative activist in California, launched the first successful major citizens' tax revolt in California with Proposition 13, a referendum question on the state ballot rolling back property tax rates. Similar antitax movements soon began in other states and eventually spread to national politics.

Proposition 13

The tax revolt helped the right solve one of its biggest problems. For more than thirty years after the New Deal, Republican conservatives had struggled to halt and even reverse the growth of the federal government. Most of those efforts had ended in futility. Attacking government programs directly, as right-wing politicians from Robert Taft to Barry Goldwater discovered, was not the way to attract majority support. Every federal program had a political constituency. The biggest and most expensive programs—Social Security, Medicare, Medicaid, and others—had the broadest support. (Goldwater was plagued throughout the 1964 campaign by fears he would dismantle Social Security.)

In Proposition 13 and similar initiatives, members of the right found a better way to discredit government than by attacking specific programs: attacking taxes. By separating the issue of taxes from the issue of what taxes supported, the right found a way to achieve the most controversial elements of its own agenda (eroding the government's ability to expand and launch new programs) without openly antagonizing the millions of voters who supported specific programs. Virtually no one liked to pay taxes, and as the economy grew weaker and the relative burden of paying taxes grew heavier, that resentment naturally rose. The right exploited that resentment and, in the process, expanded its constituency far beyond anything it had known before. The 1980 presidential election propelled it to a historic victory.

Attacking Taxes

The Campaign of 1980

By the time of the crises in Iran and Afghanistan, Jimmy Carter was in desperate political trouble—his standing in popularity polls lower than that of any president in history. Senator Edward Kennedy, younger brother of John and Robert Kennedy and one of the most magnetic (and controversial) figures in the Democratic Party, challenged him in the primaries. And while Carter managed to withstand the confrontation with Kennedy and win his party's nomination, it was an unhappy Democratic convention that heard the president's listless call to arms. Carter's campaign aroused little popular enthusiasm as he prepared to face a powerful challenge.

The Republican Party, in the meantime, had rallied enthusiastically behind the man who, four years earlier, had nearly stolen the nomination from Gerald Ford. Ronald Reagan was a sharp critic of the excesses of the federal government. He linked his campaign to the spreading tax revolt (something to which he had paid relatively little attention in the past) by promising substantial tax cuts. Equally important, he championed a restoration of American "strength" and "pride" in the world. Although he refrained from discussing the hostage situation in Iran, Reagan clearly benefitted from the continuing popular frustration at Carter's inability to resolve the crisis. In a larger sense, he benefitted as well from the accumulated frustrations of more than a decade of domestic and international disappointments.

On election day 1980, the anniversary of the seizure of the hostages in Iran, Reagan swept to victory, winning 51 percent of the vote to 41 percent for Jimmy Carter, and 7 percent for John Anderson—a moderate Republican congressman from Illinois who had mounted an independent campaign. Carter carried only five states and the District of Columbia, for a total of 49 electoral votes to Reagan's 489. The Republican Party won control of the Senate for the first time since 1952; and although the Democrats retained a modest majority in the House, the lower chamber too seemed firmly in the hands of conservatives.

1980 Election

On the day of Reagan's inauguration, the American hostages in Iran were released after their 444-day ordeal. The government of Iran, desperate for funds to support its floundering war against neighboring Iraq, had ordered the hostages freed in return for a release of billions in Iranian assets that the Carter administration had frozen in American banks. Americans welcomed the hostages home with demonstrations of joy and patriotism not seen since the end of World War II. But while the celebration in 1945 had marked a great American triumph, the euphoria in 1981 marked something quite different—a troubled nation grasping for reassurance. Ronald Reagan set out to provide it.

THE "REAGAN REVOLUTION"

Ronald Reagan assumed the presidency in January 1981 promising a change in government more fundamental than any since the New Deal of fifty years before. While his eight years in office produced a significant shift in public policy, they brought nothing so fundamental as many of his supporters had hoped or his opponents had feared. But there was no ambiguity about his purely political achievements. Reagan succeeded brilliantly in making his own engaging personality the central fact of American politics in the 1980s.

The Reagan Coalition

Reagan owed his election to widespread disillusionment with Carter and to the crises and disappointments that many voters, perhaps unfairly, associated with him. But he owed it as well to the emergence of a powerful coalition of conservative groups. That coalition was not a single, cohesive movement. It was an uneasy and generally temporary alliance among several very different movements.

The Reagan coalition included a relatively small but highly influential group of wealthy Americans associated with the corporate and financial world—the kind of people who had dominated American politics and government through much of the nation's history until the New Deal began to challenge their preeminence. What united this group was a firm commitment to capitalism and to unfettered economic growth; a belief that the market offers the

Corporate Elites

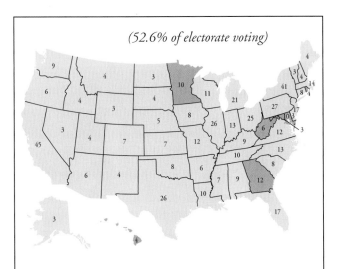

(52.6% of electorate voting)

	ELECTORAL VOTE	POPULAR VOTE (%)
Ronald Reagan *(Republican)*	489	43,901,812 (50.7)
Jimmy Carter *(Democratic)*	49	35,483,820 (41.0)
John B. Anderson *(Independent)*	—	5,719,722 (6.6)
Other candidates *(Libertarian)*	—	921,299 (1.1)

THE ELECTION OF 1980 Although Ronald Reagan won only slightly more than half of the popular vote in the 1980 presidential election, his electoral majority was overwhelming—a reflection to a large degree of the deep unpopularity of President Jimmy Carter in 1980. ◆ *What had made Carter so unpopular?*

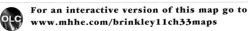

For an interactive version of this map go to www.mhhe.com/brinkley11ch33maps

best solutions to most problems; a deep hostility to most (although not all) government interference in markets; and a belief that most of what is valuable in American life depends on the health and strength of the corporate world, and thus that the corporate world is entitled to a special position of influence and privilege in society. Central to this group's agenda in the 1980s was opposition to what it considered the "redistributive" politics of the federal government (and especially its highly progressive tax structure) and hostility to the rise of what they believed were "antibusiness" government regulations. Reagan courted these free-market conservatives carefully and effectively, and in the end it was their interests his administration most effectively served.

A second element of the Reagan coalition was even smaller, but also disproportionately influential: a group of *"Neo-conservatives"* intellectuals commonly known as "neo-conservatives," who gave to the right something it had not had in many years—a firm base among "opinion leaders," people with access to the most influential public forums for ideas. Many of these people had once been liberals and, before that, socialists. But during the turmoil of the 1960s, they had become alarmed by what they considered a dangerous and destructive radicalism that was destabilizing American life, and by the weakening of liberal ardor in the battle against communism. Neo-conservatives were sympathetic to the complaints and demands of capitalists, but their principal concern was to reassert legitimate authority and reaffirm Western democratic, anticommunist values and commitments. They considered themselves engaged in a battle to regain control of the marketplace of ideas—to "win back the culture"—from the crass, radical ideas that had polluted it. Some neo-conservative intellectuals went on to become important figures in the battle against multiculturalism and "political correctness" within academia.

These two groups joined in an uneasy alliance in 1980 with the growing "new right." But several things differentiated the new right from the corporate conservatives and the neo-conservatives. Perhaps the most important was *Populist Conservatives* the new right's fundamental distrust of the "eastern establishment": a suspicion of its motives and goals; a sense that it exercised a dangerous, secret power in American life; a fear of the hidden influence of such establishment institutions and people as the Council on Foreign Relations, the Trilateral Commission, Henry Kissinger, and the Rockefellers.

These populist conservatives expressed the kinds of concerns that outsiders, non-elites, have traditionally voiced in American society: an opposition to centralized power and influence, a fear of living in a world where distant, hostile forces are controlling society and threatening individual freedom and community autonomy. It was a testament to Ronald Reagan's political skills and personal charm that he was able to generate enthusiastic support

from these populist conservatives while at the same time appealing to more elite conservative groups whose concerns were in many ways antithetical to those of the new right.

Reagan in the White House

Even many people who disagreed with Reagan's policies found themselves drawn to his attractive and carefully honed public image. Reagan was a master of television, a gifted public speaker, and—in public at least—rugged, fearless, and seemingly impervious to danger or misfortune. He turned seventy weeks after taking office and was the oldest man ever to serve as president. But through most of his presidency, he appeared to be vigorous, resilient, even youthful. He spent his many vacations on a California ranch, where he chopped wood and rode horses. When he was wounded in an assassination attempt in 1981, he joked with doctors on his way into surgery and appeared to bounce back from the ordeal with remarkable speed. He had few visible insecurities. Even when things went wrong, as they often did, the blame seldom seemed

RONALD AND NANCY REAGAN The president and the first lady greet guests at a White House social event. Nancy Reagan was most visible in her efforts to make the White House, and her husband's presidency, seem more glamorous than those of most recent administrations. But she also played an important, if quiet, policy role in the administration. *(Dirck Halstead/Getty Images)*

to attach to Reagan himself (inspiring some Democrats to begin referring to him as the "Teflon president").

Reagan was not much involved in the day-to-day affairs of running the government; he surrounded himself with tough, energetic administrators who insulated him from many of the pressures of the office and who apparently relied on him largely for general guidance, not specific decisions. At times, the president revealed a startling ignorance about the nature of his own policies or the actions of his subordinates. But Reagan did make active use of his office to generate support for his administration's programs, by appealing repeatedly to the public over television—no more frequently but much more effectively than many of his predecessors—and by fusing his proposals with a highly nationalistic rhetoric.

"Supply-Side" Economics

Reagan's 1980 campaign for the presidency had promised, among other things, to restore the economy to health by a bold experiment that became known as "supply-side" economics or, to some, "Reaganomics." Supply-side economics operated from the assumption that the woes of the American economy were in large part a result of excessive taxation, which left inadequate capital available to investors to stimulate growth. The solution, therefore, was to reduce taxes, with particularly generous benefits to corporations and wealthy individuals, in order to encourage new investments. The result would be a general economic revival that would help everyone. Because a tax cut would reduce government revenues (at least at first), it would also be necessary to reduce government expenses. A cornerstone of the Reagan economic program, therefore, was a dramatic cut in the federal budget.

"Reaganomics"

In its first months in office, accordingly, the new administration hastily assembled a legislative program based on the supply-side idea. It proposed $40 billion in budget reductions and managed to win congressional approval of almost all of them. In addition, the president proposed a bold three-year, 30 percent reduction on both individual and corporate tax rates. In the summer of 1981, Congress passed it too, after lowering the reductions to 25 percent. Not since Lyndon Johnson had a president compiled so impressive a legislative record in his first months in office. Reagan was successful because he had a disciplined Republican majority in the Senate, and because the Democratic majority in the House was weak and riddled with defectors. Shaken by the results of the 1980 election, dozens of Democrats from relatively conservative districts (mostly in the South) deserted the party's leadership; the defectors became known as "boll weevils."

Men and women whom Reagan appointed fanned out through the executive branch of government committed to reducing the role of government in American economic life. "Deregulation," an idea many Democrats had begun to embrace in the Carter years, became almost a religion in the Reagan administration. Secretary of the Interior James Watt had been a major figure in the Sagebrush Rebellion, a movement among western conservatives to fight federal environmental regulations, which they believed had a particularly devastating effect on their region's economy. Watt opened up public lands and water to development. The Environmental Protection Agency (before its directors were indicted for corruption) relaxed or entirely eliminated enforcement of major environmental laws and regulations. The Civil Rights Division of the Justice Department eased enforcement of civil rights laws. The Department of Transportation slowed implementation of new rules limiting automobile emissions and imposing new safety standards on cars and trucks. By getting government "out of the way," Reagan officials promised, they were ensuring economic revival.

"Deregulation"

By early 1982, however, the nation had sunk into the most severe recession since the 1930s. The Reagan economic program was not directly to blame for the problems, but neither did it offer a quick solution to them. In 1982 unemployment reached 11 percent, its highest level in over forty years.

The recession convinced many people, including some conservatives, that the Reagan economic program (and thus the Reagan presidency) had failed. In fact, however, the economy recovered more rapidly and impressively than almost anyone had expected. By late 1983, unemployment had fallen to 8.2 percent, and it declined steadily for several years after that. The gross national product had grown 3.6 percent in a year, the largest increase since the mid-1970s. Inflation had fallen below 5 percent. The economy continued to grow, and both inflation and unemployment remained low (at least by the new and more pessimistic standards the nation seemed now to have accepted) through most of the decade.

The recovery was a result of many things. The years of tight money policies by the Federal Reserve Board, however painful and destructive they may have been in many ways, had helped lower inflation; perhaps equally important, the Board had lowered interest rates early in 1983 in response to the recession. A worldwide "energy glut" and the virtual collapse of the OPEC cartel had produced at least a temporary end to the inflationary pressures of spiraling fuel costs. And staggering federal budget deficits were pumping billions of dollars into the flagging economy. As a result, consumer spending and business investment both increased. The stock market rose up from its doldrums of the 1970s and began a sustained and historic boom. In August 1982, the Dow Jones Industrial Average stood at 777. Five years later it had passed 2,000. Despite a frightening crash in the fall

Sources of the Recovery

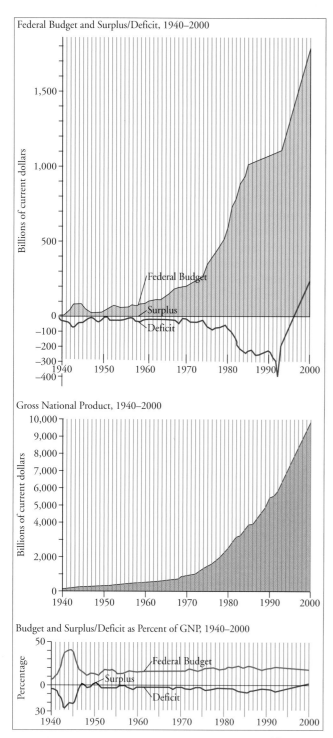

Federal Budget and Surplus/Deficit, 1940–2000

Gross National Product, 1940–2000

Budget and Surplus/Deficit as Percent of GNP, 1940–2000

FEDERAL BUDGET SURPLUS/DEFICIT, 1940 TO 2000 These charts help illustrate why the pattern of federal deficits seemed so alarming to Americans in the 1980s, and also why those deficits proved much less damaging to the economy than many predicted. The upper chart shows a dramatic increase in the federal budget from the mid-1960s on. It shows as well a corresponding, and also dramatic, increase in the size of federal deficits. Gross National Product also increased dramatically, especially in the 1980s and 1990s, as the middle chart shows. When the federal budgets and deficits of these years are calculated not in absolute numbers, but as a percentage of GNP, they seem much more stable and much less alarming. ◆ *What factors contributed to the increasing deficits of the 1980s? How were those deficits eliminated in the 1990s?*

of 1987, the market continued to grow: in early 2000, the Dow Jones average briefly passed 11,000.

The Fiscal Crisis

The economic revival did little at first to reduce the staggering, and to many Americans alarming, federal budget deficits (the gap between revenue and spending in a single year) or to slow the growth in the national debt (the debt the nation accumulates over time as a result of its annual deficits). By the mid-1980s, this growing fiscal crisis had become one of the central issues in American politics. Having entered office promising a balanced budget within four years, Reagan presided over record budget deficits and accumulated more debt in his eight years in office than the American government had accumulated in its entire previous history. Before the 1980s, the highest single-year budget deficit in American history had been $66 billion (in 1976). Throughout the 1980s, the annual budget deficit consistently exceeded $100 billion (and in 1991 peaked at $268 billion). The national debt rose from $907 billion in 1980 to nearly $3.5 trillion by 1991.

Soaring National Debt

The enormous deficits had many causes, some of them stretching back over decades of American public policy decisions. In particular, the budget suffered from enormous increases in the costs of "entitlement" programs (especially Social Security and Medicare), a result of the aging of the population and dramatic increases in the cost of health care. But some of the causes of the deficit lay in the policies of the Reagan administration. The 1981 tax cuts, the largest in American history, contributed to the deficit. The massive increase in military spending on which the Reagan administration insisted added much more to the federal budget than its cuts in domestic spending removed.

In the face of these deficits, the administration refused to consider raising income taxes (although it did agree to a major increase in the Social Security tax). It would not agree to reductions in military spending. It could not much reduce the costs of entitlement programs, and it could do nothing to reduce interest payments on the massive (and growing) debt itself. Its answer to the fiscal crisis, therefore, was further cuts in "discretionary" domestic spending, which included many programs aimed at the poorest (and politically weakest) Americans. There were reductions in funding for food stamps; a major cut in federal subsidies for low-income housing (which became one of many factors contributing to the radical increase in homelessness that by the late 1980s was plaguing virtually all American cities); strict new limitations on Medicare and Medicaid payments; reductions in student loans, school lunches, and other educational programs; and an end to many forms of federal assistance to the states and cities—which helped precipitate years of local fiscal crises as well.

Welfare Benefits Cut

MARCHING FOR DISARMAMENT In the 1960s and 1970s, protesting Americans marched for civil rights or to end war. In the 1980s, they were more likely to march for environmental causes or, in this case, an end to the arms race. The Nuclear Freeze movement spread rapidly through the United States and Europe in the early 1980s, inspiring many demonstrations such as this one down 42nd Street in New York City in 1982. *(Frank Fournier/Contact Press Images)*

CONTRAS IN TRAINING The Reagan administration's support for the Nicaraguan "contras," who opposed the leftist Sandinista regime, was the source of some of its greatest problems. Here, a small band of contras train in the Nicaraguan jungle. *(Piovano/SIPA Press)*

By the end of Reagan's third year in office, funding for domestic programs had been cut nearly as far as Congress (and, apparently, the public) was willing to tolerate, and still no end to the rising deficit was in sight. By the late 1980s, many fiscal conservatives were calling for a constitutional amendment mandating a balanced budget—a provision the president himself claimed to support. (Congress came within a few votes of passing such an amendment in 1994 and again in 1996, but by then deficits were beginning to decline and the momentum behind the amendment gradually faded.)

Reagan and the World

Reagan encountered a similar combination of triumphs and difficulties in international affairs. Determined to restore American pride and prestige in the world, he argued that the United States should once again become active and assertive in opposing communism and in supporting friendly governments whatever their internal policies.

Relations with the Soviet Union, which had been steadily deteriorating in the last years of the Carter administration, grew still more chilly in the first years of the Reagan presidency. The president spoke harshly of the Soviet regime (which he once called the "evil empire"), accusing it of sponsoring world terrorism and declaring that any armaments negotiations must be linked to negotiations on Soviet behavior in other areas. Relations with the Russians deteriorated further after the government of Poland (under strong pressure from Moscow) imposed martial law on the country in the winter of 1981 to crush a growing challenge from an independent labor organization, Solidarity.

Although the president had long denounced the SALT II arms control treaty as unfavorable to the United States, he continued to honor its provisions. But the

Reagan administration at first made little progress toward arms control in other areas. In fact, the president pro-

SDI

posed the most ambitious (and potentially most expensive) new military program in many years: the Strategic Defense Initiative (SDI), widely known as "Star Wars" (after the popular movie of that name). Reagan claimed that SDI, through the use of lasers and satellites, could provide an effective shield against incoming missiles and thus make nuclear war obsolete. The Soviet Union claimed that the new program would elevate the arms race to new and more dangerous levels (a complaint many domestic critics of SDI shared) and insisted that any arms control agreement begin with an American abandonment of SDI.

The escalation of Cold War tensions and the slowing of arms control initiatives helped produce an important popular movement in Europe and the United States calling for an end to nuclear weapons buildups. In America, the principal goal of the movement was a "nuclear freeze," an agreement between the two superpowers not to expand their atomic arsenals. In what many believed was the largest mass demonstration in American history, nearly a million people rallied in New York City's Central Park in 1982 to support the freeze. Perhaps partly in response to this growing pressure, the administration began tentative efforts to revive arms control negotiations in 1983.

It also began, rhetorically at least, to support opponents of communism anywhere in the world, whether or not the regimes or movements they were challenging had any direct con-

Reagan Doctrine

nection to the Soviet Union. This new policy became known as the Reagan Doctrine, and it meant, above all, a new American activism in the Third World. The most conspicuous examples of the new activism came in Latin America. In October 1982, the administration sent American soldiers and marines into the tiny Caribbean island of Grenada to oust an anti-American Marxist regime that showed signs of forging a relationship with Moscow. In El Salvador, where first a repressive military government and later a moderate civilian one were engaged in murderous struggles with left-wing revolutionaries (who were supported, according to the Reagan administration, by Cuba and the Soviet Union), the administration provided increased military and economic assistance. In neighboring Nicaragua, a pro-American

BREAKING PRECEDENT One of the few dramatic moments of Walter Mondale's otherwise disastrous presidential campaign in 1984 was his choice of a running mate. For the first time in American history, a woman received a major-party nomination for national office: Geraldine Ferraro, a congresswoman from New York City. She is shown here being introduced by Mondale in the House chamber of the Minnesota legislature, a few days before the start of the Democratic National Convention. *(Diana Walker/TimePix)*

dictatorship had fallen to the revolutionary "Sandinistas" in 1979; the new government had grown increasingly anti-American (and increasingly Marxist) throughout the early 1980s. The Reagan administration gave both rhetorical and material support to the so-called contras, a guerrilla movement drawn from several antigovernment groups and fighting (without great success) to topple the Sandinista regime. Indeed, support of the contras became a mission of special importance to the president, and later the source of some of his greatest difficulties.

In other parts of the world, the administration's tough rhetoric seemed to hide an instinctive restraint. In June 1982, the Israeli army launched an invasion of Lebanon in an effort to drive guerrillas of the Palestinian Liberation Organization from the country. An American peacekeeping force entered Beirut to supervise the evacuation of PLO forces from Lebanon. American marines then remained in the city, apparently to protect the fragile Lebanese government, which was embroiled in a vicious civil war. Now identified with one faction in the struggle, Americans became the targets in 1983 of a terrorist bombing of a U.S. military barracks in Beirut that left 241 marines dead. Rather than become more deeply involved in the Lebanese struggle, Reagan withdrew American forces.

The tragedy in Lebanon was an example of the changing character of Third World struggles: an increasing reliance on terrorism by otherwise powerless groups to advance their political aims. A series of terrorist acts in the 1980s—attacks on airplanes, cruise ships, commercial and diplomatic posts; the seizing of American and other Western hostages—alarmed and frightened much of the Western world. The Reagan administration spoke bravely

Combating Terrorism

about its resolve to punish terrorism; and at one point in 1986, the president ordered American planes to bomb sites in Tripoli, the capital of Libya, whose controversial leader Muammar al-Qaddafi was widely believed to be a leading sponsor of terrorism. In general, however, terrorists remained difficult to identify or control.

The Election of 1984

Reagan approached the campaign of 1984 at the head of a united Republican Party firmly committed to his candidacy. The Democrats, as had been their recent custom, followed a more fractious course. Former vice president Walter Mondale, the early frontrunner, fought off challenges from Senator Gary Hart of Colorado (who claimed to represent a "new generation" of leadership) and the magnetic Jesse Jackson, who had established himself as the nation's most prominent spokesman for minorities and the poor. Mondale brought momentary excitement to the Democratic campaign by selecting a woman, Representative Geraldine Ferraro of New York, to be his running mate and the first female candidate ever to appear on a national ticket.

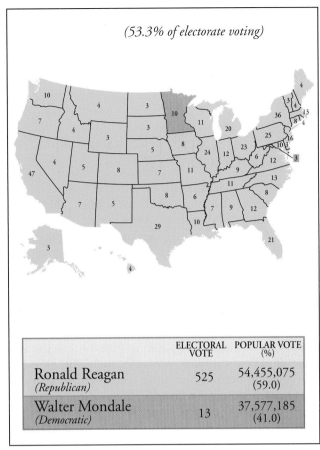

(53.3% of electorate voting)

	ELECTORAL VOTE	POPULAR VOTE (%)
Ronald Reagan *(Republican)*	525	54,455,075 (59.0)
Walter Mondale *(Democratic)*	13	37,577,185 (41.0)

THE ELECTION OF 1984 In 1984, Ronald Reagan repeated (and slightly expanded) his electoral landslide of 1980, and added to it the popular landslide that had eluded him four years earlier. As this map shows, Mondale succeeded in carrying only his home state of Minnesota and the staunchly Democratic District of Columbia. ◆ *What were some of the factors that made Reagan so popular in 1984?*

 For an interactive version of this map go to www.mhhe.com/brinkley11ch33maps

The Republican Party rallied comfortably behind its revered leader, whose triumphant campaign that fall scarcely took note of his opponents and spoke instead of what he claimed was the remarkable revival of American fortunes and spirits under his leadership. His campaign emphasized such phrases as "It's Morning in America" and "America Is Back." Reagan's victory in 1984 was decisive. He won approximately 59 percent of the vote, and carried every state but Mondale's native Minnesota and the District of Columbia. But Reagan was much stronger than his party. Democrats gained a seat in the Senate and maintained only slightly reduced control of the House of Representatives. The triumphant reelection of Ronald Reagan was the high-water mark of conservative, and Republican, fortunes in the postwar era. It reflected satisfaction with the impressive performance of the economy under the Republican economic program, and pride in the new assertiveness the United States was showing in the world. To many Reagan supporters, the 1984 election seemed to be the dawn of a new conservative era. But almost no one anticipated the revolutionary events that would change the world, and America's place in it, within a very few years. The election of 1984, therefore, was not so much the first of a new era as the last of an old one. It was the final campaign of the Cold War.

AMERICA AND THE WANING OF THE COLD WAR

Many factors contributed to the collapse of the Soviet empire. The long, stalemated war in Afghanistan proved at least as disastrous to the Soviet Union as the Vietnam War had been to America. The government in Moscow had failed to address a long-term economic decline in the Soviet republics and the Eastern-bloc nations. Restiveness with the heavy-handed policies of communist police states was growing throughout much of the Soviet empire. But the most visible factor at the time was the emergence of Mikhail Gorbachev, who succeeded to the leadership of the Soviet Union in 1985 and, to the surprise of almost everyone (probably including himself), very quickly became the most revolutionary figure in world politics in at least four decades.

The Fall of the Soviet Union

Gorbachev quickly transformed Soviet politics with two dramatic new initiatives. The first he called *glasnost*

Mikhail Gorbachev

(openness): the dismantling of many of the repressive mechanisms that had been conspicuous features of Soviet life for over half a century. The other policy Gorbachev called *perestroika* (reform): an effort to restructure the rigid and unproductive Soviet economy by introducing, among other things, such elements of capitalism as private ownership and the profit motive. He also began to transform Soviet foreign policy.

The severe economic problems at home evidently convinced Gorbachev that the Soviet Union could no longer sustain its extended commitments around the world. As early as 1987, he began reducing Soviet influence in Eastern Europe. And in 1989, in the space of a few months, every communist state in Europe—Poland, Hungary, Czechoslovakia, Bulgaria, Romania, East Germany, Yugoslavia, and Albania—either overthrew its government or forced it to transform itself into an essentially noncommunist (and in some cases, actively anticommunist) regime. The Communist Parties of Eastern Europe collapsed or redefined themselves into more conventional left-leaning social democratic parties. Gorbachev and the Soviet Union actively encouraged the changes.

The challenges to communism were not successful everywhere. In May 1989, students in China launched a mass movement calling for greater democratization. But in June, hard-line leaders seized control of the government and sent military forces to crush the uprising. The result was a bloody massacre on June 3, 1989, in Tiananmen Square in *Tiananmen Square* Beijing, in which a still-unknown number of demonstrators died. The assault crushed the democracy movement and restored the hard-liners to power. It did not, however, stop China's efforts to modernize and even westernize its economy.

But China was an exception to the worldwide movement toward democratization, which even extended to parts of the world far removed from the Soviet empire.

TIANANMEN SQUARE, 1989 The democracy movement in China accelerated rapidly in the spring of 1989 and was most visible through the vast crowds of students who began demonstrating in Tiananmen Square in Beijing. Some of them fashioned a rough replica of the American Statue of Liberty, which they called the "Goddess of Liberty," an act particularly galling to the conservative leadership of the communist regime. On June 3, the government sent troops into the square to clear out and arrest the demonstrating students. Hundreds, perhaps thousands, were killed in the violence that resulted from that decision. *(Forrest Anderson/Getty Images)*

Early in 1990, the government of South Africa, long an international pariah for its rigid enforcement of "apartheid" (a system designed to protect white supremacy), began a cautious retreat from its traditional policies. Among other things, it legalized the chief black party in the nation, the African National Congress (ANC), which had been banned for decades; and on February 11, 1990, it released from prison the leader of the ANC, and a revered hero to black South Africans, Nelson Mandela, who had been in jail for twenty-seven years. Over the next several years, the South African government repealed its apartheid laws. And in 1994, there were national elections in which all South Africans could participate. As a result, Nelson Mandela became the first black president of South Africa.

In 1991, communism began to collapse at the site of its birth: the Soviet Union itself. An unsuccessful coup by hard-line Soviet leaders on August 19 precipitated a dramatic unraveling of communist power. Within days, the coup itself collapsed in the face of resistance from the public and, more important, crucial elements within the military. Mikhail Gorbachev returned to power, but it soon became evident that the legitimacy of both the Communist Party and the central Soviet government had been fatally injured. By the end of August, many of the republics of the Soviet Union had declared independence; the Soviet government was clearly powerless to stop the fragmentation. Gorbachev himself finally resigned as leader of the now virtually powerless Communist Party and Soviet government, and the Soviet Union ceased to exist.

Dissolution of the USSR

Reagan and Gorbachev

The last years of the Reagan administration coincided with the first years of the Gorbachev regime; and while Reagan was skeptical of Gorbachev at first, he gradually became convinced that the Soviet leader was sincere in his desire for reform. At a summit meeting with Reagan in Reykjavik, Iceland, in 1986, Gorbachev proposed reducing the nuclear arsenals of both sides by 50 percent or more, although continuing disputes over Reagan's commitment to the SDI program prevented agreements. But in 1988, after Reagan and Gorbachev exchanged cordial visits to each other's capitals, the two superpowers signed a treaty eliminating American and Soviet intermediate-range nuclear forces (INF) from Europe—the most significant arms control agreement of the nuclear age. At about the same time, Gorbachev ended the Soviet Union's long and frustrating military involvement in Afghanistan.

The Fading of the Reagan Revolution

For a time, the dramatic changes around the world and Reagan's personal popularity deflected attention from a series of scandals that might well have destroyed another administration. There were revelations of illegality, corruption, and ethical lapses in the Environmental Protection Agency, the CIA, the Department of Defense, the Department of Labor, the Department of Justice, and the Department of Housing and Urban Development. A more serious scandal emerged within the savings and loan industry, which the Reagan administration had helped deregulate in the early 1980s. Many savings banks had responded by rapidly, often recklessly, and sometimes corruptly, expanding. By the end of the decade the industry was in chaos, and the government was forced to step in to prevent a complete collapse. Government insurance covered the assets of most savings and loan depositors; the cost of the debacle to the public eventually ran to more than half a trillion dollars.

Savings and Loan Crisis

But the most politically damaging scandal of the Reagan years came to light in November 1986, when the White House conceded that it had sold weapons to the revolutionary government of Iran as part of a largely unsuccessful effort to secure the release of several Americans being held hostage by radical Islamic groups in the Middle East. Even more damaging was the revelation that some of the money from the arms deal with Iran had been covertly and illegally funneled into a fund to aid the contras in Nicaragua.

In the months that followed, aggressive reporting and a highly publicized series of congressional hearings exposed a widespread pattern of covert activities orchestrated by the White House and dedicated to advancing the administration's foreign policy aims through secret and at times illegal means. The principal figure in this covert world appeared at first to be an obscure marine lieutenant colonel assigned to the staff of the National Security Council, Oliver North. But gradually it became clear that North was acting in concert with other, more powerful figures in the administration. The Iran-contra scandal, as it became known, did serious damage to the Reagan presidency—even though the investigations were never able decisively to tie the president himself to the most serious violations of the law.

Iran-Contra Scandal

The Election of 1988

The fraying of the Reagan administration helped the Democrats regain control of the United States Senate in 1986 and fueled hopes in the party for a presidential victory in 1988. Even so, several of the most popular figures in the Democratic Party refused to run, and the nomination finally went to a previously little-known figure: Michael Dukakis, a three-term governor of Massachusetts. Dukakis was a dry, even dull campaigner. But Democrats were optimistic about their prospects in 1988, largely because their opponent, Vice President George Bush, had failed to spark any real public enthusiasm. He entered the last months of the campaign well behind Dukakis.

Beginning at the Republican Convention, however, Bush staged a remarkable turnaround by making his

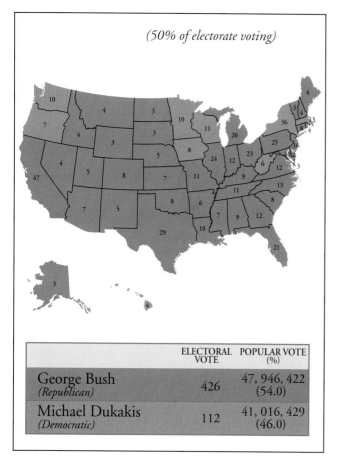

(50% of electorate voting)

	ELECTORAL VOTE	POPULAR VOTE (%)
George Bush (Republican)	426	47, 946, 422 (54.0)
Michael Dukakis (Democratic)	112	41, 016, 429 (46.0)

THE ELECTION OF 1988 Democrats had high hopes going into the election of 1988, but Vice President George Bush won a decisive victory over Michael Dukakis, who did only slightly better than Walter Mondale had done four years earlier. ◆ *What made it so difficult for a Democrat to challenge the Republicans in 1988 after eight years of a Republican administration?*

THE BUSH CAMPAIGN, 1988 Vice President George Bush had never been an effective campaigner, but in 1988 he revived his candidacy with an unabashed attack on his opponent's values and patriotism. Bush himself missed no chance to surround himself with patriotic symbols, including this red, white, and blue hot-air balloon in Kentucky. *(I. Johnson/Getty Images)*

campaign a long, relentless attack on Dukakis, tying him to all the unpopular social and cultural stances Americans had come to identify with "liberals." Indeed, the

Bush's Negative Campaign | Bush campaign was almost certainly the most negative of the twentieth century. It was also, apparently, one of the most effective, although the listless, indecisive character of the Dukakis effort contributed to the Republican cause as well. Bush won a substantial victory in November: 54 percent of the popular vote to Dukakis's 46 percent, and 426 electoral votes to Dukakis's 112. But Bush carried few Republicans into office with him; the Democrats retained secure majorities in both houses of Congress.

The Bush Presidency

The Bush presidency was notable for the dramatic developments in international affairs with which it coincided and at times helped to advance, and for the absence of important initiatives or ideas on domestic issues.

The broad popularity Bush enjoyed during his first three years in office was partly a result of his subdued, unthreatening public image. But it was primarily because of the wonder and excitement with which Americans viewed the dramatic events in the rest of the world. Bush moved cautiously at first in dealing with the changes in the Soviet Union. But like Reagan, he eventually cooperated with Gorbachev and reached a series of significant agreements with the Soviet Union in its waning years. In the three years after the INF agreement in 1988, the United States and the Soviet Union moved rapidly toward even more far-reaching arms reduction agreements.

On domestic issues, the Bush administration was less successful—partly because the president himself seemed to have little interest in promoting a domestic agenda and partly because he faced serious obstacles. His administration inherited a staggering burden of debt and a federal deficit that had been out of control for nearly a decade.

Any domestic agenda that required significant federal spending was, therefore, incompatible with the presi-

Political Gridlock

dent's pledge to reduce the deficit and his 1988 campaign promise of "no new taxes." Bush faced a Democratic Congress with an agenda very different from his own. And he was constantly concerned about the right wing of his own party and, in his eagerness to ingratiate himself with it, took divisive positions on such cultural issues as abortion and affirmative action that further damaged his ability to work with the Democratic Congress.

Despite this political stalemate, Congress and the White House managed on occasion to agree on significant measures. They cooperated in producing the plan to salvage the floundering savings and loan industry. In 1990, the president bowed to congressional pressure and agreed to a significant tax increase as part of a multiyear "budget package" designed to reduce the deficit—thus violating his own 1988 campaign pledge of "no new taxes." In 1991, after almost two years of acrimonious debate, the president and Congress agreed on a civil rights bill to combat job discrimination.

But the most serious domestic problem facing the Bush administration was one for which neither the presi-

1990 Recession

dent nor Congress had any answer: a recession that began late in 1990 and slowly increased its grip on the national economy in 1991 and 1992. Because of the enormous level of debt that corporations (and individuals) had accumulated in the 1980s, the recession caused an unusual number of bankruptcies. It also increased the fear and frustration among middle- and working-class Americans and put pressure on the government to address such problems as the rising cost of health care.

The Gulf War

The events of 1989–1991 had left the United States in the unanticipated position of being the only real superpower in the world. The Bush administration, therefore, had to consider what to do with America's formidable political and military power in a world in which the major justification for that power—the Soviet threat—was now gone.

The events of 1989–1991 suggested two possible answers, both of which had some effect on policy. One was that the United States would reduce its military strength dramatically and concentrate its energies and resources on pressing domestic problems. There was, in fact, considerable movement in that direction both in Congress and within the administration. The other was that America would continue to use its power actively, not to fight communism but to defend its regional and economic interests. In 1989, that led the administration to order an invasion of Panama, which overthrew the unpopular military leader Manuel Noriega (under indictment in the United States for drug trafficking) and replaced him with an elected, pro-American regime. And in 1990, that same impulse drew the United States into the turbulent politics of the Middle East.

On August 2, 1990, the armed forces of Iraq invaded and quickly overwhelmed their small, oil-rich neighbor, the emirate of Kuwait. Saddam Hussein, the militaristic leader

Invasion of Kuwait

of Iraq, soon announced that he was annexing Kuwait and set out to entrench his forces there. After some initial

DESERT STORM Perhaps never before in the history of warfare had an army relied as heavily on air power as did the United States and its allies during the Gulf War against Iraq in 1991. The use of ground troops was largely secondary to the heavy bombing of Iraqi positions and installations by American missiles, rockets, bombers, and artillery. *(Delabaye/SIPA Press)*

indecision, the Bush administration agreed to lead other nations in a campaign to force Iraq out of Kuwait—through the pressure of economic sanctions if possible, through military force if necessary. Within a few weeks, Bush had persuaded virtually every important government in the world, including the Soviet Union and almost all the Arab and Islamic states, to join in a United Nations-sanctioned trade embargo of Iraq.

At the same time, the United States and its allies (including the British, French, Egyptians, and Saudis) began deploying a massive military force along the border between Kuwait and Saudi Arabia, a force that ultimately reached 690,000 troops (425,000 of them American). On November 29, the United Nations, at the request of the United States, voted to authorize military action to expel Iraq from Kuwait if Iraq did not leave by January 15, 1991. On January 12, both houses of Congress voted to authorize the use of force against Iraq. And on January 16, American and allied air forces began a massive bombardment of Iraqi forces in Kuwait and of military and industrial installations in Iraq itself.

The allied bombing continued for six weeks. On February 23, allied (primarily American) forces under the command of General Norman Schwarzkopf began a major ground offensive—not primarily against the heavily entrenched Iraqi forces along the Kuwait border, as expected, but to the north of them into Iraq itself. The allied armies encountered almost no resistance and suffered only light casualties (141 fatalities). Estimates of Iraqi deaths in the war were 100,000 or more. On February 28, Iraq announced its acceptance of allied terms for a cease-fire, and the brief Persian Gulf War came to an end.

The quick and (for America) relatively painless victory over Iraq was highly popular in the United States. But the tyrannical regime of Saddam Hussein survived, in a weakened form but showing few signs of retreat from its militaristic ambitions. It would plague the United States again.

The Election of 1992

President Bush's popularity reached a record high in the immediate aftermath of the Gulf War. But the glow of that victory faded quickly as the recession worsened in late 1991, and as the administration declined to propose any policies for combating it.

Because the early maneuvering for the 1992 presidential election occurred when President Bush's popularity remained high, many leading Democrats declined to run. That gave Bill Clinton, the young five-term governor of *Bill Clinton* Arkansas, an opportunity to emerge early as the front-runner, as a result of a skillful campaign that emphasized broad economic issues instead of the racial and cultural questions that had so divided the Democrats in the past. Clinton survived a bruising primary campaign and a series

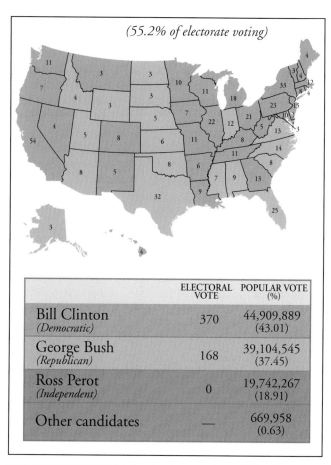

(55.2% of electorate voting)

	ELECTORAL VOTE	POPULAR VOTE (%)
Bill Clinton *(Democratic)*	370	44,909,889 (43.01)
George Bush *(Republican)*	168	39,104,545 (37.45)
Ross Perot *(Independent)*	0	19,742,267 (18.91)
Other candidates	—	669,958 (0.63)

THE ELECTION OF 1992 For the first time since 1976, a Democrat captured the White House in the 1992 election. And although the third party candidacy of Ross Perot deprived Bill Clinton of an absolute majority, he nevertheless defeated George Bush by a decisive margin in both the popular and electoral vote. ◆ *What factors had eroded President Bush's once-broad popularity by 1992? What explained the strong showing of Ross Perot?*

For an interactive version of this map go to www.mhhe.com/brinkley11ch34maps

of damaging personal controversies to win his party's nomination. And George Bush withstood an embarrassing primary challenge from the conservative journalist Pat Buchanan to become the Republican nominee again.

Complicating the campaign was the emergence of Ross Perot, a blunt, forthright Texas billionaire who became an independent candidate by tapping popular resentment of *Ross Perot* the federal bureaucracy and by promising tough, uncompromising leadership to deal with the fiscal crisis and other problems of government. At several moments in the spring, Perot led both Bush and Clinton in public opinion polls. In July, as he began to face hostile scrutiny from the media, he abruptly withdrew from the race. But early in October, he reentered and soon regained much (although never all) of his early support.

After a campaign in which the economy and the president's unpopularity were the principal issues, Clinton won a clear, but hardly overwhelming, victory over Bush and Perot. He received 43 percent of the vote in the three-way race, to the president's 38 percent and Perot's 19 percent (the best showing for a third-party or independent candidate since Theodore Roosevelt in 1912). Clinton won 370 electoral votes to Bush's 168; Perot won none. Democrats retained control of both houses of Congress.

CONCLUSION

America in the late 1970s was, by the standards of its own recent history, an unusually troubled nation: numbed by the Watergate scandals, the fall of Vietnam, and perhaps most of all the nation's increasing economic difficulties. The unhappy presidencies of Gerald Ford and Jimmy Carter provided little relief from these accumulating problems and anxieties. Indeed, in the last year of the Carter presidency, the nation's prospects seemed particularly grim in light of severe economic problems, a traumatic seizure of American hostages in Iran, and a Soviet invasion of Afghanistan.

In the midst of these problems, American conservatives were slowly and steadily preparing for an impressive revival. A coalition of disparate but impassioned groups on the right—including a large movement known as the "new right" with vaguely populist impulses—gained strength from the nation's troubles and from their own success in winning support for a broad-ranging revolt against taxes. Their efforts culminated in the election of 1980, when Ronald Reagan became the most conservative man in at least sixty years to be elected president of the United States.

Reagan's first term was a dramatic contrast to the troubled presidencies that had preceded it. He won substantial victories in Congress (cutting taxes, reducing spending on domestic programs, building up the military). Perhaps equally important, he made his own engaging personality one of the central political forces in national life. Easily reelected in 1984, he seemed to have solidified the conservative grip on national political life. In his second term, a series of scandals and misadventures—and the president's own declining energy—limited the administration's effectiveness. Nevertheless, Reagan's personal popularity remained high, and the economy continued to prosper—factors that helped his vice president, George H. W. Bush, to succeed him in 1989.

Bush's presidency was defined not by domestic initiatives, as Reagan's had been—and the perception of its disengagement with the nation's growing economic problems contributed to Bush's defeat in 1992. But a colossal historic event often overshadowed domestic concerns during Bush's term in office: the collapse of the Soviet Union and the fall of communist regimes all over Europe and in other parts of the world. The United States was to some degree a dazzled observer of this process. But the end of the Cold War also propelled the United States into the possession of unchallenged global pre-eminence—and drew it increasingly into the role of international arbiter and peacemaker. The Gulf War of 1991 was only the most dramatic example of the new global role the United States would now increasingly assume.

FOR FURTHER REFERENCE

Bruce J. Schulman, *The Seventies: The Great Shift in American Culture, Society, and Politics* (2001) is a good general history of the period. James M. Cannon, *Time and Chance: Gerald Ford's Appointment with History* (1994) is a journalist's account of the Ford presidency. Charles O. Jones, *The Trusteeship Presidency Jimmy Carter and the United States Congress* (1988) looks at Carter's frustrations in domestic policy, and Gaddis Smith, *Morality, Reason, and Power* (1986) examines his foreign policy. Steven Gillon, *The Democrats' Dilemma: Walter Mondale and the Liberal Legacy* (1992) is a good discussion of the travails of the Democrats in the 1970s. Jerome L. Himmelstein, *To the Right: The Transformation of American Conservatism* (1990) and Godfrey Hodgson, *The World Turned Upside Down: A History of the Conservative Ascendancy in America* (1996) are good introductions to the subject. E. J. Dionne, *Why Americans Hate Politics* (1991) is a perceptive discussion of the political discontents of the 1980s and early 1990s. Garry Wills, *Reagan's America* (1987) is an interesting, critical interpretation. Lou Cannon, *President Reagan: The Role of a Lifetime* (1990) and Haynes Johnson, *Sleepwalking Through History* (1991) are accounts by journalists who covered the Reagan White House. Hedrick Smith, *The Power Game* (1988) is a sweeping portrait of the culture of political Washington during the Reagan years. John Lewis Gaddis, *The United States and the End of the Cold War* (1992) and *We*

Now Know: Rethinking Cold War History (1997) examine the transformation of the world order after 1989. Thomas Crothers, *In the Name of Democracy: U.S. Foreign Policy toward Latin America in the Reagan Years* (1991) examines a controversial area of Reagan's international record, including aspects of the Iran-contra scandal. Herbert Parmet, *George*

Bush: The Life of a Lone Star Yankee (1997) is the first major scholarly study of the 41st president.

The Conservative Resurgence (1991) is a documentary film examining the growing conservative trend in American politics during the late 1970s and the 1980s.

For quizzes, Internet resources, references to additional books and films, and more, consult this book's Online Learning Center at www.mhhe.com/brinkley11.

SEPTEMBER 11, 2001 One great American symbol, the Statue of Liberty, stands against a sky filled with the thick smoke from the destruction of another American symbol, New York City's World Trade Center towers, a few hours after terrorists crashed two planes into them. *(Daniel Hulshizer/AP/Wide World Photos)*

Significant Events

1977 ·	Apple introduces first personal computer
1979 ·	Nuclear accident at Three Mile Island
1981 ·	Existence of AIDS first reported in United States
1985 ·	Crack cocaine appears in American cities
1989 ·	Human genome project launched
1991 ·	Controversy surrounds confirmation of Clarence Thomas to Supreme Court
1992 ·	Major race riot in Los Angeles
·	Bill Clinton elected president
1993 ·	Congress approves tax increase as part of deficit reduction
·	Congress ratifies North American Free Trade Agreement

CHAPTER THIRTY-FOUR

THE AGE OF GLOBALIZATION

*A*t 8:45 A.M. on the bright, sunny morning of September 11, 2001, as tens of thousands of workers—executives and financiers, secretaries and clerks, security guards and maintenance workers, chefs and waiters, citizens of dozens of nations—were beginning a day's work in lower Manhattan, a commercial airliner crashed

September 11, 2001

into the side of one of the two towers of the World Trade Center, the tallest buildings in New York. The collision created a huge explosion and a great fire of extraordinary intensity. Less than half an hour later, as thousands of workers fled the burning building, another commercial airliner rammed into the companion tower, creating a second fireball. Within an hour after that, both towers—their steel girders buckling in response to the tremendous heat—collapsed. The burning floors gave way and fell onto the floors below them, pulling one of New York's (and America's) most famous symbols to the ground. At about the same time, in Washington, another commercial airliner crashed into a side of the Pentagon—the headquarters of the nation's military—turning part of the building's facade into rubble. And several hundred miles away, still another airplane crashed in a field not far from Pittsburgh.

These four almost simultaneous catastrophes were the result of a single orchestrated plan by Islamic militants to bring terrorism—for years the bane of such nations as Israel, Turkey, Italy, Germany, Britain, Japan, and Ireland—into the United States, which had previously had relatively little recent experience of it. Similarly committed Middle Eastern terrorists had previously attacked American targets overseas—military barracks, a naval vessel, embassies, and consulates. And they had staged a less cataclysmic attack on the World Trade Center in 1993.

On September 11, groups of terrorists boarded each of the four planes armed with nothing more than box cutters and set out to use the aircraft as weapons against important buildings. In three cases, they succeeded. In the fourth, passengers—alerted by cell phone conversations to the intentions of the hijackers—apparently took over the plane and forced it down before it could reach its target. More than 3,000 people died as a result of the September 11 disasters.

The events of September 11 produced great changes in American life. They also seemed to bring to a close an extraordinary period in modern American history—a time of heady prosperity, bitter partisanship, cultural frivolity and excess, and tremendous social and economic change. And yet there was also at least one great continuity between the world of the 1990s and the world that seemed to begin on September 11, 2001. The United States, more than at any other time in its history, was becoming deeply entwined in a new age of globalism—an age that combined great promise with great peril.

- Clinton proposes national health-care system

1994
- Congress rejects health-care reform
- Republicans win control of both houses of Congress

1995
- New Republican Congress attempts to enact "Contract with America"
- Showdown between president and Congress leads to shutdown of federal government
- National crime rates show dramatic decline
- O. J. Simpson trial

1996
- Congress passes and president signs major welfare reform bill, minimum wage increase, and health-insurance reform
- Clinton reelected president; Republicans retain control of Congress

1997
- President and Congress agree on plan to balance budget
- Justice Department files antitrust suits against Microsoft

1998
- Lewinsky scandal rocks Clinton presidency
- Democrats gain in congressional elections
- Clinton impeached by House

1999
- Senate acquits Clinton in impeachment trial

2000
- George W. Bush wins contested presidential election

2001
- Terrorists destroy World Trade Center and damage Pentagon
- United States begins military action against Afghanistan

A RESURGENCE OF PARTISANSHIP

Bill Clinton took the oath of office in January 1993 as the first Democratic president since Jimmy Carter, and the first self-proclaimed activist president since Lyndon Johnson. He had a domestic agenda more ambitious than that of any president in nearly thirty years. He entered the presidency carrying the extravagant expectations of liberals who had spent a generation in exile.

William Jefferson Clinton

But Clinton also had significant political weaknesses. Having won the votes of well under half the electorate, he enjoyed no powerful mandate. Democratic majorities in Congress were frail, and Democrats in any case had grown unaccustomed to bowing to presidential leadership. The Republican leadership in Congress was highly adversarial and opposed the president with unusual unanimity on many issues. A tendency toward reckless personal behavior, both before and during his presidency, caused the president continuing problems and gave his many enemies repeated opportunities to discredit him. The Clinton years, therefore, became a time of unusually intense and bitter partisan struggles.

Launching the Clinton Presidency

The new administration compounded its problems with a series of missteps and misfortunes in its first months. The president's effort to end the longtime ban on gay men and women serving in the military met with ferocious resistance from the armed forces themselves and from many conservatives in both parties. He was forced to settle for a pallid compromise. Several of his early appointments became so controversial he had to withdraw them. A longtime friend of the president, Vince Foster, serving in the office of the White House counsel, committed suicide in the summer of 1993. His death helped spark an escalating inquiry into some banking and real estate ventures involving the president and his wife in the early 1980s; and the actions of some administration officials in handling Foster's papers after his death raised suspicions that the White House was attempting to interfere with the investigation into what became known as the Whitewater affair. An independent counsel began examining these issues in 1993.

Despite its many problems, the Clinton administration could boast of some significant achievements in its first year. The president narrowly won approval of a budget that marked a significant turn away from the policies of the Reagan-Bush years. It included a substantial tax increase on the wealthiest Americans, a significant reduction in many areas of government spending, and a major expansion of tax credits to low-income working people, designed to help lift many struggling families out of poverty.

Clinton was a committed advocate of free trade and a proponent of many aspects of what came to be known as globalism. He made that clear through his strong support of a series of new and controversial free trade agreements. After a long and difficult battle against, among others, Ross Perot, the AFL-CIO, and many Democrats in Congress,

NAFTA

he won approval of the North American Free Trade Agreement (or NAFTA), which eliminated most trade barriers among the United States, Canada, and Mexico. Later he won approval of other far-reaching trade agreements negotiated in the General Agreement on Trade and Tarriffs (or GATT).

But the administration's substantial achievements were overshadowed by a large failure. The president's most important and ambitious initiative—the project that he hoped would define his presidency—was a major reform of the nation's health-care system. Early in 1993, he appointed a task force chaired by his wife,

Failure of Health-Care Reform

Hillary Rodham Clinton, which proposed a sweeping reform designed to guarantee coverage to every American and hold down the costs of medical care. The Clinton plan relied heavily on existing institutions, most notably private insurance companies; and some critics from the left complained that the new system would be too closely tied to an undependable market. But the most substantial opposition came from the right, from those who believed the reform would transfer too much power to the government; and that well-funded opposition—combined with the determination of Republican leaders to deny the president any kind of victory on this potent issue—doomed the plan. In September 1994, after a series of compromises failed to attract majorities, Congress abandoned the health-care reform effort.

The foreign policy of the Clinton administration was at first cautious and even tentative—a reflection, perhaps, of the president's relative inexperience in international affairs, but also of the rapidly changing character of international politics. That was particularly clear in the administration's handling of one of the most troubling international questions of the early 1990s. Yugoslavia, a nation created after World War I out of a group of small Balkan countries that had once been part of the Austro-Hungarian Empire, dissolved again into several different nations in the wake of the collapse of its communist government in 1989. Bosnia was among the new nations, and it quickly became embroiled in a bloody civil war between its two major ethnic groups: one Muslim, the other Serbian and Christian backed by the neighboring Serbian republic. All efforts by the other European nations and the United States to negotiate an end to the struggle failed until 1995, when the American negotiator Richard Holbrooke finally brought the warring parties together and crafted an agreement to partition Bosnia. The United States was among the nations to send peacekeeping troops to Bosnia to police the fragile settlement, which—despite many pessimistic predictions—was still largely in place

BREAKING PRECEDENT Bill Clinton broke with precedent in 1993 when he appointed his wife, Hillary Rodham Clinton, to head a task force on health care reform. The prominent role of the First Lady in the Clinton administration surprised many Americans, pleasing some and angering others. The Clintons are shown here with Vice President Al Gore, as the First Lady talks about health care. Hillary Clinton broke precedent again in 2000 when she was elected to the United States Senate from New York. *(Wally McNamee/Corbis)*

seven years later, although terrible new conflicts soon emerged in other areas of the Balkans.

The Republican Resurgence

The trials of the Clinton administration, and the failure of health-care reform in particular, proved enormously damaging to the Democratic Party as it faced the congressional elections of 1994. Few doubted that the Republicans would make significant gains that year, but almost everyone was surprised by the dimensions of their victory. For the first time in forty years, Republicans gained control of both houses of Congress.

Several months before the election, the House Republican leader, Newt Gingrich of Georgia, released a set of campaign promises signed by almost all Republican candidates for the House and called it the "Contract with America." It called for tax reductions, dramatic changes in federal spending to produce a balanced budget, and a host of other promises consistent with the long-time goals of the

"Contract with America"

Republican Party's conservative wing. Opinion polls suggested that few voters in 1994 were aware of the "Contract" at the time they voted. But Gingrich and the new Republican congressional leadership nevertheless interpreted the election results as a mandate for their program.

Throughout 1995, the Republican Congress worked at a sometimes feverish pace to construct one of the most ambitious and even radical legislative programs in modern times. They proposed a series of measures to transfer important powers from the federal government to the states. They proposed dramatic reductions in federal spending, including a major restructuring of the once-sacrosanct Medicare program to reduce costs. They attempted to scale back a wide range of federal regulatory functions. In all these efforts, they could count on an unprecedentedly disciplined Republican majority in the House and an only slightly less united Republican majority in the Senate. The Republican agenda, if it had been successfully enacted, would have represented the most substantial shift in the distribution of public authority since the 1930s.

President Clinton responded to the 1994 election results by proclaiming that "the era of big government is over" and shifting his own agenda conspicuously to the center. He announced his own plan to cut taxes and balance the budget. Indeed, the gap between the Democratic White House and the Republican Congress on many major issues was relatively small. But because the legislative politics of 1995 was becoming part of the presidential politics of 1996, compromise between the president and Congress became very difficult. In November 1995 and again in January 1996, the federal government literally shut down for several days because the president and Congress could not agree on a budget. Republican leaders refused to pass a "continuing resolution" (to allow government operations to continue during negotiations) in hopes of pressuring the president to agree to their terms. That proved to be an epic political blunder. Public opinion turned quickly and powerfully against the Republican leadership, and against much of its agenda. Gingrich quickly became one of the most unpopular political leaders in the nation, while President Clinton slowly improved his standing in the polls.

The Election of 1996

By the time the 1996 presidential campaign began in earnest, President Clinton—who had seemed so disastrously wounded after the 1994 elections and whom many Republican leaders had come to consider almost irrelevant—was in a commanding position to win re-election. Unopposed for the Democratic nomination, he

Clinton versus Dole

faced a Republican opponent— Senator Robert Dole of Kansas— who inspired little enthusiasm even within his own party. Clinton's revival was in part a result of his adroitness in taking centrist positions that undermined the Republicans on one issue after another, and in championing traditional Democratic issues—such as raising the minimum wage— that were broadly popular. Clinton benefited even more from the disastrous errors by congressional Republicans in 1995 and early 1996. Indeed, Clinton often seemed to be campaigning more against Newt Gingrich than against his actual opponent. But his greatest strength came from the remarkable success of the American economy and the marked reduction in the federal deficit that had occurred during his presidency. Like Reagan in 1984, he could campaign as the champion of peace, prosperity, and national well-being.

As the election approached, both Democrats and Republicans grew uneasy about the failure of the 104th Congress to pass any significant measures. In a flurry of activity in the spring and summer of 1996, the Congress passed several important bills. It raised the minimum wage for the first time in more than a decade. It passed a law that required insurance companies to allow workers to retain their health insurance when they left their jobs

and that forbade the companies from denying coverage to people with "pre-existing conditions" (people who were already ill when they applied for coverage). Most dramatically of all, the Congress passed a welfare reform bill, which President Clinton somewhat uneasily signed, that marked the most important change in aid to the poor since the Social Security Act of 1935. It ended the fifty-year federal guarantee of assistance to families with dependent children and turned most of the responsibility for allocating federal welfare funds (now greatly reduced) to the states. Most of all, it shifted the bulk of welfare benefits away from those without jobs and toward support for low-wage workers. A strong economy in the first few years after the bill passed helped move many former welfare recipients into the paid workforce. But the real test of the effects of the reform awaited a recession.

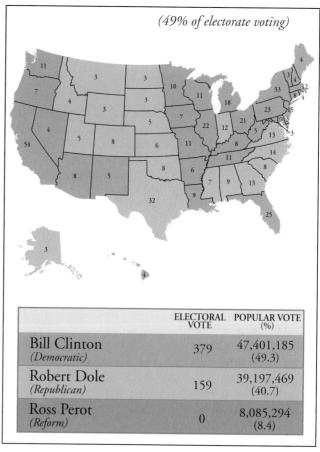

(49% of electorate voting)

	ELECTORAL VOTE	POPULAR VOTE (%)
Bill Clinton *(Democratic)*	379	47,401,185 (49.3)
Robert Dole *(Republican)*	159	39,197,469 (40.7)
Ross Perot *(Reform)*	0	8,085,294 (8.4)

THE ELECTION OF 1996 Ross Perot did much less well in 1996 than he had in 1992, and President Clinton came much closer than he had four years earlier to winning a majority of the popular vote. Once again, Clinton defeated his Republican opponent, this time Robert Dole, by a decisive margin in both the popular and electoral vote. After the 1994 Republican landslide in the congressional elections, Bill Clinton had seemed permanently weakened. ◆ *What explains his political revival?*

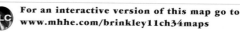

For an interactive version of this map go to www.mhhe.com/brinkley11ch34maps

Clinton's buoyant campaign flagged slightly in the last weeks before the election in the face of allegations of improper or illegal fund-raising techniques by the Democrats. But the president nevertheless won a substantial victory. He received just over 49 percent of the popular vote to Dole's 41 percent; Ross Perot, running now as the candidate of what he called the Reform Party, generated much less enthusiasm than he had in 1992 but still received over 8 percent of the vote. Clinton won 379 electoral votes to Dole's 159; Perot again won none. But the president's victory did not have much effect on other Democrats, who made only modest gains over their disastrous showing in 1994 and failed to regain either house of Congress.

Clinton Triumphant and Embattled

Bill Clinton was the first Democratic president to win two terms as president since Franklin Roosevelt, and he began his second administration with what appeared to be serene confidence. Facing a somewhat chastened but still hostile Republican Congress, he proposed a relatively modest domestic agenda, consisting primarily of tax cuts

Budget Surpluses

and tax credits targeted at middle-class Americans and designed to help them educate their children. He also negotiated effectively with the Republican leadership on a plan for a balanced budget, which passed with much fanfare late in 1997. By the end of 1998, the federal budget—transformed both by a series of changes in fiscal policy and by the long-term strength of the economy—was generating its first surplus in thirty years. The president was only partially responsible for this remarkable change. But he received significant popular credit nevertheless and finished his fifth year in office more popular than he had ever been before.

That popularity would be important to him in the turbulent year that followed, when the most serious crisis of his presidency suddenly erupted. Clinton had been bedeviled by scandals almost from his first weeks in office: the investigations into Whitewater and related issues; charges of corruption leveled against members of his cabinet and his staff; harsh accusations of illegalities in financing his 1996 campaign; and a civil suit for sexual harassment filed against the president early in his first term by a former state employee in Arkansas, Paula Jones, who charged that Clinton, while governor, had made unwanted sexual advances toward her.

In early 1998, inquiries associated with the Paula Jones case led to charges that the president had had a sexual re-

Monica Lewinsky

lationship with a young White House intern, Monica Lewinsky; that he had lied about it in his deposition before Jones's attorneys; and that he had encouraged Lewinsky to do the same. Those revelations produced a new investigation by the independent counsel in the Whitewater case,

Kenneth Starr, a former judge and official in the Reagan Justice Department.

Starr had been investigating the Whitewater matter for nearly four years without any significant results. But he suddenly resurfaced as a major threat to the president with a vigorous effort to prove that the president had lied under oath and had advised others to lie as well. Clinton forcefully denied the charges, and the public strongly backed him. His popularity soared to record levels—a 79 percent approval rating in one poll, and it remained over sixty percent throughout the year that followed. After a few weeks of frenzied speculation, the Lewinsky matter seemed to lose steam. In the meantime, a federal judge dismissed the Paula Jones case, which had launched the scandal.

But the Lewinsky scandal revived again with great force in August 1998, when Lewinsky struck a deal with the independent counsel and testified about her relationship with Clinton. Starr then subpoenaed Clinton himself, who—faced with the prospect of speaking to a grand jury—finally admitted that he and Lewinsky had had what he called an "improper relationship." A few weeks later, Starr submitted a lengthy and at times salacious report to Congress on the results of his investigation, recommending that Congress impeach the president.

The prospect of impeachment became an issue in the 1998 congressional elections. Republicans believed that the Clinton scandals would help them make substantial gains; Democrats, on the other hand, gambled that the public's strong opposition to impeachment would damage the Republicans. The Democrats

Midterm Gains for Democrats

proved right. The Republicans actually lost ten seats in the House, cutting their already thin majority to five, and gained no seats in the Senate. Once again, the president seemed to have escaped his difficulties as a result of strong popular support.

Impeachment, Acquittal, and Resurgence

But Clinton and his supporters underestimated the determination of Republican conservatives to pursue the case, apparently without regard to public opinion. House leaders resisted all calls for dismissal of the charges or compromise. First the House Judiciary Committee and then, on December 19, 1998, the full House, both voting on strictly

Impeachment

partisan lines, approved two counts of impeachment: lying to the grand jury and obstructing justice. The matter then moved to the Senate, where a trial of the president—the first since the trial of Andrew Johnson in 1868—began in early January. Even then, public opinion continued strongly to favor Clinton.

The Senate trial continued for several weeks without generating any significant public support, or even much public attention. The Senate, unlike the House, attempted to avoid partisan rancor, but with only partial success. The trial ended with a decisive acquittal of the president. Neither of the charges attracted even a majority of the votes, let alone the two-thirds necessary for conviction.

The investigation into the president's sexual behavior, and the political battle that followed it, illustrated two significant changes in the character of American public life in the 1990s. One was the expanding role of scandal in American politics, driven by an increasingly sensationalist media culture, the legal device of independent counsels, and the intensely adversarial quality of partisan politics. The other was the blurring of the distinction between public and private behavior, which made almost every facet of a politician's life a target of inquiry and exposure. This new political culture was in part a result of the increasing public cynicism about politics, politicians, and government. It was also a cause of that cynicism.

New Political Culture

The last two years of the Clinton presidency were relatively quiet ones domestically. The president recognized that he had no real hope of major domestic achievements in the face of a hostile Republican Congress and launched only modest initiatives, few of which Congress enacted. Overseas, however, he was more active than he had ever been before. Beginning in 1998, the United States found itself once again in conflict with Iraqi president Saddam Hussein, who now balked at the agreements he had signed at the end of the Gulf War and refused to permit international inspectors to examine military sites in his country. Clinton responded by ordering a series of American bombing strikes at military targets in Iraq.

In 1999, the president faced the most serious foreign policy crisis of his presidency, once again in the Balkans. This time, the conflict involved a province of Serbian-dominated Yugoslavia—Kosovo—most of whose residents were Albanian Muslims. A long-simmering conflict between the Serbian government of Yugoslavia and Kosovo separatists erupted into a savage civil war in 1998. Numerous reports of Serbian atrocities against the Kosovans, and an enormous refugee crisis spurred by Yugoslavian military action in the province, slowly roused world opinion. All efforts to negotiate a settlement of the dispute failed. And in May 1999, NATO forces—dominated and led by the United States—began a major bombing campaign against the Serbians, which after little more than a week led the leader of Yugoslavia, Slobodan Milosevic, to agree to a cease-fire. Serbian troops withdrew from Kosovo entirely, replaced by NATO peacekeeping forces. A precarious peace returned to the region.

Kosovo

Clinton finished his eight years in office with his popularity higher than it had been when he had begun. Indeed, public approval of Clinton's presidency—a presidency marked by astonishing prosperity and general world stability—was consistently among the highest of any postwar president—despite the many scandals and setbacks he suffered in the White House.

The Election of 2000

The 2000 presidential election was one of the most extraordinary in American history—not because of the campaign that preceded it, which was (in the opinion of most Americans) unusually dull and uninspiring, but because of the sensational controversy over its results, which preoccupied the nation for more than five weeks after the actual voting.

The two men who had been the frontrunners for their parties' nominations a year before the election captured those nominations with only slight difficulty. George W. Bush—son of the former president and a second-term governor of Texas—rode his famous name and his enormous campaign war chest to overcome a powerful challenge from Senator John McCain of Arizona, a maverick reformer who championed campaign finance reform. Vice President Al Gore, an even more prohibitive favorite in the Democratic race, easily beat back a challenge from former Senator Bill Bradley of New Jersey.

George W. Bush versus Al Gore

Voters found Gore and Bush rather bland—unthreatening but also unexciting. Both men ran cautious, centrist campaigns, making much of their relatively modest differences over how to use the large budget surpluses forecast for the years ahead. Although polls showed an exceptionally tight race right up to the end, no one anticipated how close the election would be. In the congressional races, Republicans maintained control of the House of Representatives by a scant five seats, while the Senate split evenly between Democrats and Republicans. (Among the victors in the Senate races was First Lady Hillary Rodham Clinton, who won a highly publicized race in New York.) In the presidential race, Gore won the national popular vote by the thin margin of about 540,000 votes out of about 100 million cast (or .05%). But on election night, both candidates remained short of the 270 electoral votes needed for victory because no one could determine who had actually won Florida.

At one point during that long night, the television networks had projected that Gore would win Florida—a victory that would have given him the presidency. Hours later, they retracted that projection. Later still, they awarded the state (and the presidency) to Bush, and Gore quickly called to concede. But as Bush's slim lead in Florida began to evaporate in the last stages of vote counting—and as Gore's motorcade was delivering him to a rally in Nashville to make his concession public—the vice president called Bush again, this time to retract his concession.

Florida

After a mandatory recount over the next two days, Bush led Gore in the state by fewer than 300 votes. (Ralph Nader, the presidential candidate of the new Green Party,

ELECTION NIGHT, 2000 The electronic billboard in New York City's Times Square, showing network coverage of the presidential contest, reports George Bush the winner of the 2000 presidential race late on election night. A few hours later, the networks retracted their projections because of continuing uncertainty over the results in Florida. Five weeks later, and then only because of the controversial intervention of the Supreme Court, Bush finally emerged the victor. *(Chris Hondros/Newsmakers)*

heavily Democratic Palm Beach County, where the ballot was especially poorly designed, thousands of confused voters punched the wrong hole, or punched two holes when they were supposed to punch one. Into this morass, the Gore campaign moved quickly with a demand—sanctioned by Florida law—for hand recounts of punch-card ballots in three critical counties.

The Bush campaign, fearing a recount that might wipe out their frail margin of victory, immediately struck back in court (where at first they failed) and through the   *Katherine Harris*
Republican Secretary of State, Katherine Harris, who had worked actively on the Bush campaign. As the official responsible for certifying elections in the state, she refused to authorize the recounts and declined to extend a deadline for making an official certification. The Gore campaign promptly petitioned the Florida Supreme Court, which voted unanimously to require Harris to permit the hand recounts and to accept the results after the deadline. Such recounts proceeded in two of those counties, but in the third and largest (Dade County, which includes Miami) the local election board—for complicated reasons, which may have included intimidation by Republican demonstrators in the municipal building—abruptly called off the recount, claiming they could not finish in time.

When the new, court-ordered deadline arrived, Harris quickly certified Bush the winner in Florida by a little more than 500 votes. The Gore campaign immediately contested the results in court, asking for the Dade County recount to be reopened. Turned down by a lower court judge, they prevailed again in the Florida Supreme Court, which ordered hand recounts of all previously uncounted ballots in all Florida counties. Once again, the laborious and controversial process of counting punch cards by hand—which required each election board to agree on its own standard for judging "voter intent," since the state Supreme Court had declined to set one—resumed.

In the meantime, the Bush campaign appealed desperately to the United States Supreme Court to stop the recounts. To the surprise of most observers, the Court issued a stay on Saturday,   *The Supreme Court's*
December 9 (by a vote of 5–4),   *Decision*
halting the recounts and calling for arguments before the Court on Monday, December 11. Late on Tuesday, the Court issued one of the most unusual and controversial decisions in its history. Voting 5–4 again, dividing sharply along party and ideological lines, the conservative majority overruled the Florida Supreme Court's order for a recount, insisted that any revised recount order be completed by December 12 (an obviously impossible demand, since the Court issued its ruling late at night on the 12th), and argued that the standards for evaluating punch-card ballots were too arbitrary and unfair to withstand constitutional scrutiny. The four-member minority bitterly protested the majority's reasoning, and

had done poorly nationally but nevertheless drew over 90,000 votes in Florida, which almost certainly denied Gore what would otherwise have been a comfortable victory there.) At that point, the long, controversial, and often bitter post-election battle began—in a state whose governor, Jeb Bush, was the Republican candidate's brother.

The technology of voting soon became central to the dispute. In a number of Florida counties, including some of the most heavily Democratic ones, votes were cast by punch-card ballots, which were then counted by machines. But punch cards are notoriously inaccurate, and many voters failed to punch out the appropriate holes adequately, leaving the machines unable to read them. In

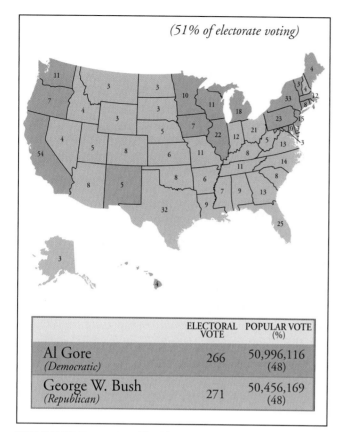

(51% of electorate voting)

	ELECTORAL VOTE	POPULAR VOTE (%)
Al Gore *(Democratic)*	266	50,996,116 (48)
George W. Bush *(Republican)*	271	50,456,169 (48)

THE ELECTION OF 2000 The 2000 presidential election was one of the closest and most controversial in American history. It also starkly revealed a new pattern of party strength, which had been developing over the previous decade. Democrats swept the Northeast and most of the industrial Midwest and carried all the states of the Pacific Coast. Republicans swept the South, the Plains States, and the Mountain States (with the exception of New Mexico) and held onto a few traditional Republican strongholds in the Midwest. Compare this map to earlier elections, and in particular the election of 1896, and ask how the pattern of party support changed over the course of the twentieth century.

the majority itself appeared deeply divided on some crucial issues. But divided or not, the Court had decided the election. Absent a recount, the original certification of Bush's victory stood—with the answer to who had actually won the election in Florida still unknown and, perhaps, unknowable. The next day, Gore gave a brief and conciliatory concession speech. Bush then delivered a subdued acknowledgment of one of the most controversial victories in the history of American presidential elections, and began to prepare for a new administration.

The Second Bush Presidency

George W. Bush assumed the presidency in January 2001 burdened both by the controversies surrounding his election and the widespread perception, even among some of his own supporters, that he was ill prepared for the office. His first eight months in the White House were notable

for some important legislative successes but also for little progress in winning over the 52 percent of the electorate that had voted against him.

Bush's principal campaign promise had been that he would use the predicted budget surplus to finance a massive tax reduction. Critics of his plan, both during and af- *Bush Tax Cuts* ter the campaign, insisted that these massive cuts would wipe out the surplus, restore deficits, and provide benefits disproportionately to the wealthiest Americans. Republicans insisted that the cuts (the largest of which were not scheduled to take effect for years) would stimulate the economy and help strengthen investment. By relying on his own party's control of both houses of Congress (Republicans controlled the 50–50 Senate because the Republican vice president, Richard Cheney, broke all ties), he won passage of the largest tax cut in American history—$1.35 trillion. Emboldened by their victory, Republicans began preparing to move other controversial legislation—dealing with education, social security reform, defense, and taxation—through Congress. But less than three months into Bush's presidency, the administration—and the Republican party—suffered a stunning setback when Senator James Jeffords of Vermont, a moderate Republican unhappy with the conservative tenor of both the administration and the Republican leadership in Congress, declared himself an independent and announced he would vote with the Democrats to organize the Senate. Suddenly, Bush's legislative road became much less promising, and over the next several months most of the bills he had proposed made little progress.

Having campaigned as a moderate adept at building coalitions across party lines, Bush spent his first months in office governing as a staunch conservative and relying on the most orthodox members of his own party for support. His popularity hovered just below 50 percent, and polls showed that if the 2000 election were held again, Bush and Gore would still be roughly tied. With its emphasis on taxes and its sensitivity to the needs of investors and corporations, it was in these early months an administration driven—as the Clinton administration had also often been—by the remarkable long-term health of the American economy.

THE ECONOMIC BOOM

The last two decades of the twentieth century saw remarkable changes in American life—some of them a result of the end of the Cold War, some of them the result of the changing character of the American population, some of them a product of a rapidly evolving culture, But most of these changes were at least in part a product of the dramatic transformation of the American economy. That transformation had begun in earnest in the early 1970s, and it continued unabated through the 1990s.

From "Stagflation" to Growth

The roots of the economic growth of the 1980s and 1990s lay in part in the troubled years of the 1970s, when the United States seemed for a time to be losing its ability to produce long-term prosperity. In the face of the sluggish growth and persistent inflation of those years, however, many American corporations began making important changes in the way they ran their businesses—changes that contributed both to the prosperity of the last decades

New Business Practices | of the twentieth century, and the growing inequality that ac-companied it. Businesses invested heavily in new technology, to make themselves more efficient and productive. Corporations began to consider mergers with other companies, to provide themselves with a more diversified basis for growth. Many enterprises—responding to the energy crises of the 1970s—created more energy-efficient plants and offices. Perhaps most of all, American businesses sought to reduce their labor costs, which were among the highest in the world and which many believed had made the United States uncompetitive against the many emerging economies that relied on low-wage workers.

Businesses cut labor costs in many ways. They took a much harder line against unions. Nonunion companies became more successful in staving off unionization drives. Companies already unionized won important concessions from their unions on wages and benefits in exchange for preserving jobs. Some companies moved their operations to areas of the country where unions were weak and wages low—some areas of the American South and West in particular. And many companies moved much of their production out of the United States entirely, to such nations as Mexico and China where there were large available labor pools willing to work for much less than American workers.

At least as important as the restructuring of existing businesses was the emergence of powerful new sectors

"Technology Industries" | of the economy—most notably what became known as the "technology industries." The growth of digital technology made possible an enormous range of new products that quickly became central to American economic life: computers, the Internet, cellular phones, digital music, video, and cameras, personal digital assistants, and many other products. The technology industries employed hundreds of thousands of people, created new consumer needs and appetites, and even spawned their own stock exchange—the NASDAQ—which enjoyed an enormous boom in the late 1990s.

For these and many other reasons, the American economy experienced astonishing growth in the last decades of the twentieth century. The Gross National Product (the total of goods and services produced by the United States) rose from $2.7 trillion in 1980 to over $9.8 trillion in 2000, quadrupling in twenty years. Inflation was low throughout these decades, never rising above 3 percent in any year and for a while in the late 1990s dropping below 2 percent. Stock prices soared to unprecedented levels, and with few interruptions, from the mid-1980s to the end of the century. The Dow Jones Industrial Average, the most common index of stock performance, stood at 1,000 in late 1980. Late in 1999, it passed 11,000. Economic growth was particularly dramatic in the last years of the 1990s. In 1997 and 1998, annual growth rates reached five percent for the first time since the 1960s. There was evidence as well of a rise not only in income but in productivity. Most impressive of all was the longevity of the boom. From 1994 to 2000, the economy recorded growth—at times very substantial growth—in every year, indeed in every quarter, something that had never before happened so continuously in peacetime since modern economic measurements began. Except for the relatively brief recession of 1992–1993, the period of dramatic growth actually extended unbroken from late 1983 until an economic downturn began in spring 2000.

Downturn

Perhaps the most powerful figure in the American economy—Alan Greenspan, chairman of the Federal Reserve Board—warned in 1999 of the "irrational exuberance" with which Americans were pursuing profits in the stock market. A few months later, the market vindicated his concerns when, in April 2001, there was a sudden and disastrous collapse of a booming new sector of the economy. For over two years, there had been tremendous optimism among investors about the possibility of new, profitable businesses making use of the Internet. Enormous sums were invested in start-up companies, known as "dot.coms," because their Internet addresses ended with ".com." Stock prices in such companies rose rapidly. But it gradually became clear that both enterpreneurs and investors had overestimated the economic potential of the Internet—or at least had not yet discovered the ways in which the Internet could be profitable. As that realization dawned, there was a sudden and dramatic sell-off of technology stocks.

At first, the bursting of the "tech bubble" seemed to have few effects on the larger economy. But by the beginning of 2001, the stock market—a great engine of growth over the previous decade—began a substantial decline, which continued for almost a year. Even when it began to recover in early 2002, it showed nothing of the booming growth of the 1990s. By the fall of 2001, the economy as a whole slipped into a recession.

In the midst of these economic troubles, a stunning corporate collapse shocked the financial world. The Enron Corporation was an energy-trading company based in

ENRON FIELD In happier days, Enron was a high-profile corporation eager to spread its reputation widely. It built a gleaming curved skyscraper in downtown Houston and was nearing completion of a second tower when bankruptcy stopped construction in December 2001. It also paid to have the new Houston baseball stadium named Enron Field. In spring 2002, as scandal tarnished the reputation of the company and its leaders, the Houston Astros paid several million dollars to allow itself to remove the now-notorious Enron name from its stadium. *(David J. Phillip/AP/Wide World Photos)*

Houston, Texas, that had claimed to be the seventh-largest company in America and the world's largest energy merchant. A model to many managers of bold innovation, it announced that it was dramatically lowering its estimates of its own revenues and net worth. Its stock price began to fall, and on December 2, 2001, the company filed for bankruptcy.

Over the following months, the Enron collapse became a major preoccupation of the media and the financial world—in part because of the extraordinary and, many charged, illegal deceptions that its failure revealed. The company had made use of unorthodox accounting practices to dramatically inflate its profits, and hence its stock price. Its auditor, the accounting firm of Arthur Andersen, had approved these unusual practices. Both Enron and Andersen, in the aftermath of the collapse, destroyed records at about the time that prosecutors and congressional committees were preparing to subpoena them. In February 2002, a parade of Enron and Arthur Andersen executives appeared before skeptical congressional committees. Most witnesses denied knowing anything of the improprieties in their companies. Others took the Fifth Amendment.

The Enron scandal, coming as it did at a time of economic difficulty, cast a harsh light on some of the aggressive practice of companies in the booming 1990s. There were calls for new and stricter regulations on accounting and auditing. Many companies began to examine their own practices to avoid similar catastrophes. Much of the public saw the Enron fiasco as an example of wider deception and corruption in the corporate world.

The Two-Tiered Economy

Although the American economy revived triumphantly from the sluggishness that had characterized it in the 1970s and early 1980s, the benefits of the new economy were less widely shared than those of earlier boom times. The increasing abundance created enormous new wealth that enriched those talented, or lucky, enough to profit from the areas of booming growth. The rewards for education—particularly in such areas as science and engineering—increased enormously. In 1995, the average annual income of a person with less than a high-school education was $14,000. For a high-school graduate, that number rose to $21,400. But a college graduate's average salary was $37,000, and the average salary of someone with an advanced degree was $56,700—four times the level of those who did not graduate from high school. Between 1980 and the mid-1990s, the average family incomes of the wealthiest 20 percent of the population grew by nearly 20 percent (to over $100,000 a year); the average family income of the next 20 percent of the population grew by more than 8 percent. Incomes remained flat for most of the remaining 60 percent of the public, and actually declined for many in the bottom 20 percent.

Rising Income Inequality

The jarring changes in America's relationship to the world economy that had begun in the 1970s—the loss of cheap and easy access to raw materials, the penetration of the American market by foreign competitors, the restructuring of American heavy industry so that it produced fewer jobs and paid lower wages—continued and in some respects accelerated through the last decades of the century. For families and individuals outside the circle of knowledgeable people benefiting from the new technologies, the results of these contractions were often devastating.

Poverty in America had declined steadily and at times dramatically in the years after World War II, so that by the end of the 1970s the percentage of people living in poverty had fallen to 12 percent (from about 20 percent in preceding decades). But the decline in poverty did not continue.

Growing Poverty Rates

In the 1980s, the poverty rate rose again, at times as high as 18 percent. By the late 1990s, it had dropped to under 13 percent again, but that was about the same as it had been twenty years before.

Globalization

Perhaps the most important economic change, and certainly the one whose impact was the most difficult to gauge, was what became known as the "globalization" of the economy. The great prosperity of the 1950s and 1960s had rested on, among other things, the relative insulation of the United States from the pressures of international competition. As late as 1970, international trade still played a relatively small role in the American economy as a whole, which thrived on the basis of the huge domestic market in North America.

By the end of the 1970s, however, the world had intruded on the American economy in profound ways, and

THE GLOBAL ECONOMY Hundreds of shipping containers, virtually all of them from China, stand waiting for delivery at the Yang Ming container terminal in Los Angeles in February 2001—an illustration of the increasing penetration of the American market by overseas manufacturers and of the growing interconnections between the United States economy and that of the rest of the world. *(Reed Saxon/AP/Wide World Photos)*

that intrusion increased unabated for the next twenty years. Exports rose from just under $43 billion in 1970 to over $789 billion in 2000. But imports rose even more dramatically: from just over $40 billion in 1970 to over $1.2 trillion in 2000. Most American products, in other words, now faced foreign competition inside the United States. America had made 76 percent of the world's automobiles in 1950 and 48 percent in 1960. By 1990, that share had dropped to 20 percent; in 2000, even after a substantial revival of the automobile industry, the American share had risen only to 21.5 percent. The first American trade imbalance in the postwar era occurred in 1971; only twice since then, in 1973 and 1975, has the balance been favorable.

Globalization brought many benefits for the American consumer: new and more varied products, and lower prices for many of them. Most economists, and most national leaders, welcomed the process and worked to encourage it through lowering trade barriers. The North American Free Trade Agreement (NAFTA) and the General Agreement on Trade and Tariffs (GATT), were the boldest of a *Costs of Globalization* long series of treaties designed to lower trade barriers stretching back to the 1960s. But globalization had many costs as well. It was particularly hard on industrial workers, who saw industrial jobs disappear as American companies lost market share to foreign competitors. American workers also lost jobs as American companies began exporting work—building plants in Mexico, Asia, and other lower-wage countries to avoid having to pay the high wages workers had won in America.

SCIENCE AND TECHNOLOGY IN THE NEW ECONOMY

The "new economy" that emerged in the last decades of the twentieth century was driven by, and in turn helped to drive, dramatic new scientific and technological discoveries. Much as in the late nineteenth century—when such technological innovations as modern manufacturing, the railroad, the telegraph, the telephone, electricity, and automobiles—transformed both society and economy, so in the late twentieth century, new technologies had profound effects on the way Americans—and peoples throughout the world—lived.

The Personal Computer

The most visible element of the technological revolution to most Americans was the dramatic growth in the use of computers in almost every area of life. Computers had been important to government and to many businesses since World War II. But their reach expanded with extraordinary speed in the 1980s and beyond. By the 1990s, most Americans were doing their banking by computer.

Most retail transactions were conducted by computerized credit mechanisms. Most businesses, schools, and other institutions were using computerized recordkeeping. Many areas of manufacturing were revolutionized by computer-driven product design and factory robotics. Scientific and technological research in almost all areas was transformed by computerized methods.

Among the most significant innovations was the development of the microprocessor, first introduced in 1971 by Intel, which represented a notable advance in the technology of integrated circuitry. A microprocessor miniaturized the central processing unit of a computer, making it possible for a small machine to perform calculations that in the past only very large machines could do. Considerable technological innovation was needed before the micro-

Development of the PC

processor could actually become the basis of what was at first known as a "minicomputer" and then a personal computer. But in 1977, Apple launched its Apple II personal computer, the first such machine to be widely available to the public. Several years later, IBM entered the personal computer market with the first "PC." IBM had engaged a small software development company, Microsoft, to design an operating system for their new computer. Microsoft produced a program known as MS-DOS (DOS for "disk operating system"). No PC could operate without it. The PC, and its software, made its debut in August 1981 and immediately became enormously successful. Three years later, Apple introduced its Macintosh computer, which marked another major innovation in computer technology, among other things because its software—very different from DOS—was much easier to use than that of the PC. But Apple could not match IBM's marketing power, and by the mid-1980s the PC had clearly established its dominance in the booming personal computer market—a dominance enhanced by the introduction of a new software package to replace DOS in 1985: Windows, also developed by Microsoft, which borrowed many concepts (most notably the Graphical User Interface, or GUI) from the Apple operating system. IBM, however, was not in the end the principal beneficiary of the dominance of its own system, as other companies began marketing their own IBM-compatible personal computers, usually at a lower price than IBM's, and seizing an increasing share of the market.

Personal computers very quickly established a presence in many areas of American life: homes, schools, businesses, universities, hospitals, government agencies, newsrooms. Computerized word processing programs replaced typewriters. Computerized spreadsheets revolutionized bookkeeping. Computerized data processing made obsolete much traditional information storage, such as filing. Some computer enthusiasts talked about the imminent coming of a "paperless" office, in which all information or communication would be stored and distributed through computers, a prediction that failed to materialize. But the emergence of ever smaller and more powerful computers—laptops, notebooks, and palm-sized devices—greatly extended the reach of computer-related technology. At the same time, however, computer scientists were creating extraordinarily powerful new forms of networking; and many were predicting that before long the stand-alone personal computer would be obsolete, that the future lay in linking many computers together into powerful networks.

The computer revolution created thousands of new, lucrative businesses: computer manufacturers themselves (IBM, Apple, Compaq, Dell, Gateway, Sun, Digital, and many others); makers of the tiny silicon chips that ran the computers and allowed smaller and smaller machines to become more and more powerful (most notably Intel); and makers of software—chief among them Microsoft, the

Microsoft

most powerful new corporation to arise in American life in generations. In the 1990s, Microsoft had a virtual monopoly on the operating systems for most personal computers in the world. It had also moved into new areas: creating other kinds of software (word processing, spreadsheets, databases, communications, personal finance, and many others) and producing software and content for the Internet. In 1997, after many abortive efforts, the Justice Department filed a series of antitrust suits against the giant corporation—a suit that in 2000 produced a strong ruling against the corporation that was later at least partly overturned by an appeals court. In the meantime, Microsoft remained one of the most profitable corporations in the country.

But if Microsoft was the most conspicuous success story of the computer age, it was only one of many. Whole regions—the so-called Silicon Valley in northern California; areas around Boston, Austin, Texas, and Seattle, Washington; even areas in downtown New York City—became centers of booming economic activity servicing the new computer age.

The Internet

Out of the computer revolution emerged another dramatic source of information and communication: the Internet. The Internet is, in essence, a vast, geographically far-flung network of computers that allows people connected to the network to communicate with others all over the world. It had its beginning in 1963, in the U.S. government's Advanced Research Projects Agency (ARPA), which funneled federal funds into scientific research projects, many of them defense-related. In the early 1960s, J. C. R.

Arpanet

Licklider, the head of ARPA's Information Processing Technique Office, was working on a project he called Libraries of the Future, through which he hoped to make vast amounts of information available electronically to people in far-flung areas. In 1963, he launched a program to link

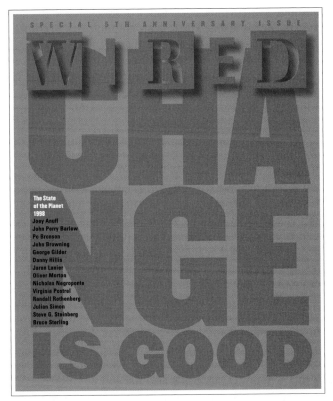

WIRED 6.01 The January 1998 issue of *Wired,* a magazine aimed at young, hip, computer-literate readers, expressed the optimistic, even visionary approach to the possibilities of new electronic technologies that was characteristic of many computer and Internet enthusiasts in the 1990s. *Wired,* which began publication in 1992, was careful to differentiate itself from the slick, commercial computer magazines that were principally interested in trumpeting new products. It tried, instead, to capture the simultaneously skeptical and progressive spirit of a generation to whom technology seemed to define much of the future. *(Designer, John Plunkett; Writer, Louis Rossetto. Copyright © 2002 by the Conde Nast Publications, Inc. All rights reserved.)*

together computers over large distances. It was known as the Arpanet. For several years, the Arpanet served mainly as a way for people to make use of what were then relatively scarce computer facilities without having to go to the site of the computer. Gradually, however, both the size and the uses of the network expanded.

This expansion was facilitated in part by two important new technologies. One was a system developed in the early 1960s at the RAND Corporation in the United States and the National Physical Laboratory in England. It was known as "store-and-forward packet switching," and it made possible the transmission of large quantities of data between computers without directly wiring the computers together. There could be a central communications backbone through which messages and information could be routed to individual computers, much as the telegraph and telephone system used centralized carriers that eventually branched off into local connections. The other technological breakthrough was the

development of computer software that would allow individual computers to handle the traffic over the network—what became known as the Interface Message Processor.

By 1971, twenty-three computers were linked together in the Arpanet, which served mostly research labs and universities. Gradually, interest in the system began to spread, and with it the number of computers connected to it. (By 2001, there were an estimated 625 million computers in use in the world, and 182 million in the United States, the great majority of them personal computers.) In the early 1980s, the Defense Department, an early partner in the development of the Arpanet, withdrew from the project for security reasons. The network, soon renamed the Internet, was then free to develop independently. It did so rapidly, especially after the invention of technologies that made possible electronic mail (or e-mail) and the emergence of the personal computer, which vastly increased the number of potential users of the Internet. As late as 1984, there remained fewer than a thousand host computers connected to the Internet. A decade later, there were over 6 million. And in 2001, an estimated 400 million people around the world were using the Internet, including 130 million in the United States.

As the amount of information on the Internet unexpectedly proliferated, without any central direction, new forms of software emerged to make it possible for individual users to navigate through the vast number of Internet sites. In 1989, a laboratory in Geneva introduced the World *World Wide Web* Wide Web, through which individual users could publish information for the Internet, which helped establish an orderly system for both the distribution and retrieval of electronic information.

The Internet is still a relatively young communications medium, and its likely impact on society is not yet fully understood. Already, however, it has revolutionized many areas of life. E-mail has replaced conventional mail, telephone calls, and even *Impact of the Internet* face-to-face conversation for millions of people. Newspapers, magazines, and other publications have begun to publish on the Internet. It has become a powerful marketing tool, through which people can purchase items as small as books and as large as automobiles. It is a site for vast amounts of documentary material for researchers, reporters, students and others. And it is, finally, a highly democratic medium—through which virtually anyone with access to a personal computer can establish a website and present information in a form that is available to virtually anyone in the world who chooses to look at it. New technologies that make it easier to transmit moving images over the Internet—and new forms of "broadband" access that give more users high-speed connections to the web—promise to expand greatly the functions that the Internet can perform.

Breakthroughs in Genetics

Aided in part by computer technology, there was explosive growth in another area of scientific research: genetics. Early discoveries in genetics by Gregor Mendel, Thomas Hunt Morgan, and others laid the groundwork for more dramatic breakthroughs—the discovery of DNA by the British scientists Oswald Avery, Colin MacLeod, and Maclyn McCarty in 1944; and in 1953, the dramatic discovery by the American biochemist James Watson and the British biophysicist Francis Crick of the double-helix structure of DNA, and thus of the key to identifying genetic codes. From these discoveries emerged the new science—and ultimately the new industry—of genetic engineering, through which new medical treatments and new techniques for hybridization of plants and animals have already become possible.

Little by little, scientists began to identify specific genes in humans and other living things that determine particular traits, and to learn how to alter or reproduce them. But the identification of genes was painfully slow; and in 1989, the federal government appropriated $3 billion to fund the National Center for the Human Genome, to accelerate the mapping of human genes. The

Human Genome Project

Human Genome Project set out to identify all of the more than 100,000 genes by 2005. But new technologies for research, and competition from other projects (some of them funded by pharmaceutical companies) drove the project forward faster than expected. In 1998, the genome project announced that it would finish its work in 2003. In the meantime, in 2000, other researchers produced a list of all the genes in the human body, even if their relationship to one another remained unmapped.

In the meantime, DNA research had already attracted considerable public attention. In 1997, scientists in Scotland announced that they had cloned a sheep—which they named Dolly—using a cell from an adult ewe; in other words, the genetic structure of the newborn Dolly was identical to that of the sheep from which the cell was taken. The DNA structure of an individual, scientists have discovered, is as unique and as identifiable as a fingerprint. DNA testing, therefore, makes it possible to identify individuals through their blood, semen, skin, or even hair. It played a major role first in the O. J. Simpson trial in 1995 and then in the 1998 investigation into President Clinton's relationship with Monica Lewinsky. Also in 1998, DNA testing appeared to establish with certainty that Thomas Jefferson had fathered a child with his slave Sally Hemings, by finding genetic similarities between descendants of both, thus resolving a political and scholarly dispute stretching back nearly 200 years. Genetic research has already spawned important new areas of medical treatment—and has helped the relatively new biotechnology industry to grow into one of the nation's most important economic sectors. Eventually, scientists expect the research to open up vast new areas for medical treatment—and also controversial new possibilities for genetically designing foods, animals, and even humans.

But genetic research was also the source of great controversy. Many people grew uneasy about the predictions that the new science might give scientists the ability to alter aspects of life that had previously seemed outside the reach of human control. Some critics feared genetic research on religious grounds, seeing it as an interference with God's plan. Others used moral arguments and expressed fears that it would allow parents, for example, to choose what kinds of children they would have. And a particularly heated controversy emerged over the way in which scientists obtained genetic material. One of the

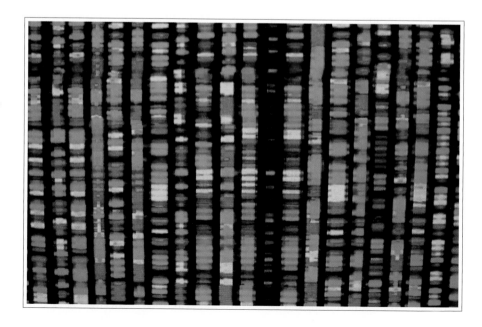

THE HUMAN GENOME This computerized image is a digital representation of part of the human genome, the constellation of genetic material that make up the human body. The Human Genome Project, one of the most ambitious in the history of science, set out in the late 1990s to chart the human genetic structure. Each color in this image represents one of the four chemical components of DNA, the principal material of genes. *(Mario Tama/Getty Images)*

most promising areas of medical research involved the use of stem cells, genetic material obtained in large part from undeveloped fetuses—mostly fetuses created by couples attempting in vitro fertilization. (In vitro fertilization is the process by which couples unable to conceive a child have a fetus conceived outside the womb using their eggs and sperm and then implanted in the mother.) Anti-abortion advocates denounced the research, claiming that it exploited (and endangered) unborn children. Supporters of stem-cell research—which showed promising signs of offering cures for Parkinson's disease, Alzheimer's disease, ALS, and other previously uncurable illnesses—argued that the stem cells they used came from fetuses that would otherwise be discarded, since in vitro fertilization always produces many more fetuses than can be used. The controversy over stem-cell research became an issue in the 2000 campaign. George W. Bush, once president, kept his promise to anti-abortion advocates and in the summer of 2001 issued a ruling barring the use of federal funds to support research using any stem cells that scientists were not already using at the time of his decision.

Moral and Ethical Dilemmas

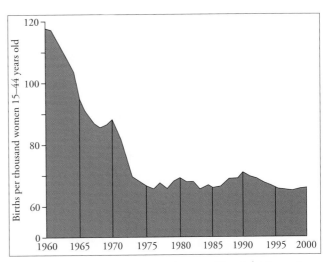

THE AMERICAN BIRTH RATE, 1960–1990 This chart shows the striking change in the pattern of the nation's birth rate from the twenty years after 1940, which produced the great "baby boom." From 1960 onward, the nation's birth rate steadily and, in the 1960s and 1970s, dramatically declined. ◆ *What effect did this declining birth rate have on the age structure of the population?*

A CHANGING SOCIETY

The changes in the economy were one of many factors producing major changes in the character of American society. By the end of the twentieth century, the American population was growing larger, older, and more racially and geographically diverse.

The Graying of America

One of the most important, if often unnoticed, features of American life in the late twentieth century was the aging of the American population. After decades of steady growth, the nation's birth rate began to decline in the 1970s and remained low through the 1980s and 1990s. In 1970, there were 18.4 births for every 1,000 people in the population. By 1996, the rate had dropped to 14.8 births. The declining birth rate and a significant rise in life expectancy produced a substantial increase in the proportion of elderly citizens. Almost 13 percent of the population was more than sixty-five years old in 2000, as compared with 8 percent in 1970. The median age in 2000 was 35.3, the highest in the nation's history. In 1970, it was 28.0.

The aging of the population had important, if not entirely predictable, implications. It was, for example, a cause of the increasing costliness of Social Security pensions. It meant rapidly increasing health costs, both for the federal Medicare system and for private hospitals and insurance companies, and was one

Impact of America's Aging Population

of the principal reasons for the anxiety about health-care costs that played such a crucial role in the politics of the early 1990s. It ensured that the elderly, who already formed one of the most powerful interest groups in America, would remain politically formidable well into the twenty-first century.

It also had important implications for the nature of the work force in the twenty-first century. In the last twenty years of the twentieth century, the number of people aged 25–54 in the native-born work force in the United States grew by over 26 million. In the first ten years of the twenty-first century, the number of workers in that age group will not grow at all. That will put increasing pressure on the economy to employ more older workers. It will also create a greater demand for immigrant workers.

New Patterns of Immigration and Ethnicity

The enormous change in both the extent and the character of immigration was one of the most dramatic social developments of the last decades of the twentieth century. The nation's immigration quotas expanded significantly in those years (partly to accommodate refugees from Southeast Asia and other nations), allowing more newcomers to enter the United States legally than at any point since the beginning of the twentieth century. In 2000, over 28 million Americans—over 10 percent of the total population—consisted of immigrants (people born outside the United States).

Equally striking was the character of the new immigration. The Immigration Reform Act of 1965 (see p. 835)

Surging Immigration

NATURALIZATION, 1996 On September 17, 1996, 10,000 people, representing 113 different countries, were sworn in as United States citizens in Texas Stadium near Dallas, the largest naturalization ceremony in the nation's history. They were part of over 1 million immigrants who became American citizens in 1996, which was also a record (and was more than twice the number naturalized in any previous year). The high number of new citizens was a result of the dramatic increase in immigration over the previous two decades. It was also a result of fears among many immigrants that restrictive new laws would deny them important benefits (including education for their children) if they did not become citizens. *(Shelly Katz/Getty Images)*

had eliminated quotas based on national origin; from then on, newcomers from regions other than Latin America were generally admitted on a first-come, first-served basis. In 1965, 90 percent of the immigrants to the United States came from Europe. By the mid-1980s, only 10 percent of the new arrivals were Europeans, although that figure rose slightly in the 1990s as emigrants from Russia and eastern Europe—now free to leave their countries—came in increasing numbers. The extent and character of the new immigration was causing a dramatic change in the composition of the American population. By the end of the twentieth century, people of white European background constituted under 80 percent of the population (as opposed to 90 percent a half-century before).

Particularly important to the new immigration were two groups: Latinos (people from Spanish-speaking nations, particularly Mexico) and Asians. Both had been significant segments of the American population for many decades—Latinos since the very beginning of the nation's history, Asians since the waves of Chinese and Japanese immigration in the nineteenth century. But both

groups experienced enormous, indeed unprecedented, growth after 1965. People from Latin America constituted more than a third of the total number of legal immigrants to the United States in every year after 1965—and a much larger proportion of the total number of illegal immigrants. Mexico alone accounted for over one-fourth of all the immigrants living in the United States in 2000. In California and the Southwest, in particular, Mexicans became an increasingly important presence. There were also substantial Latino populations in Illinois, New York, and Florida. High birth rates within Latino communities already in the United States further increased their numbers. In the 1980 census, 6 percent of the population (about 14 million) was listed as being of Hispanic origin. By 1997, census figures showed an increase to 11 percent—or 29 million people.

Latino Immigration

In the 1980s and 1990s, Asian immigrants arrived in even greater numbers than Latinos, constituting more than 40 percent of the total of legal newcomers. They swelled the already substantial Chinese and Japanese communities in California and elsewhere. And they created

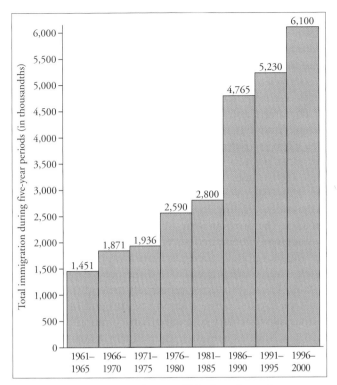

TOTAL IMMIGRATION, 1960–2000 This chart shows the tremendous increase in immigration to the United States in the decades since the Immigration Reform Act of 1965. The immigration of the 1980s and 1990s was the highest since the late nineteenth century. ◆ *What role did the 1965 Act have in increasing immigration levels?*

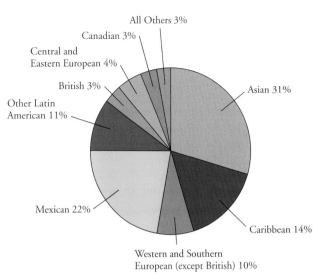

SOURCES OF IMMIGRATION, 1960–1990 The Immigration Reform Act of 1965 lifted the national quotas imposed on immigration policy in 1924 and opened immigration to large areas of the world that had previously been restricted. In 1965, 90 percent of the immigrants to the United States came from Europe. As this chart shows, by 1990 almost the reverse was true. Over 80 percent of all immigrants came from non-European sources. ◆ *What impact did this new immigration have on American politics?*

substantial new communities of immigrants from Vietnam, Thailand, Cambodia, Laos, the Philippines, Korea, and *Asian Immigrants* India. By 2000, there were more than 10 million Asian Americans in the United States (4 percent of the population), more than twice the number of fifteen years before. Like Latinos they were concentrated mainly in large cities and in the West. Many of the new Asian immigrants were refugees, including Vietnamese driven from their homes in the aftermath of the disastrous war in which the United States had so long been involved.

The Black Middle Class

The civil rights movement and the other liberal efforts of the 1960s had two very different effects on African Americans. On the one hand, there were increased opportunities for advancement available to those in a position to take advantage of them. On the other hand, as the industrial economy declined and government services dwindled, there was a growing sense of helplessness and despair among the large groups of nonwhites who continued to find themselves barred from upward mobility.

For the black middle class, which by the end of the twentieth century constituted over half of the African-American population of America, progress was remarkable in the thirty years since the high point of the civil rights movement. Disparities between black and white professionals did not vanish, but they diminished substantially. African-American families moved into *Economic Progress for African Americans* more affluent urban communities and, in many cases, into suburbs—at times as neighbors of whites, more often into predominantly black communities. The number of African Americans attending college rose by 350 percent in the decade following the passage of the civil rights acts (in contrast to a 150 percent increase among whites); African Americans made up 12 percent of the college population in the 1990s (up from 5 percent twenty-five years earlier). The percentage of black high-school graduates going on to college was virtually the same as that of white high-school graduates by the end of the twentieth century (although a far smaller proportion of blacks than whites managed to complete high school). And African Americans were making rapid strides in many professions from which, a generation earlier, they had been barred or within which they had been segregated. In increasing numbers, they were becoming partners in major law firms and joining the staffs of major hospitals and the faculties of major universities. Nearly half of all employed blacks in the United States had skilled white-collar jobs. There were few areas of American life from which blacks were any longer entirely excluded. Middle-class blacks, in other words, had realized great gains from the legislation of the 1960s, from the changing national mood on race, from the creation of controversial affirmative action programs, and from their own strenuous efforts.

Poor and Working-Class African Americans

But the rise of the black middle class also accentuated (and perhaps even helped cause) the increasingly desperate plight of other African Americans, whom the economic growth and the liberal programs of the 1960s and beyond had never reached. These impoverished people—sometimes described as the "underclass"—made up as much as a third of the nation's black population. Many of them lived in isolated, decaying, and desperately poor inner-city neighborhoods. As more successful blacks moved out of the inner cities, the poor were left virtually alone in their decaying neighborhoods. Fewer than half of young inner-city blacks finished high school; more than 60 percent were unemployed. The black family structure suffered as well from the dislocations of urban poverty. There was a radical increase in the number of single-parent, female-headed black households. In 1970, 59 percent of all black children under 18 lived with both their parents (already down from 70 percent a decade earlier). In 2000, only 38 percent of black children lived in such households, while 75 percent of white children did.

The "Underclass"

Nonwhites were disadvantaged by many factors in the changing social and economic climate of the 1980s and 1990s. Among them was a growing impatience with affirmative action and other programs designed to advance their fortunes. They suffered as well from a steady decline in the number of unskilled jobs in the economy; the departure of businesses from their neighborhoods; the absence of adequate transportation to areas where jobs were more plentiful; and failing schools that did not prepare them adequately for employment. And they suffered, in some cases, from a sense of futility and despair, born of years of entrapment in brutal urban ghettoes.

The anger and despair such conditions were creating among inner-city residents became clear in many ways. It was expressed at times artistically, as in some aspects of the most popular new black musical form of the 1980s and 1990s, rap. (See "Patterns of Popular Culture," pp. 938–939.) The anger and frustration became visible even more graphically in the summer of 1992 in Los Angeles. The previous year, a bystander had videotaped several Los Angeles police officers beating an apparently helpless black man, Rodney King, whom they had captured after an auto chase. Broadcast repeatedly around the country, the tape evoked outrage among whites and blacks alike. But an all-white jury in a suburban community just outside Los Angeles acquitted the officers when they were tried for assault. Black residents of South Central Los Angeles, one of the poorest communities in the city, erupted in anger—precipitating the largest racial disturbance of the twentieth century. There was widespread looting and arson. More than fifty people died.

Rodney King

What Americans had long called "race relations," the way in which white and black Americans viewed each other, grew increasingly sour in these difficult years. White impatience with black demands grew, as did a willingness to listen to old and long-discredited arguments about genetic differences between the races. A controversial

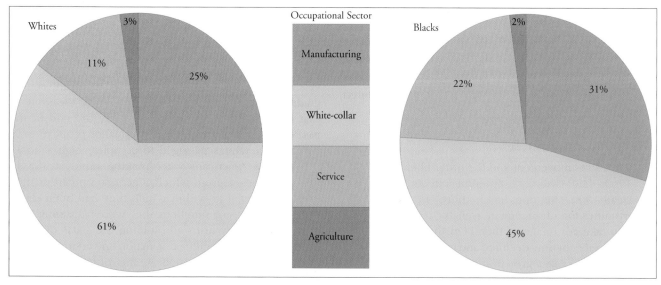

COMPARISON OF BLACK AND WHITE OCCUPATIONAL DISTRIBUTION, 1992 By the early 1990s, as this chart makes clear, the African-American middle class had grown dramatically. Nearly half of all employed black workers in the United States worked in "white-collar" jobs. Perhaps even more striking, given the distribution of the black population a half century earlier, is how few African Americans were working in agriculture by the early 1990s. But the gap between black and white workers remained wide in several areas, particularly in the percentage of each group employed in low-wage service jobs. ◆ *What factors contributed to the increase of the black middle class in the years after 1960?*

book by two white social scientists, *The Bell Curve*, published in 1994, helped reopen this bitter debate about the innate capacities of members of different races. Many African Americans, for their part, developed an intensified mistrust of the institutions of white society—of the government, the corporations, the universities, and perhaps above all the system of law enforcement.

Nowhere was this mutual suspicion more evident than in the celebrated trial of the former football star O. J. Simpson, who was accused of murdering his former wife and a young man in Los Angeles in 1994. The long and costly "O. J. trial" was an enormous media sensation for over a year. Throughout the proceedings, opinions about Simpson's guilt broke down strikingly along racial lines. A vast majority of whites believed that he was guilty, and a vast majority of blacks believed that he was innocent. Simpson's acquittal in the fall of 1995, after a trial in which the defense tried to portray him as a victim of police racism, caused celebrations in many black communities and a quiet disgust among many whites.

O. J. Simpson Trial

Modern Plagues: Drugs and AIDS

The new immigrants of the 1980s and 1990s arrived in cities being ravaged by two new and deadly epidemics. One was a dramatic increase in drug use, which penetrated nearly every community in the nation. The enormous demand for drugs, and particularly for "crack" cocaine, spawned what was in effect a multibillion-dollar industry; and those reaping the enormous profits of the illegal trade fought strenuously and often savagely to protect their positions. Political figures of both parties spoke heatedly about the need for a "war on drugs"; but in the absence of significant funding for such programs, government efforts appeared to be having little effect. Drug use declined significantly among middle-class people beginning in the late 1980s, but the epidemic showed no signs of abating in the poor urban neighborhoods where it was doing the most severe damage.

The drug epidemic was directly related to another scourge of the 1980s and 1990s: the epidemic spread of a new and lethal disease first documented in 1981 and soon named AIDS (acquired immune deficiency syndrome). AIDS is the product of the HIV virus, which is transmitted by the exchange of bodily fluids (blood or semen). The virus gradually destroys the body's immune system and makes its victims highly vulnerable to a number of diseases (particularly to various forms of cancer and pneumonia) to which they would otherwise have a natural resistance. Those infected with the virus (i.e., HIV positive) can live for a long time without developing AIDS, but for many years those who became ill were virtually certain to die.

AIDS Epidemic

"IGNORANCE = FEAR" The artist Keith Haring (whose work was inspired in large part by urban graffiti) created this striking poster in 1989, the year before he himself died of AIDS, to generate support for the battle against the disease. "ACT UP," the organization that distributed it, was among the most militant groups in demanding more rapid efforts to search for a cure. (© *The Estate of Keith Haring*)

For many generations, most of American popular music has been the product of musical forms created by African Americans: gospel, ragtime, jazz, rhythm 'n blues, rock, soul, disco, funk, and—in the 1980s and 1990s—rap. Conservative guardians of American culture have repeatedly denounced the new forms as subversive, excessively sexual, violent, dangerous. But the music has always survived the attacks.

Perhaps no musical innovation has generated as much puzzlement, dismay, and anger among its critics as rap music, which was popular in some urban African-American and Latino communities for years before becoming nationally visible beginning in the early 1980s. Unlike many earlier forms of black music that have attracted broad audiences, rap has relatively little melodic content. Indeed, many rap songs use almost identical musical and instrumental elements—sometimes even literally identical elements. Rap recordings often copy pieces of instrumental backgrounds from other recordings through a technique known as "sampling." Rap's most important element is its words. It is as much a form of language as a form of music.

Rap's musical lineage is a long and complicated one. It has elements of the disco and street funk of the 1970s; of the fast-talking jive of black radio DJs in the 1950s; of the on-stage patter of Cab Calloway and other African-American stars of the first half of the twentieth century. It contains reminders of tap and break dancing—

even of the boxing-ring poetry of Muhammad Ali. It bears a distant resemblance to some traditions of African-American pulpit oratory, which also included forms of spoken song. It draws from some of the verbal traditions of urban black street life, including the "dozens"—a ritualized trading of insults particularly popular among young black men.

But rap is also the product of a distinctive place and time: the South Bronx in the 1970s and 1980s and the hip hop culture that was born there and that soon dominated the appearance and public behavior of many young black males. "Hip hop is how you walk, talk, live, see, act, feel," one Bronx hip hopper described it. It created many of the patterns of dress and behavior that became common among inner-city youths: the popularity of athletic clothes, hats, and shoes; the practice of young men giving themselves "street names"; and—in the 1980s at least—graffiti and break dancing. In the 1990s, break dancing lost its popularity, clothes became baggier, hats became larger, and the most popular element of hip hop culture was rap, which had by then been developing for nearly twenty years.

Beginning in the early 1970s, Bronx DJs began setting up their equipment on neighborhood streets and staging block parties, where they not only played records but also put on shows of their own—performances that featured spoken rhymes, jazzy phrases, and pointed comments about the audience, the neighborhood, and themselves.

Gradually, the DJs began to bring "rappers" into shows—young men who took the DJ style and developed it into a much more elaborate form of performance, usually accompanied by dancing. As rap grew more popular in the inner city, record promoters began signing some of its new stars. In 1979, the Sugarhill Gang's "Rapper's Delight" became the first rap single to be played on mainstream commercial radio and the first to become a major hit. In the early 1980s, Run-DMC became the first national rap superstars. From there, rap moved quickly to become one of the most popular and commercially successful forms of popular music. In the 1990s, rap recordings routinely sold millions of copies.

Rap has taken many forms. There have been white rappers (Third Base, House of Pain), female rappers (Roxanne Shante, Queen Latifah), even religious rappers and children's rappers. But it has always been primarily a product of the young male culture of the inner city, and some of the most successful rap has conveyed the frustration and anger that these men have felt about their lives—"a voice for the oppressed people," one rap artist said, "that in many other ways don't have a voice." In 1982, the rap group Grandmaster Flash and the Furious Five released a rap called "The Message,"* a searing description of ghetto culture:

*Edward Fletcher, M. Glover, and S. Robinson, "The Message," recorded 1982 by Grand Master Flash & The Furious Five. Reprinted by permission of Sugar Hill Music Publishing Ltd.

The first American victims of AIDS, (and for many years the group among whom cases remained the most numerous) were homosexual men. But by the late 1980s, as the gay community began to take preventive measures, the most rapid increase in the spread of the disease occurred among heterosexuals, many of them intravenous drug users, who spread the virus by sharing contaminated hypodermic needles. In 2000, U.S. government agencies estimated that about 780,000 Americans were infected with the HIV virus and that another 427,000 had already died from the disease. But the United States represented only a tiny proportion of the worldwide total of people afflicted with AIDS, an estimated 36.1 million people at the end of 2000.

Seventy percent (over 25 million) of those cases were concentrated in Africa. Governments and private groups, in the meantime, began promoting AIDS awareness in increasingly visible and graphic ways—urging young people, in particular, to avoid "unsafe sex" through abstinence or the use of latex condoms. The success of that effort in the United States was suggested by the drop in new cases from 70,000 in 1995 to approximately 40,000 in 2000.

In the mid-1990s, AIDS researchers, after years of frustration, began discovering effective treatments for the disease. By taking a combination of powerful drugs on a rigorous schedule, among them a group known as protease inhibitors, even people with relatively advanced

RUN DMC The group Run DMC, shown here in concert, was one of rap music's first superstars. They released their first album in 1983 and remained popular fifteen years later, although by then—given the short lifespan of most groups—they were, by their own admission, senior citizens on the rap circuit. At a concert in New York in 1997, they asked the audience to "put your hands in the air if you love old-school." A critic from *Rolling Stone* wrote that "from the crowd's ecstatic reaction," the answer was clearly yes. (© Lisa Leone)

Got a bum education, double-digit inflation
Can't take the train to the job, there's a strike at the station
Don't push me, 'cause I'm close to the edge
I'm tryin' not to lose me head
It's like a jungle sometime it makes me wonder
How I keep from going under.

Similar songs by other artists came to be known as "message rap." In the late 1980s, the Compton and Watts neighborhoods of Los Angeles—two of the most distressed minority communities in the city—produced their own style, known as West Coast rap, with such groups as Ice Cube, Ice T, Tupac Shakur, and Snoop Doggy Dog. Even more than the New York version, West Coast rap often had a harsh, angry character. At its extremes (the so-called gangsta' rap), it could be strikingly violent and highly provocative. Scandals erupted again and again over controversial lyrics—Ice T's "Cop Killer," which some believed advocated murdering police; the sexually explicit lyrics of 2 Live Crew and other groups, which critics accused of advocating violence against women.

But it was not just the lyrics that caused the furor. Rap artists were almost all products of tough inner-city neighborhoods, and the rough-edged styles many took with them into the public eye made many people uncomfortable. Some rappers found themselves caught up in highly publicized trouble with the law. Several—including one of rap's biggest stars, Tupac Shakur—were murdered. The business of rap, and particularly the confrontational business style of Death Row Records (founded by Dr. Dre, a veteran of the first major West Coast rap group NWA), was a source of public controversy as well.

These controversies at times unfairly dominated the image of rap as a whole in national culture. Some rap is angry and cruel, as are many of the realities of the world from which it comes. But much of it is explicitly positive, some of it deliberately gentle. Chuck D and other successful rappers use their music to exhort young black men to avoid drugs and crime, to take responsibility for their children, to get an education. And the form, if not the content, of the original rappers has spread widely through American culture. Rap styles have made their way onto *Sesame Street* and other children's shows, into television commercials, Hollywood films, and the everyday language of millions of people, young and old, black and white. It has become another of the arresting, innovative African-American musical traditions that have shaped American culture for more than a century.

cases of AIDS experienced dramatic improvement—so much so that in many cases there were no measurable quantities of the virus left in their bloodstreams. The new drugs gave promise for the first time of dramatically extending the lives of people with AIDS, perhaps to normal life spans. The drugs were not a cure for AIDS; people who stopped taking them experienced a rapid return of the disease. And the effectiveness of the drugs varied from person to person. In addition, the drugs were very expensive and difficult to administer; poorer AIDS patients often could not obtain access to them, and they remained very scarce in Africa and other less affluent parts of the world where the epidemic was rampant.

Nevertheless, the new medications restored hundreds of thousands of desperately ill people to health and gave them realistic hopes of long and relatively normal lives.

The Decline in Crime

One of the most striking social developments of the late 1990s was also one of the least expected: a dramatic reduction in crime rates across most of the United States. The rising incidence of violent crime had been one of the most disturbing facts of American life for two generations—and a central fact of national politics since at least the 1960s. But beginning in the early 1990s, crime began to fall—in many cities, quite dramatically. The government's crime index—which measures the incidence of *Falling Crime Rates* seven serious crimes—fell by 19.5 percent between 1992 and 2000, with some of the most dramatic reductions occurring in murder and other violent crimes.

There was no agreement about the causes of this unexpected reduction. Prosperity and declining unemployment were certainly factors. So were new, sophisticated police techniques that helped deter many crimes and that led to the arrest of many criminals who would previously have escaped capture. New incarceration policies—longer, tougher sentences and fewer paroles and early releases for violent criminals—led to a radical increase in the prison population and, consequently, a reduction in the number of criminals at liberty to commit crimes.

Whatever the reason, the decline in crime—when combined with the booming prosperity of the 1990s, which (however unequally distributed) affected most Americans at least to some degree—helped produce an unusual level of social contentment, as recorded in public opinion surveys, in the late 1990s and in 2000. In stark contrast to the late 1970s, and even the 1980s, most Americans expressed general contentment with the state of their society and optimism about the future until at least September 2001.

A CONTESTED CULTURE

But American life, no matter what the level of contentment, is never without controversy. And few things created more controversy and anxiety in the 1980s and 1990s than the battles over the character of American culture. That culture had changed dramatically in many ways since World War II. It had seen a profound redefinition of the roles of women. It had produced a mobilization of many minorities and an at least partial inclusion of them into mainstream culture. It had experienced a sexual revolution. It had become much less restrained in its depiction of sex, violence, and dissent. American culture was more diverse, more open, less restrained, and more contentious than it had been in the past. One result of these changes was a series of new controversies and new issues.

Battles over Feminism and Abortion

Among the principal goals of the New Right as it became more powerful and assertive in the 1980s and 1990s, and as it focused on cultural changes it did not like, was to challenge feminism and its achievements. Leaders of the New Right had campaigned successfully against the proposed Equal Rights Amendment to the Constitution. And they played a central role in the most divisive issue of the late 1980s and 1990s: the controversy over abortion rights.

For those who favored allowing women to choose to terminate unwanted pregnancies, the Supreme Court's decision in *Roe* v. *Wade* (1973) had seemed to settle the question. By the 1980s, abortion was the most commonly performed surgical procedure in the country. But at the same *"Right-to-Life" Movement* time, opposition to abortion was creating a powerful grassroots movement. The right-to-life movement, as it called itself, found its most fervent supporters among Catholics; and indeed, the Catholic Church itself lent its institutional authority to the battle against legalized abortion. Religious doctrine also motivated the anti-abortion stance of Mormons, fundamentalist Christians, and other groups. The opposition of some other anti-abortion activists had less to do with religion than with their commitment to traditional notions of family and gender relations. To them, abortion was a particularly offensive part of a much larger assault by feminists on the role of women as wives and mothers. It was also, many foes contended, a form of murder. Fetuses, they claimed, were human beings who had a "right to life" from the moment of conception.

Although the right-to-life movement was persistent in its demand for a reversal of *Roe* v. *Wade* or, barring that, a constitutional amendment banning abortion, it also attacked abortion in more limited ways, at its most vulnerable points. In the 1970s, Congress and many state legislatures began barring the use of public funds to pay for abortions, thus making them almost inaccessible for many poor women. The Reagan and Bush administrations imposed further restrictions on federal funding and even on the right of doctors in federally funded clinics to give patients any information on abortion. Extremists in the right-to-life movement began picketing, occupying, and at times bombing abortion clinics. Several anti-abortion activists murdered doctors who performed abortions; other physicians were subject to campaigns of terrorism and harassment—part of an effort to force them to abandon serving women who wanted abortions.

The changing composition of the Supreme Court in the 1980s and early 1990s (when five new conservative justices were named by Presidents Reagan and Bush) renewed the right-to-life movements hopes for a reversal of *Roe* v. *Wade*. In *Webster* v. *Reproductive Health Services* (1989), the Court upheld a Missouri law that forbade any institution receiving state funds from performing abortions, whether or not those funds were used to finance the abortions. But the Court stopped short of overturning its 1973 decision.

Through much of the 1970s and 1980s, defenders of abortion had remained confident that *Roe* v. *Wade* protected their right to choose abortion and that the anti-abortion movement was unlikely to prevail. But the changing judicial climate of the late 1980s mobilized defenders *"Pro-Choice" Movement* of abortion as never before. They called themselves the "pro-choice" movement, because they were defending not so much abortion itself as every woman's right to

The rise of women's history in the last thirty years had produced many debates among historians. But its most important impact has been to challenge scholars to look at the past through a new lens. Historians had long been accustomed to considering the influence of ideas, of economic interests, and of race and ethnicity on the course of history. Women's history challenged them to consider as well the role of gender. Throughout history, many scholars now argue, societies have created distinctive roles for men and women. How those roles have been defined, and the ways in which the roles affect how people and cultures behave, should be central to our understanding of both the past and the present.

Women's history was not new to the 1960s. Just as women had been challenging traditional gender roles long before the 1960s, so too have women (and some men) been writing women's history for many years. In the nineteenth century, such scholarship generally stressed the unrecognized contributions of women to history—for example, Sarah Hale's 1853 *Record of All Distinguished Women from 'the Beginning' till A.D. 1850*. Work of the same sort continued into the twentieth century and, indeed, continues today. But after 1900, people committed to progressive reform movements began to produce a different kind of women's scholarship, in many ways more sociological than historical. It revealed, above all, ways in which women were victimized by a harsh new system of industrialism. In the process, it attempted to raise popular support for reform. Feminist scholars such as Edith Abbott, Margaret Byington, and Katherine Anthony examined the impact of economic change on working-class families, with a special focus on women; and they looked at the often terrible conditions in which women worked in factories, mills, and other people's homes. Their goal was less to celebrate women's contributions than to direct attention to the oppression of women by a harsh capitalist system and arouse sentiment for reform.

Feminism receded from prominence after the victory of the suffrage movement in 1920, and women's history entered a half-century of relative inactivity as well. Women continued to write important histories in many fields, and some—for example, Eleanor Flexner, whose *Century of Struggle* (1959) became a classic history of the suffrage crusade—wrote explicitly about women. Mary Beard, best known for her sweeping historical narratives written in collaboration with her husband Charles Beard, published a book of her own in 1964, *Women as a Force in History*, in which she argued for the historical importance of ordinary women as shapers of society. But such work at first had little impact on the writing of history as a whole.

As modern feminism began to sweep across society in the 1960s and 1970s, interest in women's history revived as well. Gerda Lerner, one of the pioneers of the new women's history, once wrote of the impact of feminism on historical studies: "The recognition that we had been denied our history came to many of us as a staggering insight, which altered our consciousness irretrievably." For a time, the new women's history repeated the pattern of earlier studies of women. Much of the early work was in the "contributionist" tradition, stressing the way in which women had played more notable roles in major historical events than men had usually acknowledged. Other work stressed ways in which women had been victimized by their subordination to men and by their powerlessness within the industrial economy. Increasingly, however, women's history began to question the nature of gender itself. Some scholars began to emphasize the artificiality of gender distinctions. The difference between women and men, they argued, was socially constructed. It was also superficial and (in the public world, at least) unimportant. The history of women was, therefore, the history of how men (with the unwitting help of many women) had created and maintained a set of fictions about women's capacities that late-twentieth-century women were now attempting to shatter.

By the early 1980s, some feminists had begun to make a very different argument: that there were basic differences between women and men—not just biological differences, but differences in values, sensibilities, and culture. This, of course, was what most men and many women had believed for decades (indeed centuries) before the feminist revolution. But the feminists of the 1970s and 1980s did not see these differences as evidence of women's incapacities. They saw them, rather, as evidence of an alternative female culture capable of challenging (and improving) the male-dominated world. Some historians of women, therefore, began exploring areas of female experience that revealed the special character of women's culture and values: family, housework, motherhood, women's clubs and organizations, female literature, the social lives of working-class women, women's sexuality, and many other subjects that suggested "difference" more than "contributions" or "victimization." Partly in response, some historians began to make the same argument about men—that understanding "masculinity" and its role in shaping men's lives was as important as understanding notions of "femininity" in explaining the history of women.

The notion of gender as a source of social and cultural difference was responsible for the most powerful challenge women's history has raised to the way in which scholars view the past. It is not enough simply to expand the existing story to make room for women, Joan Scott, one of the most influential theorists of gender studies, has written. Feminist history is, rather, a way of reconceptualizing the past by accepting that notions of gender have been a central force in the lives of societies.

Many historians continue to believe that other categories (race and class in particular) have in fact been more important in shaping the lives of men and women than has gender. But even those who do so are increasingly willing to accept the argument of women's historians: that understanding concepts of gender is an essential part of understanding women's (and men's) lives, even if it is not the only, or even always the most important, part.

DEMONSTRATING FOR CHOICE These women gathered in Philadelphia on the eve of the 2000 Republican convention to challenge the party—and its nominee, George W. Bush—on their anti-abortion position. The battle between those who claimed to be "pro-choice" and those who claimed to be "pro-life" accelerated after the Supreme Court's controversial 1973 decision, *Roe* v. *Wade*. *(Mark Ludak/The Image Works)*

choose whether and when to bear a child. It quickly became clear that the pro-choice movement was in many parts of the country at least as strong as, and in some areas much stronger than, the right-to-life movement. With the election of President Clinton in 1992, the immediate threat to *Roe* v. *Wade* seemed to fade. In his first week in office, he overturned several of the restrictions on federally funded abortions imposed by Reagan and Bush. And during his first two years in office, Clinton named two pro-choice justices to the Court—Ruth Bader Ginsburg and Stephen Breyer. Clinton's reelection in 1996 was, among other things, evidence that the pro-choice movement maintained considerable political strength. But abortion rights remained highly vulnerable, given the intensity of feeling among those who opposed them. And Clinton's successor, George W. Bush, openly opposed abortion.

At times the pro-choice campaign overshadowed other efforts by feminists to protect and expand the rights of women. But such efforts continued. Women's organizations and many individual women worked strenuously in the 1980s and 1990s to improve access to child care for poor women, and to win the right to caregiver leaves for parents, which a law passed by Congress and signed by President Clinton in 1993 helped secure. They also worked to raise awareness of sexual harassment in the workplace, with considerable success. Colleges, universities, the military, government agencies, even many corporations established strict new standards of behavior for their employees in dealing with members of the opposite sex and created grievance procedures for those who believed they had been harassed.

Both the achievements and the limits of their progress on this issue were evident in the sensational controversy

in 1991 over Judge Clarence Thomas, President Bush's nominee for a seat on the Supreme Court. Late in the confirmation proceedings, accusations of sexual harassment from Anita Hill, a law professor and former employee of Thomas, became public. Hill's testimony before the Senate Judiciary Committee dramatically polarized both the Senate and the nation. Feminists and others tended to believe the accusations and hailed the accuser for drawing national attention to the issue of harassment; but many Americans (and most members of the virtually all-male Senate) apparently did not believe her—or at least concluded that the alleged activities should not disqualify Thomas from serving on the Court. Thomas was ultimately confirmed by a narrow margin.

Anita Hill and Clarence Thomas

The Changing Left and the Growth of Environmentalism

The New Left of the 1960s and early 1970s did not disappear after the end of the war in Vietnam, but it faded rapidly. Many of the students who had fought in its battles grew up, left school, and entered conventional careers. Some radical leaders, disillusioned by the unresponsiveness of American society to their demands, resignedly gave up the struggle and chose instead to work "within the system." Marxist critiques continued to flourish in academic circles, but to much of the public they came to appear dated and irrelevant—particularly as, beginning in 1989, Marxist governments collapsed in disrepute.

Yet a left of sorts did survive, giving evidence in the process of how greatly the nation's political climate had changed. Where 1960s activists had rallied to protest

ENVIRONMENTALISTS PROTEST AMERICAN POLICY Early in his administration, George W. Bush announced that he would not accept the international treaty on global warning that many nations, including the United States, had negotiated in Kyoto, Japan in 1997. On his first trip to Europe, in June 2001, Bush confronted these young demonstrators protesting his repudiation of the agreement. American environmentalists were critical of the decision as well. *(J. Fistick/Imapress/The Image Works)*

racism, poverty, and war, their counterparts in the 1980s and 1990s more often worked to organize communities to fight for local concerns. A great resurgence of grass-roots organizing in many parts of the country was, in part, testament to the legacy of the New Left. Most of all, activists in the 1980s and 1990s organized to stop the proliferation of nuclear weapons and power plants, to save the wilderness, to protect endangered species, to limit reckless economic development, and to otherwise protect the environment.

The environmental movement, which had grown so dramatically in the late 1960s and early 1970s, continued to expand in the last decades of the twentieth century. Several highly visible environmental catastrophes in those years greatly increased their commitment. Among them were a major oil spill off Santa Barbara, California, in 1969; the discovery of large deposits of improperly disposed toxic waste in a residential community in upstate New York in 1978; a frightening accident at the nuclear power plant on Three Mile Island, Pennsylvania, in 1979; and the largest oil spill in American history in Alaska in 1989.

In the decades after the first Earth Day, environmental issues gained increasing attention and support. Although the federal government displayed only intermittent interest in the subject, environmentalists won a series of significant battles, mostly at the local level. They blocked the *Environmental Activism* construction of roads, airports, and other projects (including American development of the supersonic transport airplane, or SST) that they claimed would be ecologically dangerous, taking advantage of new legislations protecting endangered species and environmentally fragile regions. There was less progress in dealing with some of the most ominous environmental hazards. By the end of the 1970s, many scientists were warning that the release of certain industrial pollutants (most notably chlorofluorocarbons) into the atmosphere was depleting the ozone layer of the earth's atmosphere, which protects the globe from the sun's most dangerous rays. They warned, too, of the related danger of global warming, a rise in the earth's temperature as a result of emissions from the burning of fossil fuels (coal and oil). These problems—and such others as the pollution of the oceans and the destruction of rain forests—required international solutions, which were much more difficult to produce. International conferences—in Montreal in 1987 and in Brazil in 1992 (the celebrated "Earth Summit")—produced some broad agreements on several global environmental problems. But there was no way to enforce compliance with them; and the United States government, during the first Bush administration, publicly rejected some of the accords. In 1997, representatives of the major industrial nations met in Kyoto, Japan, and agreed to a broad treaty banning certain emissions into the atmosphere as a step toward reversing global warming. But in March 2001, under pressure from business leaders who feared the cost of such changes and claiming that the treaty penalized wealthy nations and required little of poorer ones, the second Bush administration rejected the treaty.

The concern for the environment, the opposition to nuclear power, the resistance to economic development—all were reflections of a more fundamental characteristic of the post-Vietnam left. In a sharp break from the nation's long commitment to growth and progress, many dissidents argued that only by limiting growth and curbing traditional forms of progress could society hope to survive. Some of these critics of the "idea of progress" expressed a gloomy resignation, urging a lowering of social expectations and predicting an inevitable deterioration in the quality of life. Other advocates of restraint believed that change did not require decline: human beings could live more comfortably and more happily if they learned to respect the limits imposed on them by their environment. But in either case, such arguments evoked strong opposition from conservatives and others, who ridiculed the no-growth ideology as an expression of defeatism and despair. Ronald Reagan, in particular, made an attack on the idea of "limits" central to his political success.

The rising popularity of environmental issues reflected another important shift both in the character of the American left and in the tone of American public life gen-

Shift Away from Class Politics

erally. Through much of the first half of the twentieth century, American politics had been preoccupied with debates over economic power and disparities of wealth. In the late twentieth century, even though inequality in the distribution of wealth and power was reaching unprecedented levels, such debates had largely ceased. There were, of course, economic implications to environmentalism and other no-growth efforts. But what drove such movements was less a concern about class than a concern about the quality of individual and community life.

The Fragmentation of Mass Culture

One of the most powerful cultural trends throughout much of the twentieth century was the growing power and the increasing standardization of mass culture. The institutions of the media—news, entertainment, advertising, and others—grew steadily more powerful. Almost without exception, they also strove to attract the largest

possible audience or market. In doing so, they attempted to standardize their products so that they would be familiar and accessible to everyone. This standardization began with mass merchandising in the late nineteenth century; it accelerated in the early twentieth century with the rise of Hollywood movies, national radio networks, and powerful, mass-circulation magazines; it became dramatically more important in the 1950s, with the rise of network television. It was reinforced by the philosophy of the advertising industry to promote most products for the largest possible audience.

Beginning in the 1970s, and accelerating in the 1980s and 1990s, the character of mass culture changed in some important ways. There was, of course, continued standardization in many areas. McDonald's, Burger King, and other fast-food chains became the most widely known restaurants in America (and indeed the world). Huge retail chains—Kmart, Bradlees, Wal-Mart, Barnes & Noble, Blockbuster, the Gap, and others—dominated retail sales in many communities. The most popular Hollywood films attracted larger audiences than ever before; and the most powerful media companies—most notably, Disney—produced merchandise that made their film and television characters familiar to almost everyone in the world. But there was also a very different trend at work at the same time: a tendency in both retailing and entertainment to appeal less to mass markets and more to specific segments of the market.

This segmentation was first visible in new ideas about advertising that became powerful in the 1970s, ideas known as "targeting." Instead of finding promotional techniques

Target Marketing

to appeal to everyone, advertisers sought to identify a product with a particular "segment" of the market (men, women, young people, old people, health-conscious people, the rich, people of modest means, children) and create advertisements designed to appeal to it. As if in response, the television networks began to produce programming that focused on particular segments of the audience. Some programs were aimed at women, some at African Americans, some at affluent, urban middle-class viewers, some at more rural and provincial people. Fewer and fewer programs had a truly "mass" audience; more and more aimed at a particular group within that audience.

Even more important was the rapid proliferation of media outlets. As late as the 1970s, American television audiences overwhelmingly watched programs on the three major networks: NBC, CBS, and ABC. In the 1980s, that began to change. One reason was the proliferation of video cassette recorders (VCRs), which were in well over 75 percent of all homes by 2000. Instead of watching network television, viewers could now rent or buy videotapes and watch movies or other programming of their own choosing—available in enormous variety at thousands of video stores all across the country. In the late 1990s, VCRs began to face a challenge from digital video disk players (DVDs), which spread rapidly and seemed likely eventually to displace VCRs altogether. Another reason was the increasing availability of cable and satellite television, which allowed homes to receive many more channels than ever before. The percent of television viewers watching the major networks declined steadily in the 1980s. New networks (Fox and Warner Brothers), along with specialized sports, movie, shopping, music, weather, and other channels, began to compete with the traditional leaders, distributing their programming over a combination of broadcast and cable channels. And many people turned away from television altogether and began to explore the powerful new medium of the Internet, with its huge variety of sites tailored to almost every conceivable interest and taste.

As audiences fragmented among many different stations and media, the phenomenon of the national "shared experience" declined as well. Network news, once the most important source for the vast majority of information, experienced a dramatic decline in viewership; many people now got their news from a variety of cable stations, from the increasingly powerful vehicle of talk radio, or from the new national newspaper *USA Today.* Young people found their own media world in MTV and other cable stations that focused on rock music and other elements of youth culture. Hollywood continued to turn out hugely expensive "blockbusters" in a search for a mass audience. But some filmgoers turned instead to smaller independent films, which targeted particular segments of the population.

The "Culture Wars"

As American culture became more segmented, it also became more contentious. That contentiousness was reinforced by the decline of class-based controversies in American public life, and an increasing attention to cultural battles in their place. *Battle over Multiculturalism* Indeed, few issues attracted more attention in the 1990s than the battle over what became known as "multiculturalism." Multiculturalism meant different things to different people, but at its core it was an effort to legitimize the cultural pluralism of the rapidly diversifying American population. That meant acknowledging that "American culture," which had long been defined primarily by white males of European descent, also included other traditions: female, African-American, Indian, and increasingly in the late twentieth century, Hispanic and Asian. Although such demands were often controversial, especially when they became the basis of assaults on traditional academic curricula, much greater acrimony emerged out of efforts by some revisionists to portray traditional Western culture as inherently racist and imperialistic.

A prolonged, if somewhat muted, dispute over how to commemorate the 500th anniversary of Columbus's first voyage to the New World illustrated how sharply ideas of multiculturalism had changed the way Americans discussed their past. In 1892, the Columbian anniversary had been the occasion of boisterous national celebration—and a great World's Fair in Chicago. In 1992, it produced agonizing debates over the impact of the European discovery on native peoples; and the only World's Fairs were in Italy and Spain.

Debates over multiculturalism and related issues helped produce an increasingly strained climate in academia and in the larger American intellectual world. People on the left complained that the ascendancy of conservative politics placed new and intolerable limits on freedom of expression, as efforts to restrict NEA grants to controversial artists suggested. Many on the right complained equally vigorously of a tyranny of "political correctness," by which feminists, cultural radicals, and others introduced a new form of intolerance to public discourse in the name of defending the rights of women and minorities.

The controversies surrounding multiculturalism and "political correctness" were illustrations of a painful change in the character of American society. Traditional patterns of *"Political Correctness"* authority faced challenges from women, minorities, and others. The liberal belief in tolerance and assimilation was fraying in the face of the growing cultural separatism of some ethnic and racial groups. But multiculturalism, in many of its forms, was also a way of broadening the definition of American culture to include all the nation's diverse peoples. It was an expression of confidence in society's ability to tolerate and understand its many differences.

THE PERILS OF GLOBALIZATION

The celebration of the beginning of a new millennium on January 1, 2000, was a notable moment not just because of the dramatic change in the calendar. It was notable above all as a global event—a shared and for the most part joyous experience that united the world in its exuberance. Television viewers around the world followed the dawn of the new century from Australia, through Asia, Africa, and Europe, and on into the Americas. Never had the world seemed more united. But if the millennium celebrations suggested the bright promise of globalization, other events at the dawn of the new century suggested its dark perils.

Opposing the "New World Order"

In the United States and other industrial nations, opposition to globalization—or to what President George H. W. Bush once called "the new world order"—took several forms. To many Americans on both the left and the right, the

PROTESTS IN SEATTLE, 1999 When the World Trade Organization held its annual meeting in Seattle, Washington, in late 1999, thousands of demonstrators crowded into the city to protest the WTO's role in the globalization of the economy and, they believed, the exploitation of working people in the United States and around the world. Their rowdy and at times violent demonstrations postponed the opening of the conference. In this photograph, a protester faces Seattle police in a cloud of tear gas, waiting to be arrested. Similar demonstrations disrupted other meetings of global economic organizations over the next several years, including protests in Washington and Genoa, Italy. *(Reuters NewMedia Inc./Corbis)*

nation's increasingly interventionist foreign policy was deeply troubling. Critics on the left charged that the

Critics of Intervention

United States was using military action to advance its economic interests, most notably in the 1991 Gulf War. Critics on the right claimed that the nation was allowing itself to be swayed by the interests of other nations; they opposed such supposedly humanitarian interventions as the 1993 invasion of Somalia and the American interventions in the Balkans in the late 1990s—both because they insisted no vital American interests were at stake and because they feared that the United States was ceding its sovereignty in these actions to international organizations.

But the most impassioned opposition to globalization in the West came from an array of groups that challenged the claim that the "new world order" was economically beneficial. Labor unions insisted that the rapid expansion of free-trade agreements led to the export of jobs from advanced nations to less developed ones. In the United States, the AFL-CIO was a consistent opponent of free-trade agreements in the 1990s, even though the principal champion of the treaties was Bill Clinton, a Democratic president whom they usually supported. Other groups attacked working conditions in new manufacturing countries on humanitarian grounds, arguing that the global economy was creating new classes of "slave laborers" laboring in conditions that few western nations would tolerate. Environmentalists argued that globalization, in exporting industry to low-wage countries, also exported industrial pollution and toxic waste into nations that had no effective laws to control them. And still others opposed global economic arrangements on the grounds that

they enriched and empowered large multinational corporations and threatened the freedom and autonomy of individuals and communities.

The varied opponents of globalization may have had different reasons for their hostility, but they were agreed on the targets of their discontent: not just free-trade agreements, but also the multinational institutions that policed and advanced the global economy. Among them were the World Trade Organization, which monitored the enforcement of the GATT treaties of the 1990s; the International Monetary Fund, which controlled international credit and exchange rates; and the World Bank, which made money available for development projects in many countries. In November 1999, when the leaders of the

Globalization Protested

seven leading industrial nations (and the leader of Russia) gathered for their annual meeting in Seattle, Washington, tens of thousands of protesters—most of them peaceful, but some of them violent—clashed with police, smashed store windows, and all but paralyzed the city. A few months later a smaller but still substantial demonstration disrupted meetings of the IMF and the World Bank in Washington. And in July 2001, at a meeting of the same leaders in Genoa, Italy, thousands of demonstrators clashed violently with police in a melee that left one protester dead and several hundred injured. In the days that followed, the number of protesters in Genoa rose to an estimated 50,000. The participants in the meeting responded to the demonstrations by pledging $1.2 billion to fight the AIDS epidemic in developing countries, and also by deciding to hold their next meeting at a remote resort in Canada.

Defending Orthodoxy

Outside the industrialized West, the impact of globalization created other concerns. Many citizens of nonindustrialized nations resented the way the world economy had left them in poverty and, in their view, exploited and oppressed. But in some parts of the nonindustrialized world—and particularly in some of the Islamic nations of the Middle East—the increasing reach of globalization created additional grievances, less rooted in economics than in religion and culture.

The Iranian Revolution of 1979, in which orthodox Muslims ousted a despotic government whose leaders had embraced many aspects of modern western culture,

Rise of Islamic Fundamentalism

was one of the first large and visible manifestations of a phenomenon that would eventually reach across much of the Islamic world and threaten the stability of the globe. In one Islamic nation after another, waves of fundamentalist orthodoxy emerged to defend traditional culture against incursions from the West. The new fundamentalism met considerable resistance within Islam—from established governments, from affluent middle classes that had made their peace with the modern industrial world, from women who feared the antifeminist agenda of many of these movements. But it emerged nevertheless as a powerful force—and in a few nations, among them Iran after 1979 and Afghanistan in the late 1990s—the dominant force.

Islamic fundamentalism is a complex phenomenon and takes many different forms. But among some particularly militant fundamentalists, the battle to preserve orthodoxy came to be defined as a battle against the West generally and the United States in particular. Resentment of the West was rooted in the incursion of new and, in their view, threatening cultural norms into traditional societies. It was rooted as well in resentment of the support western nations gave to corrupt and tyrannical regimes in some Islamic countries, and in opposition to western (and particularly American) economic and military incursions into the region. The continuing struggle between Palestinians and Israelis—a struggle defined in the eyes of many Muslims by American support for Israel—added further to their contempt.

One product of this combination of resentments was individuals and groups committed to using violence to fight the influence of the West. No fundamentalist movement had any advanced military capabilities. Militants resorted instead to isolated incidents of violence and mayhem, designed to disrupt societies and governments and to create fear among their peoples. Such tactics became known to the world as terrorism.

The Rise of Terrorism

The term "terrorism" was used first during the French Revolution in the 1790s to describe the actions of the radical Jacobins against the French government. It continued to be used intermittently throughout the nineteenth and early twentieth centuries to describe the use of violence as a form of intimidation against peoples and governments. But

Origins of Terrorism

the widespread understanding of terrorism as an important fact of modern life is largely a product of the second half of the twentieth century.

Acts of what we have come to call terrorism have occurred in many parts of the world. Irish revolutionaries engaged in terrorism regularly against the English through much of the twentieth century. Jews used it in Palestine against the British before the creation of Israel, and Palestinians have used it frequently against Jews in Israel—particularly in the last several decades. Revolutionary groups in Italy, Germany, Japan, and France have engaged in terrorist acts intermittently over the last thirty years.

The United States, too, has experienced terrorism for many years, much of it against American targets abroad. These included bombing of the Marine barracks in Beirut in 1983, the explosion that brought down an American airliner over Lockerbie, Scotland in 1988, the bombing of American embassies in 1998, the assault on the U.S. naval vessel *Cole* in 2000, and other events around the world. Terrorist incidents were relatively rare, but not unknown, within the United States itself prior to September 11, 2001. Militants on the American left performed various acts of terror in the 1960s and early 1970s. In February, 1993, a bomb exploded in the parking garage of the World Trade Center in New York killing six people and causing serious, but not irreparable, structural damage to the towers. Several men connected with militant Islamic organizations were convicted of the crime. In April 1995, a van containing explosives blew up in front of a federal building in Oklahoma City, killing 168 people. Timothy McVeigh, a former Marine who had become part of a militant antigovernment movement of the American right, was convicted of the crime and eventually executed in 2001.

Most Americans, however, considered terrorism a problem that mainly plagued other nations. Few thought very much about it as an important concern in their own country. One of the many results of the terrible events of September 11, 2001, was to jolt the American people out of complacency and alert them to the presence of continuing danger. That awareness increased in the weeks after September 11. New security measures began to change the way in which Americans traveled. New government regulations began to alter immigration policies and to affect the character of international banking. Warnings of possible new terrorist attacks created widespread tension and uneasiness. A puzzling and frightening epidemic of anthrax—a potent bacterial agent that can cause illness and death if not properly treated—began in the weeks after September 11 and spread through the mail to media outlets, members of Congress, and random others.

In the meantime, the United States government launched what President Bush called a "war against terrorism." The

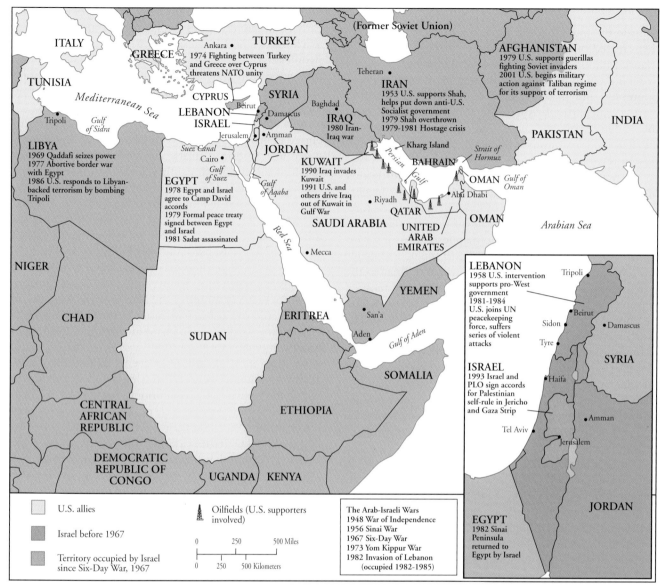

CRISES IN THE MIDDLE EAST In the 1970s and beyond, the Middle East became one of the most turbulent regions of the world and one of the regions most vital to, and difficult for, the United States. The United States intervened in the Middle East frequently during the Cold War and beyond, in ways both large and small, as this map reveals. After the events of September 2001, those interventions seemed likely to increase. ◆ *Why did the United States have so much at stake in the Middle East?*

attacks on the World Trade Center and the Pentagon, government intelligence indicated, had been planned and

"War against Terrorism"
orchestrated by Middle Eastern agents of a powerful terrorist network known as Al Qaeda. Its leader, Osama Bin Laden—until 2001 little known outside the Arab world—quickly became one of the best known and most notorious figures in the world. Fighting a shadowy terrorist network spread out among many nations of the world was a very difficult task, and the administration made clear from the beginning that the battle would be waged in many ways, not just militarily. But the first visible act of the war against terrorism was, in fact, a military one. Convinced that the militant "Taliban" government of Afghanistan had sheltered and supported Bin Laden and his organization, the United States

began a sustained campaign of bombing against the regime and sent in small numbers of ground troops to help a resistance organization overthrow the Afghan government.

This first battle in the struggle against terrorism produced a surprisingly quick military victory. Afghanistan's Taliban regime collapsed, and its leaders—along with the Al Qaeda fighters allied with them—fled the capital, Kabul. American and anti-Taliban Afghan troops pursued them into the mountains, but were, at least at first, unable to find Bin Laden and the other leaders of his organization. In the aftermath of this speedy victory, however, American forces found themselves caught up in the instability of factionalized Afghanistan. While continuing to pursue terrorists, they also had to deal with infighting among the new leaders of the nation.

GIULIANI AND THE ANTHRAX SCARE, 2001 Mayor Rudolph Giuliani of New York emerged as a national hero in the aftermath of the terrorist attacks on his city. His strong, reassuring presence helped New Yorkers to cope with the disruption of their lives and gave Americans elsewhere a sense of confidence in the capacity of the nation to deal with catastrophe. In this scene from one of his many news conferences, October 12, 2001, the mayor—who left office January 1, 2002—discusses the appearance of the dangerous bacteria anthrax in several buildings in New York City. *(AP/Wide World Photos/MSNBC)*

In his State of the Union Address to Congress in January 2002, President Bush spoke of an "axis of evil," which included the nations of Iraq, Iran, and North Korea—all nations with anti-American regimes, all nations that either possessed or were thought to be trying to acquire nuclear weapons. Although Bush did not say so, many people—both in America and elsewhere—took his words to mean that the United States would soon try to topple the government of Saddam Hussein in Iraq. But the complications in Afghanistan seemed to slow whatever expansion of the battle the American government might have been contemplating.

A New Era?

In the immediate aftermath of September 11, 2001, many Americans came to believe that they had entered a new era in their history. The instability that had plagued so much of the rest of the world for years seemed suddenly to have arrived in the United States, shattering longstanding assumptions about safety and security and opening a period of uncertainty and fear. The prospects for the future were clouded further by a significant weakening of the economy that was already well advanced before September 11 and that the events of that day helped to increase.

But fear and uncertainty were not the only results of the September 11 disasters. The reaction to the catastrophe—in New York, in Washington, and in much of the rest of the country—exposed a side of American life and culture that had always existed but that had not always been visible during the booming, self-indulgent years of the 1980s and 1990s. Americans responded to the tragedies with countless acts of courage and generosity, large and

Uncertainty and Unity

FIGHTING AND REMEMBERING An American B-52 pilot prepares for a night bombing mission in Afghanistan in November 2001, his plane carrying a symbol of the events that precipitated the conflict. *(Department of Defense Visual Information Center/US Air Force Photo by SSgt Larry A. Simmons)*

small, and with a sense of national unity and commitment that seemed, at least for a time, to resemble the unity and commitment at the beginning of World War II. The displays of courage began with the heroism of firefighters and rescue workers in New York City, who unhesitatingly plunged into the burning towers of the World Trade Center in an effort to save the people inside. Over 300 such workers died when the towers collapsed. In the weeks after the disaster, New York was flooded with volunteers—welders, metal workers, police, firefighters, medical personnel, and many others—who flocked to the city from around the country and the world to assist with rescue and recovery. Charitable donations to help the victims of the disasters exceeded $1 billion, the largest amount ever raised for a single purpose in such a short time in American history. Open

and unembarrassed displays of patriotism and national pride—things that many Americans had once scorned—suddenly became fashionable again. Faith in government and its leaders, in decline for decades, suddenly surged.

"Nothing has changed. . . . Everything has changed," wrote one prominent journalist in the weeks after September 11. In fact, no one could reliably predict whether the catastrophe would prove to be a fundamental turning point in the course of American and world history, or simply another in the countless changes and adjustments, great and small, that have characterized the nation's experience for centuries.

CONCLUSION

Americans entered the twenty-first century afflicted with many anxieties, doubts, and resentments. Faith in the nation's institutions—most notably, government—was at its lowest point in many decades. Confidence in the nation's leaders had dramatically eroded in the wake of the tawdry scandals and vicious partisanship of the Clinton years and the dispiriting controversy over the results of the 2000 election. Ugly battles over differing standards of morality and different cultural styles disturbed many communities. Vague resentments over the increasingly unequal patterns of income and wealth in the new economy, which few Americans seemed able to translate into a coherent economic agenda, increased the nation's unease.

But the United States at the end of the century was, despite its many problems, a remarkably successful society. It had made dramatic strides in improving the lives of its citizens and in dealing with many of its social problems since the end of World War II. It entered the new century

with the strongest economy in the world; with violent crime—one of its most corrosive problems for more than a generation—in a marked decline; and with its international power and stature unrivaled.

The traumatic events of September 11, 2001, changed many aspects of American life, not least the nation's sense of its isolation, and insulation, from the problems of the rest of the world. But both the many longstanding problems and the many longstanding strengths of the United States survived the attacks. It seemed safe to predict that the American people would go forward into their suddenly uncertain future not simply burdened by difficult challenges, but also armed with great wealth, great power, and perhaps most of all with the extraordinary energy and resilience that has allowed the nation—throughout its long and often turbulent history—to endure, to flourish, and to strive continually for a better future.

FOR FURTHER REFERENCE

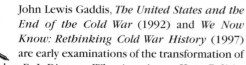

John Lewis Gaddis, *The United States and the End of the Cold War* (1992) and *We Now Know: Rethinking Cold War History* (1997) are early examinations of the transformation of the world order. E. J. Dionne, *Why Americans Hate Politics* (1991) is a perceptive discussion of the political discontents of the 1980s and early 1990s. Thomas Byrne Edsall and Mary D. Edsall, *Chain Reaction: The Impact of Race, Rights, and Taxes on American Politics* (1991) is an alternative interpretation of the changes in American politics, focusing primarily on the impact of race. David Maranis, *First in His Class: A Biography of*

Bill Clinton (1995) traces Clinton's pre-presidential career. Theda Skocpol, *Boomerang: Clinton's Health Security Effort and the Turn Against Government in U.S. Politics* (1996) is an account of one of the major setbacks of Clinton's first term. Jeffrey Toobin, *A Vast Conspiracy* (1999) is an account of the scandals that rocked the Clinton presidency. Toobin is also the author of an important account of the disputed 2000 presidential election, *Too Close to Call* (2001). Haynes Johnson, *The Best of Times: America in the Clinton Years* (2001) is an account of the politics and culture of the 1990s. David Halberstam, *War in a Time of Peace: Bush, Clinton, and the Generals* (2001) examines the foreign policy and military ventures of the Bush and Clinton years. Michael A. Bernstein and David E. Adler, *Understanding American Economic Decline* (1994) is an important collection of essays on the changes in the American economy since the 1970s. *Computer: A History of the Information Machine*, by Martin Campbell-Kelly and William Aspray (1996) is an introduction to the development of one of the critical technologies of the late twentieth century. Randy Shilts, *And the Band Played On: Politics, People, and the AIDS Epidemic* (1987) is a provocative discussion of the early years of AIDS in America. Andrew Hacker, *Two Nations: Black and White, Separate, Hostile, Unequal* (1992) and Michael Katz, *The Undeserving Poor: From the War on Poverty to the War on Welfare* (1989) are two contrasting arguments about the nature of African-American life and inner-city poverty. William Julius Wilson, *The Truly Disadvantaged* (1987) and *When Work Disappears* (1996) are important studies of the inner-city poor from one of America's leading sociologists. David A. Hollinger, *Postethnic America: Beyond Multiculturalism* (1995) is an intelligent and spirited comment on the debates over multiculturalism.

APPENDIXES

THE UNITED STATES

Seattle
Olympia ☆ Tacoma
Spokane
WASHINGTON
Portland
Salem
Eugene
OREGON
Helena
MONTANA
Billings
NORTH
Bismarck
Boise
IDAHO
WYOMING
Casper
SOUTH
Rapid City
Reno
Sacramento
Carson City
Oakland Berkeley
San Francisco Stockton
Sunnyvale San Modesto
Jose
Fresno
NEVADA
Salt Lake
City
Provo
Laramie Cheyenne
NEBR
Boulder Denver
Lakewood Aurora
Colorado
Springs
Pueblo
COLORADO
KA
UTAH
CALIFORNIA
Las
Vegas
Bakersfield
Oxnard
Glendale
Pasadena
Los Angeles San Bernardino
Torrance Riverside
Long Beach Anaheim
Huntington Beach Santa Ana
San Diego
PACIFIC
OCEAN
ARIZONA
Taos
Santa Fe
Albuquerque
Phoenix
Tempe Mesa
NEW MEXICO
Tucson
El Paso
Amarillo
O
TEXAS
Lubbock
Sa
Anton

PACIFIC OCEAN

Kauai
Oahu
Ewa Honolulu
HAWAII Maui
Hawaii
PACIFIC OCEAN
0   125 Miles

RUSSIA
ALASKA
Fairbanks
Anchorage
CANADA
Juneau
PACIFIC
OCEAN
0   500 Miles

MEXICO

CANADA

MAINE

Lake Superior

MICHIGAN

Lake Huron

WISCONSIN

Burlington

Montpelier ☆ Augusta

VT. N.H.

Portland

NEW YORK

Concord

Lake Ontario

Manchester

St. Paul

Albany

Boston

MASS. Worcester

R.I.

Milwaukee

Grand Rapids

Flint

Rochester

Syracuse

Springfield

Providence

Madison

Lansing

Buffalo

CT. Hartford

Cedar Rapids

Rockford

Ann Arbor

Warren Detroit

Lake Erie

PENN.

Bridgeport

New Haven

Stamford

Sterling Heights

Livonia

Erie

Newark

New York

WI VA

Davenport

Chicago

South Bend

Toledo

Cleveland

Allentown

Jersey City

ILLINOIS

Gary

Fort Wayne

Akron

Youngstown

Harrisburg

Trenton

Peoria

OHIO

Columbus

Pittsburgh

Philadelphia

N.J.

Independence

Urbana

Indianapolis

Dayton

Baltimore

Dover

Kansas City

Springfield

INDIANA

Cincinnati

W.VA.

Annapolis

DE.

Jefferson City

St. Louis

Louisville

Frankfort

Charleston

WASHINGTON MD.

D.C.

Springfield

Evansville

Lexington

Roanoke

Richmond

Hampton

MISSOURI

KENTUCKY

VA.

Newport News

Norfolk

Portsmouth

Virginia Beach

Chesapeake

ARKANSAS

Nashville

Knoxville

Greensboro

Durham

Winston-Salem

Raleigh

Memphis

TENNESSEE

Asheville

N.C.

Charlotte

Little Rock

Chattanooga

Greenville

Columbia

Huntsville

Atlanta

S.C.

Birmingham

Augusta

Charleston

Shreveport

Jackson

Montgomery

Macon

Savannah

LOUISIANA

Columbus

MISSISSIPPI

ALABAMA

GEORGIA

Baton Rouge

Biloxi

Pensacola

Tallahassee ☆

New Orleans

Mobile

Jacksonville

FLORIDA

ATLANTIC OCEAN

Orlando

Gulf of Mexico

Tampa

St. Petersburg

Hialeah

Fort Lauderdale

Miami

Hollywood

| 250 | 500 Miles |
| 250 | 500 Kilometers |

POPULOUS METROPOLITAN AREAS

▣ Cities over 5 million

■ Cities over 1 million

○ Cities under 1 million

☆ State Capitals

A-3

TOPOGRAPHICAL MAP OF THE UNITED STATES

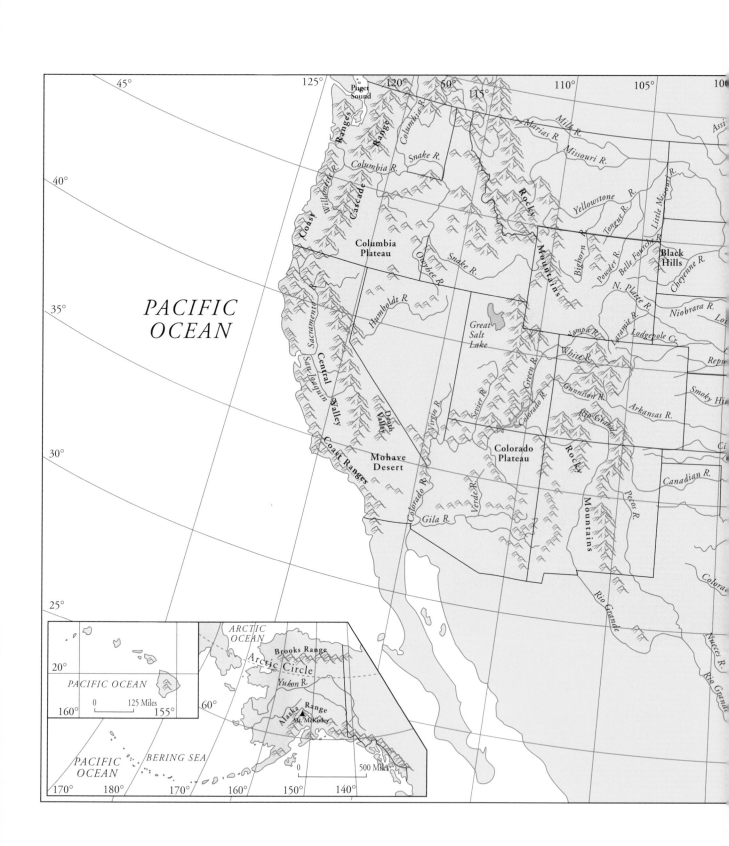

90°   85°   80°   75°   70°   65°

Lake Superior

St. Croix R.

Mississippi R.

Kennebeck R.

St. Lawrence R.

Lake Michigan

Lake Huron

Connecticut R.

Adirondack
Mts.

Cedar R.

Des Moines R.

Iowa R.

Lake Ontario

Mohawk R.

Hudson R.

Lake Erie

Rock R.

Fox R.

Kankakee R.

Delaware R.

Illinois R.

Allegheny R.

Susquehanna R.

Central   **Plains**

Scioto R.

Ohio R.

Potomac R.

Atlantic Coastal Plain

Missouri R.

Wabash R.

Mts.

Kanawha R.

Shenandoah Valley

Osage R.

Mississippi R.

James R.

•Chesapeake
Bay

Ozark Plateau

Allegheny

Roanoke R.

White R.

Tennessee R.

Cumberland R.

Appalachian Mountains

Blue Ridge Mts.

Arkansas R.

Saluda R.

Savannah R.

ATLANTIC
OCEAN

Ouachita R.

Yazoo R.

Tombigbee R.

Chattahoochee R.

Red R.

Alabama R.

Altamaha R.

Sabine R.

Pearl R.

Coastal **Plain**

•Galveston
Bay

Gulf of Mexico

| 0 | 250 | 500 Miles |

| 0 | 250 | 500 Kilometers |

THE WORLD

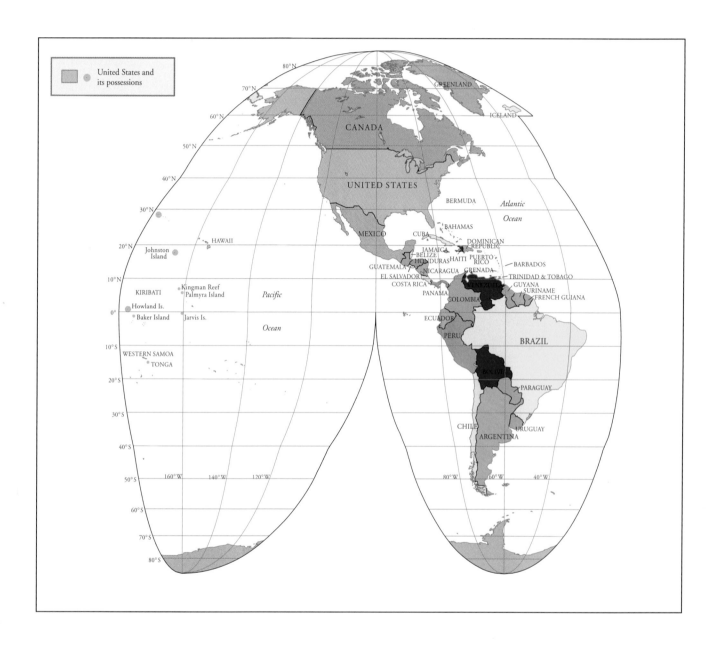

United States and
its possessions

80°N
70°N
60°N
50°N
40°N
30°N
20°N
10°N
0°
10°S
20°S
30°S
40°S
50°S
60°S
70°S
80°S

GREENLAND

ICELAND

CANADA

UNITED STATES

BERMUDA

Atlantic

Ocean

MEXICO

CUBA

BAHAMAS

DOMINICAN
REPUBLIC

HAWAII

JAMAICA

BELIZE

HAITI

PUERTO
RICO

BARBADOS

Johnston
Island

GUATEMALA

HONDURAS

NICARAGUA

GRENADA

TRINIDAD & TOBAGO

EL SALVADOR

COSTA RICA

VENEZUELA

GUYANA

KIRIBATI

Kingman Reef
Palmyra Island

Pacific

PANAMA

COLOMBIA

SURINAME

FRENCH GUIANA

Howland Is.

Baker Island

Jarvis Is.

ECUADOR

Ocean

PERU

BRAZIL

WESTERN SAMOA

TONGA

BOLIVIA

PARAGUAY

CHILE

URUGUAY

ARGENTINA

160°W 140°W 120°W

80°W 60°W 40°W

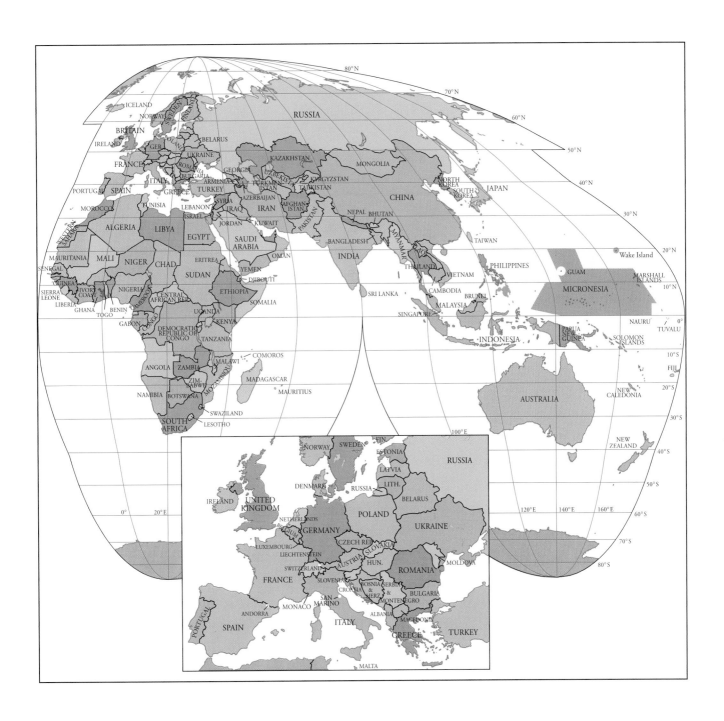

UNITED STATES TERRITORIAL EXPANSION, 1783–1898

THE DECLARATION OF INDEPENDENCE

In Congress, July 4, 1776,

THE UNANIMOUS DECLARATION OF THE THIRTEEN UNITED STATES OF AMERICA

When, in the course of human events, it becomes necessary for one people to dissolve the political bands which have connected them with another, and to assume, among the powers of the earth, the separate and equal station to which the laws of nature and of nature's God entitle them, a decent respect to the opinions of mankind requires that they should declare the causes which impel them to the separation.

We hold these truths to be self-evident, that all men are created equal; that they are endowed by their Creator with certain unalienable rights; that among these, are life, liberty, and the pursuit of happiness. That, to secure these rights, governments are instituted among men, deriving their just powers from the consent of the governed; that, whenever any form of government becomes destructive of these ends, it is the right of the people to alter or to abolish it, and to institute a new government, laying its foundation on such principles, and organizing its powers in such form, as to them shall seem most likely to effect their safety and happiness. Prudence, indeed, will dictate that governments long established, should not be changed for light and transient causes; and, accordingly, all experience hath shown, that mankind are more disposed to suffer, while evils are sufferable, than to right themselves by abolishing the forms to which they are accustomed. But, when a long train of abuses and usurpations, pursuing invariably the same object, evinces a design to reduce them under absolute despotism, it is their right, it is their duty, to throw off such government and to provide new guards for their future security. Such has been the patient sufferance of these colonies, and such is now the necessity which constrains them to alter their former systems of government. The history of the present King of Great Britain is a history of repeated injuries and usurpations, all having, in direct object, the establishment of an absolute tyranny over these States. To prove this, let facts be submitted to a candid world:

He has refused his assent to laws the most wholesome and necessary for the public good.

He has forbidden his governors to pass laws of immediate and pressing importance, unless suspended in their operation till his assent should be obtained; and, when so suspended, he has utterly neglected to attend to them.

He has refused to pass other laws for the accommodation of large districts of people, unless those people would relinquish the right of representation in the legislature; a right inestimable to them, and formidable to tyrants only.

He has called together legislative bodies at places unusual, uncomfortable, and distant from the depository of their public records, for the sole purpose of fatiguing them into compliance with his measures.

He has dissolved representative houses repeatedly for opposing, with manly firmness, his invasions on the rights of the people.

He has refused, for a long time after such dissolutions, to cause others to be elected; whereby the legislative powers, incapable of annihilation, have returned to the people at large for their exercise; the state remaining, in the meantime, exposed to all the danger of invasion from without, and convulsions within.

He has endeavored to prevent the population of these States; for that purpose, obstructing the laws for naturalization of foreigners, refusing to pass others to encourage their migration hither, and raising the conditions of new appropriations of lands.

He has obstructed the administration of justice, by refusing his assent to laws for establishing judiciary powers.

He has made judges dependent on his will alone, for the tenure of their officers, and the amount and payment of their salaries.

He has erected a multitude of new offices, and sent hither swarms of officers to harass our people, and eat out their substance.

He has kept among us, in time of peace, standing armies, without the consent of our legislatures.

He has affected to render the military independent of, and superior to, the civil power.

He has combined, with others, to subject us to a jurisdiction foreign to our Constitution, and unacknowledged by our laws; giving his assent to their acts of pretended legislation:

For quartering large bodies of armed troops among us:

For protecting them by a mock trial, from punishment, for any murders which they should commit on the inhabitants of these States:

For cutting off our trade with all parts of the world:

For imposing taxes on us without our consent:

For depriving us, in many cases, of the benefit of trial by jury:

For transporting us beyond seas to be tried for pretended offences:

For abolishing the free system of English laws in a neighboring province, establishing therein an arbitrary government, and enlarging its boundaries, so as to render it at once an example and fit instrument for introducing the same absolute rule into these colonies:

For taking away our charters, abolishing our most valuable laws, and altering, fundamentally, the powers of our governments:

For suspending our own legislatures, and declaring themselves invested with power to legislate for use in all cases whatsoever.

He has abdicated government here, by declaring us out of his protection, and waging war against us.

He has plundered our seas, ravaged our coasts, burnt our towns, and destroyed the lives of our people.

He is, at this time, transporting large armies of foreign mercenaries to complete the works of death, desolation, and tyranny, already begun, with circumstances of cruelty and perfidy scarcely paralleled in the most barbarous ages, and totally unworthy the head of a civilized nation.

He has constrained our fellow citizens, taken captive on the high seas, to bear arms against their country, to become the executioners of their friends, and brethren, or to fall themselves by their hands.

He has excited domestic insurrections amongst us, and has endeavored to bring on the inhabitants of our frontiers, the merciless Indian savages, whose known rule of warfare is an undistinguished destruction of all ages, sexes, and conditions.

In every stage of these oppressions, we have petitioned for redress, in the most humble terms; our repeated petitions have been answered only by repeated injury. A prince, whose character is thus marked by every act which may define a tyrant, is unfit to be the ruler of a free people.

Nor have we been wanting in attention to our British brethren. We have warned them, from time to time, of attempts made by their legislature to extend an unwarrantable jurisdiction over us. We have reminded them of the circumstances of our emigration and settlement here. We have appealed to their native justice and magnanimity, and we have conjured them, by the ties of our common kindred, to disavow these usurpations, which would inevitably interrupt our connections and correspondence. They, too, have been deaf to the voice of justice and consanguinity. We must, therefore, acquiesce in the necessity, which denounces our separation, and hold them as we hold the rest of mankind, enemies in war, in peace, friends.

We, therefore, the representatives of the United States of America, in general Congress assembled, appealing to the Supreme Judge of the world for the rectitude of our intentions, do, in the name, and by the authority of the good people of these colonies, solemnly publish and declare, that these united colonies are, and of right ought to be, free and independent states: that they are absolved from all allegiance to the British Crown, and that all political connection between them and the state of Great Britain is, and ought to be, totally dissolved; and that, as free and independent states, they have full power to levy war, conclude peace, contract alliances, establish commerce, and to do all other acts and things which independent states may of right do. And, for the support of this declaration, with a firm reliance on the protection of Divine Providence, we mutually pledge to each other our lives, our fortunes, and our sacred honor.

The foregoing Declaration was, by order of Congress, engrossed, and signed by the following members:

JOHN HANCOCK

New Hampshire
Josiah Bartlett
William Whipple
Matthew Thornton

Massachusetts Bay
Samuel Adams
John Adams
Robert Treat Paine
Elbridge Gerry

Rhode Island
Stephen Hopkins
William Ellery

Connecticut
Robert Sherman
Samuel Huntington
William Williams
Oliver Wolcott

New York
William Floyd
Philip Livingston
Francis Lewis
Lewis Morris

New Jersey
Richard Stockton
John Witherspoon
Francis Hopkinson
John Hart
Abraham Clark

Pennsylvania
Robert Morris
Benjamin Rush
Benjamin Franklin
John Morton
George Clymer
James Smith
George Taylor
James Wilson
George Ross

Delaware
Caesar Rodney
George Read
Thomas McKean

Maryland
Samuel Chase
William Paca
Thomas Stone
Charles Carroll, of
   Carrollton

Virginia
George Wythe
Richard Henry Lee
Thomas Jefferson
Benjamin Harrison
Thomas Nelson, Jr.
Francis Lightfoot Lee
Carter Braxton

North Carolina
William Hooper
Joseph Hewes
John Penn

South Carolina
Edward Rutledge
Thomas Heyward, Jr.
Thomas Lynch, Jr.
Arthur Middleton

Georgia
Button Gwinnett
Lyman Hall
George Walton

Resolved, That copies of the Declaration be sent to the several assemblies, conventions, and committees, or councils of safety, and to the several commanding officers of the continental troops; that it be proclaimed in each of the United States, at the head of the army.

THE CONSTITUTION OF THE UNITED STATES OF AMERICA[1]

We the People of the United States, in Order to form a more perfect Union, establish Justice, insure domestic Tranquility, provide for the common defence, promote the general Welfare, and secure the Blessings of Liberty to ourselves and our Posterity, do ordain and establish this CONSTITUTION for the United States of America.

ARTICLE 1

Section 1.

All legislative Powers herein granted shall be vested in a Congress of the United States, which shall consist of a Senate and House of Representatives.

Section 2.

The House of Representatives shall be composed of Members chosen every second Year by the People of the several States, and the Electors in each State shall have the Qualifications requisite for Electors of the most numerous Branch of the State Legislature.

No Person shall be a Representative who shall not have attained to the Age of twenty-five Years, and been seven Years a Citizen of the United States, and who shall not, when elected, be an Inhabitant of that State in which he shall be chosen.

[Representatives and direct Taxes[2] shall be apportioned among the several States which may be included within this Union, according to their respective Numbers, which shall be determined by adding to the whole Number of free Persons, including those bound to Service for a Term of Years, and excluding Indians not taxed, three fifths of all other Persons.][3] The actual Enumeration shall be made within three Years after the first Meeting of the Congress of the United States, and within every subsequent Term of ten Years, in such Manner as they shall by Law direct. The Number of Representatives shall not exceed one for every thirty Thousand, but each State shall have at Least one Representative; and until such enumeration shall be made, the State of New Hampshire shall be entitled to chuse three, Massachusetts eight, Rhode-Island and Providence Plantations one, Connecticut five, New York six, New Jersey four, Pennsylvania eight, Delaware one, Maryland six, Virginia ten, North Carolina five, South Carolina five, and Georgia three.

When vacancies happen in the Representation from any State, the Executive Authority thereof shall issue Writs of Election to fill such Vacancies.

The House of Representatives shall chuse their Speaker and other Officers; and shall have the sole Power of Impeachment.

Section 3.

The Senate of the United States shall be composed of two Senators from each State, chosen by the Legislature thereof, for six Years; and each Senator shall have one Vote.

Immediately after they shall be assembled in Consequence of the first Election, they shall be divided as equally as may be into three Classes. The Seats of the Senators of the first Class shall be vacated at the Expiration of the second Year, of the second Class at the Expiration of the fourth Year, and of the third Class at the Expiration of the sixth Year, so that one-third may be chosen every second Year; and if Vacancies happen by Resignation, or otherwise, during the Recess of the Legislature of any State, the Executive thereof may make temporary Appointments until the next Meeting of the Legislature, which shall then fill such Vacancies.

No Person shall be a Senator who shall not have attained to the Age of thirty Years, and been nine Years a Citizen of the United States, and who shall not, when elected, be an Inhabitant of that State for which he shall be chosen.

The Vice President of the United States shall be President of the Senate, but shall have no vote, unless they be equally divided.

The Senate shall chuse their other Officers, and also a President pro tempore, in the absence of the Vice President, or when he shall exercise the office of President of the United States.

The Senate shall have the sole Power to try all Impeachments. When sitting for that purpose they shall be on Oath or Affirmation. When the President of the United States is tried, the Chief Justice shall preside: And no person shall be convicted without the Concurrence of two thirds of the Members present.

Judgment in Cases of Impeachment shall not extend further than to removal from Office, and disqualification to hold and enjoy any Office of honor, Trust, or Profit under the United States: but the Party convicted shall nevertheless be liable and subject to Indictment, Trial, Judgment, and Punishment, according to Law.

[1]This version, which follows the original Constitution in capitalization and spelling, was published by the United States Department of the Interior, Office of Education, in 1935.
[2]Altered by the Sixteenth Amendment.
[3]Negated by the Fourteenth Amendment.

Section 4.

The Times, Places and Manner of holding Elections for Senators and Representatives, shall be prescribed in each State by the Legislature thereof; but the Congress may at any time by Law make or alter such Regulations, except as to the Places of Chusing Senators.

The Congress shall assemble at least once in every Year, and such Meeting shall be on the first Monday in December, unless they shall by Law appoint a different day.

Section 5.

Each House shall be the Judge of the Elections, Returns and Qualifications of its own Members, and a Majority of each shall constitute a Quorum to do Business; but a smaller number may adjourn from day to day, and may be authorized to compel the Attendance of absent Members, in such Manner, and under such Penalties, as each House may provide.

Each House may determine the Rules of its Proceedings, punish its Members for disorderly Behaviour, and, with the Concurrence of two thirds, expel a Member.

Each House shall keep a Journal of its Proceedings, and from time to time publish the same, excepting such Parts as may in their Judgment require Secrecy; and the Yeas and Nays of the Members of either House on any question shall, at the Desire of one fifth of those Present, be entered on the Journal.

Neither House, during the Session of Congress, shall, without the Consent of the other, adjourn for more than three days, nor to any other Place than that in which the two Houses shall be sitting.

Section 6.

The Senators and Representatives shall receive a Compensation for their Services, to be ascertained by Law, and paid out of the Treasury of the United States. They shall in all Cases, except Treason, Felony, and Breach of the Peace, be privileged from Arrest during their Attendance at the Session of their respective Houses, and in going to and returning from the same; and for any Speech or Debate in either House, they shall not be questioned in any other Place.

No Senator or Representative shall, during the Time for which he was elected, be appointed to any civil Office under the Authority of the United States, which shall have been created, or the Emoluments whereof shall have been increased, during such time; and no Person holding any Office under the United States shall be a Member of either House during his continuance in Office.

Section 7.

All Bills for raising Revenue shall originate in the House of Representatives; but the Senate may propose or concur with Amendments as on other bills.

Every Bill which shall have passed the House of Representatives and the Senate, shall, before it become a Law, be presented to the President of the United States; If he approve he shall sign it, but if not he shall return it, with his Objections, to that House in which it shall have originated, who shall enter the Objections at large on their Journal, and proceed to reconsider it. If after such Reconsideration two thirds of that House shall agree to pass the bill, it shall be sent, together with the objections, to the other House, by which it shall likewise be reconsidered, and if approved by two thirds of that House, it shall become a Law. But in all such Cases the Votes of both Houses shall be determined by Yeas and Nays, and the Names of the Persons voting for and against the Bill shall be entered on the Journal of each House respectively. If any Bill shall not be returned by the President within ten Days (Sundays excepted) after it shall have been presented to him, the Same shall be a Law, in like Manner as if he had signed it, unless the Congress by their Adjournment prevent its Return, in which Case it shall not be a Law.

Every Order, Resolution, or Vote to which the Concurrence of the Senate and House of Representatives may be necessary (except on a question of Adjournment) shall be presented to the President of the United States; and before the Same shall take Effect, shall be approved by him, or being disapproved by him, shall be repassed by two thirds of the Senate and House of Representatives, according to the Rules and Limitations prescribed in the Case of a Bill.

Section 8.

The Congress shall have Power To lay and collect Taxes, Duties, Imposts and Excises, to pay the Debts and provide for the common Defence and general Welfare of the United States; but all Duties, Imposts and Excises shall be uniform throughout the United States;

To borrow money on the credit of the United States;

To regulate Commerce with foreign Nations, and among the several States, and with the Indian Tribes;

To establish an uniform rule of Naturalization, and uniform Laws on the subject of Bankruptcies throughout the United States;

To coin Money, regulate the Value thereof, and of foreign Coin, and fix the Standard of Weights and Measures;

To provide for the Punishment of counterfeiting the Securities and current Coin of the United States;

To establish Post Offices and post Roads;

To promote the Progress of Science and useful Arts, by securing for limited Times to Authors and Inventors the exclusive Right to their respective Writings and Discoveries;

To constitute Tribunals inferior to the Supreme Court;

To define and punish Piracies and Felonies committed on the high Seas, and Offenses against the Law of Nations;

To declare War, grant Letters of Marque and Reprisal, and make Rules concerning Captures on Land and Water;

To raise and support Armies, but no Appropriation of Money to that Use shall be for a longer Term than two Years;

To provide and maintain a Navy;

To make Rules for the Government and Regulation of the land and naval forces;

To provide for calling forth the Militia to execute the Laws of the Union, suppress Insurrections and repel Invasions;

To provide for organizing, arming, and disciplining the Militia, and for governing such Part of them as may be employed in the Service of the United States, reserving to the States respectively, the Appointment of the Officers, and the Authority of training the Militia according to the discipline prescribed by Congress;

To exercise exclusive Legislation in all Cases whatsoever, over such District (not exceeding ten Miles square) as may, by Cession of particular States, and the acceptance of Congress, become the Seat of the Government of the United States, and to exercise like Authority over all Places purchased by the Consent of the Legislature of the State in which the Same shall be, for the Erection of Forts, Magazines, Arsenals, Dockyards, and other needful Buildings;—And

To make all Laws which shall be necessary and proper for carrying into Execution for foregoing Powers, and all other Powers vested by this Constitution in the Government of the United States, or in any Department or Officer thereof.

Section 9.

The Migration or Importation of such Persons as any of the States now existing shall think proper to admit, shall not be prohibited by the Congress prior to the Year one thousand eight hundred and eight, but a tax or duty may be imposed on such Importation, not exceeding ten dollars for each Person.

The privilege of the Writ of Habeas Corpus shall not be suspended, unless when in Cases of Rebellion or Invasion the public Safety may require it.

No bill of Attainder or ex post facto Law shall be passed.

No capitation, or other direct, Tax shall be laid unless in Proportion to the Census or Enumeration herein before directed to be taken.

No Tax or Duty shall be laid on Articles exported from any State.

No Preference shall be given by any Regulation of Commerce or Revenue to the Ports of one State over those of another: nor shall Vessels bound to, or from, one State, be obliged to enter, clear, or pay Duties in another.

No Money shall be drawn from the Treasury, but in Consequence of Appropriations made by Law; and a regular Statement and Account of the Receipts and Expenditures of all public Money shall be published from time to time.

No Title of Nobility shall be granted by the United States: And no Person holding any Office of Profit or Trust under them, shall, without the Consent of the Congress, accept of any present, Emolument, Office, or Title, of any kind whatever, from any King, Prince, or foreign State.

Section 10.

No State shall enter into any Treaty, Alliance, or Confederation; grant Letters of Marque and Reprisal; coin Money; emit Bills of Credit; make any Thing but gold and silver Coin a Tender in Payment of Debts; pass any Bill of Attainder, ex post facto Law, or Law impairing the Obligation of Contracts, or grant any Title of Nobility.

No State shall, without the Consent of the Congress, lay any Imposts or Duties on Imports or Exports, except what may be absolutely necessary for executing its inspection Laws; and the net Produce of all Duties and Imposts, laid by any State on Imports or Exports, shall be for the use of the Treasury of the United States; and all such Laws shall be subject to the Revision and Control of the Congress.

No state shall, without the Consent of Congress, lay any duty of Tonnage, keep Troops, or Ships of War in time of Peace, enter into any Agreement or Compact with another State, or with a foreign Power, or engage in War, unless actually invaded, or in such imminent Danger as will not admit of delay.

ARTICLE II

Section 1.

The executive Power shall be vested in a President of the United States of America. He shall hold his Office during the Term of four years, and, together with the Vice President, chosen for the same Term, be elected, as follows:

Each State shall appoint, in such Manner as the Legislature thereof may direct, a Number of Electors, equal to the whole Number of Senators and Representatives to which the State may be entitled in the Congress: but no Senator or Representative, or Person holding an Office of Trust or Profit under the United States, shall be appointed an Elector.

[The Electors shall meet in their respective States, and vote by Ballot for two persons, of whom one at least shall not be an Inhabitant of the same State with themselves. And they shall make a List of all the Persons voted for, and of the Number of Votes for each; which List they shall sign and certify, and transmit sealed to the Seat of the Government of the United States, directed to the President of the Senate. The President of the Senate shall, in the Presence of the Senate and House of Representatives, open all the Certificates, and the Votes shall then be counted. The Person having the greatest Number of Votes shall be the President, if such Number be a Majority of the whole Number of Electors appointed; and if there be more than one who have such Majority, and have an equal Number of Votes, then the House of Representatives shall immediately chuse by Ballot one of them for President; and if no Person have a Majority, then from the five highest on the list the said House shall in like Manner chuse the President. But in chusing the President, the Votes shall be taken by States, the Representation from each State having one Vote; a quorum for this Purpose shall consist of a Member or Members from two-thirds of the States, and a Majority of all the States shall be necessary to a Choice. In every Case, after the Choice of the President, the Person having the greatest Number of Votes of the Electors shall be the Vice President. But if there should remain two or more who have equal votes, the Senate shall chuse from them by Ballot the Vice President.][4]

The Congress may determine the Time of chusing the Electors, and the Day on which they shall give their Votes; which Day shall be the same throughout the United States.

No person except a natural-born Citizen, or a Citizen of the United States, at the time of the Adoption of this Constitution, shall be eligible to the Office of President; neither shall any Person be eligible to that Office who shall not have attained to the Age of thirty-five years, and been fourteen Years a Resident within the United States.

In Case of the Removal of the President from Office, or of his Death, Resignation, or Inability to discharge the Powers and Duties of the said Office, the same shall devolve on the Vice President, and the Congress may by Law provide for the Case of Removal, Death, Resignation, or Inability, both of the President and Vice President, declaring what Officer shall then act as President, and such Officer shall act accordingly, until the disability be removed, or a President shall be elected.

The President shall, at stated Times, receive for his Services a Compensation, which shall neither be increased nor diminished during the Period for which he shall have been elected, and he shall not receive within that Period any other Emolument from the United States, or any of them.

Before he enter on the execution of his Office, he shall take the following Oath or Affirmation:—"I do solemnly swear (or affirm) that I will faithfully execute the Office of President of the United States, and will, to the best of my Ability, preserve, protect, and defend the Constitution of the United States."

Section 2.

The President shall be Commander in Chief of the Army and Navy of the United States, and of the Militia of the several States, when called into the actual Service of the United States; he may require the Opinion, in writing, of the principal Officer in each of the executive Depart-

ments, upon any subject relating to the Duties of their respective Offices, and he shall have Power to Grant Reprieves and Pardons for Offenses against the United States, except in Cases of Impeachment.

He shall have Power, by and with the Advice and Consent of the Senate, to make Treaties, provided two-thirds of the Senators present concur; and he shall nominate, and by and with the Advice and Consent of the Senate, shall appoint Ambassadors, other public Ministers and Consuls, Judges of the supreme Court, and all other Officers of the United States, whose Appointments are not herein otherwise provided for, and which shall be established by Law: but the Congress may by Law vest the Appointment of such inferior Officers, as they think proper, in the President alone, in the Courts of Law, or in the Heads of Departments.

The President shall have Power to fill up all Vacancies that may happen during the Recess of the Senate, by granting Commissions which shall expire at the End of their next Session.

Section 3.

He shall from time to time give to the Congress Information of the State of the Union, and recommend to their Consideration such Measures as he shall judge necessary and expedient; he may, on extraordinary occasions, convene both Houses, or either of them, and in Case of Disagreement between them, with respect to the Time of Adjournment, he may adjourn them to such Time as he shall think proper; he shall receive Ambassadors and other public Ministers; he shall take care that the Laws be faithfully executed, and shall Commission all the Officers of the United States.

Section 4.

The President, Vice President and all civil Officers of the United States, shall be removed from Office on Impeachment for, and Conviction of, Treason, Bribery, or other high Crimes and Misdemeanors.

ARTICLE III

Section 1.

The judicial Power of the United States, shall be vested in one supreme Court, and in such inferior Courts as the Congress may from time to time ordain and establish. The Judges, both of the supreme and inferior Courts, shall hold their Offices during good Behaviour, and shall, at stated Times, receive for their Services, a Compensation, which shall not be diminished during their Continuance in Office.

Section 2.

The judicial Power shall extend to all Cases, in Law and Equity, arising under this Constitution, the Laws of the

[4]Revised by the Twelfth Amendment.

United States, and Treaties made, or which shall be made, under their Authority;—to all Cases affecting ambassadors, other public ministers and consuls;—to all cases of admiralty and maritime Jurisdiction;—to Controversies to which the United States shall be a Party;—to Controversies between two or more States;—between a State and Citizens of another State;[5]—between Citizens of different States—between Citizens of the same State claiming Lands under Grants of different States, and between a State, or the Citizens thereof, and foreign States, Citizens, or Subjects.

In all Cases affecting Ambassadors, other public Ministers and Consuls, and those in which a State shall be Party, the supreme Court shall have original Jurisdiction. In all the other Cases before mentioned, the supreme Court shall have appellate Jurisdiction, both as to Law and Fact, with such Exceptions, and under such Regulations as the Congress shall make.

The trial of all Crimes, except in Cases of Impeachment, shall be by Jury; and such Trial shall be held in the State where the said Crimes shall have been committed; but when not committed within any State, the Trial shall be at such Place or Places as the Congress may by Law have directed.

Section 3.

Treason against the United States, shall consist only in levying War against them, or in adhering to their Enemies, giving them Aid and Comfort. No Person shall be convicted of Treason unless on the Testimony of two Witnesses to the same overt Act, or on Confession in open Court.

The Congress shall have power to declare the Punishment of Treason, but no Attainder of Treason shall work Corruption of Blood, or Forfeiture except during the Life of the Person attained.

ARTICLE IV

Section 1.

Full Faith and Credit shall be given in each State to the public Acts, Records, and judicial Proceedings of every State. And the Congress may by general Laws prescribe the Manner in which such Acts, Records and Proceedings shall be proved, and the Effect thereof.

Section 2.

The Citizens of each State shall be entitled to all Privileges and Immunities of Citizens in the several States.

A Person charged in any State with Treason, Felony, or other Crime, who shall flee from Justice, and be found in another State, shall on demand of the executive Authority

of the State from which he fled, be delivered up, to be removed to the State having Jurisdiction of the crime.

No Person held to Service or Labour in one State, under the Laws thereof, escaping into another, shall, in Consequence of any Law or Regulation therein, be discharged from such Service or Labour, but shall be delivered up on Claim of the Party to whom such Service or Labour may be due.

Section 3.

New States may be admitted by the Congress into this Union; but no new State shall be formed or erected within the Jurisdiction of any other State; nor any State be formed by the Junction of two or more States, or parts of States, without the Consent of the Legislatures of the States concerned as well as of the Congress.

The Congress shall have Power to dispose of and make all needful Rules and Regulations respecting the Territory or other Property belonging to the United States; and nothing in this Constitution shall be so construed as to Prejudice any Claims of the United States, or of any particular State.

Section 4.

The United States shall guarantee to every State in this Union a Republican Form of Government, and shall protect each of them against Invasion; and on Application of the Legislature, or of the Executive (when the Legislature cannot be convened) against domestic violence.

ARTICLE V

The Congress, whenever two-thirds of both Houses shall deem it necessary, shall propose Amendments to this Constitution, or, on the Application of the Legislatures of two-thirds of the several States, shall call a Convention for proposing Amendments, which, in either Case, shall be valid to all Intents and Purposes, as part of this Constitution, when ratified by the Legislatures of three-fourths of the several States, or by Conventions in three-fourths thereof, as the one or the other Mode of Ratification may be proposed by the Congress; Provided that no Amendment which may be made prior to the Year One thousand eight hundred and eight shall in any Manner affect the first and fourth Clauses in the Ninth Section of the first Article; and that no State, without its Consent, shall be deprived of its equal Suffrage in the Senate.

ARTICLE VI

All Depts contracted and Engagements entered into, before the Adoption of this Constitution, shall be as valid against the United States under this Constitution, as under the Confederation.

---

[5]Qualified by the Eleventh Amendment.

This Constitution, and the Laws of the United States which shall be made in Pursuance thereof; and all Treaties made, or which shall be made, under the Authority of the United States, shall be the supreme Law of the Land; and the Judges in every State shall be bound thereby, any Thing in the Constitution or Laws of any State to the Contrary notwithstanding.

The Senators and Representatives before mentioned, and the Members of the several State Legislatures, and all executive and judicial Officers, both of the United States and of the several States, shall be bound by Oath or Affirmation to support this Constitution; but no religious Tests shall ever be required as a qualification to any Office or public Trust under the United States.

ARTICLE VII

The Ratification of the Conventions of nine States shall be sufficient for the Establishment of this Constitution between the States so ratifying the same.

Done in convention by the Unanimous Consent of the States present the Seventeenth Day of September in the Year of our Lord one thousand seven hundred and Eighty seven, and of the Independence of the United States of America the Twelfth. In Witness whereof We have hereunto subscribed our Names.[6]

George Washington
President and deputy from Virginia

New Hampshire
John Langdon
Nicholas Gilman

Massachusetts
Nathaniel Gorham
Rufus King

Connecticut
William Samuel Johnson
Roger Sherman

New York
Alexander Hamilton

Delaware
George Read
Gunning Beford, Jr.
John Dickinson
Richard Bassett
Jacob Broom

New Jersey
William Livingston
David Brearley
William Paterson
Jonathan Dayton

Pennsylvania
Benjamin Franklin
Thomas Mifflin
Robert Morris
George Clymer
Thomas FitzSimons
Jared Ingersoll
James Wilson
Gouverneur Morris

North Carolina
William Blount
Richard Dobbs Spaight
Hugh Williamson

Maryland
James McHenry
Daniel of St. Thomas Jenifer
Daniel Carroll

Virginia
John Blair
James Madison, Jr.

South Carolina
John Rutledge
Charles Cotesworth
  Pinckney
Charles Pinckney
Pierce Butler

Georgia
William Few
Abraham Baldwin

Articles in Addition to, and Amendment of, the Constitution of the United States of America, Proposed by Congress, and Ratified by the Legislatures of the Several States, Pursuant to the Fifth Article of the Original Constitution[7]

[ARTICLE I]

Congress shall make no law respecting an establishment of religion, or prohibiting the free exercise thereof; or abridging the freedom of speech, or of the press; or the right of the people peaceably to assemble, and to petition the Government for a redress of grievances.

[ARTICLE II]

A well regulated Militia, being necessary to the security of a free State, the right of the people to keep and bear Arms shall not be infringed.

[ARTICLE III]

No Soldier shall, in time of peace, be quartered in any house, without the consent of the Owner, nor in time of war, but in a manner to be prescribed by law.

[ARTICLE IV]

The right of the people to be secure in their persons, houses, papers, and effects, against unreasonable searches and seizures, shall not be violated, and no Warrants shall issue, but upon probable cause, supported by Oath or affirmation, and particularly describing the place to be searched, and the persons or things to be seized.

[ARTICLE V]

No person shall be held to answer for a capital or otherwise infamous crime, unless on a presentment or indictment of a Grand Jury, except in cases arising in the land or

---

[6]These are the full names of the signers, which in some cases are not the signatures on the document.

[7]This heading appears only in the joint resolution submitting the first ten amendments.

naval forces, or in the Militia, when in actual service in time of War or public danger; nor shall any person be subject for the same offence to be twice put in jeopardy of life or limb; nor shall be compelled in any criminal case to be a witness against himself, nor be deprived of life, liberty, or property, without due process of law; nor shall private property be taken for public use, without just compensation.

[ARTICLE VI]

In all criminal prosecutions, the accused shall enjoy the right to a speedy and public trial, by an impartial jury of the State and district wherein the crime shall have been committed, which district shall have been previously ascertained by law, and to be informed of the nature and cause of the accusation; to be confronted with the witnesses against him; to have compulsory process for obtaining witnesses in his favour, and to have the Assistance of Counsel for his defence.

[ARTICLE VII]

In suits at common law, where the value in controversy shall exceed twenty dollars, the right of trial by jury shall be preserved, and no fact tried by a jury, shall be otherwise reexamined in any Court of the United States, than according to the rules of the common law.

[ARTICLE VIII]

Excessive bail shall not be required, nor excessive fines imposed, nor cruel and unusual punishments inflicted.

[ARTICLE IX]

The enumeration in the Constitution, of certain rights, shall not be construed to deny or disparage others retained by the people.

[ARTICLE X]

The powers not delegated to the United States by the Constitution, nor prohibited by it to the States, are reserved to the States respectively, or to the people. [Amendments I-X, in force 1791.]

[ARTICLE XI][8]

The Judicial power of the United States shall not be construed to extend to any suit in law or equity, commenced or prosecuted against one of the United States by Citizens of another State, or by Citizens or Subjects of any Foreign State.

[8]Adopted in 1798.

[ARTICLE XII][9]

The Electors shall meet in their respective States and vote by ballot for President and Vice-President, one of whom, at least, shall not be an inhabitant of the same State with themselves; they shall name in their ballots the person voted for as President, and in distinct ballots the person voted for as Vice-President, and they shall make distinct lists of all persons voted for as President, and of all persons voted for as Vice-President, and of the number of votes for each, which lists they shall sign and certify, and transmit sealed to the seal of the government of the United States, directed to the President of the Senate;—The President of the Senate shall, in the presence of the Senate and House of Representatives, open all the certificates and the votes shall then be counted;—The person having the greatest number of votes for President, shall be the President, if such number be a majority of the whole number of Electors appointed; and if no person have such majority, then from the persons having the highest numbers not exceeding three on the list of those voted for as President, the House of Representatives shall choose immediately, by ballot, the President. But in choosing the President, the votes shall be taken by states, the representation from each state having one vote; a quorum for this purpose shall consist of a member or members from two-thirds of the states, and a majority of all the states shall be necessary to a choice. And if the House of Representatives shall not choose a President whenever the right of choice shall devolve upon them, before the fourth day of March next following, then the Vice-President shall act as President, as in the case of the death or other constitutional disability of the President.—The person having the greatest number of votes as Vice-President, shall be the Vice-President, if such number be a majority of the whole number of Electors appointed, and if no person have a majority, then from the two highest numbers on the list, the Senate shall choose the Vice-President; a quorum for the purpose shall consist of two-thirds of the whole number of Senators, and a majority of the whole number shall be necessary to a choice. But no person constitutionally ineligible to the office of President shall be eligible to that of Vice-President of the United States.

[ARTICLE XIII][10]

Section 1.

Neither slavery nor involuntary servitude, except as a punishment for crime whereof the party shall have been duly convicted, shall exist within the United States, or any place subject to their jurisdiction.

[9]Adopted in 1804.
[10]Adopted in 1865.

Section 2.

Congress shall have power to enforce this article by appropriate legislation.

[ARTICLE XIV][11]

Section 1.

All persons born or naturalized in the United States, and subject to the jurisdiction thereof, are citizens of the United States and of the State wherein they reside. No State shall make or enforce any law which shall abridge the privileges or immunities of citizens of the United States; nor shall any State deprive any person of life, liberty, or property, without due process of law; nor deny to any person within its jurisdiction the equal protection of the laws.

Section 2.

Representatives shall be apportioned among the several States according to their respective numbers, counting the whole number of persons in each State, excluding Indians not taxed. But when the right to vote at any election for the choice of electors for President and Vice-President of the United States, Representatives in Congress, the Executive and Judicial officers of a State, or the members of the Legislature thereof, is denied to any of the male inhabitants of such State, being twenty-one years of age, and citizens of the United States, or in any way abridged, except for participation in rebellion, or other crime, the basis of representation therein shall be reduced in the proportion which the number of such male citizens shall bear to the whole number of male citizens twenty-one years of age in such State.

Section 3.

No person shall be a Senator or Representative in Congress, or elector of President and Vice-President, or hold any office, civil or military, under the United States, or under any State, who, having previously taken an oath, as a member of Congress, or as an officer of the United States, or as a member of any State legislature, or as an executive or judicial officer of any State, to support the Constitution of the United States, shall have engaged in insurrection or rebellion against the same, or given aid or comfort to the enemies thereof. But Congress may by a vote of two-thirds of each House, remove such disability.

Section 4.

The validity of the public debt of the United States, authorized by law, including debts incurred for payment of pensions and bounties for services in suppressing insurrection or rebellion, shall not be questioned. But neither the United States nor any State shall assume or pay any debts or obligation incurred in aid of insurrection or rebellion against the United States, or any claim for the loss or emancipation of any slave; but all such debts, obligations, and claims shall be held illegal and void.

Section 5.

The Congress shall have the power to enforce, by appropriate legislation, the provisions of this article.

[ARTICLE XV][12]

Section 1.

The right of citizens of the United States to vote shall not be denied or abridged by the United States or by any State on account of race, color, or previous condition of servitude—

Section 2.

The Congress shall have power to enforce this article by appropriate legislation.

[ARTICLE XVI][13]

The Congress shall have power to lay and collect taxes on incomes, from whatever source derived, without apportionment among the several States, and without regard to any census or enumeration.

[ARTICLE XVII][14]

The Senate of the United States shall be composed of two Senators from each State, elected by the people thereof, for six years; and each Senator shall have one vote. The electors in each State shall have the qualifications requisite for electors of the most numerous branch of the State legislatures.

When vacancies happen in the representation of any State in the Senate, the executive authority of such State shall issue writs of election to fill such vacancies: *Provided,* That the legislature of any State may empower the executive thereof to make temporary appointments until the people fill the vacancies by election as the legislature may direct.

This amendment shall not be so constructed as to affect the election or term of any Senator chosen before it becomes valid as part of the Constitution.

[11]Adopted in 1868.

[12]Adopted in 1870.
[13]Adopted in 1913.
[14]Adopted in 1913.

[ARTICLE XVIII][15]

Section 1.

After one year from the ratification of this article the manufacture, sale, or transportation of intoxicating liquors within, the importation thereof into, or the exportation thereof from the United States and all territory subject to the jurisdiction thereof for beverage purposes is hereby prohibited.

Section 2.

The Congress and the several States shall have concurrent power to enforce this article by appropriate legislation.

Section 3.

This article shall be inoperative unless it shall have been ratified as an amendment to the Constitution by the legislatures of the several States, as provided in the Constitution, within seven years from the date of the submission hereof to the States by the Congress.

[ARTICLE XIX][16]

The right of citizens of the United States to vote shall not be denied or abridged by the United States or by any State on account of sex.

Congress shall have power to enforce this article by appropriate legislation.

[ARTICLE XX][17]

Section 1.

The terms of the President and Vice-President shall end at noon on the 20th day of January, and the terms of Senators and Representatives at noon on the 3d day of January, of the years in which such terms would have ended if this article had not been ratified; and the terms of their successors shall then begin.

Section 2.

The Congress shall assemble at least once in every year, and such meeting shall begin at noon on the 3d day of January, unless they shall by law appoint a different day.

Section 3.

If, at the time fixed for the beginning of the term of the President, the President elect shall have died, the Vice-President elect shall become President. If a President shall not have been chosen before the time fixed for the beginning of his term or if the President elect shall have failed to qualify, then the Vice-President elect shall act as Presi-

dent until a President shall have qualified; and the Congress may by law provide for the case wherein neither a President elect nor a Vice-President elect shall have qualified, declaring who shall then act as President, or the manner in which one who is to act shall be selected, and such person shall act accordingly until a President or Vice-President shall have qualified.

Section 4.

The Congress may by law provide for the case of the death of any of the persons from whom the House of Representatives may choose a President whenever the right of choice shall have developed upon them, and for the case of the death of any of the persons from whom the Senate may choose a Vice-President whenever the right of choice shall have developed upon them.

Section 5.

Sections 1 and 2 shall take effect on the 15th day of October following the ratification of this article.

Section 6.

This article shall be inoperative unless it shall have been ratified as an amendment to the Constitution by the legislatures of three-fourths of the several States within seven years from the date of its submission.

[ARTICLE XXI][18]

Section 1.

The eighteenth article of amendment to the Constitution of the United States is hereby repealed.

Section 2.

The transportation or importation into any State, Territory, or possession of the United States for delivery or use therein of intoxicating liquors, in violation of the laws thereof, is hereby prohibited.

Section 3.

This article shall be inoperative unless it shall have been ratified as an amendment to the Constitution by conventions in the several States, as provided in the Constitution, within seven years from the date of the submission hereof to the States by the Congress.

[ARTICLE XXII][19]

No person shall be elected to the office of the President more than twice, and no person who has held the office of President, or acted as President, for more than two years of a term to which some other person was elected

[15]Adopted in 1918.
[16]Adopted in 1920.
[17]Adopted in 1933.

[18]Adopted in 1933.
[19]Adopted in 1961.

President shall be elected to the office of the President more than once.

But this Article shall not apply to any person holding the office of President when this Article was proposed by the Congress, and shall not prevent any person who may be holding the office of President, or acting as President, during the term within which this Article becomes operative from holding the office of President or acting as President during the remainder of such term.*

This article shall be inoperative unless it shall have been ratified as an amendment to the Constitution by the legislatures of three-fourths of the several states within seven years from the date of its submission to the states by the Congress.

[ARTICLE XXIII][20]

Section 1.

The District constituting the seat of Government of the United States shall appoint in such manner as the Congress may direct:

A number of electors of President and Vice-President equal to the whole number of Senators and Representatives in Congress to which the District would be entitled if it were a State, but in no event more than the least populous State; they shall be in addition to those appointed by the States, but they shall be considered, for the purposes of the election of President and Vice-President, to be electors appointed by a State; and they shall meet in the District and perform such duties as provided by the twelfth article of amendment.

Section 2.

The Congress shall have power to enforce this article by appropriate legislation.

[ARTICLE XXIV][21]

Section 1.

The right of citizens of the United States to vote in any primary or other election for President or Vice President, for electors for President or Vice President, or for Senator or Representative in Congress, shall not be denied or abridged by the United States or any state by reason of failure to pay any poll tax or other tax.

Section 2.

The Congress shall have the power to enforce this article by appropriate legislation.

[20]Adopted in 1961.
[21]Adopted in 1964.

[ARTICLE XXV][22]

Section 1.

In case of the removal of the President from office or of his death or resignation, the Vice President shall become President.

Section 2.

Whenever there is a vacancy in the office of the Vice President, the President shall nominate a Vice President who shall take office upon confirmation by a majority vote of both Houses of Congress.

Section 3.

Whenever the President transmits to the President Pro Tempore of the Senate and the Speaker of the House of Representatives his written declaration that he is unable to discharge the powers and duties of his office, and until he transmits to them a written declaration to the contrary, such powers and duties shall be discharged by the Vice President as Acting President.

Section 4.

Whenever the Vice President and a majority of either the principal officers of the executive departments or of such other body as Congress may by law provide, transmit to the President Pro Tempore of the Senate and the Speaker of the House of Representatives their written declaration that the President is unable to discharge the powers and duties of his office, the Vice President shall immediately assume the powers and duties of the office as Acting President.

Thereafter, when the President transmits to the President Pro Tempore of the Senate and the Speaker of the House of Representatives his written declaration that no inability exists, he shall resume the powers and duties of his office unless the Vice President and a majority of either the principal officers of the executive departments or of such other body as Congress may by law provide, transmit within four days to the President Pro Tempore of the Senate and the Speaker of the House of Representatives their written declaration that the President is unable to discharge the powers and duties of his office. Thereupon Congress shall decide the issue, assembling within forty-eight hours for that purpose if not in session. If the Congress, within twenty-one days after receipt of the latter written declaration, or, if Congress is not in session, within twenty-one days after Congress is required to assemble, determines by two-thirds vote of both Houses that the President is unable to discharge the powers and duties of his office, the Vice President shall continue to discharge the same as Acting President; otherwise, the President shall resume the powers and duties of his office.

[22]Adopted in 1967.

[ARTICLE XXVI][23]

Section 1.

The right of citizens of the United States, who are eighteen years of age or older, to vote shall not be denied or abridged by the United States or by any State on account of age.

Section 2.

The Congress shall have power to enforce this article by appropriate legislation.

[ARTICLE XXVII][24]

No law varying the compensation for the services of Senators and Representatives shall take effect until an election of Representatives shall have intervened.

[23]Adopted in 1971.
[24]Adopted in 1992.

PRESIDENTIAL ELECTIONS

Year	Candidates	Parties	Popular Vote	Percentage of Popular Vote	Electoral Vote	Percentage of Voter Participation
1789	**GEORGE WASHINGTON (Va.)***				69	
	John Adams				34	
	Others				35	
1792	**GEORGE WASHINGTON (Va.)**				132	
	John Adams				77	
	George Clinton				50	
	Others				5	
1796	**JOHN ADAMS (Mass.)**	Federalist			71	
	Thomas Jefferson	Democratic-Republican			68	
	Thomas Pinckney	Federalist			59	
	Aaron Burr	Dem.-Rep.			30	
	Others				48	
1800	**THOMAS JEFFERSON (Va.)**	Dem.-Rep.			73	
	Aaron Burr	Dem.-Rep.			73	
	John Adams	Federalist			65	
	C. C. Pinckney	Federalist			64	
	John Jay	Federalist			1	
1804	**THOMAS JEFFERSON (Va.)**	Dem.-Rep.			162	
	C. C. Pinckney	Federalist			14	
1808	**JAMES MADISON (Va.)**	Dem.-Rep.			122	
	C. C. Pinckney	Federalist			47	
	George Clinton	Dem.-Rep.			6	
1812	**JAMES MADISON (Va.)**	Dem.-Rep.			128	
	De Witt Clinton	Federalist			89	
1816	**JAMES MONROE (Va.)**	Dem.-Rep.			183	
	Rufus King	Federalist			34	
1820	**JAMES MONROE (Va.)**	Dem.-Rep.			231	
	John Quincy Adams	Dem.-Rep.			1	
1824	**JOHN Q. ADAMS (Mass.)**	Dem.-Rep.	108,740	30.5	84	26.9
	Andrew Jackson	Dem.-Rep.	153,544	43.1	99	
	William H. Crawford	Dem.-Rep.	46,618	13.1	41	
	Henry Clay	Dem.-Rep.	47,136	13.2	37	
1828	**ANDREW JACKSON (Tenn.)**	Democratic	647,286	56.0	178	57.6
	John Quincy Adams	National Republican	508,064	44.0	83	
1832	**ANDREW JACKSON (Tenn.)**	Democratic	687,502	55.0	219	55.4
	Henry Clay	National Republican	530,189	42.4	49	
	John Floyd	Independent			11	
	William Wirt	Anti-Mason	33,108	2.6	7	
1836	**MARTIN VAN BUREN (N.Y.)**	Democratic	765,483	50.9	170	57.8
	W. H. Harrison	Whig			73	
	Hugh L. White	Whig	739,795	49.1	26	
	Daniel Webster	Whig			14	
	W. P. Magnum	Independent			11	
1840	**WILLIAM H. HARRISON (Ohio)**	Whig	1,274,624	53.1	234	80.2
	Martin Van Buren	Democratic	1,127,781	46.9	60	
	J. G. Birney	Liberty	7,069		—	

*State of residence at time of election.

Year	Candidates	Parties	Popular Vote	Percentage of Popular Vote	Electoral Vote	Percentage of Voter Participation
1844	**JAMES K. POLK (Tenn.)**	Democratic	1,338,464	49.6	170	78.9
	Henry Clay	Whig	1,300,097	48.1	105	
	J. G. Birney	Liberty	62,300	2.3	—	
1848	**ZACHARY TAYLOR (La.)**	Whig	1,360,967	47.4	163	72.7
	Lewis Cass	Democratic	1,222,342	42.5	127	
	Martin Van Buren	Free-Soil	291,263	10.1	—	
1852	**FRANKLIN PIERCE (N.H.)**	Democratic	1,601,117	50.9	254	69.6
	Winfield Scott	Whig	1,385,453	44.1	42	
	John P. Hale	Free-Soil	155,825	5.0	—	
1856	**JAMES BUCHANAN (Pa.)**	Democratic	1,832,955	45.3	741	78.9
	John C. Frémont	Republican	1,339,932	33.1	114	
	Millard Fillmore	American	871,731	21.6	8	
1860	**ABRAHAM LINCOLN (Ill.)**	Republican	1,865,593	39.8	180	81.2
	Stephen A. Douglas	Democratic	1,382,713	29.5	12	
	John C. Breckinridge	Democratic	848,356	18.1	72	
	John Bell	Union	592,906	12.6	39	
1864	**ABRAHAM LINCOLN (Ill.)**	Republican	2,213,655	55.0	212	73.8
	George B. McClellan	Democratic	1,805,237	45.0	21	
1868	**ULYSSES S. GRANT (Ill.)**	Republican	3,012,833	52.7	214	78.1
	Horatio Seymour	Democratic	2,703,249	47.3	80	
1872	**ULYSSES S. GRANT (Ill.)**	Republican	3,597,132	55.6	286	71.3
	Horace Greeley	Democratic; Liberal Republican	2,834,125	43.9	66	
1876	**RUTHERFORD B. HAYES (Ohio)**	Republican	4,036,298	48.0	185	81.8
	Samuel J. Tilden	Democratic	4,300,590	51.0	184	
1880	**JAMES A. GARFIELD (Ohio)**	Republican	4,454,416	48.5	214	79.4
	Winfield S. Hancock	Democratic	4,444,952	48.1	155	
1884	**GROVER CLEVELAND (N.Y.)**	Democratic	4,874,986	48.5	219	77.5
	James G. Blaine	Republican	4,851,981	48.2	182	
1888	**BENJAMIN HARRISON (Ind.)**	Republican	5,439,853	47.9	233	79.3
	Grover Cleveland	Democratic	5,540,309	48.6	168	
1892	**GROVER CLEVELAND (N.Y.)**	Democratic	5,556,918	46.1	277	74.7
	Benjamin Harrison	Republican	5,176,108	43.0	145	
	James B. Weaver	People's	1,041,028	8.5	22	
1896	**WILLIAM McKINLEY (Ohio)**	Republican	7,104,779	51.1	271	79.3
	William J. Bryan	Democratic-People's	6,502,925	47.7	176	
1900	**WILLIAM McKINLEY (Ohio)**	Republican	7,207,923	51.7	292	73.2
	William J. Bryan	Dem.-Populist	6,358,133	45.5	155	
1904	**THEODORE ROOSEVELT (N.Y.)**	Republican	7,623,486	57.9	336	65.2
	Alton B. Parker	Democratic	5,077,911	37.6	140	
	Eugene V. Debs	Socialist	402,283	3.0	—	
1908	**WILLIAM H. TAFT (Ohio)**	Republican	7,678,098	51.6	321	65.4
	William J. Bryan	Democratic	6,409,104	43.1	162	
	Eugene V. Debs	Socialist	420,793	2.8	—	
1912	**WOODROW WILSON (N.J.)**	Democratic	6,293,454	41.9	435	58.8
	Theodore Roosevelt	Progressive	4,119,538	27.4	88	
	William H. Taft	Republican	3,484,980	23.2	8	
	Eugene V. Debs	Socialist	900,672	6.0	—	
1916	**WOODROW WILSON (N.J.)**	Democratic	9,129,606	49.4	277	61.6
	Charles E. Hughes	Republican	8,538,221	46.2	254	
	A. L. Benson	Socialist	585,113	3.2	—	

Year	Candidates	Parties	Popular Vote	Percentage of Popular Vote	Electoral Vote	Percentage of Voter Participation
1920	**WARREN G. HARDING (Ohio)**	Republican	16,152,200	60.4	404	49.2
	James M. Cox	Democratic	9,147,353	34.2	127	
	Eugene V. Debs	Socialist	919,799	3.4	—	
1924	**CALVIN COOLIDGE (Mass.)**	Republican	15,725,016	54.0	382	48.9
	John W. Davis	Democratic	8,386,503	28.8	136	
	Robert M. LaFollette	Progressive	4,822,856	16.6	13	
1928	**HERBERT HOOVER (Calif.)**	Republican	21,391,381	58.2	444	56.9
	Alfred E. Smith	Democratic	15,016,443	40.9	87	
	Norman Thomas	Socialist	267,835	0.7	—	
1932	**FRANKLIN D. ROOSEVELT (N.Y.)**	Democratic	22,821,857	57.4	472	56.9
	Herbert Hoover	Republican	15,761,841	39.7	59	
	Norman Thomas	Socialist	881,951	2.2	—	
1936	**FRANKLIN D. ROOSEVELT (N.Y.)**	Democratic	27,751,597	60.8	523	61.0
	Alfred M. Landon	Republican	16,679,583	36.5	8	
	William Lemke	Union	882,479	1.9	—	
1940	**FRANKLIN D. ROOSEVELT (N.Y.)**	Democratic	27,244,160	54.8	449	62.5
	Wendell L. Willkie	Republican	22,305,198	44.8	82	
1944	**FRANKLIN D. ROOSEVELT (N.Y.)**	Democratic	25,602,504	53.5	432	55.9
	Thomas E. Dewey	Republican	22,006,285	46.0	99	
1948	**HARRY S. TRUMAN (Mo.)**	Democratic	24,105,695	49.5	304	53.0
	Thomas E. Dewey	Republican	21,969,170	45.1	189	
	J. Strom Thurmond	State-Rights Democratic	1,169,021	2.4	38	
	Henry A. Wallace	Progressive	1,156,103	2.4	—	
1952	**DWIGHT D. EISENHOWER (N.Y.)**	Republican	33,936,252	55.1	442	63.3
	Adlai E. Stevenson	Democratic	27,314,992	44.4	89	
1956	**DWIGHT D. EISENHOWER (N.Y.)**	Republican	35,575,420	57.6	457	60.6
	Adlai E. Stevenson	Democratic	26,033,066	42.1	73	
	Other	—	—		1	
1960	**JOHN F. KENNEDY (Mass.)**	Democratic	34,227,096	49.9	303	62.8
	Richard M. Nixon	Republican	34,108,546	49.6	219	
	Other	—	—		15	
1964	**LYNDON B. JOHNSON (Tex.)**	Democratic	43,126,506	61.1	486	61.7
	Barry M. Goldwater	Republican	27,176,799	38.5	52	
1968	**RICHARD M. NIXON (N.Y.)**	Republican	31,770,237	43.4	301	60.6
	Hubert H. Humphrey	Democratic	31,270,533	42.7	191	
	George Wallace	American Indep.	9,906,141	13.5	46	
1972	**RICHARD M. NIXON (N.Y.)**	Republican	47,169,911	60.7	520	55.2
	George S. McGovern	Democratic	29,170,383	37.5	17	
	Other	—	—		1	
1976	**JIMMY CARTER (Ga.)**	Democratic	40,828,587	50.0	297	53.5
	Gerald R. Ford	Republican	39,147,613	47.9	241	
	Other	—	1,575,459	2.1	—	
1980	**RONALD REAGAN (Calif.)**	Republican	43,901,812	50.7	489	52.6
	Jimmy Carter	Democratic	35,483,820	41.0	49	
	John B. Anderson	Independent	5,719,722	6.6	—	
	Ed Clark	Libertarian	921,188	1.1	—	
1984	**RONALD REAGAN (Calif.)**	Republican	54,455,075	59.0	525	53.3
	Walter Mondale	Democratic	37,577,185	41.0	13	
1988	**GEORGE BUSH (Texas)**	Republican	47,946,422	54.0	426	50.2
	Michael S. Dukakis	Democratic	41,016,429	46.0	112	

Year	Candidates	Parties	Popular Vote	Percentage of Popular Vote	Electoral Vote	Percentage of Voter Participation
1992	**WILLIAM J. CLINTON (Ark.)**	Democratic	44,908,233	43.3	370	55.2
	George Bush	Republican	39,102,282	37.7	168	
	Ross Perot	Independent	19,721,433	19.0	—	
1996	**WILLIAM J. CLINTON (Ark.)**	Democratic	47,401,185	49.3	379	
	Robert Dole	Republican	39,197,469	40.7	159	49.0
	Ross Perot	Reform	8,085,294	8.4	—	
2000	**GEORGE W. BUSH (Texas)**	Republican	50,459,211	47.89	271	51.0
	Albert Gore, Jr.	Democratic	51,003,894	48.41	266	
	Ralph Nader	Green	2,834,410	2.69	—	

VICE PRESIDENTS AND CABINET MEMBERS

The Washington Administration (1789–1797)

Vice President	John Adams	1789–1797
Secretary of State	Thomas Jefferson	1789–1793
	Edmund Randolph	1794–1795
	Timothy Pickering	1795–1797
Secretary of Treasury	Alexander Hamilton	1789–1795
	Oliver Wolcott	1795–1797
Secretary of War	Henry Knox	1789–1794
	Timothy Pickering	1795–1796
	James McHenry	1796–1797
Attorney General	Edmund Randolph	1789–1793
	William Bradford	1794–1795
	Charles Lee	1795–1797
Postmaster General	Samuel Osgood	1789–1791
	Timothy Pickering	1791–1794
	Joseph Habersham	1795–1797

The John Adams Administration (1797–1801)

Vice President	Thomas Jefferson	1797–1801
Secretary of State	Timothy Pickering	1797–1800
	John Marshall	1800–1801
Secretary of Treasury	Oliver Wolcott	1797–1800
	Samuel Dexter	1800–1801
Secretary of War	James McHenry	1797–1800
	Samuel Dexter	1800–1801
Attorney General	Charles Lee	1797–1801
Postmaster General	Joseph Habersham	1797–1801
Secretary of Navy	Benjamin Stoddert	1798–1801

The Jefferson Administration (1801–1809)

Vice President	Aaron Burr	1801–1805
	George Clinton	1805–1809
Secretary of State	James Madison	1801–1809
Secretary of Treasury	Samuel Dexter	1801
	Albert Gallatin	1801–1809
Secretary of War	Henry Dearborn	1801–1809
Attorney General	Levi Lincoln	1801–1805
	Robert Smith	1805
	John Breckinridge	1805–1806
	Caesar Rodney	1807–1809
Postmaster General	Joseph Habersham	1801
	Gideon Granger	1801–1809
Secretary of Navy	Robert Smith	1801–1809

The Madison Administration (1809–1817)

Vice President	George Clinton	1809–1813
	Elbridge Gerry	1813–1817
Secretary of State	Robert Smith	1809–1811
	James Monroe	1811–1817
Secretary of Treasury	Albert Gallatin	1809–1813
	George Campbell	1814
	Alexander Dallas	1814–1816
	William Crawford	1816–1817
Secretary of War	William Eustis	1809–1812
	John Armstrong	1813–1814
	James Monroe	1814–1815
	William Crawford	1815–1817
Attorney General	Caesar Rodney	1809–1811
	William Pinkney	1811–1814
	Richard Rush	1814–1817
Postmaster General	Gideon Granger	1809–1814
	Return Meigs	1814–1817
Secretary of Navy	Paul Hamilton	1809–1813
	William Jones	1813–1814
	Benjamin Crowninshield	1814–1817

The Monroe Administration (1817–1825)

Vice President	Daniel Tompkins	1817–1825
Secretary of State	John Quincy Adams	1817–1825
Secretary of Treasury	William Crawford	1817–1825
Secretary of War	George Graham	1817
	John C. Calhoun	1817–1825
Attorney General	Richard Rush	1817
	William Wirt	1817–1825
Postmaster General	Return Meigs	1817–1823
	John McLean	1823–1825

Secretary of Navy	Benjamin Crowninshield	1817–1818
	Smith Thompson	1818–1823
	Samuel Southard	1823–1825

The John Quincy Adams Administration (1825–1829)

Vice President	John C. Calhoun	1825–1829
Secretary of State	Henry Clay	1825–1829
Secretary of Treasury	Richard Rush	1825–1829
Secretary of War	James Barbour	1825–1828
	Peter Porter	1828–1829
Attorney General	William Wirt	1825–1829
Postmaster General	John McLean	1825–1829
Secretary of Navy	Samuel Southard	1825–1829

The Jackson Administration (1829–1837)

Vice President	John C. Calhoun	1829–1833
	Martin Van Buren	1833–1837
Secretary of State	Martin Van Buren	1829–1831
	Edward Livingston	1831–1833
	Louis McLane	1833–1834
	John Forsyth	1834–1837
Secretary of Treasury	Samuel Ingham	1829–1831
	Louis McLane	1831–1833
	William Duane	1833
	Roger B. Taney	1833–1834
	Levi Woodbury	1834–1837
Secretary of War	John H. Eaton	1829–1831
	Lewis Cass	1831–1837
	Benjamin Butler	1837
Attorney General	John M. Berrien	1829–1831
	Roger B. Taney	1831–1833
	Benjamin Butler	1833–1837
Postmaster General	William Barry	1829–1835
	Amos Kendall	1835–1837
Secretary of Navy	John Branch	1829–1831
	Levi Woodbury	1831–1834
	Mahlon Dickerson	1834–1837

The Van Buren Administration (1837–1841)

Vice President	Richard M. Johnson	1837–1841
Secretary of State	John Forsyth	1837–1841
Secretary of Treasury	Levi Woodbury	1837–1841
Secretary of War	Joel Poinsett	1837–1841
Attorney General	Benjamin Butler	1837–1838
	Felix Grundy	1838–1840
	Henry D. Gilpin	1840–1841
Postmaster General	Amos Kendall	1837–1840
	John M. Niles	1840–1841
Secretary of Navy	Mahlon Dickerson	1837–1838
	James Paulding	1838–1841

The William Harrison Administration (1841)

Vice President	John Tyler	1841
Secretary of State	Daniel Webster	1841
Secretary of Treasury	Thomas Ewing	1841
Secretary of War	John Bell	1841
Attorney General	John J. Crittenden	1841
Postmaster General	Francis Granger	1841
Secretary of Navy	George Badger	1841

The Tyler Administration (1841–1845)

Vice President	None	
Secretary of State	Daniel Webster	1841–1843
	Hugh S. Legaré	1843
	Abel P. Upshur	1843–1844
	John C. Calhoun	1844–1845
Secretary of Treasury	Thomas Ewing	1841
	Walter Forward	1841–1843
	John C. Spencer	1843–1844
	George Bibb	1844–1845
Secretary of War	John Bell	1841
	John C. Spencer	1841–1843
	James M. Porter	1843–1844
	William Wilkins	1844–1845
Attorney General	John J. Crittenden	1841
	Hugh S. Legaré	1841–1843
	John Nelson	1843–1845
Postmaster General	Francis Granger	1841
	Charles Wickliffe	1841
Secretary of Navy	George Badger	1841
	Abel P. Upshur	1841
	David Henshaw	1843–1844
	Thomas Gilmer	1844
	John Y. Mason	1844–1845

The Polk Administration (1845–1849)

Vice President	George M. Dallas	1845–1849
Secretary of State	James Buchanan	1845–1849
Secretary of Treasury	Robert J. Walker	1845–1849
Secretary of War	William L. Marcy	1845–1849
Attorney General	John Y. Mason	1845–1846
	Nathan Clifford	1846–1848
	Isaac Toucey	1848–1849
Postmaster General	Cave Johnson	1845–1849
Secretary of Navy	George Bancrocft	1845–1846
	John Y. Mason	1846–1849

The Taylor Administration (1849–1850)

Vice President	Millard Fillmore	1849–1850
Secretary of State	John M. Clayton	1849–1850
Secretary of Treasury	William Meredith	1849–1850
Secretary of War	George Crawford	1849–1850
Attorney General	Reverdy Johnson	1849–1850
Postmaster General	Jacob Collamer	1849–1850
Secretary of Navy	William Preston	1849–1850
Secretary of Interior	Thomas Ewing	1849–1850

The Fillmore Administration (1850–1853)

Vice President	None	
Secretary of State	Daniel Webster	1850–1852
	Edward Everett	1852–1853
Secretary of Treasury	Thomas Corwin	1850–1853
Secretary of War	Charles Conrad	1850–1853
Attorney General	John J. Crittenden	1850–1853
Postmaster General	Nathan Hall	1850–1852
	Sam D. Hubbard	1852–1853
Secretary of Navy	William A. Graham	1850–1852
	John P. Kennedy	1852–1853
Secretary of Interior	Thomas McKennan	1850
	Alexander Stuart	1850–1853

The Pierce Administration (1853–1857)

Vice President	William R. King	1853–1857
Secretary of State	William L. Marcy	1853–1857
Secretary of Treasury	James Guthrie	1853–1857
Secretary of War	Jefferson Davis	1853–1857
Attorney General	Caleb Cushing	1853–1857
Postmaster General	James Campbell	1853–1857
Secretary of Navy	James C. Dobbin	1853–1857
Secretary of Interior	Robert McClelland	1853–1857

The Buchanan Administration (1857–1861)

Vice President	John C. Breckinridge	1857–1861
Secretary of State	Lewis Cass	1857–1860
	Jeremiah S. Black	1860–1861
Secretary of Treasury	Howell Cobb	1857–1860
	Philip Thomas	1860–1861
	John A. Dix	1861
Secretary of War	John B. Floyd	1857–1861
	Joseph Holt	1861
Attorney General	Jeremiah S. Black	1857–1860
	Edwin M. Stanton	1860–1861
Postmaster General	Aaron V. Brown	1857–1859
	Joseph Holt	1859–1861
	Horatio King	1861
Secretary of Navy	Isaac Toucey	1857–1861
Secretary of Interior	Jacob Thompson	1857–1861

The Lincoln Administration (1861–1865)

Vice President	Hannibal Hamlin	1861–1865
	Andrew Johnson	1865
Secretary of State	William H. Seward	1861–1865
Secretary of Treasury	Salmon P. Chase	1861–1864
	William P. Fessenden	1864–1865
	Hugh McCulloch	1865
Secretary of War	Simon Cameron	1861–1862
	Edwin M. Stanton	1862–1865
Attorney General	Edward Bates	1861–1864
	James Speed	1864–1865

Postmaster General	Horatio King	1861
	Montgomery Blair	1861-1864
	William Dennison	1864-1865
Secretary of Navy	Gideon Welles	1861-1865
Secretary of Interior	Caleb B.Smith	1861-1863
	John P. Usher	1863-1865

The Andrew Johnson Administration (1865–1869)

Vice President	None	
Secretary of State	William H. Seward	1865-1869
Secretary of Treasury	Hugh McCulloch	1865-1869
Secretary of War	Edwin M. Stanton	1865-1867
	Ulysses S. Grant	1867-1868
	Lorenzo Thomas	1868
	John M. Schofield	1868-1869
Attorney General	James Speed	1865-1866
	Henry Stanbery	1866-1868
	William M. Evarts	1868-1869
Postmaster General	William Dennison	1865-1866
	Alexander Randall	1866-1869
Secretary of Navy	Gideon Welles	1865-1869
Secretary of Interior	John P. Usher	1865
	James Harlan	1865-1866
	Orville H. Browning	1866-1869

The Grant Administration (1869–1877)

Vice President	Schuyler Colfax	1869-1873
	Henry Wilson	1873-1877
Secretary of State	Elihu B. Washburne	1869
	Hamilton Fish	1869-1877
Secretary of Treasury	George S. Boutwell	1869-1873
	William Richardson	1873-1874
	Benjamin Bristow	1874-1876
	Lot M. Morrill	1876-1877
Secretary of War	John A. Rawlins	1869
	William T. Sherman	1869
	William W. Belknap	1869-1876
	Alphonso Taft	1876
	James D. Cameron	1876-1877
Attorney General	Ebenezer Hoar	1869-1870
	Amos T. Ackerman	1870-1871
	G. H. Williams	1871-1875
	Edwards Pierrepont	1875-1876
	Alphonso Taft	1876-1877

Postmaster General	John A. J. Creswell	1869-1874
	James W. Marshall	1874
	Marshall Jewell	1874-1876
	James N. Tyner	1876-1877
Secretary of Navy	Adolph E. Borie	1869
	George M. Robeson	1869-1877
Secretary of Interior	Jacob D. Cox	1869-1870
	Columbus Delano	1870-1875
	Zachariah Candler	1875-1877

The Hayes Administration (1877–1881)

Vice President	William A. Wheeler	1877-1881
Secretary of State	William M. Evarts	1877-1881
Secretary of Treasury	John Sherman	1877-1881
Secretary of War	George W. McCrary	1877-1879
	Alex Ramsey	1879-1881
Attorney General	Charles Devens	1877-1881
Postmaster General	David M. Key	1877-1880
	Horace Maynard	1880-1881
Secretary of Navy	Richard W. Thompson	1877-1880
	Nathan Goff, Jr.	1881
Secretary of Interior	Carl Schurz	1877-1881

The Garfield Administration (1881)

Vice President	Chester A. Arthur	1881
Secretary of State	James G. Blaine	1881
Secretary of Treasury	William Windom	1881
Secretary of War	Robert T. Lincoln	1881
Attorney General	Wayne MacVeagh	1881
Postmaster General	Thomas L. James	1881
Secretary of Navy	William H. Hunt	1881
Secretary of Interior	Samuel J. Kirkwood	1881

The Arthur Administration (1881–1885)

Vice President	None	
Secretary of State	F. T. Frelinghuysen	1881-1885
Secretary of Treasury	Charles J. Folger	1881-1884
	Walter Q. Gresham	1884
	Hugh McCulloch	1884-1885

Secretary of War	Robert T. Lincoln	1881–1885
Attorney General	Benjamin H. Brewster	1881–1885
Postmaster General	Timothy O. Howe	1881–1883
	Walter Q. Gresham	1883–1884
	Frank Hatton	1884–1885
Secretary of Navy	William H. Hunt	1881–1882
	William E. Chandler	1882–1885
Secretary of Interior	Samuel J. Kirkwood	1881–1882
	Henry M. Teller	1882–1885

The Cleveland Administration (1885–1889)

Vice President	Thomas A. Hendricks	1885–1889
Secretary of State	Thomas F. Bayard	1885–1889
Secretary of Treasury	Daniel Manning	1885–1887
	Charles S. Fairchild	1887–1889
Secretary of War	William C. Endicott	1885–1889
Attorney General	Augustus H. Garland	1885–1889
Postmaster General	William F. Vilas	1885–1888
	Don M. Dickinson	1888–1889
Secretary of Navy	William C. Whitney	1885–1889
Secretary of Interior	Lucius Q. C. Lamar	1885–1888
	William F. Vilas	1888–1889
Secretary of Agriculture	Norman J. Colman	1889

The Benjamin Harrison Administration (1889–1893)

Vice President	Levi P. Morton	1889–1893
Secretary of State	James G. Blaine	1889–1892
	John W. Foster	1892–1893
Secretary of Treasury	William Windom	1889–1891
	Charles Foster	1891–1893
Secretary of War	Redfield Proctor	1889–1891
	Stephen B. Elkins	1891–1893
Attorney General	William H. H. Miller	1889–1891
Postmaster General	John Wanamaker	1889–1893
Secretary of Navy	Benjamin F. Tracy	1889–1893
Secretary of Interior	John W. Noble	1889–1893
Secretary of Agriculture	Jeremiah M. Rusk	1889–1893

The Cleveland Administration (1893–1897)

Vice President	Adlai E. Stevenson	1893–1897
Secretary of State	Walter Q. Gresham	1893–1895
	Richard Olney	1895–1897
Secretary of Treasury	John G. Carlisle	1893–1897
Secretary of War	Daniel S. Lamont	1893–1897
Attorney General	Richard Olney	1893–1895
	James Harmon	1895–1897
Postmaster General	Wilson S. Bissell	1893–1895
	William L. Wilson	1895–1897
Secretary of Navy	Hilary A. Herbert	1893–1897
Secretary of Interior	Hoke Smith	1893–1896
	David R. Francis	1896–1897
Secretary of Agriculture	Julius S. Morton	1893–1897

The McKinley Administration (1897–1901)

Vice President	Garret A. Hobart	1897–1901
	Theodore Roosevelt	1901
Secretary of State	John Sherman	1897–1898
	William R. Day	1898
	John Hay	1898–1901
Secretary of Treasury	Lyman J. Gage	1897–1901
Secretary of War	Russell A. Alger	1897–1899
	Elihu Root	1899–1901
Attorney General	Joseph McKenna	1897–1898
	John W. Griggs	1898–1901
	Philander C. Knox	1901
Postmaster General	James A. Gary	1897–1898
	Charles E. Smith	1898–1901
Secretary of Navy	John D. Long	1897–1901
Secretary of Interior	Cornelius N. Bliss	1897–1899
	Ethan A. Hitchcock	1899–1901
Secretary of Agriculture	James Wilson	1897–1901

The Theodore Roosevelt Administration (1901–1909)

Vice President	Charles Fairbanks	1905–1909
Secretary of State	John Hay	1901–1905
	Elihu Root	1905–1909
	Robert Bacon	1909

Secretary of Treasury	Lyman J. Gage	1901-1902
	Leslie M. Shaw	1902-1907
	George B. Cortelyou	1907-1909
Secretary of War	Elihu Root	1901-1904
	William H. Taft	1904-1908
	Luke E. Wright	1908-1909
Attorney General	Philander C. Knox	1901-1904
	William H. Moody	1904-1906
	Charles J. Bonaparte	1906-1909
Postmaster General	Charles E. Smith	1901-1902
	Henry C. Payne	1902-1904
	Robert J. Wynne	1904-1905
	George B. Cortelyou	1905-1907
	George von L. Meyer	1907-1909
Secretary of Navy	John D. Long	1901-1902
	William H. Moody	1902-1904
	Paul Morton	1904-1905
	Charles J. Bonaparte	1905-1906
	Victor H. Metcalf	1906-1908
	Truman H. Newberry	1908-1909
Secretary of Interior	Ethan A. Hitchcock	1901-1907
	James R. Garfield	1907-1909
Secretary of Agriculture	James Wilson	1901-1909
Secretary of Labor and Commerce	George B. Cortelyou	1903-1904
	Victor H. Metcalf	1904-1906
	Oscar S. Straus	1906-1909
	Charles Nagel	1909

The Taft Administration (1909–1913)

Vice President	James S. Sherman	1909-1913
Secretary of State	Philander C. Knox	1909-1913
Secretary of Treasury	Franklin MacVeagh	1909-1913
Secretary of War	Jacob M. Dickinson	1909-1911
	Henry L. Stimson	1911-1913
Attorney General	George W. Wickersham	1909-1913
Postmaster General	Frank H. Hitchcock	1909-1913
Secretary of Navy	George von L. Meyer	1909-1913
Secretary of Interior	Richard A. Ballinger	1909-1911
	Walter L. Fisher	1911-1913
Secretary of Agriculture	James Wilson	1909-1913
Secretary of Labor and Commerce	Charles Nagel	1909-1913

The Wilson Administration (1913–1921)

Vice President	Thomas R. Marshall	1913-1921
Secretary of State	William J. Bryan	1913-1915
	Robert Lansing	1915-1920
	Bainbridge Colby	1920-1921
Secretary of Treasury	William G. McAdoo	1913-1918
	Carter Glass	1918-1920
	David F. Houston	1920-1921
Secretary of War	Lindley M. Garrison	1913-1916
	Newton D. Baker	1916-1921
Attorney General	James C. McReynolds	1913-1914
	Thomas W. Gregory	1914-1919
	A. Mitchell Palmer	1919-1921
Postmaster General	Albert S. Burleson	1913-1921
Secretary of Navy	Josephus Daniels	1913-1921
Secretary of Interior	Franklin K. Lane	1913-1920
	John B. Payne	1920-1921
Secretary of Agriculture	David F. Houston	1913-1920
	Edwin T. Meredith	1920-1921
Secretary of Commerce	William C. Redfield	1913-1919
	Joshua W. Alexander	1919-1921
Secretary of Labor	William B. Wilson	1913-1921

The Harding Administration (1921–1923)

Vice President	Calvin Coolidge	1921-1923
Secretary of State	Charles E. Hughes	1921-1923
Secretary of Treasury	Andrew Mellon	1921-1923
Secretary of War	John W. Weeks	1921-1923
Attorney General	Harry M. Daugherty	1921-1923
Postmaster General	Will H. Hays	1921-1922
	Hubert Work	1922-1923
	Harry S. New	1923
Secretary of Navy	Edwin Denby	1921-1923
Secretary of Interior	Albert B. Fall	1921-1923
	Hubert Work	1923
Secretary of Agriculture	Henry C. Wallace	1921-1923
Secretary of Commerce	Herbert C. Hoover	1921-1923
Secretary of Labor	James J. Davis	1921-1923

The Coolidge Administration (1923–1929)

Vice President	Charles G. Dawes	1925–1929
Secretary of State	Charles E. Hughes	1923–1925
	Frank B. Kellogg	1925–1929
Secretary of Treasury	Andrew Mellon	1923–1929
Secretary of War	John W. Weeks	1923–1925
	Dwight F. Davis	1925–1929
Attorney General	Harry M. Daugherty	1923–1924
	Harlan F. Stone	1924–1925
	John G. Sargent	1925–1929
Postmaster General	Harry S. New	1923–1929
Secretary of Navy	Edwin Derby	1923–1924
	Curtis D. Wilbur	1924–1929
Secretary of Interior	Hubert Work	1923–1928
	Roy O. West	1928–1929
Secretary of Agriculture	Henry C. Wallace	1923–1924
	Howard M. Gore	1924–1925
	William M. Jardine	1925–1929
Secretary of Commerce	Herbert C. Hoover	1923–1928
	William F. Whiting	1928–1929
Secretary of Labor	James J. Davis	1923–1929

The Hoover Administration (1929–1933)

Vice President	Charles Curtis	1929–1933
Secretary of State	Henry L. Stimson	1929–1933
Secretary of Treasury	Andrew Mellon	1929–1932
	Ogden L. Mills	1932–1933
Secretary of War	James W. Good	1929
	Patrick J. Hurley	1929–1933
Attorney General	William D. Mitchell	1929–1933
Postmaster General	Walter F. Brown	1929–1933
Secretary of Navy	Charles F. Adams	1929–1933
Secretary of Interior	Ray L. Wilbur	1929–1933
Secretary of Agriculture	Arthur M. Hyde	1929–1933
Secretary of Commerce	Robert P. Lamont	1929–1932
	Roy D. Chapin	1932–1933
Secretary of Labor	James J. Davis	1929–1930
	William N. Doak	1930–1933

The Franklin D. Roosevelt Administration (1933–1945)

Vice President	John Nance Garner	1933–1941
	Henry A. Wallace	1941–1945
	Harry S. Truman	1945
Secretary of State	Cordell Hull	1933–1944
	Edward R. Stettinius, Jr.	1944–1945
Secretary of Treasury	William H. Woodin	1933–1934
	Henry Morgenthau, Jr.	1934–1945
Secretary of War	George H. Dern	1933–1936
	Henry A. Woodring	1936–1940
	Henry L. Stimson	1940–1945
Attorney General	Homer S. Cummings	1933–1939
	Frank Murphy	1939–1940
	Robert H. Jackson	1940–1941
	Francis Biddle	1941–1945
Postmaster General	James A. Farley	1933–1940
	Frank C. Walker	1940–1945
Secretary of Navy	Claude A. Swanson	1933–1940
	Charles Edison	1940
	Frank Knox	1940–1944
	James V. Forrestal	1944–1945
Secretary of Interior	Harold L. Ickes	1933–1945
Secretary of Agriculture	Henry A. Wallace	1933–1940
	Claude R. Wickard	1940–1945
Secretary of Commerce	Daniel C. Roper	1933–1939
	Harry L. Hopkins	1939–1940
	Jesse Jones	1940–1945
	Henry A. Wallace	1945
Secretary of Labor	Frances Perkins	1933–1945

The Truman Administration (1945–1953)

Vice President	Alben W. Barkley	1949–1953
Secretary of State	Edward R. Stettinius, Jr.	1945
	James F. Byrnes	1945–1947
	George C. Marshall	1947–1949
	Dean G. Acheson	1949–1953
Secretary of Treasury	Fred M. Vinson	1945–1946
	John W. Snyder	1946–1953
Secretary of War	Robert P. Patterson	1945–1947
	Kenneth C. Royall	1947
Attorney General	Tom C. Clark	1945–1949
	J. Howard McGrath	1949–1952
	James P. McGranery	1952–1953

Postmaster General	Frank C. Walker	1945
	Robert E. Hannegan	1945–1947
	Jesse M. Donaldson	1947–1953
Secretary of Navy	James V. Forrestal	1945–1947
Secretary of Interior	Harold L. Ickes	1945–1946
	Julius A. Krug	1946–1949
	Oscar L. Chapman	1949–1953
Secretary of Agriculture	Clinton P. Anderson	1945–1948
	Charles F. Brannan	1948–1953
Secretary of Commerce	Henry A. Wallace	1945–1946
	W. Averell Harriman	1946–1948
	Charles W. Sawyer	1948–1953
Secretary of Labor	Lewis B. Schwellenbach	1945–1948
	Maurice J. Tobin	1948–1953
Secretary of Defense	James V. Forrestal	1947–1949
	Louis A. Johnson	1949–1950
	George C. Marshall	1950–1951
	Robert A. Lovett	1951–1953

The Eisenhower Administration (1953–1961)

Vice President	Richard M. Nixon	1953–1961
Secretary of State	John Foster Dulles	1953–1959
	Christian A. Herter	1959–1961
Secretary of Treasury	George M. Humphrey	1953–1957
	Robert B. Anderson	1957–1961
Attorney General	Herbert Brownell, Jr.	1953–1958
	William P. Rogers	1958–1961
Postmaster General	Arthur E. Summerfield	1953–1961
Secretary of Interior	Douglas McKay	1953–1956
	Fred A. Seaton	1956–1961
Secretary of Agriculture	Ezra T. Benson	1953–1961
Secretary of Commerce	Sinclair Weeks	1953–1958
	Lewis L. Strauss	1958–1959
	Frederick H. Mueller	1959–1961
Secretary of Labor	Martin P. Durkin	1953
	James P. Mitchell	1953–1961
Secretary of Defense	Charles E. Wilson	1953–1957
	Neil H. McElroy	1957–1959
	Thomas S. Gates Jr.	1959–1961
Secretary of Health, Education, and Welfare	Oveta Culp Hobby	1953–1955
	Marion B. Folsom	1955–1958
	Arthur S. Flemming	1958–1961

The Kennedy Administration (1961–1963)

Vice President	Lyndon B. Johnson	1961–1963
Secretary of State	Dean Rusk	1961–1963
Secretary of Treasury	C. Douglas Dillon	1961–1963
Attorney General	Robert F. Kennedy	1961–1963
Postmaster General	J. Edward Day	1961–1963
	John A. Gronouski	1963
Secretary of Interior	Stewart L. Udall	1961–1963
Secretary of Agriculture	Orville L. Freeman	1961–1963
Secretary of Commerce	Luther H. Hodges	1961–1963
Secretary of Labor	Arthur J. Goldberg	1961–1962
	W. Willard Wirtz	1962–1963
Secretary of Defense	Robert S. McNamara	1961–1963
Secretary of Health, Education, and Welfare	Abraham A. Ribicoff	1961–1962
	Anthony J. Celebrezze	1962–1963

The Lyndon Johnson Administration (1963–1969)

Vice President	Hubert H. Humphrey	1965–1969
Secretary of State	Dean Rusk	1963–1969
Secretary of Treasury	C. Douglas Dillon	1963–1965
	Henry H. Fowler	1965–1969
Attorney General	Robert F. Kennedy	1963–1964
	Nicholas Katzenbach	1965–1966
	Ramsey Clark	1967–1969
Postmaster General	John A. Gronouski	1963–1965
	Lawrence F. O'Brien	1965–1968
	Marvin Watson	1968–1969
Secretary of Interior	Stewart L. Udall	1963–1969
Secretary of Agriculture	Orville L. Freeman	1963–1969
Secretary of Commerce	Luther H. Hodges	1963–1964
	John T. Connor	1964–1967
	Alexander B. Trowbridge	1967–1968
	Cyrus R. Smith	1968–1969
Secretary of Labor	W. Willard Wirtz	1963–1969
Secretary of Defense	Robert F. McNamara	1963–1968
	Clark Clifford	1968–1969

Secretary of Health, Education, and Welfare	Anthony J. Celebrezze	1963-1965
	John W. Gardner	1965-1968
	Wilbur J. Cohen	1968-1969
Secretary of Housing and Urban Development	Robert C. Weaver	1966-1969
	Robert C. Wood	1969
Secretary of Transportation	Alan S. Boyd	1967-1969

The Nixon Administration (1969–1974)

Vice President	Spiro T. Agnew	1969-1973
	Gerald R. Ford	1973-1974
Secretary of State	William P. Rogers	1969-1973
	Henry S. Kissinger	1973-1974
Secretary of Treasury	David M. Kennedy	1969-1970
	John B. Connally	1971-1972
	George P. Shultz	1972-1974
	William E. Simon	1974
Attorney General	John N. Mitchell	1969-1972
	Richard G. Kleindienst	1972-1973
	Elliot L. Richardson	1973
	William B. Saxbe	1973-1974
Postmaster General	Winton M. Blount	1969-1971
Secretary of Interior	Walter J. Hickel	1969-1970
	Rogers Morton	1971-1974
Secretary of Agriculture	Clifford M. Hardin	1969-1971
	Earl L. Butz	1971-1974
Secretary of Commerce	Maurice H. Stans	1969-1972
	Peter G. Peterson	1972-1973
	Frederick B. Dent	1973-1974
Secretary of Labor	George P. Shultz	1969-1970
	James D. Hodgson	1970-1973
	Peter J. Brennan	1973-1974
Secretary of Defense	Melvin R. Laird	1969-1973
	Elliot L. Richardson	1973
	James R. Schlesinger	1973-1974
Secretary of Health, Education, and Welfare	Robert H. Finch	1969-1970
	Elliot L. Richardson	1970-1973
	Caspar W. Weinberger	1973-1974
Secretary of Housing and Urban Development	George Romney	1969-1973
	James T. Lynn	1973-1974
Secretary of Transportation	John A. Volpe	1969-1973
	Claude S. Brinegar	1973-1974

The Ford Administration (1974–1977)

Vice President	Nelson A. Rockefeller	1974-1977
Secretary of State	Henry A. Kissinger	1974-1977
Secretary of Treasury	William E. Simon	1974-1977
Attorney General	William Saxbe	1974-1975
	Edward Levi	1975-1977
Secretary of Interior	Rogers Morton	1974-1975
	Stanley K. Hathaway	1975
	Thomas Kleppe	1975-1977
Secretary of Agriculture	Earl L. Butz	1974-1976
	John A. Knebel	1976-1977
Secretary of Commerce	Frederick B. Dent	1974-1975
	Rogers Morton	1975-1976
	Elliot L. Richardson	1976-1977
Secretary of Labor	Peter J. Brennan	1974-1975
	John T. Dunlop	1975-1976
	W. J. Usery	1976-1977
Secretary of Defense	James R. Schlesinger	1974-1975
	Donald Rumsfeld	1975-1977
Secretary of Health, Education, and Welfare	Caspar Weinberger	1974-1975
	Forrest D. Mathews	1975-1977
Secretary of Housing and Urban Development	James T. Lynn	1974-1975
	Carla A. Hills	1975-1977
Secretary of Transportation	Claude Brinegar	1974-1975
	William T. Coleman	1975-1977

The Carter Administration (1977–1981)

Vice President	Walter F. Mondale	1977-1981
Secretary of State	Cyrus R. Vance	1977-1980
	Edmund Muskie	1980-1981
Secretary of Treasury	W. Michael Blumenthal	1977-1979
	G. William Miller	1979-1981
Attorney General	Griffin Bell	1977-1979
	Benjamin R. Civiletti	1979-1981
Secretary of Interior	Cecil D. Andrus	1977-1981
Secretary of Agriculture	Robert Bergland	1977-1981
Secretary of Commerce	Juanita M. Kreps	1977-1979
	Philip M. Klutznick	1979-1981
Secretary of Labor	F. Ray Marshall	1977-1981
Secretary of Defense	Harold Brown	1977-1981
Secretary of Health, Education and Welfare	Joseph A. Califano	1977-1979
	Patricia R. Harris	1979

Secretary of Health and Human Services	Patricia R. Harris	1979–1981
Secretary of Education	Shirley M. Hufstedler	1979–1981
Secretary of Housing and Urban Development	Patricia R. Harris	1977–1979
	Moon Landrieu	1979–1981
Secretary of Transportation	Brock Adams	1977–1979
	Neil E. Goldschmidt	1979–1981
Secretary of Energy	James R. Schlesinger	1977–1979
	Charles W. Duncan	1979–1981

The Reagan Administration (1981–1989)

Vice President	George Bush	1981–1989
Secretary of State	Alexander M. Haig	1981–1982
	George P. Shultz	1982–1989
Secretary of Treasury	Donald Regan	1981–1985
	James A. Baker III	1985–1988
	Nicholas F. Brady	1988–1989
Attorney General	William F. Smith	1981–1985
	Edwin A. Meese III	1985–1988
	Richard Thornburgh	1988–1989
Secretary of Interior	James Watt	1981–1983
	William P. Clark, Jr.	1983–1985
	Donald P. Hodel	1985–1989
Secretary of Agriculture	John Block	1981–1986
	Richard E. Lyng	1986–1989
Secretary of Commerce	Malcolm Baldrige	1981–1987
	C. William Verity, Jr.	1987–1989
Secretary of Labor	Raymond Donovan	1981–1985
	William Brock	1985–1987
	Ann D. McLaughlin	1987–1989
Secretary of Defense	Caspar Weinberger	1981–1987
	Frank C. Carlucci	1987–1989
Secretary of Health and Human Services	Richard Schweiker	1981–1983
	Margaret Heckler	1983–1985
	Otis R. Bowen	1985–1989
Secretary of Education	Terrel H. Bell	1981–1985
	William J. Bennett	1985–1988
	Laura F. Cavazos	1988–1989
Secretary of Housing and Urban Development	Samuel Pierce	1981–1989
Secretary of Transportation	Drew Lewis	1981–1983
	Elizabeth Dole	1983–1987
	James H. Burnley	1987–1989

Secretary of Energy	James Edwards	1981–1982
	Donald P. Hodel	1982–1985
	John S. Herrington	1984–1989

The George H. W. Bush Administration (1989–1993)

Vice President	J. Danforth Quayle	1989–1993
Secretary of State	James A. Baker III	1989–1992
	Lawrence S. Eagleburger	1992–1993
Secretary of Treasury	Nicholas F. Brady	1989–1993
Attorney General	Richard Thornburgh	1989–1991
	William P. Barr	1991–1993
Secretary of Interior	Manuel Lujan	1989–1993
Secretary of Agriculture	Clayton K. Yeutter	1989–1991
	Edward Madigan	1991–1993
Secretary of Commerce	Robert A. Mosbacher	1989–1992
	Barbara H. Franklin	1992–1993
Secretary of Labor	Elizabeth Dole	1989–1991
	Lynn M. Martin	1991–1993
Secretary of Defense	Richard B. Cheney	1989–1993
Secretary of Health and Human Services	Louis W. Sullivan	1989–1993
Secretary of Education	Laura F. Cavazos	1989–1991
	Lamar Alexander	1991–1993
Secretary of Housing and Urban Development	Jack F. Kemp	1989–1993
Secretary of Transportation	Samuel K. Skinner	1989–1992
	Andrew H. Card	1992–1993
Secretary of Energy	James D. Watkins	1989–1993
Secretary of Veterans Affairs	Edward J. Derwinski	1989–1993

The Clinton Administration (1993–2001)

Vice President	Albert Gore, Jr.	1993–2001
Secretary of State	Warren M. Christopher	1993–1997
	Madeleine Albright	1997–2001
Secretary of Treasury	Lloyd Bentsen	1993–1995
	Robert E. Rubin	1995–1999
	Lawrence H. Summers	1999–2001
Attorney General	Janet Reno	1993–2001

Secretary of Interior	Bruce Babbitt	1993–2001
Secretary of Agriculture	Mike Espy	1993–1995
	Daniel R. Glickman	1995–2001
Secretary of Commerce	Ronald H. Brown	1993–1996
	Mickey Kantor	1996–1997
	William M. Daley	1997–2000
	Norman Minetta	2001
Secretary of Labor	Robert B. Reich	1993–1997
	Alexis M. Herman	1997–2001
Secretary of Defense	Les Aspin	1993–1994
	William Perry	1994–1996
	William S. Cohen	1996–2001
Secretary of Health and Human Services	Donna E. Shalala	1993–2001
Secretary of Education	Richard W. Riley	1993–2001
Secretary of Housing and Urban Development	Henry G. Cisneros	1993–1997
	Andrew Cuomo	1997–2001
Secretary of Transportation	Federico Pena	1993–1997
	Rodney E. Slater	1997–2001
Secretary of Energy	Hazel O'Leary	1993–1997
	Federico Pena	1997–1998
	Bill Richardson	1998–2001
Secretary of Veteran Affairs	Jesse Brown	1993–1998
	Togo D. West, Jr.	1998–2000
	Hershel Gober (Acting)	2000–2001

The George W. Bush Administration (2001–   )

Vice President	Richard B. Cheney	2001–
Secretary of State	Colin Powell	2001–
Secretary of Treasury	Paul O'Neill	2001–
Attorney General	John Ashcroft	2001–
Secretary of Interior	Gale Norton	2001–
Secretary of Agriculture	Ann M. Venemean	2001–
Secretary of Commerce	Don Evans	2001–
Secretary of Labor	Elaine Chao	2001–
Secretary of Defense	Donald Rumsfeld	2001–
Secretary of Health and Human Services	Tommy Thompson	2001–
Secretary of Education	Roderick Paige	2001–
Secretary of Housing and Urban Development	Mel Martinez	2001–
Secretary of Transportation	Norman Mineta	2001–
Secretary of Energy	Spencer Abraham	2001–
Secretary of Veteran Affairs	Anthony Principi	2001–

POPULATION OF THE UNITED STATES, 1790–2000

Year	Population	Percent Increase	Population per Square Mile	Percent Urban/ Rural	Percent White/ Nonwhite	Median Age
1790	3,929,214		4.5	5.1/94.9	80.7/19.3	NA
1800	5,308,483	35.1	6.1	6.1/93.9	81.1/18.9	NA
1810	7,239,881	36.4	4.3	7.3/92.7	81.0/19.0	NA
1820	9,638,453	33.1	5.5	7.2/92.8	81.6/18.4	16.7
1830	12,866,020	33.5	7.4	8.8/91.2	81.9/18.1	17.2
1840	17,069,453	32.7	9.8	10.8/89.2	83.2/16.8	17.8
1850	23,191,876	35.9	7.9	15.3/84.7	84.3/15.7	18.9
1860	31,443,321	35.6	10.6	19.8/80.2	85.6/14.4	19.4
1870	39,818,449	26.6	13.4	25.7/74.3	86.2/13.8	20.2
1880	50,155,783	26.0	16.9	28.2/71.8	86.5/13.5	20.9
1890	62,947,714	25.5	21.2	35.1/64.9	87.5/12.5	22.0
1900	75,994,575	20.7	25.6	39.6/60.4	87.9/12.1	22.9
1910	91,972,266	21.0	31.0	45.6/54.4	88.9/11.1	24.1
1920	105,710,620	14.9	35.6	51.2/48.8	89.7/10.3	25.3
1930	122,775,046	16.1	41.2	56.1/43.9	89.8/10.2	26.4
1940	131,669,275	7.2	44.2	56.5/43.5	89.8/10.2	29.0
1950	150,697,361	14.5	50.7	64.0/36.0	89.5/10.5	30.2
1960	179,323,175	18.5	50.6	69.9/30.1	88.6/11.4	29.5
1970	203,302,031	13.4	57.4	73.5/26.5	87.6/12.4	28.0
1980	226,545,805	11.4	64.0	73.7/26.3	86.0/14.0	30.0
1990	248,718,000	9.8	70.3	77.5/22.5	83.8/16.2	32.9
2000	281,421,906	13.0	79.6	NA/NA	83.0/17.0	35.3

NA = Not Available.

EMPLOYMENT, 1870–2000

Year	Number of Workers (in millions)	Male/Female Employment Ratio	Percentage of Workers in Unions
1870	12.5	85/15	—
1880	17.4	85/15	—
1890	23.3	83/17	—
1900	29.1	82/18	3
1910	38.2	79/21	6
1920	41.6	79/21	12
1930	48.8	78/22	7
1940	53.0	76/24	27
1950	59.6	72/28	25
1960	69.9	68/32	26
1970	82.1	63/37	25
1980	108.5	58/42	23
1985	108.9	57/43	19
1990	118.8	55/45	16
2000	134.3	53/47	13.5

PRODUCTION, TRADE, AND FEDERAL SPENDING/DEBT, 1790–2000

Year	Gross National Product (GNP) (in billions $)	Balance of Trade (in billions $)	Federal Budget (in billions $)	Federal Surplus/Deficit (in billions $)	Federal Debt (in billions $)
1790	—	–3	.004	+0.00015	.076
1800	—	–20	.011	+0.0006	.083
1810	—	–18	.008	+0.0012	.053
1820	—	–4	.018	–0.0004	.091
1830	—	+3	.015	+0.100	.049
1840	—	+25	.024	–0.005	.004
1850	—	–26	.040	+0.004	.064
1860	—	–38	.063	–0.01	.065
1870	7.4	–11	.310	+0.10	2.4
1880	11.2	+92	.268	+0.07	2.1
1890	13.1	+87	.318	+0.09	1.2
1900	18.7	+569	.521	+0.05	1.2
1910	35.3	+273	.694	–0.02	1.1
1920	91.5	+2,880	6.357	+0.3	24.3
1930	90.7	+513	3.320	+0.7	16.3
1940	100.0	–3,403	9.6	–2.7	43.0
1950	286.5	+1,691	43.1	–2.2	257.4
1960	506.5	+4,556	92.2	+0.3	286.3
1970	992.7	+2,511	196.6	+2.8	371.0
1980	2,631.7	+24,088	579.6	–59.5	914.3
1985	4,087.7	–148,480	946.3	–212.3	1,827.5
1990	5,764.9	–101,012	1,251.8	–220.5	4,064.6
2000	9,860.8	–369.7	1,789.6	+237.0	5,674.2

Index

Note: Some page numbers are in *italics* and are followed by letters; these refer to illustrations (*i*), maps (*m*), or tables (*t*).

THE WORLD

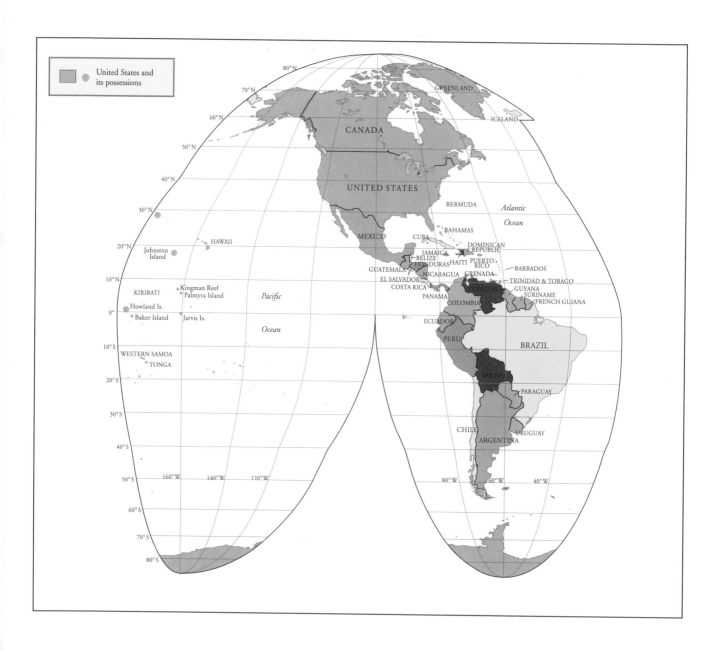

United States and
its possessions

80°N

70°N

60°N

GREENLAND

ICELAND

50°N

CANADA

40°N

UNITED STATES

BERMUDA

Atlantic

30°N

Ocean

MEXICO

BAHAMAS

CUBA

20°N

HAWAII

DOMINICAN
REPUBLIC

Johnston
Island

JAMAICA
BELIZE
HONDURAS HAITI

PUERTO
RICO

BARBADOS

GUATEMALA

GRENADA

TRINIDAD & TOBAGO

10°N

EL SALVADOR
COSTA RICA

NICARAGUA

VENEZUELA

GUYANA
SURINAME
FRENCH GUIANA

KIRIBATI

Kingman Reef
Palmyra Island

Pacific

PANAMA

COLOMBIA

0°

Howland Is.
Baker Island

Jarvis Is.

Ocean

ECUADOR

PERU

BRAZIL

10°S

WESTERN SAMOA
TONGA

20°S

BOLIVIA

PARAGUAY

30°S

CHILE

URUGUAY

40°S

ARGENTINA

160°W   140°W   120°W

80°W   60°W   40°W

50°S

60°S

70°S

80°S